Contents

THE FIRST WEST

Writing from the American Frontier
1776–1860

Edited by

Edward Watts
Michigan State University

David Rachels
Virginia Military Institute

New York   Oxford
OXFORD UNIVERSITY PRESS
2002

Oxford University Press

Oxford   New York
Athens   Auckland   Bangkok   Bogotá   Buenos Aires   Cape Town
Chennai   Dar es Salaam   Delhi   Florence   Hong Kong   Istanbul   Karachi
Kolkata   Kuala Lumpur   Madrid   Melbourne   Mexico City   Mumbai   Nairobi
Paris   São Paulo   Shanghai   Singapore   Taipei   Tokyo   Toronto   Warsaw

and associated companies in
Berlin   Ibadan

Published by Oxford University Press, Inc.
198 Madison Avenue, New York, New York, 10016
http://www.oup-usa.org

Library of Congress Cataloging-in-Publication Data

The first West : writing from the American frontier, 1776–1860 / edited by Edward Watts
and David Rachels.
    p. cm.
  Includes bibliographical references.
  ISBN 0-19-514133-4 (pbk. : acid-free paper)
    1. American literature—West (U.S.) 2. Frontier and pioneer life—West
(U.S.)—History—Sources. 3. American literature—Revolutionary period, 1775–1783. 4.
Frontier and pioneer life—Literary collections. 5. West (U.S.)—Literary collections. 6.
American literature—1783–1850. I. Watts, Edward. II. Rachels, David.

PS561 F57 2001
810.9'3278—dc21   2001018539

Printing number: 9 8 7 6 5 4 3 2 1

Printed in the United States of America
on acid-free paper

Maps

II. Different Voices

Thematic Contents

I. Thematic Connections

Introduction

By 1840, there were as many Americans living west of the Appalachian mountains as there were to their east. In 1830, Cincinnati was the fourth most productive center of the nation's publishing industry. Yet to this day, with few exceptions, the authors, texts, and literatures produced in "the West" go largely ignored. When they are noticed, it is usually for the purpose of illustrating subjects limited to regional interests, subjects thus of secondary importance in respect to the identification of "national" culture of the east. This book, *The First West,* aims to do two things: to demonstrate that eastern texts about the west must be studied in their national context, and to reveal that the west produced significant literary and cultural texts whose significance is not limited to their immediate geographical environs but which must also be considered as contributing to the diverse cultures of the antebellum United States as a whole.

Before and during the period when the texts that imagined, expressed, represented, and constructed the first west were produced, a complex array of historical circumstances led to the peculiar contexts of their production and, later, their subsequent exclusion from earlier versions of American writing and culture. After the Revolution, white Americans spilled west over the mountains and encountered a complex array of British, Algonquian, Iroquois, French, Spanish, and unaffiliated white squatters and their traditions, communities, and ideas about the region. From then until the outbreak of the Civil War, every form of literary and nonliterary expression was employed and practiced to describe the region by both eastern Americans writing about the west and, more and more, western Americans writing back to the east and about themselves.

However, the culture and literature of the Mississippi valley and Great Lakes Basin (regions combined as the "West" in virtually all antebellum references) have been dismissed as products of the frontier and thus marginal to our understanding and study of more mature versions of "American" culture being generated, mostly, in New England. As we continue to diversify our understanding of the nation's modes and practices of self-expression during this period, we must consider the inclusion of western voices. Geographical and topographical differences were important in the years before telecommunications began with the telegraph late in the period in question. The historical, geographical, and physical differences in the west did, in fact, generate divergent regional cultures in the west. The identification of a distinct "western" cultural and literary tradition would add greatly to understanding of the diversity and complexity of the era.

Such a study must begin with an understanding of the forces, then and now, that discouraged a complication or a pluralization of what we mean by "American" culture. As early as 1938, Temple Bodley identified the region whose writing we are addressing as "the first great west," but noted how cultural politics had erased it from

American history: "these eastern historians were prone to magnify the importance of events and men of their own section and to minimize, or entirely overlook, distant ones far more important." Bodley correctly noted that a paucity of materials from the Revolutionary west in particular had led to a dearth of scholarship on its role in the war. His effort, like ours, was to make available for scholars, students, and general readers versions of American self-expression that were minimized as long as we considered the east the epicenter of our national culture.

Most collections of writing from the various western frontiers of the United States retain the seventeenth-century distinction that a "frontier" is a line that separates distinct zones of cultural purity. As a result, they stress texts generated by moments of intercultural contact and conflict between Native and European Americans. The line of contact has been the essential dramatic site of encounter in the definition and the depiction of frontiers in American history. As a result, frontier literature has traditionally embraced the central conflicts between Europeans and Indians and between humans and wilderness as pitting two wholly opposed forces against each other in a struggle for dominion. From the diaries of various explorers (Lewis and Clark, Zebulon Pike, etc.) and the accounts of native "savages" published by whites (Henry Rowe Schoolcraft, George Catlin) emerged a literature of the frontier from the pens of writers like James Fenimore Cooper and William Cullen Bryant that stressed the romantic and adventurous nature of frontier experience as a thrilling allegory realizing the larger drama of "Manifest Destiny."

As such, collections of western writing have often told and retold different versions of the same story, albeit with each version set further to the west. These materials are undoubtedly crucial to understanding how the two races came together, broke apart, and ultimately formed or failed to form new communities, cultures, and identities that were suited to the regions in question. For that reason, *The First West* includes a number of such texts, which depict and represent, if not initial contact between natives and Europeans, the first contact between natives and people who thought of themselves as *American,* rather than as English, French, or Spanish. Our selections in those areas have been informed by understanding how the American Revolution caused a change from older practices of trade-based interculturalism endeavored by European colonial administrations to a more aggressive occupation-oriented American disposition.

Recent scholarship, however, has suggested that such an arrangement is historically limited in two ways. First, the natives of the *American* wests were usually already not only aware of whites, but were also in many cases intermarried and militarily allied with them. Many native groups were also thoroughly entangled with western material culture through the use of horses and guns or a reliance on the fur trade or on a number of other white-dominated trading systems. Especially in the north, Native Americans through the end of the War of 1812 had been allied with the British and the French in a long process to combat American settlement west of the Appalachians and Alleghenies. The American frontier of the early nineteenth century was not so much characterized by contact between two alien groups but rather, too often, between groups that knew each other all too well.

Second, the study of twentieth-century borders has shown that an identifiable "line" between one culture and another oversimplifies the complexities of frontier and border experiences. On the one hand, it connotes an intrinsic assymetry between the conquering culture and the conquered and assumes that, east of the frontier, indigenous culture is erased. The lingering native presence east of the Mississippi today demonstrates the failure of even such a strong assertion of a "frontier" as that embraced by the 1830 Indian Removal Act. Furthermore, such a race-based demarkation implies that the "white" communities constructed east of the frontier represented and extended a coherent and singular idea of "American" civilization that varied little from Massachusetts to Georgia. In fact, as one traveled from north to south, vastly different terms of contact and settlement prevailed and markedly divergent communities were formed in the wake of the westward-moving process of American territorial acquisition. In particular, the Northwest Ordinance (1787) and the Missouri Compromise (1820) subdivided "white" America into radically different social and political constructions.

Finally, in recent years the frontier has been more often defined as a "zone" that is not necessarily geographically or chronologically contiguous. For example, in 1803, was the frontier traveling westward to the Pacific with Lewis and Clark, or was it in northern Indiana with Tecumseh? Within the scope of *The First West,* the new communities that were formed, although technically east of the lines dividing the "settled" and "unsettled" spaces, still today exist among a complex matrix of the historical, cultural, political, and geographical ruptures, contradictions, and paradoxes that characterize "frontier" experience. Because these complexities have often either contradicted the triumphalist and, more recently, antitriumphalist versions of the frontier, many texts produced by writers in these communities have not been reprinted since their initial publication. Those that have been reprinted, furthermore, have often not been read for their description of "frontier" experience, since the line of territorial acquisition had often moved hundreds or even thousands of miles further west.

With all of the foregoing in mind, our goal has been to study what was known as the "west" in most antebellum American publications: the eastern Mississippi and Ohio valleys and the southern Great Lakes region. This excludes Texas, about which a great body of material was produced, and the far and mountain wests, both of which were brought into the United States late in the period in question. In a sense, these represent later "wests," and were imagined, administered, and represented in radically different ways in regard to the nation's intents and operations. By contrast, tracing the cultural evolution of a single region from its original occupation through the development of a self-conscious regional identity or identities would demonstrate more completely what happened after contact, colonization, and statehood: how the frontier became a settlement and how the settlements became part of the nation.

Our selections, then, are based on understanding the zone of these antebellum frontiers as a process that includes not only the drama of contact and conquest but also what came after. Dating back to Richard C. Wade's *The Urban Frontier* (1958), ideas about the antebellum frontier descended from Frederick Jackson Turner have been challenged by scholars such as Colin Calloway, Susan Gray, Elizabeth Perkins, Nicole Etcheson, Mary Grant, John Seelye, Richard White, Andrew Cayton, John Mack Faragher, and others. *The First West* is the first anthology that pulls together both their revisionist ideas and many of the primary texts on which they base their arguments and the more conventional descriptions of the frontier. Then as now, the struggle to represent the west is, at heart, a struggle over what kind of nation was extending itself westward. Was or is it a single cultural entity whose conquest of the west demonstrates its inevitable ascendence to superpower? Does the conquest of the west demonstrate a deep-seated violence in American society based in racist and genocidal impulses? Was the conquest of the west as simple as either of those images?

We have tried to assemble a group of texts which suggest that the invasion, occupation, colonization, and settlement of the first American west was a very complex process that cannot be limited to the paradigms of either triumphalism or its rejection. We document contact between Americans and natives as very different in different places and regions. We reprint texts which suggest that intraracial, as well as interracial, conflict informed frontier experience; that there were moments of multiracial cohabitation; that towns and cities as well as farms and forts characterized the frontier; that the frontier was intrinsically interwoven in larger national debates about race, class, gender, and region. Furthermore, we are mostly concerned with the public performance of these conflicts, and so have not, with rare exception, republished recovered private texts such as diaries that were not published during the years in question. As such, our selections range from political documents and treaties to poetry and short fiction. As William D. Gallagher admitted in 1844, the monthly journal was the dominant means of print culture in the Ohio valley, and those journals—in which much of the material reproduced here first appeared—published a similar array of genres ranging from fiction to geographical surveys side by side, a diversity we seek to recreate. Furthermore, we have chosen a rather limited number of texts and tried to reproduce them at length, rather than reprinting smaller fragments of a greater number of texts.

Our ending date—1860—has been selected because the frontier's entanglement in national issues changed at that time. The regional complexities we mean to identify were overwhelmed in a more strident program of nationalism connected to the war. In the national imagination, the line dividing it was now no longer the longitudinal line of the westward-moving frontier but rather the latitudinal line dividing north from south. Despite this, the west's increasing calls for regional autonomy—disregarding the eastern-drawn line of the Northwest Ordinance's division of the west—reflect a desire to be separate from the competing eastern sections, a separation bound to fail as war encroached. During and after the Civil War, the United States's attitudes toward its frontiers shifted dramatically in ways that detach the late nineteenth-century "west" from its antebellum settlement. As the nation became in the late nineteenth century what historian Richard Bensel calls the "Yankee Leviathan," older reckonings and conversations about regions and sections became a separate issue: just as the Dawes Act of 1887 erased 370 treaties between the federal government and native tribes, so too did the post–Civil War era's strident nationalism begin to generate the triumphalist narratives of the frontier that omitted many of the authors, texts, and historical and cultural complexities and regional divergences we mean to revive.

The First West documents the development of the first west as it explored it own historical peculiarities and differences from the eastern United States, a regional distinction and divergence shattered by the Civil War. Nonetheless, in the writing from the first west are many treasures and important reflections of how the various populations, traditions, cultures, and regions came together. We hope the book's readers will find in it ways of reconsidering and redefining nineteenth-century American culture in general.

J. HECTOR ST. JOHN DE CREVECOEUR

(1735–1813)

"What is an American?" This question, the subtitle to Letter III of Creve-coeur's *Letters from an American Farmer,* is often asked in an effort to dis-tinguish Americans from Europeans. However, its very asking implies ei-ther that there is or that there should be a singular and universal national identity. Crevecoeur's Letter III has been reprinted throughout the twen-tieth century to bolster claims of the historical sources of coherence and stability that superseded what were viewed as divergent claims to plural-ity from various groups excluded from Crevecoeur's construction of the American as a white, male, landowning farmer.

However, Crevecoeur was quite aware of the short-sightedness of Letter III's jingoistic optimism. Crevecoeur himself, a cosmopolitan lower-level French nobleman who settled in New York after the French and Indian War, had traveled throughout the colonies and was uniquely suited to stand apart from any specific national loyalty. Recently, Creve-coeur's Letter IX, which vividly depicts the horrors of Southern slavery, has been resurrected and placed within a rereading of *Letters* as a work of fiction. In this fiction, the Pennsylvania farmer James, Crevecoeur's narra-tor, begins the book with the blind optimism of Letters II and III, and is deeply chastened by being exposed to the brutal treatment received by slaves outside of Charleston. As a result, Crevecoeur's view has been re-considered as ironic or critical of the notion of nationalism and mono-culturalism. With that in mind, his important comments on the western frontier might be also reconsidered. Letter III represents the frontier as an outlet for civilization's "off-casts" and erects a "stage-version" of history whereby the first generation of white settlers regresses to a nearly native condition. Each succeeding generation then moves toward the national model as the frontier moves west.

In Letter XII, James himself is forced to flee west from the Revolu-tion, even as Crevecoeur himself fled to Europe. Before James leaves, he pens "Distresses of a Frontier Man" in which he seeks to regain the noble savagery he ascribes to the native Americans with whom he intends to live. His stated intent is contradicted by James's encroaching plan to re-make the west in the image of the east by introducing agriculture, Chris-tianity, and literacy, all the while recruiting more emigrants. This contra-dictory combination reflects the new nation's double-mindedness about the west: it is valued both as uncultivated wilderness and as a resource to be cultivated.

Letters has appeared in many editions and forms throughout its pub-lication history. It stands both as an articulation of the role assigned to the

western frontier in the early republic and as a criticism of that assignment and the view of the west as a permanent border protecting the east. We have reproduced here both Letter III's articulation of the hyperbolic propaganda of eastern representations of the west and the entirely of Letter XII.

Text: *Letters from an American Farmer and Sketches of 18th-Century America* (1782; rpt. ed. Albert E. Stone, 1963): 66–79, 200–227

FROM *LETTERS FROM AN AMERICAN FARMER* (1782)

LETTER III

What is an American?

I wish I could be acquainted with the feelings and thoughts which must agitate the heart and present themselves to the mind of an enlightened Englishman when he first lands on this continent. He must greatly rejoice that he lived at a time to see this fair country discovered and settled; he must necessarily feel a share of national pride when he views the chain of settlements which embellish these extended shores. When he says to himself, "This is the work of my countrymen, who, when convulsed by factions, afflicted by a variety of miseries and wants, restless and impatient, took refuge here. They brought along with them their national genius, to which they principally owe what liberty they enjoy and what substance they possess." Here he sees the industry of his native country displayed in a new manner and traces in their works the embryos of all the arts, sciences, and ingenuity which flourish in Europe. Here he beholds fair cities, substantial villages, extensive fields, an immense country filled with decent houses, good roads, orchards, meadows, and bridges where an hundred years ago all was wild, woody, and uncultivated! What a train of pleasing ideas this fair spectacle must suggest; it is a prospect which must inspire a good citizen with the most heart-felt pleasure. The difficulty consists in the manner of viewing so extensive a scene. He is arrived on a new continent; a modern society offers itself to his contemplation, different from what he had hitherto seen. It is not composed, as in Europe, of great lords who possess everything and of a herd of people who have nothing. Here are no aristocratical families, no courts, no kings, no bishops, no ecclesiastical dominion, no invisible power giving to a few a very visible one, no great manufactures employing thousands, no great refinements of luxury. The rich and the poor are not so far removed from each other as they are in Europe. Some few towns excepted, we are all tillers of the earth, from Nova Scotia to West Florida. We are a people of cultiva-

From Temple Bodley's Our First Great West *(1938)*

tors scattered over an immense territory, communicating with each other by means of good roads and navigable rivers, united by the silken bands of mild government, all respecting the laws without dreading their power, because they are equitable. We are all animated with the spirit of an industry which is unfettered and unrestrained, because each person works for himself. If he travels through our rural districts, he views not the hostile castle and the haughty mansion, contrasted with the clay-built hut and miserable cabin, where cattle and men help to keep each other warm and dwell in meanness, smoke, and indigence. A pleasing uniformity of decent competence appears throughout our habitations. The meanest of our log-houses is a dry and comfortable habitation. Lawyer or merchant are the fairest titles our towns afford; that of a farmer is the only appellation of the rural inhabitants of our country. It must take some time ere he can reconcile himself to our dictionary, which is but short in words of dignity and names of honour. There, on a Sunday, he sees a congregation of respectable farmers and their wives, all clad in neat homespun, well mounted, or riding in their own humble waggons. There is not among them an esquire, saving the unlettered magistrate. There he sees a parson as simple as his flock, a farmer who does not riot on the labour of others. We have no princes for whom we toil, starve, and bleed; we are the most perfect society now existing in the world. Here man is free as he ought to be, nor is this pleasing equality so transitory as many others are. Many ages will not see the shores of our great lakes replenished with inland nations, nor the unknown bounds of North America entirely peopled. Who can tell how far it extends? Who can tell the millions of men whom it will feed and contain? For no European foot has as yet travelled half the extent of this mighty continent!

The next wish of this traveller will be to know whence came all these people. They are a mixture of English, Scotch, Irish, French, Dutch, Germans, and Swedes. From this promiscuous breed, that race now called Americans have arisen. The eastern provinces must indeed be excepted as being the unmixed descendants of Englishmen. I have heard many wish that they had been more intermixed also; for my part, I am no wisher and think it much better as it has happened. They exhibit a most conspicuous figure in this great and variegated picture; they too enter for a great share in the pleasing perspective displayed in these thirteen provinces. I know it is fashionable to reflect on them, but I respect them for what they have done; for the accuracy and wisdom with which they have settled their territory; for the decency of their manners; for their early love of letters; their ancient college, the first in this hemisphere; for their industry, which to me who am but a farmer is the criterion of everything. There never was a people, situated as they are, who with so ungrateful a soil have done more in so short a time. Do you think that the monarchical ingredients which are more prevalent in other governments have purged them from all foul stains? Their histories assert the contrary.

In this great American asylum, the poor of Europe have by some means met together, and in consequence of various causes; to what purpose should they ask one another what countrymen they are? Alas, two thirds of them had no country. Can a wretch who wanders about, who works and starves, whose life is a continual scene of sore affliction or pinching penury—can that man call England or any other kingdom his country? A country that had no bread for him, whose fields procured him no harvest, who met with nothing but the frowns of the rich, the severity of the laws, with jails and punishments, who owned not a single foot of the extensive surface of this planet? No! Urged by a variety of motives, here they came. Everything has tended to regenerate them: new laws, a new mode of living, a new social system; here they are

become men: in Europe they were as so many useless plants, wanting vegetative mould and refreshing showers; they withered, and were mowed down by want, hunger, and war; but now, by the power of transplantation, like all other plants they have taken root and flourished! Formerly they were not numbered in any civil lists of their country, except in those of the poor; here they rank as citizens. By what invisible power hath this surprising metamorphosis been performed? By that of the laws and that of their industry. The laws, the indulgent laws, protect them as they arrive, stamping on them the symbol of adoption; they receive ample rewards for their labours; these accumulated rewards procure them lands; those lands confer on them the title of freemen, and to that title every benefit is affixed which men can possibly require. This is the great operation daily performed by our laws. Whence proceed these laws? From our government. Whence that government? It is derived from the original genius and strong desire of the people ratified and confirmed by the crown. This is the great chain which links us all, this is the picture which every province exhibits, Nova Scotia excepted. There the crown has done all; either there were no people who had genius or it was not much attended to; the consequence is that the province is very thinly inhabited indeed; the power of the crown in conjunction with the musketos has prevented men from settling there. Yet some parts of it flourished once, and it contained a mild, harmless set of people. But for the fault of a few leaders, the whole was banished. The greatest political error the crown ever committed in America was to cut off men from a country which wanted nothing but men!

What attachment can a poor European emigrant have for a country where he had nothing? The knowledge of the language, the love of a few kindred as poor as himself, were the only cords that tied him; his country is now that which gives him his land, bread, protection, and consequence; *Ubi panis ibi patria* is the motto of all emigrants. What, then, is the American, this new man? He is neither an European nor the descendant of an European; hence that strange mixture of blood, which you will find in no other country. I could point out to you a family whose grandfather was an Englishman, whose wife was Dutch, whose son married a French woman, and whose present four sons have now four wives of different nations. *He* is an American, who, leaving behind him all his ancient prejudices and manners, receives new ones from the new mode of life he has embraced, the new government he obeys, and the new rank he holds. He becomes an American by being received in the broad lap of our great Alma Mater. Here individuals of all nations are melted into a new race of men, whose labours and posterity will one day cause great changes in the world. Americans are the western pilgrims who are carrying along with them that great mass of arts, sciences, vigour, and industry which began long since in the East; they will finish the great circle. The Americans were once scattered all over Europe; here they are incorporated into one of the finest systems of population which has ever appeared, and which will hereafter become distinct by the power of the different climates they inhabit. The American ought therefore to love this country much better than that wherein either he or his forefathers were born. Here the rewards of his industry follow with equal steps the progress of his labour; his labour is founded on the basis of nature, self-interest; can it want a stronger allurement? Wives and children, who before in vain demanded of him a morsel of bread, now, fat and frolicsome, gladly help their father to clear those fields whence exuberant crops are to arise to feed and to clothe them all, without any part being claimed, either by a despotic prince, a rich abbot, or a mighty lord. Here religion demands but little of him: a small voluntary salary to the minister and gratitude to God; can he refuse these? The American is a new man, who acts upon new principles; he must therefore entertain new ideas and form new opinions. From involuntary idleness, servile dependence, penury, and useless labour, he has passed to toils of a very different nature, rewarded by ample subsistence. This is an American.

British America is divided into many provinces, forming a large association scattered along a coast of 1,500 miles extent and about 200 wide. This society I would fain examine, at least such as it appears in the middle provinces; if it does not afford that variety of tinges and gradations which may be observed in Europe, we have colours peculiar to ourselves. For instance, it is natural to conceive that those who live near the sea must be very different from those who live in the woods; the intermediate space will afford a separate and distinct class.

Men are like plants; the goodness and flavour of the fruit proceeds from the peculiar soil and exposition in which they grow. We are nothing but what we derive from the air we breathe, the climate we inhabit, the government we obey, the system of religion we profess, and the nature of our employment. Here you will find but few crimes; these have acquired as yet no root among us. I wish I were able to trace all my ideas; if my ignorance prevents me from describing them properly, I hope I shall be able to delineate a few of the outlines, which is all I propose.

Those who live near the sea feed more on fish than on flesh and often encounter that boisterous element. This renders them more bold and enterprising; this leads them to neglect the confined occupations of the land. They see and converse with a variety of people; their intercourse with mankind becomes extensive. The sea inspires them with a love of traffic, a desire of transporting produce from one place to another, and leads them to a variety of resources which supply the place of labour. Those who inhabit the middle settlements, by far the most numerous, must be very different; the simple cultivation of the earth purifies them, but the indulgences of the government, the soft remonstrances of religion, the rank of independent freeholders, must necessarily inspire them with sentiments, very little known in Europe among a people of the same class. What do I say? Europe has no such class of men; the early knowledge they acquire, the early bargains they make, give them a great degree of sagacity. As freemen, they will be litigious; pride and obstinacy are often the cause of lawsuits; the nature of our laws and governments may be another. As citizens, it is easy to imagine that they will carefully read the newspapers, enter into every political disquisition, freely blame or censure governors and others. As farmers, they will be careful and anxious to get as much as they can, because what they get is their own. As northern men, they will love the cheerful cup. As Christians; religion curbs them not in their opinions; the general indulgence leaves every one to think for themselves in spiritual matters; the law inspects our actions; our thoughts are left to God. Industry, good living, selfishness, litigiousness, country politics, the pride of freemen, religious indifference, are their characteristics. If you recede still farther from the sea, you will come into more modern settlements; they exhibit the same strong lineaments, in a ruder appearance. Religion seems to have still less influence, and their manners are less improved.

Now we arrive near the great woods, near the last inhabited districts; there men seem to be placed still farther beyond the reach of government, which in some measure leaves them to themselves. How can it pervade every corner, as they were driven there by misfortunes, necessity of beginnings, desire of acquiring large tracks of land, idleness, frequent want of economy, ancient debts; the reunion of such people does not afford a very pleasing spectacle. When discord, want of unity and friendship, when either drunkenness or idleness prevail in such remote districts, contention, inactivity, and wretchedness must ensue. There are not the same remedies to these evils as in a long-established community. The few magistrates they have are in general little better than the rest; they are often in a perfect state of war; that of man against man, sometimes decided by blows, sometimes by means of the law; that of man against every wild inhabitant of these venerable woods, of which they are come to dispossess them. There men appear to be no better than carnivorous animals of a superior rank, living on the flesh of wild animals when they can catch them, and when they are not able, they subsist on grain. He who would wish to see America in its proper light and have a true idea of its feeble beginnings and barbarous rudiments must visit our extended line of frontiers, where the last settlers dwell and where he may see the first labours of settlement, the mode of clearing the earth, in all their different appearances, where men are wholly left dependent on their native tempers and on the spur of uncertain industry, which often fails when not sanctified by the efficacy of a few moral rules. There, remote from the power of example and check of shame, many families exhibit the most hideous parts of our society. They are a kind of forlorn hope, preceding by ten or twelve years the most respectable army of veterans which come after them. In that space, prosperity will polish some, vice and the law will drive off the rest, who, uniting again with others like themselves, will recede still farther, making room for more industrious people, who will finish their improvements, convert the log-house into a convenient habitation, and rejoicing that the first heavy labours are finished, will change in a few years that hitherto barbarous country into a fine, fertile, well-regulated district. Such is our progress; such is the march of the Europeans toward the interior parts of this continent. In all societies there are off-casts; this impure part serves as our precursors or pioneers; my father himself was one of that class, but he came upon honest principles and was therefore one of the few who held fast; by good conduct and temperance, he transmitted to me his fair inheritance, when not above one in fourteen of his contemporaries had the same good fortune.

Forty years ago, this smiling country was thus inhabited; it is now purged, a general decency of manners prevails throughout, and such has been the fate of our best countries.

Exclusive of those general characteristics, each province has its own, founded on the government, climate, mode of husbandry, customs, and peculiarity of circumstances. Europeans submit insensibly to these great powers and become, in the course of a few generations, not only Americans in general, but either Pennsylvanians, Virginians, or provincials under some other name. Whoever traverses the continent must easily observe those strong differences, which will grow more evident in time. The inhabitants of Canada, Massachusetts, the middle provinces, the southern ones, will be as different as their climates; their only points of unity will be those of religion and language.

As I have endeavoured to show you how Europeans become Americans, it may not be disagreeable to show you likewise how the various Christian sects introduced wear out and how religious indifference becomes prevalent. When any considerable number of a particular sect happen to dwell contiguous to each other, they immediately erect a temple and there worship the Divinity agreeably to their own peculiar ideas. Nobody disturbs them. If any new sect springs up in Europe, it may happen that many of its professors will come and settle in America. As they bring their zeal with them, they are at liberty to make proselytes if they can and to build a meeting and to follow the dictates of their consciences; for neither the government nor any other power interferes. If they are peaceable subjects and are industrious, what is it to their neighbours how and in what manner they think fit to address their prayers to the Supreme Being? But if the sectaries are not settled close together, if they are mixed with other denominations, their zeal will cool for want of fuel, and will be extinguished in a little time. Then, the Americans become as to religion what they are as to country, allied to all. In them the name of Englishman, Frenchman, and European is lost, and in like manner, the strict modes of Christianity as practised in Europe are lost also. This effect will extend itself still farther hereafter, and though this may appear to you as a strange idea, yet it is a very true one. I shall be able, perhaps, hereafter to explain myself better; in the meanwhile, let the following example serve as my first justification.

Let us suppose you and I to be travelling; we observe that in this house, to the right, lives a Catholic, who prays to God as he has been taught and believes in transsubstantiation; he works and raises wheat, he has a large family of children, all hale and robust; his belief, his prayers, offend nobody. About one mile farther on the same road, his next neighbour may be a good, honest, plodding German Lutheran, who addresses himself to the same God, the God of all, agreeably to the modes he has been educated in, and believes in consubstantiation; by so doing, he scandalizes nobody; he also works in his fields, embellishes the earth, clears swamps, etc. What has the world to do with his Lutheran principles? He persecutes nobody, and nobody persecutes him; he visits his neighbours, and his neighbours visit him. Next to him lives a seceder, the most enthusiastic of all sectaries; his zeal is hot and fiery, but separated as he is from others of the same complexion, he has no congregation of his own to resort to where he might cabal and mingle religious pride with worldly obstinacy. He likewise raises good crops, his house is handsomely painted, his orchard is one of the fairest in the neighbourhood. How does it concern the welfare of the country, or of the province at large, what this man's religious sentiments are, or really whether he has any at all? He is a good farmer, he is a sober, peaceable, good citizen; William Penn himself would not wish for more. This is the visible character; the invisible one is only guessed at, and is nobody's business. Next, again, lives a Low Dutchman, who implicitly believes the rules laid down by the synod of Dort. He conceives no other idea of a clergyman than that of an hired man; if he does his work well, he will pay him the stipulated sum; if not, he will dismiss him, and do without his sermons, and let his church be shut up for years. But notwithstanding this coarse idea, you will find his house and farm to be the neatest in all the country; and you will judge by his waggon and fat horses that he thinks more of the affairs of this world than of those of the next. He is sober and laborious; therefore, he is all he ought to be as to the affairs of this life. As for those of the next, he must trust to the great Creator. Each of these people instruct their children as well as they can, but these instructions are feeble compared to those which are given to the youth of the poorest class in Europe. Their children will therefore grow up less zealous and more indifferent in matters of religion than their parents. The foolish vanity or, rather, the fury of making proselytes is unknown here; they have no time, the seasons call for all their attention, and thus in a few years this mixed neighbourhood will exhibit a strange religious medley that will be neither pure Catholicism nor pure Calvinism. A very perceptible indifference, even in the first generation, will become apparent; and it may happen that the daughter of the Catholic will marry the son of the seceder and settle by themselves at a distance from their parents. What religious education will they give their children? A very imperfect one. If there happens to be in the neighbourhood any place of worship, we will suppose a

Quaker's meeting; rather than not show their fine clothes, they will go to it, and some of them may perhaps attach themselves to that society. Others will remain in a perfect state of indifference; the children of these zealous parents will not be able to tell what their religious principles are, and their grandchildren still less. The neighbourhood of a place of worship generally leads them to it, and the action of going thither is the strongest evidence they can give of their attachment to any sect. The Quakers are the only people who retain a fondness for their own mode of worship; for be they ever so far separated from each other, they hold a sort of communion with the society and seldom depart from its rules, at least in this country. Thus all sects are mixed, as well as all nations; thus religious indifference is imperceptibly disseminated from one end of the continent to the other, which is at present one of the strongest characteristics of the Americans. Where this will reach no one can tell; perhaps it may leave a vacuum fit to receive other systems. Persecution, religious pride, the love of contradiction, are the food of what the world commonly calls religion. These motives have ceased here; zeal in Europe is confined; here it evaporates in the great distance it has to travel; there it is a grain of powder inclosed; here it burns away in the open air and consumes without effect.

But to return to our back settlers. I must tell you that there is something in the proximity of the woods which is very singular. It is with men as it is with the plants and animals that grow and live in the forests; they are entirely different from those that live in the plains. I will candidly tell you all my thoughts, but you are not to expect that I shall advance any reasons. By living in or near the woods, their actions are regulated by the wildness of the neighbourhood. The deer often come to eat their grain, the wolves to destroy their sheep, the bears to kill their hogs, the foxes to catch their poultry. This surrounding hostility immediately puts the gun into their hands; they watch these animals, they kill some; and thus by defending their property, they soon become professed hunters; this is the progress; once hunters, farewell to the plough. The chase renders them ferocious, gloomy, and unsocial; a hunter wants no neighbour, he rather hates them because he dreads the competition. In a little time, their success in the woods makes them neglect their tillage. They trust to the natural fecundity of the earth and therefore do little; carelessness in fencing often exposes what little they sow to destruction; they are not at home to watch; in order, therefore, to make up the deficiency, they go oftener to the woods. That new mode of life brings along with it a new set of manners, which I cannot easily describe. These new manners being grafted on the old stock produce a strange sort of lawless profligacy, the impressions of which are indelible. The manners of the Indian natives are respectable compared with this European medley. Their wives and children live in sloth and inactivity; and having no proper pursuits, you may judge what education the latter receive. Their tender minds have nothing else to contemplate but the example of their parents; like them, they grow up a mongrel breed, half civilized, half savage, except nature stamps on them some constitutional propensities. That rich, that voluptuous sentiment is gone that struck them so forcibly; the possession of their freeholds no longer conveys to their minds the same pleasure and pride. To all these reasons you must add their lonely situation, and you cannot imagine what an effect on manners the great distances they live from each other has! Consider one of the last settlements in its first view: of what is it composed? Europeans who have not that sufficient share of knowledge they ought to have in order to prosper; people who have suddenly passed from oppression, dread of government, and fear of laws into the unlimited freedom of the woods. This sudden change must have a very great effect on most men, and on that

class particularly. Eating of wild meat, whatever you may think, tends to alter their temper, though all the proof I can adduce is that I have seen it, and having no place of worship to resort to, what little society this might afford is denied them. The Sunday meetings, exclusive of religious benefits, were the only social bonds that might have inspired them with some degree of emulation in neatness. Is it, then, surprising to see men thus situated, immersed in great and heavy labours, degenerate a little? It is rather a wonder the effect is not more diffusive. The Moravians and the Quakers are the only instances in exception to what I have advanced. The first never settle singly; it is a colony of the society which emigrates; they carry with them their forms, worship, rules, and decency. The others never begin so hard; they are always able to buy improvements, in which there is a great advantage, for by that time the country is recovered from its first barbarity. Thus our bad people are those who are half cultivators and half hunters; and the worst of them are those who have degenerated altogether into the hunting state. As old ploughmen and new men of the woods, as Europeans and new-made Indians, they contract the vices of both; they adopt the moroseness and ferocity of a native, without his mildness or even his industry at home. If manners are not refined, at least they are rendered simple and inoffensive by tilling the earth. All our wants are supplied by it; our time is divided between labour and rest, and leaves none for the commission of great misdeeds. As hunters, it is divided between the toil of the chase, the idleness of repose, or the indulgence of inebriation. Hunting is but a licentious idle life, and if it does not always pervert good dispositions, yet, when it is united with bad luck, it leads to want: want stimulates that propensity to rapacity and injustice, too natural to needy men, which is the fatal gradation. After this explanation of the effects which follow by living in the woods, shall we yet vainly flatter ourselves with the hope of converting the Indians? We should rather begin with converting our back-settlers; and now if I dare mention the name of religion, its sweet accents would be lost in the immensity of these woods. Men thus placed are not fit either to receive or remember its mild instructions; they want temples and ministers, but as soon as men cease to remain at home and begin to lead an erratic life, let them be either tawny or white, they cease to be its disciples.

Thus have I faintly and imperfectly endeavoured to trace our society from the sea to our woods! Yet you must not imagine that every person who moves back acts upon the same principles or falls into the same degeneracy. Many families carry with them all their decency of conduct, purity of morals, and respect of religion, but these are scarce; the power of example is sometimes irresistible. Even among these back-settlers, their depravity is greater or less according to what nation or province they belong. Were I to adduce proofs of this, I might be accused of partiality. If there happens to be some rich intervals, some fertile bottoms, in those remote districts, the people will there prefer tilling the land to hunting and will attach themselves to it; but even on these fertile spots you may plainly perceive the inhabitants to acquire a great degree of rusticity and selfishness.

It is in consequence of this straggling situation and the astonishing power it has on manners that the back-settlers of both the Carolinas, Virginia, and many other parts have been long a set of lawless people; it has been even dangerous to travel among them. Government can do nothing in so extensive a country; better it should wink at these irregularities than that it should use means inconsistent with its usual mildness. Time will efface those stains: in proportion as the great body of population approaches them they will reform and become polished and subordinate. Whatever has been said of the four New England provinces, no such degeneracy of manners has

ever tarnished their annals; their back-settlers have been kept within the bounds of decency, and government, by means of wise laws, and by the influence of religion. What a detestable idea such people must have given to the natives of the Europeans! They trade with them; the worst of people are permitted to do that which none but persons of the best characters should be employed in. They get drunk with them and often defraud the Indians. Their avarice, removed from the eyes of their superiors, knows no bounds; and aided by a little superiority of knowledge, these traders deceive them and even sometimes shed blood. Hence those shocking violations, those sudden devastations which have so often stained our frontiers, when hundreds of innocent people have been sacrificed for the crimes of a few. It was in consequence of such behaviour that the Indians took the hatchet against the Virginians in 1774. Thus are our first steps trodden, thus are our first trees felled, in general, by the most vicious of our people; and thus the path is opened for the arrival of a second and better class, the true American freeholders, the most respectable set of people in this part of the world: respectable for their industry, their happy independence, the great share of freedom they possess, the good regulation of their families, and for extending the trade and the dominion of our mother country.

LETTER XII

Distresses of a Frontier Man

I wish for a change of place; the hour is come at last that I must fly from my house and abandon my farm! But what course shall I steer, inclosed as I am? The climate best adapted to my present situation and humour would be the polar regions, where six months' day and six months' night divide the dull year; nay, a simple aurora borealis would suffice me and greatly refresh my eyes, fatigued now by so many disagreeable objects. The severity of those climates, that great gloom where melancholy dwells, would be perfectly analogous to the turn of my mind. Oh, could I remove my plantation to the shores of the Obi, willingly would I dwell in the hut of a Samoyed; with cheerfulness would I go and bury myself in the cavern of a Laplander. Could I but carry my family along with me, I would winter at Pello, or Tobolsk, in order to enjoy the peace and innocence of that country. But let me arrive under the pole, or reach the antipodes, I never can leave behind me the remembrance of the dreadful scenes to which I have been witness; therefore, never can I be happy! Happy—why would I mention that sweet, that enchanting word? Once happiness was our portion; now it is gone from us, and I am afraid not to be enjoyed again by the present generation! Whichever way I look, nothing but the most frightful precipices present themselves to my view, in which hundreds of my friends and acquaintances have already perished; of all animals that live on the surface of this planet, what is man when no longer connected with society, or when he finds himself surrounded by a convulsed and a half-dissolved one? He cannot live in solitude; he must belong to some

community bound by some ties, however imperfect. Men mutually support and add to the boldness and confidence of each other; the weakness of each is strengthened by the force of the whole. I had never before these calamitous times formed any such ideas; I lived on, laboured and prospered, without having ever studied on what the security of my life and the foundation of my prosperity were established; I perceived them just as they left me. Never was a situation so singularly terrible as mine, in every possible respect, as a member of an extensive society, as a citizen of an inferior division of the same society, as a husband, as a father, as a man who exquisitely feels for the miseries of others as well as for his own! But alas! So much is everything now subverted among us that the very word *misery*, with which we were hardly acquainted before, no longer conveys the same ideas, or, rather, tired with feeling for the miseries of others, every one feels now for himself alone. When I consider myself as connected in all these characters, as bound by so many cords, all uniting in my heart, I am seized with a fever of the mind, I am transported beyond that degree of calmness which is necessary to delineate our thoughts. I feel as if my reason wanted to leave me, as if it would burst its poor weak tenement; again, I try to compose myself, I grow cool, and preconceiving the dreadful loss, I endeavour to retain the useful guest.

You know the position of our settlement; I need not therefore describe it. To the west it is inclosed by a chain of mountains, reaching to ———; to the east, the country is as yet but thinly inhabited; we are almost insulated, and the houses are at a considerable distance from each other. From the mountains we have but too much reason to expect our dreadful enemy; the wilderness is a harbour where it is impossible to find them. It is a door through which they can enter our country whenever they please; and, as they seem determined to destroy the whole chain of frontiers, our fate cannot be far distant: from Lake Champlain, almost all has been conflagrated one after another. What renders these incursions still more terrible is that they most commonly take place in the dead of the night; we never go to our fields but we are seized with an involuntary fear, which lessens our strength and weakens our labour. No other subject of conversation intervenes between the different accounts, which spread through the country, of successive acts of devastation, and these, told in chimney-corners, swell themselves in our affrighted imaginations into the most terrific ideas! We never sit down either to dinner or supper but the least noise immediately spreads a general alarm and prevents us from enjoying the comfort of our meals. The very appetite proceeding from labour and peace of mind is gone; we eat just enough to keep us alive; our sleep is disturbed by the most frightful dreams; sometimes I start awake, as if the great hour of danger was come; at other times the howling of our dogs seems to announce the arrival of our enemy; we leap out of bed and run to arms; my poor wife, with panting bosom and silent tears, takes leave of me, as if we were to see each other no more; she snatches the youngest children from their beds, who, suddenly awakened, increase by their innocent questions the horror of the dreadful moment. She tries to hide them in the cellar, as if our cellar was inaccessible to the fire. I place all my servants at the windows and myself at the door, where I am determined to perish. Fear industriously increases every sound; we all listen; each communicates to the other his ideas and conjectures. We remain thus sometimes for whole hours, our hearts and our minds racked by the most anxious suspense: what a dreadful situation, a thousand times worse than that of a soldier engaged in the midst of the most severe conflict! Sometimes feeling the spontaneous courage of a man, I seem to wish for the decisive minute; the next instant a message from my wife, sent by one of the children, puzzling me beside with their little questions, unmans me; away goes my courage, and

I descend again into the deepest despondency. At last, finding that it was a false alarm, we return once more to our beds; but what good can the kind of sleep of Nature do to us when interrupted by such scenes! Securely placed as you are, you can have no idea of our agitations, but by hearsay; no relation can be equal to what we suffer and to what we feel. Every morning my youngest children are sure to have frightful dreams to relate; in vain I exert my authority to keep them silent; it is not in my power; and these images of their disturbed imagination, instead of being frivolously looked upon as in the days of our happiness, are on the contrary considered as warnings and sure prognostics of our future fate. I am not a superstitious man, but since our misfortunes, I am grown more timid and less disposed to treat the doctrine of omens with contempt.

Though these evils have been gradual, yet they do not become habitual like other incidental evils. The nearer I view the end of this catastrophe, the more I shudder. But why should I trouble you with such unconnected accounts; men secure and out of danger are soon fatigued with mournful details: can you enter with me into fellowship with all these afflictive sensations; have you a tear ready to shed over the approaching ruin of a once opulent and substantial family? Read this, I pray, with the eyes of sympathy, with a tender sorrow; pity the lot of those whom you once called your friends, who were once surrounded with plenty, ease, and perfect security, but who now expect every night to be their last, and who are as wretched as criminals under an impending sentence of the law.

As a member of a large society which extends to many parts of the world, my connexion with it is too distant to be as strong as that which binds me to the inferior division in the midst of which I live. I am told that the great nation of which we are a part is just, wise, and free beyond any other on earth, within its own insular boundaries, but not always so to its distant conquests; I shall not repeat all I have heard because I cannot believe half of it. As a citizen of a smaller society, I find that any kind of opposition to its now prevailing sentiments immediately begets hatred; how easily do men pass from loving to hating and cursing one another! I am a lover of peace; what must I do? I am divided between the respect I feel for the ancient connexion and the fear of innovations, with the consequence of which I am not well acquainted, as they are embraced by my own countrymen. I am conscious that I was happy before this unfortunate revolution. I feel that I am no longer so; therefore I regret the change. This is the only mode of reasoning adapted to persons in my situation. If I attach myself to the mother country, which is 3,000 miles from me, I become what is called an enemy to my own region; if I follow the rest of my countrymen, I become opposed to our ancient masters: both extremes appear equally dangerous to a person of so little weight and consequence as I am, whose energy and example are of no avail. As to the argument on which the dispute is founded, I know little about it. Much has been said and written on both sides, but who has a judgement capacious and clear enough to decide? The great moving principles which actuate both parties are much hid from vulgar eyes, like mine; nothing but the plausible and the probable are offered to our contemplation. The innocent class are always the victims of the few; they are in all countries and at all times the inferior agents on which the popular phantom is erected; they clamour and must toil and bleed, and are always sure of meeting with oppression and rebuke. It is for the sake of the great leaders on both sides that so much blood must be spilt; that of the people is counted as nothing. Great events are not achieved for us, though it is *by* us that they are principally accomplished, by the arms, the sweat, the lives of the people. Books tell me so much that they inform me of nothing. Sophistry, the bane of freemen, launches forth in all her deceiving attire! After all, most men reason from passions; and shall such an ignorant individual as I am decide and say this side is right, that side is wrong? Sentiment and feeling are the only guides I know. Alas, how should I unravel an argument in which Reason herself has given way to brutality and bloodshed! What then must I do? I ask the wisest lawyers, the ablest casuists, the warmest patriots; for I mean honestly. Great Source of wisdom! Inspire me with light sufficient to guide my benighted steps out of this intricate maze! Shall I discard all my ancient principles, shall I renounce that name, that nation which I held once so respectable? I feel the powerful attraction; the sentiments they inspired grew with my earliest knowledge and were grafted upon the first rudiments of my education. On the other hand, shall I arm myself against that country where I first drew breath, against the playmates of my youth, my bosom friends, my acquaintance? The idea makes me shudder! Must I be called a parricide, a traitor, a villain, lose the esteem of all those whom I love to preserve my own, be shunned like a rattlesnake, or be pointed at like a bear? I have neither heroism not magnanimity enough to make so great a sacrifice. Here I am tied, I am fastened by numerous strings, nor do I repine at the pressure they cause; ignorant as I am, I can pervade the utmost extent of the calamities which have already overtaken our poor afflicted country. I can see the great and accumulated ruin yet extending itself as far as the theatre of war has reached; I hear the groans of thousands of families now ruined and desolated by our aggressors. I cannot count the multitude of orphans this war has made nor ascertain the immensity of blood we have lost. Some have asked whether it was a crime to resist, to repel some parts of this evil. Others have asserted that a resistance so general makes pardon unattainable and repentance useless, and dividing the crime among so many renders it imperceptible. What one party calls meritorious, the other denominates flagitious. These opinions vary, contract, or expand, like the events of the war on which they are founded. What can an insignificant man do in the midst of these jarring contradictory parties, equally hostile to persons situated as I am? And after all, who will be the really guilty? Those most certainly who fail of success. Our fate, the fate of thousands, is, then, necessarily involved in the dark wheel of fortune. Why, then, so many useless reasonings; we are the sport of fate. Farewell education, principles, love of our country, farewell; all are become useless to the generality of us: he who governs himself according to what he calls his principles may be punished either by one party or the other for those very principles. He who proceeds without principle, as chance, timidity, or self-preservation directs, will not perhaps fare better, but he will be less blamed. What are *we* in the great scale of events, we poor defenceless frontier inhabitants? What is it to the gazing world whether we breathe or whether we die? Whatever virtue, whatever merit and disinterestedness we may exhibit in our secluded retreats, of what avail? We are like the pismires destroyed by the plough, whose destruction prevents not the future crop. Self-preservation, therefore, the rule of Nature, seems to be the best rule of conduct; what good can we do by vain resistance, by useless efforts? The cool, the distant spectator, placed in safety, may arraign me for ingratitude, may bring forth the principles of Solon or Montesquieu; he may look on me as wilfully guilty; he may call me by the most opprobrious names. Secure from personal danger, his warm imagination, undisturbed by the least agitation of the heart, will expatiate freely on this grand question and will consider this extended field but as exhibiting the double scene of attack and defence. To him the object becomes abstracted; the intermediate glares; the perspective distance and a variety of opinions, unimpaired by affections, present to his mind but one set of ideas. Here he proclaims the high guilt of the one, and there the right of the other. But let him come and re-side with us one single month; let him pass with us through all the successive hours of necessary toil, terror, and affright; let him watch with us, his musket in his hand, through tedious, sleepless nights, his imagination furrowed by the keen chisel of every passion; let his wife and his children become exposed to the most dreadful hazards of death; let the existence of his property depend on a single spark, blown by the breath of an enemy; let him tremble with us in our fields, shudder at the rustling of every leaf; let his heart, the seat of the most affecting passions, be powerfully wrung by hear-ing the melancholy end of his relations and friends; let him trace on the map the progress of these desolations; let his alarmed imagination predict to him the night, the dreadful night when it may be his turn to perish, as so many have perished before. Observe, then, whether the man will not get the better of the citizen, whether his po-litical maxims will not vanish! Yes, he will cease to glow so warmly with the glory of the metropolis; all his wishes will be turned toward the preservation of his family! Oh, were he situated where I am, were his house perpetually filled, as mine is, with mis-erable victims just escaped from the flames and the scalping knife, telling of barbari-ties and murders that make human nature tremble, his situation would suspend every political reflection and expel every abstract idea. My heart is full and involuntarily takes hold of any notion from whence it can receive ideal ease or relief. I am informed that the king has the most numerous, as well as the fairest, progeny of children of any potentate now in the world; he may be a great king, but he must feel as we common mortals do in the good wishes he forms for their lives and prosperity. His mind no doubt often springs forward on the wings of anticipation and contemplates us as hap-pily settled in the world. If a poor frontier inhabitant may be allowed to suppose this great personage the first in our system to be exposed but for one hour to the exqui-site pangs we so often feel, would not the preservation of so numerous a family en-gross all his thoughts; would not the ideas of dominion and other felicities attendant on royalty all vanish in the hour of danger? The regal character, however sacred, would be superseded by the stronger, because more natural one of man and father. Oh! Did he but know the circumstances of this horrid war, I am sure he would put a stop to that long destruction of parents and children. I am sure that while he turned his ears to state policy, he would attentively listen also to the dictates of Nature, that great par-ent; for, as a good king, he no doubt wishes to create, to spare, and to protect, as she does. Must I then, in order to be called a faithful subject, coolly and philosophically say it is necessary for the good of Britain that my children's brains should be dashed against the walls of the house in which they were reared; that my wife should be stabbed and scalped before my face; that I should be either murthered or captivated; or that for greater expedition we should all be locked up and burnt to ashes as the family of the B———n was? Must I with meekness wait for that last pitch of deso-lation and receive with perfect resignation so hard a fate from ruffians acting at such a distance from the eyes of any superior, monsters left to the wild impulses of the wildest nature? Could the lions of Africa be transported here and let loose, they would no doubt kill us in order to prey upon our carcasses! But their appetites would not require so many victims. Shall I wait to be punished with death, or else to be stripped of all food and raiment, reduced to despair without redress and without hope? Shall those who may escape see everything they hold dear destroyed and gone? Shall those few survivors, lurking in some obscure corner, deplore in vain the fate of their fami-lies, mourn over parents either captivated, butchered, or burnt; roam among our wilds and wait for death at the foot of some tree, without a murmur or without a sigh, for

the good of the cause? No, it is impossible! So astonishing a sacrifice is not to be expected from human nature; it must belong to beings of an inferior or superior order,
actuated by less or by more refined principles. Even those great personages who are
so far elevated above the common ranks of men, those, I mean, who wield and direct
so many thunders, those who have let loose against us these demons of war, could they
be transported here and metamorphosed into simple planters as we are—they would,
from being the arbiters of human destiny, sink into miserable victims; they would feel
and exclaim as we do, and be as much at a loss what line of conduct to prosecute. Do
you well comprehend the difficulties of our situation? If we stay we are sure to perish at one time or another; no vigilance on our part can save us; if we retire, we know
not where to go; every house is filled with refugees as wretched as ourselves; and if
we remove, we become beggars. The property of farmers is not like that of merchants,
and absolute poverty is worse than death. If we take up arms to defend ourselves, we
are denominated rebels; should we not be rebels against Nature, could we be shame-
fully passive? Shall we, then, like martyrs, glory in an allegiance now become useless,
and voluntarily expose ourselves to a species of desolation which, though it ruin us
entirely, yet enriches not our ancient masters. By this inflexible and sullen attachment,
we shall be despised by our countrymen and destroyed by our ancient friends; whatever we may say, whatever merit we may claim, will not shelter us from those indiscriminate blows, given by hired banditti, animated by all those passions which urge
men to shed the blood of others; how bitter the thought! On the contrary, blows received by the hands of those from whom we expected protection extinguish ancient
respect and urge us to self-defence—perhaps to revenge; this is the path which Nature herself points out, as well to the civilized as to the uncivilized. The Creator of
hearts has himself stamped on them those propensities at their first formation; and
must we then daily receive this treatment from a power once so loved? The fox flies
or deceives the hounds that pursue him; the bear, when overtaken, boldly resists and
attacks them; the hen, the very timid hen, fights for the preservation of her chicken,
nor does she decline to attack and to meet on the wing even the swift kite. Shall man,
then, provided both with instinct and reason, unmoved, unconcerned, and passive see
his subsistence consumed and his progeny either ravished from him or murdered?
Shall fictitious reason extinguish the unerring impulse of instinct? No; my former respect, my former attachment, vanishes with my safety; that respect and attachment
were purchased by protection, and it has ceased. Could not the great nation we belong to have accomplished her designs by means of her numerous armies, by means
of those fleets which cover the ocean? Must those who are masters of two thirds of
the trade of the world, who have in their hands the power which almighty gold can
give, who possess a species of wealth that increases with their desires—must they establish their conquest with our insignificant, innocent blood!

    Must I, then, bid farewell to Britain, to that renowned country? Must I renounce
a name so ancient and so venerable? Alas, she herself, that once indulgent parent,
forces me to take up arms against her. She herself first inspired the most unhappy citizens of our remote districts with the thoughts of shedding the blood of those whom
they used to call by the name of friends and brethren. That great nation which now
convulses the world, which hardly knows the extent of her Indian kingdoms, which
looks toward the universal monarchy of trade, of industry, of riches, of power: why
must she strew our poor frontiers with the carcasses of her friends, with the wrecks
of our insignificant villages, in which there is no gold? When, oppressed by painful
recollection, I revolve all these scattered ideas in my mind, when I contemplate my

situation and the thousand streams of evil with which I am surrounded, when I descend into the particular tendency even of the remedy I have proposed, I am convulsed—convulsed sometimes to that degree as to be tempted to exclaim, "Why has the Master of the world permitted so much indiscriminate evil throughout every part of this poor planet, at all times, and among all kinds of people?" It ought surely to be the punishment of the wicked only. I bring that cup to my lips, of which I must soon taste, and shudder at its bitterness. What, then, is life, I ask myself; is it a gracious gift? No, it is too bitter; a gift means something valuable conferred, but life appears to be a mere accident, and of the worst kind: we are born to be victims of diseases and passions, of mischances and death; better not to be than to be miserable. Thus, impiously I roam, I fly from one erratic thought to another, and my mind, irritated by these acrimonious reflections, is ready sometimes to lead me to dangerous extremes of violence. When I recollect that I am a father and a husband, the return of these endearing ideas strikes deep into my heart. Alas! They once made it glow with pleasure and with every ravishing exultation; but now they fill it with sorrow. At other times, my wife industriously rouses me out of these dreadful meditations and soothes me by all the reasoning she is mistress of; but her endeavours only serve to make me more miserable by reflecting that she must share with me all these calamities the bare apprehensions of which I am afraid will subvert her reason. Nor can I with patience think that a beloved wife, my faithful helpmate, throughout all my rural schemes the principal hand which has assisted me in rearing the prosperous fabric of ease and independence I lately possessed, as well as my children, those tenants of my heart, should daily and nightly be exposed to such a cruel fate. Self-preservation is above all political precepts and rules, and even superior to the dearest opinions of our minds; a reasonable accommodation of ourselves to the various exigencies of the times in which we live is the most irresistible precept. To this great evil I must seek some sort of remedy adapted to remove or to palliate it; situated as I am, what steps should I take that will neither injure nor insult any of the parties, and at the same time save my family from that certain destruction which awaits it if I remain here much longer. Could I ensure them bread, safety, and subsistence, not the bread of idleness, but that earned by proper labour as heretofore; could this be accomplished by the sacrifice of my life, I would willingly give it up. I attest before heaven that it is only for these I would wish to live and toil, for these whom I have brought into this miserable existence. I resemble, me-thinks, one of the stones of a ruined arch, still retaining that pristine form which anciently fitted the place I occupied, but the centre is tumbled down; I can be nothing until I am replaced, either in the former circle or in some stronger one. I see one on a smaller scale, and at a considerable distance, but it is within my power to reach it; and since I have ceased to consider myself as a member of the ancient state now convulsed, I willingly descend into an inferior one. I will revert into a state approaching nearer to that of nature, unencumbered either with voluminous laws or contradictory codes, often galling the very necks of those whom they protect, and at the same time sufficiently remote from the brutality of unconnected savage nature. Do you, my friend, perceive the path I have found out? It is that which leads to the tenants of the great ———— village of ————, where, far removed from the accursed neighbourhood of Europeans, its inhabitants live with more ease, decency, and peace than you imagine; who, though governed by no laws, yet find in uncontaminated simple manners all that laws can afford. Their system is sufficiently complete to answer all the primary wants of man and to constitute him a social being such as he ought to be in the great forest of Nature. There it is that I have resolved at any rate to transport

myself and family: an eccentric thought, you may say, thus to cut asunder all former connexions and to form new ones with a people whom Nature has stamped with such different characteristics! But as the happiness of my family is the only object of my wishes, I care very little where we are or where we go, provided that we are safe and all united together. Our new calamities, being shared equally by all, will become lighter; our mutual affection for each other will in this great transmutation become the strongest link of our new society, will afford us every joy we can receive on a foreign soil, and preserve us in unity as the gravity and coherency of matter prevent the world from dissolution. Blame me not; it would be cruel in you, it would beside be entirely useless; for when you receive this, we shall be on the wing. When we think all hopes are gone, must we, like poor pusillanimous wretches, despair and die? No; I perceive before me a few resources, though through many dangers, which I will explain to you hereafter. It is not, believe me, a disappointed ambition which leads me to take this step; it is the bitterness of my situation, it is the impossibility of knowing what better measure to adopt: my education fitted me for nothing more than the most simple occupations of life; I am but a feller of trees, a cultivator of lands, the most honourable title an American can have. I have no exploits, no discoveries, no inventions to boast of; I have cleared about 370 acres of land, some for the plough, some for the scythe, and this has occupied many years of my life. I have never possessed or wish to possess anything more than what could be earned or produced by the united industry of my family. I wanted nothing more than to live at home independent and tranquil and to teach my children how to provide the means of a future ample subsistence, founded on labour, like that of their father. This is the career of life I have pursued and that which I had marked out for them and for which they seemed to be so well calculated by their inclinations and by their constitutions. But now these pleasing expectations are gone; we must abandon the accumulated industry of nineteen years; we must fly we hardly know whither, through the most impervious paths, and become members of a new and strange community. Oh, virtue! Is this all the reward thou hast to confer on thy votaries? Either thou art only a chimera, or thou art a timid, useless being; soon affrighted, when ambition, thy great adversary, dictates, when war re-echoes the dreadful sounds and poor helpless individuals are mowed down by its cruel reapers like useless grass. I have at all times generously relieved what few distressed people I have met with; I have encouraged the industrious; my house has always been opened to travellers; I have not lost a month in illness since I have been a man; I have caused upwards of a hundred and twenty families to remove hither. Many of them I have led by the hand in the days of their first trial; distant as I am from any places of worship or school of education, I have been the pastor of my family and the teacher of many of my neighbours. I have learnt them as well as I could the gratitude they owe to God, the Father of harvests, and their duties to man; I have been an useful subject, ever obedient to the laws, ever vigilant to see them respected and observed. My wife hath faithfully followed the same line within her province; no woman was ever a better economist or spun or wove better linen; yet we must perish, perish like wild beasts, included within a ring of fire!

Yes, I will cheerfully embrace that resource; it is a holy inspiration; by night and by day, it presents itself to my mind; I have carefully revolved the scheme; I have considered in all its future effects and tendencies the new mode of living we must pursue, without salt, without spices, without linen, and with little other clothing; the art of hunting we must acquire, the new manners we must adopt, the new language we must speak; the dangers attending the education of my children we must endure.

These changes may appear more terrific at a distance perhaps than when grown familiar by practice; what is it to us whether we eat well-made pastry or pounded àla-grichés, well-roasted beef or smoked venison, cabbages or squashes? Whether we wear neat homespun or good beaver, whether we sleep on feather-beds or on bearskins? The difference is not worth attending to. The difficulty of the language, the fear of some great intoxication among the Indians, finally the apprehension lest my younger children should be caught by that singular charm, so dangerous at their tender years, are the only considerations that startle me. By what power does it come to pass that children who have been adopted when young among these people can never be prevailed on to readopt European manners? Many an anxious parent have I seen last war who at the return of the peace went to the Indian villages where they knew their children had been carried in captivity, when to their inexpressible sorrow they found them so perfectly Indianized that many knew them no longer, and those whose more advanced ages permitted them to recollect their fathers and mothers absolutely refused to follow them and ran to their adoptive parents for protection against the effusions of love their unhappy real parents lavished on them! Incredible as this may appear, I have heard it asserted in a thousand instances, among persons of credit. In the village of ———, where I purpose to go, there lived, about fifteen years ago, an Englishman and a Swede, whose history would appear moving had I time to relate it. They were grown to the age of men when they were taken; they happily escaped the great punishment of war captives and were obliged to marry the squaws who had saved their lives by adoption. By the force of habit, they became at last thoroughly naturalized to this wild course of life. While I was there, their friends sent them a considerable sum of money to ransom themselves with. The Indians, their old masters, gave them their choice, and without requiring any consideration, told them that they had been long as free as themselves. They chose to remain, and the reasons they gave me would greatly surprise you: the most perfect freedom, the ease of living, the absence of those cares and corroding solicitudes which so often prevail with us, the peculiar goodness of the soil they cultivated, for they did not trust altogether to hunting—all these and many more motives which I have forgot made them prefer that life of which we entertain such dreadful opinions. It cannot be, therefore, so bad as we generally conceive it to be; there must be in their social bond something singularly captivating and far superior to anything to be boasted of among us; for thousands of Europeans are Indians, and we have no examples of even one of those aborigines having from choice become Europeans! There must be something more congenial to our native dispositions than the fictitious society in which we live; or else why should children, and even grown persons, become in a short time so invincibly attached to it? There must be something very bewitching in their manners, something very indelible and marked by the very hands of Nature. For, take a young Indian lad, give him the best education you possibly can, load him with your bounty, with presents, nay with riches, yet he would secretly long for his native woods, which you would imagine he must have long since forgot; and on the first opportunity he can possibly find, you will see him voluntarily leave behind all you have given him and return with inexpressible joy to lie on the mats of his fathers. Mr. ——— some years ago received from a good old Indian, who died in his house, a young lad of nine years of age, his grandson. He kindly educated him with his children and bestowed on him the same care and attention in respect to the memory of his venerable grandfather, who was a worthy man. He intended to give him a genteel trade, but in the spring season when all the family went to the woods to make their maple sugar, he suddenly disappeared,

and it was not until seventeen months after that his benefactor heard he had reached the village of Bald Eagle, where he still dwelt. Let us say what we will of them, of their inferior organs, of their want of bread, etc., they are as stout and well made as the Europeans. Without temples, without priests, without kings, and without laws, they are in many instances superior to us; and the proofs of what I advance are that they live without care, sleep without inquietude, take life as it comes, bearing all its asperities with unparalleled patience, and die without any kind of apprehension for what they have done or for what they expect to meet with hereafter. What system of philosophy can give us so many necessary qualifications for happiness? They most certainly are much more closely connected with Nature than we are; they are her immediate children: the inhabitants of the woods are her undefiled offspring; those of the plains are her degenerated breed, far, very far removed from her primitive laws, from her original design. It is therefore resolved on. I will either die in the attempt or succeed; better perish all together in one fatal hour than to suffer what we daily endure. I do not expect to enjoy in the village of ———— an uninterrupted happiness; it cannot be our lot, let us live where we will; I am not founding my future prosperity on golden dreams. Place mankind where you will, they must always have adverse circumstances to struggle with; from nature, accidents, constitution; from seasons, from that great combination of mischances which perpetually leads us to diseases, to poverty, etc. Who knows but I may meet in this new situation some accident whence may spring up new sources of unexpected prosperity? Who can be presumptuous enough to predict all the good? Who can foresee all the evils which strew the paths of our lives? But after all, I cannot but recollect what sacrifice I am going to make, what amputation I am going to suffer, what transition I am going to experience. Pardon my repetitions, my wild, my trifling reflections; they proceed from the agitations of my mind and the fulness of my heart; the action of thus retracing them seems to lighten the burthen and to exhilarate my spirits; this is, besides, the last letter you will receive from me; I would fain tell you all, though I hardly know how. Oh! In the hours, in the moments of my greatest anguish, could I intuitively represent to you that variety of thought which crowds on my mind, you would have reason to be surprised and to doubt of their possibility. Shall we ever meet again? If we should, where will it be? On the wild shores of ————. If it be my doom to end my days there, I will greatly improve them and perhaps make room for a few more families who will choose to retire from the fury of a storm, the agitated billows of which will yet roar for many years on our extended shores. Perhaps I may repossess my house, if it be not burnt down; but how will my improvements look? Why, half defaced, bearing the strong marks of abandonment and of the ravages of war. However, at present I give everything over for lost; I will bid a long farewell to what I leave behind. If ever I repossess it, I shall receive it as a gift, as a reward for my conduct and fortitude. Do not imagine, however, that I am a stoic—by no means: I must, on the contrary, confess to you that I feel the keenest regret at abandoning a house which I have in some measure reared with my own hands. Yes, perhaps I may never revisit those fields which I have cleared, those trees which I have planted, those meadows which, in my youth, were a hideous wilderness, now converted by my industry into rich pastures and pleasant lawns. If in Europe it is praiseworthy to be attached to paternal inheritances, how much more natural, how much more powerful must the tie be with us, who, if I may be permitted the expression, are the founders, the creators, of our own farms! When I see my table surrounded with my blooming offspring, all united in the bonds of the strongest affection, it kindles in my paternal heart a variety of tumultuous sen-

timents which none but a father and a husband in my situation can feel or describe. Perhaps I may see my wife, my children, often distressed, involuntarily recalling to their minds the ease and abundance which they enjoyed under the paternal roof. Perhaps I may see them want that bread which I now leave behind, overtaken by diseases and penury, rendered more bitter by the recollection of former days of opulence and plenty. Perhaps I may be assailed on every side by unforeseen accidents which I shall not be able to prevent or to alleviate. Can I contemplate such images without the most unutterable emotions? My fate is determined; but I have not determined it, you may assure yourself, without having undergone the most painful conflicts of a variety of passions—interest, love of ease, disappointed views, and pleasing expectations frustrated—I shuddered at the review! Would to God I was master of the stoical tranquillity of that magnanimous sect; oh, that I were possessed of those sublime lessons which Appollonius of Chalcis gave to the Emperor Antoninus! I could then with much more propriety guide the helm of my little bark, which is soon to be freighted with all that I possess most dear on earth through this stormy passage to a safe harbour, and when there, become to my fellow-passengers a surer guide, a brighter example, a pattern more worthy of imitation, throughout all the new scenes they must pass and the new career they must traverse. I have observed, notwithstanding, the means hitherto made use of to arm the principal nations against our frontiers. Yet they have not, they will not take up the hatchet against a people who have done them no harm. The passions necessary to urge these people to war cannot be roused; they cannot feel the stings of vengeance, the thirst of which alone can impel them to shed blood: far superior in their motives of action to the Europeans who, for sixpence per day, may be engaged to shed that of any people on earth. They know nothing of the nature of our disputes; they have no ideas of such revolutions as this; a civil division of a village or tribe are events which have never been recorded in their traditions; many of them know very well that they have too long been the dupes and the victims of both parties, foolishly arming for our sakes, sometimes against each other, sometimes against our white enemies. They consider us as born on the same land, and, though they have no reasons to love us, yet they seem carefully to avoid entering into this quarrel, from whatever motives. I am speaking of those nations with which I am best acquainted; a few hundreds of the worst kind mixed with whites worse than themselves are now hired by Great Britain to perpetuate those dreadful incursions. In my youth I traded with the ———, under the conduct of my uncle, and always traded justly and equitably; some of them remember it to this day. Happily their village is far removed from the dangerous neighbourhood of the whites; I sent a man last spring to it who understands the woods extremely well and who speaks their language; he is just returned, after several weeks' absence, and has brought me, as I had flattered myself, a string of thirty purple wampum as a token that their honest chief will spare us half of his wigwam until we have time to erect one. He has sent me word that they have land in plenty, of which they are not so covetous as the whites; that we may plant for ourselves, and that in the meantime he will procure us some corn and meat; that fish is plenty in the waters of ———, and that the village to which he had laid open my proposals have no objection to our becoming dwellers with them. I have not yet communicated these glad tidings to my wife, nor do I know how to do it; I tremble lest she should refuse to follow me, lest the sudden idea of this removal rushing on her mind might be too powerful. I flatter myself I shall be able to accomplish it and to prevail on her; I fear nothing but the effects of her strong attachment to her relations. I would willingly let you know how I purpose to remove my family to so great a distance, but it would become unintelligible to you because you are not acquainted with the geographical situation of this part of the country. Suffice it for you to know that with about twenty-three miles land carriage, I am enabled to perform the rest by water; and when once afloat, I care not whether it be two or three hundred miles. I propose to send all our provisions, furniture, and clothes to my wife's father, who approves of the scheme, and to reserve nothing but a few necessary articles of covering, trusting to the furs of the chase for our future apparel. Were we imprudently to encumber ourselves too much with baggage, we should never reach to the waters of ————, which is the most dangerous as well as the most difficult part of our journey, and yet but a trifle in point of distance. I intend to say to my Negroes, "In the name of God, be free, my honest lads; I thank you for your past services; go, from henceforth, and work for yourselves; look on me as your old friend and fellow-labourer; be sober, frugal, and industrious, and you need not fear earning a comfortable subsistence." Lest my countrymen should think that I am gone to join the incendiaries of our frontiers, I intend to write a letter to Mr. ———— to inform him of our retreat and of the reasons that have urged me to it. The man whom I sent to ———— village is to accompany us also, and a very useful companion he will be on every account.

You may therefore, by means of anticipation, behold me under the wigwam; I am so well acquainted with the principal manners of these people that I entertain not the least apprehension from them. I rely more securely on their strong hospitality than on the witnessed compacts of many Europeans. As soon as possible after my arrival, I design to build myself a wigwam, after the same manner and size with the rest in order to avoid being thought singular or giving occasion for any railleries, though these people are seldom guilty of such European follies. I shall erect it hard by the lands which they propose to allot me, and will endeavour that my wife, my children, and myself may be adopted soon after our arrival. Thus becoming truly inhabitants of their village, we shall immediately occupy that rank within the pale of their society, which will afford us all the amends we can possibly expect for the loss we have met with by the convulsions of our own. According to their customs, we shall likewise receive names from them, by which we shall always be known. My youngest children shall learn to swim and to shoot with the bow, that they may acquire such talents as will necessarily raise them into some degree of esteem among the Indian lads of their own age; the rest of us must hunt with the hunter. I have been for several years an expert marksman; but I dread lest the imperceptible charm of Indian education may seize my younger children and give them such a propensity to that mode of life as may preclude their returning to the manners and customs of their parents. I have but one remedy to prevent this great evil, and that is to employ them in the labour of the fields as much as I can; I have even resolved to make their daily subsistence depend altogether on it. As long as we keep ourselves busy in tilling the earth, there is no fear of any of us becoming wild; it is the chase and the food it procures that have this strange effect. Excuse a simile—those hogs which range in the woods, and to whom grain is given once a week, preserve their former degree of tameness; but if, on the contrary, they are reduced to live on ground nuts and on what they can get, they soon become wild and fierce. For my part, I can plough, sow, and hunt, as occasion may require; but my wife, deprived of wool and flax, will have no room for industry; what is she then to do? Like the other squaws, she must cook for us the nasaump, the ninchickè, and such other preparations of corn as are customary among these people. She must learn to bake squashes and pompions under the ashes, to slice and smoke the meat of our own killing in order to preserve it; she must cheerfully adopt the manners and customs of her neighbours, in their dress, deportment, conduct, and internal economy, in all respects. Surely if we can have fortitude enough to quit all we have, to remove so far, and to associate with people so different from us, these necessary compliances are but subordinate parts of the scheme. The change of garments, when those they carry with them are worn out, will not be the least of my wife's and daughter's concerns, though I am in hopes that self-love will invent some sort of reparation. Perhaps you would not believe that there are in the woods looking-glasses and paint of every colour; and that the inhabitants take as much pains to adorn their faces and their bodies, to fix their bracelets of silver, and plait their hair as our forefathers the Picts used to do in the time of the Romans. Not that I would wish to see either my wife or daughter adopt those savage customs; we can live in great peace and harmony with them without descending to every article; the interruption of trade hath, I hope, suspended this mode of dress. My wife understands inoculation perfectly well; she inoculated all our children one after another and has successfully performed the operation on several scores of people, who, scattered here and there through our woods, were too far removed from all medical assistance. If we can persuade but one family to submit to it, and it succeeds, we shall then be as happy as our situation will admit of; it will raise her into some degree of consideration, for whoever is useful in any society will always be respected. If we are so fortunate as to carry one family through a disorder, which is the plague among these people, I trust to the force of example we shall then become truly necessary, valued, and beloved; we indeed owe every kind office to a society of men who so readily offer to admit us into their social partnership and to extend to my family the shelter of their village, the strength of their adoption, and even the dignity of their names. God grant us a prosperous beginning; we may then hope to be of more service to them than even missionaries who have been sent to preach to them a Gospel they cannot understand.

As to religion, our mode of worship will not suffer much by this removal from a cultivated country into the bosom of the woods; for it cannot be much simpler than that which we have followed here these many years, and I will with as much care as I can redouble my attention and twice a week retrace to them the great outlines of their duty to God and to man. I will read and expound to them some part of the decalogue, which is the method I have pursued ever since I married.

Half a dozen of acres on the shores of ———, the soil of which I know well, will yield us a great abundance of all we want; I will make it a point to give the overplus to such Indians as shall be most unfortunate in their huntings; I will persuade them, if I can, to till a little more land than they do and not to trust so much to the produce of the chase. To encourage them still farther, I will give a quirn to every six families; I have built many for our poor back-settlers, it being often the want of mills which prevents them from raising grain. As I am a carpenter, I can build my own plough and can be of great service to many of them; my example alone may rouse the industry of some and serve to direct others in their labours. The difficulties of the language will soon be removed; in my evening conversations, I will endeavour to make them regulate the trade of their village in such a manner as that those pests of the continent, those Indian-traders, may not come within a certain distance; and there they shall be obliged to transact their business before the old people. I am in hopes that the constant respect which is paid to the elders, and shame, may prevent the young hunters from infringing this regulation. The son of ——— will soon be made acquainted with our schemes, and I trust that the power of love and the strong attachment he professes for my daughter may bring him along with us; he will make an excellent hunter; young and vigorous, he will equal in dexterity the stoutest man in the village. Had it not been for this fortunate circumstance, there would have been the greatest danger; for however I respect the simple, the inoffensive society of these people in their villages, the strongest prejudices would make me abhor any alliance with them in blood, disagreeable no doubt to Nature's intentions, which have strongly divided us by so many indelible characters. In the days of our sickness, we shall have recourse to their medical knowledge, which is well calculated for the simple diseases to which they are subject. Thus shall we metamorphose ourselves from neat, decent, opulent planters, surrounded with every conveniency which our external labour and internal industry could give, into a still simpler people divested of everything beside hope, food, and the raiment of the woods: abandoning the large framed house to dwell under the wigwam, and the featherbed to lie on the mat or bear's skin. There shall we sleep undisturbed by frightful dreams and apprehensions; rest and peace of mind will make us the most ample amends for what we shall leave behind. These blessings cannot be purchased too dear; too long have we been deprived of them. I would cheerfully go even to the Mississippi to find that repose to which we have been so long strangers. My heart sometimes seems tired with beating; it wants rest like my eyelids, which feel oppressed with so many watchings.

These are the component parts of my scheme, the success of each of which appears feasible, whence I flatter myself with the probable success of the whole. Still, the danger of Indian education returns to my mind and alarms me much; then again, I contrast it with the education of the times; both appear to be equally pregnant with evils. Reason points out the necessity of choosing the least dangerous, which I must consider as the only good within my reach; I persuade myself that industry and labour will be a sovereign preservative against the dangers of the former; but I consider, at the same time, that the share of labour and industry which is intended to procure but a simple subsistence, with hardly any superfluity, cannot have the same restrictive effects on our minds as when we tilled the earth on a more extensive scale. The surplus could be then realized into solid wealth, and at the same time that this realization rewarded our past labours, it engrossed and fixed the attention of the labourer and cherished in his mind the hope of future riches. In order to supply this great deficiency of industrious motives and to hold out to them a real object to prevent the fatal consequences of this sort of apathy, I will keep an exact account of all that shall be gathered and give each of them a regular credit for the amount of it, to be paid them in real property at the return of peace. Thus, though seemingly toiling for bare subsistence on a foreign land, they shall entertain the pleasing prospect of seeing the sum of their labours one day realized either in legacies or gifts, equal if not superior to it. The yearly expense of the clothes which they would have received at home, and of which they will then be deprived, shall likewise be added to their credit; thus I flatter myself that they will more cheerfully wear the blanket, the matchcoat, and the moccasins. Whatever success they may meet with in hunting or fishing shall be only considered as recreation and pastime; I shall thereby prevent them from estimating their skill in the chase as an important and necessary accomplishment. I mean to say to them: "You shall hunt and fish merely to show your new companions that you are not inferior to them in point of sagacity and dexterity." Were I to send them to such schools as the interior parts of our settlements afford at present, what can they learn there? How could I support them there? What must become of me; am I to proceed on my voyage and leave them? That I never could submit to. Instead of the perpetual discordant noise of disputes so common among us, instead of those scolding scenes, frequent in every house, they will observe nothing but silence at home and abroad: a singular appearance of peace and concord are the first characteristics which strike you in the villages of these people. Nothing can be more pleasing, nothing surprises an European so much, as the silence and harmony which prevail among them, and in each family, except when disturbed by that accursed spirit given them by the wood rangers in exchange for their furs. If my children learn nothing of geometrical rules, the use of the compass, or of the Latin tongue, they will learn and practise sobriety, for rum can no longer be sent to these people; they will learn that modesty and diffidence for which the young Indians are so remarkable; they will consider labour as the most essential qualification, hunting as the second. They will prepare themselves in the prosecution of our small rural schemes, carried on for the benefit of our little community, to extend them farther when each shall receive his inheritance. Their tender minds will cease to be agitated by perpetual alarms, to be made cowards by continual terrors; if they acquire in the village of ———— such an awkwardness of deportment and appearance as would render them ridiculous in our gay capitals, they will imbibe, I hope, a confirmed taste for that simplicity which so well becomes the cultivators of the land. If I cannot teach them any of those professions which sometimes embellish and support our society, I will show them how to hew wood, how to construct their own ploughs, and with a few tools how to supply themselves with every necessary implement, both in the house and in the field. If they are hereafter obliged to confess that they belong to no one particular church, I shall have the consolation of teaching them that great, that primary worship which is the foundation of all others. If they do not fear God according to the tenets of any one seminary, they shall learn to worship Him upon the broad scale of nature. The Supreme Being does not reside in peculiar churches or communities; He is equally the great Manitou of the woods and of the plains; and even in the gloom, the obscurity of those very woods, His justice may be as well understood and felt as in the most sumptuous temples. Each worship with us hath, you know, its peculiar political tendency; there it has none but to inspire gratitude and truth: their tender minds shall receive no other idea of the Supreme Being than that of the Father of all men, who requires nothing more of us than what tends to make each other happy. We shall say with them: "Soungwanèha, èsa caurounkyawga, nughwonshauza neattèwek, nèsalanga." Our Father, be thy will done in earth as it is in great heaven.

Perhaps my imagination gilds too strongly this distant prospect: yet it appears founded on so few and simple principles that there is not the same probability of adverse incidents as in more complex schemes. These vague rambling contemplations which I here faithfully retrace carry me sometimes to a great distance; I am lost in the anticipation of the various circumstances attending this proposed metamorphosis! Many unforeseen accidents may doubtless arise. Alas! It is easier for me in all the glow of paternal anxiety, reclined on my bed, to form the theory of my future conduct than to reduce my schemes into practice. But when once secluded from the great society to which we now belong, we shall unite closer together, and there will be less room for jealousies or contentions. As I intend my children neither for the law nor the church, but for the cultivation of the land, I wish them no literary accomplishments; I pray heaven that they may be one day nothing more than expert scholars in husbandry: this is the science which made our continent to flourish more rapidly than any other. Were they to grow up where I am now situated, even admitting that we were in safety; two of them are verging toward that period of their lives when they must necessarily take up the musket and learn, in that new school, all the vices which are so common in armies. Great God! Close my eyes forever rather than I should live to see this calamity! May they rather become inhabitants of the woods.

Thus then in the village of ———, in the bosom of that peace it has enjoyed ever since I have known it, connected with mild, hospitable people, strangers to *our* political disputes and having none among themselves; on the shores of a fine river, surrounded with woods, abounding with game, our little society, united in perfect harmony with the new adoptive one, in which we shall be incorporated, shall rest, I hope, from all fatigues, from all apprehensions, from our present terrors, and from our long watchings. Not a word of politics shall cloud our simple conversation; tired either with the chase or the labours of the field, we shall sleep on our mats without any distressing want, having learnt to retrench every superfluous one; we shall have but two prayers to make to the Supreme Being, that He may shed His fertilizing dew on our little crops and that He will be pleased to restore peace to our unhappy country. These shall be the only subject of our nightly prayers and of our daily ejaculations; and if the labour, the industry, the frugality, the union of men, can be an agreeable offering to Him, we shall not fail to receive His paternal blessings. There I shall contemplate Nature in her most wild and ample extent; I shall carefully study a species of society of which I have at present but very imperfect ideas; I will endeavour to occupy with propriety that place which will enable me to enjoy the few and sufficient benefits it confers. The solitary and unconnected mode of life I have lived in my youth must fit me for this trial; I am not the first who has attempted it; Europeans did not, it is true, carry to the wilderness numerous families; they went there as mere speculators, I as a man seeking a refuge from the desolation of war. They went there to study the manner of the aborigines, I to conform to them, whatever they are; some went as visitors, as travellers; I, as a sojourner, as a fellow-hunter and labourer, go determined industriously to work up among them such a system of happiness as may be adequate to my future situation and may be a sufficient compensation for all my fatigues and for the misfortunes I have borne: I have always found it at home; I may hope likewise to find it under the humble roof of my wigwam.

O Supreme Being! If among the immense variety of planets, inhabited by thy creative power, thy paternal and omnipotent care deigns to extend to all the individuals they contain, if it be not beneath thy infinite dignity to cast thy eye on us wretched mortals, if my future felicity is not contrary to the necessary effects of those secret causes which thou hast appointed, receive the supplications of a man to whom in thy kindness thou hast given a wife and an offspring; view us all with benignity, sanctify this strong conflict of regrets, wishes, and other natural passions; guide our steps through these unknown paths and bless our future mode of life. If it is good and well meant, it must proceed from thee; thou knowest, O Lord, our enterprise contains neither fraud nor malice nor revenge. Bestow on me that energy of conduct now become so necessary that it may be in my power to carry the young family thou hast given me through this great trial with safety and in thy peace. Inspire me with such intentions and such rules of conduct as may be most acceptable to thee. Preserve, O God, preserve the companion of my bosom, the best gift thou hast given me; endue her with courage and strength sufficient to accomplish this perilous journey. Bless the children of our love, those portions of our hearts; I implore thy divine assistance, speak to their tender minds and inspire them with the love of that virtue which alone can serve as the basis of their conduct in this world and of their happiness with thee. Restore peace and concord to our poor afflicted country; assuage the fierce storm which has so long ravaged it. Permit, I beseech thee, O Father of nature, that our ancient virtues and our industry may not be totally lost and that as a reward for the great toils we have made on this new land, we may be restored to our ancient tranquillity and enabled to fill it with successive generations that will constantly thank thee for the ample subsistence thou hast given them.

The unreserved manner in which I have written must give you a convincing proof of that friendship and esteem of which I am sure you never yet doubted. As members of the same society, as mutually bound by the ties of affection and old acquaintance, you certainly cannot avoid feeling for my distresses; you cannot avoid mourning with me over that load of physical and moral evil with which we are all oppressed. My own share of it I often overlook when I minutely contemplate all that hath befallen our native country.

2

WILLIAM BARTRAM

(1739–1823)

On April 20, 1739, William Bartram was born in Philadelphia, where his father was famous for the wonders of his botanical gardens. Above the door to his greenhouse, John Bartram had engraved a couplet from Alexander Pope:

> Slave to no sect, who takes no private road,
> But looks through nature up to Nature's God.

Of John Bartram's seven sons, it was William who seemed to share this sentiment. He spent his first decade and a half in the botanical gardens, and he seemed intent on following in his father's footsteps.

But John Bartram seemed less than eager to have another botanist in the family. In late 1756 William was a student at Philadelphia's Old College when his father pulled him out of school to begin an apprenticeship with a local merchant. In his spare moments, however, William clung to his life's ambition, continuing to study botany.

In 1761, Bartram left Philadelphia for an uncle's home in Cape Fear, North Carolina. Here the young man put his apprenticeship to use by establishing his own store. More importantly, though, he was now able to devote as much time as he could find to the study of nature. He left North Carolina in 1765 to join his father—now "botanist to the king of Great Britain"—on a trip to Florida. When John Bartram left Florida in 1766, his son stayed behind and quickly failed in his attempt to establish a plantation.

When William Bartram returned to Philadelphia in 1767, he was eager to return south as soon as possible. In 1770, he returned to North Carolina, and then, in 1772, Dr. John Fothergill commissioned him to travel through the deep south to collect plants and seeds and to keep an illustrated botanical journal. For his efforts he would receive an annual stipend of £50.

Though Bartram returned to Philadelphia in 1777, he did not publish *Travels through North & South Carolina, Georgia, East & West Florida, the Cherokee Country, the Extensive Territories of the Muscogulges, or Creek Confederacy, and the Country of the Chactaws* until 1791. In the introduction to this book, Bartram hoped that the "advantages" of having been raised by John Bartram would allow him "to present new as well as useful information to the botanist and zoologist." But Bartram's *Travels* is more than a dry recitation of plant habitats and soil conditions; the author saw the world as "a glorious apartment of the boundless palace of the sovereign Creator." Ralph Waldo Emerson would later praise Bartram's "wondrous kind of floundering eloquence" and remark that "American libraries ought to provide themselves with that kind of book; and keep them as a kind of *biblical* article."

After publication of his first and only book, Bartram wrote a few additional articles, but he spent most of the rest of his life gardening. He died on July 22, 1823. The site of his burial is unknown.

Text: *Travels through North & South Carolina, Georgia, East & West Florida, the Cherokee County, the Extensive Territories of the Muscogulges, or Creek Confederacy, and the County of The Chactaws* (Philadelphia, 1791): 440–466.

FROM *TRAVELS THROUGH NORTH & SOUTH CAROLINA, GEORGIA, EAST & WEST FLORIDA, THE CHEROKEE COUNTRY, THE EXTENSIVE TERRITORIES OF THE MUSCOGULGES, OR CREEK CONFEDERACY, AND THE COUNTRY OF THE CHACTAWS (1791)*

CHAP. VIII

November 27th 1777, sat off from Mobile, in a large boat with the principal trader of the company, and at evening arrived at Taensa, where were the pack-horsemen with the merchandize, and next morning as soon as we had our horses in readiness, I took my last leave of Major Farmer, and left Taensa. Our caravan consisting of between twenty and thirty horses, sixteen of which were loaded, two pack-horsemen, and myself, under the direction of Mr. Tap—y the chief trader. One of our young men was a Mustee Creek, his mother being a Chactaw slave, and his father a half breed, betwixt a Creek and a white man. I loaded one horse with my effects, some presents to the Indians, to enable me to purchase a fresh horse, in case of necessity, for my old trusty slave which had served me faithfully almost three years, having carried me on his back at least six thousand miles, was by this time almost worn out, and I expected every hour he would give up, especially after I found the manner of these traders' travelling; who seldom decamp until the sun is high and hot; each one having a whip made of the toughest cow-skin, they start all at once, the horses having ranged themselves in regular Indian file, the veteran in the van, and the younger in the rear; then the chief drives with the crack of his whip, and a whoop or shriek, which rings through the forests and plains, speaks in Indian, commanding them to proceed, which is repeated by all the company, when we start at once, keeping up a brisk and constant trot, which is incessantly urged and continued as long as the miserable creatures are able to move forward, and then come to camp, though frequently in the middle of the afternoon, which is the pleasantest time of the day for travelling: and every horse has a bell on, which being stopped when we start in the morning with a twist of grass or leaves; soon shakes out, and they are never stopped again during the day; the constant ringing and clattering of the bells, smacking of the whips, whooping and too frequent cursing these miserable quadrupeds, cause an incessant uproar and confusion, inexpressibly disagreeable.

After three days travelling in this mad manner, my old servant was on the point of giving out, and several of the company's horses were tired, but were relieved of their burthens by the led horses which attended for that purpose. I was now driven to disagreeable extremities, and had no other alternative, but either to leave my horse in the woods, pay a very extravagant hire for a doubtful passage to the Nation, or separate myself from my companions, and wait the recovery of my horse alone: the traders gave me no other comfortable advice in this dilemma, than that, there was a company of traders on the road a-head of us from the nation, to Mobile, who had a large gang of led horses with them for sale, when they should arrive; and expected from the advice which he had received at Mobile before we set off from thence, that this company must be very near to us, and probably would be up tomorrow, or at least in two or three days: and this man condescended so far as to moderate a little his mode of travelling, that I might have a chance of keeping up with them until the evening of next day; besides I had the comfort of observing that the traders and pack-horsemen carried themselves towards me, with evident signs of humanity and friendship, often expressing sentiments of sympathy, and saying I must not be left alone to perish in the wilderness.

Although my apprehensions on this occasion, were somewhat tumultuous, since there was little hope, on the principle of reason, should I be left alone, of escaping cruel captivity, and perhaps being murdered by the Chactaws; for the company of traders was my only security, as the Indians never attack the traders on the road, though they be trading with nations at enmity with them. Yet I had secret hopes of relief and deliverance, that cheered me, and inspired confidence and peace of mind.

Now I am come within the atmosphere of the illisium groves, how reanimating is the fragrance! every part of this plant above ground possesses an aromatic scent, but the large stillated pericarpes is the most fragrant part of it, which continually perspires an oleagenous sweat, as warm and vivific as Cloves or Mace, I never saw it grow naturally further North than Lat. 33°, on the Mobile river and its branches, and but one place in East Florida near Lake George, Lat. 28°.

About the middle of the afternoon, we were joyfully surprised at the distant prospect of the trading company coming up, and we soon met, saluting each other several times with a general Indian whoop, or shouts of friendship; then each company came to camp within a few paces of each other; and before night I struck up a bargain with them for a handsome strong young horse, which cost me about ten pounds sterling. I was now constrained to leave my old slave behind, to feed in rich Cane pastures, where he was to remain and recruit until the return of his new master from Mobile; from whom I extorted a promise to use him gently, and if possibly, not to make a pack-horse of him.

Next morning we decamped, proceeding again on my travels, now alert and cheerful. Crossed a brisk rivulet ripling over a gravelly bed, and winding through aromatic groves of the Illisium Floridanum, then gently descended to the high forests, leaving Deadman's creek, for at this creek a white man was found dead, supposed to have been murdered, from which circumstance it has its name.

A few days before we arrived at the Nation we met a company of emigrants from Georgia; a man, his wife, a young woman, several young children and three stout young men, with about a dozen horses loaded with their property. They informed us their design was to settle on the Alabama, a few miles above the confluence of the Tombigbe.

Being now near the Nation, the chief trader with another of our company sat off a-head for his town, to give notice to the Nation, as he said, of his approach with the merchandize, each of them taking the best horse they could pick out of the gang, leaving the goods to the conduct and care of the young Mustee and myself. Early in the evening we came to the banks of a large deep creek, a considerable branch of the Alabama: the waters ran furiously, being overcharged with the floods of rain which had fallen the day before. We discoverd immediately that there was no possibility of crossing it by fording; its depth and rapidity would have swept our horses, loads and all, instantly from our sight; my companion, after consideration, said we must make a raft to ferry over our goods, which we immediately set about, after unloading our horses and turning them out to range. I undertook to collect dry Canes, and my companion dry timber or logs and vines to bind them together: having gathered the necessary materials, and laid them in order on the brink of the river, ready to work upon, we betook ourselves to repose, and early next morning sat about building our raft. This was a novel scene to me, and I could not, until finished and put to practice, well comprehend how it could possibly answer the effect desired. In the first place we laid, parallel to each other, dry, sound trunks of trees, about nine feet in length, and eight or nine inches diameter, which binding fast together with Grape vines and withs, until we had formed this first floor, about twelve or fourteen feet in length, then binding the dry Canes in bundles, each near as thick as a man's body, with which we formed the upper stratum, laying them close by the side of each other and binding them fast; after this manner our raft was constructed: then having two strong Grape vines, each long enough to cross the river, we fastened one to each end of the raft, which now being completed, and loading on as much as it would safely carry, the Indian took the end of one of the vines in his mouth, plunged into the river and swam over with it, and the vine fixed to the other end was committed to my charge, to steady the raft and haul it back again after being unloaded; as soon as he had safe landed and hauled taught his vine, I pushed off the raft, which he drew over as quick as possible, I steadying it with my vine: in this manner, though with inexpressible danger of loosing our effects, we ferried all safe over: the last load, with other articles, contained my property, with all my clothes, which I stripped off, except my breeches, for they contained matters of more value and consequence than all the rest of my property put together; besides I did not choose to expose myself entirely naked to the alligators and serpents in crossing the flood. Now seeing all the goods safe over, and the horses at a landing place on the banks of the river about fifty yards above, I drove them all in together, when, seeing them safe landed, I plunged in after them, and being a tollerable swimmer, soon reached the opposite shore; but my difficulties at this place were not yet at an end, for our horses all landing just below the mouth of a considerable branch of this river, of fifteen or twenty feet width, and its perpendicular banks almost as many feet in height above its swift waters, over which we were obliged to carry every article of our effects, and this by no other bridge than a sapling felled across it, which is called a raccoon bridge, and over this my Indian friend would trip as quick and light as that quadruped, with one hundred weight of leather on his back, when I was scarcely able to shuffle myself along over it astride. At last having re-packed and sat off again, without any material occurrence intervening; in the evening we arrived at the banks of the great Tallapoose river, and came to camp under shelter of some Indian cabins, in expansive fields, close to the river bank, opposite the town of Savannuca. Late in the evening a young white man, in great haste and seeming confusion, joined our camp, who immediately related, that being on his journey from Pensacola, it happened that the very night after we had passed the company of emigrants, he met them and joined their camp in the evening, when, just at dark, the Chactaws surrounded them, plundered their camp and carried all the people off captive, except himself, he having the good fortune to escape with his horse, though closely pursued.

Next morning very early, though very cold and the surface of the earth as hoary as if covered with a fall of snow, the trader standing on the opposite shore entirely naked except a breech-clout, and encircled by a company of red men in the like habit, hailed us, and presently, with canoes brought us all over with the merchandize, and conducted us safe to the town of Mucclasse, a mile or two distant.

The next day was a day of rest and audience: the following was devoted to feasting, and the evening concluded in celebrating the nuptials of the young Mustee with a Creek girl of Mucclasse, daughter of the chief and sister to our trader's wife. The trader's house and stores formed a compleat square, after the mode of the habitations of the Muscogulges, that is, four oblong buildings of equal dimensions, two opposite to each other, encompassing an area of about a quarter of an acre; on one side of this a fence enclosed a yard of near an acre of ground, and at one of the farther corners of which a booth or pavilion was formed of green boughs, having two Laurel trees planted in front (Magnolia grandiflora.) This was the secret nuptial chamber. Dancing, music and feasting continued the forepart of the night, and towards morning the happy couple privately withdrew, and continued alone all the next day, no one presuming to approach the sacred, mysterious thalame.

The trader obliged me with his company on a visit to the Alabama, an Indian town at the confluence of the two fine rivers, the Tallapoose and Coosau, which here resign their names to the great Alabama, where are to be seen traces of the ancient French fortress, Thoulouse; here are yet lying, half buried in the earth, a few pieces of ordnance, four and six pounders. I observed, in a very thriving condition, two or three very large Apple trees, planted here by the French. This is, perhaps, one of the most elegible situations for a city in the world, a level plain between the conflux of two majestic rivers, which are exactly of equal magnitude in appearance, each navigable for vessels and perreauguas at least five hundred miles above it, and spreading their numerous branches over the most fertile and delightful regions, many hundred miles before we reach their sources in the Apalachean mountains.

Stayed all night at Alabama, where we had a grand entertainment at the public square, with music and dancing, and returned next day to Mucclasse, where being informed of a company of traders about setting off from Tuckabatche for Augusta, I made a visit to that town to know the truth of it, but on my arrival there they were gone, but being informed of another caravan who were to start from the Ottasse town in two or three weeks time, I returned to Mucclasse in order to prepare for my departure.

On my arrival, I was not a little surprised at a tragical revolution in the family of my friend the trader, his stores shut up, and guarded by a party of Indians: in a few minutes however, the whole affair was related to me. It appeared that this son of Adonis, had been detected in an amorous intrigue, with the wife of a young chief, the day after his arrival: the chief being out on a hunt, but arrived next day, who upon information of the affair, and the fact being confirmed, he with his friends and kindred resolved to exact legal satisfaction, which in this case is cutting off both ears of the delinquent, close to the head, which is called cropping. This being determined upon, he took the most secret and effectual methods to effect his purpose. About a dozen young Indian fellows, conducted by their chief (the injured husband) having provided and armed themselves with knotty cudgels of green Hickory, which they concealed under their mantles, in the dusk of the evening paid a pretended friendly visit to the trader at his own house; when the chief feigning a private matter of business, took him aside in the yard; then whistling through his fingers (the signal preconcerted) he was instantly surrounded, knocked down, and then stripped to his skin, and beaten with their knotty bludgeons; however he had the subtilty to feign himself speechless before they really killed him, which he supposed was their intention; when he had now lain for dead, the executioner drew out his knife with an intention of taking off his ears; this small respite gave him time to reflect a little; when he instantly sprang up, ran off, leaped the fence and had the good fortune to get into a dark swamp, overgrown with vines and thickets, where he miraculously eluded the earnest researches of his enemies, and finally made a safe retreat to the house of his father-in-law, the chief of the town; throwing himself under his protection, who gave his word that he would do him all the favour that lay in his power. This account I had from his own mouth, who hearing of my return, the next morning after my arrival, sent a trusty messenger, by whom I found means of access to him. He farther informed me that there had been a council of the chiefs of the town convened, to deliberate on the affair, and their final determination was that he must loose his ears, or forfeit all his goods, which amounted to upwards of one thousand pounds sterling, and even that forfeiture would not save his ears, unless Mr. Golphin interposed in his behalf; and after all the injured Indian declares that he will have his life. He entreated me with tears to make what speed I could to Silver Bluff, represent his dangerous situation to Mr. Golphin, and solicit that gentleman's most speedy and effectual interference; which I assured him I would undertake.

Now having all things prepared for my departure, early in the morning, after taking leave of my distressed friend the trader of Mucclasse, I sat off; passed through continued plantations and Indian towns on my way up the Tallapoose river, being every where treated by the inhabitants with marks of friendship, even as though I had been their countryman and relation. Called by the way at the beautiful town of Coolome, where I tarried some time with Mr. Germany the chief trader of the town, an elderly gentleman, but active, cheerful and very agreeable; who received and treated me with the utmost civility and friendship: his wife is a Creek woman, of a very amiable and worthy character and disposition, industrious, prudent and affectionate; and by whom he had several children, whom he is desirous to send to Savanna or Charleston, for their education, but cannot prevail on his wife to consent to it: this affair affects him very sensibly, for he has accumulated a pretty fortune by his industry and commendable conduct.

Leaving Coolome, I re-crossed the river at Tuccabache, an ancient and large town, thence continuing up the river, and at evening arrived at Attasse, where I continued near a week, waiting the preparations of the traders, with whom I was to join in company to Augusta.

The next day after my arrival, I was introduced to the ancient chiefs, at the public square or areopagus, and in the evening in company with the traders, who are numerous in this town, repaired to the great rotunda, where were assembled the greatest number of ancient venerable chiefs and warriors that I had ever beheld; we spent the evening and greater part of the night together, in drinking Caffine and smoking Tobacco. The great counsel-house or rotunda is appropriated to much the same purpose as the public square, but more private, and seems particularly dedicated to political affairs; women and youth are never admitted; and I suppose it is death for a female to presume to enter the door, or approach within its pale. It is a vast conical building or circular dome, capable of accomodating many hundred people; constructed and furnished within, exactly in the same manner as those of the Cherokees already described, but much larger than any I had seen there; there are people appointed to take care of it, to have it daily swept clean, to provide canes for fuel or to give light.

As their vigils and manner of conducting their vespers and mystical fire in this rotunda, is extremely singular, and altogether different from the customs and usages of any other people, I shall proceed to describe it. In the first place, the governor or officer who has the management of this business, with his servants attending, orders the black drink to be brewed, which is a decoction or infusion of the leaves and tender shoots of the Caffine: this is done under an open shed or pavilion, at twenty or thirty yards distance, directly opposite the door of the council-house. Next he orders bundles of dry Canes to be brought in; these are previously split and broke in pieces to about the length of two feet, and then placed obliquely crossways upon one another on the floor, forming a spiral circle round about the great centre pillar, rising to a foot or eighteen inches in height from the ground; and this circle spreading as it proceeds round and round, often repeated from right to left, every revolution encreases its diameter, and at length extends to the distance of ten or twelve feet from the centre, more or less, according to the length of time the assembly or meeting is to continue. By the time these preparations are accomplished it is night, and the assembly taken their seats in order. The exterior extremity or outer end of the spiral circle takes fire and immediately rises into a bright flame (but how this is effected I did not plainly apprehend; I saw no person set fire to it; there might have been fire left on the hearth, however I neither saw nor smelt fire or smoke until the blaze instantly ascended upwards) which gradually and slowly creeps round the centre pillar, with the course of the sun, feeding on the dry Canes, and affords a cheerful, gentle and sufficient light until the circle is consumed, when the council breaks up. Soon after this illumination takes place, the aged chiefs and warriors being seated on their cabbins or sophas, on the side of the house opposite the door, in three classes or ranks, rising a little, one above or behind the other; and the white people and red people of confederate towns in the like order on the left hand: a transverse range of pillars, supporting a thin clay wall about breast high, separates them: the king's cabbin or seat is in front, the next back of it the head warriors, and the third or last accommodates the young warriors, &c. the great war chief's seat or place is on the same cabbin with, and immediately to the left hand of the king and next to the white people, and to the right hand of the mico or king the most venerable head men and warriors are seated. The assembly being now seated in order, and the house illuminated, two middle aged men, who perform the office of slaves or servants, pro tempore, come in together at the door, each having very large conch shells full of black drink, advancing with slow, uniform and steady steps, their eyes or countenances lifted up, singing very low but sweetly, advance within six on eight paces of the king's and white people's cabbins, when they stop together, and each rests his shell on a tripos or little table, but presently takes it up again, and, bowing very low, advances obsequiously, crossing or intersecting each other about midway: he who rested his shell before the white people now stands be-

fore the king, and the other who stopped before the king stands before the white people, when each presents his shell, one to the king and the other to the chief of the
white people, and as soon as he raises it to his mouth the slave utters or sings two
notes, each of which continues as long as he has breath, and as long as these notes continue, so long must the person drink, or at least keep the shell to his mouth. These two
long notes are very solemn, and at once strike the imagination with a religious awe
or homage to the Supreme, sounding somewhat like a-hoo—ojah and a-lu—yah.
After this manner the whole assembly are treated, so long as the drink and light continues to hold out, and as soon as the drinking begins, Tobacco and pipes are brought.
The skin of a wild cat or young tyger stuffed with Tobacco is brought, and laid at the
king's feet, with the great or royal pipe beautifully adorned; the skin is usually of the
animals of the king's family or tribe, as the wild-cat, otter, bear, rattle-snake, &c. A skin
of Tobacco is likewise brought and cast at the feet of the white chief of the town, and
from him it passes on from one to another to fill their pipes from, though each person has besides his own peculiar skin of Tobacco. The king or chief smokes first in the
great pipe a few whiffs, blowing it off ceremoniously, first towards the sun, or as it is
generally supposed to the Great Spirit, for it is puffed upwards, next towards the four
cardinal points, then towards the white people in the house, then the great pipe is
taken from the hand of the mico by a slave, and presented to the chief white man, and
then to the great war chief, whence it circulates through the rank of head men and
warriors, then returns to the king. After this each one fills his pipe from his own or
his neighbours skin.

The great or public square generally stands alone, in the centre and highest part
of the town, it consists of foursquare or cubical buildings, or houses of one story, uniform, and of the same dimensions, so situated as to form an exact tetragon, encompassing an area of half an acre of ground, more or less, according to the strength or
largeness of the town, or will of the inhabitants; there is a passage or avenue at each
corner of equal width; each building is constructed of a wooden frame fixed strong
in the earth, the walls filled in, and neatly plaistered with clay mortar; close on three
sides, that is the back and two ends, except within about two feet of the wall plate or
eves, which is left open for the purpose of a window and to admit a free passage of
the air; the front or side next to the area is quite open like a piazza. One of these buildings which is properly the counsil house, where the mico, chiefs, and warriors, with
the citizens who have business, or choose to repair thither, assemble every day in
counsil, to hear, decide and rectify all grievances, complaints and contentions, arising
betwixt the citizens; give audience to ambassadors, and strangers; hear news and talks
from confederate towns, allies or distant nations; consult about the particular affairs of
the town, as erecting habitations for new citizens, or establishing young families, concerning agriculture, &c. This building is somewhat different from the other three: it is
closely shut up on three sides, that is, the back and two ends, and besides, a partition
wall longitudinally from end to end divides it into two apartments, the back part totally dark, only three small arched apertures or holes opening into it from the front
apartment or piazza, and little larger than just to admit a man to crawl in upon his
hands and knees. This secluded place appears to me to be designed as a sanctuary[1] de-
didated to religion or rather priest craft; for here are deposited all the sacred things, as
the physic pot, rattles, chaplets of deer's hoofs and other apparatus of conjuration; and

---

1. Sanctorium or sacred temple; and it is said to be death for any person but the mico, war-chief and
high priest to enter in, and none are admitted but by permission of the priests, who guard it day and night.

likewise the calumet or great pipe of peace, the imperial standard, or eagle's tail, which is made of the feathers of the white eagle's tail[2] curiously formed and displayed like an open fan on a sceptre or staff, as white and clean as possible when displayed for peace; but when for war, the feathers are painted or tinged with vermilion. The piazza or front of this building, is equally divided into three apartments, by two transverse walls or partitions, about breast high, each having three orders or ranges of seats or cabins stepping one above and behind the other, which accommodate the senate and audience, in the like order as observed in the rotunda. The other three buildings which compose the square, are alike furnished with three ranges of cabins or sophas, and serve for a banqueting-house, to shelter and accommodate the audience and spectators at all times, particularly at feasts or public entertainments, where all classes of citizens resort day and night in the summer or moderate season; the children and females however are seldom or never seen in the public square.

The pillars and walls of the houses of the square were decorated with various paintings and sculptures; which I suppose to be hieroglyphic, and as an historic legendary of political and sacerdotal affairs: but they are extremely picturesque or caricature, as men in variety of attitudes, some ludicrous enough, others having the head of some kind of animal as those of a duck, turkey, bear, fox, wolf, buck, &c. and again those kind of creatures are represented having the human head. These designs were not ill executed, the outlines bold, free and well proportioned. The pillars supporting the front or piazza of the council-house of the square, were ingeniously formed in the likeness of vast speckled serpents, ascending upward; the Otasses being of the snake family or tribe. At this time the town was fasting, taking medicine, and I think I may say praying, to avert a grievous calamity of sickness, which had lately afflicted them, and laid in the grave abundance of their citizens; they fast seven or eight days, during which time they eat or drink nothing but a meagre gruel, made of a little corn-flour and water; taking at the same time by way of medicine or physic, a strong decoction of the roots of the Iris versicolor, which is a powerful cathartic; they hold this root in high estimation, every town cultivates a little plantation of it, having a large artificial pond, just without the town, planted and almost overgrown with it, where they usually dig clay for pottery, and mortar and plaster for their buildings, and I observed where they had lately been digging up this root.

In the midst of a large oblong square adjoining this town (which was surrounded with a low bank or terrace) is standing a high pillar, round like a pin or needle, it is about forty feet in height, and between two and three feet in diameter at the earth, gradually tapering upwards to a point; it is one piece of Pine wood, and arises from the centre of a low circular, artificial hill, but it leans a little to one side. I enquired of the Indians and traders what it was designed for, who answered they knew not: the Indians said that their ancestors found it in the same situation, when they first arrived and possessed the country, adding, that the red men or Indians, then the possessors, whom they vanquished, were as ignorant as themselves concerning it, saying that their ancestors likewise found it standing so. This monument, simple as it is, may be worthy the observations of a traveller, since it naturally excites at least the following queries: for what purpose was it designed? its great antiquity and incorruptibility—what method or machines they employed to bring it to the spot, and how they raised it erect? There is no tree or species of the Pine, whose wood, i. e. so large a portion of

---

2. Vultur sacra.

the trunk, is supposed to be incorruptible, exposed in the open air to all weathers, but the long-leaved Pine (Pin. palustris) and there is none growing within twelve or fifteen miles of this place, that tree being naturally produced only on the high, dry, barren ridges, where there is a sandy soil and grassy wet savannas. A great number of men uniting their strength, probably carried it to the place on handspikes, or some such contrivance.

On the Sabbath day before I sat off from this place, I could not help observing the solemnity of the town, the silence and the retiredness of the red inhabitants, but a very few of them were to be seen, the doors of their dwellings shut, and if a child chanced to stray out, it was quickly drawn in doors again: I asked the meaning of this, and was immediately answered, that it being the white people's beloved day or Sabbath, the Indians kept it religiously sacred to the Great Spirit.

Last night was clear and cold, wind North West, and this morning January 2d, 1778, the face of the earth was perfectly white with a beautiful sparkling frost. Sat off for Augusta with a company of traders, four men with about thirty horses, twenty of which were loaded with leather and furs, each pack or load supposed to weigh one hundred and fifty pounds upon an average; in three days we arrived at the Apalachucla or Chata Uche river, crossed at the point towns Chehaw and Usseta; these towns almost join each other, yet speak two languages, as radically different perhaps as the Muscogulge's and Chinese. After leaving the river we met with nothing material, or worth particular observation, until our arrival at Oakmulge, towards evening, where we encamped in expansive ancient Indian fields, in view of the foaming flood of the river, now raging over its banks. Here were two companies of traders from Augusta, bound to the Nation, consisting of fifteen or twenty men, with seventy or eighty horses, most of which had their loads of merchandize; they crossed the river this morning and lost six horses in the attempt; they were drowned, being entangled in the vines under water at landing. But the river now falling again, we were in hopes that by next morning the waters would be again confined within the banks. We immediately sat about rigging our portable leather boat, about eight feet long, which was of thick foal leather, folded up and carried on the top of a pack of deer skins; the people soon got her rigged, which was effected after the following manner. We in the first place cut down a White-Oak sapling, and by notching this at each end, bent it up, which formed the keel, stem and stern post of one piece, this being placed in the bottom of the boat, and pretty strong hoop-poles being fixed in the bottom across the keel, and, turning up their ends, expanded the hull of the boat, which being fastened by thongs to two other poles bent round, the outside of the rim forms the gunwales, thus in an hour's time our bark was rigged, to which afterwards we added two little oars or sculls. Our boat being now in readiness, and our horses turned out to pasture, each one retired to repose, or to such exercise as most effectually contributed to divert the mind. I was at this time rather dejected, and sought comfort in retirement. Turning my course to the expansive fields, fragrant groves and sublime forests. Returned to camp by dusk, where I found my companions cheerful and thoughtless rather to an extreme. It was a calm still evening and warm, the wood-cock (scolopax) chirruping high up in the air, gently descends by spiral circular tract, and alights on the humid plain: this bird appears in Pennsylvania early in the spring, when the Elm and Maple begin to flower, and here the scarlet Maple, Elm and Alder began to shew their flowers, the yellow Jasmin just ready to open its fragrant golden blossoms, and the gay Azalea also preparing to expand its beauties.

The morning cool and pleasant, after reconnoitering the shores of the rivers, and consulting with our brethren in distress, who had not yet decamped, resolving to stay and lend their assistance in passing over this rapid gulph, we were encouraged to proceed, and launching our barke into the raging flood, after many successful trips ferried over all the goods, then drove in our horses altogether, and had the pleasure of seeing them all safely landed on the opposite shore; and lastly I embarked with three of our people, and several packs of leather, we then put off from shore, bidding adieu to our generous friends left behind, who re echoed our shouts upon our safe landing. We proceeded again, crossed the Oconne in the same manner, and with the like success, and came to camp in the fertile fields, on the banks of that beautiful river, and proceeding thence next day, in the evening came to camp on the waters of great Ogeche, and the following day, after crossing several of its considerable branches, came to camp, and next day crossed the main branch of that famous river, which being wide and very rapid proved difficult and dangerous fording, yet we crossed without any loss, but some of our pack-horses were badly bruised, being swept off their feet and dashed against the rocks, my horse too being carried away with the current, and plunging off sunken shelving rocks into deep holes, I got very wet, but I kept my seat and landed safe: however I suffered much, it being a cold freezing day. We came to camp early, and raising great fires with Pine knots and other wood, we dried ourselves and kept warm during the long night, and after two days more hard travelling we arrived at Augusta.

Being under a necessity of making two or three days stay here, in order to refit myself, for by this time my stock of cloths were entirely worn out. I took this opportunity of visiting my friend doctor Wells at his plantations near the city. And now being again new clothed and furnished with a tolerable Indian poney, I took leave of my host and prepared to depart for Savanna.

Soon after I left Augusta, proceeding for Savanna, the capital, a gentleman overtook me on the road, who was a native of Ireland, and had lately arrived in this part of America with a view of settling a plantation in Georgia, particularly for the culture of those very useful fruits and vegetables that are cultivated up the Mediterranean, and which so largely contribute towards supporting that lucrative branch of commerce, i.e. the Levant trade, viz. Vitis vinifera, for wine, Vitis Corinthiaca, for Currants, Vitis Allobrogica, for Raisins, Olives, Figs, Morus, for feeding silk-worms, Amygdalus communis, Pistachia, Capparis, Citrus aurantium, Citrus limon, Citrus verrucosa, the great sweet scented Citron, &c. He was very ingenious, desirous of information and as liberal and free of communicating his own acquisitions and discoveries in useful science, and consequently a very agreeable companion. On our journey down we stopped awhile to rest and refresh ourselves at the Great Springs, near the road, on our left hand, about midway between Augusta and Savanna. This amazing fountain of transparent, cool water, breaks suddenly out of the earth, at the basis of a moderately elevated hill or bank, forming at once a bason near twenty yards over, ascending through a horizontal bed of soft rocks, of a heterogenious composition, chiefly a testacious concretion of broken, entire and pulverised sea shells, sand, &c. constituting a coarse kind of lime-stone. The ebullition is copious, active and continual, over the ragged apertures in the rocks, which lie seven or eight feet below, swelling the surface considerably immediately above it; the waters descend swiftly from the fountain, forming at once a large brook, six or eight yards over, and five or six feet deep. There are multitudes of fish in the fountain of various tribes, chiefly the several species of bream, trout, cat-fish and garr: it was amusing to behold the fish continually ascending and descending through the rocky apertures. Observed that we crossed no stream or

brook of water within twelve or fifteen miles of this fountain, but had in view vast savannas, swamps and Cane meadows, at no great distance from our road, on our right
hand, which we may presume were the resources or reservoirs which contributed to
the supplies of this delightful grotto. Here were growing on the ascents from the
fountain, Magnolia grandiflora, Laurus Borbonia, Quercus sempervirens, Callicarpa;
at a little distance a grove of the Cassine, and in an old field, just by, are to be seen
some small Indian mounts. We travelled several miles over ridges of low swelling hills,
whose surfaces were covered with particoloured pebbles, streaked and clouded with
red, white, brown and yellow: they were mostly broken or shivered to pieces, I believe
by the ancients in forming arrow-heads, darts, knives &c. for I observed frequently
some of these misshapen implements amongst them, some broken and others spoiled
in the making. These stones seemed to be a species of jasper or agate.

On my way down I also called at Silver Bluff, and waited on the honourable G.
Golphin, Esq. to acknowledge my obligations to him, and likewise to fulfil my engagements on the part of Mr. T———y, trader of Mucclasse. Mr. Golphin assured me
that he was in a disagreeable predicament, and that he feared the worst, but said he
would do all in his power to save him.

After five days pleasant travelling we arrived at Savanna in good health.

List of the towns and tribes in league, and which constitute the powerful confederacy or empire of the Creeks or Muscogulges, viz.

Towns on the Tallapoose or Oakfuske river, viz.

Oakfuske, upper.
Oakfuske, lower.
Usale, upper.   These speak the Musco-
Usale, lower.   gulge or Creek tongue,
Sokaspoge.   called the Mother
Tallase, great.   tongue.
Coolome.

Towns on the Tallapoose or Oakfuske river, viz.

Ghuaclahatche.
Otasse.   These speak the Musco-
Cluale.   gulge or Creek tongue,
Fusahatche.   called the Mother
Tuccabatche.   tongue.
Cunhutke.
Macclasse.   Speak the Stincard tongue.
Alabama.
Savannuca.   Speak the Uche tongue.
Whittumke.   Speak the Stincard
Coosauda.   tongue.

Towns on the Coosau river, viz.

Abacooche.	Speak a dialect of Chicasaw.
Pocontallahasse.	
Hickory ground, traders	Speak the Muscogulge
name.	tongue
Natche.	Speak Muscog. and Chicasaw.

Towns on the branches of the Coosau river, viz.

Wiccakaw.	
Fish pond, traders name.	
Hillaba.	Speak the Muscogulge
Kiolege	tongue.

Towns on the Apalachucla or Chata Uche river viz.

Apalachucla.	
Tucpauska.	
Chockeclucca.	
Chata Uche.	Speak the Muscogulge
Checlucca ninne.	tongue
Hothletega.	
Coweta.	
Usseta.	

Towns on the Apalachucla or Chata Uche river, continued, viz.

Uche.	Speak the Savannuca tongue.
Hooseche.	Speak the Muscog. tongue.
Chehaw.	
Echeta.	
Occone.	Speak the Stincard.
Swaglaw, great.	
Swaglaw, little.	

Towns on Flint river, comprehending the Siminoles or Lower Creeks.

Suola-nocha.
Cuscowilla or Allachua.

Talahasochte.

Caloosahatche.

—Great island.	Traders name.
—Great hammock.	Traders name.
—Capon.	Traders name.
—St. Mark's.	Traders name.
—Forks.	Traders name.

With many others of less note.

The Siminoles speak both the Muscogulge and Stincard tongue.

In all fifty-five towns, besides many villages not enumerated, and reckoning two hundred inhabitants to each town on an average, which is a moderate computation, would give eleven thousand inhabitants.

It appears to me pretty clearly, from divers circumstances, that this powerful empire or confederacy of the Creeks or Muscogulges, arose from, and established itself upon the ruins of that of the Natches, agreeably to Monsieur Duprat. According to the Muscogulges account of themselves, they arrived from the South-West, beyond the Mississipi, some time before the English settled the colony of Carolina and built Charleston; and their story concerning their country and people, from whence they sprang, the cause of leaving their native land, the progress of their migration, &c. is very similar to that celebrated historian's account of the Natches, they might have been included as allies and confederates in that vast and powerful empire of red men. The Muscogulges gradually pushing and extending their settlements on their North-East border, until the dissolution of the Natches empire; being then the most numerous, warlike and powerful tribe, they began to subjugate the various tribes or bands (which formerly constituted the Natches) and uniting them with themselves, formed a new confederacy under the name of the Muscogulges.

The Muscogulge tongue being now the national or sovereign language, the Chicasaws, Chactaws, and even the remains of the Natches, if we are to credit the Creeks and traders, being dialects of the Muscogulge; and probably, when the Natches were sovereigns, they called their own the national tongue, and the Creeks, Chicasaws, &c. only dialects of theirs. It is uncertain which is really the mother tongue.

As for those numerous remnant bands or tribes, included at this day within the Muscogulge confederacy, who generally speak the Stincard language, (which is radically different from the Muscogulge) they are, beyond a doubt, the shattered remains of the various nations who inhabited the lower or maritime parts of Carolina and Florida, from Cape Fear, West to the Mississipi. The Uches and Savannucas is a third language, radically different from the Muscogulge and Lingo, and seems to be a more Northern tongue; I suppose a language that prevailed amongst the numerous tribes who formerly possessed and inhabited the maritime parts of Maryland and Virginia. I was told by an old trader that the Savannuca and Shawanese speak the same language, or very near alike.

3

MANASSEH CUTLER

(1742–1823)

In the years immediately following the Revolution, settlement of the west was complicated by two factors. First, intransigent native resistance was still supported and encouraged by British agents in the area. Second, without a federal government, land claims in the west made by various eastern states precluded the development of any coherent programs of land distribution. Since western lands were largely held by the federal government, it was thought that their sale could be used to pay off the debt still owed from the costs of the Revolution. With the Land Ordinance of 1785 and the passage of the Northwest Ordinance in 1787, a coherent program could be put in place even as the Constitution was still being drafted. What was then needed were investors to buy the land from the government and then develop programs for the expansion of American settlements into the region.

The Reverend Manasseh Cutler was the representative (today we might say lobbyist) of the Ohio Company of Connecticut at both the Congress's session in New York and the Constitutional Convention in Philadelphia during the summer of 1787. While there is no evidence that he intervened in the legislation of either document, each document satisfied his and his partners' ambition to develop profitable and virtuous settlement on the Muskingum River in what is now southern Ohio. Once the Ohio Company had secured contract to those lands, Cutler needed to attract settlers who would invest in the land he had bought from the government. He wrote the pamphlet, "An Explanation of the Map of Federal Lands," as advertising. In terms borrowed from generations of British colonial investors and later borrowed by generations of American land speculators, Cutler described southern Ohio as little less than a paradise, free of the corruptions of postwar America and situated on fertile lands free of threats of native violence.

The pamphlet was a success: in the fall of 1787, settlers marched from New England to Ohio and followed his plan for creating an orderly settlement defined by its piety, order, and organization. Cutler's plan was based on the assumption that other western lands were corrupted by unsystematized patterns of settlement that led to moral, economic, and political chaos. He reimagined the process of settlement as the neat replication of New England, and sought young and perhaps illiterate settlers for his purposes. While Cutler managed the colony from home in New England, it grew into Marietta, Ohio, and became the site of the university of that name, just as Cutler planned. Furthermore, Cutler's influence can be seen, domestically, in writers such as James Fenimore Cooper and Henry

Ward Beecher, or, internationally, in the work of British colonial theoreticians such as Edward Gibbon Wakefield and George Merivale.

Text: "An Explanation of the Map of Federal Lands" (Salem, 1787; rpt. 1966). 22 pp.

FROM "AN EXPLANATION OF THE MAP OF FEDERAL LANDS" (1787)

The great river Ohio is formed by the confluence of Monongahela and the Alleghany, in the State of Pennsylvania, about 290 miles west of the city of Philadelphia, and about 20 miles east of the western line of that State. In the common travelling road, the former distance is computed at 320 miles; and, by the windings and oblique direction of the Ohio, the latter is reckoned about 42. These two sources of the Ohio are large navigable streams; the former, flowing from the southeast, leaves but 30 miles portage from the navigable waters of the Potowmac, in Virginia; the latter opens a passage from the northeast, and rises not far from the head waters of the Susquehanna.

The State of Pennsylvania have already adopted the plan of opening a navigation from the Alleghany river to the city of Philadelphia, through the Susquehanna and the Delaware. In this route there will be a portage of only 24 miles.

On the junction of these rivers, or at the head of the Ohio, stands Fort Pitt, which gives name to the town of Pittsburgh, a flourishing settlement in the vicinity of the fortress. From this place the Ohio takes a southwestern course of 1188 miles, including its various windings, and discharges itself into the Missisippi; having passed a prodigious length of delightful and fertile country, and received the tribute of a large number of navigable streams. The Muskingum, the Hockhocking, the Sioto, the Miami, and the Wabash, from the northwest; the Kenhawa, the Kentucky, the Buffaloe, the Shawanee, and the Cherokee, from the southeast, all navigable from 100 to 900 miles, discharge themselves into the Ohio; and yet the Ohio itself forms but an inconsiderable part of that vast variety of congregated streams which visit the ocean through the channel of the Missisippi.

The Ohio, from Pennsylvania to the Missisippi, divides the State of Virginia from the federal lands, or the lands which do not fall within the limits of any particular State. These extend westward to the Missisippi, and northward to the boundary of the United States, excepting only the Connecticut reserve, which is a narrow strip of land, bordering on the south of Lake Erie, and stretching 120 miles west of the western limit of Pennsylvania. But a small proportion of these lands is as yet purchased of the natives, and to be disposed of by Congress. Beginning on the meridian line, which forms the western boundary of Pennsylvania, they have surveyed and laid off seven ranges of townships. As a north and south line strikes the Ohio in a very oblique direction, the termination of the seventh range falls upon that river 9 miles above the Muskingum, which is the first large river that falls into the Ohio. It forms this junction at 172 miles below Fort Pitt, including the windings of the Ohio, though in a direct line it is but 90 miles.

The lands in which the Indian title is extinguished, and which are now purchasing under the United States, are bounded as before described on the east, by the great Miami on the west, by the Ohio on the south, and extend near to the head waters of the Muskingum and Sioto on the north.

The Muskingum is a gentle river, confined by banks so high as to prevent its overflowing. It is 250 yards wide at its confluence with the Ohio, and navigable by large batteaux and barges to the *Three Legs;* and, by small ones, to the lake at its head. From thence, by a portage of about one mile, a communication is opened to Lake Erie, through the Cayahoga, which is a stream of great utility, navigable the whole length, without any obstruction from falls. From Lake Erie, the avenue is well known to the Hudson in the State of New-York. The most considerable portage in this route is at the fall of Niagara, which interrupts the communication between the lakes Erie and Ontario. From the latter you pass through the river Oswego, the Oneyda lake, Wood's creek, and find a short portage into the Mohawk, and another occasioned by a fall near the confluence of the Mohawk and the Hudson, at Albany.

The Hockhocking resembles the Muskingum, though somewhat inferior in size. It is navigable for large boats about 70 miles, and for small ones much farther. On the banks of this very useful stream are found inexhaustible quarries of free-stone, large beds of iron ore, and some rich mines of lead. Coal mines and salt springs are frequent in the neighbourhood of this stream, as they are in every part of the western territory. The salt that may be obtained from these springs will afford an inexhaustible store of that necessary article. Beds of white and blue clay, of an excellent quality, are likewise found here, suitable for the manufacture of glass, crockery and other earthen wares. Red bole and many other useful fossils have been observed on the branches of this river.

The Sioto is a larger river than either of the preceding, and opens a more extensive navigation. It is passable for large barges for 200 miles, with a portage of only 4 miles to the Sandusky, a good navigable stream that falls into the lake Erie. Through the Sandusky and Sioto lies the most common pass from Canada to the Ohio and Missisippi; one of the most extensive and useful communications that are to be found in any country. Prodigious extensions of territory are here connected; and, from the rapidity with which the western parts of Canada, lake Erie and the Kentucky countries are settling, we may anticipate an immense intercourse between them. The lands on the borders of these middle streams, from this circumstance alone, aside from their natural fertility, must be rendered vastly valuable. There is no doubt, but flour, corn, flax, hemp, &c. raised for exportation in that great country between the lakes Huron and Ontario, will find an easier outlet through lake Erie and these rivers, than in any other direction. The Ohio merchant can give a higher price than those of Quebec, for these commodities; as they may be transported from the former to Florida and the West-India islands, with less expence, risk and insurance, than from the latter; while the expence from the place of growth to the Ohio will not be one fourth of what it would be to Quebec, and much less than even to the Oneyda lake. The stream of Sioto is gentle, no where broken by falls: At some places, in the spring of the year, it overflows its banks, providing for large natural rice plantations. Salt springs, coal mines, white and blue clay, and free-stone, abound in the country adjoining this river.

The undistinguishing terms of admiration, that are commonly used in speaking of the natural fertility of the country on the western waters of the United States, would render it difficult, without accurate attention in the surveys, to ascribe a preference to any particular part; or to give a just description of the territory under consideration, without the hazard of being suspected of exaggeration: But in *this* we have the united opinion of the Geographer, the Surveyors, and every traveller that has been intimately acquainted with the country, and marked every natural object with the most scrupulous exactness—That no part of the federal territory unites so many advantages, in point of health, fertility, variety of production, and foreign intercourse, as that tract which stretches from the Muskingum to the Sioto and the Great Miami rivers.

Col. Gordon, in his journal, speaking of a much larger range of country, in which this is included, and makes unquestionably the finest part, has the following observation:—"The country on the Ohio is every where pleasant, with large level spots of rich land; and remarkably healthy. One general remark of this nature will serve for the whole tract of the globe comprehended between the western skirts of the Alleghany mountains; thence running southwesterly to the distance of 500 miles to the Ohio falls; then crossing them northerly to the heads of the rivers that empty themselves into the Ohio; thence east along the ridge that separates the lakes and Ohio's streams, to French Creek—This country may, from a proper knowledge, be affirmed to be the most healthy, the most pleasant, the most commodious and most fertile spot of earth, known to the European people."

The lands that feed the various streams above-mentioned, which fall into the Ohio, are now more accurately known, and may be described with confidence and precision. They are interspersed with all the variety of soil which conduces to pleasantness of situation, and lays the foundation for the wealth of an agricultural and manufacturing people. Large level bottoms, or natural meadows, from 20 to 50 miles in circuit, are every where found bordering the rivers, and variegating the country in the interior parts. These afford as rich a soil as can be imagined, and may be reduced to proper cultivation with very little labour. It is said, that in many of these bottoms a man may clear an acre a day, fit for planting with Indian corn; there being no under wood; and the trees, growing very high and large, but not thick together, need nothing but girdling.

The prevailing growth of timber and the more useful trees are, maple or sugar tree—sycamore—black and white mulberry—black and white walnut—butternut—chestnut—white, black, Spanish and chesnut oaks—hickory—cherry—buckwood—honey locust—elm—horse chesnut—cucumber tree—lynn tree—gum tree—iron wood—ash—aspin—sassafras—crab apple tree—paupaw or custard apple—a variety of plumb trees—nine bark spice, and leather wood bushes. General Parsons measured a black walnut tree near the Muskingum, whose circumference, at 5 feet from the ground, was 22 feet. A sycamore, near the same place, measures 44 feet in circumference, at some distance from the ground. White and black oak, and chesnut, with most of the above-mentioned timbers, grow large and plenty upon the high grounds. Both the high and low lands produce vast quantities of natural grapes of various kinds, of which the settlers universally make a sufficiency for their own consumption of rich

red wine. It is asserted in the old settlement of St. Vincent's, where they have had opportunity to try it, that age will render this wine preferable to most of the European
wines. Cotton is the natural production of this country, and grows in great perfection.

The sugar maple is a most valuable tree for an inland country. Any number of inhabitants may be forever supplied with a sufficiency of sugar, by preserving a few trees
for the use of each family. A tree will yield about ten pounds of sugar a year, and the
labour is very trifling: The sap is extracted in the months of February and March, and
granulated, by the simple operation of boiling, to a sugar equal in flavour and whiteness to the best Muscovado.

Springs of excellent water abound in every part of this territory; and small and
large streams, for mills and other purposes, are actually interspersed, as if by art, that
there be no deficiency in any of the conveniences of life.

Very little waste land is to be found in any part of the tract of country comprehended in the map which accompanies this. There are no swamps; and though the
hills are frequent, they are gentle and swelling, no where high nor incapable of tillage.
They are of a deep, rich soil, covered with a heavy growth of timber, and well adapted
to the production of wheat, rye, indigo, tobacco, &c.

The communications between this country and the sea will be principally in the
four following directions.

1. The route through the Sioto and Muskingum to lake Erie, and so to the river
Hudson; which has been already described.

2. The passage up the Ohio and Monongahela, to the portage above-mentioned,
which leads to the navigable waters of the Potowmac. This portage is 30 miles, and
will probably be rendered much less by the execution of the plans now on foot for
opening the navigation of those waters.

3. The great Kenhawa, which falls into the Ohio from the Virginia shore, between
the Hock-hocking and the Sioto, opens an extensive navigation from the southeast,
and leaves but 18 miles portage from the navigable waters of James river, in Virginia.
This communication, for the country between Muskingum and Sioto, will probably
be more used than any other, for the exportation of manufactures, and other light and
valuable articles; and, especially, for the importation of foreign commodities, which
may be brought from the Chesapeak to the Ohio much cheaper than they are now
carried from Philadelphia to Carlisle and the other thick settled back counties of
Pennsylvania.

4. But the current down the Ohio and the Missisippi, for heavy articles that suit
the Florida and West-India markets, such as corn, flour, beef, lumber, &c. will be more
frequently loaded than any streams on earth. The distance from the Sioto to the Missisippi is 800 miles; from thence to the sea is 900. This whole course is easily run in
15 days; and the passage up those rivers is not so difficult as has usually been represented. It is found, by late experiments, that fails are used to great advantage against
the current of the Ohio: And it is worthy of observation, that in all probability steamboats will be found to do infinite service in all our extensive river navigation.

Such is the state of facts relative to the natural advantages of the territory described in the annexed map. As far as observations in passing the rivers, and the transitory remarks of travellers, will justify an opinion, the lands farther down, and in
other parts of the unappropriated country, are not equal, in point of soil and other
local advantages, to the tract which is here described. This, however, cannot be accurately determined, as the present situation of these countries will not admit of that
minute inspection which has been bestowed on the one under consideration.

It is a happy circumstance, that the *Ohio Company* are about to commence the settlement of this country in so regular and judicious a manner. It will serve as a wise model for the future settlement of all the federal lands; at the same time that, by beginning so near the western limit of Pennsylvania, it will be a continuation of the old settlements, leaving no vacant lands exposed to be seized by such lawless banditti as usually infest the frontiers of countries distant from the seat of government.

The design of Congress and of the settlers is, that the settlements shall proceed regularly down the Ohio; and northward to lake Erie. And it is probable that not many years will elapse, before the whole country above Miami will be brought to that degree of cultivation, which will exhibit all its latent beauties, and justify those descriptions of travellers which have so often made it the garden of the world, the seat of wealth, and the *centre* of a great empire.

To the philosopher and the politician, on viewing this delightful part of the federal territory, under the prospect of an immediate and systematic settlement, the following observations will naturally occur.

First. The toils of agriculture will here be rewarded with a greater variety of valuable productions, than in any part of America. The advantages of almost every climate are here blended together; every considerable commodity, that is cultivated in any part of the United States, is here produced in the greatest plenty and perfection. The high and dry lands are of a deep, rich soil—producing, in abundance, *wheat, rye, Indian corn, buck wheat, oats, barley, flax, hemp, tabacco, indigo, silk, wine and cotton.* The tobacco is of a quality superior to that of Virginia; and the crops of wheat are larger than in any other part of America. The common growth of Indian corn is from 60 to 80 bushels to the acre.[1] The low lands are well suited to the production of nearly all the above articles, except wheat. Where the large bottoms are interspersed with small streams, they are well adapted to the growth of rice; which may be produced in any quantities. The borders of the large streams do not generally admit of this crop, as very few of them overflow their banks. But the scarcity of natural rice swamps is amply compensated by the remarkable healthfulness of the whole country; it being entirely free from stagnant waters. It is found, in this country, that stagnant waters are by no means necessary to the growth of rice; the common rich bottoms produce this crop in as great perfection as the best rice swamps of the southern States. Hops are the natural production of this country; as are peaches, plumbs, pears, apples, melons, and almost every fruit of the temperate zone.

No country is better stocked with wild game of every kind: Innumerable herds of deer, elk, buffaloe, and bear, are sheltered in the groves, and fed in the extensive bottoms that every where abound; an unquestionable proof of the great fertility of the soil: Turkies, geese, ducks, swans, teal, pheasants, partridges, &c. are, from observation, believed to be in greater plenty here, than the tame poultry are in any part of the old settlements in America.

The rivers are well stored with fish of various kinds, and many of them of an excellent quality. They are generally large, though of different sizes: The cat-fish, which is the largest, and of a delicious flavour, weighs from 30 to 80 pounds.

Provisions will, for many years, find a ready market on any of these rivers; as set-

---

1. General Parsons, one of the Commissioners of the treaty at Miami, in 1786, has made in his journal the following note:—"Mr. Dawson has lived two summers at the place—[*Little Beaver, near Pennsylvania west line*]—He says, his corn is from 80 to 100 bushels per acre: Last year, he planted 7 acres—plowed twice before planting, and hoed once only—and had 600 bushels."

tlers are constantly coming in from all parts of the world, and must be supplied by purchase, for one year at least, with many articles.

Second. From its situation and productions, no country is so well calculated for the establishment of manufactures of various kinds. Provisions will be forever plenty and cheap. The raw materials for fabricating most of the articles of clothing and dress, are and will be the luxuriant production of this country. Though silk, cotton and flax are valuable in themselves, yet, by being wrought into the various articles of use and ornament, the expence of transportation is proportionably lessened. The United States, and, perhaps, other countries, will be supplied from these interior parts of America.

Shipbuilding will be a capital branch of business on the Ohio and its confluent streams. The Ohio, when at the lowest, admits of four fathom of water, from the mouth of the Muskingum to its confluence with the Mississippi, except at the rapids, which, at such times, interrupt the navigation for about one mile. The descent, in that distance, is only 15 feet; and the channel, which is 250 yards wide, has, at no time, less than 5 feet of water. In freshes, the water rises 30 feet; and boats are not only rowed against the stream, but ascend the rapids by means of their fails only. It is the opinion of the Geographer, and others, who have viewed the spot, that, by cutting a canal a little more than half a mile on the south side of the river, which is low meadow ground, the rapids may be avoided, and the navigation made free at all seasons of the year. Hemp, timber and iron will be plenty and good; and the high freshes, from February to April, and frequently in October and November, will bear a vessel of any burden over the rapids, in their present state, and out to sea.

The following observations, by an English engineer, who had explored the western country, were addressed to the Earl of Hillsborough, in the year 1770, when Secretary of State for the North American department—at a time when we were British colonies, and our country considered only as the handmaid to Great Britain, in furnishing raw materials for their manufactures.

"No part of North America will require less encouragement for the production of naval stores and raw materials for manufactories in Europe; and for supplying the West-India islands with lumber, provisions, &c. than the country of the Ohio—and for the following reasons.

"1. The lands are excellent—the climate, temperate; the native grapes, silkworms, and mulberry trees, abound every where; hemp, hops and rye grow spontaneously in the vallies & low lands; lead & iron ore are plenty in the hills; salt springs are innumerable; and no soil is better adapted to the culture of tobacco, flax and cotton, than that of the Ohio.

"2. The country is well watered by several navigable rivers, communicating with each other; by which, and a short land carriage, the produce of the lands of the Ohio can, even now, be sent cheaper to the seaport town of Alexandria, on the river Potowmac, where General Braddock's transports landed his troops, than any kind of merchandise is sent from Northampton to London.

"3. The river Ohio is, at *all seasons* of the year, navigable with large boats; and, from the month of February to April, large ships may be built on the Ohio, and sent to sea, laden with hemp, iron, flax, silk, tobacco, cotton, potash, &c.

"4. Flour, corn, beef, ship-plank, and other useful articles, can be sent down the stream of Ohio to West Florida, and from thence to the West India islands, much cheaper, and in better order, than from New York or Philadelphia to those islands.

"5. Hemp, tobacco, iron, and such bulky articles, may be sent down the stream of

Ohio to the sea, at least 50 per cent. cheaper than these articles were ever carried by a land carriage of only 60 miles in Pennsylvania, where waggonage is cheaper than in any other part of North-America.

"6. The expence of transporting European manufactures from the sea to the Ohio will not be so much as is now paid, and ever must be paid, to a great part of the counties of Pennsylvania, Virginia and Maryland. Whenever the farmers or merchants of Ohio shall properly understand the business of transportation, they will build schooners, sloops, &c. on the Ohio, suitable for the West India or European markets; or, by having black walnut, cherry tree, oak, &c. properly sawed for foreign markets, and formed into rafts, in the manner that is now done by the settlers near the upper parts of the Delaware, in Pennsylvania, and thereon stow their hemp, iron, tobacco, &c. and proceed with them to New Orleans.

"It may not, perhaps, be amiss to observe, that large quantities of flour are made in the western counties of Pennsylvania, and sent, by an expensive land carriage, to the city of Philadelphia; and from thence shipped to South Carolina, and East and West Florida—there being little or no wheat raised in these provinces. The river Ohio seems kindly designed, by nature, as the channel, through which the two Floridas may be supplied with flour, not only for their own consumption, but also for carrying on an extensive commerce with Jamaica, and the Spanish settlements in the Bay of Mexico. Millstones, in abundance, are to be obtained in the hills near the Ohio; and the country is every where well watered with large and constant springs and streams for grift and other mills. The passage from Philadelphia to Pensacola is seldom made in less than a month; and 60 shillings sterling per ton freight (consisting of 16 barrels) is usually paid for flour, &c. thither. Boats, carrying 500 or 1000 barrels of flour, may go in about the same time from Pittsburgh, as from Philadelphia, to Pensacola, and for half the above freight. The Ohio merchants could deliver flour, &c. there, in much better order than from Philadelphia, and without incurring the damage and delay of the sea, and charges of insurance, &c. as from thence to Pensacola. This is not mere speculation; for it is a fact, that about the year 1746 there was a scarcity of provisions at New Orleans; and the French settlements at the Illinois, small as they then were, sent thither, in one winter, upwards of eight hundred thousand weight of flour."

If, instead of furnishing other nations with raw materials, companies of manufacturers from Europe could be introduced and established in this inviting situation, under the superintendence of men of property, it would occasion an immense addition of men and wealth to these new settlements, and serve as a beneficial example of economy to many parts of the United States.

Third. In the late ordinance of Congress, for disposing of the western lands as far down as the river Sioto, the provision that is made for schools and the endowment of an university, looks with a most favourable aspect upon the settlement, and furnishes the presentiment, that, by a proper attention to the subject of education, under these advantages, the field of science may be greatly enlarged, and the acquisition of useful knowledge placed upon a more respectable footing here, than in any other part of the world. Besides the opportunity of opening a new and unexplored region for the range of natural history, botany and the medical science, there will be one advantage which no other part of the earth can boast, and which probably will never again occur— that, in order to begin *right,* there will be no *wrong* habits to combat, and no inveterate systems to overturn—there is no rubbish to remove, before you can lay the foundation. The first settlement will inbosom many men of the most liberal minds—well versed in the world in business and every useful science. Could the necessary apparatus be procured, and funds immediately established, for founding a university on a liberal plan, that professors might be active in their various researches and employments—even now, in the infancy of the settlement, a proper use might be made of an advantage which will never be repeated.

Many political benefits would immediately result to the United States from such an early institution in that part of the country. The people in the Kentucky and Illinois countries are rapidly increasing. Their distance from the old States will prevent their sending their children thither for instruction; from the want of which they are in danger of losing all their habits of government, and allegiance to the United States: But, on seeing examples of government, science, and regular industry, follow them into the neighbourhood of their own country, they would favour their children with these advantages, and revive the ideas of order, citizenship, and the useful sciences. This attention, from these neighbouring people, would increase the wealth and population of the new proposed settlement.

Fourth. In the ordinance of Congress, for the government of the territory northwest of the Ohio, it is provided, that, after the said territory acquires a certain degree of population, it shall be divided into States. The eastern State, that is thus provided to be made, is bounded on the Great Miami on the west, and by the Pennsylvania line on the east. The centre of this State will fall between the Sioto and the Hockhocking. At the mouth of one of these rivers, will probably be the seat of government for this State: And, if we may indulge the sublime contemplation of beholding the whole territory of the United States settled by an enlightened people, and continued under one extended government—on the river Ohio, and not far from this spot, will be the seat of empire for the whole dominion. This is central to the whole; it will best accommodate every part; it is the most pleasant, and probably the most healthful.

Altho' it is an object of importance, that Congress should soon fix on a seat of government—yet, in the present state of the country, it is presumed, it will not be thought best that such seat be considered as immovably fixed. To take the range of the Alleghany mountains from north to south, it is probable 20 years will not elapse, before there will be more people on the western than on the eastern waters of the United States. The settlers ought even now to have it in view, that government will forever accommodate them as much as their brethren on the cast: This may be necessary, to prevent their forming schemes of independence, seeking other connexions, and providing for their separate convenience. As it is the most exalted and benevolent object of legislation that ever was aimed at, to unite such an amazingly extensive people, and make them happy, under one jurisdiction, every act of Congress under the new constitution, by looking forward to this object, will, we trust, inculcate and familiarize the idea. They will, no doubt, at an early period, make a reservation or purchase of a suitable tract of land for a federal town, that will be central to the whole; and give some public intimation of such intention to transfer the seat of government, on the occurrence of certain events—such as, comparative population, &c. This would render such transfer easily practicable, by preventing the occasion of uneasiness in the old States; while it would not appear to be the result of danger, or the prospect of revolt, in the new.

THOMAS JEFFERSON

(1743–1826)

Thomas Jefferson said and wrote much about the western frontier and its inhabitants during his long career. His sympathy with western settlers was rooted in their sharing of his antifederalist sympathies and demonstrated in his appointment of an accused leader of the Whiskey Rebellion of western Pennsylvania, Albert Gallatin, as his secretary of state. However, like so many things throughout his career, Jefferson's view of the west was fraught with embedded contradictions and paradoxes. In the two documents reproduced here we see each side.

Jefferson's Report of a Plan of Government for the Western Territory (1784)—obviously an early draft of the Northwest Ordinance (1787)—and his accompanying map first demonstrates his emblematic need to imagine and construct the American colonization of the west using the order-loving ideology of the Enlightenment. The absurdly cubed states and the oddly classical names he etches on the region represent an imperial gaze: the west as the tabula rasa upon which a more rational and structured community could be conceived to perfect the ideals of the eighteenth century. Moreover, Jefferson's criteria for application for statehood clearly set the terms of entry for each state in ways that secure the ascendence of the east in the nation's politics. His Plan therefore very stingently ensures the cultural and geopolitical absorption of the region into the nation, a vision shared by such cultural nationalists as Alexander Hamilton, James Fenimore Cooper, and Frederick Jackson Turner.

However, Jefferson's 1803 letter to Senator John Breckenridge of Kentucky suggests just the reverse: that the requirements of local self-determination may lead to either a decentralization or a balkanization of the different American regions. In his suggestion that the Atlantic and Mississippi regions are distinct and their alliance provisional and, perhaps, temporary, he foreshadows such later regionalists as Hugh Henry Brackenridge, Daniel Drake, and Hamlin Garland. The crux of the matter lies in what type of nation is the United States to become: a vertical and singular hierarchy of regions with the Atlantic states ascendent or a horizontal and plural collection of different populations? Jefferson's articulation of both sides of this issue early in the period when white settlers were moving west serves to set the stage for the west's confused identity in subsequent centuries.

Text: Both are in *The Portable Thomas Jefferson* (New York, 1975): Report, 254–258; Letter, 494–497.

REPORT OF A PLAN OF GOVERNMENT FOR THE WESTERN TERRITORY[1] (1784)

March 1, 1784

The Committee appointed to prepare a plan for the temporary government of the Western territory have agreed to the following resolutions.

Resolved, that the territory ceded or to be ceded by Individual states to the United states shall be formed into distinct states, bounded in the following manner as nearly as such cessions will admit, that is to say; Northwardly and Southwardly by parallels of latitude so that each state shall comprehend from South to North two de-

Bounds of States Proposed by the Report of March 1, 1784, with names assigned in territory already ceded.

---

1. The text is from a manuscript in Jefferson's hand. Although considered by Congress, it was returned to the committee, of which Jefferson was chairman, and a revised report, also of his authorship, was presented on March 22 and adopted, after amendment, on April 23, 1784. The latter report differed from the former principally in the omission of the names Jefferson wished to give to the territories. [Ed.]

grees of latitude beginning to count from the completion of thirty one degrees North of the Equator: but any territory Northwardly of the 47th. degree shall make part of the state next below. And Eastwardly and Westwardly they shall be bounded, those on the Missisipi by that river on one side and the meridian of the lowest point of the rapids of Ohio on the other; and those adjoining on the East by the same meridian on their Western side, and on their Eastern by the meridian of the Western cape of the mouth of the Great Kanhaway. And the territory Eastward of this last meridian between the Ohio, Lake Erie, and Pennsylvania shall be one state.

That the settlers within any of the said states shall, either on their own petition, or on the order of Congress, receive authority from them, with appointments of time and place for their free males of full age to meet together for the purpose of establishing a temporary government, to adopt the constitution and laws of any one of these states, so that such laws nevertheless shall be subject to alteration by their ordinary legislature, and to erect, subject to a like alteration, counties or townships for the election of members for their legislature.

That such temporary government shall only continue in force in any state until it shall have acquired 20,000 free inhabitants; when giving due proof thereof to Congress, they shall receive from them authority with appointments of time and place to call a Convention of representatives to establish a permanent constitution and government for themselves.

Provided that both the temporary and permanent governments be established on these principles as their basis. 1. That they shall for ever remain a part of the United states of America. 2. That in their persons, property and territory they shall be subject to the government of the United states in Congress assembled, and to the Articles of confederation in all those cases in which the original states shall be so subject. 3. That they shall be subject to pay a part of the federal debts contracted or to be contracted to be apportioned on them by Congress according to the same common rule and measure by which apportionments thereof shall be made on the other states. 4. That their respective governments shall be in republican forms, and shall admit no person to be a citizen who holds any hereditary title. 5. That after the year 1800 of the Christian æra, there shall be neither slavery nor involuntary servitude in any of the said states, otherwise than in punishment of crimes, whereof the party shall have been duly convicted to have been personally guilty.

That whensoever any of the said states shall have, of free inhabitants, as many as shall then be in any one the least numerous of the thirteen original states, such state shall be admitted by it's delegates into the Congress of the United states, on an equal footing with the said original states: after which the assent of two thirds of the United states in Congress assembled shall be requisite in all those cases, wherein by the Confederation, the assent of nine states is now required. Provided the consent of nine states to such admission may be obtained according to the eleventh of the articles of Confederation. Until such admission by their delegates into Congress, any of the said states, after the establishment of their temporary government, shall have authority to keep a sitting member in Congress, with a right of debating, but not of voting.

That the territory Northward of the 45th. degree that is to say, of the completion of 45°. from the Equator, and extending to the Lake of the Woods shall be called SYLVANIA:

That of the territory under the 45th and 44th degrees that which lies Westward of Lake Michigan shall be called MICHIGANIA, and that which is Eastward thereof within the peninsul formed by the lakes and waters of Michigan, Huron, St. Clair and

Erie, shall be called CHERRONESUS, and shall include any part of the peninsul which may extend above the 45th. degree.

Of the territory under the 43d and 42d degrees, that to the Westward thro' which the Assenisipi or Rock river runs shall be called ASSENISIPIA, and that to the Eastward in which are the fountains of the Muskingum, the two Miamis of Ohio, the Wabash, the Illinois, the Miami of the lake and Sandusky rivers shall be called METROPOTAMIA.

Of the territory which lies under the 41st. and 40th. degrees, the Western, thro' which the river Illinois runs, shall be called ILLINOIA; that next adjoining to the Eastward SARATOGA, and that between this last and Pennsylvania and extending from the Ohio to Lake Erie, shall be called WASHINGTON.

Of the territory which lies under the 39th. and 38th. degrees to which shall be added so much of the point of land within the fork of the Ohio and Missisipi as lies under the 37th. degree, that to the Westward within and adjacent to which are the confluences of the rivers Wabash, Shawanee, Tanissee, Ohio, Illinois, Missisipi and Missouri, shall be called POLYPOTAMIA, and that to the Eastward farther up the Ohio, otherwise called the Pelisipi shall be called PELISIPIA.

That the preceding articles shall be formed into a Charter of Compact, shall be duly executed by the President of the U.S. in Congress assembled under his hand and the seal of the United States, shall be promulgated, and shall stand as fundamental constitutions between the thirteen original states, and those now newly described, unalterable but by the joint consent of the U.S. in Congress assembled and of the particular state within which such alteration is proposed to be made.

LETTER TO JOHN BRECKINRIDGE[1] (1803)

Monticello, August 12, 1803.

DEAR SIR

The enclosed letter, though directed to you, was intended to me also, and was left open with a request, that when forwarded, I would forward it to you. It gives me occasion to write a word to you on the subject of Louisiana, which being a new one, an interchange of sentiments may produce correct ideas before we are to act on them.

Our information as to the country is very incomplete; we have taken measures to obtain it full as to the settled part, which I hope to receive in time for Congress. The boundaries, which I deem not admitting question, are the high lands on the western side of the Mississippi enclosing all its waters, the Missouri of course, and terminating in the line drawn from the northwestern point of the Lake of the Woods to the nearest source of the Mississippi, as lately settled between Great Britain and the United States. We have some claims, to extend on the seacoast westwardly to the Rio

---

1. United States Senator from Kentucky. [Ed.]

Norte or Bravo, and better, to go eastwardly to the Rio Perdido, between Mobile and Pensacola, the ancient boundary of Louisiana. These claims will be a subject of negotiation with Spain, and if, as soon as she is at war, we push them strongly with one hand, holding out a price in the other, we shall certainly obtain the Floridas, and all in good time. In the meanwhile, without waiting for permission, we shall enter into the exercise of the natural right we have always insisted on with Spain, to wit, that of a nation holding the upper part of streams, having a right of innocent passage through them to the ocean. We shall prepare her to see us practise on this, and she will not oppose it by force.

Objections are raising to the eastward against the vast extent of our boundaries, and propositions are made to exchange Louisiana, or a part of it, for the Floridas. But, as I have said, we shall get the Floridas without, and I would not give one inch of the waters of the Mississippi to any nation, because I see in a light very important to our peace the exclusive right to its navigation, and the admission of no nation into it, but as into the Potomac or Delaware, with our consent and under our police. These federalists see in this acquisition the formation of a new confederacy, embracing all the waters of the Mississippi, on both sides of it, and a separation of its eastern waters from us. These combinations depend on so many circumstances which we cannot foresee, that I place little reliance on them. We have seldom seen neighborhood produce affection among nations. The reverse is almost the universal truth. Besides, if it should become the great interest of those nations to separate from this, if their happiness should depend on it so strongly as to induce them to go through that convulsion, why should the Atlantic States dread it? But especially why should we, their present inhabitants, take side in such a question? When I view the Atlantic States, procuring for those on the eastern waters of the Mississippi friendly instead of hostile neighbors on its western waters, I do not view it as an Englishman would be procuring future blessings for the French nation, with whom he has no relations of blood or affection. The future inhabitants of the Atlantic and Mississippi States will be our sons. We leave them in distinct but bordering establishments. We think we see their happiness in their union, and we wish it. Events may prove it otherwise; and if they see their interest in separation, why should we take side with our Atlantic rather than our Mississippi descendants? It is the elder and the younger son differing. God bless them both, and keep them in union, if it be for their good, but separate them, if it be better. The inhabited part of Louisiana, from Point Coupée to the sea, will of course be immediately a territorial government, and soon a State. But above that, the best use we can make of the country for some time, will be to give establishments in it to the Indians on the east side of the Mississippi, in exchange for their present country, and open land offices in the last, and thus make this acquisition the means of filling up the eastern side, instead of drawing off its population. When we shall be full on this side, we may lay off a range of States on the western bank from the head to the mouth, and so, range after range, advancing compactly as we multiply.

This treaty must of course be laid before both Houses, because both have important functions to exercise respecting it. They, I presume, will see their duty to their country in ratifying and paying for it, so as to secure a good which would otherwise probably be never again in their power. But I suppose they must then appeal to *the nation* for an additional article to the Constitution, approving and confirming an act which the nation had not previously authorized. The Constitution has made no provision for our holding foreign territory, still less for incorporating foreign nations into our Union. The executive in seizing the fugitive occurrence which so much advances the good of their country, have done an act beyond the Constitution. The Legislature in casting behind them metaphysical subtleties, and risking themselves like faithful servants, must ratify and pay for it, and throw themselves on their country for doing for them unauthorized, what we know they would have done for themselves had they been in a situation to do it. It is the case of a guardian, investing the money of his ward in purchasing an important adjacent territory; and saying to him when of age, I did this for your good; I pretend to no right to bind you: you may disavow me, and I must get out of the scrape as I can: I thought it my duty to risk myself for you. But we shall not be disavowed by the nation, and their act of indemnity will confirm and not weaken the Constitution, by more strongly marking out its lines. . . .

5

JOHN FILSON AND DANIEL BOONE

(c. 1753–1788 and 1734–1820)

Little is known about the early life of John Filson. Family tradition places his birth in Chester County, Pennsylvania, on December 10, 1753. Historical tradition has Filson wounded during the Revolution, though his biographer, John Walton, concludes it is "somewhat doubtful" that he served in the war at all. It is uncertain as well when Filson first arrived in Kentucky, though the fall of 1783 seems most likely. A schoolmaster by trade, Filson was also an experienced surveyor, and he saw the future in Kentucky's fertile, unsettled countryside when he snapped up 12,000 acres in present-day Fayette County.

This investment appears to have prompted Filson to write the first book about Kentucky: *The Discovery, Settlement, and Present State of Kentucke: And an Essay Toward the Topography, and Natural History of That Important Country.* Writing this book proved easier than having it published. As there were no presses west of the Allegheny Mountains, Filson traveled to Wilmington, Delaware, to have the book printed. The first edition appeared on October 22, 1784.

Filson's book succeeded in drawing settlers to Kentucky, but the author did not live to enjoy the fruits of his 12,000-acre investment. In September 1788, Filson and two partners began promoting a new settlement on the banks of the Great Miami River. Late in that month, or perhaps early in October, Filson was exploring on the banks of the Great Miami when his party encountered a band of Shawnee natives. Filson fled for the settlement, which he had christened Losantiville, but he was never seen again. After his death, the name of the settlement was changed to Cincinnati.

Filson's fame rests largely on a section of his book's appendix that he titled *The Adventures of Col. Daniel Boon; Containing a Narrative of the Wars of Kentucke.* Boone was among the Kentucky settlers whom Filson interviewed for his book, and Filson wrote that he had taken Boone's words and "published them from his [Boone's] own mouth." Thus, Filson presented Boone's story as an autobiography. He wrote that it included "every important Occurrence in the political History" of the settlement. At the time Boone told Filson his story, his celebrity was only local. Filson's book changed that.

On October 22, 1734, Boone the Kentucky Indian fighter was, ironically, born into a family of Pennsylvania Quakers. His family moved twice during his teenage years: first to Virginia's Shenendoah valley in 1750 and then to the frontier country of North Carolina's Yadkin valley in 1752, where he developed his considerable skills as an outdoorsman. Hunting became, in Boone's words, his "business of life." He married Rebecca Bryan in 1756, and they made their home in Rowan County, North Carolina.

Boone first visited Kentucky on a long hunting trip in 1767–1768. He found there, he recalled as an old man, "a spot of earth where nature seem[ed] to have concentrated all her bounties." He returned in May 1769 and spent nearly two years prowling the countryside. In March 1771, he and his brother Squire packed the fruits of their long labors— mostly furs—and headed for North Carolina, but natives robbed them of all their belongings before they arrived home.

Boone's first attempt to settle his family in Kentucky was aborted en route in October 1773 after natives attacked a party sent to get supplies. Boone's sixteen-year-old son James was killed by Big Jim, a Cherokee, after the Indian tortured the boy by tearing the nails from his hands and feet. An account of this attack printed in a North Carolina newspaper marked the first publication of Boone's name.

Boone returned to Kentucky as a messenger in 1774, and in 1775 he led those cutting the Wilderness Road from the Cumberland Gap to the Kentucky River and building Fort Boonesborough. He succeeded in re-locating his family to Kentucky in September 1775. His troubles with Indians, however, continued. He rescued his daughter Jemima from her Shawnee captors in July 1776, an event that James Fenimore Cooper later immortalized in *The Last of the Mohicans* (1826), in which Natty Bumppo performs a similar rescue. In 1777, Boone was shot in the ankle when Shawnees attacked Boonesborough, and the following year, he was captured and held by Shawnees for four months. Boone escaped on June 16, 1778, after learning that an attack on Boonesborough was imminent, and he returned in time to help defend the settlement. In September came his most important triumph over the Shawnees, in which he and the residents of Boonesborough endured a twelve-day siege.

Boone turned fifty years old on the day that Filson's book was published in 1784, and he still had thirty-six years to live. As Boone aged, his lifestyle seemed not to change. In 1803, aged sixty-eight, he was badly hurt when his hand was caught in a steel hunting trap. In 1812, aged seventy-eight, he volunteered for service in the War of 1812, but his offer was declined. He died on September 26, 1820, a living legend who little realized how much his legend had yet to grow. His last words were, "I am going. My time has come."

Text: *The Discovery, Settlement, and Present State of Kentucke: And an Essay Toward the Topography, and Natural History of That Important Country* (Wilmington, 1784): on Kentucky, 7–11, 28–30; on Daniel Boone, 49–82.

FROM *THE DISCOVERY, SETTLEMENT, AND PRESENT STATE OF KENTUCKE: AND AN ESSAY TOWARD THE TOPOGRAPHY, AND NATURAL HISTORY OF THAT IMPORTANT COUNTRY* (1784)

The first white man we have certain accounts of, who discovered this province, was one James M'Bride, who, in company with some others, in the year 1754, passing down the Ohio in Canoes, landed at the mouth of Kentucke river, and there marked a tree, with the first letters of his name, and the date, which remain to this day. These men reconnoitred the country, and returned home with the pleasing news of their discovery of the best tract of land in North-America, and probably in the world. From this period it remained concealed till about the year 1767, when one John Finley, and some others, trading with the Indians, fortunately travelled over the fertile region, now called Kentucke, then but known to the Indians, by the name of the Dark and Bloody Ground, and sometimes the Middle Ground. This country greatly engaged Mr. Finley's attention. Some time after, disputes arising between the Indians and traders, he was obliged to decamp; and returned to his place of residence in North-Carolina, where he communicated his discovery to Col. Daniel Boon, and a few more, who conceiving it to be an interesting object, agreed in the year 1769 to undertake a journey in order to explore it. After a long fatiguing march, over a mountainous wilderness, in a westward direction, they at length arrived upon its borders; and from the top of an eminence, with joy and wonder, descried the beautiful landscape of Kentucke. Here they encamped, and some went to hunt provisions, which were readily procured, there being plenty of game, while Col. Boon and John Finley made a tour through the country, which they found far exceeding their expectations, and returning to camp, informed their companions of their discoveries: But in spite of this promising beginning, this company, meeting with nothing but hardships and adversity, grew exceedingly disheartened, and was plundered, dispersed, and killed by the Indians, except Col. Boon, who continued an inhabitant of the wilderness until the year 1771, when he returned home.

About this time Kentucke had drawn the attention of several gentlemen. Doctor Walker of Virginia, with a number more, made a tour westward for discoveries, endeavouring to find the Ohio river; and afterwards he and General Lewis, at Fort Stanwix, purchased from the Five Nations of Indians the lands lying on the north side of Kentucke. Col. Donaldson, of Virginia, being employed by the State to run a line from six miles above the Long Island, on Holstein, to the mouth of the great Kenhawa, and finding thereby that an extensive tract of excellent country would be cut off to the Indians, was solicited, by the inhabitants of Clench and Holstein, to purchase the lands lying on the north side of Kentucke river from the Five Nations. This purchase he compleated for five hundred pounds, specie. It was then agreed, to fix a boundary line, running from the long Island on Holstein to the head of Kentucke river: thence down the same to the mouth; thence up the Ohio, to the mouth of Great Kenhawa; but this valuable purchase the State refused to confirm.

Col. Henderson, of North-Carolina, being informed of this country by Col. Boon, he, and some other gentlemen, held a treaty with the Cherokee Indians at Wataga, in March 1775, and then purchased from them the lands lying on the south side of Kentucke river for goods, at valuable rates, to the amount of six thousand pounds, specie.

Soon after this purchase, the State of Virginia took the alarm, agreed to pay the money Col. Donaldson had contracted for, and then disputed Col. Henderson's right of purchase, as a private gentlemen of another state, in behalf of himself: However, for his eminent services to this country, and for having been instrumental in making so valuable an acquisition to Virginia, that state was pleased to reward him with a tract of land, at the mouth of Green River, to the amount of two hundred thousand acres; and the state of North-Carolina gave him the like quantity in Powel's Valley. This region was formerly claimed by various tribes of Indians; whose title, if they had any, originated in such a manner, as to render it doubtful which ought to possess it: Hence this fertile spot became an object of contention, a theatre of war, from which it was properly denominated the Bloody-Grounds. Their contentions not being likely to decide the Right to any particular tribe, as soon as Mr. Henderson and his friends proposed to purchase, the Indians agreed to sell; and notwithstanding the valuable Consideration they received, have continued ever since troublesome neighbours to the new settlers.

An accurate account is kept of all the male inhabitants above the age of sixteen, who are rated towards the expences of the government by the name of Tithables; from which, by allowing that those so enrolled amount to a fourth part of the whole inhabitants, we may conclude that Kentucke contains, at present, upwards of thirty thousand souls: So amazingly rapid has been the settlement in a few years. Numbers are daily arriving, and multitudes expected this Fall; which gives a well grounded expectation that the country will be exceedingly populous in a short time. The inhabitants, at present, have not extraordinary good houses, as usual in a newly settled country.

They are, in general, polite, humane, hospitable; and very complaisant. Being collected from different parts of the continent, they have a diversity of manners, customs and religions, which may in time perhaps be modified to one uniform. As yet united to the State of Virginia, they are governed by her wholesome laws, which are virtuously executed, and with excellent decorum. Schools for education are formed, and a college is appointed by act of Assembly of Virginia, to be founded under the conduct of trustees in Kentucke, and endowed with lands for its use. An excellent library is likewise bestowed upon this seminary, by the Rev. John Todd, of Virginia.

The Anabaptists were the first that promoted public worship in Kentucke; and the Presbyterians have formed three large congregations near Harrod's station, and have engaged the Rev. David Rice, of Virginia, to be their pastor. At Lexington, 35 miles from these, they have formed another large congregation, and invited the Rev. Mr. Rankin, of Virginia, to undertake that charge among them. At present there are no other religious societies formed, although several other sects have numerous adherents. But from these early movements it is hoped that Kentucke will eminently shine in learning and piety, which will fulfil the wish of every virtuous citizen.

THE ADVENTURES OF COL. DANIEL BOON; CONTAINING A NARRATIVE OF THE WARS OF KENTUCKE (1784)

Curiosity is natural to the soul of man, and interesting objects have a powerful influence on our affections. Let these influencing powers actuate, by the permission or disposal of Providence, from selfish or social views, yet in time the mysterious will of Heaven is unfolded, and we behold our conduct, from whatsoever motives excited, operating to answer the important designs of heaven. Thus we behold Kentucke, lately an howling wilderness, the habitation of savages and wild beasts, become a fruitful field; this region, so favourably distinguished by nature, now become the habitation of civilization, at a period unparalleled in history, in the midst of a raging war, and under all the disadvantages of emigration to a country so remote from the inhabited parts of the continent. Here, where the hand of violence shed the blood of the innocent; where the horrid yells of savages, and the groans of the distressed, founded in our ears, we now hear the praises and adorations of our Creator; where wretched wigwams stood, the miserable abodes of savages, we behold the foundations of cities laid, that, in all probability, will rival the glory of the greatest upon earth. And we view Kentucke situated on the fertile banks of the great Ohio, rising from obscurity to shine with splendor, equal to any other of the stars of the American hemisphere.

The settling of this region well deserves a place in history. Most of the memorable events I have myself been exercised in; and, for the satisfaction of the public, will briefly relate the circumstances of my adventures, and scenes of life, from my first movement to this country until this day.

It was on the first of May, in the year 1769, that I resigned my domestic happiness for a time, and left my family and peaceable habitation on the Yadkin River, in North-Carolina, to wander through the wilderness of America, in quest of the country of Kentucke, in company with John Finley, John Stewart, Joseph Holden, James Monay, and William Cool. We proceeded successfully, and after a long and fatiguing journey through a mountainous wilderness, in a westward direction, on the seventh day of June following, we found ourselves on Red-River, where John Finley had formerly been trading with the Indians, and, from the top of an eminence, saw with pleasure the beautiful level of Kentucke. Here let me observe, that for some time we had experienced the most uncomfortable weather as a prelibation of our future sufferings. At this place we encamped, and made a shelter to defend us from the inclement season, and began to hunt and reconnoitre the country. We found every where abundance of wild beasts of all sorts, through this vast forest. The buffaloes were more frequent than I have seen cattle in the settlements, browzing on the leaves of the cane, or croping the herbage on those extensive plains, fearless, because ignorant, of the violence of man. Sometimes we saw hundreds in a drove, and the numbers about the salt springs were amazing. In this forest, the habitation of beasts of every kind natural to America, we practised hunting with great success until the twenty-second day of December following.

This day John Stewart and I had a pleasing ramble, but fortune changed the scene in the close of it. We had passed through a great forest, on which stood myriads of trees, some gay with blossoms, others rich with fruits. Nature was here a series of wonders, and a fund of delight. Here she displayed her ingenuity and industry in a variety of flowers and fruits, beautifully coloured, elegantly shaped, and charmingly flavoured; and we were diverted with innumerable animals presenting themselves perpetually to our view.—In the decline of the day, near Kentucke river, as we ascended the brow of a small hill, a number of Indians rushed out of a thick cane-brake upon us, and made us prisoners. The time of our sorrow was now arrived, and the scene fully opened. The Indians plundered us of what we had, and kept us in confinement seven days, treating us with common savage usage. During this time we discovered no uneasiness or desire to escape, which made them less suspicious of us; but in the dead of night, as we lay in a thick cane-brake by a large fire, when sleep had locked up their senses, my situation not disposing me for rest, I touched my companion and gently awoke him. We improved this favourable opportunity, and departed, leaving them to take their rest, and speedily directed our course towards our old camp, but found it plundered, and the company dispersed and gone home. About this time my brother, Squire Boon, with another adventurer, who came to explore the country shortly after us, was wandering through the forest, determined to find me, if possible, and accidentally found our camp. Notwithstanding the unfortunate circumstances of our company, and our dangerous situation, as surrounded with hostile savages, our meeting so fortunately in the wilderness made us reciprocally sensible of the utmost satisfaction. So much does friendship triumph over misfortune, that sorrows and sufferings vanish at the meeting not only of real friends, but of the most distant acquaintances, and substitutes happiness in their room.

Soon after this, my companion in captivity, John Stewart, was killed by the savages, and the man that came with my brother returned home by himself. We were then in a dangerous, helpless situation, exposed daily to perils and death amongst savages and wild beasts, not a white man in the country but ourselves.

Thus situated, many hundred miles from our families in the howling wilderness, I believe few would have equally enjoyed the happiness we experienced. I often observed to my brother, You see now how little nature requires to be satisfied. Felicity, the companion of content, is rather found in our own breasts than in the enjoyment of external things: And I firmly believe it requires but a little philosophy to make a man happy in whatsoever state he is. This consists in a full resignation to the will of Providence; and a resigned soul finds pleasure in a path strewed with briars and thorns.

We continued not in a state of indolence, but hunted every day, and prepared a little cottage to defend us from the Winter storms. We remained there undisturbed during the Winter; and on the first day of May, 1770, my brother returned home to the settlement by himself, for a new recruit of horses and ammunition, leaving me by myself, without bread, salt or sugar, without company of my fellow creatures, or even a horse or dog. I confess I never before was under greater necessity of exercising philosophy and fortitude. A few days I passed uncomfortably. The idea of a beloved wife and family, and their anxiety upon the account of my absence and exposed situation, made sensible impressions on my heart. A thousand dreadful apprehensions presented themselves to my view, and had undoubtedly disposed me to melancholy, if further indulged.

One day I undertook a tour through the country, and the diversity and beauties of nature I met with in this charming season, expelled every gloomy and vexatious thought. Just at the close of day the gentle gales retired, and left the place to the disposal of a profound calm. Not a breeze shook the most tremulous leaf. I had gained the summit of a commanding ridge, and, looking round with astonishing delight, beheld the ample plains, the beauteous tracts below. On the other hand, I surveyed the famous river Ohio that rolled in silent dignity, marking the western boundary of Kentucke with inconceivable grandeur. At a vast distance I beheld the mountains lift their venerable brows, and penetrate the clouds. All things were still. I kindled a fire near a fountain of sweet water, and feasted on the loin of a buck, which a few hours before I had killed. The sullen shades of night soon overspread the whole hemisphere, and the earth seemed to gasp after the hovering moisture. My roving excursion this day had fatigued my body, and diverted my imagination. I laid me down to sleep, and I awoke not until the sun had chased away the night. I continued this tour, and in a few days explored a considerable part of the country, each day equally pleased as the first. I returned again to my old camp, which was not disturbed in my absence. I did not confine my lodging to it, but often reposed in thick cane-brakes, to avoid the savages, who, I believe, often visited my camp, but fortunately for me, in my absence. In this situation I was constantly exposed to danger, and death. How unhappy such a situation for a man tormented with fear, which is vain if no danger comes, and if it does, only augments the pain. It was my happiness to be destitute of this afflicting passion, with which I had the greatest reason to be affected. The prowling wolves diverted my nocturnal hours with perpetual howlings; and the various species of animals in this vast forest, in the day time, were continually in my view.

Thus I was surrounded with plenty in the midst of want. I was happy in the midst of dangers and inconveniences. In such a diversity it was impossible I should be disposed to melancholy. No populous city, with all the varieties of commerce and stately structures, could afford so much pleasure to my mind, as the beauties of nature I found here.

Thus, through an uninterrupted scene of sylvan pleasures, I spent the time until the 27th day of July following, when my brother, to my great felicity, met me, according to appointment, at our old camp. Shortly after, we left this place, not thinking it safe to stay there longer, and proceeded to Cumberland river, reconnoitring that part of the country until March, 1771, and giving names to the different waters.

Soon after, I returned home to my family with a determination to bring them as soon as possible to live in Kentucke, which I esteemed a second paradise, at the risk of my life and fortune.

I returned safe to my old habitation, and found my family in happy circumstances. I sold my farm on the Yadkin, and what goods we could not carry with us; and on the twenty-fifth day of September, 1773, bade a farewel to our friends, and proceeded on our journey to Kentucke, in company with five families more, and forty men that joined us in Powel's Valley, which is one hundred and fifty miles from the now settled parts of Kentucke. This promising beginning was soon overcast with a cloud of adversity; for upon the tenth day of October, the rear of our company was attacked by a number of Indians, who killed six, and wounded one man. Of these my eldest son was one that fell in the action. Though we defended ourselves, and repulsed the enemy, yet this unhappy affair scattered our cattle, brought us into extreme difficulty, and so discouraged the whole company, that we retreated forty miles, to the settlement on Clench river. We had passed over two mountains, viz. Powel's and Walden's, and were approaching Cumberland mountain when this adverse fortune overtook us. These mountains are in the wilderness, as we pass from the old settlements in Virginia to Kentucke, are ranged in a S. west and N. east direction, are of a great length and breadth, and not far distant from each other. Over these, nature hath formed passes, that are less difficult than might be expected from a view of such huge piles. The aspect of these cliffs is so wild and horrid, that it is impossible to behold them without terror. The spectator is apt to imagine that nature had formerly suffered some violent convulsion; and that these are the dismembered remains of the dreadful shock; the ruins, not of Persepolis or Palmyra, but of the world!

I remained with my family on Clench until the sixth of June, 1774, when I and one Michael Stoner were solicited by Governor Dunmore, of Virginia, to go to the Falls of the Ohio, to conduct into the settlement a number of surveyors that had been sent thither by him some months before; this country having about this time drawn the attention of many adventurers. We immediately complied with the Governor's request, and conducted in the surveyors, compleating a tour of eight hundred miles, through many difficulties, in sixty-two days.

Soon after I returned home, I was ordered to take the command of three garrisons during the campaign, which Governor Dunmore carried on against the Shawanese Indians: After the conclusion of which, the Militia was discharged from each garrison, and I being relieved from my post, was solicited by a number of North Carolina gentlemen, that were about purchasing the lands lying on the S. side of Kentucke River, from the Cherokee Indians, to attend their treaty at Wataga, in March, 1775, to negotiate with them, and, mention the boundaries of the purchase. This I accepted, and at the request of the same gentlemen, undertook to mark out a road in the best passage from the settlement through the wilderness to Kentucke, with such assistance as I thought necessary to employ for such an important undertaking.

I soon began this work, having collected a number of enterprising men, well armed. We proceeded with all possible expedition until we came within fifteen miles of where Boonsborough now stands, and where we were fired upon by a party of Indians that killed two, and wounded two of our number; yet, although surprised and taken at a disadvantage, we stood our ground. This was on the twentieth of March, 1775. Three days after, we were fired upon again, and had two men killed, and three wounded. Afterwards we proceeded on to Kentucke river without opposition; and on the first day of April began to erect the fort of Boonsborough at a salt lick, about sixty yards from the river, on the S. side.

On the fourth day, the Indians killed one of our men.—We were busily employed in building this fort, until the fourteenth day of June following, without any farther opposition from the Indians; and having finished the works, I returned to my family, on Clench.

In a short time, I proceeded to remove my family from Clench to this garrison; where we arrived safe without any other difficulties than such as are common to this passage, my wife and daughter being the first white women that ever stood on the banks of Kentucke river.

On the twenty-fourth day of December following we had one man killed, and one wounded, by the Indians, who seemed determined to persecute us for erecting this fortification.

On the fourteenth day of July, 1776, two of Col. Calaway's daughters, and one of mine, were taken prisoners near the fort. I immediately pursued the Indians, with only eight men, and on the sixteenth overtook them, killed two of the party, and recovered the girls. The same day on which this attempt was made, the Indians divided themselves into different parties, and attacked several forts, which were shortly before this time erected, doing a great deal of mischief. This was extremely distressing to the new settlers. The innocent husbandman was shot down, while busy cultivating the soil for his family's supply. Most of the cattle around the stations were destroyed. They continued their hostilities in this manner until the fifteenth of April, 1777, when they attacked Boonsborough with a party of above one hundred in number, killed one man, and wounded four.—Their loss in this attack was not certainly known to us.

On the fourth day of July following, a party of about two hundred Indians attacked Boonsborough, killed one man, and wounded two. They besieged us forty-eight hours; during which time seven of them were killed, and at last, finding themselves not likely to prevail, they raised the siege, and departed.

The Indians had disposed their warriors in different parties at this time, and attacked the different garrisons to prevent their assisting each other, and did much injury to the distressed inhabitants.

On the nineteenth day of this month, Col. Logan's fort was besieged by a party of about two hundred Indians. During this dreadful siege they did a great deal of mischief, distressed the garrison, in which were only fifteen men, killed two, and wounded one. The enemies loss was uncertain, from the common practice which the Indians have of carrying off their dead in time of battle. Col. Harrod's fort was then defended by only sixty-five men, and Boonsborough by twenty-two, there being no more forts or white men in the country, except at the Falls, a considerable distance from these, and all taken collectively, were but a handful to the numerous warriors that were every where dispersed through the country, intent upon doing all the mischief that savage barbarity could invent. Thus we passed through a scene of sufferings that exceeds description.

On the twenty-fifth of this month a reinforcement of forty-five men arrived from North-Carolina, and about the twentieth of August following, Col. Bowman arrived with one hundred men from Virginia. Now we began to strengthen, and from hence, for the space of six weeks, we had skirmishes with Indians, in one quarter or other, almost every day.

The savages now learned the superiority of the Long Knife, as they call the Virginians, by experience; being out-generalled in almost every battle. Our affairs began to wear a new aspect, and the enemy, not daring to venture on open war, practised secret mischief at times.

On the first day of January, 1778, I went with a party of thirty men to the Blue Licks, on Licking River, to make salt for the different garrisons in the country.

On the seventh day of February, as I was hunting, to procure meat for the company, I met with a party of one hundred and two Indians, and two Frenchmen, on their march against Boonsborough, that place being particularly the object of the enemy.

They pursued, and took me; and brought me on the eighth day to the Licks, where twenty-seven of my party were, three of them having previously returned home with the salt. I knowing it was impossible for them to escape, capitulated with the enemy, and, at a distance in their view, gave notice to my men of their situation, with orders not to resist, but surrender themselves captives.

The generous usage the Indians had promised before in my capitulation, was afterwards fully complied with, and we proceeded with them as prisoners to old Chelicothe, the principal Indian town, on Little Miami, where we arrived, after an uncomfortable journey, in very severe weather, on the eighteenth day of February, and received as good treatment as prisoners could expect from savages.—On the tenth day of March following, I, and ten of my men, were conducted by forty Indians to Detroit, where we arrived the thirtieth day, and were treated by Governor Hamilton, the British commander at that post, with great humanity.

During our travels, the Indians entertained me well; and their affection for me was so great, that they utterly refused to leave me there with the others, although the Governor offered them one hundred pounds Sterling for me, on purpose to give me a parole to go home. Several English gentlemen there, being sensible of my adverse fortune, and touched with human sympathy, generously offered a friendly supply for my wants, which I refused, with many thanks for their kindness; adding, that I never expected it would be in my power to recompense such unmerited generosity.

The Indians left my men in captivity with the British at Detroit, and on the tenth day of April brought me towards Old Chelicothe, where we arrived on the twenty-fifth day of the same month. This was a long and fatiguing march, through an exceeding fertile country, remarkable for fine springs and streams of water. At Chelicothe I spent my time as comfortably as I could expect; was adopted, according to their custom, into a family where I became a son, and had a great share in the affection of my new parents, brothers, sisters, and friends. I was exceedingly familiar and friendly with them, always appearing as chearful and satisfied as possible, and they put great confidence in me. I often went a hunting with them, and frequently gained their applause for my activity at our shooting-matches. I was careful not to exceed many of them in shooting; for no people are more envious than they in this sport. I could observe, in their countenances and gestures, the greatest expressions of joy when they exceeded me; and, when the reverse happened, of envy. The Shawanese king took great notice of me, and treated me with profound respect, and entire friendship, often entrusting me to hunt at my liberty. I frequently returned with the spoils of the woods, and as often presented some of what I had taken to him, expressive of duty to my sovereign. My food and lodging was, in common, with them, not so good indeed as I could desire, but necessity made every thing acceptable.

I now began to meditate an escape, and carefully avoided their suspicions, continuing with them at Old Chelicothe until the first day of June following, and then was taken by them to the salt springs on Sciotha, and kept there, making salt, ten days. During this time I hunted some for them, and found the land, for a great extent about this river, to exceed the soil of Kentucke, if possible, and remarkably well watered.

When I returned to Chelicothe, alarmed to see four hundred and fifty Indians, of their choicest warriors, painted and armed in a fearful manner, ready to march against Boonsborough, I determined to escape the first opportunity.

On the sixteenth, before sun-rise, I departed in the most secret manner, and arrived at Boonsborough on the twentieth, after a journey of one hundred and sixty miles; during which, I had but one meal.

I found our fortress in a bad state of defence, but we proceeded immediately to repair our flanks, strengthen our gates and posterns, and form double bastions, which we compleated in ten days. In this time we daily expected the arrival of the Indian army; and at length, one of my fellow prisoners, escaping from them, arrived, informing us that the enemy had an account of my departure, and postponed their expedition three weeks.—The Indians had spies out viewing our movements, and were greatly alarmed with our increase in number and fortifications. The Grand Councils of the nations were held frequently, and with more deliberation than usual. They evidently saw the approaching hour when the Long Knife would dispossess them of their desirable habitations; and anxiously concerned for futurity, determined utterly to extirpate the whites out of Kentucke. We were not intimidated by their movements, but frequently gave them proofs of our courage.

About the first of August; I made an incursion into the Indian country, with a party of nineteen men, in order to surprise a small town up Sciotha, called Paint-Creek-Town. We advanced within four miles thereof, where we met a party of thirty Indians, on their march against Boonsborough, intending to join the others from Chelicothe. A smart fight ensued betwixt us for some time: At length the savages gave way, and fled. We had no loss on our side: The enemy had one killed, and two wounded. We took from them three horses, and all their baggage; and being informed, by two of our number that went to their town, that the Indians had entirely evacuated it, we proceeded no further, and returned with all possible expedition to assist our garrison against the other party. We passed by them on the sixth day, and on the seventh, we arrived safe at Boonsborough.

On the eighth, the Indian army arrived, being four hundred and forty-four in number, commanded by Capt. Duquesne, eleven other Frenchmen, and some of their own chiefs, and marched up within view of our fort, with British and French colours flying; and having sent a summons to me, in his Britannick Majesty's name, to surrender the fort, I requested two days consideration, which was granted.

It was now a critical period with us.—We were a small number in the garrison:—A powerful army before our walls, whose appearance proclaimed inevitable death, fearfully painted, and marking their footsteps with desolation. Death was preferable to captivity; and if taken by storm, we must inevitably be devoted to destruction. In this situation we concluded to maintain our garrison, if possible. We immediately proceeded to collect what we could of our horses, and other cattle, and bring them through the posterns into the fort: And in the evening of the ninth, I returned answer, that we were determined to defend our fort while a man was living—Now, said I to their commander, who stood attentively hearing my sentiments, We laugh at all your formidable preparations: But thank you for giving us notice and time to provide for our defence. Your efforts will not prevail; for our gates shall for ever deny you admittance.—Whether this answer affected their courage, or not, I cannot tell; but, contrary to our expectations, they formed a scheme to deceive us, declaring it was their orders, from Governor Hamilton, to take us captives, and not to destroy us; but if nine of us would come out, and treat with them, they would immediately withdraw their forces from our walls, and return home peaceably. This sounded grateful in our ears; and we agreed to the proposal.

We held the treaty within sixty yards of the garrison, on purpose to divert them from a breach of honour, as we could not avoid suspicions of the savages. In this situation the articles were formally agreed to, and signed; and the Indians told us it was customary with them, on such occasions, for two Indians to shake hands with every white-man in the treaty, as an evidence of entire friendship. We agreed to this also, but were soon convinced their policy was to take us prisoners.—They immediately grappled us; but, although surrounded by hundreds of savages, we extricated ourselves from them, and escaped all safe into the garrison, except one that was wounded, through a heavy fire from their army. They immediately attacked us on every side, and a constant heavy fire ensued between us day and night for the space of nine days.

In this time the enemy began to undermine our fort, which was situated sixty yards from Kentucke river. They began at the water-mark, and proceeded in the bank some distance, which we understood by their making the water muddy with the clay;

and we immediately proceeded to disappoint their design, by cutting a trench a-cross their subterranean passage. The enemy discovering our counter-mine, by the clay we threw out of the fort, desisted from that stratagem: And experience now fully convincing them that neither their power nor policy could effect their purpose, on the twentieth day of August they raised the siege, and departed.

During this dreadful siege, which threatened death in every form, we had two men killed, and four wounded, besides a number of cattle. We killed of the enemy thirty-seven, and wounded a great number. After they were gone, we picked up one hundred and twenty-five pounds weight of bullets, besides what stuck in the logs of our fort; which certainly is a great proof of their industry. Soon after this, I went into the settlement, and nothing worthy of a place in this account passed in my affairs for some time.

During my absence from Kentucke, Col. Bowman carried on an expedition against the Shawanese, at Old Chelicothe, with one hundred and sixty men, in July, 1779. Here they arrived undiscovered, and a battle ensued, which lasted until ten o'clock, A. M. when Col. Bowman, finding he could not succeed at this time, retreated about thirty miles. The Indians, in the mean time, collecting all their forces, pursued and overtook him, when a smart fight continued near two hours, not to the advantage of Col. Bowman's party.

Col. Harrod proposed to mount a number of horse, and furiously to rush upon the savages, who at this time fought with remarkable fury. This desperate step had a happy effect, broke their line of battle, and the savages fled on all sides. In these two battles we had nine killed, and one wounded. The enemy's loss uncertain, only two scalps being taken.

On the twenty-second day of June, 1780, a large party of Indians and Canadians, about six hundred in number, commanded by Col. Bird, attacked Riddle's and Martin's stations, at the Forks of Licking River, with six pieces of artillery. They carried this expedition so secretly, that the unwary inhabitants did not discover them, until they fired upon the forts; and, not being prepared to oppose them, were obliged to surrender themselves miserable captives to barbarous savages, who immediately after tomahawked one man and two women, and loaded all the others with heavy baggage, forcing them along toward their towns, able or unable to march. Such as were weak and faint by the way, they tomahawked. The tender women, and helpless children, fell victims to their cruelty. This, and the savage treatment they received afterwards, is shocking to humanity, and too barbarous to relate.

The hostile disposition of the savages, and their allies, caused General Clark, the commandant at the Falls of the Ohio, immediately to begin an expedition with his own regiment, and the armed force of the country, against Pecaway, the principal town of the Shawanese, on a branch of Great Miami, which he finished with great success, took seventeen scalps, and burnt the town to ashes, with the loss of seventeen men.

About this time I returned to Kentucke with my family; and here, to avoid an enquiry into my conduct, the reader being before informed of my bringing my family to Kentucke, I am under the necessity of informing him that, during my captivity with the Indians, my wife, who despaired of ever seeing me again, expecting the Indians had put a period to my life, oppressed with the distresses of the country, and bereaved of me, her only happiness, had, before I returned, transported my family and goods, on horses, through the wilderness, amidst a multitude of dangers, to her father's house, in North-Carolina.

Shortly after the troubles at Boonsborough, I went to them, and lived peaceably there until this time. The history of my going home, and returning with my family, forms a series of difficulties, an account of which would swell a volume, and being foreign to my purpose, I shall purposely omit them.

I settled my family in Boonsborough once more; and shortly after, on the sixth day of October, 1780, I went in company with my brother to the Blue Licks; and, on our return home, we were fired upon by a party of Indians. They shot him, and pursued me, by the scent of their dog, three miles; but I killed the dog, and escaped. The Winter soon came on, and was very severe, which confined the Indians to their wigwams.

The severity of this Winter caused great difficulties in Kentucke. The enemy had destroyed most of the corn, the Summer before. This necessary article was scarce, and dear; and the inhabitants lived chiefly on the flesh of buffaloes. The circumstances of many were very lamentable: However, being a hardy race of people, and accustomed to difficulties and necessities, they were wonderfully supported through all their sufferings, until the ensuing Fall, when we received abundance from the fertile soil.

Towards Spring, we were frequently harassed by Indians; and, in May, 1782, a party assaulted Ashton's station, killed one man, and took a Negro prisoner. Capt. Ashton, with twenty-five men, pursued, and overtook the savages, and a smart fight ensued, which lasted two hours; but they being superior in number, obliged Captain Ashton's party to retreat, with the loss of eight killed, and four mortally wounded; their brave commander himself being numbered among the dead.

The Indians continued their hostilities; and, about the tenth of August following, two boys were taken from Major Hoy's station. This party was pursued by Capt. Holder and seventeen men, who were also defeated, with the loss of four men killed, and one wounded. Our affairs became more and more alarming. Several stations which had lately been erected in the country were continually infested with savages, stealing their horses and killing the men at every opportunity. In a field, near Lexington, an Indian shot a man, and running to scalp him, was himself shot from the fort, and fell dead upon his enemy.

Every day we experienced recent mischiefs. The barbarous savage nations of Shawanese, Cherokees, Wyandots, Tawas, Delawares, and several others near Detroit, united in a war against us, and assembled their choicest warriors at old Chelicothe, to go on the expedition, in order to destroy us, and entirely depopulate the country. Their savage minds were inflamed to mischief by two abandoned men, Captains M'Kee and Girty. These led them to execute every diabolical scheme; and, on the fifteenth day of August, commanded a party of Indians and Canadians, of about five hundred in number, against Briant's station, five miles from Lexington. Without demanding a surrender, they furiously assaulted the garrison, which was happily prepared to oppose them; and, after they had expended much ammunition in vain, and killed the cattle round the fort, not being likely to make themselves masters of this place, they raised the siege, and departed in the morning of the third day after they came, with the loss of about thirty killed, and the number of wounded uncertain.— Of the garrison four were killed, and three wounded.

On the eighteenth day Col. Todd, Col. Trigg. Major Harland, and myself, speedily collected one hundred and seventy-six men, well armed, and pursued the savages. They had marched beyond the Blue Licks to a remarkable bend of the main fork of Licking River, about forty-three miles from Lexington, as it is particularly represented in the map, where we overtook them on the nineteenth day. The savages observing us, gave way; and we, being ignorant of their numbers, passed the river. When the enemy saw our proceedings, having greatly the advantage of us in situation, they formed the line of battle, as represented in the map, from one bend of Licking to the other, about a mile from the Blue Licks. An exceeding fierce battle immediately began, for about fifteen minutes, when we, being over-powered by numbers, were obliged to retreat, with the loss of sixty-seven men; seven of whom were taken prisoners. The brave and much lamented Colonels Todd and Trigg, Major Harland and my second son, were among the dead. We were informed that the Indians, numbering their dead, found they had four killed more than we; and therefore, four of the prisoners they had taken, were, by general consent, ordered to be killed, in a most barbarous manner, by the young warriors, in order to train them up to cruelty; and then they proceeded to their towns.

On our retreat we were met by Col. Logan, hastening to join us, with a number of well armed men. This powerful assistance we unfortunately wanted in the battle; for, notwithstanding the enemy's superiority of numbers, they acknowledged that, if they had received one more fire from us, they should undoubtedly have given way. So valiantly did our small party fight, that, to the memory of those who unfortunately fell in the battle, enough of honour cannot be paid. Had Col. Logan and his party been with us, it is highly probable we should have given the savages a total defeat.

I cannot reflect upon this dreadful scene, but sorrow fills my heart. A zeal for the defence of their country led these heroes to the scene of action, though with a few men to attack a powerful army of experienced warriors. When we gave way, they pursued us with the utmost eagerness, and in every quarter spread destruction. The river was difficult to cross, and many were killed in the flight, some just entering the river, some in the water, others after crossing in ascending the cliffs. Some escaped on horse-back, a few on foot; and, being dispersed every where, in a few hours, brought the melancholy news of this unfortunate battle to Lexington. Many widows were now made. The reader may guess what sorrow filled the hearts of the inhabitants, exceeding any thing that I am able to describe. Being reinforced, we returned to bury the dead, and found their bodies strewed every where, cut and mangled in a dreadful manner. This mournful scene exhibited a horror almost unparalleled: Some torn and eaten by wild beasts; those in the river eaten by fishes; all in such a putrified condition, that no one could be distinguished from another.

As soon as General Clark, then at the Falls of the Ohio, who was ever our ready friend, and merits the love and gratitude of all his country-men, understood the circumstances of this unfortunate action, he ordered an expedition, with all possible haste, to pursue the savages, which was so expeditiously effected, that we overtook them within two miles of their towns, and probably might have obtained a great victory, had not two of their number met us about two hundred poles before we come up. These returned quick as lightening to their camp with the alarming news of a mighty army in view. The savages fled in the utmost disorder, evacuated their towns, and reluctantly left their territory to our mercy. We immediately took possession of Old Chelicothe without opposition, being deserted by its inhabitants. We continued our pursuit through five towns on the Miami rivers, Old Chelicothe, Pecaway, New Chelicothe, Will's Towns, and Chelicothe, burnt them all to ashes, entirely destroyed their corn, and other fruits, and every where spread a scene of desolation is the country. In this expedition we took seven prisoners and five scalps, with the loss of only four men, two of whom were accidentally killed by our own army.

This campaign in some measure damped the spirits of the Indians, and made them sensible of our superiority. Their connections were dissolved, their armies scattered, and a future invasion put entirely out of their power; yet they continued to practise mischief secretly upon the inhabitants, in the exposed parts of the country.

In October following, a party made an excursion into that district called the Crab Orchard, and one of them, being advanced some distance before the others, boldly entered the house of a poor defenceless family, in which was only a Negro man, a woman and her children, terrified with the apprehensions of immediate death. The savage, perceiving their defenceless situation, without offering violence to the family attempted to captivate the Negro, who, happily proved an over-match for him, threw him on the ground, and, in the struggle, the mother of the children drew an ax from a corner of the cottage, and cut his head off, while her little daughter shut the door. The savages instantly appeared, and applied their tomahawks to the door. An old rusty gun-barrel, without a lock, lay in a corner, which the mother put through a small crevice, and the savages, perceiving it, fled. In the mean time, the alarm spread through the neighbourhood; the armed men collected immediately, and pursued the ravagers into the wilderness. Thus Providence, by the means of this Negro, saved the whole of the poor family from destruction. From that time, until the happy return of peace between the United States and Great-Britain, the Indians did us no mischief. Finding the great king beyond the water disappointed in his expectations, and conscious of the importance of the Long Knife, and their own wretchedness, some of the nations immediately desired peace; to which, at present, they seem universally disposed, and are sending ambassadors to General Clark, at the Falls of the Ohio, with the minutes of their Councils; a specimen of which, in the minutes of the Piankashaw Council, is subjoined.

To conclude, I can now say that I have verified the saying of an old Indian who signed Col. Henderson's deed. Taking me by the hand, at the delivery thereof, Brother, says he, we have given you a fine land, but I believe you will have much trouble in settling it.—My footsteps have often been marked with blood, and therefore I can truly subscribe to its original name. Two darling sons, and a brother, have I lost by savage hands, which have also taken from me forty valuable horses, and abundance of cattle. Many dark and sleepless nights have I been a companion for owls, separated from the cheerful society of men, scorched by the Summer's sun, and pinched by the Winter's cold, an instrument ordained to settle the wilderness. But now the scene is changed: Peace crowns the sylvan shade.

What thanks, what ardent and ceaseless thanks are due to that all-superintending Providence which has turned a cruel war into peace, brought order out of confusion, made the fierce savages placid, and turned away their hostile weapons from our country! May the same Almighty Goodness banish the accursed monster, war, from all lands, with her hated associates, rapine and insatiable ambition. Let peace, descending from her native heaven, bid her olives spring amidst the joyful nations; and plenty, in league with commerce, scatter blessings from her copious hand.

This account of my adventures will inform the reader of the most remarkable events of this country.—I now live in peace and safety, enjoying the sweets of liberty, and the bounties of Providence, with my once fellow-sufferers, in this delightful country, which I have seen purchased with a vast expence of blood and treasure, de-

lighting in the prospect of its being, in a short time, one of the most opulent and powerful states on the continent of North-America; which, with the love and gratitude
of my country-men, I esteem a sufficient reward for all my toil and dangers.

DANIEL BOON

FAYETTE COUNTY, KENTUCKE.

GEORGE ROGERS CLARK

(1752–1818)

George Rogers Clark was born a Virginian and moved west to what would become Kentucky in 1776. Kentucky, at the time, was within the boundaries of Virginia, and so, when the Revolution began, he considered himself the leader of the western wing of the Virginia militia. During the conflict, Clark fought an eventually unsuccessful campaign to wrest the Wabash and southern Great Lakes regions from the British. Clark's situation, however, was complicated by a number of issues that were not relevant in the east. First, Clark was aware of the foreboding Spanish control of the Mississippi; second, Clark was required to secure the alliance of the French in southern Indiana and Illinois; and third, he had no way of gauging the loyalty of the Native Americans—specifically the Piankeshaw, Wea, and Shawnee tribes. When Clark wrote and traveled east for instructions, supplies, and support, he was largely met with indifference from his colleagues such as George Mason, Richard Henry Lee, and George Washington. Furthermore, many of the Kentucky settlers were more concerned with gaining access to the Mississippi than with the fate of the east. Subsequently, recruiting and retaining his troops was a constant challenge.

From 1776 until 1779, Clark was quite successful. However, his rash expedition up the Wabash in a vain hope to invade British-held Detroit was met with staunch native resistance, and the settler army retreated to Kentucky. Nonetheless, in the Treaty of Paris the British ceded the territory Clark had sought to conquer, leaving him with a very mixed historical legacy. In the section of his memoir reproduced here, Clark confronts the French and his own late arrival as an American in the region. His lack of historical awareness of the region's interracial complexities is gradually lessened during this sequence. His own creeping awareness of the Ohio valley's difference from the east is demonstrated in this description of how the Revolution was very different in the west than in the east. His description of the occupation of Vincennes begins the book's most important sequence.

Text: *The Conquest of the Illinois* (Chicago: Lakeside Classics, 1920, ed. Milo M. Quaife): 35–62.

FROM *THE CONQUEST OF THE ILLINOIS* (1788)

Knowing that spies were watching the river below the Illinois towns, I had planned to march part of the way by land. I therefore left behind all of our baggage except enough to equip the men after the Indian fashion. Our entire force, after leaving behind those who were judged unequal to the expected fatigues of the march, consisted of but four companies, under Captains Montgomery, Bowman, Helm, and Harrod. My force being so much smaller than I had expected, I found it necessary to alter my plan of operations. As Vincennes was a town of considerable strength, having four hundred militia, besides which there was an Indian town adjoining and large numbers of Indians always in the neighborhood, and since it was more important than any other from the viewpoint of Indian affairs, I had thought of attacking it first; but I now found myself too weak to undertake this, and accordingly resolved to begin operations against the Illinois towns. Although they had more inhabitants than Vincennes they were scattered in different villages. There was less danger of our being immediately overpowered by the Indians; in case of necessity, too, we could probably make good our retreat to the Spanish side of the river, while if we were successful here the way might be paved for us to take possession of Vincennes.

I was well aware of the fact that the French inhabitants of these western settlements had great influence over the Indians, by whom they were more beloved than were any other Europeans. I knew also that their commercial intercourse extended throughout the entire western and northwestern country, while the governing interest on the Great Lakes was chiefly in the hands of the English, who were not popular with the natives. These reflections, along with others of similar import, determined me to strengthen myself, if possible, by adopting such a course of conduct as would tend to attach the whole French and Indian population to our interest, and give us influence beyond the limits of the country which constituted the objective of our campaign. Such were the principles which guided my further conduct; fortunately I received at this time a letter from Colonel Campbell at Pittsburgh informing me of the contents of the treaty between France and America.

Intending to leave the Ohio at Fort Massac, three leagues below the mouth of the Tennessee, I landed on Barataria, a small island in the mouth of that river, to make preparations for our march. A few hours after our arrival here, one John Duff, coming down the river with a party of hunters, was brought to by our boats. They were originally from the states, and they expressed pleasure in the adventure, their surprise having been owing to lack of knowledge who we were. They had recently been at Kaskaskia and were able to give us all the information we desired. They told us that Governor Abbott had recently left Vincennes to go to Detroit on business of importance. Mr. Rochblave was commanding at Kaskaskia. The militia were in good order, spies were watching the Mississippi, and all hunters were instructed to keep close watch for the rebels. The fort was kept as orderly as an asylum, but our informants thought this watchfulness was due more to a fondness for parade than to any expectation of a visit from us. Should they receive timely notice of our approach, the hunters thought, they would give us a warm reception, since they had been taught to entertain horrible ideas of the barbarity of the rebels, especially so of the Virginians.

If, however, we could surprise the place, they had no doubt of our ability to master it at pleasure.

These men asked to be permitted to join our expedition, and offered to assist the guides in conducting our party across the country. This offer was accepted by me and they proved a valuable acquisition, all the more so in view of the fact that I had had no intelligence concerning the French posts since that gained from the spies I had sent a year before. No part of the information I received pleased me more than that concerning the inhabitants believing us to be more savage than their neighbors, the Indians. I resolved to make capital of this should I be fortunate enough to gain control over them, since I considered that the greater the shock I could give them in the beginning the more appreciative would they be later of my lenity, and the more valuable as friends. This I conceived to accord with human nature as I had observed it in many instances.

All things being ready, we descended the river to a little gut a short distance above Fort Massac, where we concealed our boats and began our march in a northwesterly direction. Nothing worthy of remark occurred in this portion of our route. The weather was favorable, although in some places both water and game were scarce, which entailed some suffering both from thirst and hunger. On the third day John Saunders, our principal guide, appeared to be confused, and barring some other explanation of his conduct, we perceived that he was totally lost. I asked him a number of questions and was at a loss to determine from his answers whether his confusion was due to the knowledge that he was lost, or whether he was purposely deceiving us. The men all cried out that he was a traitor. On this he asked to be permitted to go some distance into a plain which was in full view, to try to make some discovery concerning the route. I told him he might go, but that I was suspicious of his conduct. From his first engagement he had claimed to know the way perfectly but now things looked different. I saw from the nature of the country that one who had once become acquainted with it could not forget it in a short time. I told him a few men would go with him to prevent his escape, and if he did not conduct us to the hunter's road he had frequently described as leading into Kaskaskia from the east I would have him immediately put to death. This I should have done, but after searching an hour or two he came to a place that he knew perfectly, and we now perceived that the poor fellow had been genuinely bewildered.

On the evening of July fourth we arrived within a few miles of the town, where we threw out scouts in advance and lay until nearly dark. We then resumed our march and took possession of a house on the bank of the Kaskaskia River, about three-quarters of a mile above the town, occupied by a large family. We learned from the inmates that the people had been under arms a few days before but had concluded the alarm to be groundless and at present all was quiet, and that there was a large number of men in town, although the Indians were for the most part absent. We obtained from the man boats enough to convey us across the river, where I formed my force in three divisions. I felt confident the inhabitants could not now obtain knowledge of our approach in time to enable them to make any resistance. My object was now to get possession of the place with as little confusion as possible, but to have it if necessary at the loss of the whole town. I did not entirely credit the information given us at the house, as the man seemed to contradict himself, informing us among other things that a noise we heard in the town was caused by the negroes at a dance. I set out for the fort with one division, ordering the other two to proceed to different quarters of the town. If I met with no resistance, at a certain signal a general shout was to be given and a certain part of the town was to be seized immediately, while men from each detachment who were able to talk French were to run through the streets proclaiming what had happened and informing the townsmen to remain in their houses on pain of being shot down.

These arrangements produced the desired effect, and within a very short time we were in complete possession of the place, with every avenue guarded to prevent any one from escaping and giving the alarm to the other villages. Various orders not worth mentioning had been issued for the guidance of the men in the event of opposition. Greater silence, I suppose, never reigned among the inhabitants of a town than in Kaskaskia at this juncture; not a person was to be seen or a word to be heard from them for some time. Meanwhile our troops purposely kept up the greatest possible noise throughout every quarter of the town, while patrols moved around it continually throughout the night, as it was a capital object to intercept any message that might be sent out. In about two hours all the inhabitants were disarmed, and informed that anyone who should be taken while attempting to escape from the place would immediately be put to death. Mr. Rochblave was secured, but some time elapsed before he could be gotten out of his room. I suppose he delayed to tell his wife what disposition to make of his public papers, but few of which were secured by us. Since his chamber was not entered during the night, she had ample opportunity to dispose of them, but how she did it we could never learn. I do not suppose she put them in her trunks, although we never examined them. From the idea she entertained of us she must have expected the loss even of her clothes.

During the night I sent for several individuals, from whom I sought to procure information, but obtained very little that was not already known to us. We learned, however, that the conduct of several of the inhabitants indicated them to be inclined to the American cause; that a large number of Indians were in the neighborhood of Cahokia; sixty miles distant; that Mr. Cerré, a leading merchant and one of our most inveterate enemies, had left Kaskaskia with a large quantity of furs a few days before, enroute to Michilimackinac and thence to Quebec, from which place he had lately arrived at Kaskaskia; and that he was then in St. Louis, the Spanish capital, but his wife and family were still in town, together with a considerable quantity of goods which would be useful to our men.

In addition to Cerré, information was given me about numerous other individuals. I at once suspected that the object of the informers was to make their peace with me at the expense of their neighbors, and my situation demanded of me too much caution to permit giving them much satisfaction. I found Cerré to be one of the most eminent men of the country, with great influence over the people. I had some suspicion that his accusers were probably in debt to him, and hence desired to ruin him. What I had heard led me to feel that he was an object of importance to me, since he might be wavering in his opinion respecting the merits of the war; and if he should take a decisive stand in our favor, he might prove a valuable acquisition. In short, his enemies led me to desire much to see him, and as he was then out of my power I had no doubt I could bring this about by means of his family who were in my hands. I immediately caused a guard to be stationed at his house and his stores to be sealed along with all the others. I did not doubt that when he should hear of this he would be extremely anxious for an interview.

By the morning of the fifth Messrs. Richard Winston and Daniel Murray, who proved to have been attached to the American cause, had plenty of provisions prepared. After the troops had regaled themselves they were withdrawn from the town and posted in extended position on its border. Every man had been expressly forbidden to hold any conversation with the inhabitants. All was distrust; their town was in complete possession of an enemy of whom they entertained the most horrid conception, and they were unable as yet to have any conversation with one of our people. Even those I talked with were ordered not to speak to any of my men. After some time they were told they could walk freely about the town. Finding they were busily engaged in conversation, I had a few of the principal militia officers put in irons, without hinting any reason or hearing anything they had to say in their own defense. The worst was now anticipated by all. I perceived the state of consternation the inhabitants were in, and in imagination, I suppose, felt all that they were experiencing in reality; and I felt perfectly disposed to act as arbiter between them and my duty.

After some time the priest obtained permission to call on me, and came accompanied by five or six elderly gentlemen. However great the shock they had already sustained by reason of their situation, the addition when they entered the room where I was sitting with my officers was obvious and great. Having left our extra clothing at the Ohio River, we were almost naked; torn by the bushes and briers, we presented a dirty and savage aspect. So shocked were they that some time elapsed before they ventured to seat themselves, and still more before they would speak. At length we asked them what they wanted. The priest stated (after inquiring which of us was the commander) that as the townsmen expected to be separated, never, perhaps, to meet again, they had commissioned him to petition for permission to spend some time in the church taking their leave of each other. I knew that they supposed their very religion to be obnoxious to us. I carelessly told him, therefore, that I had nothing to say about his church and he might go there if he pleased; if he did, he was to tell the people not to leave the town. They attempted to introduce some other conversation, but were told that we were not at leisure; and, after answering a few questions, which I asked with a view to discouraging them from again coming to me with petitions, as they had not yet come to the state of mind I wanted, they went away. The whole populace now seemed to assemble in the church. The infants were carried along, and the houses were left for the most part without a person in them, with the exception of a few who cared little how things went and a few more who were not so much alarmed as the majority. I issued an order prohibiting the soldiers from entering the houses.

The people remained some time in the church, and, on breaking up, the priest and many of the principal citizens came to thank me for the indulgence shown them, and to beg permission to address me further on a subject dearer to them than all things else. They stated that their present situation was the fate of war and they were reconciled to the loss of their property; but they hoped I would not part them from their families, and that the women and children might keep some of their clothes and a small quantity of provisions, that they might support themselves by their industry. Their entire conduct had been influenced by their commandants, whom they had felt obliged to obey, and they were not much acquainted with the American war, as they had had but little opportunity to inform themselves. Many of them, however, had expressed themselves as strongly in favor of the Americans as they had dared. In short, they said everything that sensible men in their situation could be expected to advance, and their sole hope seemed to be to secure some lenity for their women and families, supposing their property would appease us. I felt convinced there was no finesse in all this, but that they really expressed their sentiments and the height of their expectations.

This was the point to which I had wished to bring them. I now asked them very abruptly whether they thought they were addressing savages. I told them that from the tenor of their conversation I was sure they did. Did they suppose we meant to strip the women and children or take the bread out of their mouths? Or that we would condescend to make war on women and children or the church? I informed them it was to prevent the effusion of innocent blood by the Indians, instigated thereto by their commandants and enemies, and not the prospect of plunder, that had caused us to visit them. As soon as this object was attained we would be perfectly satisfied; and as the king of France had joined the Americans (this information affected them very visibly) it was probable the war would shortly come to an end. They were at liberty to take whichever side they pleased without danger of losing their property or having their families distressed. As for their church, all religions would be tolerated in America, and so far were we from meddling with it, that any one who offered insult to it would be punished by me. To convince them we were not savages and plunderers, as they had conceived us to be, they might return to their families and tell them to conduct themselves as usual, with entire freedom and without any apprehension of danger. I told them the information I had received since my arrival so fully convinced me that they had been influenced by false information given them by their leaders I was willing to forget all that had passed. Their friends who were in confinement would be released immediately and the guards withdrawn from every part of the town except the house of Cerré, and I only required compliance with a proclamation which I should immediately issue.

Such was the substance of my reply to them. They attempted to soften my idea that they had supposed us to be a set of savages and plunderers, or that they had supposed the property in a town belonged to those who captured it. I told them I knew they had been taught to believe that we were but little better than barbarians, but that we would say no more on the subject, and that I wished them to go and relieve the anxiety of the townsmen. Their feelings may more easily be imagined than expressed. They retired and in a few minutes the scene changed from an extreme state of dejection to one of great joy. Bells were rung, the church was crowded with people returning thanks, in short, every appearance of extravagant joy was manifested.

I immediately set about preparing a proclamation to be presented to them before they should leave the church, but wishing to test the people further, I postponed it for a few days. Feeling confident that any report that might now be sent out to the surrounding country would be favorable to us, I became more careless about who should go from or come into the town; but not knowing what might yet take place, I was uneasy over Cahokia and was determined as soon as possible to make a lodgement there and gain the place by some such stratagem as I had already employed at Kaskaskia.

I ordered Major Bowman to mount his company and part of another on horses to be procured from the town, and taking with him a few townsmen to inform their friends of what had happened, to proceed without delay to Cahokia and if possible gain possession of the place before the following morning. I gave him no further instructions on the subject, leaving him free to exercise his own judgment. He gave orders for collecting the horses, whereupon a number of gentlemen came to inform me that they were aware of the design. They pointed out that the soldiers were much fatigued, and said they hoped I would not reject their offer to execute whatever I might wish to have done at Cahokia. The people there were their friends and relatives and would, they thought, follow their example. At least, they hoped, they might be permitted to accompany the detachment.

Conceiving that it might be good policy to show them that we put confidence in them (which, in fact, I desired for obvious reasons to do), I told them I had no doubt Major Bowman would welcome their company and that as many as chose might go. Although we were too weak to be other than suspicious and much on our guard, I knew we had sufficient security for their good behavior. I told them that if they went at all they ought to go equipped for war. I was in hopes that everything would be settled amicably, but as it was the first time they had ever borne arms as freemen it might be well to equip themselves and see how they felt, especially as they were about to put their friends in the same situation as themselves.

They appeared to be highly pleased at this idea, and in the evening the Major set out with a force but little inferior to the one with which we had entered the country, the Frenchmen being commanded by their former militia officers. These new friends of ours were so elated over the thought of the parade they were to make at Cahokia that they were too much concerned about equipping themselves to appear to the best advantage. It was night before the party moved and the distance being twenty leagues, it was late in the morning of the sixth before they reached Cahokia. Detaining every person they met, they entered the outskirts of the town before they were discovered. The townsmen were at first much alarmed by this sudden appearance of strangers in hostile array and being ordered even by their friends and relatives to surrender the town. As the confusion among the women and children over the cry of the Big Knives being in town proved greater than had been anticipated, the Frenchmen immediately informed the people what had happened at Kaskaskia. Major Bowman told them not to be alarmed; that although resistance was out of the question he would convince them that he would prefer their friendship to their hostility. He was authorized to inform them that they were at liberty to become free Americans as their friends at Kaskaskia had done. Any who did not care to adopt this course were free to leave the country except such as had been engaged in inciting the Indians to war.

Cries of liberty and freedom, and huzzahs for the Americans rang through the whole town. The gentlemen from Kaskaskia dispersed among their friends and in a few hours all was amicably arranged, and Major Bowman snugly quartered in the old British fort. Some individuals said the town had been given up too tamely, but little attention was paid to them. A considerable number of Indians who were encamped in the neighborhood (Cahokia was an important center of Indian trade) immediately fled. One of the townsmen who was at St. Louis, some time later wrote a letter to me excusing himself for not paying me a visit. By July 8, Major Bowman had everything settled agreeably to our wishes. All of the inhabitants cheerfully took the oath of allegiance, and he set about repairing the fort and regulating the internal police of the place.

The neighboring villages followed the example set by Kaskaskia and Cahokia, and since we made no strict inquiry concerning those who had been engaged in encouraging the Indians to war, within a few days the country appeared to be in a state of perfect harmony. Friendly correspondence which was at once commenced between the Spanish officers and ourselves added much to the general tranquillity and happiness. It was not my fortune to enjoy pleasures of this kind. I found myself embarked on an enterprise that would require close attention and all the skill of which I was master to execute that service for my country which now appeared in prospect, with honor to it and with credit to myself.

Being now in position to procure all the information I desired, I was astonished at perceiving the pains and expense the British had incurred in inciting the Indians. They had sent emissaries to every tribe throughout that vast country, even bringing the denizens of Lake Superior by water to Detroit and there outfitting them for war. The sound of war was universal, there being scarcely a nation among them but what had declared and received the bloody belt and hatchet.

Vincennes I found to be a place of infinite importance for us to gain. This was now my object, but realizing that all the force we had, joined by every man in Kentucky, would not be able to take the place, I resolved on other measures than those of arms. I determined to send no message to the Indians for the present, but wishing an interview between us to be arranged through the agency of French gentlemen, to assume the appearance of carelessness about the matter. In all the papers I wrote I referred to myself as at the Falls of the Ohio, in order that it might appear that the troops we had with us were only a detachment from that place. I sought to spread the impression that the main body of our troops were fortifying that point, and that large reinforcements were daily expected, on the arrival of which we intended to continue the war. Every man we had was instructed to talk in this strain. Indeed, from many hints and pretended information of mine, before I left that place the greater part of them believed the most of this to be true. In short, as I had early perceived, an excuse for our marching into the Illinois country with so small a force was really necessary.

I inquired particularly into the manner the people had been governed heretofore and found, much to my satisfaction, that the government had generally been as severe as though under martial law. I resolved to make capital of this, and took every step in my power to cause the people to appreciate the blessings enjoyed by an American citizen. This enabled me, as I soon discovered, to support by their own choice almost supreme authority over them. I caused a court of civil judicature, elected by the people, to be established at Cahokia. Major Bowman, to the surprise of the people, held an election for a magistracy, and was himself elected judge of the court. His policy in holding an election can easily be perceived. After this similar courts were established at Kaskaskia and Vincennes. There was an appeal to myself in certain classes of cases, and I believe no people ever had their business done more to their satisfaction than these had for a considerable time by means of this regulation.

At the time of Major Bowman's arrival at Cahokia, Mr. Cerré, whom I have already mentioned, was still in St. Louis preparing to prosecute his journey to Canada. He was deterred from this in consequence of the news of our arrival. Agreeably to my expectation, upon learning the situation of affairs he resolved to return, but hearing that there was a guard kept at his house alone, and that several persons had attempted to ruin him with their information to me, he was advised not to cross the river without a safe-conduct. He applied to the Spanish governor for a letter requesting this, and coming to Ste. Genevieve, across the river from Kaskaskia, procured another of the same tenor from the commandant of that post and sent them both to me. However, all of the intercession he could arouse through the channel of Spanish officers and the solicitation of his particular friends, whom I found to constitute a great majority of the people, could not procure him a safe-conduct. I absolutely refused it, and intimated that I wished to hear no more on the subject; nor would I hear any person who had anything to say in vindication of him. I told them I understood Mr. Cerré to be a sensible man. If he were innocent of the allegations against him he would not be afraid to surrender himself. I added that his backwardness seemed to prove his guilt, and I felt very little concern about him.

I suppose rumor immediately carried this information to him, for in a few hours he crossed over the river and, without stopping to visit his family, presented himself before me. I told him that I supposed he was aware of the charges preferred against him, particularly that of inciting the Indians to murder, a crime that ought to be punished by all people who should be fortunate enough to get such culprits into their power; and that his recent backwardness about surrendering himself convinced me of his guilt. He replied that he was merely a merchant, that he never concerned himself about affairs of state further than the interest of his trade required, and that he had not as yet enjoyed opportunity to inform himself of the principles involved in the present contest sufficiently to enable him to form an opinion about it. He said he was so remote from the seat of war that he was doubtful of having heard more than one side of the question. He had learned more within the last few days than he had ever known before, and this information had only confirmed his former impression. I read to him part of a letter from Governor Hamilton of Detroit to Mr. Rochblave, wherein he was alluded to in affectionate terms. He said that when he was at Detroit he behaved himself as became a subject, but he defined any man to prove that he had ever incited the Indians to war. Many people, on the contrary, had often heard him express his disapproval of the cruelty of such proceedings. He said there were several people in town who were deeply indebted to him, and it might be the object of some of them to extricate themselves from their debts by ruining him. In his present situation it would be inconsistent for him to offer to declare his sentiments; but with respect to his part in the war he welcomed every investigation, as he had ever detested inciting the Indians. He sought to excuse his fears about coming across the Mississippi as soon as he could have wished.

Without making any further reply, I told him to withdraw into another room. The whole town was anxious to know his fate. I sent for his accusers, who were followed by a large number of townsmen, and had Mr. Cerré called in. I perceived plainly the confusion into which they were thrown by his appearance. I stated the case to the whole assembly, telling them that I never condemned a man unheard. I said that Cerré was now present and I was ready to do justice to the world in general by punishing him if he were found guilty of inciting to murder, or by acquitting him if he proved innocent of the charge. I closed by desiring them to submit their information.

Cerré undertook to speak to them but was ordered to desist. His accusers began to whisper among themselves and to retire for private conversation. At length only one out of six or seven was left in the room, and I asked him what he had to say to the point in question. In short, I found that none of them had anything to say. I gave them a suitable reprimand and after some general conversation informed Mr. Cerré that I was happy to find he had so honorably acquitted himself of so black a charge. I told him he was now at liberty to dispose of himself and property as he pleased. If he chose to become a citizen of the United States it would give us pleasure. If he did not, he was at full liberty to do as he wished. He made many acknowledgments and concluded by saying that many doubts he had entertained were now cleared up to his satisfaction, and that he wished to take the oath of allegiance immediately. In short, he became a most valuable man to us. Simple as this transaction may appear, it had great weight with the people, and was of infinite service to us.

Everything in this section now wore a promising appearance, but Vincennes was never absent from my mind. I had reason to suspect from some things I had learned, that Mr. Gibault, the priest, had been inclined to the American interest previous to our arrival in the country. I had no doubt of his fidelity to us. Knowing he had great influence over the people, and that Vincennes was also under his jurisdiction, I sent for him and had a long conference on that subject. In response to my questions he stated that he did not think it worth my while to cause any military preparation to be made at the Falls for an attack on Vincennes although the place was strong and there was a great number of Indians in the neighborhood. He said that Governor Abbott had left the place a few weeks since on some errand to Detroit. He thought that when the inhabitants should be fully informed of what had happened at the Illinois and the present happiness of their friends there, and should be fully acquainted with the nature of the war, their sentiments concerning it would undergo a great change. He was certain that his appearance there would have great weight even among the savages. If it were agreeable to me, he would take this matter upon himself, and he had no doubt of being able to bring the place over to the American interest without my being put to the trouble of marching troops against it. His business being altogether of a spiritual character, he desired that another person might be charged with the temporal part of the embassy, and named Dr. Laffont as his associate, but he agreed that he would privately direct the whole undertaking.

This was quite in line with what I had been secretly aiming at for some days. The plan was immediately settled upon, and the two doctors with their intended retinue, among whom I placed a spy, set about preparing for their journey. On July 14 they set out with the following address, taking with them, also, a large number of letters from their friends to the inhabitants at Vincennes. Dr. Laffont's instructions are now lost. I gave Mr. Gibault verbal instructions how to act in certain contingencies. It is mentioned here that Governor Abbott's letters to Mr. Rochblave had convinced us that the inhabitants were warmly attached to the American cause. This was wholly a piece of policy on my part. No such thing had been said; but as they would naturally suppose that Governor Abbott's letters to Rochblave had fallen into our hands, we knew that if they were led to suppose he had written in that style concerning them they would the more cordially verify it. Mr. Gibault had been led to believe this, and my authorizing them to garrison their own town would convince them of the great confidence we reposed in them. All this had its desired effect. Mr. Gibault and party arrived safely, and after spending a day or two in explaining matters to the people they universally acceded to the proposal (except for a few Europeans who had been left there by Mr. Abbott and who immediately left the country) and went in a body to the church, where the oath of allegiance was administered to them in the most solemn manner. A commander was elected and the fort was immediately taken possession of and the American flag displayed, to the great astonishment of the Indians.

Thus everything was settled beyond our most sanguine hopes. The people here at once assumed a new attitude; they began to talk in a different style and to act like perfect freemen. With a United States garrison at hand their language to the Indians was immediately altered; they informed the latter that their old Father, the King of France, had come to life again, and that he had joined the Big Knives and was angry at them for fighting for the English. They advised the Indians to make peace with the Americans as soon as possible; otherwise they might expect the land to be deluged with blood. Such was now the language the natives throughout that whole region received through correspondence from their ancient friends of the Wabash and the Illinois, and throughout all those tribes they began to reflect seriously upon it.

❧ 7 ❧

HUGH HENRY BRACKENRIDGE

(1748–1816)

The late eighteenth century was a time of violent conflict on the upper Ohio River. After the Revolution, the new American forces sought to bring the region under their control despite lingering British, native, and white settler resistance. Eastern discourse, as demonstrated by Manesseh Cutler or the Northwest Ordinance, viewed the region's conquest and colonization as a fait accompli, and so the forces of local resistance were usually represented as trivial, fading, and, finally, unsuited to occupying the land.

A Princeton graduate, published poet and dramatist, Revolutionary propagandist, Presbyterian minister, and lawyer, Hugh Henry Bracken-ridge arrived in Pittsburgh in 1781. Like many such men, he came west as a Yankee, hoping to make his fortune by establishing himself among the elite of a new settlement. As founder and editor of the *Pittsburgh Gazette,* Brackenridge chronicled the region's complexities with extraordinary acuity born of his diverse experience in the public sphere of the eastern cities. This experience quickly soured him on the ways in which Americans were administering their western territories, a flaw he viewed as indicative of a more general national oversimplification in republican culture. During the constitutional convention, he became a staunch antifederalist and, in 1794, a moderate spokesman for the Whiskey Rebellion. These activities were given literary analog in his massive and multi-part novel *Modern Chivalry* (1792–1815).

Modern Chivalry is, however, little more than a series of episodes; Brackenridge was at his best writing in shorter formats. "The Trial of Mamachtaga" is among his best narratives and more precisely demonstrates his deviation, as a western writer, from eastern modes of representation. In most eastern writing during the 1780s, natives in the Ohio valley were thoroughly vilified, especially on account of their alliance with the British both during and after the Revolution and the subsequent Indian Wars. In 1785, Brackenridge published a fictionalized autobiographical narrative of his defense of Mamachtaga, a Delaware living across the river from Pittsburgh who had, while both were drunk, killed a white companion. "The Trial of Mamachtaga" tells the story of how white law was unsuited to dealing with native traditions, which are represented in the story as an equally legitimate means of pursuing justice. The evolution of the narrator's growth toward understanding the plight of his client demonstrates an important growth away from imported perceptions of the region. Brackenridge republished "Mamachtaga" in his collection *Gazette Publications* in 1806 and found a national audience for it in Loudon's *Indian Narratives* in 1808.

Brackenridge's regional awareness was also visible in his writing about the Whiskey Rebellion. Indicted by Alexander Hamilton as a leader of the riots, Brackenridge successfully defended and articulated his activities in *Incidents of the Insurrection* and was fully acquitted. *Incidents* has recently been recognized as Brackenridge's most successful sustained work: a realistic account of his own thoughts and activities, it stands out among the frontier's many narratives for its psychological depth and self-awareness. Further, in it he conjectures on the need for local self-determination within a national whole, an important meditation on the significance of regional awareness. In the section reproduced here, we see the beginnings of a "western" consciousness as distinct from the "American" identity being defined and stabilized in the east. Asking for the westerners, "If Indians can have treaties, why cannot we have one too?," Brackenridge, as early as the 1790s, understood the paradoxes of the experience of the white settler on the western frontier.

Texts: "Mamachtaga" in *Loudon's Indian Narratives* (Carlisle, 1808): vol. I, 16–38. *Incidents of the Insurrection* (Pittsburgh, 1796): vol. II, 123–153.

THE TRIAL OF MAMACHTAGA

I know the particulars of the following story well, because one of the men (Smith) was shingling a house for me in the town of Pittsburgh the evening before he was murdered by Mamachtaga, and for which murder and of some others, this Indian was tried. Smith had borrowed a blanket of me, saying that he was about to cross the river (Allegheny) to the Indian camp on the west side. Here a party of Indians, mostly Delawares, had come in it, it being just after the war and the greater part of these Indians having professed themselves friendly during the war, and their chief Killbuck with his family and that of several others having remained at the garrison or on an island in the Ohio river called Killbuck's island and under the reach of the guns of the fort. Mamachtaga had been at war against the settlements with others of the Delawares who were now at this encampment.

I went myself over to the encampment the next morning and found the Indians there. Two men had been murdered, Smith and another of the name of Evans, and two wounded, one of them a dwarf of the name of Freeman. According to the relation which I got from the wounded, there were four white men together in a cabin when Mamachtaga, without the least notice, rushed in and stabbed Smith mortally, and had stabbed Evans who had seized the Indian who was entangled with the dwarf among his feet, attempting to escape, and who [*the dwarf*] had received wounds also in the scuffle; and the other white man also had received a stab. It would appear that the Indian had been in liquor according to the account of the other Indians and of the white men who escaped. Killbuck appeared greatly cast down and sat upon a log, silent. Mamachtaga made no attempt to escape. He was now sober and gave himself up to the guard that came over, affecting not to know what had happened. The seat of justice of Westmoreland county being thirty miles distant and the jail there not being secure, he was taken to the guardhouse of the garrison to be confined until a court of Oyer and Terminer should be holden in the county. Living in the place and being of the profession of the law, said I to the interpreter Joseph Nicholas, one day, "Has that Indian any fur or peltry, or has he any interest with his nation that he could collect some and pay a lawyer to take up his defense for this homicide?" The interpreter said that he had some in the hands of a trader in town, and that he could raise from his nation any quantity of racoon or beaver provided it would answer any purpose. I was struck with the pleasantry of having an Indian for a client and getting a fee in this way, and told the interpreter to go to the Indian, and explain the matter to him. He did so, and brought me an account that Mamachtaga had forty weight of beaver, which he was ready to make over, being with a trader in town, and that he had a brother who would set off immediately to the Indian towns and procure an hundred weight or more if that would do any good, but the interpreter stipulated that he should have half of all that should be got, for his trouble in bringing about the contract. Accordingly he was dispatched to the Indian, and from whom he brought in a short time an order for the beaver in the hand of the trader, [signed by] Mamachtaga (his mark). The mark was something like a turkey's foot, as these people have no idea of an hieroglyphic merely abstract as a strait line or a curve, but it must bear some resemblance to a thing in nature. After this as it behoved, I went to consult with my client and arrange his defense, if it were possible to make one on which a probable face could be put. Accompanied by the interpreter I was admitted to the Indian so that I could converse with him. He was in what is called the black hole, something resembling that kind of hole which is depressed in the floor and which the southern people have in their cabins in which to keep their esculent roots from the frost during the winter season. Not going down into the hole as may be supposed, though it was large enough to contain two or three and was depressed about eight feet, being the place in which delinquent or refractory soldiery had been confined occasionally for punishment, but standing on the floor above, I desired the interpreter to put his questions. This was done, explaining to him the object of the inquiry, that it was to serve him and, by knowing the truth, [to] be prepared for his defense. He affected to know nothing about it, nor was he disposed to rely upon any defense that could be made. His idea was that he was giving the beaver as a commutation for his life. Under this impression it did not appear to me proper that I should take the beaver, knowing that I could do nothing for him, besides seeing the manner in which the dark and squalid creature was accommodated with but a shirt and breech-clout on, humanity dictated that the beaver should be applied to procure him a blanket and food additional to the bread and water which he was allowed. Accordingly I returned the order to the interpreter, and desired him to procure and furnish these things. He seemed reluctant, and thought we ought to keep the prerequisite we had got. On this, I thought it most advisable to retain the order and give it to a trader in town with directions to furnish these articles occasionally to the officer of the guard, which I did, taking the responsibility upon myself to the interpreter for his part of the beaver.

An Indian woman known by the name of the Grenadier Squaw was sitting doing some work by the trap door of the cell or hole in which he was confined, for the trap door was kept open and a sentry at the outer door of the guard-house. The Indian woman was led by sympathy to sit by him. I had a curiosity to know the force of abstract sentiment in preferring greater evils to what with us would seem to be less, or rather the force of opinion over pain. For knowing the idea of the Indians with regard to the disgrace of hanging, I proposed to the Indian woman, who spoke English as well as Indian and was a Delaware herself (Mamachtaga was of that nation), to ask him which he would choose, to be hanged or burned? Whether it was that the woman was struck with the inhumanity of introducing the idea of death, she not only declined to put the question, but her countenance expressed resentment. I then recollected, and have since attended to the circumstance, that among themselves when they mean to put anyone to death they conceal the determination and the time until it is about to be put in execution, unless the blacking the prisoner which is a mark upon such as about to be burned may be called an intimation; but it is only by those who are accustomed to their manners that it can be understood. However, I got the question put by the interpreter, at which he seemed to hesitate for some time but said he would rather be shot or be tomahawked.

In a few days it made a great noise through the country that I was to appear for the Indian, and having acquired some reputation in the defense of criminals, it was thought possible by some that he might be acquited by "the crooks of the law" as the people expressed it; and it was talked of publicly to raise a party and come to town and take the interpreter and me both and hang the interpreter and exact an oath from me not to appear on behalf of the Indian. It was however finally concluded to come in to the garrison and demand the Indian and hang him themselves. Accordingly a party came in a few days, and about break of day summoned the garrison and demanded the surrender of the Indian; the commanding officer remonstrated, and prevailed with them to leave the Indian to the civil authority. Upon which they retired, firing their guns as they came through the town. The interpreter, hearing the alarm, sprang up in his shirt and made for a hill above the town called Grant's Hill. On seeing him run, he was taken for the Indian that had been suffered to escape, and was pursued until the people were assured that it was not the Indian. In the meantime he had run some miles, and swimming the river, lay in the Indian country until he thought it might be safe to return.

It was not without good reason that the interpreter was alarmed, for having been some years among the Indians in early life a prisoner, and since a good deal employed in the Indian trade, and on all occasions of treaty employed as an interpreter, he was associated in the public mind with an Indian, and on this occasion considered as the abetter of the Indian from the circumstance of employing council to defend him. And before this time a party had come from the Chartiers, a settlement south of the Monongahela in the neighborhood of this town, and had attacked some friendly Indians on the island in the Ohio (Killbuck's island) under the protection of the garrison, and had killed several and among them some that had been of essential service to the whites in the expeditions against the Indian towns and on scouting parties in case of attacks upon the settlements.[1] One to whom the whites had given the name of Wilson (Captain Wilson), was much regretted by the garrison. A certain Cisna had commanded the party that committed this outrage.

A day or two after his return the interpreter came to me and relinquished all interest in the beaver that was lodged with the trader or expectant from the towns, that

---

1. In March 1783, militia from Chartiers Creek attacked Killbuck's friendly Delawares encamped on Smoky Island and killed all but a few.

he might, to use his own language, "wipe his hands of the affair, and be clear of the charge of supporting the Indian." The fact was that as to beaver from the towns I expected none, having been informed in the meantime by the friendly Indians that Mamachtaga was a bad man and was thought so by his nation, that he had been a great warrior but was mischievous in liquor, having killed two of his own people, that it would not be much regretted in the nation to hear of his death, and that except his brother, no one would give anything to get him off.

He had the appearance of great ferocity, was of tall stature [and] fierce aspect. He was called Mamachtaga, which signifies trees blown across, as is usual in a hurricane or tempest by the wind, and this name had been given him from the ungovernable nature of his passion. Having therefore no expectation of peltry or fur in the case, it was no great generosity in me to press upon the interpreter the taking half the beaver as his right in procuring the contract; but finding me obstinate in insisting upon it, he got a friend to speak to me, and at length I suffered myself to be prevailed upon to let him off and take all the beaver that could be got to myself.

It did not appear to me advisable to relinquish the defense of the Indian, fee or no fee, lest it should be supposed that I yielded to the popular impression, the fury of which, when it had a little spent itself, began to subside. And there were some who thought the Indian might be cleared, if it could be proved that the white men killed had made the Indian drunk, which was alleged to be the case but which the wounded and surviving persons denied, particularly the dwarf (William Freeman), but his testimony it was thought would not be much regarded as he could not be said to be a "man grown," and had been convicted at the quarter sessions of stealing a keg of whiskey some time before.

At a court of Oyer and Terminer holden for the county of Westmoreland before Chief Justices M'Kean[2] and Bryan, Mamachtaga was brought to trial. The usual forms were pursued. An interpreter, not Nicholas but a certain Handlyn, stood by him and interpreted in the Delaware language the indictment and the meaning of it and the privilege he had to deny the charge, that is the plea of "not guilty." But he could not easily comprehend that it was a matter of form, and that he must say "not guilty"; for he was unwilling to deny, as unbecoming a warrior to deny the truth. For though he did not confess, yet he did not like to say that he had not killed the men; but said he was drunk, and did not know what he had done but "supposed he should know when he was under the grount." The court directed the plea to be entered for him, and he was put upon his trial.

He was called upon to make his challenges, which the interpreter explained to him and which he was left to make himself and which he did, as he liked the countenances of the jury and challenged according to the sourness or cheerfulness of the countenance and what he thought indications of a mild temper. The jurors . . . were called to the book, being told in the usual form, "Prisoner, look upon the juror. Juror, look upon the prisoner at the bar. Are you related to the prisoner?" One of them, a German of a swarthy complexion and being the first called, took the question amiss, as thinking it a reflection and said with some anger that he thought "that a uncivil way to treat Dutch peoples as if he could be the brothers, or cousings of an Indian." But the matter being explained to him by another German of the jury, he was satisfied, and was sworn.

---

2. Thomas McKean, elected Governor of Pennsylvania in 1799, supported by Brackenridge.

The meaning of the jury being on oath was explained to the Indian to give him some idea of the solemnity and fairness of the trial. The testimony was positive and put the homicide beyond a doubt; so that nothing remained for me in opening his defense but the offering to prove that he was in liquor, and that this had been given to him by the white people, the traders in town. The testimony was overruled, and it was explained to the Indian that the being drunk could not by our law excuse the murder. The Indian said he hoped the good man above would excuse it.

The jury gave their verdict, guilty, without leaving the bar. And the prisoner was remanded to jail. In the meantime there was tried at the same court another person (John Bradly) on a charge of homicide but who was found guilty of manslaughter only. Towards the ending of the court these were both brought up to receive sentence. The Indian was asked what he had to say, why sentence of death should not be pronounced upon him. This was interpreted to him, and he said that he would rather "run awhile." This was under the idea of the custom among the Indians of giving time to the murderer, according to the circumstances of the case, to run, during which time if he can satisfy the relations of the deceased, buy a commutation for his life [with] a gun, a horse, fur and the like, it is in their power to dispense with the punishment; but if this cannot be done, having not enough to give, or the relations not consenting to take a commutation, he must come at the end of the time appointed to the spot assigned, and there, by a warrior of the nation, or some relative, son, brother, etc. of the deceased, be put to death, in which case the tomahawk is the usual instrument. No instance will occur in which the condemned man will not be punctual to his engagement. And I think it very probable, or rather can have no doubt, but that if this Indian had been suffered to run at this time, that is, go to his nation on the condition to return at a certain period to receive the sentence of what he would call the council, he would have come with as much fidelity as a man challenged would on a point of honor come to the place assigned . . . to risk himself to his adversary. Such is the force of opinion, from education, on the human mind.

Sentence [had] been pronounced upon the convicted [white man] of manslaughter. (In this case the first part of the sentence, as the law directs, was that of hanging, which is done until the "benefit of clergy is prayed by the prisoner";[3] but not understanding this, nothing could exceed the contortion of his muscles when a sentence contrary to what he had expected was pronounced.) Being a simple man he made a hideous outcry, and gave a most woeful look to the court and country and begged for mercy; and it was not for some time after, that having the matter explained to him and the benefit of clergy being allowed, he could be composed. Sentence of "burning in the hand" being now pronounced, at this moment the sheriff came in with a rope to bind up his hand to a beam of the low and wooden court-house in which we were in order that the hot iron might be put upon it.

Sentence of hanging had been previously pronounced upon the Indian, on which he had said that he would prefer to be shot; but it being explained to him that this could not be done, he had the idea of hanging in his mind. Accordingly, by a side glance, seeing the sheriff coming in with a rope which was a bed-cord he had procured, having nothing else in our then low state of trade and manufacturing, Mamachtaga conceived that the sentence was about to be executed presently upon him,

---

3. The sentence is imposed as a form and is changed to manslaughter when the prisoner asks for the intervention of a clergyman. Apparently the convicted man had not been informed of this legal custom.

and that the rope was for this purpose, which coming unaware upon him, he lost the command of himself for a moment. His visage grew black, his features were screwed up, and he writhed himself with horror and aversion; the surprise not having given time to the mind to collect itself, and on the acquired principle of honor to conceal its dismay, or on those of reason to bear with and compose itself to its fate. Even when undeceived and made acquainted that he was not to die then, he remained under a visible horror, the idea of immediate death and especially of hanging giving a tremor, like the refrigeration of cold upon the human frame.

Before he was taken from the bar he wished to say something, which was to acknowledge that his trial had been fair and to express a wish that his nation would not revenge his death or come to war on his account. Being asked, as he was taken off by some of those accompanying the sheriff in conducting him to jail, whom he thought the judges to be before whom he had been tried and who were on the bench in scarlet robes, which was the official custom of that time. Being of the Delaware nation, among whom Moravian missionaries had been a good deal and, as it would seem, mixing some recollections which he had derived from this source, he answered that the one, meaning the Chief Justice, was God, and the other Jesus Christ.

At the same court of Oyer and Terminer was convicted a man for the crime against nature, and at a court of Quarter Sessions a short time after, another, a young man of the name of Jack had been convicted of larceny and was now confined in the same jail, and in fact in the same room, for there was but one, with the Indian and the white man before-mentioned. And though, upon account of his youth and family connections, the jury in finding a verdict had recommended him to pardon, for which the supreme executive council of the state had been petitioned some time before, nevertheless he could not restrain the wickedness of his mind and had prevailed upon the white man, guilty of the crime against nature, as he had to die at any rate, to save the disgrace of being hanged, to consent to be murdered by the Indian. The creature [*the one condemned to death*] was extremely simple and had actually consented, and Jack had prepared a knife for the purpose. But the Indian refused, though solicited and offered liquor, but he declined, saying he had killed white men enough already.

A child of the jailor had been taken sick and had a fever. The Indian said he could cure it if he had roots from the woods which he knew. The jailor, taking off his irons which he had on his feet, took his word that he would not make his escape while he let him go to the woods to collect roots, telling him that if he did make his escape the great council, the judges, would hang him (the jailor) in his place. But for the greater security the jailor thought proper to accompany him to the woods where roots were collected, and which on their return were made use of in the cure of the child.

The warrant for the execution of the Indian and of the white man came to hand, and the morning of the execution the Indian expressed a wish to be painted that he might die like a warrior. The jailor as before unironed him and took him to the woods to collect his usual paints, which having done, he returned and prepared himself for the occasion, painting highly . . . [as] on great occasions.

A great body of people assembling at the place of execution, the white man was hung first, and afterwards the Indian ascended a ladder placed to the cross timber of the gibbet; and the rope being fastened, when he was swung off it broke and the Indian fell, and having swooned a little, he rose with a smile and went up again. A stronger rope in the meantime having been provided, or rather two put about his neck together so that his weight was supported . . . he underwent the sentence of the law and was hanged till he was dead.

This was during the Indian war, and this place on the verge of the settlement, so that if the Indian had taken a false step, and gone off from the jailor while he was looking for roots for the cure or for painting, it would have been easy for him to have made his escape. But such is the force of opinion as we have before said, resulting from the way of thinking among the Indians, that he did not seem to think that he had the physical power to go. It was nevertheless considered an imprudent thing in the jailor to run this risk. For if the Indian had made his escape it is morally certain that in the then state of the public mind, the jailor himself would have fallen a sacrifice to the resentment of the people.

[*Pittsburgh, 1785*]

FROM *INCIDENTS OF THE INSURRECTION*

[5]

Had the denounced persons left the country immediately, before it became known extensively that they were obnoxious, they could have got out of it without difficulty; but it was no easy matter afterwards. The cause of their proscription was not distinctly known, and it was thought to be some great state crime that had come to light. The people had an idea that it would be no harm to shoot them down, at least to arrest and imprison them.

Kirkpatrick was to have had an escort of two men, but one only had been able to join him; the other had been detained by the people who, not knowing the measures of the committee, were lying in wait to apprehend him. With the person that had been able to join him, he escaped by a circuitous route on the frontiers of the country as far as the Allegheny mountains and then ventured to take the road.

Prothonotary Brison had been detained a night at the house of the deputy attorney for the Commonwealth at the distance of some miles from Pittsburgh. It was rumored in the neighborhood that he was there still. A party of about forty persons had collected in the night and surrounded the house. They demanded of the attorney to give them entrance that they might search for the culprit. It could not be refused. The lady of the attorney had fainted with the fright; a mulatto woman had been dispatched to the spring hastily for a glass of cool water; and mistaking her complexion in the dark, she was taken for the prothonotary making his escape in the disguise of a night cap. She was pursued; and supposing herself obnoxious, she left the glass and took to the woods. It was thought that the prothonotary had escaped, and the resentment fell on the attorney for harboring a criminal; and it was with great difficulty and not until the mulatto woman, recovering herself, had come back that he could convince them of the truth.

Edward Day had taken the safest route and descended the river to Fort Washington.

The inspection offices through the whole survey, comprehending five counties, had at this time been burned down with the dwelling houses of the deputies. Liberty poles with inscriptions and devices [were] raised everywhere. Inscriptions such as, "an equal tax, and no excise"; devices such as a snake divided, with this motto, "united we stand, divided we fall." I met with no man that seemed to have an idea that we were to separate from the government or to overthrow it, but simply to oppose the excise law; and yet the people acted and spoke as if we were in a state of revolution. They threatened life and property familiarly. They talked of not suffering Alexander Addison, the district judge, to return to the country. He was at that time in Philadelphia.

A report that, on his way down, he had met the marshall and encouraged him to come forward with the writs had rendered him obnoxious. They proceeded to acts of violence among themselves, every man avenging his own injury. Persons consulted me on the expediency of coming to town to shelter themselves there. I dissuaded [them] from this measure, as dangerous to them and to the town both. We could not defend it; and if we could, yet whence our provisions? It was better to conceal and lie by a little, until it could be seen what arrangements could be made for the restoration of order; or if, in the meantime, any man was apprehensive of injury to himself personally, he had better cross the Ohio and be absent for a while under the pretext of discovering and improving vacant land. I was consulted by many, supposing me to have a knowledge of the times; and when I thought myself safe, I gave my real sentiments. . . . My sentiments were that the people must be brought to order by arrangements among themselves, or the government would reduce them. When I thought myself not safe, not knowing the persons or suspecting myself to be watched, my answers were evasive or equivocal.

The most delicate conduct was necessary in order to avoid giving offense. Some days after the cavalcade at Braddock's fields, I was reading an advertisement, by one who had been there, put up at a public house in Pittsburgh and laughing with some persons present at the singularity of the phraseology and orthography. Looking around, I saw two or three from the country who discovered by their countenances strong emotions of resentment; they had conceived our merriment, at the expense of the advertisement, to indicate an undervaluing of the writer and his service. I turned it off suddenly by saying that it was no matter; he did not spell well but he might be a good soldier and fight well. This restored their good humor.

I canvassed my situation fully and began more seriously to think of emigration; but in that case, I would be considered in the light of a deserter and my property become a sacrifice. I thought of disposing of my house, which was perishable, to some individual less conspicuous and under his name save it. But that would be suspected or discovered. I thought of being absent on some pretense that might be plausible; and it struck me to prevail with the people of Pittsburgh to appoint me as an envoy to the executive, to state the motives of their conduct and explain their situation. I mentioned this to James Ross, who approved of it and at my request [agreed to] sound General Wilkins to get him to favor it. Mr. Ross did so, but informed me that General Wilkins was not willing that I should leave the town. He was in the same situation himself and did not like to lose company. I have learned since that there were more in the same situation and with the same reflections elsewhere who had planned the getting out of the country by pretending to go below to purchase powder. . . .

I made up my mind now to wait the result of the meeting at Parkinson's ferry. My object was a pacification of the country by means short of force. With a view to this, I wished the government to have a just idea of the situation of the country, the magnitude and extent of the opposition. In that case, the executive might be disposed to adopt conciliatory measures. On this principle, having received a packet containing some papers from Tench Coxe of Philadelphia on agricultural subjects to be communicated to the people of the country, it struck me to communicate to the government by writing to him my impressions with regard to the disturbance. This letter was misunderstood and considered as proof that I was engaged in the insurrection. Some expressions led to this misconception, which [expressions] I had used to save myself with the more violent of the people of the country, if it should fall into their hands by the intercepting the mail, a thing constantly expected. In writing to Tench Coxe, I considered myself as writing to the government, understanding him to be in an official situation near the President.

A term had come into popular use before this time to designate the opposition to the excise law; it was that of Tom the Tinker. It was not given, as the appellation of Whig originally was, as a term of reproach by adversaries, but assumed by the people who were active in some of the masked riots which took place at an early period. A certain John Holcroft was thought to have made the first application of it. It was at the time of the masked attack on a certain William Cochran, who rendered himself obnoxious by an entry of his still, according to law. His still was cut to pieces; and this was humorously called mending his still; and the menders of course must be tinkers; and the name, collectively, became Tom the Tinker. Advertisements were now put up on trees on the highways, or on other conspicuous places, under the signature of Tom the Tinker, threatening individuals or admonishing or commanding them in measures with regard to the excise law. . . . It was not now, "Are you Whig or Tory?" But, "Are you a Tom the Tinker's man?" Every man was willing to be thought so; and some had a great deal of trouble to wipe off imputations to the contrary. Advertisements appeared in the gazettes, from individuals, appealing to the public and averring the falsehood of aspirations upon them as favoring the excise law.

I had frequently heard it said by the people of the country, since the introduction of the excise law, that it were better for them to be under the British, and at this time such language began to be very common. But I cannot say that I ever heard any person of note breathe the idea. It was said that arms and ammunition could be obtained from the British.

Reports from the east of the mountains were that the people on that side were as violent as those on this, that they had proceeded to outrages. This was alarming. I saw before me the anarchy of a period, a shock to the government and possibly a revolution—a revolution impregnated with the Jacobin principles of France, and which might become equally bloody to the principal actors. It would be bloody unavoidably to them, and to the people, destructive. Let no man suppose that I coveted revolution. I had seen the evils of one already, the American; and I had read the evils of another, the French. My imagination presented the evils of the last strongly to my view and brought them so close to probable experience at home that, during the whole period of the insurrection, I could scarcely bear to cast my eye upon a paragraph of French news. This is not a statement of sentiment invented now; they were my expressions at the time. It was not the excise law alone that was the object with the people; it was with many not the principle object. A man of some note, and whose family had been at the burning of Neville's house, was seen on horseback in Pittsburgh the day of Braddock's field, riding along with a tomahawk in his hand and raised over his head: "This is not all that I want; it is not the excise law only that must go down, [but] your high offices and salaries. A great deal more is to be done; I am but beginning yet."

There was an accidental circumstance which, independent of fixed and permanent causes in the minds of the people, contributed to the inflammation of this period. It preceded the election of sheriff and members of assembly; and without meaning anything more than to be elected, the candidate was clamorous against excises and salaries, and was for taking arms, not having the least expectation of fighting, but willing to make other people think that he would fight. This class of men were numerous and greatly vociferous. Strange as it may seem, it never once struck them that if things went on in that manner there could be no election.

I have given the state of the country previous to the meeting at Parkinson's ferry.

[6]

The meeting was opened by placing Edward Cooke in the chair and making Albert Gallatin secretary . . . there appeared to be members from Ohio county in Virginia and five counties of Pennsylvania. In the whole there [were] two hundred and sixty. Our hall was a grove and might well be called the mountain, for we were on a very lofty ground overlooking the river. We had a gallery of lying timber and stumps, and there were more people collected there than there was of the committee.

Several persons spoke on the subject of constituting magazines of arms and ammunition and seemed to wish resolutions pointedly to this. . . . Gallatin was laboring hard to divert this by attacking it in front. . . . I affected, as before, to oppose Gallatin and made an apology for those who were for providing means of war. Said I, "It may not be amiss to talk of these things and to hold out the idea of fighting with a view to avoid it, just as a general displays columns, meaning by that display to avoid engaging. This idea of our being about to fight may induce the government to accommodate with the country. But enough is done. These things will be left to the direction of the standing committee."

The apology saved the pride of the speakers and satisfied the hopes of the violent; and there was no more said. I was thought to be for war, if it should be necessary. I was applauded by the gallery, and it was said I had gained what I had lost at Mingo creek.

I lay that night at a farmhouse in the neighborhood, with a hundred or more of the gallery or committee about me. The whole cry was war. From the manner in which they understood me, I was greatly popular with them. "Stand by us," said they, "and we will stand by you."

I felt my situation with extreme sensibility. I had an attachment to the people because they had an attachment to me, and I thought of the consequence: . . . suppose that, in the prosecution of the plan I have in view, arrangements cannot be made to satisfy them and that a war must ensue; what shall I do? I am under no obligation to honor, to take part in supporting them, for I have no way contributed to produce the disturbance. And though, on principles of conscience, it may be excusable in them to make war, for they think they are right, yet it would not be so in me, for I think them wrong. But on the score of self-preservation and personal interest, what am I to do? It is a miserable thing to be an emigrant; there is a secret contempt attached to it, even with those to whom you come. They respect more the valor, though they disapprove the principle, of those that stay at home. All I have in the world is in this country. It is not in money; I cannot carry it with me; and if I go abroad, I go poor; and [I] am too far advanced in life to begin the world altogether.

But as to these people, what chance have they? They may defend the passes of the mountains; they are warlike, accustomed to the use of arms, capable of hunger and fatigue, and can lie in the water like badgers. They are enthusiastic to madness, and the effect of this is beyond calculation.

The people on the east of the mountains are, many of them, dissatisfied on the same principle and will be little disposed to disturb the people here if they should mean to defend themselves. It is true, the consequence of war, supposing the country independent of the United States, will be poverty and a miserable state of things for a long time; but still, those who stand by the country, where they are, have the best chance and the most credit in the end. Should I emigrate and the country be reduced, I cannot live in it again for a thousand reasons. I am in a quandry, and in either case the election is painful. The only thing that can suit me is an accommodation and having the matter settled without a civil war. But is there any prospect of this? Will the executive be disposed to act with mildness or rigor in this instance? The excise law is a branch of the funding system, which is a child of the Secretary of the Treasury, who is considered as the minister of the President. He will feel a personal antipathy against the opposers of it and will be inclined to sanguinary counsels. The President himself will consider it as a more dangerous case than the Indian war or the British spoilations and will be disposed to apply more desperate remedies. He will see that here the vitals are affected, whereas there the attack was upon the extremities. Nevertheless, the extreme reluctance which he must have to shed the blood of the people, with whom he is personally popular, will dispose him to overtures of amnesty. These were my reveries as I lay, with my head upon a saddle, of the flooring of a cabin.

In the morning, the committee of four having met, we proceeded to the arranging and mending the resolutions. Bradford was not satisfied with the indefinite expression of the power given to the standing committee but wished to have it in plain terms, probably with a view to get something to pass the committee that would involve all equally with himself in the treason committed. I wished to evade it, and endeavored to divert his attention by keeping him laughing. I dispensed with Craig on this occasion and made use of Herman Husband. I endeavored to amuse Bradford with him, as a person would a boy by playing bear.

I had heard of this extraordinary character many years ago, when [he was] a principal of the insurgents known by the name of Regulars in North Carolina. I had seen him in the year 1778, when he was a member of the legislature of Pennsylvania. I was present when a Quaker lady was introduced and preached before the house. Herman, who was a divine as well as a politician, thought her not orthodox and wished to controvert; but the house, willing to avoid religious controversies, would not suffer him.

I had visited him in the year 1780 at his residence in the glades of the Allegheny mountain on my way from Philadelphia to Pittsburgh. He had then just finished a commentary on a part of the prophet Ezekiel. It was the vision of the temple, the walls, the gates, the sea of glass, etc. Loggerhead divines heretofore had interpreted it of the New Jerusalem, but he conceived it to apply to the Western country, and the walls were the mountains, the gates the gaps in them by which the roads came, and the sea of glass the lake on the west of us. I had no hesitation in saying that the commentary was analogous to the vision. He was pleased and said I was the only person, except his wife, that he ever got to believe it. Thought I, your church is composed, like many others, of the ignorant and the dissembling.

It was to this topic I drew him [*Bradford*] at present, and wished him to explain his reveries. But Bradford was too intent on getting the resolution amended to an explicit provisional declaration of war; he complained of my laughing and wished me to be serious. Gallatin, not perceiving my drift, said cynically, "He laughs all by himself. . . ."

[7]

I have mentioned James Ross as a commissioner on the part of the United States. The others were William Bradford, Attorney General of the United States, and Jasper Yates, a judge of the Supreme Court of Pennsylvania. The two last had arrived at Parkinson's ferry a short time after the adjournment of the meeting; from thence they came [to] Pittsburgh. Being known to the Attorney General and the judge, I waited on them at the public house after their arrival. I found Major Craig giving them a tragical account of the cruel treatment of Kirkpatrick, Neville, and the others by the people of Pittsburgh in sending them away. I felt great indignation and addressed him before the commissioners. Said I, "The representation is not just. You are imposing upon these gentlemen. You are leading them to suppose that the people of Pittsburgh expelled these men; it was the country. We acted as their guardians in sending them away; the act was for them more than for ourselves." Here I gave a detail of the circumstances. He was silent and withdrew.

I had discovered in the commissioners unfavorable impressions towards me; I was at a loss whether to attribute them to what they had heard on the way or to the account of Craig. An expression of the Attorney General struck me much. In my observations on the account of Craig I had said that I had never considered myself as an insurgent. I was employed to negotiate for those who were, but that did not involve the fact that I was one myself. Said the Attorney General, "That will be a subject of future consideration." I was with the commissioners but a short time, finding the point of view in which I conceived myself to stand with them. The expression of the Attorney General had hurt my mind and, with the language of Craig, became the subject of very serious reflections. I considered Craig but as an automaton, and that his impressions but [to] be those with which Colonel Neville went away. That being the case, I had reason to suppose that this representation would be the same which Neville would make to the executive. The people of Pittsburgh, and in particular myself, could be held up as insurgents. After all my labor to get matters settled, this family [*Neville's*] would consider me as having injured them; and when they returned, I should be insulted by them. I had found it hard enough in the village before to support myself against them, but it would be worse now. I began to consider whether it would not be better to stand with the *sans culottes* of the country and keep these men away while they were away. But was it practicable? I could not reconcile it to myself to disturb the union; that would be a wickedness beyond all possibility of contemplation. But this country might secede from it. That is a right that is never given up in society. A part of a country, as well as an individual, may quit a government; and no doubt this country will quit the United States in due time. That may be by a consent of the union or without it. But at the present there would be no consent. The example would be dangerous to give. Common interest would not suffer it. We are bound to the union for our proportion of the public debt. We must discharge demands against the partnership before the firm, as to that, can be legally dissolved. The United States have land beyond us; they cannot suffer us to shut them out from these by an independent government between.

But is it practicable to establish and support such a government? Perhaps it might claim these lands to the westward and invite all the world to take possession of them. Collect all the bandits on the frontiers of the state to help us to fight for them; tell the Spaniards to come up to the mouth of the Ohio and give us a free trade; let the British keep the posts and furnish us with arms and ammunition; get the Indians of the woods to assist us; tell them that the people on the east of the mountains want our whiskey and their lands. We might wage war, and perhaps succeed. It is true we should succeed to misery for a while and poverty at last. But even this would be more tolerable to me than to live under any circumstances, suspected by the government and treated with contumely by these people when they had returned loaded with the favors of the government, as having been the great defenders of it.

These were the thoughts of a night. When I saw James Ross in the morning, I explained to him my chagrin of the preceding day and my reflections in consequence of it; and gave him to understand that I had half a mind to become an insurgent. He took it more seriously than I intended it. His expression was, "The force of genius is almighty. Give them not the aid of yours."

I told him that nothing but self-preservation would lead me to think of it, or the being unjustly suspected. He soothed my mind by assuring me that no suspicion could possibly fall on me, that the commissioners the preceding day were perfectly satisfied with the explanation I had given in the presence of Craig, and that what he had said had not left the least impression.

The point was now gained to which I had always looked forward, the point where the foot was to be fixed in order to make an open stand against the insurrection. This was my expression to James Ross. . . . "The point is gained," said I. "There is a basis now laid from which we can act." To this point I had always looked forward, not expecting commissioners from the government but propositions from it to commissioners . . . holding out an amnesty, which I took to be the great secret of composing the disturbance. Until that appeared, the disposition of those involved would lead them to cut throats to support themselves; and the whole country, conscious that every man had in some degree contributed by words or by actions to produce that mental opposition to the law which had terminated in actual force, could not reconcile it to their feelings to abandon those who had acted with precipitation in the late instances. But an amnesty being given, these could say to their countrymen, "You are now on a ground with us; stop, we will go no further."

I considered the appointment of commissioners on the part of the executive as a pledge of amnesty, though I had yet no information of their powers. I therefore saw the way clear for the country to get out; and now the conduct ought no longer to be a concealment of intentions and a half-way acquiescence, but an explicit avowal of opinions.

On this principle I took the first opportunity I had with Bradford and Marshall, and it was in the presence of one of the committee before any conference with the commissioners, to inform them of my real sentiments with regard to the violation of the laws which had taken place, and particularly with regard to those in which they had been implicated—the intercepting the mail and the rendezvous at Braddock's fields. Bradford looked red and angry, Marshall pale and affected.

My system from the commencement had been to take the business out of the hands of the multitude as speedily as possible by instituting an extensive committee. [It was] not to take a final question but, having enlightened that committee and rendered them moderate, to make use of them as evangelists among the people when they went home to disseminate the proper doctrines. It was on this principle that I had suggested the Parkinson's ferry meeting. The fury of the people at that meeting led me to see the necessity of reducing the country into still smaller bounds by a committee extracted from the first. It was on this principle I approved and supported the appointing of a standing committee. Even this committee was too large with which to break the business, and therefore I wished the smaller committee of twelve to be the body with which we should begin to act. Having instructed and enlightened these and gained their assent, we should come forward with them to the standing committee as so many disciples, not wounding the pride of others by having it upon them, without their concurrence, to judge, but deliberating, as if not having judged at all.

Having instructed and converted the standing committee, we should send them home to disciple as many as they could; and come forward in the original and extensive committee in order to govern the result. In the meantime . . . the gazettes and handbills [would] reach the body of the people with reasonings on the subject. If this system could have been adopted, it might have succeeded. For it is a great mistake to suppose that Bradford or Marshall or others led the people. It was the people led them. It was the mass of the people that commanded, and it was the fear of them that operated on the minds of the more conspicuous individuals. Even Bradford was the most obstinate because he was the greatest coward. He had no reach of thought to see the danger from the government, but the danger from the people was just before his nose.

The conduct of the people below contributed to deprive us of that time that was necessary to bring the public mind, among ourselves, to a proper sense of interest and duty.

In drafting [the report] which had been committed to me on the part of our committee, I had introduced our statement, at least the statement made by me, of our general grievances in this country. It was with a view to show the people that we had made the most of our case and of course must be supposed to have got the best terms that could be given; and if we, who had been thus impressed, had yielded, they might. The commissioners thought it might rather strengthen opposition in their minds, and it was struck out.

I had stated strongly, on the part of the commissioners, the sense they had expressed of the outrages committed, the burning, the expulsions, and especially the intercepting the mail and the march to Braddock's field. It was with a view to bring these strongly before the minds of the people that, sensible of the atrocity, they might the more appreciate the value of an amnesty. But I am disposed to believe that this gave offense to Marshall and Bradford, who had been implicated in the last acts. For I cannot otherwise account for the dissatisfaction they discovered towards me from this time. I cannot believe that Marshall, especially, was at all dissatisfied at being relieved from the extremely hazardous situation in which he had been involved.

Concluding the report, I added some reasons which had been suggested, at least by myself in the committee, as grounds of conceding to the propositions of the commissioners. They were such as I thought would have weight with the people. Albert Gallatin, in his speech in the legislature of Pennsylvania on the subject of the insurrection, speaking of these reasons, says, "They are, I suppose, such as, in the judgment of the author, would make the most impression upon the people. On that head, however, I think he was mistaken." I think now, as I did then, that they were the most likely to impress. But that is a matter of opinion. I am not going to dispute about it. The true democratic principle on which it should be put doubtless was that "the will of the majority should govern. The national will had made the law, and it should be obeyed." However unequal and oppressive on this part of the community we might suppose it, yet the good of the whole demanded our submission.

It is an abstract argument that must satisfy the understanding but can never reconcile the heart. It is precisely the same with the theological argument of the divines; the good of the whole requires that some should be damned, and a man cannot be a saint until he feels a disposition to be reconciled to the divine will, in this particular, even if it should fall to his lot to go to hell. A man regenerated may come to this, but a natural man never will. So an enlightened politician may comprehend and acquiesce in the principle of submission to inequality of burdens when the nation dooms him to it; but the common mind revolts, and nothing will quiet him but the consideration that he cannot help himself. My argument, therefore, chiefly contemplated the want of power; and sometimes, by introducing an idea of postponement on the ground of existing circumstances, I endeavored to get an acquiescence for the present. Using the argument with one, his answer was, "The people never can be roused again." I knew that, and it was on this principle I suggested it. It was quite safe to talk of another day, for if the devil had been once laid it would be difficult to raise him again. The people would begin to look back and be made sensible of the precipice on which they had been standing. Let the law be put in operation, and they would not find it the evil they had conceived it to be.

At the request of the commissioners, it had been urged to call a meeting of the standing committee at an earlier day than appointed. They were called to meet on the 28th of August.

[8]

Our committee of conference met at Brownsville on the morning of the 28th of August. Brownsville is on the Monongahela, at the mouth of a stream known by the name of Redstone.

The first thing that struck us was a party of men, perhaps seventy, armed with rifles, who had marched from the upper part of Washington with a view, as we understood, to take the person and burn the buildings, mill, dwelling house, etc., of Samuel Jackson, near that place, who had given offense by an expression disrespectful to the committee. Pains were taken to dissuade [them] from outrage, informing them that, by the arrangements made at Parkinson's ferry, all complaints against offenders were to come before the committee, who were to decide upon the criminality and upon the punishment. They were prevailed upon to be contented with having him brought before the committee and tried in form, but insisted upon going with a file of men to bring him.

The committee of sixty having met, which was under a shade of boards constructed for the occasion, Edward Cooke was constituted chairman and Albert Gallatin secretary.

Samuel Jackson had been, by this time, brought up and was before the committee. He was of the denomination of the people called Quakers, a tall man with a broad brim to his hat. He preserved a grave demeanor and stood with an appearance of composed submission to the sufferings that might await him.

The charge against him was that, speaking of the committee, he had called it a scrub congress. The charge was proved by two witnesses. The question now was what punishment should be inflicted if he was found guilty, in the language of scripture, of "speaking evil of dignities." By the Scottish law it was what is called "leese-making," and subjects [one] to transportation. By the common law of England, which is our law, it might be construed sedition, indictable and punishable as a misdemeanor. In the delicate situation in which the country then was, it was thought to be a dangerous language, tending to lessen the respect due to the newly constituted authorities and evincing a bad disposition towards the cause of the people. A general and sincere concern was felt for the man because it was made a serious matter by the country and especially by the body of armed men who had marched a distance of twenty or thirty miles to do execution on his person and property. There were of the committee [those] who must be supposed incensed and of course resentful of the insult.

I had recourse to my usual expedient in desperate cases, pleasantry. "I recollect," said I, "to have read that in the time of Oliver Cromwell, lord protector of England, when he was in the height of his glory, a person came to him and gave him information of words used by another, greatly contemptuous of his dignity; viz., 'he has said that your excellency may kiss his ————.' 'You may tell him,' said Oliver, 'that he may kiss mine.' This Quaker has called us a scrub congress; let our sentence be that he shall be called a scrub himself."

The story of Cromwell had produced a sudden, involuntary, and loud laugh and [had] thrown a light upon the affair of Jackson, introducing a proper sentiment with regard to him; viz., that there was more magnanimity in disregarding his expressions than in punishing them. The troop that had brought him laughed and took him off to give him the epithet. He got a bucket of whiskey and water to drink with them and we heard no more of it.

The report was now about to be read; and a number of copies having been struck off, they were distributed among the members. While it was reading, there appeared great agitation in the committee; at some sentences, a rumor as in a church at the response—not "Lord help us to keep this law," but that of "Good Lord deliver us."

The popular mind had by this time gone far beyond that idea of an amnesty and they rather thought of giving an amnesty than of taking it, passing by the injuries of government on condition that it did not repeat them. They had expected a suspension of the law or, at least, a promise of a repeal of it.

I was a good deal alarmed and saw that it would not do to come forward immediately. It would be necessary to give them time to reflect a little and to prepare the way by a general conversation out of doors. Findley, Smiley, and other popular men were on the ground and might contribute to inform the people.

It had struck Gallatin and others in the same point of view, and it was moved to adjourn until the next morning. It was with a view to give the members time to consider the report. An adjournment took place, and I heard Bradford calling for the Washington members to convene by themselves.

I had crossed the river that night and lodged at a farm house on the west side, and this not only with a view to convenience but also to be out of the way if, in consequence of dissatisfaction with our report, any personal violence to the committee of twelve, or any of them, should be meditated, a thing which I thought not at all improbable, for what avails popularity in such times as these? It is but the turning of the hand, the palm up or down, from the height of favor to the lowest point of obloquy and persecution. Was there any man in Pennsylvania more popular than John Dickinson at the commencement of the American revolution? He was to be opposed to a declaration of independence and became obnoxious. James Wilson was at the height of political fame among the people but he had disapproved of the form of constitution they had adopted in the Commonwealth and they were about to murder him in his own house. I possessed, at this present time, the best kind of popularity; viz., that obtained after much obloquy through a series of years, suffered to correct itself; a popularity obtained, doubtless, by failing a little with the popular gale, at least not opposing it, but chiefly by a steady and upright demeanor in my profession. The popular mind, though passionate, is generous; and if it becomes sensible that it has wronged a man, will repair it. I mean to explain this more fully, as far as regards myself, in the conclusion of this narrative.

But though possessing at this time a solid popularity, I knew that a breath on the subject of the excise law would put it to a temporary death. However, I had no thought now of the loss of popularity but so far as it would produce permanent danger on the ground. Gallatin was in his own country, among a people more moderate, and he might be in less danger; nevertheless, he was not without apprehensions and had reason.

In the morning, crossing the river and coming into the village, I was led to understand that at the private meeting of the Washington members the preceding evening a great warmth and talk of guillotining was heard and the clapping of hands. I met Gallatin and James Lang, a member of the committee of twelve and who was of that village and was greatly alarmed from what he had seen and heard. It was early, and the committee of sixty had not yet collected; and the gallery, of which great numbers were from the neighborhood of the Mingo meeting house, had not yet convened. I had conversed with some the preceding evening before I left the village and found strong prejudices against me, as having made use of my talents as a lawyer to persuade the committee of conference to the acquiescence with the propositions of the commissioners. It was insinuated that we had been bribed, and [I] was told myself that attorneys would take fees. I hesitated, therefore, whether I should remain or not. It might be safest to return to Pittsburgh. I thought of this, more especially as I had observed that Bradford had preserved a distance from me and appeared to be dissatisfied. I knew that the example of arresting members in the French Convention, the knowledge of which was familiar here, might lead to the arresting me or others that were obnoxious; and between an arrest and putting to death, as there so here, there would be but little interval. Gallatin acknowledged himself not insensible of the delicacy of the situation and that insult, at least, might be offered, but observed that we had bound ourselves in honor to the commissioners to come forward and support the propositions. I reflected with myself that, nevertheless, in this undertaking of our committee of conference with the commissioners it was not understood that we were to run a risk of life or even indignities in recommending their own interest to the people. However, as Gallatin was disposed to try it, I was willing. It was then considered what should be the order of our speaking; there was a reluctance with each of us to break the business. I proposed that we should get James Edgar, a member of the committee of twelve, to begin. He was an associate judge of the court of Washington and a king or a rabbi in the Presbyterian churches of the Western country, had been a presbytery or elder from his youth, had been a member of committees in the early period of the American revolution, and of legislative assemblies, executive and censorial counsels, or deliberative conventions ever since. His head was prematurely hoary with prayers and fastings and religious exercises; his face thin and puritanic, like the figures of the old republicans in the time of the long parliament in England. He was a man of sense and not destitute of eloquence. It was agreed that he should open the way for us. It was proposed by him, but he appeared reluctant, I know not on what principle. It was imposed, therefore, upon Gallatin.

The committee having convened with a formidable gallery, as the day before, Gallatin addressed the chair in a speech of some hours. It was a piece of perfect eloquence and was heard with attention and without disturbance. I shall not undertake to give the scope of this speech as I could not do it justice and probably may have misconceived and might mistake some part of it.

It was a difficulty with me to find anything new that could be advanced, and I spoke more for the sake of showing that I had courage to speak than from an idea that I could add to the argument or improve the impression that had been made. However, I exerted my invention to vary the light of the argument and to add something new. Gallatin had addressed himself chiefly to the patriotism of the audience. I addressed myself to their conscience and fears. I confess that it was in their fears that I had most confidence. Gallatin had been didactic and deliberate, though animated. I became more impassioned and declamatory. My observations were to the following effect:

"It seems to be an idea entertained by the people that we can remain a part of government and yet wage war against it. That is impossible in the nature of the case; we are known to the government by representation only and not by force. We must therefore either overthrow it or it must overthrow us. But we have sworn to support it. If we contemplate the overthrowing it, where is our oath of allegiance? But can we overthrow it? We might as well think of tossing the Allegheny mountain from its base.

"But we may obtain a repeal of the law by an exhibition of force, by possessing the mountain and making a show of arms. That is not probable after the steps taken by the President. On principle of example it would so vitally affect the safety of the government that it can never be countenanced. We are told by the commissioners, and we have no reason to doubt it, that the whole force of the union will be exerted to crush such a precedent.

"But cannot we secede from the union? Not, and remain part of the government at the same time. We must dissolve our connection with Pennsylvania before we can cease to be under the government of the United States. But have we a right to dissolve our union with both? An individual may emigrate from society and a part of a society may separate from the whole, but an individual cannot leave a state in war because he owes service for the benefits he has enjoyed in peace. He cannot leave it without discharging debts he owes to individuals or to the public. How then can a part of the community separate before it has discharged the obligations contracted by the whole?

"But is it our interest to secede?" Having no sea coast, we are at the mercy of the imposts of all around us, even for the necessaries of life. If the weight of the Union, in the scale of nations, cannot procure us the surrender of the western posts, peace with the Indians, and the navigation of the Mississippi, how shall a half uninhabited, un-commerced extent of a hundred and fifty miles square command it? There is no man-ner of question but the time will come when the Western country will fall off from the Eastern, as North will from the South, and produce a confederacy of four; but surely it is our mutual interest to remain together as long as possible, to bear with in-equalities or local and partial grievances while we enjoy general advantages and avoid general evils.

"But are you able to secede? Can you fight the United States? Can you beat the 15,000 that are in requisition by the President? Grant it. Perhaps 30,000 in the passes of the mountains, for a heat. What of that? Are you able to beat a second 15,000 or a second 30,000? . . . I know your spirit but condemn your prudence.

"But do you know that you are mistaken in your support at home? Do you think that all are sincere who have been clamoring for war? Some clamor because they are cowards and wish to be thought brave, because they [are] ignorant enough not to ex-pect a war. Others because they have not estimated the fatigues of campaigning and do not consider how soon they will be tired. Others because they have contracted for the sale of their lands, are about to remove to Kentucky or elsewhere. Others—and this class numerous—because they have nothing to lose and can make their escape by the floods. If you depend upon these, you will, by and by, have to take the same course and descend the current with the frogs.[1]

"But men affect to be for war because they are afraid to speak their real senti-ments. I have my [eye] upon those here present and could name them who are thought to be strenuous for the most violent measures, and yet in the course of our committeeing have acknowledged to me what they really think, and it is their earnest desire to get out of the scrape upon almost any terms. After what has happened, any terms short of life ought to be accepted.

"The outrages have been grievous, wanton, and useless; in construction of law, amounting to high treason. Having had no privacy with these transactions or concern in the perpetration but disapproving when and where I could speak with safety, nev-ertheless, for the sake of those involved, I have labored hard to bring them out and have ever looked forward to that amnesty which is now before you. If I, who have nothing to apprehend for myself, have been ready to embrace it, surely those in a dif-ferent predicament well may.

"I have heretofore felt myself embarrassed in [not] knowing what to do. I con-sidered the feelings of the country with partiality of heart, knowing the ground of them to be the unequal law in question. I made excuses for the breaking into acts, knowing it to be the error of judgment, not distinguishing between what feelings are and what acts ought to be. I was impressed with the reflection that the disapproba-tion of the law having been general in the country and expressed by almost every one, no man could tell how far by words he might have contributed to that current of re-sentment which, at length, swelled beyond the constitutional banks of representation and remonstrance and broke out into outrage. He must, therefore, have a disposition to repair the mischief and save those who have gone to an excess not contemplated. . . . If these terms are not accepted, I am done and consider myself as discharged in honor and in conscience from all further concern in the business. It is, therefore, the

---

1. This expression escaped me in the hurry of the speech and gave great offense. [H.H.B.]

last and only advice I have to give, that you acquiesce with the propositions of the commissioners and accept the amnesty offered you. It is the expedient left to save the country, which has been already impaired and reduced by your late history. It was improving in agriculture, replenishing with buildings, becoming an object of emigration from abroad, and is now dejected from this height to a considerable depth from what it was. The value of property is reduced from what has happened. I do not consider what I possess at this moment as of more than one half of the value of what it was three months ago, but it will be still worse unless the evils that are impending are prevented by an immediate acquiescence. . . ."

Edgar followed me, with great earnestness and with the solemnity of an evening sermon, in a discourse of great length.

Bradford now rose to speak; and contrary to his engagements with the commissioners personally and his agreement with the report of the committee, he opposed the acceptance of the propositions in direct and violent terms. Speaking of the resources of war, arms, ammunition, etc., said he, "We will defeat the first army that comes over the mountains and take their arms and baggage."

"Not so easy neither," said a man in a blue coat who was in the gallery. This, I understood afterwards, was a Colonel Crawford, a brave Indian warrior of the frontiers. He had some experience of what fighting was and an idea there might be fighting; Bradford had none. . . .

Gallatin spoke a little and moved to take the vote on the propositions of the commissioners. Objections were made to the taking any vote at all. The question was then put, "Shall a vote be taken?" This was negatived, not a single person rising but the committee of twelve who had made the report. It was again moved on our part to take a vote by ballot on the propositions, presuming that an unwillingness to let their sentiments be known on the subject was the reason of objecting to the taking the vote publicly. The question was put, "Shall a private vote by ballot be taken?" It was negatived, the twelve only, as before, rising.

Here was a moment of delicacy indeed. The taking no vote was rejecting the propositions. And what the consequence? Measures must have been taken instantly to prepare for war. Bradford would have come forward with the schedule, baffled at Parkinson's ferry, with his heads of ammunition, arms, money, provisions, etc. Gallatin and myself would have been arrested upon the spot. For the example of the terrorists, as they have been called, was in the public mind, especially with Bradford, who had some light, wandering information of French affairs as he had of other subjects, and had heard of their arresting one another after their debates and cutting off heads; and coupling the successes and the executions together, he would conceive the idea that the executions produced the successes.

Gallatin, with great presence of mind, seized the moment and proposed that we should take a final vote by ballot; not to be made a part of our answer to the commissioners but simply in order to know our own minds.

There was hesitation even at this, for every man was afraid the hand writing, even of his ballot, would be known, and by some means it might transpire in what manner he had voted.

At this instant, a member of the committee rising and having a scrap of paper in his finger with the word yea written on one part and the nay on the other, held it up and proposed that sixty scraps with the words yea and nay written in the same manner should be made out by the secretary, and a scrap given to each of the members; and let every one divide the scrap in two parts, with the yea on one and the nay on the other; and let him chew or tear the yea or the nay as he thought proper, and [put] the other piece into a hat held by the secretary. When these were drawn out, it would be seen what the private sense of the committee was, without the possibility of any-one knowing how another voted. This mode was thought sufficiently safe and adopted.

It struck me greatly to observe the carefulness of every one in dividing or put-ting in his yea or no. All having been put in and the tickets drawn out, there were found 34 yeas and 23 nays.

It verified what I had stated, that the sentiments of a great part were not privately what they publicly avowed. . . .

Bradford appeared struck on finding that the majority was with us. His counte-nance became dark and dismayed, for I remarked him with attention. The members that had been for war were pretty easily discoverable by the dissatisfaction they evinced by the countenance or by language. There were some of them considerably enraged. But the gallery were the most explicit in showing satisfaction or dissatisfac-tion with the vote. It was in general not a popular one.

However, it had changed the face of things; and, there appearing a majority in favor of adopting the propositions, it remained for the committee to go on and make up their answer to the commissioners. But having sat a long time, it was thought proper to adjourn and meet again for the purpose. During the adjournment, Brad-ford went home. . . .

No gallery, or little, had attended in the afternoon. On going out I saw clubs and clusters of those who had been the gallery in private and close conversation in dif-ferent places. Passing by some of them, I spoke with confidence, as if I suspected noth-ing, but was received with silence and with looks of indignity. These were persons who were at that time my clients in causes of moment and with whom I had been long in habits of attachment; yet notwithstanding every lien of amity, they behaved to me in this manner. A man whom I had brought with me from Pittsburgh to carry the copies of the report, a few hundred of which had been printed, gave me to under-stand that, from what he could overhear, there was something on foot. I gave him money to discharge my bill at the public house and, as speedily as I could without seeming to be in haste, crossed the river. My horses had been left in a pasture on that side. I assisted a lad in driving them up, bridled them and had them saddled, and was ready to mount, when the man whom I had left had got over. Some persons had crossed over with him; among these were four of the Allegheny members of the com-mittee. It was then dark. We rode eighteen miles that night and got through the bulk of the Mingo creek settlement.

I have learned since that nothing but a want of decision prevented them from ar-resting me after my speech in the forenoon. It was in agitation, but they wavered in attempting it. The going away of Bradford also discouraged them. They had talked of arresting Gallatin, but his speech had been more abstract and guarded and had not given so much offense as mine. It was in agitation, some days after this, to take him; and a body of men had actually collected at Fredericktown on the west of the Al-legheny for that purpose. They were dissuaded by persons who went over from Fayette County and who endeavored to remove their misconceptions.

In our company that night, of the four Allegheny members that were along, was one of the name of Miller. When he first joined us I was suspicious of him knowing that he had been a principal in the two attacks upon the house of the inspector and commanded a company upon Peter's creek in a settlement through which we had to pass. I did not know but he might have been dispatched with orders to arrest me as I went through. I communicated this to some of the other members in the company, and we took care to ride fast enough not to put it in his power to be much ahead of us. He lodged with us where we halted a few hours and slept on the planks at the house of a German.

In the morning when we had set out, which was early, on our way I kept close by him and fell into conversation. He had been in the American service during the war with Great Britain, had been employed chiefly in the Western country in the war against the Indians. [He] had distinguished himself for fidelity, activity, and bravery on every occasion. I led him to talk of his services, and he gave the history of a variety of incidents. Sliding gradually from thence, I touched upon the present affairs of the country, the coming of the marshall, the opposition to him, the attack upon the house of the inspector, etc. I knew he had been one of the delinquent distillers and that it was on leaving his house, after having served a writ, that the marshall had been fired upon, which was the first opposition he had met with in the service of process. Miller gave me, with frankness, a relation of the whole circumstances. "The federal sheriff," said he, "was reading the writ, and General Neville was on horseback in the lane when he called to the sheriff to make haste. I looked up and saw a party of men running across the field, as it were, to the head of the lane. The people fired upon them." "Do you think," said I, "they fired balls and meant to hit them?" Said he, "I believe they meant to hit them; they pursued them and would have killed them.

"That night," continued Miller, "it was concluded that we would go on to Neville's and take him and the marshall. I felt myself mad with passion. I thought 250 dollars would ruin me; and to have to go to the federal court at Philadelphia would keep me from going to Kentucky this fall, after I had sold my plantation and was getting ready.[2]

"I felt my blood boil at seeing General Neville along to pilot the sheriff to my very door. He had been against the excise law as much as anybody. When old Graham, the excise man, was catched and had his hair cut off, I heard General Neville himself say they ought to have cut off the ears of the old rascal; and when the distillers were sued some years ago for fines, he talked as much against it as anybody. But he wanted to keep in the Assembly then. But whenever he got an offer of the office himself, he took it. I am a relation of Kirkpatrick. His mother and my mother were sisters. I was always for General Neville in his elections, and it put me mad to see him coming to ruin me."

I desired him to give me the particulars of the attack upon Neville's house the first day. He did so; he said they had about thirty men with fifteen guns, six only in order. They found the general just got up. After some words, he fired first. It was from the windows. A horn was blowing in the house the time of the firing. "Was the door open?" said I. "It was," said he. "Why then did you [not] rush into the entry?" "We were afraid," said he, "that he had a swivel or a big gun there.

"The Negroes," continued Miller, "by this time fired out of their cabins upon our backs and shot several, and we got off as well as we could."

"Well, what now? Are you for war?" "No," said he, "I voted for peace, but if I was to acknowledge that, I need never go home. I will have to deny it, and I will have to

---

2. This was one of the men that was thought might be depended upon in case of a war. [H.H.B.]

do whatever my company will insist upon me doing now. But I expect to get away soon and to be clear of it."

By this time we had arrived at this house, about eight miles from Pittsburgh. As we came up, three pretty children presented themselves in the inside of the fence that enclosed the cabin; and one of them said, putting his fingers between the rails, "Daddy, I have got a little brother."[3]

I was sensibly affected with the reflection that possibly that daddy might come to be hanged and that brother fatherless before it could know that it ever had one. . . .

Such was the state of things when the commissioners, both of the United States and the state of Pennsylvania, having done all that was in their power to do, left the country.

[9]

Just after the commissioners had left the country, a certain John Galton, calling on the printer of the *Pittsburgh Gazette,* presented him with a note which he had received, signed Tom the Tinker, commanding him to have it inserted in the *Pittsburgh Gazette.* In the situation of the country, even then, the printer thought it prudent for his own personal safety to insert it. It shows the sentiments of the violent, at this time, on the question of submission:

> Poor Tom takes this opportunity to inform his friends throughout the country that he is obliged to take up his commission once more, though disagreeable to his incli- nation. I thought when I laid down my commission before that we had the country so well united that there would have been no more need for me in that line, but my friends see more need for me than ever. They chose a set of men whom they thought they could confide in but find themselves much mistaken, for the majority of them have proved traitors. Four or five big men from below has scared a great many, but few are killed yet. But I hope none of those are any that ever pretended to be a friend to poor Tom; so I would have all my friends keep up their spirits and stand to their integrity, their rights, and liberty, and you will find poor Tom be your friend. This is a fair warning; traitors take care, for my hammer is up and my ladle is hot. I cannot travel the country for nothing.
>
> FROM YOUR OLD FRIEND
>
> TOM THE TINKER

John Galton, the person who brought Tom the Tinker's letter to the printer, was a client of mine in an enactment brought for him against a certain M'Clure. He called upon me at my office and, with a freedom which he thought he could take with his lawyer who would not suspect him of personal ill will, he inveighed against me much for having consented to the propositions of the commissioners. "What?" said he, "five men scare seventy-five?" The court being at hand, he was led to inquire when his cause would come on. "Not at all," said I. "How so?" said he. "Why," said I, "the gov- ernment is gone to the devil; the courts are overthrown; all law is at an end; there can be no justice now. The strong hand must manage all things. Is this M'Clure a stout fel-

---

3. The woman had been brought to bed in his absence. [H.H.B.]

low? Has he any sons? Cannot you and your sons beat him? Take the cudgel and drive
him off." "Ah," said he, "that will not do." "It may be," said I, "there is no help for it;
that is all that can be done now, at least until some other government and other courts
of law are set up in the place of those that are overthrown." He did not appear sensible of the scope of my observations but thought it a play of fancy on my part and
laughed; and, after inveighing another while against the committee of conference, he
would return to the question, "When will my cause with M'Clure come to trial?" I
mention this incident to show the indistinct conception on the part of the people of
the connection between the state government and the federal. Though laws of the
state are not the laws of the union, yet the laws of the union are the laws of the state.
I scarcely ever met a man that I could get to comprehend this. . . .

DR. JOHN KNIGHT

(?–1838)

In many ways, the war for independence in the Ohio valley did not end until 1815. While American and British forces rarely skirmished directly, the British employed and armed the Native American tribes to obstruct the American settlement of the region. In the eighteenth century, British and French presences in the region had been more concerned with building trade networks; Americans were more concerned with occupation. As a result, the natives accepted the British as the lesser of two evils and sought their protection and arms. Every year saw new campaigns against the encroaching settlements, despite the fact that the Americans were settling lands ceded by the British in the Treaty of Paris, ending the Revolution.

Narratives of frontier adventure, violence, and melodrama were among the first ways the "west" was presented to American readers, aside from promotional tracts. In 1782, Colonel William Crawford led a campaign into the Sandusky region in Ohio against the Shawnee and their allies. Its medical officer, Dr. John Knight was one of the few to return to the settlements alive. Knight had been Crawford's company's medical officer during the Revolution and left private life in Virginia to accompany Crawford on the campaign against the Natives.

When he reached Pittsburgh, Hugh Henry Brackenridge helped him compose his "Narrative," and it was soon published in the *Freeman's Journal* in Philadelphia and in Brackenridge's *Pittsburgh Gazette*. In the first decade of the nineteenth century, a Scottish scholar, Archibald Loudon, was assembling a collection of materials relating to Native Americans to be published for both American and British readers, and Brackenridge sent him Knight's "Narrative." Knight himself left the Virginia militia after his escape, married Crawford's niece, and eventually settled in Shelbyville, Kentucky, where he died in 1838.

Brackenridge described its relation as such: "I saw Knight on his being brought into the garrison at Pittsburgh; he was weak and scarcely able to speak. When he began to be able to speak a little, his Scottish dialect was much broader than it had been when I knew him before. This I remarked as usual with persons in a fever, or sick, they return to the vernacular tongue of their earlier years" (vi). Knight's story is intriguing as well for its depiction of the chief evil presence during the torture scenes as the British agent, Simon Girty. The "Narrative's" complex interculturalism—Shawnee, Scottish, and American—makes it a particularly interesting, as well as vivid, account of frontier violence and its roots in larger issues.

Texts: "The Narrative of Dr. Knight," in *Loudon's Indian Narratives* (Carlisle, 1808; rpt. New York, 1995): 1–15.

THE NARRATIVE OF DR. KNIGHT

About the latter end of the month of March or the beginning of April, of the present year 1782, the western Indians began to make incursions upon the frontiers of Ohio, Washington, Youghagany and West-moreland counties, which has been their constant practice ever since the commencement of the present war, between the United States and Great Britain.

In consequence of these predatory invasions, the principal officers of the above mentioned counties, namely: Colonels Williamson and Marshall, tried every method in their power to set on foot an expedition against the Wyandot towns, which they could effect no other way than by giving all possible encouragement to volunteers. The plan proposed was as follows: Every man furnishing himself with a horse, a gun, and one month's provision, should be exempt from two tours of militia duty. Likewise, that every one who had been plundered by the Indians, should, if the plunder could be found at their towns, have it again, proving it to be his property, and all horses lost on the expedition by unavoidable accident were to be replaced by horses taken in the enemy's country.

The time appointed for the rendezvous, or the general meeting of the volunteers, was fixed to be on the 20th of May, and the place, the old Mingo town, on the west side of the river Ohio, about 40 miles below Fort Pitt, by land; and I think about 75 by water.

Col. Crawford was solicited by the general voice of these western counties and districts to command the expedition. He accordingly set out as volunteer, and came to Fort Pitt, two days before the time appointed for the assembling of the men. As there was no surgeon yet appointed to go with the expedition, colonel Crawford begged the favor of gen. Irvine to permit me to accompany him, (my consent having been previously asked,) to which the general agreed, provided colonel Gibson did not object.

Having obtained permission of the colonel, I left Fort Pitt on Tuesday, May 1st, and the next day about one in the afternoon, arrived at the Mingo bottom. The volunteers had not all crossed the river until Friday morning, the 24th, they then distributed themselves into eighteen companies, choosing their captains by vote. There were chosen also, one colonel commandant, four field and one brigade major. There were four hundred and sixty-five who voted.

We began our march on Saturday, May 25th, making almost a due west course, and on the fourth day reached the old Moravian town, upon the river Muskingum, about 60 miles from the river Ohio. Some of the men having lost their horses on the night preceding, returned home.

Tuesday, the 28th, in the evening, major Brenton and captain Bean went some distance from camp to reconnoitre; having gone about one-quarter of a mile they saw two Indians, upon whom they fired, and then returned to camp. This was the first place in which we were discovered, as we understood afterwards.

On Thursday, the fourth of June, which was the eleventh day of our march, about 1 o'clock we came to the spot where the town of Sandusky formerly stood; the inhabitants had moved 18 miles lower down the creek nearer the lower Sandusky; but as neither our guides or any who were with us had known any thing of their removal, we began to conjecture there were no Indian towns nearer than the lower Sandusky, which was at least forty miles distant.

However, after refreshing our horses we advanced in search of some of their settlements, but had scarcely got the distance of three or four miles from the old town when a number of our men expressed their desire to return, some of them alleging that they had only five days' provision; upon which the field officers and captains, determined in council, to proceed that afternoon, and no longer. Previous to the calling of this council, a small party of light horse had been sent forward to reconnoitre.

I shall here remark, by the way, that there are a great many extensive plains in that country. The woods in general grew very thin, free from brush and underwood; so that light horsemen may advance a considerable distance before an army without being much exposed to the enemy.

Just as the council ended, an express returned from the above mentioned party of light horse with intelligence "that they had been about three miles in front, and had seen a large body of Indians running towards them." In a short time we saw the rest of the light horse, who joined us, and having gone one mile further, met a number of Indians who had partly got possession of a piece of woods before us, whilst we were in the plains; but our men alighting from their horses and rushing into the woods, soon obliged them to abandon that place.

The enemy being by this time reinforced, flanked to the right, and part of them coming in nearer, quickly made the action more serious. The firing continued very warm on both sides from four o'clock until the dusk of the evening, each party maintaining their ground. Next morning, about six o'clock, their guns were discharged, at the distance of two or three hundred yards, which continued till day, doing little or no execution on either side.

The field officers then assembled and agreed, as the enemy were every moment increasing, and we had already a number of wounded, to retreat that night. The whole body was to form into three lines, keeping the wounded in the centre. We had four killed and twenty-three wounded, of the latter, seven very dangerously, on which account as many biers were got ready to carry them; most of the rest were slightly wounded and none so bad but they could ride on horseback. After dark the officers went on the out-posts and brought in all the men as expeditiously as they could. Just as the troops were about to form, several guns were fired by the enemy, upon which some of our men spoke out and said our intention was discovered by the Indians who were firing alarm guns. Upon which some in front hurried off and the rest immediately followed, leaving the seven men that were dangerously wounded, some of whom however got off on horseback, by means of some good friends, who waited for, and assisted them.

We had not got a quarter of a mile from the field of action when I heard col. Crawford calling for his son, John Crawford, his son-in-law, major Harrison, major Rose and William Crawford, his nephews, upon which I came up and told him I believed they were on before us.—He asked is that the doctor?—I told him it was—he then replied they were not in front, and begged of me not to leave him.—I promised him I would not.

We then waited and continued calling for these men till the troops had passed us. The colonel told me his horse had almost given out, that he could not keep up with the troops, and wished some of his best friends to remain with him: he then exclaimed against the militia for riding off in such an irregular manner, and leaving some of the wounded behind, contrary to his orders. Presently there came two men riding after us, one of them an old man, the other a lad, we enquired if they had seen any of the above persons? and they answered they had not.

By this time there was a very hot firing before us, and as we judged, near where our main body must have been. Our course was then nearly southwest, but changing it, we went north about two miles, the two men remaining in company with us. Judging ourselves to be now out of the enemy's lines, we took a due east course, taking care to keep at the distance of fifteen or twenty yards apart, and directing ourselves by the north star.

The old man often lagged behind, and when this was the case, never failed to call for us to halt for him. When we were near the Sandusky Creek he fell one hundred yards behind, and bawled out, as usual, for us to halt. While we were preparing to reprimand him for making a noise, I heard an Indian halloo, as I thought, one hundred and fifty yards from the man, and partly behind him; after this we did not hear the man call again, neither did he ever come up to us any more. It was now past midnight, and about day-break col. Crawford's and the young man's horses gave out, and they left them. We pursued our journey eastward, and about two o'clock fell in with capt. Biggs, who had carried lieut. Ashly from the field of action, who had been dangerously wounded. We then went on about the space of an hour, when a heavy rain coming on, we concluded it was best to encamp, as we were encumbered with the wounded officer. We then barked four or five trees, made an encampment and a fire, and remained there all that night. Next morning we again prosecuted our journey, and having gone about three miles found a deer which had been recently killed. The meat was sliced from the bones and bundled up in the skin, with a tomahawk lying by it. We carried all with us, and in advancing about one mile further, espyed the smoke of a fire. We then gave the wounded officer into the charge of the young man, directing him to stay behind whilst the colonel, the captain and myself walked up as cautiously as we could toward the fire. When we came to it, we concluded, from several circumstances, some of our people had encamped there the preceding night. We then went about roasting the venison, and when just about to march, observed one of our men coming upon our tracks. He seemed at first very shy, but having called to him, he came up and told us he was the person who had killed the deer, but upon hearing us come up, was afraid of Indians, hid in a thicket and made off. Upon this we gave him some bread and roasted venison, proceeded all together on our journey, and about two o'clock came upon the paths by which we had gone out. Capt. Biggs and myself did not think it safe to keep the road, but the colonel said the Indians would not follow the troops farther than the plains, which we were then considerably past. As the wounded officer rode capt. Biggs' horse, I lent the captain mine. The colonel and myself went about one hundred yards in front, the captain and the wounded officer in the centre, and the two young men behind. After we had traveled about one mile and a half, several Indians started up within fifteen or twenty steps of the colonel and me. As we at first discovered only three, I immediately got behind a large black oak, made ready my piece and raised it up to take sight, when the colonel called to me twice not to fire; upon that one of the Indians ran up to the colonel and took him by the hand. The colonel then told me to put down my gun which I did. At that instant one of them came up to me whom I had formerly seen very often, calling me doctor and took me by the hand. They were Delaware Indians of the Wingenim tribe. Captain Biggs fired amongst them but did no execution. They then told us to call these people and make them come there, else they would go and kill them, which the colonel did, but they four got off and escaped for that time. The colonel and I were then taken to the Indian camp, which was about half a mile from the place where we were captivated. On Sunday evening five Delawares who had posted themselves at some distance further on the road brought back to the camp, where we lay, captain Biggs' and lieutenant Ashley's scalps, with an Indian scalp which captain Biggs had taken in the field of action; they also brought in Biggs' horse and mine, they told us the other two got away from them.

Monday morning, the tenth of June, we were paraded to march to Sandusky, about 33 miles distant; they had eleven prisoners of us and four scalps the Indians being seventeen in number.

Colonel Crawford was very desirous to see a certain Simeon Girty, who lived among the Indians, and was on this account permitted to go to town the same night, with two warriors to guard him, having orders at the same time to pass by the place where the colonel had turned out his horse, that they might if possible, find him. The rest of us were taken as far as the old town which was within eight miles of the new.

Tuesday morning, the 11th, colonel Crawford was brought out to us on purpose to be marched in with the other prisoners. I asked the colonel if he had seen Mr. Girty?—He told me he had, and that Girty had promised to do every thing in his power for him, but that the Indians were very much enraged against the prisoners; particularly captain Pipe one of the chiefs; he likewise told me that Girty had informed him that his son-in-law, colonel Harrison, and his nephew William Crawford, were made prisoners by the Shawanese, but had been pardoned. This captain Pipe had come from the towns about an hour before colonel Crawford, and had painted all the prisoners' faces black.

As he was painting me he told me I should go to the Shawanese towns and see my friends. When the colonel arrived he painted him black also, told him he was glad to see him and that he would have him shaved when he came to see his friends at the Wyandot town. When we marched, the colonel and I were kept back between Pipe and Wyngenim, the two Delaware chiefs, the other nine prisoners were sent forward with another party of Indians. As went along we saw four of the prisoners lying by the path tomahawked and scalped, some of them were at the distance of half a mile from each other. When we arrived within half a mile of the place where the colonel was executed, we overtook the five prisoners that remained alive; the Indians had caused them to sit down on the ground, as they did also the colonel and me at some distance from them. I was there given in charge to an Indian fellow to be taken to the Shawanese towns.

In the place where we were now made to sit down there was a number of squaws and boys, who fell on the five prisoners and tomahawked them. There was a certain John M'Kinley amongst the prisoners, formerly an officer in the 13th Virginia regiment, whose head an old squaw cut off, and the Indians kicked it about upon the ground. The young Indian fellows came often where the colonel and I were, and dashed the scalps in our faces. We were then conducted along toward the place where the colonel was afterwards executed; when we came within about half a mile of it, Simeon Girty met us, with several Indians on horseback; he spoke to the colonel, but as I was about one hundred and fifty yards behind could not hear what passed between them.

Almost every Indian we met struck us either with sticks or their fists. Girty waited till I was brought up and asked, was that the doctor?—I told him yes, and went toward him reaching out my hand, but he bid me begone, and called me a damn'd rascal; upon which the fellows who had me in charge pulled me along. Girty rode up after me and told me I was to go to the Shawanese towns.

When we were come to the fire the colonel was stripped naked, ordered to sit down by the fire, and then they beat him with sticks and their fists. Presently after I was treated in the same manner. They then tied a rope to the foot of a post about fifteen feet high, bound the colonel's hands behind his back and fastened the rope to the ligature between his wrists. The rope was long enough either for him to sit down or walk round the post once or twice and return the same way. The colonel then called to Girty and asked if they intended to burn him?—Girty answered, yes. The colonel said he would take it all patiently. Upon this Captain Pipe, a Delaware chief, made a speech to the Indians, viz: about thirty or forty men, sixty or seventy squaws and boys.

When the speech was finished they all yelled a hideous and hearty assent to what had been said. The Indian men then took up their guns and shot powder into the colonel's body, from his feet as far up as his neck. I think not less than seventy loads were discharged upon his naked body. Then they crowded about him, and to the best of my observation, cut off his ears; when the throng had dispersed a little I saw the blood running from both sides of his head in consequence thereof.

The fire was about six or seven yards from the post to which the colonel was tied; it was made of small hickory poles, burnt quite through in the middle, each end of the poles remaining about six feet in length. Three or four Indians by turns would take up, individually, one of these burning pieces of wood and apply it to his naked body, already burned black with powder. These tormentors presented themselves on every side of him, so that whichever way he ran round the post they met him with the burning faggots and poles. Some of the squaws took broad boards, upon which they would carry a quantity of burning coals and hot embers and throw on him, so that in a short time he had nothing but coals of fire and hot ashes to walk upon.

In the midst of these extreme tortures, he called to Simeon Girty and begged of him to shoot him; but Girty making no answer he called to him again. Girty then, by way of derision, told the colonel that he had no gun, at the same time turning about to an Indian who was behind him, laughed heartily, and by all his gestures seemed delighted at the horrid scene.

Girty then came up to me and bade me prepare for death. He said, however, I was not to die at that place, but to be burnt at the Shawanese towns. He swore by G—d I need not expect to escape death, but should suffer it in all its extremities.

He then observed, that some prisoners had given him to understand, that if our people had him they would not hurt him; for his part, he said, he did not believe it, but desired to know my opinion of the matter; but being at that time in great anguish and distress for the torments the colonel was suffering before my eyes, as well as the expectation of undergoing the same fate in two days, I made little or no answer. He expressed a great deal of ill will for colonel Gibson, and said he was one of his greatest enemies, and more to the same purpose, to all which I paid very little attention.

Colonel Crawford at this period of his sufferings, besought the Almighty to have mercy on his soul, spoke very low, and bore his torments with the most manly fortitude. He continued in all the extremities of pain for an hour and three quarters, or two hours longer, as near as I can judge, when at last, being almost exhausted, he lay down on his belly; they then scalped him and repeatedly threw the scalp in my face, telling me "that was my great captain."—An old squaw (whose appearance every way answered the ideas people entertain of the devil) got a board, took a parcel of coals and ashes and laid them on his back and head, after he had been scalped; he then raised himself upon his feet and began to walk round the post; they next put a burning stick to him as usual, but he seemed more insensible of pain than before.

The Indian fellow who had me in charge, now took me away to captain Pipe's house, about three-quarters of a mile from the place of the colonel's execution. I was bound all night, and thus prevented from seeing the last of the horrid spectacle. Next morning, being June 12th, the Indian untied me, painted me black, and we set off for the Shawanese town, which he told me was somewhat less than forty miles from that place. We soon came to the spot where the colonel had been burnt, as it was partly in our way; I saw his bones laying amongst the remains of the fire, almost burnt to ashes; I suppose after he was dead they had laid his body on the fire.

The Indian told me that was my Big Captain, and give the scalp halloo. He was on horseback and drove me before him.

I pretended to this Indian I was ignorant of the death I was to die at the Shawanese town, assumed as cheerful a countenance as possible, and asked him if we were not to live together as brothers in one house, when we should get to town? He seemed well pleased, and said yes. He then asked me if I could make a wigwam?—I told him I could—he then seemed more friendly—we went that day as near as I can judge about 25 miles, the course partly southwest—The Indian told me we should next day come to the town, the sun being in such a direction, pointing nearly south. At night, when we went to rest, I attempted very often to unty myself, but the Indian was extremely vigilant and scarce ever shut his eyes that night. About day break he got up and untied me; he next began to mend up the fire, and as the gnats were troublesome I asked him if I should make a smoke behind him—he said, yes. I then took the end of a dogwood fork which had been burnt down to about 18 inches long; it was the longest stick I could find, yet too small for the purpose I had in view; then I picked up another smaller stick and taking a coal of fire between them went behind him; then turning suddenly about, I struck him on the head with all the force I was master of; which so stunned him that he fell forward with both his hands into the fire, but seeing him recover and get up, I seized his gun while he ran off howling in a most fearful manner.—I followed him with a determination to shoot him down, but pulling back the cock of the gun with too great violence, I believe I broke the main spring. I pursued him, however, about thirty yards, still endeavouring to fire the gun, but could not; then going back to the fire I took his blanket, a pair of new mokkisons, his hoppes, powder horn, bullet bag, (together with the gun) and marched off, directing my course toward the five o'clock mark: about half an hour before sunset I came to the plains which I think are about sixteen miles wide. I laid me down in a thicket till dark, and then by the assistance of the north star made my way through them and got into the woods before morning. I proceeded on the next day, and about noon crossed the paths by which our troops had gone out; these paths are nearly east and west, but I went due north all that afternoon with a view to avoid the enemy.

In the evening I began to be very faint, and no wonder; I had been six days prisoner; the last two days of which I had eat nothing, and but very little the first three or four; there were wild gooseberries in abundance in the woods, but being unripe, required mastication, which at that time I was not able to perform on account of a blow received from an Indian on the jaw with the back of a tomahawk. There was a weed that grew plentifully in that place, the juice of which I knew to be grateful and nourishing; I gathered a bundle of the same, took up my lodging under a large spreading beach tree and having sucked plentifully of the juice, went to sleep. Next day, I made a due east course which I generally kept the rest of my journey. I often imagined my gun was only wood bound, and tried every method I could devise to unscrew the lock but never could effect it, having no knife nor anything fitting for the purpose; I had now the satisfaction to find my jaw began to mend, and in four or five days could chew any vegetable proper for nourishment, but finding my gun only a useless burden, left her in the wilderness. I had no apparatus for making fire to sleep by, so that I could get but little rest for the gnats and musketoes; there are likewise a great many swamps in the beach ridge, which occasioned me very often to lie wet; this ridge, through which I traveled, is about twenty miles broad, the ground in general very level and rich, free from shrubs and brush; there are, however, very few springs, yet wells might easily be dug in all parts of the ridge; the timber on it is very lofty, but it is no easy matter to make a straight course through the same, the moss growing as high upon the South side of the trees as on the North. There are a great many white oaks, ash and hickory trees that grow among the beach timber; there are likewise some places on the ridge, perhaps for three or four continued miles where there is little or no beach, and in such spots, black, white oak, ash, and hickory abound. Sugar trees grow there also to a very great bulk—the soil is remarkably good, the ground a little ascending and descending with some small rivulets and a few springs. When I got out of the beach ridge and nearer the river Muskingum, the lands were more broken but equally rich with those before mentioned, and abounding with brooks and springs of water; there are also several small creeks that empty into that river, the bed of which is more than a mile wide in many places; the woods consist of white and black oak, walnut, hickory and sugar trees in the greatest abundance. In all parts of the country through which I came the game was very plenty, that is to say, deer, turkies and pheasants; I likewise saw a great many vestiges of bears and some elks.

I crossed the river Muskingum about three or four miles below Fort Laurence, and crossing all paths aimed for the Ohio river. All this time my food was gooseberries, young nettles, the juice of herbs, a few service berries, and some May apples, likewise two young blackbirds and a turripine, which I devoured raw. When my food sat heavy on my stomach, I used to eat a little wild ginger which put all to rights.

I came upon Ohio river about five miles below fort M'Intosh, in the evening of the 21st day after I had made my escape, and on the 22d about seven o'clock in the morning, being the 4th day of July, arrived safe, though very much fatigued, at the fort.

THE NORTHWEST ORDINANCE

(1787)

No document represents the east's imaginative construction of the west more than the Northwest Ordinance. Embedded in it are the paradoxes and contradictions that would at once vitalize and impede the settlement, development, and character of the northern section of the west in the decades before the Civil War. Salmon P. Chase, prominent Cincinnati abolitionist, historian, and politician of the antebellum era, referred to it as "a pillar of cloud by day, and of fire by night," reflecting the document's ambivalent reception in the west.

On the one hand, the Ordinance sets up a coherent plan for harnessing and organizing the chaos of speculating, squatting, and boundary-drawing that was going on regardless of federal regulation. The Ordinance's plan for carving states out of the territory, for banning primogeniture, for supporting public schools, for extending constitutional rights, and for banning slavery north of the Ohio all reflect a republican ideology that means to preserve and create freedom in the west. As such, as many historians have noted, it sets the groundwork for an "empire of liberty." At the same time, it sets the stage for the removal of Native Americans, installs a class hierarchy whose elite are indebted to the east, limits the number of states that might be created, and makes local self-determination difficult. That is, the terms of the colonization of the northwest are set by the east in such a way that the west might never challenge the east for a place at the center of the nation's identity.

While the Ordinance makes white male settlers Americans, the terms for their entry into the national community are based on their ability to satisfy eastern definitions of legitimacy. In brief, the ordinance reflects the east's awareness that its own colony might do what it had done—gain independence from a distant colonial metropolis—and takes steps to forestall the possibility. As a result of the Ordinance, the contemporary region defined by the Ordinance has the dual legacies of both strong public schools and a feeling of needing to look east for the meaningful signs of acceptance and legitimacy.

Text: The Northwest Ordinance, 1787, reprinted in *The Northwest Ordinance: Essays on its Formulation, Provisions, and Legacy* (East Lansing, 1988, ed. Frederick D. Williams): 119–127.

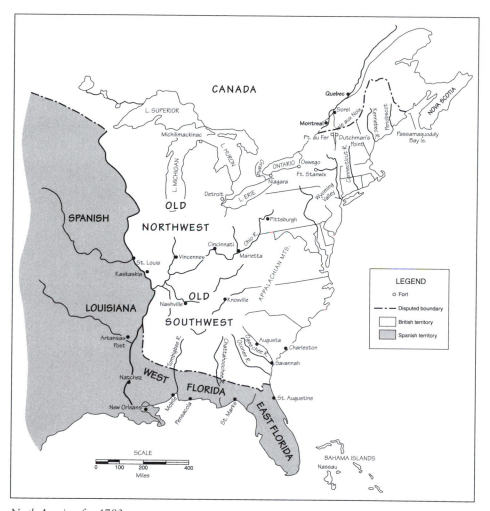

North America after 1783.

THE NORTHWEST ORDINANCE (1787)

An Ordinance for the government of the territory of the United States North West of the river Ohio

⟨ornament⟩

Be it ordained by the United States in congress Assembled that the said territory for the purposes of temporary government be one district, subject however to be divided into two districts as future circumstances may in the Opinion of Congress make it expedient.

Be it ordained by the authority aforesaid, that the estates both of resident and non resident proprietors in the said territory dying intestate shall descend to and be distributed among their children and the descendants of a deceased child in equal parts; the descendants of a deceased child or grandchild to take the share of their deceased parent in equal parts among them; and where there shall be no children or descendants then in equal parts to the next *of* kin in equal degree and among collaterals the children of a deceased brother or sister of the intestate shall have in equal parts among them their deceased parent's share *and there shall in no case be a distinction between kindred of the whole and half blood;* saving in all cases to the widow of the intestate her third part of the real estate for life, and one third part of the personal estate; and this law relative to descents and dower shall remain in full force until altered by the legislature of the district. And until the governor and judges shall adopt laws as hereinafter mentioned estates in the said territory may be devised or bequeathed by wills in writing signed and sealed by him or her in whom the estate may be, being of full age, and attested by three witnesses, and real estates may be conveyed by lease and release or bargain and sale signed, sealed and delivered by the person being of full age in whom the estate may be and attested by two witnesses provided such wills be duly proved and such conveyances be acknowledged or the execution thereof duly proved and be recorded within one year after proper magistrates, courts and registers shall be appointed for that purpose and personal property may be transferred by delivery saving however *to the french and canadian inhabitants and other settlers of the Kaskaskies, Saint Vincents and the neighbouring villages who have heretofore professed themselves citizens of Virginia, their* laws and customs now in force among them relative to the descent and conveyance of property.

Be it ordained by the authority aforesaid that there shall be appointed from time to time by Congress a governor, whose commission shall continue in force for the term of three years, unless sooner revoked by Congress; he shall reside in the district and have a freehold estate therein, in one thousand acres of land while in the exercise of his office. There shall be appointed from time to time by Congress a secretary, whose commission shall continue in force for four years, unless sooner revoked; he shall reside in the district and have a freehold estate therein in five hundred acres of land while in the exercise of his office; It shall be his duty to keep and preserve the acts and laws passed by the legislature and the public records of the district and the proceedings of the governor in his executive department and transmit authentic copies of such acts and proceedings every six months to the Secretary of Congress. There shall also be appointed a court to consist of three judges any two of whom to form a court, who shall have a common law jurisdiction and reside in the district and have each therein a freehold estate in five hundred acres of land while in the exercise of their offices, and their commissions shall continue in force during good behaviour.

The governor, and judges or a majority of them shall adopt and publish in the district such laws of the original states criminal and civil as may be necessary and best suited to the circumstances of the district and report them to Congress from time to time, which laws shall be in force in the district until the organization of the general assembly therein, unless disapproved of by Congress; but afterwards the legislature shall have authority to alter them as they shall think fit.

The governor for the time being shall be Commander in chief of the militia, appoint and commission all officers in the same below the rank of general Officers; All *general* Officers shall be appointed and commissioned by Congress.

Previous to the Organization of the general Assembly the governor shall appoint such magistrates and other civil officers in each county or township, as he shall find necessary for the preservation of the peace and good order in the same. After the general Assembly shall be organized, the powers and duties of magistrates and other civil officers shall be regulated and defined by the said Assembly; but all magistrates and other civil officers, not herein otherwise directed shall during the continuance of this temporary government be appointed by the governor.

For the prevention of crimes and injuries the laws to be adopted or made shall have force in all parts of the district and for the execution of process criminal and civil, the governor shall make proper divisions thereof, and he shall proceed from time to time as circumstances may require to lay out the parts of the district in which the indian titles shall have been extinguished into counties and townships subject however to such alterations as may thereafter be made by the legislature.

So soon as there shall be five thousand free male inhabitants of full age in the district upon giving proof thereof to the governor, they shall receive authority with time and place to elect representatives from their counties or townships to represent them in the general assembly, provided that for every five hundred free male inhabitants there shall be one representative and so on progressively with the number of free male inhabitants shall the right of representation encrease until the number of representatives shall amount to twenty five after which the number and proportion of representatives shall be regulated by the legislature; provided that no person be eligible or qualified to act as a representative unless he shall have been a citizen of one of the United States three years and be a resident in the district or unless he shall have resided in the district three years and in either case shall likewise hold in his own right in fee simple two hundred acres of land within the same; provided also that a freehold in fifty acres of land in the district having been a citizen of one of the states and being resident in the district; or the like freehold and two years residence in the district shall be necessary to qualify a man as an elector of a representative.

The representatives thus elected shall serve for the term of two years and in case of the death of a representative or removal from office, the governor shall issue a writ to the county or township for which he was a member, to elect another in his stead to serve for the residue of the term.

The general assembly or legislature shall consist of the governor, legislative council and a house of representatives. The legislative council shall consist of five members to continue in Office five years unless sooner removed by Congress any three of whom to be a quorum and the members of the council shall be nominated and appointed in the following manner, to wit; As soon as representatives shall be elected, the governor shall appoint a time and place for them to meet together, and when met they shall nominate ten persons residents in the district and each possessed of a free-hold in five hundred acres of Land and return their names to Congress; five of whom Congress shall appoint and commission to serve as aforesaid; and whenever a vacancy shall happen in the council by death or removal from office, the house of representatives shall nominate two persons qualified as aforesaid, for each vacancy, and return their names to Congress, one of whom Congress shall appoint and commission for the residue of the term, and every five years, four months at least before the expiration of the time of service of the Members of Council, the said house shall nominate ten persons qualified as aforesaid, and return their names to Congress, five of whom Congress shall appoint and commission to serve as Members of the council five years, unless sooner removed. And the Governor, legislative council, and house of representatives, shall have authority to make laws in all cases for the good government of the district, not repugnant to the principles and Articles in this Ordinance established and declared. And all bills having passed by a majority in the house, and by a majority in the council, shall be referred to the Governor for his assent; but no bill or legislative Act whatever, shall be of any force without his assent. The Governor shall have power to convene, prorogue and dissolve the General Assembly, when in his opinion it shall be expedient.

The Governor, Judges, legislative Council, Secretary, and such other Officers as Congress shall appoint in the district shall take an Oath or Affirmation of fidelity, and of Office, the Governor before the president of Congress, and all other Officers before the Governor. As soon as a legislature shall be formed in the district, the Council and house assembled in one room, shall have authority by joint ballot to elect a Delegate to Congress, who shall have a seat in Congress, with a right of debating, but not of voting, during this temporary Government.

And for extending the fundamental principles of civil and religious liberty, which form the basis whereon these republics, their laws and constitutions are erected; to fix and establish those principles as the basis of all laws, constitutions and governments, which forever hereafter shall be formed in the said territory; to provide also for the establishment of States and permanent government therein, and for their admission to a share in the federal Councils on an equal footing with the original States, at as early periods as may be consistent with the general interest,

It is hereby Ordained and declared by the authority aforesaid, That the following Articles shall be considered as Articles of compact between the Original States and the people and States in the said territory, and forever remain unalterable, unless by common consent, to *wit,*

Article the First. No person demeaning himself in a peaceable and orderly manner shall ever be molested on account of his mode of worship or religious sentiments in the said territory.

Article the Second. The Inhabitants of the said territory shall always be entitled to the benefits of the writ of habeas corpus, and of the trial by Jury; of a proportionate representation of the people in the legislature, and of judicial proceedings according to the course of the common law; all persons shall be bailable unless for capital offences, where the proof shall be evident, or the presumption great; all fines shall be moderate, and no cruel or unusual punishments shall be inflicted; no man shall be deprived of his liberty or property but by the judgment of his peers, or the law of the land; and should the public exigencies make it necessary for the common preservation to take any persons property, or to demand his particular services, full compensation shall be made for the same; and in the just preservation of rights and property it is understood and declared; that no law ought ever to be made, or have force in the said territory, that shall in any manner whatever interfere with, or affect private contracts or engagements, bona fide and without fraud previously formed.

Article the Third. Religion, Morality *and knowledge being necessary to good government and the happiness of mankind,* Schools and the means of education shall forever be encouraged. The utmost good faith shall always be observed toward the Indians, their lands and property shall never be taken from them without their consent; and in their property, rights and liberty, they never shall be invaded or disturbed, unless in just and lawful wars authorised by Congress; but laws founded in justice and humanity shall from time to time be made, for preventing wrongs being done to them, and for preserving peace and friendship with them.

Article the Fourth. The said territory, and the States which may be formed therein shall forever remain a part of this Confederacy of the United States of America, subject to the Articles of Confederation, and to such alterations therein as shall be constitutionally made; and to all the Acts and Ordinances of the United States in Congress Assembled, conformable thereto. The Inhabitants and Settlers in the said territory, shall be subject to pay a part of the federal debts contracted or to be contracted, and a proportional part of the expences of Government, to be apportioned on them by Congress, according to the same common rule and measure by which apportionments thereof shall be made on the other States; and the taxes for paying their proportion, shall be laid and levied by the authority and direction of the legislatures of the district or districts or new States, as in the original States, within the time agreed upon by the United States in Congress Assembled. The Legislatures of those districts, or new States, shall never interfere with the primary disposal of the Soil by the United States in Congress Assembled, nor with any regulations Congress may find necessary for securing the title in such soil to the bona fide purchasers. No tax shall be imposed on lands the property of the United States; and in no case shall non resident proprietors be taxed higher than residents. The navigable Waters leading into the Mississippi and St. Lawrence, and the carrying places between the same shall be common highways, and forever free, as well to the Inhabitants of the said territory, as to the Citizens of the United States, and those of any other States that may be admitted into the Confederacy, without any tax, impost or duty therefor.

Article the Fifth. There shall be formed in the said territory, not less than three nor more than five States, and the boundaries of the States, as soon as Virginia shall alter her act of cession and *consent to* the same, shall become fixed and established as follows, to wit: The Western State in *the* said territory, shall be bounded by the Mississippi, the Ohio and Wabash rivers; a direct line drawn from the Wabash and post Vincents due North to the territorial line between the United States and Canada, and by *the* said territorial line to the lake of the Woods and Mississippi. The middle State shall be bounded by the said direct line, the Wabash from post Vincents to the Ohio; by the Ohio, by direct line drawn due North from the mouth of the great Miami to *the* said territorial line, and by *the* said territorial line. The eastern State shall be bounded by the last mentioned direct line, the Ohio, Pennsylvania, and the said territorial line; provided however, and it is further understood and declared, that the boundaries of these three States, shall be subject so far to be altered, that if Congress shall hereafter find it expedient, they shall have authority to form one or two States in that part of the said territory which lies north of an east and west line drawn through the southerly bend or extreme of lake Michigan; and whenever any of the said States shall have sixty thousand free Inhabitants therein, such State shall be admitted by its Delegates into the Congress of the United States, on an equal footing with the original States, in all respects whatever; and shall be at liberty to form a permanent constitution and State government, provided the constitution and government so to be formed, shall be republican, and in conformity to the principles contained in these Articles; and so far as it can be consistent with the general interest of the Confederacy, such admission shall be allowed at an earlier period, and when there may be a less number of free Inhabitants in the State than sixty thousand.

Article the Sixth. There shall be neither Slavery nor involuntary Servitude in the said territory otherwise than in the punishment of crimes, whereof the party shall have been duly convicted; provided always that any person escaping into the same, from whom labor or service is lawfully claimed in any one of the original States, such fugitive may be lawfully reclaimed and conveyed to the person claiming his or her labor or service as aforesaid.

Be it Ordained by the Authority aforesaid, that the Resolutions of the 23^{d} of April 1784 *relative to the subject of this ordinance* be, and the same are hereby repealed and declared null and void.

10

GILBERT IMLAY

(1754?–1828?)

In 1792 and 1793, Gilbert Imlay published two books in London. The first, *A Topographical Description of the Western Territory of North America,* was a largely plagiarized collection of information regarding the Ohio valley and its prospects for settlement. It is thought that, like Manasseh Cutler, John Filson, and others, he was writing advertisements for land in which he had speculated. His novel, *The Emigrants,* likewise appeared under dubious conditions; it was thought that his lover, Mary Wollstonecraft, had written a good deal of it. Only recently has authorship been reattributed to Imlay, although the long sections advocating reform in British and American divorce laws certainly reflect her interest.

The exoneration of Imlay's authorship, however, does little to resurrect his character. W. H. Verhoeven calls Imlay "a man of many trades and talents, few of which were within the confines of what is conventionally regarded as legally and morally acceptable behavior." After the Revolution, in which his self-styled "captaincy" was based, he moved to Kentucky. By 1786, a variety of debts and other legal stresses forced him to leave the United States for Europe. Establishing himself in post revoutionary Paris, he moved in elite circles with Wollstonecraft, William Godwin, Thomas Paine, and others. The Enlightenment ideals to which he was exposed there he applied to the Ohio valley in each of his books. In *The Emigrants* in particular, we can see how literature could be used as a component in the same strategies of appropriation and reconconstruction with which Europe and the east were monopolizing the terms of the west's representation.

The Emigrants is an epistolary novel and, like most within that genre, deploys a romantic plot as a way of commenting on a variety of social issues. Set in the 1780s, the story's romantic leads are Caroline, an emigrant from London, and Captain Arl—ton, a dashing veteran of the American Revolution. Arl—ton intends to construct a new settlement, independent of the United States, on the southern banks of the Ohio river in what would become Kentucky. The new settlement, named Bellefont, was to be built on a perfect square of 256 square miles, dispersed among a like number of former officers who would constitute the colony's governing elite. Along the way, of course, plot entanglements ensue, including romantic tensions and Caroline's captivity among and rescue from Native Americans by the captain.

In the novel, a number of issues regarding the west can be perceived, all of which construct it as an extension of European civilization rather than as a unique or divergent community. From land distribution, class hierarchy, erasure of the natives, and even the thought policing of making established religion unacceptable in Bellefont, we see how Enlightenment thinking regarded the west as a glorious opportunity to reinvent European history upon more orderly and logical lines. Of the three sections here, the first is Caroline's view west from Pittsburgh; the second, Caroline and Arl—ton's adventure with the natives along the Illinois River; and the third, Arl—ton's plan for Bellefont. Although Imlay imagined that this community must be distinct from the United States, his gaze is quite similar to that of other eastern thinkers about the west, especially Thomas Jefferson, Manasseh Cutler, and James Fenimore Cooper.

Text: *The Emigrants* (New York, 1998, ed. W. M. Verhoeven and Amanda Gilroy; rpt. of 1793 edition): 50–56, 195–205, 230–236.

FROM *THE EMIGRANTS*

LETTER XIV

Miss Caroline to Mrs. F———

Pittsburg, Oct.

MY DEAR SISTER,

As George sets out this evening for Philadelphia, I embrace with the greatest pleasure the opportunity of complying with my promise.

Every season has its charms, and every pleasure its alloy; but I shall ever feel the sensations of sorrow when I look toward the east, particularly as it will always afford me the image of my kind Eliza, in a distant prospective; and while my heart eagerly pants after the substance, I shall be tantalized with the shadow.

O cruel fate! how hard is the situation of poor Caroline?—Every day brings fresh proofs to her that the loss of her Eliza is irreparable.

There is something in the decrees of heaven which forbids us to examine too nicely into the object of Providence; but how can I forbear complaining, when I seem to stand insulated and deserted, at a time I want most the advice and support of my once kind protectress?

O Eliza! how shall I tell you?—my innocent heart diffuses the crimson over my face at the very thought—There was something too interesting, at the first sight of Capt. Arl———ton, for me, not to feel the most lively emotions;—but the time and place of his overtaking me, and his manner of assisting our helpless family, so conspired to make impressions upon my fond foolish heart, that it has ever since caused me considerable uneasiness; but what I have most cause to lament is of a very recent date.

Walking has hitherto formed my principal amusement, and as I had been taking a view of some of the picturesque scenes of this romantic country, accompanied by a female companion, Capt. Arl————ton and his friend, on our return I was alarmed at the sight of three of the natives, which quite overcame me; and when I recovered I found myself in the arms of Capt. Arl————ton, and frightened as I was, I could discover all the signs of solicitude and anxiety, so strongly pourtrayed in his countenance, that it was impossible for me to mistake the emotions of his heart.—His full eyes seemed to have caught the flame of sympathy, and emitted such a radiance of expression and tenderness, that I am afraid my feelings, which were in unison with nature, and ever true to the dictates of gratitude, which I felt anew for his attempt to preserve me against the fury of the sanguinary Indians, betrayed the situation of my heart; for he scarcely allowing me time to recover, he declared in the most ardent manner the existence of his passion.

Heavens! how was my soul agitated between hope and fear? but fortunately our company coming up before I had time to have spoken, which would have been impossible, my embarrassment in a degree subsided: and in that situation I returned home, and have ever since, more from anxiety than from any harm I experienced from my fright, been obliged to keep my room. He has been several times to enquire after my health, and has sent his servant much oftener.—He came this morning and insisted upon seeing me, and told Mary that it was unkind to deny him that satisfaction, after the intimacy which had for some time subsisted between him and our family; particularly since he had been my fellow traveller.—But recollecting himself he begged pardon if there was an impropriety in the request, and said he presumed I was not confined to my bed; and as Mary formally assured him that provided I was better in the evening he should be permitted to see me; I am afraid, it gave him offence. For she says he departed with signs of displeasure.

Mary is at a loss to know what to make of such rudeness, for such she terms it, and you know, my dear Eliza, that there is so little affinity of disposition between us, that it is impossible for me to communicate to her the real cause of his importunities. However, you know that she possesses all that kind of penetration which is necessary to develope such mysteries—I both fear and wish for the *rencontre* this evening, but as Mary will be sure to be *present* I hope to be collected.

I find, as usual, I have wandered from the subject I intended to have began; but I know you will forgive the egotism after so ingenuous a confession; but not to have made it to you, my Eliza, would have been criminal.—Would to God it could have been oral! and when I again clasped you to my tender heart, you would be sensible how much I love you—but avaunt, treason!—I will not doubt your confidence in that; but let me pray that you will continue to love your Caroline as usual.

Now for Pittsburg and its inhabitants.—How shall I talk of things which are inanimate or indifferent?—But I will rouse my senses from their torpor, for every thing here is interesting, and many of the citizens are amiable, and possess the most exalted virtues.

Pittsburg stands in the fork of the Allegany and Monongahala rivers, which intermingle their waters, and form the Ohio—Ohio, in the Indian language signifies fair, and perhaps nothing can be more applicable than the name of this beautiful river.

The Monongahala is about the breadth of the Thames at London,—its current gentle,—its waters limpid,—and its banks on the opposite shore are high and steep, which are said to be a body of coal, and for many years were on fire, which exhibited the image of a Volcano.

The Allegany is not so broad as the Monogahala, but its current is much more impetuous, and from the fierceness of its aspect, and the wildness which lowers over its banks, it appears to be what it really is, the line between civilization and barbarism. So that you see, my dear Sister, I have passed from the most populous city in the world—a city embellished with all the beauty that art and ingenuity can furnish, and which the accumulated industry of ages have produced, to the remote corner of the empire of reason and science.

But here are charms as well as at masquerades, operas, or the dusty rides in Hyde Park.—Here is a continual feast for the imagination—here every thing is new, and when you contemplate a frowning wilderness, and view the shades or gradations of the polish of manners, which the blandishments of science has produced, and then compare this scene with what must have been the state of Great Britain, and the manners of the Aborigines of that island, when it was first invaded by the more polished Romans, what a comprehensive and sublime subject is it for the human mind? How familiar does it make you with the appearance of things at an event so remote, and to form an adequate idea of which, requires a scene like this? and in what an estimable point of view does it place those geniuses, who by their labour and talents have produced the astonishing contrast?—I must pause for a moment at the stupendous thought.

On one side of us lie the wild regions of the Indian country; on the other our prospect is obstructed by the high banks of the Monongahala, beyond which lies a beautiful country that is well peopled and cultivated—behind us a considerable plain that is laid out in orchards and gardens, and which yields a profusion of delicious fruits,—and in our front the Ohio displays the most captivating beauty, and after shooting forward for about a mile it abruptly turns round a high and projecting point, as if conscious of its charms, and as if done with an intent to elude the enraptured sight.

From the various picturesque scenes with which this country abounds, I have derived the most lively amusements; and perhaps they have been made more agreeable from my having been continually attended by Capt. Arl————ton, which gave a zest to them, without my being sensible of the cause.

I will not fatigue your attention by repeating the whole history of this place; but you may recollect it was a fort erected previous to the last war by the French called fort Du Quesne, and was taken by the British forces in the course of that war—since which period it has been a garrisoned town by the name of Fort Pitt, or Pittsburg, in honour of the splendid virtues and talents of that great man, during whose administration it was taken.

The Americans keep a considerable force at this place, and as it is the rendezvous for a great number of emigrants, who are continually passing down the Ohio, it affords a great variety in our society.

But I must tell you of two accomplished and amiable beings, whose virtues and goodness would serve as a patron for half the world. General W———— had felt a juvenile tenderness for his lady, and had given every proof of it during his services in the army, and after having acquired much honour at Saratoga in actions fought against our brave and unfortunate forces, he returned with his brows incircled with laurels, to repose in the bosom of love, after the fatigues and perils of three campaigns.

During his first overtures which were made upon the eve of that ill-fated war, she wrote a sonnet, in which she chided him in so delicate a manner, yet so pathetically, that I will transcribe a part of it, as it will afford you an opportunity of estimating the qualities of this charming woman.

"Full well dear youth,
I know thy truth,
And all thy arts to please;—
But ah! is this
A time for bliss,
Or things so soft as these.—
Whilst all around
We hear no sound
But war's terrific strain,
Our martial bands,
The drum commands,
And chides each tardy swain?"

They continued for some time after their marriage to be the admiration of the gay circles of Philadelphia; but, finding that the dissipation which the English and French manners had introduced during the late war, and knowing that their fortune was not equal to a continuation of that extravagance, which the times and their rank in society had made unavoidable, they came to a resolution of retiring to this country, which seems to be the asylum of all unfortunate people; but at the same time it has a large proportion of rational characters among them; which to be sure, is not often the case with such persons as have been the cause of their own troubles. But in the case of the disappointed persons who find their way here, the most of them are men of high spirit, who have consumed their estates in the service of their country.

The General has in addition to the graces of person, those of the mind—he is an accomplished gentleman, an affectionate husband, a fond father, a cheerful and pleasant companion; but above all he is a good and useful citizen.

Mrs. W——— appears to be about five and twenty, which may be two or three years younger than the General; and is one of those happy women whom we seldom meet in England, i.e. to derive her greatest pleasure from the General's attention, the care of her children, the free intercourse of her friends, and from sharing her hospitable board with strangers.

As to her character as a mere woman, I cannot give you a better idea of it, than adopting that, which Cardinal De Retz has given Madam De Longueville; who he said, "had a great store of natural wit, and which was more, took great pains to refine and give it a pleasing turn.

"Her capacity which was not helped by her laziness, could never reach so far as state affairs. She had a languishing air that touched the heart more than the vivacity even of a more beautiful woman—she had even a certain indolence of mind which had its charms; because she was now and then awaked out of it by starts of fancy surprizingly fine."

George is hurrying me to finish my letter.—O my dear Eliza! how does my poor heart beat? How powerfully do the ties of nature call upon me to tell you how sincerely I love you? and at the very moment when I expect—O my kind sister, George must write you from Philadelphia respecting the family. I can only say that we are all well. Adieu! I was very near omitting to mention, that Capt. Arl———ton and myself had a curious adventure with an old gentleman as we were crossing the mountain; for such he proved himself by his manners and conversation, though his garb and employment was that of a yeoman. He promised to call upon me when he should return, and I assure you, such are my expectations of the pleasure I shall derive from this curious character, that I am quite impatient to see him.

GOD BLESS YOU.

CAROLINE

LETTER LIX

Capt. Arl———ton, to Mr. Il———ray

Kaskaskia, Sept.

MY DEAR FRIEND,

From St. Vincent's we crossed the immense Buffalo plains, and then making our course north-westerly, towards the head waters of the Illinois river, we fell in upon it about one hundred and fifty miles above its mouth, according to the computation of my guide, where we encamped in order to prepare rafts to transport our baggage across the river; and during which time, the hunters would have an opportunity to secure provisions for the party until we should arrive at St. Anthony's falls: As we were falling more into the track of the Indians, I thought it prudent that we should move as compact as possible; and that could not be done in case the hunters should be frequently in pursuit of game: Besides, firing would have been a signal for the savages to discover us; a consideration sufficient to induce me to lay in a plentiful stock before I left the buffalo country, to supply us to the limits of our journey, and, it was my intention after crossing the Illinois, not to suffer a gun to be fired.

It was early in the morning of the 30th ult., that one of my hunters, who had been absent the whole of the preceding day, returned to camp in great haste, and informed me, that morning, immediately after the break of day, as he was watching for Buffalos, at a crossing about ten miles above where we lay, he saw a party of Indians put off from the shore, upon a raft, who appeared to have charge of prisoners; and the moment that he had seen them land upon the opposite bank, he had posted back to the party.

I instantly ordered the baggage to be packed up, when I crossed to the other side of the river, where it was deposited with the provisions we had secured, and then forcing a march to the place where the hunter had seen the Indians land, we took their track, which we followed with all possible celerity; and I think it was about two in the afternoon, when my advanced man returned to inform me, they were then ascending a hill, not distant half a mile.

I halted my party for a moment to instruct them how to act, and desired them to follow about three hundred yards in my rear, and taking with me two men, I went rapidly forward until I obtained sight of them; when I saw their number was double ours, and, that they had only one female prisoner.—

How to rescue the prisoner, without endangering her life, was a difficulty I could not contrive to surmount—at length, I thought the only chance would be to wait until night, and in case they kept no guard, for they were now far removed from an enemy's country, and when they should be sleeping we might retake her, before they would have time to hear, or perceive us.—However that scheme was frustrated by their vigilance; when I devised the following stratagem:—

At the dawn of day I dispatched four of my men, keeping only the mountaineer with me, with orders to advance about one quarter of a mile in front of the Indians, there to discharge their pieces irregularly twice, as quick as possible, and then to make a small circuit, and return with the greatest expedition. The plan succeeded—The Indians were in an instant up, and hastened towards the place where the firing appeared, leaving only two men to guard their prisoner. This was the moment for action—I rushed forward followed by my mountaineer, who had orders to carry off the prisoner in his arms, while I encountered the men, as I expected every instant my people would return to my assistance.

They came—but not until I had knocked one down, and was engaged with the other, who I had aimed a blow at, but my feet slipping, I missed him, when he levelled his piece at me, but it having flashed in the pan, I had recovered myself, and was aiming a second blow when my four men returned and made the two Indians prisoners.

It was my intention not to fire, as had the Indians heard a firing in their rear, they would doubtless have been back upon us, before we could effect our escape with the prisoners.

Fortunately my blows did not prove mortal, or in the least dangerous, and as my men instantly bound the prisoners, we retreated to join my mountaineer, who had fallen back with the rescued captive to the place appointed for our *rendezvous.*

Our peril was not yet over, for the number of Indians being still so much superior to us, it was not only necessary to make a precipitate retreat; but it was an object of the greatest moment to baffle their vigilance in the pursuit, which there was no doubt they would make.

Accordingly I dispatched my guide, with orders to conduct the mountaineer with his captive, by the shortest route, to the place where we had deposited our baggage; who were to prepare the rafts, and put on board the baggage against our arrival, without any regard to any more of the provisions, than would be necessary to last us for a day or two; and then mounted the prisoners behind the two hunters, who had orders to follow the track of the guide, while my brave servant and friend Andrew, who had led the party in the execution of the stratagem, and myself, brought up the rear.

We had travelled in the course of the preceding day upwards of forty miles beyond the Illinois, so that it was nearly 3 P.M. before we regained the bank of the river.

My active guide and mountaineer had embarked the baggage the moment of our arrival, when I first had an opportunity of recognizing our captive.

Ah! Il————ray how did my swelling heart beat with joy, which was instantly succeeded by sorrow, when I first caught a glance from the brilliant eyes of the most divine woman upon earth, torn into shatters by the bushes and briars, with scarcely covering left to hide the transcendency of her beauty, which to be seen by common eyes is a profanation, and it was only by the effulgence of her æthereal looks, that I could have known her?

Caroline has fallen into my hands!—she is at this moment decorating the gardens of this place while I am writing to you, and seems to give enchantment to the whispering breezes that are wafted to my window, and which in their direction as they pass her, collect from her sweets the fragrance of ambrosia, and the exhilirating charms of love itself.

She was sitting upon the bank of the river half harrassed to death when I arrived, which from the horrors of a wilderness was converted into elysium; when I, regardless of every appearance, fell at her feet, and then embracing her, I felt all the transports that the circumstances of our meeting and the divinity of feminine charms can inspire.

I was for a minute regardless of the danger we were still in, when my faithful Andrew came with a *surtoute,* covered Caroline, and then carried and placed her upon a seat which he had prepared upon the raft.

We instantly put off from the shore, when this honest fellow brought us some refreshment, and a bottle of Italian cordial which he carried with him as a *bon bouche.* Neither of us could taste of them, though we had not eat or drank any one thing during the day.

I now believed that we were safe, without ever thinking;—but I was soon roused by the appearance of the Indians, who were arrived upon the shore we had left, before we had fallen a league down the river.

The weather was very fine, and as my rafts were well constructed, I ordered them to be brought along side of each other, and lashed together; in order to render us more compact in case we should be followed: which was not very likely, as it would take them too long to prepare a raft, and it was impossible for them to procure a canoe—but it was not unlikely they would cross and follow down upon the opposite shore, under an idea that we might encamp at night, which would give them an opportunity of coming up with us; for that reason I determined to float the whole night, as it would give us such an advantage, that we should by the morning be out of all danger: accordingly I had a canopy stretched in such a manner as to secure Caroline a place to sleep, who I knew must be much fatigued from our rapid movements, independent of the perils and hardships she must have undergone during her captivity.

Indeed I wondered that she was alive—but she was not only alive, my friend! but she looked more lovely than ever—the lustre of her eyes was like the torch of love— her smiles like the genial hours of May when nature blooms in all its eradiated charms; and though her beauteous face had been lacerated with brambles, still the little loves seemed to vie with each other, as if to prove, which of her features were the most fascinating.

The sun had declined below the horizon, and the bird of Minerva had resumed its nightly vigils, when Andrew told Caroline, that a pallet was prepared for her under the canopy, and that she must retire to rest; for said he, my good mistress, master would keep you up half the night, and I am sure you cannot have spirits or strength to support such fatigue. Andrew was in the right.

When Venus lies sleeping on the couch of night, and one half of the world is cheered by the brilliancy of her charms, so looked my Caroline when Somnus had sealed up her eye-lids; and while Morpheus, his minister of dreams, was agitating her tender heart, her bosom disclosed the temple of bliss, while her lips distilled nectareous sweets.

I was already distracted with the potency of the bewitching joys which I had snatched in my embrace upon the river bank; and while I was constrained to watch as she slept, it was impossible for me to withstand the reflection of the taper, that Andrew had lighted, and which cast its rays upon a bosom more transparent than the effulgence of Aurora, when robed in all her charms, and more lovely than a poetical imagination can paint, when influenced by all its enthusiasm;—and which was now half naked. I was obliged to extinguish the light, to preserve my reason.

> Oh! how I could for ever her adore,
> By tasting sweets new beauties to explore,
> Then to entangle in her lovely arms,
> And drown ev'ry sense in unrivall'd charms?

The current had wafted us down by the morning nearly fifty miles from the place we embarked, so that we were secure from all danger from those Indians; and as Caroline had slept very little, and was then awake, I immediately put to shore in order that we might prepare some refreshment for her; after which we proceeded down the river, upon its banks, with an expectation that we might see a batteaux from Cohoes, which I meant to hire to take Caroline and myself to this place, while my men should continue their route by land.

We were fortunate; for it was not yet mid-day when we espied a batteaux with people in it, to whom we made a signal, when they instantly came to us and most readily complied with my wishes.

They were the French of Louissiana, who had been upon a hunting excursion, and as they were well acquainted with the country, and the nature of Indian affairs, I felt my anxiety for Caroline's safety entirely removed.

We arrived that evening about eleven o'clock at Cohoes, and the next morning set out for this place, where we arrived yesterday at four P.M. Here I have been able to procure all the little articles of dress my lovely Caroline you must suppose wanted, after the wonderful journey she had travelled; for according to the best of her recollection, she was taken the twentieth ult. and it must be nearly four hundred miles upon a straight line, from Clarkeville to the place where I overtook her.

What a change has happened in the fortune of your friend?—Every thing conspires to make me the happiest man living—I have been almost three days alone, as it were, with Caroline—She is the most charming woman alive, and as ingenuous as she is lovely—she asked me what I alluded to by the note?—Divine creature! She never knew any thing of the matter.—It must have been a transaction almost equal in blackness to the conduct of S——— towards you, in the business of Mr. R———.

Fly to us if you are sufficiently recovered, that you may participate in our happiness, and that we together may return and consummate those joys, which can only be equalled in heaven.

We shall remain here until Caroline has recovered from her fatigue, and if we should set out before you reach us, we shall certainly meet you on the road between this place and St. Vincent's.

I have a thousand little trifles to relate to you, but I must reserve them until we meet, as I am anxious to dispatch a runner to relieve the distress of our friends, and ease the corroding sorrows of Caroline's affectionate and generous uncle; who I reverence for his age and virtues, and esteem for his courage and understanding.

Caroline has this moment entered with a humming bird that a little French lad caught and gave to her;—behold, said she, as she came into the room where I was writing, and look at the little captive, how sad it looks, because it has lost its mate—and was you sad, my Caroline, said I, taking hold of her hand and tenderly pressing it, when you was hurried a prisoner from your friends?—Her cheek was resting upon my breast—Ah! Il————ray, her murmuring accents, for she could not articulate, expressed the most unutterable things—go thou little innocent thing, said she to the bird, putting her hand out of the window at the same time to facilitate its escape, you shall not be a moment longer confined, for perhaps, already have I robbed thee of joys, which the exertions of my whole life could not repay—Ah! Caroline, said I, and who is to restore to us the rapturous pleasures of which we have been robbed?—or shall we find, my charming girl, a compensation for such a sequestration in our future endearments?—O Il————ray! I dare not repeat another sentence!

Caroline writes with her own hand, her wishes for the immediate restoration of your health, and is very sorry to add, that she has cause to lament your valetudinary habit prevented her from meeting you upon the head branches of the Illinois; which she has been exploring, and hopes when she has the pleasure to meet you, that she shall be able to give you a good account of that delectable region.

ADIEU!

J. ARL————TON

LETTER LX

Mr. Il————ray to P. P————, Esq.

St. Vincent's, October

MY DEAR SIR,

I was so overjoyed at the reception of my friend's letter, announcing his having retaken your niece, the charming Caroline, that I was scarcely able to write a line, and which I hope will appear a sufficient excuse for my having written you so crude a letter upon the event.

The instant I dispatched the runner to you with Arl————ton's letter, I posted to Kaskaskia, to assure Caroline and my friend, how very sincerely I participated in the propitious events of their meeting, and the happy development of the cause of their long and cruel sufferings.

I experienced every sensation that friendship and esteem can inspire, when I first recognized the amiable and affectionate Caroline; she appeared to be recovered from her recent fatigue, though there were still vestiges upon her fair face, of the lacerations she had received in the course of her wonderful journey: But as they were superficial, they are now no longer visible.

Never could she appear to so much advantage. All the sweetness that beauty can give, was heightened by the graces with which she received me, by the cheerfulness of the most ingenuous heart, and which was rendered more delightful, by the ineffable brilliancy of thought, that so peculiarly characterizes her imagination, when she is happy, so that I must leave you to judge, what was my satisfaction, again, to see your affectionate niece, and to find my friend restored to his reason.

After remaining with them a short time at Kaskaskia, we set out together for this place on our return, where we arrived last evening; and here I have induced them to rest for some days, in order that they may see a place, upon which nature has lavished so many favours; and which has been improved by the hospitable French, who are its inhabitants. I was more anxious upon the subject, as I discovered in them both, such an eagerness to return to Louisville, and as I was apprehensive for Caroline's health; for however extraordinary her strength must have been, to have supported her through the rapid and rough journey she was carried by the savages, it was not reasonable to suppose, that she could support such expeditious movement under any other circumstances.

Two things in Caroline's account of her captivity are very extraordinary; they are, that she never felt in the least harassed, or alarmed for her safety, as she had, from the moment she was captured, a *presentiment* that Arl————ton would retake her; and, that the Indians treated her the whole time with the most distant respect, and scrupulous delicacy.

The first appears to be natural, when we consider the enthusiasm of the human mind when it is in love; and the latter is corroborated, by the testimony of all decent looking women, who have been so unfortunate as to fall into their hands. Indeed, I have been told of instances, where women have been treated with such tenderness and attention by them, that they have from gratitude become their wives.

Every thing seemed to be enchantment as we passed the extensive plains of the Illinois country. The zephyrs which had gathered on their way the fragrance of the flowery riches which bespangle the earth, poured such a torrent of voluptuous sweets upon the enraptured senses, that my animation was almost overpowered with their delicious and aromatic odours. The fertile and boundless Savannas were covered with flocks of buffalo, elk, and deer, which appeared to wanton in the exuberance of their luxurious pastures, and which were sporting in the cool breezes of the evening; while the sun descending below the horizon was gilding some remote clumps of trees, it brought to my imagination, the charms of old ocean, when she receives into her bosom the luminary by which we live, as if to renovate in her prolific element his exhausted powers. But when the scene was embellished by an image so fair and beauteous as that of Caroline's, we seemed to have regained Paradise, while all the golden fruits of autumn hung pending from their shrubs, and seemed to invite the taste, as though they were jealous of each others delicious sweets.

Yes! my dear sir, we have had the most delectable journey perhaps that ever was made. The circumstances attending it, and the season and weather altogether conspired to give us such spirits, that instead of appearing to be in an uninhabited waste, we seemed to want only our friends to have determined us, there to have taken up our residence, for the remainder of our lives.

It is impossible for any country to appear to advantage after you have seen the Illinois; but still there are a variety of charms at this place, and could you see the *naiveté* of the inhabitants, which has united with it, all the sprightliness of the country, from whom they descended, you would believe you was living in those Arcadian days, when the tuneful shepherd used to compose sonnets to his mistress, and when the charms of love, were propitiated in sequestered groves, and smiling meads.

Here we find all the cheerful idleness that plenty gives; and while the sprightly youth in festive dance, chase away the gloom of the surrounding forests, the neighbouring plantations are cultivated to a perfection, that I have scarcely seen equalled in any part of America; and the hospitality of the inhabitants, who make large quantities of wine, renders it one of the most interesting places I ever knew.—for,

Here the well covered board is enrich'd by the vine,
And friendship is season'd with goblets of wine:—
When nectar is sparkling the joys of the bowl,
With rapture inspiring give zest to the soul;
And mirth laughing wit, upon fancy's swift wings,
Bedecks us with myrtle, and endless bliss brings;
While Venus, whose charms most effulgent at night,
Awakes us to reason, when love gives delight.

I have this instant received a letter from General W————, and as I shall have the pleasure to see you in a few days, I hope you will pardon me for not being more particular. Caroline bids me tell you she has so many things to relate, that she does not know how to begin a letter; besides she thinks they will prove more agreeable to you to be communicated by word of mouth. The truth is, both Caroline and Arl————ton are so totally absorbed in each other, that for either of them to write, is a thing not to be expected.

They both desire me to assure you of their utmost friendship and esteem, and permit me to request that you will believe, I am

YOUR FRIEND, AND MOST

OBEDIENT SERVANT,

G. IL————RAY

LETTER LXVII

Capt. Arl————ton to Mr. Il————ray

Louisville, March

During the delirium of my distempered brain, which the violence of my passions, and the circumstances attending my love for Caroline produced, I sometimes forgot, my dear Il————ray, the important duties I owe both to my friends, to myself, and above all to my country.—And it is to your regard for my welfare that I am indebted for the felicity I now enjoy.

The flexible temper of the human mind is capable of being wrought to a polish so elegantly fine, that the most delicate touches makes the most lasting impressions; and perhaps it was owing to the refined and judicious lessons upon morality you have so repeatedly given me, which now makes me feel a glow of gratitude for the benefits I have experienced—and nothing can more effectually prove to me the advantages resulting from a permanent and reciprocal friendship like ours, than a retrospect to the dangers I have escaped, and a view of the gilded prospect by which I am now surrounded.

It was to your active zeal for my honour and health which prevented me from falling a victim to my impetuous disposition and propensity to dissipation, at an early period. It was by your council and advice I learned to distinguish between virtue and vice, which have become so confounded, that it is no difficult task to instruct the understanding of men whose minds have received a false bias—and it was your watchful solicitude for the happiness of Caroline and myself, that led to the unraveling the mystery of our love and unbosomed its sweets in all its blushing charms, which otherwise would have withered, untasted, and unenjoyed.

How can I describe to you our mutual happiness?—The fleeting season seems to have hurried round his course, and has left me the image of a banquet that floats in my imagination, where beauty at rest, lies embraced by love, while the rosy hours are dancing with enchantment to the mellifluous tones of desire.

Every preparation having been adjusted shortly after your departure, that was necessary to the consummation of our wishes, and Caroline's excellent uncle having no objection to our alliance, declared he would never be the cause of procrastinating, by a regard to idle ceremony, the completion of our joys:—and though it was not at that season of which Thompson speaks where he so beautifully describes the glowing charms of the virgin, yet Caroline.

"Flushed by the spirit of the genial hour
Then from her virgin's cheek a fresher bloom
Shot less, and less, the live carnation round;—
Her lips blush'd deeper sweets; she breath'd of youth;
The shining moisture swell'd into her eyes,
In brighter flow.—Her wishing bosom heav'd,
With palpitations wild;—kind tumult seiz'd
Her veins, and all her yielding soul was love."

Be so good as to excuse this slight alteration.

When the ruthless hand of barbarous war has in many places desolated the fairest country upon the face of the globe,—a country which Voltaire said "if ever the golden age existed, it was in the middle provinces of America." Who can help feeling an indignation against such gothic practices?

When I recollect the once smiling meads of the gentle Pacaic, which are now untilled—when I reflect upon the plenty that prolific region once produced, which is now a waste; and then figure to my mind the innocent wiles of a growing progeny that used to gladden the fields with the rude songs of the uncultivated bard, which the horrors of a sanguinary warfare have turned into gloom and heaps of ruins, how can I help reprobating a system pregnant with evils the most monstrous?

We can scarcely cast our eyes upon a page of history which is not stained with the relation of some bloody transaction—the sacrifice of innocence—the proscription of the virtuous, or the triumph of a villain; which is sufficient to convince every unprejudiced man, that the greater part of the world has hitherto been governed by barbarians: and which must prove to all men of sentiment and humanity, that it is high time to inquire into the cause which has so often destroyed the repose of the world, and stained the annals of mankind with indelible disgrace.

Such were the considerations, you know my friend, that first induced me to turn my thoughts towards the western territory of this continent, as its infancy affords an opportunity to its citizens of establishing a system conformable to reason and humanity, and thereby extend the blessings of civilization to all orders of men.—And if a circumstance that at first distracted my brain, and debarred me from thinking of living in a country that contained the most lovely woman in the world, but which now affords me such undescribable joy, for a time frustrated my object, and induced me to determine to leave the country; I now assure you that I am more than ever attached to an object interesting to every human being.

I have not the vanity to suppose my exertions will materially tend to effect this important end;—but I have the satisfaction to know I shall be entitled to the reputation of a good, if not a very useful citizen; an honour, in my opinion, that has more real splendour annexed to it than all the inflated eulogiums which have been lavished upon vain and inhuman conquerors, or intriguing and unprincipled ministers of state.

As the government of this district is not organized, it is my intention to form in epitome the model of a society which I conceive ought to form part of the polity of every civilized commonwealth;—for which purpose I have purchased a tract of country lying upon the Ohio from the rapids or Louisville, and extending above Diamond island to a point sixteen miles from its beginning, and running back an equal distance, which will constitute an area of two hundred and fifty-six square miles, or nearly, making an allowance for the bends of the river.

This tract I have laid out into two hundred and fifty-six parcels, upon which I am settling men who served in the late war, giving to each a fee-simple in the soil he occupies, who shall be eligible to a seat in a house of representatives consisting of twenty members, who are to assemble every Sunday in the year, to take into consideration the measures necessary to promote the encouragements of agriculture and all useful arts, as well to discuss upon the science of government and jurisprudence.

Every male being of the age of twenty-one, and sound in his reason, is intitled to a vote in the nomination of a member to represent them, and every member is intitled to the rewards and honours which the institution may think proper to bestow. And in order that their debates shall be perfectly free and uncontrouled, the right of electing their president is invested in them also, every member being eligible to the office; but not to the dignity for more than one year; and he must then remain out of office for seven years before he can be eligible again; by which means all unwarrantable views will be frustrated, and the object of every member will be limited to the ambition of meriting the thanks of his country: and thus by the fundamental laws of the society, every expectation of aggrandizement will fall to the ground, and love, and harmony, must consequently be productive of every generous advantage; and the respectability of every citizen be established upon that broad basis—the dignity of man.

Mr. P——— thinks the object is laudable, and he has promised to lend his assistance in framing the particular instructions immediately necessary to give order and motion to the machine; and he has moreover promised, if they will do him the honour to elect him president, to serve the first year, and give them every information in his power.

He has also offered to build a house for the assembly with galleries large and capacious enough to contain all the inhabitants of the district; for he says, every thing of this sort ought to have the greatest publicity—and by that means the people will be edified by hearing what passes, and will also be prevented from listening to those itinerant preachers who travel about the country under a pretence of propagating the pure christian religion, but who are, in truth, the disturbers of domestic felicity,—the harbingers of hypocrisy, and whose incoherent sermons are a cloud of ignorance that too often spreads a gloom over the understanding of the uninformed, which nothing but the rays of reason can dispel, and which have too long darkened the intellect of mankind, and produced an obscurity of ideas that is truly lamentable.

The plan I am determined shall not be merely theoretical, for it is in great part already carried into execution.—The land is not only purchased and parcelled out, but there is upwards of one hundred families settled, and Mr. P——— is making preparations for the public building. Therefore you see, my friend, if I have been folded in the arms of love, I have not been idle as to what ought to be the object of every human being, i. e. promoting the good of his fellow creatures.

Caroline has not either been unemployed for she has paid constant visits to the wives of these brave men, my fellow soldiers, and brothers, and has instructed them in various and useful employments, which must tend not a little to promote their comfort.

Such, you see, is my prospect of happiness after a tempestuous and dangerous conflict that was so near destroying my happiness for ever: and which I have the greater pleasure of repeating as it is a tribute I owe to your unparalleled worth and philanthrophy.

You are too well convinced, I am certain, of the advantages this sort of system will produce, to make it necessary for me to be elaborate upon the subject:—but if you will forgive me, I shall observe that while the embellishment of manners, and the science of politics, have been engrossed by the higher orders of society, the bulk of mankind have been the mere machines of states;—and they have acted with a blind zeal for the promotion of the objects of tyrants, which has often desolated empires, while the once laughing vineyards have been changed into scenes of butchery; and the honest and industrious husbandmen, those supporters of all our wealth and all our comfort, have mourned for the sad havock of their cruel depradations.

The intercourse of men and nations has tended, not a little, to accelerate the advancement of civilization, and I am convinced the only cause why philanthropy is so uncommon a virtue, is owing to the want of a just knowledge of the human heart.

Small societies of this kind established throughout a great community would help to soften the manners of the vulgar, correct their idle and vicious habits—extend their knowledge—ameliorate their judgement—and afford an opportunity to every genius or man of sense of becoming useful to his country, who often lie obscured, uncultivated, unknown, and their talents unappropriated while the state has suffered: and at the time tyrants would be effectually prevented from trampling upon the laws of reason and humanity.

Our society, as one, beg leave to express to you, that they sincerely wish for your happiness, and to assure you they anxiously wish for your return. Caroline has the ambition to aspire at a preeminence in your esteem.

Do not omit to mention us affectionately to Mrs. F———, and inform her, that Caroline will write to her, as soon as we are settled, which will be in the district I have mentioned.

GOD BLESS YOU MY FRIEND. ADIEU!

J. ARL———TON

11

SELECTED TREATIES BETWEEN THE UNITED STATES AND NATIVE AMERICAN TRIBES

Literally hundreds of treaties were formed between Native Americans and white Americans between the Revolution and the Civil War. The usual arrangement was a coerced exchange of lands for money and supplies. Many white westerners, such as Benjamin Drake and James Hall, were deeply critical of the policies of treaty writing and publicized what they viewed as unjust and tyrannical claims by the government. The four treaties we have reproduced here reflect in particular a need to write treaties that accounted for greater complexities as the region in question aged.

The first, the 1791 Treaty with the Cherokees, came a few years after the initial Treaty of Hopewell. Unlike that treaty, however, this one initiates a developing pattern between the natives and the whites: that assimilation would be written into the treaties. In Article XIV, the Cherokees are rewarded for foregoing traditional lifeways. During the early nineteenth century, the Cherokees met these terms and farmed, owned slaves, and lived in the manner of European Americans. When they were unjustly removed on the Trail of Tears, the circumstances of their plight are that much more complex, as noted by Cherokee writers such as John Ross and Elias Boudinot.

The Treaty of Greenville in 1795 represented the first major victory by American forces in the Old Northwest. After major setbacks in 1790 and 1791, finally in 1794 General Anthony Wayne had defeated a combined force of Shawnees, Wyandots, Miamis, Weas, Sauks, and many others at Fallen Timbers, near present-day Toledo, Ohio. To that point, these tribes, armed and encouraged by British agents in the region contrary to the Treaty of Paris, which ceded these lands from Great Britain to the United States in 1783, had violently resisted American settlement. The treaty reflects the ideals of the Northwest Ordinance's hope to gain native lands by rule of law, not force.

In 1804, four Sauk elders were called to St. Louis to aid one of their tribesmen accused of murder. While there, they were encouraged to drink, and then to sign away most of the Illinois River valley, according to Black Hawk, a Sauk war chief who did not sign the treaty, a finding corroborated by Issac Galland in *Chronicles of the North American Savages* (1834) and by Benjamin Drake in his *Life of Black Hawk* (1838). This treaty, and its dubious origins, was the source of trouble in the Black Hawk War. The American government failed to prevent settlers from squatting on Sauk lands and then refused to punish squatters who committed crimes on native lands.

The Treaty of Prairie du Chien in 1829 is notable for its treatments of mixed-blood denizens of the region. At the treaty's conclusion, the Ojibways and the local officials agreed on certain payments for these mixed-bloods in land and money. These white commissioners, with the exception of Zachary Taylor, who was not a primary signatory, were all settlers; usually, treaties were negotiated by generals in the American army, usually easterners. When the treaty was sent to Washington for ratification, the cessions to the mixed-bloods were stricken, according to both the historical record and William Warren. The mixed-bloods were then grouped by the federal government with the Ojibway.

Recently, scholars and activists have been able to use the status of treaties as contracts in perpetuity between two sovereign peoples to hold the government to some very old promises. Despite their often coerced origins, today old treaties such as these have provided Native Americans with access to greater empowerment and self-determination.

Texts: All are in volume 2 of *Indian Affairs: Laws and Treaties,* ed. Charles J. Kappler (Washington, 1972): 29–33, 39–45, 74–77, 297–300.

TREATY WITH THE CHEROKEE (1791)

A Treaty of Peace and Friendship made and concluded between the President of the United States of America, on the Part and Behalf of the said States, and the undersigned Chiefs and Warriors of the Cherokee Nation of Indians, on the Part and Behalf of the said Nation.

July 2, 1791.
7 Stat., 39.
Proclamation, Feb. 7, 1792.

The parties being desirous of establishing permanent peace and friendship between the United States and the said Cherokee Nation, and the citizens and members thereof, and to remove the causes of war, by ascertaining their limits and making other necessary, just and friendly arrangements: The President of the United States, by William Blount, Governor of the territory of the United States of America, south of the river Ohio, and Superintendant of Indian affairs for the southern district, who is vested with full powers for these purposes, by and with the advice and consent of the

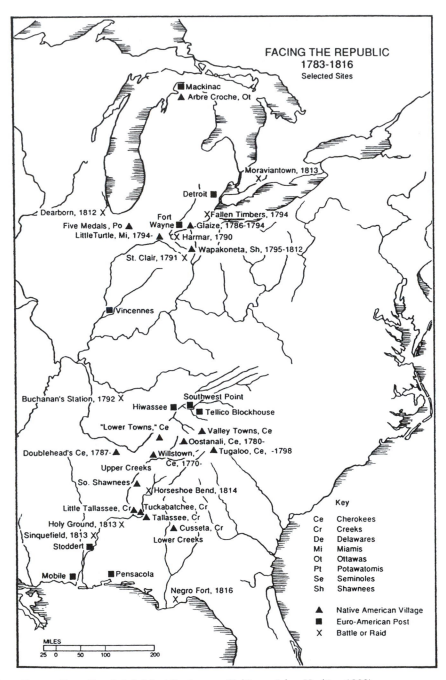

FACING THE REPUBLIC
1783-1816
Selected Sites

■ Mackinac
▲ Arbre Croche, Ot

Moraviantown, 1813
X

Detroit ■

Dearborn, 1812 X

Fort
Wayne ■ ▲ Glaize, 1786-1794
Five Medals, Po ▲
LittleTurtle, Mi, 1794- ▲ X Harmar, 1790
▲ Wapakoneta, Sh, 1795-1812
St. Clair, 1791 X

X Fallen Timbers, 1794

■ Vincennes

Buchanan's Station, 1792 X
Southwest Point
Hiwassee ■ ■ Tellico Blockhouse

"Lower Towns," Ce
▲ Valley Towns, Ce
▲ ▲ Oostanali, Ce, 1780-
Doublehead's Ce, 1787- ▲ ▲ Tugaloo, Ce, -1798
▲ Willstown,
Ce, 1770-

Upper Creeks
So. Shawnees ▲
X Horseshoe Bend, 1814
Little Tallassee, Cr ▲ ▲ Tuckabatchee, Cr
▲ Tallassee, Cr
Holy Ground, 1813 X
Sinquefield, 1813 X ▲ Cusseta, Cr
Stoddert ■ Lower Creeks

Mobile ■ ■ Pensacola

Negro Fort, 1816
X

Key

Ce	Cherokees
Cr	Creeks
De	Delawares
Mi	Miamis
Ot	Ottawas
Pt	Potawatomis
Se	Seminoles
Sh	Shawnees

▲ Native American Village
■ Euro-American Post
X Battle or Raid

MILES
25 0   50   100   200

From Gregory Evans Dowd, A Spirited Resistance *(Baltimore: Johns Hopkins, 1992).*

Senate of the United States: And the Cherokee Nation, by the undersigned Chiefs and Warriors representing the said nation, have agreed to the following articles, namely:

Article I.

Peace and friendship perpetual.

There shall be perpetual peace and friendship between all the citizens of the United States of America, and all the individuals composing the whole Cherokee nation of Indians.

Article II.

Indians acknowledge protection of United States.

The undersigned Chiefs and Warriors, for themselves and all parts of the Cherokee nation, do acknowledge themselves and the said Cherokee nation, to be under the protection of the said United States of America, and of no other sovereign whosoever; and they also stipulate that the said Cherokee nation will not hold any treaty with any foreign power, individual state, or with individuals of any state.

Article III.

Prisoners to be restored.

The Cherokee nation shall deliver to the Governor of the territory of the United States of America, south of the river Ohio, on or before the first day of April next, at this place, all persons who are now prisoners, captured by them from any part of the United States: And the United States shall on or before the same day, and at the same place, restore to the Cherokees, all the prisoners now in captivity, which the citizens of the United States have captured from them.

Article IV.

Boundaries.

The boundary between the citizens of the United States and the Cherokee nation, is and shall be as follows: Beginning at the top of the Currahee mountain, where the Creek line passes it; thence a direct line to Tugelo river; thence northeast to the Occunna mountain, and over the same along the South-Carolina Indian boundary to the North-Carolina boundary; thence north to a point from which a line is to be extended to the river Clinch, that shall pass the Holston at the ridge which divides the waters running into Little River from those running into the Tennessee; thence up the river Clinch to Campbell's line, and along the same to the top of Cumberland mountain; thence a direct line to the Cumberland river where the Kentucky road crosses it; thence down the Cumberland river to a point from which a south west line will strike the ridge which divides the waters of Cumberland from those of Duck river, forty miles above Nashville; thence down the said ridge to a point from whence a south west line will strike the mouth of Duck river.

And in order to preclude forever all disputes relative to the said boundary, the same shall be ascertained, and marked plainly by three persons appointed on the part of the United States, and three Cherokees on the part of their nation.

And in order to extinguish forever all claims of the Cherokee nation, or any part thereof, to any of the land lying to the right of the line above described, beginning as aforesaid at the Currahee mountain, it is hereby agreed, that in addition to the consideration heretofore made for the said land, the United States will cause certain valuable goods, to be immediately delivered to the undersigned Chiefs and Warriors, for the use of their nation; and the said United States will also cause the sum of one thousand dollars to be paid annually to the said Cherokee nation. And the undersigned Chiefs and Warriors, do hereby for themselves and the whole Cherokee nation, their heirs and descendants, for the considerations above-mentioned, release, quit-claim, relinquish and cede, all the land to the right of the line described, and beginning as aforesaid.

Article V.

Stipulation for a road.

It is stipulated and agreed, that the citizens and inhabitants of the United States, shall have a free and unmolested use of a road from Washington district to Mero district, and of the navigation of the Tennessee river.

Article VI.

United States to regulate trade.

It is agreed on the part of the Cherokees, that the United States shall have the sole and exclusive right of regulating their trade.

Article VII.

Guarantee.

The United States solemnly guarantee to the Cherokee nation, all their lands not hereby ceded.

Article VIII.

No citizen to settle on Indian lands.

If any citizen of the United States, or other person not being an Indian, shall settle on any of the Cherokees' lands, such person shall forfeit the protection of the United States, and the Cherokees may punish him or not, as they please.

Article IX.

Nor hunt on the same.

No citizen or inhabitant of the United States, shall attempt to hunt or destroy the game on the lands of the Cherokees; nor shall any citizen or inhabitant go into the Cherokee country, without a passport first obtained from the Governor of some one of the United States, or territorial districts, or such other person as the President of the United States may from time to time authorize to grant the same.

Article X.

Indians to deliver up criminals.

If any Cherokee Indian or Indians, or person residing among them, or who shall take refuge in their nation, shall steal a horse from, or commit a robbery or murder, or other capital crime, on any citizens or inhabitants of the United States, the Cherokee nation shall be bound to deliver him or them up, to be punished according to the laws of the United States.

Article XI.

Citizens of United States committing crimes in Indian territory to be punished.

If any citizen or inhabitant of the United States, or of either of the territorial districts of the United States, shall go into any town, settlement or territory belonging to the Cherokees, and shall there commit any crime upon, or trespass against the person or property of any peaceable and friendly Indian or Indians, which if committed within the jurisdiction of any state, or within the jurisdiction of either of the said districts, against a citizen or white inhabitant thereof, would be punishable by the laws of such state or district, such offender or offenders, shall be subject to the same punishment, and shall be proceeded against in the same manner as if the offence had been committed within the jurisdiction of the state or district to which he or they may belong, against a citizen or white inhabitant thereof.

Article XII.

Retaliation restrained.

In case of violence on the persons or property of the individuals of either party, neither retaliation or reprisal shall be committed by the other, until satisfaction shall have been demanded of the party of which the aggressor is, and shall have been refused.

Article XIII.

Cherokees to give notice of designs against United States.

The Cherokee shall give notice to the citizens of the United States, of any designs which they may know, or suspect to be formed in any neighboring tribe, or by any person whatever, against the peace and interest of the United States.

Article XIV.

United States to make presents.

That the Cherokee nation may be led to a greater degree of civilization, and to become herdsmen and cultivators, instead of remaining in a state of hunters, the United States will from time to time furnish gratuitously the said nation with useful implements of husbandry, and further to assist the said nation in so desirable a pursuit, and at the same time to establish a certain mode of communication, the United States will send such, and so many persons to reside in said nation as they may judge proper, not exceeding four in number, who shall qualify themselves to act as interpreters. These persons shall have lands assigned by the Cherokees for cultivation for themselves and their successors in office; but they shall be precluded exercising any kind of traffic.

Article XV.

Animosities to cease.

All animosities for past grievances shall henceforth cease, and the contracting parties will carry the foregoing treaty into full execution with all good faith and sincerity.

Article XVI.

Ratification.

This treaty shall take effect and be obligatory on the contracting parties, as soon as the same shall have been ratified by the President of the United States, with the advice and consent of the Senate of the United States.

In witness of all and every thing herein determined between the United States of America and the whole Cherokee nation, the parties have hereunto set their hands and seals, at the treaty ground on the bank of the Holston, near the mouth of the French Broad, within the United States, this second day of July, in the year of our Lord one thousand seven hundred and ninety-one.

William Blount, governor in and over the territory of the United States of America south of the river Ohio, and superintendent of Indian Affairs for the southern district, ...[L. S.]

Chuleoah, or the Boots, his x mark, ...[L. S.]

Squollecuttah, or Hanging Maw his x mark, ...[L. S.]

Occunna, or the Badger, his x mark, ...[L. S.]

Enoleh, or Black Fox, his x mark, ...[L. S.]

Nontuaka, or the Northward, his x mark, ...[L. S.]

Tekakiska, his x mark, ...[L. S.]

Chutloh, or King Fisher, his x mark, ...[L. S.]

Tuckaseh, or Terrapin, his x mark, ...[L. S.]

Kateh, his x mark, ...[L. S.]

Kunnochatutloh, or the Crane, his x mark, ...[L. S.]

Cauquillehanah, or the Thigh, his x mark, ...[L. S.]

Chesquotteleneh, or Yellow Bird, his x mark, ...[L. S.]

Chickasawtehe, or Chickasaw Killer, his x mark, ...[L. S.]

Tuskegatehe, Tuskega Killer, his x mark, ...[L. S.]

Kulsatehe, his x mark, ...[L. S.]

Tinkshalene, his x mark, ...[L. S.]

Sawutteh, or Slave Catcher, his x mark, ...[L. S.]

Aukuah, his x mark, ...[L. S.]

Oosenaleh, his x mark, ...[L. S.]

Kenotetah, or Rising Fawn, his x mark, ...[L. S.]

Kanetetoka, or Standing Turkey, his x mark, ...[L. S.]

Yonewatleh, or Bear at Home, his x mark, ...[L. S.]

Long Will, his x mark, ...[L. S.]

Kunoskeskie, or John Watts, his x mark, ...[L. S.]

Nenetooyah, or Bloody Fellow, his x mark, ...[L. S.]

Chuquilatague, or Double Head, his x mark, ...[L. S.]

Koolaquah, or Big Acorn, his x mark, ...[L. S.]

Toowayelloh, or Bold Hunter, his x mark, ...[L. S.]

Jahleoonoyehka, or MiddleStriker, his x mark, ...[L. S.]

Kinnesah, or Cabin, his x mark, ...[L. S.]

Tullotehe, or Two Killer, his x mark, ...[L. S.]

Kaalouske, or Stopt Still, his x mark, ...[L. S.]

Kulsatche, his x mark, ...[L. S.]

Auquotague, the Little Turkey's Son, his x mark, ...[L. S.]

Talohteske, or Upsetter, his x mark, ...[L. S.]

Cheakoneske, or Otter Lifter, his x mark, ...[L. S.]

Keshukaune, or She Reigns, his x mark, ...[L. S.]

Toonaunailoh, his x mark, ...[L. S.]

Teesteke, or Common Disturber, his x mark, ...[L. S.]

Robin McClemore, ...[L. S.]

Skyuka, ...[L. S.]

John Thompson, Interpreter.

James Cery, Interpreter.

Done in presence of—

Dan'l Smith, Secretary Territory United States south of the river Ohio.

Thomas Kennedy, of Kentucky.

Jas. Robertson, of Mero District.

Claiborne Watkins, of Virginia.

Jno. McWhitney, of Georgia.

Fauch, of Georgia.

Titus Ogden, North Carolina.

Jno. Chisolm, Washington District.

Robert King.

Thomas Gegg.

Additional Article To the Treaty made between the United States and the Cherokees on the second day of July, one thausand seven hundred and ninety-one.

Feb. 17, 1792.
7 Stat., 42.
Proclamation, Feb. 17, 1792.
Increase of annual payment to Indians.

It is hereby mutually agreed between Henry Knox, Secretary of War, duly authorized thereto in behalf of the United States, on the one part, and the undersigned chiefs and warriors, in behalf of themselves and the Cherokee nation, on the other part, that the following article shall be added to and considered as part of the treaty made between the United States and the said Cherokee nation on the second day of July, one thousand seven hundred and ninety-one; to wit:

The sum to be paid annually by the United States to the Cherokee nation of Indians, in consideration of the relinquishment of land, as stated in the treaty made with them on the second day of July, one thousand seven hundred and ninety-one, shall be one thousand five hundred dollars instead of one thousand dollars, mentioned in the said treaty.

In testimony whereof, the said Henry Knox, Secretary of War, and the said chiefs and warriors of the Cherokee nation, have hereunto set their hands and seals, in the city of Philadelphia, this seventeenth day of February, in the year of our Lord, one thousand seven hundred and ninety-two.

H. Knox, Secretary of War, ...[L. S.]

Iskagua, or Clear Sky, his x mark (formerly Nenetooyah, or Bloody Fellow), ...[L. S.]

Nontuaka, or the Northward, his x mark, ...[L. S.]

Chutloh, or King Fisher, his x mark, ...[L. S.]

Katigoslah, or the Prince, his x mark, ...[L. S.]

Teesteke, or Common Disturber, his x mark, ...[L. S.]

Suaka, or George Miller, his x mark, ...[L. S.]

In presence of—

Thomas Grooter.

Jno. Stagg, jr.

Leonard D. Shaw.

James Cery, sworn intrepreter to the Cherokee Nation.

TREATY OF GREENVILLE (1795)

A treaty of peace between the United States of America and the Tribes of Indians, called the Wyandots, Delawares, Shawanoes, Ottawas, Chipewas, Putawatimes, Miamis, Eel-river, Weea's, Kickapoos, Piankashaws, and Kaskaskias.

Aug. 3, 1795.
7 Stat., 49.
Proclamation, Dec. 2, 1795.

To put an end to a destructive war, to settle all controversies, and to restore harmony and a friendly intercourse between the said United States, and Indian tribes; Anthony Wayne, major-general, commanding the army of the United States, and sole commissioner for the good purposes above-mentioned, and the said tribes of Indians, by their Sachems, chiefs, and warriors, met together at Greeneville, the head quarters of the said army, have agreed on the following articles, which, when ratified by the President, with the advice and consent of the Senate of the United States, shall be binding on them and the said Indian tribes.

Article I.

Peace established.

Henceforth all hostilities shall cease; peace is hereby established, and shall be perpetual; and a friendly intercourse shall take place, between the said United States and Indian tribes.

Article II.

Prisoners on both sides to be restored.

All prisoners shall on both sides be restored. The Indians, prisoners to the United States, shall be immediately set at liberty. The people of the United States, still remaining prisoners among the Indians, shall be delivered up in ninety days from the date hereof, to the general or commanding officer at Greeneville, Fort Wayne or Fort Defiance; and ten chiefs of the said tribes shall remain at Greeneville as hostages, until the delivery of the prisoners shall be effected.

Article III.

Boundary line established.
Cession of particular tracts of land by the Indians.
Cession of passages in certain places by the Indians.

The general boundary line between the lands of the United States, and the lands of the said Indian tribes, shall begin at the mouth of Cayahoga river, and run thence up the same to the portage between that and the Tuscarawas branch of the Muskingum; thence down that branch to the crossing place above Fort Lawrence; thence westerly to a fork of that branch of the great Miami river running into the Ohio, at or near which fork stood Loromie's store, and where commences the portage between the Miami of the Ohio, and St. Mary's river, which is a branch of the Miami, which runs into Lake Erie; thence a westerly course to Fort Recovery, which stands on a branch of the Wabash; then south-westerly in a direct line to the Ohio, so as to intersect that river opposite the mouth of Kentucke or Cuttawa river. And in consideration of the peace now established; of the goods formerly received from the United States; of those now to be delivered, and of the yearly delivery of goods now stipulated to be made hereafter, and to indemnify the United States for the injuries and expenses they have sustained during the war; the said Indians tribes do hereby cede and relinquish forever, all their claims to the lands lying eastwardly and southwardly of the general boundary line now described; and these lands, or any part of them, shall never hereafter be made a cause or pretence, on the part of the said tribes or any of them, of war or injury to the United States, or any of the people thereof.

And for the same considerations, and as an evidence of the returning friendship of the said Indian tribes, of their confidence in the United States, and desire to provide for their accommodation, and for that convenient intercourse which will be beneficial to both parties, the said Indian tribes do also cede to the United States the following pieces of land; to-wit. (1.) One piece of land six miles square at or near Loromie's store before mentioned. (2.) One piece two miles square at the head of the navigable water or landing on the St. Mary's river, near Girty's town. (3.) One piece six miles square at the head of the navigable water of the Au-Glaize river. (4.) One piece six miles square at the confluence of the Au-Glaize and Miami rivers, where

Fort Defiance now stands. (5.) One piece six miles square at or near the confluence of the rivers St. Mary's and St. Joseph's, where Fort Wayne now stands, or near it. (6.) One piece two miles square on the Wabash river at the end of the portage from the Miami of the lake, and about eight miles westward from Fort Wayne. (7.) One piece six miles square at the Ouatanon or old Weea towns on the Wabash river. (8.) One piece twelve miles square at the British fort on the Miami of the lake at the foot of the rapids. (9.) One piece six miles square at the mouth of the said river where it empties into the Lake. (10.) One piece six miles square upon Sandusky lake, where a fort formerly stood. (11.) One piece two miles square at the lower rapids of Sandusky river. (12.) The post of Detroit and all the land to the north, the west and the south of it, of which the Indian title has been extinguished by gifts or grants to the French or English governments; and so much more land to be annexed to the district of Detroit as shall be comprehended between the river Rosine on the south, lake St. Clair on the north, and a line, the general course whereof shall be six miles distant from the west end of lake Erie, and Detroit river. (13.) The post of Michillimackinac, and all the land on the island, on which that post stands, and the main land adjacent, of which the Indian title has been extinguished by gifts or grants to the French or English governments; and a piece of land on the main to the north of the island, to measure six miles on lake Huron, or the strait between lakes Huron and Michigan, and to extend three miles back from the water of the lake or strait, and also the island De Bois Blanc, being an extra and voluntary gift of the Chipewa nation. (14.) One piece of land six miles square at the mouth of Chikago river, emptying into the south-west end of Lake Michigan, where a fort formerly stood. (15.) One piece twelve miles square at or near the mouth of the Illinois river, emptying into the Mississippi. (16.) One piece six miles square at the old Piorias fort and village, near the south end of the Illinois lake on said Illinois river: And whenever the United States shall think proper to survey and mark the boundaries of the lands hereby ceded to them, they shall give timely notice thereof to the said tribes of Indians, that they may appoint some of their wise chiefs to attend and see that the lines are run according to the terms of this treaty.

And the said Indian tribes will allow to the people of the United States a free passage by land and by water, as one and the other shall be found convenient, through their country, along the chain of posts herein before mentioned; that is to say, from the commencement of the portage aforesaid at or near Loromie's store, thence along said portage to the St. Mary's, and down the same to Fort Wayne, and then down the Miami to lake Erie: again from the commencement of the portage at or near Loromie's store along the portage from thence to the river Au-Glaize, and down the same to its junction with the Miami at Fort Defiance: again from the commencement of the portage aforesaid, to Sandusky river, and down the same to Sandusky bay and lake Erie, and from Sandusky to the post which shall be taken at or near the foot of the rapids of the Miami of the lake: and from thence to Detroit. Again from the mouth of Chikago, to the commencement of the portage, between that river and the Illinois, and down the Illinois river to the Mississippi, also from Fort Wayne along the portage aforesaid which leads to the Wabash, and then down the Wabash to the Ohio. And the said Indian tribes will also allow to the people of the United States the free use of the harbors and mouths of rivers along the lakes adjoining the Indian lands, for sheltering vessels and boats, and liberty to land their cargoes where necessary for their safety.

Article IV.

Relinquishment of certain lands by United States.
Exceptions.
Annual allowance to be made to the Indians.
Proviso.

In consideration of the peace now established and of the cessions and relinquish-
ments of lands made in the preceding article by the said tribes of Indians, and to
manifest the liberality of the United States, as the great means of rendering this
peace strong and perpetual; the United States relinquish their claims to all other
Indian lands northward of the river Ohio, eastward of the Mississippi, and westward
and southward of the Great Lakes and the waters uniting them, according to the
boundary line agreed on by the United States and the king of Great-Britain, in the
treaty of peace made between them in the year 1783. But from this relinquishment
by the United States, the following tracts of land, are explicitly excepted. 1st.
The tract of one hundred and fifty thousand acres near the rapids of the river Ohio,
which has been assigned to General Clark, for the use of himself and his warriors.
2d. The post of St. Vincennes on the river Wabash, and the lands adjacent, of which
the Indian title has been extinguished. 3d. The lands at all other places in possession
of the French people and other white settlers among them, of which the Indian
title has been extinguished as mentioned in the 3d article; and 4th. The post of
fort Massac towards the mouth of the Ohio. To which several parcels of land so
excepted, the said tribes relinquish all the title and claim which they or any of them
may have.

And for the same considerations and with the same views as above mentioned,
the United States now deliver to the said Indian tribes a quantity of goods to the value
of twenty thousand dollars, the receipt whereof they do hereby acknowledge; and
henceforward every year forever the United States will deliver at some convenient
place northward of the river Ohio, like useful goods, suited to the circumstances of
the Indians, of the value of nine thousand five hundred dollars; reckoning that value
at the first cost of the goods in the city or place in the United States, where they shall
be procured. The tribes to which those goods are to be annually delivered, and the
proportions in which they are to be delivered, are the following.

1st. To the Wyandots, the amount of one thousand dollars. 2d. To the Delawares,
the amount of one thousand dollars. 3d. To the Shawanese, the amount of one thousand dollars. 4th. To the Miamis, the amount of one thousand dollars. 5th. To the Ottawas, the amount of one thousand dollars. 6th. To the Chippewas, the amount of one
thousand dollars. 7th. To the Putawatimes, the amount of one thousand dollars. 8th.
And to the Kickapoo, Weea, Eel-river, Piankashaw and Kaskaskias tribes, the amount
of five hundred dollars each.

Provided, That if either of the said tribes shall hereafter at an annual delivery of
their share of the goods aforesaid, desire that a part of their annuity should be furnished in domestic animals, implements of husbandry, and other utensils convenient
for them, and in compensation to useful artificers who may reside with or near them,
and be employed for their benefit, the same shall at the subsequent annual deliveries
be furnished accordingly.

Article V.

Indians have right to hunt on lands relinquished by United States, etc.

To prevent any misunderstanding about the Indian lands relinquished by the United States in the fourth article, it is now explicitly declared, that the meaning of that relinquishment is this: The Indian tribes who have a right to those lands, are quietly to enjoy them, hunting, planting, and dwelling thereon so long as they please, without any molestation from the United States; but when those tribes, or any of them, shall be disposed to sell their lands, or any part of them, they are to be sold only to the United States; and until such sale, the United States will protect all the said Indian tribes in the quiet enjoyment of their lands against all citizens of the United States, and against all other white persons who intrude upon the same. And the said Indian tribes again acknowledge themselves to be under the protection of the said United States and no other power whatever.

Article VI.

Indians may expel settlers from their lands.

If any citizen of the United States, or any other white person or persons, shall presume to settle upon the lands now relinquished by the United States, such citizen or other person shall be out of the protection of the United States; and the Indian tribe, on whose land the settlement shall be made, may drive off the settler, or punish him in such manner as they shall think fit; and because such settlements made without the consent of the United States, will be injurious to them as well as to the Indians, the United States shall be at liberty to break them up, and remove and punish the settlers as they shall think proper, and so effect that protection of the Indian lands herein before stipulated.

Article VII.

Indians may hunt on lands ceded to United States.

The said tribes of Indians, parties to this treaty, shall be at liberty to hunt within the territory and lands which they have now ceded to the United States, without hindrance or molestation, so long as they demean themselves peaceably, and offer no injury to the people of the United States.

Article VIII.

Trade to be opened with the Indians.

Trade shall be opened with the said Indian tribes; and they do hereby respectively engage to afford protection to such persons, with their property, as shall be duly licensed to reside among them for the purpose of trade, and to their agents and servants; but no person shall be permitted to reside at any of their towns or hunting camps as a trader, who is not furnished with a license for that purpose, under the hand and seal of the superintendent of the department north-west of the Ohio, or such other person as the President of the United States shall authorize to grant such licenses; to the end, that the said Indians may not be imposed on in their trade. And if any licensed trader shall abuse his privilege by unfair dealing, upon complaint and proof thereof, his license shall be taken from him, and he shall be further punished according to the laws of the United States. And if any person shall intrude himself as a trader, without such license, the said Indians shall take and bring him before the superintendent or his deputy, to be dealt with according to law. And to prevent impositions by forged licenses, the said Indians shall at least once a year give information to the superintendent or his deputies, of the names of the traders residing among them.

Article IX.

Retaliation restrained.
Indians to give notice of designs against United States.

Lest the firm peace and friendship now established should be interrupted by the misconduct of individuals, the United States, and the said Indian tribes agree, that for injuries done by individuals on either side, no private revenge or retaliation shall take place; but instead thereof, complaint shall be made by the party injured, to the other: By the said Indian tribes, or any of them, to the President of the United States, or the superintendent by him appointed; and by the superintendent or other person appointed by the President, to the principal chiefs of the said Indian tribes, or of the tribe to which the offender belongs; and such prudent measures shall then be pursued as shall be necessary to preserve the said peace and friendship unbroken, until the Legislature (or Great Council) of the United States, shall make other equitable provision in the case, to the satisfaction of both parties. Should any Indian tribes meditate a war against the United States or either of them, and the same shall come to the knowledge of the before-mentioned tribes, or either of them, they do hereby engage to give immediate notice thereof to the general or officer commanding the troops of the United States, at the nearest post. And should any tribe, with hostile intentions against the United States, or either of them, attempt to pass through their country, they will endeavor to prevent the same, and in like manner give information of such attempt, to the general or officer commanding, as soon as possible, that all causes of mistrust and suspicion may be avoided between them and the United States. In like manner the United States shall give notice to the said Indian tribes of any harm that may be meditated against them, or either of them, that shall come to their knowledge; and do all in their power to hinder and prevent the same, that the friendship between them may be uninterrupted.

Article X.

Former treaties void.

All other treaties heretofore made between the United States and the said Indian tribes, or any of them, since the treaty of 1783, between the United States and Great Britain, that come within the purview of this treaty, shall henceforth cease and become void.

In testimony whereof, the said Anthony Wayne, and the sachems and war chiefs of the beforementioned nations and tribes of Indians, have hereunto set their hands and affixed their seals.

Done at Greenville, in the territory of the United States northwest of the river Ohio, on the third day of August, one thousand seven hundred and ninety-five.

Anthony Wayne Wyandots: . . .[L. S.]

Tarhe, or Crane, his x mark, . .[L. S.]

J. Williams, jun. his x mark, . .[L. S.]

Teyyaghtaw, his x mark, ...[L. S.]

Haroenyou, or half king's son, his x mark, ...[L. S.]

Tehaawtorens, his x mark, . . .[L. S.]

Awmeyeeray, his x mark, ...[L. S.]

Stayetah, his x mark, ...[L. S.]

Shateyyaronyah, or Leather Lips, his x mark, ...[L. S.]

Daughshuttayah, his x mark, .[L. S.]

Shaawrunthe, his x mark, Delawares: . . . .[L. S.]

Tetabokshke, or Grand Glaize King, his x mark, ...[L. S.]

Lemantanquis, or Black King, his x mark, ...[L. S.]

Wabatthoe, his x mark, ...[L. S.]

Maghpiway, or Red Feather, his x mark, ...[L. S.]

Kikthawenund, or Anderson, his x mark, ...[L. S.]

Bukongehelas, his x mark, . . .[L. S.]

Peekeelund, his x mark, ...[L. S.]

Peewanshemenogh, his x mark, ...[L. S.]

Weymegwas, his x mark, ...[L. S.]

Gobmaatick, his x mark, Ottawa: . . . .[L. S.]

Chegonickska, (an Ottawa from Sandusky,) his x mark, Pattawatimas of the river St Joseph: . . . .[L. S.]

Thupenebu, his x mark, ...[L. S.]

Nawac, (for himself and brother Etsimethe,) his x mark, ...[L. S.]

Nenanseka, his x mark, ...[L. S.]

Keesass, or Run, his x mark, ...[L. S.]

Kabamasaw, (for himself and brother Chisaugan,) his x mark, ...[L. S.]

Sugganunk, his x mark, ...[L. S.]

Wapmeme, or White Pigeon, his x mark, ...[L. S.]

Wacheness, (for himself and brother Pedagoshok,) his x mark, ...[L. S.]

Wabshicawnaw, his x mark, ...[L. S.]

La Chasse, his x mark, ...[L. S.]

Meshegethenogh, (for himself and brother Wawasek,) his x mark, . . .[L. S.]

Hingoswash, his x mark, ...[L. S.]

Wellebawkeelund, his x mark, [L. S.]

Peekeetelemund, or Thomas Adams, his x mark, ...[L. S.]

Kishkopekund, or Captain Buffalo, his x mark, ...[L. S.]

Amenahehan, or Captain Crow, his x mark, ...[L. S.]

Queshawksey, or George Washington, his x mark, ...[L. S.]

Weywinquis, or Billy Siscomb, his x mark, ...[L. S.]

Moses, his x mark, Shawanees: . . . .[L. S.]

Misquacoonacaw, or Red Pole, his x mark, ...[L. S.]

Cutthewekasaw, or Black Hoof, his x mark, ...[L. S.]

Kaysewaesekah, his x mark, . .[L. S.]

Weythapamattha, his x mark, .[L. S.]

Nianymseka, his x mark, ...[L. S.]

Waytheah, or Long Shanks, his x mark, ...[L. S.]

Weyapiersenwaw, or Blue Jacket, his x mark, ...[L. S.]

Nequetaughaw, his x mark, . .[L. S.]

Hahgooseekaw, or Captain Reed, his x mark, Ottawas: . . . .[L. S.]

Augooshaway, his x mark, . . .[L. S.]

Keenoshameek, his x mark, . .[L. S.]

La Malice, his x mark, ...[L. S.]

Machiwetah, his x mark, ...[L. S.]

Thowonawa, his x mark, ...[L. S.]

Secaw, his x mark, Chippewas: . . . .[L. S.]

Mashipinashiwish, or Bad Bird, his x mark, ...[L. S.]

Nahshogashe, (from Lake Superior,) his x mark, ...[L. S.]

Kathawasung, his x mark, ...[L. S.]

Masass, his x mark, ...[L. S.]

Nemekass, or Little Thunder, his x mark, ...[L. S.]

Anewasaw, his x mark, ...[L. S.]

Nawbudgh, his x mark, ...[L. S.]

Missenogomaw, his x mark, ...[L. S.]

Waweegshe, his x mark, ...[L. S.]

Thawme, or Le Blanc, his x mark, ...[L. S.]

Geeque, (for himself and brother Shewinse,) his x mark, Pattawatimas of Huron: . . . .[L. S.]

Okia, his x mark, ...[L. S.]

Chamung, his x mark, ...[L. S.]

Segagewan, his x mark, ...[L. S.]

Nanawme, (for himself and brother A. Gin,) his x mark, ...[L. S.]

Marchand, his x mark, ...[L. S.]

Wenameac, his x mark, Miamis: . . . .[L. S.]

Nagohquangogh, or Le Gris, his x mark, ...[L. S.]

Meshekunnoghquoh, or Little Turtle, his x mark, Miamis and Eel Rivers: . . . .[L. S.]

Peejeewa, or Richard Ville, his x mark, ...[L. S.]

Cochkepoghtogh, his x mark, Eel River Tribe: . . . .[L. S.]

Shamekunnesa, or Soldier, his x mark, Miamis: . . . .[L. S.]

Wapamangwa, or the White Loon, his x mark, Weas, for themselves and the Piankeshaws: . . . .[L. S.]

Amacunsa, or Little Beaver, his x mark, ...[L. S.]

Acoolatha, or Little Fox, his x mark, ...[L. S.]

Francis, his x mark, Kickapoos and Kaskaskias: . . . .[L. S.]

Keeawhah, his x mark, ...[L. S.]

Nemighka, or Josey Renard, his x mark, ...[L. S.]

Paikeekanogh, his x mark, Delawares of Sandusky: . . . .[L. S.]

Hawkinpumiska, his x mark, ...[L. S.]

Peshawkay, or Young Ox, his x mark, ...[L. S.]

Nanguey, his x mark, ...[L. S.]

Meenedohgeesogh, his x mark, ...[L. S.]

Peyamawksey, his x mark, ...[L. S.]

Reyntueco, (of the Six Nations, living at Sandusky,) his x mark, ...[L. S.]

In presence of (the word "goods" in the sixth line of the third article; the word "before" in the twenty-sixth line of the third article; the words "five hundred" in the tenth line of the fourth article, and the word "Piankeshaw" in the fourteenth line of the fourth article, being first interlined)—

H. De Butts, first aid de camp and secretary to Major General Wayne.

Wm. H. Harrison, aid de camp to Major General Wayne.

T. Lewis, aid de camp to Major General Wayne.

James O'Hara, quartermaster general.

John Mills, major of infantry and adjutant general.

Caleb Swan, P. M. T. U. S.

Geo. Demter, lieutenant artillery.

Vigo.

P. Frs. La Fontaine.

Ant. Lasselle.

H. Lasselle.

Jn. Beau Bien.

David Jones, chaplain U. S. S.

Lewis Beaufait.

R. Lachambre.

Jas. Pepen.

Baties Coutien.

P. Navarre.

  Sworn interpreters:

Wm. Wells.

Jacques Lasselle.

M. Morins.

Bt. Sans Crainte.

Christopher Miller.

Robert Wilson.

Abraham Williams, his x mark.

Isaac Zane, his x mark.

TREATY OF ST. LOUIS (1804)

A treaty between the United States of America and the United tribes of Sac and Fox Indians.

Nov. 3, 1804.
7 Stat., 84.
Ratified Jan. 25, 1805.
Proclaimed Feb. 21, 1805.

Articles of a treaty made at St. Louis in the district of Louisiana between William Henry Harrison, governor of the Indiana territory and of the district of Louisiana, superintendent of Indian affairs for the said territory and district, and commissioner plenipotentiary of the United States for concluding any treaty or treaties which may be found necessary with any of the north western tribes of Indians of the one part, and the chiefs and head men of the united Sac and Fox tribes of the other part.

Article 1.

Indians taken under protection of United States.

The United States receive the united Sac and Fox tribes into their friendship and protection, and the said tribes agree to consider themselves under the protection of the United States, and of no other power whatsoever.

Article 2.

Boundaries.

The general boundary line between the lands of the United States and of the said Indian tribes shall be as follows, to wit: Beginning at a point on the Missouri river opposite to the mouth of the Gasconade river; thence in a direct course so as to strike the river Jeffreon at the distance of thirty miles from its mouth, and down the said Jeffreon to the Mississippi, thence up the Mississippi to the mouth of the Ouisconsing river and up the same to a point which shall be thirty-six miles in a direct line from the mouth of the said river, thence by a direct line to the point where the Fox river (a branch of the Illinois) leaves the small lake called Sakaegan, thence down the Fox river to the Illinois river, and down the same to the Mississippi. And the said tribes, for and in consideration of the friendship and protection of the United States which is now extended to them, of the goods (to the value of two thousand two hundred and thirty-four dollars and fifty cents) which are now delivered, and of the annuity herein-after stipulated to be paid, do hereby cede and relinquish forever to the United States, all the lands included within the above-described boundary.

Article 3.

Goods to be delivered to the Indian tribes at St. Louis every year.

In consideration of the cession and relinquishment of land made in the preceding article, the United States will deliver to the said tribes at the town of St. Louis or some other convenient place on the Mississippi yearly and every year goods suited to the circumstances of the Indians of the value of one thousand dollars (six hundred of which are intended for the Sacs and four hundred for the Foxes) reckoning that value at the first cost of the goods in the city or place in the United States where they shall be procured. And if the said tribes shall hereafter at an annual delivery of the goods aforesaid, desire that a part of their annuity should be furnished in domestic animals, implements of husbandry and other utensils convenient for them, or in compensation to useful artificers who may reside with or near them, and be employed for their benefit, the same shall at the subsequent annual delivery be furnished accordingly.

Article 4.

Indians to be secured in their possessions, etc.

The United States will never interrupt the said tribes in the possession of the lands which they rightfully claim, but will on the contrary protect them in the quiet enjoyment of the same against their own citizens and against all other white persons who may intrude upon them. And the said tribes do hereby engage that they will never sell their lands or any part thereof to any sovereign power, but the United States, nor to the citizens or subjects of any other sovereign power, nor to the citizens of the United States.

Article 5.

Retaliation restrained.
Offenders on both sides to be apprehended and punished.
Stolen horses to be restored to the proper owner.

Lest the friendship which is now established between the United States and the said Indian tribes should be interrupted by the misconduct of individuals, it is hereby agreed that for injuries done by individuals no private revenge or retaliation shall take place, but, instead thereof, complaints shall be made by the party injured to the other—by the said tribes or either of them to the superintendent of Indian affairs or one of his deputies, and by the superintendent or other person appointed by the President, to the chiefs of the said tribes. And it shall be the duty of the said chiefs upon complaint being made as aforesaid to deliver up the person or persons against whom the complaint is made, to the end that he or they may be punished agreeably to the laws of the state or territory where the offence may have been committed; and in like manner if any robbery, violence or murder shall be committed on any Indian or Indians belonging to the said tribes or either of them, the person or persons so offending shall be tried, and if found guilty, punished in the like manner as if the injury had been done to a white man. And it is further agreed, that the chiefs of the said tribes shall, to the utmost of their power exert themselves to recover horses or other property which may be stolen from any citizen or citizens of the United States by any individual or individuals of their tribes, and the property so recovered shall be forthwith delivered to the superintendent or other person authorized to receive it, that it may be restored to the proper owner; and in cases where the exertions of the chiefs shall be ineffectual in recovering the property stolen as aforesaid, if sufficient proof can be obtained that such property was actually stolen by any Indian or Indians belonging to the said tribes or either of them, the United States may deduct from the annuity of the said tribes a sum equal to the value of the property which has been stolen. And the United States hereby guarantee to any Indian or Indians of the said tribes a full indemnification for any horses or other property which may be stolen from them by any of their citizens; provided that the property so stolen cannot be recovered and that sufficient proof is produced that it was actually stolen by a citizen of the United States.

Article 6.

Intruders on Indian lands to be removed.

If any citizen of the United States or other white person should form a settlement upon lands which are the property of the Sac and Fox tribes, upon complaint being made thereof to the superintendent or other person having charge of the affairs of the Indians, such intruder shall forthwith be removed.

Article 7.

Indians may hunt on lands ceded to United States.

As long as the lands which are now ceded to the United States remain their property, the Indians belonging to the said tribes, shall enjoy the privilege of living and hunting upon them.

Article 8.

None but authorized traders to reside among the Saukes and Foxes.

As the laws of the United States regulating trade and intercourse with the Indian tribes, are already extended to the country inhabited by the Saukes and Foxes, and as it is provided by those laws that no person shall reside as a trader in the Indian country without a license under the hand [and] seal of the superintendent of Indian affairs, or other person appointed for the purpose by the President, the said tribes do promise and agree that they will not suffer any trader to reside amongst them without such license; and that they will from time to time give notice to the superintendent or to the agent for their tribes of all the traders that may be in their country.

Article 9.

Trading house or factory to be established.

In order to put a stop to the abuses and impositions which are practiced upon the said tribes by the private traders, the United States will at a convenient time establish a trading house or factory where the individuals of the said tribes can be supplied with goods at a more reasonable rate than they have been accustomed to procure them.

Article 10.

Peace to be made between certain tribes under the direction of United States.

In order to evince the sincerity of their friendship and affection for the United States and a respectful deference for their advice by an act which will not only be acceptable to them but to the common Father of all the nations of the earth; the said tribes do hereby solemnly promise and agree that they will put an end to the bloody war which has heretofore raged between their tribes and those of the Great and Little Osages. And for the purpose of burying the tomahawk and renewing the friendly intercourse between themselves and the Osages, a meeting of their respective chiefs shall take place, at which under the direction of the above-named commissioner or the agent of Indian affairs residing at St. Louis, an adjustment of all their differences shall be made and peace established upon a firm and lasting basis.

Article 11.

Cession of land for the establishment of a military post.
Traders, etc., to be free from any toll or exaction.

As it is probable that the government of the United States will establish a military post at or near the mouth of the Ouisconsing river; and as the land on the lower side of the river may not be suitable for that purpose, the said tribes hereby agree that a fort may be built either on the upper side of the Ouisconsing or on the right bank of the Mississippi, as the one or the other may be found most convenient; and a tract of land not exceeding two miles square shall be given for that purpose. And the said tribes do further agree, that they will at all times allow to traders and other persons travelling through their country under the authority of the United States a free and safe passage for themselves and their property of every description. And that for such passage they shall at no time and on no account whatever be subject to any toll or exaction.

Article 12.

Treaty, when to take effect.

This treaty shall take effect and be obligatory on the contracting parties as soon as the same shall have been ratified by the President by and with the advice and consent of the Senate of the United States.

In testimony whereof, the said William Henry Harrison, and the chiefs and head men of the said Sac and Fox tribes, have hereunto set their hands and affixed their seals.

Done at Saint Louis, in the district of Louisiana, on the third day of November, one thousand eight hundred and four, and of the independence of the United States the twenty-ninth.

William Henry Harrison, ...[L. S.]

Layauvois, or Laiyurva, his x mark, ...[L. S.]

Pashepaho, or the giger, his x mark, ...[L. S.]

Quashquame, or jumping fish, his x mark, ...[L. S.]

Outchequaka, or sun fish, his x mark, ...[L. S.]

Hahshequarhiqua, or the bear, his x mark, ...[L. S.]

In presence of (the words "a branch of the Illinois," in the third line of the second article, and the word "forever," in the fifth line of the same article, being first interlined)—

Wm. Prince, secretary to the commissioner,

John Griffin, one of the judges of the Indiana Territory,

J. Bruff, major artillery, United States,

Amos Stoddard, captain, Corps Artillerists,

P. Chouteau,

Vigo,

S. Warrel, lieutenant, United States Artillery,

D. Delamay.

Joseph Barron,

Hypolite Bolen, his x mark,

    Sworn interpreters.

Additional Article.

It is agreed that nothing in this treaty contained, shall affect the claim of any individual or individuals who may have obtained grants of land from the Spanish government, and which are not included within the general boundary line laid down in this treaty, provided that such grant have at any time been made known to the said tribes and recognized by them.

TREATY OF PRAIRIE DU CHIEN (1829)

Articles of a treaty made and concluded at Prairie du Chien, in the Territory of Michigan, between the United States of America, by their Commissioners, General John McNeil, Colonel Pierre Menard, and Caleb Atwater, Esq, and the United Nations of Chippewa, Ottawa, and Potawatamie Indians, of the waters of the Illinois, Milwaukee and Manitoouck Rivers.

July 29, 1829.
7 Stat., 320.
Proclamation, Jan. 2, 1830.

Article I.

Certain lands ceded to United States.

The aforesaid nations of Chippewa, Ottawa, and Potawatamie Indians, do hereby cede to the United States aforesaid, all the lands comprehended within the following limits, to wit: Beginning at the Winnebago Village, on Rock river, forty miles from its mouth, and running thence down the Rock river, to a line which runs due west from the most southern bend of Lake Michigan to the Mississippi river, and with that line to the Mississippi river opposite to Rock Island; thence, up that river, to the United States' reservation at the mouth of the Ouisconsin; thence, with the south and east lines of said reservation, to the Ouisconsin river; thence, southerly, passing the heads of the small streams emptying into the Mississippi, to the Rock River aforesaid, at the Winnebago Village, the place of beginning. And, also, one other tract of land, described as follows, to wit: Beginning on the Western Shore of Lake Michigan, at the northeast corner of the field of Antoine Ouitmette, who lives near Gross Pointe, about twelve miles north of Chicago; thence, running due west, to the Rock River, aforesaid; thence, down the said river, to where a line drawn due west from the most southern bend of Lake Michigan crosses said river; thence, east, along said line, to the Fox River of the Illinois; thence, along the northwestern boundary line of the cession of 1816, to Lake Michigan; thence, northwardly, along the Western Shore of said Lake, to the place of beginning.

Article II.

Consideration therefor.

In consideration of the aforesaid cessions of land, the United States aforesaid agree to pay to the aforesaid nations of Indians the sum of sixteen thousand dollars, annually, forever, in specie: said sum to be paid at Chicago. And the said United States further agree to cause to be delivered to said nations of Indians, in the month of October next, twelve thousand dollars worth of goods as a present. And it is further agreed, to deliver to said Indians, at Chicago, fifty barrels of salt, annually, forever; and further, the United States agree to make permanent, for the use of the said Indians, the black-smith's establishment at Chicago.

Article III.

Certain lands reserved.

From the cessions aforesaid, there shall be reserved, for the use of the undernamed Chiefs and their bands, the following tracts of land, viz:

For *Wau-pon-eh-see,* five sections of land at the Grand Bois, on Fox River of the Illinois, where *Shaytee's* Village now stands.

For *Shab-eh-nay,* two sections at his village near the Paw-paw Grove. For *Awn-kote,* four sections at the village of *Saw-meh-naug,* on the Fox River of the Illinois.

Article IV.

Certain tracts to be granted to certain descendants from the Indians.

There shall be granted by the United States, to each of the following persons, (being descendants from Indians,) the following tracts of land, viz: To Claude Laframboise, one section of land on the Riviere aux Pleins, adjoining the line of the purchase of 1816.

To François Bourbonné, Jr. one section at the Missionary establishment, on the Fox River of the Illinois. To Alexander Robinson, for himself and children, two sections on the Riviere aux Pleins, above and adjoining the tract herein granted to Claude Laframboise. To Pierre Leclerc, one section at the village of the As-sim-in-eh-Kon, or Paw-paw Grove. To Waish-kee-Shaw, a Potawatamie woman, wife of David Laughton, and to her child, one and a half sections at the old village of Nay-ou-Say, at or near the source of the Riviere aux Sables of the Illinois. To Billy Caldwell, two and a half sections on the Chicago River, above and adjoining the line of the purchase of 1816. To Victoire Pothier, one half section on the Chicago River, above and adjoining the tract of land herein granted to Billy Caldwell. To Jane Miranda, one quarter section on the Chicago River, above and adjoining the tract herein granted to Victoire Pothier. To Madeline, a Potawatamie woman, wife of Joseph Ogee, one section west of and adjoining the tract herein granted to Pierre Leclerc, at the Paw-paw Grove. To Archange Ouilmette, a Potawatamie woman, wife of Antoine Ouilmette, two sections, for herself and her children, on Lake Michigan, south of and adjoining the northern boundary of the cession herein made by the Indians aforesaid to the United States. To Antoine and François Leclerc, one section each, lying on the Mississippi River, north of and adjoining the line drawn due west from the most southern bend of Lake Michigan, where said line strikes the

Mississippi River. To Mo-ah-way, one quarter section on the north side of and adjoining the tract herein granted to Waish-Kee-Shaw. The tracts of land herein stipulated to be granted, shall never be leased or conveyed by the grantees, or their heirs, to any persons whatever, without the permission of the President of the United States.

Article V.

United States to pay claims against Indians.

The United States, at the request of the Indians aforesaid, further agree to pay to the persons named in the schedule annexed to this treaty, the sum of eleven thousand six hundred and one dollars; which sum is in full satisfaction of the claims brought by said persons against said Indians, and by them acknowledged to be justly due.

Article VI.

United States to survey boundary line of cession.

And it is further agreed, that the United [States] shall, at their own expense, cause to be surveyed, the northern boundary line of the cession herein made, from Lake Michigan to the Rock River, as soon as practicable after the ratification of this treaty, and shall also cause good and sufficient marks and mounds to be established on said line.

Article VII.

Right to hunt reserved.

The right to hunt on the lands herein ceded, so long as the same shall remain the property of the United States, is hereby secured to the nations who are parties to this treaty.

Article VIII.

Treaty binding when ratified.

This treaty shall take effect and be obligatory on the contracting parties, as soon as the same shall be ratified by the President of the United States, by and with the advice and consent of the Senate thereof.

In testimony whereof, the said John NcNiel, Pierre Menard, and Caleb Atwater, commissioners as aforesaid, and the chiefs and warriors of the said Chippewa, Ottawa, and Potawatamie nations, have hereunto set their hands and seals, at Prairie du Chein, as aforesaid, this twenty-ninth day of July, in the year of our Lord one thousand eight hundred and twenty-nine.

John McNiel, ...[L. S.]

Pierre Menard, ...[L. S.]

Caleb Atwater,
Commissioners. . . . .[L. S.]

Sin-eh-pay-nim, his x mark, .[L. S.]

Kawb-suk-we, his x mark, . . .[L. S.]

Wau-pon-eh-see, his x mark, .[L. S.]

Naw-geh-say, his x mark, ...[L. S.]

Shaw-a-nay-see, his x mark, . .[L. S.]

Naw-geh-to-nuk, his x mark, [L. S.]

Meek-say-mauk, his x mark, .[L. S.]

Kaw-gaw-gay-shee, his
x mark, ...[L. S.]

Maw-geh-set, his x mark, . . .[L. S.]

Meck-eh-so, his x mark, ...[L. S.]

Awn-kote, his x mark, ...[L. S.]

Shuk-eh-nay-buk, his
x mark, ...[L. S.]

Sho-men, his x mark, ...[L. S.]

Nay-a-mush, his x mark, ...[L. S.]

Pat-eh-ko-zuk, his x mark, . .[L. S.]

Mash-kak-suk, his x mark, . . .[L. S.]

Pooh-kin-eh-naw, his x mark, [L. S.]

Waw-kay-zo, his x mark, ...[L. S.]

Sou-ka-mock, his x mark, ...[L. S.]

Chee-chee-pin-quay, his
x mark, ...[L. S.]

Man-eh-bo-zo, his x mark, ...[L. S.]

Shah-way-ne-be-nay, his
x mark, ...[L. S.]

Kaw-kee, his x mark, ...[L. S.]

To-rum, his x mark, ...[L. S.]

Nah-yah-to-shuk, his
x mark, ...[L. S.]

Mee-chee-kee-wis, his
x mark, ...[L. S.]

Es-kaw-bey-wis, his x mark, ...[L. S.]

Wau-pay-kay, his x mark, ...[L. S.]

Michel, his x mark, ...[L. S.]

Nee-kon-gum, his x mark, ...[L. S.]

Mes-quaw-be-no-quay, her
x mark, ...[L. S.]

Pe-i-tum, her x mark, ...[L. S.]

Kay-wau, her x mark, ...[L. S.]

Wau-kaw-ou-say, her x mark, ...[L. S.]

Shem-naw, her x mark. . . . .[L. S.]

In presence of—

Charles Hempstead, secretary to the commission,

Alex. Wolcott, Indian agent,

Jos. M. Street, Indian agent,

Thomas Forsyth, Indian agent,

A. Hill,

Henry Gratiot,

Richard Gentry,

John Messersmith,

Wm. P. Smith,

John H. Kinzie, subagent Indian affairs,

R. B. Mason, captain, First Infantry,

John Garland, major, U. S. Army,

H. Dodge,

Jesse Benton, Jr.,

J. L. Bogardus,

Antoine Le Claire, Indian interpreter,

Jon. W. B. Mette, Indian interpreter,

C. Chouteau,   Sogee,

James Turney,   John W. Johnson.

Z. Taylor, Lieutenant-Colonel
U.S. Army,

Schedule of claims and debts to be paid by the United States for the Chippewa, Ottawa, and Pottawatamie Indians, under the fifth article of the treaty of the 29th July, 1829, with said tribe.

July 29, 1829.
7 Stat., 604.

To Francis Laframboise, for a canoe-load of merchandise taken by the Chippewa and Ottowata Indians of Chab-way-way-gun and the neighboring villages, while frozen up in the lake in the winter of the year 1799, two thousand dollars **$2,000 00**

To Antoine Ouilmett, for depredations committed on him by the Indians at the time of the massacre of Chicago and during the war, eight hundred dollars **800 00**

To the heirs of the late John Kinzie, of Chicago, for depredations committed on him at the time of the massacre of Chicago and at St. Joseph's, during the winter of 1812, three thousand five hundred dollars **3,500 00**

To Margaret Helm, for losses sustained at the time of the capture of Fort Dearborn, in 1812, by the Indians, eight hundred dollars **800 00**

To the American Fur Company, for debts owed to them by the United Tribes of Chippewas, Ottowas, and Pottawatamies, three thousand dollars **3,000 00**

To Bernardus Laughton, for debts owed to him by same tribes, ten hundred and sixteen dollars **1,016 00**

To James Kinzie, for debts owed to him by same, four hundred and eighty-five dollars **485 00**
                                                          $11,601 00

MERIWETHER LEWIS AND WILLIAM CLARK

(1774–1809 and 1770–1838)

In the years after the United States won its independence from Great Britain, Thomas Jefferson recognized the importance of exploring the west. He was motivated, in part, by practical concerns: It was vital that his country gain a foothold lest France or Britain or some other country should establish colonies there. Jefferson was motivated as well by the Enlightenment value of knowledge: What might western exploration discover of practical use? Jefferson initiated three early expeditions, all of which ended in failure. The last of these came in 1793, when Jefferson learned that his man in the field, botanist André Michaux, was a secret agent for France.

For the next decade, Jefferson seemed to give up on the west, but then a young man named Alexander Mackenzie lit a spark. Setting out from Fort Fork (near the Peace River in western Canada), Mackenzie and his party crossed the Continental Divide and eventually made their way to the Strait of Georgia. There he wrote on a rock, "Alexander Mackenzie, from Canada, by land, the twenty-second of July, one thousand seven hundred and ninety-three."

News of Mackenzie's journey did not reach now-President Jefferson until after a narrative of the explorer's exploits was published in London in 1801. Jefferson did not receive his copy until the summer of 1802. Upon reading the book, Jefferson had the consolation of learning that Mackenzie had not found a practical trade route—that is, a navigable waterway—through the west. Book in hand, Jefferson began planning yet another western expedition, now with a sense of urgency. This time he worked with the conviction that he had the right man to oversee the mission: his personal secretary, Meriwether Lewis. In fact, Lewis had volunteered to lead the ill-fated Michaux expedition, but Jefferson had passed over the eighteen-year-old. Now Lewis was nearly thirty, and Jefferson thought him ready for the challenge.

Meriwether Lewis and his eventual partner, William Clark, came from similar backgrounds. Both were born in Virginia to well-off but not well-to-do families. Neither Lewis nor Clark had much education, though Lewis had some private tutoring as a boy. Jefferson explained his choice of Lewis for the job: "It was impossible to find a character who to a compleat science in botany, natural history, mineralogy & astronomy, joined the firmness of constitution & character, prudence, habits adapted to the woods, & a familiarity with the Indian manners & character, requisite for this undertaking. All of the latter qualifications Capt. Lewis has." Jefferson tried to make up for Lewis's lack of education with a year of personal instruction before the journey began.

As young men, both Lewis and Clark ended up in the army where they met and became friends. Clark left the army in 1796 to help his family. Lewis was summoned from the army in 1801 to become the president's private secretary. When Clark came to Washington to visit Lewis in 1802, he met Jefferson as well. Jefferson may then have mentioned the possibility of his joining Lewis on the expedition. Clark wrote to Lewis, when he accepted the job the next year, "The enterprise &c. is Such as I have long anticipated."

In May 1804, Lewis and Clark embarked up the Missouri River on a journey that would last twenty-eight months over the course of which they would write more than a million words. Their journals were a central part of their mission. Lewis and Clark had specific instructions from Jefferson to record most everything they saw from flora and fauna to soil and rainfall to the Indians and their nations to volcanoes and dinosaur bones. All this, of course, in addition to the possibility of finding a viable trade route.

Though there was only one death—probably from appendicitis— among the twenty-five men whom Lewis and Clark enlisted for their expedition, the going was often rough. Some nights the men would wake up choking on mosquitoes; other nights the men would sleep standing rather than lie on the rain-flooded ground. Despite such conditions, morale remained mostly high and there were only two desertions. After winding up the Missouri, the expedition crossed the Rocky Mountains and traveled the Snake and Columbia rivers to the coast. They reached the Pacific Ocean in November 1805.

The selection that follows, from a week early in Clark's journal, finds the explorers making their way across present-day Missouri. The text is from Reuben Gold Thwaites's 1904 edition *Original Journals of the Lewis and Clark Expedition, 1804–1806*. The bracketed clarifications in the journal entries are by Thwaites.

Text: *Original Journals of the Lewis and Clark Expedition, 1804–1806*, vol. 1 (New York, 1904): 46–52.

FROM *ORIGINAL JOURNALS OF THE LEWIS AND CLARK EXPEDITION, 1804–1806*

[William Clark]

12ᵗʰ June. Tuesday 1804

Set out early passed Some bad Placies, and a Small Creek on the L. S. called *plumb Creek* at abᵗ. 1 Mˡ. at 1 oClock we brought too [to,] two Chaussies on loaded with furs & Pelteries, the other with Greece [*buffalow grease & tallow*] we purchased 300ˡᵇˢ of Greese, and finding that old Mʳ. Durioun was of the party we questioned him un-till it was too late to Go further, and Concluded to Camp for the night, those people inform nothing of much information.

Concluded to take old Durioun [*who went acc'*] back as fur as the Soux nation with a view to get some of their Chiefs to visit the Presdᵗ. of the United S. (This man being a verry confidential friend of those people, he haveing resided with the Nation 20 odd years) and to accompany them on [Sentence incomplete.—Eᴅ.]

Course & Distance June 12ᵗʰ
    N. 25° W. 3½ Mˢ. to L. S. passed Plumb C.
    N 70 W 2½ Mˢ. to pᵗ. on S. S.
    N. 60° W 3 Mˢ. to pᵗ. on S. S.
         ──
         9

13ᵗʰ June Wednesday 1804—

We Set out early passed a round bend to the S. S. and two Creeks Called the round bend Creeks between those two Creeks and behind a Small Willow Island in the bend is a Prarie in which the Missouries Indians once lived and the Spot where 300 [*200*] of them fell a sacrifise to the fury of the *Saukees,* this nation (Missouries) once the most numerous nation in this part of the Continent now reduced to about 30 fᵉˢ [fires, i.e., families—Eᴅ.] and that fiew under the protection of the *Otteaus* [*Ottoes*] on R Platt who themselves are declining, passed some willow Isᵈˢ. and bad Sand bars, Took Medⁿ. Altitude with Octent back observation it gave for altᵈ. on its Loʷ L. 36° 58′ 0″ the E [Error] Enstrement 2° 00′ − 00″ +. the Hills or high land for Several days past or above the 2 Charletons does not exceed 100 foot, passed a Batteau on Sand rolling where the Boat was nearly turning over by her Strikeing & turning on the Sand. We came too in the mouth of Grand River on S. S. and Camped for the night, this River is from 80 to 100 yards wide at its mouth and navagable for Perogues a great distance, this river heads with the R. Dumoine, below its mouth is a butifull Plain of bottom land, the hills rise at 1/2 a mile back, the lands about this place is either Plain or over flown bottom. Capᵗ Lewis and myself walked to the hill, from the top of which we had a butifull prospect of Serounding countrey, in the open Prarie we caught a racoon, our hunter brought in a Bear & Deer, we took some Lunar observations this evening.

Course & Distance 13ᵗʰ June 1804
    N. 40° W 2½ Mˢ. to a pᵗ. L. S.

S. 39   W. 3   M^s. to a p^t. S. S. ps^d. 2 Creeks
N. 28, W   1½   M^s. to a p^t. Stb^d. S.
N. 30   W   2   M^s. to a p^t. L. S. ops^d. G^d. R
           ___
           9 M^s.

14th June Thursday—

We Set out at 6 oClock, after a thick fog passed thro: a narrow pass on the S. S. which forms a large Is^d. opposit the upper point of this Island on the L. S. is one of the worst quick or moveing sand bars Which I have Seen, notwithstanding all our precaustons to Clear the Sands and pass between them (which was the way we were comp^d. to pass, from the immence Current & falling banks on the S. S.) the Boat Struck the point of one from the active exertions of the men, prevented her turning, if She had turned she must have overset. We met a *Causseu* [Cajaux, or raft—ED.] from the Pania [Paunee] on the River Platt, we detained 2 hours with a view of engageing one of the hands to go to the Pania nation with a view to get those people to meet us on the river, (I went out & Shot a Deer) We passed a high land, & clay bluff on the S. S. Called the Snake bluff from the number of Snakes about this place, we passed a Creek above the Bluff about 18 yd^s. wide, this Creek is Called Snake Creek, a bad Sand bar just below, which we found Dificullty in passing & Camp^d. above, our Hunters came in. George Drewyer, gives the following ac^t. of a Pond, & at ab^t. 5 Miles below here S. S. Passed a Small Lake in which there was many Deer feeding. he heard in this Pond a Snake makeing goubleing noises like a turkey. he fired his gun & the noise was increased, he has heard the indians mention this Species of Snake, one Frenchman gives a Similar account

Course & Distance June 14th
    S. 33°   W   2   M^s. to Low^r. p^t. on an Is^d. S. S.
    S. 60°   W   1   M^l. thro: a chanil on S. S.
    S. 70°   W   2   M^s. to p^t. L. S. passed a bad Sand
    S. 5   E   3   M^s. to a p^t. on S. S. passed a Creek S. S.
            ___
             8

15th June, Friday 1804—

Set out early and had not proceeded far e'er we wheeled on a Sawyer which was near injuring us verry much, passed a plain on the L. S. a Small Is^d. in the middle, the river riseing, water verry swift Passed a Creek on the L. S. passed between two Islands, a verry bad place, moveing Sands, we were nearly being swallowed up by the rolling Sands over which the Current was so Strong that we could not Stem it with our Sales under a Stiff breese in addition to our ores, we were compelled to pass under a bank which was falling in, and use the Toe rope occasionally, Continued up pass two other Small Islands and Camped on the S. S. nearly opposit the *antient Village* of the *Little Osarges* and below the ant.^{t} *Village* of the *Missouries* both Situations in view and within three M^s. of each other, the Osage were Settled at the foot [of] a hill in a butifull Plain, which extends back quite to the Osage River, in front of the Vilg: next to the river is an ellegent bottom Plain which extends several miles in length on the river in this low Prarie the *Missouries* lived after they were reduced by the *Saukees* at their Town Some Dist^e. below. The little osage finding themselves much oppressed by the Saukees & other nations, left this place & built a village 5 M^s. from the Grand *Osarge Town,* about   years ago a fiew of the Missouries accompanied them, the remainder of that Nation went to the Otteaus on the River Platt. The River at this place is about 3 [*one*] M^s. wide. our hunters did not come in this evening the river beginning to fall

Course & Distance June 15th
    S. 35°   W. 2   M^s. along S. S.
    S. 50°   W. 1½   M^s. p^t. L. S. passed a pra: & Creek L. S.
    S. 51°   W. 2½   M^s. a p^t. S. S. ps^d. a Willow Is^d.
    S. 8°   W. 3/4 M^s. to a p^t. L. S. pass^d. Low p^t. 2 Isd^s.
    S. 80°   W. 2   M^s. to up^r. P^t. Is^d. S. S. ps^d. bad place
    S. 5°   W. 2   M^s. to a p^t. S. S. passed bad place
    S. 12°   W. 1½   M^s. to a p^t. S. S. ps^d. a Is^d. in Mid^l ops^d. old village
               ——
               12¼   Lit: Osage.

16th June Satturday 1804—
Set out at 7 oClock at about a mile ½ we came to the Camp of our hunters, they had two Bear & two Deer, proceeded on pass a Island on the S. S. a heavy rain came on & lasted a Short time, we came to on the S. S. in a Prarie at the place where M^r. Mackey lais down a old french fort, I could See no traces of a Settlement of any kind, in the plain I discovered a kind of Grass resembling Timothey which appeared well Calculated for Hay. this Plain is verry extensive in the evening I walked on the S. S. to see if any timber was conv^t. to make Oars, which we were much in want of, I found some indifferent timber and Struck the river above the Boat at a bad Sand bar, the worst I had Seen which the boat must pass or Drop back Several Miles & Stem a Swift Current on the ops^d. side of an Is^d. the Boat however assended the middle of the Streem which was difficult Dangerious We came to above this place at Dark and Camped in a bad place, the Mosquitoes and Ticks are noumerous & bad.

Course & Distance June 16th
    N. 68°   W. 2½   M^s. to a p^t. L. S. pass Is^d. S. S.
    West   2   M^s. to a ^{lg}. in Snag Is^d. L. S.
    S. 85   W. 1   M^l. on L. S. a bad Sand Mid.
    S. 61   W. 1   M^l. on L.S.   do   do   and 2 sm. Is^{ds}
    S. 30   W. 2½   M^s to a p^t. S. S. passed up^r. S^d. Is^{ds}.
    S. 40   W   1   M^l. alg. S. S. an Is^d. Md^l. & bad p^s
               ——
               10

June 17th Sunday 1804 (S. 65° W. 1 M^l. S. Side.)—
Cloudy morning wind from the S. E we Set out early and proceeded on one mile & came too to make oars, & repair our cable & toe rope &c. &c. which was necessary for the Boat & Perogues, Sent out Sj^t. Pryor and Some men to get ash timber for ores, and Set some men to make a Toe Rope out of the Cords of a *Cable* which had been provided by Capt. Lewis at Pittsburg for the Cable of the boat. George Drewyer our hunter and one man came in with 2 Deer & a Bear, also a young Horse, they had found in the Prarie, this horse has been in the Prarie a long time and is fat, I Suppose, he has been left by Some war party against the *Osage,* This is a Crossing place for the war parties against that nation from the *Saukees, Aiaouez,* [*Ayauways*] & *Souix.* The

party is much aflicted with *Boils,* and Several have the Deassentary, which I contribute
to the water [*which is muddy.*] The Countrey about this place is butifull on the river
rich & well timbered on the S. S. about two miles back a Prarie com^s. [commences]
which is rich and interspursed with groves of timber, the count^y rises at 7 or 8 miles
Still further back and is rolling. on the L. S. the high lands & Prarie com^s. in the bank
of the river and and continus back, well watered and abounds in Deer Elk & Bear The
Ticks & Musquiters are verry troublesome.

June 18th Monday

Some rain last night, and Some hard Showers this morning which delay our work
verry much, Send out Six hunters in the Prairie on the L. S. they kill 5 Deer & Coht
[caught] a Bear, which verry large & fat, the party to wok at the oars, make rope, &
jurk their meat all Day Dry our wet Sales &c. in the evening, The Musquiters verry
bad

13

BLACK HAWK (MA-KA-TAI-ME-SHE-KIA-KIAK)

(1767–1838)

Both Black Hawk and the book he narrated about himself have long and complicated histories, each revealing much about the cultural and racial politics of the antebellum west. Black Hawk himself was born a Sauk on the Rock River in what is now western Illinois. At the time, the territory was only recently in British hands, after decades of French alliance. The Spanish occupied the region's largest population center, St. Louis. During the American Revolution, the Sauk allied themselves with the British and stayed largely in their employ through the War of 1812. Black Hawk, as war chief, aligned himself with Tecumseh, and, in fact, claimed to have been with the Shawnee leader at his death at the Battle of Malden.

In 1831, after sixteen years of relative calm, the Sauk were displaced from their village at the mouth of the Rock River, which broke the disputed Treaty of St. Louis (1804). Many of the Sauk followed Keokuk, accepted removal, and moved to Iowa. Black Hawk and his band, however, resisted the move, and the subsequent Black Hawk War, which Black Hawk conducted having been lied to about British support, began. After some initial success, Black Hawk was captured, forced to surrender, and, ultimately, taken on a tour of the eastern cities to be awed and intimidated by the whites' civilization.

Upon his exile to Iowa, Black Hawk narrated his life story to Antoine Le Clair, a prominent mixed-race leader, who translated it for John B. Patterson, who edited it for subsequent publication in Cincinnati. The layers of translation and transcription put the authenticity of the text in doubt until 1964, when Donald Jackson edited a new edition and established the reliability of Le Clair and Patterson and the faithfulness of their work. The sections reproduced here refer to the period between the War of 1812 and the commencement of the Black Hawk War. During these years, under the terms of the 1804 treaty, Black Hawk's band remained in their village and tolerated the unlawful white settlement of lands that were still theirs. Black Hawk also describes a visit to his village by James Hall and Thomas Cole, deposed Whig politicians who confessed their inability to maintain the status quo now that Removalists were in office. In the end, Hall could aid Black Hawk only by helping his autobiography find its way to publication and by contributing to Benjamin Drake's sympathetic biography. In the end, Black Hawk must be understood as more than merely a native voice; he represents the preremoval west in many ways that transcend race.

Text: *Black Hawk: An Autobiography* (Cincinnati, 1833; rpt. Urbana, Illinois: 1964, ed. Donald Jackson): 82–113.

FROM *THE LIFE OF BLACK HAWK* (1833)

Soon after I returned from my wintering ground, we received information that *peace* had been made between the British and Americans, and that *we* were required to make peace also—and were invited to go down to Portage des Sioux, for that purpose. Some advised that we should go down—others that we should not. No-mite, our principal civil chief, said he would go, as soon as the Foxes came down from the Mines. They came, and we all started from Rock river. We had not gone far, before our chief was taken sick. We stopped with him at the village on Henderson river. The Foxes went on, and we were to follow as soon as our chief got better; but he continued to get worse, and died. His brother now became the principal chief. He refused to go down—saying, that if he started, he would be taken sick and die, as his brother had done—which was reasonable! We all concluded, that none of us would go at this time.

The Foxes returned. They said they "had smoked the *pipe of peace* with the Americans, and expected that a war party would be sent against us, because we did not go down. This I did not believe; as the Americans had always *lost* by their war parties that came against us.

La Gutrie, and other British traders, arrived at our village on Rock river, in the fall. La Gutrie told us, that we must go down and make peace—that it was the wish of our English father. He said he wished us to go down to the Two-River country to winter—where game was plenty, as there had been no hunting there for several years.

Having heard that a principal war chief, with troops, had come up, and commenced building a fort near Rapids des Moines, we consented to go down with the traders, to see the American chief, and tell him the reason why we had not been down sooner. We arrived at the head of the rapids. Here the traders left their goods and boats, except one, in which they accompanied us to the Americans. We visited the war chief, (he was on board of a boat,) and told him what we had to say—explaining the reason we had not been down sooner. He appeared angry, and talked to La Gutrie for some time. I inquired of him, what the war chief said? He told me that he was threatening to hang him up on the yard-arm of his boat. "But," said he, "I am not afraid of what he says. He dare not put his threats into execution. I have done no more than I had a right to do, as a British subject."

I then addressed the chief, asking permission for ourselves and some Menomonees, to go down to the Two-River country to hunt. He said, *we* might go down, but must return before the ice made, as he did not intend that we should winter below the fort. "But," said he, "what do you want the Menomonees to go with you for?" I did not know, at first, what reply to make—but told him that they had a great many *pretty squaws* with them, and we wished them to go with us on that account! He consented. We all started down the river, and remained *all winter,* as we had no intention of returning before spring, when we asked leave to go. We made a good hunt. Having loaded our traders' boats with furs and peltries, they started to Mackinac, and we returned to our village.

There is one circumstance which I omitted to mention in its proper place. It does not relate to myself or people, but to my friend Gomo, the Pottowatomie chief. He came to Rock river to pay me a visit. During his stay, he related to me the following story:

"The war chief at Peoria is a very good man; he always speaks the truth, and treats our people well. He sent for me one day, and told me that he was nearly out of provision, and wished me to send my young men out to hunt, to supply his fort. I promised to do so; and immediately returned to my camp, and told my young men the wishes and wants of the war chief. They readily agreed to go and hunt for our friend; and soon returned with about twenty deer. They carried them to the fort, laid them down at the gate, and returned to our camp. A few days afterwards, I went again to the fort to see if they wanted more meat. The chief gave me some powder and lead, and said he wished me to send my hunters out again. When I returned to my camp, and told my young men that the chief wanted more meat, Má-ta-táh, one of my principal braves, said he would take a party and go across the Illinois, about one day's travel, where game was plenty, and make a good hunt for our friend, the war chief. He took eight hunters with him; his wife and several other squaws accompanied them. They had travelled about half the day in the prairie, when they discovered a party of white men coming towards them with a drove of cattle. Our hunters apprehended no danger, or they would have kept out of the way of the whites, (who had not yet perceived them.) Má-ta-táh changed his course, as he wished to meet and speak to the whites. As soon as the whites saw our party, some of them put off at full speed, and came up to our hunters. Má-ta-táh gave up his gun to them, and endeavored to explain to them that he was friendly, and was hunting for the war chief. They were not satisfied with this, but fired at and wounded him. He got into the branch of a tree that had been blown down, to keep the horses from running over him. He was again fired on by several guns and badly wounded. He found that he would be murdered, (if not mortally wounded already,) and sprung at the nearest man to him, seized his gun, and shot him from his horse. He then fell, covered with blood from his wounds, and almost instantly expired!

"The other hunters, being in the rear of Má-ta-táh, seeing that the whites had killed him, endeavored to make their escape. They were pursued, and nearly all the party *murdered!* My youngest brother brought me the news in the night, he having been with the hunters, and got but slightly wounded. He said the whites had abandoned their cattle, and gone back towards the settlement. The remainder of the night was spent in lamenting for the death of our friends. At day-light, I blacked my face, and started to the fort to see the war chief. I met him at the gate, and told him what had happened. His countenance changed; I could see sorrow depicted in it for the death of my people. He tried to persuade me that I was mistaken, as he 'could not believe that the whites would act so cruelly.' But when I convinced him, he told me that those 'cowards who had murdered my people should be punished.' I told him that my people would have *revenge*—that they would not trouble any of his people of the fort, as we did not blame him or any of his soldiers—but that a party of my braves would go towards the Wabash to avenge the death of their friends and relations. The next day I took a party of hunters and killed several deer, and left them at the fort gate as I passed."

Here Gomo ended his story. I could relate many similar ones that have come within my own knowledge and observation; but I dislike to look back and bring on sorrow afresh. I will resume my narrative.

The great chief[1] at St. Louis having sent word for us to go down and confirm the treaty of peace, we did not hesitate, but started immediately, that we might smoke the *peace-pipe* with him. On our arrival, we met the great chiefs in council. They explained to us the words of our Great Father at Washington, accusing us of heinous crimes and divers misdemeanors, particularly in not coming down when first invited. We knew very well that *our Great Father had deceived us,* and thereby *forced* us to join the British, and could not believe that he had put this speech into the mouths of these chiefs to deliver to us. I was not a civil chief, and consequently made no reply: but our chiefs told the commissioners that "what they had said was a *lie!*—that our Great Father had sent no such speech, he knowing the situation in which we had been placed had been *caused by him!*" The white chiefs appeared very angry at this reply, and said they "would break off the treaty with us, and *go to war,* as they would not be insulted."

Our chiefs had no intention of insulting them, and told them so—"that they merely wished to explain to them that *they had told a lie,* without making them angry; in the same manner that the whites do, when they do not believe what is told them!" The council then proceeded, and the pipe of peace was smoked.

Here, for the first time, I touched the goose quill to the treaty—not knowing, however, that, by that act, I consented to give away my village. Had that been explained to me, I should have opposed it, and never would have signed their treaty, as my recent conduct will clearly prove.

What do we know of the manner of the laws and customs of the white people? They might buy our bodies for dissection, and we would touch the goose quill to confirm it, without knowing what we are doing. This was the case with myself and people in touching the goose quill the first time.

We can only judge of what is proper and right by our standard of right and wrong, which differs widely from the whites, if I have been correctly informed. The whites *may do bad* all their lives, and then, if they are *sorry for it* when about to die, *all is well!* But with us it is different: we must continue throughout our lives to do what we conceive to be good. If we have corn and meat, and know of a family that have none, we divide with them. If we have more blankets than sufficient, and others have not enough, we must give to them that want. But I will presently explain our customs, and the manner we live.

We were friendly treated by the white chiefs, and started back to our village on Rock river. Here we found that troops had arrived to build a fort at Rock Island. This, in our opinion, was a contradiction to what we had done—"to prepare for war in time of peace." We did not, however, object to their building the fort on the island, but we were very sorry, as this was the best island on the Mississippi, and had long been the resort of our young people during the summer. It was our garden (like the white people have near to their big villages) which supplied us with strawberries, blackberries, gooseberries, plums, apples, and nuts of different kinds; and its waters

---

1. William Clark.

supplied us with fine fish, being situated in the rapids of the river. In my early life, I spent many happy days on this island. A good spirit had care of it, who lived in a cave in the rocks immediately under the place where the fort now stands, and has often been seen by our people. He was white, with large wings like a *swan's*, but ten times larger. We were particular not to make much noise in that part of the island which he inhabited, for fear of disturbing him. But the noise of the fort has since driven him away, and no doubt a *bad spirit* has taken his place!

Our village was situate on the north side of Rock river, at the foot of its rapids, and on the point of land between Rock river and the Mississippi. In its front, a prairie extended to the bank of the Mississippi; and in our rear, a continued bluff, gently ascending from the prairie. On the side of this bluff we had our corn-fields, extending about two miles up, running parallel with the Mississippi; where we joined those of the Foxes whose village was on the bank of the Mississippi, opposite the lower end of Rock island, and three miles distant from ours. We had about eight hundred acres in cultivation, including what we had on the islands of Rock river. The land around our village, uncultivated, was covered with blue-grass, which made excellent pasture for our horses. Several fine springs broke out of the bluff, near by, from which we were supplied with good water. The rapids of Rock river furnished us with an abundance of excellent fish, and the land, being good, never failed to produce good crops of corn, beans, pumpkins, and squashes. We always had plenty—our children never cried with hunger, nor our people were never in want. Here our village had stood for more than a hundred years, during all which time we were the undisputed possessors of the valley of the Mississippi, from the Ouisconsin to the Portage des Sioux, near the mouth of the Missouri, being about seven hundred miles in length.

At this time we had very little intercourse with the whites, except our traders. Our village was healthy, and there was no place in the country possessing such advantages, nor no hunting grounds better than those we had in possession. If another prophet had come to our village in those days, and told us what has since taken place, none of our people would have believed him. What! to be driven from our village and hunting grounds, and not even permitted to visit the graves of our forefathers, our relations, and friends?

This hardship is not known to the whites. With us it is a custom to visit the graves of our friends, and keep them in repair for many years. The mother will go alone to weep over the grave of her child! The brave, with pleasure, visits the grave of his father, after he has been successful in war, and re-paints the post that shows where he lies! There is no place like that where the bones of our forefathers lie, to go to when in grief. Here the Great Spirit will take pity on us!

But, how different is our situation now, from what it was in those days! Then we were as happy as the buffalo on the plains—but now, we are as miserable as the hungry, howling wolf in the prairie! But I am digressing from my story. Bitter reflection crowds upon my mind, and must find utterance.

When we returned to our village in the spring, from our wintering grounds, we would finish trading with our traders, who always followed us to our village. We purposely kept some of our fine furs for this trade; and, as there was great opposition among them, who should get these skins, we always got our goods cheap. After this trade was over, the traders would give us a few kegs of rum, which was generally promised in the fall, to encourage us to make a good hunt, and not go to war. They would then start with their furs and peltries for their homes. Our old men would take a frolic, (at this time our young men never drank.) When this was ended, the next thing to be done was to bury our dead, (such as had died during the year.) This is a great *medicine feast*. The relations of those who have died, give all the goods they have purchased, as presents to their friends—thereby reducing themselves to poverty, to show the Great Spirit that they are humble, so that he will take pity on them. We would next open the cashes, and take out corn and other provisions, which had been put up in the fall,—and then commence repairing our lodges. As soon as this is accomplished, we repair the fences around our fields, and clean them off, ready for planting corn. This work is done by our women. The men, during this time, are feasting on dried venison, bear's meat, wild fowl, and corn, prepared in different ways; and recounting to each other what took place during the winter.

Our women plant the corn, and as soon as they get done, we make a feast, and dance the *crane* dance, in which they join us, dressed in their best, and decorated with feathers. At this feast our young braves select the young woman they wish to have for a wife. He then informs his mother, who calls on the mother of the girl, when the arrangement is made, and the time appointed for him to come. He goes to the lodge when all are asleep, (or pretend to be,) lights his matches, which have been provided for the purpose, and soon finds where his intended sleeps. He then awakens her, and holds the light to his face that she may know him—after which he places the light close to her. If she blows it out, the ceremony is ended, and he appears in the lodge the next morning, as one of the family. If she does not blow out the light, but leaves it to burn out, he retires from the lodge. The next day he places himself in full view of it, and plays his flute. The young women go out, one by one, to see who he is playing for. The tune changes, to let them know that he is not playing for them. When his intended makes her appearance at the door, he continues his *courting* tune, until she returns to the lodge. He then gives over playing, and makes another trial at night, which generally turns out favorable. During the first year they ascertain whether they can agree with each other, and can be happy—if not, they part, and each looks out again. If we were to live together and disagree, we should be as foolish as the whites. No indiscretion can banish a woman from her parental lodge—no difference how many children she may bring home, she is always welcome—the kettle is over the fire to feed them.

The crane dance often lasts two or three days. When this is over, we feast again, and have our *national* dance. The large square in the village is swept and prepared for the purpose. The chiefs and old warriors, take seats on mats which have been spread at the upper end of the square—the drummers and singers come next, and the braves and women form the sides, leaving a large space in the middle. The drums beat, and the singers commence. A warrior enters the square, keeping time with the music. He shows the manner he started on a war party—how he approached the enemy—he strikes, and describes the way he killed him. All join in applause. He then leaves the square, and another enters and takes his place. Such of our young men as have not been out in war parties, and killed an enemy, stand back ashamed—not being able to enter the square. I remember that I was ashamed to look where our young women stood, before I could take my stand in the square as a warrior.

What pleasure it is to an old warrior, to see his son come forward and relate his exploits—it makes him feel young, and induces him to enter the square, and "fight his battles o'er again."

This national dance makes our warriors. When I was travelling last summer, on a steam boat, on a large river, going from New York to Albany, I was shown the place where the Americans dance their national dance [West Point]; where the old warriors recount to their young men, what they have done, to stimulate them to go and do likewise. This surprised me, as I did not think the whites understood our way of making braves.

When our national dance is over—our corn-fields hoed, and every weed dug up, and our corn about knee-high, all our young men would start in a direction towards sun-down, to hunt deer and buffalo—being prepared, also, to kill Sioux, if any are found on our hunting grounds—a part of our old men and women to the lead mines to make lead—and the remainder of our people start to fish, and get mat stuff. Every one leaves the village, and remains about forty days. They then return: the hunting party bringing in dried buffalo and deer meat, and sometimes *Sioux scalps,* when they are found trespassing on our hunting grounds. At other times they are met by a party of Sioux too strong for them, and are driven in. If the Sioux have killed the Sacs last, they expect to be retaliated upon, and will fly before them, and vice versa. Each party knows that the other has a right to retaliate, which induces those who have killed last, to give way before their enemy—as neither wish to strike, except to avenge the death of their relatives. All our wars are predicated by the relatives of those killed; or by aggressions upon our hunting grounds.

The party from the lead mines bring lead, and the others dried fish, and mats for our winter lodges. Presents are now made by each party; the first, giving to the others dried buffalo and deer, and they, in exchange, presenting them with lead, dried fish and mats.

This is a happy season of the year—having plenty of provisions, such as beans, squashes, and other produce, with our dried meat and fish, we continue to make feasts and visit each other, until our corn is ripe. Some lodge in the village makes a feast daily, to the Great Spirit. I cannot explain this so that the white people would comprehend me, as we have no regular standard among us. Every one makes his feast as he thinks best, to please the Great Spirit, who has the care of all beings created. Others believe in two Spirits: one good and one bad, and make feasts for the Bad Spirit, *to keep him quiet!* If they can make peace with him, the Good Spirit will not hurt them! For my part, I am of opinion, that so far as we have *reason,* we have a right to use it, in determining what is right or wrong; and should pursue that path which we believe to be right—believing, that "whatever is, is right." If the Great and Good Spirit wished us to believe and do as the whites, he could easily change our opinions, so that we would see, and think, and act as they do. We are *nothing* compared to His power, and we feel and know it. We have men among us, like the whites, who pretend to know the right path, but will not consent to show it without *pay!* I have no faith in their paths—but believe that every man must make his own path!

When our corn is getting ripe, our young people watch with anxiety for the signal to pull roasting-ears—as none dare touch them until the proper time. When the corn is fit to use, another great ceremony takes place, with feasting, and returning thanks to the Great Spirit for giving us corn.

I will here relate the manner in which corn first came. According to tradition, handed down to our people, a beautiful woman was seen to descend from the clouds, and alight upon the earth, by two of our ancestors, who had killed a deer, and were sitting by a fire, roasting a part of it to eat. They were astonished at seeing her, and concluded that she must be hungry, and had smelt the meat—and immediately went to her, taking with them a piece of the roasted venison. They presented it to her, and she eat—and told them to return to the spot where she was sitting, at the end of one year, and they would find a reward for their kindness and generosity. She then ascended to the clouds, and disappeared. The two men returned to their village, and explained to the nation what they had seen, done, and heard—but were laughed at by their people. When the period arrived, for them to visit this consecrated ground, where they were to find a reward for their attention to the beautiful woman of the clouds, they went with a large party, and found, where her right hand had rested on the ground, *corn* growing—and where the left hand had rested, *beans*—and immediately where she had been seated, *tobacco.*

The two first have, ever since, been cultivated by our people, as our principal provisions—and the last used for smoking. The white people have since found out the latter, and seem to relish it as much as we do—as they use it in different ways, viz. smoking, snuffing and eating!

We thank the Great Spirit for all the benefits he has conferred upon us. For myself, I never take a drink of water from a spring, without being mindful of his goodness.

We next have our great ball play—from three to five hundred on a side, play this game. We play for horses, guns, blankets, or any other kind of property we have. The successful party take the stakes, and all retire to our lodges in peace and friendship.

We next commence horse-racing, and continue our sport and feasting, until the corn is all secured. We then prepare to leave our village for our hunting grounds. The traders arrive, and give us credit for such articles as we want to clothe our families, and enable us to hunt. We first, however, hold a council with them, to ascertain the price they will give us for our skins, and what they will charge us for goods. We inform them where we intend hunting—and tell them where to build their houses. At this place, we deposit part of our corn, and leave our old people. The traders have always been kind to them, and relieved them when in want. They were always much respected by our people—and never since we have been a nation, has one of them been killed by any of our people.

We disperse, in small parties, to make our hunt, and as soon as it is over, we return to our traders' establishment, with our skins, and remain feasting, playing cards and other pastimes, until near the close of the winter. Our young men then start on the beaver hunt; others to hunt raccoons and muskrats—and the remainder of our people go to the sugar camps to make sugar. All leave our encampment, and appoint a place to meet on the Mississippi, so that we may return to our village together, in the spring. We always spent our time pleasantly at the sugar camp. It being the season for wild fowl, we lived well, and always had plenty, when the hunters came in, that we might make a feast for them. After this is over, we return to our village, accompanied, sometimes, by our traders. In this way, the year rolled round happily. But these are times that were!

On returning, in the spring, from our hunting ground, I had the pleasure of meeting our old friend, the trader of Peoria, at Rock Island. He came up in a boat from St. Louis, not as a trader, as in times past, but as our *agent.* We were all pleased to see him. He told us, that he narrowly escaped falling into the hands of Dixon. He remained with us a short time, gave us good advice, and then returned to St. Louis.

The Sioux having committed depredations on our people, we sent out war parties that summer, who succeeded in killing *fourteen.* I paid several visits to fort Armstrong during the summer, and was always well treated. We were not as happy then in our village as formerly. Our people got more liquor than customary. I used all my influence to prevent drunkenness, but without effect. As the settlements progressed towards us, we became worse off, and more unhappy. Many of our people, instead of going to their old hunting grounds, where game was plenty, would go near to the set-tlements to hunt—and, instead of saving their skins to pay the trader for goods fur-nished them in the fall, would sell them to the settlers for whisky! and return in the spring with their families, almost naked, and without the means of getting any thing for them.

About this time my eldest son was taken sick and died. He had always been a du-tiful child, and had just grown to manhood. Soon after, my youngest daughter, an in-teresting and affectionate child, died also. This was a hard stroke, because I loved my children. In my distress, I left the noise of the village, and built my lodge on a mound in my corn-field, and enclosed it with a fence, around which I planted corn and beans. Here I was with my family alone. I gave every thing I had away, and reduced myself to poverty. The only covering I retained, was a piece of buffalo robe. I resolved on blacking my face and fasting, for two years, for the loss of my two children—drink-ing only of water in the middle of the day, and eating sparingly of boiled corn at sun-set. I fulfilled my promise, hoping that the Great Spirit would take pity on me.

My nation had now some difficulty with the Ioways, with whom we wished to be at peace. Our young men had repeatedly killed some of the Ioways; and these breaches had always been made up by giving presents to the relations of those killed. But the last council we had with them, we promised that, in case any more of their people were killed by ours, instead of presents, we would give up the person, or per-sons, that had done the injury. We made this determination known to our people; but, notwithstanding, one of our young men killed an Ioway the following winter.

A party of our people were about starting for the Ioway village to give the young man up. I agreed to accompany them. When we were ready to start, I called at the lodge for the young man to go with us. He was sick, but willing to go. His brother, however, prevented him, and insisted on going to die in his place, as he was unable to travel. We started, and on the seventh day arrived in sight of the Ioway village, and when within a short distance of it, halted and dismounted. We all bid farewell to our young brave, who entered the village alone, singing his *death-song,* and sat down in the square in the middle of the village. One of the Ioway chiefs came out to us. We told him that we had fulfilled our promise—that we had brought the brother of the young man who had killed one of their people—that he had volunteered to come in his place, in consequence of his brother being unable to travel from sickness. We had no further conversation, but mounted our horses and rode off. As we started, I cast my eye towards the village, and observed the Ioways coming out of their lodges with spears and war clubs. We took our trail back, and travelled until dark—then encamped and made a fire. We had not been here long, before we heard the sound of horses com-ing towards us. We seized our arms; but instead of an enemy, it was our young brave with two horses. He told me that after we had left him, they menaced him with death for some time—then gave him something to eat—smoked the pipe with him—and made him a present of the two horses and some goods, and started him after us. When we arrived at our village, our people were much pleased; and for the noble and gen-erous conduct of the Ioways, on this occasion, not one of their people has been killed since by any of our nation.

That fall I visited Malden with several of my band, and were well treated by our British father, who gave us a variety of presents. He also gave me a medal, and told me there never would be war between England and America again; but, for my fidelity to the British during the war that had terminated sometime before, requested me to come with my band every year and get presents, as Col. Dixon had promised me.

I returned, and hunted that winter on the Two-Rivers. The whites were now set-tling the country fast. I was out one day hunting in a bottom, and met three white men. They accused me of killing their hogs; I denied it; but they would not listen to me. One of them took my gun out of my hand and fired it off—then took out the flint, gave back my gun, and commenced beating me with sticks, and ordered me off. I was so much bruised that I could not sleep for several nights.

Some time after this occurrence, one of my camp cut a bee-tree, and carried the honey to his lodge. A party of white men soon followed, and told him that the bee-tree was theirs, and that he had no right to cut it. He pointed to the honey, and told them to take it; they were not satisfied with this, but took all the packs of skins that he had collected during the winter, to pay his trader and clothe his family with in the spring, and carried them off!

How could we like such people, who treated us so unjustly? We determined to break up our camp, for fear that they would do worse—and when we joined our peo-ple in the spring, a great many of them complained of similar treatment.

This summer our agent came to live at Rock Island. He treated us well, and gave us good advice. I visited him and the trader very often during the summer, and, for the first time, heard talk of our having to leave my village. The trader explained to me the terms of the treaty that had been made, and said we would be obliged to leave the Illinois side of the Mississippi, and advised us to select a good place for our village, and remove to it in the spring. He pointed out the difficulties we would have to en-counter, if we remained at our village on Rock river. He had great influence with the principal Fox chief, (his adopted brother,) and persuaded him to leave his village, and go to the west side of the Mississippi river, and build another—which he did the spring following.

Nothing was now talked of but leaving our village. Ke-o-kuck had been per-suaded to consent to go; and was using all his influence, backed by the war chief at fort Armstrong, and our agent and trader at Rock Island, to induce others to go with him. He sent the crier through the village to inform our people that it was the wish of our Great Father that we should remove to the west side of the Mississippi—and recommended the Ioway river as a good place for the new village—and wished his party to make such arrangements, before they started out on their winter's hunt, as to preclude the necessity of their returning to the village in the spring.

The party opposed to removing, called upon me for my opinion. I gave it freely—and after questioning Quàsh-quà-me about the sale of the lands, he assured me that he "never had consented to the sale of our village." I now promised this party to be their leader, and raised the standard of opposition to Ke-o-kuck, with a full de-termination not to leave my village. I had an interview with Ke-o-kuck, to see if this difficulty could not be settled with our Great Father—and told him to propose to give other land, (any that our Great Father might choose, even our *lead mines*,) to be peaceably permitted to keep the small point of land on which our village and fields were situate. I was of opinion that the white people had plenty of land, and would never take our village from us. Ke-o-kuck promised to make an exchange if possible; and applied to our agent, and the great chief at St. Louis, (who has charge of all the agents,) for permission to go to Washington to see our Great Father for that purpose. This satisfied us for some time. We started to our hunting grounds, in good hopes that something would be done for us. During the winter, I received information that three families of whites had arrived at our village, and destroyed some of our lodges, and were making fences and dividing our corn-fields for their own use—*and were quarrel-*

ing among themselves about their lines, in the division! I immediately started for Rock river, a distance of ten day's travel, and on my arrival found the report to be true. I went to my lodge, and saw a family occupying it. I wished to talk with them, but they could not understand me. I then went to Rock Island, and (the agent being absent,) told the interpreter what I wanted to say to those people, viz: "Not to settle on our lands—nor trouble our lodges or fences—that there was plenty of land in the country for them to settle upon—and they must leave our village, as we were coming back to it in the spring." The interpreter wrote me a paper, and I went back to the village, and showed it to the intruders, but could not understand their reply. I expected, however, that they would remove, as I requested them. I returned to Rock Island, passed the night there, and had a long conversation with the trader. He again advised me to give up, and make my village with Ke-o-kuck, on the Ioway river. I told him that I would not. The next morning I crossed the Mississippi, on very bad ice—but the Great Spirit made it strong, that I might pass over safe. I travelled three days farther to see the Winnebago sub-agent, and converse with him on the subject of our difficulties. He gave me no better news than the trader had done. I started then, by way of Rock river, to see the prophet, believing that he was a man of great knowledge. When we met, I explained to him every thing as it was. He at once agreed that I was right, and advised me never to give up our village, for the whites to plough up the bones of our people. He said, that if we remained at our village, the whites would not trouble us—and advised me to get Ke-o-kuck, and the party that had consented to go with him to the Ioway in the spring, to return, and remain at our village.

I returned to my hunting ground, after an absence of one moon, and related what I had done. In a short time we came up to our village, and found that the whites had not left it—but that others had come, and that the greater part of our corn-fields had been enclosed. When we landed, the whites appeared displeased because we had come back. We repaired the lodges that had been left standing, and built others. Ke-o-kuck came to the village; but his object was to persuade others to follow him to the Ioway. He had accomplished nothing towards making arrangements for us to remain, or to exchange other lands for our village. There was no more friendship existing between us. I looked upon him as a coward, and no brave, to abandon his village to be occupied by strangers. What *right* had these people to our village, and our fields, which the Great Spirit had given us to live upon?

My reason teaches me that *land cannot be sold.* The Great Spirit gave it to his children to live upon, and cultivate, as far as is necessary for their subsistence; and so long as they occupy and cultivate it, they have the right to the soil—but if they voluntarily leave it, then any other people have a right to settle upon it. Nothing can be sold, but such things as can be carried away.

In consequence of the improvements of the intruders on our fields, we found considerable difficulty to get ground to plant a little corn. Some of the whites permitted us to plant small patches in the fields they had fenced, keeping all the best ground for themselves. Our women had great difficulty in climbing their fences, (being unaccustomed to the kind,) and were ill-treated if they left a rail down.

One of my old friends thought he was safe. His corn-field was on a small island of Rock river. He planted his corn; it came up well—but the white man saw it!—he wanted the island, and took his team over, ploughed up the corn, and re-planted it for himself! The old man shed tears; not for himself, but the distress his family would be in if they raised no corn.

The white people brought whisky into our village, made our people drunk, and cheated them out of their horses, guns, and traps! This fraudulent system was carried to such an extent that I apprehended serious difficulties might take place, unless a stop was put to it. Consequently, I visited all the whites and begged them not to sell whisky to my people. One of them continued the practice openly. I took a party of my young men, went to his house, and took out his barrel and broke in the head and turned out the whisky. I did this for fear some of the whites might be killed by my people when drunk.

Our people were treated badly by the whites on many occasions. At one time, a white man beat one of our women cruelly, for pulling a few suckers of corn out of his field, to suck, when hungry! At another time, one of our young men was beat with clubs by two white men for opening a fence which crossed our road, to take his horse through. His shoulder blade was broken, and his body badly bruised, from which he soon after *died!*

Bad, and cruel, as our people were treated by the whites, not one of them was hurt or molested by any of my band. I hope this will prove that we are a peaceable people—having permitted ten men to take possession of our corn-fields; prevent us from planting corn; burn and destroy our lodges; ill-treat our women; and *beat to death* our men, without offering resistance to their barbarous cruelties. This is a lesson worthy for the white man to learn: to use forbearance when injured.

We acquainted our agent daily with our situation, and through him, the great chief at St. Louis—and hoped that something would be done for us. The whites were *complaining* at the same time that *we* were *intruding* upon *their rights!* THEY made themselves out the *injured* party, and *we* the *intruders!* and called loudly to the great war chief to protect *their* property!

How smooth must be the language of the whites, when they can make right look like wrong, and wrong like right.

During this summer, I happened at Rock Island, when a great chief arrived, (whom I had known as the great chief of Illinois, [governor Cole,] in company with another chief, who, I have been told, is a great writer, [judge Jas. Hall.] I called upon them and begged to explain to them the grievances under which me and my people were laboring, hoping that they could do something for us. The great chief, however, did not seem disposed to council with me. He said he was no longer the great chief of Illinois—that his children had selected another father in his stead, and that he now only ranked as they did. I was surprised at this talk, as I had always heard that he was a good, brave, and great chief. But the white people never appear to be satisfied. When they get a good father, they hold councils, (at the suggestion of some bad, ambitious man, who wants the place himself,) and conclude, among themselves, that this man, or some other equally ambitious, would make a better father than they have, and nine times out of ten they don't get as good a one again.

I insisted on explaining to these two chiefs the true situation of my people. They gave their assent: I rose and made a speech, in which I explained to them the treaty made by Quàsh-quà-me, and three of our braves, according to the manner the trader and others had explained it to me. I then told them that Quàsh-quà-me and his party *denied,* positively, having ever sold my village; and that, as I had never known them to *lie,* I was determined to keep it in possession.

I told them that the white people had already entered our village, *burnt our lodges, destroyed our fences, ploughed up our corn, and beat our people:* that they had brought *whisky* into our country, *made our people drunk,* and taken from them their *horses, guns,* and *traps;* and that I had borne all this injury, without suffering any of my braves to raise a hand against the whites.

My object in holding this council, was to get the opinion of these two chiefs, as to the best course for me to pursue. I had appealed in vain, time after time, to our agent, who regularly represented our situation to the great chief at St. Louis, whose duty it was to call upon our Great Father to have justice done to us; but instead of this, we are told *that the white people want our country, and we must leave it to them!*

I did not think it possible that our Great Father wished us to leave our village, where we had lived so long, and where the bones of so many of our people had been laid. The great chief said that, as he was no longer a chief, he could do nothing for us; and felt sorry that it was not in his power to aid us—nor did he know how to advise us. Neither of them could do any thing for us; but both evidently appeared very sorry. It would give me great pleasure, at all times, to take these two chiefs by the hand.

That fall I paid a visit to the agent, before we started to our hunting grounds, to hear if he had any good news for me. He had news! He said that the land on which our village stood was now ordered to be sold to individuals; and that, when sold, *our right* to remain, by treaty, would be at an end, and that if we returned next spring, we would be *forced* to remove!

We learned during the winter, that *part* of the lands where our village stood had been sold to individuals, and that the *trader* at Rock Island had bought the greater part that had been sold. The reason was now plain to me, why *he* urged us to remove. His object, we thought, was to get our lands. We held several councils that winter to determine what we should do, and resolved, in one of them, to return to our village in the spring, as usual; and concluded, that if we were removed by force, that the *trader*, agent, and others, must be the cause; and that, if found guilty of having us driven from our village, they should be *killed!* The trader stood foremost on this list. He had purchased the land on which my lodge stood, and that of our *grave yard* also! Ne-a-pope promised to kill him, the agent, interpreter, the great chief at St. Louis, the war chief at fort Armstrong, Rock Island, and Ke-o-kuck—these being the principal persons to blame for endeavoring to remove us.

Our women received bad accounts from the women that had been raising corn at the new village—the difficulty of breaking the new prairie with hoes—and the small quantity of corn raised. We were nearly in the same situation in regard to the latter, it being the first time I ever knew our people to be in want of provision.

I prevailed upon some of Ke-o-kuck's band to return this spring to the Rock river village. Ke-o-kuck would not return with us. I hoped that we would get permission to go to Washington to settle our affairs with our Great Father. I visited the agent at Rock Island. He was displeased because we had returned to our village, and told me that we *must* remove to the west of the Mississippi. I told him plainly that we *would not!* I visited the interpreter at his house, who advised me to do as the agent had directed me. I then went to see the trader, and upbraided him for buying our lands. He said that if he had not purchased them, some person else would, and that if our Great Father would make an exchange with us, he would willingly give up the land he had purchased to the government. This I thought was fair, and began to think that he had not acted as badly as I had suspected. We again repaired our lodges, and built others, as most of our village had been burnt and destroyed. Our women selected small patches to plant corn, (where the whites had not taken them within their fences,) and worked hard to raise something for our children to subsist upon.

I was told that, according to the treaty, we had no *right* to remain upon the lands *sold,* and that the government would *force* us to leave them. There was but a small portion, however, that *had been sold;* the balance remaining in the hands of the government, we claimed the right (if we had no other) to "live and hunt upon, as long as it remained the property of the government," by a stipulation in the same treaty that required us to evacuate it *after* it had been sold. This was the land that we wished to inhabit, and thought we had the best right to occupy.

I heard that there was a great chief on the Wabash, and sent a party to get his advice. They informed him that we had not sold our village. He assured them then, that if we had not sold the land on which our village stood, our Great Father would not take it from us.

I started early to Malden to see the chief of my British Father, and told him my story. He gave the same reply that the chief on the Wabash had given; and in justice to him, I must say, that he never gave me any bad advice: but advised me to apply to our American Father, who, he said, would do us justice. I next called on the great chief at Detroit, and made the same statement to him that I had to the chief of our British Father. He gave the same reply. He said, if we had not sold our lands, and would remain peaceably on them, that we would not be disturbed. This assured me that I was right, and determined me to hold out, as I had promised my people.

I returned from Malden late in the fall. My people were gone to their hunting ground, whither I followed. Here I learned that they had been badly treated all summer by the whites; and that a treaty had been held at Prairie du Chien. Ke-o-kuck and some of our people attended it, and found out that our Great Father had exchanged a small strip of the land that was ceded by Quàsh-quà-me and his party, with the Pottowatomies, for a portion of their land, near Chicago; and that the object of this treaty was to get it back again; and that the United States had agreed to give them *sixteen thousand dollars a year forever,* for this small strip of land—it being less than the twentieth part of that taken from our nation, for *one thousand dollars a year!* This bears evidence of something I cannot explain. This land, they say, belonged to the United States. What reason, then, could have induced them to exchange it with the Pottowatomies, if it was so valuable? Why not keep it? Or, if they found that they had made a bad bargain with the Pottowatomies, why not take back their land at a fair proportion of what they gave our nation for it? If this small portion of the land that they took from us for *one thousand dollars* a year, be worth *sixteen thousand dollars a year forever,* to the Pottowatomies, then the whole tract of country taken from us ought to be worth, to our nation, *twenty times* as much as this small fraction.

Here I was again puzzled to find out how the white people reasoned; and began to doubt whether they had any standard of right and wrong!

Communication was kept up between myself and the Prophet. Runners were sent to the Arkansas, Red river and Texas—not on the subject of our lands, but a secret mission, which I am not, at present, permitted to explain.

It was related to me, that the chiefs and headmen of the Foxes had been invited to Prairie du Chien, to hold a council to settle the differences existing between them and the Sioux. That the chiefs and headmen, amounting to *nine,* started for the place designated, taking with them one woman—and were met by the Menomonees and Sioux, near the Ouisconsin, and all *killed,* except one man. Having understood that the whole matter was published shortly after it occurred, and is known to the white people, I will say no more about it.

I would here remark, that our pastimes and sports had been laid aside for the last two years. We were a divided people, forming two parties. Ke-o-kuck being at the head of one, willing to barter our rights merely for the good opinion of the whites; and cowardly enough to desert our village to them. I was at the head of the other party, and was determined to hold on to my village, although I had been *ordered* to leave it. But, I considered, as myself and band had no agency in selling our country—and that as provision had been made in the treaty, for us all to remain on it as long as it belonged to the United States, that we could not be *forced* away. I refused, therefore, to quit my village. It was here, that I was born—and here lie the bones of many friends and relations. For this spot I felt a sacred reverence, and never could consent to leave it, without being forced therefrom.

When I called to mind the scenes of my youth, and those of later days—and reflected that the theatre on which these were acted, had been so long the home of my fathers, who now slept on the hills around it, I could not bring my mind to consent to leave this country to the whites, for any earthly consideration.

The winter passed off in gloom. We made a bad hunt, for want of the guns, traps, &c. that the whites had taken from our people for whisky! The prospect before us was a bad one. I fasted, and called upon the Great Spirit to direct my steps to the right path. I was in great sorrow—because all the whites with whom I was acquainted, and had been on terms of friendship, advised me so contrary to my wishes, that I begun to doubt whether I had a *friend* among them.

Ke-o-kuck, who has a smooth tongue, and is a great speaker, was busy in persuading my band that I was wrong—and thereby making many of them dissatisfied with me. I had one consolation—for all the women were on my side, on account of their corn-fields.

On my arrival again at my village, with my band increased, I found it worse than before. I visited Rock Island. The agent again ordered me to quit my village. He said, that if we did not, troops would be sent to drive us off. He reasoned with me, and told me, it would be better for us to be with the rest of our people, so that we might avoid difficulty, and live in peace. The *interpreter* joined him, and gave me so many good reasons, that I almost wished I had not undertaken the difficult task that I had pledged myself to my brave band to perform. In this mood, I called upon the *trader,* who is fond of talking, and had long been my friend, but now amongst those advising me to give up my village. He received me very friendly, and went on to defend Ke-o-kuck in what he had done, and endeavored to show me that I was bringing distress on our women and children. He inquired, if some terms could not be made, that would be honorable to me, and satisfactory to my braves, for us to remove to the west side of the Mississippi? I replied, that if our Great Father would do us justice, and would make the proposition, I could then give up honorably. He asked me "if the great chief at St. Louis would give us six thousand dollars, to purchase provisions and other articles, if I would give up peaceably, and remove to the west side of the Mississippi?" After thinking some time, I agreed, that I could honorably give up, by being paid for it, according to our customs; but told him, that I could not make the proposal myself, even if I wished, because it would be dishonorable in me to do so. He said he would do it, by sending word to the great chief at St. Louis, that he could remove us peaceably, for the amount stated, to the west side of the Mississippi. A steam boat arrived at the island during my stay. After its departure, the *trader* told me that he had "requested a war chief, who is stationed at Galena, and was on board of the steam boat, to make the offer to the great chief at St. Louis, and that he would soon be back, and bring his answer." I did not let my people know what had taken place, for fear they would be displeased. I did not much like what had been done myself, and tried to banish it from my mind.

After a few days had passed, the war chief returned, and brought for answer, that "the great chief at St. Louis would give us *nothing!*—and said if we did not remove immediately, we should be *drove off!*"

I was not much displeased with the answer brought by the war chief, because I would rather have laid my bones with my forefathers, than remove for any consideration. Yet if a friendly offer had been made, as I expected, I would, for the sake of my women and children, have removed peaceably.

I now resolved to remain in my village, and make no resistance, if the military came, but submit to my fate! I impressed the importance of this course on all my band, and directed them, in case the military came, not to raise an arm against them.

About this time, our agent was put out of office—for what reason, I never could ascertain. I then thought, if it was for wanting to make us leave our village, it was right—because I was tired hearing him talk about it. The interpreter, who had been equally as bad in trying to persuade us to leave our village, was retained in office—and the young man who took the place of our agent, told the same old story over, about removing us. I was then satisfied, that this could not have been the cause.

Our women had planted a few patches of corn, which was growing finely, and promised a subsistence for our children—but the *white people again commenced ploughing it up!*

I now determined to put a stop to it, by clearing our country of the *intruders.* I went to the principal men and told them, that they must and should leave our country—and gave them until the middle of the next day, to remove in. The worst left within the time appointed—but the one who remained, represented, that his family, (which was large,) would be in a starving condition, if he went and left his crop—and promised to behave well, if I would consent to let him remain until fall, in order to secure his crop. He spoke reasonably, and I consented.

We now resumed some of our games and pastimes—having been assured by the prophet that we would not be removed. But in a little while it was ascertained, that a great war chief, [Gen. Gaines,] with a large number of soldiers, was on his way to Rock river. I again called upon the prophet, who requested a little time to see into the matter. Early next morning he came to me, and said he had been *dreaming!* "That he saw nothing bad in this great war chief, [Gen. Gaines,] who was now near Rock river. That the *object* of his mission was to *frighten* us from our village, that the white people might get our land for *nothing!*" He assured us that this "great war chief dare not, and would not, hurt any of us. That the Americans were at peace with the British, and when they made peace, the British required, (which the Americans agreed to,) that they should never interrupt any nation of Indians that was at peace—and that all we had to do to retain our village, was to *refuse* any, and every offer that might be made by this war chief."

The war chief arrived, and convened a council at the agency. Ke-o-kuck and Wà-pel-lo were sent for, and came with a number of their band. The council house was opened, and they were all admitted. Myself and band were then sent for to attend the council. When we arrived at the door, singing a *war song,* and armed with lances, spears, war clubs and bows and arrows, as if going to battle, I halted, and refused to enter—as I could see no necessity or propriety in having the room crowded with those who were already there. If the council was convened for us, why have others there in our room? The war chief having sent all out, except Ke-o-kuck, Wà-pel-lo, and a few of their chiefs and braves, we entered the council house, in this war-like appearance, being desirous to show the war chief that we were *not afraid!* He then rose and made a speech.

He said:

"The president is very sorry to be put to the trouble and expense of sending a

large body of soldiers here, to remove you from the lands you have long since ceded
to the United States. Your Great Father has already warned you repeatedly, through
your agent, to leave the country; and he is very sorry to find that you have disobeyed
his orders. Your Great Father wishes you well; and asks nothing from you but what is
reasonable and right. I hope you will consult your own interest, and leave the country you are occupying, and go to the other side of the Mississippi."

I replied: "That *we* had never sold our country. *We* never received any annuities
from our American father! And *we* are determined to hold on to our village!"

The war chief, apparently angry, rose and said:—"Who is *Black Hawk?* Who is
Black Hawk?"

I responded:

"I am a *Sac!* my forefather was a SAC! and all the nations call me a SAC!!"

The war chief said:

"I came here, neither to *beg* nor *hire* you to leave your village. My business is to
remove you, peaceably if I can, but *forcibly* if I must! I will now give you two days to
remove in—and if you do not cross the Mississippi within that time, I will adopt measures to *force* you away!"

I told him that I never could consent to leave my village, and was determined not
to leave it!

The council broke up, and the war chief retired to the fort. I consulted the
prophet again: He said he had been dreaming, and that the Great Spirit had directed
that a woman, the daughter of Mat-ta-tas, the old chief of the village, should take a
stick in her hand and go before the war chief, and tell him that she is the daughter of
Mat-ta-tas, and that he had always been the *white man's friend!* That he had fought their
battles—been wounded in their service—and had always spoke well of them—and
she had never heard him say that he had sold their village. The whites are numerous,
and can take it from us if they choose; but she hoped they would not be so unfriendly.
If they were, she had one favor to ask: she wished her people to be allowed to remain
long enough to gather the provisions now growing in their fields: that she was a
woman, and had worked hard to raise something to support her children! And, if we
are driven from our village without being allowed to save our corn, many of our little children must perish with hunger!"

14

ZADOK CRAMER

(1773–1813)

Zadok Cramer's *The Navigator* was the book bought by travelers going downriver from Pittsburgh in the early nineteenth century. In fourteen editions in twenty-five years, Cramer and his literary executors provided pioneers with an extensive and astonishingly detailed guide to the rivers on which they would be traveling, mostly on flatboats. Along the way, Cramer offers commentary on the natural landscape, the history of the waters between Pittsburgh and New Orleans, and the people the travelers would find. Generations of westerners, from Daniel Drake in the early nineteenth century to Scott Russel Sanders in the late twentieth century, have recognized the utility, depth, and ubiquity of *The Navigator*. The eighth edition published posthumously in 1814 was the last Cramer personally supervised.

In the sections reproduced here describing the Allegheny and Ohio rivers, Cramer's concern is mostly with navigational practicality. Seemingly oblivious to the surrounding crises with the region's natives, Cramer writes as and for a common traveler. *The Navigator* was not written for or about the elite, the politicians, or the soldiers. Cramer reminds us that most settlers were of the yeoman class, and what they needed was not indoctrination, in the manner of Manasseh Cutler, but rather instruction in the skills needed to survive the trip west and the attendant difficulties concerning markets and conditions. Cramer provides, then, a wealth of common wisdom drawn from a fundamental familiarity with the nature of the western waters.

Near the end of his description of the Ohio, Cramer ponders the changes on the rivers coming with the arrival of steamboats in the next decades. Cramer waxes nostalgic for the days of the solitary trader working out of a canoe, and how such labors provided a steppingstone to prosperity and social acceptance. At the same time, he sees steam as the product of a uniquely American genius that will accelerate the development of the west in new ways. Cramer, seeing both the loss and the gain created by the industrialization of shipping, embodies much of the westerner's ambivalence toward the region's rapid transformations early in the nineteenth century.

Text: *The Navigator* (Pittsburgh, 1801–1826; 8th ed., 1814): 18–40.

Of the Allegheny.[1]

This is a beautiful, large, and navigable river, taking its rise in Lycoming county, Pennsylvania, within a few miles of the head waters of Sinemahoning creek, a navigable stream that falls into the Susquehanna river, to which there is a portage of 23 miles. Thence pursuing a north course, passes into New York state, winding to the N.W. about 20 miles, turns gradually to the S.W. enters Pennsylvania, and meandering in about that direction 180 miles, joins the Monongahela at Pittsburgh.

Few rivers and perhaps none excel the Allegheny for the transparency of its water, or the beauty of its bottom, having a fine gravelly bed, clear of rocks and uninterrupted by falls. Its surface is unbroken, and its mean velocity is about $2\frac{1}{2}$ miles an hour; when high it runs at the rate of four miles an hour, being a little more rapid in its course than the Monongahela. Its waters in some instances have proved medicinal; and the fish caught in it are allowed to be superior to those of the Monongahela.

The Allegheny in its windings receives many large and tributary streams: among these are the Kiskiminetas, which is navigable for batteaux 40 or 50 miles, and good portages are found between it and the Juniata; it enters the Allegheny about 14 miles below Kittanning, the county town of Armstrong county, Pa. lat. 40° 40'—45 miles above Pittsburgh. The Kiskiminetas receives in its course Little Conemaugh and Stone creek, which forms its head waters; after their junction it is called Conemaugh river;[2] it then receives Black Lick from the N.E. and 17 miles from its mouth Loyalhanna creek enters from the S.S.E.—Muhulbuctitum, another branch of the Allegheny, 20 miles above, is passable in small crafts to the settlements in Northumberland county; Wheeling is its northern branch. Toby's creek enters the Allegheny 20 miles below Fort Franklin, may be navigated in flat bottomed boats a considerable way up, thence by a short portage to the west branch of the Susquehanna, by which a valuable communication is formed between the Ohio country and the eastern parts of Pennsylvania. French creek is a N. Western branch of the Allegheny, and enters it at Fort Franklin, 80 miles N.E. of Pittsburgh; it is navigable to Le Bœuf, now called Waterford, from whence to Erie there is a portage of 15 miles, on which a turnpike is now erected.

The Allegheny affords another communication to Lake Erie by way of the Conewango creek, at whose head is a small lake called Chatauque, thence to Portland, a new town laid off by Mr. John M'Mahon, on the bank of lake Erie, there is a

---

1. The word *Allegheny* seems to have been derived from an ancient tribe of Indians, called the *"Tallegawe,"* who, though represented to have been a tall and stout race of men, were totally routed and extirpated by the Delawares and those of their stock. The Delaware Indians do not say, "Allegheny"—but "Allegawe," and again "Allegawenink," which signifies with them, as much as to say, "in the country of the Tallegawe—or the country inhabited by the Tallegawe, or Allegawe people."

2. Salt water lately discovered itself oozing through the bed of this river, about half a mile above its junction with the Loyalhanna, 17 miles from the Allegheny by the Kiskiminetas, and 7 miles from New Alexandria in Westmoreland county, Penn.—Works for making salt have been erected, and are successfully conducted.

The Ohio River Basin. From Elizabeth Perkins, Border Life, *(Chapel Hill: University of North Carolina, 1997).*

good portage of but 9 miles. A small creek, called Chatauque, enters lake Erie at Portland, which is about thirty miles below the town of Erie, in the state of New York.

The trade carried on between the lakes and the Ohio, by way of the Allegheny and its branches, is at this time [1810] very considerable, and must in a few years become of great importance. There are about 4000 or 5000 barrels, and sometimes more, of Onondago salt brought down to Pittsburgh annually, worth per barrel 9 dollars, making an average of about 40,000 dollars worth of traffic in this one article. Exclusive of the article salt, there are an immense number of boards, shingles, and lumber of different kinds, floated down to Pittsburgh and the country below on the Ohio. The quantity of boards and lumber that arrive yearly at Pittsburgh from the Allegheny and French creek, is supposed to be about 3,000,000 feet,[3] averaging about 9 dollars per 1000 feet, amounting to 27,000 dollars; this added to the amount of the salt, makes the handsome sum to domestic trade of 67,000 dollars.

In the fall and spring of 1809–10, the quantity of Onondaga salt had increased in our market to the amount of between 12, and 14,000 barrels averaging eight dollars per barrel, amounting to about 104,000 dollars. So great a quantity, however, may not again be expected from that quarter, since the owners of the Kenhawa salt works say they can deliver at this place any quantity at from five to six dollars per barrel, a price

---

3. Mr Lambden, one of our board inspectors for the borough, informs that for the year 1812, about seven million feet of boards and scantling passed inspection. The average price of lumber this spring, 1814, is $15 per 1000 feet.

at which it is thought impossible to deliver Onondaga salt, owing to the great distance it has to come, and the frequent reshipments, storages, land carriage, &c.

In return, the keel boats ascend loaded with whiskey, iron and castings, cider, apples, bacon, and many other articles of home production—and merchandise of foreign importation.—As long as the water keeps good, that is, neither too high nor too low, boats are ascending and descending continually, making a trip up in 17 days, and down in 5 days.

It has been suggested that goods might be brought by water from New York to Pittsburgh by way of the lakes and this river, for three cents a pound, which is one half less than is generally given from Philadelphia to Pittsburgh. By this Northern route, which would certainly be a very long and tedious one, there would be a portage of 15 miles from Albany on the Hudson or North river to Schenectada on the Mohawk, thence up that river and through Wood creek into lake Ontarie, thence up Niagara river to the falls, thence 10 miles around Niagara falls, thence by water up Erie lake to the town of Erie, thence 15 miles portage to Waterford or Le Bœuf, thence down French creek and Allegheny river, making in all a land carriage of 40 miles from New York to Pittsburgh, a distance by this route of not less than 850 miles.

The brig Dean, Galley Ross, and several other vessels of burden, were built on the Allegheny, and we hope to see many more borne down by the current of this beautiful stream. A brig of 160 tons burden was put on the stocks at the mouth of Plumb creek, on the Allegheny river, 12 miles above Pittsburgh, in the fall of 1809, and launched in the uncommonly high freshet[4] of November 11, (Sunday) 1810. She was constructed and built by Nathan Jones, shipcarpenter, and is owned by Brintley Robbins, an enterprising farmer. The brig is calculated for a double-decker, and will serve either for peace or war. She is of handsome construction, and perhaps has not been exceeded for beauty or durability by any that have left the western waters.

The Allegheny river joins the Monongahela nearly at right angles, and its current being more rapid, it generally marks its course across the mouth of the latter river, and forces the current of the Monongahela on the opposite shore with great impetuosity. Though their streams are now united, the clear and transparent water of the one and the muddy appearance of the other, form a singular contrast, and this difference is plainly observable ten or fifteen miles below their junction.

---

4. The Allegheny and Monongahela rivers rose at this place at a most rapid rate from about sunset Saturday evening until Sunday 12 o'clock at night, when they appeared at a stand, and soon began to give signs of withdrawing their floods from the already injured and alarmed inhabitants of their banks. The waters rose about 37 feet above the common level of the rivers, and both streams seemed equally strong, for neither appeared detained by the other in their sweeping courses. The water of the Monongahela was within eight feet of the level of Market street, and ascended Wood street gutters to Front street, and measured four feet on the ground floor of Mr Graham's tavern, corner of Wood and Water streets, and about the same depth in Messrs. T. & J. Cromwell's warehouse. The public wharf on the Allegheny river, opposite Fort Fayette, was carried off. Penn and Liberty streets were inundated, and the first floor of James Robinson, Esq's house, which stands on a second bank on the west side of the Allegheny, is said to have been covered with water.

A curious circumstance took place at Marietta. The Ohio had backed up the Muskingum for 12 miles, and occasioned a considerable retrogade current, into which some New Orleans boats got, and being enveloped in a heavy fog they discovered their mistake by being hailed as ascending the Muskingum.

This flood appears to have been about five feet three inches higher at Pittsburgh than those of 1807 8, which were at that time considered to have been the highest known for 20 or 30 years.

The Allegheny is about 400 yards wide at its mouth, and when Smoky island, lying to the N. W. is washed away, it will be nearer eight.—It runs through an immense tract of country, much of it rough and hilly land, the greater part of which is yet to be settled.—This river as well as the Ohio, are known and called by the name of Allegheny river by the Seneca, and other tribes of the Six Nations of Indians, from its head waters until it enters the Mississippi.

Among the natural advantages of the waters of the Allegheny, is *Oil* creek, which empties into that river about 100 miles from Pittsburgh. This creek issues from a spring on the top of which floats an oil similar to that called Barbadoes tar, and is found in such quantities that a person may gather several gallons a day. The oil is said to be very efficacious in rheumatic pains, rubbed on the parts affected. The troops sent to guard the Western posts, halted at this spring, collected some of the oil and bathed their joints with it; this gave them great relief from the rheumatic complaints, with which they were afflicted. They also drank freely of the water, which operated on them as a gentle cathartic.

This oil is called *Seneca Oil* in Pittsburgh, probably from its first having been discovered and used, by a nation of Indians of that name.

It is wise plan in Nature, to generally place an antidote where she has planted a poison.—No climate perhaps is more subject to pains of the rheumatic kind than ours, arising from the sudden transitions of heat to cold, and vice versa—and if it be true that the qualities of this oil are so effectual in the cure of diseases to which we are more or less subject, from the nature of our climate—it is equally true that Nature in her wisdom, has not been unmindful of her general plan of providing a good for an evil in this particular instance.

On the Allegheny and French creek, there are large bodies of low lands, covered with fine white pine and hemlock. These are noble trees, measuring from three to five feet in diameter at the butt; are remarkably tall and straight, and without limbs to near the top. They are well calculated for masts of ships, and can be floated down in high water with ease to Pittsburgh, thence down the Ohio and Mississippi; the heavy sediment of the latter river however, would perhaps tend to sink them and make them troublesome to float.—These white pine swamps afford also an immense number of excellent boards, and shingles, and lumber of different kinds, for Pittsburgh, and towns on the Ohio. Boats go loaded with pine boards even to New Orleans, where they sell for about 3 dollars per 100 feet.

Among the numerous advantages of the Allegheny river, there is one which may have escaped general observation, and this of immense value. Pittsburgh is badly situated for water courses giving fall sufficient for millscats, and such as afford water all the year. The Allegheny presents a remedy for this deficiency. By taking the water out of the river ten or fifteen miles above the town, and conduct it in a canal along the side of the hill down to the point of Grant's Hill, there may be had a fall of from 12 to 15 feet, and water in abundance at all seasons to turn as many works and mills as could stand together in the distance of two miles or more. This to be sure would cost a handsome capital. But no matter, since there is a security of that capital being expended in a stock which would probably yield 15 or 20 per cent, and a stock too as permanent as the running of the waters of the Allegheny itself. The thing at present may be thought visionary, but I should not be surprised, were life to last, to see some of the children now shouting about the streets of Pittsburgh, engaged in this project some 20 or 30 years hence,

Of the Ohio.[5]

The junction of the Allegheny and Monongahela rivers form the Ohio, and this discharges itself into the Mississippi, (in N. lat. 36° 43′ Hutchins—37° 0′ 23″ and W. long. 5° 55′ 38″ according to Mr. Ellicot[6]) about 1188 computed miles from Pittsburgh. The Ohio in its passage to the Mississippi, glides through a pleasant, fruitful, and healthy country, and carries a great uniformity of breadth, from 400 to 600 yards, except at its confluence with the Mississippi and for 100 miles above it, where it is 1000 yards wide; about 100 miles above the falls, which are 705 miles below Pittsburgh, it is 700 yards wide.

The Ohio has been described, as "beyond all competition, the most beautiful river in the universe, whether we consider it for its meandering course through an immense region of forests, for its clean and elegant banks, which afford innumerable delightful situations for cities, villages and improved farms: or for those many other advantages, which truly entitle it to the name originally given it by the French, of *"La Belle Riviere,"* that is, "the Beautiful river." This description was penned several years since, and it has not generally been thought an exaggerated one. Now the immense forests recede, cultivation smiles along its banks, towns every here and there decorate its shores, and it is not extravagant to suppose, that the day is not very far distant when its whole margin will form one continued village.

The reasons for this supposition are numerous—the principal ones are, the immense tracts of fine country that have communication with the Ohio by means of the great number of navigable waters that empty into it; the extraordinary fertility, extent, and beauty of the river bottoms, generally high, dry, and with few or no exceptions, remarkably healthy, and the superior excellence of its navigation, through means of which, the various productions of the most extensive and fertile parts of the United States must eventually be sent to market.

For 30 miles below Pittsburgh it takes a N. W. course, then turns gradually to the W. S. W. and pursuing that course for about 500 miles, turns to the S. W. for nearly 170 miles, then it turns westward 280 miles, thence S. W. 180 miles, and empties itself into the Mississippi, in a flat and swampy country, where there are no hills to variegate the scene, nor mountains to overtop the union of these two noble streams.

The numerous islands that are interspersed in this river, in many instances, add much to the grandeur of its appearance, but they embarrass the navigation considerably, particularly in low water, as they occasion a great many shoals and sandbars. The soil of the islands for the most part is rich, timber luxuriant, and the extent of many

---

5. This name is said to signify in some of the Indian languages, Bloody; so that the Ohio may be translated the River of Blood.

Brackenridge's Gazette Publication.

6. Mr. Ellicot in his Journal down the Ohio, having arrived at the mouth of that river, observes, "On the top of the stump of a large tree, to which the zenith sector was fixed, a plate of lead was laid, containing the latitude and longitude of that place.—The stump was then covered by a mound of earth of considerable magnitude; but which will probably be demolished in a few years by the annual inundations" Mr Ellicot and his party were detained at the mouth of the Ohio, in consequence of the inclemency of the season, from the 18th Dec. 1796, to the 31st of Jan. following, during which period, he ascertained from accurate observations, the latitude and longitude of the junction of the Ohio and Mississippi rivers, as above stated. It may be proper to inform the reader that Mr And. Ellicot was appointed commissioner on the part of the U. S. for determining the boundary between them and the possessions of his Catholic majesty, from the year 1796 till 1800.

of them considerable. Fruit is raised to great perfection on them, and seldom fail of a crop, as is generally the case in all the river bottoms.

In low water the navigation of the Ohio is difficult to the old Mingo-town,[7] about 75 miles below Pittsburgh; from thence to the Mississippi it is good for keel boats or barges carrying from 100 to 200 tons burden; up from thence it may be navigated with smaller crafts. In times of high water, vessels of 400 tons burden can descend with ease, except the difficulty arising from managing so unwieldy a bulk at the points of islands and short turns in the channel of the river. Vessels of this tonnage have descended from Pittsburgh to Orleans in safety, but the chance of good water renders the undertaking a little hazardous. The Falls, however, are much the greatest impediment, for, unless vessels happen to hit the time of the highest stage of water, they are either detained, perhaps till the next season, or, if they attempt a passage over them, a wreck in part or in whole may be the consequence, in either case, putting in jeopardy property to an amount that few individuals can bear the loss of. A lock-canal round the Falls would remove this difficulty, and be of an immense advantage to the Ohio trade, and to the people on or near the river from the Falls up to the head of the Allegheny and Monongahela rivers.—There has been some talk of attempting the commencement of this lock-canal. What jarring and clashing interests prevent the undertaking, are not easily to be found out. It can scarcely be supposed to be the want of a publick spirit in the Kentuckians or their legislature.

There are many smaller impediments, however, in the river from Pittsburgh to the Mingo-town, which may be as long getting removed as even the Falls themselves: these consist of rocks that might be blown to pieces, and ripples that might be easily cleared out in such a way as to make the channel good through them. This is certainly an important national concern, but the people must begin to act first, before their representatives will bring the thing forward in the house of general assembly. It must be done by grants of monies from the state, aided by subscriptions from the people; both must be liberal and vigilant, or the object will never be accomplished.

The consideration for opening the navigation of the Ohio, has become a matter of greater importance and necessity for the interest of Pennsylvania now than ever before. The United States' road from Cumberland on the Potomack, to Wheeling on the Ohio, when completed, will naturally draw a great deal of the trade of the northern states to the states of Ohio, Kentucky, Tennessee, and to Louisiana, through that channel, thereby abridging very much the trade from those states through Pennsylvania. Therefore, if Pennsylvania looks closely to her own interests, she will find that the completing the turnpike road from Harrisburgh to Pittsburgh, and opening the navigation of the Ohio, are the two principal objects which will tend to secure to her, her usual commercial, foreign and domestick, advantages. Exclusive of the probability of the United States' road drawing the trade to the south of Pennsylvania, New York state, on the north, is pushing her inland navigation, and opening easy communications from one end of the state to the other, by way of turnpikes, canals, &c. to an extent unparalleled in any other state in the Union. The spirit of the people in the back part of the state of New York is peculiarly turned to this point, and no exertions seem to be lacking in the industry of the one class; or money wanting from the other. The purses of the one and the labour of the other seem to be happily united for the

---

7. This was the only Indian village in 1766 on the banks of the Ohio from that place to Fort Pitt; it contained at that time 60 families.
Hutchins.

good of the whole. When this is the case, a state must flourish in her internal improvements, and of course advance to wealth and independence.

The Ohio river has on its left in descending, Pennsylvania as far as the mouth of Mill creek; Virginia to the mouth of Big Sandy river; and the state of Kentucky about 60 miles below the mouth of the Ohio. On the right, Pennsylvania to the line crossing just below the mouth of Little Beaver; the state of Ohio from thence to the mouth of the Great Miami; and below this the Indiana to the mouth of the Wabash; thence to the Mississippi, the Illinois territory.

It receives in its course many large and navigable streams, the principal of which are; on the right, Big and Little Beaver, Muskingum, Sciota, Little and Great Miami, and the Wabash. On the left, Little and Great Kanhawa, Sandy, Licking, Kentucky, Green, Cumberland, and Tennessee rivers:—These will be more particularly mentioned as we go on with directions for navigating the Ohio.

The fish of the Ohio are numerous and of various kinds: the black and yellow cat, weighing from 3 to 100 pounds; the buffaloe, from 5 to 30 pounds; the pike from 4 to 15 pounds; the sturgeon from 4 to 40; the perch from 3 to 12 pounds; the sucker from 1 to 6 pounds; a few herrings sometimes caught, and in the spring of 1805, several shad were caught and sold in the Pittsburgh market, weighing about two pounds; eels and soft shelled turtles are sometimes caught.—These ascend the Allegheny and Monongahela rivers, and their principal branches, and are caught in seines, baskets, pots, and with trot-lines, hooks and lines, &c. The different species of the wild duck are numerous, and a few geese, brant, &c. are seen on the river, and the swan has sometimes been seen stemming the current. Turkies, pheasant and partridges, are numerous on its banks; these, with the opportunity of sometimes shooting bears and deer swimming across the river, afford much pleasure to the navigator, and form sumptuous meals to the boat's crew. Boats, to take advantage of this profitable amusement, are generally well provided with ammunition and fire-arms.

The principal articles constituting loading for the boats trading on the Ohio and Mississippi, are; flour, whiskey, apples, cider, peach and apple brandy, bar iron and castings, tin and copper wares, glass, cabinet work, windsor chairs, mill stones, grind stones, nails, &c. &c. And the principal articles brought up the Ohio in keel boats, are cotton, lead, furs and peltry, and hemp and tobacco from Kentucky. This traffick is carried on briskly at this time and no doubt a few years will greatly increase it, and much to the advantage of the adventurers.

Exclusive of the trading boats, there are many loaded altogether with merchandise of foreign importation, destined to Kentucky, Tennessee, Ohio and the territories. Many others are family boats, seeking places of settlement in these new countries, where their posterity may rest in safety, having plenty of all the necessaries, and many of the luxuries of life, where their children's children may enjoy the rich and prolifick productions of the land, without an over degree of toil or labour, where the climate is mild and the air salubrious,[8] where each man is a prince in his own kingdom, and may without molestation, enjoy the frugal fare of his humble cot; where the

---

8. The following observations on the soil and climate are taken from the Journal of a col. Gordon, who passed down the Ohio as early as 1760.—"The country on the Ohio, &c. is every where pleasant, with large level spots of rich land, remarkably healthy. One general remark of this nature may serve for the whole tract of the globe, comprehended between the western skirts of the Allegheny mountains, beginning at Fort Ligonier, thence bearing southwesterly to the distance of 500 miles opposite to the Ohio falls, then crossing them northerly to the heads of the rivers that empty themselves into the Ohio; then east along the ridge that separates the Lakes and Ohio streams to French-creek, which is opposite the above mentioned Fort Ligonier, northerly. This country may, from a proper knowledge, be affirmed to be

clashing and terrifick sounds of war are not heard; where tyrants that desolate the earth dwell not; where man, simple man, is left to the guidance of his own will, subject only to laws of his own making, fraught with mildness, operating equally just on all, and by all protected and willingly obeyed.

The hills on both sides of the Ohio, as low as Grave creek, below Wheeling, are filled with excellent coal.[9] Below this coal grows scarce, and what is found, is not of so good a quality. Coal has been boated down from Grave creek to Marietta, Limestone, falls of the Ohio, &c. where it sells for 12 cents per bushel. Even at this price, it is not a very advantageous article of trade. It is also boated to Natchez from mines above the falls, and sells in that market to the blacksmiths at from 25 to $37\frac{1}{2}$ cents per bushel, and is preferred at that advanced price to the charcoal of that country. A mine of mineral coal has been observed lately at the Yellow banks on the Ohio. The hills of the Allegheny and Monongahela rivers, are also filled with good coal mines up to their head waters; and in some places valuable iron ores are found in them.

The lands of the Ohio, and its branches, are differently timbered according to their quality and situation. The high and dry lands are covered with red, white and black oak, hickory, walnut, red and white mulberry, ash, poplar, dogwood, some yellow pine, cucumber tree, sassafras, chesnut, and patches of grape vines are sometimes to be found on the south side of the hills. The low and bottom lands produce butternut, tulip tree, papaw, black willow, locust, honey-locust, buckeye, cherry, mulberry; beech, elm, aspen, maple or sugar-tree, plum tree, hickory, walnut, grape pine, remarkably large, spice wood, black alder, &c. And below or southwardly of the Falls, are several cedar and cypress swamps, where the cedar and cypress trees grow remarkably large, and where also are great abundance of canes, such as grow in South Carolina, and on the Mississippi.

The *Sycamore* seems to be the king of the forest on the banks of the Ohio. Their monstrous growth, towering height, and extended branches really fill the beholder with awe and astonishment. Between Wheeling and Marietta I measured several from 10 to 16 feet over, four feet above ground, and this seems to be but their common size. A gentleman of Marietta told me he knew of one 60 feet in circumference, and that in the hollow of another he had turned himself around with a ten feet pole in his hands, sweeping it at right angles with himself. And there is one of these huge trees in Scioto county, Ohio, on the land of a Mr. Abraham Miller, into whose hollow thirteen men rode on horse back, June 6, 1808, the fourteenth did not enter, his horse being skittish and too fearful to advance into so curious an apartment, but there was room enough for two more.

In the fall of the leaf, and when the year's growth of bark begins to peal off these trees, the rays of the bright moon playing through their white branches, form a scene uncommonly brilliant, and quite cheering and amusing to the nightly traveller.

The growth of the grape vines on the banks of the Ohio astonish the beholder not less than that of the sycamores. It is not uncommon to find them measure from seven to eleven inches over, and so numerous, that in many places for 250 yards in circuit they form a complete canopy or covering of a great body and thickness, in which

---

the most healthy, the most pleasant, the most commodious, and most fertile spot of earth, known to European people."

Hutchins.

9. A coal mine was opened in the year 1760, opposite to Fort Pitt on the Monongahela, for the use of that garrison.

Ibid.

the tops of the trees are left in the entwining branches and umbrageous vine leaves. The number and manner of their hanging 60 or 80 feet from the tops of the tallest trees without touching the trunk, rather puzzles the spectator how they could thus fix themselves. A sailor might say they were first planted in the tops of the trees, as he first fastens his ropes to the mast head, and then grew downwards and fastened into the ground at their leisure; they have this appearance, but the principle does not answer the order of nature.

There is now on foot a new mode of navigating our western waters, particularly the Ohio and Mississppi rivers. This is with boats propelled by the power of steam. This plan has been carried into successful operation on the Hudson river at New York, and on the Delaware between New Castle and Burlington.—It has been stated that the one on the Hudson goes at the rate of four miles an hour against wind and tide on her route between New York and Albany, and frequently with 500 passengers on board. From these successful experiments there can be but little doubt of the plan succeeding on our western waters, and proving of immense advantage to the commerce of our country. A Mr. Rosewalt, a gentleman of enterprise, and who is acting it is said in conjunction with Messrs. Fulton and Livingston of New York, has a boat of this kind now (1810) on the stocks at Pittsburgh, of 138 feet keel, calculated for 300 or 400 tons burden.[10] And there is one building at Frankfort, Kentucky, by citi-

---

10. This steam boat called the New Orleans, was launched in March and descended the Ohio and Mississippi, and landed at Natchez in December 1811, where she took in loading and passengers for the first time, and passed on to New Orleans, in which route she has been successfully employed ever since. Her accommodations are good, and her passengers generally numerous; seldom less from Natchez than from 10 to 20, at 18 dollars per head, and when she starts from New Orleans, generally from 30 to 50, and sometimes as many as 80 passengers, at 25 dollars each to Natchez. According to the observations of captain Morris, of New Orleans, who attended her as pilot several trips, the boat's receipts for freight upwards, has averaged the last year 700 dollars; passage money $900—downwards $300 freight, $500 for passengers—That she performs 13 trips in the year, which at 2,400 per trip, amounts to $31,200. Her expenses are, 12 hands at 30 dollars per month, $4,320, captain, one thousand dollars; 70 cord of wood each trip, at $1-25, which amounts to $1,586, in all $6,906. It is presumed that the boat's extra trips for pleasure or otherwise, out of her usual route, has paid for all the expenses of repairs, and with the profits of the bar-room, for the boat's provisions.—In which case, there will remain a nett gain of $24,294 for the first year. The owners estimate the boat's value at $40,000, which give an interest of $2,400, and by giving $1,894 more for furniture &c. we have the clear gain of 20,000 dollars for the first year's labour of the Steam Boat "New Orleans." A revenue superior to any other establishment in the United States, and what is equally gratifying, arising out of a capital whose application is of singular benefit to the whole community, and particularly so as it respects the navigation of the western waters, whose resources in wealth is unknown, and whose enterprising inhabitants, we doubt not, will soon see the advantage of steam power over that of the oars and poles, and ere long have steam boats of all sizes and fashions, running up and down our numerous rivers, with as much ease and facility as does the common canoe under the direction of its skilful, original masters, the Indians.

The steam boat goes up in about seven or eight days, and descends in two or three, stopping several times for freight, passengers, &c. She stays at the extreme of her journey, Natchez and New Orleans, about four or five days, to discharge and take in loading. By pushing her, it is thought she is capable and ought to make a trip in every three weeks throughout the year, in which case her nett gain would be considerably more than stated, three weeks to each trip giving seventeen trips, four more than she performed the first year.

I have descended twice in the steam boat from Natchez to New-Orleans, the first time she ran it in thirty two hours, that is, throwing off the time she stopped for wood, freight, &c. the second time in thirty one hours, making about nine miles an hour. She passes floating wood on the river, as you pass objects on land when on a smart trotting horse.

When we consider that England has had in use the steam power for upwards of one hundred years, and that it was left to Americans to apply its force to the propelling of boats against wind, tide, and the most powerful currents in our rivers, we cannot but rejoice, and for a moment, believe America possesses that happy kind of superior genius, willing to embrace all the better parts of the old, and capacitated to invent new principles, and, by combining the experience of former ages, with the inventive genius of the present day, it is not wonderful that something extraordinary is produced, especially when genius from

zens who no doubt will push the enterprise. It will be a novel sight, and as pleasing as novel to see a huge boat working her way up the windings of the Ohio, without the appearance of sail, oar, pole, or any manual labour about her—moving within the secrets of her own wonderful mechanism, and propelled by power undiscoverable!— This plan if it succeeds, must open to view flattering prospects to an immense country, an interior of not less than two thousand miles of as fine a soil and climate, as the world can produce, and to a people worthy of all the advantages that nature and art can give them, a people the more meritorious, because they know how to sustain peace and live independent, among the crushing of empires, the falling of kings, the slaughter and bloodshed of millions, and the tumult, corruption and tyranny of all the world beside. The immensity of country we have yet to settle, the vast riches of the bowels of the earth, the unexampled advantages of our water courses, which wind without interruption for thousands of miles, the numerous sources of trade and wealth opening to the enterprising and industrious citizens, are reflections that must rouse the most dull and stupid. Indeed the very appearance of the placid and unbroken surface of the Ohio invite to trade and enterprise, and from the canoe, which the adventurer manages with a single pole or paddle, he advances to a small square ark boat, which he loads at the head waters with various wares, liquors, fruits, dry goods and small groceries, and starts his bark for the river traffic, stopping at every town and village to accommodate the inhabitants with the best of his cargo.—This voyage performed, which generally occupies three months, and the ark sold for half its first cost, the trader returns doubly invigorated, and enabled to enlarge his vessel and cargo, he sets out again; this is repeated, until perhaps getting tired of this mode of merchandising, he sets himself down in some town or village as a wholesale merchant, druggist or apothecary, practising physician or lawyer, or something else, that renders himself respectable in the eyes of his neighbors, where he lives amidst wealth and comforts the remainder of his days—nor is it by any known that his fortune was founded in the paddling of a canoe, or trafficking in apples, cider-royal and peach brandy, whiskey, &c. &c. &c. From the canoe, we now see ships of two or three hundred tons burden, masted and rigged, descending the same Ohio, laden with the products of the country, bound to New Orleans, thence to any part of the world.—Thus, the rise and progress of the trade and the trader on the western waters; thus, the progress of our country from infancy to manhood; and thus, the flattering prospects of its future greatness through the channels of the Ohio and Mississippi rivers.

Instructions and Precautions, Necessary to Be Attended to by Strangers and Others About Descending the Ohio River.

The first thing to be attended to by emigrants or traders wanting to descend the river, is to procure a boat, to be ready so as to take advantage of the times of flood, and to be careful that the boat be a good one: For many of the accidents that happen in nav-

---

the cradle, has, perhaps, above any other country in the world, an uncurbed reign, an open expanse, to work in—where the mind is as free as the air of heaven—where oppression is unknown—and where the tyranny of the parent, and of the government, would be equally disposed, and equally guarded against— where in fact we are one people, equally free from the taunts of the one, or depraved duplicity of the other—where each man feels a pride in being the first to assist the oppressed, to reward merit, encourage genius, free of prejudice, or partiality, for name or nation—the whole united with a *love of country,* a glow of patriotism, that makes man brother to man in all countries and in all situations.

igating the Ohio, are owing to the unpardonable carelessness or penuriousness of the boat builders, who will frequently slight their work, or make their boats of injured plank.[11] in either case, putting the lives and properties of a great many people at manifest hazard. This egregious piece of misconduct, should long before this time have been rectified, by the appointment of boat inspectors at the different places, where boats are built. But as this has never been done, it behoves every purchaser of a Kentucky boat, which is the sort here alluded to, to get it narrowly examined before the embarkation, by persons who are well acquainted with the strength and form of a boat suitable for a voyage of this kind.

The principal places where families and merchants stop to prepare for embarkation, are Brownsville, (or Redstone) Pittsburgh, and Wheeling. There are people in each of those places that make it their business to accommodate strangers descending the river with every article they may want, either in provisions, farming utensils, boats, or other crafts, &c. at a cheap and reasonable price. There are large boat-yards at each of these places, and their boats are generally well made and strong, the price of which varies according to their make, length, and strength; one convenient for a family, between 30 and 40 feet in length, costs from 1 dollar to 1 dollar and 25 cents per foot, making perhaps 35 dollars for a comfortable family boat, well boarded up on the sides, and roofed to within seven or eight feet of the bow; exclusive of this expense, is the price of a cable, pump, and fire place, perhaps ten dollars more. Boats may also be had sometimes at New Geneva, Williamsport, Elizabethtown, and M'Keesport, on the Monongahela; and at some places on the Youghiogheny river; also at the mouth of Big Beaver, and Charlestown, on the Ohio, and perhaps a few other places. The Allegheny is now beginning to furnish boats, which descend that river in high water loaded with salt, boards, and lumber, and sell at Pittsburgh generally at a reduced price.

The number of embarkations, and their conveniences, which take place at Brownsville, Pittsburgh, and Wheeling, depend much on the different stages of the water in the different reasons: The first place is about 10 miles the nearest to the western waters from the eastward; and when the waters will suit, it saves length of road to take water there;—but the waters must be pretty well up to make embarkation sale at Brownsville; therefore, stopping there when the waters are really low, is attended with much loss of time, and of course expense.—Boats can go from Pittsburgh at a much lower stage of the water than they can from Brownsville; yet there are periods, and these generally happen from about the middle of July until the beginning of October, when embarkation at either place would be attended with considerable detention. Wheeling, therefore, is the safest point to strike at in very low stages of the water, and from thence boats may go at all seasons of the year. It is about 58 miles by land from Brownsville. Pittsburgh is preferred as a place of embarkation to Wheeling, when boats can descend from it, for two reasons: first, it is about 45 miles nearer Philadel-

---

11. We were in hopes that these observations were no longer necessary, but a recent circumstance proves their truth and applicability; Some time in the last of October or beginning of November, 1807, a Mr Winchester's boat struck a rock a few miles below Pittsburgh, and one of the bottom planks being stove in, the boat sunk immediately; and the loading, consisting of dry goods, was materially injured, to the amount of several thousand dollars. The proprietor, not being with the boat at the time, immediately, on his hearing of the accident, conceived that it must have arisen from the carelessness of the person to whom he had entrusted the care of the boat and cargo; and in consequence, brought suit against the man for damages. The man, however, to prove his innocence, produced before the justice of the peace, (Doctor Richardson, of Pittsburgh, since deceased,) the broken plank, which proved to be rotten in the part where it was broken; and the justice discharged him as not being culpable for damages in this case.

phia or Baltimore; and secondly, merchants and travellers say they are better accommodated here with storage for their goods, and all other conveniences they may stand in need of, than they could be at Wheeling; therefore, they seldom go there, except in cases of very low water, embarking either at Brownsville or Pittsburgh. But families wishing to cross the Ohio, with their wagons, generally cross at Wheeling, Charlestown, Georgetown, and Big Beaver, according to the direction of the country they are about to remove to. Those destined to the country N. W. of the Allegheny river, and on lake Erie, and bordering the boundary between Pennsylvania and Ohio, generally cross the Allegheny at Pittsburgh.

The best seasons for navigating the Ohio, are in spring and autumn. The spring season commences at the breaking up of the ice, which generally happens about the middle of February, and continues good for about three months and sometimes four. The fall season generally commences in October, and continues good until the first of December, and sometimes all through that month; when the ice begins to form and the river close. But the seasons of high water can scarcely be called periodical, as they vary considerably, according to the wetness or dryness of the season, or earliness or lateness of the setting in, or breaking up of winter.

But freshes in the rivers are not entirely confined to the spring and fall; heavy rains frequently happen, during the summer months, in the mountains, and at the sources of the Allegheny and Monongahela rivers, which give a sufficiency of water to render the navigation of the Ohio perfectly eligible. Those freshes however are not to be depended on, and when they occur, must be taken immediate advantage of, as the waters subside rapidly.

When provided with a good boat, and strong cable of at least 40 feet long, there is little danger in descending the Ohio in high freshes, when proper care is taken, unless at such times as when the river is full of floating ice. In this case it is safest to permit your boat to have pretty much her own way, as rowing may tend to throw you out of the current or on the points of islands, before you are aware of it; in which case, nothing but presence of mind and great exertions will save you. Therefore, prevent yourself being caught on the river among floating ice if possible, unless indeed, when it is very thin and thawing very fast; and even in this case, it would be better to detain until the river is clear of ice.

As frequent landing is attended with considerable loss of time and some hazard, you should contrive to land as seldom as possible; you need not even lie by at night, provided you trust to the current, and keep a good look out: If you have moon light so much the better. When you come to, the strength of your cable is a great safeguard. A quantity of fuel, and other necessaries should be laid in at once, and every boat ought to have a canoe or skiff along side, to send on shore, when necessary, or as a relief in case of accident.

Although the labour of navigating the Ohio in times of high water is very inconsiderable to what it is when it is low, when continual rowing is necessary, it is always best to keep a good look out, and be strong handed. The wind will sometimes drive you too near the points of islands, or on projecting parts of the main shore, or into a bend where there is but little current, in either case considerable exertions are necessary to get you under way again, and keep you clear of danger either on the one side or the other. You will frequently meet with head winds, the river being so very crooked as that which is in your favour one hour, may be directly against you the next; and when contrary winds contend with a strong current, it is attended with considerable inconvenience, and requires careful and circumspect management, or you may be driven on shore in spite of all your efforts. One favorable circumstance is, that the wind commonly abates about sun-set, particularly in summer.

Boats, have frequently passed from Pittsburgh to the mouth of the Ohio in 15 days in high water; but in general, 10 days to the falls is reckoned a quick passage; but sometimes a boat will be 2 weeks in going to Limestone, and in a very low state of water, 20 days.

One other precaution perhaps is necessary in case you are on the river in time of ice, which above all other seasons is certainly the most perilous:—If at any time you are obliged to bring to, on account of ice, great circumspection should be used in the choice of a place to lie in. There are many places where the shore, projecting to a point, throws off the cakes of ice towards the middle of the river, and forms a kind of harbour below. By bringing to, in such a situation, and fixing your canoe above the boat, with one end strongly tied to the shore, and the other out in the stream, sloping downwards, so as to drive off the cakes of ice, which would otherwise accumulate, and tend to sink or drive your boat from her moorings, you may lie with a tolerable degree of safety.

This is a much better way than that of feeling a tree above the boat so as to fall partly into the river; for if the tree does not strongly adhere to the stump, ten to one but the masses of ice carry it down against your boat, and put you in imminent danger, much worse than if the precaution had not been taken.

The reflection here naturally occurs, how easy it would be, and how trifling the expense, in different places on the river where boats are accustomed to land, to project a sort of pier into the river, inclining downwards, which would at all times ensure a safe mooring below. The expenses of such erections would soon be repaid by the place becoming famous for a safe and convenient stopping place for boats.

The best mode perhaps in descending the Ohio, in time of low water, is in keel boats. These seem to be more at immediate command in navigating the river; and as they are always strongly manned, they go with greater expedition. They draw little water and require but a narrow channel. Merchants are beginning to prefer this method for safety and expedition; and instead of purchasing boats and taking charge of them themselves, they get their goods freighted down from Pittsburgh in keel boats by the persons who make them, and who make it their business to be prepared, with good boats and experienced hands, for such engagements.

This method is the safest, if not the cheapest, for this special reason: the cargo is consigned to the care of an experienced and careful man, who perhaps descends and ascends the river twice or thrice in the course of one season, and of course must be well acquainted with all the difficulties in navigating it—On the contrary, when merchants are young, and inexperienced, they do not, often enough, as the Scotch phrase goes, *"Look before they loup."* They, being flushed with the idea of a fortune before them, hastily buy a boat, load, jump into it themselves, fly to the steering oar, and halloo to the hands to *pull out*. Now swimming in good water, and unapprehensive of the bad, they think themselves safe, until alarmed by the rumbling of the boat on a ripple, or shoving herself into the mud on a sandbar.—And until now they believed themselves from having gone down the river once or twice, to have been master navigators, and capable of conducting a ship of 400 tons with equal ease and safety as a common Indian canoe—Such are the mistaken calculations of the extent of our own knowledge and abilities.—And in common life, it does not unfrequently happen, that we run our ship aground, when we think she has most water to ride in.

As the trimming your boat, that is, loading her in such a manner as to draw an equal depth of water all around, is of considerable consequence to her safety, you ought to be careful to have it done before departure with a circumspect eye. For though the construction of our boats does not render them liable to overset, yet when loaded irregularly, and one corner sunken more than another, a stroke on a rock, or a log on the diagonal corner, subjects her to fill in that quarter much sooner than if properly trimmed.

There is another precaution which ought not to be neglected; that is, to see that your boat is kept afloat while loading, and when you bring to over night; for if the cable corner should rest on the shore, and during the night, the river should fall much, ten to one but before morning your boat would be filled with water. From a neglect of this kind I have seen a valuable cargo of dry goods sunk and much injured, before the boat was completely loaded.

The caulking of a boat ought to be well attended to before embarkation; for if she has been long built, her timbers and plank may have shrunk, and the caulking got loose. Boats are seldom caulked above the gunnel joint. I think this a great error, and an unsafe finishing. The next joint at least ought to be well caulked all around. And for fear of accident, it would be well that every boat was furnished with a few pounds of oakum, together with a mallet and caulking iron. These precautionary provisions might sometimes be the means of saving in part, if not in whole, a loading worth many thousand dollars. For the greater part of the accidents that happen on the Ohio, arise from a want of a proper knowledge of the means that ought to be taken to prevent them.—Some, indeed, possessing the knowledge, unpardonably neglect their duty, until sad experience puts them in mind of it, by a loss which perhaps they are little able to bear.

Having given some general and preparatory instructions which we presume will be found useful if attended to, and a cursory view of the rivers, we now commence the more particular directions how to navigate them. The distances from place to place, except those marked *(M. D.)* not having been ascertained from actual survey, may not in all cases be found absolutely correct, yet it is hoped they will not be found so materially erroneous, as to militate against the utility of the work.

15

JAMES KIRKE PAULDING

(1778–1860)

Though James Kirke Paulding wrote important works of frontier literature in four genres—travel writing (*Letters from the South* [1817]), poetry
(*The Backwoodsman* [1818]), drama (*The Lion of the West* [1830]), and fiction (*Westward Ho!* [1832])—he lived most of his life in New York. Paulding was born in Great Nine Partners, New York, during the Revolutionary War. He grew up awash in anti-British sentiments, which soon
became his own and which led to his interest in the literary possibilities
afforded by the American west.

Paulding's first important writings were the *Salmagundi* papers
(1807–1808), satiric essays that he wrote with the Irving brothers, Washington and William, in the vein of Addison and Steele. Paulding would
build his career, however, by attacking the British, not imitating them. His
anti-British writings began in 1812 with *The Diverting History of John Bull
and Brother Jonathan,* which he followed in 1813 with a parody of Sir Walter Scott, *The Lay of the Scottish Fiddle.* Later came *The United States and
England* (1815), *A Sketch of Old England by a New-England Man* (1822), and
John Bull in America: or, The New Munchausen (1825).

While Paulding attacked Britain, the British, and British literature, he
also strove to elevate the United States and American letters. In so doing,
he hoped to help establish "a distinct and characteristic national literature." He realized, however, that this would be difficult, given that Americans shared their language with the British and that American writers
looked to British writers for their literary heritage. Paulding thought that
these problems might be overcome if American writers turned to distinctly American subjects for inspiration.

Paulding's tentative first steps in this direction came in *Letters from the
South,* which he based on his 1816 travels through Virginia. He drew on
these travels again in writing *The Backwoodsman,* though this long poem
(3306 lines) is set on the Ohio frontier. In his preface, he explained the
poem's purpose: "His object was to indicate to youthful writers of his native country, the rich poetic resources with which it abounds, as well as to
call their attention *home,* for the means of attaining to novelty of subject,
if not to originality in style or sentiment."

In 1830 American actor James H. Hackett offered a prize of $300 for
"an original comedy whereof an American should be the leading character," and Paulding responded with *The Lion of the West.* When Paulding
was announced as the winner, the *New-York Mirror* lauded his "noble ambition to second the efforts of our indigenous comedian [Hackett] in laying the foundation for a national drama." The central character of *The

Lion of the West—played by Hackett, of course—was Colonel Nimrod Wildfire, an apparent caricature of Tennessee senator David Crockett. Though Paulding denied that Wildfire was Crockett, few believed him. When *The Lion of the West* was performed in Washington, Crockett sat in the front row. When Hackett came onto the stage, he bowed to Crockett, and Crockett, to the delight of the audience, bowed in return. Ironically, the text of the original *The Lion of the West* is lost, with only a British adaptation surviving.

Westward Ho!, Paulding's last major frontier work, chronicles the westward migration of Colonel Cuthbert Dangerfield, a debt-plagued Virginia gentleman. Here Paulding based his portrayal of the west on Timothy Flint's *Recollections of the Last Ten Years Passed in the Valley of the Mississippi* (1826). Paulding's later literary output includes a biography of George Washington (*A Life of Washington* [1835]), a defense of slavery (*Slavery of the United Sates* [1836]), and an historical romance of early America (*The Puritan and His Daughter* [1849]). Though Paulding was a prolific writer, he did not earn his living with his pen. In 1841 he retired from a career in government service that culminated with a term as secretary of the navy for the Martin Van Buren administration. He died on April 6, 1860, at his farm north of Hyde Park, New York.

Text: *The Backwoodsman* (Philadelphia, 1818): 7–23, 88–92, 118–121, 165–171.

FROM *THE BACKWOODSMAN*

BOOK I

My humble theme is of a hardy swain,
The lowliest of the lowly rural train,
Who left his native fields afar to roam,
In western wilds, in search of happier home.
5 Simple the tale I venture to rehearse,
For humble is the Muse, and weak her verse;
She hazards not, to sing in lofty lays,
Of steel-clad knights, renown'd in other days,
For glorious feats that, in this dastard time,
10 Would on the gallows make them swing sublime;
Or tell of stately dames of royal birth,
That scorn'd communion with dull things of earth,
With fairies leagu'd, and dwarfs of goblin race,
Of uncouth limbs, and most unseemly face,

15 Tremendous wights! that erst in nursery-keep
   Were used to scare the froward babe to sleep.

      Neglected Muse! of this our western clime,
   How long in servile, imitative rhyme,
   Wilt thou thy stifled energies impart,
20 And miss the path that leads to every heart?
   How long repress the brave decisive flight,
   Warm'd by thy native fires, led by thy native light?
   Thrice happy he who first shall strike the lyre,
   With homebred feeling, and with homebred fire;
25 He need not envy any favour'd bard,
   Who Fame's bright meed, and Fortune's smiles reward;
   Secure, that wheresoe'er this empire rolls,
   Or east, or west, or tow'rd the firm fixed poles,
   While Europe's ancient honours fade away,
30 And sink the glories of her better day,
   When, like degenerate Greece, her former fame
   Shall stand contrasted with her present shame,
   And all the splendours of her bright career
   Shall die away, to be relighted here,
35 A race of myriads will the tale rehearse,
   And love the author of the happy verse.
   Come then, neglected Muse! and try with me
   The untrack'd path—'tis death or victory;
   Let Chance or Fate decide, or critics will,
40 No fame I lose—I am but nothing still.

      From Hudson—oft, and well remember'd name!—
   Led by the star of Hope, our hero came;
   Here was he born, and here perchance had died,
   But Fate ordain'd he other scenes should bide;
45 For BASIL, like true Yankee lad, a wife
   Took to himself ere settled half in life,
   And soon began, in sober truth to prove,
   The cares that often break the heart of love.
   For, well-a-day! the offspring's sweetest smile,
50 And wife's caress, may fail to sweeten toil;
   Nor can the gentlest nature always stem
   The thought, that all these cares are brav'd for them.
   Each morn we saw him, ere the rising sun,
   And saw him, when his golden course was run,
55 Toiling, through all the livelong tedious day,
   To chase the scarecrow Poverty away;
   And when the sacred day of rest came round,
   Nor rest, nor village church by him was found;
   Along the river's bank still forc'd to roam,
60 To catch a meal for wife and babes at home.

Thus all his days in one long toil were past,
And each new day seem'd heavier than the last,
While the keen thought that his hard sinewy hand
Was blister'd, labouring on another's land;
65 That the rich products which he toil'd to rear,
To others' boards gave plenty through the year,
While he and his, at home, but half supplied,
Shar'd all the ills that poverty betide,
To many an hour of bitterness gave birth,
70 And smote his mounting spirit to the earth.

O! Independence! man's bright mental sun,
With blood and tears by our brave country won,
Parent of all, high mettled man adorns,
The nerve of steel, the soul that meanness scorns,
75 The mounting wind that spurns the tyrant's sway,
The eagle eye that mocks the God of day,
Turns on the lordly upstart scorn for scorn,
And drops its lid to none of woman born!
With blood, and tears, and hardships thou wert bought,
80 Yet rich the blessings thy bright sway has wrought;
Hence comes it that a gallant spirit reigns
Unknown among old Europe's hapless swains,
Who slaves to some proud lord, himself a slave,
From sire to son from cradle to the grave,
85 From race to race, more dull and servile grow,
Until at last they nothing feel or know.
Hence comes it, that our meanest farmer's boy
Aspires to taste the proud and manly joy
That springs from holding in his own dear right
90 The land he plows, the home he seeks at night;
And hence it comes, he leaves his friends and home,
Mid distant wilds and dangers drear to roam,
To seek a competence, or find a grave,
Rather than live a hireling or a slave.
95 As the bright waving harvest field he sees,
Like sunny ocean rippling in the breeze,
And hears the lowing herd, the lambkins' bleat,
Fall on his ear in mingled concert sweet,
His heart sits lightly on its rustic throne,
100 The fields, the herds, the flocks are all his own.

But BASIL tasted not this sober bliss,
A diff'rent and a sterner lot was his;
Years pass'd away, and every year that past
Brought cares and toils still heavier than the last;
105 For still, each passing year, his fruitful wife
Brought a new burthen struggling into life,

Till, sooth to say, his house became too small,
Within its narrow walls to hold them all,
And all the struggles of our hardy swain
110 Could scarcely keep from want the lusty train.
At last, one winter came,—relentless time!—
Fear'd by the wretched in this pinching clime,
Where driving sleets and piercing whistling wind
Through every cranny a rude entrance find,
115 Chilling the cottage hearth, whose stinted blaze
Half warms the urchin that around it plays.
The trying season came, and, sad to tell,
Rheumatic agonies on BASIL fell,
And with a rude, unsparing, withering hand
120 Cast him a wreck on Life's hard frozen strand.
No more his vigorous arm can strike the blow
That lays the monarch of the woodland low;
No more, alas! no more his daily toils
Feed his poor babes, and wake their grateful smiles;
125 For when the poor man sickens, all is gone,
Health, food, and all his comforts—every one;
The hand that fed the little whitehair'd race,
Lies motionless, in one sad resting place,
And keen varieties of wo combin'd
130 Prey on his flesh, and lacerate his mind.
But when the rich one suffers—happy wealth!
He feels no want, but the one want of health;
And all those precious comforts that impart
Such soothings to the sad and sinking heart,
135 Still in his cup with plenteous current flow
And half create oblivion of his wo;
No anxious cares molest his weaken'd mind
For starving wife and children left behind,
Who, when the sire that fed them shall be dead,
140 Will pine in anguish for their daily bread,
And meet no succour, save from that good Hand
Which fed the prophet in a desert land.

Were I to tell what BASIL suffer'd now,
What agonizing drops roll'd down his brow,
145 As sad he lay upon his stinted bed,
Fearing to die, yet wishing he were dead;
How through that endless winter, Want and Pain,
Like rival fiends, tugg'd at his heart and brain;
How when his wife to distant neighbour's home,
150 For work or charity each day would roam;
Alone he lay, all desolate the while,
Sooth'd by no kind caress, or offspring's smile;

While other sounds there never met his ear,
But moans for food, that smote his heart to hear,
155 However sad the story, or how true,
The tale, alas! were neither strange nor new;
For even in this—man's chosen resting place,—
This nestling corner of the human race;—
This new Medina of the glowing West—
160 Where want finds plenty, and the exile rest,
Such scenes in real life, we sometimes see,
That blunt the keener edge of sympathy,
And teach, that rich and poor, the wise and fool,
Take lessons, soon or late, in Misery's school.

165   But time, as wise ones say, can all things cure,
Or what's as well, can teach us to endure;
For ever tasting, our enjoyment cloys—
For ever suffering, half our pain destroys;
The prosperous, fear to lose what they possess,
170 The poor man, hopes some future hour will bless;
The happy, live in constant fear to die,
The wretched, hope for immortality;
Fear to the one, paints danger from afar,
Hope, is the other's bright and blessed star.
175 Now laughing Spring came on, and birds, in pairs,
Chirp'd in the lively woods, while balmy airs
And warming beams, no more with frosts at strife,
Wak'd from its trance the genial tide of life,
That as it flow'd through Nature's swelling veins,
180 Freed every pulse from Winter's icy chains,
Tinted her mantling cheek with rosy hue,
And call'd her vernal beauties all to view;
The swelling buds forth from their coverts sprung,
And push'd away the wither'd leaves that hung
185 Whispering through many a shivering wint'ry blast,
To fall in the first breath of Spring at last.
Like dead men, in their graves forgot, they lie,
Unmark'd by all, save some lone musing eye
That marvels much, and idly, on its way,
190 Men, with such cause to weep, should be so gay.

Who can resist the coaxing voice of Spring,
When flowers put forth and sprightly songsters sing?
He is no honest son of mother Earth,
And shames the holy dame that gave him birth;
195 We are her children, and when forth she hies,
Dress'd in her wedding suit of varied dyes,
Beshrew the churl that does not feel her charms,
And love to nestle in her blooming arms;

He has no heart, or such a heart as I
200 Would not possess for all beneath the sky:
For thus to sit upon the clover'd brow
Of some full bosom'd hill as I do now,
And see the river, wind its happy way,
Round jutting points, with Spring's blest verdure gay,
205 Bearing upon its broad expansive brim
A flock of little barques that gayly skim
Backward and forth, as wayward zephyrs blow,
Like buoyant swans, all white as wint'ry snow;
And hear the distant waves so faintly roar
210 On the white sand, or whiter pebbled shore,
Mix'd with the whip-poor-will, and warbling train,
That hail the evening with their mingled strain;
And, over all, to see the Sun's last rays
Gild the glad world, and make the forests blaze.—
215 Yes—thus to sit in some gay solitude,
And call around him Memory's shadowy brood,
By turning to the folded leaf to look
For some sweet record, in Time's sacred book,
That brings to mind a train of gentle themes,
220 Ideal joys, and sprites of long past dreams
Of happy times, I never may forget,
That thrill with no sharp pang of keen regret,
But like the splendours of a summer day,
Amid the western clouds more sweetly play,
225 Reflected in the skies when day is past,
Each varying hue still softer than the last—
This is my happiness—and those who know
A surer path to peace on Earth below,
May keep it to themselves—I lack it not,
230 Content with what I am—and with my lot.

     Even BASIL, as all desolate he lay,
Felt the bland influence of Spring's newborn sway;
The Sun's warm beams like oil of gladness came,
And pour'd fresh vigour through his wasted frame;
235 Relax'd his rigid muscles like a charm,
And now a leg, and now a helpless arm,
Reviv'd to motion, life, and liberty,
Till in good time his wasted frame was free;
Life through his wither'd trunk resistless flow'd,
240 And his brown cheek with Health's own colour glow'd.
Yet though Health came, and in her jocund train
Brought all his wonted comforts back again,
Still anxious cares would throng his manly breast,
And poison many an hour of toil and rest.

245 The thought, when wint'ry frosts again came round,
    And dash'd the forest's honours to the ground,
    Its chilling influence might again renew
    The scene that cleft his stubborn heart in two;
    That once again himself, his babes, his wife,
250 Might be indebted for a niggard life,
    To those who had but little to bestow,
    Wak'd in his heart anticipated wo,
    And rous'd his spirit to go any where,
    Rather than such a beggar'd lot to share.
255 At last there reach'd his eager listening ear,
    A tale that made his heart leap light to hear;
    'Twas said that o'er the hills, and far away,
    Towards the setting sun, a land there lay,
    Whose unexhausted energies of soil
260 Nobly repaid the hardy lab'rer's toil;
    Where men were worth full twice their weight in gold,
    And goodly farms for almost nought were sold;
    Prairies of flowers, and grassy meads abound,
    And rivers every where meander round.

265   The news like music came to BASIL's ear,
    And mov'd his mind to seek a refuge here;
    What though long tedious miles did intervene,
    And dangers lurk his hopes and him between;
    What if he bade a long, nay last adieu,
270 To scenes his earliest feelings fondly knew,
    Bright Independence could the loss repay,
    And make him rich amends some other day;
    Better to leave all these, and friends most dear,
    Than live a pining pauper half the year.
275 His trembling wife, when this resolve was known,
    Shrunk from the journey to these regions lone,
    But sooth'd, at last, by Hope's persuasive wile,
    Consented gayly with a tearful smile;
    Brac'd every nerve to meet the parting day,
280 When they to distant lands should speed away,
    And, like right trusty dame, resolv'd to share
    The good man's lot, how hard soe'er it were.

    Soon all was ready, for but little they
    To such far distant wilds could move away,
285 And if they could, their store of goods was small,
    And little time it took to pack them all:
    A little cover'd cart held all their store,
    And, sooth to say, it might have held much more:
    A sturdy nag, right rugged, rough, and strong,
290 Fitted to drag such equipage along,

"Stood ready dight," as minstrel poets say,
To speed the little bevy on their way:—
Such was their outfit in this journey lone,
To distant wilds, and haunts to man unknown.

295   Now all was ready—but ere starting day
To village church poor BASIL bent his way,
To ask of Him whose goodness ne'er denies
The prayers from honest poverty that rise,
Whose help is ever ready for the man
300 That helps himself, when help himself he can—
To ask for steady firmness to pursue
The honest purpose which he had in view;
That health would hover round his lonely way,
And GOD protect him through each passing day.
305 He begg'd no more—and all was freely given
By the sweet bounty of approving Heav'n.

    And now the simple morning service o'er,
The neighbours throng'd round BASIL at the door;
For they had heard his vent'rous project told—
310 Some thought him mad, some desperately bold;—
For 'twas not then as now—and such a plan,
Like a strange wonder, through the country ran,
And people star'd that he should leave his home,
Among the western wilds afar to roam.
315 The pastor bless'd him sadly as he past,
The young ones look'd as though they'd look their last,
While aged grandsires many a story told,
That made the breathless list'ners' blood run cold;
Of troops of howling wolves aye prowling round,
320 Of shaggy bears that every where abound,
And bloody Indian, whose infernal yell,
Of torture, death, and scalping tells full well;
Who hated blood of white-man never spares,
Women, nor babes, nor reverend snow white hairs.
325 They conjur'd up each story that they knew,
And car'd not, so 'twas strange, if it were true—
Of woodmen shot outright, in open day,
By prowling Indian watching for his prey;
Of sleeping wife and babes, rous'd by the yell
330 Of him whose voice is Death's shrill howling knell,
Consum'd in midnight flames, as lone they lay,
The father and protector far away.

    Chill horror curdled every list'ner's blood,
And stiff on end the urchins' light hair stood,
335 But BASIL still his manly heart sustain'd,
And to his daring purpose firm remain'd;

Hope was his guide, and led by that bright lure,
Man can the keenest rubs of life endure.
He was no haughty lordling's humble slave,
340 Stript of the mantle that his Maker gave;
No dull unletter'd hireling, whose starv'd mind
Just leaves, and hardly leaves, the beast behind;
Who chains and stripes with equal calmness bears,
And, so he eats enough, for neither cares;
345 Fit tenant for some little lord, who serves
Some little king, and, what he gives, deserves.
No! though the poorest of a poor man's race,
Our BASIL was not born to such disgrace;
He felt that he was free, and that one word,
350 In his proud heart, a noble spirit stirr'd,
Whose gallant thrilling through his pulses ran,
And made him feel, and know himself a man.
He shook their outstretch'd hands, and bade them pray
That Heaven would speed him on his lonely way;
355 Then sought the aged tree, beneath whose shade
His sire, and mother, side by side were laid,
Leant o'er the simple mounds that mark'd the spot,
By all, save him, full many a year forgot,
And pray'd to live a life of honest fame,
360 And leave behind, like them, a spotless name.

FROM BOOK IV

Far in a dismal glen whose deep recess,
The Sun's life-giving ray did never bless,
35 Beside a lone and melancholy stream,
That never sparkled in the spritely beam,
Sever'd from all his copper-colour'd race,
A moody Indian made his biding place;
Here mid green carpets of dew dripping moss,
40 And solemn pines, that lock'd their arms across
The foam-crown'd brook, and with their gloomy shade
An everlasting dusky twilight made,
With hurrying steps, like maniac oft he trod,
And curs'd the white-man, and the white-man's God.
45 Once the proud painted chief of warriors brave,
Whose bones now bleaching lay without a grave,
A thousand red-men own'd his savage sway,
And follow'd on where'er he led the way,

Rang'd the wide forest many a countless mile,
50 And hail'd him lord of cruelty and wile—
Now, like a girdled tree, unleaf'd he stood,
The only relick of a stately wood;
The last of all his race—he lived alone,
His name, his being, and his haunts unknown.

55   Amid a sunless vegetation here,
Fungus, and mildew'd rottenness so drear,
He nurs'd his spleen, and studied day and night
How he his nation's wrongs might best requite,
Tear every white-man's offspring limb from limb,
60 And do to them, as they had done to him;
For no deep casuist, alas! was he,
The justice of the white-man's claims to see,
Or comprehend, why the pale slave of toil,
Who turns to gold the fruits of every soil,
65 A better claim had to this smiling earth,
Than those who rang'd it from their nation's birth.
Oft would he roam the pathless woods by night,
When star and moon refus'd their cheering light,
Invoke the shadows of his fallen race,
70 That howl about the world from place to place,
Or call dark spirits from their dread repose,
To sooth his vengeance and strike down his foes,
And when the echoes answer'd loud and near,
Would fancy that they throng'd around him here.
75 The passions that in other breasts bear sway,
And lead the race of man a different way,
He never knew, or if he e'er had known,
Before one master feeling they had flown.
The love of woman, glory, or of gain,
80 Ne'er caus'd a pang, or sooth'd an hour of pain,
All were condens'd in one intense desire,
That scorch'd his brain and heart with quenchless fire;
His very life and being it had grown,
He liv'd, he breath'd, in that, and that alone.

85   Thus long time brooding o'er one bloody theme,
That fill'd his daily musings, and his dream,
His brain to moody madness was beguil'd,
And broke into a chaos dark and wild—
Forsaken haunts unknown to the clear Heav'n,
90 Caves in the dripping rocks by torrents riv'n,
At eve he sought, and with half-smother'd breath,
Woo'd fell Revenge, and hungry white-ribb'd Death,
"Hark!" would he mutter, "every thing is still,
"The screech-owl, wolf, and boding whip-poor-will!

95 "Now is your time—come forth I prithee now—
   "Come my pale darlings, fan my burning brow.
   "If in the air ye hover—blessed things!—
   "Come like the raven with his coal-black wings;
   "If in the worthless, man-encumber'd earth,
100 "Like forked adders, crawl ye hissing forth;
    "Come with an apple in your coiling train,
    "And blast these ague-cheeks yet once again;
    "Or if beneath the Ocean's mad'ning foam,
    "Ye find your dark and melancholy home,
105 "Rise, with its ugliest monsters in your train,
    "And give me vengeance for my people slain;
    "So shall the blue detested wave that bore,
    "The book-learn'd fiend, the white-man to this shore,
    "With tardy justice help me to repay,
110 "The wrongs that eat my very heart away."

FROM BOOK V

   The maniac Prophet, whose infuriate hate,
   Disdain'd the lagging steps of War to wait,
   Set forth on lonely ramble to descry,
   If yet, perchance, the adverse foe was nigh,
195 Or haply free from dreary War's alarm,
   He staid at home, nor dream'd of coming harm.
   Alone he hied him—for his gloomy soul,
   Sicken'd at fellowship, and scorn'd control;
   His humour was to roam, no one knew where,
200 Mutt'ring and murm'ring to the lonely air.
   With cautious step, the wily Indian went
   Like prowling thief on villanous intent,
   Lay on his face, and listen'd to the breeze,
   Whose whisper'd greetings woo'd the waving trees,
205 And if an acorn fell, he quail'd with fear,
   For now the white-man's dangerous haunts were near.
   Nearer, and nearer still the Prophet hied,
   And now the curling smoke far off descry'd,
   Above the woods in waving volumes rise,
210 Mingling its lighter tints with pale blue skies.
   A little nearer, and the village spire,
   Rose every moment higher yet and higher,
   Until, at last, the peaceful hamlet scene,
   Burst on his view, along the level green;

215 The Sun's last rays upon the spire top gleam'd,
    The ev'ning purple on the still wave beam'd,
    The lazy herds tinkled their evening bell,
    The measur'd oar upon the river fell,
    As swift the light canoe, from side to side,
220 Flitting like Indian barque was seen to glide,
    The boatman ty'd his boat to root of tree,
    And sung, or whistled there, right merrily—
    And every sound upon the ear that broke,
    The hour of rural relaxation spoke;
225 Nothing was seen, but comfort every where,
    And nothing heard, that seem'd the voice of Care.

       Back shrunk the madbrain'd wand'rer stung with spleen,
    And sick'ning at this peaceful village scene;
    It minded him of times he once had known,
230 Ere doom'd to wander through the earth alone,
    For on this spot he once had reign'd a king,
    O'er man and beast, and every living thing;
    In this fair haunt, from boy to man he grew,
    And tasted all the bliss the savage knew;
235 Here had he seen his people happy dwell,
    Here had they fought, were conquer'd, and all fell.
    A flood of tenderness rush'd on his mind,
    And for one moment the poor wretch grew blind;
    A thrill, for many, and many a year unknown,
240 Cut through his heart, though harden'd into stone,
    A tear, the only one that e'er had stain'd
    His manhood's cheek, unbrush'd away remain'd,
    And, for one breath, his lone and wretched lot,
    Was in the mem'ry of the past forgot.
245 But 'twas a moment only that engag'd
    His tender thoughts—the next his bosom rag'd;
    Indignantly he brush'd the tear away,
    And as more hotly glows the Sun's bright ray,
    When past the Summer shower that soon is o'er,
250 And leaves it brighter than it was before,
    His swelling heart with keener vengeance burn'd,
    And all his tenderness to fury turn'd.

       "Aye—rest ye safe awhile"—he madly cried;
    "Bask in the sunshine on *my* river's side,
255 "While the true lord of wave and wood and soil,
    "Skulks from his home, and howls and starves the while.
    "Sleep soundly yet, ye curs'd—devoted train,
    "Ere long ye'll slumber ne'er to wake again,
    "Or wake to hear the death-denouncing yell,
260 "Rouse for the last time, with its echoing swell,

"To see your dwellings wrapt in midnight flames,
"Hear helpless babes, and wives invoke your names,
"And call upon the Christian God in vain,
"To be their safeguard, yet, yet once again.
265 "How silent all around—how mild the eve!
"Farewell awhile—a little while I leave
"These gentle haunts, which when again I see,
"Wo to the white-man—he'll remember me!"

FROM BOOK VI

Why then should I luxuriate in gore,
And tell of horrors often told before?
How Christian groans, and Pagan's fearful yell,
As fled the one, or as the other fell,
500 And made the stoutest bosom quake with fear?
Why should I free my Muse from her restraint,
And with unfeeling coolness pause, to paint
The quiv'ring limb, the bleeding bosom bare,
The dripping head, reft of its honour'd hair,
505 The writhing struggle in the last sad hour,
When Death and fainting Nature try their power;
The wounded victim, now bereft alike,
Of strength to crawl, or energy to strike,
Rolling and weltering in his smoking gore,
510 By friends and foes alike now trampled o'er,
Unheeded in the bloody, busy strife,
Where each man fought to save, or win a life?
Why should I—but enough, alas! and more—
We are no vampyres thus to live on gore;
515 Man 's not a wolf, o'er carnag'd fields to prowl,
And snuff the scent of blood, and lap, and howl;
Nor vulture hov'ring in the blessed air,
Watching, the dying victim's heart to tear,
That he should thus delight in blood and strife,
520 And hang with rapture o'er the woes of life.

. . . .

All now is silent, in the scene so lone,
Save ever and anon a feeble moan,
That at each repetition dies away,
Like the last echoes of some plaintive lay.
655 The watchful wolf that hears the welcome sound,
Lur'd by the signal, prowls the field around,

Licking the earth, and yelling forth the while,
His horrid joy at such a glorious spoil;
Sad music to the dying victim's ear,
660 Whose fainting heart still throbs such notes to hear.
What ghastly spectre, near yon heap of slain,
Wak'd by the music, comes to life again,
With desp'rate effort bravely seeks to rise,
Then sinks in silence, and in silence dies?
665 It is the maniac Prophet!—lo, once more
He strives to rise, but falls e'en as before,
His waning strength that heart no more sustains,
And drop by drop the life blood slowly drains.
But see! supported by that groaning wretch,
670 I see him toward the heav'ns his red arm stretch,
And hark! his last words tremble on mine ear,
Just faintly heard, amid the silence drear.

     "'Tis past—no more I hail the rising sun—
"'Tis past—and yet the work is left undone!
675 "The white man triumphs, the poor Indian bleeds,
"The good cause suffers, and the bad succeeds.
"Yet how yon heavens do smile, as if in scorn
"Of wretched man, from life and kindred torn,
"As if they car'd not for the right or wrong,
680 "Or sided ever with the righteous strong.
"'Twas always thus—for I remember well,
"Long time ago, when my brave nation fell,
"No signs appear'd that those who dwell above,
"For one or other in the conflict strove;
685 "No Indian spirits battled on our side,
"To curb the bold invader's towering pride,
"Or bolster up the tottering cause of right,
"Man, man alone, decided that last fight,
"While earth, and skies smil'd at the bloody scene,
690 "And Nature pitiless, look'd on serene.
"Then why should I to these direct my pray'r,
"They never listen, or they never care?
"Great Spirit! ev'n in this my dying hour,
"I do defy thee, fearless of thy power,
695 "Be it thy want of might, or lack of will,
"Or one or both, I do defy thee still.
"Thou did'st deceive me in thy promis'd aid,
"First rais'd our hopes, and then those hopes betray'd,
"Sold us to whitemen, battled on their side,
700 "Else we had not been beat, nor had I died.
"If thou hadst power, why then refuse thine aid,
"If not, then have thy vot'ries idly pray'd;

"Thou art a cheat that in the heav'ns dost dwell,
"Take my defiance, and so fare thee well.

705   "Yet if there be among ye one that cares
        "For Indian wrongs, to thee I lift my prayers.
        "Alas!—'tis now too late for me to pray
        "For victory on some propitious day,
        "The time is past, our rights and lands to save,
710   "Nor canst thou wake the tenants of the grave.
        "Yet oh! if e'er their groans have reach'd thine ear,
        "Hear my last adjuration—Spirit, hear!
        "Let slip a race of powerful demons forth
        "From the deep bosom of the blasted earth,
715   "To wage eternal vengeance in our name,
        "To wrap the world, in one wide wasting flame,
        "Sweep from their lands usurp'd the whiteman's race,
        "And plant still bloodier monsters in their place.
        "But if within the bounds of Earth or Hell,
720   "No bloodier fiends than they are found to dwell,
        "Bring thou one half of that detested race
        "Against the other, marshall'd face to face,
        "There let them murder, till of all the train,
        "But one gash'd wretch alone like me remain,
725   "The venom'd spleen of all his race to nurse,
        "And breathe it forth, in one last dying curse."

        Down on the bleeding wretch he sunk again,
        Who groan'd, as if with agonizing-pain;
        "Silence! thou woman"—scornfully he cried,
730   "Art thou the first hast suffer'd, bled, or died?
        "Pale whiteman—for I know thee by thy groans,
        "If thou want'st pity, go and ask yon stones;
        "Or tell me over slowly, one by one,
        "The favours ye to our wild race have done—
735   "Tell how ye sought our haunts with pious care,
        "Show'd us thy way to heav'n, and pack'd us there,
        "And when ye found us roving in the wood,
        "Baptiz'd us Christians in our smoking blood.
        "But"—and the dying energy that still
740   "Obey'd the impulse of his master will,
        New strung his arm—"One pleasure yet remains,
        "There's yet some blood left in thy Christian veins,
        "There's yet one nerve within thy treacherous heart,
        "Where I may wake one keen and mortal smart;
745   "Come let me practise knowledge clearly bought,
        "And christen thee, as I by thee was taught.

"Whoe'er thou art, I neither care, or know,
"Thou art a whiteman, and of course my foe."

    Then as the speechless victim rais'd his arm,
750 To supplicate, or haply shield from harm,
    Deep in his bloodless heart he plung'd the knife,
    And freed the last remains of struggling life—
    Heav'n still is just, it was the Renegade
    That suffer'd by the hand he had betray'd!
755 Delirious laughter rattled in his throat,
    As thus the guilty caitiff dead he smote,
    And ere the dying victim sunk to rest,
    The murd'rer breath'd his last upon his breast.

ᔙ 16 ᔖ

CHARLES BALL

(c. 1781–?)

The full title of Charles Ball's autobiography, published in 1837, gives a fair idea of its contents: *Slavery in the United States: A Narrative of the Life and Adventures of Charles Ball, a Black Man, Who Lived Forty Years in Maryland, South Carolina and Georgia, As a Slave, under Various Masters, and Was One Year in the Navy with Commodore Barney, During the Late War. Containing an Account of the Manners and Usages of the Planters and Slaveholders of the South—A Description of the Condition and Treatment of the Slaves, with Observations from the State of Morals amongst the Cotton Planters, and the Perils and Sufferings of a Fugitive Slave, Who Twice Escaped the Cotton Country.* As was commonly the case with antislavery narratives, Ball's story and its overlong title were ghostwritten. His ghostwriter, a Mr. Fisher, assured readers that "the narrative is taken from the mouth of the adventurer himself; and if the copy does not retain the identical words of the original, the sense and import, at least, are faithfully preserved."

Ball's grandfather was kidnapped from Africa and sold into slavery in Calvert County, Maryland, around 1730. When Ball knew him, his grandfather was a slave near Leonardtown, Maryland. Ball's father also lived in this vicinity. Circa 1785, when Ball was about four, his mother's owner, a tobacco planter, died. Soon thereafter, Ball, his mother, and his numerous siblings were sold to different masters. He would never see any of them again. In the selection below, we join Ball's story in 1806. A resident of South Carolina, he sets out with a wagon to build a new home in the west. But the wagon and the home are not his. Indeed, Ball does not even own himself. Thus, he tells a common story from an unusual perspective.

Text: *Slavery in the United States: A Narrative of the Life and Adventures of Charles Ball* (New York, 1837): 337–346.

FROM *SLAVERY IN THE UNITED STATES:*

A Narrative of the Life and Adventures of Charles Ball, a Black Man (1837)

CHAPTER XVII.

An affair was now in progress, which, though the persons who were actors in it were far removed from me, had in its effects a great influence upon the fortunes of my life. I have informed the reader that my master had three daughters, and that the second of the sisters was deemed a great beauty. The eldest of the three was married about the time of which I now write, to a planter of great wealth, who resided near Columbia; but the second had formed an attachment to a young gentleman whom she had frequently seen at the church attended by my master's family. As this young man, either from want of wealth, or proper persons to introduce him, had never been at my master's house, my young mistress had no opportunity of communicating to him the sentiments she entertained towards him, without violating the rules of modesty in which she had been educated. Before she would attempt any thing which might be deemed a violation of the decorum of her sex, she determined to take a new method of obtaining a husband. She communicated, to her father, my master, a knowledge of the whole affair, with a desire that he would invite the gentleman of her choice to his house. This the father resolutely opposed, upon the ground that the young man upon whom his daughter had fixed her heart was without property, and consequently destitute of the means of supporting his daughter in a style suitable to the rank she occupied in society. A woman in love is not easily foiled in her purposes; my young mistress, by continual entreaties, so far prevailed over the affections, or more probably the fears of her father, that he introduced the young man to his family, and about two months afterwards my young mistress was a bride; but it had been agreed amongst all the parties, as I understood, before the marriage, that as the son-in-law had no land or slaves of his own, he should remove with his wife to a large tract of land that my master owned in the new purchase in the state of Georgia.

In the month of September, 1806, my master came to the quarter one evening, at the time of our return from the field, in company with his son-in-law, and informed me that he had given me, with a number of others of his slaves, to his daughter; and that I, with eight other men and two or three women, must set out on the next Sunday with my new master, for his estate in Georgia, whither we were to go, to clear land, build houses, and make other improvements, necessary for the reception of the newly-married lady, in the following spring.

I was much pleased with the appearance and manners of my new master, who was a young man apparently about twenty-seven or eight years old, and of good figure. We were to take with us, in our expedition to Georgia, a wagon, to be drawn by six mules, and I was appointed to drive the team. Before we set off my young mistress came in person to the quarter, and told us that all those who were going to the new settlement must come to the house, where she furnished each of us with two full suits of clothes, one of coarse woollen, and the other of hempen cloth. She also gave a hat to each of us, and two pairs of shoes, with a trifle in money, and enjoined us to be good boys and girls, and get things ready for her, and that when she should come to live with us we should not be forgotten. The conduct of this young lady was so different from that which I had been accustomed to witness since I came to Carolina, that I considered myself highly fortunate in becoming her slave, and now congratulated myself with the idea that I should, in future, have a mistress who would treat me kindly, and if I behaved well, would not permit me to want.

At the time appointed we set out for Georgia, with all the tools and implements necessary to the prosecution of a new settlement. My young master accompanied us, and travelled slowly for several days to enable me to keep up with him. We continued our march in this order until we reached the Savannah river at the town of Augusta, where my master told me that he was so well satisfied with my conduct, that he intended to leave me with the team to bring on the goods and the women and children; but that he would take the men and push on, as fast as possible, to the new settlement, and go to work until the time of my arrival. He gave me directions to follow on and inquire for Morgan county Court House, and said that he would have a person ready there on my arrival to guide me to him and the people with him. He then gave me twenty dollars to buy food for the mules and provisions for myself and those with me, and left me on the high road master of myself and the team. I was resolved that this striking proof of confidence on the part of my master should not be a subject of regret to him, and pursued my route with the greatest diligence, taking care to lay out as little money as possible for such things as I had to buy. On the sixth day, in the morning, I arrived at our new settlement in the middle of a heavy forest of such timber as is common to that country, with three dollars and twenty-five cents in my pocket, part of the money given to me at Augusta. This I offered to return, but my master refused to take it, and told me to keep it for my good conduct. I now felt assured that all my troubles in this world were ended, and that, in future, I might look forward to a life of happiness and ease; for I did not consider labour any hardship, if I was well provided with good food and clothes, and my other wants properly regarded.

My master, and the people who were with him, had, before our arrival with the wagon, put up the logs of two cabins, and were engaged, when we came, in covering one of them with clapboards. In the course of the next day we completed both these cabins, with puncheon floors and small glass windows, the sash and glass for which I had brought in the wagon. We put up two other cabins, and a stable for the mules, and then began to clear land. After a few days, my master told me he meant to go down into the settlements to buy provisions for the winter, and that he should leave me to oversee the hands, and carry on the work in his absence. He accordingly left us, taking with him the wagon and two boys, one to drive the team, and another to drive cattle and hogs, which he intended to buy and drive to our settlement. I now felt myself almost proprietor of our new establishment, and believe the men left under my charge did not consider me a very lenient overseer. I in truth compelled them to work very hard, as I did myself. At the end of a week my master returned with a heavy load of meal and bacon, with salt and other things that we needed, and the day following a white man drove to our station several cows, and more than twenty hogs, the greater part of which were breeders. At this season of the year neither the hogs nor the cattle required any feeding at our hands. The woods were full of nuts, and the grass was abundant; but we gave salt to our stock, and kept the hogs in a pen, two or three days, to accustom them to the place.

We now lived very differently from what we did on my old master's plantation.

We had as much bacon every day as we could eat; which, together with bread and sweet potatoes which we had at will, constituted our fare. My master remained with us more than two months; within which time we had cleared forty acres of ground, ready for the plough; but, a few days before Christmas, an event took place, which, in its consequences, destroyed all my prospects of happiness, and totally changed the future path of my life. A messenger one day came to our settlement, with a letter, which had been forwarded in this manner, by the postmaster at the Court House, where the post-office was kept. This letter contained intelligence of the sudden death of my old master; and that difficulties had arisen in the family which required the immediate attention of my young one. The letter was written by my mistress. My master, forthwith, took an account of the stock of provisions, and other things that he had on hand, and putting the whole under my charge, gave me directions to attend to the work, and set off on horseback that evening; promising to return within one month at furthest. We never saw him again, and heard nothing of him until late in the month of January, 1807, when the eldest man of my late master came to our settlement, in company with a strange gentleman. The son of my late master informed me, to my surprise and sorrow, that my young master, who had brought us to Georgia, was dead, and that he and the gentleman with him, were administrators of the deceased, and had come to Georgia for the purpose of letting out on lease, for the period of seven years, our place, with all the people on it, including me.

To me, the most destroying part of the years, was the death of my young master, and I was still more sorry when I learned, that he had been killed in a duel. My young mistress, whose beauty had drawn around her numerous suiters, many of whom were men of base minds and cowardly hearts, had chosen her husband, in the manner I have related; and his former rivals, after his return from Georgia, confederated together, for the dastardly purpose of revenging themselves, of both husband and wife, by the murder of the former.

In all parts of the cotton country, there are numerous taverns, which answer the double purpose of drinking and gambling houses. These places are kept by men who are willing to abandon all pretensions to the character and standing of gentlemen, for the hope of sordid gain; and are frequented by all classes of planters; though it is not to be understood, that all the planters resort to these houses. There are men of high and honourable virtue amongst the planters, who equally detest the mean cupidity of the men who keep these houses, and the silly wickedness of those who support them. Billiards is the game regarded as the most polite amongst men of education and fashion; but cards, dice, and every kind of game, whether of skill or of hazard, are openly played in these sinks of iniquity. So far as my knowledge extends, there is not a single district of ten miles square, in all the cotton region, without at least one of these vile ordinaries, as they are frequently and justly termed. The keeping of these houses is a means of subsistence resorted to by men of desperate reputation, or reckless character; and they invite, as guests, all the profligate, the drunken, the idle, and the unwary of the surrounding country. In a community, where the white man never works, except at the expense of forfeiting all claim to the rank of a gentleman, and where it is beneath the dignity of a man, to oversee the labour of his own plantation, the number of those who frequent these gaming houses, may be imagined.

My young master, fortunately for his own honour, was of those who kept aloof from the precincts of the tavern, unless compelled by necessary business to go there; but the band of conspirators, who had resolved on his destruction, invited him through one of their number, who pretended to wish to treat with him concerning his property, to meet them at an ordinary, one evening. Here a quarrel was sought with him, and he was challenged to fight with pistols, over the table around which they sat.

My master, who, it appears, was unable to bear the reproach of cowardice even amongst fools, agreed to fight and as he had no pistols with him, was presented with a pair belonging to one of the gang; and accepted their owner as his friend, or second in the business. The result was as might have been expected. My master was killed at the first fire by a ball which passed through his breast, whilst his antagonist escaped unharmed.

A servant was immediately despatched with a letter to my mistress, informing her of the death of her husband. She was awakened in the night, to read the letter, the bearer having informed her maid that it was necessary for her to see it immediately. The shock drove her into a feverish delirium; from which she never recovered. At periods, her reason resumed its dominion; but in the summer following, she became a mother and died in child bed of puerperal fever. I obtained this account from the mouth of a black man who was the travelling servant of the eldest son of my old master, and who was with his master at the time he came to visit the tenant to whom he let his sister's estate in Georgia in the year 1807.

The estate to which I was now attached was advertised to be rented for the term of seven years, with all the stock of mules, cattle, and so forth upon it—together with seventeen slaves, six of whom were too young to be able to work at present. The price asked, was one thousand dollars for the first year, and two thousand dollars for each of the six succeeding years; the tenant to be bound to clear thirty acres of land annually.

Before the day on which the estate was to be let, by the terms of the advertisement, a man came up from the neighbourhood of Savannah, and agreed to take the new plantation, on the terms asked. He was immediately put into possession of the premises, and from this moment, I became his slave for the term of seven years.

❧ 17 ❧

TIMOTHY FLINT

(1780–1840)

Timothy Flint began his career as a New England minister and ended up one of the first major writers of the American west. Flint was born July 11, 1780, near North Reading, Massachusetts, and was graduated from Harvard in 1800. He served twelve unhappy years as pastor of the Congregational church in Lunenburg, Massachusetts, before resigning in 1814. Inertia seems to have kept Flint in church work; beginning in 1815 he served as a missionary in western states including Ohio, Indiana, Kentucky, and Missouri. Flint was no happier, so he quit missionary work in 1818.

Flint now settled near St. Charles, Missouri, where his misery continued as he attempted unsuccessfully to support his family as a farmer. He finally found a measure of happiness and financial security in 1823 when he relocated to Alexandria, Louisiana, to take the helm of a small college. But then his health caught up with him. Plagued by illness throughout his life, Flint was convinced that the end had come, and he returned alone to New England to die. Instead, his cousin, the Reverend James Flint, nursed him back to health and convinced him to start writing.

The result was Flint's first book, the travel memoir *Recollections of the Last Ten Years in the Valley of the Mississippi* (1826). Drawing on his decade of travel beginning with his years as a missionary, Flint framed his narrative as a series of letters written to his cousin from the various locations he had visited: Pittsburgh, Wheeling, Marietta, Cincinnati, Lexington, and so on. In 1826 Flint also published the first English-language novel set in the American southwest, *Francis Barrian; or, The Mexican Patriot,* which takes place during the Mexican Revolution. Flint had begun the most productive period of his career. Between 1826 and 1833, he would write eleven books and translate a twelfth. He wrote short stories as well, including "The Indian Fighter" and "Nimrod Buckskin, Esq.," which appeared in the literary annual *The Token.*

A Condensed Geography and History of the Western States, or the Mississippi Valley, perhaps Flint's most ambitious work, appeared in 1828 and ran for more than 1,000 pages. It attempted to catalog everything that its author could learn about Florida, Alabama, Mississippi, Louisiana, the Arkansas Territory, Tennessee, Missouri, Illinois, Indiana, Kentucky, and Ohio. Flint's purpose here, as in most of his writings, was not to celebrate the west for its own sake, but to celebrate and encourage the taming of the west. Referring to himself in the third person, Flint explained the origins of this work:

The general amenity of [the country's] aspect, its boundless woods and prairies, its long and devious streams, and its unparalleled advancement in population and improvement, filled his imagination. He had seen the country, in some sense, grow up under his eye. He saw the first steam boat, that descended the Mississippi. He had seen much of that transformation, as if of magic, which has converted the wilderness to fields and orchards. He has wished to transfer to others some of the impressions, which have been wrought on his own mind by witnessing those changes.

As part of his campaign to promote the west and western writers, Flint founded and edited the *Western Monthly Review* (1827–1830) in Cincinnati, the first successful literary periodical published west of the Allegheny mountains. Though Flint claimed more than 1,000 subscribers, he could not claim more than 1,000 *paying* subscribers, and financial losses forced the magazine's early demise. Flint probably made his money back, however, with his most popular work, *Biographical Memoir of Daniel Boone* (1833), which, like John Filson's original biography of Boone, was widely reprinted under a variety of titles. Predictably, Flint's Boone was not a natural man glorying in the wilderness but an agent of civilization.

In 1833, Flint returned east to serve as editor of *The Knickerbocker; or, New-York Magazine,* but continuing ill health forced him to resign in January 1834. Believing that his health would improve in the west, he returned to Louisiana to be near his children. He spent much time traveling during his last years. In the end, it may have been traveling that killed him. Not long after a cold and wet accident on a Mississippi steamboat, Flint died on August 16, 1840.

Texts: *Recollections of the Last Ten Years in the Valley of the Mississippi* (Boston, 1826): 219–228. "The Indian Fighter" in *The Token* (Boston, 1830): 38–58. "Nimrod Buckskin, Esq." in *The Token* (Boston, 1832): 249–274.

FROM *RECOLLECTIONS OF THE LAST TEN YEARS IN THE VALLEY OF THE MISSISSIPPI* (1826)

LETTER XXI.

New Madrid

The county of New Madrid is the southern limit of the state of Missouri, which here bounds upon the territory of Arkansas. I expected to have found this little village a most abandoned and disagreeable place, and it was my object to have made my way with my family by land to St. Charles. But we were still feeble from sickness. We arrived about the middle of December, 1819. The winter was commencing with severity, and the Mississippi was so low, that the boat which brought my family from Arkansas,—although it drew only thirty inches of water,—was continually striking on the shoal sand-bars. And to add to the difficulty, the ice was beginning to run in the Mississippi, so as to preclude any possibility of going up safely. We concluded to spend the winter at New Madrid, and we were delighted to find a few amiable and well-informed families, with whom we passed a few months very pleasantly, in the interchange of kind and affectionate offices. A congregation attended divine service on the Sabbath with perseverance and attention. A venerable lady of the name of Gray, who was as well-informed as she was devout, a part of whose house my family occupied, assisted me in my labours, and formed herself a Sabbath school, which she has continued some years with uninterrupted success. The winter passed pleasantly. The region is interesting in many points of view. It is a fine tract of country, principally alluvial, very rich and pleasant, and chiefly timbered land. In this respect, the country south of the Missouri, and west of the Mississippi, differs essentially from the country north of the Missouri. From the Mississippi, for two hundred miles west it is almost entirely woodland. A few small alluvial prairies make the only exceptions. There is much land covered with shrubs and very poor, which differs much from prairie land. And then, beyond that, there are vast tracts of country covered with flint-knobs. With the exception of what is called the Great Prairie, near New Madrid, the country, for many miles on all sides, is covered with heavy timber of all the descriptions common to that country; and in addition there is the yellow poplar,—*tulipifera liriodendron,*—one of of the grandest and loftiest trees of the forest.

You first begin to discern in new species of trees,—in new classes of *lianes,* or creeping vines in the bottoms, and in a few classes of most beautiful shrubs, approaches to a new and more southern climate. This region also is interesting from the singularly romantic project of colonizing a great town and country under the Spanish *régime.* In listening to the details of this singular attempt, under a certain General Morgan, of New Jersey, I have heard particulars alternately ludicrous and terrible, exciting laughter and shuddering, which if they were narrated without any colouring, would emulate the stories of romance. A hundred and a hundred scenes have been exhibited in these regions, which are now incapable of being rescued from oblivion, which possessed, to me at least, a harrowing degree of interest, in the disappointments and sufferings of these original adventurers, enticed away by coloured descriptions, which represented these countries as terrestrial paradises. Many of the families were respectable, and had been reared in all the tenderness of opulence and plenty. There were highly cultivated and distinguished French families,—and here, among the bears and Indians, and in a sickly climate, and in a boundless forest, surrounded by a swamp, dotted with a hundred dead lakes, and of four hundred miles extent, they found the difference between an Arcadian residence in the descriptions of romance, and actual existence in the wild woods. There were a few aged chroniclers of these days still surviving, when I was there, particularly two French families, from whom I obtained many of these details. The settlement had almost expired, had been resuscitated, and had again exhibited symptoms of languishment, a number of times.

But up to the melancholy period of the earthquakes, it had advanced with the slow but certain progress of every thing that feels the influence of American laws and habits. By these terrible phenomena, the settlement again received a shock which portended at first entire desertion, but from which, as the earthquakes have lessened in frequency and violence, it is again slowly recovering. From all the accounts, corrected one by another, and compared with the very imperfect narratives which were published, I infer that the shock of these earthquakes in the immediate vicinity of the centre of their force, must have equalled in their terrible heavings of the earth, any thing of the kind that has been recorded. I do not believe that the public have ever yet had any adequate idea of the violence of the concussions. We are accustomed to measure this by the buildings overturned, and the mortality that results. Here the country was thinly settled. The houses, fortunately, were frail and of logs, the most difficult to overturn that could be constructed. Yet, as it was, whole tracts were plunged into the bed of the river. The grave-yard at New Madrid, with all its sleeping tenants, was precipitated into the bend of the stream. Most of the houses were thrown down. Large lakes of twenty miles in extent were made in an hour. Other lakes were drained. The whole country, to the mouth of the Ohio in one direction, and to the St. Francis in the other, including a front of three hundred miles, was convulsed to such a degree as to create lakes and islands, the number of which is not yet known,—to cover a tract of many miles in extent, near the Little Prairie, with water three or four feet deep; and when the water disappeared, a stratum of sand of the same thickness was left in its place. The trees split in the midst, lashed one with another, and are still visible over great tracts of country, inclining in every direction and in every angle to the earth and the horizon. They described the undulation of the earth as resembling waves, increasing in elevation as they advanced, and when they had attained a certain fearful height, the earth would burst, and vast volumes of water, and sand, and pit-coal were discharged, as high as the tops of the trees. I have seen a hundred of these chasms, which remained fearfully deep, although in a very tender alluvial soil, and after a lapse of seven years. Whole districts were covered with white sand, so as to become uninhabitable. The water at first covered the whole country, particularly at the Little Prairie; and it must have been, indeed, a scene of horror, in these deep forests and in the gloom of the darkest night, and by wading in the water to the middle, to fly from these concussions, which were occurring every few hours, with a noise equally ter-

rible to the beasts and birds, as to men. The birds themselves lost all power and disposition to fly, and retreated to the bosoms of men, their fellow sufferers in this general convulsion. A few persons sunk in these chasms, and were providentially extricated. One person died of affright. One perished miserably on an island, which
retained its original level in the midst of a wide lake created by the earthquake. The
hat and clothes of this man were found. A number perished, who sunk with their
boats in the river. A bursting of the earth just below the village of New Madrid, arrested this mighty stream in its course, and caused a reflux of its waves, by which in a
little time a great number of boats were swept by the ascending current into the
mouth of the *Bayou,* carried out and left upon the dry earth, when the accumulating
waters of the river had again cleared their current.

There was a great number of severe shocks, but two series of concussions were
particularly terrible; far more so than the rest. And they remark that the shocks were
clearly distinguishable into two classes; those in which the motion was horizontal, and
those in which it was perpendicular. The latter were attended with the explosions, and
the terrible mixture of noises, that preceded and accompanied the earthquakes, in a
louder degree, but were by no means so desolating and destructive as the other. When
they were felt, the houses crumbled, the trees waved together, the ground sunk, and
all the destructive phenomena were more conspicuous. In the interval of the earthquakes there was one evening, and that a brilliant and cloudless one, in which the
western sky was a continued glare of vivid flashes of lightning, and of repeated peals
of subterranean thunder, seeming to proceed, as the flashes did, from below the horizon. They remark that the night, so conspicuous for subterranean thunder, was the
same period in which the fatal earthquakes at Carraccas occurred, and they seem to
suppose these flashes and that event parts of the same scene.

One result from these terrific phenomena was very obvious. The people of this
village had been noted for their profligacy and impiety. In the midst of these scenes
of terror, all, Catholics and Protestants, praying and profane, became of one religion,
and partook of one feeling. Two hundred people, speaking English, French, and Spanish, crowded together, their visages pale, the mothers embracing their children,—as
soon as the omen that preceded the earthquakes became visible, as soon as the air became a little obscured, as though a sudden mist arose from the east,—all, in their different languages and forms, but all deeply in earnest, betook themselves to the voice
of prayer. The cattle, as much terrified as the rational creation, crowded about the assemblage of men, and seemed to demand protection, or community of danger. One
lady ran as far as her strength would permit, and then fell exhausted and fainting, from
which she never recovered. The general impulse, when the shocks commenced, was
to run; and yet when they were at the severest point of their motion, the people were
thrown on the ground at almost every step. A French gentleman told me that in escaping from his house, the largest in the village, he found he had left an infant behind,
and he attempted to mount up the raised piazza to recover the child, and was thrown
down a dozen times in succession. The venerable lady in whose house we lodged, was
extricated from the ruins of her house, having lost every thing that appertained to her
establishment, which could be broken or destroyed. The people at the Little Prairie,
who suffered most, had their settlement,—which consisted of a hundred families, and
which was located in a wide and very deep and fertile bottom,—broken up. When I
passed it, and stopped to contemplate the traces of the catastrophe which remained
after seven years, the crevices where the earth had burst were sufficiently manifest, and

the whole region was covered with sand to the depth of two or three feet. The surface was red with oxided pyrites of iron, and the sand-blows, as they were called, were abundantly mixed with this kind of earth, and with pieces of pit-coal. But two families remained of the whole settlement. The object seems to have been in the first paroxysms of alarm to escape to the hills at the distance of twenty-five miles. The depth of the water that covered the surface soon precluded escape.

The people without an exception were unlettered backwoodsmen, of the class least addicted to reasoning. And yet it is remarkable how ingeniously, and conclusively they reasoned from apprehension sharpened by fear. They remarked that the chasms in the earth were in direction from southwest to northeast, and they were of an extent to swallow up not only men, but houses, "down quick into the pit." And these chasms occurred frequently within intervals of half a mile. They felled the tallest trees at right angles to the chasms, and stationed themselves upon the felled trees. By this invention all were saved. For the chasms occurred more than once under these felled trees. Meantime their cattle and their harvests, both here and at New Madrid, principally perished. The people no longer dared to dwell in houses. They passed this winter, and the succeeding one in bark booths and camps, like those of the Indians, of so light a texture as not to expose the inhabitants to danger in case of their being thrown down. Such numbers of laden boats were wrecked above, and the lading driven by the eddy into the mouth of the *Bayou,* at the village, which makes the harbour, that the people were amply supplied with every article of provision. Flour, beef, pork, bacon, butter, cheese, apples, in short, every thing that is carried down the river, was in such abundance, as scarcely to be matters of sale. Many boats, that came safely into the *Bayou,* were disposed of by their affrighted owners for a trifle. For the shocks still continued every day; and the owners, deeming the whole country below to be sunk, were glad to return to the upper country, as fast as possible. In effect, a great many islands were sunk, new ones raised, and the bed of the river very much changed in every respect.

After the earthquake had moderated in violence, the country exhibited a melancholy aspect of chasms of sand covering the earth, of trees thrown down, or lying at an angle of forty-five degrees, or split in the middle. The earthquakes still recurred at short intervals, so that the people had no confidence to rebuild good houses, or chimnies of brick. The Little Prairie settlement was broken up. The Great Prairie settlement, one of the most flourishing before on the west bank of the Mississippi, was much diminished. New Madrid again dwindled to insignificance and decay; the people trembling in their miserable hovels at the distant and melancholy rumbling of the approaching shocks. The general government passed an act, allowing the inhabitants of this country to locate the same quantity of lands, that they possessed here, in any part of the territory, where the lands were not yet covered by any claim. These claims passed into the hands of speculators, and were never of any substantial benefit to the possessors. When I resided there, this district, formerly so level, rich, and beautiful, had the most melancholy of all aspects of decay, the tokens of former cultivation and habitancy, which were now mementos of desolation and desertion. Large and beautiful orchards, left uninclosed, houses uninhabited, deep chasms in the earth, obvious at frequent intervals,—such was the face of the country, although the people had for years become so accustomed to frequent and small shocks, which did no essential injury, that the lands were gradually rising again in value, and New Madrid was slowly rebuilding, with frail buildings, adapted to the apprehensions of the people.

THE INDIAN FIGHTER (1830)

That hermit hath gone to his last narrow cell,
And his bosom at length has forgotten to swell.
The couch, where he slept, is all crusted with mould,
And the fire on his hearth is extinguished and cold.

Whoever has travelled far, and seen many men, has seen much sorrow. That lonely man of singular habits, so well known, by those who navigate the Upper Mississippi, by the name of Indian Fighter, or the Hermit of Cap au Gris, has at length paid his last debt; and I am released from my promise, not to relate the passages of his life, until he was no more. I well know that the life of man is everywhere diversified with joy and wo; and that his story is but one of countless millions, varied only in the lights and shades. But it seemed right to me, to declare to the proud inhabitants of cities, that scenes of tragic interest, and incidents of harrowing agony, rise on the vision and pass away unrecorded in the desert. As I sojourned on the prairies of Illinois, I experienced, for one night, the well known and ample hospitality of the hermit, and over his cheerful autumnal fire heard the following narrative of the more prominent events of his life.

'The pride of life hath long since passed away from me. But it is due to the simplicity of fact, to declare, that my family in Britain was patrician, of no ignoble name, or stinted possessions. A hereditary lawsuit deprived us of all but the mere wreck of our fortunes. We came over the seas, to escape from the scene of our pride and humiliation. We crossed the western mountains. We were borne down the forests of the beautiful Ohio. We ascended the majestic father of waters, and debarked on the devious and secluded Maccoupin, which, after winding through the central woods and prairies of Illinois, pays its tribute to the Upper Mississippi, some leagues above the mouth of the Missouri.

'With us emigrated a band of backwoodsmen, who sought their homes on these fair and untrodden plains. As friends knit by the ties of common pursuits, and the strong bond of intending to be fellow dwellers in the desert, we selected contiguous farms on the open grass plains; and our cabins rose under the peccans and sugar maples, that formed a skirt of deep and beautiful forest on the banks of the stream. We were fresh from the fastidious creations of luxury and art. I well remember the day when our tents were first pitched in the wild. Here all was fresh nature, as in our forsaken home all had been marked with the labor of men. The sky was beautifully blue and cloudless; and the mild south gently rustled the trees, as it bore fragrance in soft whispers along the flowering wilderness. The huge, straight trees were all moss-covered; and their gray trunks rose proudly, like columns. The starting hares, and deers, and the wild denizens of the woods bounded away from our path. Eagles and carrion vultures soared above our heads. Birds with brilliant plumage of red, green, and gold, sang among the branches. The countless millions of water dwellers, awakened from the long sleep of winter, mingled their cries in the surrounding waters. We added to this promiscuous hymn of nature the clarion echoes of our bugles, the baying of our dogs, all the glad domestic sounds of animals that have joined partnership with man, the hearty blows of the woodcutter's axe, the crash of falling trees, and the reckless wood notes of the first songs which these solitudes had heard from the creation. I look back upon these pleasant, and too fond remembrances, as a green island in the illimitable darkness of the past.

'We consecrated our cabin in this forest with the affecting and tender name of home. I have seen many a spot since, where nature is beautiful in privacy and seclusion, as it should seem, for her own solitary joy; but none more like Eden than this. I had scarcely lived twenty years. I had seen the richly dressed and haughty fair of my native country and of American cities, as an equal, and all with the same indifference. It may be that the heart has more tender sentiments, the eye keener perceptions, and the imagination more vivid and varied combinations, in places like these, than amidst the palling and commonplace associations of art. Little had I dreamed that in these wild forests I was to see a vision of loveliness, which will forever remain impressed upon my memory and my heart, like the stamp of the seal upon wax. Here is the image of the loved one, I hope innocently worn along with that of my Saviour. I pass my eye from one to the other; and while I remember that they are both in heaven, I long to rejoin them.'

His voice failed for a moment; and he took from his bosom, where it hung with a crucifix, on which, engraven on a gem, was the head of a Jesus, a miniature of a beautiful girl, with raven locks, and radiant eyes of piercing blackness. It showed a countenance of uncommon loveliness even to me, who saw with impartial view. But the eye of a lover discovers perfection where less entranced vision sees only common beauty. As I intensely viewed the miniature in different lights, he proceeded, in the luxuriant amplification of a lover's poetry, to paint his beloved with a pencil dipped in sunbeams. The ambrosial curls, the divine expression of a melting eye, the lily and the rose in her cheek, the snowy neck, the majestic form, in short, the usual illustrations of that vocabulary were all put in requisition.

'She, too,' he resumed, replacing the miniature in his bosom, 'before she had seen sixteen summers, had seen reverses; and her piercing eye sometimes swam in a languor, which told a tale of sorrow. Her father had ventured all on the seas; and his wealth had been merged in the fickle element. His proud spirit, like mine, brooked not the affected pity of those who had shared in the hospitality of his better days. He sought repose in the same forests, and had selected his home on the same stream a few leagues above. In passing near our cabin, his horse, affrighted by the starting of a hare from his path, had thrown him. I found him, bore him home, and nursed him, during his lameness, till he was able to return to his own house. Next time we saw him, he brought his lovely daughter with him on a visit to our settlement. I no longer complained of the tedium of slumbering affections, or spoke in derision of the mock torments of love.

'The time of her visit was a sweet April evening; and the place an extensive sugar camp, near our cluster of cabins. The greater portion of our settlement were gathered round the caldrons and the blazing fires in that pleasant valley. The sugar maple poured its rich syrup abundantly; and the tree itself, the fairest of the American forest, had begun to start the germs of its leaves beneath its brilliant red flowers. The fresh air told that the snow had not yet all melted from the higher hills. But violets, columbines, the white clover, the cornel, and red bud already mingled their fragance in the evening breeze. A requiem to departing day was lulling the song birds to rest among their branches. A number of black servants, engaged in the work, sang, in the strain of their spicy native groves, songs, at once gay and plaintive, which breathed remembrances of the Lote and the Palm. Steaming above the bright fires arose the fragrance of the forming crystals. The aged parents sat under the trees, and told their feats of hunting buffaloes and bears, and their still sterner contests with the Indians. The young men and their elected maidens were grouped apart. A fat and joyous black, as laughing and as reckless as though he had neither heard nor known the import of the word slave, scraped his violin. At the note the scattered groups left their satisfying privacy for the more exciting sport of the dance. The Africans, meanwhile, enacted their own under plot of still more boisterous gladness; and, when weary with laughter, sipped the syrup, and, imitating the phrase of the adjacent dancers, talked of their dusky loves as still sweeter than the forest nectar.

'It was at such a time and place that the father and Emma dismounted from their horses and joined us. It was, as if Diana had descended amidst the rustic assemblage. I no longer had indistinct visions of grace, and loveliness, and dignity, which all stood embodied before me. The time and the place added their charmed influence to the impression. The father named me to his daughter as one to whom he owed a debt of grateful obligation. At her home the maple was not found; and this scene, and the process of preparing the sugar, had for her all the charm of novelty. She seemed no ways disinclined to make the circuit of the camp with me, nor to repose herself on a rustic bench at a spring fountain, whence the whole gay scene was surveyed below, and which was beautifully illumined by the hundred bright fires. Her reserve wore away with mine; and I became bold, as she turned her melting eye upon me, as if to inquire, why a being as unlike the rest as herself, had been cast in these woods. I talked of the charming country, and of the unlimited selection in these fertile solitudes. I spoke of the peace of those who are far from the corroding passions and the venal motives of crowded cities, and who live in guileless peace, content, and privacy; and, I added, that the poet's song, in the days of primeval innocence, had peopled such scenes with gods and nymphs; but that I had not dreamed to find, as I now did, the fable true in these iron days. A smile slightly ironical gave me no omens of displeasure. We named over our stores of books; and in the course of this delightful evening she incidentally expressed the hope that our fathers might be acquainted. The song and the dance and our fathers' colloquy and ours ceased not until the moon in the centre of the concave told us, that it was the noon of night; and yet much remained for us both to say.

'Her father came for her, complaining, in the usual phrase, of the unperceived lapse of the hours. They mounted, and rode towards their home. I followed them with my eyes and my thoughts, as the yet unabated and boisterous mirth around rung upon my ear. The tempest of war had begun to rage along our immense line of frontier; and the fierce and ruthless northern savages were abroad among the commencing settlers of the Illinois plains. We began to hear of their desolations of fire and blood. I neither affirm nor deny the wisdom of believing in presentiment in the case of others. It may be I followed the leading of a new train of thoughts; but it seemed to me as if a mysterious intimation warned me to follow in their course. I moved over the hills until our fires had faded upon my eye, and the mirth around them upon my ear. One height drew me on to another, until I heard a sharp and piercing scream, preceded by a rifle shot, in a thicket but a little way before me. An instant brought me to the place. The father lay on the ground, apparently lifeless, and covered with his blood. A half-suppressed groan, as of one flying away among the fallen trees, directed me to the daughter. She, too, was on the earth; but whether in faintness or death, appeared not;

though, reclined in her white dress, my dark thoughts viewed her as lying in her shroud. In springing to reach her, I stumbled over a fallen tree. It providentially saved me from the unerring aim of an Indian hatchet, which gleamed past the point, to which I should otherwise have advanced. The sender instantly after grasped me in deadly strife. Then first I knew by experience the fierce encounter of the red man. Providence or love endowed me with more than mortal powers. While I felt in the tremendous clutch of my adversary, as exerting the weak efforts of man against the brute and irresistible powers of nature, I had, I scarcely know how, inflicted such a wound, that I felt his spasmodic grasp relax. His arms sunk away nerveless; and the sternness of disappointed vengeance was sealed upon his grim brow in death.

'I need not prolong my tale. Water from a neighbouring spring restored Emma. She had fled unharmed, and fallen in faintness and terror. Her father had been wounded, but not severely, by a rifle shot. He was removed to my father's cabin; and nursed, I need not say, with tenderness. While a firm friendship grew up between the fathers, a compact of another sort had been unalterably ratified between their children. There was no glade, spring source, or cool and sequestered bower of the broad-leaved grape, that had not been consecrated by the repetition of our vows, and our words of love. The days fled, and we counted not how fast; for the sun, moon, stars, and seasons were not our remembrancers. Alas! the memory of these halcyon days alone remains to me; but even the memory is pleasant. It is like a calm and sweet dream in a feverish night of pain.

'The time of our union was fixed. Our parents would not separate until it had taken place. Ample provision had been made for our commencing a farming establishment in rustic abundance and comfort. Earth can furnish no happier anticipations than were ours.

'A savage that we had deemed friendly, and who often brought us venison for sale, came in one evening, when a number of our neighbours were paying us a social visit. He begged my father to send some one to help him bring in a deer, which, he said, he had killed near the house. The greater number of the men, and I among them, improvidently set forth to see the game. An ambush of hostile Indians rose between them and the house. The yells of the savages, the dying groans of our neighbours, the sharp reports of the rifles, all ring in my ears as I think of the past. I was stunned and struck down, remote from the rest, with a rifle blow. The fathers and mothers, the brothers and sisters, the husbands and wives fell together. Savage knives spilled the blood of the young infants. They exerted themselves even to kill our house dogs. To render the ruin complete, conflagration glared upon their murders. With horrid dexterity, they composed a pyramidal pile of bodies; the longer laid at the base, the shorter forming another tier, and the little infants, lying in their innocent blood, crowned the pile. By this pile they held their infernal orgies, dancing and yelling, as they circled round it, by the glare of the burning buildings. I should have made one, had they found me. I remained awhile insensible at a distance among the brush; and awoke to consciousness with this shocking scene in full view, though it was my fortune not to be myself discovered.

'In the midst of their horrid rites of blood and drunkenness, the clarion notes of the rangers' bugles awakened the night echoes. The murderous foe cowered and fled, like wolves from the sheepfold. Had it been heard an hour before, I had not passed from hope to despair; and many a brave heart had palpitated with the joy of welcome, which would now beat no more. The rangers soon came up in measured gallop, and, clad in steel, alighted to survey the work of death. I called them to my aid. They carried me to a cabin which the savages had spared; and I speedily recovered of my bruises. Revenge burned at my bosom, and for that alone I wished to live. Besides, the body of Emma had not been found among the dead. Might not the loved and forlorn orphan be a captive to these ruthless invaders? To seek for her, and to measure back to the murderers the cup of retaliation, these were motives for which to cherish life. All uncertainty touching Emma's fate, was soon dispelled. A single captive, with her, sole survivors of the massacre of my father's house, escaped them, rejoined our settlement, and reported, that they were carrying the lovely captive to Rock Fort, near Peonia of the Illinois.

'The rangers had gone on their ordered destination, in another direction. But, stimulated by the sympathy of common feelings, and urged by my despair, a few gallant friends from the vicinity joined me in pursuit of the captive. They were brave and determined spirits, who knew how to find a home in the forest, to whom rivers and forests, and prairies and distance, and danger and death were familiar objects. They were men of robust body and unconquerable mind. We mounted our horses, heedless of provisions, as long as we had powder and lead, and as long as the prairies and the forests alike afforded food for our horses. We bounded away through the wood, stream, prairie, and over hill and dale. On the third night of our march we saw the watch fires of our foe gleaming afar through the forests. So far away from the scene of their murders without pursuit, they now reposed in reckless riot. Gorged with food, most of them slept in drunkenness. One trusty sentinel slept not; and his dismal guttural song occasionally chimed in with the hoot of the owls, the long dismal cry of the wolves, and the distant crash of trees, falling in the forests under the weight of time.

'I felt that my motives impelled me to confront the first dangers; and they detached me to reconnoitre, or, if I chose, to enter the camp in secret. I almost suppressed my breath, the beatings of my heart I could not suppress, as, panther-like, I crept upon the foe. The tall, grim sentinel, with half blinking eyes, nodded erect over a decaying fire. A fallen tree interposed on his flank, as a screen, and I crept undiscovered by him. Unheeded, as I crawled, I surveyed many a brawny warrior in deep sleep; and one, as I passed near him, half started up, and commenced a dozing note of his habitual "Cheowanna! ha! ha!" and sunk back to his visions. Providence, that watches over innocence, guided me to the very tent where Emma lay, feeding upon her sleepless tears. A start of joy marked her instant recognition. "Hush! A word is death. Follow me. We are free, or fall together!" I waited in breathless impatience. In sounds inaudible by any but a lover's ear, she whispered, "I am bound." I cut the vile bonds from her swollen and tender limbs. I felt at my heart the full and confiding pressure of her pledged hand. We stole away, as noiseless as the footstep of time. Our devious course was often changed by seeing a gigantic body, first in this direction, and then in that. More than one turned in his sleep, as we passed, with a half waking spasm, and settled back with a long drawn sigh to his repose again. The warrior sentinel seemed to have caught in his ear the rustle of our feet among the leaves; for he raised himself fully erect, and cast a keen and searching glance on every side. We sunk unmarked behind a briar tangle. Our hearts palpitated equally with love and terror during this suspense of horror. The grim Argus, having scrutinized the whole scene with a detail of survey, stirred his fire, passed his dusky form twice around it, uttered in his most lugubrious tones, "Cheowanna! ha! ha!" and, as if ashamed of his fears, seemed to court his former dozing apathy.

'This dreadful suspense elapsed, we fled; and I safely brought back the captive orphan to my friends. We saw most clearly that the foe was too numerous for prudent attack. We whispered a moment in earnest debate. Having secured the chief object of pursuit, we concluded to return with all possible speed to our settlement. We commenced our march by the uncertain light of the moon, now dimmed by clouds and mists. Morning dawned upon our forest march in crimson splendor and dewy freshness. The glad sounds of matin music showed that every living thing rejoiced in the renovated day but ourselves. We would have chosen the sheltering darkness that was the scourge of Egypt; for, from the hills behind us, the Indian yell of pursuit was heard. Behind us was this loud and appalling war song of the foe; before us a prairie, gay with flowers, dripping and sparkling in the freshness of morning dew, but measureless to vision, and offering only the unsheltered nakedness of a level plain.

'To fight, retreat, or seek shelter, were our only alternatives. The foe outnumbered us ten to one. Their horses were fresh; ours fatigued. We were unwilling that the rescued orphan should sustain the same chance from their rifles as ourselves. One of those immense elliptical, concave basins, so common on the verge of the western prairies, offered itself before us. The general voice was to descend the basin, take down our horses, and, if we might, lie there concealed until the storm of pursuit should be past. If the foe had not tracked us, our chances were good. The basin was a hundred feet in perpendicular depth; and the descent so prone, that our horses slid from the summit to the base. Briars and thorns and bushes and small shrubs sheltered the rim as a kind of hedge. At the base a cool spring trickled across the limestone floor.

'Here we stood in breathless suspense, while Emma clung fast to my side. Alas! we soon heard the measured trample of their horses at hand; and, as if to preclude all chances of concealment, our horses, scenting theirs, neighed vehemently, and were instantly answered by theirs. Our basin was surrounded in a moment. The rifle's sharp clang was heard, again and again, followed by the heavy sigh of my falling comrades; while our return fire upon those who stood high above, and showed only their heads at the moment of discharge, took little effect. Emboldened by impunity, and impatient at the slowness of their work, the foe soon came howling down the basin. Then we fought at bay, and with desperation; and the blood of more than one of their number mingled with ours. Emma fell on my bosom. "Henry," said she, "we die together." Stout frames, and noble minds, and fearless hands availed nothing against numbers. Emma was slain in my arms; and her last look mingled in strange union love, terror, and death. Darkness came over my own eyes; and the last sensation of a heavy and iron sleep, was, that our released spirits were making the last journey together.

'But life returned to me, and brought with it bitter and distinct consciousness, and rayless despair. The morning sun had just emerged from the mists when we entered this basin. It was now burning noon. I lay on the stone floor. The pale, cold face of Emma was near me. Her eye, lately so piercing, was fixed and glassy. I was bound in various points by thongs, which a giant could not have broken. I struggled madly with them, until I was exhausted, and nature would go no further. Then I cried to Heaven from the depths, and called aloud on God for mercy. When I paused in the intervals of my groans, what a spectacle! There were my companions, lying as they fell. My brain began to madden. I strove to dash my head on the stone floor. Bright, broad gleams of light, in all the colors of the prism, filled the heavens in my view, and I fondly hoped that my last hour had come. But I was not permitted thus to lay down my loathed life.

'The sun seemed, for a whole age, to remain suspended high in the heavens only to concentre his radiance on my head. But after the scorching of that long period, the burning orb declined. I was in darkness, wet with the chill dews of night, and constantly enduring the benumbing torture of my cords. First I heard the hooting of owls. The panther's harsh scream next grated on my ear. The sharp bark and the hungry howl of the wolves commenced, and still drew nearer. I soon heard their menacing growl, and their stealthy and cat-like tread. Immediately after a whole troop, emboldened by numbers, rushed down the den, licking their greedy jaws, as they fell at once upon their horrid feast. The bodies were torn, and in their rabid eagerness, they often turned their rage upon each other. Could they have instantly destroyed my own life, I had been content. But, when I saw them tearing the form of my beloved, all my associations with life arose; and I unconsciously raised such a cry of horror, as drove the satiated and coward prowlers in rapid retreat from the den.

'The morn returned. The hot sun once more illumined the summit of the basin. Corruption had commenced its appropriate work; and a new evil, more insupportable than all the rest, crowned my miseries. I burned with the mad thirst of fever, and my mouth and throat were as parchment. Then I knew the truth of all that I had heard of the agony of thirst. Mere physical thirst expelled all horrors of the mind, and reigned sole object of my thoughts. Drink! Give me drink! I cried, till I heard the wild echoes calling for drink. I had no conception of any misery but thirst, or of any joy in earth or heaven, but to quaff water forever from a cool spring.

'Then I felt that time is a relation of the mind, and the creation of thought. I looked up at the sun. Roll on, I cried in my despair; roll on, and bring me death. But it seemed as though the voice that suspended his course in Ajalon had renewed the mandate. Worn down and exhausted, I slept, as I knew by a waking start, that broke off a dream that myself and my beloved had passed our mortal agonies and were safe landed in heaven. The cool evening was drawing on, convincing me, that in joy or sorrow, time never stands still. I had long seen the carrion vultures wheeling their droning flight above the basin, allured by the scent of carnage. The effluvia now directed them to their mark. They settled down by hundreds.

'But God, who is rich in mercy, heard my cry in the bottom of this deep basin. The corps of mounted rangers was scouring the prairie in search of the bodies of their friends. Their practised eyes were directed in a moment, by the wheeling circles of these birds of evil omen. They found me; and in the madness of my thirst, I struggled with them in wrath, to be allowed to quaff my fill, and drink death at the spring. But by kindly violence they held me back. Some washed my swollen limbs, while others with manly tears committed decently to the earth the mangled remains of my friends.

'All my purposes and affections were now concentered in the insatiate desire of retaliation and vengeance. At the head of a volunteer corps of rangers, I vowed to the shade of Emma, that I would expiate her murder by copious libations of Indian blood. I faithfully redeemed my pledge. When a daring assault was to be made on one of their villages, or a body of their warriors, I was the first in attack, and the last to spare. My companions saw that I took no counsel from distance, toil, exposure, or danger. My only inquiry was, where is the foe? My corps emulated my example; and many a burning village testified to the deluded miscreants that we knew how to retaliate. So terrible had my name become to them, that I bore in their language an appellation which imports Indian Fighter.

'At length we met the same band that destroyed my father's family and Emma. They retreated, after a short fight, to the same basin where she fell. It was filled with the high grass of autumn. We sent down flames among them, and drove them howling upon the plain. We destroyed many of them there. The remnant fled before us to their lair, their summer residence near the Illinois. Here were their wives and children, and the mounds that contained the bones of their forefathers. Here they turned and stood at bay. Why should I recal these scenes of vengeance and blood? Their warriors agreed to kill their women and children, and then despatch each other. We heard the aged warriors singing the death song, as the work of destruction went on. Our rangers were affected, and the reports of their rifles ceased. All had fallen but the leader of the band. He fired the village, and came forth. "Indian Fighter," he said to me, "I killed thy father and mother. I killed the maiden of thy love. If thou art indeed a warrior, and a warrior's son, seek thy revenge now." Nor was I one to refuse that invitation. We struggled long for mastery, for life and death. These scars remain, as durable memorials of that strife. But as I was weak with loss of blood, I shouted Emma! and my arm was renerved. He rolled on the grass, and I saw, not without a strange feeling of respect, the look of defiance and the denial of triumph fixed on his stern brow, after his spirit had passed.

'Peace has revisited these plains many years past; and it is not long since I made a pilgrimage to the ruins of the Indian village. I should say to thee, stranger, that I trust I have long since become a Christian. Anger, revenge, despair are alike merged in my immortal hopes, and the new tempers of a better mind. I stand amazed at myself, and ask, is this quiet and forgiving bosom the same, where such a whirlwind of vengeance and wrath so lately raged? I shed tears of pity and forgiveness over these affecting ruins. There were the scathed peach and plum trees. There were the dilapidated remains of the few cabins that had escaped the fire. There were the clumps of hazel bushes covered with the wild hop. There were patches of the green velvet sward of blue grass, indicating that human habitancy had introduced it among the wild grass of the prairies. I remembered to have seen this sward covered with the business and bustle of life. I remembered the bench at the head of the village, where I had beheld the aged council chiefs smoking their calumets in silent gravity. Their bones were now bleaching around me. In their sculls the ground rattlesnake had gathered up his coil, and waited for his prey. But the robin redbreast and the purple cardinal, birds that love the shorn sward of blue grass, picked their seeds upon it, and now and then started a few mellow notes, as if singing the dirge of the dead.

'That whole race is wasting away about me, like the ice in the vernal brooks. I shall soon be with them. But, stranger, when thou goest thy way, say to those that come after me, that it is wise, as well as christian, to stay the storm of wrath, and leave vengeance to Him, who operateth by the silent and irresistible hand of time, and will soon subdue all our enemies under our feet.'

NIMROD BUCKSKIN, ESQ. (1832)

I have not seen a fairer sample of the respectable and opulent western pioneers in the bygone days, than Nimrod Buckskin, Esq., of West Virginia. He lived, for, I regret to say, he lives no longer, on the main branch of the Kenhawa, not far below the point, where it pours its pure mountain-tribute upon the plain. Impetuous and wild in its foaming descent, an emblem of the inhabitants of the West, as soon as it rolls upon level and arable soil, it becomes calm. It winds through a grove of those gigantic and noble tulip-trees, that are the glory of the western forest, and emerges, from the dark green shade, or yellow sands and polished pebbles, into a wide and fertile alluvial tract, which constituted the estate of this gentleman. He was the fortunate heir, with this fine tract and fifty negroes, to a rich Saline, which, without parsimony or speculation, had enabled him to accumulate a hundred thousand dollars in ready money. Opulent, intelligent, high-minded, not wholly unlettered, though rustic from the circumstances of his life, he practised that simple and noble hospitality peculiar to the western country, of which the inhabitants of towns could form no adequate idea, but by inspection. His house was in the still favorite style of an ancient western man; an ample, double log house, not without its indications of the opulence and comfort of the owner. The perfect uniformity of the lines of logs, and the white parallels of plaster, showed the curious transition medium between a German stone house and a cabin. Around it the village of negro quarters, barns, horse-mill, spring-house, cribs, and shops, presented an unique aspect in the distance, not unlike a large community of beehives. The whole was shaded by noble forest-trees, which the owner had had the good taste to spare. Vigorous and thrifty orchards were spread beyond. Beside the barns ranged domestic animals and fowls, for number and variety, recalling the beautiful bible picture of the ancient man of Uz. I suspect man is a hunter by instinct. At least he seems always such, where circumstances allow him the pastime. No appetite fastens deeper upon the heart, and Mr Buckskin would tell you, with an indescribable enthusiasm, that no man ought to talk of high enjoyment, who had not hunted in the western forests, in the days of Daniel Boone. But bears grew scarce; even venison and turkeys were no longer obtained with sufficient ease and regularity, to furnish a constant supply of these forest dainties for his patriarchal table. The time was a kind of interregnum between hunting and municipal life.

A considerable village had grown up, at the distance of half a mile from this house. It was, what is called in the West, a country-seat, a place of some importance. The chief inn had the word 'Hotel' on a prodigious sign, which bore a most ferocious caricature of Washington. The arm chair of the ordinary of this establishment was regularly assigned to Squire Buckskin, by prescription; although the villagers were, for the most part, recent emigrants, half unconscious of the claims of an old *residenter*. Among these people, the most natural themes of interest were the arrival and departure of steamboats, and the internal improvements of turnpikes and canals. In these conversations, the Squire seldom bore any part; and a discussion of them generally brought over his countenance a kind of stern sadness. Some one of the company, who divined that an unpleasant string of comparison had been harped within him, and wished to gain his favorable ear, would digress from modern improvements to the bulletin of a night bear-hunt, in the times of the Indians and first settlers. They then had a story of Herculean and skin-clad men, in energetic phrase, in keeping with the scenes and incidents of the narrative. It presented ancient and boundless forests, as yet untouched by the axe, illumined by the blaze of the hunter's fire, the chiming cry of the dogs, the hearty shouts of the hunters, the clang of the rifles, ringing through the night stillness, and the sullen bruin driven to his last retreat in the huge, hollow sycamore, followed by the elastic shout of triumph in surveying the dimensions of the fallen forest prowler. The countenance of Squire Buckskin would then lighten with a peculiar expression. The memory of joys that were past, was recalled. It was as the narrative of Austerlitz, told by a companion in arms to Napoleon, on the far rock of the seas.

'Bears,' or, as he called them, 'bar,' the patriarch would add, with a peculiar into-
nation of sadness, 'are getting so scarce, that the pleasure of a night-hunt is dead out.
The forests have become thin. Hunting-shirts are disappearing. Old times are gone.
Keel-boats are going out of use, and it is no great matter that I am going with the rest.
All I wish, is, that they, who live in the days of steamboats, extravagant fashions, and
the everlasting grinding of politics, may be as honest and happy, as the true old west
country *Cohoes.*'

Exposure, and the indulgence of a hunter's appetite, at the age of seventyfive,
brought on rheumatism, and general morbid derangement of the system. Mountain
herbs, Indian doctors, sweating doctors, and quack patents, were all tried in succession; but all alike failed to remove the complaint. During his illness, an honored young
Tuckahoe relative, a gem of the Virginia aristocracy of the first water, made him a visit
from Norfolk, and furnished him an ample budget of the freshest modern news, and
imbued him with the history of the last half century, brought down to the present
time. Among other things, he vaunted the waters of Saratoga, and instanced many
Southerners, who had been completely restored by them from complaints not unlike
his. He earnestly recommended the experiment to him.

The old gentleman listened, without signs of visible impatience, to the fluent
speech and modern phrases of his young friend. But internally he hated steamboats,
unshaded turnpikes, and modern changes. He had a particular dislike, compounded
of prejudice and dread, towards Yankees; about whose tin wares, wooden clocks, and
ingenious knaveries, he told many pleasant second hand stories. He considered the
whole generation instinctively inclined to cheat, even where honesty was most gain-
ful, and least laborious. Not having been east of the mountains, since the glorious affair of Yorktown, in which he had borne an honorable part, his antipathy to Yankees,
and his views of modern improvements, connected sufficiently revolting associations
with such a journey. But circumstances gave to the words of his young friend oracu-
lar importance. Pain, too, has a tongue of strong persuasion, and he was discouraged
at the thought of repeating former experiments, that had so entirely failed. Situated
as he was, the expense of the journey need not be an element in settling the question.
His loneliness, after the departure of his young friend, fixed his purpose. Having completed his preparations, he held a solemn conversation with his only son and child, in
presence of two nieces, whom he had brought up, as children. 'Nimrod,' said he, 'it is,
perhaps, probable that I shall die on this journey. The world has not been overly happy
to me since the death of your dear mother. Game, too, is getting scarce. Most of my
old acquaintances in the low lands are gone; and, somehow, the ways of the times seem
more calculated for the new comers, than for me. I shall leave you a fine estate, and a
solemn charge to be faithful to these young girls. If I die away, I would rather my
bones should not be left in the Yankee country. Let me be buried at the bend of the
branch, where it looks out upon the mountains.' Two trusty body servants attended
him, and his carriage drove away for a steamboat at the Saline, in which he had engaged a passage to Pittsburg.

Though strongly imbued with prejudice, he was deficient neither in intelligence
nor good feeling. As he experienced a new kind of exercise, and his thoughts were led
out of their gloomy circle of habit, his health and spirits improved, and he became
gradually reconciled to modern changes. He frankly admitted, that steamboats were
better than keel-boats; Reeside's carriages, than Kentucky wagons; and a good turnpike, than an Indian trail, or a forest quagmire. Still further onward, the civility of the
attendants at the hotels astonished him, and gradually wore away his dislike to east-

ern people. Though the waters of Saratoga were of service to him, yet cotillions and concerts and the gaiety of the unthinking young, and the tawdry affectation of rich and ignorant *parvenus,* and the incessant noise and whirl of movement, neutralized their beneficial effect. His patience was exhausted in a fortnight, and he was already contemplating some change of place, when he met a west country acquaintance, who, like him, had been travelling for his health, and was now on his return from Nahant, immensely improved by sea-bathing. He spoke with enthusiasm of his trip. Some of Squire Buckskin's prejudices resumed their ancient vigor. 'I should like to try it,' said he, 'I have never seen the sea but once in my life, and it is one of the few spectacles that I can never forget. I am told that the summer air from the blue water is cool and refreshing; and this place is like a cobler's room heated by a stove, and the everlasting din more annoying than that of spring black-birds. But then to get there, I must pass through the whole land of wooden clocks; confound the tin-pedling knaves!' But dissatisfaction with the springs, uniting with the impulse of unquenched native ardor and curiosity, overcame even this obstacle; and he was whirled away through Albany, New Lebanon, the impressive scenery of the Green Mountains, so like the blue hills at the sources of the Kenhawa, and the neat, white villages beyond. He saw towns, spires, and rosy faces, in continual succession; and such was his impression from what he saw, and from his intercourse with the people, that here, in the very centre of Yankee land, his prejudices against them loosened their hold faster than ever.

He reached the beautiful peninsula, washed by the summer surge, in safety; and inhaled the health-giving breeze, charged with the elastic coolness of the immeasurable wave; and meditated on his far home, as the traces of the carriage wheels were pencilled on the polished strand, whence the tide had just ebbed. This retirement, change of diet, air, and sea-bathing, completely restored him; and he became almost a New Englander in his admiration of the climate and people. 'If they have the cool sea,' said he, 'and sea fish, and handsomer and better taught children, we ought not, in pure envy, to calumniate them with clumsy falsehoods about their cheating; but be satisfied with our more fertile country, and train our children to equal quickness.'

On his return homeward, caught by a shower, as he was riding on horseback over the Berkshire mountains, he experienced a relapse of his rheumatism from sudden cold. The severity of the complaint brought him up, as it happened, in a quiet and neat inn, where he was attended with the most unwearied assiduity and consideration. Beside the general attendance of the inn, he had a particular nurse in Katharine Spooner, a charming girl, of the very best pattern of Yankee neatness, cleverness, and kindness of character. She not only nursed him, but read and sung to him, and cheered the loneliness of his confinement by her intelligent and lively conversation. Gratitude and an affectionate interest were awakened for her, not diminished by learning that she was an orphan, brought up by the landlord; that she had gained all her advantages at the common school of the village, and was entirely dependent on her own exertions. He was struck with astonishment. 'Why,' said he, 'after all the expense and trouble of sending our daughters to fashionable schools in the Atlantic country, we seldom see them return instructed as she is.' So strong a liking did the old gentleman manifest for his favorite, that more than one of her young acquaintances, half in jest, half in earnest, bantered her on her chances of marrying the ancient and rich widower, and coming forth, after a short discipline of penance, a young widow with a fortune. Nor were there wanting envious minds, who seriously suspected her of such sordid views. But they as little divined the character of the west country man, as the pure kindness and the simple integrity of the high spirited girl. Good minds know each other by instinct. The frank manners, and the blunt honesty of her invalid charge, had won her kind feelings; and her display of intelligent and benevolent resources, to amuse and restore him, had gained his warm heart. It is true, these attributes were none the less effective, for being displayed in a buoyant and beautiful girl of seventeen. But no thoughts, beyond filial sanctity on the one part, and parental affection on the other, had been elicited between them.

Squire Buckskin had regained his usual health, and had no longer even a pretext for delay. Having paid the landlord's bill, with a handsome gratuity to the other attendants, he requested to speak with Katharine Spooner by herself. Almost affected to tears, he held out a fifty dollar note.

'My pretty Yankee girl,' said he, 'I can never repay your kindness to me. If this'—

'No, Sir,' she answered, promptly; 'I am already paid for all I have done. I take no money for what I have not earned.'

He paused, in a slight revulsion of astonishment. 'What! a Yankee, and act in this style? Fifty dollars would not go begging in some other parts of the country. You are above taking money, then? Perhaps you are right. God Almighty has given you, in your head, heart, and pretty face, what no money could buy you. I shall tell of this when I hear the Yankees traduced.'

Her cheek crimsoned, as she replied, 'But I have no relatives here. I think I could keep a good school, and'—

'I understand you; I will think of it, my dear girl,' said he. 'I hope you will hear from your old western friend, whom your nursing has restored; and, if we meet not again, may He be your recompense, who never permits virtue to go unrewarded.' In the style of his country, he saluted her on her polished cheek, and turned away to conceal his tears.

The return of Squire Buckskin to his estate, in good health, was an era of general gladness in the vicinity, as well as particular joy to his family. Like another Robinson Crusoe, he was continually reciting the incidents of his journey to Yankee land, mingling almost unconscious eulogy of the people and country with his descriptions. 'He had seen,' he said, 'with his own eyes, the stupid misrepresentations of them so current in the west and south.' He was particularly emphatic in his praise of New England schools, and the efficient training which the children acquired there. On an election eve, in which the candidate had been carried unanimously, he made a kind of harangue, and concluded by saying, 'We must have a better female school in this village.' The hearts of the people were warm, and in concert. They requested him to draw up a subscription list. He did so, and headed it with a hundred dollars, adding, that for the advantage of having his nieces instructed at home, he would board the mistress, beside his subscription. Five hundred dollars a year, for two years, were subscribed on the spot; and Squire Buckskin was elected committee man, with full power to offer the place to whom he chose. His feelings at once prompted him to write to Katharine Spooner. He offered her the place, and enclosed a hundred dollar note, to pay her travelling expenses, 'which,' he added, 'she was not to consider a gift, but a kind of gratuity, along with her board, for which he should expect particular attention to his nieces, at home.'

After due reflection, Katharine determined to accept the proposition, which was, indeed, far beyond her highest expectations. Fitting herself out, with the neatness and taste indicative of her character, and taking a tender, filial leave of the protector of her early years, as well as a general farewell of her many friends, she was handed into the stage. A couple of well-dressed young gentleman gave her place on the back seat, with that officious civility, which a pretty person, similarly invested, is sure to exact.

Katharine was not one of your over-delicate ladies, who either shrink from the observations of a male stranger, or obtrude themselves upon it, and who seem terrified at the thought of venturing a step, without reclining daintily on the arm of a protector. But purity of thought and character was written on every lineament of her countenance. A virtuous education had impressed, upon every step, visible propriety and self-respect. If her innocent loveliness sometimes attracted the gaze of lawless admiration, a second view repelled all thought of any improper advances to her acquaintance. She took the steamboat at Pittsburg, and once or twice a trader dandy, on his return from Philadelphia, ventured to survey her through his eye-glass. A calm look of easy and yet indignant defiance, at once settled the terms of relationship between them. Such is the ultimate triumph of the better kind of New England education, inspiring the most winning modesty, in the form of self-reliance and self-respect. A girl, who has it, will pass, unprotected and alone, without a stain of suspicion upon her, from Maine to the Sabine; and so would she. On all the long way from Berkshire to Kenhawa, she never failed receiving considerate civility, and respectful attention.

She arrived safely at her destination, and was welcomed by the elder Buckskin with fatherly kindness. Nimrod Buckskin, junior, looked in her glowing face, as she received his father's salute, and never forgot the spectacle; being that he had never dreamed of such a Yankee before. As she passed by him to her seat, he bent his form of six feet and two inches with an odd kind of awkward respect. He felt that he had received a sure shaft, notwithstanding all his preconceived associations with tin-ware, and pit-coal Indigo. He was now turned of twentyone, and would have been a fine young man, if a higher education, and more enlarged acquaintance with society, had developed his native endowments. His first exclamation to a young friend, on returning from the interview, was, 'Gemini! is this the daughter of a tin pedlar? To a dead certainty, she's the severest bird I ever saw.'

Behold her forthwith charged, at home in particular, with the two little favorite nieces, and bending her youthful beauty and gaiety to the stern requisitions upon patience, discretion, and the difficult task of governing, as she put on the thorny crown of a village school. The next process was to pass through the furnace of trial by the tongue. One critical mother, her children furnishing the allegations, espied one defect, and another an opposite and incompatible one; but, on the whole, she passed the first ordeal with uncommon good fortune, and there was a decided balance of estimation in her favor. However, some of the young ladies demurred, and entered certain pleas in abatement; after her first appearance in church, the gentlemen carried the vote for her by acclamation.

To settle her place in society was a matter of somewhat more pith and moment. Beside the family of Augustus Fillagree, Esq., almost a counterpoise in importance to that of Squire Buckskin, there were some five or six others, that, from comparative opulence, or other adventitious circumstances, constituted the aristocracy of that circle. The question of admitting the schoolmistress a formal member of this high society, was earnestly debated in private, and family by family. The point long hung in doubtful suspense, and was only settled, as the sage Panza arranged it for Don Quixote, by a palpable conviction, that wherever she was, would be the head. The aristocracy of nature carried it over that of prescription. The question was decided in her favor, and she became forthwith free of the high privileges and immunities of the social circle.

Anne Maria Theresa Fillagree, of Fillagree Grove, was only daughter of Augustus Fillagree, Esq.; between whom and Squire Buckskin there was a strong coincidence of condition. The former was a *Tuckahoe*. So had been the father of the latter. Both were unquestioned scions of Virginia aristocracy. The one had an only son, the other an only daughter, and both were widowers. In one essential respect they differed. The one was rich, far beyond his show and expenditure. The other had squandered a large patrimonial estate in the low country, with two hundred and fifty negroes, and was compelled to move west of the mountains, to this hereditary tract, with only thirty negroes, the wreck of his former means; where he sustained, as he might, the heart-wearing struggle between poverty and pride, former habits of lavish show, and present desperate expedients, to satisfy their craving. Still, his condition and pretensions placed him far above all other competition in that quarter, except with Squire Buckskin, and over him he had no slight advantage, in being a *Tuckahoe,* when the latter would claim only the honors of being a *Cohoe.*

Miss Anne, as she was called, we omit her remaining pastoral appellations, had been showily educated at Norfolk; danced, played the piano, and had even taken lessons on the harp; had attended lectures, and became possessed of some fifty technicals, and had been heard to say *donnez moi du café* at the breakfast table. She was tall, a good figure, a little sallow, listless in her manners, affecting a kind of yawning ennui; and, when she walked, a negro girl preceded, and another followed her, whose duty required, that each should draw off one of her stockings, when she retired to bed. She was, of course, the undisputed belle and fine lady of the country. Indifferent and listless as she seemed, she was awake to any infraction of her dignity, and exacted her tithe of homage to a tittle.

A kind of family compact between the widowed fathers, had destined her for Nimrod Buckskin, junior. Both the parties had so understood it, so long and so early, that the connexion had come to be contemplated by them with as much indifference, as though it had actually taken place half a dozen years. Although she had not a particle of predilection for anything appertaining to him but his negroes and wealth, yet her optics wanted not the keenness to discern the immense importance of these. Moreover, a certain spice of bitterness, it is presumed, a heritage from the first mother, arose in her bosom, in surveying the Yankee schoolmistress, blooming, buoyant, and erect, moving over the dewy sward in the conscious pride of usefulness, with her numerous fair-haired family skipping onwards, like spring lambs, towards the schoolhouse. A feverish presentiment of danger darted into her mind. A possession, which seemed valueless when there was no competitor, assumed in her eye a fearful importance, as soon as symptoms of contingent loss were descried in the distance.

Before the first quarter of Katharine's services had expired, with an acuteness of tact in that line, as I think, appropriate to the better half of the species, Miss Anne understood precisely what the schoolmistress was; and, without appearing as the accredited source of the information, contrived, that everybody should know, that Katharine was a poor orphan, and that there would be no want of an efficient leader of an opposition to her. With intuitive sagacity, Katharine divined the current that would be likely to spring from this undertow. But, partly from the conviction, that the straight and upright course is the safest; partly from knowing, that little sympathy is won by complaining; and partly from the pride of conscious worth and integrity, she made no inquiries nor confidants, complained not, managed not; but left events to take the natural chances in favor of simple truth, in conflict with intrigue.

Whenever there was a walk or a party, a horse race or a meeting, young Buckskin continued to achieve his prescribed duty of beau to Miss Anne, dragged to it, to use his own words, like a dog in a string. Katharine, interdicted by her employment from many of these interviews, wisely evaded appearing at the remainder, whenever there was a decent pretext. Miss Anne keenly comprehended what a bitter infliction this was to her swain. As they took a morning ride, they often passed the fair young mistress, thoughtfully wending her way to her noisy domain. As their proud coursers pranced by her, 'See,' Miss Anne would pronounce, with a scornful toss of the head, 'where Mr Buckskin's thoughts are wandering! Strange, that the daughter of a strolling tin-pedlar, a mere Yankee rustic, should have so subdued the proud heart of a bear slayer, and heir expectant!' On such occasions young Nimrod gnawed his whip-handle, but word spake not, precisely because the predicament was perplexing beyond his powers of dialogue. But as she proceeded, excited by temper beyond her purpose, to asperse Katharine's character and motives, generosity and justice would have produced a recoil within him, if love had not. Such efforts reacted upon the agent far more than the object. All helped to fan the flame in the young hunter's bosom, until the blind urchin had done the work most effectually for the heir. Love, to him entirely a new disease, raged in his powerful frame, like a tropical epidemic; and most palpably did he manifest the spasms of this terrible malady.

His grand object now was to make known his deplorable case to the schoolmistress. Night and day was he vexing his brain to invent schemes and pretexts, that might bring on a private interview. His purpose was too palpable, not to be as fully comprehended by her as himself. But, although the house was large, a grove near at hand, a few inmates, except negro servants, to act as spies; and, although young Buckskin's authority, over everything within and about the house, was next to despotic, she countervailed his project with such dexterous cleverness, as to defeat all his calculations, without any apparent effort to do so. When, as sometimes happened, they were casually cast together in the same circle, Miss Anne imperatively held her beau to close attendance by a kind of centripetal attraction, while the schoolmistress repelled him by managing firmness. The fierce and proud young heir felt like a caged lion; and it was no circumstance to soothe his agony, to see the loved young schoolmistress followed by the eyes and the homage of the finest young men present.

But Miss Anne began to perceive, with terror, that the stern and independent young hunter was in daily danger of bursting his manacles. She saw, that he had already forgotten, that she was an aristocrat, and heiress of thirty negroes; and her rival an orphan and a Yankee. She had a presentiment, that the crisis of her absolute abandonment could not be distant. The scale of pride sank, as that of real alarm arose; and she repaired to her father, with an ample and undisguised statement of the aspect of the emergency.

The intelligence fell upon her father like a thunder-stroke. He had never dreamed of the possibility, that the compact between him and his neighbor could fail. The consummation had been his anticipated resource for replenishing his purse. He perceived, in a moment, that it was a case that called for prompt action. He was forthwith closeted with the elder Buckskin, who trembled to be informed, what he had half conjectured before, that his son evidently slighted Miss Anne, and loved the schoolmistress, who was represented, as having brought about this issue by the customary management of the Yankees. Squire Fillagree adverted, with due solemnity, to the patrician taint that would be contracted by this misalliance. 'Be true to your honor,' said he, vehemently, 'and your pledged word. Drive away the girl. Inform your son, that he must marry my daughter at once, or never. You both know, that neither my daughter nor myself are to be trifled with.'

Squire Buckskin wrung his hands, in agony. 'I am afraid you have laid out more work than I can accomplish. Both my son and your daughter have always had their will. If the son is like his father, you may as well turn over the Bald Mountain, as change his purposes. This all comes of letting young people have their own heads.'

After much discussion, complaint, and even menace, in which Buckskin indignantly repelled some of the charges against the schoolmistress, it was agreed to attempt the union by persuasion and gentle means. Buckskin could not deny, that his word was pledged, and that he had constantly regarded the union, as though it were already accomplished. He had never imagined, more than his unsuspecting neighbor, that obstacles, like the present, could arise. It was an astounding dilemma to prepare himself to remonstrate with that son, whom he had suffered to grow up as unyielding as a gnarled oak. Nevertheless, he promised his neighbor that he would attempt it, and he sent a servant to summon him, that morning, to prepare for a private conversation with him on particular business.

The son, though neither courtier nor jesuit, discerned how the land laid. True, he sincerely loved his father, but had never been taught to pay much attention to any other will than his own, even in indifferent things, much less, when his whole heart was involved in the issue. 'Am I then a nose of wax?' said he, to himself. 'Is the only advantage of being rich, and an only child, to be transferred to a wife, like a sack of salt? I am strong, and can labor, thank God. I had rather marry the schoolmistress, and settle on Congress land, than Anne Fillagree, with three such estates as my father's. He may make her his heiress, but never me her husband.'

I say not, whether Katharine had been most influenced to her studious avoidance of being alone with him, by a wish to escape the charge of design upon him, by her innate sense of right, or by a keen perception, that the surest mode of drawing such a spirit on, was to hold him back; or whether, as is more probable, she acted from some mixture of all these motives together. At any rate, young Buckskin had hitherto languished for privacy with her, to no purpose. The message in question immediately screwed his courage up to carrying his point at all risks. It is true, she had found means to inspire him, who feared nothing else, with a most reverend dread of her. The cold sweat started at the thought of compelling an interview, the circumstances of which he strove to premeditate, much as the victim on the scaffold looks up at the glittering axe, that hangs over his head.

The morning of the message was one of the brightest of Indian summer, which precede the final fall of the leaves. The echo of the baying dogs, apparently in pursuit of deer, was abroad in the mountains, on whose summits curled the morning mists, just illumined by the early sun. All the glad voices of animated nature came mingled upon the ear in sweet confusion. Even the little school girls bounded for pure gladness of heart. The young mistress had set forth on her daily promenade to her little kingdom, and her children were swinging their satchels a few rods in advance of her. 'She shall not escape me this time,' said Nimrod, in desperation, 'unless she can outrun me;' and he made towards her in a gait betwixt walking and running, but sufficiently indicating, that she could not avoid meeting him, just as she entered a thick grove on her way. His strange approach inclined her to turn round.

'My mind is up to it, Miss Katharine,' said he, in a husky tone of voice. 'Nothing shall balk me. I hope you will not fly the track, for I have something very particular to say to you.'

Though actually terrified herself, she assumed a playful calmness, as she replied,

'Mr Buckskin, these lands, I believe, belong to your father. You have, at least, an equal right to walk here with me. You seem to be flurried. If you have anything to say, I am ready to hear. Only use despatch, and avoid frightening the children.'

Nimrod was at length in the position so earnestly desired, alone in the wood with her, and permitted to communicate what he had to say. But a sudden palsy seemed to have struck at once his faculties and his speech; and the more self-possessed Katharine felt divided between pity and laughter, as she witnessed his ludicrous torment. At length, sidling towards her, as she recoiled, he said, in the hesitating manner of a stammerer, and with a face alternately crimson and pale;—

'A fine morning this, and the deer are down from the mountains.'

'I am no hunter, Sir.'

'Well, I admire a deer-hunt above everything.'

'Very like. It does not follow that I should, though.'

'But you might have the civility to seem to like it. I know nothing that you love, but what I will love too.'

'You are exceedingly complaisant. You do not know, perhaps, that we cannot always love what we would.

'Yes, I do, with a vengeance; and that it is just as impossible not to love—you smile, as though you had no heart. You look, at this moment, just as Miss Anne calls you, proud and cruel.'

'Does she charge me so?'

'Yes, and worse than that.'

'For the rest, I cannot say; but she is just in her charges so far. I am both proud and cruel.'

'There's a woman for you! Miss Katharine. Whoever heard of accusing one's-self? It is not true, begging your pardon, and I told Miss Anne so, when she said it; told her, that Heaven might as soon be proud and cruel as you. Then she went on to asperse you; and I told her, that the more she hated, the more I loved you. I told her, I would give all the deer in the mountains, all I expect beside in the world, and seven such lives as mine, if I could be sure that you returned my love.'

'Indeed, Mr Buckskin, you have such strange ways of talking, here in the West, that I am not quite sure I understand you. Under correction, Mr Buckskin, in New England, we should call this sort of conversation mere folly.'

'Miss Katharine, laugh at me, as you will; your eyes, after all, are not so cruel as your words. I love'—

'Hush, Mr Buckskin. My children will hear. You forget your well known engagement with Miss Fillagree; your feelings are no concern of mine. Please to terminate this conversation, and let me go on to my school.'

'You cannot stop, or silence me, now. You may as well chain up the wind. By thunder! I will never marry Miss Anne, disinherited or not, that's flat.'

'I am not your guardian, and have no power to compel you. But I always considered you a man of honor, and true to your engagement.'

'Thank you a thousand times, for thinking so; and so I am. The person lives not, who can charge me, either by word, look, or action, with intentional deception. I never gave her any expectations that I would offer myself.'

'I have never charged you with it. What is all this to me? Hush, I say; don't you see the children close at hand?'

'I am above fearing children, or anything else. I will never marry her. I love'—

'Good morning, Mr Buckskin. To repay your declarations by equal frankness, be assured, I will never think, for a moment, of aiding a son in disobedience to his father.'

Saying this, she hurried into the school; and, while he stood in a kind of quandary as to what was to be done next, she gathered in her flock, shut the door, and locked it upon the inside. He surveyed the premises a moment, as a warrior does a besieged city, and then went off, soliloquizing, 'that's a severe bird, any how. The daughter of a Yankee is up to anything;' and he fell to abusing the country in all the vigor of vexation.

But while materials for thickening the plot were thus collecting, whether from the chagrin superinduced by the furious uproar of Squire Fillagree and daughter, or whether from listening to the earnest expostulations of his son, or from a return of his old complaint, can never be certainly known; but so it was, that at this juncture, Squire Buckskin fell dangerously sick. His deportment was devout and edifying. He absolved his son from all engagements made by him with Squire Fillagree. He seemed never so calm, as when Katharine Spooner was his nurse. Before he died, when they happened to be together beside his bed, he joined their hands, and bade them love, and be happy, when he should be no more. He died after a short illness.

Soon after the funeral, the young mourner waited on his neighbor Fillagree, peremptorily assuring him, that he had never, in any way, paid any serious court to his daughter, and adding, that he never should. Fillagree suppressed his rising rage, and urged that the reputation of his daughter was committed, that his own honor was bound to his father's contract, and various other considerations, not forgetting the contamination of blood, and the selfish intrigue and management of the school-mistress. Buckskin remained immoveable. High words then ensued, and Fillagree talked of settling the difficulty with rifles. But Buckskin continued cool and invincible. Seeing that nothing was gained in this way, Fillagree fell to cursing the whole generation of Yankees, man, woman, and child. The race were born with an instinctive appetite to cheat and deceive. They would always go to their point by a crooked way, if there were an alternative between a straight and crooked one. He capped his climax of curses with a more vehement tirade against Katharine.

Buckskin coolly replied, that he was led to believe, that most of the stale calumnies against the Yankees had been invented in a state of mind not unlike his. As to what he had said of Katharine, had it been any other man, he would have given him the lie in his throat.

But to shorten my tale, the proud and pastoral Miss Fillagree, foreseeing the probable issue of her hopes with Mr Buckskin, had cast an anchor to the windward, in a private marriage with a Yankee steamboat captain, who had visited Mr Buckskin for a load of salt. Her father was more outrageous than ever; but, in the midst of his paroxysm, the wedded pair silently slipped off, and passed the honeymoon in a trip to New Orleans.

Nimrod Buckskin, Esq. had now fewer obstacles in the way of private interviews with Miss Spooner. Not that she was too easy at driving the terms of the contract; not that she did not, as he complained, sometimes *yankee* him. But she was not cruel enough to break down the impetuous spirit of the young hunter, and the negotiation ended in marriage. The schoolmistress gave up her fifty scholars, and confined herself to this single, tall pupil, and a most docile subject he became; though he, his father before him, and the whole generation, had been noted for the most immoveable perseverance in their way. It was a proverb in the place, that a common fence might as well turn a deer, as anything, but his own will, a Buckskin. It now goes near to amuse the family dog under the table, to see his master sit down so gently, beside his beautiful bride, to dictionaries, grammars, a globe, and the like, speaking in a soft and subdued tone, as though he were a schoolboy. In less than six months after their marriage, Buckskin not only began to talk about literature, reviews, and the fine arts, but he actually perpetrated a *blank* verse sonnet to his wife's curls.

The politics of the village and county are Yankee and Anti-Yankee. Buckskin leads the former, and Fillagree the latter; though he has a son-in-law of that people. But his interest clearly kicks the beam. Mr Buckskin has been the chief agent in building a handsome church and schoolhouse, and in establishing a village library. Under the new spirit, and the higher regulations that have arisen in the village, everything wears a new aspect. Mr Buckskin is the ostensible agent in these improvements. But an eye, that traces effects to their causes, sees all these happy results developing from the germ of a New England free school. Mrs Buckskin is, in fact, an admirable example of the good that may be done by a single person, uniting beauty, intelligence, opulence, and goodness.

Mr Buckskin sometimes colors a little, as an Anti-Yankee slyly insinuates the proverb, about the *grey nag*. But he replies by saying, that he is as wilful as ever; but that his wife has the secret of divining his thoughts, and is so invariably of his mind, that he can find no chance to contradict her, if he would.

18

JOHN TANNER

(1780–1847?)

John Tanner was born near Fort Washington, the future site of Cincinnati, in 1780, to a pioneer family. At the age of nine, he was captured by Shawnees and sold to the Ojibways in Detroit, at a British trading post. For most of the next thirty years, Tanner was an Ojibway, for all intents and purposes. He remembered little English and wholly adapted to a life of hunting and trapping in the upper Great Lakes region. While he was excluded from the trappings of power which should have accompanied his prowess as a hunter on account of his race, Tanner was allowed to marry, to lead his own hunting parties, and to join war parties against the Sioux further to the west. As such, despite its title, the *Narrative* is not a captivity narrative, but rather something more resembling an Ojibway autobiography.

However, being an Ojibway in areas controlled by the large British and Canadian fur companies before the War of 1812 meant contact with other whites. Some never noticed his race; others tried to bring him back into white society. After the War of 1812, Tanner's position became increasingly untenable, as American trading companies, Indian agents, and settlers showed themselves to be less tolerant toward flexible racial identities. Dislodged from his identity as an Ojibway, who had now grown suspicious of him, Tanner was forced to try to live as a white man.

The sections reproduced here describe Tanner's difficulty in finding a new identity at middle age. Leaving the Ojibways in 1820, Tanner was confused and depressed and wandered the west pursuing various occupations during the 1820s, before finally settling at Henry Rowe Schoolcraft's agency at Sault Ste. Marie, Michigan. There, with the chaplain Edwin James, he transcribed his *Narrative* and then traveled to New York to secure publication. While the book ends with a promise of assimilation, in fact, Tanner's life became only more complicated. Ultimately unable to find a home in the white world, sometime in the early 1840s Tanner reentered the world of the Ojibway and the northern fur trade and disappeared from the written record. Tanner left mixed-race children in each world. Those who remained with the Ojibway settled at the White Earth Reservation in Minnesota; a son raised in Michigan died in the Civil War. Tanner's legacy, then, is ultimately to the enormous mixed-race population of the Great Lakes region.

Text: *A Narrative* (New York, 1830; rpt. Minneapolis, 1956): 172–198, 223–240.

FROM *A NARRATIVE OF THE CAPTIVITY AND ADVENTURES OF JOHN TANNER* (1830)

CHAPTER XI

Rapacity of the traders—revelation of Manito-o-geezhik—pretensions of As-kaw-ba-wis—credulity of the Indians—colony at Red River, planted by the Hudson's Bay traders—large war-party assembled at Turtle Mountain—want of discipline.

Mr. Henry had traded ten years at Pembinah. He was succeeded by a Mr. M'Kenzie, who remained but a short time, and after him came Mr. Wells, called by the Indians Gah-se-moan, (a sail,) from the roundness and fulness of his person. He built a strong fort on Red River, near the mouth of the Assinneboin. The Hudson's Bay Company had now no post in that part of the country, and the Indians were soon made conscious of the advantage which had formerly resulted to them from the competition between rival trading companies. Mr. Wells, at the commencement of winter, called us all together, gave the Indians a ten gallon keg of rum and some tobacco, telling them, at the same time, he would not credit one of them the value of a single needle. When they brought skins, he would buy them, and give in exchange such articles as were necessary for their comfort and subsistence during the winter. I was not with the Indians when this talk was held. When it was reported to me, and a share of the presents offered me, I not only refused to accept any thing, but reproached the Indians for their pusillanimity in submitting to such terms. They had been accustomed for many years to receive credits in the fall. They were now entirely destitute not of clothing merely, but of ammunition, and many of them of guns and traps. How were they, without the accustomed aid from the traders, to subsist themselves and their families during the ensuing winter? A few days afterwards, I went to Mr. Wells, and told him that I was poor, with a large family to support by my own exertions, and that I must unavoidably suffer, and perhaps perish, unless he would give me such a credit as I had always, in the fall, been accustomed to receive. He would not listen to my representation and told me, roughly, to be gone from his house. I then took eight silver beavers, such as are worn by the women, as ornaments on their dress, and which I had purchased the year before at just twice the price that was commonly given for a capote. I laid them before him on the table, and asked him to give me a capote for them, or retain them as a pledge for the payment of the price of the garment, as soon as I could procure the peltries. He took up the ornaments, threw them in my face, and told me never to come inside of his house again. The cold weather of the winter had not yet set in, and I went immediately to my hunting ground, killed a number of moose, and set my wife to make the skins into such garments as were best adapted to the winter season, and which I now saw we should be compelled to substitute for the blankets and woollen clothes we had been accustomed to receive from the traders.

I continued my hunting with good success, but the winter had not half passed when I heard that Mr. Hanie, a trader for the Hudson's Bay people, had arrived at Pembinah. I went immediately to him, and he gave me all the credit I asked, which was to the amount of seventy skins. Then I went to Muskrat River, where I hunted the remainder of the winter, killing great numbers of martens, beavers, otters, etc.

Early in the spring, I sent word by some Indians to Mr. Hanie, that I would go down to the mouth of the Assinneboin, and meet him there to pay my credit, as I had skins more than enough for this purpose.

When I arrived at the Assinneboin, Mr. Hanie had not yet passed, and I stopped to wait for him opposite Mr. Well's trading house. An old Frenchman offered me a lodging in his house, and I went in and deposited my peltries under the place he gave me to sleep in. Mr. Wells, having heard of my arrival, sent three times, urging me to come and see him. At last, I yielded to the solicitations of my brother-in-law and crossed over with him. Mr. Wells was glad to see me, and treated me with much politeness. He offered me wine and provisions, and whatever his house afforded. I had taken nothing except a little tobacco, when I saw his Frenchman come in with my packs. They carried them past me into Mr. Well's bed room. He then locked the door, and took out the key. Immediately his kindness and attentions to me relaxed. I said nothing, but felt not the less anxious and uneasy, as I was very unwilling to be deprived of the means of paying Mr. Hanie his credit, still more so to have my property taken from me by violence, or without my consent. I watched about the house, and at length found an opportunity to slip into the bed room, while Mr. Wells was then taking something from a trunk. He tried to drive me, and afterwards to push me out, but I was too strong for him. After he had proceeded to this violence, I did not hesitate to take up my packs, but he snatched them from me. Again I seized them, and in the struggle that ensued, the thongs that bound them were broken, and the skins strewed about the floor. As I went to gather them up, he drew a pistol, cocked it, and presented it to my breast. For a moment I stood motionless, thinking he would certainly kill me, as I saw he was much enraged. Then I seized his hand, and turned it aside, at the same moment drawing from my belt a large knife, which I grasped firmly in my right hand, still holding him by my left. Seeing himself thus suddenly and entirely in my power, he called first for his wife, then for his interpreter, and told them to put me out of the house. To this, the interpreter answered, "You are as able to put him out as I am." Some of the Frenchmen were also in the house, but they refused to give him any assistance. Finding he was not likely to intimidate or overcome me by violence, he had recourse once more to milder measures. He offered to divide with me, and to allow me to retain half my peltries for the Hudson's Bay people. "You have always," said he, "belonged to the North West; why should you now desert us for the Hudson's Bay?" He then proceeded to count the skins, dividing them into two parcels, but I told him it was unnecessary, as I was determined he should not have one of them. "I went to you," said I, "last fall, when I was hungry and destitute, and you drove me, like a dog, from your door. The ammunition with which I killed these animals, was credited to me by Mr. Hanie, and the skins belong to him but if this was not the case, you should not have one of them. You are a coward. You have not so much courage as a child. If you had the heart of a squaw, you would not have pointed your pistol at my breast, and have failed to shoot me. My life was in your power, and there was nothing to prevent your taking it, not even the fear of my friends, for you know that I am a stranger here, and not one among the Indians would raise his hand to avenge my death. You might have thrown my body into the river, as you would a dog, and no one would have asked you what you had done, but you wanted the spirit to do even this." He asked me if I had not a knife in my hand. I then showed him two, a large and a small one, and told him to beware how he provoked me to use them. At last, wearied with this altercation, he went and sat down opposite me in the large room. Though he was at considerable distance, so great was his agitation that I could distinctly hear his heart beat. He sat awhile, then went and began to walk back and forth in the yard. I collected my skins together, and the interpreter helped me to tie them up; then taking them on my back, I walked out, passed close by him, put them in my canoe, and returned to the old Frenchman's house on the other side.

Next morning, it appeared that Mr. Wells had thought better of the subject than to wish to take my property from me by violence, for he sent his interpreter to offer me his horse, which was a very valuable one, if I would think no more of what he had done. "Tell him," said I, to the interpreter, "he is a child, and wishes to quarrel and forget his quarrel in one day, but he shall not find I am like him. I have a horse of my own, I will keep my packs, nor will I forget that he pointed his pistol at my breast when he had not the courage to shoot me."

On the following morning, one of the clerks of the North West Company arrived from the trading-house at Mouse River, and he, it appeared, told Mr. Wells when he heard what had passed that he would take my packs from me, and though Mr. Wells cautioned him against it, he determined on making the attempt. It was near noon when the old Frenchman, after looking out of his house, said to me, "My friend, I believe you will lose your packs now. Four men are coming this way, all well armed; their visit, I am sure, is for no good or friendly purpose." Hearing this, I placed my packs in the middle of the floor, and taking a beaver trap in my hand, sat down on them. When the clerk came in, accompanied by three young men, he asked me for my packs. "What right have you," said I, "to demand them?" "You are indebted to me," said he. "When did I owe the North West any thing, that was not paid at the time agreed on?" "Ten years ago," said he, "your brother, Wa-me-gon-a-biew, had a credit from me, which he paid all but ten skins. Those are still due, and I wish you to pay them." "Very well," said I, "I will pay your demand, but you must, at the same time, pay me for those four packs of beaver we sent to you from the Grand Portage. Your due bill was, as you know, burned with my lodge at Ke-mu-kaw-ne-she-wa-bo-ant, and you have never paid me, or any member of our family, the value of a single needle for those one hundred and sixty beaver skins." Finding this method would not succeed, and knowing, though he disregarded it, the justice of my reply, he tried the effect of violent measures, like those used on the preceding day by Mr. Wells; but when he perceived these were and would be equally unavailing, he returned to the fort without having taken a single marten skin from me.

When I ascertained that it would be some time before Mr. Hanie would arrive, I went down to Dead River, and while I was waiting there, killed four hundred muskrats. At last, Mr. Hanie arrived at the place where I, with another man, had been waiting for him. He told me that he had passed Mr. Wells' trading-house at the mouth of the Assinneboin, in the middle of the day, with his crew singing. Mr. Wells, on seeing him, had immediately started after him, with a canoe strongly manned and armed. On perceiving this pursuit, Mr. Hanie went on shore, and leaving his men in his canoe, went up about twenty yards into a smooth prairie. Hither Mr. Wells followed him, attended by several armed men, but Mr. Hanie made him stop at the distance of ten yards, and a long dispute followed, which ended in his permitting Mr. Hanie to pass down. I related to him my story of the treatment I had received, and paid him his credit. I traded with him for the remainder of my peltries, and after we had finished, he gave me some handsome presents, among which was a valuable gun, and then went on his way. As I was re-ascending Red River, I met Mr. Wells. He was destitute of fresh game, and asked me for some, which I should have given, had it been in my power, but he attributed my refusal to ill will. Afterwards, though I was living at a distance from him, he sent his horse to me, and again subsequently to Pembinah, but I constantly refused to accept it. Notwithstanding my steady and repeated refusal, I was informed he always said the horse belonged to me, and after his death, which happened three years later, the other traders told me I ought to take the horse, but I would not, and it fell into the hands of an old Frenchman. After the death of Mr. Wells, I returned to the North West Company, and traded with them, as before, but never while he lived. If he had shot me, and wounded me ever so severely, I should have been less offended with him, than to have him present his pistol, as he did, to my breast, and take it away without firing.

Esh-ke-buk-ke-koo-sa, a chief of Leech Lake, came after this to Pembinah with about forty young men, and I went, by invitation, from the Be-gwi-o-nus-ko, with others, to hear him give some account of the recent revelation from the Great Spirit to Manito-o-geezhik. We were all assembled one night in a long lodge, erected for the purpose, to dance and feast, and listen to the discourse of the chief, when suddenly we heard two guns, in quick succession, in the direction of the North West Company's trading-house, now unoccupied, except by two Frenchmen who had that day arrived. The old men looked at each other in doubt and dismay. Some said the Frenchmen are killing wolves, but Esh-ke-buk-ke-koo-sa said, "I know the sound of the guns of the Sioux." The night was very dark, but all the young men took their arms and started immediately, and I among the foremost. Many getting entangled among logs and stumps, made but little progress. I kept the path, and was still foremost, when a dark figure shot past me, and at the same moment I heard the voice of the Black Duck, saying, neen-dow-in-nin-ne, (I am a man.) I had often heard of the prowess of this man, and in one instance had seen him at the Sioux village at Chief Mountain, lead in what we all supposed would be an attack. Now I determined to keep near him. We had advanced within about gun shot of the fort when he began to leap, first to one side, and then to the other, thus moving in a zigzag line, though rapidly, towards the gate of the fort. I followed his example, and when he leapt into the open gate of the fort, it was with a surprising effort of activity, which carried his feet near two yards from the ground. We saw within the fort a house, at the window and door of which we perceived a bright light. The Black Duck had a buffalo robe over his shoulders, the dark colour of which enabled him to pass the window undiscovered by the man who was watching within, but my white blanket betraying me, the muzzle of a gun was instantly presented to my head, but not discharged, for the Black Duck at that instant caught in his arms the affrighted Frenchman, who had mistaken me for one of the Sioux, and was in the act of firing upon me. The second Frenchman was with the women and children, who were all lying in a heap in the corner of the room, crying through fear. It appeared that the one who was watching by the window, who was the most manly of the two, had, a few minutes before, been driving his horse out of the fort, to give him water, when the animal had been shot dead in the gate by some men concealed near at hand. He at first thought we were the people who had shot his horse, but he was soon convinced of his error, as we did not even know that the body of the horse was lying at the gate, having jumped entirely over it when we entered. This Frenchman would not leave the fort, but the Black Duck, who was a relative of one of the women, insisted that they should be taken to the Indian camp. Others of our young men had by this time come up, and we determined to watch in the fort all night. Next morning we found the trail of the two men who had crossed the Pembinah river, a considerable war party having been concealed on the other side. The two men were the celebrated Yanktong chief, Wah-ne-tow, and his uncle. They had concealed themselves near the gate of the fort, with the determination to shoot down whatever came out or went in. The first that passed, happening to be the Frenchman's horse, he was shot down; and the two men, proba-bly without knowing whether they had killed man or beast, fled across the river.

When it was ascertained that the Sioux war party was not a very large one, many were disposed to pursue after it, but Esh-ke-buk-ke-koo-sha said, "not so, my brethren. Manito-o-geezhik, whose messenger I am to you, tells us we must no more go against our enemies. And is it not manifest that in this instance the Great Spirit has protected us. Had the Sioux come about our lodge when we were feasting in secu-rity, without our arms in our hands, how easily might they have killed all of us, but they were misled, and made to mistake a Frenchman's horse for an Ojibbeway. So will it continue to be if we are obedient to the injunctions we have received." I began to be apprehensive for my family, having left them at home, and fearing that the Sioux might visit them on their way to their own country. "Go," said Esh-ke-buk-ke-koo-sha, when I told him of my anxiety, "but do not fear that the Sioux can do any injury to your wife or children, but I wish you to go that on your return you may bring me your medicine bag, and I shall show you what to do with the contents." I did ac-cordingly, and he ordered the contents of my medicine bag, except the medicines for war and hunting, to be thrown into the fire. "This," said he, "is what we must hence-forth do. If any one is sick, let them take a bowl of birch bark, and a little tobacco; the sick person himself, if he is able to walk, otherwise his nearest relative, and let them go to the nearest running water. Let the tobacco be offered to the stream, then dip-ping the bowl in the same direction in which the water runs, let them take a little, and carry it home, for the sick person to drink. But if the sickness be very severe, then let the person that dips up the water, plunge the bowl so deep that the edge of it shall touch the mud in the bottom of the stream." He then gave me a small hoop of wood to wear on my head like a cap. On one half of this hoop was marked the figure of a snake, whose office, as the chief told me, was to take care of the water; on the other half, the figure of a man, to represent the Great Spirit. This band, or fillet, was not to be worn on ordinary occasions—only when I should go to bring water for some of my family or friends who should be sick. I was much dissatisfied at the destruction of the contents of my medicine bag, many of them being such roots and other substances as I had found useful in the disorders incident to my situation, and I was still more displeased that we were not, henceforth, to be allowed to use these remedies, some of which I knew to be of great value. But all the Indians of the band were in the same situation with myself, and I was compelled to submit.

When the spring came on, I went to fulfil an appointment I had made the pre-ceding fall with Sha-gwaw-ko-sink, to meet him at a certain place. I arrived on the spot at the time appointed, and shortly afterwards, the old man came, on foot and alone, to search for me. He had encamped about two miles distant, where he had been for two days, and they had plenty of fresh meat, which was particularly grateful to me as for some time past I had killed but little.

I lived with him during the summer. Sha-gwaw-ko-sink was now too old and fee-ble to hunt, but he had some young men with him, who kept him supplied while game was to be had, but late in the fall the hunting grounds about us became poor. The weather was very cold, and the ground hard frozen, but no snow fell so that it was diffi cult to follow the tracks of the moose and the noise of our walking on hard ground and dry leaves, gave the animals timely warning of our approach. This state of things con tinuing for some time, we were all reduced nearly to starvation, and had recourse, as a last resort, to medicine hunting. Half the night I sung and prayed, and then lay down to sleep. I saw in my dream a beautiful young man come down through the hole in the top of my lodge, and he stood directly before me. "What," said he, "is this noise and crying that I hear? Do I not know when you are hungry and in distress? I look down upon you at all times, and it is not necessary you should call me with such loud cries." Then point ing directly towards the sun's setting, he said, "do you see those tracks?" "Yes," I answered, "they are the tracks of two moose." "I give you those two moose to eat." Then pointing in an opposite direction, towards the place of the sun's rising, he showed me a bear's track, and said, "that also I give you." He then went out at the door of my lodge, and as he raised the blanket, I saw that snow was falling rapidly.

I very soon awoke, and feeling too much excited to sleep, I called old Sha-gwaw-ko-sink to smoke with me, and then prepared my Muz-zin-ne-neen-suk,[1] as in the

---

1. *Muz-zin-ne-neen, muz-zin-ne-neen-sug*—singular and plural. *Meshe-nin-ne-shah, Meshe-nin-ne-shuk*—Menomonie dialect. These little images, or drawings, for they are called by the same names, whether of carved wood, or rags, or only rudely sketched on birch bark, or even traced in sand, are much in use among several, and probably all the Algonkin tribes. Their use is not confined to hunting, but extends to the making of love, and the gratifiction of hatred, revenge, and all malignant passions.

It is a prevailing belief, to which the influence of established superstition has given an astonishing power, that the necromancers, men and women of medicine, or those who are acquainted with the hid den powers of their *wusks*, can, by practising upon the Muz-zin-ne-neence, exercise an unlimited control over the body and mind of the person represented. As it may have been, in former times, among the peo ple of our race, many a simple Indian girl gives to some crafty old squaw her most valued ornaments, or whatever property she may possess, to purchase from her the love of the man she is most anxious to please. The old woman, in a case of this kind, commonly makes up a little image of stained wood and rags, to which she gives the name of the person whose inclinations she is expected to control; and to the heart, the eyes, or to some other part of this, she, from time to time, applies her medicine, or professes to have done so, as she may find necessary to dupe and encourage her credulous employer.

But the influence of these images and conjurations, is more frequently tested in cases of an opposite character; where the inciting cause is not love, but hatred, and the object to be attained, the gratification of a deadly revenge. In cases of this kind, the practices are similar to those above mentioned, only differ ent medicines are used. Sometimes the Muz-zin-ne-neence is pricked with a pin, or needle, in various parts, and pain or disease is supposed to be produced in the corresponding part of the person practiced upon. Sometimes they blacken the hands and mouth of the image, and the effect expected, is the change which marks the near approach of death.

In the sanguinary chapter of the Calica Puran, we find reference to a similar superstition among the Asiatics.

"Let a figure be made, either of barley meal or earth, representing the person with whom the sac rificer is at variance, and the head of the figure struck off. After the usual texts have been used, the fol lowing is to be used in invoking the axe on the occasion: *Effuse, effuse blood! be terrific, be terrific! seize, seize! destroy, for the love of Ambica, the head of this enemy.* Having struck off the head let him present it, using the texts laid down hereafter for the occasion, concluding with the word PHAT. Water must be sprinkled on the meal or earthen victim, which represents the sacrificer's enemy, using the text commencing with *Racta draibaih,* (i. e. by streams of blood,) and marks must be made on the forehead with red sanders; garlands of red flowers must be put round the neck of the image, and it must be dressed in red garments, tied with red cords, and girt with a red girdle. Then placing the head towards the north, let it be struck off with an axe, using the *Scanda* text."

So general and prevalent, among the Indians, is the confidence in the efficacy of these charms, and of those practised by means of a hair from the head of the intended victim, that the belief in them has ex tended to many of the more ignorant of the Canadians who reside with the Indians, and even to some of the traders. Instances in which a hair is used in place of the image, or mus-zin-ne-neence, are frequently those of young women; and various, and sometimes dreadful, are the consequences supposed to result. So confident are the representations of whites, and those even of some shrewdness, and so strong the belief

subjoined sketch, to represent the animals whose tracks had been shown me in my dream. At the earliest dawn, I started from the lodge in a heavy fall of snow, and taking the course pointed out to me, long before noon I fell on the track of two moose, and killed them both, a male and a female, and extremely fat.

The songs used on occasion of these medicine hunts have relation to the religious opinions of the Indians. They are often addressed to Na-na-boo-shoo, or Na-Na-bush, whom they intreat to be their interpreter, and communicate their requests to the Supreme. Oftentimes, also, to Me-suk-kum-mik O-kwi, or the earth, the great-grandmother of all. In these songs, they relate how Na-na-bush created the ground in obedience to the commands of the Great Spirit, and how all things for the use, and

---

of the Indians, in the power of these drawings, as to enforce the conviction that effects have been produced in connection with these mummeries, either by the influence of imagination, or the still more powerful and certain operation of poison, administered secretly. Poisoning is a crime of perhaps greater frequency among the Indians than could have been expected from their situation; and they attribute equal guilt to the poisoner, whether he actually and craftily administers some powerful drug, or whether, at the distance of one or two hundred miles, or at any place, however remote, he so applies medicine to the Muz-zin-ne-neence, or to a hair, as to produce pain, sickness, death, or other suffering, in his enemy. The influence of these superstitions and absurd fears is boundless, and would, perhaps, surpass comprehension and belief if we could not look back to the time when the minds of our own race were similarly enthralled, and when the dread of supernatural powers in the hands of the malicious or the envious, formed one among the most serious and real evils in the life even of the most enlightened and independent. Many cases of sudden sickness occur among them, and many deaths happen entirely in the way of nature, which they, being ignorant of the true cause, attribute to poison, or more frequently to bad medicine; but enough of well authenticated instatnces exist to prove that they, in some cases, practice upon each other by poison; sometimes using such noxious plants, or other substances as their own country affords, and in other instances procuring arsenic, or other drugs, from the whites. To destroy life in this way is perfectly in accordance with their ideas of bravery, or toughness of heart, (Soug-ge-da-win;) he being often esteemed the bravest man who destroys his enemy with least risk to his own life.

The Chippewyans, whose bleak and inhospitable country, affords neither birch bark nor other similar article, indeed nothing from the vegetable kingdom to serve as a substitute for the birch bark, and whose extreme rudeness has left them ignorant of any method of preparing from stones or earth any things suitable to write or delineate figures upon, use, in their preparations for the medicine hunt, the scapular bone of the rein deer, or such other animals as are found in their country. With an apparent poverty of language, corresponding to the meagerness of their soil, and the bluntness of their intellects, they denominate the drawing used in this kind of hunting, *El-kul-lah ke-eet-ze,* (the shoulder blade bone.) It would appear, also, that the accompanying ceremonies of this superstition are proportionately rude and inartificial. After awkwardly sketching the rein deer, or whatever animal they may happen to consider as indicated to them by their dream, they cast the bone on which the drawing is made into the fire, if, by chance, they happen to have one, and this fulfills all those important ends, which, in the imagination of the Ojibbeway hunter, are dependent upon the proper application of his medicines, and the patient chanting of his prayers.

to supply the wants of the uncles and aunts of Na-na-bush, (by which are meant men and women,) were committed to the care and keeping of the great mother. Na-na-bush, ever the benevolent intercessor between the Supreme Being and mankind, procured to be created for their benefit the animals whose flesh should be for their food, and whose skins were for their clothing. He sent down roots and medicines of sovereign power to heal their sicknesses, and in times of hunger, to enable them to kill the animals of the chase. All these things were committed to the care of Me-suk-kum-mik O-kwi, and that his uncles and aunts might never call on her in vain, the old woman was directed to remain constantly at home in her lodge. Hence it is that good Indians never dig up the roots of which their medicines are made, without at the same time depositing in the earth something as an offering to Me-suk-kum-mik O-kwi. They sing also, how, in former times, the Great Spirit having killed the brother of Na-na-bush, the latter was angry, and strengthened himself against the Supreme. Na-na-bush waxed stronger and stronger, and was likely to prevail against Gitch-e-manito, when the latter, to appease him, gave him the Me-tai. With this, Na-na-bush was so pleased, that he brought it down to his uncles and aunts on the earth.

Many of these songs are noted down by a method probably peculiar to the Indians, on birch bark, or small flat pieces of wood, the ideas being conveyed by emblematic figures somewhat like those before mentioned, as used in communicating ordinary information.

Two years previous to this time, a man of our band called Ais-kaw-ba-wis, a quiet and rather insignificant person, and a poor hunter, lost his wife by death, and his children began, even more than formerly, to suffer of hunger. The death of his wife was attended with peculiar circumstances, and Ais-kaw-ba-wis became melancholy and despondent, which we attributed to the sluggishness of his disposition, but he at length called the chiefs together, and with much solemnity announced to them that he had been favoured by a new revelation from the Great Spirit. He showed them a round ball of earth, about four or five inches in diameter, or more than half as large as a man's head, rolled round and smooth, and smeared with red paint. "The Great Spirit," said he, "as I sat, from day to day, crying, and praying, and singing in my lodge, at last called to me, and said, 'Ais-kaw-ba-wis, I have heard your prayers, I have seen the mats in your lodge wet with your tears, and have listened to your request. I give you this ball, and as you see it is clean and new, I give it to you for your business to make the whole earth like it, even as it was when Na-na-bush first made it. All old things must be destroyed and done away; every thing must be made anew, and to your hands, Ais-kaw-ba-wis, I commit this great work.'"

I was among those whom he called in to listen to this first annunciation of his mission. It was not until after he dismissed us that I said any thing, but then, in conversation with my companions, I soon betrayed my want of credulity. "It is well," said I, "that we may be made acquainted with the whole mind and will of the Great Spirit at so cheap a rate. We have now these divinely taught instructors springing up among ourselves, and fortunately, such men as are worth nothing for any other purpose. The Shawnee prophet was far off. Ke-zhi-ko-we-ninne and Manito-o-geezhik, though of our own tribe, were not with us. They were also men. But here we have one too poor, and indolent, and spiritless, to feed his own family, yet he is made the instrument, in the hand of the Great Spirit, as he would have us believe, to renovate the whole earth." I had always entertained an unfavourable opinion of this man, as I knew him to be one of the most worthless among the Indians, and I now felt indignant at his attempt to pass himself upon us as a chosen and favoured messenger of the Supreme

Spirit. I hesitated not to ridicule his pretensions wherever I went, but notwithstanding that bad luck constantly attended him, he gained a powerful ascendancy over the minds of the Indians. His incessant beating of his drum at night scared away the game from our neighbourhood, and his insolent hypocrisy made him offensive to me at all times, but he had found the way to control the minds of many of the people, and all my efforts in opposition to him were in vain.

On one occasion, while we remained at this place, and had been suffering some days from hunger, I went out to hunt and wounded a moose. On my return, I related this, and said I believe the moose was so badly wounded that he must die. Early next morning, Ais-kaw-ba-wis came to my lodge, and with the utmost seriousness in his manner, said to me that the Great Spirit had been down, and told him of the moose I had wounded. "He is now dead," said he, "and you will find him in such a place. It is the will of the Great Spirit that he should be brought here and cooked for a sacrifice." I thought it not improbable that the moose was killed, and went in search of him accordingly, but I found he was not dead. This afforded me another opportunity to ridicule the pretensions of Ais-kaw-ba-wis, but all seemed in no degree to impair the confidence of the Indians. Very shortly afterwards, it happened that I again wounded a moose, and went home without getting it. "This," said Ais-kaw-ba-wis, "is the moose which the Great Spirit showed me." So I went out and brought him in, and as I knew many of the Indians were hungry, I was willing to make a feast, though not out of deference to Ais-kaw-ba-wis. As we were too few in number to consume all the meat, we cut it off the bones, and these were heaped up before Ais-kaw-ba-wis, care being taken that not one of them should be broken. They were afterwards carried to a safe place, and hung up out of the reach of the dogs or wolves, as no bone of an animal offered in this way must, by any means, be broken. On the following day, I killed another fat moose, on which occasion Ais-kaw-ba-wis made a long address to the Great Spirit, and afterwards said to me, "You see, my son, how your goodness is rewarded. You gave the first you killed to the Spirit. He will take care you shall not want." Next day I went with my brother-in-law, and we killed each one, and now Ais-kaw-ba-wis exulted much in the efficacy of the sacrifice he had caused me to make, and his ascendancy over the superstitious minds of the Indians was confirmed. Notwithstanding this high degree of favour he had obtained by his cunning, he was a man who, once in his life, had eaten his own wife for hunger, and whom the Indians would then have killed as one unworthy to live.

When the snow began to harden on the top at the approach of the spring, the men of our band, Sha-gwaw-koo-sink, Wau-zhe-gaw-maish-koon, Ba-po-wash, Gish-kau-ko, myself and some others, went to make a hunting camp at some distance for the purpose of making dry meat, and left only Ais-kaw-ba-wis at home with the women. We killed much game, as it is very easy to take moose and elk at that season. The crust on the snow, while it will bear a man, almost deprives them of the power of motion. At length, Gish-kau-ko went home to see his family, and on his return he brought me a little tobacco from Ais-kaw-ba-wis, with this message. "Your life is in danger." "My life," said I, "belongs neither to Ais-kaw-ba-wis nor myself. It is in the hands of the Great Spirit, and when he sees fit to place it in danger, or bring it to an end, I shall have no cause to complain, but I cannot believe that he has revealed any part of his intentions to so worthless a man as Ais-kaw-ba-wis." But this intimation alarmed all the Indians who were with me, and they made the best of their way to the place where Ais-kaw-ba-wis was encamped with the women. I took a circuitous route by myself to visit some of my traps, and having caught an otter, I took him on my back, and arrived at home some time after them. Here I found all our lodges converted into one large one. The women and children together with the men who had arrived long before me, were shivering with cold by a fire in the open air. When I inquired the meaning of all this, they told me that Ais-kaw-ba-wis was preparing for some important communication to be given through him from the Great Spirit. He had been a long time in preparing the lodge, during which every one was excluded, and he had arranged that at a certain signal Ba-po-wash, who was to lead the dance, should enter, and the others were to follow him, and after having danced four times around the lodge, to sit down, each in his place. Hearing this, I immediately entered the long lodge, and throwing down my otter, seated myself by the fire. Ais-kaw-ba-wis gave me one angry and malicious look, then closed his eyes, and affected to go on with a prayer that I had interrupted. After some time, he began to drum and sing aloud, and at the third interval of silence, which was the signal agreed upon with Ba-po-wash, the latter came dancing in, followed by men, women, and children, and after circling the lodge four times, they all sat down in their places. For a few moments all was silence, while Ais-kaw-ba-wis continued sitting with his eyes closed, in the middle of the lodge, by a spot of smooth and soft ground which he had prepared, like that used by the war chiefs in their Ko-zau-bun-zitch-e-kun. Then he began to call the men, one by one, to come and sit down by him. Last of all, he called me, and I went and sat down as he directed. Then addressing himself to me, he said, "Shaw-shaw-wa ne-ba-se, my son, it is probable you will now be frightened, as I have very unpleasant information to give you. The Great Spirit has, as you, my friends, all know, in former times favoured me with the free communication of his mind and will. Lately he has been pleased to show me what is to happen to each of us in future. For you, my friends, (to Sha-gwaw-go-nuck and the other Indians,) who have been careful to regard and obey the injunctions of the Great Spirit, as communicated by me, to each of you he has given to live to the full age of man; this long and straight line is the image of your several lives. For you, Shaw-shaw-wa ne-ba-se, who have turned aside from the right path, and despised the admonitions you have received, this short and crooked line represents your life. You are to attain only to half of the full age of man. This line, turning off on the other side, is that which shows what is determined in relation to the young wife of Ba-po-wash." As he said this, he showed us the marks he had made on the ground, as below. The long, straight line, A, representing, as he said, the life of the Indians, Sha-gwaw-koo-sink, Wau-zhe-gaw-maish-koon, etc. The short crooked one, B, showing the irregular course and short continuance of mine, and the abruptly

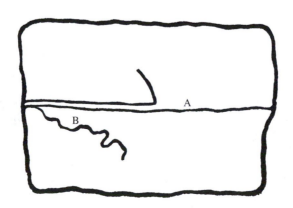

terminating one on the other side, showing the life of the favourite wife of Ba-po-wash. It happened that Ba-po-wash had dried the choice parts of a fat bear, intending in the spring to make a feast to his medicine, and a few days previous to this time, while we were absent at our hunting camp, Ais-kaw-ba-wis had said to the old woman, the mother of Ba-po-wash's wife, "The Great Spirit has signified to me that all things are not as they should be. Send out and see, therefore, if the fat bear which your son has hung up for a feast to his medicine is all where it was left." She went out accordingly, and found that the feet of the bear were gone, Ais-kaw-ba-wis himself, who was a great glutton, having stolen them. This was now made known to Ba-po-wash, who was much alarmed at the threatened evil, and to avert it he not only gave Ais-kaw-ba-wis the remainder of the bear, but a large quantity of marrow he had saved for his feast, and other valuable presents.

After this, we started to come to an island called Me-nau-zhe-taw-naun, in the Lake of the Woods, where we had concluded to plant corn, instead of our old fields at Dead River. On our way we stopped at a place to make sugar, then we went to visit the traders, leaving Ais-kaw-ba-wis with our women. It happened that the wife of Gish-kau-ko had left her kettle at the sugar camp, some distance from the place where they were to wait for our return. Some time after the men had gone, Ais-kaw-ba-wis, who lived by himself in a little lodge, pretending to be too holy to go into a common house, or to mingle with men in their ordinary pursuits, sent for the wife of Gish-kau-ko, and when she came to him, he said, "The Great Spirit is not pleased that you should abandon and lose your property. Go, therefore, and get the kettle that you have left at the sugar camp." The woman obeyed, and he, soon after she had left the camp, took his gun, and under the pretence of going to hunt, went out in a different direction. But he had no sooner got out of sight of the lodges than he turned, and by circuitous route came upon the track of the wife of Gish-kau-ko. She, who had been before annoyed by his particular attentions, and surmised the real object he had in view in sending her for the kettle, kept a look out behind her, and when she saw him come running after her, she began to run also. Just at this time I was returning from the trading-house with the other Indians, when we descried this chase at a distance. It occasioned us much alarm when we saw first a woman, then a man, running with so much apparent earnestness. We thought nothing less than that the Sioux had come to the country, and were murdering our women and children. But when we came a little nearer, the pretended prophet gave over his pursuit of the woman, and came and sat down with us, to drink of the rum which the Indians had brought from the trading-house, and which they gave him very liberally. The woman was, however, after her arrival at home, compelled to give some account of the race, and she acknowledged that Ais-kaw-ba-wis had often sought similar opportunities to be alone with her, though such was her fear of him that she never dared make any disclosure, or offer any other resistance than an attempt to escape by flight. This discovery occasioned no disturbance, and seemed in no degree to diminish the influence of Ais-kaw-ba-wis. A large proportion of the rum we had brought from the trading-house was set apart for him, but when the principal man among us sent for him to come and receive it, he returned for answer, that he could not come. "Tell the chief," said he, "that if he has any business with me, he can come to my lodge." The liquor was accordingly carried to him, but its effect seemed to render his disposition somewhat more social and condescending, for about the middle of the night he came staggering into the lodge where I was without the least covering on any part of his body. To me his appearance was ludicrous in the extreme, and I did not refrain from a good deal of irreverent merriment on the occasion.

After this we came to the Lake of the Woods, where I hunted for about a month, then went back into the country I had left, all the Indians remaining behind to clear the ground where they intended planting corn at Me–nau–zhe–tau–naung. I now began to experience the inconveniences resulting from having incurred the ill will of Ais–kaw–ba–wis. He it was who prejudiced the Indians so much against me, and particularly the relatives of my wife, that my situation at Me–nau–zhe–tau–naung was uncomfortable, and I was compelled to return to Red River.

It was about this time that the Scots people, to the number of one hundred or more, arrived to settle at Red River, under the protection of the Hudson's Bay Company, and among these I saw, for the first time in many years, since I had become a man, a white woman. Soon after my arrival, I was taken into the employment of the Hudson's Bay Company, and Mr. Hanie, the agent, sent me, accompanied by Mr. Hess, an interpreter, and some men, to kill buffalo. The buffalo were at that time, at a great distance, and the Scots people in great distress for want of provisions. I happened to find and kill two bulls near home, and after sending back the meat, I went on to the herds.

I had hunted here a few days, when our number was increased to four clerks and about twenty men, the latter employed in bringing in the meat I killed to my lodge, whence it was carried in carts to the settlement. All of these lived in my lodge, but one of the clerks named M'Donald was very abusive to my wife and children. Mr. Hess repeatedly checked him for this conduct, but as he continued it, he complained to Mr. Hanie, who sent M'Donald to a place several miles distant where the Indians had killed about twenty buffaloes, which it was not convenient, at present, to bring out, and there he remained by himself for two months, having no other occupation or amusement than to scare the wolves away from the meat. Mr. M'Kenzie was one of the three remaining clerks who lived in my lodge, and he was so different from M'Donald, that at the end of four months, when the greater part of the people were called in to the settlement, he solicited and obtained from Mr. Hanie permission to remain longer with me, to improve himself in the Ojibbeway language, and he did not leave me until after the sugar season.

I killed, in the four months that I hunted for the Hudson's Bay Company, about one hundred buffaloes, but as part, or all of many of these were eaten in my own lodge, I delivered only forty entire and fat ones to the company's people, for which Mr. Hanie paid me, in the spring, three hundred and ten dollars. Those Scots labourers who were with me, were much more rough and brutal in their manners than any people I had before seen. Even when they had plenty, they ate like starved dogs, and never failed to quarrel over their meat. The clerks frequently beat and punished them, but they would still quarrel.

Mr. Hanie, and the governor for the Hudson's Bay Company, proposed to me to build me a house, and engage me permanently in their employment, but I delayed accepting their offer, as I thought it doubtful whether their attempt at settling the country would finally succeed. Some of the Indians whom I had left at the Lake of the Woods had followed me out, spent the winter with me, and returned long ago. I was still by myself at Red River, when Wa–ge–tote came from Me–nau–zhe–tau–naung with a message from my father and mother-in-law. They had lost several of their children by death, and feeling lonely, they sent for me to come to them. This message Wa–ge–tote delivered to me in the presence of the traders, and some other persons, but afterwards he called me out by myself, and said to me, "Do not believe that your father-in-law calls you to Me–nau–zhe–tau–naung, to be at peace, or with any kind intention. When the children were sick, they called Ais–kaw–ba–wis to do something for them, and he having made a chees–suk–kon, said he had called you into his enclosure, and made you confess that you had shot bad medicine at the children, though you were at that time at Red River. He made your father-in-law believe that you had the power of life and death over his children, and he continues to believe, as do most of the Indians of the band, that it was your medicine which killed them. Be assured, therefore, that they call you thither with the design of killing you." Notwithstanding this admonition, I started immediately, as I knew if I did not they would be but the more confirmed in their unfounded opinion of my culpability.

I had bought a shirt from some of the Scots people at Red River, which I put on as I was about to start on this journey. Probably it was from this I contracted a disease of the skin, which became so troublesome and violent that I was compelled to stop at the Be-gwi-o-nus-ko River. Here I remained for a month, being for a long time unable to move. When I first stopped I set up my lodge on the brink of the river, and after I was unable to walk, I subsisted myself and family by lying in my canoe and fishing. After being placed in my canoe, sometimes I lay there for three or four days without being moved, covering myself with a mat at night. My wife was not so severely affected, being, though very sick, still able to walk. When I began to get a little better, I tried all sorts of medicines I could procure, but none seemed to do me so much good as gun powder, moistened a little, and rubbed upon the sores, which were very large. This disorder, caught originally from the Scotch people, spread among the Indians and killed numbers of them.

After I had recovered, I went up the Be-wi-o-nus-ko, to the small lake of the same name, where I stopped to hunt, and killed plenty of meat. While I remained here, there came one day to my lodge, four young men from our village at Me-nau-zhe-tau-naung. In one of them, who was painted black, I recognized my brother-in-law. The three other children being dead, grief, and a feeling of loneliness, influenced him to leave his father, and start in search of some war party, that he might accompany them against their enemies, and thus have an opportunity of sacrificing, honourably, a life that had become irksome to him. The three young men his companions, being unwilling to see him depart alone, had voluntarily accompanied him. I gave him my horse, and then went up to the Lake of the Woods to my father-in-law, where I remained a few days. As it was then the time when the wild geese, having cast their quills, are unable to fly, we caught great numbers of them.

After four days, I said to the old people, "I cannot remain here, while my little brother has gone crying about, with none to protect him. I know there is danger in the path he will walk, and I ought to follow to show him where it lies. He wishes to join a war party, that he may walk in a dangerous road, but there is often danger where we least expect it." I knew that Wa-me-gon-a-biew would fall upon this boy, and insult or perhaps kill him on account of his remote relationship to the man who wounded Taw-ga-we-ninne, at Mackinac, or at least with this pretence. Sha-gwaw-koo-sink, hearing my determination, and the reasons I gave for it, said he would accompany me. We started together, and on our arrival at Red River, we heard that Wa-me-gon-a-biew had taken from the boy the horse I gave him, and had already threatened to kill him. I went immediately to Wa-me-gon-a-biew, and a quarrel would probably have taken place at once on account of the young man, had not old Net-no-kwa come between and separated us, as we were about to come to blows. We were all now about to join the Crees and Assinneboins to go against the Sioux, and I cautioned my young brother-in-law to be, on this journey, always watchful of the movements of Wa-me-gon-a-biew. We were about forty men in number when we started from Red River. As we passed along through the Cree and Assinneboin encampments and villages on our route, our party was augmented to the number of two hundred men long before we arrived at Turtle Mountain. While we were encamped near one of the Cree villages, Wa-ge-tote and the principal chiefs being called away to a feast, Wa-me-gon-a-biew began to talk of my brother-in-law, and as I did not like to hear him, I went out and walked about at a distance from the camp. When I thought the chiefs had returned from the feast, I re-entered the camp, but from the expression of concern and interest visible in the faces of those about me, I immediately comprehended that something had happened. I went to search for the young man on whose account particularly I felt anxious, and finding him safe, was returning to my own place, when I discovered in the hands of an old man, who was trying to replace them in their original shape, the splinters and fragments of my new gun. I was at no loss to comprehend the nature of the accident which had deprived me of the use of my gun at a time when it was likely to prove so important to me, and in the first moment of irritation, I seized the barrel, and was walking towards Wa-me-gon-a-biew to beat him with it, when I met Wa-ge-tote, who interfered to prevent me from striking him, though Wa-ge-tote himself, as well as the other chiefs, expressed the greatest dissatisfaction at what he had done.

But notwithstanding the loss of my gun, I did not turn back. Arming myself with my gun barrel in place of war club and spear, I went on. In two days from this camp, we arrived at the head of Turtle Mountain, being now about four hundred men. This was the place agreed upon for the assembling of all who should join in the party, and we had supposed that those we should meet here would be few in number in comparison with ourselves. We were therefore somewhat surprised when we found already on the ground, one thousand Assinneboins, Crees, and Ojibbeways.

We stopped at a little distance, and some communication took place between the chiefs, respecting the ceremony of salutation to be used. It is customary for war parties engaged in the same cause, or friendly to each other, when they meet, to exchange a few shots by way of a sham battle, in which they use all the jumping, the whooping, and yelling of a real fight. But on this occasion both bands were so large, and one so much larger than the other, that the chiefs thought it more prudent to use a different method of exchanging compliments in meeting. It was agreed, on the part of Match-a-to-ge-wub,[2] the principal chief, that his young men should all remain in their lodges, and that twenty warriors of our band should salute their encampment by practising the manoeuvres of attacking a village. A large lodge was set up for them to cut in pieces by their firing. I was one of the twenty selected for this performance, having supplied myself with a gun which I procured from a man who turned back. It was not without the utmost exertion of all my strength that I kept even pace with my companions, in running, leaping, loading, and yelling, and though we rested four times, when we arrived at the chief's lodge, and had blown it to fragments, I was entirely exhausted with fatigue. A man of our own party, imprudently, and without any authority, exposed himself in the village while this salute was in progress, but his clothes were blown and scorched off his back, his lodge shot down, and himself much hurt. But as the exposure had been altogether voluntary on his part, and the notice taken of him rather honourable than otherwise, he had no cause of complaint.

On the first night after we came together, three men of the Ojibbeways were killed. On the next, two horses belonging to the Assinneboins, and on the third, three more. When such numbers of men assemble from different and remote parts of the country, some must be brought into contact between whom old grudges and enmities exist, and it is not surprising that the unstable power and influence of the chiefs

---

2. *Match-a-to-ge-wub,* (in the Cree, *Mait-cha-to-ke-wab,*) in the Ojibbeway, means nearly "Many Eagles sitting."

should be insufficient to prevent disturbances and bloodshed. On this occasion, men were assembled from a vast extent of country, of dissimilar feelings and dialects, and of the whole fourteen hundred, not one who would acknowledge any authority superior to his own will. It is true that ordinarily they yield a certain deference, and a degree of obedience to the chief each may have undertaken to follow, but this obedience, in most instances, continues no longer than the will of the chief corresponds entirely with the inclination of those he leads. In this party were some who had been a year on their journey to reach this place. Two hundred lodges had their women with them.

Soon after we joined the main body at Turtle Mountain, a Cree of Prairie Fort, adopted me into his family, taking my baggage, and inviting me into his lodge. He called me constantly Ne-je,[3] (my friend,) and treated me with great kindness. Many other men who were without lodges, were in like manner taken into the families of those that had.

But a few days had passed, when the little boys commenced, in the first instance a very small number, by kicking at each other in playfulness merely, but it happened that on one side were Assinneboin children only, and on the other Crees and Ojibbeways. By degrees larger and larger boys, and at last men joined in on either side, and what had commenced in play, was like to terminate in a serious and bloody brawl. Match-a-to-ge-wub ran between the combatants, exerted his voice and his hands; afterwards Wa-ge-tote and all the other principal chiefs, but the young men paid little or no regard to them. The excitement which had kindled among them was maddening to rage, and the chiefs were running about in the utmost distress and fear, when an old man, whose head was white as snow, and who was so bent down with age that he walked on two sticks, and looking more like a dog than a man, came out, and though his voice was too feeble to be heard at any distance, he no sooner appeared, than all the Assinneboins desisted entirely from their violence, and the quarrel ended. Of those that were wounded and injured in this affair, only two died immediately, but many were so much injured that they were sent back to their own country. Had not the greater number entered into the affray without their arms, more extensive mischief would have resulted. Though I inquired much, I could neither learn the name, or hear any thing satisfactory of the history of the old man, by whose interference this affair was brought so timely to an end. Vague, and probably very extravagant reports, circulated among us respecting him.

CHAPTER XIII

Suffering of the Ojibbeways from hunger—persecutions of Waw-be-be-nai-sa, and unkindness of my Indian relatives—journey to Detroit—Governor Cass—Council at St. Mary, on the Miami.

All the men who were still able to walk now determined to start after buffalo, which we knew could not then be very near us. For my own part, I chose to remain, as did

---

3. *Ne-je,* my friend, used to males; and *nin-dong-gwa,* used by females to one another.

one good hunter besides, who knew that the prospect of getting buffaloes was not good. We remained behind, and in a short time killed five moose, all the flesh of which being immediately distributed among the suffering women and children, afforded some relief, and checked the progress of death which was making extensive havoc among us. The men returned one after another, more worn out and reduced than when they had left us. Only a single buffalo had been killed. As the most incessant, and the most laborious exertions alone could save us from perishing, I went immediately out to hunt again, and having started a bear, I pursued him for three days without being able to come up with him. At the end of this time I found myself so exhausted, that I knew I could never overtake the bear, and I should not have reached home, had not some Indians, little less miserable and hungry than myself, happened to meet with me. I had stopped at night, and being unable to make a camp, or kindle a fire, I was endeavouring to reconcile myself to the immediate approach of death which I thought inevitable, when these people unexpectedly found me, and helped me to return to camp. This is but a fair specimen of the life which many of the Ojibbeways of the north lead during the winter. Their barren and inhospitable country affords them so scantily the means of subsistence, that it is only with the utmost exertion and activity that life can be sustained, and it not unfrequently happens that the strongest men, and the best hunters, perish of absolute hunger.

Now the Indians again determined to move all together, towards the buffaloes, and endeavour to reach them with their families. Only Oon-di-no, the man who had remained with me before, wished to stay, that his women might dry the skin of the last moose he had killed, so that they might carry it with them to be eaten in case of the failure of all other supplies. I concluded to remain with him, but in the middle of the first night after the Indians left, the distress of my children became so great that I could no longer remain in my lodge. I got up and started, and told him that if I could kill or procure any game, I would return to his relief. I pursued, rapidly as my strength would permit, the path of the Indians, and about morning came up with their camp. I had no sooner arrived then I heard the sounds of a feast and going up to the lodge, I heard the voice of an old man, thanking the Great Spirit for the supply that had been bestowed in the time of their necessity. He did not mention the animal by name that had been killed, only calling it Manito-wais-se, which means nearly "Spirit beast." From this I could not ascertain what had been killed, but from another source, I learned it was an old and poor buffalo. From this I inferred that herds must be near, and two young men being willing to join me, we went immediately in the direction in which we believed the herd would be found, and after having walked about three hours, ascended a little hill, and saw before us the ground black with buffaloes. We crawled up, and I killed immediately two fat cows. As I was cutting these up, I began to hear the guns of the men of our party, they having followed me on, and being now arrived among the buffaloes. It was somewhat late when I was ready to go to our camp, most of the men were in before me. I had expected to have heard the sounds of feasting and rejoicing, but when I entered the camp, not a voice was to be heard. No women and children were running about, all was silent and sad. Can it be, thought I, that this relief has come too late, and that our women and children are all dead. I looked into one lodge after another. In all, the people were alive, but none had any thing to eat. The men having most of them come from a forest country, and having never hunted buffalo before, all failed to kill except myself. The supply I had brought, I having loaded the two young men that were with me, somewhat allayed the hunger that was prevailing.

There was at this time with us a man called Waw-bebe-nai-sa, (White Bird,) with whom I had formerly been somewhat acquainted, and whose jealousy and ill will against me, seemed to be excited and irritated by my success in hunting. It was on account of this man, and because I wished to avoid all ostentation, that I now forbore to make a feast in my own lodge, as would have been proper for me to have done on this occasion. Nevertheless, one of the young men who had been with me made a feast, and I, after reserving sufficient food to allay the pressing hunger of my own children, sent the remainder to the families about me. The young man who made the feast, called, among others, Waw-bebe-nais-sa, the man I have mentioned. In the course of the evening, he said, as I understood, much to prejudice me in the opinion of the Indians, accusing me of pride, insolence, and of having in various ways done mischief among them. But I remained in my own lodge, and at present took no notice of this, farther than to contradict his unfair statements.

Next morning, long before the dawn, the women started for the remains of the two buffalo I had killed, and several of the men, most of them having obtained from me some instruction about the part to be aimed at, again went in pursuit of the herds, and this day several of them killed. We soon had plenty of meat, and all that were sick and near death recovered, except one woman, who having gone mad with hunger, remained in a state of derangement for more than a month.

The principal man of this band was called O-poih-gun,[1] (the pipe.) He, with three lodges, remained with me, the others scattered here and there in pursuit of the buffalo. One of the men who remained back with me, was Waw-bebe-nais-sa, and another his son-in-law. I killed great numbers of fat buffalo, and the choice parts of forty of them I had dried. We had suffered so much from hunger that I wished to secure my family against a return of it. I also still had it in contemplation to make my way to the States when I knew it would be necessary for me to leave them for some time without any one to hunt for them. I made twenty large sacks of pemmican. Ten kegs of ten gallons each, which I procured from the Indians, I filled with tallow, and preserved, besides, a considerable number of tongues, etc.

It was not immediately that I discovered Waw-bebe-nais-sa's design in remaining near my camp, which was solely to annoy and molest me. I had such large quantities of meat to carry when we came finally to move, that I was compelled to return with my dogs four times, to carry forward to my camping place, one load after another. One day he contrived to meet me alone at the place where I deposited my loads, and I had no sooner stopped, than he thrust both his hands into my long hair, which then hung down on both sides of my head. "This," said he, "is the head of your road, look down and see the place where the wolves and the carrion birds shall pick your bones." I asked him why he offered me this violence. "You are a stranger," said he, "and have no right among us, but you set yourself up for the best hunter, and would make us treat you as a great man. For my own part, I have long been weary of your insolence, and I am determined you shall not live another day." Finding that remonstrance was likely to have no effect upon him, but that he was proceeding to beat my head against a poplar tree that stood there, by a sudden exertion of strength, I threw him upon the ground, and disengaged my head at the expense of part of my hair. But in the struggle, he caught three of the fingers of my right hand between his teeth. Having sunk his strong teeth quite to the bones of my fingers, I could not draw them out of his

---

1. O-poih-gun—pipe; O-poih-gun-nun—pipes.

mouth, but with my left hand aimed a blow at one of his eyes. His jaws flew open, and he leapt instantly to his feet. My tomahawk was lying near me, and his eye happening to fall upon it, he caught it in his hand, and aimed so hearty a blow at my head, that as I eluded it, his own violence brought him to the ground. I jumped upon him, wrenched the tomahawk from his hand, and threw it as far as I could, while I continued to hold him fast to the ground. I was much enraged at his unprovoked and violent attack upon me; nevertheless I would not kill him, but seeing there a piece of a stout lodge pole, I caught it in my hands, and told him to get up. When he did so, I commenced beating him, and as he fled immediately, I followed, and continued to beat him while he ran two or three hundred yards.

When I returned to my load, his son-in-law and two other young men belonging to him, having heard his cries, had come up. One of them said angrily to me, "What is this you have done?" and immediately the three rushed upon me, and I being already overcome with fatigue, they threw me upon the ground. At this time Waw-bebe-nais-sa had returned, and he caught me by a black silk handkerchief that I wore about my neck, strangled, kicked, and beat me, and thrust me down in the snow. I remember hearing one of them say, "he is dead," and as I knew I could not hope while I was down, to make resistance against four, I endeavoured to encourage this opinion. When they took their hands off me, and stood at a little distance, I sprang upon my feet, and seized a lodge pole, probably very contrary to their expectations. Whether through surprise or fear I know not, they all fled, and seeing this, I pursued Waw-bebe-nais-sa, and gave him another severe beating with my pole. For this time they left me, and I returned once more to hang up the meat I had brought. But Waw-bebe-nais-sa and his people returned to the lodges, where my dogs, which my wife had taken back, were lying, much fatigued, before the door. He drew his knife, and stabbed one of them. My wife hearing the noise, ran out, but he threatened to kill her also.

Next day, as Waw-bebe-nais-sa was much bruised and sore, and his face in particular very badly swollen, I thought probable he would remain in his lodge, and apprehending danger to my wife if she should be left alone in the lodge, I sent her to carry forward meat, and remained myself at home. But I was much fatigued, and being alone in my lodge, about the middle of the day I fell asleep. Suspecting, or perhaps knowing this, Waw-bebe-nais-sa crept slyly in with his knife in his hand, and was almost near enough to strike me, when I awoke and sprang up. As I was not unarmed, he started back and fled, but I did not pursue him. He still continued to threaten and molest me. Whenever he met me in the path, he would not turn aside, though he was unloaded, and I might have a heavy burthen on my back. His eye was for many days so swollen that he could not see out of it, and his whole appearance very ludicrous, he being at best but an awkward and homely man. Once, after an unsuccessful attempt to stab me, he went home, and in the impatience of his baffled rage, made the squaw's gesture of contempt towards my lodge,[2] which exposed him to the ridicule even of his own friends among the Indians.

His persecutions were, however, troublesome to me, and I endeavoured to avoid him. One day I had preceded the party, and as we were travelling in a beaten path which I knew they would follow, I turned a little out of it to place my camp where I should not necessarily be in the way of seeing him. But when he came to the fork of

---

2. *Nin-us-kun-je-ga kwi-uk we-ke-wah-mik.* See note at the end of the volume on the Menominio word *Ke-kish-kosh-kaw-pe-nin.*

my road, with his little son twelve years old, I heard him say to the lad, "stop here while I go and kill this white man." He then threw down his load, and though his son entreated him not to do any thing, he came up within about fifty yards of me, drew his gun from its case, cocked it, and pointed it at me. Having held it in this position some time, and seeing he did not excite my fears, he began to approach me, jumping from side to side, and yelling in the manner of warriors when they approach each other in battle. He continued pointing his gun at me, and threatening me so loudly that I was at last irritated, and caught up my own gun. The little boy ran up, and throwing his arms about me, entreated me to spare his father, though he was a fool. I then threw down my gun, seized the old man, and took his from him. I reproached him for his obstinate perseverance in such foolish practices. "I have," said I, "put myself so often in your power, that you ought by this time to know you have not courage to kill me. You are not a man. You have not the heart even of a squaw, nor the courage of a dog. Now for the first time I speak to you. I wish you to know that I am tired of your foolishness, and that if you trouble me any more hereafter, it will be at the hazard of your own life."

He then left me, and with all the others, except my own family, went on in advance. Next day I followed, drawing a loaded sled myself, and driving my dogs with their loads before me. As we approached a thicket of bushes, I cautioned my daughter Martha, that Waw-bebe-nais-sa might probably be lying in ambush somewhere among them. Presently I saw her leap several feet from the ground, then she came running towards me, with her hands raised, and crying, "*My father! My father!*" I seized my gun and sprang forward, examined every place for concealment, passed the lodge poles, and the almost extinguished fires of their last encampment, and returned without having discovered any thing. When I inquired of my daughter what had occasioned her alarm, she said she had "smelt fire." So great was the terror and apprehension with which her mind was agitated on account of the annoyances Waw-bebe-nais-sa had given us.

I was so glad to be released from the persecutions of this troublesome man that I now resolved to stop at Rush Lake and remain there by myself, as I thought it was the intention of Waw-bebe-nais-sa and the other Indians to proceed immediately to the Lake of the Woods. So I selected a place where I intended to establish my camp for the remainder of the winter. Here I left my children to take care of the lodge, and my wife and myself returned to bring up loads of meat. On coming home at night, the children told us their grandmother had in our absence been to see them, and had left word that her daughter must come on the following day to see her, and that there were, in that place, three or four lodges of our friends encamped together. I readily gave my consent to this arrangement, and as my mother-in-law had left a message particularly for me, I consented to accompany her, saying that we could bring up the remainder of the meat after we should return. But that night I dreamed, and the same young man whom I had repeatedly seen in the preparations for my medicine hunts came down as usual through the hole in the top of my lodge, and stood directly before me. "You must not go," said he, "to the place you propose to visit to-morrow. But if you persist, and will disregard my admonition, you shall see what will happen to you there. Look there," said he, pointing in the opposite direction, and I saw She-gwaw-koo-sink, Me-zhuk-ko-naun, and others of my friends coming. Then pointing upwards, he told me to look, and I saw a small hawk with a banded tail, flying about over my head. He said no more, but turned and went out at the door of my lodge. I awoke much troubled in my mind, and could sleep no more. In the morning, I told my wife I could not go with her. "What is the reason," said she, "you cannot accompany me as you promised yesterday?" I told her my dream, but she accused me of fear, and as she continued her solicitations, I finally consented to go.

In the morning, I told my children that their uncle and other Indians would come to the lodge that day. That they must tell them, if I returned at all, it would be by noon. If I did not come then, they might conclude I was dead. I then started with my wife, but I had not gone two hundred yards when I looked up and saw the same small hawk that had appeared to me in my dream. I knew that this was sent to forewarn me of evil, and again I told my wife I could not go. But though I turned back to go towards my own lodge, she again reproached me with fear, and pretended to ridicule my apprehensions. I knew, also, the strong prejudice that existed against me in the family of my mother-in-law, and the tendency of my refusing, in this case, to visit her, would be to confirm and make them stronger. I therefore, though contrary to my better judgment, consented to go on.

When I arrived at the lodge of my mother-in-law, I left my gun at the door, went in, and took a seat between two of the sisters of my wife who were the wives of one man. They had young children, and I was playing with two of these, with my head down, when I heard a loud and sudden noise, and immediately lost my senses. I saw no one, and I remembered nothing till I began to revive. Then I found several women holding my hands and arms, and I saw the expression of terror and alarm in the faces of all about me. I could not comprehend my situation, and knew nothing of what had happened, until I heard on the outside of the lodge, a loud and insulting voice, which I knew to be that of Waw-bebe-nais-sa. I now began to feel something like warm water on my face, and putting my hand to my head, I laid my fingers on my naked skull. I at length broke away from the women who held me, and pursued after Waw-bebe-nais-sa, but I could not overtake him as the Indians assisted him in keeping out of my way. Towards night I returned to my lodge, though very severely wounded, and, as I believed, with the bones of my skull broken. A very little blood had run down upon my face when I was first wounded, but for a considerable time afterwards none flowed, and though I heard strange noises in my head, I did not faint or fall down until I reached my own lodge. My gun Waw-bebe-nais-sa had taken from the door of the lodge of my mother-in-law, and I had to return without it.

At my lodge, I found She-gwaw-koo-sink, Me-zhuk-ko-naun, and Nah-gaun-esh-kaw-waw, a son-in-law of Wa-ge-tote, more commonly called Oto-pun-ne-be. The moment I took She-gwaw-koo-sink by the hand, the blood spouted in a stream from my head. "What is the matter, my son?" said he. "I have been at play with another man, and the water of the Be-gwi-o-mus-ko having made us drunk, we have played rather roughly." I wished to treat the matter lightly, but as I immediately fainted away, they saw the extent of the wound I had received. Oto-pun-ne-be had formerly been an acquaintance of mine, and had always shown a friendly disposition towards me. He now seemed much affected at my misfortune, and of his own accord undertook to punish Waw-bebe-nais-sa for his unjust violence. This man, to whom I was often under obligation for the kindnesses he bestowed upon me, has since experienced the fate which overtakes so many of all characters and descriptions of people among the Ojibbeways of that country: he has perished of hunger.

When I had entered the lodge of my mother-in-law, I had omitted to pull off the hood of my thick moose-skin capote, and it was this which prevented me from noticing the entrance of Waw-bebe-nais-sa into the lodge, or seeing, or hearing his approach towards me. It is probable also, that had not my head been thus covered, the blow, had it been made, would have proved instantly fatal to me, as the force of it must have been somewhat broken by this thick covering of leather. But as it was, the skull was fractured, and there is still a large ridge upon that part of it where the edge of the tomahawk fell. It was very long before I recovered from this wound, though the immediate confinement which followed it did not last so long as I had feared it must.

Waw-bebe-nais-sa fled immediately to our village at Me-naw-zhe-tau-naung, and the remainder of the people, having never hunted in the prairie before now became panic struck at the idea that the Sioux would fall upon their trail and pursue them. I was too weak to travel, and moreover I knew well we were in no danger from the Sioux, but my mother-in-law found much fault because I was not willing to start with the Indians. I knew that my mother-in-law, and I had reason to suppose that my wife, had been willing to aid Waw-bebe-nais-sa in his attempt on my life, and I therefore told them both to leave me if they wished. They went accordingly, and took all my children with them. The only person who did not desert me at this time was Oto-pun-ne-be, as he was called from his bear totem, with his cousin, a lad of fourteen years old. These two remained and performed for me those offices of attention and kindness which my situation required, while those who should have been my friends abandoned me to my fate. After the fourth day, I became much worse, and was unable to sit up, and almost to move, until the tenth day, when I began to recover.

After I had gained a little strength, we left the lodges as they had been abandoned by the Indians in their fright, all standing, some of them filled with meat, and other valuable property, and started together for the village. Our trader lived at some distance from the village, and when we arrived at the place where the roads forked, I agreed with Oto-pun-ne-be that I would meet him at an appointed place, on the day which he named, as that on which he would return from the village. I went accordingly to the trader's, and he to the Indian's camp. We met again at the time and place agreed on, when he related to me, that he went to the village, entered the lodge of one of the principal chiefs, and sat down. He had not been long there, when Waw-bebe-nais-sa came in and sat down opposite him. After regarding each other for some time, Waw-bebe-nais-sa said to him, "You, Oto-pun-ne-be, have never been in our village before, and I am not ignorant of the occasion which has brought you so far to see us. You have no brothers of your own, the Long Knives having killed all of them, and you are now so foolish as to call the man whom I beat the other day your brother." "It is not true," said Oto-pun-ne-be, "that the Long Knives have killed any brother of mine. But if they had, I would not suffer you to fall upon my friend, who is as one of us, and abuse and injure him, as you have done, without cause or provocation. It is true, I call him my brother, and I will avenge his cause as if he were such, but I will not spill blood in the lodge of this chief, who has received me as a friend." So saying, he took Waw-bebe-nais-sa by the hand, dragged him out of the lodge, and was about to plunge the knife to his heart, when the chief, who was a strong man, caught his hand, took away the knife, and broke it. In the scuffle which ensued, three or four men were at once upon Oto-pun-ne-be, but he being a powerful man, and not forgetting the object of his journey, kept fast his grip upon Waw-bebe-nais-sa, and did not quit him until two of his ribs were broken, and he was otherwise severely injured. Oto-pun-ne-be was a quiet man, even when drunk, and if he ever entered into a quarrel, it was more commonly, as in this case, in the cause of his friend, rather than his own.

I was content with the punishment that had been thus bestowed upon Waw-bebe-nais-sa, as I thought two broken ribs about equal to the broken head he had given me. We feasted together on game I had killed, so rapid had been my recovery, and then returned to the deserted camp where we found the lodges all standing as we had left them. After about ten days more, the people began to come back to look after their property. Oto-pun-ne-be took my canoe and returned to Red River, where he lived.

All our people returned, and removed their lodges and their property to Me-naw-zhe-tau-naung. I had now a great store of meat, sufficient as I knew, to supply the wants of my family for a year or more. After making the best disposition I could of all my affairs, I took a small canoe, and started by myself with the intention of coming to Mackinac, intending to go thence to the states, and endeavour to find some of my relatives, if any remained.

At Rainy Lake, I fell in with Mr. Giasson and others in the employ of the Hudson's Bay Company, who told me it would not be safe for me to suffer myself to be seen by any of the North West Company's people, as they were all much enraged against me on account of the course I had taken. Nevertheless, I knew well that the Hudson's Bay people, having no occasion to go to the lower end of Lake Superior, could not conveniently aid me themselves, and that if I attempted to go alone, I must unavoidably fall in with some of the North West. I went, therefore, directly to the trading-house at Rainy Lake, where I found my old trader, Mr. Tace. He was standing on the bank when I came up with my little canoe. He told me to come into the house, and I followed him in accordingly. He then asked me, rather sternly, what I had come to him for. "Why do you not go," said he, "to your own people of the Hudson's Bay Company?" I told him I was now wishing to go to the states. "It would have been well," he replied, "had you gone long ago." I waited there twenty days, receiving all the time the kindest treatment from Mr. Tace. He then brought me in his own canoe to Fort William, whence Dr. M'Laughlin sent me in one of his boats to the Saut De St. Marie, and thence Mr. Ermatinger brought me to Mackinac. All the people of the North West Company, whom I saw on this journey, treated me kindly, and no one mentioned a word of my connection with the Hudson's Bay.

Major Puthuff, the United States Indian Agent at Mackinac gave me a birch bark canoe, some provisions, and a letter to Gov. Cass at Detroit. My canoe was lashed to the side of the schooner, on board which I sailed for Detroit under the care of a gentleman whose name I do not recollect, but who, as I thought, was sent by Major Puthuff expressly to take care of me on the way. In five days we arrived, and the gentleman telling me to wait until he could go on shore and return, he left me, and I heard no more of him. Next day I went on shore by myself, and walking up into the street I stood for some time gazing around me. At length, I saw an Indian, and going up to him, asked who he was, and where he belonged. He answered me, "An Ot-tawwaw, of Saw-ge-nong." "Do you know Gish-kaw-ko?" said I. "He is my father." "And where," said I, "is Manito-o-geezhik, his father, and your grand-father?" "He died last fall." I told him to go and call his father to come and see me. He called him, but the old man would not come.

Next day, as I was again standing in the street, and looking one way and the other, I saw an old Indian, and ran after him. When he heard me coming, he turned about, and after looking anxiously at me for a few moments, caught me in his arms. It was Gish-kaw-ko, but he looked very unlike the young man who had taken me prisoner so many years before. He asked me, in a hurried manner, many questions, inquired what had happened to me, and where I had been since I left him, and many such questions. I tried to induce him to take me to the house of Gov. Cass, but he appeared afraid to go. Finding I could not prevail upon him, I took Major Puthuff's letter in my hand, and having learned from the Indians in which house the governor lived, I went toward the gate, till a soldier, who was walking up and down before it, stopped me. I could not speak English so as to be at all understood, but seeing the governor sitting in his porch, I held up the letter towards him. He then told the soldier to let me pass in. As soon as he had opened the letter, he gave me his hand, and having sent for an interpreter, he talked a long time with me. Gish-kaw-ko having been sent for, confirmed my statement respecting the circumstances of my capture, and my two years residence with the Ottawwaws of Saw-ge-nong.

The governor gave me clothing to the amount of sixty or seventy dollars value, and sent me to remain, for the present, at the house of his interpreter more than a mile distant, where he told me I must wait till he should assemble many Indians and white men, to hold a council at St. Mary's on the Miami, whence he would send me to my relatives on the Ohio.

I waited two months or more, and becoming extremely impatient to go on my way, I started with Be-nais-sa, the brother of Gish-kaw-ko, and eight other men who were going to the council. I went without the knowledge of Gov. Cass, and was therefore destitute of any supply of provisions. We suffered much from fatigue, and still more from hunger, particularly after we passed the rapids of the Miami where we left our canoe. The Indians among whom we passed oftentimes refused to give us any thing, though they had plenty. Sometimes we stopped to sleep near a white man's corn field, and though the corn was now fit to roast, and we almost perishing with hunger, we dared not take any thing. One night, we stopped near a good looking house, where was a large and fine corn field. The Indians, being very hungry, said to me, "Shaw-shaw-was ne-ba-se, you have come very far to see your relations, now go in and see whether they will give you any thing to eat." I went and stood in the door, but the people within, who were then eating, drove me away, and on my return the Indians laughed at me.

Some time after this, as we were sleeping one night in the road, some one came up on horseback, and asked us, in the Ottawwaw dialect, who we were. One of the Indians answered, "We are Ottawwaws and Ojibbeways, and have with us one Long Knife from Red River, who was taken prisoner many years ago by Gish-kaw-ko." He told us, after he understood who we were, and where we were going, that his name was Ah-koo-nah-goo-zik. "If you are brisk travellers," said he, "you may reach my house next day after to-morrow at noon, and then you will find plenty to eat. It is necessary that I should travel on all night, that I may reach home to-morrow." And thus he left us. Next day, my strength failed so much that I was only able to keep up by being released from my load. One took my gun, another my blanket, and we reached that night the forks of the Miami, where was a settlement of Indians and a trading-house, as well as several families of whites. I applied to the trader, and stated my situation, and that of the Indians with me, but we could obtain no relief, and on the next day I was totally unable to travel. We were indebted to the Indians for what relief we obtained, which was sufficient to enable us the day after to reach the hospitable dwelling of Ah-ko-nah-goo-zik.

This man had two large kettles of corn and venison ready cooked, and awaiting our arrival. One he placed before me, with some wooden dishes, and spoons; the other before Be-nais-sa. After we had eaten, he told us we had better remain with him ten or fifteen days, and refresh ourselves from our long journey, as he had plenty of corn, and fat venison was abundant about him. I told him that for my own part I had for many years been wishing to make the journey I had now so nearly accomplished, and that I was extremely impatient to see whether or not any of my own relatives were still alive, but that I should be glad to rest with him two or three days, and afterwards to borrow one of his horses to ride as far as Kau-wis-se-no-ki-ug, or St. Mary's. "I will tell you," said he. After two or three days, as we were early one morning making up our loads to start, he came to me, leading a fine horse and putting the halter in my hand, he said, "I give you this for your journey." I did not again tell him I would leave it at Kau-wis-se-no-ki-ug, as I had already told him this, and I knew that in such cases the Indians do not wish to hear much said. In two days I arrived at the place appointed for the council. As yet no Indians had assembled, but a man was stationed there to issue provisions to such as should come. I had been but a short time at this place when I was seized with fever and ague, which, though it did not confine me all the time, was yet extremely painful and distressing.

After about ten days, a young man of the Ottawwaws, whom Be-nais-sa had given me to cook for me and assist about me in my sickness, went across the creek to a camp of the Po-ta-wa-to-mies who had recently arrived and were drinking. At midnight he was brought into the lodge drunk, and one of the men who came with him, said to me, as he pushed him in, "Take care of your young man. He has been doing mischief." I immediately called Be-nais-sa to kindle a fire, when we saw, by the light of it, the young man standing with his knife in his hand, and that, together with his arm and great part of his body covered with blood. The Indians could not make him lie down, but when I told him to, he obeyed immediately and I forbade them to make any inquiries about what he had done, or take any notice of his bloody knife. In the morning, having slept soundly, he was perfectly unconscious of all that had passed. He said he believed that he had been very drunk, and as he was now hungry, he must hurry and get ready something to eat. He was astonished and confounded when I told him he had killed a man. He remembered only that in his drunkenness he had began to cry for his father, who had been killed on that spot several years before by white men. He expressed much concern, and went immediately to see the man he had stabbed, who was not yet dead. We learned from the Po-ta-wa-to-mies that he had found the young man sleeping, or lying in a state of insensibility from intoxication, and had stabbed him without any words having been exchanged, and apparently without knowing who he was. The relations of the wounded man said nothing to him, but the interpreter of Gov. Cass reproved him very sharply.

It was evident to all that the young man he had wounded could not recover; indeed, he was now manifestly near his end. When our companion returned, we had made up a considerable present, one giving a blanket, one a piece of strouding, some one thing, and some another. With these he immediately returned, and placing them on the ground beside the wounded man, he said to the relatives who were standing about, "My friends, I have, as you see, killed this, your brother; but I knew not what I did. I had no ill will against him, and when, a few days since, he came to our camp, I was glad to see him. But drunkenness made me a fool, and my life is justly forfeited to you. I am poor, and among strangers, but some of those who came from my own country with me, would gladly bring me back to my parents. They have, therefore, sent me with this small present. My life is in your hands, and my present is before you, take which ever you choose. My friends will have no cause to complain." He then sat down beside the wounded man, and stooping his head, hid his eyes with his hands, and waited for them to strike. But the mother of the man he had wounded, an old woman, came a little forward and said, "For myself and my children, I can answer, that we wish not to take your life; but I cannot promise to protect you from the resentment of my husband, who is now absent; nevertheless, I will accept your present, and whatever influence I may have with him, I shall not fail to use it in your behalf. I know that it was not from design, or on account of any previous hatred that you have done this, and why should your mother be made to cry as well as myself?" She took the presents, and the whole affair being reported to Gov. Cass, he was satisfied with the course that had been taken.

On the following day the wounded man died, and some of our party assisted the young man who had killed him in making his grave. When this was completed, the governor gave the dead man a valuable present of blankets, cloth, etc. to be buried with him, according to the Indian custom, and these were brought and heaped up on the brink of the grave. But the old woman, instead of having them buried, proposed to the young men to play for them. As the articles were somewhat numerous, various games were used, as shooting at the mark, leaping, wrestling, etc. but the handsomest piece of cloth was reserved as the prize for the swiftest in the foot race, and was won by the young man himself who had killed the other. The old woman immediately afterwards called him to her, and said, "Young man, he who was my son, was very dear to me, and I fear I shall cry much and often for him. I would be glad if you would consent to be my son in his stead, to love me and take care of me as he did, only I fear my husband." The young man, who was grateful to her for the anxiety she showed to save his life, immediately consented to this arrangement, and entered heartily upon it. But the governor had heard that some of the friends of the deceased were still determined to avenge his death, and he sent his interpreter to the young man, to direct him, without loss of time, to make his escape, and fly to his own country. He was unwilling to go, but as Be-nais-sa and myself concurred with the governor in his advice, and assisted him in his preparations, he went off in the night; but instead of going immediately home, as he had been directed to do, he lay concealed in the woods only a few hundred yards from our lodge.

Very early next morning, I saw two of the friends of the young man that was killed coming towards our lodge. At first I was somewhat alarmed, as I supposed they came with the intention of doing violence; but I soon perceived they were without arms. They came in, and sat a long time silent. At last one of them said, "Where is our brother? We are sometimes lonely at home, and we wish to talk with him." I told them he had but lately gone out, and would soon return. As they remained a long time, and insisted on seeing him, I went out, with the pretence of seeking for him, but without the remotest expectation that he would be found. He, however, had observed from his hiding place the visit of the two young men to our lodge, and not believing it to have been made with any unfriendly design, discovered himself to me and we returned together. They shook hands with him, and treated him with great kindness, and we soon afterwards ascertained that all the reports of their wishing to kill him were false.

19

ROBERT BRECKENRIDGE MCAFEE

(1784–1849)

Many Americans found out about the west and its Native Americans in histories of the various wars in the region. Many writers worked within this genre, some writing autobiographically, such as Arthur St. Clair and George Rogers Clark; others writing as historians, such as Francis Parkman and Benjamin Drake. Robert Breckenridge McAfee wrote as both. After serving in the War of 1812, McAfee, from Kentucky, returned to Lexington to write about the war in a book that combined personal experience with documentary evidence. The result was the massive *A History of the War in the Western Country*. McAfee published his book in Lexington, an act representative of his view that his work was meant primarily for western readers.

McAfee begins with the notion that, in the west, the revolution against the British had never ended. Instead, the British, in addition to refusing to relinquish their forts on the Great Lakes, in fact had been the instigators of the so-called Indian Wars waged by various native tribes against the American settlers. McAfee suggests that native leaders from Little Turtle to Tecumseh fought because they were paid to do so and thus must be considered primarily as British agents rather than as indigenes: the region was not wrested from the natives but rather from the British. The War of 1812 is often considered a rather trivial conflict in American history—an epilogue to the Revolution, finishing old business. However, in the west, the War of 1812, more than the Revolution, removed the threat of European recolonization. This threat had not mitigated since the end of the Revolution; the War of 1812 cut the natives off from the British payments for their resistance to American settlement.

In the sections reproduced here, McAfee describes conflicts between the Americans and the natives both before and during the War of 1812. His representation of natives as dupes allowed for a postwar reconciliation of the races—the source of evil was the British, who had exploited the natives' savagery for their own selfish ends. Like many other westerners, McAfee knew that the native presence was intractible and hoped for an eventual transfer of native loyalty to the Americans. McAfee's text is thus far more complicated and layered than most representations of the conflicts that plagued the first west. Furthermore, McAfee, foreshadowing later regional writers, understood the region as running from Mississippi to Minnesota: he included chapters on the conflicts with the Creeks in the south and the Shawnee in the north as components of the same struggle to purge the west of British corruption and exploitation. Furthermore, the volume concludes with a note that General Robert Winches-

ter, the New Yorker who led the army in the northwest, had objected to
certain passages. Leaving these objections unanswered, McAfee's un-
apologetic refutation of the eastern version of American history places
him at the beginnings of western writing.

Text: *A War in the Western Country* (Lexington, Kentucky, 1816; rpt. March of America Facsimile
Series, 1966): chapter 1 (1–49); chapter 7 (283–315).

FROM *HISTORY OF THE LATE WAR IN THE WESTERN COUNTRY* (1816)

CHAPTER I.

Preliminary views. . . . Causes of the War. . . . Battle of Tippecanoe.

At the close of the American revolution, many persons in England entertained an
opinion, that the American colonies were not irretrievably lost to the mother country. They hoped that Great Britain would be able, at some favorable moment, to regain the sovereignty of these states; and in this hope it is highly probable the British
ministry participated.

From calculations and sentiments like these, as well as from the irritation caused
by the failure of their arms, may have proceeded their unjustifiable conduct, on the
interior frontiers of the new states. The military posts of Niagara, Detroit, and Mackinaw, were detained under various pretences, for many years, in violation of the treaty
of peace. The Indian tribes on our borders, were at the same time supplied with munitions of war, and instigated to commit depredations and hostilities on the frontiers
of Kentucky, and the settlements northwest of the Ohio. This fact is fully established
by the letters of colonel M'Kee, the British commandant of fort Miami at the foot of
the Rapids, written previous to the visit of general Wayne to that place in '94, and
published during the late war in the American journals, the originals having then
fallen into the hands of our government.

This unwarrantable interference with the Indians, residing within the limits of
the United States, was continued by the British from the peace of '83, quite down to
the commencement of the late war. During a great part of that time, they kept the
Indians in hostility with our western settlements: and when the probability of a new
war between the two countries, became very strong, they so excited the savages, as to
make a battle with them the necessary prelude to general hostilities. Although this interference with the Indians, was not an obvious and ostensible cause of the war; yet it
may fairly be considered as a very efficient cause. Much of that resentment against the

British, which prevailed so strongly in the western states, the principal advocates for the war, may fairly be attributed to this source.

President Washington was apprised of the intrigues of the English agents, and endeavored by negotiation to obtain redress: and nothing but the exhausted state of the country after the revolutionary war, prevented that great man from resorting to arms to punish British perfidy. His policy however was wise; it was consistent with the genius of our government, and the condition of our country. It would certainly have been hazardous, to venture on a new war, so soon after we had established our independence, and instituted an untried form of government.

Several campaigns however, were conducted against the Indians northwest of the Ohio. General Harmer commanded one, in the year 1790, against the Miami village, at the junction of the rivers St. Marys and St. Josephs, where fort Wayne was subsequently built. It eventuated in burning the town; and afterwards in the defeat of several detachments of his army, with the loss of many of his men.

In the following year another army was conducted in the same direction, from Kentucky and the back parts of Pennsylvania and Virginia, by general Arthur St. Clair. The object of this expedition, was to destroy the Miami and Shawanoe settlements, on the Auglaize and Miami rivers: but it was late in the season before the necessary arrangements were made, and the Indians having received intelligence of his march, and anticipating his views, advanced and met him near the place where fort Recovery now stands. On the 7th of November, they attacked his army in its encampment, when a total rout ensued, and the greater part of the army was destroyed. The Indian mode of warfare was not well understood by this general, and the panic produced by the savage yells in the time of action, threw the whole into confusion.

For several years previous to this disastrous campaign, the people of Kentucky had remonstrated against the manner in which the general government was conducting the war against the Indians: and President Washington had so far regarded their representations, as to authorise certain eminent citizens, Messrs. Scott, Innes, Brown, Logan, and Shelby, to send expeditions against the Indians in their own way. Accordingly in the spring and summer preceding the defeat of general St. Clair, two expeditions of volunteer militia from the district of Kentucky, were sent by those gentlemen against the Indians on the Wabash—the first under the command of general Charles Scott, and the other under general James Wilkinson. They were both completely successful. The Indian country was laid waste, many lives were destroyed, and many prisoners were taken, without much loss on the part of the Kentuckians. Yet in the autumn of the same year, the old method of sending regulars, under a general unskilled in savage warfare, was again employed in the case of St. Clair's campaign, with the disastrous consequence of a total defeat.

After this disaster, affairs with the Indians wore a gloomy aspect. It was extremely difficult to procure supplies, from the scattered settlements of the frontiers, to subsist a regular army sufficient to humble the savages. General Washington hence determined to attempt a negotiation with them; and colonel Hardin was accordingly sent to them with a flag. All that is known about him after his departure, is that he was met and massacred by the Indians. A predatory, skirmishing warfare was then continued for several years, without any important and decisive action being fought, until in the year '94 a formidable and successful expedition was conducted against the savages by general Anthony Wayne, a distinguished revolutionary officer from Pennsylvania, who was then commander in chief of the American army. He was accompanied by generals Wilkinson and Scott of the same character from Kentucky. The principal part of the troops were assembled at Cincinnati in the month of June, and thence marched by the way of forts Hamilton, Greenville, Recovery, Adams, and Defiance, which had been built by the regulars under Wayne, during several preceding years of preparation for this decisive campaign.

In the mean time, the British commandant at Detroit, had seized a commanding spot, in the American territory, on the north side of the Miami of the lakes, below the Rapids, where he had erected a strong fort, from which the Indians were notoriously fed and supplied with ammunition, under the pretence of paying them annuities. They also were secretly counselled, in relation to their management of the war. The following extracts from the letters of colonel M'Kee, the superintendant of Indian affairs for the districts of Detroit and Mackinaw, which were addressed from this fort to colonel England, the military commandant at Detroit, are worthy to be preserved as evidence of the conduct of the British government in this case. The letters were written from one *British officer* to another, and were endorsed "*on his Majesty's service.*"

'Rapids, July 2d, '94.

'By the same channel I learn that a large body of troops, supposed to be 3000, with wagons &c. crossed the Ohio some days ago and marched towards the forts in the Indian country.

'I am much pressed for tobacco and ammunition *(for the Indians)* which I hope I may receive by the return of the boat.'

'Rapids, July 5th, '94.

'Sir—I send this by a party of Saganas, who returned yesterday from fort Recovery, where the whole body of Indians, except the Delawares, who had gone another route, imprudently attacked the fort on Monday the 30th of last month, and lost 16 or 17 men, besides a good many wounded.

'Every thing had been settled, prior to their leaving the Fallen Timber, and it had been agreed upon to confine themselves to taking convoys, and attacking at a distance from the forts, if they should have the address to entice *the enemy out;* but the impetuosity of the Mackinaw Indians, and their eagerness to begin with the nearest, prevailed with the others to alter their system, the consequences of which, from the present appearance of things, may most materially injure the interest of these people; both the Mackinaw and Lake Indians seeming resolved on going home again, having completed the belts they carried with scalps and prisoners, and having no provision there, or at the Glaze to subsist upon; so that his *Majesty's post* will derive *no security* from the late great *influx of Indians* into this part of the country, should they persist in their resolution of returning so soon.

'Capt. Elliott writes that they are immediately to hold a council at the Glaze, in order to try if they can *prevail on the Lake Indians to remain; but without provisions, ammunition &c. being sent to that place, I conceive it will be extremely difficult to keep them together.*'

'Rapids, August 13th, '94.

Sir—I was honored last night with your letter of the 11th, and am extremely glad to find you are making *such exertions to supply the Indians with provisions.*

'Capt. Elliott arrived yesterday; *what he has brought will greatly relieve us,* having been obliged all day yesterday to take the corn and flour which the traders had there.'

'Scouts are sent-up to view the situation of the army, *and we now muster 1000 In-*

dians. All the Lake Indians from Sagana downwards *should not loose one moment in join-ing their brethren,* as every accession of strength is an addition to their spirits.'

'*Camp near Fort Miami, August 30, '94.*
'Sir, I have been employed several days *in endeavoring to fix the Indians,* (who have been driven from their villages and corn fields) between the fort and the bay. Swan creek is generally agreed upon, and will be a very convenient place for the delivery of pro-vision &c.'

As general Wayne advanced, the Indians retired, leaving their villages and corn, on the Miami and Auglaize rivers, to be burnt and destroyed. Through the medium of his spies, the general often tendered them terms of peace, which they as often rejected. They at length determined on making a stand about two miles above the British gar-rison to give Wayne battle. An engagement accordingly took place on the 20th of Au-gust, '94—the result was a complete discomfiture of the Indians. A number of British Canadians fought with the Indians in this battle. On the next day, the general recon-noitred the British fort, and demanded in peremptory terms the reasons for their in-trusion. The British officer commanding, replied that he was there by the orders of his government, and would abandon the place as soon as he was ordered to do so by his superiors; and that he hoped the general would not proceed to extremities till their respective governments were consulted. General Wayne then retired up the Miami and erected fort Wayne.

This victory over the Indians laid the foundation of a general peace with them. They had believed, that the British would protect them; but they found themselves deceived; for the gates of the British fort were shut against them as they retreated after the battle. In the following year, '95, general Wayne held a general council, with all the Indians northwest of the Ohio, at Greenville, which eventuated in a treaty, by which they ceded us an extensive tract of country, as an indemnity for past injuries, and in consideration of annuities to be paid to them by the United States.

In the year '94, a treaty was also negotiated by Mr. Jay with the British govern-ment. It was signed on the 19th November, a few months after Wayne's battle with the Indians. In pursuance of this treaty, in the year '96, all the military posts, held by the British, on the American side of the lakes, were given up to the American authorities.

These treaties and events secured our interior frontiers from the active hostility of the Indians, and promoted the commercial enterprise of our citizens on the ocean. Our western settlements in consequence, rapidly advanced in population and the im-provement of their country, while our Atlantic citizens were fast accumulating wealth by their trade with foreign nations. This prosperity however, was not permitted to ad-vance uninterrupted by British aggressions. The British continued their intercourse with the Indians within our limits, so as to keep them attached to British interests, and hostile in their feelings towards the United States. But the evils we experienced on the ocean, were now infinitely more intolerable than those of the interior.

The war in Europe, which had originally been instigated by the British against the revolution in France, continued to rage with unabated violence. England and France, the leading parties in the war, used every species of artifice and violence, to involve all other nations in the contest. Orders and decrees were published, by which the mar-itime rights of neutral nations were infringed, and extensive coasts declared in a state of blockade, without any adequate means of enforcement. By the British orders in council, our vessels were required, under the penalty of being liable to capture, to call at a British port, on their way to any place belonging to France and her allies. By way of retaliation, Bonaparte decreed, that all vessels which had submitted to this British regulation, should be subject to capture by his cruisers. And thus no vessel of the United States could sail, either to Britain or France, or to any of their allies including all Europe, without being subject to capture by one or the other of the belligerents. At the same time the British naval officers carried on the practice of impressing American seamen, in a manner so extensive and vexatious, as to cause much distress among our seafaring people, and much inconvenience and risk to our merchants.

An endless course of negotiation was pursued, on these different subjects of complaint, without the prospect of success becoming any brighter. The American government could obtain in this way neither indemnity for the past nor security for the future. No alternative was left, but a resort to arms, to vindicate our honor and our rights, and to protect our interests on the ocean. Our losses by captures and impressments nearly equalled the expenses of a war in men and money. A formal declaration of war was accordingly made on the 18th of June, 1812. But previous to this declaration, hostilities had commenced with the Indians, and the battle of Tippecanoe had been fought.

A preliminary view of Indian affairs will enable us to understand this commencement of the war. By the combined counsels and schemes of the British agents, and some of the principal chiefs among the Indians, the seeds of hostility were sown among them soon after the peace of Greenville, and were gradually nurtured into war. At that time, Little Turtle and Blue Jacket were the leading chiefs among the northwestern tribes. They had disagreed about the manner of opposing Wayne's army. The plan of Blue Jacket was adopted, and eventuated in the total defeat of the Indians, as predicted by the other. After this event, Little Turtle continued friendly to the United States. He was of opinion, that the Indian tribes were unable to contend against the Americans; that no material aid would be furnished them by the British: and that war would only be the means of their losing more of their lands. Blue Jacket had more confidence in the British; he thirsted for revenge against the Americans; and he wished to regain the lands which had been ceded by the treaty of Greenville. His influence increased, whilst the Little Turtle became unpopular. He found in Tecumseh, a Shawanoese Indian, whom he associated with him in his views and projects, an able and persevering coadjutor. The leading principles in their policy were, to combine all the tribes together in one confederacy; to prevent the sale of their lands by any single tribe; and to join the British in the event of war, with a view to revenge and the recovery of their lands. They contended, that by the treaty of Greenville, the United States had acknowledged the right to their lands to reside jointly in all the tribes; and that of course the United States had no right to purchase lands from any single tribe, without the consent of the others. Blue Jacket did not live to execute his schemes; but they were diligently pursued by Tecumseh, in which he was encouraged and supported by the British agents.

The various tribes, who were in the habit of visiting Detroit and Sandwich, were annually subsidised by the British. When the American agent at Detroit gave one dollar by way of annuity, the British agent on the other side of the river Detroit would give them ten. This course of iniquity had the intended effect: the Indians were impressed with a great aversion for the Americans; and disregarding the treaty of Greenville, they desired to recover the lands which they had ceded, and for which they had annually received the stipulated annuity. They wished also to try their strength again with the "Big Knife." as they called the Kentuckians, in order to wipe away the disgrace of their defeat by general Wayne. And they were still promised the aid of the British, in the event of a war between the British and Americans. Their natural temper for war was thus inflamed, and they were held in readiness at any moment to commence the contest.

About the year 1804, a Shawanoese Indian, the brother of Tecumseh, proclaimed himself a Prophet, alleging that he had been commanded by the Great Spirit, who made the red people, and who was not the same that made the white people, and whom the latter worshipped, to inform his red children, that the misfortunes which had fallen upon them, proceeded from their having abandoned the mode of life which he had prescribed for them, and adopted the manners and dress of the white people; and that he was commanded to tell them, that they must return to their former habits, leave off the use of whiskey, and as soon as possible clothe themselves in skins instead of blankets.

The Prophet fixed himself at Greenville, the spot which had been so noted from the cantonment of general Wayne's army, and from the treaty made by him with the Indian tribes at that place in the year 1795. The fame of the Prophet spread through the surrounding Indian tribes, and he soon found himself at, the head of a considerable number of followers, composed principally however of the most abandoned of the young men of the Shawanoese Delawares, Wyandots, Potawatamies, Ottowas, Chippewas and Kickapoos. Besides these he was visited by an immense concourse of men, women and children from the tribes of the Mississippi and Lake Superior. The most absurd stories were told, and believed by the Indians, of his power to perform miracles, and no fatigue or suffering was thought too great to be endured to get a sight of him. The people of Ohio became much alarmed at the great assemblage of the Indians upon their frontier; and a mission was sent by the governor to insist upon their removal. The United States' agent at fort Wayne also joined in the remonstrance, against his forming a permanent settlement at Greenville, which was within the boundary of the United States. Accordingly, in 1808, he removed to the Wabash, and fixed his residence on the north bank of that river, near the mouth of the Tippecanoe. This land was the property of the Miami tribe, who made strong remonstrances against it, but were not strong enough to effect his removal by force, as he had collected around him a considerable body of the most daring and unprincipled young men, of all the neighbouring tribes. The chiefs of the latter were almost unaminously opposed to him, as they discovered that he was constantly endeavouring to destroy their influence, or to prevail on the warriors to take the authority into their own hands. Several of the most influential chiefs were put to death by the young men, under the pretence of their practising magic. Teteboxke, the venerable chief of the Delawares, with several of his friends, were condemned to the flames. The loss of their chiefs began however to be regretted, and those that survived made a common cause, in opposing the extension of the Prophet's influence. He was only able to retain about 40 warriors of his own tribe, the chiefs of which hated him most cordially. In the year 1809, he had not more than 250 or 300 warriors with him. They had suffered much for provisions, and the greater part of them perhaps would have perished, if they had not been supplied with corn by governor Harrison, from Vincennes. In September, 1809, a treaty was made at fort Wayne, by the governor, as commissioner upon the part of the United States, for the extinguishment of the title to a considerable tract of land, extending about 60 miles up the Wabash above Vincennes. The Delawares, Miamies and Potawatamies were parties to this treaty; but the Prophet and his followers were not invited; because, as the governor says in his address to the legislature of Indiana, "it never had been suggested, that they could plead even the title of occupancy to the lands which were then conveyed to the United States," and it was well known they were the rightful property of the Miamies, who had possessed them from the time of the first arrival of the white people among them. The Shawanoese tribe made no pretensions to those lands. Their principal chief attended the treaty, and recommended to the Miami chiefs to make the cession. About the time that the treaty was made, the affairs of the Prophet were at a low ebb. In the course of the succeeding winter, however, the intrigues and negotiations of his brother Tecumseh, procured a large accession of strength. They were joined by a considerable number of Winnebagoes or Puants, the greater part of the Kickapoo tribe, and some of the Wyandots. Although the affairs were managed in the name of the Prophet, Tecumseh was in fact the director of every thing. This extraordinary man had risen into consequence, subsequently to the treaty of Greenville in the year 1795. He had been considered an active warrior in the war which was terminated by that treaty, but possessed no considerable influence. The principal object of his labors, by which he obtained distinction, was to unite all the tribes upon the continent in one grand confederacy for the purpose of opposing the encroachments of the whites. Tecumseh was on a mission for this purpose, when the treaty was concluded in 1809. Upon his return, he threatened to kill the chiefs who had signed it, and declared his determination to prevent the lands from being surveyed and settled.

Governor Harrison, upon being informed of his proceedings, sent him a message, informing him "that any claims he might have to the lands which had been ceded, were not affected by the treaty; that he might come to Vincennes and exhibit his pretensions, and if they were found to be solid, that the land would either be given up, or an ample compensation made for it." Accordingly in the month of August, 1810, he came down to Vincennes, attended by several hundred warriors. A day was appointed to hear his statement, which it took him many hours to make. He asserted, that the Great Spirit had made the continent for the use of the Indians exclusively— that the white people had no right to come here, and take it from them—that no particular part of it was given to any tribe, but that the whole was the common property of all; and that any sale of lands, made without the consent of all, was not valid. In his answer, the governor observed, that the Indians, like the white people, were divided into different tribes or nations, and that the Great Spirit never intended that they should form but one nation, or he would not have taught them to speak different languages, which put it out of their power to understand each other—and that the Shawanoese, who emigrated from Georgia, could have no claim to the lands on the Wabash, which had been occupied far beyond the memory of man by the Miamies. The governor having proceeded thus far, sat down for the purpose of giving the interpreters time to explain what he had said, to the different tribes that were present. As soon as it was interpreted in Shawanoese, Tecumseh interrupted the interpreter, and said that it was all false, and giving a signal to his warriors, they seized their tomahawks and war clubs and sprang upon their feet.

For some minutes the governor was in the most imminent danger: he preserved his presence of mind however, and disengaging himself from an arm-chair in which he was sitting, seized his sword to defend himself. A considerable number of the citizens of Vincennes were present, all unarmed. At a little distance however, there was a guard of a sergeant and 12 men, who were immediately brought up by an officer. The governor then told Tecumseh, that he was a bad man, and he would have no further intercourse with him; and directed him to retire to his camp and set out immediately on his return home. As the Indians with Tecumseh greatly outnumbered the citizens of the town, and the regular troops there, two companies of militia were brought in during the night, and a large number the next day. Early however on the following morning, Tecumseh sent for the interpreter, made an apology for his conduct, and earnestly requested that he might have another conference with the governor. His request was at length granted; but the governor took care to be attended by a number of his friends, well armed, and to have the troops in the town ready for action. In his speech Tecumseh said, that he had been advised by some white persons, to act as he had done; but that it was not his intention to offer any violence to the governor. The latter then inquired, whether he had any other grounds for claiming the lands, that had been ceded to the United States, but those which he had stated; and he answered in the *negative*. The governor then observed to him, that so great a warrior should disdain to conceal his intentions, and desired to know whether he really intended to make war upon the United States, if the lately purchased lands were not relinquished by them. He answered that it was decidedly his determination, and that he would never rest, until he brought all the tribes upon the continent, to unite in one confederacy. The activity and perseverance, which he manifested in the prosecution of this scheme, are most wonderful. He visited all the tribes west of the Mississippi, and on lakes Superior, Huron, and Erie repeatedly, before the year 1811. So sanguine were his followers about this time, and so much were they encouraged by the British agents, that in the event of a war between England and America, they believed the confederated tribes, with the aid of the British, would be able to drive the Americans over the Ohio river to the south side, and thus regain all the country on the northwest of that river: And from the *sine qua non,* advanced by the British commissioners in the negotiation at Ghent, it would appear, that the British ministry had indulged a delusion not much less extravagant.

It was the intention of Tecumseh, to avoid hostilities with the whites, until he should effect a combination strong enough to resist them, or until the expected war with Great Britain should commence. Whether the British were really the authors of this plan, for forming a general confederacy amongst the tribes, or whether the scheme originated with Blue Jacket and Tecumseh themselves, is not certain; but from the papers found in the baggage of the British army taken on the Thames, it appears more than probable, that the former was the case—at least it is certain, that an intimate communication was kept up, between the Prophet and Tecumseh, and the British Indian department, from their first establishment at Greenville; and that they were constantly supplied with arms, ammunition and clothing, from the King's stores at Malden. In the winter and spring of the year 1811, many depredations and several murders were committed upon the inhabitants of the frontiers of the Indiana, Illinois, and Missouri territories. The perpetrators were demanded of the respective chiefs, but no satisfaction could be obtained. A militia officer was sent by governor Harrison to demand the delivery of some horses, that had been stolen from the settlements, and which were discovered with the Indians: no satisfaction was however obtained; and Tecumseh and his brother informed the officer, that they would pay a visit in person to the governor. They were told that they would be well received, provided they came with not more than 30 followers. This was acceded to. The governor however caused their motions to be watched, and was soon informed, that they were descending the river with several hundred warriors. The same officer was dispatched to meet them, and to forbid their approach to Vincennes with that body. Compliance was again promised, and Tecumseh came on with a few canoes only, but was soon followed by all the rest, who joined and encamped with him a mile from the town of Vincennes. The inhabitants were much alarmed, and there is little doubt, but that it was the intention of the Indians, to surprise and plunder the town. The governor was however on his guard. The militia of the town were kept under arms, and some companies were brought in from the country. Tecumseh demanded an interview. The governor agreed to it, and asked whether it was the intention of the Indians to come armed to the council. Tecumseh replied that he would be governed by the conduct of the white people; if they attended the council armed, his warriors would be armed also, but if the white people would come unarmed, his would come in the same way. The governor informed him, that he would be attended by a troop of dragoons, dismounted, who would have only side arms, and that the Indians might bring their war clubs, tomahawks, and knives. The meeting took place in a large arbour, on one side of which were placed the dragoons, 80 in number, seated in rows; on the other side, the Indians. Besides their swords, the dragoons had their pistols stuck in their belts. The Indians were evidently alarmed, and when the governor, who was seated in front of the front row of dragoons, began to address them, Tecumseh complained that he could not hear him, and desired him to remove his seat to an open space near himself. The governor complied. In his speech he complained of the constant depredations, which were committed by the Indians of Tippecanoe. The refusal on their part to give satisfaction—and the constant accumulation of force at that place, for the avowed purpose of obliging the United States to give up lands, which they had fairly purchased of the rightful owners. In his answer Tecumseh denied that he had taken the murderers under his protection; but admitted his design of forming a grand confederacy of all the nations and tribes of Indians upon the continent, for the purpose of putting a stop to the encroachments of the white people. He said, that "the policy which the United States pursued, of purchasing their lands from the Indians, he viewed as a *mighty water,* ready to overflow his people, and that the confederacy which he was forming among the tribes, to prevent any individual tribe from selling without the consent of the others, was the *dam* he was erecting to resist this mighty water." And he added, "your great father may sit over the mountains and drink his wine, but if he continues this policy, you and I will have to fight it out." He admitted, that he was then on his way to the Creek nation for the purpose of bringing them over to his measures; and he actually did, two days afterwards, set out on this journey with 12 or 15 of his warriors. Having visited the Creeks, Choctaws, and Chickasaws, he crossed the Mississippi and continued his course northwardly, as high as the river Demoins. Having obtained, it is believed, the promise of assistance from all the tribes in that direction, he returned to the Wabash by land, across the heads of the Illinois river. In his absence his affairs had sustained a sad reverse. His town was consumed, his large deposit of provisions destroyed, his bravest followers killed, and the rest dispersed. Upon his departure to visit the southern Indians, the Prophet his brother, was left in charge of the temporal as well as spiritual concerns of the establishment. It is believed that he received from Tecumseh, positive instructions to avoid coming to extremities with the white people, and to restrain his followers from committing depredations, which might lead to the commencement of hostilities before his plans were ripe. The Prophet however wanted the inclination as well as the authority necessary to follow the direction. Murders and other depredations followed in quick succession; no redress could be obtained; the people upon the frontiers became exceedingly alarmed, as well as the citizens of Vincennes, at which place a large meeting was held, which passed a number of resolutions indicating their sense of the danger they were in, and warmly approbating the measures, which had been taken by the governor for their defence. These resolutions, with a strong remonstrance against the propriety of suffering this banditti to continue their depredations, were forwarded to the President of the United States. They produced the desired effect, and the 4th regiment commanded by colonel Boyd, which was at that time at Pittsburgh, was ordered to repair immediately to Vincennes, and was placed under the command of governor Harrison. The governor was also directed to add to them a body of militia, to take measures for the defence of the citizens, and as a last resort to remove the Prophet and his followers by force.

As soon as it was known in Kentucky, that Harrison was authorized to march with an army against the Indians, a number of volunteers went over to join his standard. Many of them were men of high standing at home, as military, civil, and literary characters. Of this number were Samuel Wells, a major general of the militia, who had been an active soldier in former wars with the Indians—Joseph H. Daveiss esq. a very eminent attorney, who had great military ambition—Col. Abraham Owen, a veteran in Indian warfare—and Col. Keiger, who raised a small company of young men near Louisville, including among them Messrs. Croghan, O'Fallon, Shipp, Chum and Edwards, who afterwards distinguished themselves as officers in the army of the United States.

In the latter part of September, the governor commenced his march up the Wabash, with a force of about *nine hundred effective men,* composed of the 4th regiment, a body of militia, and about 130 volunteer dragoons. The 4th regiment had been raised for some time, and was well trained and well officered. The militia too, who were all volunteers, had been trained with great assiduity by the governor, in those particular evolutions which had been practised by general Wayne's army, and which had been found useful in a covered country, and operating against Indians. Conformably to his orders from the president, the governor halted within the boundary of the United States, and endeavoured by the intervention of the Delaware and Miami tribes, to induce the Prophet to deliver up the murderers and the stolen horses. These messengers of peace were received and treated with great insolence, and the demands made by them rejected with disdain by the Prophet and his council. To put an end to all hopes of accommodation, a small war party was detached for the purpose of commencing hostilities. Finding no stragglers about the camp, they fired upon one of the sentinels, and wounded him severely; the Delaware chiefs informed the governor of the object of the party, and that it was in vain to expect, that any thing but force could obtain either satisfaction for the injuries done, or security for the future. He learned also from the same source, that the strength of the Prophet was daily increasing by the ardent and giddy young men from every tribe, and particularly from the tribes on and beyond the Illinois river. The governor was at this time busily engaged, in erecting a fort on the southeast side of the Wabash, some miles within the boundary of the United States, and in preparing ammunition, and disciplining his men for the expected conflict, which from the character of the enemy, he knew would be a desperate one. His little army had been much weakened by sickness, the effect of fresh food without vegetables and a sufficient quantity of bread. The governor finding his flour growing short, had early in October put the troops upon half allowance of that article—this regulation extended to the officers of every rank, and was rigidly conformed to in the family of the general. The sick having been deposited in the fort; which the officers, in compliment to their commander, had requested might be called Fort Harrison; and the weak and convalescent being drawn out to form the garrison; the troops on the 29th of October took up the line of march: the infantry in two columns in single file on each side of the trace, and capable by a single conversion, of being formed into two lines, to receive the enemy on any point he might attack, or of being reduced into a hollow square.

The country through which the army passed was occasionally open, beautiful prairie, intersected by thick woods, deep creeks, and ravines. The cavalry and mounted riflemen, of the latter of which there were two companies, covered the advance, the flanks and the rear, and were made to exchange positions with each other, as the ground varied—so as to keep them upon that which best suited the mode of fighting which they respectively practised. The Indians being perfectly master of the art of ambuscading, every precaution was used to guard against surprise, and prevent the army from being attacked in a disadvantageous position. At some distance above fort Harrison, two routes for approaching the Prophet's town presented themselves to the choice of the governor. The one passing up the south side of the Wabash, was much shorter than the other, but it led through an uneven woody country. To the north of the river, the prairies are very extensive, affording few situations for the kind of warfare peculiar to the savages. To deceive the enemy, the governor caused the route to be reconnoitred on the south side and a wagon road laid out, and having advanced upon it a short distance, he suddenly changed his direction and gained the right bank of the Wabash, by crossing it above the mouth of Racoon creek. Here the army was joined by some of the volunteers from Kentucky, amongst whom were major general Wells, and colonels Owen and Keiger. To general Wells the command of the mounted riflemen was assigned with the rank of major. Colonel Owen was appointed aid-de-camp to the governor; and the rest of the volunteers with a detachment of the Indiana militia under major Beck were formed into a company, and placed under the command of colonel Keiger as captain. To colonel Daveiss the command of the dragoons had been given with the rank of major. In passing the large prairies, the army was frequently halted, and made collectively to perform the evolutions, which they had been taught in smaller bodies, during their stay at fort Harrison, at which place, the governor had manœuvred the relieving guards every day in person, and had required the attendance of the field officers on those occasions.

The Indians not expecting the army on the north side of the river, no signs of them were seen, until it approached Pine creek, a very dangerous pass, where a few men might successfully oppose a whole army. The appearance of this creek forms a singular exception to the other water courses of this country. It runs for the distance of 15 or 20 miles above its mouth, between immense cliffs of rock, upon whose summits are found considerable quantities of pine and red cedar, the former of which is rare, and the latter no where else to be found near the Wabash. The ordinary crossing place, to which the trace led that the army was pursuing, was represented by the traders, who served as guides, to be extremely difficult, if not impassable for wagons, and that it was no doubt the spot where the Indians would make their attack, if they had determined to meet the army in the field. It had been twice selected by them for that purpose—once in the year 1780, when general Clarke undertook a campaign against the Indians of the Wabash; but their design was then frustrated by a mutiny of a part of his troops 70 or 80 miles above Vincennes—and a second time in the year 1790, when colonel Hamtramack penetrated with a small force as high as the Vermillion, to make a diversion in favor of general Harmer's expedition to the Miami of the Lake. The governor had no intention of encountering the enemy in a place like this. He accordingly, in the course of the night preceding his approach to the creek, dispatched captain Prince, of the Indiana militia, with an escort of forty men, to reconnoitre the creek some miles above, and endeavour to find a better fording. About 10 o'clock next day, this excellent officer met the army in its advance, and informed the general, that at the distance of six or eight miles, he had found a trace, used by the Illinois Indians in travelling to Tippecanoe, which presented an excellent ford, at a place where the prairie skirted the creek. This prairie which they were now crossing, excited the admiration and astonishment of the officers and soldiers, who had never been on the north west side of the Wabash. To the north and west the prospect was unbounded—from the highest eminence no limit was to be seen, and the guides asserted, that the prairie extended to the Illinois river. On the evening of the 5th November, the army encamped at the distance of nine or ten miles from the Prophet's town. It was ascertained that the approach of the army had been discovered before it crossed Pine creek. The traces of reconnoitring parties were very often seen, but no Indians were discovered until the troops arrived within 5 or 6 miles of the town on the 6th November. The interpreters were then placed with the advanced guard, to endeavour to open a communication with them. The Indians would however return no answer to the invitations that were made to them for that purpose, but continued to insult our people by their gestures. Within about three miles of the town, the ground became broken by ravines and covered with timber. The utmost precaution became necessary, and every difficult pass was examined by the mounted riflemen before the army was permitted to enter it. The ground being unfit for the operation of the squadron of dragoons, they were thrown in the rear. Through the whole march, the precaution had been used of changing the disposition of the different corps, that each might have the ground best suited to its operations. Within about two miles of the town, the path descended a steep hill, at the bottom of which was a small creek running through a narrow wet prairie, and beyond this a level plain partially covered with oak timber, and without under-brush. Before the crossing of the creek, the woods were very thick and intersected by deep ravines. No place could be better calculated for the savages to attack with a prospect of success, and the governor apprehended that the moment the troops descended into the hollow, they would be attacked. A disposition was therefore made of the infantry, to receive the enemy on the left and rear. A company of mounted riflemen was advanced a considerable distance from the left flank to check the approach of the enemy; and the other two companies were directed to turn the enemy's flanks, should he attack from that direction. The dragoons were ordered to move rapidly from the rear and occupy the plain in advance of the creek, to cover the crossing of the army from an attack in front. In this order the troops were passed over; the dragoons were made to advance to give room to the infantry, and the latter having crossed the creek, were formed to receive the enemy in front in one line, with a reserve of three companies—the dragoons flanked by mounted riflemen forming the first line. During all this time, Indians were frequently seen in front and on the flanks. The interpreters endeavoured in vain to bring them to a parley. Though sufficiently near to hear what was said to them, they would return no answer, but continued by gestures to menace and insult those who addressed them. Being now arrived within a mile and a half of the town, and the situation being favorable for an encampment, the governor determined to remain there and fortify his camp, until he could hear from the friendly chiefs, whom he had dispatched from fort Harrison, on the day he had left it, for the purpose of making another attempt to prevent the re-

currence to hostilities. Those chiefs were to have met him on the way, but no intelligence was yet received from them. Whilst he was engaged in tracing out the lines of
the encampment, major Daveiss and several other field officers approached him, and
urged the propriety of immediately marching upon the town. The governor answered
that his instructions would not justify his attacking the Indians, as long as there was a
probability of their complying with the demands of the government, and that he still
hoped to hear something in the course of the evening from the friendly Indians,
whom he had dispatched from fort Harrison.

To this it was observed, that as the Indians seen hovering about the army, had
been frequently invited to a parley by the interpreters, who had proceeded some distance from the lines for the purpose; and as these overtures had universally been answered by menace and insult, it was very evident that it was their intention to fight;
that the troops were in high spirits and full of confidence; and that advantage ought
to be taken of their ardour to lead them immediately to the enemy. To this the governor answered, that he was fully sensible of the eagerness of the troops; and admitting the determined hostility of the Indians, and that their insolence was full evidence
of their intention to fight, yet he knew them too well to believe, that they would ever
do this, but by surprise, or on ground which was entirely favorable to their mode of
fighting. He was therefore determined not to advance with the troops, until he knew
precisely the situation of the town, and the ground adjacent to it, particularly that
which intervened between it and the place where the army then was—that it was
their duty to fight when they came in contact with the enemy—it was his to take care
that they should not engage in a situation where their valor would be useless, and
where a corps upon which he placed great reliance would be unable to act—that the
experience of the last two hours ought to convince every officer, that no reliance
ought to be placed upon the guides, as to the topography of the country—that relying on their information, the troops had been led into a situation so unfavorable, that
but for the celerity with which they changed their position, a few Indians might have
destroyed them: he was therefore determined not to advance to the town, until he had
previously reconnoitred, either in person, or by some one, on whose judgment he
could rely. Major Daveiss immediately replied, that from the right of the position of
the dragoons, which was still in front, the opening made by the low grounds of the
Wabash could be seen; that with his adjutant D. Floyd, he had advanced to the bank,
which descends to the low grounds, and had a fair view of the cultivated fields and
the houses of the town; and that the open woods, in which the troops then were, continued without interruption to the town. Upon this information, the governor said
he would advance, provided he could get any proper person to go to the town with
a flag. Captain T. Dubois of Vincennes having offered his services, he was dispatched
with an interpreter to the Prophet, desiring to know whether he would now comply
with the terms, that had been so often proposed to him. The army was moved slowly
after in order of battle. In a few moments a messenger came from captain Dubois, informing the governor that the Indians were near him in considerable numbers, but
that they would return no answer to the interpreter, although they were sufficiently
near to hear what was said to them, and that upon his advancing, they constantly endeavored to cut him off from the army. Governor Harrison during this last effort to
open a negotiation, which was sufficient to shew his wish for an accommodation, resolved no longer to hesitate in treating the Indians as enemies. He therefore recalled
captain Dubois, and moved on with a determination to attack them. He had not proceeded far however before he was met by three Indians, one of them a principal coun-

sellor to the Prophet. They were sent, they said, to know why the army was advancing upon them—that the Prophet wished if possible to avoid hostilities; that he had sent a pacific message by the Miami and Potawatamie chiefs, who had come to him on the part of the governor—and that those chiefs had unfortunately gone down on the south side of the Wabash. A suspension of hostilities was accordingly agreed upon; and a meeting was to take place the next day between Harrison and the chiefs, to agree upon the terms of peace. The governor further informed them, that he would go on to the Wabash, and encamp there for the night. Upon marching a short distance further he came in view of the town, which was seen at some distance up the river upon a commanding eminence. Major Daveiss and adjutant Floyd had mistaken some scattered houses in the fields below, for the town itself. The ground below the town being unfavorable for an encampment, the army marched on in the direction of the town, with a view to obtain a better situation beyond it. The troops were in an order of march, calculated by a single conversion of companies, to form the order of battle, which it had last assumed, the dragoons being in front. This corps however soon became entangled in ground, covered with brush and tops of fallen trees. A halt was ordered, and major Daveiss directed to change position with Spencer's rifle corps, which occupied the open fields adjacent to the river. The Indians seeing this manœuvre, at the approach of the troops towards the town, supposed that they intended to attack it, and immediately prepared for defence. Some of them sallied out, and called to the advanced corps to halt. The governor upon this rode forward, and requested some of the Indians to come to him, assured them, that nothing was farther from his thoughts, than to attack them—that the ground below the town on the river, was not calculated for an encampment, and that it was his intention to search for a better one above. He asked if there was any other water convenient beside that which the river afforded; and an Indian with whom he was well acquainted, answered, that the creek, which had been crossed two miles back, ran through the prairie to the north of the village. A halt was then ordered, and some officers sent back to examine the creek, as well as the river above the town. In half an hour, brigade major Marston Clarke and major Waller Taylor returned, and reported that they had found on the creek, every thing that could be desirable in an encampment—an elevated spot, nearly surrounded by an open prairie, with water convenient, and a sufficiency of wood for fuel. An idea was propagated by the enemies of governor Harrison, after the battle of Tippecanoe, that the Indians had forced him to encamp on a place, chosen by them as suitable for the attack they intended. The place however was chosen by majors Taylor and Clark, after examining all the environs of the town: and when the army of general Hopkins was there in the following year, they all united in the opinion, that a better spot to resist Indians, was not to be found in the whole country.

The army now marched to the place selected, and encamped late in the evening, on a dry piece of ground, which rose about ten feet above the level of a marshy prairie in front towards the town, and about twice as high above a similar prairie in the rear; through which, near the bank, ran a small stream clothed with willows and brush wood. On the left of the encampment, this bench of land became wider; on the right it gradually narrowed, and terminated in an abrupt point, about 150 yards from the right flank. The two columns of infantry occupied the front and rear. The right flank, being about eighty yards wide, was filled with captain Spencer's company of eighty men. The left flank, about 150 yards in extent, was composed of three companies of mounted riflemen, under major general Wells, commanding as a major. The front line was composed of one battalion of United States' infantry, under the command of major

Floyd, flanked on the right by two companies of militia infantry, and on the left by one company of the same troops. The rear line consisted of a battalion of United States infantry, under captain Baen, commanding as a major; and four companies of militia infantry, under lieut, colonel Decker; the regulars being stationed next the riflemen under Wells, and the militia on the other end of the line adjoining Spencer's company. The cavalry under Daveiss were encamped in the rear of the front line and the left flank. The encampment was not more than three fourths of a mile from the town.

The order given to the army, in the event of a night attack, was for each corps to maintain its ground at all hazards till relieved. The dragoons were directed in such a case, to parade dismounted, with their swords on and their pistols in their belts, and to wait for orders. The guard for the night consisted of two captains' commands of 42 men and 4 non-commissioned officers each; and two subalterns' guards of twenty men and non-commissioned officers—the whole under the command of a field officer of the day.

The night was dark and cloudy: the moon rose late, and after midnight there was a drizzling rain. Many of the men appeared to be much dissatisfied: they were anxious for a battle, and the most ardent regretted, that they would have to return without one. The army generally had no expectation of an attack; but those who had experience in Indian affairs suspected some treachery. Colonel Daveiss was heard to say, he had no doubt but that an attack would be made before morning.

It was the constant practice of governor Harrison to call up the troops an hour before day, and keep them under arms till it was light. After 4 o'clock in the morning, the governor, general Wells, colonel Owen, and colonel Daveiss had all risen, and the governor was going to issue his orders for raising the army; when the treacherous Indians had crept up so near the sentries, as to hear them challenge when relieved. They intended to rush upon the sentries and kill them before they could fire: but one of them discovered an Indian creeping towards him in the grass, and fired. This was immediately followed by the Indian yell, and a desperate charge upon the left flank. The guard in that quarter gave way, and abandoned their officer without making any resistance. Capt. Barton's company of regulars and capt. Keiger's company of mounted riflemen, forming the left angle of the rear line, received the first onset. The fire there was excessive; but the troops who had lain on their arms, were immediately prepared to receive, and gallantry resist the furious savage assailants. The manner of the attack was calculated to discourage and terrify the men; yet as soon as they could be formed and posted, they maintained their ground with desperate valor, though but very few of them had ever before been in battle. The fires in the camp were extinguished immediately, as the light they afforded was more serviceable to the Indians than to our men.

As soon as the governor could mount his horse, he proceeded towards the point of attack, and finding the line much weakened there, he ordered two companies from the centre of the rear line to march up and form across the angle in the rear of Barton's and Keiger's companies. General Wells immediately proceeded to the right of his command; and colonel Owen, who was with him, was proceeding directly to the point of attack, when he was shot on his horse near the lines, and thus bravely fell among the first victims of savage perfidy. A heavy fire now commenced all along the left flank, upon the whole of the front and right flank, and on a part of the rear line.

In passing through the camp, towards the left of the front line, the governor met with colonel Daveiss and the dragoons. The colonel informed him that the Indians, concealed behind some trees near the line, were annoying the troops very severely in that quarter; and he requested permission to dislodge them, which was granted. He immediately called on the first division of his cavalry to follow him, but the order was not distinctly heard, and but few of his men charged with him. Among those who charged, were two young gentlemen who had gone with him from Kentucky, Messrs. Meade and Sanders, who were afterwards distinguished as captains in the United States' service. They had not proceeded far out of the lines, when Daveiss was mortally wounded by several balls and fell. His men stood by him, and repulsed the savages several times, till they succeeded in carrying him into camp.

In the mean time the attack on Spencer's and Warwick's companies on the right, became very severe. Captain Spencer and his lieutenants were all killed, and captain Warwick was mortally wounded. The governor in passing towards that flank, found captain Robb's company near the centre of the camp. They had been driven from their post; or rather, had fallen back without orders. He sent them to the aid of captain Spencer, where they fought very bravely, having seventeen men killed during the battle. Capt. Prescott's company of United States' infantry had filled up the vacancy caused by the retreat of Robb's company. Soon after colonel Daveiss was wounded, captain Snelling at the head of his company charged on the same Indians and dislodged them with considerable loss. The battle was now maintained on all sides with desperate valor. The Indians advanced and retreated by a rattling noise made with deer hoofs: they fought with enthusiasm, and seemed determined on victory or death.

As soon as day light appeared, captain Snelling's company, captain Posey's, under lieutenant Albright, and captain Scott's, were drawn from the front line, and Wilson's from the rear, and formed on the left flank; while Cook's and Baen's companies were ordered to the right. General Wells took command of the corps formed on the left, and with the aid of some dragoons, who were now mounted and commanded by captain Parke, made a successful charge on the enemy in that direction, driving them into an adjoining swamp through which the cavalry could not pursue them. At the same time Cook's and lieutenant Laribiè's companies, with the aid of the riflemen and militia on the right flank, charged on the Indians and put them to flight in that quarter, which terminated the battle.

During the time of this contest, the Prophet kept himself secure, on an adjacent eminence, singing a war song. He had told his followers, that the Great Spirit would render the army of the Americans unavailing, and that their bullets would not hurt the Indians, who would have light, while their enemies were involved in thick darkness. Soon after the battle commenced, he was informed that his men were falling. He told them to fight on, it would soon be as he had predicted, and then began to sing louder.

Colonel Boyd commanded as a brigadier general in this engagement; and the governor in his letter to the war department, speaks highly of him and his brigade, and of Clarke and Croghan who were his aids. Col. Decker is also commended for the good order in which he kept his command: and of general Wells, it is said, that he sustained the fame which he had acquired in almost every campaign since the first settlement of Kentucky.

The officers and soldiers generally, performed their duties well. They acted with a degree of coolness, bravery and good order, which was not to be expected from men unused to carnage, and in a situation so well calculated to produce terror and confusion. The fortune of war necessarily put it in the power of some officers and their men, at the expense of danger, wounds and death, to render more service and acquire more honor than others: but to speak of their particular merits, would be to detail again the operations of the conflict.

Of colonels Owen and Daveiss, the governor speaks in the highest terms. Owen joined him as a private in Keiger's company at fort Harrison, and accepted the place of volunteer aid. He had been a representative in the legislature of Kentucky. His character was that of a good citizen and a brave soldier. He left a wife and a large family of children, to add the poignancy of domestic grief to the public regret for his loss.

Colonel Daveiss also joined the army as a private, and was promoted on the recommendation of the officers of the dragoons; his conduct as their commander fully justified their choice. Never was there an officer possessed of more military ardor, nor more zeal to discharge all his duties with punctilious propriety: and never perhaps did any man, who had not been educated for the profession of arms, possess a richer fund of military information at his entrance on a military life. All that books and study could furnish, all the preparation the closet could make for the field, was his. He was a man of great talents—of genius—and indefatigable industry. In Kentucky he stood among the foremost in the profession of the law. His elocution was singularly attractive and forcible. Wit and energy, acuteness and originality of thought, were the characteristics of his eloquence. But as an orator he was very unequal. Some times he did not rise above mediocrity, whilst some of his happiest efforts were never surpassed in America—never perhaps in any age or country. Such at least was the opinion of men, whose talents, acquirements and taste, had qualified them to judge. He had much eccentricity in his manners and his dress. In his disposition he was generous; and in his friendship he was ardent. His person was about six feet high, well formed and robust—his countenance open and manly. He had acquired fortune and fame by his own exertions—neither his patrimony nor his education having been very ample. Being in the prime of life, and possessing great military ambition and acquirements, he was destined perhaps, had he lived, to become one of the first military characters of America. He died a few hours after the battle had closed. As soon as he was informed, that the Indians were repulsed, and the victory was complete, he observed, he could die satisfied—that he had fallen in defence of his country. He left a wife but no children.

Capt. Baen, who fell early in the action, had the character of an able officer and a brave soldier. Capt. Spencer was wounded in the head—he exhorted his men to fight on. He was then shot through both thighs and fell—still he continued to encourage his men. He was then raised up, and received a ball through his body which immediately killed him. His lieuts. M. Mahan and Berry, fell bravely encouraging their men. Warwick was shot through the body, and was taken to the surgery to be dressed: as soon as it was over, being a man of much bodily strength and still able to walk, he insisted on going back to his post, though it was evident, he had but a few hours to live. Col. White, formerly U. S. agent at the Saline, was also killed in the action. The whole number killed, with those who died soon of their wounds, was upwards of fifty: the wounded were about double that number. Governor Harrison himself narrowly escaped, the hair on his head being cut by a ball.

The Indians left 38 warriors dead on the field, and buried several others in the town, which with those who must have died of their wounds, would make their loss at least as great as that of the Americans. The troops under the command of governor Harrison of every description, amounted on the day before the battle, to something more than 800. The ordinary force, that had been at the Prophet's town, through the preceding summer, was about 450. But they were joined a few days before the action, by all the Kickapoos of the Prairie, and by many bands of Potawatamies from the Illinois river, and the St. Josephs of Lake Michigan. They estimated their number after the battle, to have been 600; but the traders who had a good opportunity of knowing, made them at least 800, and some as many as 1000. However it is certain, that no victory was ever before obtained over the northern Indians, where the numbers were any thing like equal. The number of killed too was greater, than was ever before known. It is their custom always to avoid a close action, and from their dexterity in hiding themselves, but few of them can be killed, even when they are pouring destruction into the ranks of their enemy. It is believed that there were not ten of them killed at St. Clair's defeat, and still fewer at Braddock's. At Tippecanoe, they rushed up to the bayonets of our men, and in one instance, related by capt. Snelling, an Indian adroitly put the bayonet of a soldier aside, and clove his head with his war club, an instrument on which there is fixed a triangular piece of iron, broad enough to project several inches from the wood. Their conduct on this occasion, so different from what it usually is, was attributed to the confidence of success, with which their prophet had inspired them, and to the distinguished bravery of the Winebago warriors.

The Indians did not determine to attack the American camp till late at night. The plan that was formed the evening before, was to meet the governor in council the next day, and agree to the terms he proposed. At the close of the council, the chiefs were to retire to the warriors, who were to be placed at a convenient distance. The governor was then to be killed by two Winebagoes, who had devoted themselves to certain death to accomplish this object. They were to loiter about the camp, after the council had broken up; and their killing the governor and raising the war whoop, was to be the signal for a general attack. The Indians were commanded by White Loon, Stone Eater, and Winemac, a Potawatamie chief, who had been with the governor on his march, and at fort Harrison, making great professions of friendship.

The 4th regiment was about 250 strong, and there were about 60 volunteers from Kentucky in the army. The rest of the troops were volunteers from the Indiana militia. Those from the neighbourhood of Vincennes had been trained for several years by the governor, and had become very expert in the manœuvres which he had adopted for fighting the Indians. The greater part of the territorial troops followed him as well from personal attachment as from a sense of duty. Indeed a greater degree of confidence and personal attachment has rarely been found in any army towards its commander, than existed in this; nor has there been many battles in which the dependence of the army on its leader was more distinctly felt. During the whole action the governor was constantly on the lines, and always repaired to the point which was most hardly pressed. The reinforcements drawn occasionally from the points most secure, were conducted by himself and formed on the spot, where their services were most wanted. The officers and men who believed that their ultimate success depended on his safety, warmly remonstrated against his so constantly exposing himself. Upon one occasion as he was approaching an angle of the line, against which the Indians were advancing with horrible yells, lieut. Emmerson of the dragoons seized the bridle of his horse, and earnestly entreated that he would not go there; but the governor putting spurs to his horse, pushed on to the point of attack, where the enemy were received with firmness and driven back.

The army remained in camp on the 7th and 8th November, to bury the dead and dress the wounded; and to make preparations for returning. During this time, gen. Wells was permitted with the mounted riflemen to visit the town, which he found evacuated by all, except a chief whose leg was broke. The general burnt their houses, destroyed their corn and brass kettles, and returned to camp unmolested. The town was well prepared for an attack, and no doubt but the Indians fully expected it; for they had determined to agree to no terms which could be offered. The wounds of the chief being dressed, and provision made for him, he was left with instructions to tell his companions, that if they would abandon the Prophet and return to their respective tribes, they should be forgiven.

On the 9th November the return of the army was commenced. It marched slowly, on account of the wounded, the difficulty of transportation, and some apprehensions of another attack. As the army had come up the river, a block house had been built on its bank, where some boats and heavy baggage had been left. The wounded were now put in the boats as the army returned, and were taken to fort Harrison and Vincennes by water. Capt. Snelling and his company were left at fort Harrison; and the governor arrived at Vincennes on the 18th, having been met and welcomed back by a concourse of two hundred citizens.

The battle of Tippecanoe has been the subject of much speculation, both as to its object, and the manner of its execution and final issue. Gov. Harrison was censured by some, for not making an attack upon the Indians, on the evening of the 6th November, and for not fortifying his camp with a breast work. It was erroneously said by some, that indulging a false security, he had suffered his camp to be surprised. He was also blamed by the friends of col. Daveiss, for directing him with his dragoons only, to dislodge the Indians, who were sheltered near the line, and doing much execution in safety. Many other complaints of less magnitude were also made by men, who were wise after the transaction was over. There were indeed more able generals in the United States, who could tell what ought to have been done after the battle was fought, than the governor had soldiers in his army to fight it. Col. Boyd who commanded the regulars, wishing to monopolize all the honor to himself and his regiment, concluded the governor had not sufficiently noticed him in his report; and he therefore made a separate communication to the war department; and also made many round assertions respecting the conduct of the militia—which was promptly explained, and the charges in general disproved by governor Harrison. Col. Boyd however had his partizans, and some of them still persist in attributing the salvation of the army to him; though all the troops, regulars as well as militia, with the exception of only three or four individuals, united in attributing the victory to the governor. Most of the officers publickly united in attesting his merits. Without intending to impeach col. Boyd with any dereliction of duty, we can positively aver, that he did not give a single order, nor perform a single act, that contributed in any perceptible way to the issue of the contest. All the arrangements and orders before the action and during its continuance, came direct from gov. Harrison.

After much altercation, by which the battle of Tippecanoe was fought over again and fully investigated, in all the public circles of the western country, the public opinion preponderated greatly in favor of the governor. All the material accusations of his enemies were disproved; and after all the testimony had been heard, the common opinion seemed to be, that the army had been conducted with prudence, and that the battle had been fought as well as it could have been by any general, considering the time and manner of the attack. If the governor had made the attack himself on the evening of the 6th, after a chief had informed him, that the Indians were desirous of an accommodation, and had sent a messenger three days before to meet him for that purpose, his conduct would have had the appearance of rashness and cruelty. His enemies and the opposition in general, would have vilified him and the executive as murderers, who had first provoked, and then massacred those *"innocent people"* in their own dwellings. Hence a regard for his own character and for the dictates of humanity required, that he should not make an attack while any prospect of accommodation remained. The principal error consisted in not fortifying his camp, when so near the enemy and so likely to be attacked; but this he excuses by stating, that the army had scarcely a sufficient number of axes to procure firewood. It is not the object of this history however to justify or condemn, but to relate facts correctly and leave the reader to judge for himself.

In December, the month after the battle, the legislature of Kentucky, on the motion of J. H. Hawkins esq. went into mourning for the loss of cols. Daveiss, Owen, and others, who had fallen at Tippecanoe; and in the same session, while this battle was the subject of much discussion, the following resolution, moved by J. J. Crittenden esq. was adopted with only two or three dissenting votes—"Resolved &c. That in the late campaign against the Indians on the Wabash, governor W. H. Harrison has, in the opinion of this legislature, behaved like a hero, a patriot, and a general; and that for his cool, deliberate, skillful and gallant conduct in the late battle of Tippecanoe, he well deserves the warmest thanks of the nation."

The veteran soldier, governor Charles Scott, approved this resolution, which at once gave tone to the popularity of Harrison, effectually turning the tide in his favor, and reducing the clamor of his enemies to private murmurs.

On the 22d November, the annual meeting of the Indians to receive their annuities took place at fort Wayne, where several of those who had fought in the battle, had the effrontery to present themselves and claim their respective portions. They had the address completely to deceive our Indian agent at that place, John Johnson esq. They represented, that the Prophet's party had him in confinement and were determined to kill him; that they blamed him for all their misfortunes; with many other deceptive stories, which induced Mr. Johnson to inform the government, that the Indians were all inclined for peace, and that no further hostilities should be committed against them. Yet at this very time, in most of the nations there assembled, a British faction was boiling to the brim, and ready to overflow on our devoted frontiers, whenever the perfidious British agents might think proper to increase the fire of their hostility. The Prophet instead of being in confinement, was at perfect liberty at Mississineway, a village about 70 miles southwest from fort Wayne. Previous to the battle, the Governor General of the Canadas, had given our government information, that some of the Indians were hostile to the U. States: but this was evidently done to remove suspicion, and to render the British more secure and successful in their intrigues with the savages.

The Indians, assembled at this place, were the chiefs and head men of the Delawares, Miamies, Potawatamies, and Shawanoese. The agent delivered them a speech, in which he explained to them, that the President wished to live in peace and friendship with them, and promised pardon to any of the hostile Indians who would lay down their arms. An answer was returned on the part of all the tribes present, by Black-Hoof a Shawanoe chief, in which they professed the strongest desire to live in peace and friendship with the United States. The profession was sincere on the part of the Shawanoese, and a great majority of the Delawares; but the Potawatamies and Miamies had no intention to be peaceable after receiving their annuities. The Little Turtle of the Miamies, now in the decline of life and of influence, was the strenuous advocate of peace, but the majority of his people followed the counsels of Tecumseh.

On the Wabash, after the battle of Tippecanoe, the Indians remained quiet, and in a few days many of them returned to their towns. Before Christmas, Stone Eater, with two Winebagoes, one Kickapoo, and a Piankishaw, came to fort Harrison, and delivered a talk to capt. Snelling, in which they professed much contrition for what had happened, with a desire to be at friendship. The same fellow had defended the cause of Tecumseh in a council at Vincennes, shortly before the march of the expedition; and he now wished to go there again, to make deceptious offers of friendship to the governor. He pretended, that the Prophet was despised, and had escaped from them to the Huron Indians. After receiving orders from governor Harrison, capt. Snelling permitted them to go on to Vincennes, where they renewed their professions of friendship, and promised to punish the Prophet, or deliver him to the U. States, as soon as they could catch him. They returned once more to their own country, determined not to commit hostilities again—till a favorable opportunity should occur.

During the winter 1811–12, a number of Indians from various tribes came to fort Harrison and Vincennes; but Tecumseh, the Prophet, and others known to be the most hostile, staid behind—hence little reliance could be placed on the professions of those who came in. After Tecumseh returned from the south, he visited fort Wayne, and was still haughty, and obstinate in the opinions he had embraced. He made bitter reproaches against Harrison; and at the same time had the presumption to demand ammunition from the commandant, which was refused him. He then said he would go to his British father, who would not deny him—he appeared thoughtful a while, then gave the war whoop and went off.

Early in the spring 1812, Tecumseh and his party began to put their threats into execution. Small parties began to commit depredations on the frontiers of the Indiana and Illinois Territories, and part of Ohio. Twenty scalps were taken in the Indiana alone before the 1st June. The people were thus compelled to protect themselves by going into forts along the frontiers. Volunteer companies of militia were organised, and the marauders were frequently pursued, but generally without success, as they fled immediately after doing mischief. Governor Harrison requested permission from the war department, to raise a mounted force and penetrate to their towns to chastise them. They occupied Tippecanoe, and had commenced raising corn. But the governor was not permitted to march against them, and the frontiers continued to suffer in every direction. Had a strong mounted army been permitted to scour the Wabash as far as Mississine-way, the settlements of the savages would have been completely destroyed, and their depredations would have ceased. The government appears to have pursued a mistaken policy of forbearance, lest the Indians should join the British in the expected war. But this forbearance only inspired them with a belief, that we were weak and pusillanimous, and tended to ensure their alliance with the British, had any thing been necessary for that purpose. By vigorous measures we might easily have beaten them into peaceable deportment and respect. Mr. Secretary Eustis of the war department, thought differently; and while he was attempting to soothe them with good words, they were laughing at his credulity. To maintain peace with an Indian, it is necessary to adopt his own principles and punish every aggression promptly, and thus convince him that you are a *man* and not a *squaw.*

In May governor Harrison made considerable arrangements towards organising a corps of mounted volunteers, to chastise the Indians on the Wabash. A company of mounted volunteers was raised in Franklin county, Ky. containing about 70 gentlemen of respectability, under the command of Capt. John Arnold, and Col. Anthony Crocket, who had distinguished themselves not only in the revolution, but in most of the Indian wars at an early period in Kentucky. This company remained at Vincennes only 10 days; during which time several parties made excursions up the Wabash, and protected the inhabitants while planting their corn. The governor being disappointed in receiving orders for the expedition from the war department, the company was dismissed; and all measures for offensive operations being abandoned, the Indians pursued their course of robbery and murder on the frontiers unresisted.

It will no doubt be interesting to the reader, to conclude the present chapter with the following letter from general Harrison to the war department, respecting the northwestern Indians. It contains, says the general, in a different letter to the secretary—"a sketch of the situation of each of the tribes bordering on this frontier; and an abstract of the policy, which has been pursued in the negotiations, which have been conducted by me, for the extinguishment of their title to lands, since the year 1801; and which you could only otherwise obtain, by wading through a most voluminous correspondence in the archives of your office." It will further explain the causes of Indian hostility, and enable the reader to understand more correctly many parts in the following history.

H. Q. Cincinnati, March 22nd, 1814.

Sir—The tribes of Indians upon this frontier and east of the Mississippi, with whom the U. S. have been connected by treaty, are the Wyandots, Delawares, Shawanoese, Miamies, Potawatamies, Ottawas, Chippewas, Piankashaws, Kaskaskias, and Sacs. All but the two last were in the confederacy, which carried on the former Indian war against the United States, that was terminated by the peace of Greenville. The Kaskaskias were parties to the treaty, but they had not been in the war. The Wyandots are admitted by the others to be the leading tribe. They hold the grand *calumet,* which unites them and kindles the council fire. This tribe is nearly equally divided between the *Crane* at Sandusky, who is the grand Sachem of the nation, and Walk-in-the-Water at Brownstown near Detroit. They claim the lands, bounded by the settlements of this state, southwardly and eastwardly; and by lake Erie, the Miami river, and the claim of the Shawanoese upon the Auglaize, a branch of the latter. They also claim the lands they live on near Detroit, but I am ignorant to what extent.

The Wyandots of Sandusky have adhered to us through the war. Their chief, the Crane, is a venerable, intelligent, and upright man. Within the tract of land claimed by the Wyandots a number of Senecas are settled. They broke off from their own tribe six or eight years ago, but receive a part of the annuity granted that tribe by the U. States, by sending a deputation for it to Buffaloe. The claim of the Wyandots to the lands they occupy, is not disputed, that I know of by any other tribe. Their residence on it however, is not of long standing, and the country was certainly once the property of the Miamies.

Passing westwardly from the Wyandots, we meet with the Shawanoese settlement at Stony creek, a branch of the big Miami, and at Wapockaunata on the Auglaize. These settlements were made immediately after the treaty of Greenville, and with the consent of the Miamies, whom I consider the real owners of those lands. The chiefs of this band of Shawanoese, Blackhoof, Wolf, and Lewis, are attached to us from principle as well as interest—they are all honest men.

The Miamies have their principal settlements at the forks of the Wabash, thirty miles from fort Wayne; and at Mississineway, thirty miles lower down. A band of them under the name of Weas, have resided on the Wabash sixty miles above Vincennes; and another under the Turtle on Eel river, a branch of the Wabash, twenty miles northwest of fort Wayne. By an artifice of the Little Turtle, these three bands were passed on general Wayne as distinct tribes, and an annuity was granted to each. The Eel river and Weas however to this day call themselves Miamies, and are recognised as such by the Mississineway band. The Miamies, Manmees, or Tewicktovies, are the undoubted proprietors of all that beautiful country which is watered by the Wabash and its branches; and there is as little doubt, that their claim extended at least as far east as the Scioto. They have no tradition of removing from any other quarter of the country; whereas all the neighboring tribes, the Piankishaws, excepted, who are a branch of the Miamies, are either intruders upon them, or have been permitted to settle in their country. The Wyandots emigrated first from lake Ontario, and subsequently from lake Huron—the Delawares, from Pennsylvania and Maryland—the Shawanoese from Georgia—the Kickapoos and Potawatamies from the country between lake Michigan and the Mississippi—and the Ottawas and Chippewas from the peninsula formed by the lakes Michigan, Huron, and St. Clair, and the streight connecting the latter with Erie. The claims of the Miamies were bounded on the north and west by those of the Illinois confederacy, consisting originally of five tribes, called Kaskaskias, Cahokias, Peorians, Michiganians, and Temarois, speaking the Miami language, and, no doubt branches of that nation.

When I was first appointed governor of Indiana Territory, these once powerful tribes were reduced to about thirty warriors, of whom twenty-five were Kaskaskias, four Peorians, and a single Michiganian. There was an individual lately alive at St. Louis, who saw the enumeration made of them by the Jesuits in the year 1743, making the number of their warriors four thousand. A furious war between them and the Sacs and Kickapoos, reduced them to that miserable remnant, which had taken refuge amongst the white people of the towns of Kaskaskia and St. Genevieve. The Kickapoos had fixed their principal village at Peoria, upon the south bank of the Illinois river, whilst the Sacs remained masters of the country to the north.

During the war of our revolution, the Miamies had invited the Kickapoos into their country to assist them against the whites, and a considerable village was formed by that tribe on the Vermillion river near its junction with the Wabash. After the treaty of Greenville, the Delawares had with the approbation of the Miamies, removed from the mouth of the Auglaize to the head waters of White river, a large branch of the Wabash—and the Potawatamies without their consent had formed two villages upon the latter river, one at Tippecanoe, and the other at Chippoy twenty-five miles below.

The Piankishaws lived in the neighbourhood of Vincennes, which was their ancient village, and claimed the lands to the mouth of the Wabash, and to the north and west as far as the Kaskaskians claimed. Such was the situation of the tribes, when I received the instructions of President Jefferson, shortly after his first election, to make efforts for extinguishing the Indian claims upon the Ohio, below the mouth of the Kentucky river, and to such other tracts as were necessary to connect and consolidate our settlements. It was at once determined, that the community of interests in the lands amongst the Indian tribes, which seemed to be recognised by the treaty of Greenville, should be objected to; and that each individual tribe should be protected in every claim that should appear to be founded in reason and justice. But it was also determined, that as a measure of policy and liberality, such tribes as lived upon any tract of land which it would be desirable to purchase, should receive a portion of the compensation, although the title might be exclusively in another tribe. Upon this principle the Delawares, Shawanoese, Potawatamies, and Kickapoos were admitted as parties to several of the treaties. Care was taken however, to place the title to such tracts as it might be desirable to purchase hereafter, upon a footing that would facilitate the procuring of them, by getting the tribes who had no claim themselves, and who might probably interfere, to recognise the titles of those who were ascertained to possess them.

This was particularly the case with regard to the lands watered by the Wabash, which were declared to be the property of the Miamies, with the exception of the tract occupied by the Delawares on White river, which was to be considered the joint property of them and the Miamies. This arrangement was very much disliked by Tecumseh, and the banditti that he had assembled at Tippecanoe. He complained loudly, as well of the sales that had been made, as of the principle of considering a particular tribe as the exclusive proprietors of any part of the country, which he said the Great Spirit had given to all his red children. Besides the disaffected amongst the neighboring tribes, he had brought together a considerable number of Winebagoes and Folsovoins from the neighborhood of Green Bay, Sacs from the Mississippi, and some Ottawas and Chippewas from Abercrosh on lake Michigan. These people were better pleased with the climate and country of the Wabash, than with that they had left.

The Miamies resisted the pretensions of Tecumseh and his followers for some time, but a system of terror was adopted, and the young men were seduced by eternally placing before them a picture of labor, and restriction as to hunting, to which the system adopted would inevitably lead. The Potawatamies and other tribes inhabiting the Illinois river and south of lake Michigan, had been for a long time approaching gradually towards the Wabash. Their country, which was never abundantly stocked with game, was latterly almost exhausted of it. The fertile regions of the Wabash still afforded it. It was represented, that the progressive settlements of the whites upon that river, would soon deprive them of their only resource, and indeed would force the Indians of that river upon them, who were already half starved.

It is a fact, that for many years the current of emigration, as to the tribes east of the Mississippi, has been from north to south. This is owing to two causes: the diminution of those animals from which the Indians procure their support; and the pressure of the two great tribes, the Chippewas and Sioux to the north and west. So long ago as the treaty of Greenville, the Potawatamies gave notice to the Miamies, that they intended to settle upon the Wabash. They made no pretensions to the country, and their only excuse for the intended aggression, was that "they were tired of eating fish, and wanted meat." It has been already observed that the Sacs had extended themselves to the Illinois river, and that the settlement of the Kickapoos at the Peorias was of modern date. Previously to the commencement of the present war, a considerable number had joined their brethren upon the Wabash. The Tawas from the Des Moins river have twice made attempts to get a footing there.

From these facts it will be seen, that it will be nearly impossible to get the Indians south of the Wabash to go beyond the Illinois river. The subject of providing an outlet to such of the tribes as it might be desirable to remove, has been under consideration for many years. There is but one. It was long since discovered by the Indians themselves, and but for the humane policy, which has been pursued by our government, the Delawares, Kickapoos, and Shawanoese would long since have been out of our way. The country claimed by the Osages abounds with every thing that is desirable to a savage. The Indians of the tribes above mentioned have occasionally intruded upon them—a war was the consequence, which would soon have given a sufficient opening for emigration. But our government interfered and obliged the hostile tribes to make peace.

I was afterwards instructed to endeavour to get the Delawares to join that part of their tribe, which is settled on the west side of the Mississippi near Cape Girardeau. The attempt was unsuccessful at the time. I have no doubt however, that they could be prevailed on to move; but it ought not in my opinion to be attempted in a general council of the tribes.

The question of the title to the lands south of the Wabash has been thoroughly examined: every opportunity was afforded to Tecumseh and his party to exhibit their pretensions, and they were found to rest upon no other basis, than that of their being the common property of all the Indians. The Potawatamies and Kickapoos have unequivocally acknowledged the Miami and Delaware title. The latter as I before observed can I think be induced to remove. It may take a year or eighteen months to effect it. The Miamies will not be in our way. They are a poor, miserable, drunken set, diminishing every year. Becoming too lazy to hunt, they feel the advantage of their annuity. The fear of the other Indians has alone prevented them from selling their whole claim to the United States; and as soon as there is peace, or the British can no longer intrigue, they will sell. I know not what inducements can be held out to the Wyandots to remove; they were not formerly under my superintendence, but I am persuaded that a general council would not be the place to attempt it.

I HAVE THE HONOR &C. &C.

WM. H. HARRISON.

HON. J. ARMSTRONG,

SECRETARY OF WAR.

From this able and interesting review of Indian settlements, rights, and politics—the result of an intimacy, for 20 years, with those affairs—we are enabled to judge of the justice of the cause advocated by Tecumseh. His scheme of policy was certainly well calculated to secure and promote the best interests of the Indians as savages; but to render it just in theory, and efficient in practice, it was necessary that it should receive the undivided sanction and support of all the tribes concerned. This, all the talents and persevering industry of Tecumseh, aided by the intrigues and bribes of the British, were unable to effect. To form a confederacy out of so many and such various tribes, required a degree of civilisation to which the Indians had not attained. If such a union were actually effected, it is improbable that any purchase of lands could ever afterwards be accomplished by the United States. The consent of all the tribes in a general council, to the cession of any part of their country, was considered by the advocates of the scheme as a thing unattainable. On the contrary, while no such confederacy existed *in fact,* had our government acknowledged the principle of Tecumseh, that a community of interest in their lands was a matter of *natural right,* we should have been subjected to great inconvenience in the extension of our settlements. As soon as one tribe had sold us a parcel of land, other hordes might settle on it in succession, and by the mere temporary occupancy of the soil, compel our government to purchase it again twenty times over.

It is doubtless true, that scarcely any tribe has lands appropriated to itself by exact and special boundaries. Its villages and the lands immediately around them, may be considered as clearly its exclusive property; but the remote wilderness, between the more distant settlements of the different tribes, is not partitioned with any precision, except where nature may have done it, by a water course or some such striking limit. The wandering nature of their occupation renders a more exact appropriation impracticable. This vagueness of their claims however, is no foundation for the doctrine of a common property. The Miamies appear to have been the original occupants and real owners of all the lands northwest of the Ohio; but other tribes have gradually intruded, and formed settlements with or without their consent, till they are at last reduced to narrow limits and insignificance themselves.

CHAPTER VII

Colonel Richard M. Johnson's mounted regiment; with various other incidents.

In the early part of the campaign of 1812, colonel R. M. Johnson had personally witnessed the great efficiency and usefulness of mounted riflemen, employed against the Indians—and was hence induced, when he returned to congress, to lay before the war department, a plan for a mounted expedition against the Indians during the ensuing winter. The object of the expedition, was to destroy the subsistence of the Indians and otherwise disable them, so as to prevent their committing depredations in the spring to revenge the destruction of their villages on the Wabash and Elk Hart rivers. The good effect to be expected from its execution were more distinctly stated to be— security to the northwestern frontiers from fort Wayne to the Mississippi—safety to the convoys of provisions for the northwestern army, when its force was diminished in the spring—and the neutrality of the savages in future, from the powerful impression that would be made on their fears. It was believed, that the winter season would favor the enterprise, by enabling the horsemen, while snow was on the ground and the leaves off the bushes, to hunt up and destroy the sculking Indians.

The force to be employed and its organization, were proposed to be two regiments, including in each eight companies of eighty privates, and making altogether 1280 men. This was deemed amply sufficient to traverse the whole Indian country, from fort Wayne past the lower end of lake Michigan, round by the Illinois river, and back to the Ohio near Louisville; and to disperse and destroy all the tribes of Indians and their resources to be found within that compass. The proposition was also communicated by colonel Johnson to the governor of Kentucky, and was submitted by the secretary of war to general Harrison, in a letter dated 26th December, 1812, from which the following is an extract. "The President has it in contemplation, to set on foot an expedition from Kentucky of about 1000 mounted men, to pass by fort Wayne, the lower end of lake Michigan, and round by the Illinois back to the Ohio near Louisville, for the purpose of scouring that country, destroying the provisions collected in the Indian villages, scourging the Indians themselves, and disabling them from interfering with your operations. It is expected that this expedition will commence in February; and it will terminate in a few weeks. I give you the information, that you may take it into consideration in the estimate of those arrangements, you may find it necessary to make, for carrying into effect the objects of the government. I send you a copy of the proposed plan, on which I wish to hear from you without delay. You will particularly state, whether you can effect these objects in the manner which is suggested, by adequate portions of the force now in the field; and in that case, whether it will be better to suspend the movement of this force until the spring." *Monroe.*

General Harrison had already anticipated in part, the objects of the proposed expedition, by sending colonel Campbell to Mississiniway; and was dissuaded by that experiment from attempting any thing more extensive during the winter. It was also already so late in the season, that the hard freezing would be over, before the proposed force could be raised and marched through the Indian country; and its progress would therefore be arrested by impassable swamps during the wet weather in the spring. The general intended however to follow up the blow on the Mississiniway, by striking at the main village farther down that river, and had visited Chillicothe to engage governor Meigs to organize a new corps of mounted men, to act with the dragoons then in service. The governor promptly cooperated in the measure; but on ascertaining the situation of the dragoons, they were found to be so frost bitten, and their horses so reduced, that they were wholly unfit for farther service during the winter; and the intended stroke was afterwards abandoned. The following are the views of general Harrison, respecting the proposition of colonel Johnson, which are extracted from letters to the war department of the 4th and 8th January. "I am sorry not to be able to agree with my friend, colonel Johnson, upon the propriety of the contemplated mounted expedition. An expedition of this kind directed against a particular town will probably succeed. The Indian towns cannot be surprised in succession, as they give the alarm from one to the other with more rapidity than our troops can move. In the months of February, March, and April, the towns are all abandoned. The men are hunting, and the women and children, particularly to the north of the Wabash, are scattered about making sugar. The corn is in that season universally hid in small parcels in the earth, and could not be found. There are no considerable villages in that direction. Those that are there, are composed of bark huts, which the Indians do not care for, and which during the winter are entirely empty. The detachment might pass through the whole extent of country to be scoured, without seeing an Indian, except at the first town they struck, and it is more than probable, that they would find *it* empty. But the expedition is impracticable to the extent proposed. The horses, if not the men, would perish. The horses that are now to be found, are not like those of the early settlers, and such as the Indians and traders now have. They have been accustomed to corn, and must have it. Colonel Campbell went but 70 or 80 miles from the frontiers, and the greater part of his horses could scarcely be brought in. Such an expedition in the summer and fall would be highly advantageous, because the Indians are then at their towns, and their corn can be destroyed. An attack upon a particular town in the winter, when the inhabitants are at it, as we know they are at Mississiniway, and which is so near as to enable the detachment to reach it without killing their horses, is not only practicable, but if there is snow on the ground is perhaps the most favorable."

January 8th—The expedition contemplated from Kentucky may supercede the necessity of that which I was proposing. But I am still of the opinion given in my last, that no attempt on the enemy beyond Mississiniway would be attended with any advantage, if it did not end in the destruction of the detachment employed to execute it. I repeat that the Indians are not at this season to be found in their towns, that they invariably take their families with them upon their hunting excursions, and that their provisions are always buried in small parcels, each family hiding its own."

In consequence of these suggestions, the winter expedition was abandoned, and the attention of the government was directed to the organization of a mounted corps for the spring. Accordingly general Armstrong who was now secretary of war, gave the following authority to colonel Johnson on the 26th of February, 1813. "Sir, you are hereby authorized to organize and hold in readiness, a regiment of mounted volunteers—the organization as to the number of officers and men, to be conformable to the military establishment of the United States. The governor of the state of Kentucky will be required to commission the officers when selected, to serve four months after being called into actual service; and six months if required by the United States—the pay of officers and men to commence from the actual service and march of the corps, under the direction of the war department. After marching orders, the contractors and commissaries' agents in the different districts through which it passes, will supply the regiment with forage for the horses, and provision for the men, if required so to do. The keepers of military stores, will also furnish said corps with ammunition on regular returns of the effective force of the regiment. If any difficulty arises as to rank, the commanding general will settle the same, after the corps shall have reached its place of destination. *Armstrong.*

As soon as congress adjourned, colonel Johnson hastened to Kentucky with feelings of indignation at the cruelties inflicted on his fellow citizens at the river Raisin; and on the 22nd of March published the above authority, accompanied by an address on the subject of raising the men, in which he appealed to the patriotism of the citizens, and detailed the terms, equipments, and prospects of the service. He immediately selected individuals to raise companies in different parts of the state—the platoon and other officers to be chosen by the men who enroled themselves, as this mode was deemed most consistent with the principle of volunteering. The service was exactly of that kind, which suited the habits and views of the Kentuckians; and as much zeal to avenge the wrongs they had endured, was now prevalent among the people, the regiment was soon filled, and in a few weeks was ready to take the field, although the personal enemies of colonel Johnson, and the opposers of the administration, made considerable opposition to the measure, which they represented as an irregular and unconstitutional exercise of authority. The organization was submitted to governor Shelby, who aided in procuring the necessary funds to enable the colonel to accommodate his men. Captain James Johnson, his brother, a man of sterling merit and undaunted bravery, received the appointment of lieutenant colonel of the regiment—the honorable Samuel M'Kee, a representative in congress, and colonel Duval Payne, were selected as majors. Mr. M'Kee declined the appointment, and colonel D. Thompson accepted it. They were all men of high standing and genuine patriots.

After the discharge of the regiment under Cox and Caldwell, the public attention was fixed on the mounted regiment, as the only efficient corps in Kentucky, by which fort Meigs could be relieved and the frontiers protected; and colonel Johnson, young, ardent and enterprising, anxiously wished for a theatre, on which he might distinguish himself in the cause of his country; and was much pleased, soon after the intelligence of the siege had arrived, to receive a letter from governor Shelby from which the following are extracts. "The information received from various sources, of an attack on fort Meigs, by a large body of the British and Indians, justifies a belief, that a reinforcement ought to be sent to the aid of general Harrison. The enemy can be met only by horsemen; and as you have a regiment of mounted infantry nearly organised, the crisis will in my opinion justify its immediate march to the scene of operations. You have my entire approbation and sanction to do so. I will in conformity with the wishes of the secretary of war, expressed in his order of the 26th February, under which the regiment was raised, issue commissions to the officers; and as far as depends on the executive of this state, the men who march under you shall be allowed tours of duty, according to the time they may be in service. Captains Whitaker, Coleman, and Payne, have each raised a company of cavalry, and reported themselves for service this season. As I do not expect a call for cavalry, they have my approbation to join your regiment, and in case they do so, will be commissioned accordingly."

"The officers and men must look to the general government alone for a compensation for their services." *Shelby.*

Upon the authority of the above letter, colonel Johnson immediately issued an order for his regiment to assemble. The regiment of mounted volunteers was organised under the authority of the war department, to await its call, or to meet any crisis which might involve the honor, the rights and the safety of the country. "That crisis has arrived. Fort Meigs is attacked. The northwestern army is surrounded by the enemy, and under the command of general Harrison is nobly defending the cause of the country against a combined enemy, the British and Indians. They will maintain their ground till relieved. The intermediate garrisons are also in imminent danger, and may fall a bleeding sacrifice to savage cruelty, unless timely reinforced. The frontiers may be deluged in blood. The mounted regiment will present a shield to the defenceless; and united with the forces now marching, and the Ohio volunteers for the same purpose, will drive the enemy from our soil. Therefore on Thursday the 20th of May, the regiment will rendezvous at the Great Crossings in Scott county, except the companies &c. which will rendezvous on the 22d at Newport;—at which place, the whole corps will draw arms, ammunition &c." *R. M. Johnson.*

In pursuance of this order, the companies of captains Stucker, M'Afee, Davidson, Ellison, and Combs, and several small fractions, rendezvoused in Scott on the 20th; and captains Matson, Coleman, Payne, Warfield and Craig met at Newport on the 22d. As the former companies were marching on the 21st towards Newport, they met John T. Johnson esq. volunteer aid to general Harrison, with the following general order. "Head Quarters, Franklinton, May 16th, 1813. The commanding general has observed with the warmest gratitude, the astonishing exertions, which have been made by his excellency governor Meigs, and the generals and other militia officers of this state, in collecting and equipping a body of troops for the relief of camp Meigs. But the efforts of these men would have been unavailing, had they not been seconded by the patriotic ardor of every description of citizens, which has induced them to leave their homes, at a most critical season of the year, regardless of every consideration, but that of rendering service to their country. The general found the road from Lower Sandusky to this place literally covered with men, and amongst them many who had shared in the toils and dangers of the revolutionary war, and on whom of course there existed no legal claims for military services. The general has every reason to believe, that similar efforts have been made in Kentucky. He offers to all these brave men from both states, his sincere acknowledgments; and is happy to inform them, that there is at present no necessity for their longer continuance in the field. The enemy has fled with precipitation from camp Meigs, and that is in a much better situation to resist an attack, than when the last siege was commenced.

"BY ORDER OF THE GENERAL,

"R. GRAHAM, *AID.*"

This order excited considerable murmurs in the state of Ohio. The volunteers had marched under the expectation of being led immediately against the enemy; and they reflected on general Harrison and the government for being too tardy in their movements. Those who understood the situation of the country, and the difficulty of supplying a large army through a swampy wilderness of 140 miles in extent, were however satisfied that nothing better could be done. There being a necessity in the first instance for obtaining the command of the lake, for which the greatest exertions were making, it would have been extravagant folly to retain so large a mounted force in service at fort Meigs, or to have led them through the wilderness against the enemy.

When the order met the front companies in Johnson's regiment, it was understood as disbanding that regiment also, and produced much depression and chagrin among the men. Some of the companies turned back a few miles, and at length a halt was called till colonel Johnson should arrive, who had been detained a few hours in the rear. When he came up, he did not consider the order as even discharging the regiment from present service, and determined to march on at least, till he received the positive orders of general Harrison on that subject. This determination restored harmony and cheerfulness to the ranks, and the march was resumed with new devotion to their leader.

Colonel Johnson went on before them to Newport, to organize the balance of the regiment, and receive orders from general Harrison, who had returned to Cincinnati on a visit to his family: and on the next day, these companies were ordered by the lieutenant colonel to proceed by way of the north bend of Ohio river, above the mouth of the Big Miami, where they arrived on the 24th, and received information, that the regiment was received into the service of the United States by general Harrison. Their colonel was ordered by general Harrison to take command of fort Wayne and the posts on the Auglaize, to scour the northwestern frontiers, to make incursions into the country of the Indians, and if possible to cut off small parties, who might infest the forts, or be marching from the Illinois and Wabash towards Malden and Detroit; and never to remain at one place more than three days. As the regiment would be employed in this manner for some time, before the expedition against Malden could be put in motion, colonel Johnson now gave his captains permission to send back an officer from each company, to raise more men. They were to meet the regiment at fort Winchester on the 18th of June, at which time it was believed the fleet would certainly have command of the lake. Three lieutenants returned on this recruiting service, and the balance then crossed the river and marched up the Big Miami on the 26th. They arrived and formed a junction with the other part of the regiment, on the 28th at Dayton.

The organization of the regiment was here finally completed as follows:

R. M. Johnson, colonel. James Johnson lieutenant colonel.

1st battalion. Duval Payne major. R. B. M'Afee, Richard Matson, Jacob Elliston, Benjamin Warfield, John Payne, (cavalry) Elijah Craig, captains.

2nd battalion. David Thompson, major. Jacob Stucker, James Davidson, S. R. Combs, W. M. Price, James Coleman, captains.

Staff. Jeremiah Kertly, adjutant. B. S. Chambers, quarter master. Samuel Theobalds, judge advocate. L. Dickinson, sergeant major.

James Suggett, chaplain, and major of the spies. L. Sandford, quarter master sergeant. Afterwards was added, doctor Ewing, surgeon—doctors Coburn and Richardson, surgeon's mates.

From this place the regiment proceeded in a few days towards St. Marys, and arrived there on the 1st of June. This march was very much incommoded by high waters and bad roads. At this season of the year there are marshes and quagmires in every quarter of the country, which are extremely difficult to pass. As soon as the troops had all arrived, the colonel issued a general order, establishing the police of the camp, requiring the companies to be regularly mustered and drilled, and appointing a day for their inspection.

From St. Marys colonel Johnson went to the village of Wopogliconata on the Auglaize, to procure some Shawanoe Indians to act as guides and spies. During his absence, the regiment was employed in training under the superintendence of the lieutenant colonel, and in making other necessary arrangements for their future service. In a few days the colonel returned with 12 or 13 Indians, among whom was the celebrated Anthony Shane, a half blood whose father was a Frenchman. In his integrity, and fidelity to our cause, the utmost confidence was placed. He had been an active partizan in the war against general Wayne; but since the treaty of Greenville he had become unalterably attached to the Americans.

An order of march and battle was now issued, and it was enjoined on the officers to understand it as soon as possible, and be able to execute it correctly. It is certainly the duty of every general, or commandant of an independent corps, to give his men an order of battle as early as possible after taking the field, which may afterwards be varied as circumstances may require. The officers and men of every army, ought to be well acquainted with the manner of forming and with the duty of each corps, previous to their being led into action. It will tend to preserve them from confusion and consequent disaster. Hence the general who fails entirely to give an order of battle, or who defers it until a few minutes before a battle, is guilty of the most criminal neglect. This is particularly the case in militia, and other raw troops, where the state of discipline does not enable the commander with facility and certitude, to throw his army on any emergency into the necessary form. Colonel Johnson seemed to be well apprised of its importance, and faithfully discharged his duty in this respect.

On the 5th the regiment marched towards fort Wayne, with a view to protect some boats loaded with flour and bacon, which had been sent down the St. Marys by general Wingate of the Ohio militia, who was stationed with a small guard at St. Marys. When the troops arrived at a handsome prairie about half way to Shane's crossing, they were halted and practised in forming the line of battle, till every man was well acquainted with his place and his particular duties. The men were also abundantly supplied with ammunition, and well prepared for action.

A very heavy rain having fallen to-day, the St. Marys was found impassable when the regiment arrived at Shane's crossing in the evening. On the next day by felling trees into it from both banks, a rude bridge was constructed, over which the men passed with their baggage, while their horses were crossed by swimming. The rest of the way to fort Wayne was found very difficult, all the flats and marshes being covered with water, and the roads very miry. They arrived on the evening of the 7th, and found that all the boats had reached the fort in safety but one, which had struck on a bar in sight of the fort. While the boatmen were endeavoring to get her off, a party of Indians fired on and killed two of them, and the other in attempting to swim over the river was drowned. Colonel Johnson with his staff and a few men had just arrived at the fort and stript their horses. As soon as they could make ready they mounted and crossed to the boat. The Indians fired upon the advance and then retreated. The spies being of opinion, that the party of Indians was much stronger, than that with the colonel, he deferred the pursuit till the regiment all arrived. He then took a strong detachment and pursued them about ten miles, when a rainy night coming on, he returned to the fort. Next morning the 8th, a council of officers was held, which determined, after collecting all the information they could from the spies, to make an excursion towards the southeast end of lake Michigan, and visit the Indian villages in that direction. In the evening the regiment deposited their heavy baggage in the fort, drew ten days provision, and crossed the St. Marys to encamp in the forks. This stream was now just beginning to rise at the fort, though on the evening of the 5th it had been at the top of its banks at Shane's crossing, but 40 miles from its mouth by land. Hence if we suppose the current to run three miles an hour, which is near the truth, the distance by water would be upwards of 200 miles, so extremely crooked is the course of the river.

On the next day, the regiment marched early on the trail of the Indians, which led towards the village of Five Medals, that had been destroyed last year, but which it was believed had been rebuilt. They had marched forty miles before night, and the colonel intended after grazing and resting a while, to resume the march and attack that village at daylight in the morning. But a heavy rain came on, and prevented him from executing this plan. In the morning they proceeded, and after encountering many obstacles in crossing high waters and marshes, they arrived at the Elkhart river, before it had risen so as to be impassable, and in half an hour afterwards the village of Five Medals was again surrounded. But it was not occupied at present. Colonel Johnson now determined to visit a town called Paravash on the other side of the St. Josephs of the lake; and in the morning of the 11th, the line of march was resumed in that direction; but on arriving at the St. Josephs it was found to be impassable, and the intention of reaching that place was abandoned. The colonel then determined to advance with rapidity to the White Pigeon's town, at which place he arrived in the afternoon, having seen a few Indians on his route, who made their escape in a canoe over a stream which the horsemen could not pass. The village which had been the most considerable in that region of the country, was also unoccupied at present. The main trace of the Indians, from Chicago and the Illinois country to Detroit, passes through this town. It appeared to have been but little travelled this spring. The regiment remained encamped near it till next day; and as colonel Johnson had now fulfilled his instructions to visit this trace, and intercept the enemy if now making use of it; and as the provisions of the troops had been much damaged by the rain, he determined to return to fort Wayne. There is an Indian path leading directly to that place from the village, on which the regiment returned, and reached the fort on the 14th, having performed a march of near 200 miles, with heavy rains every day, and in a region never before traversed by so large a force of Americans. By this excursion, our knowledge of the country was enlarged, and it was ascertained that all the Indians in the British service, who had been at the siege of fort Meigs, were still kept in the vicinity of Malden, as no considerable body of them had returned to their country.

In the mean time the savages were committing many depredations on the Illinois and Missouri territories, where a skirmishing warfare was carried on, very much to the annoyance of the frontier settlers. It would be too tedious to enter on a detail of all the little transactions of this kind in that quarter: we shall only mention a few of the most prominent incidents. Much apprehension was entertained, that all the Indians on the Missouri and Mississippi rivers would be induced by the intrigues of the British and Tecumseh to join in the general confederacy against us. In April the Mississippi Indians invested fort Madison, though many of the tribes professed to be friendly. They did but little execution there, and soon afterwards formally besieged fort Mason, a post which had been established on the Mississippi by governor Howard, about 80 miles above St. Louis. Captain Boone who commanded a company of rangers succeeded in getting into the fort, by which it was rendered completely secure against their forces. They remained before it for 8 or 10 days, and succeeded once in setting fire to some of the cabins, which were burnt down, and at the same time a violent assault was made on the fort, which was gallantly repulsed by the garrison without much loss.

A war with the powerful Osage nation was now apprehended. During the winter governor Howard had been absent at the City of Washington, and before his return authority had been given to raise three companies of rangers in his territory. This being known to the Osage Indians, they applied to Mr. secretary Bates for permission to furnish one of the companies, which was granted; and on their appearance at St. Louis, they were supplied with arms and ammunition for the service. But when the governor returned he disapproved of employing the Indians in any way, and sent them home. Anxious to engage in the war, they shewed evident symptoms of displeasure at this treatment, and said they would have satisfaction of the Americans for it. It was hence supposed, that they also would be induced to attack the frontiers. Fort Madison had already been evacuated, as too remote from the settlements to be maintained; and under the apprehension of an attack from the Osages, the officers at fort Mason held a council, and determined to abandon that place also, and retire to fort Howard, within 40 miles of St. Louis; which they effected about the 1st of May. A chain of posts was then established from fort Howard across the country to the Missouri; and about the same time the governor received the appointment of brigadier general in the army of the United States, and was succeeded in the former office by William Clarke esq. who had explored the country westward to the Pacific ocean with captain Lewis.

Early in the spring, the celebrated Robert Dickson, a British trader and emissary, had been sent among the Indians on the frontiers of those territories, to excite them to war, and raise recruits for the service under Procter and Tecumseh. He visited all the tribes on the Illinois and Mississippi rivers from Prairie de Chien to Green bay, and in the neighborhood of Chicago, at which place a general rendezvous was to be held, professedly for the purpose of descending the Illinois river, and attacking that territory. By making great promises of presents and plunder, he succeeded in collecting nearly one thousand warriors at Chicago early in June; and after exciting considerable alarm in the mind of governor Edwards of the Illinois territory, he led them in separate detachments towards Detroit, along the main trace which passes by the White Pigeon's town. They passed that village but a few days after the regiment of colonel Johnson had left it; by which the latter missed a glorious opportunity to meet the enemy and distinguish themselves.

The followers of Dickson were a horde of as wild and cruel savages as ever disgraced human nature. They were the most worthless and abandoned desperadoes from all the tribes he had visited; and were worthy to be the accomplices of the humane and honorable Procter, by whom Dickson had been sent to collect them. Among the chiefs who commanded them, was the great Potawatamie, *Mai-Pock,* a monster who was distinguished by a girdle, sewed full of human scalps, which he wore round his waist, and strings of bear's claws and the bills of owls and hawks, round his ancles—as the trophies of his prowess in arms, and as a terror to his enemies. It is remarkable that after these savages joined the British standard, to combat for the "defender of the faith," victory never again declared for the allies in the northwest. For the cruelties they had already committed, and those which were threatened by this inhuman association, a just God frowned indignant on all their subsequent operations.

It is a fact, that in July and August, the British by their unparalleled exertions had collected nearly all the warriors of the north and northwest into the neighborhood of Malden, where they were regularly supplied with rations by their employers. Their camps extended from Brownstown to Detroit, besides a number on the east side of the straight. As they neither hunted nor labored for their subsistence, their support was a heavy burthen on the British contractors and commissaries. The number of warriors was about 2,500—but including the subsistence of the women and children they had brought with them, the amount of rations issued exceeded seven thousand. As the British expected an attack from the American army, and as this assemblage of savages constituted their main force, it was necessary to keep them well supplied with the means of subsistence and the munitions of war. Dickson who had been so instrumental in collecting this horde of barbarians was a Scotchman by birth, and certainly proved his loyalty, and deserved well of his employers, by his great zeal, industry and address in this service.

After the return of the mounted regiment to fort Wayne, they remained there a few days and then proceeded down the river with an escort of provisions to fort Winchester. A sufficient number of men were put in the boats containing the provisions to man them well, and the balance of the men proceeded down the road opened by Winchester on the north side of the Miami, encamping every night with the boats. After they had arrived at fort Winchester, colonel Johnson received a dispatch from general Harrison, recommending him to make an attack on the enemy at Raisin and Brownstown. Although the general only recommended this movement, yet it was done in such a way, that colonel Johnson as a gallant soldier felt himself bound to execute it. General Harrison had just heard of the success of our arms against the enemy below, and that general Procter was ordered in that direction to assist in repelling the invaders. Believing that Procter had left Malden with a considerable portion of his force, the general supposed that an excellent opportunity had offered, to attack his savage allies in the Michigan Territory, by a coup de main with the mounted regiment. Colonel Johnson however was unable to execute this plan immediately. His horses were so exhausted by their late expedition, that some rest was necessary before they could perform another march so difficult as that to Brownstown. A considerable detachment of his men were also engaged in escorting provisions from St. Marys, and could not be collected for this service immediately. A strong reinforcement was also daily expected from Kentucky, the expedition was therefore deferred for a few days.

The service recommended by the general was considered extremely hazardous. For a mounted regiment about 700 strong, with worndown horses destitute of forage, to march at least 100 miles through swamps and marshes, and over difficult rivers, with guides not very well acquainted with the country, to attack a body of Indians who could in a few hours raise more than double the force of the regiment, would have been a bold and perilous enterprise, and might have ended in their total discomfiture. For had they succeeded in battle, it is very doubtful whether they could have made good their retreat encumbered with wounded and obstructed by swamps, while a strong force of the enemy could have pursued and been ready at every advantageous place to attack them. Colonel Johnson however resolved to attempt it, as soon as his troops could be put into a condition, which promised vigorous exertions.

But fortunately for the regiment, on the next day an express arrived from general Clay commanding at fort Meigs, with information that the British and Indians threatened to invest that place again, and with a request that colonel Johnson would march his regiment there immediately for its relief. Orders to march were given without delay; and such was the zeal and promptitude of both officers and men, that in half an hour they were all ready to march, and commenced crossing the Miami opposite the fort. The provision boats were manned, and those who were unfit for duty, or had horses unfit to travel, were left with the garrison. That night they proceeded no farther after crossing the river, than Winchester's old camps; but in the morning they advanced in order and celerity, and arrived at the head of the Rapids at five in the evening, where colonel Johnson was met by another express from general Clay, advising him to be very cautious in his advance to the fort. The heads of the columns were then drawn up in close order, and the colonel in a short and impressive address, instructed them in their duties. If an enemy were discovered, the order of march was to be in two lines, one parallel to the river, and the other in front, stretching across from the head of the former to the river on the right. He concluded with saying "We must fight our way thro' any opposing force, let what will be the consequences, as no retreat could be justifiable. It is no time to flinch—we must reach the fort or die in the attempt." Every countenance responsive to the sentiments of the speaker, indicated the same desperate determination. The ground on which the enemy had gained their barbarous triumph over Dudley, was again to be traversed; and the allies would doubtless hope to realise another 5th of May, in another contest with Kentucky militia. The march was again resumed, and the regiment arrived at ten o'clock in the night opposite fort Meigs without molestation, and encamped in the open plain between the river and the hill on which the British batteries had been erected. The boats were left at the head of the Rapids, as it was deemed hazardous in the present state of the water to bring them down in the night.

At day light, when the morning gun fired, the horses of the regiment were frightened, and ran through the camp, running over several of the men and hurting them badly. They proceeded down the river a considerable distance, and with much trouble and risk to the men were caught and brought back. About 10 o'clock the regiment crossed to the fort, and encamped above it in a handsome plain clothed with blue grass. General Clay who commanded in the fort, was very cautious and vigilant, and daily sent spies down the river to reconnoitre and watch for the enemy.

Since he had been in command, he had repaired all the injuries, which the fort had sustained during the siege, and had cleared off the timber to a greater distance from it, burning that which was lying down, and erasing the works where the British batteries had stood. He had also assisted in bringing down a considerable portion of the provisions from the posts on the Auglaize and St. Marys. His troops at the same time had suffered excessively by sickness. During the month of June and a part of July, a most fatal epidemic prevailed in the camp, which carried off from three to five, and sometimes as many as ten in a day. It was computed that near 200 fell a sacrifice to it, within the space of six weeks, which was a dreadful mortality for the number of men in the garrison. The disease had been caused in the commencement, most probably by the exposure of the men during the siege; but the bad water which they had to use, and the flat, marshy, putrescent condition of all that region of country, was well calculated to destroy an army of men, who were alike unused to such a climate, and to the life of a soldier.

The apprehension of an attack at this time, was caused by information which general Clay had received from a Frenchman and a private of colonel Dudley's regiment, who came to fort Meigs on the 20th of June from Detroit. The latter had been a prisoner with the Indians. They stated that the allies had determined to renew the attack on the fort, and were to march about the time they had arrived. From the circumstantial information which they possessed, no doubt was left on the minds of the officers in the garrison, but that an attack was in preparation. The force of the Indians was estimated at near four thousand—and reinforcements of regulars from the Niagara were expected to the amount of one thousand. The Canadian militia had been disbanded as unfit for the service. When this information was received, it was immediately communicated by an express to general Harrison, and duplicates of the despatch were sent to the governors of Ohio and Kentucky.

General Harrison was at Franklinton when the intelligence reached him. He determined to set out the next morning for Lower Sandusky, and immediately addressed a letter to the war department and another to governor Meigs on this subject, in which he stated that he did not believe fort Meigs to be the object of the attack, but that it would be Lower Sandusky, Cleveland, or Erie. The 24th regiment, United States' infantry, under the command of colonel Anderson, was now at Upper Sandusky, and was ordered to proceed immediately to Lower Sandusky. Major Creghan with a part of the 17th was ordered to the same place, and also colonel Ball with his squadron of cavalry, who had been stationed at Franklinton.

Immediately before general Harrison was called to the outposts by the impending attack, he held a council at Franklinton, with the chiefs of the friendly Indians, consisting of the Delaware, Shawanoe, Wyandot, and Seneca tribes. He informed them that circumstances had come to his knowledge, which induced him to suspect the fidelity of some of the tribes, who seemed disposed to join the enemy in case they succeeded in capturing fort Meigs—that a crisis had arrived, which required all the tribes who remained neutral, and who were willing to engage in the war, to take a decided stand either for us or against us—that the President wanted no false friends—that the proposal of general Procter to exchange the Kentucky militia for the tribes in our friendship, indicated that he had received some hint of their willingness to take up the tomahawk against us—and that to give the United States a proof of their good disposition, they must either remove with their families into the interior, or the warriors must accompany him in the ensuing campaign and fight for the United States. To the latter condition, the chiefs and warriors unanimously agreed; and said they had long been anxious for an invitation to fight for the Americans. TAHE, the oldest Indian in the western country, who represented all the tribes, professed in their name the most indissoluble friendship for the United States. General Harrison then told them he would let them know, when they would be wanted in the service—"but you must conform to our mode of warfare. You are not to kill defenceless prisoners, old men, women, or children." He added that by their conduct he would be able to tell, whether the British could restrain their Indians from such horrible cruelty. For if the Indians fighting with him would forbear such conduct, it would prove, that the British could also restrain theirs if they wished to do it. He humorously told them he had been informed, that general Procter had promised to deliver him into the hands of Tecumseh, if he succeeded against fort Meigs, to be treated as that warrior might think proper. "Now if I can succeed in taking Procter, you shall have him for your prisoner, provided you will agree to treat him *as a squaw,* and only put petticoats upon him; for he must be a coward who would kill a defenceless prisoner."

The government of the United States at last reluctantly agreed to employ Indians in their army, against the savages employed by the British. The thing was perfectly justifiable, as a measure of self defence: yet there is only one reason which reconciles me to it. We thus demonstrated, that the north American savage is not such a cruel and ferocious being, that he cannot be restrained by civilized man within the bounds of civilized warfare. In several instances, subsequent to the present period, strong corps of Indians fought under the American standard, and were uniformly distinguished by their orderly and humane conduct. Had the Indians been employed by the British on the condition that they must conform to the rules of civilized warfare, no instance of savage cruelty in this war, would now be recorded against them, in the page of history, and in the celestial register of human crimes; but they employed the savages on a different principle—and I repeat that if the British officers in Upper Canada did not directly instigate, they at least very willingly permitted, the savages to massacre the prisoners, who had surrendered, not to the savages, but to themselves after receiving a solemn promise of protection.

On the evening of the 26th, general Harrison overtook the 24th regiment on its way to Lower Sandusky; and immediately selected all the men who were able to make a forced march. They amounted to 300, and were pushed forward for fort Meigs under the command of colonel Anderson. The general arrived at the fort on the evening of the 28th, and in a few hours afterwards the detachment under Anderson also made its appearance. As no farther information had been received, respecting the designs of the enemy, general Harrison ordered a detachment of Johnson's regiment to proceed the next day to the river Raisin to procure intelligence. Colonel Johnson took command of the detachment himself, and was accompanied also by the lieutenant colonel, the whole being 150 strong. They left the fort about 11 o'clock, and although the high water obliged them to go considerably out of their way to get over some of the creeks, they reached Frenchtown that night after 12 o'clock, and searched the whole town in hopes of taking a prisoner; but none of the enemy could be found. All the inhabited houses were visited by the colonel, and enquiry made respecting the enemy. The intelligent part of the citizens all agreed in stating, that they had heard of no reinforcements of regulars arriving at Malden, nor any considerable number of Indians, since the siege of fort Meigs—that the Indians had pressed general Procter to make another attack, and were much dissatisfied at his putting it off—that the success of our arms below had been kept from their knowledge some time, but was at last divulged to them by a trader, for which he was seized by Procter, but afterwards released at the demand of the Indians—that they held councils, the proceedings of which were kept secret from the British—and that 100 warriors of the Ottawa tribe had passed the river Raisin in boats to take scalps in the vicinity of Lower Sandusky.

Colonel Johnson on the next day returned to fort Meigs, taking with him two Frenchmen, one of them a citizen of Michigan, and the other a British subject. He had learnt that about 20 Indians had proceeded towards fort Meigs with a view to steal the horses of the army; and on his return he struck their trail, and pursued them. But in a few miles he found, that they had altered their minds and changed their course, having probably got intelligence of his excursion. On his arrival at the fort his regiment was reinforced by 100 men, brought by lieutenants Cardwell, White, Branham, and Lapsley from Kentucky.

General Harrison now deemed it unnecessary for him to remain any longer at fort Meigs, and on the 1st of July proceeded to Lower Sandusky with an escort of 70 mounted men commanded by captain M'Afee, at which place they arrived by dark, although the road was a continued and deep swamp. General Harrison expected with this escort and colonel Ball's squadron, to be ready to oppose the party of Indians, of whose expedition colonel Johnson had brought intelligence; but on the morning of that day they had been in the vicinity of the fort, and had killed at a farm house 3 men, a woman, and two children, and then made their escape in view of the garrison. Colonel Ball had not yet arrived, and there was of course no troops at the place, who could move with sufficient speed to intercept them, nor was the whole number there sufficient to make the attempt. Colonel Wells commanded, and the garrison consisted of 140 Ohio volunteers, whose term of service having expired, they were anxious to go home. General Harrison however prevailed upon them to remain some time longer.

On the evening of the 2nd colonel Ball's squadron arrived at Lower Sandusky, and on the next day proceeded with general Harrison to Cleveland. The object of the general in going to that place, was to make arrangements for the better security of the provisions, and of the boats which were constructing at that post. They were now guarded by a few regulars, and a small but excellent company of militia called the Chillicothe guards. General Harrison caused a small fort to be erected on the bank of the lake, drew a company of artillery, and another of 12 months' infantry from the interior, directed the boats to be sunk in a deep part of the Cayago river, as fast as they were finished, and had the magazine of provisions, which was at some distance from the town, prepared for conflagration, should the enemy land with a force, which our troops could not meet in the field. When the general afterwards left the place, colonel Ball remained there in command.

The mounted regiment had been ordered to proceed by Lower Sandusky to the river Huron, where it was intended, that they should remain a while to recruit their horses. They marched on the 2nd from fort Meigs, but did not arrive at Sandusky until the evening of the 3rd. THE FOURTH OF JULY, the anniversary of independence, was celebrated by the garrison and mounted men together, in great harmony and enthusiasm. Colonel Johnson delivered an appropriate address; and a number of toasts, breathing sentiments of the republican soldier were then drank, and cheered by the shouts of the men, the firing of small arms, and the discharge of a six pounder from the fort. The militia soldier whose patriotism was satisfied with going to the boundary line and looking at the enemy, while he refused to cross and fight them, was strongly reprobated in one of their toasts.

Considerable exertions were now making to finish the works of fort Stephenson, which had been planned and commenced in April by major Wood. They were soon afterwards completed, so as to contain a larger garrison and make a more formidable resistance. On the 6th colonel Johnson's regiment proceeded in detachments to Huron, and encamped on the shore of the lake, where they were supplied with forage by boats from Cleveland on the next day; and on the 8th lieutenant colonel J. Johnson returned in the boats with a party of 50 men to procure more forage. On the morning of the 9th a despatch was received from general Harrison which the colonel immediately answered, sending captain Payne for that purpose in a barge with a few men, though the lake was at that time extremely rough. The object of these expresses not being explained at the time, considerable curiosity and uneasiness were excited among the men, by the haste and secrecy observed.

General Harrison had just received the following letter from the war department, which he enclosed to colonel Johnson with orders to act accordingly. The letter had been delayed by being sent to Cincinnati and from thence following the movements of the general.

'*War Department, June 9th, 1813.*

'Sir, General Howard and governor Edwards urge the necessity of more troops in that quarter; and there being no other disposable force for that purpose at this time, the president directs that you order colonel Johnson with his regiment of mounted volunteers directly to Kaskaskias, to report to general Howard.

'I HAVE THE HONOR, &C.

'JOHN ARMSTRONG.

'GENERAL HARRISON.'

In reply colonel Johnson remonstrated against the order—he did not insist on the wishes of his men, which however to be indulged among friends in social life, were not to be mentioned against a military command; but represented his inability to comply, with any advantage to the country, or honor to the corps. He stated that his horses were in such a situation, that it would require ten days to put them in a condition for a journey of 400 miles to Kaskaskias—that it would require 30 days to perform it through the swamps they must traverse—that allowing 20 days more, to recruit the horses after their arrival, and to reach the frontiers, they would then have but 20 days left for service till their time would expire—that so many of his men were already dismounted, he could not expect after leaving captain Payne's cavalry as directed, to reach that place with more than 400—that he would hence arrive there with a reduced corps too late for the service—that governor Edwards was unnecessarily alarmed, his territory not being in danger, as the greater part of the Indians were collected at Malden—that the present position and circumstances of the regiment could not be known to the president at the time the order was given—that they would have an opportunity of rendering important services and acquiring laurels by remaining in the northwestern army, and would be rendered wholly useless by going to the west. On these grounds he entreated the general to detain him, or to leave to him the responsibility under existing circumstances of disobeying the order. In addition to these, many other considerations were pressed by lieutenant colonel Johnson, who was at head quarters. But the general replied that the order from the war department was so peremptory, that he could not authorize the suspension of the march even for a day; although he regretted extremely that the regiment would be separated from him in his contemplated movements against Upper Canada.

The following letter from colonel Johnson to general Harrison, which was written on the fourth of July, will exhibit the condition, the sentiments, and views of the regiment, from which the reader may imagine their feelings on this occasion, recollecting that the colonel was a distinguished partizan of the administration in congress, and that his regiment included a number of prominent characters in Kentucky.

'Camp at Lower Sandusky, July 4th, 1813.

'DEAR SIR—I arrived at this place last evening with a part of the mounted regiment, after two days march from camp Meigs, leaving two companies four miles in the rear, who were unable to reach this place; besides about twenty horses left on the way, which I am in hopes will be able to get back to camp Meigs or come to this place in a few days, where we can keep them together and recruit them. Having been in the most active service for upwards of forty days, and having travelled upwards of 700 miles, much of it forced marching, it is natural to conclude, that most of the horses are weak; and we feel great pleasure, and obligations to you, in finding your arrangements such as to enable us to recruit the horses of the regiment. To be ready to move with you, to Detroit and Canada, against the enemies of our country, is the first wish of our hearts. Two great objects induced us to come—first, to be at the regaining of our own territory and Detroit, and at the taking of Malden—and secondly, to serve under an officer in whom we have confidence. We could not have engaged in the service without such a prospect, when we recollected what disasters have attended us for the want of good generals. We did not want to serve under cowards, drunkards, old grannies, nor traitors, but under one who had proved himself to be wise, prudent and brave. The officers of the mounted regiment had some idea of addressing you on their anxiety to be a part of your army in the campaign against Canada, and of giving you a statement of the importance of having an opportunity to make the regiment efficient for such a campaign by recruiting their horses. As to the men, they are active, healthy and fond of service. This morning I have sent out 100 on foot to scour the surrounding country; and wherever we are we wish continual service. Our regiment is about 900 strong when all together. I have left 100 at Defiance to regain some lost horses, and to guard that frontier.

'You have not witnessed the opposition I encountered in raising the regiment. Every personal enemy, every traitor and tory, and your enemies, all combined—but in vain. Nothing but the hurry which attended our march prevented me from having 1500 men. Nothing but the importance of the service, which I thought we could render, would have justified my absence from the present catch penny congress. (The great object of the session was to raise a revenue.) My enemies, your enemies, the enemies of our cause, would exult if the mounted regiment should from any cause, be unable to carry a strong arm against the savages and British, when you strike the grand blow.

'It is with much diffidence I write you any thing touching military matters; but the desires of my soul and the situation of the regiment, have induced me thus freely and confidentially to express myself. In the morning we shall leave this place for Huron, ready to receive your orders, which will always he cheerfully executed at every hazard.

'YOUR OBEDIENT SERVANT,

'RH: M. JOHNSON.'

Little did the colonel expect, when winding up this letter, that he was going to Huron to receive an order of banishment to the wilds of the west. When he did receive it finally however, by the return of his express, it was "cheerfully executed at every hazard," and without a murmur. His men would "not disgrace him and themselves by any unsoldierly opposition to the orders of the president," however contrary to their views and wishes. The only service they were expected to render by this counterplot movement, was to aid governor Edwards who was continually representing to the government, that Dickson would certainly invade his territory with several thousand Indians; when in fact Dickson had been recruiting only for general Procter, and was now at Malden with all the Indians he could raise, intending to fight general Harrison as soon as Procter could make his arrangements. Both the secretary of war and general Harrison had constantly been of the opinion, that while the enemy had Malden to protect and the northwestern army to destroy, they would attempt no considerable movement against the western territories; and their opinion proved to be correct. General Harrison immediately informed the war department of the situation of colonel Johnson's regiment, and of the great anxiety which they had shewn to remain in the northwestern service.

After receiving the final orders of the general on the 13th, and having selected the route by Upper Sandusky, fort M'Arthur, St. Marys, Greenville, Delaware towns on White river, fort Harrison and Vincennes, as the most eligible of those recommended by the general, the troops marched by detachments and arrived at Upper Sandusky on the 16th. Some of the companies passed by Lower Sandusky, at which place major Croghan had arrived with part of the 17th regiment and taken command of the fort. At Upper Sandusky colonel Johnson ascertained that it was indispensably necessary to change his route so as to pass Urbana, for the purpose of procuring grain and other necessaries for the regiment. They proceeded again in detachments and ar-

rived at that place in a very unfavorable condition on the 19th and 20th. A considerable number of horses had been lost already, and many of the men were sick with the
measles and other fevers. The prospect of marching through the wilderness to Vincennes became every day more gloomy; and it was now evident, that if that route was
pursued, but a small portion of the regiment could be expected to reach their destination, on account of sickness and the loss of horses. A meeting of the officers was
therefore held, and an address drawn up and presented to the colonel, in which they
solicited him to change their route and allow them to pass through Kentucky. They
represented the cheerfulness and promptitude, with which the regiment had to this
moment, executed the orders of the government and their commandant; and had performed a march of near 800 miles in the whole, over roads of the worst description,
swimming the numerous streams they had to cross, and generally proceeding by
forced marches from 30 to 50 miles a day—that the regiment was very much reduced
and scattered by the loss of horses; and by the time it reached Kaskaskias would be
rendered wholly inefficient, and perhaps entirely useless—and that by going through
Kentucky they would be able to raise more men, and remount those who had lost
their horses, or had rendered them unfit for the expedition, and would ultimately
reach their destination as soon as by the more direct route through the wilderness,
and be in a condition to render efficient service. In reply the colonel remarked, that
"It was not until the arrival of the regiment at this place, that the entire impractica-
bility of carrying to Kaskaskias one half the horses was certainly known, without recruiting many days, or changing the route to Kentucky. Under the whole view of the
subject, no hesitation exists as to the propriety and evident necessity of granting the
request of the officers." The regiment was therefore ordered to march through Kentucky for the above purposes, and to rendezvous at Vincennes on the 20th of August.
To justify this step in violation of his positive orders, the colonel relied on its evident
propriety; and it proved in fact to be the salvation of the regiment.

While the regiment was at Urbana, intelligence was received that colonel William
Russell was preparing an expedition against the Indians from the Indiana territory;
and he was at this time marching through their country with a strong mounted corps
of rangers and volunteer militia. An excursion had also been previously made by
colonel Bartholomew, which it will be proper in this place to notice. In the spring the
Indians had committed many depredations on the frontiers of Indiana, in the way of
murdering the inhabitants and stealing their horses and cattle. The Delawares were
strongly suspected of either secretly aiding in the mischief, or of committing it themselves. Colonel Bartholomew of that territory hence determined to visit their towns
on White river with a military force, and if any proofs of their hostility could be discovered, to retaliate and chastise them effectually for it. He accordingly assembled
three companies of mounted men at Valonia, commanded by captains Peyton, Biggers
and Dunn, and amounting to 140 men. Having selected majors Tipton and Owen for
his aids, he proceeded up the country till he had reached the upper Delaware towns,
which he found uninhabited; and returning by the lower towns he found them in the
same condition. Some Indian sign was discovered, but only one Indian was seen during the whole excursion. Those who had not gone to reside in the interior of the state
of Ohio, had left the villages where they formerly resided for some other region.

Soon after this excursion, colonel Russell of the United States army, who commanded the rangers of Indiana, which had been raised under the act of congress, authorizing ten additional companies for the protection of the western territories, projected another expedition to penetrate as far as the Mississiniway villages. He requested

Joseph Allen esq. of Kentucky to raise a company and join him at Valonia early in July; and also invited major general Thomas, and brigadier general Cox of the Kentucky militia, to join in the expedition. They repaired accordingly to that place, which is about 50 miles from Louisville near White river, and carried about 100 volunteers, to the standard of colonel Russell, whose whole force then amounted to 500 men. The colonel determined to march this force in five lines with an officer having the rank of major at the head of each line. Generals Thomas and Cox, colonels Evans and Wilson, and major Zach. Taylor, were assigned to these posts; and the corps then proceeded directly to the Delaware towns which were found still unoccupied. He then marched towards the Mississiniway, intending if possible to surprise any Indians who might be found in the villages on that river. In five days he reached the main village at the mouth of that river, which he found vacant; and from every appearance, it was supposed the Indians had been gone about two months. There were nearly two hundred houses in this village, which extended about a mile in length; and two miles further up the river, there were the remains of a large encampment, and a block house with several port holes large enough for a six pounder. This had been erected by Tecumseh in the preceding autumn with a view to resist the progress of general Hopkins, and had been a place of general rendezvous for the concentration of his forces. The encampment had apparently been large enough to contain one thousand Indians. It was now abundantly evident, that all the Indians of the Wabash were gone to Malden to serve under the banners of general Procter. Colonel Russell therefore proceeded down the Wabash by Tippecanoe to fort Harrison, having taken a circuit of more than 400 miles through the Indian country, without having seen an Indian or lost a man.

❧ 20 ❧

JOHN JAMES AUDUBON

(1785–1851)

Today many people associate John James Audubon with the conservationist organization that bears his name. Ironically, Audubon was a lifelong hunter of all sorts of animals, including the birds that made him famous. In fact, his wildlife paintings are sometimes criticized for the unrealistic appearances of their birds—a result of the unnatural ways in which Audubon posed their corpses.

Audubon was born on April 26, 1785, in Les Cayes, Santo Domingo (now Haiti), the illegitimate son of a French sea merchant and a French chambermaid. From the age of six, he was raised and educated in France, where he did not, as he later claimed, study with French classicist painter Jacques-Louis David. Audubon's father sent him to Philadelphia in 1803 so that he might avoid service in the Napoleonic wars.

In the birds and other wildlife of America, Audubon discovered an unlimited outlet for his artistic talents. His study of nature was well under way by 1804 when he became perhaps the first person to band birds for identification. In 1807 Audubon moved to Kentucky to pursue business opportunities, but art and nature remained his priorities. His business career ended in 1819 with the ignominy of a brief term in jail for debt.

In 1820 Audubon began pursuing the project that would make him famous: *The Birds of America* (1827–1838), whose 435 color plates featured life-sized illustrations of 1,065 birds representing 498 species. That year he took his first trip down the Mississippi River, from Cincinnati to New Orleans, collecting and painting birds. To accompany *The Birds of America,* Audubon published *Ornithological Biography* (1831–1839), which included not only descriptions of American birds, plants, insects, and the like, but also sixty brief essays covering a variety of Audubon's experiences on the American frontier. Four of these essays are presented here.

Text: Essays from Audubon's *Ornithological Biography* (1831–1839) are reprinted in *Delineations of American Scenery and Character* (New York, 1926): "The Prairie," 14–18; "Kentucky Sports," 56–63; "Colonel Boon," 111–116; "The Squatters of the Mississippi," 137–142.

THE PRAIRIE (1831)

On my return from the Upper Mississippi, I found myself obliged to cross one of the wide Prairies, which, in that portion of the United States vary the appearance of the country. The weather was fine, all around me was as fresh and blooming as if it had just issued from the bosom of nature. My knapsack, my gun, and my dog, were all I had for baggage and company. But, although well moccasined, I moved slowly along, attracted by the brilliancy of the flowers, and the gambols of the fawns around their dams, to all appearance as thoughtless of danger as I felt myself.

My march was of long duration; I saw the sun sinking beneath the horizon long before I could perceive any appearance of woodland, and nothing in the shape of man had I met with that day. The track which I followed was only an old Indian trace, and as darkness overshadowed the prairie, I felt some desire to reach at least a copse, in which I might lie down to rest. The Night-hawks were skimming over and around me, attracted by the buzzing wings of the beetles which form their food, and the distant howling of wolves gave me some hope that I should soon arrive at the skirts of some woodland.

I did so, and almost at the same instant a fire-light attracting my eye, I moved towards it, full of confidence that it proceeded from the camp of some wandering Indians. I was mistaken:—I discovered by its glare that it was from the hearth of a small log cabin, and that a tall figure passed and repassed between it and me, as if busily engaged in household arrangements.

I reached the spot, and presenting myself at the door, asked the tall figure, which proved to be a woman, if I might take shelter under her roof for the night. Her voice was gruff, and her attire negligently thrown about her. She answered in the affirmative. I walked in, took a wooden stool, and quietly seated myself by the fire. The next object that attracted my notice was a finely formed young Indian, resting his head between his hands, with his elbows on his knees. A long bow rested against the log wall near him, while a quantity of arrows and two or three raccoon skins lay at his feet. He moved not; he apparently breathed not. Accustomed to the habits of the Indians, and knowing that they pay little attention to the approach of civilized strangers (a circumstance which in some countries is considered as evincing the apathy of their character), I addressed him in French, a language not unfrequently partially known to the people in that neighborhood. He raised his head, pointed to one of his eyes with his finger, and gave me a significant glance with the other. His face was covered with blood. The fact was, that an hour before this, as he was in the act of discharging an arrow at a raccoon in the top of a tree, the arrow had split upon the cord, and sprung back with such violence into his right eye as to destroy it for ever.

Feeling hungry, I inquired what sort of fare I might expect. Such a thing as a bed was not to be seen, but many large untanned bear and buffalo hides lay piled in a corner. I drew a fine time-piece from my breast, and told the woman that it was late, and that I was fatigued. She had espyed my watch, the richness of which seemed to operate upon her feelings with electric quickness. She told me that there was plenty of venison and jerked buffalo meat, and that on removing the ashes I should find a cake. But my watch had struck her fancy, and her curiosity had to be gratified by an immediate sight of it. I took off the gold chain that secured it from around my neck, and presented it to her. She was all ecstasy, spoke of its beauty, asked me its value, and put the chain round her brawny neck, saying how happy the possession of such a watch should make her. Thoughtless, and, as I fancied myself, in so retired a spot, secure, I paid little attention to her talk or her movements. I helped my dog to a good supper of venison, and was not long in satisfying the demands of my own appetite.

The Indian rose from his seat, as if in extreme suffering. He passed and repassed me several times, and once pinched me on the side so violently, that the pain nearly brought forth an exclamation of anger. I looked at him. His eye met mine; but his look was so forbidding, that it struck a chill into the more nervous part of my system. He again seated himself, drew his butcher-knife from its greasy scabbard, examined its edge, as I would do that of a razor suspected dull, replaced it, and again taking his tomahawk from his back, filled the pipe of it with tobacco, and sent me expressive glances whenever our hostess chanced to have her back towards us.

Never until that moment had my senses been awakened to the danger which I now suspected to be about me. I returned glance for glance to my companion, and rested well assured that, whatever enemies I might have, he was not of their number.

I asked the woman for my watch, wound it up, and under pretence of wishing to see how the weather might probably on the morrow, took up my gun, and walked out of the cabin. I slipped a ball into each barrel, scraped the edges of my flints, renewed the primings, and returning to the hut, gave a favourable account of my observations. I took a few bearskins, made a pallet of them, and calling my faithful dog to my side, lay down, with my gun close to my body, and in a few minutes was, to all appearance, fast asleep.

A short time had elapsed, when some voices were heard, and from the corner of my eyes I saw two athletic youths making their entrance, bearing a dead stag on a pole. They disposed of their burden, and asking for whisky, helped themselves freely to it. Observing me and the wounded Indian, they asked who I was, and why the devil that rascal (meaning the Indian, who, they knew, understood not a word of English) was in the house. The mother—for so she proved to be, bade them speak less loudly, made mention of my watch, and took them to a corner, where a conversation took place, the purport of which it required little shrewdness in me to guess. I tapped my dog gently. He moved his tail, and with indescribable pleasure I saw his fine eyes alternately fixed on me and raised towards the trio in the corner. I felt that he perceived danger in my situation. The Indian exchanged a last glance with me.

The lads had eaten and drunk themselves into such condition, that I already looked upon them as *hors de combat;* and the frequent visits of the whisky bottle to the ugly mouth of their dam I hoped would soon reduce her to a like state. Judge of my astonishment, reader, when I saw this incarnate fiend take a large carving-knife, and go to the grindstone to whet its edge. I saw her pour the water on the turning machine, and watched her working away with the dangerous instrument, until the sweat covered every part of my body, in despite of my determination to defend myself to the last. Her task finished, she walked to her reeling sons, and said, "There, that'll soon settle him! Boys, kill yon ———, and then for the watch."

I turned, cocked my gun-locks silently, touched my faithful companion, and lay ready to start up and shoot the first who might attempt my life. The moment was fast approaching, and that night might have been my last in this world, had not Providence made preparations for my rescue. All was ready. The infernal hag was advancing slowly, probably contemplating the best way of despatching me, whilst her sons should be engaged with the Indian. I was several times on the eve of rising and shooting her on the spot:—but she was not to be punished thus. The door was suddenly opened, and there entered two stout travellers, each with a long rifle on his shoulder. I bounced up on my feet, and making them most heartily welcome, told them how well it was for me that they should have arrived at that moment. The tale was told in a minute. The drunken sons were secured, and the woman, in spite of her defence and vociferations, shared the same fate. The Indian fairly danced with joy, and gave us to understand that, as he could not sleep for pain, he would watch over us. You may suppose we slept much less than we talked. The two strangers gave me an account of their once having been themselves in a somewhat similar situation. Day came, fair and rosy, and with it the punishment of our captives.

They were now quite sobered. Their feet were unbound, but their arms were still securely tied. We marched them into the woods off the road, and having used them as Regulators were wont to use such delinquents, we set fire to the cabin, gave all the skins and implements to the young Indian warrior, and proceeded, well pleased, towards the settlements.

During upwards of twenty-five years, when my wanderings extended to all parts of our country, this was the only time at which my life was in danger from my fellow creatures. Indeed, so little risk do travellers run in the United States, that no one born there ever dreams of any to be encountered on the road; and I can only account for this occurrence by supposing that the inhabitants of the cabin were not Americans.

Will you believe, reader, that not many miles from the place where this adventure happened, and where fifteen years ago, no habitation belonging to civilized man was expected, and very few ever seen, large roads are now laid out, cultivation has converted the woods into fertile fields, taverns have been erected, and much of what we Americans call comfort is to be met with. So fast does improvement proceed in our abundant and free country.

KENTUCKY SPORTS (1831)

It may not be amiss, before I attempt to give some idea of the pleasures experienced by the sportsmen of Kentucky, to introduce the subject with a slight description of that State.

Kentucky was formerly attached to Virgina, but in those days the Indians looked upon that portion of the western wilds as their own, and abandoned the district only when forced to do so, moving with disconsolate hearts farther into the recesses of the unexplored forests. Doubtless the richness of its soil, and the beauty of its borders, situated as they are along one of the most beautiful rivers in the world, contributed as much to attract the Old Virginians, as the desire so generally experienced in America, of spreading over the uncultivated tracts, and bringing into cultivation lands that have for unknown ages teemed with the wild luxuriance of untamed nature. The conquest of Kentucky was not performed without many difficulties. The warfare that long existed between the intruders and the Redskins was sanguinary and protracted;

but the former at length made good their footing, and the latter drew off their shattered bands, dismayed by the mental superiority and indomitable courage of the white men.

This region was probably discovered by a daring hunter, the renowned Daniel Boon. The richness of its soil, its magnificent forests, its numberless navigable streams, its salt springs and licks, its saltpetre caves, its coal strata, and the vast herds of buffaloes and deer that browsed on its hills and amidst its charming valleys, afforded ample inducements to the new settler, who pushed forward with a spirit far above that of the most undaunted tribes, which for ages had been the sole possessors of the soil.

The Virginians thronged towards the Ohio. An axe, a couple of horses, and a heavy rifle, with store of ammunition, were all that were considered necessary for the equipment of the man, who, with his family, removed to the new State, assured that, in that land of exuberant fertility, he could not fail to provide amply for all his wants. To have witnessed the industry and perseverance of these emigrants must at once have proved the vigour of their minds. Regardless of the fatigue attending every movement which they made, they pushed through an unexplored region of dark and tangled forests, guiding themselves by the sun alone, and reposing at night on the bare ground. They had to cross numberless streams on rafts, with their wives and children, their cattle and their luggage, often drifting to considerable distances before they could effect a landing on the opposite shores. Their cattle would often stray amid the rice pasturage of these shores, and occasion a delay of several days. To these troubles add the constantly impending danger of being murdered, while asleep in their encampments, by the prowling and ruthless Indians; while they had before them a distance of hundreds of miles to be traversed, before they could reach certain places of rendezvous called *stations*. To encounter difficulties like these must have required energies of no ordinary kind; and the reward which these veteran settlers enjoy was doubtless well merited.

Some removed from the Atlantic shores to those of the Ohio in more comfort and security. They had their wagons, their Negroes, and their families. Their way was cut through the woods by their own axemen, the day before their advance, and when night overtook them, the hunters attached to the party came to the place pitched upon for encamping, loaded with the dainties of which the forest yielded an abundant supply, the blazing light of a huge fire guiding their steps as they approached, and the sounds of merriment that saluted their ears assuring them that all was well. The flesh of the buffalo, the bear, and the deer, soon hung in large and delicious steaks, in front of the embers; the cakes already prepared were deposited in their proper places, and under the rich drippings of the juicy roasts, were quickly baked. The wagons contained the bedding, and whilst the horses which had drawn them were turned loose to feed on the luxuriant undergrowth of the woods, some perhaps hoppled, but the greater number merely with a light bell hung to their neck, to guide their owners in the morning to the spot where they might have rambled, the party were enjoying themselves after the fatigues of the day.

In anticipation all is pleasure; and these migrating bands feasted in joyous sociality, unapprehensive of any greater difficulties than those to be encountered in forcing their way through the pathless woods to the land of abundance; and although it took months to accomplish the journey, and a skirmish now and then took place between them and the Indians, who sometimes crept unperceived into their very camp, still did the Virginians cheerfully proceed towards the western horizon, until the various groups all reached the Ohio, when, struck with the beauty of that magnificent stream, they at once commenced the task of clearing land, for the purpose of establishing a permanent residence.

Others, perhaps encumbered with too much luggage, preferred descending the stream. They prepared *arks* pierced with port-holes, and glided on the gentle current, more annoyed, however, than those who marched by land, by the attacks of the Indians, who watched their motions. Many travellers have described these boats, formerly called *arks,* but now named *flat-boats.* But have they told you, reader, that in those times a boat thirty or forty feet in length, by ten or twelve in breadth, was considered a stupendous fabric; that this boat contained men, women and children, huddled together, with horses, cattle, hogs and poultry for their companions, while the remaining portion was crammed with vegetables and packages of seeds? The roof or deck of the boat was not unlike a farm-yard, being covered with hay, ploughs, carts, wagons, and various agricultural implements, together with numerous others among which the spinning wheels of the matrons were conspicuous. Even the sides of the floating mass were loaded with the wheels of the different vehicles, which themselves lay on the roof. Have they told you that these boats contained the little all of each family of venturous emigrants, who, fearful of being discovered by the Indians, under night moved in darkness, groping their way from one part to another of these floating habitations, denying themselves the comfort of fire or light, lest the foe that watched them from the shore should rush upon them and destroy them? Have they told you that this boat was used, after the tedious voyage was ended, as the first dwelling of these new settlers? No, such things have not been related to you before. The travellers who have visited our country have had other objects in view.

I shall not describe the many massacres which took place among the different parties of White and Red men, as the former moved down the Ohio; because I have never been very fond of battles, and indeed have always wished that the world were more peaceably inclined than it is; and shall merely add, that, in one way or other, Kentucky was wrested from the original owners of the soil. Let us, therefore, turn our attention to the sports still enjoyed in that now happy portion of the United States.

We have individuals in Kentucky, that even there are considered wonderful adepts in the management of the rifle. To *drive a nail* is a common feat, not more thought of by the Kentuckians than to cut off a wild turkey's head, at a distance of a hundred yards. Others will *bark* off squirrels one after another, until satisfied with the number procured. Some, less intent on destroying game, may be seen under night *snuffing a candle* at the distance of fifty yards, off-hand, without extinguishing it. I have been told that some have proved so expert and cool, as to make choice of the eye of a foe at a wonderful distance, boasting beforehand of the sureness of their piece, which has afterwards been fully proved when the enemy's head has been examined!

Having resided some years in Kentucky, and having more than once been witness of rifle sport, I will present you with the results of my observation, leaving you to judge how far rifle-shooting is understood in that State.

Several individuals who conceive themselves expert in the management of the gun, are often seen to meet for the purpose of displaying their skill, and betting a trifling sum, put up a target, in the centre of which a common-sized nail is hammered for about two-thirds of its length. The marksmen make choice of what they consider a proper distance, which may be forty paces. Each man cleans the interior of his tube, which is called *wiping* it, places a ball in the palm of his hand, pouring as much powder from his horn upon it as will cover it. This quantity is supposed to be sufficient for any distance within a hundred yards. A shot which comes very close to the nail is

considered as that of an indifferent marksman; the bending of the nail is, of course,
somewhat better; but nothing less than hitting it right on the head is satisfactory. Well,
kind reader, one out of three shots generally hits the nail, and should the shooters
amount to half a dozen, two nails are frequently needed before each can have a shot.
Those who drive the nail have a further trial amongst themselves, and the two best
shots of these generally settle the affair, when all the sportsmen adjourn to some
house, and spend an hour or two in friendly intercourse, appointing, before they part,
a day for another trial. This is technically termed *Driving the Nail*.

   Barking off squirrels is delightful sport, and in my opinion requires a greater degree
of accuracy than any other. I first witnessed this manner of procuring squirrels whilst
near the town of Frankfort. The performer was the celebrated Daniel Boon. We
walked out together, and followed the rocky margins of the Kentucky River, until we
reached a piece of flat land thickly covered with black walnuts, oaks and hickories. As
the general mast was a good one that year, squirrels were seen gambolling on every
tree around us. My companion, a stout, hale, and athletic man, dressed in a homespun
hunting-shirt, bare-legged and moccasined, carried a long and heavy rifle, which, as
he was loading it, he said had proved efficient in all his former undertakings, and
which he hoped would not fail on this occasion, as he felt proud to show me his skill.
The gun was wiped, the powder measured, the ball patched with six-hundred-thread
linen, and the charge sent home with a hickory rod. We moved not a step from the
place, for the squirrels were so numerous that it was unnecessary to go after them.
Boon pointed to one of these animals which had observed us, and was crouched on
a branch about fifty paces distant, and bade me mark well the spot where the ball
should hit. He raised his piece gradually, until the *bead* (that being the name given by
the Kentuckians to the *sight*) of the barrel was brought to a line with the spot which
he intended to hit. The whip-like report resounded through the woods and along the
hills in repeated echoes. Judge of my surprise, when I perceived that the ball had hit
the piece of the bark immediately beneath the squirrel, and shivered it into splinters,
the concussion produced by which had killed the animal, and sent it whirling through
the air, as if it had been blown up by explosion of a powder magazine. Boon kept up
his firing, and before many hours had elapsed, we had procured as many squirrels as
we wished; for you must know, that to load a rifle requires only a moment, and that
if it is wiped once after each shot, it will do duty for hours. Since that first interview
with our veteran Boon, I have seen many other individuals perform the same feat.

   The *snuffing of a candle* with a ball, I first had an opportunity of seeing near the
banks of Green River, not far from a large pigeon-roost, to which I had previously
made a visit. I heard many reports of guns during the early part of a dark night, and
knowing them to be those of rifles, I went towards the spot to ascertain the cause. On
reaching the place, I was welcomed by a dozen of tall stout men, who told me they
were exercising, for the purpose of enabling them to shoot under night at the reflected light from the eyes of a deer or wolf, by torch-light, of which I shall give you
an account somewhere else. A fire was blazing near, the smoke of which rose curling
among the thick foliage of the trees. At a distance which rendered it scarcely distinguishable, stood a burning candle, as if intended for an offering to the goddess of
night, but which in reality was only fifty yards from the spot on which we all stood.
One man was within a few yards of it, to watch the effects of the shots, as well as to
light the candle should it chance to go out, or to replace it should the shot cut it
across. Each marksmen shot in his turn. Some never hit either the snuff or the candle, and were congratulated with a loud laugh; while others actually snuffed the can-

dle without putting it out, and were recompensed for their dexterity by numerous hurrahs. One of them, who was particularly expert, was very fortunate, and snuffed the candle three times out of seven, whilst all the other shots either put out the candle, or cut it immediately under the light.

Of the feats performed by the Kentuckians with the rifle, I could say more than might be expedient on the present occasion. In every thinly peopled portion of the State, it is rare to meet one without a gun of that description, as well as a tomahawk. By way of recreation they often cut off a piece of the bark of a tree, make a target of it, using a little powder wetted with water or saliva for the bull's eye, and shoot into the mark all the balls they have about them, picking them out of the wood again.

After what I have said, you may easily imagine with what ease a Kentuckian procures game, or dispatches an enemy, more especially when I tell you that every one in the State is accustomed to handle the rifle from the time when he is first able to shoulder it until near the close of his career. That murderous weapon is the means of procuring them subsistence during all their wild and extensive rambles, and is the source of their principal sports and pleasures.

COLONEL BOON (1831)

Daniel Boon, or, as he was usually called in the western country, Colonel Boon, happened to spend a night with me under the same roof, more than twenty years ago. We had returned from a shooting excursion, in the course of which his extraordinary skill in the management of the rifle had been fully displayed. On retiring to the room appropriated to that remarkable individual and myself for the night, I felt anxious to know more of his exploits and adventures than I did, and accordingly took the liberty of proposing numerous questions to him. The stature and general appearance of this wanderer of the western forests approached the gigantic. His chest was broad and prominent; his muscular powers displayed themselves in every limb; his countenance gave indication of his great courage, enterprise and perseverance; and when he spoke, the very motion of his lips brought the impression that whatever he uttered could not be otherwise than strictly true. I undressed, whilst he merely took off his hunting shirt, and arranged a few folds of blankets on the floor, choosing rather to lie there, as he observed, than on the softest bed. When we had both disposed of ourselves, each after his own fashion, he related to me the following account of his powers of memory, which I lay before you, kind reader, in his own words, hoping that the simplicity of his style may prove interesting to you.

"I was once," said he, "on a hunting expedition on the banks of the Green River, when the lower parts of this State (Kentucky) were still in the hands of nature, and none but the sons of the soil were looked upon as its lawful proprietors. We Virginians had for some time been waging a war of intrusion upon them, and I, amongst the rest, rambled through the woods in pursuit of their race, as I now would follow the tracks of any ravenous animal. The Indians outwitted me one dark night, and I was as unexpectedly as suddenly made a prisoner by them. The trick had been managed with great skill; for no sooner had I extinguished the fire of my camp, and laid me down to rest, in full security, as I thought, than I felt myself seized by an indistinguishable number of hands, and immediately pinioned, as if about to be led to the scaffold for execution. To have attempted to be refractory, would have proved useless and dangerous to my life; and I suffered myself to be removed from my camp to theirs a few miles distant, without uttering even a word of complaint. You are aware, I dare say, that to act in this manner was the best policy, as you understand that by so doing, I proved to the Indians at once, that I was born and bred as fearless of death as any of themselves.

"When we reached the camp, great rejoicings were exhibited. Two squaws and a few papooses appeared particularly delighted at the sight of me, and I was assured, by very unequivocal gestures and words, that, on the morrow, the mortal enemy of the Red-skins would cease to live. I never opened my lips, but was busy contriving some scheme which might enable me to give the rascals the slip before dawn. The women immediately fell a searching about my hunting-shirt for whatever they might think valuable, and, fortunately for me, soon found my flask filled with *monongahela* (that is, reader, strong whisky). A terrific grin was exhibited on their murderous countenances, while my heart throbbed with joy at the anticipation of their intoxication. The crew immediately began to beat their bellies and sing, as they passed the bottle from mouth to mouth. How often did I wish the flask ten times its size, and filled with aqua-fortis! I observed that the squaws drank more freely than the warriors, and again my spirits were about to be depressed, when the report of a gun was heard at a distance. The Indians all jumped on their feet. The singing and drinking were both brought to a stand, and I saw, with inexpressible joy, the men walk off to some distance and talk to the squaws. I knew that they were consulting about me, and I foresaw that in a few moments the warriors would go to discover the cause of the gun having been fired so near their camp. I expected that the squaws would be left to guard me. Well, Sir, it was just so. They returned; the men took up their guns, and walked away. The squaws sat down again, and in less than five minutes had my bottle up to their dirty mouths, gurgling down their throats the remains of the whisky.

"With what pleasure did I see them becoming more and more drunk, until the liquor took such hold of them that it was quite impossible for these women to be of any service. They tumbled down, rolled about, and began to snore: when I, having no other chance of freeing myself from the cords that fastened me, rolled over and over towards the fire, and, after a short time, burned them asunder. I rose on my feet, stretched my stiffened sinews, snatched up my rifle, and, for once in my life, spared that of Indians. I now recollected how desirous I once or twice felt to lay open the skulls of the wretches with my tomahawk; but when I again thought upon killing beings unprepared and unable to defend themselves, it looked like murder without need, and I gave up the idea.

"But, Sir, I felt determined to mark the spot, and walking to a thrifty ash sapling, I cut out of it three large chips, and ran off. I soon reached the river, soon crossed it, and threw myself deep into the cane-brakes, imitating the track of an Indian with my feet, so that no chance might be left for those from whom I had escaped to overtake me.

"It is now nearly twenty years since this happened, and more than five since I left the Whites' settlements, which I might probably never have visited again, had I not been called on as a witness in a law-suit that was pending in Kentucky, and which I really believe would never have been settled, had I not come forward, and established the beginning of a certain boundary line. This is the story, Sir.

"Mr. ——— moved from Old Virginia into Kentucky, and having a large tract granted to him in the new State, laid claim to a certain parcel of land adjoining Green River, and as chance would have it, took for one of his corners the very Ash tree on which I had made my mark, and finished his survey of some thousands of acres, beginning, as it expressed in the deed, 'at an Ash marked by three distinct notches of the tomahawk of a white man.'

"The tree had grown much, and the bark had covered the marks; but somehow or other, Mr. ——— heard from some one all that I have already said to you, and thinking that I might remember the spot alluded to in the deed, but which was no longer discoverable, wrote for me to come and try at least to find the place or the tree. His letter mentioned that all my expenses should be paid, and not caring much about once more going back to Kentucky, I started and met Mr. ———. After some conversation, the affair with the Indians came to my recollection. I considered for a while, and began to think that after all I could find the very spot, as well as the tree, if it was yet standing.

"Mr. ——— and I mounted our horses, and off we went to the Green River Bottoms. After some difficulties, for you must be aware, Sir, that great changes have taken place in those woods, I found at last the spot where I had crossed the river, and waiting for the moon to rise, made for the course in which I thought the Ash tree grew. On approaching the place, I felt as if the Indians were there still, and as if I was still a prisoner among them. Mr. ——— and I camped near what I conceived the spot, and waited until the return of day.

"At the rising of the sun, I was on foot, and after a good deal of musing, thought that an Ash tree then in sight must be the very one on which I had made my mark. I felt as if there could be no doubt of it, and mentioned my thought to Mr. ———. "Well, Colonel Boon," said he, "if you think so, I hope it may prove true, but we must have some witnesses; do you stay here about, and I will go and bring some of the settlers whom I know." I agreed. Mr. ——— trotted off, and I, to pass the time, rambled about to see if a deer was still living in the land. But ah! Sir, what a wonderful difference thirty years makes in the country! Why, at the time when I was caught by the Indians, you would not have walked out in any direction for more than a mile without shooting a buck or a bear. There were then thousands of Buffaloes on the hills in Kentucky; the land looked as if it never would become poor; and to hunt in those days was a pleasure indeed. But when I was left to myself on the banks of Green River, I dare say for the last time in my life, a few *signs* only of a deer were to be seen, and, as to a deer itself, I saw none.

"Mr. ——— returned, accompanied by three gentlemen. They looked upon me as if I had been Washington himself, and walked to the Ash tree, which I now called my own, as if in quest of a long lost treasure. I took an axe from one of them, and cut a few chips off the bark. Still no signs were to be seen. So I cut again until I thought it was time to be cautious, and I scraped and worked away with my butcher knife, until I *did* come to where my tomakawk had left an impression in the wood. We now went regularly to work, and scraped at the tree with care, until three hacks as plain as any three notches ever were, could be seen. Mr. ——— and the other gentlemen were astonished, and, I must allow, I was as much surprised as pleased myself. I made affidavit of this remarkable occurrence in presence of these gentlemen. Mr. ——— gained his cause. I left Green River for ever, and came to where we now are; and, Sir, I wish you a good night."

I trust, kind reader, that when I again make my appearance with another volume of Ornithological Biography, I shall not have to search in vain for the impression which I have made, but shall have the satisfaction of finding its traces still unobliterated. I now withdraw, and, in the words of the noted wanderer of the western wilds, "WISH YOU A GOOD NIGHT."

THE SQUATTERS OF THE MISSISSIPPI (1833)

Although every European traveller who has glided down the Mississippi, at the rate of ten miles an hour, has told his tale of the Squatters, yet none has given any other account of them than that they are "a sallow, sickly-looking sort of miserable beings," living in swamps, and subsisting on pignuts, Indian corn and bear's flesh. It is obvious, however, that none but a person acquainted with their history, manners, and condition, can give any real information respecting them.

The individuals who become squatters choose that sort of life of their own free will. They mostly remove from other parts of the United States, after finding that land has become too high in price; and they are persons who, having a family of strong and hardy children, are anxious to enable them to provide for themselves. They have heard from good authorities, that the country extending along the great streams of the West, is of all parts of the Union the richest in its soil, the growth of its timber, and the abundance of its game; that, besides, the Mississippi is the great road to and from all the markets in the world; and that every vessel borne by its waters, affords to settlers some chance of selling their commodities, or of exchanging them for others. To these recommendations is added another, of ever greater weight with persons of the above denomination, namely, the prospect of being able to settle on land, and perhaps to hold it for a number of years, without purchase, rent or tax of any kind. How many thousands of individuals in all parts of the globe would gladly try their fortune with such prospects, I leave to you, reader, to determine.

As I am not disposed too highly to colour the picture which I am about to submit to your inspection, instead of pitching on individuals who have removed from our eastern boundaries, and of whom certainly there are a good number, I shall introduce to you the members of a family from Virginia, first giving you an idea of their condition in that country, previous to their migration to the west. The land which they and their ancestors have possessed for a hundred years, having been constantly forced to produce crops of one kind or other, is now completely worn out. It exhibits only a superficial layer of red clay, cut up by deep ravines, through which much of the soil has been conveyed to some more fortunate neighbour, residing in a yet rich and beautiful valley. Their strenuous efforts to render it productive have failed. They dispose of every thing too cumbrous or expensive for them to remove, retaining only a few horses, a servant or two, and such implements of husbandry and other articles as may be necessary on their journey, or useful when they arrive at the spot of their choice.

I think I see them at this moment harnessing their horses, and attaching them to their waggons, which are already filled with bedding, provisions, and the younger children; while on their outside are fastened spinning-wheels and looms; and a bucket, filled with tar and tallow, swings between the hind wheels. Several axes are secured to the bolster, and the feeding trough of the horses contains pots, kettles, and pans. The servant, now become a driver, rides the near saddled horse, the wife is mounted on another, the worthy husband shoulders his gun, and his sons, clad in plain substantial homespun, drive the cattle ahead, and lead the procession, followed by the hounds and other dogs. Their day's journey is short and not agreeable:—the cattle, stubborn or wild, frequently leave the road for the woods, giving the travellers much trouble; the harness of the horses here and there gives away, and needs immediate repair; a basket, which has accidentally dropped, must be gone after, for nothing that they have can be spared; the roads are bad, and now and then all hands are called to push on the waggon, or prevent it from upsetting. Yet by sunset they have proceeded perhaps twenty miles. Rather fatigued, all assemble round the fire, which has been lighted, supper is prepared, and a camp being erected, there they pass the night.

Days and weeks, nay months, of unremitting toil, pass before they gain the end of their journey. They have crossed both the Carolinas, Georgia, and Alabama. They have been travelling from the beginning of May to that of September, and with heavy hearts they traverse the State of Mississippi. But now, arrived on the banks of the broad stream, they gaze in amazement on the dark deep woods around them. Boats of various kinds they see gliding downwards with the current, while others slowly ascend against it. A few inquiries are made at the nearest dwelling, and, assisted by the inhabitants with their boats and canoes, they at once cross the Mississippi, and select their place of habitation.

The exhalations arising from the swamps and morasses around them, have a powerful effect on these new settlers, but all are intent on preparing for the winter. A small patch of ground is cleared by the axe and the fire, a temporary cabin is erected, to each of the cattle is attached a jingling-bell before it is let loose into the neighbouring cane-brake, and the horses remain about the house, where they find sufficient food at that season. The first trading boat that stops at their landing, enables them to provide themselves with some flour, fish-hooks, and ammunition, as well as other commodities. The looms are mounted, the spinning-wheels soon furnish some yarn, and in a few weeks the family throw off their ragged clothes, and array themselves in suits adapted to the climate. The father and sons meanwhile have sown turnips and other vegetables; and from some Kentucky flat boat a supply of live poultry has been procured.

October tinges the leaves of the forest, the morning dews are heavy, the days hot, the nights chill, and the unacclimated family in a few days are attacked with ague. The lingering disease almost prostrates their whole faculties, and one seeing them at such a period might well call them sallow and sickly. Fortunately the unhealthy season soon passes over, and the hoar-frosts make their appearance. Gradually each individual recovers strength. The largest ash trees are felled; their trunks are cut, split, and corded in front of the building; a large fire is lighted under night on the edge of the water, and soon a steamer calls to purchase the wood, and thus add to their comforts during the winter.

This first fruit of their industry imparts new courage to them; their exertions multiply, and when spring returns, the place has a cheerful look. Venison, bear's flesh, wild turkeys, ducks, and geese, with now and then some fish, have served to keep up their strength, and now their enlarged field is planted with corn, potatoes, and pumpkins. Their stock of cattle, too, has augmented; the steamer, which now stops there as if by preference, buys a calf or a pig, together with the whole of their wood. Their store of provisions is renewed, and brighter rays of hope enliven their spirits.

Who is he of the settlers on the Mississippi that cannot realize some profit? Truly none who is industrious. When the autumnal months return, all are better prepared to encounter the ague, which then prevails. Substantial food, suitable clothing, and abundant firing, repel its attacks; and before another twelvemonth has elapsed, the family is naturalized.

The sons by this time have discovered a swamp covered with excellent timber, and as they have seen many great rafts of saw logs, bound for the mills of New Orleans, floating past their dwelling, they resolve to try the success of a little enterprise. Their industry and prudence have already enhanced their credit. A few cross-saws are purchased, and some broad-wheeled "carry-logs" are made by themselves. Log after log is hauled to the bank of the river, and in a short time their first raft is made on the shore, and loaded with cord-wood. When the next freshet sets it afloat, it is secured by long grape-vines or cables, until the proper time being arrived, the husband and sons embark on it, and float down the mighty stream.

After encountering many difficulties, they arrive in safety at New Orleans where they dispose of their stock, the money obtained for which may be said to be all profit; supply themselves with such articles as may add to their convenience or comfort, and with light hearts, procure a passage on the upper deck of a steamer, at a very cheap rate, on account of the benefit of their labour in taking in wood or otherwise.

And now the vessel approaches their home. See the joyous mother and daughters as they stand on the bank! A store of vegetables lies around them, a large tub of fresh milk is at their feet, and in their hands are plates filled with rolls of butter. As the steamer stops, three broad straw-hats are waved from its upper deck; and soon, husband and wife, brothers and sisters, are in each other's embrace. The boat carries off the provisions, for which value has been left, and as the captain issues his orders for putting on the steam, the happy family enter their humble dwelling. The husband gives his bag of dollars to the wife, while the sons present some token of affection to their sisters. Surely, at such a moment, the Squatters are richly repaid for all their labours.

Every successive year has increased their savings. They now possess a large stock of horses, cows, and hogs, with abundance of provisions, and domestic comfort of every kind. The daughters have been married to the sons of neighbouring Squatters, and have gained sisters to themselves by the marriage of their brothers. The government secures to the family the lands, on which, twenty years before, they settled in poverty and sickness. Larger buildings are erected on piles, secure from the inundations; where a single cabin once stood, a neat village is now to be seen; warehouses, stores, and work-shops, increase the importance of the place. The Squatters live respected and in due time die regretted, by all who knew them.

Thus are the vast frontiers of our country peopled, and thus does cultivation, year after year, extend over the western wilds. Time will no doubt be, when the great valley of the Mississippi, still covered with primeval forests, interspersed with swamps, will smile with corn-fields and orchards, while crowded cities will rise at intervals along its banks, and enlightened nations will rejoice in the bounties of Providence.

$$\text{\qquad}\mathcal{C} \qquad 21 \qquad \mathcal{C}$$

MINOR NATIVE VOICES

Tecumseh (c. 1771–1813), Jane Johnston Schoolcraft (1800–1841), George W. Harkins (?–?)

The following selections were composed by Native Americans who wrote or published little else in their lifetimes. Each is an historically significant figure but for reasons other than their literary efforts. Nonetheless, the texts reproduced here represent significant and articulate expressions of Native American sentiments and experience.

The first, Tecumseh, a Shawnee, was a major leader of Native American forces throughout the Ohio valley early in the nineteenth century. While Tecumseh was not literate, he was noted by figures from both races for his articulate composition and clarity of expression. In this speech, his final one before his death, Tecumseh addresses General William Proctor on the eve of the Battle of Malden in the War of 1812. Tecumseh's own coalition had been decimated in 1811 when his brother, the Prophet (Tenskatawa), rashly led his forces into battle at Tippecanoe against William Henry Harrison while Tecumseh was in the south rallying support for his coalition among the Choctaws and the Creeks. Tecumseh's accusation of cowardice at the fleeing British reveals his profound disappointment in the fact that, after fighting for years with their aid, the British had only used the Natives as mercenaries and were, in the end, concerned only with selfish ends.

Jane Johnston Schoolcraft was the mixed-blood Ojibway wife of Henry Rowe Schoolcraft, for twenty years Indian agent at Sault Ste. Marie and major author of books on Native American history and languages. She was also the daughter of John Johnston, a white trader, and the granddaughter of noted Ojibway chief Waub Ojeeg, whose story she sets to print here. Her husband had earlier transcribed a prose biography of Waub Ojeeg, reproduced in this volume. However, while Henry Schoolcraft used the story to demonstrate the natives' coming disappearance, his wife expresses a more resisting attitude.

Finally, George W. Harkins, about whom little is known, published this articulate farewell to the United States in 1832. The Choctaw were in the process, like the Creeks and the Cherokees, of being forcibly removed west of the Mississippi. In the South, the exposive growth of the cotton industry accelerated the removal of natives. Harkins is notable for his lack of rancor and his awareness of the tragedy of removal.

Texts: Tecumseh, in Benjamin Drake, *Life of Tecumseh* (Cincinnati, 1841): 188–189. Schoolcraft, *The Literary Voyager or Muzzeniegun* (Sault Ste. Marie, Michigan, 27 March 1827), rpt. *The Literary Voyager or Muzzeniegun,* ed. Philip P. Mason (East Lansing, Michigan: 1962): 138–143. Harkins, in *Great Documents in American Indian History,* ed. Wayne Moquin (New York: Da Capo, 1993): 151–153.

TECUMSEH, SPEECH AT MALDEN (1813)

"Father, listen to your children! you have them now all before you.

"The war before this, our British father gave the hatchet to his red children, when our old chiefs were alive. They are now dead. In that war our father was thrown on his back by the Americans; and our father took them by the hand without our knowledge; and we are afraid that our father will do so again at this time.

"Summer before last, when I came forward with my red brethren and was ready to take up the hatchet in favor of our British father, we were told not to be in a hurry, that he had not yet determined to fight the Americans.

"Listen! when war was declared, our father stood up and gave us the tomahawk, and told us that he was then ready to strike the Americans; that he wanted our assistance, and that he would certainly get our lands back, which the Americans had taken from us.

"Listen! you told us at that time, to bring forward our families to this place, and we did so; and you promised to take care of them, and they should want for nothing, while the men would go and fight the enemy; that we need not trouble ourselves about the enemy's garrisons; that we knew nothing about them, and that our father would attend to that part of the business. You also told your red children that you would take good care of your garrison here, which made our hearts glad.

"Listen! when we were last at the Rapids, it is true we gave you little assistance. It is hard to fight people who live like ground-hogs.

"Father, listen! our fleet has gone out; we know they have fought; we have heard the great guns; but we know nothing of what has happened to our father with one arm.[1] Our ships have gone one way, and we are much astonished to see our father tying up every thing and preparing to run away the other, without letting his red children know what his intentions are. You always told us to remain here and take care of our lands; it made our hearts glad to hear that was your wish. Our great father, the king, is the head, and you represent him. You always told us you would never draw your foot off British ground; but now, father, we see that you are drawing back, and we are sorry to see our father doing so without seeing the enemy. We must compare our father's conduct to a fat dog, that carries his tail on its back, but when affrighted, drops it between its legs and runs off.

"Father, listen ! the Americans have not yet defeated us by land; neither are we sure that they have done so by water; *we, therefore, wish to remain here and fight our enemy, should they make their appearance.* If they defeat us, we will then retreat with our father.

"At the battle of the Rapids, last war, the Americans certainly defeated us; and when we returned to our father's fort at that place, the gates were shut against us. We were afraid that it would now be the case; but instead of that, we now see our British father preparing to march out of his garrison.

"Father, you have got the arms and ammunition which our great father sent for his red children. If you have an idea of going away, give them to us, and you may go and welcome, for us. Our lives are in the hands of the Great Spirit. We are determined to defend our lands, and if it be his will, we wish to leave our bones upon them."

---

1. Commodore Barclay, who had lost an arm in some previous battle.

In northern climes there liv'd a chief of fame,
LaPointé his dwelling, and Ojeeg his name,
Who oft in war had rais'd the battle cry,
And brav'd the rigors of an Arctic sky;
Nor less in peace those daring talents shone,
That rais'd him to his simple forest throne,
Alike endow'd with skill, such heaven's reward,
To wield the oaken sceptre, and to guard.
Now round his tent, the willing chieftain's wait,
10 The gathering council, and the stern debate—
Hunters, & warriors circle round the green,
Age sits sedate, & youth fills up the scene,
While careful hands, with flint & steel prepare,
The sacred fire—the type of public care.

15   Warriors and friends'—the chief of chiefs oppress'd,
With rising cares, his burning thoughts express'd.
'Long have our lands been hem'd around by foes,
Whose secret ire, no check or limit knows,
Whose public faith, so often pledg'd in vain,
20 'Twere base for freemen e'er to trust again.
Watch'd in their tracks our trusting hunters fall,
By ambush'd arrow, or avenging ball;
Our subtil foes lie hid in every pass,
Screen'd in the thicket, shelter'd in the grass,
25 They pierce our forests, & they cross our lines,
No treaty binds them, & no stream confines
And every spring that clothes the leafy plain,
We mourn our brethren, or our children slain.
Delay but swells our woes, as rivers wild,
30 Heap on their banks the earth they first despoil'd.
Oh chieftains! listen to my warning voice,
War—war or slavery is our only choice.
No longer sit, with head & arms declin'd,
The charms of ease still ling'ring in the mind;
35 No longer hope, that justice will be given
If ye neglect the proper means of heaven:
Fear—and fear only, makes our foemen just
Or shun the path of conquest, rage or lust,
Nor think the lands we own, our sons shall share,
40 If we forget the noble rites of war.
Choose then with wisdom, nor by more delay,

Put off the great—the all important day.
Upon yourselves alone, your fate depends,
'Tis warlike acts that make a nation friends
45 'Tis warlike acts that prop a falling throne,
And makes peace, glory, empire, all our own.
Oh friends! think deeply on my counsel—words
I sound no peaceful cry of summer birds!
No whispering dream of bliss without allay
50 Or idle strain of mute, inglorious joy
Let my bold voice arouse your slumb'ring hearts,
And answer warriors—with uplifted darts,
Thick crowding arrows, bristled o'er the plain,
And joyous warriors rais'd the battle strain.

55   All but Camudẃa, join'd the shouting throng,
Camudẃa, fam'd for eloquence of tongue
Whose breast resolv'd the coming strife with pain,
And peace still hop'd, by peaceful arts to gain.
'Friends'—he reply'd—'our ruler's words are just,
60 Fear breeds respect and bridles rage or lust,
But in our haste, by rude and sudden hate,
To prop our own, or crush our neighbors state
Valor itself, should not disdain the skill
By pliant speech, to gain our purpos'd will.
65 The foe may yet, be reason'd into right.
And if we fail in speech—we still may fight.
At least, one further effort, be our care,
I will myself, the daring message bear,
I give my body, to the mission free,
70 And if I fall, my country, 'tis for thee!
The wife and child, shall lisp my song of fame,
And all who value peace, repeat my name!

        'Tis well—Baimwáwa placidly replied,
'To cast our eyes, with care to either side,
75 Lest in our pride, to bring a rival low,
Our own fair fields shall fall beneath the foe.
Great is the stake, nor should we lightly yield,
Our ancient league by many a battle seal'd.
The deeds of other days before my eyes,
80 In all their friendship, love and faith arise,
When hand in hand with him we rov'd the wood,
Swept the long vale, or stem'd the boiling flood.
In the same war path, march'd with ready blade,
And liv'd, and fought, and triumph'd with his aid.
85 When the same tongue, express'd our joys and pains,
And the same blood ran freely thro' our veins?

'Not we—not we'—in rage Keewaydin spoke,
'Strong ties have sever'd, or old friendships broke,
Back on themselves the baseless charge must fall,
90 They sunder'd name, league, language, rites and all.
They, with our firm allies, the Gallic race,
First broke the league, by secret arts and base,
Then play'd the warrior—call'd our bands a clog,
And earn'd their proper title, Fox and Dog.
95 Next to the false Dacota gave the hand,
And leagued in war, our own destruction plan'd.
Do any doubt the words I now advance,
Here is my breast'—he yelled & shook his lance.

'Rage'—interposed the sage Canowakeed,
100 Ne'er prompted wit, or bid the council speed
For other aims, be here our highest end,
Such gentle aims as rivet friend to friend.
If harsher fires, in ardent bosoms glow,
At least restrain them, till we meet the foe,
105 Calm judgment here, demands the care of all,
For if we judge amiss, ourselves shall fall.
Beside, what boasts it, that ye here repeat,
The current tale of ancient scaith or heat,
Love, loss, or bicker, welcome or retort,
110 Once giv'n in earnest, or return'd sport
Or how, or when, this hapless feud arose,
That made our firmest friends, our firmest foes.
That so it is, by causes new or old,
There are no strangers present, to be told,
115 Each for himself, both knows & feels & sees,
The growing evils of a heartless peace,
And the sole question, of this high debate,
Is—shall we longer suffer—longer wait,
Or, with heroic will, for strife prepare,
120 And try the hazard of a gen'ral war!

HARKINS, FAREWELL LETTER TO THE AMERICAN PEOPLE (1832)

[In December, 1830, the Choctaws had signed away their last remaining territory in the state of Mississippi and faced the prospect of moving west to Indian Territory. It was with much regret that the tribe members left their old homes; and the move, ill-provided for by the U.S. Government, came in midwinter. As the journey was about to take place, one of the tribal leaders voiced the sentiments of his people regarding the treaty and the decision to go west.]

TO THE AMERICAN PEOPLE.

It is with considerable diffidence that I attempt to address the American people, knowing and feeling sensibly my incompetency; and believing that your highly and well improved minds could not be well entertained by the address of a Choctaw. But having determined to emigrate west of the Mississippi river this fall, I have thought proper in bidding you farewell, to make a few remarks of my views and the feelings that actuate me on the subject of our removal.

Believing that our all is at stake and knowing that you readily sympathize with the distressed of every country, I confidently throw myself on your indulgence and ask you to listen patiently. I do not arrogate to myself the prerogative of deciding upon the expediency of the late treaty, yet I feel bound as a Choctaw, to give a distinct expression of my feelings on that interesting, (and to the Choctaws) all important subject.

We were hedged in by two evils, and we chose that which we thought least. Yet we could not recognize the right that the state of Mississippi had assumed to legislate for us. Although the legislature of the state were qualified to make laws for their own citizens, that did not qualify them to become law makers to a people who were so dissimilar in manners and customs as the Choctaws are to the Mississippians. Admitting that they understood the people, could they remove that mountain of prejudice that has ever obstructed the streams of justice, and prevented their salutary influence from reaching my devoted countrymen? We as Choctaws rather chose to suffer and be free, than live under the degrading influence of laws, where our voice could not be heard in their formation.

Much as the state of Mississippi has wronged us, I cannot find in my heart any other sentiment than an ardent wish for her prosperity and happiness.

I could cheerfully hope that those of another age and generation may not feel the effects of those oppressive measures that have been so illiberally dealt out to us; and that peace and happiness may be their reward. Amid the gloom and honors of the present separation, we are cheered with a hope that ere long we shall reach our destined home, and that nothing short of the basest acts of treachery will ever be able to wrest it from us, and that we may live free. Although your ancestors won freedom on the fields of danger and glory, our ancestors owned it as their birthright, and we have had to purchase it from you as the vilest slaves buy their freedom.

Yet it is said that our present movements are our own voluntary acts—such is not the case. We found ourselves like a benighted stranger, following false guides, until he was surrounded on every side, with fire or water. The fire was certain destruction, and feeble hope was left him of escaping by water. A distant view of the opposite shore encourages the hope; to remain would be utter annihilation. Who would hesitate, or would say that his plunging into the water was his own voluntary act? Painful in the extreme is the mandate of our expulsion. We regret that it should proceed from the mouth of our professed friend, and for whom our blood was commingled with that of his bravest warriors, on the field of danger and death.

But such is the instability of professions. The man who said that he would plant a stake and draw a line around us, that never should be passed, was the first to say he could not guard the lines, and drew up the stake and wiped out all traces of the line. I will not conceal from you my fears, that the present grounds may be removed—I have my foreboding—who of us can tell after witnessing what has already been done, what the next force may be.

I ask you in the name of justice, for repose for myself and my injured people. Let us alone—we will not harm you, we want rest. We hope, in the name of justice, that another outrage may never be committed against us, and that we may for the future be cared for as children, and not driven about as beasts, which are benefitted by a change of pasture.

Taking an example from the American government, and knowing the happiness which its citizens enjoy, under the influence of mild republican institutions, it is the intention of our countrymen to form a government assimilated to that of our white breathern in the United States, as nearly as their condition will permit.

We know that in order to protect the rights and secure the liberties of the people, no government approximates so nearly to perfection as the one to which we have alluded. As east of the Mississippi we have been friends, so west we will cherish the same feelings with additional fervor; and although we may be removed to the desert, still we shall look with fine regard, upon those who have promised us their protection. Let that feeling be reciprocated.

Friends, my attachment to my native land is strong—that cord is now broken; and we must go forth as wanderers in a strange land! I must go—let me entreat you to regard us with feelings of kindness, and when the hand of oppression is stretched against us, let me hope that every part of the United States, filling the mountains and valleys, will echo and say stop, you have no power, we are the sovereign people, and our friends shall no more be disturbed. We ask you for nothing that is incompatible with your other duties.

We go forth sorrowful, knowing that wrong has been done. Will you extend to us your sympathizing regards until all traces of disagreeable oppositions are obliterated, and we again shall have confidence in the professions of our white brethern.

Here is the land of our progenitors, and here are their bones; they left them as a sacred deposit, and we have been compelled to venerate its trust; it is dear to us yet we cannot stay, my people are dear to me, with them I must go. Could I stay and forget them and leave them to struggle alone, unaided, unfriended, and forgotten by our great father? I should then be unworthy the name of a Choctaw, and be a disgrace to my blood. I must go with them; my destiny is cast among the Choctaw people. If they suffer, so will I; if they prosper, then I will rejoice. Let me again ask you to regard us with feelings of kindness.

22

DANIEL DRAKE

(1785–1852)

Known during his lifetime as the "Franklin of the West," Dr. Daniel Drake's importance to the trans-Appalachian west during the antebellum decades can hardly be understated. First and foremost, he was a doctor, specifically an epidemiologist whose research helped eliminate malaria in the region. He also helped found medical colleges throughout the region in Tennessee, Kentucky, and Ohio. His publications in these areas make up the majority of his bibliography and earned him a place in the American Philosophical Society and offers to teach at a number of prestigious eastern medical colleges. This culminated in his monumental *Systematic Treatise on the Principal Diseases of the Interior Valley of North America* (1850), a landmark in nineteenth-century American medical scholarship. However, Drake was also a successful businessman, journalist, editor, and, of immediate interest, advocate of western regional culture.

The Drake family (including younger brother Benjamin) emigrated from New Jersey to northern Kentucky in 1788. At age fifteen, Drake was apprenticed to a local doctor and was sent to Philadelphia in 1805 to complete his training. By 1807, he was established as a doctor in the rapidly growing city of Cinicinnati, the place that would serve as the base of his operations for the rest of his life. Drake's medical career would move him around the region as his increasing insistence on studying specifically local medical problems contrasted with the more classical orientations of many of his colleagues.

By the mid-1820s, his interests grew from this interest to larger cultural issues in the region, and he started a literary salon (the Buck-Eye Club) in his home for similar advocates of local self-determination in political and cultural matters. By contrast, Cincinnati's "Semi-Colon Club" was started by eastern immigrants such as Henry Ward Beecher to accomplish just the reverse. Aside from his brother, now editor of *The Cincinnati Chronicle,* Drake gathered around him such western intellectuals as Timothy Flint, James Hall, Edward Mansfield, William Davis Gallagher, Amelia Welby, Salmon P. Chase, and others interested in exploring nonsectional forms of regional differentiation from the metropolitan culture of the eastern seaboard. His advocacy of their work cultivated the city's extensive literary scene, at the time the fourth most productive center of the nation's publishing industry.

The pieces reprinted here reflect Drake's alienation from the east and his view of a resulting need for "western" regional cultural self-exploration. Suggesting that "no western man" could read Cooper's *The Prairie* without laughing, Drake was among the first to recognize his region's

340

misrepresentation in the national media. Furthermore, his view of the "west," like Flint's, runs along the rivers, and disregards the regional distinctions promulgated by both northern and southern sectionalists during the antebellum era. By contrast, more like Brackenridge, Drake perceived the west as a third component that could moderate between north and south in the approaching conflict but argued that, to do so, it must first know itself.

The two addresses—"Remarks" and "Discourse"—articulate one of the most important tenets of American regionalism in general: that regionalism and nationalism were compatible. That is, especially in the northeast during this period, a single "national" culture was being identified as a model on which local communities could measure their own legitimacy—a vertical scale with the "Universal Yankee nation" ascendent. Drake's recognition that one could be an American without being a Yankee serves as a model for recognizing and celebrating the diversity at the heart of the nation's life that Yankee-ism sought to conceal.

Texts: Both are available in *Physician to the West: Selected Writings of Daniel Drake* (Athens, Ohio 1975): "Remarks," 223–238; "Discourse," 240–259.

REMARKS ON THE IMPORTANCE OF PROMOTING LITERARY AND SOCIAL CONCERT IN THE VALLEY OF THE MISSISSIPPI (1833)

About three years ago, several respectable teachers in the valley of the Ohio River, most of whom reside in Cincinnati, projected and organized a society, which they denominated, "THE WESTERN LITERARY INSTITUTE, AND COLLEGE OF PROFESSIONAL TEACHERS." Its second annual meeting was held in Cincinnati, in the month of September last, and was attended by a number of teachers and professors of Ohio, Kentucky and Illinois. Several interesting topics connected with education, it is understood, were discussed by these gentlemen, and a number of public lectures, by themselves and others invited to that task, were delivered to large audiences of ladies and gentlemen.

Before the Institute adjourned, it was thought advisable to enlarge its limits, both as to the objects on which it should in future exert itself, and also to the qualifications of membership. Accordingly the following resolution was adopted:

"*Resolved,* That a Central Committee be appointed to devise a plan of a Society for the Improvement of Education and the diffusion of useful knowledge, which shall include the citizens of all classes, in the several Western States, and be calculated to exert an influence on the whole mass of the people; and that said committee shall make its report at a General Convention of the Citizens of the Western States and Territories, in this City, (Cincinnati,) on the second Monday in April next."

In the first week of November, by the efforts of the Rev. B. O. PEERS, acting President of Transylvania University, a similar Convention, for the State of Kentucky alone, was held at Lexington, and attended by several gentlemen from Cincinnati, invited thither by Mr. PEERS. The Author of this pamphlet was among the number, and was one of those whom the Convention honored with the request to address them. The subject which he chose, was the Physical, Intellectual and Moral Education, *appropriate to the two sexes, respectively.*

The lecture being concluded, he deemed the occasion a suitable one for promoting the *general* literary meeting just referred to, and accordingly offered the following resolution, which was ultimately adopted by a unanimous vote.

"*Resolved, as the sense of this body,* That the State of Kentucky should be represented in the proposed meeting of delegates, from the different States of the Valley of the Mississippi, in April next."

After the Convention adjourned, a respectable number of its members, did him the honor to ask a copy of both the *Lecture* and the *Remarks* for publication. Expecting, at no distant time, to be able to present the former to the public, in a different way, he has complied with their flattering request, in reference to the latter only.

His remarks were chiefly extempore or from brief and hasty notes; and in writing them out for the press, he has extended them on certain points, so as to present the subject more fully than it was then displayed.

He is not a statesman, nor even a politician, but a naturalist; and has applied his geographical and geological observations, to the discussion of certain questions of patriotic and social duty. By this application he hopes in some degree to promote uniformity and elevation of character in the Valley of the Mississippi, and thereby contribute to the preservation of the Union; which, however, he regards in no present, and believes, by the West alone, may be preserved from all future danger.

CINCINNATI, (OHIO,) DECEMBER 15, 1833.

Our happy UNION enjoys unlimited sovereignty among the nations of the earth, but over its own people, and the different states to which they belong, its powers are restricted. On many points the states are sovereign, in relation to the confederacy, but they have few attributes of sovereignty in reference to each other, individually, and still fewer, in regard to foreign governments. This complex political organization, the only one perhaps that could enable the inhabitants of an *extensive* territory to establish union, and at the same time enjoy the blessings of laws adapted to their respective wants, like every thing complicated, is liable to decomposition. At a period when such a catastrophe is spoken of by all, and apprehended by many, it cannot be unprofitable for the people of the different states, to consider what they may do to avert it. As a citizen of the valley of the Mississippi, addressing those who dwell in the same region, I propose to say something on the means of prevention which lie within *our* reach; and hope to show, that the intellectual and moral elevation which it is our absolute duty to promote, is precisely that which would most effectually perpetuate the UNION.

In past ages of the world, such a union would, perhaps, have conferred but few benefits on those who might have formed it, and could not, in fact, have been sustained. To the discoveries and inventions of modern science—physical, mechanical, political and moral—applied to national objects, we are indebted for the means of its preservation in our own case. But even these might be ineffectual, if nature did not favor their application. Thus guided, it is, I think, the coldest scepticism, to doubt their perfect efficiency.

Before the means of diffusing knowledge, favoring personal intercourse, and facilitating an exchange of productions, between the remote sections of a great empire, were invented, the ties which bound them together, were woven and sustained by the hand of military power; and when it became convulsed or paralyzed, decomposition was the inevitable consequence. The natural objects and operations which might have promoted union, or which required to be controlled for the purpose of maintaining it, were too often overlooked. In the United States the case is far different. A profound policy of the people, exerted at the same time through the federal and state governments, has laid the foundations of union on the plan of nature. Where she favors intercourse between the different portions of the country, the hand of art lends its cultivation; and when she opposes it, the same hand is successfully raised against her power. Let them persevere in this policy and the UNION is perpetual.

To understand how the natural configuration of our country, under the influence of science, must of *necessity* give permanence to the UNION, we need but turn our eyes upon its map, and contemplate the different great valleys or basins into which it is naturally divisible.

The seaboard presents a range of states, the "Old Thirteen"; the whole of which, except Vermont, are connected with the Atlantic ocean. Each has its navigable rivers, its bays, harbors, and wharves, enabling it to establish and maintain an independent commercial intercourse with every other state, and with all the world. Most of their rivers originate in the Alleghany Mountains; which, commencing in the north of Georgia, terminate in the state of New York, traversing the states of North Carolina, Virginia, Maryland, and Pennsylvania. The average distance of these mountain ranges from the ocean, is about two hundred miles. Large portions of two of the states extend beyond them into the interior. Between the extremities of these mountains and the gulf of Mexico, towards the south and Lake Ontario, towards the north, the land is low and level. New England, separated from this Alpine range, by the valleys of Lake Champlain and the Hudson river, has its own mountains. Such is the maritime or Atlantic basin of the Union; and the states which it comprehends, extending from East Florida to Maine, form a sort of arch, of which New York is regarded, as the keystone, though nearer to one extremity than the other. New England is the northern buttress of this arch.

The original states, lying in this basin, were settled in a great degree, by separate colonies from Europe; and if *they* composed the *whole* union, it might, at any time be dissolved; for there is among them no physical tie of paramount influence. Indeed, I think it a fair presumption, that before this time, the Chesapeake bay would have politically divided them into a northern and a southern confederacy. But, happily there rests on the arch a weight, which, unremoved must forever preserve it. This weight is the superstructure of trans-alpine states and territories, which stretch from the western foot of the Alleghanies to the wilds of Missouri, in prospect even to the Chippewan mountains; and from the Lakes to the gulf of Mexico, in *natural* association. The waters of this extensive inland region, flow off to the sea in two opposite channels; the Niagara and the Mississippi, dividing it physically into two great valleys or basins. Let us consider them separately.

The southwest corner of New York, the adjacent parts of Pennsylvania, the northern portions of Ohio, Indiana, and Illinois, a part of the Northwest Territory, and the whole of Michigan, lie in the Niagara basin; and are, commercially, connected with the city of New York by the Clinton Canal, and the Hudson river. The connexion of the west with that city, is not, however, limited to the states just enumerated, for the Grand Canal of the enterprizing state of Ohio, has recently extended the water communication between New York and the West, quite into the valley of the Mississippi; and Indiana, and Illinois have similar works in contemplation or actual progress.

The connexion between the Niagara basin thus enlarged and the Atlantic states, is not limited to New York, but extends to New England, especially to Connecticut, Rhode Island, and Massachusetts. Thus the northern parts of the United States present a natural zone, which reaches from the eastern extremity of Maine to the Upper Mississippi, through nearly thirty degrees of longitude. This is our lake country, an interior maritime basin, of twice the length of the Atlantic, and four times its fertility. The states which it comprehends, form, like the thirteen, a kind of arch, of which New York again is the keystone, and New England the eastern abutment. The two lines of states, indeed, meet in New York, which is common to both and the "land of the pilgrims" constitutes the point of the angle which they form. The long chain of northern lakes with their connecting rivers and canals facilitate emigration from east to west; and, as man never migrates in numbers from a warmer to a colder climate, the predominant population of this great zone will be *Yankee*. The manners and customs, the literature, religion, arts, sciences, and institutions of New England, and its derivative Western New York, are destined to prevail throughout its whole extent. All this is the offspring of *natural* causes; which, whenever enterprize is left free, and laws are enacted for the public good, will be found to guide emigration, govern the investment of capital, and direct legislation.

Every friend of the Union must look with pleasure and confidence on the interest which the eastern and western halves of this zone must forever have, in maintaining their various mutual relations. The focus of these relations is the city of New York. In her resides the centripetal power, which can never cease to attract the whole. This power has increased a hundred fold within the last twenty years; and cannot be annihilated. Nature has decreed that she should be the commercial capital of the northern belt of the Union. All the states and parts of states, which it naturally comprehends, will be brought under her paramount influence; and she, on the other hand, will never cease to perceive, that her prosperity rests upon theirs, and that if her connection with them were dissolved, the gorgeous visions of future greatness which cheer her enterprising citizens, would vanish in an hour. Of the vast, and already populous region which administers to her wealth, that part which stretches from the Falls of Niagara into the wilderness, will soon be the most important, and, in her wisdom, will be especially cherished. In prosperity or adversity—in her days of pride and exultation, of conscious superiority over many of her humbler sisters of the Sea-coast—in the calm of political peace or amidst the schemes and ragings of faction—she will never be so mad as to disconnect herself, if indeed, she could, from her western resources.

Such is the northern girdle of the UNION, extending from the Bay of Fundy to the Lake of the Woods. New York is the link which connects its opposite parts, and until there arise a power strong enough to displace her, it cannot be broken. A fruitful fancy may conjure up undefined images of such a power, shooting forth from the midst of possible revolutions;—the speculative politician may have his reveries of the future, and the hypochondriac his forebodings—but the naturalist, who quietly contemplates the overruling influence of physical causes on the political and social relations of a free and enlightened people, will confide in their power, and continue a firm believer in the stability of the north.

The integrity of that commercial and social confederacy being preserved, the *Union* itself could scarcely be dissolved. The western portions of that zone, must forever exert an attraction on the northern parts of the valley of the Mississippi, while its eastern half, composed of New York and New England will act with equal power on Pennsylvania and New Jersey. Physically, the north of Pennsylvania, and the south of New York, are one region. The great rivers of the former originate in the latter, and there is between the two no natural line of separation. The north-west of Pennsylvania, moreover, has a direct interest in the Erie basin and the canal which connects it with the ocean. The connection between my native state and New York, is still closer. New Jersey, in truth, must forever remain in political, as she is in commercial, association with the great emporium. It is, however, East Jersey only, that feels this influence. West Jersey is allied in trade and social relations to Philadelphia, and hence, that little state must, at all times, constitute a link of union between the valleys of the Hudson and the Delaware. But dismissing the influence of the basin of the Lakes, let us turn to that of the Mississippi.

It is said by Dr. Goldsmith in his Natural History, that however large one fancies an Elephant to be, from reading the description, it always appears larger, still, when seen by him. I would apply a similar remark to the valley of the Mississippi. Whatever ideas may be formed of its extent and importance, from the ordinary notices of it, they will always be found too limited, when a profound examination is made. Compared with it, the maritime and lake basins dwindle into insignificance. They are but belts, and at many points narrow ones. Their united area does not greatly exceed that part of the valley lying east of the Mississippi; which is itself, much less than the portion situated beyond that river. This great region extends through thirty degrees of longitude and twenty of latitude, and no part is as far north as England. It is at least equal in area to Europe south of the Baltic and west of the Black Sea.—Bounded on the east by the Alleghanies; on the west by the Chippewan mountains, its numerous rivers meet in the channel of the Mississippi through a distance of more than two thousand miles. To the north, the sources of these rivers blend themselves, on an elevated plain, with the shorter streams which flow into the lakes. To the east, from New York to Georgia, originating on the slopes of the Alleghany mountains, they interlock with the Delaware, the Susquehanna, the Potomac, James River, the Roanoke, the Santee and the Savannah. It is no exaggeration to say, that considered in reference to area, soil, aspect, and climate, this valley is superior to any other on the globe. Its only natural highway to the sea is the river Mississippi;—New Orleans constitutes its mart; and between that city—the New York of the south—and the vast country above, there is and must ever be an action and reaction still more natural and powerful than that between the city just named and the basin of the lakes. Let us consider the civil divisions of the valley, with a reference to the influence it is exerting, and must continue to exert, on the whole union.

Several states, as Missouri, Kentucky, Tennessee, and Arkansas, lie wholly within its limits. Of Illinois, Indiana, Ohio, Mississippi and Louisiana, the greater portions are included in it. A part of New York, a larger one of Pennsylvania, and a still larger of Virginia, with a small portion of Maryland, North Carolina, Georgia, and Alabama, dip into the same basin. Thus twenty states and territories out of twenty-nine, the latter of which are of vast extent and destined to sub-division, are embraced wholly or in part in the Great Valley; the inhabitants of which already make one-third of the entire population of the Union, and are daily augmenting by emigration from every quarter.

As the extent to which the old states run into the Mississippi valley is very different, so there must be degrees in their influence on the stability of the union.

The participation of Pennsylvania and Virginia is most extensive, and to this we may look for a permanent effect. The Western portions of these great states, are, in truth, natural and unalienable elements of the Mississippi community; united to the true and proper *West,* by ties not to be dissolved; dependent on our great river; familiar with its banks; and proud of its name. They can never consent to become a distinct people from their brethren below, through whom they must forever wish to pass to the ocean; and among whom, it must always be their interest, to distribute their mountain forests of pine and cedar, their beds of iron ore, their banks of coal, and the products of their salt springs. So intimate, indeed, is the *physical* relation of the western declivities of these states, with the other parts of the Mississippi basin, that no influence of the maritime portions could ever draw them from the West. Sooner shall we see them, respectively, broken asunder along the spine of the Alleghenies, than their western extremities detached from the Ohio states.

With respect to Pennsylvania, especially, what motive can ever madden her into a desire to leave the West? Certainly none. She has the same interest in the West as New York. It has contributed largely to make her what she is. To facilitate intercourse with it, she has even anticipated the resources of generations to come: she is turning her rivers into artificial channels, reducing her mountains, and perforating her hills; in short, she is laboring to bind herself with the West and the West to her. Thus we see that the commonwealth of William Penn, populous, orderly, respectable, and situated in the centre of the maritime zone, is equally bound to the North and the West, and must forever maintain her position in the confederacy.

Her neighbor Maryland, united to her by many natural and artificial ties, will not consent to see them broken; and although, more remote from the Great Valley than Pennsylvania, she is deeply impressed with the importance of participating in its trade, and has for years been stretching towards it her enterprizing arms.

The public sentiment of Virginia is moulding itself on the same plan. The Atlantic can never think of a separation from the Ohio portions of that state. I assume that the two halves will remain united; but the western, for the reasons I have just assigned, will adhere politically to the Valley with which it is naturally associated; and thus, the whole is permanently bound to the West by physical causes.

Would North Carolina leave Virginia? Contemplate the imaginary line which separates them. The waters of the same fountain may bubble up on the territories of the two states, and the fallen tree which lies across the stream below may serve as a bridge to connect them. Virginia, moreover, the greater in extent and physical resources, must forever be superior in political and moral power, and would be a dangerous rival. Would North Carolina withdraw from her daughter, Tennessee, estranged from her by no impassable barrier; and prepared, under a proper system of internal improvement to administer to her wealth and power? She can never willingly consent to such a separation.

What of our high-minded and palmy South Carolina; the brightest orb in our southern constellation, will she seek a new zodiac, and become the lost star of our political heavens? Of all the states she has the least of natural and commercial connexion with the valley of the Mississippi, and, as if to afford a negative evidence of the over-ruling influence of physical causes, she alone has shown symptoms of secession. But she will not wander off by herself, and none of the sisterhood *can* accompany her. The geographical cords by which she is united to her twin sister on the north, and her younger sister on the south, are too strong to be snapt assunder, and those states are bound to others by ties of equal strength and durability.

The participation of Georgia in the valley of the Mississippi, is small, but her natural relations with Tennessee are intimate and profitable, and those with Alabama and Florida permanently controlling. She cannot disconnect herself from the union, without the concurrence of Alabama, and the prospective co-operation of Florida. But Alabama is naturally associated with Louisiana, Tennessee and Mississippi, and is not therefore, politically separable from them. Moreover, New Orleans exerts on the entire region immediately east of it, an effect precisely similar to that of New York on the south of New England; and, therefore the maritime portions of Mississippi, Alabama, and Florida, are commercially under its control, and cannot become politically detached from the West, till Louisiana shall secede; an event that may happen when the Mississippi finds some other route to the ocean, or is swallowed up in the sands of its own delta.

Thus, in travelling along the Atlantic coast of the union from the St. Lawrence to the Balize, we find such natural connexions and dependencies of its states on the valleys of the Niagara and the Mississippi, as must forever set the spirit of disunion at defiance. Within these basins, together constituting the West, lies the centre of gravity of the union. Here dwells the conservative power. The cement of future adhesion among all the states exudes, to speak figuratively, from the soil of the West. To borrow a metaphor from my own profession, it is the interior of the sovereign body politic, embracing the vital organs, which distribute nourishment through the outer parts. Once more to change the figure, it is the part, where the cords of union are wound into a Gordian knot, which, cut assunder by the sword, would, under proper treatment, reunite, *by the first intention,* and not even leave a scar behind. Conventional regulations may be annulled, treaties abrogated and political confederacies dissolved, when they are not based on nature; but give them this foundation; rest the political and social upon the physical; and they will be preserved from all serious revolutions, but those which change the surface of the earth itself.

But to produce this effect on the union, the west must become and remain united with itself. Whatever retards or diminishes this subordinate but central and natural confederacy, weakens the general union; whatever strengthens it, invigorates the whole. The federal constitution cannot be overthrown while the Mississippi states remain in connection and harmony. To my own mind, this opinion is so conclusive and cheering, that I wish, most earnestly, to commend the grounds on which it rests, to the consideration of every intelligent patriot, who may apprehend our political dissolution.

Under these views, let us proceed to inquire into the duties of the people of the interior. They must weave among themselves a firm web of brotherhood, and become still more closely united in social feeling, literary institutions, and manners and customs; and then, no temporary or partial suffering, no conflicting interests, or state aspirations; no lawless ambition, no military power, nor reign of faction among their elder brethren of the sea-coast, can ever jostle from its place, a single column of the great temple of union. The objects thus presented to the people of the west are of the highest and noblest kind. In laboring to promote harmony among themselves, they are working for the harmony and happiness of the whole union. They have a holy task of patriotism to perform. The palladium of the Constitution is committed to them by nature, and they should faithfully preserve it. The destinies of brethren widely separated are confided to their care—let them not betray the trust.

But their own prospective interests should prompt them to action. Suppose they should neglect these labors, and the Union dissolve:—how deplorable then would be their own condition—geographically united—bound inseparably together like the Siamese twins—but attached by no civil ties—no pervading sentiments of kindness— no general plans of education—no common bonds of social harmony! Nature demanding union, but reciprocal prejudices—local animosities—contrarieties of education, and diversities of manners and customs, conspiring to array them against each other. It requires but few lessons from history, but a limited knowledge of our common dependence on the Mississippi to foresee, that should such a melancholy event ever happen, without social preparation on our part, the west would crumble with the rest into its political elements, and the immense valley, where brethren dwell together in peace, would become the Flanders of the new world in war, as it now is in corn. "Ploughs would be turned into swords, and pruning hooks into spears." The drum and trumpet would echo along our fertile valleys, and the midnight cry of hostile sentinels fall on the ear from the opposing banks of our beautiful rivers. The teeming steamboat would no longer depart from Pittsburgh or Cincinnati for New Orleans, but to a neighboring port within the limited jurisdiction to which it belonged. Never again would its decks present an epitome of the Union; a concourse of passengers from every state; greeting each other as brethren and sisters; originating plans of business, contracting new friendships, and forming the alliances of love, while the noble steamer held its way for a thousand miles, through peaceful and happy lands, which each might call his own. Fortifications would then frown from the magnificent cliffs on which the eye of the voyager now dwells with delight. The smoke of artillery would poison our evening mists, and contaminate the morning fogs, which rising from our plains, curl around the summits of the green hills. A sulphurous odour would blend itself with the aroma of our flowers. Armed steamboats would traverse all our rivers, and the glorious stripes and stars of our Union, be replaced by the hostile flags of every device. To the dangers of navigation would be added those of war; a brother's hand would apply the torch of battle, and a brother's blood mingle with our waters.

Would we, through all coming ages, avert these vast calamities, we must in due time, and at all times, labor to preserve ourselves in domestic harmony; make ourselves one brotherhood in our customs, affections, and feelings, however, distinct in political power: let us, in short, establish among the people of the Mississippi valley a literary and social communion, like that which New England presents, and then, should the old, the parent states; respectively, set up for themselves; should the demagogue undermine the foundations of the republic, or the reeking sword of the desperado cut assunder its bands, the West would go together; the largest mass of the ruin, the least mutilated in the fall, the most powerful, the most respected, the most prosperous! She might, as she would, mourn over the catastrophe; her daughters, like the damsels of Jerusalem weep fountains of tears, and her sons as those of Judea, clothe themselves in sackcloth and ashes; but they would still be safe and happy, compared with their brethren of the other states.

Thus, whether we seek to perpetuate the Union, or would prepare for its possible dissolution at some remote epoch, our duty is the same; to commune together from every part of the mighty West; to make acquaintanceship with each other; to correct each other's faults; sympathise in each other's joys and sorrows, and mould ourselves into one great social brotherhood as our flowing waters mingle and roll onward to the ocean. To these labors of love we are exhorted or commanded, by more considerations than ever prevailed among the people of any other land.

The millions who already flourish in the valleys of the Mississippi and the lakes, are chiefly emigrants. They have entered it on every side, and are derived, not only from all the original states of the Union, but from western and even central Europe. Bringing with them various national peculiarities, the common good requires that they should be speedily amalgamated into one social compound. On this will their stability and moral power depend. Every movement of the air or waters drifts about the loose sand; but consolidated into rock, it resists the action of the "winds and waves," and is fitted for permanent use. A community formed out of such elements would exert an attraction on the whole Union. But little emigration takes place between New England and Pennsylvania, New York and Virginia, Maryland or New Jersey and the Carolinas. There is no region east of the mountains, where natives of all the states congregate, and cherishing their early attachments, constitute a *Union Society*. It was reserved for the west to exhibit this interesting concourse. Elsewhere, general patriotism may be the offspring of policy or interest—in the west it must always be a sentiment of the heart.

In the character of the materials for Western society, there is much to encourage those who would labor to construct it. I believe them the best which ever came to the hands of the social architect. The old states were peopled by Europe, when she was far from the elevated grade of civilization she now exhibits, and which belongs equally to those states. Those who are emigrating to the west, have more knowledge and refinement than ever before belonged to any moving population. Even the pioneers of Kentucky, Tennessee, and Ohio, were, in part, composed of men who would have been respected in any community. Our *Clarkes, Boons, Todds, Logans, Scotts, Marshalls, Shelbys, Putnams, Cutlers, Symmes, Ludlows, Benhams, Worthingtons, Lytles, Harrisons, St. Clairs, Robertsons, Seviers, Buchhanons, Jacksons, McNairys,* are but a small portion of the honored patriarchs of the three sister states; and those who accompanied them as associates or followers, possessed, like themselves, the sagacity, courage, and high aspiration which gave a good earnest in the infancy of the west of what we already see it in youth. The emigrants to the original states, were chiefly from Great Britain, and frequently in masses or streams which flowed and settled together. When the continent made contributions, it was done in colonies, which too often continued as such after they reached the shores of America. Thus the original materials of society in the Atlantic states were less diversified, and *therefore* inferior to those which past and present emigration has distributed over the region we inhabit. With such ingredients in the moral crucible, the resulting compound must, ultimately, have less alloy than is found in most communities, should those who watch over and direct the process of union, be diligent, harmonious, and persevering.

Other considerations press themselves on the mind; address themselves to the heart. Western Pennsylvania, Western Virginia, Kentucky, Tennessee, and Ohio, young as they are, compared with the seaboard, have long been emigrating states. From the unsettled feelings of a new community, their people have passed incessantly from one to the other, still, however, advancing into the wilderness. Thus, Western Pennsylvania has scattered its sons over Ohio, while the latter has peopled Indiana and Illinois with thousands, and Tennessee sent her children to Alabama, Mississippi, Missouri and Arkansas. But above all, Kentucky, the land of my earliest recollections, has spread herself over Ohio, Indiana, Illinois, and Missouri. Of all the new states, she has, indeed, been the longest an emigrating state. Even the plan and settlement of Cincinnati, which the orator of the West has pronounced the unrivalled queen of the West, were arranged in Lexington, at that time the infant metropolis of all the new settlements.

Thus, all the states and territories of the Great Valley contain the germs of a natural brotherhood. Every where we meet with men and women, whose feelings turn instinctively to some other spot of the interior, where in the may day of life, when filled with the love of nature, they joyfully collected the lilies of the untrodden valley, or rambled, without care, among its pawpaw groves. While the grandfather smokes his pipe in the wide hall of a Kentucky double cabin, his son follows the plough in Ohio, and his grandson opens a new farm in Indiana. Two brothers embark on the Ohio river; one will stop in Missouri, the other plant himself in Louisiana. Two sisters marry in the same week; one to be taken to Alabama, the other to Illinois. These unrestrained and apparently capricious migrations, so familiar to all the inhabitants of Ohio, Kentucky, and Tennessee, must inspire the people of those states with an imperishable interest in the entire West. They predispose to union. They invite the western patriot to action, and point out the delightful task, which love of country, and love of liberty, and love of offspring, alike call upon him to execute. Seizing upon these scattered elements of union, he should bind them together, nourish them with one blood, and harmonize them with a single nervous system. Thus they will come to work together, like the different organs of the living body endowed with the same sensibility, reciprocally sympathizing, and obedient to the same laws of morality, religion, and social order.

Other considerations still, arise to the mind while intent on this subject. The territory which is now divided into Kentucky, Ohio, Indiana, and Illinois, was once a part of Virginia. The recollection of this should inspire the inhabitants of the whole, with a feeling of affection for each other. At that time, all except Kentucky was an unpeopled wilderness. The history of their early settlement fills the heart with emotion. The region between the Ohio and the Lakes, *belonged* to the Ancient Dominion, but Kentucky was the child—a daughter settled in the wilderness, and exposed to every kind of peril and privation. Participating in the glory of the Cavaliers, her sons established their claims to such a heritage, by a chivalrous devotion to the younger sisterhood of the west, which posterity will never cease to admire. For years, Kentucky was a living barrier to Tennessee, against the tribes of the north; and when did Ohio, Indiana, Illinois, and even Michigan raise the cry of alarm, that the gallant state did not, by spontaneous impulse, send forth the choicest of her sons? Their battle cry has resounded through all the forests of the north—their blood has fertilized the plains of the Wabash, the Maumee, the Raisin, and the Thames; their bones still moulder among the rank weeds, from the banks of the Ohio to Lake Superior. Their fall in the defence of their younger brethren, has more than once clothed the mothers of their native state in mourning, and spread through the city where we are now assembled, a voice of lamentation more sorrowful than even pestilence could raise. Kentucky must even cherish towards those for whom she has thus fought and bled, the good will which kind offices create for those on whom they are bestowed; and the children of the people for whom she thus suffered, can never be unmindful of her gallantry. Here then we have another chain of friendship; one which applies itself to the heart, encloses its best affections, is alloyed with no selfishness, and may be brightened through all future ages, should our literature prove true to its charge, and our men of influence devote themselves to the great cause of civil union.

But let us leave the history and resume the physical and political geography of the West, for the purpose of considering the relations of its different regions—not to the *Atlantic States,* but to *each other.* In reviewing their boundaries and connections, we find much to excite reflection and inspire us with deep emotion. The geography of the interior, in truth, admonishes us to live in harmony, cherish uniform plans of education, and found similar institutions.

The relations between the upper and lower Mississippi States, established by the collective waters of the whole valley, must forever continue unchanged. What the towering oak is to our climbing winter grape, the "Father of waters" must ever be to the communities along its trunk and countless tributary streams—an imperishable support, an exhaustless power of union. What is the composition of its lower coasts and alluvial plains, but the soil of all the upper states and territories, transported, commingled, and deposited by its waters? Within her own limits, Louisiana has, indeed, the rich mould of ten sister states, which have thus contributed to the fertility of her plantations. It might almost be said, that for ages this region has sent thither a portion of its soil, where, in a milder climate, it might produce the cotton, oranges and sugar, which, through the same channel, we receive in exchange for the products of our corn fields, work shops, and mines. Facts which prepare the way, and invite to perpetual union between the West and South.

The state of Tennessee, separated from Alabama and Mississippi on the south and Kentucky on the north, by no natural barrier, has its southern fields overspread with floating cotton, wafted from the two first by every autumnal breeze; while the shade of its northern woods, lies for half the summer day on the borders of the last. The songs and uproar of a Kentucky *husking* are answered from Tennessee; and the midnight raccoon-hunt that follows, beginning in one state, is concluded in the other. The Cumberland on whose rocky banks the capital of Tennessee rises, in beauty, begins and terminates in Kentucky—thus bearing on its bosom at the same moment the products of the two states descending to a common market. Still further, the fine river Tennessee drains the eastern half of that state, dips into Alabama, recrosses the state in which it arose, and traverses Kentucky to reach the Ohio river; thus uniting the three into one natural and enduring commercial compact.

Further north, the cotton trees which fringe the borders of Missouri and Illinois, throw their images towards each other in the waters of the Mississippi—the toiling emigrant's axe, in the depths of the leafless woods, and the crash of the falling rail-tree on the frozen earth, resound equally among the hills of both states—the clouds of smoke from their burning prairies, mingle in the air above, and crimson the setting sun of Kentucky, Indiana and Ohio.

The Pecan tree sheds its fruit at the same moment among the people of Indiana and Illinois, and the boys of the two states paddle their canoes and fish together in the Wabash, or hail each other from opposite banks. Even villages belong equally to Indiana and Ohio, and the children of the two commonwealths trundle their hoops together in the same street.

But the Ohio river forms the most interesting boundary among the republics of the West. For a thousand miles its fertile bottoms are cultivated by farmers, who belong to the different states, while they visit each other as friends or neighbors. As the school boy trips or loiters along its shores, he greets his playmates across the stream, or they sport away an idle hour in its summer waters. These are to be among the future, perhaps the opposing statesmen of the different commonwealths. When, at low water, we examine the rocks of the channel, we find them the same on both sides. The plants which grow above, drop their seeds into the common current, which lodges them indiscriminately on either shore. Thus the very trees and flowers emigrate from one republic to another. When the bee sends out its swarms, they as often seek a habitation beyond the stream, as in their native woods. Throughout its whole extent, the hills of Western Virginia and Kentucky, cast their morning shadows on the plains of Ohio, Indiana, Illinois, and Missouri. The thunder cloud pours down its showers on different commonwealths; and the rainbow resting its extremities on two sister states, presents a beautiful arch, on which the spirits of peace may pass and repass in harmony and love.

Thus connected by nature in the great valley, we must live in the bonds of companionship, or imbrue our hands in each other's blood. We have no middle destiny. To secure the former to our posterity, we should begin while society is still tender and pliable. The saplings of the woods, if intertwined, will adapt themselves to each other and grow together; the little bird may hang its nest on the twigs of different trees, and the dew-drop fall successively on leaves which are nourished by distinct trunks. The tornado strikes harmless on such a bower, for the various parts sustain each other; but the grown tree; sturdy and set in its way; will not bend to its fellow, and when uprooted by the tempest, is dashed in violence against all within its reach.

Communities, like forests, grow rigid by time. To be properly trained they must be moulded while young. Our duty, then, is quite obvious. All who have moral power, should exert it in concert. The germs of harmony must be nourished, and the roots of present contrariety or future discord torn up and cast into the fire. Measures should be taken to mould an uniform system of manners and customs, out of the diversified elements which are scattered over the West. Literary meetings should be held in the different states; and occasional conventions in the central cities of the great valley, be made to bring into friendly consultation, our enlightened and zealous teachers, professors, lawyers, physicians, divines, and men of letters, from its remotest sections. In their deliberations the literary and moral wants of the various regions might be made known, and the means of supplying them devised. The whole should successively lend a helping hand to all the parts, on the great subject of education from the primary school to the University. Statistical facts, bearing on this absorbing interest, should be brought forward and collected; the systems of common school instruction should be compared, and the means of different school books, foreign and domestic, freely canvassed. Plans of education, adapted to the natural, commercial, and social condition of the interior should be invented; a correspondence instituted among all our higher seminaries of learning, and an interchange established of all local publications on the subject of education. In short, we should foster western genius, encourage western writers, patronize western publishers, augment the number of western readers, and create a western heart.

When these great objects shall come seriously to occupy our minds, the union will be secure, for its centre will be sound, and its attraction on the surrounding parts irresistible. Then will our state governments emulate each other in works for the common good; the people of remote places begin to feel as the members of one family; and our whole intelligent and virtuous population unite, heart and hand, in one long, concentrated, untiring effort, to raise still higher the social character, and perpetuate forever, the political harmony of the green and growing WEST.

DISCOURSE ON THE HISTORY, CHARACTER, AND PROSPECTS OF THE WEST[1] (1834)

In appearing among classical scholars, within the walls of a university, as your orator on this academical occasion, I find myself in the situation of a Haw tree of the woods, left standing in the cleared ground, and planted about with foreign fruit trees. Being improved by grafting and the various labors of art, their products are savory, and by persons of good taste, are, of course preferred; but still the Haw is not useless, for it serves as a term of comparison, and shows the necessity and value of early cultivation.

In consenting, at a late period, to supply the place of the able civilian on whom you at first relied,[2] I felt all the embarrassment that could arise from the consciousness of my incapacity to discuss a theme of pure literature; but I have, finally, chosen a topic which commends itself to my own feelings, and will not, I hope, be unacceptable to yours—it is the character, history, and prospects of the WEST.

The ancient and venerable maxim, KNOW THYSELF, has been generally addressed to individuals, but is equally applicable to communities; who should be familiar with the natural resources of their country, and the genius and tendency of their social, literary, religious, and political institutions; or they cannot cherish the good, and successfully cast out the evil. This self-knowledge of nations, is especially necessary for one of recent origin, where everything is still green, and must be fashioned according to the skill of those who regulate its growth.

Society in these BACKWOODS, even in the most thickly settled parts, is but in its forming state; and we are, therefore, invited to scrutinize, with care, the principles which control its development; for otherwise its maturity may offer less of perfection, than is found in communities which sprang up at an earlier period, instead of displaying, in its own strength and beauty, the beneficial fruits of their experience and wisdom.

It may be asked, however, whether it is consistent with the peace and perpetuity of the UNION, to inculcate a devotion to one of its parts? I shall not give a general answer to this question, but reply, that a devotion to the WEST, is manifestly compatible with both, and indeed the most efficient means of promoting both. This results from the geographical relations between the Valley of the Mississippi and the Atlantic states; relations, which being founded on nature, cannot be dissolved by the hand of art, but are daily acquiring new strength, as the ligaments of the body bind its different organs more closely together in each succeeding year of its natural growth.

I do not propose, however, to go into the analysis of our young institutions; but in the spirit of the West, shall wander to and fro, expatiating on whatever may seem attractive, but still keeping within its ample bounds.

---

1. *Discourse on the History, Character, and Prospects of the West: Delivered to the Union Literary Society of Miami University, Oxford, Ohio, at their Ninth Anniversary, September 23, 1834.* By Daniel Drake, M.D. Cincinnati: Truman and Smith. 1834. Pp. 5–17, 28–34, 40–45.

2. JUDGE LANE, of the Supreme Court of Ohio.

The first thing which strikes our attention, is the difference between the opportunities for intellectual and moral improvement, in old and new states of society, and their influence on the character of the people.

As the flavor of the grape depends greatly on the soil by which it is nourished, so the temperament of individuals is modified by the intellectual aliment on which their minds subsist in childhood and youth; and of course, in studying national character, it is of great service to know the different circumstances under which the people of different places have been educated.

Children who are born in old and compactly organized communities, are surrounded from infancy, with all the means of improvement which the inventive genius of civilization can create. Books adapted to every age and all varieties of taste—established institutions of learning, from the infant school to the ancient and venerable university—professional teachers of every grade of erudition—ingenious toys, which, in the very creaking of their wheels, speak instruction—full cabinets of the works of nature and art,—public lectures in lyceums—and laws of action, for the morning, noon and night of every day throughout the year, are but a part of the means of their education and discipline. They are thus made the objects of a sleepless superintendence; which not only supplies their minds with rich materials of thought, but lays down the rules by which their growth in intellect shall proceed. Educated under these advantages, they acquire a copious and varied learning, and exhibit, in manhood, a conformity more or less striking, to the standards of excellence which have been held up for their imitation.

Most of what gives them this excellence, is either imperfect or entirely wanting, in a new country; but are there no substitutes for these artificial advantages? I think there are several, and shall proceed to offer some of them to your consideration, leaving it with yourselves to assign the value of each.

Precious as may be the benefits which good establishments of learning afford, they are not the only means of intellectual improvement; for the pathless wilderness may be made a schoolbook, and nature is the institution, in which many of the ancients were chiefly educated, whose works of taste and genius, constitute an important part of your college course. It would be an error to say, that all children of the woods, are thus instructed; for all are not educated where the best institutions have been established; and many are incapable of being taught: but none, even for mere pastime, can roam over hill and dale, descend the precipice, and stray in the cavern that opens underneath, wade through the matted herbage, and part the tangled bushes, without acquiring knowledge at every step; as the bee which buzzes round him, loads its limbs with the *materiel* of its cells, while it flits from flower to flower to feast upon their honey. To derive substantial advantage from this intercourse with nature, the youth must give scope to his curiosity, and be fully aware that its gratification will bring a rich harvest of knowledge. He should, also, cultivate the faculty of observation; which, beyond every other, can be made to supply him with valuable information, in whatever situation he may be placed; and must be exercised early, or it will remain inactive and unproductive through life. An acute and vigilant observer finds improvement in the smallest object or humblest event, as well as in those impressive phenomena, which only can arouse the attention of the dull and heedless. He suffers nothing to pass without inspection; and from habit, connects all he sees, with the memory of something he has seen before. Even in his moments of deepest study, he glances on what surrounds him, and recognizes the new and curious; he unites contemplation with his observation, or passes from one to the other, with a facility that confounds those who cannot think, except they be secluded from every external influence. He supplies his mind with fresh materials of thought, instead of ruminating on the old; and nourishes it with food collected by himself, in place of what has passed through a hundred intellects, and been subjected to as many distinct concoctions; finally, he perceives new qualities, relations and functions, in the objects that lie along his path, and thus becomes original and inventive. Indeed, with a small number of exceptions, every branch of knowledge and all the duties of life, call for the active and accurate exercise of this faculty; and the world has had but few distinguished and useful men, in whom it was not cultivated and powerful. The WEST, as already intimated, presents an endless variety of new objects and operations, to stimulate and reward this faculty; and hence, our young men *may* attain strength of intellect, and treasures of useful knowledge, although comparatively destitute of the means of academical instruction. Here then have been, and still are, a number of sources of mental improvement, which may compensate, to a small extent, at least, for the want of those which abound in older nations.

The extended limits of the WEST, and the broad navigable rivers which traverse it in every direction, exert on the mind that expanding influence, which comes from the contemplation of vast natural objects; while the distant visits and long migrations, to which this condition invites, and the wide, reciprocal commerce, which it suggests and facilitates, perpetually call its inhabitants from place to place, opening new sources of observation, and establishing fresh and profitable modes of intellectual communion.

The want of those arts and inventions, by which the inhabitants of older countries accomplish their ends, renders it necessary for the people of a new state, to invent and substitute others, as emergencies may arise; whereby their faculties are strengthened, and a spirit of self-dependence is awakened, which comes, at length, to preside over all their actions.

The many opportunities for bold enterprize, compared with the population, which a new country presents, constitute a kindred source of improvement; for occasions call forth ingenuity, and where the mind is left free to execute its schemes according to its own suggestions, it becomes fertile in expedients, and even failure does not bring discouragement; while success inspires a taste for higher undertakings, and contributes to develop the power requisite to their achievement.

In old countries, the employments of men divide them into *castes,* and while each becomes distinguished in the business to which he is confined, and which he can seldom relinquish for any other, his mind is narrowed down to the limited circle of his employments, and like the rail-road car, he moves always on the one path. But in a country like the WEST, the same person is compelled to do many different things, and often tempted to change his pursuits. A high degree of perfection in any, is impracticable under this variety of objects; but the intellect, by such various training, expands in many directions, and the aggregate of its powers, is greater than when it is compelled to extend itself in one only.

In a new country, the restraints employed by an old social organization, do not exist—the government of fashion is democratic—and a thousand corporations,—literary, charitable, political, religious, and commercial, have not combined into an oligarchy, for the purpose of bringing up to one set of artificial and traditional standards, the feelings, opinions, and actions of the rising generation; and thus the mind of each individual is allowed, in a great degree, to form on its own constitutional principles;

whence result those exhibitions of original character, of which the country has always been more prolific than the city, and which are oftener seen in new than old states of society.

When an individual from the depths of a compressing population, builds his cabin in the WEST, of the trees which grew on the spot selected for his future home, being speedily released from the requisitions of the society he left behind, he permits his children, like the bushes among which they ramble, to vegetate, almost unmoulded by the hand of art. Deep and enduring ignorance might be thought the lot of all who thus grow up in the forest; but observation has shown, that this condition of the mind is far more favorable to the reception of new truths, than that which prevails in the youth of older states of society. Hence, the WEST is pre-eminently the place where discoveries and new principles of every kind, are received with avidity, and promptly submitted to the test of experiment. The mental sensibility is alive to innovations, and the growth of intellect which they impart, has a corresponding activity.

It is the peculiar distinction of the institutions, and the public sentiment of the United States, that a youth of talents and virtue, may rise from the lowest to the highest walks of society, without being obstructed or frowned upon as he advances.—This is especially the case in the Western States, where the feelings of the people are in sympathy with young men of poor parentage; and the knowledge of this facility, arouses the emulation, strengthens the purpose, and enlarges the views of our native population.

For the first quarter of a century after the settlement of the WEST began, it had but few post roads, and its scattered inhabitants seldom saw a newspaper. In this comparative destitution of a political press, it became necessary for the candidates for office to visit the people, and address them, when assembled for that purpose in central situations. On these occasions, opposing aspirants often met each other in fierce or earnest debate; and departed from the arena, improved both in logic and the art of stirring up the passions; while the people themselves were instructed on subjects of legislation, and warmed in their political sensibilities. The practice has survived the necessity from which it was at first adopted, and may still be regarded as a valuable school of oratory and political knowledge.

The itinerant clergy are important teachers in a new country; for they present to the observation of the people, a perpetual succession of ministers, who lodge in their houses, converse with their families, and, from the pulpit, promulgate every variety of Christian doctrine, explained by the aid of as many different modes of illustration.

The emigration to the West is a perennial stream. The fertility and beauty of the Great Valley, have been proclaimed on both sides of the Atlantic, and the subjects of European despotism have started from their slumbers and felt new impulses to action. Captivated by the story of our social and political freedom, our native luxuries, and the amplitude of our unsettled territories, the mind of the peasant and the villager, has been raised above the venal condition of their forefathers, and fired with the desire of emigration; the cottage of three generations, and the overshadowing elm of a hundred years, have lost their spell, and the friendships of childhood their charm; brother has bid farewell to brother, the father has pronounced his blessing on the son, impatient to be gone, and the mother shed the tear of love and sorrow, on the daughter she was to see no more; compacts of emigration have been formed, and departing companies have thinned the population of the lordly estate, or left entire streets of the village unpeopled and deserted. Thus, day after day has brought into the WEST, the enterprising and ambitious from other realms; and each has been a schoolmaster to our native population—presenting them with strange manners and customs; arts, opinions, and prejudices, not seen before; and traits of individual and national character, as numerous as the kingdoms which have poured their little colonies into the bosom of our young society. Many of the advantages of foreign travel, are thus experienced by those who could never go abroad; the Atlantic states and the west of Europe have come to us; and without leaving our native woods we have seen specimens well fitted to enlarge our conceptions of character, and diminish the necessity of hazardous voyages, for the purpose of studying human nature, in its development under political institutions entirely different from our own.

The emigrants, themselves, generally the most enterprising members of the families to which they belonged, are improved by the change of place, for it affords new objects and associations; their curiosity is awakened, and their powers of observation are rendered more acute; their minds are thrown into fermentation and become heated; purer standards of excellence float before their eyes and lead them on, while brighter hopes illuminate the paths they are to tread—thus they aspire to a better rank in society, and the aspiration brings the means of its attainment.

The addition to the Union, of Louisiana, with its French and Spanish population, opened to the inhabitants of the Valley, a new source of intellectual improvement; for the trade between the Upper States and Lower Louisiana, has made thousands acquainted with the manners and customs and character, of a different people from ourselves, and thus augmented our knowledge of human nature. In the state of Missouri, the number of French inhabitants was very considerable, and even Indiana and Illinois had masses of the same population, whose intercourse with the Anglo-American emigrants contributed to the same effect.

The near neighborhood, the wars, and the monuments, insignificant as the last may be, of the Indians, have exerted a similar effect on the mental improvement of our young population, because they have been led, intently to observe and contemplate a peculiar variety of the human race, having a number of striking features, and far removed, in most of their qualities, from our own.

Additional means of intellectual improvement, which, like these, are in some degree peculiar to the WEST, may have been recognized by other observers; but a sufficient number have been enumerated to show, that new countries are not wholly deficient in substitutes for the academies and colleges of the old. It is true, that sound scholarship, in the present era of the world, is conferred only by institutions of learning, supplied with the requisite books, and confided to able professors; but much valuable knowledge, adapted to the immediate purposes of human life, may be amassed by observation alone, if the objects and wants which stimulate and satisfy that faculty are brought within its reach. In regard to the varieties of national character, that may spring from this diversity in modes of education, the estimate of a person who has not been familiar with both, may not, perhaps, be according to the fact; but I feel strong in the conviction, that with all its deficiencies in literature and science, the mind of the WEST is at least equal to that of the East and of Europe, in vigor of thought, variety of expedient, comprehensiveness of scope, and general efficiency of execution; while in perspicacity of observation, independence of thought, and energy of expression, it stands on ground unattainable by the more literary and disciplined population of older nations.

But it would be great injustice to the subject before us to stop here. We have considered some of the beneficial effects of new countries on the mind, but their influences are, perhaps, still more salutary on the heart. Without aiming at metaphysical accuracy, we may recognize in the human character, a love of nature for the enjoyment derived from contemplating her beauties, sublimities, and eccentricities—a feeling of romance and enthusiasm—a keen sensibility to whatever is touching or magnanimous in the human character—a taste, in short, for all which the natural and moral world can present, to stir the imagination, and warm and elevate the feelings. This susceptibility constitutes the true poetical temperament, although it may not often express itself in numbers. To do this it must be associated with an imagination, that is not merely effervescent but creative, and an understanding, that will enable that imagination to embody and put forth, in beauty and natural order, those images which, in common minds, play in a lively confusion among themselves, like fairies sporting amid the violets in the darkness of the night, but never moving in procession after the dawn of day. The influence of this temperament on the character of the individual is impressive, and, within proper limits, every way admirable. It is the animating power of the inquiring and reasoning faculties—the soul of the intellect—the vital fire of genius, and the fountain which encircles, with a halo of light, not a few of the noblest forms of human greatness. The influence of this temperament may be seen, *must* indeed manifest itself, in the opinions and actions of the individual, whatever may be his rank or pursuits; and when its intensity does not make him a visionary, it throws about his character an irresistible charm. Would you have examples of it, take the man of business, who stops in the street to admire a curious or beautiful object, or listen with delight to the story of a new act of generosity or self-devotion by one whom, perhaps, he never saw; and then, by a redoubled effort, overtakes the object from which his attention had been withdrawn; or take the young farmer, who turns away his scythe from a clump of sweet-williams, that may stand smiling in his meadow; or the student, who hastens on with his problem or his translation, that he may stray for an hour in the genial air, and register the forms of the passing clouds. The soul that was never warmed by this vivifying flame, like unbaked clay of the potter, is destitute of transparency, and will not vibrate to any stroke; and the greatest intellect in which it may have been quenched, resembles the half extinguished volcano, that obscures with volumes of murky smoke, the heavens which it once illuminated with sheets of fire.

Now it must be admitted, that new countries are more favorable than old, to the preservation and active influence of this temperament; and I cannot doubt, that their inhabitants have greater freshness of feeling, more lively impulses and deeper enthusiasm, than those who grow up and die, in the midst of a dense and struggling population.

Young Gentlemen: let me exhort you to cherish this temperament by every means within your power. Like the other dispositions of the mind, it may be nourished and exalted; or depressed, degraded, and even extinguished. By exercise it grows in strength, and by receiving a direction upon proper objects it acquires dignity. The means of its gratification and improvement are always at your command:—

Watch attentively the conduct of little children, for in them you see the workings of nature; be wide awake to the eccentric movements of those around you, for the human character is known by its extravagant flights, as the corruscations of the clouds reveal to us, that they are charged with electricity; treasure up the great and good actions that fall under your observation, for they will warm your own hearts, and fortify them against the mildew of a frigid selfishness; recall perpetually and dwell upon the memory of your young friendships; foster all your early local attachments, and cherish the wild and airy superstitions of your childhood. When opportunities offer plunge into the depths of the forest, alone, or with friends of kindred taste, and establish a familiar intercourse with nature—drink out of your hand at her gushing fountains, and wade in the pebbly brook below; bathe in the deeper stream, and give yourselves up to musing on the lonely banks of the majestic river; now cast your eyes through the green canopy of maples, and gaze at the vulture poised high in the regions above; then chase the humming–bird, as it glides among the flowers which dress out our prairies in the dyes of the rainbow, or watch the worm as it slowly penetrates the trunk of the fallen tree; seek a spot still more silent and retired, people it with the creations of your own heated imagination, and then hold converse with the spirits which you may fancy are dwelling in gaiety or gloom beneath its embowering trees; as the thunder-cloud rolls onward, emerge from the woods and contemplate the warring hosts of heaven; sympathize with the ancient and venerable oak when you see him scathed by the thunderbolt; take sides with the conflicting elements, and soothe your feelings with a view of the mild glories of the setting sun, when the west wind has swept away the angry and contending clouds.

Who is he that will sneer at this advice, and call it rhapsody; and guard you against its seductions; and tell you, "the soft grass waves smilingly, but the copperhead lurks beneath?"—Who is he that would subdue your admiration of nature, put out the fires of your enthusiasm, and plunge the ice bolt into your warm hearts? The man who forgets the divine command,—"Take no thought for your life, what ye shall eat, or what ye shall drink; nor yet for your body, what ye shall put on."—Who can *not* exclaim, with the inspired poet—"Praise ye the Lord. Praise ye the Lord from the heavens: Praise him in the heights: Praise ye him, sun and moon: Praise him, all ye stars of light. Praise the Lord from the earth, ye dragons and all deeps: fire and hail; snow and vapor; stormy wind fulfilling his word: mountains and hills: fruitful trees and all cedars: beasts and cattle: creeping things, and flying fowl: Let them praise the name of the Lord." Who is he that would dry up your fountains of sympathy, with all that is grand and lovely in man, or beautiful and inspiring, in the great field of external nature? It is he, whose feelings never rise above mean heat; whose idols lie on his work bench; and whose delight is in the music of the saw; who passes, heedless, by the tender leaves of the young ash, and looks with exstacy on those of his ledger; who counts his gold by day, and dreams upon it by night; plants in the morning, and hopes to reap at noon; talks only of profitable results; and would make the earth a great work shop, and convert the human family into a vast body of operatives—instigated by avarice and abandoned to deeds of rapacity: The self-styled utilitarian, whose scope of vision takes in but the lowest part of human nature; provides chiefly for the gratification of his animal wants, hoards up the excess of his earnings, and feels no pang in the hour of death, but that of separation from the stores which a life of toil and eagerness, had enabled him to gather into his vaults.

A cherished sensibility to all that is admirable in nature, is in no degree incompatible, with the acquisition of all that is necessary or useful in life. The sluggard, the glutton, and the drunkard, no less than the miser, do not, it is true, find time to indulge themselves in hours of fervent contemplation among the works of God; but all who are not delivered over to the tyranny of one, out of the many desires which belong to human nature, are enabled in the midst of business, to send forth their imaginations upon the world of matter and of man, and take into the warm embrace of their feelings, whatever is touching and noble in both.

He who fosters this sensibility, retains a youthfulness of taste, that keeps him in sympathy with the generations, which, like saplings that spring up around the aged and decaying tree, are at last to succeed him in society. This amiable condescension, spreads an irresistible charm over the character of age. Its maxims of wisdom become a law to the erring footsteps of youth; while the dark and dreary hours from which the most favored cannot escape, are lighted up by the flashes of gayety and innocent mirth, which beam from the eye in the springtime of life. On the contrary, the sullen old man lives only in the past, and dwelling alone in his dotage, goes down towards the grave, as the sun in winter descends through the mists and fogs of our western mountains, which extinguish his fires, while he still lingers on the verge of the horizon.

Dismissing, for the present, our inquiry into some of the intellectual and moral advantages, which our new country offers, as substitutes for the establishments of older states, let us proceed to speak of the duties and labors which it enjoins upon its sons.

In the first place, we should transmit to posterity a graphic description of the Great Valley, as it appeared in primitive loveliness to the eyes of the pioneers, as many of us remember to have seen it, and as it still smiles in spots unviolated by man. Civilization is a transforming power, and wherever its wand is raised, the surface of the earth assumes a new aspect. The native trees, cut down and consumed, are replaced by the apple and orange; the wild grape, which united their limbs, is succeeded by an exotic, resting on trestles; the rivers are constrained within narrower channels, or turned into canals; and the mossy rocks of their margins, are broken with the sledge or exploded with gunpowder; hills are leveled and valleys filled up; a macadamized road usurps the bed of the little brook, and the rumbling of the coach wheel falls upon the ear, instead of the soft music of its rippling waters; fields of wheat undulate, where the prairie grass waved before, and tobacco and cotton, are nourished on the wreck of the cane-brake, which formerly spread its green leaves over the snows of winter. Thus the teeming and beautiful landscape of nature, fades away like a dream of poetry, and is followed by the useful but awkward creations of art. Before this transformation is finished, a portrait should be taken, that our children may contemplate the primitive physiognomy of their native land, and feast their eyes on its virgin charms.

Young Gentlemen: The scenery, history, and biography, of the Valley of the Mississippi, constitute the very elements of our literature, and their retrospect naturally leads us to inquire into its resources, and the character it will probably assume. When the young planter, on the banks of the Yazoo or the Illinois, clears away the forest, and prepares his lands for tillage, his taste and judgment are displayed in the plan on which he marks out his fields, and the seeds with which he sows them. It will depend on himself, whether his farm be beautiful in its arrangement and varied in its products, or irregular, unsightly, and more prolific in weeds and briars, than the useful and elegant productions of agriculture. Thus must it be with the scholars of the Great Valley. They have a vast field to cultivate, but small portions of which are as yet laid off and planted, and its future beauty and abundance, will be according to their skill and industry.

As a part of the generation, to which are confided the rudiments of our infant literature, I would exhort you to study profoundly the elements you are to control, and labor to combine them according to the principles of taste and science. If the germs are deformed and sickly, the future plants must be shapeless, feeble, and unproductive of salutary fruit.

The materials placed at your command, and the age of the world in which you come up to the task, confer upon you many important advantages. When we contemplate the history, condition, and prospects, of the West, we cannot fail to perceive, that its literature will ultimately prove not only opulent in facts and principles, but peculiar in several of its qualities. Let us inquire into some of its present and prospective characteristics.

In the first place—The time is remote, when language in the West, will acquire a high degree of purity, in nomenclature and idiom. Many of our writers have received but little education, and are far more anxious about results, than the polish of the machinery by which they are to be effected. They write for a people, whose literary attainments are limited and imperfect; whose taste is for the strong rather than the elegant; and who are not disposed or prepared to criticize any mode of expression, that is striking or original, whatever may be the deformities in its drapery;—consequently, but little solicitude is felt by our authors, about classical propriety. Moreover, the emigration into the Valley being from every civilized country, new and strange forms of expression are continually thrown into the great reservoir of spoken language; whence they are often taken up by the pen, transferred to our literature, and widely disseminated. For many years to come, these causes will prevent the attainment either of regularity or elegance; but, gradually, the heterogeneous rudiments will conform to a common standard, and finally shoot into a compound of rich and varied elements; inferior in refinement, but superior in force, variety, and freshness, to the language of the mother country.

Second. Our literature, at present, is but slightly imbued with allusions and illustrations drawn from the classics; and although it may possess a portion of their temperament, they have not infused it; for they are cultivated by a small part of our scholars only, and seldom read, even in translation, by a majority of our educated people. I shall not prophecy on this subject, but nothing indicates, that the number of devotees to classical learning will be greater in proportion to our population, hereafter, than at the present time. I see as little to admire in this neglect, as in that preposterous idolatry to the ancients, which would substitute the study of their literature for that of modern times. A genuine scholar extends his researches as far as his opportunities will permit, and drawing from the literature of all nations—ancient and modern—whatever is good and beautiful in spirit, applies it to the embellishment and elevation of his own.

Third. Our literature will be tinctured with the thoughts and terms of business. The mechanic arts have become locomotive, both in temper and capacity—they travel abroad, and exhibit themselves in every department of society. To a certain degree, they modify the public mind; supply new topics for the tongue and pen; generate strange words and phrases, as if by machinery; suggest novel modes of illustration, and manufacture figures of speech by steam power. They afford canal transportation to the ponderous compiler of statistics; a turnpike to the historian; a tunnel to the metaphysician; a scale of definite proportions to the moral philosopher; a power loom and steam press to the novelist; fulminating powder to the orator; corrosive acids to the satirist; a scalpel to the reviewer; a siesta chair to the essayest; a kaleidescope to the dramatist; a balloon to the poet; a railroad to the enthusiast, and nitrous oxide to the dunce. While we devoutly indulge the hope, that our literature will not depend for its elevation on the lever of the arts, there can be no objection to a fellowship between them; nor any reason why it should not adopt, whatever they may offer, to diversify its objects and enrich its resources.

Fourth. The absence, in the Valley of the Mississippi, of those ancient and decaying edifices, which are scattered over Europe, and were once the seats of great political, military, or social events, must deprive our literature of an element of solemn and touching grandeur. It might be thought, that our own antiquities would supply the place of those; but we know nothing of the people by whom these were erected, and consequently, they inspire but little of that romantic and tender feeling, which results from associating the history of a people with the ivy-covered ruins of their former taste and industry.

Fifth. In the West there is no prevailing love or talent for music, the most delightful of all the liberal arts; and, of course, its softening and refining influences will not be exerted on our literature. To what extent a musical taste might, hereafter, be created by pressing the study of this science, as a branch of popular education, cannot be foreseen; but the interesting results that would flow from success, should animate us to a vigorous effort in the experiment. I have little doubt, that the musical temperament of Germany, is one reason why, on having her mind directed to the creation of a national literature, she so speedily and gracefully accomplished the object.

Sixth. A religious spirit animates the infancy of our literature, and must continue to glow in its maturity. The public taste calls for this quality, and would relish no work in which it might be supplanted by a principle of infidelity. Our best authors have written under the influence of Christian feeling; but had they been destitute of this sentiment, they would have found it necessary to accommodate themselves to the opinions of the people, and follow Christian precedents. The beneficent influence of religion on literature, is like that of our evening sun, when it awakens in the clouds those beautiful and burning tints, which clothe the firmament in gold and purple. It constitutes the heart of learning—the great source of its moral power. Religion addresses itself to the highest and holiest of our sentiments—benevolence and veneration; and their excitement stirs up the imagination, strengthens the understanding, and purifies the taste. Thus, both in the mind of the author and the reader, Christianity and literature act and react on each other, with the effect of elevating both, and carrying the human character to the highest perfection which it is destined to reach. Learning should be proud of this companionship, and exert all her wisdom to render it perpetual.

Seventh. The literature of the West is now, and will continue to be, ultra-republican. If we compare the constitutions of the new states with the old, we find that when republicans transfer themselves into the free and expanded solitudes of the wilderness, and proceed to organize new institutions, they display an increasing disposition to retain the political power in their own hands. It is possible to run into excesses in this respect, but that error is safer than the opposite; unless, indeed, they should carry their democratic principles so far, as to generate anarchy. Liberal political institutions favor the growth of literature; and, in turn, when its powerful energies are exerted in the great cause of personal freedom, the liberties of a reading people are placed beyond the grasp of tyranny.

Eighth. The literature of a young and a free people, will of course be declamatory, and such, so far as it is yet developed, is the character of our own. Deeper learning will, no doubt, abate its verbosity and intumescence; but our natural scenery, and our liberal political and social institutions, must long continue to maintain its character of floridness. And what is there in this that should excite regret in ourselves, or raise derision in others? Ought not the literature of a free people to be declamatory? Should it not exhort and animate? If cold, literal, and passionless, how could it act as the handmaid of improvement? In absolute governments all the political, social, and literary institutions, are supported by the monarch—here they are originated and sustained by public sentiment. In despotisms, it is of little use to awaken the feelings or warm the imagination of the people—here an excited state of both, is indispensable to those popular movements, by which society is to be advanced. Would you rouse men to voluntary action, on great public objects, you must make their fancy and feelings glow under your presentations; you must not merely carry forward their reason, but their desires and their will; the utility and loveliness of every object must be displayed to their admiration; the temperature of the heart must be raised, and its cold selfishness melted away, as the snows which buried up the fields when acted on by an April sun; then—like the budding herb which shoots up from the soil—good and great acts of patriotism will appear. Whenever the literature of a new country loses its metaphorical and declamatory character, the institutions which depend on public sentiment will languish and decline; as the struggling boat is carried back, by the impetuous waves of the Mississippi, as soon as the propelling power relaxes. In this region, low pressure engines are found not to answer—high steam succeeds much better; and, although an orator may now and then explode and go off in vapor, the majority make more productive voyages, than could be performed under the influence of a temperate heat.

Ninth. For a long time the oration, in various forms, will constitute a large portion of our literature. A people who have fresh and lively feelings, will always relish oratory; and a demand for it will of course bring a supply. Thus auditors create orators, and they, in turn, increase the number of hearers. In a state of society where an indefinite number of new associations, political, religious, literary, and social, are to be organized, it is far more effective to assemble men together and address them, personally, than through the medium of the press. If an excitement can be raised in a few, it spreads sympathetically among the many; and is often followed by immediate results of greater magnitude, than the pen could produce in years. Hence, I regard the study of oratory, as among the most important objects of an academical and collegiate course; and would earnestly commend it to your consideration. None of you should assume, that he will never be called upon to speak in public, and may, therefore, omit the cultivation of eloquence. In this country, occasions for doing good by public speaking come up when little expected; and are not confined to the learned professions of theology and law. The opportunities and calls are numerous beyond computation; and the variety of objects so great, as to extend to every intelligent man in society. Even the merchant, the mechanic, and the agriculturist, are often placed in situations where an expression of their opinions, before assemblies of their own brethren, may be followed by beneficial effects to themselves, as well as to those whom they may address. I am so far from wishing to discourage this practice, that I would promote it by every argument, as an instrument of social advancement, a method of popular instruction on specific subjects, and a means of preserving our free institutions.

Tenth. The early history, biography, and scenery of the Valley of the Mississippi, will confer on our literature a variety of important benefits. They furnish new and stirring themes for the historian, the poet, the novelist, the dramatist, and the orator. They are equally rich in events and objects for the historical painter. As a great number of those who first threaded the lonely and silent labyrinths of our primitive woods, were men of intelligence, the story of their perils and exploits, has a dignity which does not belong to the early history of other nations. We should delight to follow their footsteps and stand upon the spot where, at night, they lighted up the fire of hickory bark to frighten off the wolf; where the rattlesnake infused his deadly poison into the foot of the rash intruders on his ancient domain; where, in the deep grass, they laid prostrate and breathless, while the enemy, in Indian file, passed unconsciously on his march. We should plant willows over the spots once fertilized with their blood; and the laurel tree where they met the unequal war of death, and remained conquerors of the little field.

Eleventh. Our literature cannot fail to be patriotic, and its patriotism will be American—composed of a love of country, mingled with an admiration for our political institutions. The slave, whose very mind has passed under the yoke, and the senseless ox, whom he goads onward in the furrow, are attached to the spot of their animal companionship, and may even fight for the cabin and the field where they came into existence; but this affection, considered as an ingredient of patriotism, although the most universal, is the lowest; and to rise into a virtue it must be discriminating and comprehensive, involving a varied association of ideas, and embracing the beautiful of the natural and moral world, as they appear around us. To feel in his heart, and infuse into his writings, the inspiration of such a patriotism, the scholar must feast his taste on the delicacies of our scenery, and dwell with enthusiasm on the genius of our constitution and laws. Thus sanctified in its character, this sentiment becomes a principle of moral and intellectual dignity—an element of fire, purifying and subliming the mass in which it glows. As a guiding star to the will, its light is inferior only to that of Christianity. Heroic in its philanthropy, untiring in its enterprises, and sublime in the martyrdoms it willingly suffers, it justly occupies a high place among the virtues which ennoble the human character. A literature, animated with this patriotism, is a national blessing, and such must be the literature of the West. That of all parts of the Union must be richly endowed with this spirit; but a double portion will be the lot of the interior, because the foreign influences, which dilute and vitiate this virtue in the extremities, cannot reach the heart of the continent, where all that lives and moves is American. Hence a native of the West may be confided in as his country's hope. Compare him with the native of a great maritime city, on the verge of the nation,— his birthplace the fourth story of a house, strangulated by the surrounding edifices, his play-ground a pavement, the scene of his juvenile rambles an arcade of shops, his young eyes feasted on the flags of a hundred alien governments, the streets in which he wanders crowded with foreigners, and the ocean, common to all nations, forever expanding to his view: estimate his love of country, as far as it depends on local and early attachments, and then contrast him with the young backwoodsman, born and reared amidst objects, scenes, and events, which you can all bring to mind;—the jutting rocks in the great road, half alive with organic remains, or sparkling with crystals; the quiet old walnut tree, dropping its nuts upon the yellow leaves, as the morning sun melts the October frost; the grape vine swing; the chase after the cowardly black snake, till it creeps under the rotten log; the sitting down to rest upon the crumbling trunk, and an idle examination of the mushrooms and mosses which grow from its ruins; then the wading in the shallow stream, and upturning of the flat stones, to find bait with which to fish in the deeper waters; next, the plunder of a bird's nest, to make necklaces of the speckled eggs, for her who has plundered him of his young heart; then the beech tree with its smooth body, on which he cuts the initials of her name interlocked with his own; finally, the great hollow stump, by the path that leads up the valley to the log school-house, its dry bark peeled off, and the stately polk-weed growing from its centre, and bending with crimson berries; which invite him to sit down and write upon its polished wood, how much pleasanter it is to extract ground squirrels from underneath its roots, than to extract the square root, under that labor-saving machine, the ferule of a pedagogue! The affections of one who is blest with such reminiscences, like the branches of our beautiful trumpet flower, strike their roots into every surrounding object, and derive support from all which stand within their reach. The love of country is with him a constitutional and governing principle. If he be a mechanic, the wood and iron which he moulds into form, are dear to his heart, because they remind him of his own hills and forests; if a husbandman, he holds companionship with the growing corn, as the offspring of his native soil; if a legislator, his dreams are filled with sights of national prosperity, to flow from his beneficent enactments; if a scholar, devoted to the interests of literature, in his lone and excited hours of midnight study, while the winds are hushed and all animated nature sleeps, when the silence is so profound, that the stroke of his own pen grates, loud and harsh, upon his ear, and fancy, from the great deep of his luminous intellect, draws up new forms of smiling beauty and solemn grandeur; the genius of his country hovers nigh, and sheds over his pages an essence of patriotism, as sweet as the honey-dew which the summer night distills upon the leaves of our forest trees.

Young Gentlemen: I have directed your attention to some of the circumstances that will exert an influence on the character of our literature. It is for you and your cotemporaries to recognize others, and so control and animate the action of the whole, as to bring out results in harmony with the nature that surrounds you. To do this, successfully, you must study that nature and comprehend its temperament. With the elements of learning and science, conferred by your honored *alma mater,* you should go forth, and make acquaintance with the aspects, productions, and people of your native land. Few of you can travel in foreign countries, but all may explore their own; and I do not hesitate to say, that the latter confers greater benefits than the former; though both should be enjoyed by those who possess the means. But to render traveling beneficial, it must not be performed in steam boats and railroad cars, darting with the flight of the wild pigeon before the north wind, and cutting through whole states in the darkness of a single night. Thus borne impetuously onward, you see only the great commercial points, which, from their constant intercourse, become so assimilated, as to afford but little variety. The *diversities* in aspect and productions; in natural curiosities; in works of art, both elegant and useful; in public improvements and resources; in political, literary, social, and religious establishments, and in personal and national character, the study of which should be the chief end of travel, are found in places remote from the commercial highways of the nation, not less than in those which lie upon them; and can only be seen and studied, by him who departs from the beaten track, and views every spot with the eye of a curious and disciplined observer. The copious stores of knowledge, and the vigor of intellect, which may thus be acquired, are not the only advantages which traveling in your own country can yield; for it will confirm your native tastes and feelings, preserve your love of home, and strengthen your nationality—so often impaired by premature or protracted residence abroad. Hence you will become better qualified as writers; and, when time shall ripen your judgments into perfect maturity, you will be able to lend important aid to your countrymen, in the formation of an American literature; that shall be rich in illustrations drawn from your native land, glowing in its patriotism, attractive by its freshness, and intense in its strength and fervor.

MY YOUNG FRIENDS: When you return home as men, you will find that other duties await you, than those which relate to our literature. Your fathers have done little more than clear the ground, and scatter the first seeds of society; and you must not only weed and water the young plants, but enrich the soil with others, to which their limited means could not extend. Thus you, and even the next generation, will be pioneers, like the last; but your pioneering will be less difficult and arduous. I cannot indicate all the labors and enterprises which lie before you; but as specimens may say, that new political constitutions are to be formed, and the older remodeled, as experience may dictate; laws adapted to the character and genius of a varying population, and to the wants and productions of different parts of the Valley, are to be devised; a machinery of civil and municipal government, and systems of jurisprudence, in unison with the taste and temper of our rising communities, are to be instituted; inventions and manufactures, appropriate to our various situations, are to be naturalized, or brought forth on the spots where required, and put into operation; our plans of internal improvement must be extended, and made to unite with each other, in such manner as to spread over and connect all parts of the Valley; institutions of learning, from common schools up to universities, must be organized where they do not exist, and re-organized and improved where they do; public hospitals on all our great rivers should be erected, for the relief of our trading population; new associations, for purifying the morals of the great mass of the people, should be formed; and religious societies constituted, wherever they are rendered necessary, by the extension of our settlements.

Thus, you will be called to participate in grand and noble objects, and enjoy the high prerogative of creating—of giving the first impulse—of prescribing the direction, and laying down the rule of action. In performing these momentous functions, you will fix the course of future events, as far as human agency can regulate them. A great responsibility rests upon you—the destinies of millions will be lodged in the hands of your fellow laborers and yourselves. Keep those hands free from stain; look into your own hearts, and cast out all unholy selfishness; chasten your ambition; cherish your benevolence, till it shall expand over every object of philanthropy; cultivate your religious feelings; preserve your simplicity of manners; rebel against the tyranny of fashion; study profoundly the character of your countrymen, that you may know how to supply their intellectual and moral wants; enrich your minds with the maxims of wisdom furnished by other ages, and modify them to suit your own; learn to concentrate your thoughts, successively, on every scheme of public utility; mould yourselves into practical patriots; declare a war of extermination against the whole class of demagogues; finally, school all your faculties and affections, till you can come to feel powerful in your *country's* strength, exalted in *her* greatness, and bright in *her* glory.

With this preparation of mind, and willing devotion of heart, you will labor, in harmony, till the monuments of your skill and industry shall cover the land, from Michigan to Louisiana—from the mountain rivulets of our own unrivaled Ohio, to the grassy fountains of the savage Arkansas. You will contribute to raise up a mighty people, a new world of man, in the depths of the new world of history, and the friends of liberty, literature, and religion, in all nations, will look upon it with love and admiration: composed of the descendants of emigrants from every country, its elements will be as various as the trees which now attire our hills; but its beauties as resplendent as the hues of their autumn foliage.

Then, in the hour of death, when your hearts shall pour out the parting benediction, and your eyes are soon to close, eternally, on the scene of your labors, you will enjoy the conscious satisfaction, of having contributed to rear in your native Valley, a lovely sisterhood of states, varying from each other, as the flowers of its numerous climates differ in beauty and fragrance; but animated with the same spirit of patriotism, instinct with one sentiment of rising glory, and forever united by our Great River, as the Milky-way, whose image dances on its rippling waters, combines the stars of the sky into one broad and sparkling firmament.

23

HENRY MARIE BRACKENRIDGE

(1786–1871)

At the age of eight, Henry Marie Brackenridge was sent from Pittsburgh to Missouri by his father Hugh Henry Brackenridge to be raised by friends on the frontier. Despite this unorthodox upbringing, Henry Marie became a successful businessman, journalist, travel writer, and public advocate of unpopular causes. His loyalty to his father and his father's notion of western cultural separatism is demonstrated in his vigorous and exhaustively researched defense of his father's activities in the Whiskey Rebellion in his 1859 book *History of the Western Insurrection*. There he articulated his belief in the necessity of accurate reporting. Referring to the lasting "sinister effect of these misrepresentations," he explained how the east sought to denigrate the west as a whole in its suppression of the rebellion: "Because the interests, the pride, and the passions of party would not permit the truth to be told. It would reflect too seriously on the existing administration. Its defense was silence; and it was the only way in which it could be met, except by gross and unmeasured contumely cast on the western people. . . . How hard to turn the current of obloquy when it has once received a wrong direction?" (328).

Even in his first book, *Views of Louisiana* (1814), Henry Marie was aware that representation carried powerful weight in establishing the public imaginative, cultural, and political position of a people or a place. Most of *Views* describes his trip up the Missouri in the summer of 1810 and records the topography, resources, and native inhabitants of the region, much in the manner of Zebulon Pike or Lewis and Clark. As such, his observations of the far west are beyond the scope of this collection. However, at the end of the book, he appended a few chapters on southern Illinois, a region he called "the American bottom." His interest there was describing and contemplating the various populations that had inhabited the region prior to white arrival. In many texts, French (such as in Imlay's *The Emigrants*) and native populations had been constructed as alien to the American settlers, as primitive, premodern groups easily displaced or absorbed.

Henry Marie, however, ventures a more complicated exploration of French and Native presences and, all the while, reflects upon the politics of representation and the relations of colonies to nations and the fate of these populations in the histories of empires. The first section of *Views* addresses the French of the region and their lack of ambition to dominate and occupy the region the way Americans would. The second studies native archeology and origins. In both cases, the non-Anglo-American is not represented as "other" but simply as representative of the region's complex history, one that cannot be erased with the imposition of what Cooper would call "our language, our religion, and our institutions."

Text: *Views of Louisiana* (Pittsburgh, 1814): 132–146, 181–195.

FROM *VIEWS OF LOUISIANA*

CHAPTER VI

Historical Character of the Ancient Inhabitants—Change of Government . . .

There is scarcely any thing more difficult and consequently more rare, than correct delineation of character:—This task is usually undertaken by friends or enemies, and the result is either panegyrick or satire.—Even amongst such as are unbiassed, how few the happy copyists, who can paint nature with her own colors, so as to be recognized by every beholder!

Conscious of this difficulty, I entertain humble hopes of success, in being able to satisfy the expectation and inquiries of the intelligent reader. And, particularly where there are no striking and prominent features, but the traits of an infant colony delicately marked.

A colony will not remain long separated from the parent stock, until it exhibits a peculiar and distinct character. Climate, situation, and country, although not exclusively the agents in forming this character, must nevertheless, be admitted to have great influence. Nor do the manners of the parent country continue invariable; other times, other men, other circumstances, produce the most surprising changes, while the colony, beyond the sphere of their influence, retains its pristine customs and manners. The Spaniards of Mexico are said to bear a stronger resemblance to their ancestors of the fifteenth century, than to their present brethren of Old Spain:—The French inhabitants of the Mississippi, have little resemblance to the gay, and perhaps frivolous, Frenchmen of Louis the fifteenth and sixteenth, and still less to those who have felt the racking storm of the revolution.

To the country on both sides of the Mississippi, the general name, *Les Illinoix,* was given. It was inhabited by a powerful Indian nation of that name, at present reduced to a handful of miserable creatures. After the discovery of the Mississippi, by Mons. Joliet and the priest Marquette, from Canada, a number of Canadian traders, about the year 1680 settled in Kaskaskia, a large Indian town. By degrees, a number of families were induced to quit Canada, for a country represented as much more desirable. A monastery of Jesuits was established here, which succeeded in converting a number of the Indians to christianity. I am credibly informed, that they had at one time, five hundred catechumens. In time, these people, as it has ever been the case, were found to degenerate and diminish, from their intercourse with the whites: and the French were left the possessors and proprietors of their village.

About the beginning of the last century, the celebrated scheme of *Law, and Company,* was set on foot, and supported by the high reputation for wealth and fertility, which Louisiana had already required. To further this delusion, it was represented in still more glowing colors, and it became the paradise of Frenchmen. The Illinois was regarded as of immense importance; the attention of the nation was turned towards it, and notwithstanding the failure of Law's project, this remote colony flourished surprisingly. Besides Kaskaskia, which became a considerable place, there were several large villages, a lucrative fur trade was carried on, and an extensive agriculture.— These settlements sent to New Orleans in one year, (1746) eight hundred thousand weight of flour. But, at this time there was not one permanent establishment on the west side of the Mississippi, although resorted to by traders, and the lead mines were known and worked. Twenty-five or thirty years after the failure of Law, the French, with something more substantial in view, had formed the plan of securing the great valley of the Mississippi, and of connecting it with Canada; immense sums of money were expended. Fort Chartres, which is said to have cost the crown, nine millions of livres, was built, and the village of Fort Chartres rose by its side; but alas! such are the reverses of fortune, even in this newly peopled region, the gay and sprightly village has disappeared forever, and the fort is but a noble ruin. This fort was deemed an important one, at which there was stationed an officer of rank, with a suitable command. Much of the elegance and refinement of the officers was communicated to the susceptible inhabitants.

The war between France and England, which broke out about the year 1754, deprived France of her possessions in this part of the world. In consequence of this, les Illinoix experienced a sudden and rapid decay; which was again accelerated by the conquest of general Clark for the United States, in 1779. The greater number of the wealthy and respectable inhabitants descended the Mississippi, and settled in New Orleans, and the lower country. Others crossed the Mississippi, and established St. Louis and St. Genevieve. Scarcely any but natives of the country remained. The foreigners chiefly returned to the countries from whence they first emigrated.

Such then, is the origin of the greater part of that class of the population of this territory, which I have denominated the ancient inhabitants. They are chiefly natives of the country; but few families are immediately from France, or even from New Orleans or Canada.

In the character of these people, it must be remembered, that they are essentially Frenchmen; but, without that restlessness, impatience and fire, which distinguishes the European. There is, even in their deportment, something of the gravity of the Spaniard, though gay, and fond of amusements. From the gentle and easy life which they led, their manners, and even language, have assumed a certain degree of softness and mildness: the word *paisible,* expresses this characteristic. In this remote country, there were few objects to urge to enterprise, and few occasions to call forth and exercise their energies. The necessaries of life were easily procured, and beggary was unknown. Hospitality was exercised as in the first ages, for there were no taverns. Ambition soared far hence, for here there was no prey. Judges, codes of law, and prisons, were of little use, where such simplicity of manners prevailed, and where every one knew how far to confide in his neighbour. In such a state of things, to what end is learning or science? The schools afforded but slender instruction; the better sort of people acquired in them reading, writing, and a little arithmetic. The number of those who were lovers of knowledge, and made it a profession, was small. From the habits of these people, it would naturally be expected, that they would have been unaccustomed to reason on political subjects; they were in fact, as ignorant of them, as children are of life and manners. These inhabitants were as remarkable for their tame and peaceable disposition, as the natives of France are for the reverse.

Amongst their virtues, we may enumerate honesty and punctuality in their dealings, hospitality to strangers, friendship and affection amongst relatives and neighbours. Instances of abandonment on the female side, or of seduction, are extremely rare. The women make faithful and affectionate wives, but will not be considered secondary personages in the matrimonial association. The advice of the wife is taken on all important, as well as on less weighty concerns, and she generally decides. In opposition to these virtues, it must be said, that they are devoid of public spirit, of enterprise or ingenuity, and are indolent and uninformed.

They are catholics, but, very far from being bigoted or superstitious, as some travellers have said. They were perhaps more strict observers, formerly, of the rules and discipline of their church, and of the different holy days in the calender. Their *fetes,* or celebration of these days, were considered, as the most interesting occasions; the old and young engaged in them with the greatest delight, and they doubtless contributed to their happiness. Of late, this attention to the ceremonies of their religion is considerably relaxed, since other objects of pursuit and interest have been opened to their view. The catholic worship is the only one yet known in the territory, except in private families, and in a few instances of itinerant preachers.

There was scarcely any distinction of classes in the society. The wealthy or more intelligent, would of course be considered as more important personages, but there was no difference clearly marked. They all associated, dressed alike, and frequented the same ball room. They were in fact nearly all connected by the ties of affinity or consanguinity: and so extensive is it, that I have seen the carnival, from the death of a common relation, pass by cheerless and unheeded. The number of persons excluded was exceedingly small. What an inducement to comport ones self with propriety and circumspection! The same interest at stake, the same sentiments that in other countries influence the first classes of society, were here felt by all its members. Perhaps as many from unmerited praise have been formed into valuable characters, as others from having been unjustly despised have become truly despicable.

Their wealth consisted principally in personal property, lands were only valuable when improved. Slaves were regarded in the light of *bien foncier,* or real property, and in fact, as the highest species. Lead and peltry were frequently used as the circulating medium.

There was but little variety in their employments. The most enterprising and wealthy were traders, and had at the same time trifling assortments of merchandise for the accommodation of the inhabitants, but there were no open shops or stores, as in the United States. There were no tailors or shoemakers; such as pursue these occupations at present, are from the United States. The few mechanics, exercising their trades, principally carpenters and smiths, scarcely deserved the name. The lead mines, I have already observed, engaged a considerable number. The government gave employment to but few, and those principally at St. Louis. By far the greater proportion of the population was engaged in agriculture; in fact, it was the business of all, since the surplus produce of the country was too inconsiderable to be depended upon. A number of the young men for some time, embraced the employment of boatmen, which was by no means considered degrading; on the contrary, it was desirable for a young man to have it to say, that he had made a voyage in this capacity: and they appeared proud of the occupation, in which they certainly are not surpassed by any people in dexterity. It is highly pleasing to see them exerting themselves, and giving encouragement to each other, by their cheering songs—

———adductis spumant freta vesa lacertis.
Infindunt pariter sulcos; totumque dehiscit
Convulsum remis, rostrisque tridentibus aequor.

But this occupation, amongst many other changes, has been reduced to the same footing as with the Americans. Arising probably from the simple cause, of there having arisen objects of more generous emulation.

What is somewhat strange, there were no domestic manufactures among them; the spinning wheel and the loom were alike unknown. So deficient were they in this respect, that although possessed of numerous herds, they were not even acquainted with the use of the churn, but made their butter by beating the cream in a bowl, or shaking it in a bottle.

Their amusements, were cards, billiards, and dances: this last of course the favorite. The dances, were cotillions, reels, and sometimes the minuet. During the carnival, the balls follow in rapid succession. They have a variety of pleasing customs, connected with this amusement. Children have also their balls, and are taught a decorum and propriety of behavior, which is preserved through life. They have a certain ease and freedom of address, and are taught the secret of real politeness, *self-denial;* but which by the apes of French manners, is mistaken for an affected grimace of complaisant regard, and a profusion of bows, scrapes and professions.

Their language, every thing considered, is more pure than might be expected; their manner of lengthening the sound of words, although languid, and without the animation which the French generally possess, is by no means disagreeable. They have some new words, and others are in use, which in France have become obsolete.

In their persons, they are well formed, of an agreeable pleasant countenance; indicating cheerfulness and serenity. Their dress was formerly extremely simple; the men wore a blanket coat, of coarse cloth or coating, with a cape behind, which could be drawn over the head; from which circumstance it was called a *capote*. They wore a blue handkerchief on their heads: but no hats, or shoes, or stockings; moccasins, or the Indian sandals, were used by both sexes. The dress of the females was likewise simple, and the variations of fashion, few: though they were dressed in a much better taste than the other sex. These manners will soon cease to exist, but in remembrance and description: every thing has changed. The American costume is generally introduced, amongst the first families, and amongst the young girls and young men universally. I never saw any where greater elegance of dress than at the balls of St. Louis. We still see a few of both sexes in their ancient habiliments; capots, moccasins, blue handkerchiefs on the head, a pipe in the mouth, and the hair tied up in a long queue. These people exhibit a striking difference when compared with the unconquerable pertinacity of the Pennsylvania Germans, who adhere so rigidly to the customs, manners, and language of their fathers. A few years have effected more change with the inhabitants of this territory than has been brought about amongst the Germans in fifty years.

The *government,* of the province, though a mixture of the civil and military, was simple. Each district had its commandant, or syndic. These were the judges in civil matters under a certain amount, and had also command of the militia. They received their appointment from the intendant at New Orleans, to whom there was an appeal, from their decisions, and where were also referred such matters as exceeded their jurisdiction. Arbitrators under the direction of the commandant, in some degree obviated his want of authority. The mode of proceeding is singular enough; the party complaining obtained a notification from the commandant to his adversary of the complaint, accompanied by a command from the commandant, to render the complainant justice. If this had no effect he was notified to appear before the commandant on a particular day, and answer the complaint; and if this last notice was neglected, a sergeant, with a file of men, was sent to bring him.

The lieut. governor, who resided at St. Louis, was the commander of the militia, and had a general superintendance of the public works and property, but I do not know the exact extent of his powers. The laws of Spain were in force here: but it does not appear that any others had been in practice, besides those, which related to lands and the municipal arrangements. Laws regulating civil contracts, are so intimately interwoven with the manners of a people, that it is no easy task to separate them: here *la coutume de Paris,* the common law of France, was the system by which their contracts were governed. The judges, in administering justice according to the American jurisprudence, are often perplexed by the article of Session, which provides, that respect should be paid to the usages and customs of the country. A few troops were kept up in each district, throughout the province, but too inconsiderable to afford much protection to the inhabitants. This country being so remote from the main possessions of Spain, was not regarded with much attention, when we consider its natural importance. The rod of government was so light as scarcely to be felt; the worst of the governors, were content, with imposing on their king, by exorbitant charges for useless fortifications, or for supplies never furnished. I have heard of some oppressions practised on strangers, but I have been informed by a number of Americans settled here before the change, that the Spanish government treated them with particular attention and respect. I believe, instances of individual oppressions on the part of the governors, were few: but this is to be attributed, not to the government, but to the state of society.

The present government appears to be operating a general change: its silent but subtle spirit is felt in every nerve and vein, of the body politic. The United States, acting upon broad principles, cannot be influenced by contemptible partialities between their own sons and their adopted children. They do not want colonies—they will disdain to hold others in the same state, which they themselves so nobly despised. They are in fact, both natives of the same land, and both can claim *Freedom* as their birth right.

It requires many hands to work the complicated machinery of our government; the object of which, is to enable men, as much as possible, to govern themselves. Each of the principal towns, has its officers, its legislature, in which the ancient inhabitants have the principal voice. They have been placed on the bench, they are jurors and magistrates; commissions are distributed, which, although not regarded of much importance in time of peace, yet they make a man feel that he counts something in his country; for instance, in the militia, there are generals, colonels, majors, captains, &c. Thus, one might suppose that their manners and habits of thinking were gradually preparing for the reception of a free government. The Americans have communicated to them, their industry and spirit of enterprise, and they in turn, have given some of their more gentle and amiable customs. Upon the whole, the American manners, and even language, begin to predominate. The young men have already been formed by our government, and those growing up will have known no other. A singular change has taken place, which, one would think, ought not to be the result of a transition from a despotism to a republican government: luxury has increased in a wonderful degree, and there exists something like a distinction in the classes of society. On the other hand, more pains are taken with the education of youth; some have sent their sons to the seminaries of the United States, and all seem anxious to attain this desirable end. Several of the young men have entered the army of the United States, and have discovered talents. The females are also instructed with more care, and the sound of the Piano is now heard in their dwellings for the first time.

Personal property, a few articles excepted, has fallen on an average, two hundred per cent in value, and real property risen at least five hundred. But the prices of merchandise had no proportion to the price of produce. Five bushels of corn were formerly necessary for the purchase of a handkerchief, which can now be had for one. The cultivators raised little produce beyond what was necessary for their own subsistence, it was therefore held at high prices, but fell far short of the present proportion to the price of imported articles; the petty trade was the principal dependence for these supplies. Their agriculture was so limited, that instances have been known, of their having been supplied by the king, on the failure of their crops from the inundation of the Mississippi. The low value of lands naturally arose from the great quantities lying waste, and unoccupied, in proportion to the extent of the population, or of its probable increase, and the consequent facility with which it could be obtained. Rent was scarcely known.

It may be questioned, whether the poorest class has been benefited by the change. Fearless of absolute want, they always lived in a careless and thoughtless manner; at present the greater part of them obtain a precarious subsistence. They generally possess a cart, a horse or two, a small stock of cattle, and cultivate small plots of ground. At St. Louis they have more employment than in the other villages; they make hay in the prairies, haul wood for sale, and are employed to do trifling jobs in town; some are boatmen or patrons. At St. Genevieve they depend more upon their agriculture, and have portions in the great field, but this will probably soon be taken from them by the greater industry of the American cultivators, who are continually purchasing, and who can give double the sum for rent; they are sometimes employed in hauling lead from the mines, but it will not be sufficient for their support. A number have removed to the country, and, in imitation of the Americans, have settled down on public lands, but here they cannot expect to remain long. Those who live in the more remote villages, are less affected by the change, but there is little prospect of their being better situated. But few of them have obtained permission, from the commandant, to settle on lands; in fact, there was no safety from the depredations of the Indians, in forming establishments beyond the villages. Land was only valued for what it could produce, and any one could obtain as much as he chose to cultivate.

Until possession was taken of the country by us, there was no safety from the robberies of the Osage Indians. That impolitic lenity, which the Spanish and even the French government have manifested towards them, instead of a firm though just course, gave rise to the most insolent deportment on their part. I have been informed by the people of St. Genevieve, who suffered infinitely the most, that they were on one occasion left without a horse to turn a mill. The Osages were never followed to any great distance or overtaken; this impunity necessarily encouraged them. They generally entered the neighourhood of the villages, divided into small parties, and during the night, stole in and carried away every thing they could find, frequently breaking open stables, and taking out the horses. After uniting at a small distance, their place of rendezvous, they marched leisurely home, driving the stolen horses before them, and without the least dread of being pursued. They have not dared to act in this manner under the present government; there have been a few solitary instances of robberies by them, within these three or four years, but they are sufficiently acquainted with the Americans to know, that they will be instantly pursued, even into their villages and compelled to surrender. The following well attested fact, will serve to show the insolence of the Osages under the former government. A young couple on their way from the settlement, just then formed on Big river, to St Genevieve, accompanied by a number of their friends, with the intention of having the matrimonial knot tied by the priest, were met by sixty Osages, robbed of their horses, and the whole party actually stripped! What serves, however, to lessen the atrocity of these outrages, it has been remarked, that they are never known to take away the lives of those who fall into their hands. The insolence of the other nations who came openly to their villages, the Piorias, Loups, Kickapoos, Chickasas. Cherokees, &c. is inconceivable. They were sometimes perfectly masters of the villages, and excited general consternation. I have seen the houses on some occasions closed up, and the doors barred by the terrified inhabitants; they were not always safe even there. It is strange how these people have entirely disappeared within a few years, there are at present scarcely a sufficient number to supply the villages with game.

The historical epocha of this territory, are few and simple. Shortly after the first formation of the settlement, it was ceded by the treaty of '63; the secret treaty between Spain and France of 1762, was not known, and perhaps never would have been, if France had proved successful in her contest with Britain. The history of Louisiana, generally, until it came into the hands of the United States, is the history of this territory. By the treaty of Ildefonso, of Oct 1800, this country was receded by Spain to France; the situation of France at that period not permitting her to take possession, she ceded it to the U. States. The fear of its falling into the hands of her enemy was a strong inducement.

On the part of the United States, possession was taken of this territory in 1804, by capt. (now major Stoddard) who was our first civil commandant. In pursuance of the act of congress, which separated it from the district of Orleans, with the name of the district of Louisiana, it was placed for the moment, under the government of the territory of Indiana. Governor Harrison, of that territory, accordingly, organized the government, and put it in motion. In 1805, it was elected into a territorial government similar to that of the other territories, by the name of the *Territory of Louisiana*.[1] For these things I must refer the reader to the different acts of congress on the subject. Two important treaties were formed with the Indians, one with the Sacs and Foxes, and the other with the Great and Little Osages.

If I am asked, whether the ancient inhabitants are more contented, or happy, under the new order of things, or have reason to be so, I should consider the question a difficult one, and answer it with hesitation. It is not easy to know the secret sentiments of men, and happiness is a relative term. It is true, I have heard murmurings against the present government, and something like sorrowing after that of Spain, which I rather attributed to momentary chagrin, than to real and sincere sentiment;

---

1. The territory of Orleans has now become the "state of Louisiana" and the "territory of Louisiana" has been changed to the "territory of the Missouri."

besides, this generally proceeds from those who were wont to bask in the sunshine of favor. Yet I have not observed those signs which unequivocally mark a suffering and unhappy people. The principal source of uneasiness arises from the difficulties of settling the land claimed by the commissioners on the part of the United States. The principal inhabitants have lost much of that influence which they formerly possessed, and are superseded in trade and in lucrative occupations by strangers; their claims therefore constitute their chief dependence. The subject of those claims embraces such a variety of topics, that it is not possible to give any correct idea of them in this cursory view. It is a subject on which the claimants are feelingly alive. This anxiety is a tacit compliment to our government, for under the former their claims would be scarcely worth attention. The general complaint is, the want of sufficient liberality in determining on the claims. There is perhaps too great a disposition to lean against the larger concessions, some of which are certainly very great, but when we consider the trifling value of lands under the Spanish government, there will appear less reason for this prepossession against them. For many reasons, it would not be to the honor of the United States, that too much strictness should be required in the proof, or formalities of title, particularly of a people who came into their power with out any participation on their part, and without having been consulted. Six years have passed away without the final adjustment of the claims, and even those that have been decided upon, will give rise to lawsuits; it is probable there will be as copious a harvest of these as ever was furnished by any of the states.

The lower class have never been in the habit of thinking beyond what immediately concern themselves; they cannot therefore, be expected to foresee political consequences. They were formerly under a kind of dependence, or rather vassallage, to the great men of villages, to whom they looked up for their support and protection. Had they been more accustomed to think it possible, that by industry it was in their power to become rich, and independent also, the change would have been instantly felt in their prosperity. But they possess a certain indifference and apathy, which cannot be changed till the present generation shall pass away. They are of late observed to become fond of intoxicating liquors. There is a middle class, whose claims or possessions were not extensive, but sure, and from the increased value of their property, have obtained since the change of government, a handsome competence. They, upon the whole, are well satisfied; I have heard many of them express their approbation of the American government, in the warmest terms. They feel and speak like freemen, and are not slow in declaring, that formerly the field of enterprise was occupied by the monopolies of a few, and it is now open to every industrious citizen.

There are some things in the administration of justice, which they do not yet perfectly comprehend; the trial by jury, and the multifarious forms of our jurisprudence. They had not been accustomed to distinguish between the slow and cautious advances of *even-handed justice,* and the despatch of arbitrary power.[2] In their simple state of society, when the subjects of litigation were not of great value, the administration of justice might be speedy and simple; but they ought to be aware, that when a society becomes extensive, and its occupations, relations and interests, more numerous, people less acquainted with each other, the laws must be more complex. The trial by jury, is foreign to the customs and manners of their ancestors; it is therefore not to be expected that they should at once comprehend its utility and importance.

---

2. Some of the more important lawsuits, however, where more extensive bribery could be carried on, are known to have slept for fifteen years.

The chief advantages which accrued from the change of government, may be summed up in a few words. The inhabitants derived a security from the Indians; a more extensive field, and a greater reward was offered to industry and enterprise; specie became more abundant, and merchandise cheaper.—Landed property was greatly enhanced in value. In opposition, it may be said, that formerly they were more content, had less anxiety; there was more cordiality and friendship, living in the utmost harmony, with scarcely any clashing interests. This perhaps, is not unlike the notions of old people, who believe that in their early days every thing was more happily ordered.

The idea of their becoming extinct, by dissolving before a people of a different race, and of losing their *moeurs cheries,* might excite unhappy sensations. Already the principal villages look like the towns of the Americans. Are not the customs and manners of our fathers, and of our own youth, dear to us all? Would it not fill our hearts with bitterness, to see them vanish as a dream? Sentiments like these, doubtless, sometimes steal into their hearts. They awake, and their HOME has disappeared.

But is it likely that this state of society could have been of long continuance? The policy which had been commenced of encouraging American settlers, would by this time have overwhelmed them with a torrent of emigration. Isolated as they were, they could not have withstood this accumulating wave of population. Had they been transferred to France, they would have suffered from exactions and conscriptions; had they remained attached to Spain, what miseries might not have assailed them from the convulsed state of the Spanish monarchy!—And is it nothing to exchange the name of colonists, creoles, for that of AMERICANS, for that of a citizen of an independent state, where they can aspire to the highest employments and honors. There are some, who can feel what it is to be exalted to the dignity of freemen; to the base and ignoble mind which cannot appreciate this blessing, my writings are not addressed. Louisianians, you have now become truly Americans; never will you again be transferred from one nation to another; IF YOU ARE EVER SOLD AGAIN, IT WILL BE FOR BLOOD.

At the same time, let us allow, for those emotions which must naturally be felt. Like two streams that flow to each other from remote and distant climes, although at length, included in the same channel, it is not all at once that they will unite their contributary waters, *and mingle into one.*

CHAPTER X

Antiquities in the Valley of the Mississippi.

Si Quid Novisti Rectius Istis, Candidus Imperti, Si Non, His Utere Mecum.

CONSIDERABLE curiosity has been excited by appearances on the Mississippi and its tributary waters, supposed to prove a more ancient and advanced population, than the state of the country, or the character of the tribes inhabiting it, when first visited by

Europeans, would seem to indicate. I need make no apology for devoting a chapter to a subject, which has been dignified by the pens of Mr. Jefferson, Dr. Barton, and a Bishop Madison. Yet, with all possible deference to these respectable names, I cannot but think their theories founded on a very imperfect acquaintance with these remains: having never themselves, visited any but the least considerable, and but few having been described by others with accuracy. The subject is still new, and I know of none which opens a wider field for interesting and amusing speculation.

Many, without considering the astonishing number and variety of these remains, have attributed them to a colony of Welsh, or Danes, who are supposed to have found their way by some accident to this country, about the ninth century. Without recurring to the reasoning of doctor Robertson against the probability of such a colony, I will observe, that it is absolutely impossible that they could have gained such a footing as these vestiges indicate, without at the same time, leaving others less equivocal. Excepting a wall said to be discovered in North Carolina, but which, on examination, proved to be a volcanic production, I have not heard of a single work of brick or stone north of Mexico. The fortifications in the western country are devoid of those marks which have characterised the European mode of fortifying almost time immemorial; they are mere enclosures, without angles or bastions, and seldom surrounded by a ditch. The place is usually such as convenience would dictate, or as is best adapted to the ground: two miles below Pittsburgh, on a kind of promontory called M'Kee's Rocks, nearly inaccessible on three sides, there is a fortification formed by a single line on the land side. They are sometimes, it is true, laid off with regularity, in the form of a parallelogram, semicircle, or square, but most commonly they are irregular.

We are often tempted by a fondness for the marvellous, to seek out remote and improbable causes, for that which may be explained by the most obvious. In the eagerness to prove the existence of the Welsh colony, by attributing to them these remains, we forget that the natives of the country when first discovered by Europeans, were universally in the habit of fortifying. In the early wars of the New England colonists with the Indians, we are informed, that Philip, chief of the Niphet tribe, defended himself in a fort which he had constructed, and sufficiently large to contain two thousand men. Charlevoix, du Pratz, and others, relate the particulars of several sieges. A fortification is one of the first things that would naturally suggest itself in a war: they have been known to all people; the same mind which would invent means of protection for the person of a single individual, would also devise the means of security to large bodies of men. It is no difficult matter to account for the disuse of fortifications amongst the Indians, when we consider the incredible diminution of their numbers, and the little use of their forts against the whites; yet in the two last sieges of mons. Perier, in the war of the Natchez (1729), that unfortunate people, were able to withstand the approaches and cannon of the enemy for nearly two months. Imlay, in his fanciful description of Kentucky, asserts, that the Indians were not acquainted with the use of fortifications. Carver is the first who notices these fortifications, and considers them as beyond the ingenuity of the Indians. The French writers, who most probably observed them, do not speak of them, a proof that they had no doubt as to their origin, nor thought of attributing them to any others than the natives of the country. On my voyage up the Missouri, I observed the ruins of several villages which had been abandoned twenty or thirty years, and which, in every respect resembled the vestiges on the Ohio and Mississippi. On my arrival at the Arikara and Mandan villages, I found them surrounded by palisades. I have supposed these vestiges to be nothing more than the sites of pallisadoed towns or villages, and not mere fortifications. This custom of pallisadoing, appears to have been general among the northern tribes; it is mentioned by the earliest travellers. In the library of New Orleans, I found two works at present out of print, which contributed in removing all doubt from my mind; the one is by Lapiteau, a learned Jesuit, and which is sometimes quoted by Dr. Robertson, the other is a singular mixture of fable and fact, by one La Houton, published 1678, before the discovery of the Mississippi in its full extent. This writer pretends to have travelled on the part which is above the Missouri. Both these works contain a number of curious engravings, in which, amongst other things, the fortified towns are represented.

That no Welsh nation exists at present on this continent, is beyond a doubt. Dr. Barton has taken great pains to ascertain the languages spoken by those tribes, east of the Mississippi, and the Welsh finds no place amongst them; since the cession of Louisiana, the tribes west of the Mississippi have been sufficiently known; we have had intercourse with them all, but no Welsh are yet found. In the year 1798, a young Welshman of the name of Evans, ascended the Missouri, in company with Makey, and remained two years in that country; he spoke both the ancient and modern Welsh, and addressed himself to every nation between that river and New Spain, but found no Welshmen. When we reflect upon the difficulties that such a colony would have to encounter amidst ferocious savages, is it probable, that isolated and unassisted, they could have been able to exist? The history of all the European establishments, inform us, that they were opposed by the natives with great ferocity. The Welsh would certainly either form considerable establishments, or be totally annihilated; to exist in a distinct and separate tribe, without preserving any of their arts, and without gaining a superiority over the Indians, but on the contrary adopting their manners, is absolutely impossible.

Besides the fortifications, there are other remains scattered throughout the western country, much more difficult to account for, and to which the Welsh can lay no claim. It is worthy of observation, that all these vestiges invariably occupy the most eligible situations for towns or settlements; and on the Ohio and Mississippi, they are most numerous and considerable.—There is not a rising town or a farm of an eligible situation, in whose vicinity some of them may not be found. I have heard a surveyor of the public lands observe, that wherever any of these remains were met with, he was sure to find an extensive body of fertile land. An immense population has once been supported in this country. These vestiges may be classed under three different heads—1, the walled towns or fortifications, of which I have already spoken; 2, barrows, or places of interment; 3, mounds or pyramids.

2. Barrows, such as described by Mr. Jefferson, are extremely numerous in every part of the western country. The traces of a village may be always found near them, and they have been used exclusively, as places of interment, at least of deposit for the dead. The height is usually eight or ten feet above the surrounding ground, the shape manifesting little or no design.—These accumulations may be attributed to the custom prevalent amongst the American tribes, of collecting the bones of such as expired at a distance from their homes, in battle, or otherwise, and at stated periods placing them in some common tomb. The barrows were not the only receptacles; caverns were also used, and places, which, from being extraordinary, were considered the residence of Manatoos or spirits.

3. The mounds or pyramids appear to me to belong to a period different from the others. They are much more ancient, and are easily distinguished from the barrows, by their size and the design which they manifest. Remains of palisadoed towns are

found in their vicinity, which may be accounted for from the circumstance of the mounds occupying the most eligible situations for villages, or from the veneration of the Indians, for whatever appears extraordinary. From the growth of trees on some of them, they show an antiquity of at least several hundred years. The Indians have no tradition as to the founders of them, though there is no doubt but that when we first became acquainted with those people, they were used as places of defence. The old chief of the Kaskaskia Indians, told Mr. Rice Jones, that in the wars of his nation with the Iroquois, the mounds in the American bottom were used as forts. In one of the plates of Lapiteau's work, there is a representation of an attack on an Indian fort, which is evidently constructed upon one of the mounds: its form is circular, the enclosure of large pickets, and heavy beams on the outside, extending to the ground on which the mound stands. Those inside defend themselves with stones, arrows, &c. while the assailants are either aiming their arrows at such as appear above the wall, or endeavoring to set fire to the fort. Until I saw this engraving, I had frequently doubted whether these elevations of earth were intended for any other purpose than places of interment for their great chiefs, or as sites for temples. These were probably the first objects, but experience, at the same time, taught them that they might also answer as forts; perhaps the veneration for these sacred places might induce the Indians, when invaded, to make their final stand in their temples, which therefore became strong holds.—This is conformable to the history of most nations of the world.

The mounds at Grave creek and Marietta have been minutely described, but in point of magnitude they fall far short of others which I have seen.

To form a more correct idea of these, it will be necessary to give the reader some view of the tract of country in which they are situated. The *American bottom,* is a tract of rich alluvion land, extending on the Mississippi, from the Kaskaskia to the Cahokia river, about eighty miles in length, and five in breadth; several handsome streams meander through it; the soil of the richest kind, and but little subject to the effects of the Mississippi floods. A number of lakes are interspersed through it, with high and fine banks; these abound in fish, and in the autumn are visited by millions of wild fowl. There is, perhaps, no spot in the western country, capable of being more highly cultivated, or of giving support to a more numerous population than this valley. If any vestige of ancient population were to be found, this would be the place to search for it—accordingly, this tract, as also the bank of the river on the western side,[1] exhibits proofs of an immense population. If the city of Philadelphia and its environs, were deserted, there would not be more numerous traces of human existence. The great number of mounds, and the astonishing quantity of human bones, every where dug up, or found on the surface of the ground, with a thousand other appearances, announce that this valley was at one period, filled with habitations and villages. The whole face of the bluff, or hill which bounds it to the east, appears to have been a continued burial ground.

But the most remarkable appearances, are two groupes of mounds or pyramids, the one about ten miles above Cahokia, the other nearly the same distance below it, which in all, exceed one hundred and fifty, of various sizes. The western side, also, contains a considerable number.

---

1. The Saline, below St. Genevieve, cleared out some time ago, and deepened, was found to contain wagon loads of earthen ware, some fragments bespeaking vessels as large as a barrel, and proving that the salines had been worked before they were known to the whites.

A more minute description of those above Cahokia, which I visited in the fall of 1811, will give a tolerable idea of them all.

I crossed the Mississippi at St. Louis, and after passing through the wood which borders the river, about half a mile in width, entered an extensive open plain. In 15 minutes, I found myself in the midst of a group of mounds, mostly of a circular shape, and at a distance, resembling enormous haystacks scattered through a meadow. One of the largest which I ascended, was about two hundred paces in circumference at the bottom, the form nearly square, though it had evidently undergone considerable alteration from the washing of the rains. The top was level, with an area sufficient to contain several hundred men.

The prospect from this mound is very beautiful; looking towards the bluffs, which are dimly seen at the distance of six or eight miles, the bottom at this place being very wide, I had a level plain before me, varied by *islets* of wood, and a few solitary trees; to the right, the prairie is bounded by the horizon, to the left, the course of the Cahokia may be distinguished by the margin of wood upon its banks, and crossing the valley diagonally, S. S. W. Around me, I counted forty-five mounds, or pyramids, besides a great number of small artificial elevations; these mounds form something more than a semicircle, about a mile in extent, the open space on the river.

Pursuing my walk along the bank of the Cahokia, I passed eight others in the distance of three miles, before I arrived at the largest assemblage. When I reached the foot of the principal mound, I was struck with a degree of astonishment, not unlike that which is experienced in contemplating the Egyptian pyramids. What a stupendous pile of earth! To heap up such a mass must have required years, and the labors of thousands.—It stands immediately on the bank of the Cahokia, and on the side next it, is covered with lofty trees. Were it not for the regularity and design which it manifests, the circumstances of its being on alluvial ground, and the other mounds scattered around it, we could scarcely believe it the work of human hands—The shape is that of a parallelogram, standing from north to south; on the south side there is a broad apron or step, about half way down, and from this, another projection into the plain about fifteen feet wide, which was probably intended as an ascent to the mound. By stepping round the base I computed the circumference to be at least eight hundred yards, and the height of the mound about ninety feet. The step, or apron, has been used as a kitchen garden, by the monks of La Trappe, settled near this, and the top is sowed with wheat. Nearly west there is another of a smaller size, and forty others scattered through the plain. Two are also seen on the bluff, at the distance of three miles. Several of these mounds are almost conical. As the sward had been burnt, the earth was perfectly naked, and I could trace with ease, any unevenness of surface, so as to discover whether it was artificial or accidental. I every where observed a great number of small elevations of earth, to the height of a few feet, at regular distances from each other, and which appeared to observe some order; near them I also observed pieces of flint, and fragments of earthen vessels. I concluded, that a very populous town had once existed here, similar to those of Mexico, described by the first conquerors. The mounds were sites of temples, or monuments to the great men. It is evident, this could never have been the work of thinly scattered tribes. If the human species had at any time been permitted in this country to have increased freely, and there is every probability of the fact, it must, as in Mexico, have become astonishingly numerous. The same space of ground would have sufficed to maintain fifty times the number of the present inhabitants, with ease; their agriculture having no other object than mere sustenance. Amongst a numerous population, the power of the chief

must necessarily be more absolute, and where there are no laws, degenerates into despotism. This was the case in Mexico, and in the nations of South America; a great
number of individuals were at the disposal of the chief, who treated them little better than slaves. The smaller the society, the greater the consequence of each individual. Hence, there would not be wanting a sufficient number of hands to erect mounds
or pyramids.

Hunter and Dunbar describe a mound at the junction of the Catahoula, Washita
and Tensa rivers, very similar in shape to the large one on the Cahokia. I saw it last
summer: it has a step or apron, and is surrounded by a group of ten or twelve other
mounds of a smaller size. In the vicinity of New Madrid, there are a number; one on
the bank of a lake, is at least four hundred yards in circumference, and surrounded by
a ditch at least ten feet wide, and at present, five feet deep; it is about forty feet in
height, and level on the top. I have frequently examined the mounds at St. Louis: they
are situated on the second bank just above the town, and disposed in a singular manner; there are nine in all, and form three sides of a parallelogram, the open side towards the country, being protected, however, by three smaller mounds, placed in a circular manner. The space enclosed is about four hundred yards in length, and two
hundred in breadth. About six hundred yards above there is a single mound, with a
broad stage on the river side; it is thirty feet in height, and one hundred and fifty in
length; the top is a mere ridge of five or six feet wide. Below the first mounds there
is a curious work, called the Falling Garden. Advantage is taken of the second bank,
nearly fifty feet in height at this place, and three regular stages or steps, are formed by
earth brought from a distance. This work is much admired—it suggests the idea of a
place of assembly for the purpose of counselling, on public occasions. The following
diagram may convey a more precise idea.

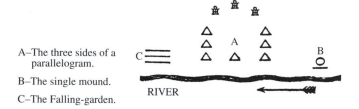

A–The three sides of a
   parallelogram.

B–The single mound.

C–The Falling-garden.

In tracing the origin of institutions or inventions amongst men, we are apt to forget, that nations, however diversified by manners and languages, are yet of the same
species, and that the same institutions may originate amongst twenty different people. Adair takes great pains to prove a similarity of customs between the American
tribes and the Jews; Lapiteau shews the existence of a still greater number common
to the Greeks and Romans; the result to the philosophic mind is no more than this,
that the American tribes belong to the human race, and that men, without any intercourse with each other, will, in innumerable instances, fall upon the same mode of
acting. The wonder would be, that they should not shew a resemblance. Man is every
where found in societies, under governments, addicted to war, hunting, or agriculture, and fond of dances, shows, and distinction. Perhaps the first employment of a
numerous population when not engaged in war, would be in heaping up piles of
earth, the rudest and most common species of human labor. We find these mounds in
every part of the globe; in the north of Europe, and in Great Britain, they are numerous, and much resemble ours, but less considerable. The pyramids of Egypt are

perhaps the oldest monuments of human labor in that country, so favorable to the production of a numerous population. The pyramids of Mexico, which are but little known, and yet scarcely less considerable, like those of Egypt have there origin hid in the night of oblivion. Humboldt is of opinion, that "these edifices must be classed with the pyramidal monuments of Asia, of which traces were found even in Arcadia; for the conical mausoleum of Callistus was a true tumulus, covered with fruit trees, and served for a base to a small temple consecrated to Diana." The Greeks, who were successful in the chariot races at the Olympic games, to shew their gratitude to their horses, gave them an honorable burial, and even erected pyramids over their graves. The great altar of Jupiter, at Olympia, was nothing more than a huge mound of earth, with stone steps to ascend. Humboldt remarks with astonishment, the striking similarity of the Asiatic and Egyptian pyramids, to those of Mexico. The similarity of those which he describes, to the mounds or pyramids on the Mississippi, is still more striking, but not a matter of so much wonder. The only difference is, that a few of the Mexican pyramids are larger, and some appear to have been faced with stone or brick. Like those of Mexico, wherever there has been a considerable town, we find two large pyramids, supposed to represent the sun and moon, and a number of smaller ones, to represent the stars. There is very little doubt but that they originated with the same people, for they may be considered as existing in the same country. What is the distance between Red river and the northern part of the intendancy of Vera Cruz, in which the pyramid of Papantla is situated? little more than ten or fifteen days journey. Even supposing there were no mounds in the intermediate space, the distance is not such, as to preclude the probability of intercourse. There is no obstruction in the way; a coach and four has been driven from Mexico to Nacogdoches.

The Mexican histories give uncertain accounts of the origin of those works, nor are the antiquarians able to form any satisfactory hypothesis. They are attributed by some to the Toultec nation, as far back as the ninth century, who emigrated to Mexico from the north, perhaps from the banks of the Mississippi; and by others, to the Olmec nation, still more ancient, who came to Mexico from the east. A curious discovery, made a few years ago in the state of Tennessee, proves beyond a doubt, that at some remote period the valley of the Mississippi had been inhabited by a much more civilized people, than when first known to us. Two human bodies were found in a copperas cave, in a surprising state of preservation. They were first wraped up in a kind of blanket, supposed to have been manufactured of the lint of nettles, afterwards with dressed skins, and then a mat of nearly sixty yards in length. They were clad in a beautiful cloth, interwoven with feathers, such as was manufactured by the Mexicans. The flesh had become hard, but the features were well preserved. They had been here, perhaps, for centuries, and certainly were of a different race from the modern Indians. They might have belonged to the Olmec, who overran Mexico about the seventh century, to the Toultec, who came centuries afterwards, or to the Aztecs, who founded the great city of Mexico, in the thirteenth century.

These subjects can only bewilder; every nation, in tracing back its history, must finally lose itself in fable. The Aztec (Mexican) mode of preserving their chronicles, must necessarily have been defective; the Egyptians could lay but little better claim to authenticity. The simple fact of the emigration to the country of the Olmecs, or Toultecs, may be relied on, but as to the time and circumstances, we must look for very slender accounts. It is only since the invention of letters that we can form a well grounded hope of the permanency of human institutions, of the certainty of history, and of the uninterrupted progress of improvements. Had this noble invention been unknown, how many of our most useful arts would have been lost during that night of barbarism, called the dark ages!

A French writer has fancifully observed, that civilization arises, *de la fermentation dune nombreuse peuplade,* and that it would be as idle to expect this result without a numerous population, as to think of making wine by the fermentation of a single grape. Experience shews, that a numerous population will always be attended with some degree of improvement, because, as Mr. Jefferson observes, the chances of improvement are multiplied. It is not without reason, that the Creator gave his command to increase and multiply, since many of the intellectual faculties would not otherwise be completely unfolded. It is not every country, however, which can of itself attain the full extent of the population of which it may be rendered susceptible. In unfriendly soils and climates, nature must be forced by the arts and labors of agriculture, to afford sustenance for a numerous population. The inhabitants of such have therefore been usually found in wandering tribes, engaged in constant wars, and probably unable ever to *originate* their own civilization. A mighty warrior, at the head of his own tribe, might subdue the tribes around him, and form a little empire, and peace being secured to a great proportion of his subjects, their numbers would increase, but it would fall into fragments, long before the useful arts could be invented. It has ever been in the mildest climates, gifted by nature with plenty, that civilization has had its origin. Egypt and fruitful Asia, first became possessed of a numerous population, and first cultivated the arts and sciences. In America civilization first appeared, in similar climates, where nature, with little help from man, produces abundance of food. In both the old and the new world, the celestial spark kindled in those happy climes, would be carried to less favored regions. But the human race has every where experienced terrible revolutions. Pestilence, war, and the convulsions of the globe, have annihilated the proudest works, and rendered vain the noblest efforts. Ask not the sage, by whom, and when, were erected those lingering ruins, the "frail memorials" of ages which have long since been swallowed up in the ocean of time; ask not the wild Arab, where may be found the owner of the superb palace, within whose broken walls he casts his tent; ask not the poor fisherman, as he spreads his nets, or the ploughman, who whistles over the ground, where is Carthage, where is Troy, of whose splendor, historians and poets have so much boasted! Alas! "they have vanished from the things that be," and have left but the melancholy lesson, of the instability of the most stupendous labors, and the vanity of immortality on earth!

In the wanderings of fancy, I have sometimes conceived this hemisphere, like the other, to have experienced the genial ray of civilization, and to have been inhabited by a numerous, polite, and enlightened people.[2] Why may not great revolutions have been experienced in America? Is it certain, that Mexico, Peru, and Chili, when first

---

2. Even this idea, strange and novel as it may seem, might, by an ingenious theorist, have an air of importance given to it, by bringing into view, some vague passages of ancient authors. Plato, in one of his dialogues, speaks of a people, who had come from the Atlantic in great numbers, and overran the greater part of Europe and Asia. Many circumstances related of the island of the Atlantic, correspond with America. This occurrence, to which Plato alludes, was considered of great antiquity, and preserved by obscure tradition. The island was said to have been sunk by an earthquake. The fact is certain, that amongst the Greeks, there prevailed a belief of the existence of another continent, in the Atlantic ocean, and inhabited by a powerful people, who, in remote antiquity, had invaded the old world. Amongst the Romans, who borrowed the greater part of their learning from the Greeks, the same belief prevailed. Seneca has this remarkable passage: "In ages to come, the seas will be traversed, and in spite of the wind and waves, avarice and pride will discover a New World, and Thule shall be no longer considered the extreme part of the

visited by Europeans, exhibited only the dawn of civilization? Perhaps it was the fiftieth approach doomed to suffer a relapse, before the sacred flame could be extended to other portions of the continent: perhaps, at some distant period the flame had been widely spread, and again extinguished by the common enemies of the human race. But I am asked, if this had been the case, should we not see indubitable proofs, in the remains of antiquity, edifices of stone, mines, and laborious works of human hands. I answer, that nature is ever laboring to restore herself, she is ever engaged in replacing in its primitive state, whatever changes the hand of man may effect in her appearance. Excavations of the earth would be filled up by the hand of time, and piles of stone when separated from the living rock, would crumble into dust. America may have been less fortunate than Europe in those happy inventions which serve in some measure to perpetuate improvements, and yet, in some of the arts she may have attained a greater excellence. The character of her civilization may have been different from any of which we have a knowledge, and her relapse produced by causes of which we can form no conjecture.

Who will assign, as the age of America, a period of years different from that allowed to, what has been denominated, the old world? A multiplicity of proofs contradict the recency of her origin; deeply imbedded stores of carbonated wood, the traces of ancient volcanoes! I could appeal on this subject to her time-worn cataracts, and channels of mighty rivers, and to her venerable mountains, which rose when the Creator laid the foundations of the earth! When the eye of Europe first beheld her, did she appear but lately to have sprung from the deep? No, she contained innumerable and peculiar plants and animals, she was inhabited by thousands of Indians, possessing different languages, manners, and appearances. Grant then, that America may have existed a few thousand years; the same causes prevailing, like effects will be produced; the same revolutions as have been known in the old world may have taken place here.

Before the invention of letters, there would be a constant succession of advances to civilization, and of relapses to barbarism. The Chaldeans, through the glimmer of ancient history, are represented to us as the first inventors of the arts; but may not those people have been preceded by the same revolutions as have succeeded them. In long and arduous advances, they might attain to a great height in civilization, and wars, pestilence, or other calamities, precipitate them to the state of the barbarian or the savage. It is true, the traces of art would long remain undefaced; but they would not remain *forever:* Time would obliterate them.

> "He grasp'd a hero's antique bust,
> The marble crumbled into dust,
> And sunk beneath the shade."
> —SELLECK OSBORNY.

---

globe." Mons. Peyroux has in a very ingenious essay, rendered it even probable, that the ancients had been acquainted with America in very remote antiquity. Plato places the destruction of the Atlantides, at nine thousand years before his time.

24

LYDIA B. BACON

(1786–1853)

The overwhelming majority of early western travel narratives were written and published by men. One exception is the journal kept by Lydia B. Bacon in 1811–1812 and first published three years after her death. A native of Boston, Lydia Stetson married Josiah Bacon, a childhood playmate, in the spring of 1807. Soon after their marriage, Josiah accepted an army commission. He became a lieutenant and a quartermaster of the fourth regiment of the United States infantry. When he received traveling orders, his wife would travel with him.

Beginning in May of 1811, the couple traveled from Fort Independence on Boston Harbor's Castle Island to Vincennes in the Indiana Territory. On November 7, 1811, Lydia waited in Vincennes while Josiah fought with William Henry Harrison against the Shawnees in the Battle of Tippecanoe. After this battle, the Bacons were en route to Detroit when Lydia and other wives were captured by British troops. The women were soon released, but, less than six weeks later, Lydia and Josiah were taken together as prisoners.

Lydia Bacon endured much in her travels with her husband, but she found compensation in the landscape around her. As a young woman, she worshipped God only as she saw Him in Nature. Lydia often explained, according to a friend,

> I *thought* I loved God when I was a child, and indeed I should then have been very much grieved had any one questioned it, but it was the *God of Nature,* only, or perhaps rather *the God of my own imagination* whom I loved. I was an enthusiastic admirer of Nature, and knowing it to be the handiwork of God, I loved him as its author. Sometimes, too, I admired Him as the God of providence, particularly when I saw some striking manifestation of his interposing hand in my own favor, or in that of my friends. But *the God of the gospel*—a Being infinitely holy, hating sin and bound to punish the guilty—such a God was not at all in my thoughts.

When their war travels were done, the Bacons returned to Boston for three years before settling in Sackett's Harbor, New York, where Lydia experienced her religious awakening.

Josiah worked as a commission merchant in Sackett's Harbor until 1829, when his business failed, and he and Lydia relocated to Sandwich, Massachusetts. He held several minor political offices before his death in 1852. Just before Josiah died, Lydia wrote to a sister, "We have neared the time allotted to man in this world." She followed him in death the next year.

Biography of Mrs. Lydia B. Bacon, the source of the present text, was cobbled together from her letters and journals and published by the Massachusetts Sabbath School Society in 1856. Bacon's original manuscript chronicling her travels in 1811–1812 is held by the New York Historical Society.

Text: *Biography of Mrs. Lydia B. Bacon* (Boston, 1856): 9–41.

FROM *BIOGRAPHY OF MRS. LYDIA B. BACON* (1811–1812, 1856)

"*June 1st,* 1811. The troops took up the line of march from Philadelphia for Pittsburgh, and Mrs. P., Mrs. G. and myself went in the stage-coach, under the care of a nephew of Col. Boyd's who was traveling for his health. The weather was serene, the roads were good, and all nature appeared in its richest dress. The land from Philadelphia to Chambersburgh, (which lies at the foot of the Alleghany mountains,) is rich and highly cultivated. Large farms with barns of spacious dimensions, built of stone, meet the eye in every direction. But our attention was particularly attracted by the sight of Dutch girls performing the labor of men in the fields, and we were greatly amused by seeing large numbers of swine feeding in rich clover up to their backs. I had often *heard* of '*pigs in clover,*' but never *saw it realized* before.

"*Pittsburgh, June 26th.* We arrived here ten days since, after a somewhat tedious but delightful journey—tedious on account of the extreme roughness of the roads over the mountains, which did not fulfill the promise of the commencement of our ride. And yet we found great delight in the beauty of the landscape by which we were continually surrounded. For on every side was exhibited to our admiring gaze a constant succession of scenery at once grand, sublime, awful and sweet. A variety of emotions filled my mind at these surveys of God's works; every thing seemed calculated for instruction, comfort and pleasure. And while contemplating these wonders and beauties our sense of dependence on their Divine Author seemed more firmly fixed in our hearts. Oh, could we be sensible of his goodness to us we should not let a murmuring thought arise, but should be wholly resigned to his will, whatever that will might be.

"The stages over the mountains were very bad, the roads equally so; and we were obliged to walk the horses in the ascent for several miles together. Sometimes for a change we would all get out and walk, and during the roughest of the way the seats were taken out from our vehicle, straw spread upon the bottom of it, and the passengers stowed in like baggage. But to those who desired to view the landscape as we passed along, the last arrangement was most unsatisfactory, and we resolved that we would rather endure the jolting upon our seats than be deprived of this pleasure. So the seats were restored, and you may just imagine to yourself Lydia seated at the coach window, to which she was obliged to hold on with both hands, straining every nerve and muscle to maintain her equilibrium.

"On one side my neighbor's elbow was constantly pounding me, on the other the stage, which was neither lined or stuffed, was bruising me, while my head was often thrown against the top till I feared my brains would be dashed out. But all this I bravely endured for the sake of beholding the scenery.

"At a distance the mountains towered to the clouds, and in some instances the tops were lost in them. On one side, and within a foot or two of the carriage wheels fell an awful precipice, at whose base a beautiful river quietly glided along, unmindful alike of the danger or the admiration of the travelers. After a little turning we would ride through this stream and then again cross it upon a rude bridge, and often afterward it would be seen in the distance. We were obliged to lock the wheels upon descending the mountains, and when we came to a narrow place in the road the driver would *blow his tin horn* vociferously to warn any teams which might be approaching to avoid danger by stopping where we could safely pass them. The distance across the mountains by the road which we traveled was one hundred and sixty miles, and this it took us several days to accomplish.

"There are some pretty and thrifty villages among the mountains, where we passed the nights during our journey. The one which pleased me most was called Bedford. We lodged there the second night. It was situated in a beautiful valley, which was watered by a very lovely stream—the Juniata. I was reminded of Johnson's Rasselas, who was born in a similar valley, and like it so entirely surrounded by mountains that he lived to the age of man ere he learned there was any other world beside the spot he inhabited."

The following description of Pittsburgh, to which place Mrs. Bacon's journey had now brought her, it will be recollected, was written more than forty years ago. Its appearance as described here, is, of course, in striking contrast with its *present* aspect, and may not only afford amusement but instruction, as indicating the rapid strides of our Young America:

"Pittsburgh is *a pleasant village* surrounded by mountains. On one side the Monongahela river laves its banks, on the other the pure waters of the Alleghany unite and mingle with the beautiful Ohio. This village is famed for its manufactories; the people appear very industrious and engrossed in the *all important* business of accumulating wealth. A great deal of coal is used here, which gives the village a very dirty appearance. The children's faces (as you see them in the street) look as if they were strangers to water, though so many beautiful rivers are running by their doors.

"We have seen a number of factories and a *large flour mill,* the labor of which is expedited by STEAM, the flour being carried by this means through all its different grades until it is snugly packed in the barrel! There is also a fine glass factory here. We saw some of the cut glass—the first ever done in our country. The first steamboat ever built for these waters has just been launched; if it were now ready we might have the pleasure of going in it. We visited Grant's Hill, a place conspicuous not so much from the loftiness of its summit as from its having been a scene of battle during the Revolutionary war. We had a terrible thunder-storm to-day; the thunder was tremendous, accompanied with vivid lightning and with rain, which drenched the streets like a flood. I believe the thunder is always more violent among the mountains than in a level country. The heat is oppressive, but it does not make us sick. All kinds of provisions are cheap and of a good quality.

"The military quarters are small and will not accommodate all our regiment. The Colonel resides with his staff at the quarters, with the exception *of my husband, who prefers to live with his wife,* the rest board or live in hired houses. Lieut. G. and wife, Josiah and myself, with some of our brother officers, have hired a new brick house on Market street, and all live at one table. For this my husband provides, and sees that our fare is cooked and served in good order. This is but little trouble, as we have plenty of servants, and those that are pretty fair, though all *men.*

"The military quarters here were built by General Wilkinson, and resemble an elegant country seat. In the rear of the house (which is both commodious and splendid,) is a large garden arranged with much taste. All kinds of fruit trees, shrubbery and flowers charm the eye and please the palate, while the odors which perfume the air leave nothing wanting which a refined taste could desire. A canal runs through this garden, over which is a Chinese bridge with seats around it. The Colonel has tea-parties frequently, and entertains his company in the garden, while an excellent band at a distance and unseen discourses fine music. The whole appears like enchantment. At one of these parties a few days since I was sitting on the bridge under the shade of a beautiful tree in conversation with some of the company. Happening to cast my eye into a walk at some little distance, I saw our gallant Colonel upon his knees presenting to a beautiful damsel her glove which she had let fall, perhaps on purpose. This chivalrous incident amused me much, especially in connection with their difference in age, the gentleman being more than fifty and the young maiden I should judge about sixteen.

"*July 27th.* Since writing the above we have received orders to proceed to Newport, Kentucky, on the Ohio River, about five hundred miles from this place. We are to descend the river in keel-boats, covered like houses; the sides we can open or close as we please, and stop at night if we choose. The river is narrow, and in many places you can call across it and be heard quite plain. We are told that it is very pleasant sailing on the river, but we should greatly prefer stopping here for the present. We are comfortably quartered, are much pleased with the people, who are both attentive and hospitable, *but go we must.* The evenings here are delightful after the excessive heat of the day. Soon as the sun retires, the families sit at their doors, or walk with uncovered heads, that they may enjoy the soft breezes of twilight. Sometimes our band, in a boat, will navigate each side of the village and send forth exquisite strains of music. These echoing among the mountains produce a charming effect, reminding me of something which I have read of but never expected to realize. All this is truly delightful, but we must leave it. The Indians are committing depredations upon the white inhabitants located upon our Western frontier, and the Governor of Indiana has requested some regular troops to assist in keeping them quiet. This is the cause of our removal at this time.

"*August 2d,* 10 A. M. Embarked on board the boats for Newport. The fleet, (if I may so call it,) consisted of eleven boats. *Our* party consists of Mr. and Mrs. A———— with her two young brothers, Mr. G———— and wife, husband and self. We went forty miles to-day, and at night stopped at Custard Island. The ground not being good we slept in the boats, and a curious figure we made indeed. We were obliged to place our beds on the floor of the cabin, and we ladies slept there together, while our husbands spread blankets upon the seats or lockers at the sides of the cabin, and all thus enjoyed comfortable repose, after the novelty of the scene allowed us composure to court the drowsy god. This is a very pleasant way of traveling. We are as comfortable as if in a house, have our regular meals cooked and served in good style by our own servants, and our reading, conversation and needlework, together with our admiration of the passing scenery, fills up the time pleasantly and profitably.

"This river is very winding, and in some places the bends are so peculiar that you seem to be sailing upon a pond with no outlet, and wonder how you are ever to find your way out. And at such times I cannot help fancying the Indians with their tomahawks and scalping knives peeping at us from behind the trees and bushes, and ready to raise their murderous yells.

"*August 3d.* We were awoke at daylight by the reveille, and left Custard Island about five o'clock in the morning. We passed the towns of Steubenville and Charleston, both of which are handsome places. The weather is fair and there is a fine breeze on the water.

"*Eight o'clock, P. M.* It is a lovely moonlight evening, and we have stopped at the foot of a beautiful bank on which are several log houses swarming with children, who seem as merry and happy as possible. The soldiers have pitched their tents, made their fires and are preparing their suppers. The ladies are making their husband's beds, and every thing is lively around me. How I wish my distant friends could take a peep at us and help me laugh.

"*August 4th.* We were aroused this morning by the drums beating the tune which accompanies these words:

'Don't you hear your General say,
Strike your tents and march away.'

Our pilot plays well upon the bugle, and the echoes and re-echoes among the hills are wonderful and delightful. One infant has died to-day; happy child, thus early escaped from this world of sin and sorrow, and gone where there will be no more sickness and no more death! It was a soldier's babe; the officers have no children with them. We are having a pleasant time. The river is perfectly smooth, and we are going *with* the stream; of course we pass along very rapidly. Our boat is seventy feet long, twelve wide and seven high. It has no sails, and is propelled by twenty-two oars. There are many small islands in the river, which add much to its beauty.

"We were obliged to stop at one o'clock on account of a squall coming on. For awhile the prospect seemed rather gloomy; but the tempest soon passed by, doing us no damage, and we proceeded on our way. The weather was most delightful after the shower, and I longed to have my friends here to enjoy the scene with me.

"*August 5th, P. M.* Stopped at Marietta, which lies upon the Ohio and Muskingum rivers. The inhabitants are principally New Englanders, who were engaged in the employment of building vessels. This they found very lucrative; but the embargo came and put a stop to their business, and of course injured the place very much. My husband and myself, in walking about the streets, were struck with the *stillness* which prevailed. In consequence of the dullness of business many of the inhabitants have moved away; in some of the streets we found the clover quite high, and in others there was hardly a footpath. I was forcibly reminded of Goldsmith's Deserted Village. The place is beautifully situated and well laid out, and we walked until fatigue compelled *me* to return to our boat. But my husband with some of his brother officers rambled farther to visit some Indian mounds in the vicinity.

"I hoped to have gone ashore at Blennerhasset Island, but the rain prevented me. It must be well worth seeing, if the description of it which I have just read from 'The Western Tour' be correct. A short extract from that account I will here copy for the benefit of my friends:

"'On ascending the bank from the landing, one quarter of a mile below the Eastern end of the island, we entered a handsome double gate with pillars of hewn stone. A graveled walk led us about one hundred and fifty paces to the house. This was situated with a meadow on the left, and a shrubbery on the right, separated by a low hedge, through which we could see innumerable flowers displaying themselves to the sun. The house is large and handsome. The shrubbery before mentioned was well stocked with all manner of flowers, and a variety of evergreens, (not only those natural to the climate, but exotics,) surrounded the walks, which were graveled and wound in labyrinthine style, through this enchanted spot. The garden is not large but seems to have every variety of fruit, flowers and vegetables which this fine climate and luxurious soil could produce. In short, Blennerhasset's Island is a most charming retreat for a man of fortune fond of retirement, and is perhaps not exceeded in beauty by any situation in this Western world. It lacks, however, the variety of mountains, precipice, cataract, distant prospect, &c., which constitute the grand and sublime.'

"The foregoing description was given several years ago. Since then the unfortunate owner was concerned with Aaron Burr in his treasonable designs against the Union, and was obliged to abscond from this charming retreat. At present its inhabitants are a few slaves, who raise hemp. The entrance is choked with bushes, yet the whole has a romantic appearance. The farther we proceed down this river the more level the country becomes and the more cultivated; indeed, we have almost lost sight of the mountains.

"*August 6th, A. M.* Our boats, last night, were locked two together, yet the current drifted us forty miles. It was a dark, rainy night, but the Colonel being anxious to reach Newport as soon as possible thought best to continue on instead of stopping for the night as heretofore. We went over L——— Falls, but I did not see them, because old Morpheus had blinded my eyes. We ladies experienced no inconvenience from this arrangement, but our poor husbands were obliged to take their watch on deck, and in consequence were wet to the skin. We are at this moment opposite a log house situated in a cornfield, and *the corn is actually higher than the house.* We can just see a troop of children playing about the door.

"*August 7th.* We drifted much last night, and this morning stopped half an hour and landed at a thrifty farm. Here we found a son of old Justice G———, of Boston. In early life he married a young lady in St. Domingo, and they were happily residing on that island when an insurrection among the blacks obliged him to flee with his wife and mother. They succeeded in reaching this country with a remnant of their property, and settled upon the Ohio. Here they have remained twelve years; they *work hard* but *sleep sound.* Their greatest trouble is the want of educational privileges for their children, who are very intelligent and promising. Having heard of a good school about twenty miles from their location, (this was the nearest within their reach,) the father with two of his children accompanied us in our boat. We found him a very intelligent and agreeable companion.

"*August 8th.* Although our boats were lashed together last night, yet two ran ashore in consequence of the fog, and a soldier sleeping on deck, encumbered with a heavy watch coat, &c., fell overboard and sunk to rise no more. Poor fellow! he was summoned in an unexpected moment into an unknown world, and left some hearts to bleed, no doubt, for his untimely end. Our boat got on to what they call a *sawyer*. These are trees carried by freshets into the river, and catching to the bottom. When the water is low, (which is generally the case at this season of the year,) these sawyers are very dangerous. The tops being just above water, boats often catch in them and are much damaged, and sometimes sunk. When we struck, the jar and noise awoke us from a sound sleep, and alarmed us not a little; but a kind Providence preserved us from destruction, and we received no material damage.

"We stopped this evening at a beautiful place without a name, and took a pleasant walk along the bank. We are in the habit of buying butter, eggs, &c., as we go along, and have found them abundant, cheap and good. Needing some butter now, we called at a house hoping to have our wants supplied; but the good housewife very carelessly told us that she had been making *soap* that day, and not having sufficient *grease* had supplied the deficiency with *butter*. What a country, thought I, where people can afford to use sweet butter for soap grease!

"*August 9th*. Arrived at Newport and found decent quarters in a comfortable location. This is a military depot. Cincinnati lies directly opposite, *and is said to be a flourishing town*. I intend going to see it to-day.

"The view, as seen from this side of the river reminds me more of Boston than any place that I have yet seen. Thirty years ago it was almost a wilderness. I can only account for its rapid growth by the fact that the settlers are principally Yankees. I long much to see my dear mother and sisters, and New England friends, but as my beloved husband was obliged to come here, I have never for a moment regretted that I accompanied him. It is a great comfort that we can be together, and I have the satisfaction of feeling that I am performing my duty. This place is healthy, we are both well, the season is delightful, and we have an abundance of fruit, which is here both plenty and cheap. How long we shall be allowed to remain here is altogether uncertain. We are now awaiting farther orders. I hope they may be to stay here or to return to Pittsburgh, but fear we shall be destined still farther west."

At Newport, Capt. and Mrs. Bacon formed the acquaintance of a family by the name of Taylor. The gentleman was a brother of General Taylor, afterwards President of the United States. He owned a beautiful plantation a short distance from the military quarters, upon the bank of the river, and treated Mr. and Mrs. B. with the utmost attention and hospitality. He often sent them delicious fruit, and frequently invited them to his house. Years afterward, Mrs. Bacon writes, "Very pleasant is the recollection of the hours passed in their society. Sweet was our social converse when seated in the calm twilight, on the front piazza, overlooking the splendid lawn which spread its green carpet to the edge of the river. The fruit trees on either side of the mansion were loaded with their rich treasures which not only delighted the eye but regaled the palate."

"*Sept. 2d*, 1811. Our fears are realized; we are ordered still farther west, and again find ourselves in our boats upon the Ohio. We have much to engage our attention, but my thoughts often recur to my absent friends, whom I fondly love, and I trust that neither time or distance will ever diminish my affection. I have no female companion with me on the boat now. Our family consists of Col., Capt. S., husband and self. Our cabin is quite large, and we are very well accommodated. On account of the lowness of the water, which renders navigation dangerous by night, our boats stop at evening, and those who choose, can sleep in tents on shore.

"*Sept. 3d*. Last night the boats were anchored under a high bank, and as the summit presented nothing very inviting, we hardly thought it worth while to ascend it.

But our minds were soon changed by the report of some of the gentlemen whose curiosity led them to reconnoitre a little distance. They brought with them some beautiful straw hats which they had purchased of a Swiss family, whom they found located a short distance from the river. About thirty families had taken up their residence here, being driven from their own country by the troubles in France. They fled to our peaceful shores, and purchasing some land of our government, planted vineyards, the produce of which enables them to realize the comfort and independence which they fondly anticipated.

"We purchased some of their wine made from Madeira and other grapes, and those who considered themselves judges of the article pronounced it excellent. But for my part, I much prefer the grapes *unpressed*. We went into one of the vineyards; it was a charming sight. The house was pleasantly situated, and the yard laid out with good taste. We approached the front door through rows of vines (supported by poles five or six feet high) loaded with clusters of ripe grapes, while the peach and nectarine trees swept the ground, so heavily were they laden with the delicious fruit. The family were neatly dressed; a number of fine, healthy children *adorned* the front yard, the grass of which having been newly mown, perfumed the air with its fragrance. It was one of the finest twilights I ever saw. We tarried until the full-orbed moon warned us that it was time to depart. We left with great reluctance, and like our mother Eve, on leaving her beautiful Eden, we cast a long and lingering look behind. I had often read of such charming spots; but thought they existed only in the author's brain, yet I must say that my eyes here beheld a sight equal to any thing of which I ever read. This place is called Vevay, in Indiana.

"*Sept. 4th.* We arrived at Jeffersonville this morning at nine o'clock, and now the boats are preparing to go through the Rapids. The water is very low and it is found necessary to take all the baggage out, and send it round by land. The distance is three miles and it takes only thirteen minutes to go by water. Lieut. G's boat with himself and wife, and Mr. and Mrs. A. has gone over safely. *We could go by land,* inasmuch as my husband being quarter-master, has charge of the property. But we prefer to run all risks which are necessary for the rest of the officers and their wives. It is rather critical navigation here; we are obliged to have two pilots, one at the bow and the other at the stern.

"*Sept. 4th.* We are safe over the Rapids; it was frightful indeed. It seemed like being at sea in a storm, surrounded by breakers. The clouds were heavy, the wind was high, and a thunderstorm threatening us which burst upon us just as we got into port. We had no passengers in our boat except Capt P. and lady, and ourselves, the soldiers having gone by land. We *stood,* while passing the Rapids, with our eyes stretched to their utmost width, that we might see the whole in its perfection; although hardly daring to take a long breath under the fear that our boat might strike the rocks.

"We have laid below the falls these two days, and have been highly interested, viewing the petrifactions which are abundant and extremely curious. I have taken some specimens along with me that I may show them to my friends some future day should I ever have the good fortune to meet them. Indeed, I often wish that I could transport them here, that they might behold with me the wonderful works of nature. We are fast approaching the lowlands. From Pittsburgh thus far, there has been a constant succession of hills and vales; but in a few hours a vast extent of level country will open to our view. We are come to the lowlands. The contrast is great; not a mountain or hill now meets the eye. This is a pleasant way of traveling—every thing goes on as regular as if at housekeeping. Our cook prepares his food well, and does the laundry work admirably. We drink the river water; it tastes very well, but I do not like to think of the dirt that is thrown into it. Last night we had a *recruit* added to our number, in the shape of a bit of female mortality born in a tent on the banks of the Wabash, which river we are now ascending. Our progress is slow and very difficult, the current, which is against us, being very strong. We could go as far in *two* days with the current in our favor, as we can in *twelve* with it setting against us. To add to our difficulties, the River Wabash is full of snags, sawyers, and sand-bars, and the night air is so damp that if exposed to it we are in danger of fever and ague. And here I must record a *furious* account of an attack of that disease which I heard from a western settler: 'You see, ma'am,' said he, 'we had just got moved into our new house; when I was took down with that pesky ague. First came the chills, and I shook so hard that all the plasterin' fell off my walls; next the fever riz, and made my room so hot that the *lathes ketched afire,* and I should have been burnt to death hadn't the *sweatin' turn* come on so powerful as to drench the room with water, and *quinch* the flames.'

"*Oct. 1st.,* 1811. We arrived at Vincennes, Indiana Territory, and find all engaged for a campaign against the Indians. Our health is very good at present, although my dear Josiah has been burnt with gun-powder, which might have destroyed life had not a kind Providence prevented. He was priming his gun, for the sake of shooting some wild fowl which are plenty on the river. The flint of the gun being rather long, struck fire into the powder, in the pan by coming in contact with it in shutting. The flask, which contained nearly half a pound of powder exploded, throwing the contents into his face, burning his eyebrows and lashes close. He shrieked, and putting his hands to his face took the skin entirely off. He could not see at all for a fortnight, and we sometimes feared that he never would see again. But a simple curd made of new milk and vinegar cured his eyes, and an application of oil and brandy alternately applied to his face healed it rapidly.

"Just after he was burnt, I took a violent cold by being out to view the comet, which had just made its appearance, and was quite sick in consequence. We were two pitiable objects, neither able to help the other and yet both needing assistance. When we arrived at Vincennes, no carriage could be procured, although I was hardly able to step, from debility, and my poor Josiah could not see at all; so we both had to be led. The night was dark and rainy, but amid all these difficulties we reached our lodgings at the only public house in the village. It proves to be a very good house, although overcrowded at present. But we shall be better accommodated when the officers from Ohio and Kentucky are gone.

"Gov. Harrison called upon me to-day, previous to his departure for his Indian campaign. He had on a hunting-shirt (as they call it here,) of calico, trimmed with fringe. In form it resembled a woman's short-gown; only the ends were pointed instead of being square, and were tied in a hard knot to keep the garment snug. On his head sat a round beaver, gracefully ornamented with a white ostrich plume. He is tall and slender, with dark, piercing eyes, and most pleasing manners, and certainly exhibited not only *politeness* but benevolence, in thus noticing *a poor sick stranger.* It made an impression upon my mind which will never be effaced."

Little did Mrs. Bacon think when thus describing the person and manners of Gov. Harrison that she spoke of the future President of these United States. And as little did she foresee that distant future when his kind remembrance of herself and husband should secure to them a position of usefulness and comfort in their declining years. But we will not anticipate.

"*Oct.* 5th. The troops have left Vincennes to-day. It was a sad sight to see them depart for war. A number of fine young men, volunteers from Ohio and Kentucky, left their studies in college to participate in this campaign. How many of them will return in safety to their homes and kindred none but God can tell! My husband's sight continuing very weak, it was not thought prudent for him to go on with the troops. So the charge of Fort Knox is assigned him together with the care of the invalid soldiers.

"*Oct. 8th.* So here we are at Fort Knox, a stockade or military depot on the banks of the Wabash. I have not a single female associate, but *I have my husband* and so *all is well.* I venture alone sometimes outside the pickets, but although a soldier's wife, I lay no claim to heroism. And as I do not relish the idea of being scalped by our red brethren, I never venture far, but strive to content myself with those sources of enjoyment which are within my reach. I read, write, sew, converse, and think of absent friends whom it seems to me I never loved better than now. Josiah's eyes are getting strong fast, and he is impatient to rejoin his regiment. Indeed, he has besought the physician to pronounce him well enough, and has besides written to his colonel, requesting that he will order him to join him.

"*Oct. 9th.* My husband has received the order to rejoin his regiment. This is very much to his satisfaction, though not exactly to mine. Inglorious ease suits me better than it does him. Although we have been here only a week, we must pack up and be off to Vincennes again.

"*Oct. 10th.* My dear husband is gone to the army, and I am boarding at Vincennes, with a Mrs. Jones. I have a very pleasant companion in Mrs. Witlock, the wife of an officer commanding another regiment. They are Virginians. I have had a return of the fever and ague, and Mrs. W. has nursed me like a sister. The troops are eighty miles from this place, building a fort. The Indians in that neighborhood have as yet manifested no decided hostility towards them, but they are so deceitful and treacherous that no reliance can be placed upon their good will. The British furnish them with arms, ammunition, and rations. I hear that Colonel Miller has been very ill, and was obliged while sick to lie upon the ground in a tent. He is now better. I should like very much to ask him and the rest (who were so impatient to go) how they like their new situation. We have had no cold weather here yet, though it is now November. Indeed, I have not once sat by a fire during the past six months. We expect to stay here all winter, which is a disagreeable prospect to me, for I do not much fancy the place or the people. Dear New England, I love thee better than ever. Oh, shall I be so happy as to visit thy blest scenes once more, for blest indeed they are to me.

"This place (Vincennes) was settled about one hundred years since by the French. Judging by the present appearance of the place, its original inhabitants could not have had much enterprise or industry. The people are mostly Roman Catholic, and in their habits not much superior to the Indians. The local situation of the place is very pleasant. It lies upon a clear stream of water which affords a variety of fish, besides the more important facilities of easy intercourse with the neighboring states and territories. The village is perfectly level with the exception of three mounds which are situated at the rear of the place. These are supposed to have been raised by the Indians some centuries since, but for what purpose we can only conjecture. They are quite ornamental, and the centre mound is easy of access, having a foot-path winding up on the back side. I rode to the top of it on horseback. Perhaps future generations may see this a flourishing place. There are now a few American families here, and those are emigrants chiefly from Virginia and Kentucky. Slavery has been tolerated here, but I am happy to say that it is being removed. Land in this western country needs but little labor to prepare it for cultivation compared with ours at the east, but then produce does not command so good a price here."

The writer hopes that our western neighbors will not feel scandalized by this meagre description of a place now so important and flourishing as Vincennes. If the reader will bear in mind that this account was penned more than forty years ago, they will not need to be told that it can in no respect (except that of location) accurately describe the present aspect of this thrifty and beautiful place. American emigration and American enterprise have far outstripped even the eager anticipations of the most sanguine, and left the sober calculations of the prudent at a marvelous distance.

But we must return to the journal of Mrs. B. which carries us back to an event that long after its accomplishment lingered like a spell upon the nation's lips, and became the watchword of political combatants, and the talisman of their success. This was *the battle of Tippecanoe.*

"*Nov. 30th,* 1811. Have been for some days very desirous to hear from our regiment, as my imagination oft pictures my dear husband in the midst of danger and death. Oh, may he be mercifully spared. News—news from the army has just arrived! My precious Josiah, after being exposed to that most horrid of all battles—an Indian attack—has been preserved in safety. I cannot describe my feelings—words cannot do justice to them. I hope that this new, this great mercy, may be the means of raising our thoughts to God, our Creator and Preserver, who has watched over us ever since we had a being, and has done us good, and only good, continually. Oh, is it not strange that beings so dependent should so little realize their utter weakness. And stranger still, that creatures so undeserving should live, daily recipients of the divine bounty, and feel no corresponding emotions of love and gratitude.

"I do not regret that Josiah was in this battle, for I trust that the goodness of God in thus saving his life, has made impressions on both our hearts which will not easily be effaced. His duty as quarter-master was particularly arduous, of course, on a march. And although he was not attached to any particular company, yet he was equally exposed to danger with those who were. While bridling his horse, one ball went through his hat, and another passed through the skirt of his coat, just hitting his boot and the hoofs of his horse. The army was encamped in a hollow square, on a rising piece of ground, the tents all facing outward, beyond which a guard was placed. Suspicious of the Indians, (although they were apparently friendly,) the troops had retired to their tents with their clothes on, and their weapons of war by their side. Thus they tried to sleep, but I am sure their slumbers could not have been very sweet or refreshing. The Indians attacked them a little before day which is their usual method. The first gun was heard, and the regulars were at their post in a moment. The enemy had their faces painted black, which is their usual custom in an attack. This our troops could only see by the light afforded at the flashing of the guns, but accompanied by their tremendous war-whoop and the groans of the wounded, it rendered the scene terrific indeed. Yet amidst it all our troops never faltered, but answered the whoop with three hearty cheers. This dreadful battle lasted until daylight, when the Indians were completely routed and compelled to retire with great loss.

"Lieutenant Peters relates an affecting incident of this battle. Among the militia from Kentucky was a Captain Spencer who had been in *twelve* Indian campaigns. He was accompanied in this expedition by his son, an intelligent boy about twelve years of age. This brave little fellow had a gun adapted to his size, went on guard in his turn, and fought like a man. During the fight the darkness prevented any one from knowing who had fallen. Each feared for his fellow. As soon as the fight was over, this poor boy sought his father, but alas! he was not among the living—the hero of so many battles had at last met his fate. And a gentleman searching for his friends found this afflicted child weeping over the mangled body of his father. My heart aches for him, and for his distressed mother, who is left poor, with a large family of children to be supported by her own exertions. Alas! many others are made widows and orphans by this dreadful fight. Oh, when will brother cease to lift his hand against his brother, and nations learn war no more!

"Oh, what a day was that when we at Vincennes heard of this battle of Tippecanoe. Receiving at first a mere report of the attack and victory without any official communication, and of course without any details, each of us expected to hear sad news from our dear ones, and for hours our souls were harrowed to the quick, and agonized with suspense and dread. At length the express arrived with letters, yet his feelings were so excited, that he could not select and deliver them, but poured them out indiscriminately into my lap. I was so overcome with apprehensions for my husband that I could neither see nor read, and passed them into the hands of a lady who stood by me. Her husband not being in the war, she was more calm and composed, and soon was enabled to find me my letter. When told that the address was in Josiah's own handwriting, I could hardly believe it. My bodily weakness was great, being just recovering from the ague and fever, and this, aggravated by my intense anxiety respecting my dear husband, caused me to sink fainting upon the nearest chair. Recovering soon, however, with Mrs. G——— kneeling on one side of me, Mrs. W——— on the other, and Mrs. J——— in front of me. I opened the letter and began to read it aloud. I had proceeded only to the third or fourth line, which contained the assurance of his safety, when we all burst into tears and thus relieved our aching hearts. Then I was able to finish the precious document, and found that my beloved husband (now more dear than ever) and those whom we most valued had escaped without serious injury. There were but two married men killed from our regiment, and they were soldiers. Only one married officer from the 4th was wounded. How often have I heard or read of Indian fights until my blood chilled in my veins, without thinking that I should ever be so personally interested in one.

"Our situation at Vincennes was very much exposed while the troops were absent, for every body left that could handle a sword or carry a musket, and we women remained without even a guard. Mrs. W——— and myself had loaded pistols at our bedside, but I very much doubt whether we should have had presence of mind enough to use them, had we found it necessary. If the Indians had been aware of our situation, a few of them could have burnt the village, and massacred the inhabitants. But a kind Providence watched over us, and kept us from so dreadful a fate.

"Another letter brings intelligence of the death of Capt. Bean who was tomahawked in a shocking manner. It is thought by the distance at which he was found from camp that the Indians attempted to take him prisoner, and that he chose death rather than submit to what he knew would be prolonged torture. He was a man of great personal beauty, and a most excellent officer, and commanded the love and esteem of his brother officers in an eminent degree. It was my husband's painful duty to see him interred. This he did, and disguised the grave that his poor body might not be disturbed, and his bones left to bleach upon the plain. The others who died during this murderous attack were all buried in one grave. But the Indians dug up the remains and left them a prey to the beasts of the forests, who by the way, are scarcely more savage than themselves. Our regiment (the 4th,) acquitted themselves with much honor in this engagement, and it is said materially contributed to secure the victory. But victories even are dearly bought with the loss of human life, that life which God gave, and which man may destroy but cannot restore.

"Some Indian chiefs have been to Gov. Harrison since the battle, and seem very desirous of peace. They are much exasperated with one whom they call their prophet, who, it seems, stimulated them to the fight with the assurance that they should be victorious. The result having proved him but man, their confidence in him is of course greatly shaken. We are keeping house with Mr. and Mrs. Whitlock, and are very comfortably and pleasantly situated, as much so as is possible among entire strangers. We eat together, but have our separate parlors, with plenty of other room, and shall not therefore necessarily fatigue each other by being too much together.

"A number of soldiers have died of their wounds since their return to Vincennes. Funerals are of daily occurrence. Very solemn is the sight and sound, for the coffins are followed to the grave by soldiers with arms reversed, marching to the tune of 'Roslyn Castle,' with muffled drums. Poor fellows! they have paid the debt of nature, with no kind mother, sister, or wife to soothe their sorrows, or alleviate their distress, or wipe the death-sweat from their brow. Strangers have performed the last sad offices, and with them their dust shall rest until summoned by the last trump to stand before the Judge of the quick and dead."

A letter from Mrs. Bacon to her mother is here inserted, as it seems to take up the thread of her narrative and bridge over a chasm in her Journal. It is dated Vincennes, January 29th, 1812.

"I cannot describe to you, my dear mother, how anxiously I look forward to the time when I may once more behold you. God only knows whether that will ever take place. May He spare your precious life and permit us yet to pass many happy hours together. It is now nine months since I left you. This is a long time for us to be separated: but the variety of scenes through which I have passed has caused it to fly rapidly.

"There is an excellent preacher of the gospel here. We (with the friends who reside with us) attend upon his ministry, and are much pleased with him. He is a good man and has an interesting family. The Sabbath here is very little observed, most of the people being wholly engrossed with this world.

"We were very much alarmed a few nights since by a shock of an earthquake. We were roused from a sound sleep by the house shaking in an unusual manner. My first impression was that the Indians were assaulting the house, but we soon discovered our mistake. It was truly alarming. We have had several shocks since, some chimneys have been thrown down and ceilings cracked. This exhibition of Almighty power has excited feelings in my breast different from any which I ever before experienced. It impresses me with the uncertainties of life, the fallibility of all earthly enjoyment and the necessity of religion to give peace and happiness here and prepare us for a solemn hereafter. My dear sister, *youth* is the time to make that preparation for eternity. Piety is delightful in the young, and the poet says,

'Religion never was designed
To make our pleasures less.'

"I felt a little vexed, dear mother, with those wives whom you mentioned in your last letter. So *they* would prefer staying at home rather than suffer such inconveniences. Pray, why did they get married ? Never, no, never for a single instant, have *I* been sorry *that I accompanied my husband.* On the contrary, I feel grateful to the Author of all our blessings that I was permitted to come, to be with him when sick, and to encourage and comfort him under the various ills which flesh is heir to. Some may say this is enthusiasm; but really I think we have been married long enough to find out whether the attachment which has grown with our growth and strengthened with our strength is real or imaginary."

Surely no one can read this genuine outburst of devoted conjugal affection, without thoroughly admiring its author both as a woman and a wife.

Her love though possessing all the tenderness and fervor of romance, was not of that sentimental kind which expands itself in fine words or endearing caresses. She was eminently *practical;* and while some wives (though eloquently bewailing their husband's absence) preferred their pleasant parlors and the gayeties of fashionable life, to the discomforts of travel and hardship in their husband's company. She chose the latter, and (as she so feelingly wrote) never regretted the sacrifice. But we must return to her journal which is continued under date of Vincennes, March 11th, 1812.

"We expect to leave this place soon; but where our destination is to be we know not. We can only hope it will be towards home; but of this there is, I suppose, little prospect. The boats are now being prepared to convey us hence. We still continue to feel repeated strokes of the earthquake. I often rise in the night to examine the weather, having learned by observation that our most severe shocks have been experienced in still, lowering weather.

"There was an Indian Council held here last week which curiosity prompted me to attend. There were about seventy of these hideous creatures painted most grotesquely, and profusely ornamented. I have no doubt but to their admiring eyes they looked charmingly; for 'there is no accounting for the difference in tastes.' One side of their faces was painted red and the other green. They were bedecked with nose and ear-jewels, and some of them wore silver bands upon their arms, and medals suspended from their necks. One still more fantastically arrayed had a pair of cow's horns upon his head. They are good, natural orators, but all they said had to be interpreted. After the Council, the calumet of peace was smoked. This is a long pipe made especially for the purpose, and each one takes their turn in smoking it. Mrs. G——— smoked with them; but I kept out of sight in an adjoining room, as I had no inclination to taste it after its being so richly spiced with the breath of so many red and white brethren. Had I showed myself in the room where the Indians sat, I should have been compelled to smoke 'the pipe of peace,' or else have incurred their suspicion and hatred. So I acted upon the old adage, 'an ounce of prevention is better than a pound of cure.'

"Before the Indians left our village they gave the inhabitants a specimen of their agility, by dancing before each house. Their music was made by means of *a keg with deer-skins* drawn over it. This they strike rapidly, but most unskillfully, making a doleful humdrum noise. Their entire dress while dancing, consists of a piece of cotton cloth around their waist. Their squaws and pappooses came with them. When the squaws are allowed to ride (which by the way is very seldom,) they ride upon their horses in the same manner as the men. Their little ones are lashed to a board and carried upon their backs. When they stop, they suspend them to the bough of a tree.

"We visited what is called a sugar-camp last week, and were much gratified with witnessing the process of sugar-making. This part of the country abounds in sugar-maples. Large trees are selected in which holes are bored and tubes inserted. These tubes convey the liquor which runs from the trees into a trough prepared for its reception. It is very clear, and pleasant to the taste. This is boiled in large kettles, or caldrons; and when sufficiently done (which those who make it seem intuitively to know,) it is made into sugar by being constantly stirred while cooling. This article is most delicious, as all who have tasted it will testify. The labor of making it here is performed by blacks, superintended closely *by their mistress*. The lady whom we saw doing it in this instance, was a person of great respectability and abundant wealth. I enjoyed my ride to the sugar-camp very much. It was a beautiful afternoon; the air was mild and sweet, the weather delightful, and my pony upon whose back I rode, stepped along with a springy gait which seemed to say that he enjoyed it too.

"This climate is so mild that I have put on no extra clothing this winter except when walking or riding. And then a large shawl was sufficient even in the coldest days. Only a very little snow has fallen, and this disappeared as soon as it touched the ground. Trees bloomed in February, and the gardens are now quite forward. Lettuce, radishes and asparagus we have already, and this without the assistance of hotbeds.

"*March 31st.* We have received orders to proceed at once to Detroit. I shall go the rounds, I dare say, ere I am permitted to see my dear mother and sisters. The troops are *to go by land,* and not *by water,* as was at first thought. The distance from Vincennes to Detroit by the route we are to take is six hundred miles, and we are to sleep on the ground in tents. It will take some days to accomplish this journey. We are to proceed to Newport, Kentucky, from thence cross the river to Cincinnati, and go through Ohio to Michigan. We shall pass through some thriving villages, but mostly through woods and prairies, where none but the hunter and the Indian have penetrated. The journey looks formidable in prospect. Mrs. F———, Mrs. G——— and myself are to ride on horseback. My husband being on the staff, will have the same privilege. So I shall be spared the distress of seeing him encounter the hardships which those who march must necessarily endure. I have been learning to ride on horseback, and like it much; but how I shall succeed in riding through swamps and fording rivers, experience alone will determine.

25

DAVID CROCKETT

(1786–1836)

Davy Crockett, King of the Wild Frontier. Thanks to his eventful life, his romantic death, and Walt Disney, he stands as the archetypal American frontiersman. Crockett was born on August 17, 1786, in present-day Greene County in eastern Tennessee. At the age of twelve, he left home for the first time when his father, plagued by debt, bound him to a Dutchman, Jacob Siler, who was driving a herd of cattle to Rockbridge County, Virginia. David helped to drive those cattle for 400 miles, and then stayed for several weeks as an indentured servant before running for home. Home life, however, proved little more agreeable, so David ran once more. For three years he worked as a herdsman and a wagoneer. He was sixteen when he returned home again, this time to pay off his father's debts.

In 1811 Crockett, now married with children, moved further west into middle Tennessee, edging along with the frontier where game would be more plentiful. He proved a poor farmer but a good hunter, once killing 105 bears in a single season. After Creek Indians slaughtered the residents of Fort Mims, Alabama, in 1813, Crockett volunteered for Andrew Jackson's army. He fought with Jackson against the Creeks at the Battles of Tallussahatchee and Talledega.

In 1815, soon after Crockett returned home from the Creek War, his first wife died. Crockett remarried within the year, and moved further west again, this time to Lawrence County, Tennessee. There he was elected to the state legislature in 1821 and reelected in 1823. As a politician, Crockett became known as a champion of the common man for his passionate defense of squatters' rights, a position that would later put him at odds with President Andrew Jackson. He ran unsuccessfully for Congress as a Jacksonian in 1825 but was elected in 1827.

Now that Crockett was on the national political stage, his fame increased with the help of a popular play and a number of best-selling books. In 1830 James Kirke Paulding wrote *The Lion of the West,* a play whose main character, Colonel Nimrod Wildfire, lampooned Crockett. James H. Hackett, the actor who played Wildfire, was the first to wear a coonskin cap as Crockett's headgear. In 1833 the first Crockett biography appeared, *The Life and Adventures of Colonel David Crockett of West Tennessee;* it was republished that same year as *Sketches and Eccentricities of Colonel David Crockett of West Tennessee.* This book was attributed to Crockett but was actually written by either Matthew St. Clair Clarke, the clerk of the House of Representatives, or James Strange French, a Virginian who gathered his material from Clarke and others.

Crockett responded with his own version of his life, which he wrote with the help of Thomas Chilton. In his preface to *A Narrative of the Life of David Crockett* (1834), Crockett wrote of the spurious earlier autobiography, "I have met with hundreds, if not with thousands of people, who have formed their opinions of my appearance, habits, language, and every thing else from that descriptive work. They have almost in every instance expressed the most profound astonishment at finding me in human shape, and with the *countenance, appearance,* and *common feelings* of a human being. It is to correct all these false notions, and to do justice to myself, that I have written."

Crockett broke with President Jackson most strongly over the issue of Indian removal. Jackson's infamous Indian Removal Bill of 1830, which Crockett loudly criticized, called for the relocation of all natives to west of the Mississippi River. Crockett's opposition to this proposal led to his defeat in the election of 1831, though he was successful in the election of 1833. When he lost again in 1835, he made good on his promise to his constituents. He had told them that if they reelected him, he would "serve them to the best of [his] ability; but if they did not, they [could] go to hell, and [he] would go to Texas."

When the forty-nine-year-old Crockett arrived in Texas, he seemed intent on proving that he was a frontiersman first, not a politician. His role in the Texas Revolution ended, of course, at the Alamo. For nearly two weeks, Crockett and roughly 150 others held Antonio Lopez de Santa Anna and his men at bay, though the Mexicans outnumbered the Americans by a ratio of 15 to 1. Santa Anna and his men stormed the Alamo at 6 a.m. on March 6, 1836. Ninety minutes later, only six or seven of the Americans were still alive, Crockett among them. They were summarily executed.

Text: *A Narrative of the Life of David Crockett* (Philadelphia, 1834): 13–27, 71–113.

FROM *A NARRATIVE OF THE LIFE OF DAVID CROCKETT* (1834)

CHAPTER I

As the public seem to feel some interest in the history of an individual so humble as I am, and as that history can be so well known to no person living as to myself, I have, after so long a time, and under many pressing solicitations from my friends and acquaintances, at last determined to put my own hand to it, and lay before the world a narrative on which they may at least rely as being true. And seeking no ornament or colouring for a plain, simple tale of truth, I throw aside all hypocritical and fawning apologies, and, according to my own maxim, just *"go ahead."* Where I am not known,

I might, perhaps, gain some little credit by having thrown around this volume some of the flowers of learning; but where I am known, the vile cheatery would soon be detected, and like the foolish jackdaw, that with a *borrowed* tail attempted to play the peacock, I should be justly robbed of my pilfered ornaments, and sent forth to strut without a tail for the balance of my time. I shall commence my book with what little I have learned of the history of my father, as all *great men* rest many, if not most, of their hopes on their noble ancestry. Mine was poor, but I hope honest, and even that is as much as many a man can say. But to my subject.

My father's name was John Crockett, and he was of Irish descent. He was either born in Ireland or on a passage from that country to America across the Atlantic. He was by profession a farmer, and spent the early part of his life in the state of Pennsylvania. The name of my mother was Rebecca Hawkins. She was an American woman, born in the state of Maryland, between York and Baltimore. It is likely I may have heard where they were married, but if so, I have forgotten. It is, however, certain that they were, or else the public would never have been troubled with the history of David Crockett, their son.

I have an imperfect recollection of the part which I have understood my father took in the revolutionary war. I personally know nothing about it, for it happened to be a little before my day; but from himself, and many others who were well acquainted with its troubles and afflictions, I have learned that he was a soldier in the revolutionary war, and took part in that bloody struggle. He fought, according to my information, in the battle at Kings Mountain against the British and tories, and in some other engagements of which my remembrance is too imperfect to enable me to speak with any certainty. At some time, though I cannot say certainly when, my father, as I have understood, lived in Lincoln county, in the state of North Carolina. How long, I don't know. But when he removed from there, he settled in that district of country which is now embraced in the east division of Tennessee, though it was not then erected into a state.

He settled there under dangerous circumstances, both to himself and his family, as the country was full of Indians, who were at that time very troublesome. By the Creeks, my grandfather and grandmother Crockett were both murdered, in their own house, and on the very spot of ground where Rogersville, in Hawkins county, now stands. At the same time, the Indians wounded Joseph Crockett, a brother to my father, by a ball, which broke his arm; and took James a prisoner, who was still a younger brother than Joseph, and who, from natural defects, was less able to make his escape, as he was both deaf and dumb. He remained with them for seventeen years and nine months, when he was discovered and recollected by my father and his eldest brother, William Crockett; and was purchased by them from an Indian trader, at a price which I do not now remember; but so it was, that he was delivered up to them, and they returned him to his relatives. He now lives in Cumberland county, in the state of Kentucky, though I have not seen him for many years.

My father and mother had six sons and three daughters. I was the fifth son. What a pity I hadn't been the seventh! For then I might have been, by *common consent,* called *doctor,* as a heap of people get to be great men. But, like many of them, I stood no chance to become great in any other way than by accident. As my father was very poor, and living as he did *far back in the back woods,* he had neither the means nor the opportunity to give me, or any of the rest of his children, any learning.

But before I get on the subject of my own troubles, and a great many very funny things that have happened to me, like all other historians and booagraphers, I should not only inform the public that I was born, myself, as well as other folks, but that this important event took place, according to the best information I have received on the subject, on the 17th of August, in the year 1786; whether by day or night, I believe I never heard, but if I did I, have forgotten. I suppose, however, it is not very material to my present purpose, nor to the world, as the more important fact is well attested, that I was born; and, indeed, it might be inferred, from my present size and appearance, that I was pretty *well born,* though I have never yet attached myself to that numerous and worthy society.

At that time my father lived at the mouth of Lime Stone, on the Nola-chucky river; and for the purpose not only of showing what sort of a man I now am, but also to show how soon I began to be a *sort of a little man,* I have endeavoured to take the *back track* of life, in order to fix on the first thing that I can remember. But even then, as now, so many things were happening, that as Major Jack Downing would say, they are all in "a pretty considerable of a snarl," and I find it "kinder hard" to fix on that thing, among them all, which really happened first. But I think it likely, I have hit on the outside line of my recollection; as one thing happened at which I was so badly scared, that it seems to me I could not have forgotten it, if it had happened a little time only after I was born. Therefore it furnishes me with no certain evidence of my age at the time; but I know one thing very well, and that is, that when it happened, I had no knowledge of the use of breeches, for I had never had any nor worn any.

But the circumstance was this: My four elder brothers, and a well-grown boy of about fifteen years old, by the name of Campbell, and myself, were all playing on the river's side; when all the rest of them got into my father's canoe, and put out to amuse themselves on the water, leaving me on the shore alone.

Just a little distance below them, there was a fall in the river, which went slap-right straight down. My brothers, though they were little fellows, had been used to paddling the canoe, and could have carried it safely anywhere about there; but this fellow Campbell wouldn't let them have the paddle, but, fool like, undertook to manage it himself. I reckon he had never seen a water craft before; and it went just any way but the way he wanted it. There he paddled, and paddled, and paddled—all the while going wrong,—until, in a short time, here they were all going, straight forward, stern foremost, right plump to the falls; and if they had only had a fair shake, they would have gone over as slick as a whistle. It was'ent this, though, that scared me; for I was so infernal mad that they had left me on the shore, that I had as soon have seen them all go over the falls a bit, as any other way. But their danger was seen by a man by the name of Kendall, but I'll be shot if it was Amos; for I believe I would know him yet if I was to see him. This man Kendall was working in a field on the bank, and knowing there was no time to lose, he started full tilt, and here he come like a cane brake afire; and as he ran, he threw off his coat, and then his jacket, and then his shirt, for I know when he got to the water he had nothing on but his breeches. But seeing him in such a hurry, and tearing off his clothes as he went, I had no doubt but that the devil or something else was after him—and close on him, too—as he was running within an inch of his life. This alarmed me, and I screamed out like a young painter. But Kendall didn't stop for this. He went ahead with all might, and as full bent on saving the boys, as Amos was on moving the deposites. When he came to the water he plunged in, and where it was too deep to wade he would swim, and where it was shallow enough he went bolting on; and by such exertion as I never saw at any other time in my life, he reached the canoe, when it was within twenty or thirty feet of the falls; and so great was the suck, and so swift the current, that poor Kendall had a hard time of it to stop them at last, as Amos will to stop the mouths of the people about his stockjobbing. But he hung on to the canoe, till he got it stop'd, and then draw'd it out of danger. When they got out, I found the boys were more scared than I had been, and the only thing that comforted me was, the belief that it was a punishment on them for leaving me on shore.

Shortly after this, my father removed, and settled in the same county, about ten miles about Greenville.

There another circumstance happened, which made a lasting impression on my memory, though I was but a small child. Joseph Hawkins, who was a brother to my mother, was in the woods hunting for deer. He was passing near a thicket of brush, in which one of our neighbours was gathering some grapes, as it was in the fall of the year, and the grape season. The body of the man was hid by the brush, and it was only as he would raise his hand to pull the bunches, that any part of him could be seen. It was a likely place for deer; and my uncle, having no suspicion that it was any human being, but supposing the raising of the hand to be the occasional twitch of a deer's ear, fired at the lump, and as the devil would have it, unfortunately shot the man through the body. I saw my father draw a silk handkerchief through the bullet hole, and entirely through his body; yet after a while he got well, as little as any one would have thought it. What become of him, or whether he is dead or alive, I don't know; but I reckon he did'ent fancy the business of gathering grapes in an out-of-the-way thicket soon again.

The next move my father made was to the mouth of Core creek, where he and a man by the name of Thomas Galbreath undertook to build a mill in partnership. They went on very well with their work until it was nigh done, when there came the second epistle to Noah's fresh, and away went their mill, shot, lock, and barrel. I remember the water rose so high, that it got up into the house we lived in, and my father moved us out of it, to keep us from being drowned. I was now about seven or eight years old, and have a pretty distinct recollection of every thing that was going on. From his bad luck in that business, and being ready to wash out from mill building, my father again removed, and this time settled in Jefferson county, now in the state of Tennessee; where he opened a tavern on the road from Abbingdon to Knoxville.

His tavern was on a small scale, as he was poor; and the principal accommodations which he kept, were for the waggoners who travelled the road. Here I remained with him until I was twelve years old; and about that time, you may guess, if you belong to Yankee land, or reckon, if like me you belong to the back-woods, that I began to make up my acquaintance with hard times, and a plenty of them.

An old Dutchman, by the name of Jacob Siler, who was moving from Knox county to Rockbridge, in the state of Virginia, in passing, made a stop at my father's house. He had a large stock of cattle, that he was carrying on with him; and I suppose made some proposition to my father to hire some one to assist him.

Being hard run every way, and having no thought, as I believe, that I was cut out for a Congressman or the like, young as I was, and as little as I knew about travelling, or being from home, he hired me to the old Dutchman, to go four hundred miles on foot, with a perfect stranger that I never had seen until the evening before. I set out with a heavy heart, it is true, but I went ahead, until we arrived at the place, which was three miles from what is called the Natural Bridge, and made a stop at the house of a Mr. Hartley, who was father-in-law to Mr. Siler, who had hired me. My Dutch master was very kind to me, and gave me five or six dollars, being pleased, as he said, with my services.

This, however, I think was a bait for me, as he persuaded me to stay with him, and not return any more to my father. I had been taught so many lessons of obedience by my father, that I at first supposed I was bound to obey this man, or at least I was afraid openly to disobey him; and I therefore staid with him, and tried to put on a look of perfect contentment until I got the family all to believe I was fully satisfied. I had been there about four or five weeks, when one day myself and two other boys were playing on the roadside, some distance from the house. There came along three waggoners. One belonged to an old man by the name of Dunn, and the others to two of his sons. They had each of them a good team, and were all bound for Knoxville. They had been in the habit of stopping at my father's as they passed the road, and I knew them. I made myself known to the old gentleman, and informed him of my situation; I expressed a wish to get back to my father and mother, if they could fix any plan for me to do so. They told me that they would stay that night at a tavern seven miles from there, and that if I could get to them before day the next morning, they would take me home; and if I was pursued, they would protect me. This was a Sunday evening; I went back to the good old Dutchman's house, and as good fortune would have it, he and the family were out on a visit. I gathered my clothes, and what little money I had, and put them all together under the head of my bed. I went to bed early that night, but sleep seemed to be a stranger to me. For though I was a wild boy, yet I dearly loved my father and mother, and their images appeared to be so deeply fixed in my mind, that I could not sleep for thinking of them. And then the fear that when I should attempt to go out, I should be discovered and called to a halt, filled me with anxiety; and between my childish love of home, on the one hand, and the fears of which I have spoken, on the other, I felt mighty queer.

But so it was, about three hours before day in the morning I got up to make my start. When I got out, I found it was snowing fast, and that the snow was then on the ground about eight inches deep. I had not even the advantage of moonlight, and the whole sky was hid by the falling snow, so that I had to guess at my way to the big road, which was about a half mile from the house. I however pushed ahead and soon got to it, and then pursued it, in the direction to the waggons.

I could not have pursued the road if I had not guided myself by the opening it made between the timber, as the snow was too deep to leave any part of it to be known by either seeing or feeling.

Before I overtook the waggons, the earth was covered about as deep as my knees; and my tracks filled so briskly after me, that by daylight, my Dutch master could have seen no trace which I left.

I got to the place about an hour before day. I found the waggoners already stirring, and engaged in feeding and preparing their horses for a start. Mr. Dunn took me in and treated me with great kindness. My heart was more deeply impressed by meeting with such a friend, and "at such a time," than by wading the snow-storm by night, or all the other sufferings which my mind had endured. I warmed myself by the fire, for I was very cold, and after an early breakfast, we set out on our journey. The thoughts of home now began to take the entire possession of my mind, and I almost numbered the sluggish turns of the wheels, and much more certainly the miles of our travel, which appeared to me to count mighty slow. I continued with my kind protectors, until we got to the house of a Mr. John Cole, on Roanoke, when my impatience became so great, that I determined to set out on foot and go ahead by myself, as I could travel twice as fast in that way as the waggons could.

Mr. Dunn seemed very sorry to part with me, and used many arguments to prevent me from leaving him. But home, poor as it was, again rushed on my memory, and it seemed ten times as dear to me as it ever had before. The reason was, that my parents were there, and all that I had been accustomed to in the hours of childhood and infancy was there; and there my anxious little heart panted also to be. We remained at Mr. Coles that night, and early in the morning I felt that I couldn't stay; so, taking leave of my friends the waggoners, I went forward on foot, until I was fortunately overtaken by a gentleman, who was returning from market, to which he had been with a drove of horses. He had a led horse, with a bridle and saddle on him, and he kindly offered to let me get on his horse and ride him. I did so, and was glad of the chance, for I was tired, and was, moreover, near the first crossing of Roanoke, which I would have been compelled to wade, cold as the water was, if I had not fortunately met this good man. I travelled with him in this way, without any thing turning up worth recording, until we got within fifteen miles of my father's house. There we parted, and he went on to Kentucky and I trudged on homeward, which place I reached that evening. The name of this kind gentleman I have entirely forgotten, and I am sorry for it; for it deserves a high place in my little book. A remembrance of his kindness to a little straggling boy, and a stranger to him, has however a resting place in my heart, and there it will remain as long as I live.

CHAPTER V

I was living ten miles below Winchester when the Creek war commenced; and as military men are making so much fuss in the world at this time, I must give an account of the part I took in the defence of the country. If it should make me president, why I can't help it; such things will sometimes happen; and my pluck is, never "to seek, nor decline office."

It is true, I had a little rather not; but yet, if the government can't get on without taking another president from Tennessee, to finish the work of "retrenchment and reform," why, then, I reckon I must go in for it. But I must begin about the war, and leave the other matter for the people to begin on.

The Creek Indians had commenced their open hostilities by a most bloody butchery at Fort Mines. There had been no war among us for so long, that but few, who were not too old to bear arms, knew any thing about the business. I, for one, had often thought about war, and had often heard it described; and I did verily believe in my own mind, that I couldn't fight in that way at all; but my after experience convinced me that this was all a notion. For when I heard of the mischief which was done at the fort, I instantly felt like going, and I had none of the dread of dying that I expected to feel. In a few days a general meeting of the militia was called for the purpose of raising volunteers; and when the day arrived for that meeting, my wife, who had heard me say I meant to go to the war, began to beg me not to turn out. She said she was a stranger in the parts where we lived, had no connexions living near her, and that she and our little children would be left in a lonesome and unhappy situation if I went away. It was mighty hard to go against such arguments as these; but my countrymen had been murdered, and I knew that the next thing would be, that the Indians would be scalping the women and children all about there, if we didn't put a stop to it. I reasoned the case with her as well as I could, and told her, that if every man would wait till his wife got willing for him to go to war, there would be no fighting done, until we would all be killed in our own houses; that I was as able to go as any man in the world; and that I believed it was a duty I owed to my country. Whether she was satisfied with this reasoning or not, she did not tell me; but seeing I was bent on it, all she did was to cry a little, and turn about to her work. The truth is, my dander was up, and nothing but war could bring it right again.

I went to Winchester, where the muster was to be, and a great many people had collected, for there was as much fuss among the people about the war as there is now about moving the deposites. When the men were paraded, a lawyer by the name of Jones addressed us, and closed by turning out himself, and enquiring, at the same time, who among us felt like we could fight Indians? This was the same Mr. Jones who afterwards served in Congress, from the state of Tennessee. He informed us he wished to raise a company, and that then the men should meet and elect their own officers. I believe I was about the second or third man that step'd out; but on marching up and down the regiment a few times, we found we had a large company. We volunteered for sixty days, as it was supposed our services would not be longer wanted. A day or two after this we met and elected Mr. Jones our captain, and also elected our other officers. We then received orders to start on the next Monday week; before which time, I had fixed as well as I could to go, and my wife had equip'd me as well as she was able for the camp. The time arrived; I took a parting farewell of my wife and my little boys, mounted my horse, and set sail, to join my company. Expecting to be gone only a short time, I took no more clothing with me than I supposed would be necessary, so that if I got into an Indian battle, I might not be pestered with any unnecessary plunder, to prevent my having a fair shake with them. We all met and went ahead, till we passed Huntsville, and camped at a large spring called Bealy's spring. Here we staid for several days, in which time the troops began to collect from all quarters. At last we mustered about thirteen hundred strong, all mounted volunteers, and all determined to fight, judging from myself, for I felt wolfish all over. I verily believe the whole army was of the real grit. Our captain didn't want any other sort; and to try them he several times told his men, that if any of them wanted to go back home, they might do so at any time, before they were regularly mustered into the service. But he had the honour to command all his men from first to last, as not one of them left him.

Gen'l. Jackson had not yet left Nashville with his old foot volunteers, that had gone with him to Natchez in 1812, the year before. While we remained at the spring, a Major Gibson came, and wanted some volunteers to go with him across the Tennessee river and into the Creek nation, to find out the movements of the Indians. He came to my captain, and asked for two of his best woodsmen, and such as were best with a rifle. The captain pointed me out to him, and said he would be security that I would go as far as the major would himself, or any other man. I willingly engaged to go with him, and asked him to let me choose my own mate to go with me, which he said I might do. I chose a young man by the name of George Russell, a son of old Major Russell, of Tennessee. I called him up, but Major Gibson said he thought he hadn't beard enough to please him,—he wanted men, and not boys. I must confess I was a little nettled at this; for I know'd George Russell, and I know'd there was no mistake in him; and I didn't think that courage ought to be measured by the beard, for fear a goat would have the preference over a man. I told the major he was on the wrong scent; that Russell could go as far as he could, and I must have him along. He saw I was a little wrathy, and said I had the best chance of knowing, and agreed that it should be as I wanted it. He told us to be ready early in the morning for a start; and so we were. We took our camp equipage, mounted our horses, and, thirteen in number, including the major, we cut out. We went on, and crossed the Tennessee river at a place called Ditto's Landing; and then traveled about seven miles further, and took up camp for the night. Here a man by the name of John Haynes overtook us. He had been an Indian trader in that part of the nation, and was well acquainted with it. He went with us as a pilot. The next morning, however, Major Gibson and myself concluded we should separate and take different directions to see what discoveries we could make; so he took seven of the men, and I five, making thirteen in all, including myself. He was to go by the house of a Cherokee Indian, named Dick Brown, and I was to go by Dick's father's; and getting all the information we could, we were to meet that evening where the roads came together, fifteen miles the other side of Brown's. At old Mr. Brown's I got a half blood Cherokee to agree to go with me, whose name was Jack Thompson. He was not then ready to start, but was to fix that evening, and overtake us at the fork road where I was to meet Major Gibson. I know'd it wouldn't be safe to camp right at the road; and so I told Jack, that when he got to the fork he must holler like an owl, and I would answer him in the same way; for I know'd it would be night before he got there. I and my men then started, and went on to the place of meeting, but Major Gibson was not there. We waited till almost dark, but still he didn't come. We then left the Indian trace a little distance, and turning into the head of a hollow, we struck up camp. It was about ten o'clock at night, when I heard my owl, and I answered him. Jack soon found us, and we determined to rest there during the night. We staid also next morning till after breakfast: but in vain, for the major didn't still come.

I told the men we had set out to hunt a fight, and I wouldn't go back in that way; that we must go ahead, and see what the red men were at. We started, and went to a Cherokee town about twenty miles off; and after a short stay there, we pushed on to the house of a man by the name of Radcliff. He was a white man, but had married a Creek woman, and lived just in the edge of the Creek nation. He had two sons, large likely fellows, and a great deal of potatoes and corn, and, indeed, almost every thing else to go on; so we fed our horses and got dinner with him, and seemed to be doing mighty well. But he was bad scared all the time. He told us there had been ten painted warriors at his house only an hour before, and if we were discovered there, they would kill us, and his family with us. I replied to him, that my business was to hunt for just such fellows as he had described, and I was determined not to gack until I had done it. Our dinner being over, we saddled up our horses, and made ready to start. But some of my small company I found were disposed to return. I told them, if we were to go back then, we should never hear the last of it; and I was determined to go ahead. I knowed some of them would go with me, and that the rest were afraid to go back by themselves; and so we pushed on to the camp of some of the friendly Creeks, which was distant about eight miles. The moon was about the full, and the night was clear; we therefore had the benefit of her light from night to morning, and I knew if we were placed in such danger as to make a retreat necessary, we could travel by night as well as in the day time.

We had not gone very far, when we met two negroes, well mounted on Indian ponies, and each with a good rifle. They had been taken from their owners by the Indians, and were running away from them, and trying to get back to their masters again. They were brothers, both very large and likely, and could talk Indian as well as English. One of them I sent on to Ditto's Landing, the other I took back with me. It was after dark when we got to the camp, where we found about forty men, women, and children.

They had bows and arrows, and I turned in to shooting with their boys by a pine light. In this way we amused ourselves very well for a while; but at last the negro, who had been talking to the Indians, came to me and told me they were very much alarmed, for the "red skins," as they called the war party of the Creeks, would come and find us there; and, if so, we should all be killed. I directed him to tell them that I would watch, and if one would come that night, I would carry the skin of his head home to make me a mockasin. When he made this communication, the Indians laughed aloud. At about ten o'clock at night we all concluded to try to sleep a little; but that our horses might be ready for use, as the treasurer said of the drafts on the United States' bank, on certain "contingences," we tied them up with our saddles on them, and every thing to our hand, if in the night our quarters should get uncomfortable. We lay down with our guns in our arms, and I had just gotten into a dose of sleep, when I heard the sharpest scream that ever escaped the throat of a human creature. It was more like a wrathy painter than any thing else. The negro understood it, and he sprang to me; for tho' I heard the noise well enough, yet I wasn't wide awake enough to get up. So the negro caught me, and said the red sticks was coming. I rose quicker then, and asked what was the matter? Our negro had gone and talked with the Indian who had just fetched the scream, as he come into camp, and learned from him, that the war party had been crossing the Coosa river all day at the Ten islands; and were going on to meet Jackson, and this Indian had come as a runner. This news very much alarmed the friendly Indians in camp, and they were all off in a few minutes. I felt bound to make this intelligence known as soon as possible to the army we had left at the landing; and so we all mounted our horses, and put out in a long lope to make our way back to that place. We were about sixty-five miles off. We went on to the same Cherokee town we had visited on our way out, having first called at Radcliff's, who was off with his family; and at the the town we found large fires burning, but not a single Indian was to be seen. They were all gone. These circumstances were calculated to lay our dander a little, as it appeared we must be in great danger; though we could easily have licked any force of not more than five to one. But we expected the whole nation would be on us, and against such fearful odds we were not so rampant for a fight.

We therefore staid only a short time in the light of the fires about the town, preferring the light of the moon and the shade of the woods. We pushed on till we got again to old Mr. Brown's, which was still about thirty miles from where we had left the main army. When we got there, the chickens were just at the first crowing for day. We fed our horses, got a morsel to eat ourselves, and again cut out. About ten o'clock in the morning we reached the camp, and I reported to Col. Coffee the news. He didn't seem to mind my report a bit, and this raised my dander higher than ever; but I knowed I had to be on my best behaviour, and so I kept it all to myself; though I was so mad that I was burning inside like a tarkiln, and I wonder that the smoke hadn't been pouring out of me at all points.

Major Gibson hadn't yet returned, and we all began to think he was killed; and that night they put out a double guard. The next day the major got in, and brought a worse tale than I had, though he stated the same facts, so far as I went. This seemed to put our colonel all in a fidget; and it convinced me, clearly, of one of the hateful ways of the world. When I made my report, it wasn't believed, because I was no officer; I was no great man, but just a poor soldier. But when the same thing was reported by Major Gibson!! why, then, it was all as true as preaching, and the colonel believed it every word.

He, therefore, ordered breastworks to be thrown up, near a quarter of a mile long, and sent an express to Fayetteville, where General Jackson and his troops was, requesting them to push on like the very mischief, for fear we should all be cooked up to a cracklin before they could get there. Old Hickory-face made a forced march on getting the news; and on the next day, he and his men got into camp, with their feet all blistered from the effects of their swift journey. The volunteers, therefore, stood guard altogether, to let them rest.

CHAPTER VI

About eight hundred of the volunteers, and of that number I was one, were now sent back, crossing the Tennessee river, and on through Huntsville, so as to cross the river again at another place, and to get on the Indians in another direction. After we passed Huntsville, we struck on the river at the Muscle Shoals, and at a place on them called Melton's Bluff. This river is here about two miles wide, and a rough bottom; so much so, indeed, in many places, as to be dangerous; and in fording it this time, we left several of the horses belonging to our men, with their feet fast in the crevices of the rocks. The men, whose horses were thus left, went ahead on foot. We pushed on till we got to what was called the Black Warrior's town, which stood near the very spot where Tuscaloosa now stands, which is the seat of government for the state of Alabama.

This Indian town was a large one; but when we arrived we found the Indians had all left it. There was a large field of corn standing out, and a pretty good supply in some cribs. There was also a fine quantity of dried leaves, which were very acceptable to us; and without delay we secured them as well as the corn, and then burned the town to ashes; after which we left the place.

In the field where we gathered the corn we saw plenty of fresh Indian tracks, and we had no doubt they had been scared off by our arrival.

We then went on to meet the main army at the fork road, where I was first to have met Major Gibson. We got that evening as far back as the encampment we had made the night before we reached the Black Warrior's town, which we had just destroyed. The next day we were entirely out of meat. I went to Col. Coffee, who was then in command of us, and asked his leave to hunt as we marched. He gave me leave, but told me to take mighty good care of myself. I turned aside to hunt, and had not gone far when I found a deer that had just been killed and skinned, and his flesh was still warm and smoking. From this I was sure that the Indian who had killed it had been gone only a very few minutes; and though I was never much in favour of one hunter stealing from another, yet meat was so scarce in camp, that I thought I must go in for it. So I just took up the deer on my horse before me, and carried it on till night. I could have sold it for almost any price I would have asked; but this wasn't my rule, neither in peace nor war. Whenever I had any thing, and saw a fellow being suffering, I was more anxious to relieve him than to benefit myself. And this is one of the true secrets of my being a poor man to this day. But it is my way; and while it has often left me with an empty purse, which is as near the devil as any thing else I have seen, yet it has never left my heart empty of consolations which money couldn't buy,—the consolations of having sometimes fed the hungry and covered the naked.

I gave all my deer away, except a small part I kept for myself, and just sufficient to make a good supper for my mess; for meat was getting to be a rarity to us all. We had to live mostly on parched corn. The next day we marched on, and at night took up camp near a large cane brake. While here, I told my mess I would again try for some meat; so I took my rifle and cut out, but hadn't gone far, when I discovered a large gang of hogs. I shot one of them down in his tracks, and the rest broke directly towards the camp. In a few minutes, the guns began to roar, as bad as if the whole army had been in an Indian battle; and the hogs to squeal as bad as the pig did, when the devil turned barber. I shouldered my hog, and went on to the camp; and when I got there I found they had killed a good many of the hogs, and a fine fat cow into the bargain, that had broke out of the cane brake. We did very well that night, and the next morning marched on to a Cherokee town, where our officers stop'd, and gave the inhabitants an order on Uncle Sam for their cow, and the hogs we had killed. The next day we met the main army, having had, as we thought, hard times, and a plenty of them, though we had yet seen hardly the beginning of trouble.

After our meeting we went on to Radcliff's, where I had been before while out as a spy; and when we got there, we found he had hid all his provisions. We also got into the secret, that he was the very rascal who had sent the runner to the Indian camp, with the news that the "red sticks" were crossing at the Ten Islands; and that his object was to scare me and my men away, and send us back with a false alarm.

To make some atonement for this, we took the old scroundrell's two big sons with us, and made them serve in the war.

We then marched to a place, which we called Camp Mills; and here it was that Captain Cannon was promoted to a colonel, and Colonel Coffee to a general. We then marched to the Ten Islands, on the Coosa river, where we established a fort; and our spy companies were sent out. They soon made prisoners of Bob Catala and his warriors, and, in a few days afterwards, we heard of some Indians in a town about eight miles off. So we mounted our horses, and put out for that town, under the direction of two friendly Creeks we had taken for pilots. We had also a Cherokee colonel, Dick Brown, and some of his men with us. When we got near the town we divided; one of our pilots going with each division. And so we passed on each side of the town, keeping near to it, until our lines met on the far side. We then closed up at both ends, so as to surround it completely; and then we sent Captain Hammond's company of rangers to bring on the affray. He had advanced near the town, when the Indians saw him, and they raised the yell, and came running at him like so many red devils. The main army was now formed in a hollow square around the town, and they pursued Hammond till they came in reach of us. We then gave them a fire, and they returned it, and then ran back into their town. We began to close on the town by making our files closer and closer, and the Indians soon saw they were our property. So most of them wanted us to take them prisoners; and their squaws and all would run and take hold of any of us they could, and give themselves up. I saw seven squaws have hold of one man, which made me think of the Scriptures. So I hollered out the Scriptures was fulfilling; that there was seven women holding to one man's coat tail. But I believe it was a hunting-shirt all the time. We took them all prisoners that came out to us in this way; but I saw some warriors run into a house, until I counted forty-six of them. We pursued them until we got near the house, when we saw a squaw sitting in the door, and she placed her feet against the bow she had in her hand, and then took an arrow, and, raising her feet, she drew with all her might, and let fly at us, and she killed a man, whose name, I believe, was Moore. He was a lieutenant, and his death so enraged us all, that she was fired on, and had at least twenty balls blown through her. This was the first man I ever saw killed with a bow and arrow. We now shot them like dogs; and then set the house on fire, and burned it up with the forty-six warriors in it. I recollect seeing a boy who was shot down near the house. His arm and thigh was broken, and he was so near the burning house that the grease was stewing out of him. In this situation he was still trying to crawl along; but not a murmur escaped him, though he was only about twelve years old. So sullen is the Indian, when his dander is up, that he had sooner die than make a noise, or ask for quarters.

The number that we took prisoners, being added to the number we killed, amounted to one hundred and eighty-six; though I don't remember the exact number of either. We had five of our men killed. We then returned to our camp, at which our fort was erected, and known by the name of Fort Strother. No provisions had yet reached us, and we had now been for several days on half rations. However we went back to our Indian town on the next day, when many of the carcasses of the Indians were still to be seen. They looked very awful, for the burning had not entirely consumed them, but given them a very terrible appearance, at least what remained of them. It was, somehow or other, found out that the house had a potatoe cellar under it, and an immediate examination was made, for we were all as hungry as wolves. We found a fine chance of potatoes in it, and hunger compelled us to eat them, though I had a little rather not, if I could have helped it, for the oil of the Indians we had burned up on the day before had run down on them, and they looked like they had been stewed with fat meat. We then again returned to the army, and remained there for several days almost starving, as all our beef was gone. We commenced eating the beef-hides, and continued to eat every scrap we could lay our hands on. At length an Indian came to our ground one night, and hollered, and said he wanted to see "Captain Jackson." He was conducted to the general's markee, into which he entered, and in a few minutes we received orders to prepare for marching.

In an hour we were all ready, and took up the line of march. We crossed the Coosa river, and went on in the direction to Fort Taladega. When we arrived near the place, we met eleven hundred painted warriors, the very choice of the Creek nation. They had encamped near the fort, and had informed the friendly Indians who were in it, that if they didn't come out, and fight with them against the whites, they would take their fort and all their ammunition and provision. The friendly party asked three days to consider of it, and agreed that if on the third day they didn't come out ready to fight with them, they might take their fort. Thus they put them off. They then immediately started their runner to General Jackson, and he and the army pushed over, as I have just before stated.

The camp of warriors had their spies out, and discovered us coming, some time before we got to the fort. They then went to the friendly Indians, and told them Captain Jackson was coming, and had a great many fine horses, and blankets, and guns, and every thing else; and if they would come out and help to whip him, and to take his plunder, it should all be divided with those in the fort. They promised that when Jackson came, they would then come out and help to whip him. It was about an hour by sun in the morning, when we got near the fort. We were piloted by friendly Indians, and divided as we had done on a former occasion, so as to go to the right and left of the fort, and, consequently, of the warriors who were camped near it. Our lines marched on, as before, till they met in front, and then closed in the rear, forming again into a hollow square. We then sent on old Major Russell, with his spy company, to bring on the battle; Capt. Evans' company went also. When they got near the fort, the top of it was lined with the friendly Indians, crying out as loud as they could roar, "How-dy-do, brother, how-dy-do?" They kept this up till Major Russel had passed by the fort, and was moving on towards the warriors. They were all painted as red as scarlet, and were just as naked as they were born. They had concealed themselves under the bank of a branch, that ran partly around the fort, in the manner of a half moon. Russel was going right into their circle, for he couldn't see them, while the Indians on the top of the fort were trying every plan to show him his danger. But he couldn't understand them. At last, two of them jumped from it, and ran, and took his horse by the bridle, and pointing to where they were, told him there were thousands of them lying under the bank. This brought them to a halt, and about this moment the Indians fired on them, and came rushing forth like a cloud of Egyptian locusts, and screaming like all the young devils had been turned loose, with the old devil of all at their head. Russel's company quit their horses, and took into the fort, and their horses ran up to our line, which was then in full view. The warriors then came yelling on, meeting us, and continued till they were within shot of us, when we fired and killed a considerable number of them. They then broke like a gang of steers, and ran across to our other line, where they were again fired on; and so we kept them running from one line to the other, constantly under a heavy fire, until we had killed upwards of four hundred of them. They fought with guns, and also with their bows and arrows; but at length they made their escape through a part of our line, which was made up of drafted militia, which broke ranks, and they passed. We lost fifteen of our men, as brave fellows as ever lived or died. We buried them all in one grave, and started back to our fort; but before we got there, two more of our men died of wounds they had received; making our total loss seventeen good fellows in that battle.

We now remained at the fort a few days, but no provision came yet, and we were all likely to perish. The weather also began to get very cold; and our clothes were nearly worn out, and horses getting very feeble and poor. Our officers proposed to Gen'l. Jackson to let us return home and get fresh horses, and fresh clothing, so as to be better prepared for another campaign; for our sixty days had long been out, and that was the time we entered for.

But the general took "the responsibility" on himself, and refused. We were, however, determined to go, as I am to put back the deposites, *if I can*. With this, the general issued his orders against it, as he has against the bank. But we began to fix for a start, as provisions were too scarce; just as Clay, and Webster, and myself are preparing to fix bank matters, on account of the scarcity of money. The general went and placed his cannon on a bridge we had to cross, and ordered out his regulars and drafted men to keep us from crossing; just as he has planted his Globe and K. C. to alarm the bank men, while his regulars and militia in Congress are to act as artillery men. But when the militia started to guard the bridge, they would holler back to us to bring their knapsacks along when we come, for they wanted to go as bad as we did; just as many a good fellow now wants his political knapsack brought along, that if, when we come to vote, he sees he has a *fair shake to go,* he may join in and help us to take back the deposites.

We got ready and moved on till we came near the bridge, where the general's men were all strung along on both sides, just like the officeholders are now, to keep us from getting along to the help of the country and the people. But we all had our flints ready picked, and our guns ready primed, that if we were fired on we might fight our way through, or all die together; just as we are now determined to save the country from ready ruin, or to sink down with it. When we came still nearer the bridge we heard the guards cocking their guns, and we did the same; just as we have had it in Congress, while the "government" regulars and the people's volunteers have all been setting their political triggers. But, after all, we marched boldly on, and not a gun was fired, nor a life lost; just as I hope it will be again, that we shall not be afraid of the general's Globe, nor his K. C., nor his regulars, nor their trigger snapping; but just march boldly over the executive bridge, and take the deposites back where the law placed them, and where they ought to be. When we had passed, no further attempt was made to stop us; but the general said, we were "the damned'st volunteers he had ever seen in his life; that we would volunteer and go out and fight, and then at our pleasure would *volunteer* and go home again, in spite of the devil." But we went on; and near Huntsville we met a reinforcement who were going on to join the army. It consisted of a regiment of volunteers, and was under the command of some one whose name I can't remember. They were sixty-day volunteers.

We got home pretty safely, and in a short time we had procured fresh horses and a supply of clothing better suited for the season; and then we returned to Fort Deposite, where our officers held a sort of a *"national convention"* on the subject of a message they had received from General Jackson,—demanding that on our return we should serve out *six months.* We had already served three months instead of two, which was the time we had volunteered for. On the next morning the officers reported to us the conclusions they had come to; and told us, if any of us felt bound to go on and serve out the six months, we could do so; but that they intended to go back home. I knowed if I went back home I couldn't rest, for I felt it my duty to be out; and when out was, somehow or other, always delighted to be in the very thickest of the danger. A few of us, therefore, determined to push on and join the army. The number I do not recollect, but it was very small.

When we got out there, I joined Major Russel's company of spies. Before we reached the place, General Jackson had started. We went on likewise, and overtook him at a place where we established a fort, called Fort Williams, and leaving men to guard it, we went ahead; intending to go to a place called the Horse-shoe bend of the Talapoosa river. When we came near that place, we began to find Indian sign plenty, and we struck up camp for the night. About two hours before day, we heard our guard firing, and we were all up in little or no time. We mended up our camp fires, and then fell back in the dark, expecting to see the Indians pouring in; and intending, when they should do so, to shoot them by the light of our own fires. But it happened that they did not rush in as we had expected, but commenced a fire on us as we were. We were encamped in a hollow square, and we not only returned the fire, but continued to shoot as well as we could in the dark, till day broke, when the Indians disappeared. The only guide we had in shooting was to notice the flash of their guns, and then shoot as directly at the place as we could guess.

In this scrape we had four men killed, and several wounded; but whether we killed any of the Indians or not we never could tell, for it is their custom always to

carry off their dead, if they can possibly do so. We buried ours, and then made a large
log heap over them, and set it on fire, so that the place of their deposite might not be
known to the savages, who, we knew, would seek for them, that they might scalp
them. We made some horse litters for our wounded, and took up a retreat. We moved
on till we came to a large creek which we had to cross; and about half of our men had
crossed, when the Indians commenced firing on our left wing, and they kept it up
very warmly. We had left Major Russel and his brother at the camp we had moved
from that morning, to see what discovery they could make as to the movements of
the Indians; and about this time, while a warm fire was kept up on our left, as I have
just stated, the major came up in our rear, and was closely pursued by a large number
of Indians, who immediately commenced a fire on our artillery men. They hid themselves behind a large log, and could kill one of our men almost every shot, they being
in open ground and exposed. The worst of all was, two of our colonels just at this trying moment left their men, and by *a forced march,* crossed the creek out of the reach
of the fire. Their names, at this late day, would do the world no good, and my object
is history alone, and not the slightest interference with character. An opportunity was
now afforded for Governor Carroll to distinguish himself, and on this occasion he did
so, by greater bravery than I ever saw any other man display. In truth, I believe, as
firmly as I do that General Jackson is president, that if it hadn't been for Carroll, we
should all have been genteely licked that time, for we were in a devil of a fix; part of
our men on one side of the creek, and part on the other, and the Indians all the time
pouring it on us, as hot as fresh mustard to a sore shin. I will not say exactly that the
old general was whip'd; but I will say, that if we escaped it at all, it was like old Henry
Snider going to heaven, "mita tam tite squeeze." I think he would confess himself, that
he was nearer whip'd this time than he was at any other, for I know that all the world
couldn't make him acknowledge that he was *pointedly* whip'd. I know I was mighty
glad when it was over, and the savages quit us, for I had begun to think there was one
behind every tree in the woods.

   We buried our dead, the number of whom I have also forgotten; and again made
horse litters to carry our wounded, and so we put out, and returned to Fort Williams,
from which place we had started. In the mean time, my horse had got crippled, and
was unfit for service, and as another reinforcement had arrived, I thought they could
get along without me for a short time; so I got a furlough and went home, for we had
had hard times again on this hunt, and I began to feel as though I had done Indian
fighting enough for one time. I remained at home until after the army had returned
to the Horse-shoe bend, and fought the battle there. But not being with them at that
time, of course no history of that fight can be expected of me.

CHAPTER VII

Soon after this, an army was to be raised to go to Pensacola, and I determined to go
again with them, for I wanted a small taste of British fighting, and I supposed they
would be there.

Here again the entreaties of my wife were thrown in the way of my going, but all in vain; for I always had a way of just going ahead, at whatever I had a mind to. One of my neighbours, hearing I had determined to go, came to me, and offered me a hundred dollars to go in his place as a substitute, as he had been drafted. I told him I was better raised than to hire myself out to be shot at; but that I would go, and he should go too, and in that way the government would have the services of us both. But we didn't call General Jackson "the government" in those days, though we used to go and fight under him in the war.

I fixed up, and joined old Major Russel again; but we couldn't start with the main army, but followed on, in a little time, after them. In a day or two, we had a hundred and thirty men in our company; and we went over and crossed the Muscle Shoals at the same place where I had crossed when first out, and where we burned the Black Warriors' town. We passed through the Choctaw and Chickasaw nations, on to Fort Stephens, and from thence to what is called the Cut-off, at the junction of the Tom-Bigby with the Alabama river. This place is near the old Fort Mimms, where the Indians committed the great butchery at the commencement of the war.

We were here about two days behind the main army, who had left their horses at the Cut-off, and taken it on foot; and they did this because there was no chance for forage between there and Pensacola. We did the same, leaving men enough to take care of our horses, and cut out on foot for that place. It was about eighty miles off; but in good heart we shouldered our guns, blankets, and provisions, and trudged merrily on. About twelve o'clock the second day, we reached the encampment of the main army, which was situated on a hill, overlooking the city of Pensacola. My commander, Major Russel, was a great favourite with Gen'l. Jackson, and our arrival was hailed with great applause, though we were a little after the feast; for they had taken the town and fort before we got there. That evening we went down into the town, and could see the British fleet lying in sight of the place. We got some liquor, and took a "horn" or so, and went back to the camp. We remained there that night, and in the morning we marched back towards the Cut-off. We pursued this direction till we reached old Fort Mimms, where we remained two or three days. It was here that Major Russel was promoted from his command, which was only that of a captain of spies, to the command of a major in the line. He had been known long before at home as old Major Russel, and so we all continued to call him in the army. A Major Childs, from East Tennessee, also commanded a battalion, and his and the one Russel was now appointed to command, composed a regiment, which, by agreement with General Jackson, was to quit his army and go to the south, to kill up the Indians on the Scamby river.

General Jackson and the main army set out the next morning for New Orleans, and a Colonel Blue took command of the regiment which I have before described. We remained, however, a few days after the general's departure, and then started also on our route.

As it gave rise to so much war and bloodshed, it may not be improper here to give a little description of Fort Mimms, and the manner in which the Indian war commenced. The fort was built right in the middle of a large old field, and in it the people had been forted so long and so quietly, that they didn't apprehend any danger at all, and had, therefore, become quite careless. A small negro boy, whose business it was to bring up the calves at milking time, had been out for that purpose, and on coming back, he said he saw a great many Indians. At this the inhabitants took the alarm, and closed their gates and placed out their guards, which they continued for a few days. But finding that no attack was made, they concluded the little negro had lied; and again threw their gates open, and set all their hands out to work their fields. The same boy was out again on the same errand, when, returning in great haste and alarm, he informed them that he had seen the Indians as thick as trees in the woods. He was not believed, but was tucked up to receive a flogging for the supposed lie; and was actually getting badly licked at the very moment when the Indians came in a troop, loaded with rails, with which they stop'd all the port-holes of the fort on one side except the bastion; and then they fell in to cutting down the picketing. Those inside the fort had only the bastion to shoot from, as all the other holes were spiked up; and they shot several of the Indians, while engaged in cutting. But as fast as one would fall, another would seize up the axe and chop away, until they succeeded in cutting down enough of the picketing to admit them to enter. They then began to rush through, and continued until they were all in. They immediately commenced scalping, without regard to age or sex; having forced the inhabitants up to one side of the fort, where they carried on the work of death as a butcher would in a slaughter pen.

The scene was particularly described to me by a young man who was in the fort when it happened, and subsequently went on with us to Pensacola. He said that he saw his father, and mother, his four sisters, and the same number of brothers, all butchered in the most shocking manner, and that he made his escape by running over the heads of the crowd, who were against the fort wall, to the top of the fort, and then jumping off, and taking to the woods. He was closely pursued by several Indians, until he came to a small byo, across which there was a log. He knew the log was hollow on the under side, so he slip'd under the log and hid himself. He said he heard the Indians walk over him several times back and forward. He remained, nevertheless, still till night, when he came out, and finished his escape. The name of this young man has entirely escaped my recollection, though his tale greatly excited my feelings. But to return to my subject. The regiment marched from where Gen'l. Jackson had left us to Fort Montgomery, which was distant from Fort Mimms about a mile and a half, and there we remained for some days.

Here we supplied ourselves pretty well with beef, by killing wild cattle which had formerly belonged to the people who perished in the fort, but had gone wild after their massacre.

When we marched from Fort Montgomery, we went some distance back towards Pensacola; then we turned to the left, and passed through a poor piny country, till we reached the Scamby river, near which we encamped. We had about one thousand men, and as a part of that number, one hundred and eighty-six Chickesaw and Choctaw Indians with us. That evening a boat landed from Pensacola, bringing many articles that were both good and necessary; such as sugar and coffee, and liquors of all kinds. The same evening, the Indians we had along proposed to cross the river, and the officers thinking it might be well for them to do so, consented; and Major Russell went with them, taking sixteen white men, of which number I was one. We camped on the opposite bank that night, and early in the morning we set out. We had not gone far before we came to a place where the whole country was covered with water, and looked like a sea. We didn't stop for this, tho', but just put in like so many spaniels, and waded on, sometimes up to our armpits, until we reached the pine hills, which made our distance through the water about a mile and a half. Here we struck up a fire to warm ourselves, for it was cold, and we were chilled through by being so long in the water. We again moved on, keeping our spies out; two to our left near the bank of the river, two straight before us, and two others on our right. We had gone in this way about six miles up the river, when our spies on the left came to us leaping the brush like so many old bucks, and informed us that they had discovered a camp of Creek Indians, and that we must kill them. Here we paused for a few minutes, and the prophets pow-wowed over their men awhile, and then got out their paint, and painted them, all according to their custom when going into battle. They then brought their paint to old Major Russell, and said to him, that as he was an officer, he must be painted too. He agreed, and they painted him just as they had done themselves. We let the Indians understand that we white men would first fire on the camp, and then fall back, so as to give the Indians a chance to rush in and scalp them. The Chickasaws marched on our left hand, and the Choctaws on our right, and we moved on till we got in hearing of the camp, where the Indians were employed in beating up what they called chainy briar root. On this they mostly subsisted. On a nearer approach we found they were on an island, and that we could get to them. While we were chatting about this matter, we heard some guns fired, and in a very short time after a keen whoop, which satisfied us, that whereever it was, there was war on a small scale. With that we all broke, like quarter horses, for the firing; and when we got there we found it was our two front spies, who related to us the following story:—As they were moving on, they had met with two Creeks who were out hunting their horses; as they approached each other, there was a large cluster of green bay bushes exactly between them, so that they were within a few feet of meeting before either was discovered. Our spies walked up to them, and speaking in the Shawnee tongue, informed them that General Jackson was at Pensacola, and they were making their escape, and wanted to know where they could get something to eat. The Creeks told them that nine miles up the Conaker, the river they were then on, there was a large camp of Creeks, and they had cattle and plenty to eat; and further, that their own camp was on an island about a mile off, and just below the mouth of the Conaker. They held their conversation and struck up a fire, and smoked together, and shook hands, and parted. One of the Creeks had a gun, the other had none; and as soon as they had parted, our Choctaws turned round and shot down the one that had the gun, and the other attempted to run off. They snapped several times at him, but the gun still missing fire, they took after him, and overtaking him, one of them struck him over the head with his gun, and followed up his blows till he killed him.

The gun was broken in the combat, and they then fired off the gun of the Creek they had killed, and raised the war-whoop. When we reached them, they had cut off the heads of both the Indians; and each of those Indians with us would walk up to one of the heads, and taking his war club would strike on it. This was done by every one of them; and when they had got done, I took one of their clubs, and walked up as they had done, and struck it on the head also. At this they all gathered round me, and patting me on the shoulder, would call me "Warrior—warrior."

They scalped the heads, and then we moved on a short distance to where we found a trace leading in towards the river. We took this trace and pursued it, till we came to where a Spaniard had been killed and scalped, together with a woman, who we supposed to be his wife, and also four children. I began to feel mighty ticklish along about this time, for I knowed if there was no danger then, there had been; and I felt exactly like there still was. We, however, went on till we struck the river, and then continued down it till we came opposite to the Indian camp, where we found they were still beating their roots.

It was now late in the evening, and they were in a thick cane brake. We had some few friendly Creeks with us, who said they could decoy them. So we all hid behind trees and logs, while the attempt was made. The Indians would not agree that we should fire, but pick'd out some of their best gunners, and placed them near the river. Our Creeks went down to the river's side, and hailed the camp in the Creek language. We heard an answer, and an Indian man started down towards the river, but didn't come in sight. He went back and again commenced beating his roots, and sent a squaw. She came down, and talked with our Creeks until dark came on. They told her they wanted her to bring them a canoe. To which she replied, that their canoe was on our side; that two of their men had gone out to hunt their horses and hadn't yet returned. They were the same two we had killed. The canoe was found, and forty of our picked Indian warriors were crossed over to take the camp. There was at last only one man in it, and he escaped; and they took two squaws, and ten children, but killed none of them, of course.

We had run nearly out of provisions, and Major Russell had determined to go up the Conaker to the camp we had heard of from the Indians we had killed. I was one that he selected to go down the river that night for provisions, with the canoe, to where we had left our regiment. I took with me a man by the name of John Guess, and one of the friendly Creeks, and cut out. It was very dark, and the river was so full that it overflowed the banks and the adjacent low bottoms. This rendered it very difficult to keep the channel, and particularly as the river was very crooked. At about ten o'clock at night we reached the camp, and were to return by morning to Major Russell, with provisions for his trip up the river; but on informing Colonel Blue of this arrangement, he vetoed it as quick as General Jackson did the bank bill; and said, if Major Russell didn't come back the next day, it would be bad times for him. I found we were not to go up the Conaker to the Indian camp, and a man of my company offered to go up in my place to inform Major Russell. I let him go; and they reached the major, as I was told, about sunrise in the morning, who immediately returned with those who were with him to the regiment, and joined us where we crossed the river, as hereafter stated.

The next morning we all fixed up, and marched down the Scamby to a place called Miller's Landing, where we swam our horses across, and sent on two companies down on the side of the bay opposite to Pensacola, where the Indians had fled when the main army first marched to that place. One was the company of Captain William Russell, a son of the old major, and the other was commanded by a Captain Trimble. They went on, and had a little skirmish with the Indians. They killed some, and took all the balance prisoners, though I don't remember the numbers. We again met those companies in a day or two, and sent the prisoners they had taken on to Fort Montgomery, in charge of some of our Indians.

I did hear, that after they left us, the Indians killed and scalped all the prisoners, and I never heard the report contradicted. I cannot positively say it was true, but I think it entirely probable, for it is very much like the Indian character.

26

JAMES FENIMORE COOPER

(1789–1851)

In 1834, Dr. Daniel Drake of Cincinnati claimed that "No western man reads Cooper." His criticism was based on what he viewed as the false picture of the west presented in *The Prairie*. Foreshadowing Mark Twain's exposition of Cooper's habit of bending reality, Drake saw in the novel more than simple inaccuracy; he also saw a successful and popular eastern writer misrepresenting his region to an international audience in ways that erased local divergence from the nationalist ideology Cooper announced himself as promulgating.

In chapter 1, Cooper announces his own motive in creating a fiction that policed the west's divergence from the east. While, like Brackenridge and Jefferson, he admits that a multiregional nation might not endure, he perceives that, regardless of politics, what matters most is extending "our language, our religion, our institutions, and it is also to be hoped, our sense of political justice." By "our" he means the social institutions of the northeast, and, in so doing, he erases great divergence from this singularized national identity throughout the nation. Cooper's *The Prairie,* then, openly advocates a form of cultural colonialism that imagines a domesticated west and discourages a divergent west.

The ideology is played out by telling the story of the last chapter of the life of Cooper's mythic frontiersman, Natty Bummpho. Like Crevecoeur, Cooper imagined such backwoodsmen as having a hybrid white and native identity. While Crevecoeur disparaged this, Cooper celebrated it as representing white access to the nobility of savagery. Nonetheless, both saw this figure as the first stage in a multistage narrative of contact, occupation, and settlement. As the book opens, two frontier types, Natty and Ishmael Bush, are alone on the trans-Mississippi prairie, a place Cooper had never seen. The latter, a kidnapper who also spouts the kind of anti-institutional and anti-imperialist rhetoric of the Whiskey Rebellion, represents the chaos of the unpoliced frontier. Two white men eventually emerge in the novel, Duncan Middleton and Paul Hover, who come to represent the new west's elite and middle classes, respectively, a more orderly replication of Cooper's own Cooperstown in upstate New York.

Excluded from the new west are both the Pawnees and the Sioux—noble and ignoble savages respectively who flee west as the novel ends—and Bush. Cooper's conflation of contrarian thinking and crime misrepresents dissidence as malfeasance. Drake's refusal of this plot identifies the core of Cooper's agenda to remake the west in the image of the east. Natty's death as the book ends culminates a longer history Cooper would

trace throughout his five books featuring this character. Cooper's drama-
tization of the plight of the Native Americans must be understood as
tragedy but, ironically a tragedy necessary to create a context for the
greater good of expanding the ideals of "our" civilization.

Text: *The Prairie* (New York: 1987; rpt. of 1832 edition): chapters 1, 2, 34.

FROM *THE PRAIRIE* (1832)

CHAPTER I

"I pray thee, shepherd, if that love or gold
Can in this desert place buy entertainment,
Bring us where we may rest ourselves and feed."

—*AS YOU LIKE IT,* II. iv. 71–73

Much was said and written, at the time, concerning the policy of adding the vast regions of Louisiana, to the already immense, and but half-tenanted territories of the
United-States. As the warmth of the controversy however subsided, and party considerations gave place to more liberal views, the wisdom of the measure began to be
generally conceded. It soon became apparent, to the meanest capacity, that, while nature had placed a barrier of desert to the extension of *our* population in the west, the
measure had made *us* the masters of a belt of fertile country, which, in the revolutions
of the day, might have become the property of a rival nation. *It gave the sole command
of* the great thoroughfare of the interior, and placed the countless tribes of savages,
who lay along *our* borders, entirely within *our* controul; it reconciled conflicting
rights, and quieted national distrusts; it opened a thousand avenues to the inland
trade, and to the waters of the Pacific; and, if ever time or necessity shall require a
peaceful division of this vast empire, it assures *us* a neighbour that will possess *our* language, *our* religion, *our* institutions, and it is also to be hoped, *our* sense of political
justice.

   Although the purchase was made in 1803, the spring of the succeeding year was
permitted to open, before the official prudence of the Spaniard, who held the
province for his European master, admitted the authority, or even of the entrance, of
its new proprietors. But the forms of the transfer were no sooner completed, and the
new government acknowledged, than swarms of that restless people, which is ever
found hovering on the skirts of American society, plunged into the thickets that
fringed the right bank of the Mississippi, with the same careless hardihood, as had al-

ready sustained so many of them in their toilsome progress from the Atlantic states, to the eastern shores of the "Father of rivers."[1]

Time was necessary to blend the numerous and affluent colonists of the lower province with their new compatriots; but the thinner and more humble population, above, was almost immediately swallowed in the vortex which attended the tide of instant emigration. The inroad from the east was a new and sudden out-breaking of a people, who had endured a momentary restraint, after having been rendered nearly resistless by success. The toils and hazards of former undertakings were forgotten, as these endless and unexplored regions, with all their fancied as well as real advantages, were laid open to their enterprise. The consequences were such as might easily have been anticipated, from so tempting an offering, placed as it was before the eyes of a race long trained in adventure and nurtured in difficulties.

Thousands of the elders, of what were then called the *New*-States,[2] broke up from the enjoyment of their hard-earned indulgencies, and were to be seen leading long files of descendants, born and reared in the forests of Ohio and Kentucky, deeper into the land, in quest of that which might be termed, without the aid of poetry, their natural and more congenial atmosphere. The distinguished and resolute forester, who first penetrated the wilds of the latter state, was of the number. This adventurous and venerable patriarch was now seen making, his last remove; placing the "endless river" between him and the multitude his own success had drawn around him, and seeking for the renewal of enjoyments which were rendered worthless in his eyes, when trammelled by the forms of human institutions.[3]

In the pursuit of adventures, such as these, men are ordinarily governed by their habits or deluded by their wishes. A few, led by the phantoms of hope, and ambitious of sudden affluence, sought the mines of the virgin territory; but by far the greater portion of the emigrants were satisfied to establish themselves along the margins of the larger water-courses, content with the rich returns that the generous alluvial bottoms of the rivers never fail to bestow on the most desultory industry. In this manner were communities formed with magical rapidity; and most of those who witnessed the purchase of the empty empire, have lived to see already a populous and sovereign state, parcelled from its inhabitants, and received into the bosom of the national Union, on terms of political equality.

The incidents and scenes which are connected with this legend, occurred in the earliest periods of the enterprises which have led to so great and so speedy a result.

The harvest of the first year of our possession had long been passed, and the fading foliage of a few scattered trees was, already, beginning to exhibit the hues and tints of autumn, when a train of wagons issued from the bed of a dry rivulet, to pursue its course across the undulating surface of what, in the language of the country of which we write, is called a "rolling Prairie." The vehicles, loaded with household goods and

---

1. The Mississippi is thus termed in several of the Indian languages. The reader will gain a more just idea of the importance of this stream, if he recall to mind the fact, that the Missouri and the Mississippi are properly the same river. Their united lengths cannot be greatly short of four thousand miles. [1832]

2. All the states admitted to the American Union, since the revolution are called *New*-States, with the exception of Vermont that had claims before the war which were not, however, admitted until a later day. [1832]

3. Col. Boon, the patriarch of Kentucky. This venerable and hardy pioneer of civilization emigrated to an estate three hundred miles west of the Mississippi, in his ninety second year, because he found a population of ten to the square mile, inconveniently crowded! [1832]

implements of husbandry, the few straggling sheep and cattle that were herded in the
rear, and the rugged appearance and careless mien of the sturdy men who loitered at
the sides of the lingering teams, united to announce a band of emigrants seeking for
the Eldorado of the West. Contrary to the usual practice of the men of their caste, this
party had left the fertile bottoms of the low country, and had found its way, by means
only known to such adventurers, across glen and torrent, over deep morasses and arid
wastes, to a point far beyond the usual limits of civilized habitations. In their front
were stretched those broad plains, which extend, with so little diversity of character,
to the bases of the Rocky Mountains; and many long and dreary miles in their rear,
foamed the swift and turbid waters of La Platte.

The appearance of such a train, in that bleak and solitary place, was rendered the
more remarkable by the fact, that the surrounding country offered so little, that was
tempting to the cupidity of speculation, and, if possible, still less that was flattering to
the hopes of an ordinary settler of new lands.

The meagre herbage of the Prairie promised nothing, in favor of a hard and unyielding soil, over which the wheels of the vehicles rattled as lightly as if they travelled on a beaten road; neither wagons nor beasts making any deeper impression, than
to mark that bruised and withered grass, which the cattle plucked, from time to time,
and as often rejected, as food too sour, for even hunger to render palatable.

Whatever might be the final destination of these adventurers, or the secret causes
of their apparent security in so remote and unprotected a situation, there was no visible sign of uneasiness, uncertainty, or alarm among them. Including both sexes, and
every age, the number of the party exceeded twenty.

At some little distance in front of the whole, marched the individual who, by his
position and air, appeared to be the leader of the band. He was a tall, sun-burnt man,
past the middle age, of a dull countenance and listless manner. His frame appeared
loose and flexible; but it was vast, and in reality of prodigious power. It was only at
moments, however, as some slight impediment opposed itself to his loitering progress,
that his person, which, in its ordinary gait seemed so lounging and nerveless, displayed
any of those energies which lay latent in his system, like the slumbering and unwieldy,
but terrible, strength of the elephant. The inferior lineaments of his countenance were
coarse, extended and vacant; while the superior, or those nobler parts which are
thought to affect the intellectual being, were low, receding and mean.

The dress of this individual was a mixture of the coarsest vestments of a husbandman, with the leathern garments, that fashion as well as use had in some degree
rendered necessary to one engaged in his present pursuits. There was, however, a singular and wild display of prodigal and ill-judged ornaments blended with his motley
attire. In place of the usual deer-skin belt, he wore around his body a tarnished silken
sash of the most gaudy colours; the buck-horn haft of his knife was profusely decorated with plates of silver; the marten's fur of his cap was of a fineness and shadowing
that a queen might covet; the buttons of his rude and soiled blanket-coat were of the
glittering coinage of Mexico; the stock of his rifle was of beautiful mahogany, riveted
and banded with the same precious metal, and the trinkets of no less than three
worthless watches dangled from different parts of his person. In addition to the pack
and the rifle which were slung at his back, together with the well-filled, and carefully
guarded pouch and horn, he had carelessly cast a keen and bright wood-axe across his
shoulder, sustaining the weight of the whole with as much apparent ease as if he
moved, unfettered in limb, and free from incumbrance.

A short distance in the rear of this man, came a groupe of youths very similarly
attired, and bearing sufficient resemblance to each other, and to their leader, to dis-

tinguish them as the children of one family. Though the youngest of their number
could not much have passed the period, that, in the nicer judgment of the law, is called
the age of discretion, he had proved himself so far worthy of his progenitors as to have
reared already his aspiring person to the standard height of his race. There were one
or two others, of different mould, whose descriptions must however be referred to the
regular course of the narrative.

Of the females, there were but two who had arrived at womanhood; though several white-headed, olive-skinn'd faces were peering out of the foremost wagon of the
train, with eyes of lively curiosity and characteristic animation. The elder of the two
adults was the sallow and wrinkled mother of most of the party, and the younger was
a sprightly, active girl of eighteen, who in figure, dress and mien, seemed to belong to
a station in society several gradations above that of any one of her visible associates.
The second vehicle was covered with a top of cloth so tightly drawn, as to conceal its
contents, with the nicest care. The remaining wagons were loaded with such rude furniture and other personal effects as might be supposed to belong to one ready, at any
moment to change his abode, without reference to season or distance.

Perhaps there was little in this train, or in the appearance of its proprietors, that
is not daily to be encountered on the highways of this changeable and moving country. But the solitary and peculiar scenery, in which it was so unexpectedly exhibited,
gave to the party a marked character of wildness and adventure.

In the little vallies which, in the regular formation of the land, occurred at every
mile of their progress, the view was bounded, on two of the sides, by the gradual and
low elevations, which give name to the description of Prairie we have mentioned;
while on the others, the meagre prospect ran off in long, narrow, barren perspectives,
but slightly relieved by a pitiful show of coarse, though somewhat luxuriant vegetation. From the summits of the swells, the eye became fatigued with the sameness and
chilling dreariness of the landscape. The earth was not unlike the ocean, when its restless waters are heaving heavily, after the agitation and fury of the tempest have begun
to lessen. There was the same waving and regular surface, the same absence of foreign
objects, and the same boundless extent to the view. Indeed so very striking was the
resemblance between the water and the land, that, however much the geologist might
sneer at so simple a theory, it would have been difficult for a poet not to have felt that
the formation of the one had been produced by the subsiding dominion of the other.
Here and there a tall tree rose out of the bottoms, stretching its naked branches
abroad, like some solitary vessel; and, to strengthen the delusion, far in the distance,
appeared two or three rounded thickets, looming in the misty horizon like islands
resting on the waters. It is unnecessary to warn the practised reader, that the sameness
of the surface, and the low stands of the spectators exaggerated the distances; but, as
swell appeared after swell, and island succeeded island, there was a disheartening assurance that long, and seemingly interminable, tracts of territory must be passed, before the wishes of the humblest agriculturist could be realized.

Still the leader of the emigrants steadily pursued his way, with no other guide
than the sun, turning his back resolutely on the abodes of civilization, and plunging,
at each step, more deeply if not irretrievably, into the haunts of the barbarous and savage occupants of the country. As the day drew nigher to a close however, his mind,
which was, perhaps, incapable of maturing any connected system of forethought, beyond that which related to the interests of the present moment, became, in some slight
degree, troubled with the care of providing for the wants of the hours of darkness.

On reaching the crest of a swell that was a little higher than the usual elevations,
he lingered a minute, and cast a half curious eye on either hand, in quest of those well-

known signs, which might indicate a place, where the three grand requisites of water, fuel and fodder were to be obtained in conjunction.

It would seem that his search was fruitless; for after a few moments of indolent and listless examination, he suffered his huge frame to descend the gentle declivity, in the same sluggish manner that an over-fatted beast would have yielded to the downward pressure.

His example was silently followed by those who succeeded him, though not until the young men had manifested much more of interest, if not of concern, in the brief inquiry which each, in his turn, made on gaining the same look-out. It was now evident, by the tardy movements both of beasts and men, that the time of necessary rest was not far distant. The matted grass of the lower land presented obstacles which fatigue began to render formidable, and the whip was becoming necessary to urge the lingering teams to their labour. At this moment, when, with the exception of the principal individual, a general lassitude was getting the mastery of the travellers, and every eye was cast, by a sort of common impulse, wistfully forward, the whole party was brought to a halt, by a spectacle as sudden as it was unexpected.

The sun had fallen below the crest of the nearest wave of the Prairie, leaving the usual rich and glowing train on its track. In the centre of this flood of fiery light a human form appeared, drawn against the gilded background, as distinctly, and seemingly as palpable, as though it would come within the grasp of any extended hand. The figure was colossal; the attitude musing and melancholy, and the situation directly in the route of the travellers. But embedded, as it was, in its setting of garish light, it was impossible to distinguish its just proportions or true character.

The effect of such a spectacle was instantaneous and powerful. The man in front of the emigrants came to a stand, and remained gazing at the mysterious object, with a dull interest, that soon quickened into superstitious awe. His sons, so soon as the first emotions of surprise had a little abated, drew slowly around him, and, as they who governed the teams gradually followed their example, the whole party was soon collected in one silent and wondering groupe. Notwithstanding the impression of a supernatural agency was very general among the travellers, the ticking of gun-locks was heard, and one of two of the bolder youths cast their rifles forward, in readiness for service.

"Send the boys off to the right," exclaimed the resolute wife and mother, in a sharp, dissonant voice; "I warrant me Asa or Abner will give me some account of the creature!"

"It may be well enough to try the rifle," muttered a dull looking man, whose features, both in outline and expression, bore no small resemblance to the first speaker, and who loosened the stock of his piece and brought it dexterously to the front, while delivering this opinion; "the Pawnee Loups are said to be hunting by hundreds in the plains; if so, they'll never miss a single man from their tribe."

"Stay!" exclaimed a soft-toned but alarmed female voice, which was easily to be traced to the trembling lips of the younger of the two women; "we are not all together; it may be a friend!"

"Who is scouting, now?" demanded the father, scanning, at the same time, the cluster of his stout sons, with a displeased and sullen eye. "Put by the piece, put by the piece;" he continued diverting the other's aim with the finger of a giant, and with the air of one it might be dangerous to deny. "My job is not yet ended; let us finish the little that remains in peace."

The man, who had manifested so hostile an intention, appeared to understand the other's allusion, and suffered himself to be diverted from his object. The sons turned their inquiring looks on the girl, who had so eagerly spoken, to require an explanation; but, as if content with the respite she had obtained for the stranger, she sunk back in her seat, and chose to affect a maidenly silence.

In the mean time the hues of the heavens had often changed. In place of the brightness, which had dazzled the eye, a gray and more sober light had succeeded, and, as the setting lost its brilliancy, the proportions of the fanciful form became less exaggerated, and finally distinct. Ashamed to hesitate, now that the truth was no longer doubtful, the leader of the party resumed his journey, using the precaution, as he ascended the slight acclivity, to release his own rifle from the strap, and to cast it into a situation more convenient for sudden use.

There was little apparent necessity, however, for such watchfulness. From the moment when it had thus unaccountably appeared, as it were, between the heavens and the earth, the stranger's figure had neither moved nor given the smallest evidence of hostility. Had he harboured any such evil intention, the individual who now came plainly into view, seemed but little qualified to execute them.

A frame, that had endured the hardships of more than eighty seasons, was not qualified to awaken apprehension in the breast of one as powerful as the emigrant. Notwithstanding his years, and his look of emaciation, if not of suffering, there was that about this solitary being however, which said that time, and not disease, had laid his hand heavily on him. His form had withered, but it was not wasted. The sinews and muscles, which had once denoted great strength, though shrunken, were still visible; and his whole figure had attained an appearance of induration, which, if it were not for the well-known frailty of humanity, would have seemed to bid defiance to the further approaches of decay. His dress was chiefly of skins, worn with the hair to the weather; a pouch and horn were suspended from his shoulders; and he leaned on a rifle of uncommon length, but which, like its owner exhibited the wear of long and hard service.

As the party drew nigher to this solitary being, and came within a distance to be heard, a low growl issued from the grass at his feet, and then a tall, gaunt, toothless hound arose lazily from his lair, and shaking himself made some show of resisting the nearer approach of the travellers.

"Down! Hector, down!" said his master, in a voice that was a little tremulous and hollow with age. "What have ye to do, pup, with men who journey on their lawful callings?"

"Stranger, if you ar' much acquainted in this country," said the leader of the emigrants, "can you tell a traveller where he may find necessaries for the night."

"Is the land filled on the other side of the Big River!" demanded the old man, solemnly, and without appearing to hearken to the other's question; "or why do I see a sight I had never thought to behold again?"

"Why there is country left, it is true, for such as have money, and ar' not particular in the choice," returned the emigrant; "but to my taste it is getting crowdy. What may a man call the distance from this place to the nighest point on the main river?"

"A hunted deer could not cool his sides, in the Mississippi, without travelling a weary five hundred miles."

"And what may you name the district, hereaway?"

"By what name," returned the old man pointing significantly upward, "would you call the spot, where you see yonder cloud?"

The emigrant looked at the other, like one who did not comprehend his meaning and who half suspected he was trifled with, but he contended himself by saying—

"You ar' but a new inhabitant, like myself, I reckon, stranger, otherwise you wouldn't be backward in helping a traveller to some advice; words cost but little, and sometimes lead to friendships."

"Advice is not a gift, but a debt that the old owe to the young. What would you wish to know?"

"Where I may 'camp for the night. I'm no great difficulty maker, as to bed and board, but all old journeyers, like myself, know the virtue of sweet water, and a good browse for the cattle."

"Come then with me, and you shall be master of both; and little more is it that I can offer on this hungry Prairie."

As the old man was speaking, he raised his heavy rifle to his shoulder, with a facility a little remarkable for his years and appearance, and without further words led the way over the acclivity into the adjacent bottom.

CHAPTER II

"Up with my tent: here will I lie to night;
But where, to-morrow?—Well, all's one for that."

—*RICHARD III*, V.iii. 7, 9.

The travellers soon discovered the usual and unerring evidences, that the several articles necessary to their situation were not far distant. A clear and gurgling spring burst out of the side of the declivity, and joining its waters to those of other similar little fountains in its vicinity, their united contributions formed a run, which was easily to be traced, for miles along the Prairie, by the scattering foliage and verdure which occasionally grew within the influence of its moisture. Hither, then, the stranger held his way, eagerly followed by the willing teams, whose instinct gave them a prescience of refreshment and rest.

On reaching what he deemed a suitable spot, the old man halted, and with an enquiring look he seemed to demand if it possessed the needed conveniences. The leader of the emigrants cast his eyes understandingly about him, and examined the place with the keenness of one competent to judge of so nice a question, though in that dilatory and heavy manner which rarely permitted him to betray precipitation.

"Ay, this may do," he said, when satisfied with his scrutiny, "boys, you have seen the last of the sun; be stirring."

The young men manifested a characteristic obedience. The order, for such in tone and manner it was, in truth, was received with respect; but the utmost movement was the falling of an axe or two from the shoulder to the ground, while their owners continued to regard the place with listless and incurious eyes. In the mean time, the elder traveller, as if familiar with the nature of the impulses by which his children were governed, disencumbered himself of his pack and rifle, and, assisted by the man already mentioned as disposed to appeal so promptly to the rifle, he quietly proceeded to release the cattle from the gears.

At length the eldest of the sons stepped heavily forward, and, without any apparent effort, he buried his axe to the eye in the soft body of a cotton-wood tree. He stood, a moment, regarding the effect of the blow, with that sort of contempt with which a giant might be supposed to contemplate the puny resistance of a dwarf, and then flourishing the implement above his head, with the grace and dexterity with which a master of the art of offense would wield his nobler though less useful weapon, he quickly severed the trunk of the tree, bringing its tall top crashing to the earth, in submission to his prowess. His companions regarded the operation with indolent curiosity, until they saw the prostrate trunk stretch'd on the ground, when, as if a signal for a general attack had been given, they advanced in a body to the work, and in a space of time, and with a neatness of execution that would have astonished an ignorant spectator, they stripped a small but suitable spot of its burthen of forest, as effectually, and almost as promptly, as if a whirlwind had passed along the place.

The stranger had been a silent, but attentive observer of their progress. As tree after tree came whistling down, he cast his eyes upward, at the vacancies they left in the heavens, with a melancholy gaze, and finally turned away, muttering to himself with a bitter smile, like one who disdained giving a more audible utterance to his discontent. Pressing through the groupe of active and busy children, who had already lighted a cheerful fire, the attention of the old man became next fixed on the movements of the leader of the emigrants and of his savage looking assistant.

These two had already liberated the cattle, which were eagerly browsing the grateful and nutritious extremities of the fallen trees, and were now employed about the wagon, which has been described, as having its contents concealed with so much apparent care. Notwithstanding this particular conveyance appeared to be as silent, and as tenantless as the rest of the vehicles, the men applied their strength to its wheels, and rolled it apart from the others, to a dry and elevated spot, near the edge of the thicket. Here they brought certain poles, which had seemingly been long employed in such a service, and fastening their larger ends firmly in the ground, the smaller were attached to the hoops that supported the covering of the wagon. Large folds of cloth were next drawn out of the vehicle, and after being spread around the whole, were pegged to the earth in such a manner as to form a tolerably capacious and an exceedingly convenient tent. After surveying their work with inquisitive, and perhaps jealous eyes, arranging a fold here and driving a peg more firmly there, the men once more applied their strength to the wagon, pulling it, by its projecting tongue, from the centre of the canopy, until it appeared in the open air, deprived of its covering, and destitute of any other freight than a few light articles of furniture. The latter were immediately removed, by the traveller into the tent with his own hands, as though to enter it were a privilege to which even his bosom companion was not entitled.

Curiosity is a passion that is rather quickened than destroyed by seclusion, and the old inhabitant of the Prairies did not view these precautionary and mysterious movements, without experiencing some of its impulses. He approached the tent, and was about to sever two of its folds, with the very obvious intention of examining, more closely, into the nature of its contents, when the man, who had once already placed his life in jeopardy, seized him by the arm, and with a rude exercise of his strength threw him from the spot he had selected as the one most convenient for his object.

"It's an honest regulation, friend," the fellow drily observed, though with an eye that threatened volumes, "and sometimes it is a safe one, which says, mind your own business."

"Men seldom bring any thing to be concealed into these deserts," returned the old man, as if willing, and yet a little ignorant how to apologize for the liberty he had been about to take, "and I had hop'd no offence, in examining your comforts."

"They seldom bring themselves, I reckon though this has the look of an old country, to my eye it seems not to be overly peopled."

"The land is as aged as the rest of the works of the Lord, I believe; but you say true, concerning its inhabitants. Many months have passed since I have laid eyes on a face of my own colour, before your own. I say again, friend, I meant no harm; I did not know, but there was something behind the cloth, that might bring former days to my mind."

As the stranger ended his simple explanation, he walked meekly away, like one who felt the deepest sense of the right which every man has to the quiet enjoyment of his own, without any troublesome interference on the part of his neighbour; a wholesome and just principle, that he had, also, most probably imbibed from the habits of his secluded life. As he passed towards the little encampment of the emigrants, for such the place had now become, he heard the voice of the leader calling aloud, in its hoarse tones, the name of—

"Ellen Wade."

The girl, who has been already introduced to the reader, and who was occupied with the others of her sex, around the fires, sprang willingly forward at this summons, and passing the stranger with the activity of a young antelope, she was instantly lost behind the forbidden folds of the tent. Neither her sudden disappearance, nor any of the arrangements we have mentioned, seemed, however, to excite the smallest surprise among the remainder of the party. The young men, who had already completed their tasks with the axe, were all engaged after their lounging and listless manner; some in bestowing equitable portions of the fodder among the different animals; others in plying the heavy pestle of a moveable hommany-mortar,[1] and one or two, in wheeling the remainder of the wagons aside and arranging them in such a manner as to form a sort of outwork for their otherwise defenceless bivouac.

These several duties were soon performed, and, as darkness now began to conceal the objects on the surrounding Prairie, the shrill-toned termagant, whose voice since the halt had been diligently exercised among her idle and drowsy offspring, announced in tones that might have been heard at a dangerous distance, that the evening meal waited only for the approach of those who were to consume it. Whatever may be the other qualities of a border-man, he is seldom deficient in the virtue of hospitality. The emigrant no sooner heard the sharp call of his wife, than he cast his eyes about him in quest of the stranger, in order to offer him the place of distinction, in the rude entertainment to which they were so unceremoniously summoned.

"I thank you, friend," the old man replied to the rough invitation to take a seat nigh the smoking kettle; "you have my hearty thanks; but I have eaten for the day, and I am not one of them who dig their graves with their teeth. Well; as you wish it, I will take a place, for it is long sin' I have seen people of my colour eating their daily bread."

"You ar' an old settler, in these districts, then?" the emigrant rather remarked than inquired, with a mouth filled nearly to overflowing with the delicious hommany, prepared by his skillful, though repulsive spouse. "They told us below we should find settlers something thinnish, hereaway, and I must say, the report was mainly true; for, unless, we count the Canada traders on the big river, you ar' the first white face I have met, in a good five hundred miles; that is calculating according to your own reckoning."

"Though I have spent some years in this quarter, I can hardly be called a settler,

---

1. Hommany, is a dish composed chiefly of cracked corn, or maize. [1832]

seeing that I have no regular abode, and seldom pass more than a month, at a time, in the same range."

"A hunter, I reckon?" the other continued, glancing his eyes aside, as if to examine the equipments of his new acquaintance; "your fixen seem none of the best, for such a calling."

"They are old, and nearly ready to be laid aside, like their master," said the old man regarding his rifle, with a look in which affection and regret were singularly blended; "and I may say they are but little needed, too. You are mistaken, friend, in calling me a hunter; I am nothing better than a trapper."[2]

"If you ar' much of the one, I'm bold to say you ar' something of the other; for the two callings go mainly together, in these districts."

"To the shame of the man who is able to follow the first be it so said!" returned the trapper, whom in future we shall choose to designate by his pursuit; "for more than fifty years did I carry my rifle in the wilderness, without so much as setting a snare for even a bird that flies the heavens;—much less a beast, that has nothing but legs, for its gifts."

"I see but little difference whether a man gets his peltry by the rifle or by the trap," said the ill-looking companion of the emigrant, in his rough manner. "The 'arth was made for our comfort; and, for that matter, so ar' its creatur's."

"You seem to have but little plunder,[3] stranger, for one who is far abroad," bluntly interrupted the emigrant, as if he had a reason for wishing to change the conversation. "I hope you ar' better off for skins."

"I make but little use of either," the trapper quietly replied. "At my time of life, food and clothing be all that is needed, and I have little occasion for what you call plunder, unless it may be, now and then, to barter for a horn of powder or a bar of lead."

"You ar' not, then, of these parts, by natur', friend?" the emigrant continued, having in his mind the exception which the other had taken to the very equivocal word, which he himself, according to the custom of the country, had used for "baggage" or "effects."

"I was born on the sea-shore, though most of my life has been passed in the woods."

The whole party now looked up at him, as men are apt to turn their eyes on some unexpected object of general interest. One or two of the young men, repeated the words "sea-shore," and the woman tendered him one of those civilities with which, uncouth as they were, she was little accustomed to grace her hospitality, as if in deference to the travelled dignity of her guest. After a long, and seemingly a meditating silence, the emigrant, who had, however, seen no apparent necessity to suspend the functions of his masticating powers, resumed the discourse.

"It is a long road, as I have heard, from the waters of the west to the shores of the main sea?"

---

2. It is scarcely necessary to say, that this American word means one who takes his game in a trap. It is of general use on the frontiers. The beaver, an animal too sagacious to be easily killed, is oftener taken in this way than in any other. [1832]

3. The cant word for luggage in the western States is "plunder." The term might easily mislead one as to the character of the people, who, notwithstanding their pleasant use of so expressive a word, are, like the inhabitants of all new settlements hospitable and honest. Knavery of the description conveyed by "plunder," is chiefly found in regions more civilized. [1832]

"It is a weary path, indeed, friend; and much have I seen, and something have I suffered in journeying over it."

"A man would see a good deal of hard travel in going its length?"

"Seventy and five years I have been upon the road, and there are not half that number of leagues in the whole distance, after you leave the Hudson, on which I have not tasted venison of my own killing. But this is vain boasting! of what use are former deeds, when time draws to an end!"

"I once met a man, that had boated on the river he names," observed the eldest son, speaking in a low tone of voice, like one who distrusted his knowledge, and deemed it prudent to assume a becoming diffidence in the presence of a man who had seen so much; "from his tell, it must be a considerable stream, and deep enough for a keelboat, from top to bottom."

"It is a wide and deep water-course, and many sightly towns are there growing on its banks," returned the trapper; "and yet it is but a brook, to the waters of the endless river!"

"I call nothing a stream, that a man can travel round," exclaimed the ill-looking associate of the emigrant; "a real river must be crossed; not headed, like a bear in a county hunt."[4]

"Have you been far towards the sun-down, friend?" interrupted the emigrant, as if he desired to keep his rough companion, as much as possible out of the discourse. "I find it is a wide tract of clearing, this, into which I have fallen."

"You may travel weeks, and you will see it the same. I often think the Lord has placed this barren belt of Prairie, behind the States, to warn men to what their folly may yet bring the land! Ay, weeks if not months, may you journey in these open fields, in which there is neither dwelling, nor habitation for man or beast. Even the savage animals travel miles on miles to seek their dens. And yet the wind seldom blows from the east, but I conceit the sounds of axes, and the crash of falling trees are in my ears."

As the old man spoke with the seriousness and dignity that age seldom fails to communicate even to less striking sentiments, his auditors were deeply attentive, and as silent as the grave. Indeed the trapper was left to renew the dialogue, himself, which he soon did by asking a question, in the indirect manner so much in use by the border inhabitants.

"You found it no easy matter to ford the water-courses, and to make your way so deep into the Prairies, friend, with teams of horses, and herds of horned beasts?"

"I kept the left bank of the main river," the emigrant replied, "until I found the stream leading too much to the north, when we rafted ourselves across, without any great suffering. The woman lost a fleece or two from the next year's sheering, and the girls have one cow less to their dairy. Since then, we have done bravely, by bridging a creek every day or two."

"It is likely you will continue west, until you come to land more suitable for a settlement?"

"Until I see reason to stop, or to turn ag'in," the emigrant bluntly answered, rising at the same time, and cutting short the dialogue, by the suddenness of the movement. His example was followed by the trapper, as well as the rest of the party, and then, without much deference to the presence of their guest, the travellers proceeded

---

4. There is a practice, in the new countries, to assemble the men of a large district, sometimes of an entire county, to exterminate the beasts of prey. They form themselves into a circle of several miles in extent, and gradually draw nearer, killing all before them. The allusion is to this custom, in which the hunted beast is turned from one to another. [1832]

to make their dispositions to pass the night. Several little bowers, or rather huts, had already been formed of the tops of trees, blankets of coarse country manufacture, and the skins of buffaloes, united without much reference to any other object than temporary comfort. Into these covers the children with their mother soon drew themselves, and where, it is more than possible, they were all speedily lost in the oblivion of sleep. Before the men, however, could seek their rest, they had sundry little duties to perform; such as completing their works of defence; carefully concealing the fires; replenishing the fodder of their cattle, and setting the watch that was to protect the party, in the approaching hours of night.

The former was effected by dragging the trunks of a few trees into the intervals left by the wagons, and along the open space, between the vehicles and the thicket, on which, in military language, the encampment would be said to have rested; thus forming a sort of chevaux-de-frise on three sides of the position. Within these narrow limits (with the exception of what the tent contained), both man and beast were now collected; the latter being far too happy in resting their weary limbs, to give any undue annoyance to their scarcely more intelligent associates. Two of the young men took their rifles, and, first renewing the priming and examining the flints with the utmost care, they proceeded, the one to the extreme right and the other to the left of the encampment, where they posted themselves, within the shadows of the thicket, but in such positions, as enabled each to overlook a portion of the Prairie.

The trapper loitered about the place, declining to share the straw of the emigrant, until the whole arrangement was completed; and then, without the ceremony of an adieu, he slowly retired from the spot.

It was now in the first watch of the night, and the pale, quivering, and deceptive light, from a new moon, was playing over the endless waves of the Prairie, tipping the swells with gleams of brightness, and leaving the interval land in deep shadow. Accustomed to scenes of solitude like the present, the old man, as he left the encampment proceeded alone into the waste, like a bold vessel leaving its haven to enter on the trackless field of the ocean. He appeared to move for some time, without object, or indeed, without any apparent consciousness, whither his limbs were carrying him. At length, on reaching the rise of one of the undulations, he came to a stand, and for the first time, since leaving the band, who had caused such a flood of reflections and recollections to crowd upon his mind, the old man became aware of his present situation. Throwing one end of his rifle to the earth, he stood leaning on the other, again lost in deep contemplation for several minutes, during which time his hound came and crouched at his feet. A deep, menacing growl from the faithful animal, first aroused him from his musing.

"What now, dog?" he said, looking down at his companion, as if he addressed a being of an intelligence equal to his own, and speaking in a voice of great affection. "What is it, pup? ha! Hector; what is it noseing, now? It won't do, dog; it won't do; the very fa'ns play in open view of us, without minding so worn out curs, as you and I. Instinct is their gift, Hector; and they have found out how little we are to be fear'd, they have!"

The dog stretched his head upward, and responded to the words of his master by a long and plaintive whine, which he even continued after he had again buried his head in the grass, as if he held an intelligent communication with one who so well knew how to interpret his dumb discourse.

"This is a manifest warning, Hector!" The trapper continued, dropping his voice, to the tones of caution and looking warily about him. "What is it, pup; speak plainer, dog; what is it?"

The hound had, however, already laid his nose to the earth, and was silent; appearing to slumber. But the keen quick glances of his master, soon caught a glimpse of a distant figure, which seemed, through the deceptive light, floating along the very elevation on which he had placed himself. Presently its proportions became more distinct, and then an airy, female form appeared to hesitate, as if considering whether it would be prudent to advance. Though the eyes of the dog were now to be seen glancing in the rays of the moon, opening and shutting lazily, he gave no further signs of displeasure.

"Come nigher; we are friends," said the trapper, associating himself with his companion by long use, and, probably, through the strength of the secret tie that connected them together; "we are your friends; none will harm you."

Encouraged by the mild tones of his voice, and perhaps led on by the earnestness of her purpose, the female approached, until she stood at his side; when the old man perceived his visiter to be the young woman, with whom the reader, has already become acquainted by the name of Ellen Wade.

"I had thought you were gone," she said, looking timidly and anxiously around. "They said you were gone; and that we should never see you again. I did not think it was you!"

"Men are no common objects in these empty fields," returned the trapper, "and I humbly hope, though I have so long consorted with the beasts of the wilderness, that I have not yet lost the look of my kind."

"Oh! I knew you to be a man, and I thought I knew the whine of the hound, too," she answered hastily, as if willing to explain she knew not what, and then checking herself, like one fearful of having already said too much.

"I saw no dogs among the teams of your father," the trapper remarked.

"Father!" exclaimed the girl, feelingly, "I have no father! I had nearly said no friend."

The old man, turned towards her, with a look of kindness and interest, that was even more conciliating than the ordinary, upright, and benevolent expression of his weather-beaten countenance.

"Why then do you venture in a place where none but the strong should come?" he demanded. "Did you not know that, when you crossed the big river, you left a friend behind you that is always bound to look to the young and feeble, like yourself."

"Of whom do you speak?"

"The law—'Tis bad to have it, but, I sometimes think, it is worse to be entirely without it. Age and weakness have brought me to feel such weakness, at times. Yes—yes, the law is needed, when such as have not the gifts of strength and wisdom are to be taken care of. I hope, young woman, if you have no father, you have at least a brother."

The maiden felt the tacit reproach conveyed in this covert question, and for a moment she remained in an embarrassed silence. But catching a glimpse of the mild and serious features of her companion, as he continued to gaze on her with a look of interest, she replied, firmly, and in a manner that left no doubt she comprehended his meaning:

"Heaven forbid that any such as you have seen, should be a brother of mine, or any thing else near or dear to me! But, tell me, do you then actually live alone, in this desert district, old man; is there really none here besides yourself?"

"There are hundreds, nay, thousands of the rightful owners of the country, roving about the plains; but few of our own colour."

"And have you then met none who are white, but us?" interrupted the girl, like one too impatient to await the tardy explanation of age and deliberation.

"Not in many days—Hush, Hector, hush," he added in reply to a low, and nearly inaudible growl from his hound. "The dog scents mischief in the wind! The black bears from the mountains sometimes make their way, even lower than this. The pup is not apt to complain of the harmless game. I am not so ready and true with the piece as I used-to-could-be, yet I have struck even the fiercest animals of the Prairie, in my time; so, you have little reason for fear, young woman."

The girl raised her eyes, in that peculiar manner which is so often practised by her sex, when they commence their glances, by examining the earth at their feet, and terminate them by noting every thing within the power of human vision; but she rather manifested the quality of impatience, than any feeling of alarm.

A short bark from the dog, however, soon gave a new direction to the looks of both, then the real object of his second warning became dimly visible.

CHAPTER XXXIV

"Methought, I heard a voice—"

—*MACBETH*, II. ii. 35.

The water-courses were at their height, and the boat went down the swift current like a bird. The passage proved prosperous and speedy. In less than a third of the time that would have been necessary for the same journey by land, it was accomplished by the favor of those rapid rivers. Issuing from one stream into another, as the veins of the human body communicate with the larger channels of life, they soon entered the grand artery of the western waters and landed safely, at the very door of the father of Inez.

The joy of Don Augustin, and the embarrassment of the worthy Father Ignatius may be imagined. The former wept and returned thanks to Heaven, the latter returned thanks, and did not weep. The mild provincials were too happy to raise any questions on the character of so joyful a restoration, and, by a sort of general consent it soon came to be an admitted opinion that the bride of Middleton had been kidnapped by a villain and that she was restored to her friends by human agency. There were as respects this belief, certainly a few sceptics, but then they enjoyed their doubts in private, with that species of sublimated and solitary gratification that a miser finds in gazing at his growing, but useless, hoards.

In order to give the worthy priest something to employ his mind, Middleton made him the instrument of uniting Paul and Ellen. The former consented to the ceremony, because he found that all his friends laid great stress on the matter, but shortly after he led his bride into the plains of Kentucky, under the pretence of paying certain customary visits to sundry members of the family of Hover. While there, he took occasion to have the marriage properly solemnized, by a justice of the peace of his acquaintance, in whose ability to forge the nuptial chain he had much more faith than in that of all the gownsmen within the Pale of Rome. Ellen who appeared conscious that some extraordinary preventives might prove necessary to keep one of so erratic a temper, as her partner, within the proper matrimonial boundaries, raised no objections to these double knots, and all parties were content.

The local importance Middleton had acquired by his union with the daughter of so affluent a proprietor as Don Augustin, united to his personal merit, attracted the attention of the Government. He was soon employed in various situations of responsibility and confidence, which both served to elevate his character in the public estimation and to afford the means of patronage. The bee-hunter was among the first of those to whom he saw fit to extend his favor. It was far from difficult to find situations suited to the abilities of Paul in the state of society that existed three and twenty years ago in those regions. The efforts of Middleton and Inez in behalf of her husband were warmly and sagaciously seconded by Ellen, and they succeeded, in process of time, in working a great and beneficial change in his character. He soon became a landholder, then a prosperous cultivator of the soil, and shortly after a town-officer. By that progressive change in fortune, which in the republicks is often seen to be so singularly accompanied by a corresponding improvement in knowledge and self-respect, he went on, from step to step, until his wife enjoyed the maternal delight of seeing her children placed far beyond the danger of returning to that state from which both their parents had issued. Paul is, actually, at this moment, a member of the lower branch of the Legislature of the State where he has long resided, and he is even notorious for making speeches, that have a tendency to put that deliberative body in good humour, and which as they are based on great practical knowledge suited to the condition of the country, possess a merit that is much wanted in many more subtle and fine spun theories that are daily heard in similar assemblies, to issue from the lips of certain instinctive politicians. But all these happy fruits were the results of much care, and of a long period of time. Middleton, who fills, with a credit better suited to the difference in their educations, a seat in a far higher branch of Legislative Authority, is the source from which we have derived most of the intelligence necessary to compose our legend. In addition to what he has related of Paul, and of his own continued happiness, he has added a short narrative of what took place in a subsequent visit to the Prairies, with which, as we conceive it a suitable termination to what has gone before, we shall judge it wise to conclude our labors.

In the autumn of the year that succeeded the season in which the preceding events occurred, the young man, still in the military service, found himself on the waters of the Missouri, at a point not far remote from the Pawnee towns. Released from any immediate calls of duty, and strongly urged to the measure by Paul, who was in his company, he determined to take horse and cross the country, to visit the Partisan and to inquire into the fate of his friend the trapper. As his train was suited to his functions and rank, the journey was effected, with the privations and hardships that are the accompanyments of all travelling in a wild, but, without any of those dangers and alarms that marked his former passage through the same regions. When within a proper distance, he dispatched an Indian runner belonging to a friendly tribe, to announce the approach of himself and party, continuing his route at a deliberate pace, in order that the intelligence might as was customary precede his arrival. To the surprise of the travellers their message was unanswered. Hour succeeded hour, and mile after mile was passed without bringing either the signs of an honorable reception or the more simple assurances of a friendly welcome. At length the cavalcade, at whose head rode Middleton and Paul, descended from the elevated plain, on which they had long been journeying, to a luxuriant bottom, that brought them to the level of the village of the Loups.

The sun was beginning to fall, and a sheet of golden light was spread over the placid plain, lending to its even surface, those glorious tints and hues that, the human imagination is apt to conceive, form the embellishment of still more imposing scenes. The verdure of the year yet remained and herds of horses and mules were grazing peacefully in the vast natural pasture, under the keeping of vigilant Pawnee boys. Paul pointed out, among them, the well known form of Asinus, sleek, fat and luxuriating in the fulness of content, as he stood with reclining ears and closed eye-lids, seemingly musing on the exquisite nature of his present indolent enjoyment.

The route of the party led them at no great distance from one of those watchful youths, who was charged with a trust heavy as the principal wealth of his tribe. He heard the trampling of the horses and cast his eye aside, but instead of manifesting curiosity or alarm, his look instantly returned, whence it had been withdrawn, to the spot where the village was known to stand.

"There is something remarkable in all this," muttered Middleton, half offended at what he conceived to be not only a slight to his rank, but offensive to himself, personally; "yonder boy has heard of our approach, or he would not fail to notify his tribe; and yet he scarcely deigns to favor us with a glance. Look to your arms, men, it may be necessary to let these savages feel our strength!"

"Therein, Captain, I think you're in an error," returned Paul. "If honesty is to be met on the Prairies at all, you will find it in our old friend, Hard-Heart; neither is an Indian to be judged of by the rules of a white—see, we are not altogether slighted for here comes a party at last to meet us, though it is a little pitiful as to show and numbers."

Paul was right in both particulars. A groupe of horsemen were, at length, seen wheeling round a little copse and advancing across the plain directly towards them. The advance of this party was slow and dignified. As it drew nigh the Partisan of the Loups was seen at its head, followed by a dozen younger warriors of his tribe. They were all unarmed, nor did they even wear any of those ornaments or feathers, which are considered testimonials of respect to the guest an Indian receives, as well as evidence of his own importance.

The meeting was friendly though a little restrained on both sides. Middleton, jealous of his own consideration no less than of the authority of his government, suspected some undue influence on the part of the agents of the Canadas, and, as he was determined to maintain the authority of which he was the representative, he felt himself constrained to manifest an hauteur that he was far from feeling. It was not so easy to penetrate the motives of the Pawnees. Calm, dignified and yet far from repulsive, they set an example of courtesy blended with reserve, that many a diplomatist of the most polished court might have strove in vain to imitate.

In this manner the two parties continued their course to the town. Middleton had time, during the remainder of the ride, to revolve in his mind, all the probable reasons which his ingenuity could suggest for this strange reception. Although he was accompanied by a regular interpreter, the chiefs made their salutations in a manner that dispensed with his services. Twenty times, the Captain turned his glance on his former friend endeavoring to read the expression of his rigid features. But every effort and all conjectures proved equally futile. The eye of Hard-Heart was fixed, composed, and a little anxious, but as to every other emotion, impenetrable. He neither spoke himself, nor seemed willing to invite discourse in his visitors. It was therefore necessary for Middleton to adopt the patient manners of his companions, and to await the issue for the explanation.

When they entered the town, the whole of its inhabitants were seen collected in an open space where they were arranged with the customary deference to age and rank. The whole formed a large circle, in the centre of which were perhaps a dozen of the principal chiefs. Hard-Heart waved his hand as he approached, and, as the mass of bodies opened, he rode through, followed by his companions. Then they dismounted, and as the beasts were led apart, the strangers found themselves environed by a thousand, grave, composed but solicitous faces.

Middleton gazed about him, in growing concern, for no cry, no song, no shout, welcomed him among a people, from whom he had so lately parted with regret. His uneasiness, not to say apprehensions, was shared by all his followers. Determination and stern resolution began to assume the place of anxiety in every eye, as each man silently felt for his arms, and assured himself that his several weapons were in a state for service. But there was no answering symptom of hostility on the part of their hosts. Hard-Heart beckoned for Middleton and Paul to follow, leading the way towards the cluster of forms that occupied the centre of the circle. Here the visiters found a solution of all the movements which had given them so much reason for apprehension.

The trapper was placed on a rude seat, which had been made, with studied care to support his frame, in an upright and easy attitude. The first glance of the eye told his former friends that the old man was, at length, called upon to pay the last tribute of nature. His eye was glazed, and apparently as devoid of sight, as of expression. His features were a little more sunken and strongly marked, than formerly, but there all change so far as exterior was concerned, might be said to have ceased. His approaching end was not to be ascribed to any positive malady but had been a gradual and mild decay of the physical powers. Life it is true still lingered in his system, but it was as if at times, entirely ready to depart, and then it would appear to reanimate the sinking form as if reluctant to give up the possession of a tenement that had never been corrupted by vice or undermined by disease. It would have been no violent fancy to have imagined, that the spirit fluttered about the placid lips of the old woodsman, reluctant to depart from a shell that had so long given it an honest and an honourable shelter.

His body was placed so as to let the light of the setting sun, fall full upon the solemn features. His head was bare, the long, thin, locks of gray, fluttering lightly in the evening breeze. His rifle lay upon his knee, and the other accoutrements of the chase were placed at his side, within reach of his hand. Between his feet lay the figure of a hound, with its head crouching to the earth as if it slumbered, and so perfectly easy and natural was its position, that a second glance was necessary to tell Middleton he saw only the skin of Hector stuffed by Indian tenderness and ingenuity, in a manner to represent the living animal. His own dog was playing at a distance, with the child of Tachechana and Mahtoree. The mother herself, stood at hand holding in her arms a second offspring that might boast of a parentage no less honorable than that which belonged to a son of Hard-Heart. Le Balafré was seated nigh the dying trapper, with every mark about his person that the hour of his own departure, also, was not far distant. The rest of those immediately in the centre, were aged men, who had apparently drawn near, in order to observe the manner in which a just and fearless warrior would depart on the greatest of his journeys.

The old man was reaping the rewards of a life so remarkable for temperance and activity, in a tranquil and placid death. His vigor had in a manner endured, to the very last. Decay when it did occur, was rapid, but free from pain. He had hunted with the tribe in the spring, and even throughout most of the summer, when his limbs suddenly refused to perform their customary offices. A sympathysing weakness took possession of all his faculties, and the Pawnees believed that they were going to lose, in this un-expected manner, a sage and counsellor whom they had begun both to love and to re-spect. But, as we have already said, the immortal occupant seemed unwilling to desert its tenement. The lamp of life often flickered, without becoming extinguished. On the morning of the day on which Middleton arrived, there was a general reviving of the powers of the whole man. His tongue was again heard in wholesome maxims, and his eye, from time to time, recognised the persons of his friends. It merely proved to be a brief and final intercourse with the world on the part of one who had already been considered, as to mental communion, to have taken his leave of it forever.

When he had placed his guests in front of the dying man, Hard-Heart after a pause that proceeded as much from sorrow as decorum, leaned a little forward, and demanded—"Does my Father hear the words of his son?"

"Speak," returned the trapper, in tones that issued from his chest, but which were rendered awfully distinct by the stillness that reigned in the place. "I am about to de-part from the village of the Loups, and, shortly shall be beyond the reach of your voice."

"Let the wise chief have no cares for his journey!" continued Hard-Heart, with an earnest solicitude that led him to forget, for the moment, that others were waiting to address his adopted parent. "A hundred Loups shall clear his path from briars."

"Pawnee, I die, as I have lived, a christian man," resumed the trapper with a force of voice, that had the same startling effect on his hearers as is produced by the trum-pet, when its blast rises suddenly and freely on the air, after its obstructed sounds have been heard struggling in the distance. "As I came into life, so will I leave it. Horses and arms are not needed to stand in the Presence of the Great Spirit of my people! He knows my colour, and according to my gifts will he judge my deeds."

"My father will tell my young men, how many Mingoes he has struck, and what acts of valour and justice he has done, that they may know how to imitate him."

"A boastful tongue is not heard in the heaven of a white man!" solemnly returned the old man. "What I have done, he has seen. His eyes are always open. That which has been well done will he remember. Wherein I have been wrong, will he not for-get to chastise, though he will do the same in mercy. No, my son; a pale-face may not sing his own praises, and hope to have them acceptable before his God!"

A little disappointed, the young partisan stepped modestly back, making way for the recent comers to approach. Middleton took one of the meagre hands of the trap-per, and struggling to command his voice, he succeeded in announcing his presence. The old man listened like one, whose thoughts were dwelling on a very different sub-ject, but when the other had succeeded in making him understand that he was pres-ent, an expression of joyful recognition passed over his faded features.

"I hope you have not so soon forgotten those whom you so materially served!" Middleton concluded. "It would pain me to think my hold on your memory was so light."

"Little that I have ever seen is forgotten," returned the trapper, "I am at the close of many weary days, but there is not one among them all that I could wish to over-look. I remember you, with the whole of your companions; ay, and your gran'ther, that went before you. I am glad that you have come back upon these plains, for I had need of one, who speaks the English, since little faith can be put in the traders of these regions. Will you do a favor, to an old and dying man?"

"Name it," said Middleton. "It shall be done."

"It is a far journey to send such trifles," resumed the old man, who spoke at short intervals, as strength and breath permitted. "A far and weary journey is the same! But kindnesses and friendships are things not to be forgotten. There is a settlement among the Otsego hills."

"I know the place," interrupted Middleton, observing that he spoke with increasing difficulty. "Proceed to tell me what you would have done."

"Take this rifle, and pouch, and horn, and send them to the person whose name is graven on the plates of the stock. A trader cut the letters with his knife, for it is long that I have intended to send him such a token of my love."

"It shall be so. Is there more that you could wish?"

"Little else have I to bestow. My traps I give to my Indian son; for honestly and kindly has he kept his faith. Let him stand before me."

Middleton explained to the chief what the trapper had said and relinquished his own place to the other.

"Pawnee," continued the old man, always changing his language to suit the person he addressed, and not unfrequently according to the ideas he expressed, "it is a custom of my people for the Father to leave his blessing with the son, before he shuts his eyes forever. This blessing I give to you. Take it, for the prayers of a Christian man will never make the path of a just warrior to the blessed Prairies, either longer, or more tangled. May the God of a white man look on your deeds with friendly eyes, and may you never commit an act that shall cause him to darken his face. I know not whether we shall ever meet again. There are many traditions concerning the place of good Spirits. It is not for one like me, old and experienced though I am, to set up my opinions against a nation's. You believe in the blessed Prairies, and I have faith in the sayings of my fathers. If both are true, our parting will be final; but if it should prove that the same meaning is hid under different words, we shall yet stand together, Pawnee, before the face of your Wahcondah who will then be no other than my God. There is much to be said in favor of both religions, for each seems suited to its own people, and no doubt it was so intended. I fear I have not altogether followed the gifts of my colour, inasmuch as I find it a little painful to give up forever the use of the rifle, and the comforts of the chase. But then the fault has been my own, seeing that it could not have been His. Ay, Hector," he continued leaning forward a little and feeling for the ears of the hound, "our parting has come at last, dog, and it will be a long hunt. You have been an honest, and a bold and a faithful hound. Pawnee, you cannot slay the pup on my grave, for where a christian dog falls there he lies forever, but you can be kind to him, after I am gone, for the love you bear his Master?"

"The words of my father, are in my ears," returned the young Partisan, making a grave and respectful gesture of assent.

"Do you hear what the chief has promised, dog?" demanded the trapper making an effort to attract the notice of the insensible effigy of his hound. Receiving no answering look, nor hearing any friendly whine, the old man felt for the mouth and endeavored to force his hand between the cold lips. The truth then flashed upon him, although he was far from perceiving the whole extent of the deception. Falling back in his seat, he hung his head like one who felt a severe and unexpected shock. Profiting by this momentary forgetfulness, two young Indians removed the skin, with the same delicacy of feeling that had induced them to attempt the pious fraud.

"The dog is dead!" muttered the trapper, after a pause of many minutes, "a hound has his time as well as a man; and well has he filled his days! Captain," he added making an effort to wave his hand for Middleton. "I am glad you have come, for, though kind, and well meaning according to the gifts of their colour, these Indians are not the sort of men to lay the head of a white man in his grave. I have been thinking too, of this dog at my feet: it will not do to set forth the opinion that a christian can expect to meet his hound, again, still there can be little harm in placing what is left of so faithful a servant nigh the bones of his master?"

"It shall be done as you desire."

"I'm glad you think with me in this matter. In order then to save labor, lay the pup at my feet—or for that matter put him, side by side. A hunter need never be ashamed to be found in company with his dog!"

"I charge myself with your wish."

The old man made a long and, apparently, a musing pause. At times he raised his eyes, wistfully, as if he would again address Middleton, but some innate feeling appeared ever to suppress his words. The other, who observed his hesitation, enquired in a way most likely to encourage him to proceed, whither there was aught else that he could wish to have done.

"I am without kith or kin in the wide world!" the trapper answered. "When I am gone there will be an end of my race. We have never been chiefs; but honest and useful in our way, I hope it cannot be denied we have always proved ourselves. My father lies buried near the sea, and the bones of his son will whiten on the Prairies."

"Name the spot and your remains shall be placed by the side of your father," interrupted Middleton.

"Not so, not so, Captain. Let me sleep where I have lived, beyond the din of the settlements! Still I see no need why the grave of an honest man should be hid, like a red-skin in his ambushment. I paid a man in the settlements to make and put a graven stone at the head of my father's resting-place. It was of the value of twelve beaver-skins; and cunningly and curiously was it carved! Then it told to all comers that the body of such a christian lay beneath, and it spoke of his manner of life, of his years and of his honesty. When we had done with the Frenchers in the old war, I made a journey to the spot, in order to see that all was rightly performed, and glad I am to say the workman had not forgotten his faith."

"And such a stone you would have at your grave?"

"I! no, no, I have no son, but Hard-Heart, and it is little that an Indian knows of white fashions and usages. Besides I am his debtor, already, seeing it is so little I have done since I have lived in his tribe. The rifle might bring the value of such a thing— but then I know it will give the boy pleasure to hang the piece in his hall, for many is the deer and the bird that he has seen it destroy. No, no, the gun must be sent to him whose name is graven on the lock."

"But there is one who would gladly prove his affection in the way you wish. He who owes you not only his own deliverance from so many dangers, but who inherits a heavy debt of gratitude from his ancestors. The stone shall be put at the head of your grave."

The old man extended his meagre hand, and gave the other a squeeze of thanks.

"I thought you might be willing to do it, but I was backward in asking the favour," he said, "seeing that you are not of my kin. Put no boastful words on the same; but just the name, the age, and the time of the death, with something from the holy book. No more, no more. My name will then not be altogether lost on 'arth; I need no more."

Middleton intimated his assent, and then followed a pause that was only interrupted by distant and broken sentences from the dying man. He appeared now to have closed his accounts with the world, and to wait merely for the final summons to quit it. Middleton and Hard-Heart placed themselves on the opposite sides of his seat, and watched with melancholy solicitude, the variations of his countenance. For two hours there was no very sensible alteration. The expression of his faded and time-worn features was that of a calm and dignified repose. From time to time, he spoke, uttering some brief sentence in the way of advice, or asking some simple question concerning those in whose fortunes he still took a friendly interest. During the whole of that solemn and anxious period each individual of the tribe kept his place, in the most self-restrained patience. When the old man spoke, all bent their heads to listen; and when his words were uttered they seemed to ponder on their wisdom and usefulness.

As the flame drew nigher to the socket, his voice was hushed, and there were moments when his attendants doubted whether he still belonged to the living. Middleton, who watched each wavering expression of his weather-beaten visage with the interest of a keen observer of human nature softened by the tenderness of personal regard, fancied that he could read the workings of the old man's soul, in the strong lineaments of his countenance. Perhaps what the enlightened soldier took for the delusion of mistaken opinion did actually occur, for who has returned from that unknown world to explain by what forms and in what manner he was introduced into its awful precincts. Without pretending to explain what must ever be a mystery to the quick, we shall simply relate facts as they occurred.

The trapper had remained nearly motionless for an hour. His eyes, alone, had occasionally opened and shut. When opened his gaze seemed fastened on the clouds which hung around the western horizon, reflecting the bright colours and giving form and loveliness to the glorious tints of an American sunset. The hour—the calm beauty of the season—the occasion all conspired to fill the spectators with solemn awe. Suddenly, while musing on the remarkable position in which he was placed, Middleton felt the hand which he held, grasp his own, with incredible power, and the old man, supported on either side by his friends, rose upright to his feet. For a moment, he looked about him, as if to invite all in presence to listen, (the lingering remnant of human frailty) and then, with a fine military elevation of the head, and with a voice that might be heard in every part of that numerous assembly he pronounced the word—

"Here!"

A movement so entirely unexpected, and the air of grandeur and humility which were so strikingly united in the mien of the trapper, together with the clear and uncommon force of his utterance, produced a short period of confusion in the faculties of all present. When Middleton and Hard-Heart, each of whom involuntarily extended a hand to support the form of the old man, turned to him again, they found that the subject of their interest, was removed forever beyond the necessity of their care. They mournfully placed the body in its seat, and Le Balafré arose to announce the termination of the scene, to the tribe. The voice of the old Indian, seemed a sort of echo from that invisible world to which the spirit of the honest trapper had just departed.

"A valiant, a just, and a wise warrior has gone on the path which will lead him to the blessed grounds of his people!" he said. "When the voice of the Wahcondah called him, he was ready to answer. Go: my children; remember the just chiefs of the Pale-faces, and clear your own tracks from briars."

The grave was made beneath the shade of some noble oaks. It has been carefully watched to the present hour by the Pawnees of the Loup, and is often shown, to the traveller and the trader, as a spot where a just white-man sleeps. In due time the stone was placed at its head, with the simple inscription, which the trapper had himself requested. The only liberty taken by Middleton, was to add, "*May no wanton hand ever disturb his remains.*"

DANIEL BRYAN

(c. 1790–1866)

In the December 1841 issue of *Graham's Magazine,* Edgar Allan Poe praised a little-known poet from Alexandria, Virginia: "Mr. Bryan has written some very excellent poetry, and is appreciated by all admirers of 'the good old Goldsmith school.'" Today Daniel Bryan is most often remembered for having exchanged letters with Poe the following year. The men were on friendly terms in part because Bryan had been, in his words, "an intimate acquaintance" of William Henry Leonard Poe, Edgar's older brother, who had drunk himself to death at the age of twenty-four. In the Poe-Bryan correspondence, each man wanted something. Poe wanted Bryan to enlist subscribers for a new literary journal, and Bryan wanted Poe to publish his poetry. Bryan sent Poe a collection of poems titled "May-Day Rhymes." Unfortunately, the manuscript never reached him.

Daniel Bryan was born about 1790 in Rockingham, Virginia. He attended Washington Academy, now Washington and Lee University, without earning a degree. He later served as a colonel in the War of 1812, and, perhaps flushed with patriotism as a result, the next year he published *The Mountain Muse,* which included his best known poem: the seven-book, 5,635-line *The Adventures of Daniel Boone.* The elaborate, romantic exposition of Book I begins with God's creation of the universe. Books II and III are given over to Boone's heroism in the adventure of the "Allegany Robbers and the Lost Maid." Much of the rest of Bryan's epic is based on John Filson and Daniel Boone's *The Discovery of Kentucke and the Adventures of Daniel Boon* (1784). But Bryan's poem also contains information that *The Discovery* does not. It is possible that Bryan got some of this information from Boone himself: Boone was Bryan's uncle and perhaps his namesake.

In 1826 Bryan published two more books of poetry: *The Lay of Gratitude, Consisting of Poems Occasioned by the Recent Visit of Lafayette to the United States* and *The Appeal for Suffering Genius: A Poetical Address for the Benefit of the Boston Bard; and The Triumph of Truth.* Also in 1826 he began his twenty-five years as the postmaster of Alexandria, Virginia. Despite his belief that the New England literary establishment did not take southern poetry seriously, he continued to write, but his "humble muse," as he liked to call it, slowly dried up. He died in Washington, D.C., on December 22, 1866.

Text: *The Mountain Muse: Comprising The Adventures of Daniel Boone; and The Power of Virtuous and Refined Beauty* (Harrisonburg, 1813): 43–48, 144–149, 171–175, 227–228, 231–232.

FROM BOOK I

Through all the hall
A vote of cheerful approbation ran.
Then rose the guardian Spirit of Enterprise,
795 And thus address'd the Angelic convocation.
　　"Benevolent ministers of love! we well,
On this momentous era of our reign,
With gratulations may each other greet.
In fascinating perspective I see
800 Refinement's golden temple spread
Its softly-temper'd blaze, o'er all th'expanse,
Which from th'Alleganean Mountain's base,
Westward to the Pacific deeps extend—
I see its brilliance beaming from the Lakes,
805 Whose billows beat the cold Canadian shores
Along Ohio's smooth majestic stream,
And Mississippi's mighty flood to where,
In statelier pomp their mingled currents roll,
　　O'er distant Mexico's blue-bosom'd bay.
810 　With sun-brown'd check, and brow with odorous wreaths
Of clover bloom engarlanded, I see,
Young Agriculture smiling o'er the west;
While Labor's healthful sons around him flock,
And wait his mild commands. I see rich fields,
815 Green-waving Meads, and flosculous Gardens spread
Beneath his gladden'd eye, their copious stores:
While Plenty, Happiness, and Peace, and Joy,
Religion, Science, Truth, and Love, and all
The Virtues vivify, illume, refine,
820 Exalt, and sublime, the NEW-BORN WORLD!
　　Th'enrapturing scenes we soon shall realize,
Which warm prophetic Fancy here depicts,
If in pursuit of the benevolent end,
On which we have resolved, we delegate
825 To the high charge, a Hero, whom I long
Have train'd, with cheerful ease to undergo
Privations, dangers, pain, and solitude.
When oft thro' frigid storms, and forest-snows,

444

Without a friend, or fire, or even food,
830 Save what the desert gave, I've seen swift speed
To rouse from his thick lair, the antler'd Buck;
Or from their dark and solitary dens,
In dingles deep, or wildly-jutting cliffs,
To startle forth the grim predaceous Beasts;
835 The bounding Catamount, and meagre Wolf,
The surly Bear, and slaughter-hungering Panther:
A Hero whom no terrors can appal:
Whose bosom feels no fear, when lost in woods
The wildest that in all the mountain waste
840 By wintry winds are swept:—whose sinewy limbs
Can scale the roughest mountain's rocky steeps
With vigorous ease, nor feel a fibre fail,
Nor quicken'd breath, nor fluttering pulse, bespeak
Fatigue. But in his breast there beats a heart,
845 In which the warmest blood of Pity flows.
For though to him the chace affords delight,
As warranted by the Almighty's grant,
Within a limited extent; yet such
The Hero's tenderness, his soul revolts
850 From needless cruelty, to meanest life
He would not crush with wanton tread a fly,
Nor e'en with useless agonies of pain
Torment the poisonous snake. The tear of woe
Draws from his breast the sympathetic sigh,
855 And Sorrow's plaintive tale, and mournful mien,
Commisseration's tender throb awakes
Within his feeling heart. No passion reigns,
Tyrannic o'er his reason, Patriot love
With daring majesty his soul inspires,
860 And would with equal valor make him brave
The lurking dangers of the savage wild;
Or face in open field the frowning front
Of thundering Battle. Generous, guileless, kind,
The gripe of sneaking Avarice ne'er compress'd
865 His princely heart. No mean dissembling smiles,
Nor smooth, deceitful speech, his views conceal,
Nor form a feint his unsuspecting friends,
Within a venal snare to lure. He gives
To modest indigence, with bounteous will,
870 A liberal portion of his little store.
The ostentatious pageantry of power,
The moon-shine splendors of high-titled birth,
And fluttering Fashion's vain, fantastic pomp;
For his sage mind, no more attractions have,
875 Than shining gossamer upon the winds,

Or glittering froth, upon the turbid streams.
In fine, no Hero whom I've e'er inspir'd;
With more or higher Virtues is endued,
Or better qualified to fill the place,
880 For which we are about to make a choice,
Than DANIEL BOONE, th'adventurous Hunter, whom
I recommend. And he, by knowing well
The human heart, and having friends, whose souls
Like his, can dauntless, brave the stormy wilds;
885 Who th'anguish'd plaint attend, and kindly soothe
With sweet condolence Misery's bleeding woes—
Whose souls with magnanimity expand,
Sublimely soaring o'er the tinseled swarms,
Of Pride, and Fashion. With such means possess'd
890 Companions for the tour he can enlist,
Adapted well to such divine emprise,
If then, Angelic Peers! your judgments deem
Him worthy of the trust, so will you say."
      With undivided suffrage, the Divan,
895 The enterprising Angel's choice, approv'd:
And by their solemn institution gave,
To him, protection of the new-made CHIEF—
To him, by secret inspiration t'excite
The Hero's valorous soul, to undertake
900 The glorious enterprise, the task they gave.
Their great design for action, thus matur'd,
Th'enraptur'd convocation ere they rose,
Their praise in loud seraphic peans pour'd,
To that transcendently tremendous God,
905 Whose frown, an UNIVERSE, in gloom can shroud;
Whose smile, Illumination's purest blaze
Through an infinitude of Night can spread;
And with Refinement's ever-living blooms,
Creation's wildest WILDERNESS can clothe!——
910   RELIGIONS's sacred Seraph next, gave sign,
His hallow'd MAJESTY in prayer t'address—
When bowing low in suppliant attitude,
Their animated adorations forth,
The reverential congregation breathed:
915 And in a tone of warm pathetic zeal
Effused from lips bedewed with melting sweets;
With the nectarean quintessence of Love!
And honied balm of holy Eloquence!
Th'Almighty's kindly prospering smile implored,
920 Around the Hero's dreary path to beam,
And light him safely through each winding maze,
Until success his great adventure crowned.

Their pious service clos'd, the kneeling host
Arose; and nought their Session to prolong
925 Remaining now, the holy Synod was dissolv'd.
    Each Seraph spread his sparkling pinions wide;
And from the plume-bespangled portico,
Light bounded on the gently buoyant gales,
And swiftly sail'd to his appropriate Sphere.
930   So from their anchorage launch'd, majestic Ships,
The liquid deeps, in gallant beauty skim;
And seek o'er Wilds of Ocean far remote,
In various distant Realms, their native ports.

FROM BOOK V

    Again at length,
  A BROTHER's presence animates, with smiles
And sentimental solace, the dark WILDS;
85 Which they with mutual industry explore,
Until another Spring her bloom unveils.
Then Daniel Boone the mountains reascends,
Hies onward to his rural Domicil,
And meets once more, his rapture-swooning Wife,
90 And the endearing transports of sweet Babes.
He tells his wonder-kindling tales, while tears
And kind caresses speak the silent joys,
And melting admiration, which transport,
Intenerate, and thrill the tingling hearts
95 Of his dear Daughters and dove-bosom'd spouse.
While he the various scenes enumerates
Of perilous emprise, through which he'd passed,
The dawning valor of his youthful sons
Illume the trembling tears of filial love,
100 That gather in their agure-beaming eyes.
But most the account of his captivity,
And his companion Stewart's hapless doom,
Their ardor rous'd, and kindled the keen thirst
Of vengeance in their danger-daring breasts.
105 Like two young Lions in some desert Den,
When first their instinct fires begin to flame,
Impelling them to range the roaring Waste,
And try the vigor of their supple limbs

In valiant feats of blood; Boone's manly James
110 And Israel panted for the power to prove
    Their prowess, and avenge their Father's wrongs.
    Their minds dilated with the expanded view
    His strong descriptions gave of the rich WILDS;
    While prospects of magnanimous emprise,
115 And Fancy-pictur'd scenes of patriot fame;
    Establishing pure FREEDOM's prosperous States,
    Upon a base as lasting as the Hills,
    Their youthful souls with animation rapt.
       Quiescent, on the lap of PEACE and LOVE,
120 The three succeeding summers Boone repos'd,
    And then, preliminaries first arrang'd,
    The peaceful Yadkin left, and with his Wife,
    His Children, and five venturous Families more;
    Bidding adieu to Friends and scenes endear'd
125 By tenderest incidents of Love and Joy;
    Began, through gloomy wilds, the WESTERING MARCH.
      While on their weary way through Bowel's Vale,
    Two score Adventurers joined their jocund band.
    Dark labyrinthian Deserts, mountain Crags
130 Stupendous, frowning in the invaded clouds,
    And howling Monsters raging round for blood,
    Could not, with all their mingled glooms appall
    The spirits, or chill the animating Hopes
    That fir'd those gallant Sons of glorious Peril,
135 And urg'd them on their hazardous emprise.
    Unharm'd, they pass o'er two tremendous LIMBS
    Of branching Allegany—POWEL's MOUNT
    And WALDEN's named—There Nature's rudest wrath
    Seemed to have rag'd with wild disordering power—
140 Seem'd whilom to have op'd in warring fray,
    Her magazines of elemental ire—
    Her Tempests, Thunders, Lightnings, Earthquakes, Flames
    And rock-uprooting, furious WATER-SPOUTS!—
    Dark yawning ravines choak'd with broken crags,
145 Hoar rocks, in horror-frowning grandeur pil'd,
    Or pyramidical, transpiercing deep
    The thunder-bearing Tempests' cloudy breasts—
    And ragged Ridges high on Ridges heap'd!
    All seem'd memorials of Her phrenzied Mood.
150 These high colossal Hills securely pass'd,
    Their mazy course the Adventurers cheerly kept,
    Until with deathful yell, a savage Host
    Poured on their weak unguarded rear, the storms
    Of flaming murder. Then, oh gallant Boone!

155 With Battle-swaying Mars thy prowess vied!
    Thy Guardian Seraph's inspirations then
    Thou neededst not. Thy fallen fellows' blood
    The safety of thy Wife, thy Babes, and Friends,
    Were for thy valor stimulant enough!
160 The assailing Demons soon in wild dismay,
    Fled wounded, bleeding, from the torrent flames,
    Through which swift-flying bullets sought their lives.
    For well the ruthless onset was return'd;
    And dearly were its blood-effusions bought.
165 But ah! six valiant sons of enterprise,
    By its death-dealing, unsuspected blast,
    Were from their relatives and comrades torn!
    'Till then, such scene of Grief and Woe
    Had ne'er been witnessed in those spectral wilds.
170 Friends, Mothers, Fathers, Brothers, Sisters, all
    In doleful sadness weeping o'er the slain!—
    Uncoffin'd in the sun-unmellowed ground,
    'Neath gloomy Hemlock and dark-shaded spruce,
    Their noble corses colorless and cold,
175 With Sorrow's tearful streamlets were inter'd.
    Conspicuous fell our Hero's eldest son,
    His valiant James! The cruel ball that rent
    The tendrils of his blooming life in twain,
    And scattered on the waste its flow'ry charms,
180 Tore from the prospering PLANT of LIBERTY
    A germ, whose rich expanding beauties soon,
    Would have unfolded o'er the ample West;
    Diffusing round delectable perfumes,
    And dropping healthful fruitage on the lap
185 Of its luxuriant Land. That merciless ball,
    In its disaster-dealing impetus,
    Was not content, the crimson citadel
    Of human life, and the unsullied shrine
    Of fond affection only, to invade;
190 COLUMBIA's angel bosom felt its force,
    And bleeding at the pungent wound it trench'd,
    She sorrow'd o'er her youthful Hero's fate.
    And she had cause to sorrow; for in him
    She lost the promise of a patriot son,
195 Of an intrepid, wise and virtuous man!
    Irradiated with the expanding rays
    Of Erudition, his untarnished mind,
    With eye intent on Truth's effulgent disk,
    Was soaring o'er the clouds of groveling life.
200 His fellows in the *Intellectual* flight

Can well attest, with what ascending strength
He scal'd the intervening steeps, and shot
His genius-plumed pinions through the blaze
That pour'd upon his soul-subliming path;
205 That still in more resplendent torrents stream'd
As nearer to the lambent Orb he drew.
But ah! the whizzing pellet, bearing death,
Relaxed his wing, and drown'd his flight in blood!
Behold the snowy plumage sinking now,
210 All stain'd and dripping with the purp'ling streams!
Yet see! 'tis not the *Spirit's* plumes that fall;
It is the weaker wing of *mortal life*!
The wing, which buoys the encumbering clog of clay!
The soul, in all its bright embellishment,
215 Is free, and flies, with unimpeded speed.
To the supernal goal that caught its ken
From earth, the flaming fount of holy Truth!—

FROM BOOK VI

The Western Wilderness had now begun
To pour its fragrance with attractive power,
Wide o'er Columbia's cultivated states;
And several families to its solitudes
5   Had charm'd. Innumerous were the dangers, pains,
Perplexities, and hardships, which beset
On every side the infant settlers. Boone,
With warm benevolence their wants relieved;
And his protecting shield before them threw,
10   When DANGER menacing their daring breasts,
Drew from its quiver'd side the gory shafts
Of Death. The sick, the poor, the timid, all,
His friendship and significence partook.
Fatigue-emaciated females, babes
15   With hunger, wan and weeping, often own'd
His generous aid, and with their tear-dew'd smiles,
And looks of tender gratitude repaid
His bounteous kindness. Furiously incensed
With the incursions on their rude domain,

20 And by the caitiff fiends of nether Night impel'd;
    The ruthless natives marshal'd all their might,
    The feeble *colony* to mar; to tear,
    Divine Refinement's pullulating plants
    From their destruction-compass'd beds, and blast
25 Their little tender blooms! Ah! much indeed
    By the rude rage of barbarous violence,
    The fragrant germs were ravaged torn and chill'd!
    But still their bold protector's guardian arm
    The extirpation-threatening powers repel'd.
30 Ofttimes the feeble Fortresses, the brunt
    Of fierce assault sustain'd; and often fell,
    Behind the startled team, the murder'd swain;
    The family's laboring stay! and bleeding died,
    In the unsupported plough's unfinish'd trench.
35 Hostilities of minor moment thus were waged,
    Until the opening of another spring.
    Then savage WAR's blood-streaming orb began,
    With more portentous terror o'er the wild,
    To lift its awful disk. Assembled hordes
40 Of the horrific foe, our Hero's Fort
    With furious rage attack'd. The well wrought walls
    Indignantly the thundering shock withstood:
    Its fires the gallant garrison return'd,
    With triple execution. Costea led
45 The tawny bands, and saw with painful rage,
    Their bleeding ranks cut down. Reluctantly
    At length the siege was raised; and through the brakes,
    The fallen Indians' breathless bodies drag'd,
    To where the howling Squaws with anguish mourn'd
50 Their lifeless warriors' fate. Defeat but fired
    The fiends with hotter fury. Costea's soul
    For dreadful vengeance flamed. From breast to breast,
    The burning passions spread their kindling rage
    And soon the yell and war-hoop shook the hills,
55 And echoed o'er the forests' drear expanse.
    Like clouds electric scatter'd round the Heavens,
    In small detachments ireful, dusky, red,
    When the discordant wrath and tumults fierce
    Of jarring matter, into masses drive
60 Their angry bands; so rush'd the savage hordes,
    By fury urged, and form'd a direful Host.
    Their Chiefs in short harangue, the ills portray'd
    That o'er their heads in threatening horrors hung.
    They bade them save from WHITEMEN's plundering grasp
65 Their ground, their game, their fruit, their fish, their streams,

Their Freedom, Peace, their Children, Wives and ALL
   To break their strength, the different Forts
By the divided ruffians were besieg'd.
On either side much blood the conflicts mark'd;
70 But such the valor, energy and skill
Of the advent'rous Settlers, that their guns
The plumes of daring confidence shot off,
Which proudly wav'd above the savage heads,
And drove again the bleeding legions back
75 To their rude huts. The flaming tempest hurl'd
Its heaviest bolts against the garrison
Of Boone. Two days and nights the volley'd blasts
Upon the bastion'd fortress ceaseless beat.
But, from the little Bulwark's guarded band,
80 A counter storm, on which death-dealing rode
Destruction's Angel terrible and dark,
Incessantly was driv'n, until the foe,
In bloody ghastliness, and sullen rage,
Retir'd—But still their ire was not allay'd—
85 Their savage armies every week assail'd
The suffering Settlers. Logan's Station stood,
With valorous strength, a fierce distressful siege;
And Harrod's too repel'd the roaring shocks
Of many a powerful assault. At length,
90 From Carolina and Virginia came
To their relief a timely aid; and strung
With nerves of more intrepid enterprise
Their sinking spirits. Strengthen'd thus, their power
For months, in each succeeding battle blaz'd,
95 In hotter torrents on the assailants heads;
And hurried headlong into the deep gurge
Of dark Eternity, the yelling ghosts
Of many a ghastly corse.
     The foe thus foil'd,
Began to feel and dread the conquering force
100 Of the "LONG KNIFE." Its anger-sharpen'd edge
They found resistless as the scythe of Death!—
The blood-polluted glooms that dim'd the West,
Now 'gan a more propitious face to wear;
And from the attenuated Darkness broke,
105 At intervals, bright gleams. But Boone not long
In the benignant coruscations bask'd.
All times dispos'd and sedulous to serve
The Settlers, he to Licking River went,
With a small party of industrious men,
110 To explore and chrystallize the saline streams,

And salt for the brave Garrisons procure.
Through Winter's *bleakest* reign, alternately
In the kind task his coajuvancy
Was giv'n, by labor at the evaporating fires,
115 And procuration of the forest food,
On which himself and comrades were sustain'd.

FROM BOOK VII

Columbia's Western Star in splendors now,
Through an unclouded azure streaming, sheds
On drooping hearts, the beams of sweetest Hope;
795 And withers to a scroll the grumous flag
Of groaning War. His labors, Boone beholds
Unfolding their rich Comforts o'er the West:
While Amity's restrictive bonds confine
The nerves of savage Slaughter. Happy now,
800 In contemplation of the brightening scene,
He to AFFECTION's sweet embrace retires;
And reaps the Harvest of his useful toils.
Immortal Founder of stupendous States!
While generous prowess wakes the soul's applause;
805 While consecration to a Nation's weal
Of all the energies of Mind and Nerve,
Enkindles warm sensations of regard;
Thy name, in Freedom's sun-crown'd Fane enshrined,
With the rich incense of a Million's love
810 Embalmed, shall live. How rapturous to thy heart,
Thou venerable Hero! How sublime,
How beauteous, how divine! the prospect now
Of that Republic, which thy patriot hand
Implanted in the direful Wilderness.
815 Lo! flourishing uncankered, and Immense,
It strengthens, rises, spreads and blooms to Heaven!
Its branches mingle with the stars; and crown'd
With Harps Angelic, wave mid purest gales
Celestial; animate with melody,
820 By Freedom's Seraph Martyrs sweetly made;
And fragrant as the fruits of Paradise.

. . . .

My patriotic Sisters of the West!
Accept this humble plaudit of a heart
910 That loves you dearly. High indeed the praise,
And happily received; could you approve
For Freedom's sake my unpresuming Song
Oft through admiring, Fancy's eye, I've seen
Your lilly fingers, form the Warrior's robe;
915 And sorely wounded with the piercing steel,
The honored garment with pure crimson stain;
Leaving expressive emblems of the Deeds
He should achieve; and symbols of the love
Your bosoms for the gallant soldier bore.
920 Oft too your tender bodings I have seen
And anxious Hopes; while undecided yet
Remained the destiny of those ye loved,
Your valiant Countrymen! Oh! when arrived
The agonizing tidings of defeat—
925 Of the *perfidious* Massacres that stained
With infamy a butchering foe; and tore
From many a noble head the streaming scalp;
Where fell those dearer far perhaps than life;
How were your anguished and indignant breasts
930 With keen and violent emotions pained;
But when the joyous news of Conquest came,
How changed your feelings; how divinely sweet;
How glowing then with thankful extacies!
And when the honored soldier home returned,
935 What kind, what tender welcomes ye bestowed!
How carefully his rankling wounds deterged;
And with attentions bland and smiles benign,
Rewarded all his dangers, pains and toils.—
This magic theme could long my Muse detain,
940 But lo! her desultorious song draws nigh
Its beckoning goal; and we, sweet Fair, must part!
Perennial as the charms of the rich land,
Whose healthful gales your honied breath perfumes,
May your bright Virtues bloom; to crown with bliss
The gallant Boone's the shields of Honors's shrine!
946 Who share the mild dominions of your Love,
And drive the Myrmidons of Tyrant thrones
From their ensanguined Cars. And ye pure States,
The Western Pillars of Columbia's Dome,
950 The Dome of Liberty! Still may ye stand
With glories of ten thousand Boones emblazed;
Sustaining with distinguished eminence.
Your portion of the Edifice sublime;

While Kingdoms disappear in floods of gore
955 And Revolutions rock the reeking globe:
Yea, till the pageant Bubbles of the World
Are into dread Annihilation blown;
And Oceans, Suns and Spheres before the blaze
Of Heaven's avenging Anger, are consumed!——

28

AUGUSTUS BALDWIN LONGSTREET

(1790–1870)

Augustus Baldwin Longstreet spent the first decade of his life in Augusta, Georgia. His earliest schooling was at Augusta's Richmond Academy, but that school closed in 1798. Longstreet's mother was determined "to give [her children] a good education as it [was] all [their family could] do for them." This may explain the Longstreet family's move across the Savannah River to Edgefield District, South Carolina, where Longstreet might attend Gumtree Academy. The boy flourished in Edgefield—but not in the ways that his mother had hoped.

Longstreet described the closing of Richmond Academy as "a joyous release." In the rough-and-tumble frontier town of Edgefield, his "highest ambition was to out-run, out-jump, out-shoot, throw down and whip, any man in the district." In time he became "expert as a cotton picker, a wrestler, and a marksman." But Longstreet's "joyous release" would be short-lived. Richmond Academy reopened in late 1802, and sometime thereafter Longstreet received "the heart-sinking order" that he must return to his "hated penitentiary." He would not forget, however, the frontier life that he so enjoyed.

After attending Moses Waddel's famous academy in Willington, South Carolina, Longstreet matriculated at Yale in 1811. His career as a storyteller seems to have begun here. While in college, Longstreet regaled his teachers and fellow students with stories of life on the southern frontier. Many of these would later appear in his first and most famous book: *Georgia Scenes, Characters, Incidents, Etc. in the First Half Century of the Republic* (1835).

After Yale, Longstreet attended Tapping Reeve's law school in Litchfield, Connecticut. He returned to Georgia in 1814 and passed the bar in 1815. By his own account, he "was especially distinguished for his efforts and successes in criminal cases," and he served a successful term as a superior court judge. But Longstreet had a restless ambition. He dabbled in a variety of other careers, including state senator, newspaper editor, minister, political propagandist, and—most extensively—college president.

Today Longstreet is remembered most often for another of his dabblings: fiction writing. Though he is often classified as a humorist, Longstreet thought of himself as a social historian. When he realized that the frontier world of his youth was disappearing around him, he felt compelled to put his stories on paper. Longstreet wrote, "I have chosen [as my subject] the first fifty years of our republic in the course of which short space of time the society of the Southern States underwent almost an entire revolution, and at this date hardly a trace of the society of the first thirty years of the republic is to be found."

Longstreet lived for thirty-five years after the publication of *Georgia Scenes*. In that time he published only a handful of new short stories and one novel: the mediocre *Master William Mitten: or, A Youth of Brilliant Talents, Who Was Ruined by Bad Luck* (1864). Most of Longstreet's later writings were political. He defended slavery; he tried to avoid a civil war; and when the war came, he supported the Confederate cause. When, in 1862, federal troops reached Oxford, Mississippi, they burned Longstreet's house with his papers as their kindling. Longstreet and his family fled Oxford, but they returned after the war. Longstreet died there on July 9, 1870.

Text: *Georgia Scenes, Characters, Incidents, Etc. in the First Half Century of the Republic* (Augusta, 1835): "The Fight," 53–66; "The Shooting Match," 215–235.

THE FIGHT (1833, 1835)

In the younger days of the Republic, there lived in the county of ——, two men, who were admitted on all hands to be the very *best men* in the county—which, in the Georgia vocabulary, means they could flog any other two men in the county. Each, through many a hard fought battle, had acquired the mastery of his own battalion; but they lived on opposite sides of the Court House, and in different battalions: consequently they were but seldom thrown together. When they met, however, they were always very friendly; indeed, at their first interview, they seemed to conceive a wonderful attachment to each other, which rather increased than diminished, as they became better acquainted; so that, but for the circumstance which I am about to mention, the question which had been a thousand times asked "Which is the best man, Billy Stallions, (Stallings,) or Bob Durham?" would probably never have been answered.

Billy ruled the upper battalion, and Bob the lower. The former measured six feet and an inch, in his stockings, and without a single pound of cumbrous flesh about him weighed a hundred and eighty. The latter, was an inch shorter than his rival, and ten pounds lighter; but he was much the most active of the two. In running and jumping, he had but few equals in the county; and in wrestling, not one. In other respects they were nearly equal. Both were admirable specimens of human nature in its finest form. Billy's victories had generally been achieved by the tremendous power of his blows; one of which had often proved decisive of his battles; Bob's, by his adroitness in bringing his adversary to the ground. This advantage he had never failed to gain, at the onset, and when gained, he never failed to improve it to the defeat of his adversary. These points of difference, have involved the reader in a doubt, as to the probable issue of a contest between them. It was not so, however, with the two battalions. Neither had the least difficulty in determining the point by the most natural and irresistible deductions *a priori:* and though, by the same course of reasoning, they arrived at directly opposite conclusions, neither felt its confidence in the least shaken by this circumstance. The upper battalion swore "that Billy only wanted one lick at him to knock his heart, liver and lights out of him; and if he got two at him, he'd knock him into a cocked hat." The lower battalion retorted, "that he would'nt have time to double his fist, before Bob would put his head where his feet ought to be; and that, by the time he hit the ground, the meat would fly off his face so quick, that people would think it was shook off by the fall." These disputes often lead to the *argumentum ad hominem;* but with such equality of success on both sides, as to leave the main question just where they found it. They usually ended, however, in the common way, with a bet; and many a quart of old Jamaica, (whiskey had not then supplanted rum,) were staked upon the issue. Still, greatly to the annoyance of the curious, Billy and Bob continued to be good friends.

Now there happened to reside in the county, just alluded to, a little fellow, by the name of Ransy Sniffle: a sprout of Richmond, who, in his earlier days, had fed copiously upon red clay and blackberries. This diet had given to Ransy a complexion that a corpse would have disdained to own, and an abdominal rotundity that was quite unprepossessing. Long spells of the fever and ague, too, in Ransy's youth, had conspired with clay and blackberries, to throw him quite out of the order of nature. His shoulders were fleshless and elevated; his head large and flat; his neck slim and translucent; and his arms, hands, fingers and feet, were lengthened out of all proportion to the rest of his frame. His joints were large, and his limbs small; and as for flesh, he could not with propriety be said to have any. Those parts which nature usually supplies with the most of this article—the calves of the legs for example—presented in him the appearance of so many well drawn blisters. His height was just five feet nothing; and his average weight in blackberry season, ninety-five. I have been thus particular in describing him, for the purpose of showing what a great matter a little fire sometimes kindleth. There was nothing on this earth which delighted Ransy so much as a fight. He never seemed fairly alive, except when he was witnessing, fomenting, or talking about a fight. Then, indeed, his deep sunken grey eye, assumed something of a living fire; and his tongue acquired a volubility that bordered upon eloquence. Ransy had been kept for more than a year in the most torturing suspense, as to the comparative manhood of Billy Stallings and Bob Durham. He had resorted to all his usual expedients to bring them in collision, and had entirely failed. He had faithfully reported to Bob all that had been said by the people in the upper battalion "agin him," and "he was sure Billy Stallings started it. He heard Bill say himself, to Jim Brown, that he could whip him, *or any other man in his battalion;*" and this he told to Bob—adding, "Dod durn his soul, if he was a little bigger, if he'd let any man *put upon* his battalion in such a way." Bob replied, "If he, (Stallings) thought so, he'd better come and try it." This Ransy carried to Billy, and delivered it with a spirit becoming his own dignity, and the character of his battalion, and with a coloring well calculated to give it effect. These, and many other schemes which Ransy laid, for the gratification of his curiosity, entirely failed of their object. Billy and Bob continued friends, and Ransy had began to lapse into the most tantalizing and hopeless despair, when a circumstance occurred, which led to a settlement of the long disputed question.

It is said that a hundred game cocks will live in perfect harmony together, if you will not put a hen with them: and so it would have been with Billy and Bob, had there been no women in the world. But there were women in the world, and from them, each of our heroes had taken to himself a wife. The good ladies were no strangers to the prowess of their husbands, and strange as it may seem, they presumed a little upon it.

The two battalions had met at the Court House, upon a regimental parade. The two champions were there, and their wives had accompanied them. Neither knew the other's lady, nor were the ladies known to each other. The exercises of the day were just over, when Mrs. Stallings and Mrs. Durham stept simultaneously into the store of Zepheniah Atwater, from "down east."

"Have you any Turkey-red?" said Mrs. S.

"Have you any curtain calico?" said Mrs. D. at the same moment.

"Yes, ladies," said Mr. Atwater, "I have both."

"Then help me first," said Mrs. D., "for I'm in a hurry."

"I'm in as great a hurry as she is," said Mrs. S., "and I'll thank you to help me first."

"And pray, who are you, madam!" continued the other.

"Your betters, madam," was the reply.

At this moment Billy Stallings stept in. "Come," said he, "Nancy, lets be going; it's getting late."

"I'd o' been gone half an hour ago," she replied, "if it had'nt o' been for that impudent huzzy."

"Who do you call an impudent huzzy? you nasty, good-for-nothing, snaggle-toothed gaub of fat, you," returned Mrs. D.

"Look here woman," said Billy, "have you got a husband here? If you have, I'll *lick* him till he learns to teach you better manners, you *sassy* heifer you." At this moment something was seen to rush out of the store, as if ten thousand hornets were stinging it; crying "Take care—let me go—don't hold me—where's Bob Durham?" It was Ransy Sniffle, who had been listening in breathless delight, to all that had passed.

"Yonder's Bob, setting on the Court-house steps," cried one. "What's the matter?"

"Don't talk to me!" said Ransy. "Bob Durham, you'd better go long yonder, and take care of your wife. They're playing h—l with her there, in Zeph. Atwater's store. Dod deternally durn my soul, if any man was to talk to my wife as Bill Stallions is talking to yours, if I did'nt drive blue blazes through him in less than no time."

Bob sprang to the store in a minute, followed by a hundred friends; for the bully of a county never wants friends.

"Bill Stallions," said Bob, as he entered, "what have you been saying to my wife?"

"Is that your wife?" inquired Billy, obviously much surprised, and a little disconcerted.

"Yes, she is, and no man shall abuse her, I don't care who he is."

"Well," rejoined Billy, "it an't worth while to go over it—I've said enough for a fight: and if you'll step out, we'll settle it!"

"Billy," said Bob, "are you for a fair fight?"

"I am," said Billy. "I've heard much of your manhood, and I believe I'm a better man than you are. If you will go into a ring with me, we can soon settle the dispute."

"Choose your friends," said Bob; "make your ring, and I'll be in it with mine, as soon as you will."

They both stept out, and began to strip very deliberately; each battalion gathering round its champion—except Ransy, who kept himself busy, in a most honest endeavor to hear and see all that transpired in both groups, at the same time. He ran from one to the other, in quick succession—peeped here, and listened there—talked to this one—then to that one—and then to himself—squatted under one's legs, and another's arms; and in the short interval between stripping and stepping into the ring, managed to get himself trod on by half of both battalions. But Ransy was not the only one interested upon this occasion:—the most intense interest prevailed every where. Many were the conjectures, doubts, oaths and imprecations uttered, while the parties were preparing for the combat. All the knowing ones were consulted as to the issue; and they all agreed to a man, in one of two opinions: either that Bob would flog Billy, or Billy would flog Bob. We must be permitted, however, to dwell for a moment upon the opinion of 'Squire Thomas Loggins; a man, who it was said, had never failed to predict the issue of a fight, in all his life. Indeed, so unerring had he always proved, in this regard, that it would have been counted the most obstinate infidelity, to doubt for a moment, after he had delivered himself. 'Squire Loggins was a man who said but little; but that little was always delivered with the most imposing solemnity of look and cadence. He always wore the aspect of profound thought, and you could not look at him without coming to the conclusion, that he was elaborating truth from its most intricate combinations.

"Uncle Tommy," said Sam Reynolds, "you can tell us all about it, if you will—how will the fight go?"

The question immediately drew an anxious group around the 'Squire. He raised his teeth slowly from the head of his walking cane, on which they had been resting—pressed his lips closely and thoughtfully together—threw down his eye brows—dropped his chin—raised his eyes to an angle of twenty three degrees—paused about half a minute, and replied: "Sammy, watch Robert Durham close in the beginning of the fight—take care of William Stallions in the middle of it ——— and see who has the wind at the end." As he uttered the last member of the sentence, he looked slily at Bob's friends, and winked very significantly; whereupon they rushed, with one accord, to tell Bob what uncle Tommy had said. As they retired, the 'Squire turned to Billy's friends, and said, with a smile: "Them boys think I mean that Bob will whip."

Here the other party kindled into joy, and hastened to inform Billy how Bob's friends had deceived themselves as to Uncle Tommy's opinion. In the meantime, the principals and seconds, were busily employed in preparing themselves for the combat. The plan of attack and defence, the manner of improving the various turns of the conflict, "the best mode of saving wind," &c. &c. were all discussed and settled. At length, Billy announced himself ready, and his crowd were seen moving to the centre of the Court House Square; he and his five seconds in the rear. At the same time, Bob's party moved to the same point, and in the same order. The ring was now formed, and for a moment the silence of death reigned through both battalions. It was soon interrupted, however, by the cry of "clear the way!" from Billy's seconds; when the ring opened in the centre of the upper battalion, (for the order of march had arranged the centre of the two battalions on opposite sides of the circle,) and Billy stept into the ring from the east, followed by his friends. He was strip to the trowsers, and exhibited an arm, breast and shoulders, of the most tremendous portent. His step was firm, daring and martial; and as he bore his fine form a little in advance of his friends, an involuntary burst of triumph broke from his side of the ring; and at the same moment, an uncontrollable thrill of awe, ran along the whole curve of the lower battalion.

"Look at him!" was heard from his friends—"just look at him."

"Ben, how much you ask to stand before that man two seconds?"

"Pshaw, don't talk about it! Just thinkin' about it's broke three o'my ribs a'ready!"

"What's Bob Durham going to do, when Billy let's that arm loose upon him?"

"God bless your soul, he'll think thunder and lightning a mint julip to it."

"Oh, look here men, go take Bill Stallions out o' that ring, and bring in Phil Johnson's stud horse, so that Durham may have some chance! I don't want to see the man killed right away."

These and many other like expressions, interspersed thickly with oaths of the most modern coinage, were coming from all points of the upper battalion, while Bob was adjusting the girth of his pantaloons, which walking had discovered, not to be exactly right. It was just fixed to his mind, his foes becoming a little noisy, and his friends a little uneasy at his delay, when Billy called out, with a smile of some meaning, "Where's the bully of the lower battalion? I'm getting tired of waiting."

"Here he is," said Bob, lighting, as it seemed from the clouds in the ring, for he had actually bounded clear of the head of Ransy Sniffle, into the circle. His descent was quite as imposing as Billy's entry, and excited the same feelings, but in opposite bosoms.

Voices of exultation now rose on his side.

"Where did he come from?"

"Why," said one of his seconds, (all having just entered,) "we were girting him up, about a hundred yards out yonder, when he heard Billy ask for the bully; and he fetched a leap over the Court House, and went out of sight; but I told them to come on, they'd find him here."

Here the lower battalion burst into a peal of laughter, mingled with a look of admiration, which seemed to denote their entire belief of what they had heard.

"Boys widen the ring, so as to give him room to jump."

"Oh, my little flying wild cat, hold him if you can! and when you get him fast, hold lightning next."

"Ned what you think he's made of?"

"Steel-springs and chicken-hawk, God bless you!"

"Gentlemen," said one of Bob's seconds, "I understand it is to be a fair fight; catch as catch can, rough and tumble:—no man touch 'till one or the other hollos."

"That's the rule," was the reply from the other side.

"Are you ready?"

"We are ready."

"Then blaze away my game cocks!"

At the word, Bob dashed at his antagonist at full speed; and Bill squared himself to receive him with one of his most fatal blows. Making his calculation from Bob's velocity, of the time when he would come within striking distance, he let drive with tremendous force. But Bob's onset was obviously planned to avoid this blow; for contrary to all expectations, he stopt short just out of arms reach; and before Billy could recover his balance—Bob had him "all under-hold." The next second, sure enough, "found Billy's head where his feet ought to be." How it was done, no one could tell; but as if by supernatural power, both Billy's feet were thrown full half his own height in the air, and he came down with a force that seemed to shake the earth. As he struck the ground, commingled shouts, screams and yells burst from the lower battalion, loud enough to be heard for miles. "Hurra my little hornet!"—"Save him!"—"Feed him!—Give him the Durham physic till his stomach turns!" Billy was no sooner down than Bob was on him, and lending him awful blows about the face and breast. Billy made two efforts to rise by main strength, but failed. "Lord bless you man, don't try to get up!—*Lay* still and take it!—you *bleege* to have it."

Billy now turned his face suddenly to the ground, and rose upon his hands and knees. Bob jerked up both his hands and threw him on his face. He again recovered his late position, of which Bob endeavored to deprive him as before; but missing one arm, he failed, and Billy rose. But he had scarcely resumed his feet before they flew up as before, and he came again to the ground. "No fight gentlemen!" cried Bob's friends, "the man can't stand up!—Bouncing feet are bad things to fight in." His fall, however, was this time comparatively light; for having thrown his right arm round Bob's neck, he carried his head down with him. This grasp, which was obstinately maintained, prevented Bob from getting on him, and they lay head to head, seeming, for a time, to do nothing. Presently they rose, as if by mutual consent; and as they rose, a shout broke from both battalions. "Oh, my lark!" cried the east, "has he foxed you? Do you begin to feel him! He's only beginning to fight—He ain't got warm yet."

"Look yonder!" cried the west—"did'nt I tell you so! He hit the ground so hard, it jarred his nose off. Now ain't he a pretty man as he stands? He shall have my sister Sall just for his pretty looks. I want to get in the breed of them sort o' men, to drive ugly out of my kin folks."

I looked and saw that Bob had entirely lost his left ear, and a large piece from his left check. His right eye was a little discolored, and the blood flowed profusely from his wounds.

Bill presented a hideous spectacle. About a third of his nose, at the lower extremity, was bit off, and his face so swelled and bruised, that it was difficult to discover in it any thing of the human visage—much more the fine features which he carried into the ring.

They were up only long enough for me to make the foregoing discoveries, when down they went again, precisely as before. They no sooner touched the ground than Bill relinquished his hold upon Bob's neck. In this, he seemed to all, to have forfeited the only advantage which put him upon an equality with his adversary. But the movement was soon explained. Bill wanted this arm for other purposes than defence; and he had made arrangements whereby he knew that he could make it answer these purposes; for when they rose again, he had the middle finger of Bob's left hand in his mouth. He was now secure from Bob's annoying trips; and he began to lend his adversary most tremendous blows, every one of which was hailed by a shout from his friends. "Bullets!—*Hoss* kicking!—Thunder!—"—"That'll do for the face—now feel his short ribs, Billy!"

I now considered the contest settled. I deemed it impossible for any human being to withstand for five seconds, the loss of blood which issued from Bob's ear, cheek, nose and finger, accompanied with such blows as he was receiving. Still he maintained the conflict, and gave blow for blow with considerable effect. But the blows of each became slower and weaker, after the first three or four; and it became obvious, that Bill wanted the room, which Bob's finger occupied, for breathing. He would therefore, probably, in a short time, have let it go, had not Bob anticipated his politeness, by jerking away his hand, and making him a present of the finger. He now seized Bill again, and brought him to his knees—but he recovered. He again brought him to his knees; and he again recovered. A third effort, however, brought him down, and Bob on top of him. These efforts seemed to exhaust the little remaining strength of both; and they lay, Bill undermost, and Bob across his breast, motionless, and panting for breath. After a short pause, Bob gathered his hand full of dirt and sand, and was in the act of grinding it in his adversary's eyes, when Bill cried "ENOUGH!"—Language cannot describe the scene which followed—the shouts, oaths, frantic jestures, taunts, replies and little fights; and therefore I shall not attempt it. The champions were borne off by their seconds, and washed; when many a bleeding wound, and ugly bruise, was discovered on each, which no eye had seen before.

Many had gathered round Bob, and were in various ways congratulating and applauding him, when a voice from the centre of the circle cried out: "Boys, hush and listen to me!" It proceeded from Squire Loggins, who had made his way to Bob's side, and had gathered his face up into one of its most flattering and intelligible expressions. All were obedient to the Squire's command. "Gentlemen, continued he, with a most knowing smile, "is—Sammy—Reynold—in—this—company—of—gentlemen." "Yes," said Sam, "here I am." "Sammy," said the Squire, winking to the company, and drawing the head of his cane to his mouth with an arch smile, as he closed, "I—wish—you—to tell—cousin—Bobby—and—these—gentlemen here present—what—your—uncle—Tommy—said—before—the—fight—began?" "Oh! get away, uncle Tom," says Sam, smiling, (the Squire winked,) "you don't know nothing about *fighting*." (The 'Squire winked again.) "All you know about it, is how it 'll begin; how it 'll go on; how it 'll end; that's all. Cousin Bob, when you going to fight again, just go to the old man, and let him tell you all about it. If he can't, don't ask nobody else nothing about it, I tell you." The Squire's foresight was complimented in many ways by the by-standers; and he retired, advising "the boys to be at peace, as fighting was a bad business."

Durham and Stallings kept their beds for several weeks, and did not meet again for two months. When they met, Billy stepped up to Bob and offered his hand, saying: "Bobby you've *licked* me a fair fight; but you would'nt have done it, if I had'nt been in the wrong. I ought'nt to have treated your wife as I did; and I felt so through the whole fight, and it sort o' cowed me."

"Well Billy," said Bob, let's be friends. Once in the fight, when you had my finger in your mouth, and was pealing me in the face and breast, I was going to hollo; but I thought of Betsy, and knew the house would be too hot for me, if I got whipt, when fighting for her, after always whipping when I fought for myself."

"Now, that's what I always love to see," said a bystander: "It's true, I brought about the fight; but I would'nt have done it, if it had'nt o' been on account of *Miss,* (Mrs.) Durham. But dod deternally durn my soul, if I ever could stand by and see any woman put upon—much less *Miss* Durham. If Bobby had'nt been there, I'd o' took it up myself, be durned if I would'nt, even if I'd o' got whipt for it—But we're all friends now." The reader need hardly be told, this was Ransy Sniffle.

Thanks to the Christian religion, to schools, colleges, and benevolent associations, such scenes of barbarism and cruelty, as that which I have been just describing, are now of rare occurrence: though they may still be occasionally met with in some of the new counties. Wherever they prevail, they are a disgrace to that community. The peace officers who countenance them, deserve a place in the Penitentiary.

HALL.

THE SHOOTING MATCH (1835)

Shooting matches are probably nearly coeval with the colonization of Georgia. They are still common throughout the Southern States; though they are not as common as they were twenty-five or thirty years ago. Chance led me to one about a year ago. I was travelling in one of the north-eastern counties, when I overtook a swarthy, bright-eyed, smerky little fellow, riding a small poney, and bearing on his shoulder a long heavy rifle, which, judging from its looks, I should say had done service in Morgan's corps.

"Good morning, sir!" said I, reining up my horse as I came beside him.

"How goes it stranger?" said he, with a tone of independence and self-confidence, that awaked my curiosity to know a little of his character.

"Going driving?" inquired I.

"Not exactly," replied he, surveying my horse with a quizical smile, "I haven't been a driving *by myself* for a year or two, and my nose has got so bad lately I can't carry a cold trail *without hounds to help me.*"

Alone, and without hounds, as he was, the question was rather a silly one; but it answered the purpose for which it was put, which was only to draw him into conversation, and I proceeded to make as decent a retreat as I could.

"I didn't know," said I, "but that you were going to meet the huntsmen, or going to your stand."

"Ah, sure enough," rejoined he, "that *mout* be a bee, as the old woman said when she killed a wasp. It seems to me I ought to know you."

"Well, if you *ought*, why *don't* you?"

"What *mout* your name be?"

"It *might* be any thing," said I, with borrowed wit; for I knew my man, and knew what kind of conversation would please him most.

"Well, what *is* it then?"

"It *is*, Hall," said I; "but you know it might as well have been any thing else."

"Pretty digging!" said he. "I find you're not the fool I took you to be; so here's to a better acquaintance with you."

"With all my heart," returned I; "but you must be as clever as I've been, and give me your name."

"To be sure I will, my old coon—take it—take it, and welcome. Any thing else about me you'd like to have?"

"No," said I, "there's nothing else about you worth having."

"Oh, yes there is, stranger! Do you see this?" holding up his ponderous rifle with an ease that astonished me. "If you will go with me to the shooting match, and see me knock out the *bull's-eye* with her a few times, you'll agree the old *Soap-stick's* worth something when Billy Curlew puts his shoulder to her."

This short sentence was replete with information to me. It taught me that my companion was *Billy Curlew*; that he was going to a *Shooting match*; that he called his rifle the *Soap-stick*, and that he was very confident of winning beef with her; or, which is nearly, but not quite the same thing, *driving the cross with her.*

"Well," said I, "if the shooting match is not too far out of my way, I'll go to it with pleasure."

"Unless your way lies through the woods from here," said Billy, "it'll not be much out of your way; for it's only a mile ahead of us, and there is no other road for you to take, till you get there; and as that thing you're riding in, an't well suited to fast travelling, among brushy knobs, I reckon you won't lose much by going by. I reckon you hardly ever was at a shooting match, stranger, from the cut of your coat?"

"Oh yes," returned I, "many a time. I won beef at one, when I was hardly old enough to hold a shot-gun off-hand."

"*Children* don't go to shooting matches about here," said he, with a smile of incredulity. "I never heard of but one that did, and he was a little *swinge-cat.*—He was born a shooting, and killed squirrels before he was weaned."

"Nor did *I* ever hear of but one," replied I, "and that one was myself."

"And where did you win beef so young, stranger?"

"At Berry Adams'."

"Why stop, stranger, let me look at you good! Is your name *Lyman* Hall?"

"The very same," said I.

"Well, dang my buttons, if you an't the very boy my daddy used to tell me about. I was too young to recollect you myself; but I've heard daddy talk about you many a time. I believe mammy's got a neck-handkerchief now, that daddy won on your shooting at Collen Reid's store, when you were hardly knee high. Come along Lyman, and I'll go my death upon you at the shooting match, with the old Soap-stick at your shoulder."

"Ah, Billy," said I, "the old Soap-stick will do much better at your own shoulder. It was my mother's notion, that sent me to the shooting match at Berry Adams'; and to tell you the honest truth, it was altogether a chance shot that made me win beef; but that wasn't generally known; and most every body believed that I was carried there on account of my skill in shooting; and my fame was spread far and wide, I well remember. I remember too, perfectly well, your father's bet on me, at the store. *He* was at the shooting match, and nothing could make him believe, but that I was a great shot with a rifle, as well as a shot-gun. Bet he would, on me, in spite of all I could say; though I assured him, that I had never shot a rifle in my life. It so happened too, that there were but two bullets, or rather, a bullet and a half; and so confident was your father in my skill, that he made me shoot the half bullet; and, strange to tell, by another chance shot I like to have drove the cross, and won his bet."

"Now I know you're the very chap; for I heard daddy tell that very thing about the half bullet. Don't say any thing about it, Lyman, and durn my old shoes it I don't tare the lint off the boys with you at the shooting match. They'll never 'spect such a looking man as you are of knowing any thing about a rifle. I'll risk your *chance* shots."

I soon discovered that the father had eaten sour grapes, and the son's teeth were on edge; for Billy was just as incorrigibly obstinate, in his belief of my dexterity with a rifle, as his father had been before him.

We soon reached the place appointed for the shooting match. It went by the name of Sims' Cross Roads; because, here two roads intersected each other; and because, from the time that the first had been laid out, Archibald Sims had resided there. Archibald had been a Justice of the Peace in his day; (and where is the man of his age in Georgia who has not?) consequently he was called '*Squire* Sims. It is the custom in this State, when a man has once acquired a title, civil or military, to force it upon him as long as he lives; hence the countless number of titled personages, who are introduced in these sketches.

We stopt at the 'Squire's door. Billy hastily dismounted, gave me the shake of the hand which he had been reluctantly reserving for a mile back; and, leading me up to the 'Squire, thus introduced me: "Uncle Archy, this is Lyman Hall; and for all you see him in these fine clothes, he's a *swinge*-cat—a darn sight cleverer fellow than he looks to be. Wait till you see him lift the old Soap-stick, and draw a bead upon the bull's-eye. You *gwine* to see fun here to-day—Don't say nothing about it."

"Well, Mr. Swinge-cat," said the 'Squire, "here's to a better acquaintance with you," offering me his hand.

"How goes it, uncle Archy?" said I, taking his hand warmly; (for I am always free and easy with those who are so with me; and in this course I rarely fail to please)— "How's the old woman?"

"Egad," said the 'Squire, chuckling, "there you're too hard for me; for she died two and twenty years ago, and I haven't heard a word from her since."

"What! and you never married again!"

"Never, as God's my Judge!" (a solemn asseveration truly, upon so light a subject.)

"Well, that's not my fault."

"No, nor it's not mine *nither*," said the 'Squire.

Here we were interrupted by the cry of another Rancey Sniffle—"Hello here! All you as wish to put in for the shoot'n match, come on here! for the putt'n in's *riddy* to begin."

About sixty persons, including mere spectators, had collected; the most of whom were more or less obedient to the call of Mealy Whitecotton—for that was the name of the self-constituted commander-in-chief. Some hastened, and some loitered, as they desired to be first or last on the list; for they shoot in the order in which their names are entered.

The beef was not present, nor is it ever upon such occasions; but several of the company had seen it, who all concurred in the opinion that it was a good beef, and well worth the price that was set upon it—eleven dollars. A general enquiry ran round, in order to form some opinion as to the number of shots that would be taken; for, of course, the price of a shot is cheapened in proportion to the increase of that number. It was soon ascertained that not more than twenty persons would take chances; but these twenty agreed to take the number of shots, at twenty-five cents each.

The competitors now began to give in their names; some for one, some for two, three, and a few for as many as four shots.

Billy Curlew hung back to the last; and when the list was offered to him, five shots remained undisposed of.

"How many shots left?" inquired Billy.

"Five:" was the reply.

"Well, I take 'em all. Put down four shots to me, and one to Lyman Hall, paid for by William Curlew."

I was thunder struck—not at his proposition to pay for my shot, because I knew that Billy meant it as a token of friendship, and he would have been hurt if I had refused to let him do me this favor; but at the unexpected announcement of my name as a competitor for beef, at least one hundred miles from the place of my residence. I was prepared for a challenge from Billy to some of his neighbors for a *private* match upon me; but not for this.

I therefore protested against his putting in for me, and urged every reason to dissuade him from it, that I could, without wounding his feelings.

"Put it down!" said Billy, with the authority of an Emperor, and with a look that spoke volumes intelligible to every by-stander—"Reckon I don't know what I'm about?" Then wheeling off, and muttering in an under, self-confident tone—"Dang old Roper," continued he, "if he don't knock that cross to the north corner of creation and back again before a cat can lick her foot."

Had I been the king of the cat tribe, they could not have regarded me with more curious attention than did the whole company from this moment. Every inch of me was examined with the nicest scrutiny; and some plainly expressed by their looks, that they never would have taken me for such a bite. I saw no alternative but to throw myself upon a third chance shot; for though by the rules of the sport I would have been allowed to shoot by proxy, by all the rules of good breeding I was bound to shoot in person. It would have been unpardonable, to disappoint the expectations, which had been raised on me. Unfortunately too, for me, the match differed in one respect from those which I had been in the habit of attending in my younger days. In olden time the contest was carried on chiefly with *shot-guns,* a generic term which, in those days, embraced three descriptions of fire-arms—*Indian-traders,* (a long, cheap, but sometimes excellent kind of gun, that mother Britain used to send hither for traffic with the Indians,) *the large Musket,* and the *Shot-gun,* properly so called. Rifles were, however, always permitted to compete with them, under equitable restrictions. These were, that they should be fired off-hand, while the shot-guns were allowed a rest, the distance being equal; or that the distance should be one hundred yards for the rifle, to sixty, for the shot-gun, the mode of firing being equal.

But this was a match of rifles exclusively; and these are by far the most common at this time.

Most of the competitors fire at the same target; which is usually a board from nine inches to a foot wide, charred on one side as black as it can be made by fire without impairing materially the uniformity of its surface; on the darkened side of which is *pegged,* a square piece of white paper, which is larger or smaller, according to the distance at which it is to be placed from the marksmen. This is almost invariably sixty yards, and for it, the paper is reduced to about two and a half inches square. Out of the centre of it is cut a rhombus of about the width of an inch, measured diagonally— this is the *bull's-eye,* or *diamond,* as the marksmen choose to call it: in the centre of this is the cross. But every man is permitted to fix his target to his own taste; and accordingly, some remove one fourth of the paper, cutting from the centre of the square to the two lower corners; so as to leave a large angle opening from the centre downwards; while others reduce the angle more or less: but it is rarely the case that all are not satisfied with one of these figures.

The beef is divided into five prizes, or, as they are commonly termed, five *quarters*—the hide and tallow counting as one. For several years after the revolutionary war, a sixth was added; the *lead* which was shot in the match. This was the prize of the sixth best shot; and it used to be carefully extracted from the board, or tree, in which it was lodged, and afterwards remoulded. But this grew out of the exigency of the times, and has, I believe, been long since abandoned every where.

The three master shots, and rivals, were Moses Firmby, Larkin Spivey and Billy Curlew—to whom was added, upon this occasion, by common consent, and with awful forebodings—your humble servant.

The target was fixed, at an elevation of about three feet from the ground; and the judges (Captain Turner and Squire Porter) took their stands by it, joined by about half the spectators.

The first name on the catalogue was Mealy Whitecotton. Mealy stept out, rifle in hand, and toed the mark. His rifle was about three inches longer than himself, and near enough his own thickness to make the remark of Darby Chislom, as he stept out, tolerably appropriate—"Here comes the corn-stock and the sucker!" said Darby.

"Kiss my foot!" said Mealy. "The way I'll creep into that bull-eye's a fact."

"You'd better creep into your hind-sight," said Darby. Mealy raised, and fired.

"A pretty good shot! Meal" said one. "Yes, a blamed good shot!" said a second. "Well done Meal!" said a third.

I was rejoiced when one of the company enquired, "Where is it?" for I could hardly believe they were founding these remarks upon the evidence of their senses. "Just on the right hand side of the bull's-eye," was the reply.

I looked with all the power of my eyes; but was unable to discover the least change in the surface of the paper. Their report, however, was true—so much keener is the vision of a practiced than unpracticed eye.

The next in order was Hiram Baugh. Hiram was like some race-horses which I have seen—he was too good, not to contend for every prize, and too good for nothing ever to win one.

"Gentlemen," said he, as he came to the mark, "I don't say that I'll win beef; but if my piece don't blow, I'll eat the paper; or be mighty apt to do it, if you'll b'lieve my racket. My powder are not good powder, gentlemen—I bought it *thum* (from) Zeb. Daggett, and gin him three quarters of a dollar a pound for it; but it are not what I call good powder, gentlemen; but if old Buck-killer burns it clear, the boy you call Hiram Baugh eats paper, or comes mighty near it."

"Well, blaze away," said Mealy, "and be —— to you, and Zeb. Daggett and your powder and Buck-killer, and your powder-horn and shot-pouch to boot! How long you gwine stand thar talking 'fore you shoot?"

"Never mind," said Hiram, "I can talk a little and shoot a little too; but that's nothin'—Here goes!"

Hiram assumed the figure of a note of interrogation—took a long sight, and fired.

"I've eat paper," said he, at the crack of the gun, without looking, or seeming to look towards the target. "Buck-killer made a clear racket. Where am I, gentlemen?"

"You're just between Mealy and the diamond," was the reply.

"I said I'd eat paper, and I've done it; have'nt I, gentlemen?"

"And 'spose you have!" said Mealy, "what do that 'mount to? You'll not win beef, and never did."

"Be that as it mout be, I've beat Meal. 'Cotton mighty easy; and the boy you call Hiram Baugh are able to do it."

"And what do that 'mount to? Who the devil an't able to beat Meal. 'Cotton! I don't makes no pretense of bein' nothin' great, no how: but you always makes out as if you were gwine to keep 'em makin' crosses for you constant; and then do nothin' but '*eat paper*' at last; and that's a long way from *eatin' beef,* 'cordin' to Meal. 'Cotton's notions, as you call him."

Simon Stow was now called on.

"Oh Lord!" exclaimed two or three: "Now we have it. It'll take him as long to shoot as it would take Squire Dobbins to run round a *track* o' land."

"Good-by, boys," said Bob Martin.

"Where you going Bob?"

"Going to gather in my crop—I'll be back agin though by the time Sime. Stow shoots."

Simon was used to all this, and therefore it did not disconcert him in the least. He went off and brought his own target, and set it up with his own hand.

He then wiped out his rifle—rubbed the pan with his hat—drew a piece of tow through the touch-hole with his wiper—filled his charger with great care—poured the powder into the rifle with equal caution—shoved in with his finger the two or three vagrant grains that lodged round the mouth of his piece—took out a handful of bullets—looked them all over carefully—selected one without flaw or wrinkle—drew out his patching—found the most even part of it—sprung open the grease-box in the breech of his rifle—took up just so much grease—distributed it with great equality over the chosen part of his patching—laid it over the muzzle of his rifle, grease side down—placed his ball upon it—pressed it a little—then took it up and turned the neck a little more perpendicularly downward—placed his knife-handle on it—just buried it in the mouth of the rifle—cut off the redundant patching just above the bullet—looked at it, and shook his head, in token that he had cut off too much or too little, no one knew which—sent down the ball—measured the contents of his gun with his first and second fingers, on the protruding part of the ramrod—shook his head again, to signify there was too much or too little powder—primed carefully—placed an arched piece of tin over the hind sight to shade it—took his place—got a friend to hold his hat over the fore-sight to shade it—took a very long sight—fired—and did'nt even eat the paper.

"My piece was badly *loadned,*" said Simon, when he learned the place of his ball.

"Oh, you did'nt take time," said Mealy. "No man can shoot that's in such a hurry as you is. I'd hardly got to sleep 'fore I heard the crack o' the gun."

The next was Moses Firmby. He was a tall, slim man, of rather sallow complexion; and it is a singular fact, that though probably no part of the world is more healthy than the mountainous region of Georgia, the mountaineers have not generally robust frames or fine complexions: they are, however, almost inexhaustible by toil.

Moses kept us not long in suspense. His rifle was already charged, and he fixed it upon the target, with a steadiness of nerve and aim that was astonishing to me and alarming to all the rest. A few seconds, and the report of his rifle broke the deathlike silence which prevailed.

"No great harm done yet," said Spivey, manifestly relieved from anxiety by an event which seemed to me better calculated to produce despair. Firmby's ball had cut out the lower angle of the diamond, directly on a right line with the cross.

Three or four followed him without bettering his shot; all of whom, however, with one exception, "eat the paper."

It now came to Spivey's turn. There was nothing remarkable in his person or manner. He took his place, lowered his rifle slowly from a perpendicular, until it came on a line with the mark—held it there like a vise for a moment, and fired.

"Pretty *sevigrous,* but nothing killing yet," said Billy Curlew, as he learned the place of Spivey's ball.

Spivey's ball had just broken the upper angle of the diamond; beating Firmby about half its width.

A few more shots, in which there was nothing remarkable, brought us to Billy Curlew. Billy stept out with much confidence; and brought the Soap-stick to an order, while he deliberately rolled up his shirt sleeves. Had I judged of Billy's chance of success from the looks of his gun, I should have said it was hopeless. The stock of Soap-stick seemed to have been made with a case knife; and had it been, the tool would have been but a poor apology for its clumsy appearance. An augur hole in the breech, served for a grease-box—a cotton string assisted a single screw in holding on the lock; and the thimbles were made, one of brass, one of iron, and one of tin.

"Where's Lark. Spivey's bullet?" called out Billy to the judges, as he finished rolling up his sleeves.

"About three quarters of an inch from the cross," was the reply.

"Well, clear the way! the Soap-stick's coming, and she'll be along in there among 'em presently."

Billy now planted himself astraddle, like an inverted V—shot forward his left hip—drew his body back to an angle of about forty-five degrees with the plane of the horizon—brought his cheek down close to the breech of old Soap-stick, and fixed her upon the mark with untrembling hand. His sight was long, and the swelling muscles of his left arm led me to believe that he was lessening his chance of success, with every half second that he kept it burdened with his ponderous rifle; but it neither flagged nor wavered until Soap-stick made her report.

"Where am I?" said Billy, as the smoke rose from before his eye.

"You've jist touched the cross on the lower side," was the reply of one of the judges.

"I was afraid I was drawing my bead a *leetle* too fine," said Billy. "Now, Lyman, you see what the Soap-stick can do.—Take her, and show the boys how you used to do when you was a baby."

I begged to reserve my shot to the last; pleading, rather sophistically, that it was in point of fact, one of Billy's shots. My plea was rather indulged than sustained, and the marksmen who had taken more than one shot, commenced the second round. This round was a manifest improvement upon the first. The cross was driven three times: once by Spivey, once by Firmby, and once by no less a personage than Mealy Whitecotton, whom chance seemed to favor for this time, merely that he might retaliate upon Hiram Baugh; and the bull's-eye was disfigured out of all shape.

The third and fourth rounds were shot. Billy discharged his last shot, which left the rights of parties thus: Billy Curlew first and fourth choice, Spivey second, Firmby third, and Whitecotton fifth. Some of my readers may perhaps be curious to learn, how a distinction comes to be made between several, all of whom drive the cross. The distinction is perfectly natural and equitable. Threads are stretched from the uneffaced parts of the once intersecting lines, by means of which the original position of the cross is precisely ascertained. Each bullet-hole being nicely pegged up as it is made, it is easy to ascertain its circumference. To this, I believe they usually, if not invariably, measure, where none of the balls touch the cross; but if the cross be driven, they measure from it to the centre of the bullet-hole. To make a draw shot, therefore, between two, who drive the cross, it is necessary that the centre of both balls should pass directly through the cross—a thing that very rarely happens.

The Bite alone remained to shoot. Billy wiped out his rifle carefully, loaded her to the top of his skill, and handed her to me. "Now," said he, "Lyman draw a fine bead, but not too fine; for Soap-stick bears up her ball well. Take care and don't touch the trigger, until you've got your bead; for she's spring-trigger'd and goes mighty easy: but you hold her to the place you want her, and if she don't go there dang old Roper."

I took hold of Soap-stick, and lapsed immediately into the most hopeless despair. I am sure I never handled as heavy a gun in all my life. "Why Billy," said I, "you little mortal you! what do you use such a gun as this for?"

"Look at the bull's-eye yonder!" said he.

"True," said I, "but *I* can't shoot her—it is impossible."

"Go long, you old coon!" said Billy, "I see what you're at"—intimating that all this was merely to make the coming shot the more remarkable—"Daddy's little boy don't shoot any thing but the old Soap-stick here to-day, I know."

The judges, I knew, were becoming impatient, and withal, my situation was growing more embarrassing every second; so I e'en resolved to try the Soap-stick without further parley.

I stept out, and the most intense interest was excited all around me, and it flashed like electricity around the target, as I judged from the anxious gaze of all in that direction.

Policy dictated that I should fire with a falling rifle, and I adopted this mode; de-

termining to fire as soon as the sights came on a line with the diamond, *bead* or no
bead. Accordingly I commenced lowering old Soap-stick; but, in spite of all my muscular powers, she was strictly obedient to the laws of gravitation, and came down with
a uniformly accelerated velocity. Before I could arrest her downward flight, she had
not only passed the target, but was making rapid encroachments on my own toes.

"Why, he's the weakest man in the arms I ever seed," said one in a half whisper.

"It's only his fun," said Billy: "I know him."

"It may be fun," said the other; "but it looks mightily like yearnest to a man up a
tree."

I now, of course, determined to reverse the mode of firing, and put forth all my
physical energies to raise Soap-stick to the mark. The effort silenced Billy, and gave
tongue to all his companions. I had just strength enough to master Soap-stick's obstinate proclivity, and consequently my nerves began to exhibit palpable signs of distress
with her first imperceptible movement upward. A trembling commenced in my
arms—increased, and extended rapidly to my body and lower extremities; so that by
the time that I brought Soap-stick up to the mark, I was shaking from head to foot,
exactly like a man under the continued action of a strong galvanic battery. In the
mean time my friends gave vent to their feelings freely.

"I swear poin' blank," said one, "that man can't shoot."

"He used to shoot well," said another; "but can't now nor never could."

"You better *git* away from 'bout that mark!" bawled a third, "for I'll be dod durned
if Broadcloth don't give some of you the dry gripes if you stand too close thare."

"The stranger's got the *peedoddles*,"[1] said a fourth, with humorous gravity.

"If he had bullets enough in his gun, he'd shoot a ring round the bull's-eye big as
a spinning-wheel," said a fifth.

As soon as I found that Soap-stick was high enough, (for I made no further use
of the sights than to ascertain this fact,) I pulled trigger, and off she went. I have always found that the most creditable way of relieving myself of derision, was to
heighten it myself as much as possible. It is a good plan in all circles, but by far the
best which can be adopted among the plain rough farmers of the country. Accordingly I brought old Soap-stick to an order, with an air of triumph—tipt Billy a wink,
and observed, "Now Billy's your time to make your fortune—Bet 'em two to one that
I've knocked out the cross."

"No, I'll be dod blamed if I do," said Billy; "but I'll bet you two to one you han't
hit the plank."

"Ah, Billy," said I, "I was joking about *betting,* for I never bet; nor would I have
you to bet: indeed I do not feel exactly right in shooting for beef; for it is a species of
gaming at last: but I'll say this much—if that cross is'nt knoked out, I'll never shoot
for beef again as long as I live."

"By dod," said Mealy Whitecotton, "you'll lose no great things at that."

"Well," said I, "I reckon I know a little about wabbling. Is it possible, Billy, a man
who shoots as well as you do, never practiced shooting with the double wabble? It's
the greatest take in, in the world, when you learn to drive the cross with it. Another

---

1. This word was entirely new to me; but like most, if not all words, in use among the common people, it is doubtless a legitimate English word, or rather a compound of two words, the last a little corrupted, and was very aptly applied in this instance. It is a compound of "*pee*," to peep with one eye, and
"*daddle*," to totter, or wabble.

sort for getting bets upon, to the drop-sight, with a single wabble! And the Soap-stick's the very yarn for it."

"Tell you what, stranger," said one, "you're too hard for us all here. We never *hearn* o' that sort o' shoot'n in these parts."

"Well," returned I, "you've seen it now, and I'm the boy that can do it."

The judges were now approaching with the target, and a singular combination of circumstances had kept all my party in utter ignorance of the result of my shot. Those about the target had been prepared by Billy Curlew for a great shot from me; their expectations had received assurance from the courtesy which had been extended to me; and nothing had happened to disappoint them, but the single caution to them against the "dry gripes," which was as likely to have been given in irony as in earnest; for my agonies under the weight of the Soap-stick, were either imperceptible to them at the distance of sixty yards, or, being visible, were taken as the flourishes of an expert who wished to "astonish the natives." The other party did not think the direction of my ball worth the trouble of a question; or, if they did, my airs and harangue had put the thought to flight before it was delivered. Consequently they were all transfixed with astonishment when the judges presented the target to them, and gravely observed—"It's only second best after all the fuss." "Second best!" exclaimed I, with uncontrollable transports. The whole of my party rushed to the target to have the evidence of their senses before they would believe the report: but most marvellous fortune decreed that it should be true. Their incredulity and astonishment were most fortunate for me; for they blinded my hearers to the real feelings with which the exclamation was uttered, and allowed me sufficient time to prepare myself for making the best use of what I had said before, with a very different object.

"Second best!" reiterated I, with an air of despondency, as the company turned from the target to me.—"Second best only!" Here Billy, my son, take the old Soap-stick; she's a good piece, but I'm getting too old and dim sighted to shoot a rifle; especially with the drop-sight and double wabbles.

"Why good Lord a'mighty!" said Billy, with a look that baffles all description, "an't you *driv* the cross!"

"Oh, driv the cross!" rejoined I, carelessly. "What's that! Just look where my ball is! I do believe in my soul its centre is a full quarter of inch from the cross. I wanted to lay the centre of the bullet upon the cross, just as if you'd put it there with your fingers."

Several received this palaver with a contemptuous but very appropriate curl of the nose; and Mealy Whitecotton offered to bet a half-pint, "that I could'nt do the like agin with no sort o' wabbles, he did'nt care what." But I had already fortified myself on this quarter, by my morality. A decided majority, however, were clearly of opinion that I was serious; and they regarded me as one of the wonders of the world. Billy increased the majority by now coming out fully with my history, as he had received it from his father; to which I listened with quite as much astonishment as any other one of his hearers. He begged me to go home with him for the night, or as he expressed it, "to go home with him and swap lies that night, and it should'nt cost me a cent:" the true reading of which, is, that if I would go home with him, and give him the pleasure of an evening's chat about old times, his house should be as free to me as my own. But I could not accept his hospitality without retracing five or six miles of the road which I had already passed; and therefore I declined it.

"Well, if you won't go, what must I tell the old woman for you? for she'll be mighty glad to hear from the boy that won the silk handkerchief for her, and I expect she'll lick me for not bringing you home with me."

"Tell her," said I, "that I send her a quarter of beef, which I won, as I did the handkerchief, by nothing in the world but mere good luck."

"Hold your jaw, Lyman!" said Billy, "I an't a gwine to tell the old woman any such lies; for she's a *rael* reg'lar built Meth'dist."

As I turned to depart, "Stop a minute, stranger!" said one: then lowering his voice to a confidential but distinctly audible tone, "what you offering for?" continued he. I assured him I was not a candidate for any thing—that I had accidentally fallen in with Billy Curlew, who begged me to come with him to the shooting match, and as it lay right on my road, I had stopped. "Oh," said he, with a conciliatory nod, "if you're up for any thing you need'nt be mealy-mouthed about it, 'fore us boys; for we'll all go in for you here up to the handle." "Yes," said Billy, "dang old Roper if we don't go our death for you, no matter who offers. If ever you come out for any thing, Lyman, jist let the boys of Upper Hogthief know it, and they'll go for you, to the hilt, against creation, tit or no tit, that's the tatur." I thanked them kindly, but repeated my assurances. The reader will not suppose that the district took its name from the character of the inhabitants. In almost every county in the State, there is some spot, or district, which bears a contemptuous appellation, usually derived from local rivalships, or from a single accidental circumstance.

HALL.

29

HENRY ROWE SCHOOLCRAFT

(1793–1864)

Henry Rowe Schoolcraft first came west to survey the territories taken from the British after the War of 1812. He surveyed lead mines in Missouri and is credited with being the first white man to discover Lake Itasca, a claim disputed by William Warren, among others. From 1822 until 1841, he was an Indian agent at Sault Ste. Marie at the confluence of the entire Great Lakes fur trade. There, he married into the powerful mixed-race Ojibway Johnston family and worked with virtually every prominent white and native figure in the region. Periodically, he published materials in the east from his experience in the west, most notably his *Algic Researches* (1839) and his *Historical and Statistical Information Respecting the History, Conditions, and Prospects of the Indian Tribes of the United States* (1851). Well known in the east, Schoolcraft was very familiar to American readers, who trusted his authority as a specialist in native issues, a relationship also reflected in his seamless support for popular policies of removal and paternalism.

The first selection reproduced here is from his early book *Travels.* In it, his initial prejudice against natives is apparent; he had been raised with the myth of natives as savages. However, in its place, despite close contact, grows the image of natives as children of the forest. Nonetheless, Schoolcraft's interest in recording accurately the history and the languages of the peoples he encountered in the west set him apart from most eastern writers. During his early years in Sault Ste. Marie, Schoolcraft published a weekly newspaper, *The Literary Voyager or Muzzeniegun,* in which he rehearsed many of the materials he would later publish in the east. He also printed many of his wife's writings and what he considered the best writing of the Ojibway students from the school he opened. Reprinted here is the story of the legendary Ojibway (Chippewa) leader Waub Ojeeg, his wife's grandfather. The story originally appeared in three installments and is purportedly a direct transcription of his mother-in-law's account. Unfortunately, Schoolcraft imposed the myth of the vanishing Indian on Waub Ojeeg, despite his wife's and children's link to him.

Upon returning east, Schoolcraft announced his entry into the eastern republic of letters with the poem, "The Rise of the West." As in his earlier work, Schoolcraft espoused a vision of the west that excluded Native Americans. Furthermore, unlike James Hall, an easterner who stayed west, Schoolcraft rearticulated the vision of the organized and settled west as a clone of the east, similar to the vision of Manasseh Cutler and James Fenimore Cooper. The hackneyed verse Schoolcraft employed reflects the unoriginality of his vision.

Schoolcraft's influence on eastern writers such as Henry Wadsworth Longfellow has been well documented. His eminence as a source of information on natives and western lands is inestimable. Restrained, however, by a vision of race and nation bound by the conventions of his time, Schoolcraft remained an eastern traveler in the west.

Text: *Travels* (New York, 1821): 304–313. "Waub Ojeeg" (orig. in *The Literary Voyager or Muzzeniegun,* Sault Ste. Marie, 1826–1827; rpt. East Lansing, 1962, ed. Philip P. Mason): 23–26, 39–43, 50–56. "The Rise of the West" (New York, 1841).

FROM *TRAVELS* (1820)

LXX. Day.—(*August 1st.*)—A treaty of peace was this day concluded between the Sioux and Chippeways in the presence of Governor Cass, Colonel Leavenworth, Mr. Tallifierro, the Indian agent at St. Peter's, and a number of the officers of the garrison. These two nations have been at war from the earliest times, and the original causes of it are entirely forgotten, but still the ancient enmity is carefully transmitted from father to son. It is supposed to have arisen from a dispute respecting the limits of their territories, and favourite hunting grounds, but if so, nothing was agreed upon in the present instance to obviate the original causes of enmity. It was only stipulated that hostilities should immediately cease on both sides. Several of the chiefs delivered their opinions upon the subject, and the Sioux appeared to manifest some indifference to the treaty, but finally consented to drop the hatchet; and the ceremony concluded with smoking the pipe of peace and shaking hands. In this nearly every individual present united. The Sioux who attended the council were numerous, having been gathering in from the different villages from the time of our arrival; on the part of the Chippeways there were only present the deputies who accompanied us for that purpose from the sources of the Mississippi. The conduct of the latter, on our approach to St. Peter's, manifested the anxiety they felt on the subject, at the same time that it reveals a new trait in the character and customs of the Indian tribes. During the first two or three days after our departure from Sandy Lake, they proceeded very much at their ease, sometimes ahead of the expedition, at others in the rear—very seldom with us, and at night they usually encamped by themselves three or four hundred yards off. But the moment we entered the Sioux territories, they made it a point to keep close with the expedition, never venturing ahead, or lagging much in the rear, and at night they formed their encampment in the midst of ours. As we approached the falls of St. Anthony they requested of Governor Cass, a flag for their canoe, which was granted, and during the whole of that day they kept a peace-pipe hoisted on the bow of their canoe. When we embarked below the falls of St. Anthony, they commenced beating upon their drum, singing, whooping, and frequently firing into the air, increasing the tumult as we came near to the fort, that the Sioux might be advertised of their approach; but the principal object of these ceremonies was to let their enemies know, that they came unto their territories upon a mission of peace—openly and boldly— and expected to be received by them with sentiments of corresponding liberality, frankness, and conciliation. Nor were they disappointed; they were taken by the hand in a friendly manner by those Sioux who had collected on our first landing at the garrison, and the pipe of peace immediately smoked between them, and this ceremony continued as fast as the Sioux arrived, so that the object of the public treaty held at the department of the Indian agent, where these ceremonies were repeated, was more with a view of having it witnessed by the agents of the United States, than to render binding upon their respective tribes, a pacification which had already been privately and individually determined upon. It has, however, been mentioned, that there was some indifference manifested to this treaty on the part of the Sioux, and those chiefs and warriors who discovered this unconquerable spirit of animosity, could not be induced to smoke the pipe of peace, although the cessation of hostilities had their tacit consent. Whether the peace will prove a permanent one, may be doubted. All their ancient prejudices will urge them to a violation of it, while past experience abundantly shews how difficult it has been to preserve a lasting peace between two powerful rival tribes of savages, whose predominant disposition is war, and if a durable peace should result from the laudable exertions of the agents of government in effecting this pacific conference, it will probably be owing in a great measure to a continuance of those exertions, supported as they are, by the influence of the garrisons at St. Peter's, Prairie du Chien, Council Bluffs, Green Bay, and other minor posts along our extensive Indian frontiers. In 1805, a treaty of peace was concluded between the Sioux and Chippeways at the instance of Lieutenant Pike. It continued *as long as he remained among them.* In the fall of 1818, a pacification took place at St. Louis under the auspices of Governor Clark, between the Osages and the Cherokees. The latter renewed hostilities *before they reached their homes.* This only proves, that treaties of peace between Indian tribes, like those between civilized nations, only amount to a momentary cessation of hostilities, unless the limits of their territories, and other subjects of dispute, are accurately defined, and satisfactorily settled.

The numerical strength of the Sioux nation was stated by the late General Pike at 21,675, three thousand eight hundred of whom are warriors. This is the most powerful Indian tribe in North America. It consists of seven bands, namely, the Minokantongs, the Yengetongs, the Sissitongs, the Wahpetongs, the Titongs, the Mendewacantongs, and the Washpecoutongs. These are independent bands, under their own chiefs, but united in a confederacy for the protection of their territories, and send deputies to a general council of the chiefs and warriors whenever the concerns of their nation require it. If one of the tribes is attacked, the others are expected to assist in the repulsion of the enemy. They inhabit all the country between the Mississippi and Missouri rivers, from north latitude about 46° to the junction of these rivers near St. Louis, with trifling exceptions in favour of some scattered bands of Foxes, Sacs, and Kickapoos. Their country also extends south of the Missouri, where the principal part of the Titongs reside, and east of the Mississippi to the territories of the Chippeways—the Winnebagoes, and the Menomonies. The greatest chief of the nation, at present, is Talangamane, or the Red wing.

The Minokantongs, or people of the waters, are located at St. Peter's, and along the banks of the Mississippi towards Prairie du Chien. They reside in four principal villages, distinguished by the names of their respective chiefs; Chatawaconamie, or La Petit Corbeau—Talangamane, or the Red wing—Tatamane, or the wind-that-walks, and Wabashaw.

The Yengetongs and the Sissitongs inhabit the upper parts of the river St. Peter's, and are sometimes called the Sioux of the Plains. Their traffic is principally in Buffalo robes. The first chief is Muckpeanutah, or the Red Cloud. The Wahpetongs, or people of the Leaves, are the most erratic in their dispositions of all the Sioux. They inhabit the St. Peter's between the Prairie De François and the White Rock, during a part of the year, and generally go out to hunt above the falls of St. Anthony towards the sources of the river De Corbeau, and upon the plains which give origin to the Crow, Sac, and Elk rivers. Their principal chief is Wakunska, or the Rolling Thunder.

The Titongs inhabit both banks of the Missouri, and rove in quest of game over an immense extent of country. They are said to be related to the Mahas, and some other bands south of the Missouri.

The Mendewacantongs, or people of the Medicine Lake,—the Washpecoutongs, or people of the Leaves *who have ran away,* and some other scattered bands whose names are unknown, inhabit the country generally, from the St. Peter's south to the mouth of the Missouri, and are chiefly located upon the sources of the rivers Ocano, Iowa, and Desmoines.

The Sioux are generally represented as a brave, spirited, and generous people, with proud notions of their origin as a tribe, and their superiority as hunters and warriors, and with a predominant passion for war. They speak the Narcotah language, which is peculiar to themselves, and appears to have little affinity with any other Indian tongue. It is not so soft and sonorous as the Algonquin which abounds in labials, but more so, than the Winnebago, which is the most harsh and gutteral language in America. The Narcotah sounds to an English ear, like the Chinese, and both in this, and other respects, the Sioux are thought to present many points of coincidence. It is certain that their manners and customs differ essentially from those of any other tribe, and their physiognomy, as well as their language, and opinions, mark them as a distinct race of people.—Their sacrifices and their supplications to the unknown God— their feasts after any signal deliverance from danger—their meat, and their burnt offerings—the preparation of incense, and certain customs of their females, offer too striking a coincidence with the manners of the Asiatic tribes before the commencement of the christian era, to escape observation, while their paintings and hieroglyphics bear so much analogy to those of the Azteeks of Mexico, as to render it probable that the latter are of Naudowessian origin. But these hints are merely thrown out for the investigation of the future enquirer, as my limited opportunities of observation, and the short period of our sojournment among them, forbid any thing like systematic research, which is the more to be regretted as this tribe has recently assumed a more interesting attitude with respect to the United States, and as the time for conducting these enquiries with any probability of success, is rapidly receding under the pressure of an enterprizing European population. It is to be hoped that some spirited traveller, possessed of the necessary qualifications, will select their territories as the theatre of his researches, and I doubt not, that he would find more among them to elucidate the origin and history of the aborigines of our country, than among any other tribe upon the continent.

"From my knowledge of the Sioux nation," observes Lieutenant Pike, "I do not hesitate to pronounce them the most warlike and independent nation of Indians within the boundaries of the United States, their every passion being subservient to that of war; but at the same time their traders feel themselves perfectly secure of any combination being made against them, but it is extremely necessary to be careful not to injure the honour of an individual, which is certainly the cause of the many broils which occur between them. But never was a trader known to suffer in the estimation of the nation by resenting any indignity offered him; even if he went to taking the life of the offender. Their gutteral pronunciation—high cheek bones—their visages, and distinct manners, together with their own traditions, supported by the testimony of neighbouring nations, put it in my mind beyond the shadow of a doubt, that they have emigrated from the northwest point of America, to which they had come across the narrow streights, which in that quarter, divide the two continents; and are absolutely descendants of a Tartarean tribe."[1]

As an instance of the generosity of this nation, the following anecdote is related. La Petit Corbeau, chief of a small band of Sioux, located upon the banks of the Mississippi, towards the confines of the Chippeway territories, going out one morning to examine his beaver trap, found a Sauteur in the act of stealing it. He had approached without exciting alarm, and while the Sauteur was engaged in taking the trap from the water, he stood maturely surveying him with a loaded rifle in his hands. As the two nations were at war, and the offence was in itself one of the most heinous nature, he would have been justified in killing him upon the spot, and the thief looked for nothing else, on finding himself detected. But the Sioux chief walking up to him discovered a nobleness of disposition which would have done honour to the most enlightened of men. "Take no alarm, said he, at my approach; I only come to present to you the trap of which I see you stand in need. You are entirely welcome to it. Take my gun also, as I perceive you have none of your own, and depart with it to the land of your countrymen, but linger not here, lest some of my young men who are panting for the blood of their enemies, should discover your foot steps in our country, and fall upon you." So saying, he delivered him his gun and accoutrements, and returned unarmed to the village of which he is so deservedly the chief.

There are several antique mounds and circumvallations upon the banks of the St. Peter's, which are said to indicate an industrious population, and an intimate acquaintance with geometrical solids, which are still to be traced among the full-grown trees of the forest which now overshadows these enigmatical works. The most remarkable of these, are stated to be about forty miles above the mouth of the St. Peter's, near the junction of that branch which is denominated Carver's river. I regret that I can say nothing concerning them from actual inspection.—They are among the number of interesting traits, the examination and description of which, would so richly reward an exploration of this important river.

About six miles west of the new cantonement there are several beautiful little lakes, situated in the prairies. They consist of the purest water and are surrounded with a handsome beach of yellow sand and water-worn pebbles, among which are to be found fragments of the most highly coloured carnelians, and ribband agates. The largest of these lakes is about four miles in circumference, and is called Calhoun lake. It is stored with the most exquisite flavoured black bass and several other varieties of fish, and has become a fashionable resort for the officers of the garrison. The intermediate country is a prairie, and is travelled in all directions on horseback. It is not, however, a level plain, but consists of gentle slopes and ascents, and the clumps of trees which are scattered over it, give a pleasing variety to the scene. In the season of verdure, the waving heath-grass,—the profusion of wild flowers, and the sweet-scented Indian grass, while they fill the air with a refreshing fragrance, delight the eye with the richness and never-ending variety of their colours; and viewed under the influ-

---

1. Pike's Expeditions.

ence of a gentle western breeze, which is seldom wanting, leave nothing to complete the picture of the most enchanting rural beauty.

Among the animated productions of nature which serve to enliven and diversify the scene, there is a new species of burrowing squirrel, something larger than the common striped ground squirrel, with an elongated body and short legs, approaching in shape the mustela nivalis, or brown weasel. But the most striking difference is found in its colour, which is a reddish brown with four longitudinal black stripes upon the back, spotted with yellow, and resembling in this respect, the skin of the African leopard. It is a beautiful little animal—burrows in the ground, and feeds upon ground nuts and esculent roots. It has been found destructive to the gardens at St. Peter's.

THE LEGEND OF WAUB OJEEG (1826–1827)

Waub Ojeeg or The Tradition of the Outagami and Chippewa History No. 1

The following tradition is related by Oshaguscodawaqua, a female of Chegoimegon on lake Superior, the ancient capitol of the Chippewa nation. A grand daughter of the reigning chief of that place,—possessing a high opinion of the origin, bravery and position of her tribe, with every means of learning their traditions, full credence appears to be due, to the general incidents of her narrative. Having at sixteen become the wife of a gentleman of information, polite manners, and warm susceptibility, she was removed, at this early age to the comforts and conveniences of a civilized dwelling—a change of life which gives the narrative a striking similarity to that of Pochahontas. But, although raising a family of children, by this union, she remained firmly attached to the traditions of her people, and continued to speak only the Indian language.

Chippewa tradition affirms, that their ancient council fire—and capitol was on the island of Chegoimegon in lake Superior. They were governed by a chief officer, called Mujekiwis, who was, always, the eldest son of the reigning OGIMAU, or Chief. At this place, they maintained their ancient mode of worshipping the Great Spirit, whom they propitiated by hymns, prayers, and sacrifices, offered especially to the Sun.

The chieftain's wife had long been settled in the line of the **Totem** of the Reindeer, and the mark of this animal was the authoritative sign of the ruler, wherever it was placed. Waub Ojeeg succeeded by birth to this authority about the middle of the seventeenth century. But his father, Ma Mongazida, did not die and give up the entire rule, till a later period. The French supremacy had then been long established, and rumors only began to be heard, of the coming of the Saganooks—the Algonquin

name for the British. The latter were at first distasteful to the Indians, who passionately loved the French rule, & the French manners. Braddock's defeat in 1755, and the
various triumphs by which the French & Indians had kept back the British colonies,
were events heard by the lake Indians, with pleasure.

The fall of Quebec in 1759, of Montreal in 1760, and of all Canada, in a short
time following, was dreadful news to the Indians. They did not believe, what they did
not like, and determined not to give up the country without a struggle. Pontiac placed
himself at the head of their effort, and made most vigorous & bloody efforts, to repel
the Saxon race. But these efforts proved vain, & the year 1763, saw the whole nation
power prostrate, & the British flag triumphant.

Ma Mongazida, did not die, & give up his authority at Chegoimegon till about
1790. This event, left Waub Ojeeg the sole rulership, a right to which he lent claim by
his vigors and skill as a huntsman, & his bravery & diplomatic talents as a warrior.

The same period saw a young gentleman from the north of Ireland, come to the
capitol of British North America, to recruit the rental of an exhausted estate, by engaging in the half Quixotic and chivalrous enterprize of the Fur Trade. The tale is simply told. A few years saw the ardent son of Erin at the death bed of Ma Mongazida,
and the fast friend of his brave and talented son, Waub Ojeeg.

Centuries have elapsed since hostilities commenced between the Chippewas and
Sioux. They lived on terms of amity, so long as the abundance of game rendered precise limits an object of little consequence, and while their leaders saw no cause to apprehend that they were, at a future day, to become rivals; and earn the hated name of
Nadowasieu, or Rattlesnake in the grass.

The Sioux felt little uneasiness at the inroads made by the Chippewas into those
remote and woody borders of their extensive hunting grounds, which stretch around
the head of lake Superior. They had few inducements to penetrate far towards the
north, while the fertility and mildness of the Mississippi plains, and the facility of
procuring food operated to confine their villages to the banks of that river. But when
their new neighbors, on that quarter, began to sally from their inhospitable woods
into the plains, in quest of the larger animals, which at certain seasons, quit the forests
altogether, and when their numbers and power began to make them formidable; it is
reasonable to conclude that a strong jealousy was created.

Hostilities once begun, there is nothing in the institutions of Indian society, that
would induce them to preserve any connected details of its impelling causes. Nor
should we feel surprized that these original causes of enmity have been nearly forgotten, when we reflect, that every season has been supplying fresh fuel to the flame.

Tradition represents that the Chippewa bands who first settled themselves at
Shogwoinecan, or *LaPointe,* on lake Superior, had the lands bestowed upon them by
the Outagamis, who were temporarily fixed there; but had resolved on migrating further west. A greater proof of the perfect amity existing between these two tribes could
not, perhaps, be given. They were, in fact, descended from a common ethnological
stock, spoke dialects of the same language, and practised the same general customs.
They were brother-tribes. Whenever, they met, they lived together as one and the
same people, and mutually sympathized in each other's reverses, or well-being.

Between the Outagamis and Sioux, a good understanding existed, which had
been matured, till, it seems, mutual aid was expected to be given to each other, in
cases of emergency. Through this alliance, the Chippewas were well received on their
first arrival at LaPointe, and for many years afterwards the Sioux regarded them as
friends. Offices of civility were exchanged, and visits and intermarriages took place;

and they tacitly acceded to the arrangement made by the Outagamis, respecting the lands.

In process of time the intimacy, which had bound together the Outagamis and Chippewas, during their weak and migratory state, cooled; they no longer looked upon each other as friends, and they soon quarrelled for the possession of a country, which they had, at first, shared in amity.

The Outagamis, who had retired from the lake to the table lands intermediate between the Mississippi, lake Michigan, and lake Superior, envying the increasing power and strength of the Chippewa settlement at LaPointe, commenced inroads into their best hunting grounds, depriving them of means of subsistence which had become, more important, as their numbers were augmented.

Before resenting this conduct, the Chippewa chiefs held a council, and determined on demanding an explanation. When the messengers employed on this mission entered the camp of the Outagamis, they found them in council, and immediately proclaimed their errand.

They asked the Outagamis, what wrong, or injustice they had ever done them; they declared that the lands they occupied had been freely given their fathers by the Outagamis; and that they had made no encroachments. They concluded by saying, that they had always regarded each other as brothers; that they were so in reality, they would be very sorry to shed their blood on the graves of their forefathers, who had been so generous towards them. But, that if they did not put a stop to their young men's depredations, they were determined to defend themselves, as several of their young hunters had already been decoyed and slain.

The Outagamis answered; that they (the Chippewas) were the aggressors; that they had wrongfully wrested the lands from their forefathers; and that far from stopping the attempts which had been already made, they would encourage their young men in every effort to drive them off the land. The council broke up with this threat, and the messengers, with difficulty, returned to their town.

Open hostilities soon commenced on either side, and although the Sioux sided with the Outagamis, and united with them in battle, yet the Chippewas totally defeated them in several bloody recontres; they broke up their villages at the Flambeau and Ottowa lakes, and compelled the remnant of the tribe to quit the sources of the Wisconsin, Chippewa, and Bad rivers, and ultimately to seek shelter behind their allies, the Sioux.

In this war the Chippewas were first brought into contact with the Sioux, and from that period they have scarcely ever enjoyed a moment's peace.

Waub Ojeeg or The Tradition of the Outagami and Chippewa History No. 2

A short time before the breaking out of the Outagami war, and while the Sioux and Chippewas were on friendly terms, a Chippewa girl was demanded in marriage by a Sioux chief of some distinction in his nation, and she accordingly, became his wife, and bore two sons—the eldest of whom became the father of the celebrated Sioux chief, Wabasha. These boys were in their infancy, when hostilities began. These Outagamis and Sioux who had intermarried with Chippewas and lived with them, precipitately retired to their respective countries. Some of the Chippewa women went with their husbands, others remained.

Among the latter, was the wife of the Sioux chief; and the chief himself remained, for a short time; but animosity displaying itself in more daring acts every day, it was deemed best that a separation should take place.

In this step the parents of the wife concurred, and even urged the execution of it. As they did not think their child safe in the country of the Sioux, neither did they think their son-in-law safe in their own;—for if once he should incur the ill-will of the Chippewas, no authority could restrain them from murdering him. The two little boys were thought equally unsafe in the mother's hands, as the blood of the Sioux flowed in their veins. It was therefore determined they should accompany the father. The relatives conducted them on their way till they were out of danger.

The young woman remained a long time inconsolable for the loss of her husband and children; and it was not till the lapse of several years, that she consented to become the wife of a Chippewa of Shogwaimican [Chequamegon], of the Totem of the Reindeer, being of the family who had borne sway at that place from the earliest times.

Her first child by this second marriage was Ma Mongazida, otherwise called Mashickeeoshe, who became a man of considerable note, and was the principal chief in authority at that place, when the Canadas fell into the possession of the English—an event that was distinctly remembered, from the part which the Indians of that quarter took in the wars which led to it.

'Mongazida was therefore a half-brother of the elder Sioux chief, the father of Wabasha; and in this manner the family became related to the Sioux; but 'Mongazida was not himself a Sioux, as has been erroneously asserted.

'Mongazida was strongly attached to the French, who were the first Europeans that ventured with goods into lake Superior. As a proof of this attachment, and at the same time, of the influence which they had acquired over the minds of the Indians, it deserves to be mentioned that he took a decided part in the warfare which was carried on against the English colonies, and was at Quebec with a party of warriors, when that place surrendered to the army under Gen. Wolfe. (Oct. 18, 1759)

He carried a short speech from Montcalm to his band, said to have been dictated by that general after receiving his mortal wound. At Quebec he first shook hands with the English, and he afterwards visited Sir William Johnson at Niagara, by whom he was well received and presented with a yellow gorget, and a broad belt of blue wampum with white figures.

The occasion of this visit formed an era in the affairs of LaPointe, which its inhabitants had cause to remember. For two years after the taking of old Mackinac by the Indians, no traders had visited that place. The convenience of this traffic was, even at that day, too highly estimated, not to make the Indians severely feel and regret the temporary loss of it. And it was to solicit that the English would send them traders, as the French had done, that 'Mongazida visited the Superintendent General of Indian Affairs.

The belt and gorget were a long time preserved in the family. Waub Ojeeg took from the former, the wampum he employed to muster his war parties, till only a narrow strip remained. On his death, this strip and the gorget went to his younger brother Camudwa, who being overtaken by famine near the mouth of the Broulé river, was, with all his family, except a little girl, starved to death. With him these testimonies were lost.

Waub Ojeeg was the second son of 'Mongazida. An incident which occurred in his childhood is related as presaging his future eminence as a warrior. 'Mongazida generally went to make his fall hunts on the middle grounds towards the Sioux territory, taking with him all his near relatives, amounting usually to 20 persons, exclusive of children. Early one morning, while the young men were preparing for the chase, they were startled by the report of several shots, directed towards the lodge. As they had thought themselves in security, the first emotion was that of surprize, but they had scarcely time to fly to their arms when another volley was fired. This second volley wounded one man in the thigh, and killed a dog. 'Mongazida immediately sallied out, with his young men, and pronounced his name aloud in Sioux. He demanded, if Wabasha or his brother were among the assailants. The firing instantly ceased—a pause ensued, when a tall figure in a war dress, with a profusion of feathers on his head, stepped forward and presented his hand. It was his half-brother. The Sioux peaceably followed their leader into the lodge, upon which they had the moment before directed their shots. At the moment the Sioux chief entered, where, it was necessary to stoop a little, he received a blow from a club wielded by a small boy who had placed himself near the door for that purpose. It was the young Waub Ojeeg. Wabasha, pleased with this early indication of courage, took the little lad in his arms, caressed him, and pronounced that he would become a brave man, and prove an inveterate enemy of the Sioux. These words were regarded as prophetic.

The border warfare in which his father was constantly engaged, early initiated him in the arts and preparatory ceremonies, which pertain to the character of the warrior. While quite a youth he joined these war parties, and gave convincing proofs of his courage. Possessing a tall and commanding person, and evincing sense, shrewdness, and a dauntless behavior, he soon became a leader, and by his success fixed the eyes of the Chippewa bands upon himself, as the person destined to protect their frontiers against the inroads of a powerful enemy. He was seven times a leader against the Outagamis [sic] and Sioux. The eighth war party he mustered, went no farther than the environs of Ottowa lake, where he was met by a deputation of old men from that village, who advised him to return, saying, they wished repose. With this request he complied.

Waub Ojeeg and The Tradition of the Outagami and Chippewa War No. 3

He had received three wounds in battle. One, in his thigh, another in his right shoulder, and a third in his side and breast, being a glancing shot. His war parties consisted of volunteers, raised in the different villages on the shores of the lake, to each of which he sent tobacco and wampum. His first war party consisted of 40 men, and his largest mustered three hundred.

This war party was made up of warriors from Shogwoimican, Fond du Lac, Ontonagan, Keweena bay, Grand Island, and Sault Ste. Marie. They assembled at La-Pointe, and danced the war dance on the shores of the lake between LaPointe and Bad river. They went up Bad river, and crossed a portage to a tributary of the St. Croix, called Namacagon. From the time they struck this river until they discovered the enemy, they passed six nights.

They went but a short distance each day, moving with great caution, and had always scouts ahead. On the evening of the seventh day the scouts discovered a large body of Outagamis and Sioux. They were encamped at the lower end of a portage around a fall, or rapid. The four Chippewa scouts who had made this discovery, did not however get off undiscovered themselves. The Foxes being on the alert, fired on them. A skirmish ensued. The White Fisher arrived with his whole force in season, and a bloody battle was fought, in which the allied Foxes and Sioux were defeated with the loss of nearly every man. They fought however with bravery against superior numbers; but the Chippewas had extended themselves in a circle across the small peninsula of the portage, and escape was next to impossible.

This great battle decided the long struggle between the Chippewas and Outagamis; and the latter have never ventured to renew the contest. It also had the effect to raise the fame of Waub Ojeeg, to its climax, and he was from this time regarded as the head of the nation. His war songs were repeated in every village, and some of them are yet remembered. The lofty sentiments and the unconquerable spirit which they breathed, have seldom been surpassed. The following beautiful versification of one of these songs, from the pen of Mr. [John] Johnston, preserves the prominent ideas operating upon the mind of the warrior under circumstances of a temporary discomfiture.

WAR SONG

I.

On that day when our heroes lay low—lay low,
    On that day when our heroes lay low;
I fought by their side, and thought ere I died,
Just vengeance to take on the foe—the foe,
    Just vengeance to take on the foe.

II.

On that day when our Chieftains lay dead—lay dead,
    On that day when our chieftains lay dead,
I fought hand to hand, at the head of my band,
And here on my breast have I bled—have I bled,
    And here on my breast have I bled.

III.

Our chiefs shall return no more—no more,
    Our chiefs shall return no more,
Nor their brothers of war, who can show scar for scar,
Like women their fates shall deplore—deplore,
    Like women their fates shall deplore.

IV.

Five winters in hunting we'll spend—we'll spend,
    Five winters in hunting we'll spend,
Till our youth grown to men, we'll to war lead again,
And our days like our fathers we'll end—we'll end,
    And our days like our fathers we'll end.

The carrying on of the Sioux war, did not withdraw the attention of the White Fisher, from the chase. His war excursions were generally made in the leisure of spring and summer. His followers were hastily assembled, and the whole expedition was generally terminated in a few weeks.

Large bodies of Indians can seldom be kept long together. Were it possible for the Indians to submit to the necessary restraints for a great length of time, the difficulty of subsistence must always have opposed the most serious obstacle to long campaigns. In fact, they generally lived upon very little, submitted to fatigues and privations of every kind without a murmur, and when success had crowned their efforts, they eagerly sought refreshment and repose in the security of their villages. Then, as now, the whole efficacy of a war party, consisted as much in the expedition with which it could be mustered, marched and dispersed, as in the valor they displayed before the enemy.

After the leaves have begun to fall, and during the whole winter and early part of spring, seasons the most valuable for hunting, no war party was ever conducted. The severity of the climate, and the facility with which scouting parties may track each other on the snow, forbid all attempts of the kind. And hence it is, that the care and business of war, scarcely, ever interrupted the pursuits of the chase. Waub Ojeeg was, in fact as much noted for his skill as a hunter, as for his prowess and daring as a warrior.

His hunting grounds extended along the shores of lake Superior, from the Montreal river to the Broule of Fond du Lac—a district abounding in moose, bear, beaver, marten and muskrat. Besides these, the mink, lynx, and smaller furs were also taken, and the woodlands stretching east of the Mississippi plains afforded the Virginia deer, during certain seasons. A more favorable position for the employment of hunting could hardly have been selected; and nothing equal to it, existed along the entire borders of the lake. In addition to this, the climate was favorable, that curve of the lake including Fond du Lac extending farthest south and west, and approaching nearest to the skirts of the Mississippi valley. The LaPointe Indians were able to raise corn, beans and pumpkins, articles which were annually cultivated in their gardens. The waters of that part of the lake also produced fish of various kinds, particularly white fish, trout and sturgeon.

Superadded to these advantages, the entrance of three principal rivers into the lake near that point, together with numerous smaller ones, presented so many avenues, which like radii, penetrated the interior, and opened channels of approach, enjoyed by no other spot on the southern coast of the lake. That the original settlement of the Chippewas at that place, had been determined by observing these advantages can not be doubted, and it may be regarded as the principal cause of its soon becoming one of the most flourishing and populous parts of the Chippewa territories. For we find, that so late as 1790, this was the great mart of the Indian trade on the southern shores of lake Superior, where the Mackinac traders annually resorted to exchange their goods for the valuable furs of those shores.

A consideration of the causes which have led to the dispersion of the LaPointe Indians into the department of lac de Flambeau, Folle Avoine &[c]. and the consequent decline of the parent settlement, would carry us into portions of history connected with the lives of cotemporary chiefs, and lead to the development of principles which have operated in all parts of the Indian country.

The amount of furs and skins usually taken by Waub Ojeeg during the year, fell little short of four Indian packs, averaging probably, sixty pounds each. Of this quantity, about one pack and a half consisted of beaver, one of bear, the remainder otter, marten, muskrat, and other small furs; worth, estimating within bounds, $360. With this sum he amply clothed himself and family, purchased arms, ammunition, traps, axes and knives, and had usually a sum left, which he appropriated to silver ornaments, ver-million and other extra, and ornamental articles.

As a hunter he was expert, and diligent, guarding with jealousy his rights to hunt in certain parts of the country, and esteeming the intrusion of others a trespass which he on one occasion in particular, punished in an exemplary manner. In his sales he evinced method and prudence.

He had attained nearly the heighth of his reputation before he married, which was not till he had reached nearly the age of thirty; and he then married a widow, with whom, however, he lived but two years, and had a son. He then married a girl of fourteen of the Totem of the Bear, by whom he had six children.

In his domestic habits he was affectionate and forbearing. When the hunting sea-son was over, he could never bear to be idle, and employed those moments in adding to the comforts and conveniences of his lodge; thus uniting qualities of mind, which have been supposed incompatible with the hunter state. His industry proceeded from forecast, added to a strong sense of obligation to his family. His views, were enlight-ened, compared with the mass of Indians who surrounded him. He saw the true situ-ation, not only of his relatives, but of the whole nation; and he resolved to use all his influence to rouse them to a true sense of it. With this view he admonished them to be active and diligent. To hunt well, and to fight well, were the cardinal maxims of his life, upon which he believed the happiness and independence of the nation to depend.

He possessed respectable powers as an orator, and he frequently addressed his people during those short seasons of leisure and festivity, which always succeed the close of the hunting seasons. To a ready flow of words, he united the all-powerful per-suasive of personal fame. He possessed a stature of 6 feet 6 inches in height, with a keen searching black eye, and a countenance and bearing commanding high respect. His movements were lofty and dignified; he swayed as much by his air and manner as by his words. Custom had rendered his decisions a law; and although all the govern-ment exercised by Chippewa chiefs, is that of mere opinion, he ruled his village with a power almost absolute.

Such is the effect of great personal prowess, and a reputation for bravery and sagac-ity, among savage nations. The whole power and destiny of such nations hinges upon the private character of a few great men, who start up, at long intervals, rouse and di-rect the energies of their followers to a few favorite points, and when they have suc-ceeded in moulding them to purposes of activity and combined action and feeling, die, and leave them to fall back into their former state of apathy and indolence. Where nothing is written, nothing is long remembered with accuracy; and hence, in a few years, their very history is lost, or involved in the inextricable labyrinth of fiction.

Waub Ojeeg had fixed his residence permanently at LaPointe, upon the main. His lodge was of an oblong shape, about 60 feet long, formed of posts fixed in the ground, and covered with the rind of the betula. From the centre, rose a stout post, reaching above the roof some feet—on the top of which was the carved figure of an owl, so placed as to turn with the wind, and serve the purposes of a weather-cock. When he went to his wintering ground, this lodge was shut up, and re-occupied again on his return. During the short excursions, made in spring and summer, the family retained possession of the lodge.

In one of these excursions, he had a most singular contest with a moose. He went out early one morning, to make marten traps; and had set about forty, and was returning, when he encountered a large animal of this species in his path, who evinced a disposition to attack him. As he was armed with only a small hatchet and knife, he tried to avoid him. But the moose came towards him in a furious manner. He took shelter behind a tree, shifting his place from tree to tree, as the enraged animal pressed upon him. At length as he fled, he picked up a pole, and quickly untying his moccasin strings, tied his knife to the end of it. He then placed himself in a favorable position behind a tree, and when the moose came up, stabbed him several times in the throat and breast. At length the animal fell. He then cut out the tongue as a trophy of victory, and returning to his lodge, related, to his family, the singular encounter he had had, and *where* they would find the animal. When they came to the spot, they found the snow trampled down in a wide circle, sprinkled with blood, and resembling a field of battle. The animal proved to be one of uncommon size.

A frame slender in proportion to his extraordinary height, together with great exposure of his person in his numerous war excursions, brought on a premature decay. He lingered several years with a pulmonary complaint, attended with spitting of blood. He lived long enough to see his eldest daughter and child united to Mr. Johnston, and died in 1793—aged about 45 years.

THE RISE OF THE WEST

or a Prospect of the Mississippi Valley.

From Helder's shades I take my lengthened way,
O'er hills that glitter in the evening ray;
By groves that stretch on sweet Owasco's side,
Or, bright Ontario's oceanic tide,
Where, far around while nature's charms are spread,
Niagara drowns the solitary tread.
Gay, pictur'd scenes of water, woods, and light,
Spread as I go, and as I view delight;
Islands and shores, and groves and lakes abound,
10   And nature blooms a new Arcadia round.

West—westward, are my footsteps onward led,
Where half the land, the waters overspread;
Where Huron gleams—a sea of liquid blue,
And the plumed Indian plies his light canoe:
15   Or where, in light, beneath a broader sky,
August Superior breaks upon the eye:
And many a cliff, impending from its brow,
Glooms o'er the waste of crystal waves below.

A sterner toil the prospect now demands,
20 Where dark Okaug or lone Itasca stands;
Commingling glooms besetting all the way,
The day's hard toil, the night's more still dismay—
Woods—where the sun is scarcely seen on high,
And streams, that haste to quit a polar sky—
25 Lakes choked with reeds—the beaver hunter's pride!
And grassy wastes, immeasurably wide,
Where life's best toil a scanty pittance brings,
And Mississippi, draws his infant springs.

Proud, swelling stream! from sources such as these,
30 Thou gatherest force to pierce remotest seas;
Sublime example, to the sons of fate,
How small effects are gathered into great.
Pride of the land! unequall'd in thy course,
What matchless waters swell thy onward force!
35 Ohio, teeming with a thousand floods,
Missouri, nurtured in Pacific woods!
The rolling Arkansas, whose wreck and tide,
From Ozark hills, and Mexic mountains glide.
These, are but parts of the wide-gather'd stores
40 That swell thy current, and augment thy shores.
What ocean-plains, illimitably great,
Spread from thy banks, and raise thy sullen state;
What cataracts tremble, and what lakes abound!
A maze of waters, peerless and profound.
45 A thousand miles the voyager may go,
Adown thy stream, yet find it onward flow;
A thousand more, and still his course shall be,
A thousand miles from thy recipient sea;
Where spreading out o'er reedy marshes wide,
50 Unrescued Hollands lie beneath the tide.

Swift as my bark along thy waters flies,
Cliffs, grottos, forests, dance before my eyes—
A varied picture starts at once to view,
Replete with tints for ever fresh and new.
55 At first, far distant in the icy zone,
Broad woods, and silver lakes thy fountains own!
Where bounds the roe-buck, or his antler dry,
Hung up to view, denotes th' Algonquin nigh.
Soon, nobler waters rush to swell the tide,
60 Falls glitter—rapids murmur—rivers glide;
And as the moving mass pervades the land,
Rocks rent apart, like giant castles stand.
Day after day, the swelling torrent grows,
Still broader, deeper, stronger as it flows;

65 Like some huge monster of the serpent kind,
That o'er the plain, at random, seems to wind;
But if a foe within his path arise,
Coiled in his might, he hisses and defies.
So chafed by rocks each cliff augments thy force,
70 Till states are sundered by thy royal course;
The wide, wild on-rush, puts each coast in fear,
For e'en Missouri is a tribute here.
The sea, as if respectful of the foe,
O'er many a league, hath ceased to ebb and flow,[1]
75 Choked by rent plains, and forests headlong hurled,
The continental dregs of half a world.

Across thy vale, the traveller may tread,
While a whole season whispers o'er his head,
And still, a summer's moon shall wax and wane,
80 Before he scales the broad Columbic chain.
Oft in his way, he hears the panther's cry,
Or sees the bison in disorder fly;
Oft stops to view, in lowland dark and lone,
The massy tusk, or huge protruding bone;
85 Uncouth remains of nature's early reign,
When the big mammoth stalk'd across the plain.
Happy perchance, if he escapes to meet,
Along the sands, the brown bear's grizzly feet;
Or shuns betimes, upon the desert mart,
90 The Pawnee lance, or wild Aurick'ree dart.
And frequent in his path, he stops to view,
The spreading plain, and distant mountain blue;
Or starts to see, amid the forest shade,
The open cavern, or the broad cascade,
95 Fountains that hiss, or sport a twinkling flame,
Streams all unsung, and falls without a name.

    Yet, though no rhyme, thy banks to fame prolong,
Beyond the warrior's chaunt, the boatman's song,
More happy in thy fate, than Ganges' tide,
100 No purblind millions kneel upon thy side.
Beyond the Nile—beyond the Niger blest,
No bleeding Parke—no dying Ledyard prest;
Or if one fate, foredoomed the Gaul[2] to bleed,
Success o'erpaid, and cancelled half the deed.
105 Not in hot sands, or savage deserts lost,
A healthful vigor blooms along thy coast,

---

1. The protrusion of the alluvions of the Mississippi, into the Gulf of Mexico, has been remarked by travellers.
2. La Salle.

And ever blest, above the orient train,
No crouching serf here clanks the feudal chain.
E'en the poor Indian, who in nature's pride,
110 Serenely scans thy long descending tide,
Turns in his thoughts, thy course 'twixt sea and sea.
And shouts to think his noble sons are free.

Here, as I stand upon the midland plain,
That gives to either gulf its ample drain;
115 Here, hemm'd by waters, on the polar shore,
Baffin behind and Mexico before.
Though distance spreads her veil before my eyes,
I see in fancy, half the world arise,
Mountains and gulfs, and distant sea and sail,
120 And each bold trait that bounds the mighty vale
On either hand a chain of mountains rude,
Shoots high above the waving sea of wood,
And shining waters, sands, and desert plains,
Where in his might, the roving Indian reigns.
125 This, bars approach along th' Atlantic side,
And that heaves back the vast Pacific tide;
While bold in front, the yellow Indies plac'd,
Like golden islands, gild the watery waste.
The true Hesperides! where crowned with fame,
130 Columbus first, in glory set his name;
Dark oceans past—a monarch's flag unfurled,
And gave to wondering man, another world.

Far to the left, the glorious lakes expand,
In bright effulgence o'er the fruitful land,
135 Huron and Erie—wild Igoma^3 free,
And pendant Michigan itself a sea.
With all the softer, lesser, lovelier train,
That fill th' illimitable watery chain,
Pure, bright, and clear, they stretch—a shining span,
140 Sublime Niagara, glittering in the van;
Pouring, as oft the traveller stops to hear,
An Illiad of waters on the ear.

The statesman as he hither turns his eyes,
Sees only marts, towns, cities, states arise,
145 And smiling points the yet unpeopled shore,
That opens still an ample space for more.
The stranger, from beyond the distant main,
Whom gust of fame impels, or search of gain,
Casts in his mind what home's sweet scenes recal,

---

3. An abbreviation of the Indian name for Superior.

150 And sighs to think his native streams so small;
No more his hopes, the Rhone, or Rhine fulfil,
And classic Thames, seems dwindled to a rill.
Far other aims the man of God inspires,
Whose bosom swells with philanthropic fires,
155 He sees what future millions here shall stand,
To spread Messiah's kingdom in the land.

O'er all the scene, incomparably great,
Kind airs are wafted, and a temper'd heat,
Soils, deep, and fattened with unnumbered floods,
160 Expanding plains, and green aspiring woods—
Cliffs,—where the eye surveys a length of ground,
And falls, that spread in spangled showers around;
Waters, to drive the wheel, or sport the sail,
And winds, that still with measured force prevail.
165 Nature in vigor strong, here kindly warms,
Each fruitful shape, and glows in ample forms,
Bird, beast and plant, are seen of shapely size,
And the deep forest all its tribes supplies;
Full, fair, luxuriant; strong of wing and foot,
170 From the fierce falcon, to the hoof armed brute.
But chief, the waters charm the wondering soul,
A mazy mass, that wanders o'er the whole,
Joins place to place, magnificent of plan,
And nought seems unreplenished here, but man.

175　And man is here! man in affliction tried,
A sufferer from beyond th' Atlantic tide,
Who left his land, his own lov'd Albion's shore,
That he, his God unshackled might adore;
Without the form—the pomp of book and stole,
180 Free as the aspirations of his soul,
A weary pilgrim o'er the briny waste,
Whom depth of woods, and savage men embrac'd.
Still ceased not tyranny, with poison'd spear,
To vex this man with tasks and burdens here,
185 Tasks of the mind and body, taste, sight, sound—
That bow'd, and bow'd, and prest him to the ground,
However courteous, loyal, wise, or brave,
And still would scourge and bind him as a slave.
Ah! England hide the secret as you can,
190 Thy monarchs here, but ruled to shackle man.

Oppressed he rose—but rose in hope and fear,
Against the parent proud, to wield the spear,
And feign would yet have dropt it, but still—still
Might claimed a blind assent to despot will;

195 That test broke off, what love had long delay'd
     And Freedom rose, and shook the shining blade.
     That freedom, nurst of yore in Cato's breast,
     Found other Catoes in the distant west,
     Flash'd in its ire, from Warren's battle sword,
200 And Laurens, rais'd superior to a lord,
     Taught Lafayette to cast his land behind,
     And burn'd unquench'd in Washington's great mind.

     Man, thus afflicted—thus in peril schooled,
     Cast forth from Europe, hated and misruled,
205 Forsaking all, that binds in every age,
     His home, his country, and his heritage.
     Not long delayed to prove—so heaven designed,
     The innate vigor of the free born mind;
     Calm he arose, when seven long years were o'er,
210 A sovereign, where a suppliant before;
     Truth's starry wreath with liberty entwined,
     And made the West, a refuge for mankind.

     Wide o'er the land, the race athletic spread,
     They wooed each science, plied each busy trade,
215 And by the needle led, or star-lit sail,
     Explored each coast, and rode in every gale,
     Nor less intent, to fill th' expectant hour,
     By well aimed thought, revealed the springs of power,
     Each verdant vale, displayed the murmuring mill,
220 Spires, villas, temples, rose on every hill,
     Till swelling numbers peopled every shore,
     And still new numbers deeper woods explore;
     O'er Alleghany's summit swept the band,
     War in their front, and war on either hand;
225 For now another foe arose in might,
     And filled the land with terror and affright.
     E'en the proud Indian—fugitive of God!
     Who seas and lands, still vainly treads, or trod,
     The Mongol of the West—light armed he stood,
230 Lord of the plains, the mountains and the wood,
     To him opposed advanced the Saxon line,
     Calm in their might, and fixed in their design.

     Again the rage of ire and battle burns,
     Sword, axe, and plow engage the hand by turns,
235 Forever ready in their skill and might,
     Stern at the plow, unyielding in the fight.
     As seasons wane, the arrowy foe retires,
     Dim, and more dim become his battle fires,
     Faint, and more faint, his piercing yells arise,

240 Till, deep desponding, westward fast he flies;
    Oft as he goes, he casts in fond review,
    The dear loved scenes his youthful vigor knew;
    And sadly chants as fast their hues decline,
    "These, oh my children, these fair lands were mine!
245 "Here in my youth, I drew the warlike bow,
    "Pierced the proud hind, or struck the lurking foe;
    "Here, rest my father's bones, by this marked stone,
    "And here, at last, I hoped to lay my own;
    "But fate denies the boon—I go—I go
250 "With yon bright sun, far off to lay me low."

    Now poised on yonder mountains rocky brow,
    In bitter thought, he scans the vale below,
    Aghast, he sees, far gleaming to the skies,
    That rushing stream, whence all his fears arise,
255 The great, the bold, the proud, the boast of all—
    Told in one word, we Mississippi call;
    Awhile he stands, mute, gazing on the shore,
    Then plies across, with half reluctant oar.

    'Tis done! the Indian is no more opprest,
260 Free, on the bounding prairies of the west;
    No longer bound to pine in want and woe,
    Around his door the flowers of plenty grow;
    No longer doomed to feel the legal glave,
    And bitter taunt that marked him for a slave,
265 His mind expatiates o'er a scene of rest,
    With equal laws, and independence blest.
    Yet, think not these, are gifts the chance imparts,
    Fame's forest lures, or war's barbaric arts,
    Arts that chained down to misery obscure,
270 His manly race, and kept them bound and poor;
    Ah no! his grasp relaxes spear and bow,
    Taught now to guide the shuttle and the plow,
    Flocks claim his care, and herds his pastures yield,
    And all the bounties of the furrowed field;
275 These fix his skill, awake sublimer aims,
    And light his altars up, with purer flames,
    For these, he scouts each idol from his sight,
    And Zion's hymns replace the horrid rite.
    Joy claps his hands, the sounds of mirth prevail,
280 And peace and population fill the vale;
    Such, are the scenes, o'er which the good man still,
    In joy exults, and trusts in heaven to fill.

    All ranks, all nations here securely meet,
    Led from afar, and find a bland retreat,

285 From Arno's cliffs, the frugal herdsman hies,
    Alps sternest tops; or Gallia's kindlier skies,
    From England's vales, where art and nature smile,
    The winding Elb, or Erin's verdant isle;
    Together mingling under western skies,
290 Wealth owns their toils, and bids the nation rise.
    State builds on state, to mark the growing vale,
    The shout of millions mingles in the gale.
    E'en now, although but few decades be ran,
    Hope thrills with heaven-born destinies for man,
295 And casting far behind the deeds of yore,
    Sees radiant glories crown the western shore.

    These are they hopes Columbia—these to fill,
    Be the just aim of sage and patriot still,
    To what new triumphs man shall here attain,
300 What arts shall grace, or arms deface the plain;
    What gifts shall bless or judgments shade with woe;
    Ill may the past, the hidden future show,
    Such is the rapid, such the bright career,
    That marks the rise of population here.
305 Perhaps the busy march that erst began,
    From Eden's gates; the pilgrimage of man;
    Spreading from bower to bower, from shade to shade,
    From land to land, shall here at last be stayed;
    Closed the last age in war's malign career,
310 And peace begin her blissful empire here.

    But ah, forbid, whate'er my country's end,
    One freeborn hand should tyrant power defend,
    Forbid, whate'er its pathway may afford,
    Her triumphs should be triumphs of the sword.
315 Dire, bloody feats, that elder states have tried,
    Rose, glittered, triumphed, tottered, sunk and died.
    Ah, rather let her spirit and increase,
    Shine in the glorious energies of peace;
    Arts, science, letters, be her aim and vow,
320 The pen and pencil, anchor, square, and plow,
    The tube and glass by which the starry train,
    Are brought to prove how worlds their laws maintain.
    Be ours, the forms of nature to unfold,
    Her gems of crystal, and her flowers of gold;
325 To mark the laws that rivet grain to grain,
    Shoot through the skies or govern in the plain;
    To lead the mind, as by a silken thread,
    O'er fields where learning's brightest flowers are spread,
    Scan moral truth, and fit mankind to rise,
330 In wisdom's scales, and ripen for the skies.

Nor shall the muse, a pensive wanderer roam,
Without an altar, and without a home,
But winning new-found glories for her lyre,
Rouse all the land, with truth's and virtue's fire.
335 Greece built her temples, Rome in purple shone,
Be man our temple, and the mind our throne,
So shall the West, her brightest crown receive,
And shine with jewels, kings could never give.

30

JAMES HALL

(1793–1868)

The Hall family of Philadelphia had worked in literary circles for fifty years when the youngest son of the first postrevolutionary generation came west as a soldier in the War of 1812. Following the war he returned east to train as a lawyer, and finally moved to Illinois to settle in 1820. Throughout the decade he sent his writing east, where his brothers published it in vaious journals. His first book, *Letters from the West* (1828), used an Irvingesque perspective to describe his own transition to western sensibilities. Nonetheless, more than most other western writers, Hall had access to eastern and European publication, and so *Letters* marked the beginning of a remarkable career as a writer of fiction, history, travel writing, and essays which was conducted in tandem with a successful career as a banker and judge.

After the success of *Letters,* Hall started *Illinois Monthly Magazine,* which openly announced itself as designed to develop western readers and writers to resist the misrepresentation of the region in the "national" publishing circles of the east. Nowhere is that more apparent than in the short story reproduced here, "Three Hundred Years Hence." Although Hall was, in the early 1830s, the second most successful American writer of short stories (behind Irving), this story is atypical of his style. Most of his stories depict various aspects of the settlement of the west, and range from the violence of "Harpe's Head" to the generic romance of "The Emigrants." This story, on the other hand, offers a rather apocalyptic vision of the west if industrialism is not checked. Hall elsewhere linked industrialism to Yankee materialism (such as in his essays on Black Hawk) as a source of corruption. Here, after pages describing what appears to be a utopian west in 2130, a class war erupts, and the west is shown to be ruined beyond redemption by its uncitical embrace of capitalism.

Hall's increasingly anti-Yankee sensibility is demonstrated in his pamphlet war with Lyman Beecher. Hall moved to Cincinnati in 1832 and succeeded Timothy Flint as editor of the *Western Monthly Review.* In 1835, Beecher published "A Plea for the West," in which he disparaged westerners for deviating from the New England model of American identity. In particular, Beecher was appalled by how western Protestants tolerated the Catholicism of the many western emigrants from Ireland, Germany, and Central Europe. Hall's eloquent and devastating response upholds standards of western difference and, more importantly, pluralism, and even multiculturalism, in contrast to the east's monoculturalism and close-mindedness.

This attitude is also apparent in many of Hall's writings about Native

Americans. Hall co-authored with Thomas McKenney the massive *History of the Indian Tribes* (1842), a three-volume folio that has often been accused of furthering removalist and racist ideas. However, the essays reproduced here suggest that Hall may have not been to blame for those aspects of the *History.* Appended to the eighth edition of the late Benjamin Drake's *Life of Black Hawk* (which Hall may well have edited), these essays suggest a vision of the west that, like those of his earlier writings, imagines a region whose various populations had cohabited in peace prior to and apart from the encroachments of the "Universal Yankee nation." Despite the fact that he had come west as a Yankee, perhaps no writer better demonstrates how a distinct culture and perspective had developed in the west than Hall.

Texts: "Three Hundred Years Hence," *Illinois Monthly Magazine,* ed. Hall (Shawneetown, Illinois, November 1830): 49–55. "The Catholic Question and a Plea for the West" (Cincinnati, 1838). Hall's essays on Black Hawk are included in the eighth edition of Benjamin Drake's *Life of Black Hawk,* ed. Hall Cincinnati, 1848: 249–257.

THREE HUNDRED YEARS HENCE (1830)

But ye!—ye are chang'd since I saw ye last,
The shadow of ages has round you been cast:
Ye are chang'd;—ye are chang'd; and I see not here,
What I once saw in the long vanish'd year.

—*MRS. HEMANS.*

Where is the American that feels a deep interest in the fate of his country, who has not sometimes wished, like Dr. Franklin, that he could "burst the cerements of the grave," and revisit his native land, after the lapse of a few centuries? Such a wish is certainly pardonable in a citizen of the United States, for his government is yet an experiment, and his native land but just started in the career of glory;—he sees the splendor of its morning sun, and it is natural that he should desire to awake, when it has climbed to the meridian. But, alas! the power of return is not given us, and we can only *conjecture* from the present march of improvement, the future population and resources of our country. For myself, I never feel so strongly the wish to return, as I do while riding over one of our Illinois prairies, with no boundary before me but the blue horizon. The stillness that reigns over these wide regions of verdure and flowers, will one day be broken, and the hum of a busy population be heard, where the deer now graze in fearless security. The improvements which the last twenty years have wrought in the west, are truly surprising;—what, then, may we not expect from two or three *centuries,* with all the increase of means that will exist?

While on a visit to a friend who resides on the high table land that extends be-

yond that part of the American bottom which lies opposite the county of St. Louis, I
took a solitary walk, one afternoon, in that wild, uncultivated region. The scattered
forest tress, the oak shrubs, the wild flowers, and the grass, had "felt the warm breath
of spring." The birds were busy in preparing their nests, and the joyful song of returning spring, was mingled with their labors.

In no part of our extensive country, is spring a more lovely season than in Illinois. There is something in the pure, bland air;—in the deep blue of the heavens, over
which a single cloud is sailing, and throwing its long and moving shadow on the
earth;—in the ceaseless plaint of the mourning-dove;—there is something in all this,
joined with the stillness and solitude of our boundless prairies, that finds its way to
the heart.

Wearied with my walk, I sat down at the foot of an oak, on one of the high
ridges that commands an extensive prospect of the table land. In the edge of the
landscape was an Indian mound, of the largest dimensions, crowned with trees equal
in size to those that grew around it. As I gazed upon the mound, a fit of dreamy musing came over me. I thought of the people who reposed in that sepulchre of other
years. "The flood of ages" had rolled over them, and its unceasing wave was still
sweeping on. What changes, thought I, have been wrought upon this spot, wild as it
now is, and what changes are yet to follow! In *three hundred years,* the shortest date
ever assigned to the most recent of these mounds, how changed will be this landscape! I was attempting to pierce through the intervening ages, and behold, with "my
mind's eye," the landscape as it would appear THREE HUNDRED YEARS HENCE, when
a tall, majestic figure, stood before me. A long snowy beard swept his bosom, and the
furrows of countless years were on his forehead. I felt my hair stand erect as I gazed
upon him. He waved the wand which he held in his hand, and addressed me, in a
tone that thrilled on every nerve. "Child of clay," said he, "I am the GENIUS of this
valley! From the time this globe rolled from the hand of Omnipotence, I have been
its *Guardian*, and directed its destiny. From my throne on the Rocky Mountains, I
have seen the whale spouting in the ocean that once covered its surface. The destined
period when it was to be drained for the residence of man, at length arrived. Since
that period, I have seen powerful nations rise and fall. The schemes of war and ambition, the yell of victory, the soft strains of peace and domestic love, have been here;
but all that belongs to man, soon joins itself to years and scenes that never have been.
The white man has come, and the light of science beams on his track;—the volume
of destiny is now rapidly unfolding its pages. Son of mortals! I have heard your wish
to behold this region as it will appear THREE HUNDRED YEARS HENCE. It is granted.
For you, I have rolled the tide of ages three centuries onward! Arise, and behold
this region as it will be THREE HUNDRED YEARS HENCE!" He touched me with his
wand, and I sprang to my feet! The oak, at whose foot I had just sat, was no longer
there; the forest trees, the shrubs and the wild flowers had disappeared, and I found
myself in the midst of a luxuriant-vineyard. I cast my eye over the tract which I had
so lately traversed, but not a feature was left of its former appearance. My first
impulse was to return to the house of my friend; but I soon recollected that he, and
all whom I had known, were, long since, mingled with their native dust; and in the
beautiful language of scripture, *"the places that once knew them, would know them no more
forever."* I bent my steps to a cottage which I saw at no great distance. As I passed
along, I heard the simple song of a vine dresser, in a language which, at first, I did
not recognize as English. I reached the hedge that enclosed the field, and passed

through a gate, near the cottage, into a broad and paved highway. The people stared upon me with astonishment, and the children set up a shout of surprise at my strange dress. In the streets was a stream of people, some on foot, and some in carriages of every description, loaded with various commodities, all going to, or returning from the west. This was a sufficient indication that St. Louis, or some other town west of me, had become the emporium of an immense commerce. I followed the moving mass of human beings in that direction. The road on either side, was bounded by a hedge, and as far as the eye could extend its vision, houses and cottages, gardens and vineyards, were thickly sprinkled. The small portion into which the soil was divided, showed that no law of primogeniture, giving all to the favored eldest, had yet prevailed.

From extreme old age to childhood, all were busy. Before the doors, children were seen platting straw, or picking leaves for the silkworms, and old men preparing the bands to confine the grape-vine to the stake. Next to the road, the country was almost one continued village. As I journeyed on, I saw nothing to remind me of the former appearance of that region;—even the natural features of the country, hill and dale, had changed under the all-subduing hand of human industry. A few miles onward, I came to a large village, and lingered there to admire the new and strange commodities suspended at the windows of the shops. A troop of boys soon followed me, attracted by the oddness of my dress. To avoid future inconvenience, I entered a clothes-shop, and exchanged mine for a suit of such as were worn by others. I could not avoid smiling at the strange appearance I made in my new costume.

I now passed on to the west, without further interruption, and saw the denseness of the population constantly increasing. The cultivated lands resembled one continued garden; and the passing throng received new accession from every road that led into the great high-way. At length I reached a spot which I recognized in a moment;—the bluff that overlooks the great AMERICAN BOTTOM! How beautiful a prospect was presented! The deep forest that once covered it had disappeared, and, as far as I could distinguish from the heights of the bluff, whole bottom was teeming with population. "Every rood maintained its man." The little squares of land, bounded by a green hedge row, with a house or cottage to each, looked beautifully in the distance. At intervals, columns of smoke were thrown up from the chimnies of large manufactories, and the sound of the steam engine was heard in every direction. Industry is not among the virtues of a slave, and I knew by the busy throng of old and young around the low, straw-thatched, but neat cottages, that my native land was yet free.

My thoughts reverted to St. Louis, and I was ruminating upon the various changes that had probably taken place in its wealth and population, when that city, with its thousand spires, burst upon my view! How glorious was the sight presented by "THE GREAT FATHER OF WATERS!" A forest of masts lined both shores, for miles, and every flag of Europe waved at the mast head of the steam ships that ploughed its waters. I entered the city by one of the iron bridges that spanned the river. The streets near the water first excited my attention. The bustle of loading and unloading the vessels;—the constant discharge of cannon from steam ships arriving and departing, carrying on commerce with every portion of the globe;—the various costumes and dialects of merchants and sailors from China, Japan, and the islands of the Pacific, prepared me to learn, without surprise, that St. Louis, in the interior of the most fer-

tile region of the globe, far exceeded, in wealth and population, the largest city of the
eastern hemisphere.

The language of the city bore a much nearer affinity to my own than that of the
country. Many new words had been introduced, and others had acquired a new definition and pronunciation; but I had less difficulty in understanding those who appeared to be the educated. Subsequently I was informed that the English language
was divided into three distinct dialects, differing from each other in writing and in
sound;—that of the British Islands—that of America, and that of India; produced by
the difference of climate, governments, customs, and the languages of the people in-
termingling with each other.

I left the streets near the wharves, and passed a great distance beyond the former
boundary of the city, yet all was still dense. The display of merchandize from the lofty
buildings that lined the streets, was rich beyond description. The stream of passing
people—the rattling of carriages on the pavement—the cries of people vending their
commodities in the street, and the din of the artizans' hammer, were all mingled together in one, confused sound. I was gratified that so large a proportion of buildings
were devoted to religious worship.

I was particularly anxious to learn the state of American literature, and the relative esteem in which English and American authors were held. For that purpose I entered one of the immense book-stores, and obtained permission to survey their
shelves. My curiosity was fully gratified, but I will not reveal too many "secrets of my
prison-house." I inquired for your SOUVENIR, but the bookseller was interrupted by
another customer, and my inquiry not answered. I obtained much information of past
ages from an antiquary, whom I found in the store; but was astonished at the many
gross errors into which he had fallen, about the times in which I had first lived. I asked
of him the estimation in which some of our present great men were held. Alas! their
very names were unknown—they had followed those of the "vulgar mass" into the
gulf of "blank oblivion." Man, brief in his mortal existence, is yet more brief in the
remembrance of others. The shouts of the mob at the success of a political partizan,
is not the voice of after ages. Superiority of mind only, is immortal.

The sun was now setting over this wilderness of houses. His parting beams flamed
on the gilded spires of this metropolis, and reminded me of the years when I had beheld him sinking behind an unbroken line of forest. I remembered the friend with
whom I had often walked, at that hour, on the banks of a romantic little lake in the
environs of the city. I wished once more to tread the spot, hallowed by the memory
of a long lost friend. With some difficulty I reached the vicinity of the lake. A thick
cloud of smoke hung over that portion of the city, caused by the thousand fires of the
steam engines, which the lake supplied with water. Here was the theatre of the most
extensive manufactures of the west. I would gladly have entered these manufactories,
but the labors of the day were closed, and I heard only the expiring sound of business, and saw the fading wreathes of smoke. The artizans were retiring to their houses
in the high buildings of the dirty and narrow streets. I rejoiced, as I saw this multitude
of all ages and sexes, that employment and sustenance was afforded to so numerous a
population, and I remembered with exultation, that I had warmly advocated every
plan that was suggested, to induce emigration to the west, even that of giving the lands
which belonged to all, as a bribe to entice settlers. Now was the good policy of these
measures apparent wherever I went, in the overflowing population of country and
town.

I lingered in this section of the city till the broad full moon rose, and threw her beams from Illinois, in a long track of light, which the broken surface of the river sent back in a thousand glittering fragments. I thought of the years when I had gazed upon the same moon that now looked down with a smile upon the graves of all who had lived in the same age with me. Absorbed with these meditations, I leaned against the corner of a manufactory. Presently, an indistinct murmur arose, and broke the spell that bound me. I listened with a vague presentiment that all was not right, and removed for concealment, into the shade of a building. People were gliding quickly along, like spectres, evidently wishing to be unobserved. I had not remained long in that place, when a wild cry arose from every quarter of the manufacturing section, and the bells from every spire pealed an ALARM. Multitudes of enraged manufacturers immediately arranged themselves under the command of their leaders, and the cry of "BREAD! BREAD! BREAD!" was heard in every terrific tone that the human voice can give it. An attempt was made by the insurgents to demolish the buildings of the most obnoxious of their employers, but the labor, was too great, and the cry "FIRE THEM!" scarcely had died away, when a thousand fires glared on the sky. A scene of plunder commenced, that baffles description; women and children of the manufacturers, squalid with hunger and rage, rushed with frantic yells into the buildings, for food and plunder. While this was acting, the government of the town had declared martial law, the city guards were ordered to the disaffected quarter, and the militia summoned to arms. The noise of the approaching troops sounded nearer and nearer, and the insurgents posted themselves in the most advantageous position for battle. Their chiefs rushed among them, animating them to the most deadly resistance, by reminding them of their starving families, and of the ignominious death that awaited all who were taken. The whole section was now red with conflagration, and the insurgents, as the flames glared on their faces, looked like a horde of demons, just escaped from the gulf.

I found myself directly between the city troops and the insurgents, with no chance of escaping either way. The artillery of both parties was just ready to discharge, and sweep through the street in which I stood. But one hope was left me; that of joining the city troops, and watching my opportunity of deserting their ranks. I ran towards them, but as I approached, a soldier seized me and declared I was one of the insurgents. My loud protestations of innocence availed not; the voice of reason and humanity were unheard, and vengeance was the cry. An officer ordered me to be instantly put to death. The soldier was prompt in obedience. He drew his sword. Horror seized all my faculties when I saw its glittering edge descending upon my naked head, with a force that—that—AWOKE ME! Yes, awoke me; for I had fallen asleep at the root of a large oak.

The trees were sending large shadows to the east, the cattle were returning homeward, and the tinkling of their bells, and the evening carols of the birds had taken the place of the late noise of approaching conflict. The vineyards and hedges, the thronged highway and crowded population, had vanished with my waking, and the country had assumed all its former wildness.

Now, gentle reader, peradventure, thou art not pleased with this dream, which I have related unto thee; albeit, before thou venturest to say ought against it, lean thine head against an oak, and see if thou canst dream a better; and if thou findest that thou canst, then, verily, thou hast my consent to do thine own dreaming.

BLUFFDALE

THE CATHOLIC QUESTION (1836)

This question has become so important in the United States, that it is time to begin to enquire into its bearings, and to know whether the public are really interested in the excitement which has been gotten up with unusual industry, and has been kept alive with a pertinacity that has seldom been equalled. For several years past the religious Protestant papers of our country, with but few exceptions, have teemed with virulent attacks against the Catholics, and especially with paragraphs charging them substantially with designs hostile to our free institutions, and with a systematic opposition to the spread of all free inquiry and liberal knowledge. These are grave charges, involving consequences of serious import, and such as should not be believed or disbelieved, upon mere rumor, or permitted to rest upon any vague hypothesis; because they are of a nature which renders them susceptible of proof. The spirit of our institutions requires that these questions should be thus examined. We profess to guaranty to every inhabitant of our country, certain rights, in the enjoyment of which he shall not be molested, except through the instrumentality of a process of law which is clearly indicated. Life, liberty, property, reputation, are thus guarded—and equally sacred in the right secured to every man, to 'worship God according to the dictate of his own conscience.'

But it is idle to talk of these inestimable rights as having any efficacious existence, if the various checks . . . thrown around them by our constitution and laws, are now evaded, and a lawless majority, . . . take them by force from a few individuals who may be effectually outlawed by a perverted public opinion, produced by calumny and clamor. It is worse than idle, it is wicked, to talk of liberty, while a majority, having no other right than that of the strongest, persist in blasting the character of unoffending individuals by calumny, and in oppressing them by direct violence upon their persons and property not only without evidence of their delinquency, but against evidence, not only without law, but in violation of law—and merely because they belong to an unpopular denomination.

The very fact that the Roman Catholics are, and can be with impunity, thus trampled upon, in a country like ours, affords in itself the most conclusive evidence of the groundlessness of the fears, which are entertained by some respecting them. Without the power to protect themselves, in the enjoyment of the ordinary rights of citizenship, and with a current of prejudice setting so strongly against them, that they find safety only in bending meekly to the storm, how idle, how puerile, how disingenuous is it, to rave as some have done, of the danger of Catholic influence!

We repeat that this is a question which must rest upon testimony. The American people are too intelligent, too just, too magnanimous, to suffer the temporary delusion by which so many have been blinded, to settle down into a permanent national prejudice, and to oppress one christian denomination at the bidding of others without some proof, or some reasonable argument.

We have not yet seen any evidence in the various publications that have reached us, of any unfairness on the part of the Catholics, in the propagation of their religious doctrines. If they are active, persevering, and ingenious, in their attempts to gain converts, and if they are successful in securing the countenance and support of those who maintain the same form of belief in other countries, these, we imagine, are the legitimate proofs of christian zeal and sincerity. In relation to Protestant sects, they are certainly so estimated; and we are yet to learn, why the ordinary laws of evidence are to be set aside in reference to this denomination, and why the missionary spirit which is so praiseworthy in others, should be thought so wicked, and so dangerous, in them.

Let us inquire into this matter calmly. Why is it that the Catholics are pursued with such pertinacity, with such vindictiveness, with such ruthless malevolence! Why cannot their peculiar opinions be opposed by argument, by persuasion, by remonstrance, as one christian sect should oppose another. We speak kindly of the Jew, and even of the heathen; there are those that love a Negro or a Cherokee even better than their own flesh and blood; but a Catholic is an abomination, for whom there is no law, no charity, no bond of christian fraternity.

These reflections rise naturally out of the recent proceedings in relation to the Roman Catholics. A nunnery has been demolished by an infuriated mob—a small community of refined and unprotected females, lawfully and usefully engaged in the tuition of children, whose parents have voluntarily committed them to their care, have been driven from their home—yet the perpetrators have escaped punishment, and the act, if not openly excused, is winked at, by Protestant christians. The outrage was public, extensive, and undeniable; and a most respectable committee, who investigated all the facts, have shown that it was unprovoked, a mere wanton ebullition of savage malignity. Yet the sympathies of a large portion of the Protestant community are untouched. On the other hand, when an individual stated in one of our papers, that he had been forced at a Catholic meeting to take off his hat—a circumstance unsupported by any proof, and if proved, perfectly immaterial—the religious papers took up the matter in high dudgeon, the affair was magnified into a Catholic mob, and the most severe animadversions were made upon this supposed instance of Catholic domination. There was a perfect storm in a tea-kettle over Mr. Alexander Duncan's hat, and Cincinnati was supposed, by persons at a distance, to be in a state of civil commotion, when in fact the legend of the hat had not been heard of by a majority of its citizens, and to this day there are thousands who doubt the story. Now let the dispassionate reader mark the difference. In the one case, admitting the printed statement to be true, a piece of rudeness is practiced by uncourteously taking a hat from the head of an ill-mannered person, who chose to wear it irreverently in the presence of a religious assembly—in the other, there is actual crime—riot, robbery, and arson. Yet there are editors whose judgments are so completely warped on this subject, that the outrage upon the Ursulines, which should cause the spirit of every American freeman to kindle into indignation, is coldly stated by them as an item of news, while the rape of the hat is a tremendous affair, which is thought fit to be noised forth in the shrillest notes of the trumpet of party discord.

Is another instance required, of the pervading character of this prejudice? How common has been the expedient, employed by missionaries from the west, in the eastern states, of raising money for education or for religion upon the allegation that it was necessary to prevent the ascendancy of the Catholics. How often has it been asserted, throughout the last ten years, that this was the chosen field on which the papists had erected their standard, and where the battle must be fought for civil and religious liberty. What tales of horror have been poured into the ears of the confiding children of the pilgrims—of young men emigrating to the west, marrying Catholic ladies, and collapsing without a struggle into the arms of Romanism—of splendid edifices undermined by profound dungeons, prepared for the reception of heretic republicans—of boxes of fire-arms secretly transported into hidden receptacles, in the very bosoms of our flourishing cities—of vast and widely ramified European conspiracies by which Irish Catholics are suddenly converted into lovers of monarchy, and obedient instruments of kings!

If further evidence of the extent of this infatuation was required, it might be found in the astonishing circulation of the absurd and mischievous book of Miss Reed and the unanimity with which it is attempted to be sustained by a certain class of editors. That volume bore upon its face internal evidence of its utter worthlessness. No discriminating person could read it without arriving at the conclusion, that its author was weak, prejudiced, ignorant, and devoid of rectitude. If ever there was an apt illustration of that remarkable solecism in language, 'uneducated mind is educated vice' it seems to be found in the production of this noted person, whose uneducated mind has exhibited a fecundity in the conception of cunning stratagems, to deceive her patroness, and to gull the public, for which a parallel can scarcely be found in the annals of deception. If the book was true, there is little in it, except the singular display of credulity and deceit on the part of the author; if false, which it is now proved to be by irrefragable testimony, it is a wicked affair: yet thousands of copies have been sold, and scores of gentlemen, who would not themselves be guilty of perpetrating a falsehood, and whose personal integrity is above reproach, continue to laud the book and to sustain its author.

A prejudice so indomitable and so blind, could not fail, in an ingenious and enterprising land like ours, to be made the subject of pecuniary speculation; accordingly we find such works as the 'Master Key to Popery,' 'Secrets of Female Convents,' and 'Six Months in a Convent,' manufactured with a distinct view to making a profit out of this diseased state of the public mind. The abuse of the Catholics therefore is not merely matter of party rancor, but is a regular trade, and the compilation of anti-catholic books of the character alluded to, has become a part of the regular industry of the country, as much as the making of nutmegs, or the construction of clocks.

The elements of this prejudice may therefore be readily traced. Much of it is inherited, is interwoven with our nature, has been ingrained by education, and has grown with our growth. The consequences of the Reformation were momentous, and widely spread; and we look back to that period as the dawn of many of the principles of liberty which we cherish dearly, and of privileges which we now hold to be as inviolate as they are valuable. Of course we involuntarily regard the Catholics as the adversaries with whom we have combatted, and from whom have been wrested, both power and the acknowledgment of principles. The history of that contest is rendered familiar by our early studies, and impressed upon the mind throughout, the whole courses of education; the books that we read of children, and those which employ the more mature reflection of manhood, teem alike with the details of this controversy. But unfortunately the studies of the man receive a tinge from the prejudices of the child, and certain propositions are assumed gratuitously by each party against the other, not because they are true, but because we have been accustomed to believe them. We read of the corruptions of the Catholic church previous to the Reformation, and we assume that they still exist, as a characteristic and component part of the Romish system. We discover arrogance, intolerance, rapacity, cruelty, and laxity of morals, pervading the action of a church, which was the *only church,* during an era of violence and moral darkness; and we do not inquire whether any other church similarly situated would not have become equally depraved—whether the same causes would not have produced the same effects, upon any other equal number of individuals who should have been placed in like circumstances. Philosophy sanctions the belief, that power held by any set of men without restraint or competition, is liable to abuse; and history teaches the humiliating fact that power thus held has always been abused. To inquire who has been the greatest aggressor against the rights of human nature, when all who have been tempted have evinced a common propensity to trample upon the laws of justice and benevolence, would be an unprofitable procedure. The reformers punished heresy by death as well as the Catholics; and the murders perpetrated by intolerance, in the reign of Elizabeth, were not less atrocious than those which occurred under 'the bloody Mary.' We might even come nearer home, and point to colonies on our own conti-nent, planted by men professing to have fled from religious persecution, who not only excluded from all civil and political rights those who were separated from them by only slight shades of religious belief, but persecuted many even to death, for heresy and witchcraft. Yet these things are not taken into the calculation, and the Catholics are as-sumed, without examination, to be exclusively and especially prone to the sins of op-pression and cruelty. The remarkably tasteful engraving to the primmer, which pres-ents the Rev. John Rogers and the afflicted Mrs. John Rogers, surrounded by their interesting little family of ten small children including one at the breast, with the ac-companying horrors of the stake, and the myrmidons of power armed with battle-axes, has settled the belief of many a child in regard to the horrors of popery, and closed every avenue of his mind against the ingress of light and knowledge. Sectarians have taken advantage of this perversion of feeling—not because their own form of belief really required such adventitious support, but because some men choose to accomplish their ends, by indirect methods; some require excitement and can only operate effi-ciently on others by playing on the passions, while a large number have identified the devil and the pope, and made up of the two a personification of sin, against which they feel conscientiously bound to do battle even unto death. Thus men, who in their hearts despise the littleness of these proceedings, give into them from considerations of ex-pediency—the end sanctifying the means. Experience has proved that men are most prodigal of their money when in a state of excitement, and that they will give more, freely to gratify passion, than in the practice of abstract benevolence. If, therefore, money is needed to build a college, the approved plan of asking it is not, 'we need such an institution to educate our youth,' but, 'the Catholics are erecting colleges—if we do not educate our youth, they will do it for us'—if a church is to be erected, the phrase is not, 'aid us with your substance to build a house for the worship of God,' but 'help us to fight the Catholics.' Thus the vulgar prejudice against this sect of christians is per-petuated, by holding them up as the enemies of religion and education; and there are individuals who devote themselves to the office of deepening the impressions of dis-like against them which were engraved on our hearts in childhood, with a zeal less ami-able, but quite as ardent, and almost as respectable, as that of the Scottish enthusiast, who devoted his whole life to the task of retouching the inscriptions on the tomb-stones of the Cameroneans.

There are unhappily persons enough in this world, who have sufficient wis-dom—speaking after the manner of men to know that wherever there is delusion, there is money to be made; and there is no hallucination which has furnished a richer harvest than the one now under discussion. The printer, the engraver, the book ped-lar, have thriven upon it. Every corner of the Union has been visited by the itinerant vender of books—a person of grave deportment, professing himself the disinterested messenger of benevolence, entering the dwelling of the farmer with demure aspect, and breaking to him in scarcely audible whispers, the intelligence, that he brings to

him an invaluable volume, which discloses all the dark and dreadful secrets of the inquisition—illustrated with elegant engravings, price one dollar—*only*. The farmer
hates the Catholics, suspects the book pedlar, and dislikes to part company with the
dollar; but the curiosity of the wife, or peradventure his own, prevails, and as the volume usually turns out to be a cheat, he takes out the worth of his money in heartily
hating both priest and pedlar, during the remainder of his natural life. Not so his children. To them the books thus actively disseminated through the lead by a legion of
unprincipled mercenaries, are rank poison. They agonize over the sufferings of the
martyrs, and stand aghast as they contemplate the engines of torture—the thumb-
screws, the gridirons, the pincers, and the red hot pokers, which decorate these delectable volumes; and they grow up with inveterate prejudices, unjust to others and
injurious to themselves. Even the affair to which we have alluded, as having been supposed to have taken place in Cincinnati, has been the means of turning an honest
penny for an ingenious artist in New York, who has executed an engraving representing that persecuted young gentleman, Alexander Duncan, in the hands of a
Catholic mob. In the foreground stands the suffering martyr, clinging, for conscience
sake, close to his hat, which a furious, two-fisted Irish Catholic, is endeavoring to force
from his head—a priest holds up the cross, and an armed mob are rushing upon the
devoted heretic—while the gallows in the back ground shows the fate that awaited
the unfortunate Alexander Duncan had he not been rescued by the civil authority
from the hands of the infuriated papists!

There is another description of opposition against the Catholics, which is laudable, and which we should be the last, either to condemn or treat with levity—the
lawful war of principle, waged against their tenets, or their practice, and conducted
according to the established usages of courtesy, and christian forbearance. Those who
believe this form of belief to be unscriptural, to be pernicious in its tendencies, to be
inefficient in its code of morality, or to be unsafe as a guide to salvation, have an undoubted right to erect a barrier of moral antagonism against it, and to oppose it with
all the weapons which may be used consistently with truth and fairness. To combat
error is a duty incumbent on every man whose sphere of action is such as to give him
away over the minds of others; but it is not allowable to oppose even error, by artifice
or injustice, by violating private right, or disturbing the public peace.

It will be perceived that in all we have said, we have not touched the question,
whether the Catholics are, in fact, theologically, or politically, in error. We have not
the slightest partiality for their form of belief, their mode of worship, or the practicable operation of their system. We like our own faith and practice better. But these
questions are not material to the issue now under discussion. However wrong they
may be, they have a right to be considered as being conscientiously wrong, and to be
treated with kindness.

We come then to the point, and inquire, is there any part of the present or past
conduct of the catholics, which would authorize us to thrust them out of the pale of
christian charity, and carry on a controversy with them on principles different from
those which regulate the intercourse of other christian sects. We have shown that
much of the prejudice against them had its origin in historical reminiscences, partially
and injudiciously preserved—much of it is mere fanaticism—a great deal is sheer pretence got up on speculation—and a respectable portion is founded on honest difference of opinion.

In examining into the character of the catholics as a body, it is absurd to appeal
to those atrocities which throw a gloom over the history of past centuries. The

catholics of the present day are no more responsible for those acts, than we are for the execution of Servetus, or for the decapitation of Charles I. and an inference to their prejudice, drawn from the acts of the church in the dark ages, would be just as unfair as to charge any part of the American people of the present day with the intolerance and superstition of the puritans. In both cases, the errors were those which were peculiar to the times, rather than to a class of actors. The misdeeds of the catholic church in the days when it was both corrupt and intolerant, should be viewed now anly as abstractions, with which living individuals cannot be properly connected, and which can only be referred to as points of history, affording evidence of the depravity of the human mind, humiliating to all alike, who are liberal enough to look at such matters in a calm spirit of philosophy.

It is with the catholics of our own time, and country that we have to do, and especially in reference to the liberality of their civil, political, and religious opinions. At a period nearly contemporaneous with the settlement of the British colonies in America, the French began to settle Canada and Louisiana; and if we compare the early colonists, we find decidedly more toleration and benevolence on the part of the French catholics than on that of the English puritans. In the treatment of the Indian tribes, the French were, with a few exceptions in lower Louisiana, just, kind, and considerate, while the English colonists, all but the followers of Penn, were decidedly reckless, cruel, and unjust. We are not aware that catholicism produced, in this instance, any difference; the disparity between the policy of the two nations arose out of the native amiability of the one, and the natural ruggedness of the other; but it is worth while to show that papacy, if not more efficacious than other forms of faith, was not less so, in the forming stage of our society, so far as either influenced the political relations of the colonists.

The French catholics, at a very early period, commenced a system of missions for the conversion of the Indians, and were remarkably successful in gaining converts, and conciliating the confidence and affections of the tribes. While the Pequods and other northern tribes were becoming exterminated, or sold into slavery, the more fortunate savage of the Mississippi was listening to the pious counsels of the catholic missionary.—This is another fact, which deserves to be remembered, and which should be weighed in the examination of testimony. It shows that the catholic appetite for cruelty is not quite so keen as it is usually imagined, and that they exercised, of choice, an expensive benevolence, at a period when protestants, similarly situated, were blood-thirsty and rapacious.

Advancing a little further in point of time, we find a number of colonies advancing rapidly towards prosperity, on our Atlantic sea board. In point of civil government they were somewhat detached, each making its own municipal laws, and there being in each a predominance of the influence of one religious denomination. We might therefore expect to see the political bias of each sect carried out into practice, and it is curious to examine how far such was the fact. It is the more curious, because the writers and orators of one branch of this family of republics, are in the habit of attributing to their own fathers, the principles of religious and political toleration, which became established throughout the whole, and are now the boast and pride of our nation. The impartial record of history affords on this subject a proof alike honorable to all, but which rebukes alike the sectional or sectarian vanity of each. New-England was settled by English puritans, New-York by Dutch protestants, Pennsylvania by Quakers, Maryland by Catholics, Virginia by the Episcopalian adherents of the Stuarts, and South Carolina by a mingled population of roundheads and cavaliers from

England, and of French huguenots—yet the same broad foundations of civil and political liberty were laid simultaneously in them all, and the same spirit of resistance animated each community, when the oppressions of the mother country became intolerable. Religious intolerance prevailed in early times only in the eastern colonies, but
the witchcraft superstition, though most strongly developed there, prevaded some
other portions of the new settlements. We shall not amplify our remarks on this topic;
it is enough to say, that if the love of monarchy was a component principle of the
catholic faith, it was not developed in our country when a fair opportunity was offered for its exercise; and that in the glorious struggle for liberty, for civil and religious
emancipation—when our fathers arrayed themselves in defence of the sacred principles involving the whole broad ground of contest between liberty and despotism, the
catholic and the protestant stood side by side on the battle field, and in the council,
and pledged to their common country, with equal devotedness, their lives, their fortunes, and their sacred honor. Nor should it be forgotten, that in a conflict thus peculiarly marked, a catholic king was our ally, when the most powerful of protestant
governments was our enemy.

The intelligent reader will draw his own inferences from these facts. To our mind
they bear incontestible evidence, that whatever catholicism may once have been, and
whatever it now is in countries where it is the established religion, and stands connected with despotic governments, the American catholics have become imbued with
the spirit of the atmosphere and the age in which they live, and being men of like passions with ourselves, are equally devoted to the land which cherishes and the laws
which protect them.

Nor do we believe that the American catholic church exerts any systematic influence, either to keep its people in ignorance, or to instil into them opinions hostile
to freedom. We are satisfied, as to the first branch of this proposition, by the zeal which
they have shown in the establishment of seminaries of learning, upon the most sound
and liberal foundation, for the education of their youth of both sexes, and by the high
degree of refinement and erudition which prevails among the gentlemen of that denomination, both lay and clerical. And we state here, upon unquestionable authority,
the corroborative fact, that the discussion between the Rev. Mr. Breckenridge and
Mr. Hughes, relative to the fundamental tenets of the catholic creed, and which the
former was acknowledged, even by his opponents, to have managed with great address and ability, was republished, *in extenso*, in the catholic papers of the United
States, and the forcible arguments of Mr. Breckenridge against their form of belief,
placed in the hands of the whole catholic community.

The other point is, we think, equally clear of difficulty; catholic gentlemen have
served our country in various civil and military stations, and have not proved less
faithful than others—they are found among our writers, and are not less pure in the
tone of their moral sentiment, nor less orthodox in the character of their political
faith, than their contemporaries. In the party contests which have involved dogmas
more or less liberal, we have in no case seen the influence of that abused church concentrated upon one or the other side; nor have we the slightest evidence of any concerted action on the part of the priests, to arrange an organization for political action,
or to keep up the details of party discipline.—And none who are familiar with the
workings of the human mind, and are acquainted with the multitudinous and perplexing difficulties which interfere with the regular action of *a party*—especially of a
party thinly scattered over a country so wide as ours—can believe that a *cunning*
priesthood would suffer their people to become accustomed to a separate and inde-

pendent action, and to habits of liberal thought; if they possessed the power and had conceived the plan, of eventually arranging over them a regular scheme of party subordination. But above all, we can scarcely comprehend the amazing fatuity of that intellect, which can imagine that such a plan could be seriously attempted in the bosom of a country like ours, at the bidding of foreign potentates hostile to liberty; and that the indigent catholic foreigners, who have fled the lash of oppression, and come among us breathing hot and bitter curses against the despots of the old world, are destined to become the willing instruments in establishing the same pollutions in the new! We can imagine no motive which could induce the Pope to employ his clergy in so hopeless a task, unless it were that which constrained the wizard Michael Scott, to engage one of his subordinate spirits in the endless and fruitless work of making ropes of sea sand—the want of other employment.

But supposing the catholics to be anti-republican, anti-religious, anti-social, as they are represented—is there any real danger to be apprehended from their influence? Gentlemen, who are excited by partizan feelings may not believe our statements, in opposition to their own exaggerated estimate of the power of the catholics, but they will hardly deny the results drawn from authentic statistical tables. In the American Almanac, a work published at Boston, under the direction of Dr. Worcester, a learned and excellent gentleman, who is neither a Jesuit nor an emissary of Metternick,—in the volume for 1829, at page 168—is a table showing the comparative numerical strength of the religious denominations of the United States, in which sectarian influence in supposed to be divided as follows:

Those who are attached directly or indirectly to the various *protestant* sects, compose an aggregate of	11,646,453
Those under Catholic influence,	500,000
Jews and others not included above,	50,000
	12,196,453
The whole population in 1830 was	12,856,171

The Catholics then in 1832 formed a minority of less than one twenty-fifth part of the population of the United States; and it is this little body, scattered over the whole territory of the union, and existing nowhere in any concentrated body capable of a vigorous action, that is held up as so formidable to the liberty of the nation! And this, too, while the grent elements of power, physical and moral, such as the wealth, the literature, the education, the press, the government of the country, are almost exclusively in Protestant hands. It is useless to accumulate arguments on such premises.

But there is another question which must be disposed of. The editor of a religious paper in this city, for whose talents and piety we entertain a sincere respect, but who has in this matter permitted his zeal to outstrip his judgment, has lately used the following language:

"With due respect for literary and political editors, we would humbly inquire, whether it is their province to hold a supervision over the religious press of the country. Some literary and some political editors, have deemed it their duty to step in to rebuke the acerbities of religious papers. Most unfortunately, for the *effect* of their reproofs, they have been uttered in a spirit of supercilious dictation and bitter rebuke, for which scarce a parallel can be found in any political or religious discussion. Uttered with a spirit of kindness, and with that *modesty which becomes all men interfering with the appropriate business of others,* these reproofs might avail much to soothe down the waves of religious controversy. But when these reproofs develope the very spirit rebuked, they will only excite a smile al the inconsistency of gentlemen, who while, they write bitterly upon politics, are so *furious for peace,* in the religious world, that they give their admonitions to religious editors in the language of sweeping denunciation.

Does this tend to promote peace!

As every religious sect, in this country, is furnished with channels for communicating with the public, and can rebuke wrongs when they exist, would it not best promote the peace of society, to leave religious matters to the keeping of *professedly religious men,* while politicians attend to their own appropriate and important duties? These duties they have studied practically. They can perform them without outraging the religious sensibilities of any portion of their patrons, and without bringing any suspicion upon the integrity of their motives. For us to attempt to correct every supposed evil in the political press, would savor of arrogance.—And when we see a political editor rushing into religious discussions, which must bring him into direct and hostile collision with his political friends, we think he has mistaken the proper sphere of his duty. Are we wrong?"

From other paragraphs in the same paper, as well as from the language quoted, we assume that we are included in the 'some literary' editors, whose misdeeds have drawn forth this reproof, and that our chief offence consists in having reviewed in our last number, a geographical, statistical, political, anti-catholic sermon. Now let us argue this matter coolly. We have never urged as an objection against the learned divine who wrote that sermon, that he discussed topics not strictly theological, on the contrary, we should rejoice to see his vigor of intellect and great stores of attainment, poured out copiously, upon any useful train of thought in which he might choose to engage. But when he comes within our jurisdiction, shall he not be held responsible to the laws of criticism? When Metternich, and the catholics, senator Benton, and the 'Great West,' are the subjects of discussion, and the main point of the whole argument is to prove a vast political conspiracy, shall the political heresy of the writer be cloaked under his theological garb, and the shield of his clerical character be interposed between himself and the critic? This position is not tenable.

Again, if the religious papers unite in a conspiracy against a sect of christian directed against their religious sects, but their moral character, and their supposed political bias, are the literary and political presses to be muzzled, and shall it not be lawful for us to say, 'we believe these men to be peaceable and patriotic citizens?' Are not Theresa Reed, and the Cambridge mob, and the proprietor of the hat, fair subjects of criticism, or do their doings involve recondite questions in theology, which cannot be understood by laymen?

But we have rebuked 'the acerbities of religious papers.' Very well—if the editors of religious papers forget their sacred and peaceful, vocation, and convert the sheets that should be messengers of good tidings, into vehicles of abuse and slander, shall they not be rebuked? We do not rebuke the editor of such a paper, when acting within his sphere; let him remain within the sacred precincts of his vocation, and he will not be molested—let him take sanctuary under the hallowed influence of the altar, and none will pursue him there. It is only when he steps out of his office, that we assail him. When he throws off his black coat and flourishes a cudgel, we treat him as we would a friend that we find engaged in a brawl in the street—we make him put on his coat, and go home.

But this has been done 'in a spirit of supercilious dictation, for which scarce a parallel can be found in any political or religious discussion.' This we imagine is not meant for us—we are not aware of any distinct self-application; but if we are called upon to reply to it, we shall ask the favor of the editor to lend us a file of his back papers.

As to all the rest of this paragraph, wherein literary and political editors are admonished not to interfere with the appropriate duties of others, lest the *integrity of their motives* should be suspected, &c. we advise the writer, when he returns from his present absence, 'with a mind invigorated by rest, and enriched by observation,' to take it under revision. The *infallibility of the church is not a protestant doctrine;* the popish hierarchy, in the plenitude of its power, never aspired at a higher exercise of authority, than that which forbade laymen from meddling in the affairs of the church. Alas! for poor human nature! Little did Luther and Calvin and other great lights of the Reformation imagine, that in the year 1835, a protestant minister would be standing up for the infallibility of the clergy, and rebuking laymen for looking too curiously into the affairs of the church!

But we are willing to do as our friend suggests, provided we be allowed to do it of our own free will; we will not be forced to turn volunteer in this matter. If we choose to write about religion, we shall do so, and if not, we shall let it alone. If the religious editors feel any vocation for reviewing literary works, we freely concede to them the privilege; we are not so selfish as to covet the monopoly of worrying delinquent authors, and would not consider it a pleasure to have the sole right of darting out, like a ravenous spider, upon an unhappy writer, and bearing him away to our solitary cell to be devoured in secret; nor do we think, that our clerical contemporaries should desire to enjoy the exclusive luxury, of revelling upon the agony of tortured catholics, or of reaping instruction from the delectable pages of the inimitable Rebecca Theresa Reed.

We apprehend, however, that the vexed subject of the catholics, may be compromised, upon principles to which none ought to object, and least of all, the editor whose language we have quoted, and who has indicated to us, the course which we shall recommend to him. Let the religious papers cease to treat the subject, except as a theological question, confining their strictures to the religious tenets of the catholics; and treating those points with the gravity and decorum proper to such a controversy. We have no doubt, that the catholic papers would conform to a conduct so obviously proper, and so calculated to restore harmony; and that the whole discussion might be either suffered to drop, or be carried on with a becoming spirit of courtesy. If the protestants consider it a duty to allure the catholics to a better faith, let them use the arts of persuasion, which they address to others; let them labor to surround those they would win, by good influences, moral, intellectual, and religious; and let them cease to use the poisoned weapons of abuse and sarcasm, which inflict incurable wounds, and produce mutual alienation. Let Metternich, and the emperor of Austria, be turned over to the politicians, and we will engage, that clever as they may be, they will find their match. As to the priests, if they attempt any extra flourishes, and endeavor to introduce the gentlemanly crime of treason into our sober country, we can have the *second section* amended for their particular benefit. Any literary peccadillos which may be committed under the auspices of the pope, will be punctually attended to, by some of the numerous journals which deal in such matters—we have a volume before us now, which, although it is without a title, we suspect to be of popish origin, and to which we shall show no mercy. We hardly know how to include the nuns, who are non-combatants, in any regular treaty, but we recommend, when any convent in future, shall be taken by assault, that the garrison, if consisting of not more than half a dozen females, shall be permitted to march out with the honors of war, with colors flying, and that they tarry not at such a place—assured as they may be, that neither laws nor ramparts will avail, in any land where female weakness is not its own best protection.

From the Western Monthly Magazine, by James Hall, Esq. Critical Notices A Plea for the West: By Lyman Beecher, D. D. Cincinnati. Truman and Smith. 1835.

This is called a Plea for the West, but is intended to be a plea for Lane Seminary, and is in fact a plea against the catholics. It is comprised in a book of one hundred and seventy-two pages, and is said to be 'a discourse delivered by the writer in several Atlantic cities last season, while on an agency for Cincinnati Lane Seminary.' If this be so, we must acknowledge that tho people of Atlantic cities are remarkably polite listeners, for it would have required at least three hours to declaim all that is set down in this volume, and nothing but the novelty of its topics could have compensated for the tediousness of its details. These topics are the greatness of the West, and the wickedness of the catholics; the first of which occupies one third of the volume, and the latter the whole of the remainder.

The very important proposition, that 'the West is destined to be the great controling power of the nation,' is argued by Dr. Beecher with his usual force of language; and as this *very* original idea has not been advanced more than about fifty-two times a year, throughout the last twenty years, the doctor has properly supported it by facts, which must have been quite new to his audiences. Such, for instance, as that the territory of the West 'is eight thousand miles in circumference, extending from the Allegheny to the Rocky mountains, and from the gulf of Mexico to the lakes of the north'—that 'it is the largest territory, and most beneficent in climate, and soil, and mineral wealth, and commercial facilities, ever prepared for the habitation of man'—together with a variety of other statements equally novel and instructive.

The magnitude of the West, and its giant strides to greatness, are indeed noble themes—but as we happen to have seen them treated in nearly a hundred books, and to have heard them reiterated from the pulpit times out of number, we must be excused from following our learned author thro' the thousandth plagiarism upon the fortunate man, who first found out that the West was very big, and was growing bigger very fast.

Indeed we should not think it worth while to notice at all, a discourse which is but the echo, still living upon the ears of all our readers, if it was not for some curious facts attending its history, which require disclosure.

It will be recollected that in December last, we published an extract from the Lowell Journal, a highly respectable newspaper, published in Massachusetts, in which the sermon preached by Dr. Beecher, in behalf of Lane Seminary, was represented in the following language:

'In the course of his remarks, he alluded to the diversity of character in the West, the larger portion of their society being emigrants from different parts of this and other countries; spoke of their limited means of education, and of the importance of introducing the social and religious principles of New England among them—New England principles, the matchless bounty of a bountiful Providence! He dwelt upon the importance of early and immediate action—the importance of sowing the seeds of virtue before vice had taken root among them—bade us remember that uncultivated virtue was cultivated vice!—and called upon New England's sons to go among them—not in a mass, to excite an envious feeling—but to mix with them as *leaven* in the loaf, and thus produce a saving and enduring influence.'

The same sentiments were attributed to Dr. Beecher in the Annals of Education, published at Boston.

Believing these sentiments to be both pernicious and absurd, we commented upon them in the terms we thought they deserved. They were pernicious, because they drew a broad line of distinction between the east and the west, assigning a degree of moral purity and elevation to the one, and of darkness and degradation to the other, not justified by the actual condition of either; and the remarks, if true, were calculated to awaken jealous and unkind feelings. But we thought it not improbable, that Dr. Beecher was sincere in his admiration of the 'matchless' principles of New England, as well as in the exaggerated picture which he drew of the 'uncultivated vice' of our western states—for we could well imagine that a man who had spent a long life in the goodly land of the pilgrims, where there is much that is pure and noble, and whose two years' residence in the West had been passed chiefly at Cincinnati, and in the society of New England people, might honestly admire the land of his birth, and as honestly depreciate, from the representations of others, that which he knew nothing about. We chose, therefore, to treat the matter with ridicule—and to place the man, who would publicly advocate such narrow and puerile notions, in the position which would naturally be assigned to him by every person of common sense. We supposed the error of the writer to lie, in the mistaken vanity of advancing dogmas, in relation to a country whose threshold he had barely passed, whose laws and institutions he seemed not to have examined, and with whose population he could have but a slender acquaintance; and we imagined that none would have greater reason to rejoice in the exposure of those fallacies, than the recent emigrants from New England, whose interests alone were jeoparded, by such unjust and injudicious sectional comparisons.

Some of the better class of our readers, however, took it into their wise heads to be very much offended—not at any thing said of them or their country—for we did not utter a disparaging word in reference to either; but because we had the hardihood to use the weapon of sarcasm against a grave doctor of divinity, who chose, for the purpose of advancing his own ends, to flatter one people at the expense of another.

Some of the newspapers, edited by gentlemen from that much lauded region, railed at us in good set terms, as if we had desecrated the graves of the pilgrims, or treated with irreverence 'the matchless bounties of a bountiful Providence;' and a sedate personage who holds an office in Lane Seminary, to which the faculty have attached the ambitious prefix of 'honorable,' honored us with half a column of scurrility in the Cincinnati Journal—a paper devoted to Dr. Beecher—in which it was clearly shown that a man may be an honorable officer of Lane Seminary, without possessing the homely virtue of veracity—for he said of us what was not true.

But during all this complaint and vituperation, not a whisper was heard from Dr. Beecher. He never, on any occasion, *publicly disclaimed the sentiments reported to have been uttered by him,* at Lowell and at Boston, by the editors of the Lowell Journal, and the Annals of Education; and while his friends were endeavoring to defend the sentiments thus imputed to him, *he was silent.*

Under these circumstances, it was with no small degree of surprise that we read this discourse, which purports to be the one 'delivered by the writer in several of the Atlantic cities last season, while on an agency for Cincinnati Lane Seminary,' and is asserted to be '*as it was delivered,* with a little enlargement on a few points which demand more ample illustration;' but which does not contain a syllable of the objectionable matter alleged to have been delivered by its author at Lowell and Boston. On the contrary, Dr. Beecher now adopts the views advanced by us in the article which gave so much offence to his friends; and argues against the positions attributed to him by the Lowell and Boston Editors, and so zealously defended by his friends. How this discrepancy will be reconciled between him and them, is not for us to decide. It is a matter *between them,* with which we shall not interfere, further than to show that however they may differ among themselves, we have been consistent. It is enough for us to know, that we have converted the doctor to the true faith, in reference to our social and religious principles, and that the idea of bringing out people to mix with us *as leaven,* was either a humbug invented at Lowell, or has been abandoned, as being not exactly consonant with the republican feelings of the western people.

To show the sincerity of his conversion, or the difference between his sentiments as delivered, and the narrow-minded partyism imputed to him by the Lowell editor, Dr. Beecher assumes some of the positions in relation to the western people which we have always maintained, and which are too well known to our readers to need repetition; and then adds, in a note:

'I am happy since my return, to find myself so ably sustained by my friend, Judge Hall, late of Illinois, whose long residence at the West, and extensive opportunities for observation, entitle his opinions on this' subject to great respect. In the Illinois Monthly of 1831, speaking of emigration, he says:

'We have heard lately of several colonies which have been formed in the eastern states, for the purpose of emigrating to Illinois: and we always hear such information with regret. Not that we have any objections to emigration itself; on the contrary, few have done more than we, to encourage and promote it. We ardently long to see the fertile plains of Illinois covered with an industrious, an enterprising, and an intelligent population; we shall always be among the first to welcome the farmer, the mechanic, the school teacher, the *working man,* in short, of any trade, mystery or profession, and we care not from what point of the compass he may come; but wish to see them come to Illinois, with a manly confidence in us, and with feelings, not of New Englanders, or of Pennsylvanians, but of Americans.'

The quotation of that paragraph places Dr. Beecher before the public in a position by no means enviable. When we objected to the language held by him at Lowell, in which he called upon New England's sons to go to the West, to introduce the social and religious principles of New England, 'and to mix with the people as leaven, and thus produce a saving and enduring influence,' directing our satire at the narrow-mindedness exhibited by the speaker, Dr. Beecher and his friends asserted that *we* had used the same sentiments, and we were threatened with the publication of our own words. How has that pledge been redeemed? Dr. Beecher abandons the language and sentiments to which we objected, adopts our views, writes a text to suit a certain passage of ours, and then introduces that passage as a note, to support his text! Nothing could be more disingenuous than such a course. Our language had reference to an emigration by which the physical strength of the country should be improved—and not the slightest allusion was made by us to the social and religious principles of New England. We indicate no preference in favor of New England people, but said that we should be among the first to welcome the farmer, the mechanic, the school teacher—the working man, in short, of any trade mystery, or profession, *from any point of the compass.*' We spoke not of 'the West,' but of Illinois alone, into which a valuable population was pouring from Ohio, Kentucky, Virginia, Pennsylvania, and New York, as well as from New England; and the application of our language to one of those classes, in exclusion of the others, is a perversion of its meaning.

Nor is this all: Dr. Beecher *has not quoted our language correctly;* that which he gives as a connected paragraph, is taken from different places, and arranged together to suit his own purposes. The first part is taken from page 417, and the rest from page 421, of the first volume of the Illinois Monthly Magazine. The doctor is perfectly welcome to quote the language of '*his friend,* Judge Hall,' whenever he pleases, but not to alter it.

In reference to another note, in which the language of the editor of this work is quoted, it is only necessary to remind the reader that it was written with reference to *Illinois,* four years ago, and can have no application, whatever, to the condition of the whole West, nor to the present time.

We now leave this subject, which we should not have touched, but for the abuse formerly lavished on us by the partizans of Dr. Beecher, and the unauthorized liberty taken by himself, in misquoting our language, and perverting its meaning to a purpose which he knew we could not approve.

When we say that this discourse includes none of the objectionable matter contained in the remarks reported in the Lowell Journal, we should except that anomalous proposition, '*uneducated mind is educated vice,*' which we find repeated, and italicised, to render it emphatic. We are still unable to discover the slightest glimmering of common sense in this remark. Uneducated mind is not only, not necessarily educated in vice, but is absolutely not educated in anything. It is certainly the most palpable *non sequitur,* ever uttered by the president of a college, and we should be tempted to doubt the value of the education which taught such logic. Dr. Beecher's dreams about Rome, and Vienna, and Metternich, have unsettled the usually steady balance of his mind, and raised up images which have neither form nor comeliness. We are happy to learn, however, that he did not neglect, in his great love for 'the West,' and his terror of Austria, and ignorance, and papacy, and the wild Irish, the main object of his visit to New England, which was to raise money for Lane Seminary, but produced by an appeal to party feelings, that which would as cheerfully have been given to benevolence.

About two-thirds of the latter portion of this volume are filled with a labored argument against the catholics and the emigrants from foreign countries. Dr. Beecher attempts seriously to show that 'this emigration, self-moved and slow in the beginning, is now rolling its broad tide, at the bidding of the powers of Europe, hostile to free institutions, and associated in holy alliance to arrest and put them down.' The evidence should be ample, indeed, upon which a christian minister undertakes thus to denounce a whole class of laborious foreigners, who have chosen our country as their home, and have quietly submitted themselves to our laws. It is a charge of conspiracy against our liberties, which includes in its denunciation, the whole body of Catholics in the United States, whether native-born or foreign. It is a charge made without the support of a single title of testimony—without the production of a single overt act of hostility, towards our government on the part of the Roman Catholics. It is a charge made against a body, in which were numbered many of the patriots of the revolution, and of those who, at a later period, have participated in the councils of the nation, or have bared their breasts in battle to the enemies of our country, and among whom are found thousands of reputable, industrious citizens, whose integrity is above suspicion, and whose love of country is too pure and elevated to be tainted by the breath of a calumny so gratuitous and unfounded.

Will any person in his senses believe that a native American, who happens to have been educated in the Roman catholic faith, would on that account, blast his reputation, barter away his birthright, sell his country, and submit himself and those who are dear to him to the withering grasp of a despot, in obedience to the mandate of the pope, or the Emperor of Austria? Can it be credited that the Irish who have fled from a ruthless tyranny, could be prevailed upon to forget their hatred of kings, and forge new chains for their own hands? Did they come 'at the bidding of the powers of Europe hostile to free institutions! Are the illiterate, hard-working Germans, who are scattered over our lands as peaceful cultivators of the soil, the secret conspirators sent hither by the pope? Or are the French, whose own king can scarcely keep his head on his shoulders, so besotted with the love of monarchy, as to be engaged in the promising design of giving us a kingly Ruler? If it were possible to believe that the pope and despots of Europe were so weak as to imagine such a design, it is difficult to see where, in this country, they could find the materials for the party. The last place we should look for royalists, would be among our catholic population, a large proportion of whom are poor, and inclined to the most radical school of democracy.

The absurdity of this alarm about the catholics, is not more monstrous than some of the arguments used to support it—as for instance, the following:

'The simple fact that the clergy of the catholic denomination could wield in mass the suffrage of their confiding people, could not fail, in the competition of ambition and party spirit, to occasion immediately an eager competition for their votes, placing them at once in the attitude of the most favored sect: securing the remission of duties on imported church property, and copious appropriations of land for the endowment of their institutions.' To this text is appended the following marginal note: 'Senator Benton of Missouri, we understand, has introduced a bill to give two thousand sores of land to a catholic college.'

Here it is assumed, that the catholic clergy could wield, in mass, the suffrage of their people, and that this power, in the competition of party spirit, &c., would place them in the attitude of the most favored sect.—This is taking for granted both cause and consequence—it is supposing that the catholics would suffer their priests to control their votes, which never can be the case in a free country, & it is also supposing them to derive legislative favor from this cause, which is prohibited by the constitution. And the writer entirely overlooks the fact, that the catholic priesthood have always held the same influence over their people which they now possess—yet we have no evidence that they ever controlled the votes of their people in mass, nor that they have been favored as a sect; and we know no reason why the writer should assume that these consequences *would* flow from the catholic church, which have not yet appeared in the half century during which they have lived peaceably under our government. The note about senator Benton, needs no commentary to explain what would be the conduct of some protestants that might be mentioned, if they possessed the power which is attributed to the catholics. Why should not the catholics share the munificence of congress with other sects? Would congress dare, with that clause of the constitution before them which guaranties *equal* rights to all sects, to make a distinction? And if other colleges are endowed with land, why not a catholic college? In all the western states, land has been given largely for education; the college lands under the fair operation of that rule of republics which gives power to the majority, have fallen solely into the hands of the protestants.—The catholics have supported their own colleges. Yet they have higher claims than any other sect. They were the first settlers of all that is now Louisiana, Mississippi, and Missouri. They first introduced education into our valley, and their schools and colleges were, for a series of years, the only nurseries of learning, west of the mountains. They have not proved less patriotic than any other denomination. At the college at Bardstown, hundreds of young natives of the west have been educated, and among them the sons of some of our most distinguished men. It will not be contended that those gentlemen are less estimable as men, or less true to their country as citizens, than others, who were educated elsewhere. With these facts in view, the denunciation of this sect, and the attempt to hold up a member of congress to public indignation, by an insinuation of impure motives, for doing that for a portion of his constituents, to which they conceived they had a fair claim, is most ungenerous. It is an appeal to the most unkind feelings and narrow prejudices of our nature and seeking to rob a large body of unoffending citizens of those rights which are guarantied to them by the constitution of our country.

Dr. Beecher says: 'Let the catholics mingle with us as Americans, and come with their children under the full action of our common schools and republican institutions, and the various powers of assimilation, and we are prepared cheerfully to abide the consequences.'

This is an instance of the mystification, in which this author sometimes indulges, when he attempts to dress his thoughts in language which will bear one construction to the world, and another to the initiated. To the latter this means, let the catholics cease to be catholics, and we will be satisfied, but not till then; to the world it addresses a specious proposition, rounded off with great apparent candor, but which, when touched, proves to be mere sound. The catholics do already nearly all that Dr. Beecher asks of them in that sentence. They do mingle with us as American citizens, and come under the full action of our republican institutions and various powers of assimilation. They have their own schools, and have a right to have them; and no sect could with less propriety complain of this, than that to which Dr. Beecher belongs, which has grasped at the control of schools and colleges beyond any other sect, and done more for the cause of learning.

We have gone into this subject because it is one which imperiously demands the attention of those editors who are friendly to peace and good order. The recent excitement of the public mind against the catholics, founded in ignorance, error, and gross prejudice, is greatly, to be deplored; and it is with the deepest regret that we see such a man as Dr. Beecher lending the sanction of his name to an illiberal cabal of demagogues, who under the name of religion, are disturbing the peace of the country, with their own ambitious intrigues. What candid man, what liberal christian, can read without astonishment such language as the following:

'For what was the city of Boston for five nights under arms—her military upon the alert—her citizens enrolled, and a body of five hundred men constantly patroling the streets? Why were the accustomed lectures for public worship, and other public secular meetings suspended? Why were the citizens at sound of Bell, convened at midday in Faneuil Hall! to hear catholociam eulogized, and thanksgivings offered to his reverence the bishop, for his merciful protection of the children of the pilgrims! And why, in the cradle of liberty, and under the shadow of Bunker's Hill, did men turn pale, and whisper, and look over their shoulders, and around, to ascertain whether it were safe to speak aloud, or meet to worship God? Has it come to this? that the capital of New England has been thrown into consternation by the threats of a Catholic mob, and that her temples and mansions stand only through the forbearance of a catholic bishop? There can be no liberty in the presence of such masses of dark mind, and of such despotic power over it in a single man.—Safety on such terms is not the protection of law, but of single-handed despotism."

Plea for the West. p. 91

What reader unacquainted, with the history of passing events, would imagine that this inflammatory appeal to the most vindictive passions of the human breast, was elicited by the occurrence of a most brutal and cowardly outrage, in which the catholics were sufferers, and the protestants aggressors? by an event, in which a religious house was desecrated by violence and crime—when an infuriated mob rushed under cover of night, upon the sleeping inmates of a convent—upon a society of unprotected females—whose sex, whose religious character, whose threshold, were alike insufficient safe-guards, and in whose defence neither benevolence, nor law, nor gallantry, interposed a shield! Would it be believed, if the facts had not transpired within our own knowledge, that the offence of 'his reverence the bishop,' consisted in his restraining the natural feelings of resentment, aroused by persecution in the bosoms of his people, and in exercising the proper function of his holy office, by admonishing them to the practice of forgiveness and forbearance? In a protestant minister, such conduct would have been termed christian meekness—in a catholic bishop, it is *despotic power,* and *single handed despotism,* and is tauntingly spoken of as *his merciful protection of the children of the pilgrims!*—Can any one read without amazement, such logic from a venerable and veteran minister of the gospel who has no condemnation for the mob that destroyed a convent, not a word of censure for the community whose laws become inert, when the catholic claims their protection, yet can pour out bitter sarcasm upon the catholic bishop, whose piety or whose good sense, induces him to obey literally, the mandate of our Saviour, by restraining his flock from resenting such flagitious injury—who passes over in silence, the atrocities of robbery and arson, which caused the very consternation that he describes in such glowing language, and can indulge himself in the exclamation, how 'felicitous the condition of American citizens, who depend gratefully upon the hand and will of a catholic bishop to protect them from clubs, and conflagration, and the knife!

There must be a reaction of the public mind on this subject. No people have ever yet been persecuted, who have not gained strength by oppression, and in a free country like ours—in a country of generous feeling, and liberal opinion, intolerance cannot long stalk abroad unrebuked. The incessant stream of vituperation poured out upon the catholics in our religious papers has wearied out the patience of the public. The appeals to the passions of the ignorant, by which mobs have been arrayed against them, have opened the eyes of reflecting men to the true nature of the controversy; and the public sentiment will not sustain any body of men in a course of conduct which is unjust in itself, and which brings religion into discredit, while it stirs up an angry fanaticism, awakens the fierce antipathies of a past age, and brings disorder into the bosom of a peaceful country.

We might add many arguments to show the danger to our country from the violence of sectarian controversy; but we hope they are not now necessary. We have said that which the occasion demanded of us—we have given our suffrage against that iniquitous warfare, which men professing to worship the same God, and acknowledging the same Redeemer, are waging against each other, to the disturbance of the public tranquility, and the destruction of vital religion. The whole land is fretted into high excitement by irritating dissentions in politics and religion, and it becomes those who are for the country, the *whole country,* to shake off the fetters of party, and throw their influence in favor of an universal peace. Let patriots and christians unite in frowning down these discreditable brawls. Let protestants and catholics alike abstain from these unchristian contests, which block their several churches to the approach of sinners who would be taught the way of peace, and makes infidels laugh who imagine there is no religion where there is neither meekness, nor charity, nor forgiveness.

ON BLACK HAWK (1836, 1848)

"I have just returned from a delightful voyage. I have explored a portion of the exquisitely beautiful shores of the upper Mississippi, and am ready to confess that until now, I had little idea of the extent, the grandeur, or the resources of the west. The world cannot produce such another country as this great valley of ours. Yet to understand its value, one must ascend the Mississippi and the Illinois, and see the noble prairies of the two states which are destined to eclipse all others. I cannot convey to you in adequate language, my admiration of this attractive region. The traveller who visits the western country, and fancies he has acquired *any* knowledge of it—I say *any,* by simply tracing the meanders of the Ohio, or spending weeks, or years, if you please, at Cincinnati or Louisville, is very much mistaken. There is much to admire in western Pennsylvania and Virginia; Kentucky and Ohio are full of attraction; but the man who is really an admirer of nature, and would witness the most splendid exhibitions of the creative power, must go to Illinois and Missouri.

"I visited this region for the first time four years ago, while the Sacs and Foxes were at peace with the whites, and before Black Hawk had got to be a great man. They were friendly and well-disposed, and the white people residing near them, would almost as soon have distrusted or disturbed each other, as those peaceful red men. I took great interest in noticing their dwellings, and remarking their deportment, as it was the first occasion I had ever enjoyed of seeing the savage in his own wild home. I had embarked on board a steamboat at St. Louis, intending to take a pleasant excursion to the falls of St. Anthony. The weather was very delightful, only a little too warm; and the river was unfortunately so low, that on arriving at the *Des Moines* rapids, we found it difficult to ascend them, and above that point, our progress was continually impeded by the difficulty of the navigation. This circumstance, though vexatious to such of the passengers as had business ahead, or families at home, was not disagreeable to one who, like myself, travelled only for amusement, as it afforded opportunities of exploring the romantic shores. We spent a day at the Lower Rapids, and I have seldom seen a more attractive country. The land is high on both sides, and rises gradually in beautiful swells. I saw hundreds of acres covered with the native buckeye, the most beautiful tree of the forest—if, indeed, any can be entitled to that distinction among so great a variety of noble and majestic trees. Beneath, was a rich undergrowth of wild gooseberry bushes. Add to these the beautiful creeper, and the wild honeysuckle, which were occasionally seen, and it is impossible to imagine a vegetation more splendidly luxuriant and ornamental. The whole country is based on rock, and the springs which burst out from the hill sides are clear as crystal and delightfully cold. The shores of the river are plentifully strewed with crystalizations and petrifactions. We picked up some fine specimens of cornelian, and saw a vast number of geodes of every size, from one inch in diameter to fifteen.

"It was Sunday. Have you ever experienced the singular and pleasing associations connected with a sabbath passed in the wilderness? I have often enjoyed these feelings, but never felt them with such force as on this day. It was calm and sultry. The brilliant sunbeams were brightly reflected from the broad bosom of the Mississippi, and the deep green outline of the forest was splendidly illumined, while the deep shadows underneath the foliage afforded an attractive appearance of coolness and seclusion. The passengers and crew were scattered about singly or in small parties, so that when I wandered but a small distance from the vessel, and seated myself on a hill which commanded a view of the river and its banks, I found myself perfectly alone. Not a living object was visible, not a sound was heard, not a leaf or a limb stirred. How different from the streets of a city upon a sabbath morn, when crowds of well-dressed persons are seen moving in every direction; when the cheerful bells are sounding, and the beautiful smiling children are hurrying in troops to Sunday school! Here I was in solitude. I saw not the laborer resting from toil, nor the smile of infancy, nor the christian bowing before his God; but Nature proclaimed a sabbath by the silence that reigned abroad, and the splendor with which she had adorned her works.

"It is natural that these recollections of my first visit to the frontier should mingle with the observations made in my recent tour through the same scenes; I shall therefore not attempt to separate the remarks made on either occasion, but give some of the results of both voyages.

"I can scarcely describe the sensations with which I first saw the solitary lodge of an Indian hunter, on the shore of the Mississippi. In my childhood I had read with thrilling interest, the tales of border warfare; but I had not learned to hate an Indian with mortal hatred. I verily believe they have souls. People may think differently in certain places, which shall be nameless, but I cannot be persuaded to the contrary. You cannot imagine any thing more frail than an Indian wigwam—a mere shelter of poles and mats, so small, so apparently inadequate to any purpose of security or comfort, that it is hardly possible to believe it to be intended for the residence of human beings. In such habitations reside the Indian warrior, whose name is a terror to his enemies; and the dark maiden, whose story supplies the poet with rich materials, with which to embellish the page of fiction. In such wretched hovels reside the aboriginal lords of the soil.

"I *have* seen in this region, evidences of persecution perpetrated by our people upon this unhappy race, such as the American people would scarcely believe; and I am satisfied that if the events of the late war could be traced to their true source, every real philanthropist in the nation would blush for his country."

"I could relate many anecdotes, to show the friendly feelings entertained towards our government and people by the Sacs—feelings which, whether of fear or of kindness, have rendered them wholly submissive, and which nothing but the most unprovoked aggression on our side, could have kindled into hostility. I will only, at this time, repeat one, which occurred during my first voyage, reserving others for a future letter.

"One day, when the boat stopped to take in wood, some of us strolled up to the house of a Mr. D., a respectable farmer from Pennsylvania. He had been living here several years, at a spot distant from any settlements, and without a single neighbor. Upon our inquiring whether he felt no alarm in residing thus alone in the vicinity of the Indians, he replied that his family had formerly experienced much uneasiness, but that they had long since become satisfied that there was no ground for apprehension. He was convinced that the Sacs, their nearest neighbors, so far from being disposed to injure the whites, were cautious and timid of giving offence. In support of this opinion, he related the following anecdote.

"His house stands on a high bank of the Mississippi, and the family were one day much alarmed by discovering a large number of Indians passing up the river in canoes. They passed along in a most disorderly manner, some paddling their little vessels, and others strolling along the shore, but the majority evidently intoxicated. It was the latter circumstance which caused alarm. The Indians had been to St. Louis to receive their annuities, and had procured a sufficient supply of whisky to render them unsafe visitors. They continued, however, straggling along in larger or smaller parties all day, without stopping. At night, one of them, a young warrior of prepossessing appearance, came to the house, and in the most respectful manner, asked permission to sleep upon the floor of the cabin. Mr. D., although by no means pleased with his guest, knew not how to refuse. The Indian warrior was invited to supper. A plentiful meal, such as composed the ordinary repast of the family, was placed before him, and having satisfied his hunger, he wrapped himself in his blanket, threw himself on the floor before the fire, and went to sleep. In the course of the night, Mr. D. happening to go out, discovered some Indians lying in the bushes not far from the house; without disturbing them, he proceeded in a different direction, where he found another party; they were strewed, in short, entirely around his dwelling. The fact of being thus surrounded, the concealment, and the silence of the Indians, all conspired to awaken suspicion, and he passed the night in no small degree of uneasiness. He rose early in the morning; his Indian guest also started up, gathered his blanket around him, and took leave; first, however, explaining to Mr. D. that he belonged to a party of Sacs who were returning from St. Louis, and that many of them being intoxicated, it had been thought proper to station a guard round Mr. D.'s house, to protect him and his property from injury. He added, that if any depredation should be discovered to have been committed by the Indians, the chiefs would pay Mr. D. the full amount. Such an example of the care taken by the chiefs of this tribe to avoid giving umbrage to the whites, affords the highest testimony, either of their friendship for our people, or their respect for our power.

"The Sac and Fox tribe inhabited, at that time, a beautiful tract of country in Illinois, upon the borders of Rock river. These two tribes are usually mentioned in conjunction, because the Foxes, many years ago, having been nearly exterminated in a war

with some of their neighbors, the remnant of the nation, too feeble to exist as a separate tribe, sought refuge in the Sac villages, and have remained ever since incorporated with the latter people. They are a fine looking race of people, and are well disposed towards the whites. They have long been divided, however, into two parties,
one of which is friendly towards our government, while the other, called the *British
band,* is under the influence of the British traders. It has always been the policy of the
latter, to keep the Indians upon the western frontier in a state of disaffection towards
the American people, and by these means, to secure to themselves an undue proportion of the fur trade. So long as it should remain difficult upon our part to gain access to the tribes, and our intercourse with them be liable to interruption, jealousy,
and distrust, so long would the British trader possess an advantage over us in relation
to this traffic. The British fur companies, whose agents are numerous, intelligent, and
enterprising, have always acted upon this policy, and the English officers in Canada,
both civil and military, have given it their sanction. Almost all the atrocities which
have been committed on our frontiers by the Indians, within the last fifty years, have
been directly or indirectly incited by the incendiary agents of that mercenary government. The *British band* of the Sacs and Foxes have been in the habit of visiting
Malden annually, and receiving valuable presents—presents, which being made to a
disaffected portion of a tribe residing not only within the United States, but within
the limits of a state, could be viewed in no other light than as bribes,—the wages of
disaffection. Black Hawk, though not a chief, is one of the most influential individuals of the *British band.*"

[1838; 1848]
"Most of our readers have become familiarly acquainted with the name of the re-
doubted Black Hawk, whose adventures are detailed in this volume and whose fame
has been spread from Maine to Florida. There was a time when he shared the eager
attention of the public with Fanny Kemble and the cholera, and was one of the lions
of the day; and as regularly talked about as the weather, the last new novel, or the candidates for the presidency. The war in Illinois, though of brief duration, and not
marked by any stirring events, came suddenly upon us after a long series of peaceful
years upon the northwestern border. The savages, weary of fruitless conflicts, or
quelled by the superior numbers of a gigantic and growing foe, seemed to have submitted to their fate, and the pioneer had ceased to number the war-whoop among
the inquietudes of the border life. The plains of Illinois and Missouri were rapidly becoming peopled by civilized men. A race less hardy than the backwoodsmen were
tempted by the calm to migrate to those delightful solitudes, that bloomed with more
than Arcadian fascinations of fruitfulness and beauty. The smoke of the settler's cabin
began to ascend from the margin of every stream in that wide region, and the cattle
strayed through rich pastures, of which the buffalo, the elk, and the deer, had long enjoyed a monopoly—an unchartered monopoly—wondering, no doubt, at their good
luck in having their lives cast in such pleasant places.

It was the writer's lot to ramble over that beautiful country while these interesting scenes were presented; while the wilderness still glowed in its pristine luxuriance:
while the prairie-grass and the wild flowers still covered the plain, and the deer continued to frequent his ancient haunts, and while the habitations of the new settlers were
so widely and so thinly scattered, that the nearest neighbors could scarcely have exchanged the courtesy of an annual visit without the aid of the seven-leagued boots of
ancient story. But though in solitude, they lived without fear. There were none to mo-

lest nor make them afraid. If they had few friends, they had no enemies. If the Indian halted at the settler's door, it was to solicit hospitality, not to offer violence. But more frequently he stalked silently by, timid of giving offence to the white man, whom he doubtless regarded as an intruder upon his own ancient heritage, but whose possession he had been taught to respect, because he had ever found it guarded by a strong and swift arm, that had never failed to repay aggression with ten-fold vengeance. Suddenly, however, a change came over this cheering scene. The misconduct of a few white men disturbed the harmony of a wide region. The Indians were oppressed and insulted to the last point of forbearance, and a small but restless band, regarded as insubordinate and troublesome even by their own nation, seized upon the occasion to rush to war.

It is wonderful to look back upon this eventful history. The country over which Black Hawk, with a handful of followers, badly armed, and destitute of stores or munitions of war, roamed for hundreds of miles, driving off the scattered inhabitants, is now covered with flourishing settlements, with substantial houses, and large farms—not with the cabins and clearings of bordermen—but with the comfortable dwellings and the well-tilled fields of independent farmers. Organized counties and all the subordination of social life are there; and there are the noisy school-house, the decent church, the mill, the country store, the fat ox, and the sleek plough-horse. The yankee is there with his notions and his patent-rights, and the travelling agent with his subscription book; there are merchandise from India and from England, and, in short, all the luxuries of life, from Bulwer's last novel down to Brandreth's pills. And all this has been done in six years—in less than half the time of Jacob's courtship. In 1832 the Saukie warriors ranged over that fertile region, which is now (1838) covered with an industrious population; while the Territories of Wisconsin and Iowa, and vast settlements in Missouri, have since grown up, beyond the region which was then the frontier and the seat of war.

31

REBECCA BURLEND

(1793–1872)

Many British and European travelers ventured to the western frontier of the United States and returned to London to describe it, including Harriet Martineau and Charles Dickens. Moreover, many American women traveled through the region before returning east to publish their travels, such as Eliza Farnham, Caroline Kirkland, and Margaret Fuller, each reprinted in the present collection. For the most part, their common perspective is that of the privileged observer. Rarely was the voice of a woman of the less privileged socioeconomic classes heard, let alone one reflecting the differing perspective of the non-native-born American.

In Rebecca Burlend's *A True Picture of Emigration,* the voice of former peasant woman from the north of England describes her family's settlement in Pike County, Illinois, in 1831. While many families and many women like Burlend could have written such stories, few made it into print. As a poor English woman, Burlend has things to say about settlement experience that have not been noted. Her consistent observation of the differences between American and British agriculture and class systems reveals much about how the west had not and could not accommodate a wholesale transfer of values from either old or new Englands. At the same time, her consistent reference to American "peasantry" reminds the reader that American freeholders were often such in name alone, held to the land by debt rather than by vassalage. By 1831, most natives had been removed from southern Illinois, and Burlend has little to say of them. At the same time, it might be said that she describes the settlers as a new tribe whose contact and entanglement with their natural environment are a source of legitimate connection with the place to which they had recently moved. As the Burlends learn these ways, they become successful farmers and come to own their land outright.

One of Burlend's sons, John, moved back to England in the late 1830s and established himself as a minor poet and editor. When his mother briefly visited York in 1846, he encouraged her to write her story. The text he then edited was published at London in 1848 and was soon republished in the United States. To his credit, John Burlend did little to sanitize his mother's story: she is not converted to a gentlewoman to suit the genres of Victorian letters. Just as Kirkland chafed against the frontier's tendency to demolish the lines between male and female spheres in nineteenth-century America, Burlend in her text embraces the labor and strains she has enduring in helping her family create its farm.

Text: *A True Picture of Emigration, or Fourteen Years in the Interior of North America* (London, 1848; rpt. Lakeside Classics, 1935, ed. and annotated by Milo M. Quaife): 33–88.

FROM *A TRUE PICTURE OF EMIGRATION* (1848)

CHAPTER 3

As I intimated in the preceding chapter, we reached New Orleans on Sunday morning; but when I came to survey the town more leisurely, I could scarcely believe it was the Lord's day. I remembered that frequently on our passage I had heard it remarked that the time varied with the time in England a few hours, and for a moment I supposed that the Sabbath varied also. The reader will perceive the cause of my surprise, when he is told that the shops were every where open, stalls set out in all directions, and the streets thronged with lookers-on more in the manner of a fair than a Christian Sabbath. This I was told was the general method of spending that day in New Orleans. With regard to the inhabitants, their appearance was exceedingly peculiar, their complexions varying almost as much as their features; from the deep black of the flat-nosed negro to the sickly pale hue of the American shopman. This city is a regular rendezvous for merchants and tradesmen of every kind, from all quarters of the globe. Slavery is here tolerated in its grossest forms. I observed several groups of slaves linked together in chains, and driven about the streets like oxen under the yoke. The river, which is of immense width, affords a sight not less unique than the city. No one, except eye-witnesses, can form an adequate idea of the number and variety of vessels there collected, and lining the river for miles in length. New Orleans being the provision market for the West Indies and some of the Southern States, its port is frequented not merely by foreign traders, but by thousands of small craft, often of the rudest construction, on which the settlers in the interior bring down the various produce of their climate and industry.[1] The town itself, from its low marshy situation, is very unhealthy; the yellow fever is an everlasting scourge to its inhabitants, annually carrying off great numbers. As a trading port, New Orleans is the most famous and the best situated of any in America; but whoever values a comfortable climate or a healthy situation, will not, I am sure, choose to reside there.

But to resume my narrative: having arrived at the port, it was our intention to proceed immediately up the river to St. Louis; but as no steam vessel left till the next day, we remained on board in front of the town. The custom-house officers had not yet been on board to examine the ship, but as we had nothing for which duty would be required, our captain gave my husband a document to present to the inspectors, by which we were allowed to pass early the next morning. Before entering the steam vessel, we got the remainder of our money, all in English sovereigns, exchanged into American dollars. We found that our expenses, since leaving home, amounted to

---

1. The flatboat commerce by which the surplus produce of the upper Mississippi Valley was brought to New Orleans flourished for a generation or more, until the era of railroad construction which immediately preceded the Civil War. An Illinois youth of recent adoption who made the long journey to New Orleans the year preceding Mrs. Burlend's arrival in America bore the name of Abraham Lincoln. The journey he made was typical of thousands of similar ones performed in the period here alluded to.

about twenty-three pounds. On leaving the ship I felt a renewal of my home-sickness, to use a quaint expression; it seemed to be the only remaining link between me and England. I was now going to be an alien among strangers. Hitherto I had been accompanied by persons, who when my pain on leaving home manifested itself, could sympathize with me. I should have preferred the meanest passenger on the ship to any I saw on the packet. As, however, we were all in haste to be on our way, I had little time to spend on those tender associations. I certainly left the ship with an aching heart; the captain and cabin passengers had been very kind to us during the voyage, and on going away my children were severally presented with small tokens of appro-bation, of which they were not a little proud.

I must now leave the ship to pursue my route up the stream of the Mississippi to St. Louis, a distance of not less than thirteen hundred miles. The country on each side of the river is of a dead level, but to all appearance exceedingly productive, and cul-tivated with considerable pains. On account of the heat which prevails in these dis-tricts, the productions of tropical regions are here grown in great abundance. The ex-tensive plantations, notwithstanding their flat appearance, are exceedingly beautiful; and if any thing could have made me forget that I was an unsettled exile, the scenery of the country bordering this river must have done it. There was, nevertheless, one drawback: these beautiful plantations are cultivated by slaves, many of whom we saw as we passed along. As we had regularly to stop by the way to obtain timber for our fires, that being the fuel invariably used by the steamers on this river, we had frequent opportunities of stepping ashore. On one occasion a passenger seeing a negro smok-ing his pipe by his little cabin, which was just at hand, took the liberty of going up to him for the purpose of begging a little fruit, which hung in plenty on the trees around. The negro, without hesitation, granted his request; and our hero immediately mounted a tree, which he partially stripped of its juicy burden. This little incident might have passed unnoticed, had not the intruder on descending from the tree made use of a kind of box, which was underneath, to break his fall; its structure was too slen-der for so unusual a load, and in consequence he burst in the top to the terror of the negro, who immediately darted across the orchard, leaving our companion to make the best of his misfortune. The latter was soon convinced that he had committed a blunder, as the box was a bee-hive, and its occupants, aware they had been insulted, would accept no apology, but drawing their sabres attacked their foe with tremendous fury. Poor Yankee was no Leonidas; but with all the speed his heels could muster be-took himself to the packet, where he was greeted with roars of laughter by his less en-terprising associates.

As we proceeded up the river the country assumed a more rude and uncultivated appearance: the date and plantain tree of the lower regions were exchanged for ma-jestic forest trees and untrodden wilds. Further down it was delightfully pleasant; here magnificently grand eternal forests, in appearance as interminable as the universe, with here and there a patch of ground rudely cultivated by the hand of a lonely set-tler, constitute the scenery for thousands of miles contiguous to this matchless stream. As to the river itself, I shall not attempt a description of it; what has already been said proves its magnitude to be immensely great; even some of its branches, as the Ohio and the Missouri, are to be classed among the largest rivers in the world. The former[2] is noted for being very muddy, and hurrying in its ungovernable career vast quanti-

---

2. The river here alluded to is obviously the Missouri, rather than the Ohio.

ties of floating timber, which, decayed by age or other causes, fall into it so as often to render it dangerous for the steamers to pass along. Of these the Mississippi contains acres, that coming from above, have in the lapse of years gradually settled together in places where the current is least active.

Proceeding with my narrative, I must confess I liked the packet much better than I expected. We had engaged to find our own provisions, but on account of their cheapness, or partly because I acted the part of matron to such as needed my assistance, we were frequently presented with young fowls, coffee, rice, &c., so that our food cost us very little on the river. During this transit we obtained considerable information respecting Illinois, which tended in some degree to lessen our disquietude. We were nevertheless very far from being at ease; our unsettled condition was ever the uppermost in our thoughts, and shed a settled gravity over our conduct. Whilst thus the subjects of painful uncertainty, we were one night much alarmed by the following attempt to rob us: my husband and I were in our berths; I was fast asleep, but he was awake, musing upon our situation, when a black man, one of the crew, knowing we were going to settle in the country, and thinking no doubt we should have money with us, came to the side of our berths and began to search under my pillow, so softly indeed as not to awake me; he was going to examine under my husband's likewise, but as he was awake, he told him he could get him anything he wanted; such unexpected kindness was immediately understood, and the villain disappeared in a moment. Although this attempt proved a complete failure, we were induced to give up our money to the captain the following day, which he kept till we arrived at St. Louis. As my husband kept the money under his pillow, I have never looked back on this circumstance but with feelings of gratitude to Almighty God for his protecting providence, for had he succeeded, we should have been in a most miserable situation, not even able to reach the end of our journey;—destitute and penniless in a strange land, without friends and without home.

The time occupied in passing from New Orleans to St. Louis was about twelve days. We reached the latter place about noon, and found another steamer ready to convey us forward to the situation at which we purposed to remain. I had little opportunity of surveying the town, and therefore can say little respecting it; but was somewhat surprised to find that this noted city should be built principally of wood; its situation is not the most eligible as it regards health, being near the confluence of the Missouri and the Illinois. It is however on that very account likely to become a large and wealthy city, and is indeed by some described as such already.[3] On entering the second steamer I found I had made a poor exchange; the weather was beginning to feel uncommonly chill, and our accommodation was here very inferior, so that we felt exceedingly anxious to be at our journey's end.

The place at which we intended to leave the river was not more than one hundred and twenty miles from St. Louis; we therefore comforted ourselves with the idea that we should soon be there. We were finally to disembark at Phillip's Ferry, according to the directions sent by the aforementioned Mr. B. to his brother. We should then be within two miles of his residence. Mr. B., therefore, and Phillip's Ferry, occupied

---

3. Although St. Louis dates from 1764, the increase in population was extremely slow for several decades. Upon incorporation as a city in 1823, there were only a few hundred inhabitants. By 1830, the year prior to Mrs. Burlend's visit, the number had increased to almost 5,000. One hundred years later (1930) the U. S. census revealed a population of 821,960, amply fulfilling the forecast of the humble English immigrant of 1831.

our thoughts almost to the exclusion of every other subject. We had already travelled nearly seven thousand miles. Our food had been principally dried provisions. For many long weeks we had been oppressed with anxious suspense; there is therefore no cause for wonder, that, jaded and worn out as we were, we felt anxious to be at our destined situation. Our enquiries of the sailors 'how much further we had to go,' almost exhausted their patience. Already we had been on the vessel twenty-four hours, when just at nightfall the packet stopped: a little boat was lowered into the water, and we were invited to collect our luggage and descend into it, as we were at Phillip's Ferry,[4] we were utterly confounded: there was no appearance of a landing place, no luggage yard, nor even a building of any kind within sight; we, however, attended to our directions, and in a few minutes saw ourselves standing by the brink of the river, bordered by a dark wood, with no one near to notice us or tell us where we might procure accommodation or find harbour. This happened, as before intimated, as the evening shades were rapidly settling on the earth, and the stars through the clear blue atmosphere were beginning to twinkle. It was in the middle of November, and already very frosty. My husband and I looked at each other till we burst into tears, and our children observing our disquietude began to cry bitterly. Is this America, thought I, is this the reception I meet with after my long, painfully anxious and bereaving voyage? In vain did we look around us, hoping to see a light in some distant cabin. It was not, however, the time to weep: my husband determined to leave us with our luggage in search of a habitation, and wished us to remain where we then stood till he returned. Such a step I saw to be necessary, but how trying! Should he lose himself in the wood, thought I, what will become of me and my helpless offspring? He departed: I was left with five young children, the youngest at my breast. When I survey this portion of my history, it looks more like fiction than reality; yet it is the precise situation in which I was then placed.

After my husband was gone I caused my four eldest children to sit together on one of our beds, covered them from the cold as well as I could, and endeavoured to pacify them. I then knelt down on the bare ground, and committed myself and little ones to the Father of mercies, beseeching him 'to be a lantern to my feet, a light unto my path, and to establish my goings.' I rose from my knees considerably comforted, and endeavoured to wait with patience the return of my husband. Above me was the

---

4. Philips Ferry is still conducted, on or near the original site, at Valley City, where the present Editor utilized it late in the month of August, 1936. The ferry was established by Garret Van Dusen in 1822, who two years later transferred it to Nimrod Philips.

The latter had come from Kentucky to Pike County about 1821; he died here a decade later. By his will, made in 1826, he bequeathed the ferry to his son, Andrew. This document, still on file in the Court House at Pittsfield, we copy in full for the entertainment of the reader:

"Illinois pike County in the name of God Amen I Nimrod Philips of the State and County aforesaid inten to travel and Not knowing but I may die before I return do make this my last will and testament first I give to Zerrelda Jean my youngest child five head of Cattle a cow cald Cherry and her Caves a horse Cald Jack three beds and furniture and all the kitchen furniture and utensils this I give to my youngest child by Nancy Philips onst Nancy Norris Zerrelda Jean Philips is her name I give to Nancy Philips my wife one loom and its furniture 3 breeding Sows and their pigs six barrows for her meat She is to have her choise of the above named Hoggs She is to live where I now live at the ferry My part of the crop of corn that has been on the place this year to be hers She is to live on the place until Zerrelda is of age and have the benefit of the improved land Zerrelda is to have six dolers for 3 years Scholling 18 dollers

I give to Elizabeth Elledge my oldest daughter one doller the rest of my estate and property is to be equaly divided between my 3 children Andrew Philips, Selah Philips, Asa Philips except Andrew is to have the ferry this is my last will and testament

chill blue canopy of heaven, a wide river before me, and a dark wood behind. The first sound we heard was that of two dogs that came barking towards us, so as greatly to increase our alarm; the dogs came up to us, but did us no harm, and very soon after I beheld my dear husband, accompanied by a stranger, who conducted us to his habitation, whither our luggage was shortly afterwards removed in a waggon.

My husband had followed a sort of cattle track, which led him to the house, which had been concealed by trees and underwood growing around it. And now, for the first time in my life, did I fairly see the interior of a log-house, which, however rude I might think it, I felt, as the reader will readily believe, most happy to enter. It was much more comfortable to sleep on a bed laid on the floor before a fire of glowing embers, than it would have been on the cold ground, which a short time before I feared would be my lodging. The following morning, after a comfortable night's repose, we felt our health and spirits improved. My husband began to examine the soils and produce of the country, and I to collect what information I could respecting American housewifery, manners, religion, &c. Our hostess was a little woman, exceedingly fond of smoking, as the Americans generally are, particularly the females. Before leaving England I had heard a great deal said in behalf of American hospitality, but these encomiums certainly require to be qualified: they are exceedingly hospitable to gentlemen who may be making a tour, likewise amongst themselves as neighbours; but when they know a person really must trouble them, they appear to be aware they are conferring a favour, and expect an equivalent. The little lady I have been describing knew little of generosity; we understood very soon that we should be expected to pay for our harbour, although we used our own provisions. I am forgetting that on one occasion she generously told me I might give my children the broth in which she had boiled some cabbage, if I thought they would drink it; I told her they had not been accustomed to such fare. We remained here three days, during which I became tolerably conversant in the theory of American housekeeping, and as Mrs. Phillips[5] (that was the name of our hostess) was very loquacious, she initiated me into the peculiarities of Illinois politeness. No person, however slender his pretensions to knighthood, or how long so-ever the time since his small-clothes were new, is addressed without the courteous epithet of 'Sir;' and this practice is observed by the members of the same family in their intercourse with each other; of course the females are in like manner honoured with 'Madam,' *Ubi tu Caius, ego Caia.* It is not etiquette in Illinois to sit at the table after you have done eating; to remain after you have finished your meal implies that you have not had sufficient. This custom I subsequently found a very convenient one.

But I am forgetting the house. It was a fair specimen of a log-house, and therefore a description of it will give the reader a pretty correct idea of the American peasantry. There were two rooms, both on the ground floor, separated from each other with boards so badly joined, that crevices were in many places observable. The rooms were nearly square, and might contain from thirty to forty square yards each; beneath one of the rooms was a cellar, the floor and sides of which were mud and clay, as left when first dug out; the walls of the house consisted of layers of strong blocks of tim-

---

5. The will of Nimrod Philips seems to indicate that the Mrs. Philips whom Mrs. Burlend knew was a second wife of Nimrod, whose maiden name was Nancy Norris. Of her we have learned nothing apart from the vivacious picture limned by our author. An earlier wife of Philips who was a member of the Elledge family intermarried with the Boones, and on coming to Illinois settled in Scott County on the east side of the Illinois River from Pike.

ber, roughly squared and notched into each other at the corners; the joints filled up
with clay. The house had two doors, one of which is always closed in winter, and open
in summer to cause a draught. The fire was on the floor at the end of the building,
where a very grotesque chimney had been constructed of stones gathered out of the
land, and walled together with clay and mud instead of cement. It was necessarily a
great width, to prevent the fire from communicating with the building. The house
was covered with oak shingles; that is to say, thin riven boards nailed upon each other,
so as just to over-reach. The floors of the house were covered with the same material,
except a large piece near the fire, which was paved with small stones, also gathered
from the land. There was no window to the house I am describing, although many
log-houses may now be found having glass windows. This inconvenience I pointed
out to my hostess, who replied, 'upon the whole it was as well without, for in winter
the house was warmer and in summer they had always the door open, which was better than any window.' It is in reality true, that the want of light is felt very little in a
log-house; in winter they are obliged to keep fine blazing fires, which, in addition to
the light obtained from their low wide chimneys, enable the inmates to perform any
business that is requisite.

It is however by no means to be understood that an American log house equals
in comfort and convenience a snug English cottage. It is quite common to see, at least,
one bed in the same room as that in which the fire is kept; a practice which invariably gives both the bed and house a filthy appearance. There was no chamber, only a
sort of loft, constructed rather with a view to make the house warmer, than to afford
additional room. Adjoining one side were a few boards nailed together in the form of
a table, and supported principally by the timber in the wall. This was dignified with
the name 'side-board.' In the centre of the room, stood another small table, covered
with a piece of coarse brown calico; this was the dining table. The chairs, four in number, were the most respectable furniture in the house, having bark of ichory platted
for bottoms. Besides these there were two stools and a bench for common use,—a
candlestick made from an ear of Indian corn, two or three trenchers and a few tin
drinking vessels. One corner of the house was occupied with agricultural implements, consisting of large hoes, axes, &c., for stubbing, called in America grubbing,
flails and wooden forks, all exhibiting specimens of workmanship rather homely. Various herbs were suspended from the roof with a view of being medicinally serviceable, also two guns, one of them a rifle. There were also several hams and sides of
bacon, smoked almost till they were black; two or three pieces of beef, &c. Under one
of the beds were three or four large pots filled with honey, of which Mrs. P. was not
a little lavish, as she used it to every meal along with coffee. The furniture in the other
room consisted of two beds and a hand-loom, with which the family wove the greater
part of their own clothes. In the cellar I observed two or three large hewn tubs, full
of lard, and a lump of tobacco, the produce of their own land, in appearance sufficient
to serve an ordinary smoker his life.

During our sojourn at Mr. Phillips', my husband found Mr. B., and on the third
day after our arrival, brought that gentleman's team, two stiff oxen yoked to a clumsy
sledge; on which we placed our beds, boxes, &c. and bid good by to Mrs. P., who, as
we paid her for our harbour, contrived to shed a tear or two at the thoughts of parting. After arriving at Mr. B.'s house, I certainly felt I had been a little cajoled. My husband had seen him the day before, but had made no mention of his condition. He was
in the fields when we arrived; but as the door was unlocked, or rather lockless, we

took the liberty of introducing ourselves and luggage. Mr. B. was at once a bachelor and solitaire. He had left England precipitately, and what is more unusual, a great part of his money, which at this time he was daily expecting by a remittance. The property he had taken with him was all expended in land and cattle, so that a little money was a desideratum. Shortly after our arrival, Mr. B. made his appearance, which, as I before intimated, was rather mysterious. In his letters sent to England, he had spoken of his situation as 'a land flowing with milk and honey'; but I assure you patient reader, his appearance would have led any one to suppose that he gathered his honey rather from thorns than flowers. He was verily as ragged as a sheep: too much so for decency to describe. And his house was more like the cell of a hermit who aims at super-excellence by enduring privations than the cottage of an industrious peasant. The bed on which he slept was only like a bolster which he had used on shipboard, and laid upon a kind of shelf of his own constructing. Then again the walls of his house were of hewn timber as others, but the joinings or interstices were left quite open. The first night I passed in this miserable abode I was almost perished. My husband was obliged to heat a flat iron, and after wrapping it in flannel, apply it to my feet, so little were we protected from the inclemency of the weather. Finding our comforts here so few, we determined to have a home of our own as soon as possible. Mr. B. was too busy in his farm to render my husband much assistance in selecting a piece of ground. Besides the condition of his *haut-de-chausse*[6] rendered it almost imperative upon him to keep near home, especially as he was a bachelor.

Before I proceed any further with my narrative, perhaps it will be of advantage to the reader to explain the method of purchasing land in the United States. The land in the various states has all been surveyed by direction of the government, and divided into portions of eighty acres each. For the sale of the land thus surveyed and laid down on large plans, a land-office is established in various central situations, where all the allotments of a certain district are sold, and the purchasers' names registered. Any person, therefore, who wishes to purchase one or more of these subsections, can see the plan, and select any that are unsold. They will even sell as small a quantity as forty acres; but as they do this merely to accommodate new settlers, no person already possessing eighty acres, can purchase a smaller quantity than that at a time. In some of the older states the government lands are all sold off. It must there be bought of private owners; but in Illinois and other new states there is plenty unsold. The government price everywhere is one hundred dollars for eighty acres. As there are myriads of acres yet in its native luxuriant wildness, any person may with impunity cultivate as much as he chooses without paying anything; and, as a further inducement, when a person begins thus to cultivate, no other person can legally purchase that land, till four years have expired from the time of his beginning to cultivate. By obtaining what is termed a pre-emption the improvement arising from his own industry is as secure to him for four years as if he was the actual owner. Should, however, he fail to pay for the land before the term expires, an indifferent person may then purchase it; but this seldom happens. Every person purchasing land at the office, must declare upon oath, if required, that no other party has an improvement on it. And, if it be proved to be otherwise, such purchase is in every case invalid; and the fraudulent party liable to a heavy fine.

---

6. Meaning, his trousers.

An improved eighty acres was the first land we purchased: we obtained it in the following manner:—A person named Mr. Oakes[7] having heard that a family about to settle was sojourning at Mr. B.'s came to invite my husband to buy some venison, which he had killed with his rifle just before. My husband went with him, and in conversation found he was disposed to sell his improvement right; for the four years were not expired, and he had not entered it at the land office. For this right he wanted sixty dollars. My husband told him he would call upon him the next day, and returned to Mr. B.'s after buying a quantity of nice venison at a halfpenny per pound. The following day, my husband and I visited at Mr. Oakes's, who took us round the estate, shewed us the boundaries, which were marked out by large stones set at each corner, termed the corner stones.

On the land there were about four hundred sugar maples which Mr. Oakes had tapped the preceding year. These trees grow plentifully in the United States, and promise with proper culture to supersede the use of West Indian sugar in America. They like a low situation and a deep soil, and grow to a larger size than any trees in this country. They are said to thrive the better the oftener they are pierced. The method of obtaining sugar from them is very simple. A small cabin, or, as it is there termed, camp, is built in the midst of the trees; two or three large coppers, holding from five to ten gallons each, are set within it, to boil the liquor, which being drained from the trees into hewn wooden troughs, is carried into the camp. The incisions are made with an auger in the beginning of March, when the sap is beginning to rise. Into each of these holes a tube is inserted, about an inch in diameter, so as just to fill the hole, through this the liquor flows as through a spout. The tree from which these tubes are made, is admirably adapted for the purpose, growing somewhat like the elder, only its branches are straighter and contain more pith. It is usually called in Illinois the shoemaker's tree, its botanical name I do not know. The most suitable weather for the discharge of this liquor is when the days are fine and the nights frosty. After the liquor is thus collected, it is boiled down to the consistency of thin treacle. It is then strained through a coarse woollen cloth, and afterwards boiled again at a slower fire till it becomes hard and firm like raw sugar. It is at present much used in the United States, and always sells at a higher rate than that from the West Indies. On the land now under consideration, Mr. Oakes, had broken up about twelve acres, three of which were sown with wheat, and the remaining nine ready to be sown with Indian corn, oats, &c. the following spring. As we liked the situation and land very much and were wishful to be settled, the agreement was completed that evening, and the money paid and possession obtained the following day. The reader is aware that the sixty dollars given to Mr. Oakes, were only for his house, improvement right, sugar-making utensils, &c. One hundred more we paid at the land office, at Quincy, and we obtained the usual certificate or title deeds; and thus by the first of December, having

---

7. There were, commonly, three waves of migration in the settlement of any given portion of the frontier. First of all came the traders, hunters, and trappers, with no particular intention of improving the country. Second came the "squatters," who occupied (without troubling to buy legal title) a tract of land and made some slight improvements on it, frequently building a cabin and reducing one or more acres to cultivation, but relying largely upon hunting and on the natural products of the forest for their support. In the wake of the squatter came the permanent settler, who acquired legal title to the soil and developed a home with the intention of passing it on to his children. Oakes, the individual here noted, was evidently a squatter, who has left no record of his sojourn in the community. Of him and his kind, Mr. Jess M. Thompson, local historian, observes, "All seem to have vanished from the community at an early day."

spent about thirty pounds in travelling, thirty-five more in land, &c. we were the rightful owners of a farm of eighty acres, with a log house in the centre of it.[8] What more could we require? The reader will perceive in the next chapter.

CHAPTER 4

During the time we were at lodgings we had felt ourselves dependent, and looked forward with anxious expectation to the time when we might again taste the sweets and independence of home, and those enjoyments which are only to be expected at one's own fireside. That period had now arrived. We had indeed a house such as I have already described, but we had no furniture except two large boxes, two beds, and a few pots and cooking utensils; besides, our provisions were just finished. Till this time we had been using principally the remains of biscuits, &c., purchased at New Orleans. The first wants of nature must be first attended to: whether we had a chair to sit on or not, something to eat we must have. Our nearest neighbour lived about half-a-mile from us, and we were at least two miles and a-half from any place at which flour was sold; thither, however, my husband went, and as our money was growing scarce, he bought a bushel of ground Indian corn, which was only one-third the price of wheaten flour; it was there sold for thirty cents a bushel. Its taste is not pleasant to persons unaccustomed to it; but as it is wholesome food, it is much used for making bread. We had now some meal, but no yeast, nor an oven; we were therefore obliged to make sad paste, and bake it in our frying pan on some hot ashes. We procured a little milk of our nearest neighbour, Mr. Paddock, which, on account of the severe frosts that prevail in Illinois, we generally received in lumps of ice.

Thus we lived the first few weeks at our new estate. Hasty pudding, sad bread, and a little venison which we had left, were our ordinary food. The greater part of my husband's time was spent in cutting and preparing wood for our fires. About this time we made further purchases of a cow and calf, for which we paid fourteen dollars, a young mare, which cost us twenty dollars, two pigs, and a shallow flat-bottomed iron pan, with a cover to it, to bake in. This is the common, and indeed almost the only kind of oven used in Illinois. It is vulgarly called a skellit. To make it hot it is immersed in glowing embers, the lid is then removed till the dough is put in; it is then replaced and ashes again thrown over it, till the cake is baked. Hence it will be perceived that a quantity of bread beforehand is unknown in Illinois: their custom is to bake a cake to each meal, which is generally very good; eggs and milk being so plentiful, are regularly used in their bread, along with a little celeraturs to lighten it, whereby it becomes very rich and nutritive.

---

8. The farm which the immigrants thus obtained for their home is legally known as the northeast 1/4 of the northeast 1/4 of Section 6, Twp. 5 S, R. 2 W. of the Fourth P. M. It lies about two miles east of Bethel Cemetery, and about three miles north of the village of Detroit, in northwestern Detroit Township. Three miles to the northeast lies Valley City, formerly Philips Ferry. The approach of the Burlends to the farm site was, of course, by way of Philips Ferry. The original cabin site was on the face of a sloping hillside, a few rods from a spring which still gives forth a stream of clear, cool water.

The Illinois settlers live somewhat differently from the English peasantry; the former have only three meals a–day, and not much variety in them: bread, butter, coffee, and bacon, are always brought to the table, but fresh meat is a rarity, and is never obtained as in England by going to a butcher for it. In Illinois the farmers all kill their own cattle, and salt what is not used immediately; sometimes, however, they distribute portions among their neighbours, with the view of receiving as much again when they kill theirs. It is by no means uncommon for an old settler to have a couple of fowls, ducks, a goose, or a turkey to dinner; and, generally speaking, everybody has plenty of plain good food. [The object contemplated in this work requires that I should occasionally leave my own history, to render more complete the information I have to impart; I hope, therefore, the reader will not think me incoherent. To proceed:] we bought the live stock above described of Mr. Oakes, and as it was winter, we wanted something with which to feed them. Indian corn is nearly the only winter food used in Illinois; and as the culture and management of it occupy a great portion of the farmer's time and industry, it may be not out of place to explain the method of cultivating it: the land intended for Indian corn should be ploughed and harrowed once or twice to make the earth loose and mellow, that the roots may strike with greater freedom; furrows are then made at the distance of about a yard from each other: these are afterwards crossed by other furrows made at right angles to the first, and about the same distance apart; by this means the field appears divided into numberless little square portions, each somewhat less than a square yard as if hollowed at the centre; into each of these crossings four seeds are thrown, and slightly covered with a hoe; this is done in the beginning of March, and after the young blades make their appearance the plough is occasionally drawn along between the rows, for the purpose of checking weeds and keeping the mould as light as possible; as these groups of plants are so far apart, kidney beans, melons, and pumpkins are frequently sown among them, for which the strong stems of the corn are excellent supports.

Indian corn usually ripens about the beginning of October, and is of an immense produce. There are commonly four or five ears to each stem, each ear having from five hundred to a thousand grains in it.[1] As the ears ripen they gradually assume a pendent form, and are in that position severally overhung with the leaves of the plant, which form a sort of sheath, securely protecting them from rain; in this manner, when properly ripened, it will remain in perfect safety all winter uncut; and it is by no means uncommon to sow the land with wheat before the corn crop is all removed. It is not always allowed to ripen; part of the crop is often cut, when the corn is about half-fed, which being dried in the sun, the stem and leaves make excellent hay; in this state it is both hay and corn, and is in fact the only hay the farmer preserves for winter, of which he makes small stacks of a peculiar construction, so as not to require thatching. Nothing can be more beautiful than a field of Indian corn in full blossom, and perhaps nothing in nature displays the munificence of Providence more strikingly than this matchless plant. In order to supply our cattle with winter meat, we applied to Mr. Paddock, our nearest neighbour, who sold us part of a field unreaped; some of it we cut down and took home, the rest we allowed to stand and turned our cattle to it. The reader may think it strange that we should turn cattle into the fields in the

---

1. It seems probable that Edward Burlend, who never saw America, misunderstood what his mother actually told him concerning the corn crop. A yield of four or five ears of corn to a single stalk is so uncommon that the Editor, who grew up on an Iowa farm cannot remember ever having seen a single example. The Illinois River bottom land is very rich and still produces splendid crops of corn, but the statement that a yield of four or five ears to the stalk was common, even a century ago, is evidently erroneous.

depth of winter, especially as the winters are there more severe than in England; it is however the regular custom: the cattle are inured to it, as they are never kept up any part of the year, either day or night. The two pigs we had bought we were obliged to kill shortly after we purchased them, as we wanted them for our own use, and we wished to spare the small stock of Indian corn we had on hand. The reader must also know our money was nearly done: I believe we had not more than four or five dollars remaining; part of it we were obliged to spend in sulphur, to cure what is called the Illinois mange, from which we were all suffering.

This complaint invariably attacks new settlers, shortly after their arrival, and is a complete scourge until it is removed. The body breaks out all over in little spots, attended with intolerable itching. It is generally attributed to the change of water, but as theirs possesses no peculiarity of taste, I cannot understand how that can be the cause. We were soon cured after using the sulphur, and never felt anything more of it.[2]

It has already been said that when we entered our house we had no furniture; this inconvenience my husband, although no joiner, had undertaken to remove, by making for himself and me each a stool, and a low bench for our children, or more properly a log of wood, squared and laid across the hearth for a seat. He had also contrived to make a table, which if not as neat as those used in England, was quite as substantial: having met with a section of a strong tree about two feet long, he rolled it into the house, and set it upon its end; had it been a little longer, its upper surface would have been just what we wanted; we however nailed a few boards upon it, making them fit as well as we could, and having covered it with a cloth to conceal its roughness, it was far from being contemptible, at least for persons like us, who had been some days without any. As to bedsteads, we were a few weeks before we got any; of course we had them to make ourselves, and as we were ill furnished with tools and unaccustomed to such employment, when they were finished they served rather to shew how little ornament is absolutely necessary, than our skill as expert carpenters.

Hitherto the light of the fire had served us instead of a candle, which was very inconvenient, as I wished to sew a little in the evenings. It is certainly true that days are never so short as in England, nevertheless we were very wishful to have some candles. The inhabitants commonly make their own, in tin moulds; but as we had neither moulds nor tallow, we were obliged to put a little lard into a saucer, and light a piece of rag previously inserted in it; by this we could see to sew and read pretty well; but as the rag frequently got immersed in the melted lard it was very troublesome, and by constant use we had three or four saucers broken with the heat, a circumstance much to be regretted, as pots of all kinds are dear in Illinois. To prevent a recurrence of this misfortune we ultimately made use of our kettle lid, inserting the knob or holder into a piece of board to make it stand.

Our next great inconvenience was want of soap: having however learnt from Mrs. Phillips the method of making it, we were by this time in a state of readiness for supplying ourselves. The reader will remember we had before this time killed two

---

2. The "Illinois Mange," a well-known pioneer affliction, as the name itself indicates, seems not to trouble present-day denizens of Pike County. Mr. Francis Allen, a grandson of our author and now eighty years of age, who has lived his entire life in the county, informed the Editor that he had never heard of the disease. Jess M. Thompson, however, local historian (and a great-grandson of Mrs. Burlend) is familiar with its early-day prevalence in the county. He relates that local opinion attributed its occurrence to the rotting of plowed-under vegetation. Another theory attributed its ravages to the decayed fish which perished with the drying-up of ponds along the river bottoms. At Atlas, Pike County, the disease assumed the proportions of an epidemic in 1821, when many of the settlers died from it.

pigs, the entrails of which we had cleaned and preserved, along with the bits of offal, rendering, scraps, &c., and now the finest of our ashes were collected and put into a large wooden trough, and boiling water poured over them, whence we obtained a strong solution of potash, which we poured off and boiled down; fresh ashes were then used as before, and a fresh solution obtained; the whole was next boiled down to about one third of the original quantity, by which means the solution became so caustic, that it would have taken the skin off one's fingers in a moment. In this state the waste meat and entrails were mixed with it, which it very soon assimilated. After it had obtained the consistency of soft soap, it was poured into a vessel appropriated for the purpose, to be ready for use.

This is the manner the American Peasantry supply themselves with soap. Their practice of burning wood furnishes them with potash, which they saturate with other ingredients as above described. Since we were thus obliged to provide necessaries for ourselves in a manner very different from that to which we had been accustomed in England, it may be asked if there are no shops in that country. Illinois, it must be known, is very thinly populated, and on that account it is not the situation for shop-keepers. There are, however, in various places, what are termed store keepers, who supply the settlers with articles the most needed, such as food, clothing, implements of husbandry, medicine, and spirituous liquors: for which they receive in exchange the produce of their farms, consisting of wheat, Indian corn, sugar, beef, bacon, &c. As these storekeepers exercise a sort of monopoly over a certain district, their profits are great, and they often become wealthy. Besides their store, they often have a saw-mill and a cornmill, at which they grind the corn they obtain from the farmers, for the purpose of sending it to New Orleans, or some other place where it can be readily sold. Stores therefore are in Illinois, nearly what markets are in England, only there is more barter in the former country. The mills in that neighbourhood are chiefly turned by water.

We were destined to be unfortunate with the young mare we had purchased of Mr. Oakes. Having been accustomed to run in the fields with other horses, she would not settle with our cow and calf. Every day she was lost; no fences could turn her. We were therefore obliged to sell her, or rather exchange for one not near so good; only she was expected to have a foal the following spring. Shortly after we had parted with the young mare, my husband found two strange horses in the field feeding upon our corn, he turned them out and returned home. On going to the field again they were there a second time; he felt assured some one had turned them in, as the fences were all good. The next morning explained the circumstance, for the horses being in the field as before, he was about to drive them out, when a tall man hastened towards him, and bade him desist, telling him that the horses were his and he intended them to be there. My husband remonstrated with him on the injustice of such behaviour, and per-severed in his attempts to drive them out; at which the person, whose name was Brevet, went up to him, and struck him a blow on the forehead with his fist, and threatened further violence if he did not allow them to remain. Seeing that physical force was the only available argument, my husband began to prepare for resistance; but calling to mind the situation of his family, and not knowing what perfidy might be resorted to, he wisely concluded to leave the man and his horses where they were. I mention this circumstance principally to shew how much we were indebted to an over-ruling Prov-idence for the preservation of my husband's life on this occasion. We afterwards learnt that Brevet was a pest to the neighbourhood, and that he had told one of his acquain-tances of this interview, and declared he would have stabbed my partner with a large dirk which he always carried with him, if he had resisted. In a short time afterwards he left the neighbourhood, dreaded or detested by all who knew him.

We have already seen that considerable labour is required to prepare fuel, as a good fire in America is essential during the winter season. The frosts are intensely keen, a wide river is sometimes iced over in a single night, so as to be unnavigable. Every thing of a fluid nature, exposed to the weather, is formed into a solid. For two or three months the milk freezing as soon as it is taken from the cows, affords no cream, consequently no butter. It is nevertheless possible to obtain butter, by keeping the churn near the fire, and churning cream and milk both together; but as this method is exceedingly trouble-some it is seldom practised. The nights in winter are at once inexpressibly cold, and poetically fine. The sky is almost invariably clear, and the stars shine with a brilliancy entirely unknown in the humid atmosphere of England. Cold as it was, often did I, during the first winter, stand at the door of our cabin, admiring their lustre and listening to the wolves, whose howlings, among the leafless woods at this season, are almost unceasing. These animals are numerous in America; and, unless the sheep be regularly folded, their depredations are extensively injurious, as they lacerate the throats of nearly all the flock; sometimes also they will seize young pigs, but as they fear the old ones, unless they are impelled by hunger, these animals are not in much danger. The timid submissive sheep is always their favourite prey.

The reader will perceive we had not much intercourse with the rest of the world. For a while no one seemed to notice us, except Mr. B., our neighbour Mr. Paddock, and one Mr. Burns, who lived about two miles off, (all are *Misters* in America.) But indeed the villainous conduct of Mr. Brevet had made us so suspicious, that we scarcely knew whether to wish for an increased circle of acquaintance, or entire seclusion. One thing was very afflictive, our being deprived of Christian Sabbath ordinances. We always honoured that day, by abstaining from our accustomed labour; we read our Bible, and meditated thereon: but Sabbath after Sabbath passed away without our once being able to assemble with those who 'keep holy day,' or in the great congregation to unite our tribute of praise, with the aspirations of those whose sentiments are 'how amiable are thy tabernacles O Lord of Hosts!' At this time we were five miles from any place where public worship was regularly conducted; subsequently preaching-houses much nearer were opened, the character of which will be noticed in its proper place.

The motives which occasioned this work to be written require that a strict regard to truth be maintained; and, in matters of fact, that nothing be introduced calculated to mislead, either by deterring or alluring; this rule has hitherto been carefully observed. Am I then asked if we thus far were satisfied with the step we had taken, my answer is, we regretted it very much. We had indeed plenty of corn-bread and milk, but neither beer nor tea; coffee was our chief beverage, which we used very sparingly, for want of money. All the water we wanted we had to thaw, and during the nights, on account of the severe frosts, we were very cold indeed; although we always kept the fire burning. Our bed-clothes we had taken with us from England, and we were unable to procure any more, as they were dear, and our means almost exhausted. We had indeed some good land, but it was nearly all uncultivated, and we had nothing to sell except our cattle, which we wanted. The only ground of hope we had was in our industry and perseverance. My husband worked very hard; the little time we had to spare, after feeding the cattle and procuring fuel, was spent in splitting trees to make rails. All the fences here are made of rails, there are no thorns in the neighbourhood. The method of fencing is peculiar: they use no posts; but having prepared their rails, they lay one down on the ground, where they wish to make a fence; not precisely in the same direction as the line of their intended fence, but making a small angle with it. Another rail is then laid down with its end overreaching the first, with which it forms a cross like the letter X, only instead of the crossing being at the centre, it is near the end of each rail. A third is then made to cross the second as before, and so on to an indefinite length. On each side of these several crossings a stake is driven into the ground to prevent their being removed. Other rails are then placed upon these, crossing each other in a similar manner, till the fence is as high as it is required. Generally they are about nine rails high. From the description here given, the reader will perceive that the fences are not straight as in England, but in a continued zig-zag. The reason for this difference is, timber and land are of comparatively little value in America, while their method requires less labour than ours.

In this manner we spent our first winter; we had plenty of work; our amusements even tended to advantage. Great numbers of quails frequented our home-stead to feed on our small stock of Indian corn; we caught several of them with snares, which were excellent eating. My husband also shot a few rabbits, of which there are vast numbers in America. We likewise saw several deer, but as we had no rifle, we could not kill any. We observed several kinds of birds, which we had not before seen, one in particular, which we took to be a species of turkey, engaged our attention; my husband tried several times to kill one, without effect. One Saturday, however, he was successful, and brought home his game with as much apparent consciousness of triumph, as if he had slain some champion hydra of the forest. The following day we expected Mr. B., who by this time had received his money, to dine with us. We accordingly dressed our bird, and congratulated ourselves with the idea of having our countryman to dine with us on a fine boiled turkey. Sunday morning arrived, and in due time our turkey was in the pot boiling for dinner. Mr. B. came; we told him how happy we were on account of the treat we were going to give him. He was surprised at our story, as those birds are difficult to obtain with a common fowling-piece, and desired to see the feet and head. But the moment he saw them, he exclaimed 'it's a buzzard,' a bird which, we subsequently learnt, gormandizes any kind of filth or carrion, and consequently is not fit to be eaten. We were sorely disappointed; our turkey was hoisted into the yard, and we were obliged to be contented with a little bacon, and a coarse Indian corn pudding, for which our stomachs were not altogether unprepared, although recently in anticipation of more sumptuous fare. The reader may think we were stupid not to know a turkey; the bird in question is very much like one, and indeed on that account is called in Illinois a turkey-buzzard.

As spring approached we felt some symptoms of those hopes which had animated us in England with reference to our success as emigrants. Man's career in prospective is always brilliant; and it is providentially ordered that it should be so. Could we have foreseen our destiny, the prospect would have thrown us into despair. It would have robbed us of much present enjoyment, and unfitted our minds for the difficulties with which we had to struggle. I am, however, anticipating my history. The symptoms to which I referred originated with the idea of being the cultivators of our own land. How those prospects were realized, the sequel will explain. By the beginning of March our Indian corn was done, and it had served so long only through the greatest care. There was however by this time a little fresh grass in the woods, to which we were very glad to turn our little stock, consisting as before stated of a cow and calf, and a mare near foaling. As this method of summering cattle in America is peculiar to that country, and affords to the farmer considerable advantages, I shall endeavour to be explicit in the account of it, which I am about to give. I must then premise that all unenclosed lands, whether purchased of government or otherwise, are considered common pasturage; and as there are in Illinois thousands of acres in that state, any person can keep as many cattle during summer as he chooses. They are turned out at spring, and thus run where they please. A person unacquainted with these habits would naturally be afraid of losing them in such immeasurable regions. This, however, seldom happens. There are few animals having a sufficiency of food that are fond of ranging over strange domains. Even in this country we observe foxes and hares to have their favourite haunts, from which it is difficult to break them. Domesticated animals a manifest this principle of attachment still more strongly. Hence no American farmer, having his cattle on the range, would fear being able to find them in a few hours; and indeed a person unacquainted with the haunts of any certain herd, would most probably go directly towards them. Rivers and smaller streams have certainly some confining influence, but independent of that, their habits are to frequent those situations only to which they are accustomed. In that country cattle have a great liking for salt, and indeed it seems essential to their health, particularly in summer. An English farmer would smile to see a herd of cattle contending with each other over a few handfuls of dry salt which had been thrown on the floor for them. This is seen every day in America. The milch cows require more of it than the rest, and unless they are regularly served with it, their milk becomes unpleasant. This induces them to come to their stand to be milked twice-a-day. Oxen and heifers will take no harm if they have a little twice-a-week, or even not so often. Where so many different herds of cattle run at large, there is a greater danger of their intermixing than of their being lost. To prevent this, great care is taken by each grazier at the spring to mark his own. Some cut their ears in various ways. Others burn certain marks on their horns with a hot iron. There is not, however, much confusion. The cattle which have been fed together during winter, most generally associate with each other in summer; all having an unaccountable attachment to the master beast of the herd, apparently considering his presence a source of protection or honour. For this reason the owner usually suspends a bell round this animal's neck, which enables him to find his cattle with greater ease. Hence the phrase, 'bear the bell,' is common even in this country. In this manner the cattle graze during summer, and when the pasturage fails, they cease to range; but besetting their master's cabin with incessant lowings remind him that winter is approaching, and that their claims to his bounty deserve attention, and must have it. At this time if any strange cattle have joined the herd, the law requires that the farmer cause them to be valued, and their mark to be taken down and sent to four of the nearest mills for publicity; if they are not owned within a year they belong to the herd.

I must now leave our small herd of cattle running in the woods, to acquaint the reader with our first summer's performances and success. The first fruits of our industry were derived from our sugar orchard, the care of which devolved principally on me. We were in want of nearly all kinds of implements of husbandry, without the means of procuring them, except by running into debt, a practice which we felt reluctant to adopt. Our sugar trees therefore at this time afforded us a seasonable boon. The weather was favourable, and by hard working we made nearly three hundred weight, besides a barrel of molasses. We disposed of the greater part of it to a storekeeper named Mr. Varley, at the rate of seven or eight cents per pound. It must not be understood that we got money for it. Business is seldom transacted after that manner in Illinois. My meaning is we were allowed to take anything we wanted from the store by paying for it with sugar at the above rate. Our first care was to have some Indian corn for seed, and some more meal for our own use, which at that time we wanted. We likewise obtained a little coffee, two or three hoes, and a Yankee axe, which is much larger and broader than the one used in this country, and better adapted for the every-day business of hewing large blocks of timber for fuel and other purposes.

And now, kind reader, if thou hast any intentions of being an emigrant, I cordially wish thee success; but before thou forsakest the endearments of thy present home, consider the situation in which we were placed with a helpless family dependent upon us. Thou hast seen us expend our little money with the utmost frugality; thou art acquainted with our possessions, real and personal. It was now the middle of March, when Indian corn, the most useful produce of that country, must be sown, or the season would be past. We had land and seed, but no plough, nor any team, except an old mare, that we feared would scarcely live while she foaled, and consequently we could not yoke her. What could we do? If we did not sow we could not reap; we should have nothing to feed our cattle with the ensuing winter. *Labor omnia vincit* was our motto. We set to work with our hoes; I, husband, and son, the latter under ten years of age, and day after day, for three successive weeks, did we toil with unwearied diligence till we had sown and covered in nearly four acres. We should probably have sown more, had not the rains which fall in torrents at this season prevented us. Whilst referring to the weather, it will be proper to observe that during the month of April in Illinois, a great quantity of rain usually falls, accompanied almost invariably with thunder storms of a most awful character. A person who has lived only in England can have but an imperfect conception of these electrical phenomena. They happen most frequently in the night, which considerably increases their power of striking terror through the most intrepid bosom. The weather is at this time close and sultry, and as the sun declines the sky becomes gradually overcast; midnight arrives, a pitchy darkness overhangs the earth; by and by the wind begins to roar in the trees, and the hoarse thunder in the distance announces the coming of the storm. As it approaches the thunder claps wax louder and louder, while the lightning begins to play across the gloomy firmament, in a most awful and terrific manner. Every moment the voice of the thunder acquires additional compass, never ceasing even for a moment; but before one peal has well broken on the ear, it is drowned by another still more tremendous and loud. The lightning is even more overpowering than the thunder. One moment all is in obscurity, a second the heavens seem rent asunder, the bright blue lightning dancing in all directions with a frightful and deadly velocity; meanwhile the rain descends in torrents, threatening to sweep away the foundation of the dwelling. The length of time these storms continue is generally about an hour. The first I witnessed made an impression on my mind that will never be forgotten; my senses were completely disordered: I became alarmed at the slightest noise, and for a while felt more afraid of a thunder storm than of any calamity which appeared in the power of misfortune to inflict upon me. Probably my late anxieties and bereavement preying on my mind had indisposed my nerves for such phenomena, at once terrific, awful, and sublime. But whatever was the cause, I have great pleasure in stating that I soon got the better of my timidity. Trees have frequently been struck near our house, but hitherto no accident has befallen us. We now consider these storms rather as annoying than dangerous; one reason perhaps is that a dry log house is a bad conductor of the electric fluid.

About this time we were sorely tormented with another scourge, which unlike the one just noticed, possessed exceedingly little of a poetical or sublime character. It certainly operated on the nerves powerfully enough, but that in a manner rather calculated to move the lower than the more elevated passions of our nature. I refer to the musquitoes; swarms of which infest that country during spring and autumn, much to the annoyance of its inhabitants. This troublesome insect is not unlike the gnat, which in this country so often terminates its existence by flying into the candle. Its bite is slightly venomous, causing small blisters somewhat like those occasioned by the sting of a nettle, only the pain attending it is more acute. They are the most numerous in low situations, or among thick woods where the heat is less oppressive. This insect cannot bear great heats, and on that account is never seen during the hottest weather, except in very shady places. It is always most troublesome in the nights; and as it makes a constant humming when it flies, it is a most noisy as well as a most unwelcome guest in a lodging room. I do assure the reader I have lain for hours together with a handkerchief in my hand, fanning them from my face, when a little sleep would have been a more seasonable relaxation. Various methods are practised to drive them off or avoid them. We frequently made a fire at the door, and covered it with green leaves to make as much smoke as possible, and thereby to banish them from the neighbourhood; but the moment the smoke was dissipated they again made their appearance as numerous as flies in England on a summer day. Many persons make what are termed musquito hangings for their beds; these are constructed of laths strung together so closely as not to allow a space for them to pass through. They seldom are seen on the prairies, or indeed in any place remote from thick shady woods; thus some of our neighbours have been quite free from them, while we were tortured incessantly. We however had the advantage of being near fuel, a consideration of great importance in that country, especially as the soil of wood land is always more valuable than that of the prairies, and when cleared is likewise free from musquitoes.

Having referred to the prairies, it may perhaps be necessary to be a little more explicit. Many persons in England have a wrong idea of the uncultivated lands in America, imagining they are all wood. This is by no means the case. In Illinois there are thousands of acres with not a tree upon it, but covered with a sort of strong wild grass, growing sometimes three or four feet high. These lands are termed prairies, and require only to be broken up with a prairie plough, and they become at once fine arable land. As I before intimated, this kind of land, though the soonest cultivated, is not the most productive being, as the farmers term it, of a stronger quality than the other. The soil of both prairies and woodland is quite black, probably owing to the vegetable matter, which for ages has decayed thereon. At the season of the year now under notice, these prairies present to the eye a most charming appearance. Let the reader imagine himself by the side of a rich meadow, or fine grass plain several miles in diameter, decked with myriads of flowers of a most gorgeous and varied description, and he will have before his mind a pretty correct representation of one of these prairies. Nothing can surpass in richness of colour, or beauty of formation many of the flowers which are found in the most liberal profusion on these extensive and untrodden wilds. The naturalist would here meet with abundance of materials for his genius to arrange, while the poet, reminded of his elegies, would perceive how—

"Many a flower is born to blush unseen,
And waste its sweetness on the desert air."

In contrasting the hues of flowers grown in America with those in England, I must acknowledge that the former country presents the more splendid; but if they are superior in colour, they are much inferior in odour. Perhaps the superabundance of light and heat, which produces such fine colour, is prejudicial to the production of odoriferous plants, as any thing at all approaching the fragrance of the honey suckle or sweet briar, I never witnessed in America. In the woody districts, the trees most commonly

met with are the oak, ichory, walnut and sugar maple, besides a great deal of underwood and wild fruit trees of the plum family. As all these grow in a wild state, it is not
to be supposed that the trees are as numerous as they are in the plantations of this country. The strong timber trees grow at various distances from each other, sometimes being
as near to each other as they can possibly grow, at others twenty or thirty yards apart.
They not only vary considerably in this respect, but also in magnitude and age. Not a
few are to be found in the last stage of decay, their patriarchal dignity gradually submitting to the all-subduing influence of time. Numbers more are quite hollow, in
which bees, owls, and rabbits severally find shelter and propagate their species. Every
thing here bears the mark of ancient undisturbed repose. The golden age still appears,
and when the woodman with his axe enters these territories for the first time, he cannot resist the impression that he is about to commit a trespass on the virgin loveliness
of nature, that he is going to bring into captivity what has been free for centuries.

In resuming the thread of my narrative, I have to state, that as soon as we had sown
our Indian corn, and planted a few potatoes, we began to prepare for taking in more
land, although we had four or five acres unsown of that which Mr. Oakes had broken
up. We hoped, nevertheless, that before another season we should be able to plough
and sow in a regular manner. Accordingly my husband worked hard every day with
his grubbing hoe and axe, tearing up the roots of underwood and cutting down some
of the largest trees. When trees are cut down in America, as little regard is paid to the
timber, they do not cut them off level with the ground as in England, but about three
feet from it. The remaining part is burnt after it has been exposed to the sun's rays a
few months. Many trees however are allowed to remain standing, after the bark has
been cut, to cause them to die. In this state they remain even after the land is sown,
for, being destitute of foliage, they do no harm to the crop.

While my husband was thus engaged I frequently went to him, and, assisted by
our little boy, gathered the most portable pieces of brushwood, and took them to our
cabin to be ready for fuel; thus, by continued exertions, we had cleared three or four
acres by the end of May, and made a fence half round the piece we intended to enclose as our next field, consisting of about eight acres. Before this time our old mare
had foaled, and as we partly expected, only survived that event a few weeks. Near our
house there is a sort of rivulet, termed in Illinois a branch, in which one Sunday
evening, after we had walked ten miles in going to and from the chapel, we found her
laid; we got her out with the help of a rope, and after a while she appeared little worse;
a week or two afterwards, however, her foal came by itself neighing to our door; we
were immediately assured that something had befallen its mother, and set out in
search of her, whither the foal, going before, led us as naturally as if it had been endowed with reason; she had again fallen into the branch, and was quite dead. The foal,
notwithstanding its loss, throve very well, and subsequently became a very valuable
brood mare.

In the month of June, notwithstanding our economy, we were obliged to purchase some meal on credit. Mr. Varley, the storekeeper, very willingly allowed us to
have as much as we wanted, and indeed offered to sell us anything else on the same
terms. His miller, however, as soon as he knew we were not giving ready money, only
partly filled the bushel, thereby making it dearer to us than before, and we dared not
complain to his master for fear he should refuse it altogether. The debt we contracted
was very small,—not a dollar—for which we had bread for the family not less than
six weeks; the expiration of which brings us to the end of our first wheat harvest, a
season conspicuous in my history on account of the severe trials I then experienced.

32

GIDEON LINCECUM

(1793–1874)

Early in 1861 Charles Darwin received a strange letter from Texas. The writer, who was previously unknown to Darwin, noted that he had been "raised and [had] always been a dweller in the wild border countries." He wrote to offer his observations about a species of large brownish-red ants. Remarkably, he had determined that this species of ant annually planted and harvested a small crop of rice. While Darwin found the letter "extraordinary," he could "almost believe the statements" that it contained. At the very least he was "impressed with the belief that the man does not *intentionally* tell lies."

Darwin's correspondent, whose crop-planting ants have since been discredited, was Gideon Lincecum. Born in Hancock County, Georgia, on April 22, 1793, Lincecum's formal education was limited by his father's frontier wanderlust. He later wrote to Darwin,

> Except for five month's schooling, at a deserted log cabbin in the backwoods of Georgia, by an old drunkard, my mind has not been biased by training of any kind from designing man. In the canebrakes and unhacked forests on the boarders of the above named state, with the muscogee Indian boys for my class mates, I learned my first lessons, in natures grand seminary.

Lincecum's boyhood investigations of the natural world and his friendships with Indians led to his avocations of naturalism and ethnography.

Lincecum served in the War of 1812, then married Sarah Bryan, with whom he had thirteen children. Lincecum, like his father, was restless, and in 1818 he and his family moved to Mississippi. There he helped to organize Monroe County and to develop both Columbus and Cotton Gin Port, Mississippi. In 1830 Lincecum embarked on a medical career that he pursued until 1848, when he decided to move farther west. In Texas he founded Long Point and continued his naturalistic pursuits. He left Texas and the United States in 1868 to join a group of Confederate expatriates in Mexico, but he returned to Long Point before his death in 1874.

Most of Lincecum's writings—including an important collection of Indian lore and a 1,500-page manuscript on the medicinal uses of plants found in Texas and Mexico—were left unpublished at the time of his death. Some of his autobiographical writings were first published in *The American Sportsman* magazine in 1874–1875. *Autobiography of Gideon Lincecum* appeared in the *Publications of the Mississippi Historical Society* for

1904, the source of the present text. In the selection here, we join Lincecum and his peripatetic father, Hezekiah Lincecum, in about 1804.

Text: *Autobiography of Gideon Lincecum* (*Publications of the Mississippi Historical Society,* 1904):
453–476.

FROM *AUTOBIOGRAPHY OF GIDEON LINCECUM* (1872, 1904)

He again became restless, and selling his place, put his wagon in good repair, set out
on this third attempt to get to Tennessee. This time his cargo, besides the beds, trunks,
etc., consisted of grandmother, four white and four black children. He had also two
white children and one negro child walking. The weather was fine, and we made good
progress. I was delighted that we were on the road. Being in my twelfth year, I was an
expert with a bow and arrow, and could run far ahead, shooting and killing many birds
in the course of a day.

Father hired a straggling old fellow to drive for this trip, and we rolled on bravely
until we came to Saluda river. There was there a store and a blacksmith shop, and we
stopped until the smith nailed a pair of shoes on the out-riding horse. Father and his
teamster became somewhat intoxicated and got two bottles of whiskey to carry with
them. The river was wide and swift, but shallow. We forded it, and in the course of two
hours were all safely landed on the border of South Carolina again. After going about
five miles my father and the driver became more deeply intoxicated. The latter fell off
the wagon and frightened the horses. They ran away and tore up the wagon, hurting
all who were in it. My grandmother was very seriously wounded. It became necessary for us to remain at this place three weeks before my grandmother was able to
travel again. At the end of this time my father told us that he had decided to purchase
a place from a man by the name of Hamilton, who lived on a hill nearby. My father
gave him some money and his wagon and two horses for the place. This was in
Pendleton district, S. C.

We had on this place a large orchard. There were in it fifty peach trees, said to be
forty-four years old. They made a very fine crop of peaches, which my father gathered and carried to a still, where he had them made into brandy. This, with all of his
corn and fodder that he could spare, he sold to travelers for ready money at a good
price. It was an easy place to make a living, and my father seemed to be quieting down
to a settled state of mind. All of the family were satisfied and willing to remain there.
Unfortunately my uncle, Tyre Kelly, who had been living in Tennessee, stopped with
us on his way to Georgia. He and his eight motherless children remained with us a
month. After they left my father became restless again, and sold his place at the first
opportunity.

We were soon on the road again. The next time we stopped it was at a place a
mile from where we lived the previous year.

The lands beyond the Oconee river had been obtained by the United States from the Muskogee Indians. No one had moved into this new purchase, and as father intended to settle there as soon as the Indians had completed the twelve months' hunting which had been by a stipulation in the treaty with the United States reserved to them, he took an overseer's place instead of purchasing land.

There came a man by the name of Young Gill, with his family, and made up a school, which was to be kept in a little old log cabin, a mile and a half from our home. Father entered my sister, brother and me as day scholars at the rate of $7.00 each per annum. We three started the next day and did not miss a day until father moved to the new purchase five months later. I was fourteen years old, and it was the first schoolhouse I had ever seen. I began in the alphabet. There were some very small boys, seven years old, who could read.

Whenever Mr. Gill would storm out, "Mind your book," the scholars would strike up a loud, blatant confusion of tongues, which surpassed anything I had ever heard before. There I sat in a sea of burning shame, while the clatter and glib clap of tongues rattled on. I soon accustomed myself to this method of studying aloud and felt myself very much at home. In accordance with the instructions of the master to come up and recite as soon as I was ready, I managed to say a lesson about every fifteen or twenty minutes during the first day. I was then spelling words of four letters. By hard study at night I was able to spell words of two syllables on the morning of the second day. I had one of Dillworth's spelling books at first, but there was so much talk about the new spelling book,—Webster's—that father got me one. The teacher soon told me to bring paper and ink to school. He made me a pen and told me that after every lesson I must write two lines. He marked a place on the writing bench that was to be called mine, and said "Here you are to keep your paper, ink, pens, books, etc., and no one shall interfere with them." I felt very proud of my writing place, though it was nothing more than a wide two inch plank laid on some slanting pins or pegs, driven into two inch auger holes, in one of the pine logs that was a part of the wall of the house. The log above this had been cut out its whole length, leaving a long narrow window immediately above the writing bench. The seat consisted of another two inch plank, placed on the top of some stakes driven in the ground,— the house had a dirt floor—and this concludes the inventory of that seminary except some split timbers laid on blocks for seat.

The rule was that he who got to the schoolhouse first said his lesson first; and when the teacher came in—which was never later than an hour by sun—he took his seat and immediately repeated "Come, First." This meant that he who had got there first should come and recite his lesson. The school hours were from an hour by sun in the morning to an hour by sun in the evening.

At the end of the five months I could read, the master said, "very well," could write a pretty fair hand by a copy, had progressed in the arithmetic to the double root of three, and had committed Webster's spelling book entirely to memory, besides many pieces of poetry which the teacher gave me for night lessons, many of which I remember yet.

When the Indians had finished their year of hunting and retired from the new purchase my father took me with him to explore the country. We crossed the Oconee river and traversed the lands of the new purchase ten or twelve days. He preferred the country on Little river, selected a place and we returned home to make ready for the removal as soon as possible. The newly acquired land belonged to the State, and the Legislature enacted that it should be surveyed into lots of 202½ acres each, and have it drawn for by her citizens in general lottery. Men having families were entitled to two tickets; single men and women of age, and sets of orphaned children, one ticket, each. My father had been moving and shackling about so much that he was not entitled to a chance in the lottery,—and the place he had selected on Little river had been drawn by a man who would not part with it. This discovery was not made until we had moved on to it. Father then found a place belonging to Thomas McLellon, with a double cabin on it. For this place he gave all the money he had, with "Mammy Pat" and two of her children. It was situated in the wild woods, on a beautiful clear running creek, in one mile of where Eatonton now stands.

Great numbers of people flocked into the country, and the next year after we came there the county seat was laid off and named Eatonton. I was one of the chain carriers to survey the streets and lots though I was but fourteen years old. We had cleared and planted ten acres of ground the year before, and this year we cleared fifteen acres more. About this time my father and I had a misunderstanding and I decided to leave home. I hired to a man by the name of William Wilkins, a merchant at Eatonton. I worked for him two years remaining in his home during this time. At the end of the first year I had a serious difficulty with a man by the name of Clark, who had insulted me several times. He was discharged by Mr. Wilkins, who put me in entire charge of his business. After my second year with Mr. Wilkins I was employed by Mr. Thompson, a more prosperous merchant, who paid me a salary of $500.00 a year.

In the meantime I had studied medicine during odd moments. The War of 1812 was approaching. I left the store and confined myself entirely to the study of medicine until the declaration of war. I then enlisted in a company of volunteers, but as the people of Putnam county had elected me tax collector, I could enlist for only five months. I had to begin collecting in January, and it was in the month of August when I went into the army. I served until the first of January; then went home, collected the taxes, paid the money into the treasury and married. I served another period of three months after I was married, and in the spring of 1815 went home and gave my father a faithful year's work.

The next year I joined forces and farmed with Judge Strong. He had three hands and sixty acres of open land. I had forty acres of open land and two hands. He was to furnish all the provisions, smithing, etc. I was to superintend the farm and we were to make an equal division of the proceeds of the crop. I planted sixty acres in cotton and forty in corn. I cultivated the ground carefully and both crops were very good. That year cotton was worth 31½ cents a pound, but I became restless and did not feel like staying in that country until the crop could be gathered. The Alabama, Black Warrior, Tombecbee, and Chattahoochie countries had all been acquired by conquest, and I was determined to seek a home in the wilderness. My father had made up his mind to go to the new country with his large family and he had been insinuating to me the propriety of breaking up to go with him. There was another *little thing* that increased my restlessness. My wife's relations were all wealthy and my wife said they had been mean enough to cast little slurs at her and her poverty. She also persuaded me to sell out and go with my father to the new country. All these influences confirmed me in the resolution to get ready and bid adieu to my native State.

Father and I sold out our possessions and were soon on the road to the new country. We had proceeded about forty-five miles when we came to the Ocmulgee river, which at that time was a dividing line between the Georgians and the Creek Indians. A man by the name of Ferguson came to our camp and getting a little "tight" with my father, in a kind of prolic, sold my father his land and cattle. All along the river the people owned herds of cattle which they kept in the range on the Indian side of it. There was plenty of deer over there, too; and being satisfied that my father would not remain more than a year, I concluded to stop also and do what I had never done in my life; idle away the time until he got tired of his bargain and made ready to move again.

I could continue my medical reading, fish in the river, and hunt the deer beyond it; and in this way have a pleasant time. I had made two or three very successful hunting excursions, had been fishing at my baited hole, and caught some fine fat red horse, and was highly pleased at the prospects for a pleasant year's amusement.

The country near the river was densely settled. At a little gathering one day I heard some of the men say that the boys had turned out and ducked and abused White, their school-master, so badly that he had quit the school. Some of the men remarked that their children were so bad that they feared they could never find a man that would be able to manage them. In reply to a remark which I inadvertently made one of the gentlemen asked me if I could manage them, saying that if I would undertake it they would furnish me with forty pupils and give me ten dollars a piece to teach them until the first of December, which would be nine and a half months and they would pay me the cash when the term expired. It struck me at once that this would be a more profitable employment than hunting and fishing, and I told them to make out their articles, appoint a school committee, and tell me where and when to go and I would undertake it.

They immediately made out the school articles, requiring me to teach only reading, writing and arithmetic. I signed them, and they told me to meet the scholars they would furnish me the ensuing Monday morning at the mineral springs, two miles from where I resided.

According to appointment I was there at eight o'clock, and I was astonished at the number of people I found there. The committee consisted of five men. There were forty-five pupils—fifteen grown young men, five of them married, five grown young ladies, and boys and girls of all sizes and ages to make up the forty-five. All entered for the full term.

After sitting till I had examined their books and set the lessons, the committee rose up and remarked: "We feel well pleased at your method of setting your classes to work, and, sir, you see what you have before you, we wish and believe that you will succeed." They bowed a good day and left.

These children had been born and raised to the age I found them among the cows and drunken cowdrivers on the outer borders of the State, and they were positively the coarsest specimens of the human family I had ever seen. I saw very distinctly that no civil or ordinary means would be applicable to their conditions.

In the course of the first day they had half a dozen fights in the house; talking and laughing went on incessantly; and at play time the cry of look what this one or that one is doing to me rang out from every part of the play ground. Those married and grown up young men participated in the devilment and seemed to enjoy it hugely. At the expiration of one hour, I called them to books, and one of the men as he came in at the door remarked, "You give but short play time, Mistofer." I replied good humoredly, as I should, "You will please recollect, my young friend, that this is my first day with you. I may learn to suit you better after a while." I further remarked to the young man that my intention was to make it the most pleasant and most instructive school that had ever been instituted in that country, and that I should, when the proper time arrived, call upon him and his companions to aid me in the prosecution of a scheme I had arranged in my mind to make it so. "Hurrah for you! Boys he is the fellow we ought to have had here all the time," was his reply.

They got their books and had a long talk about what I had said. They wondered what I could do to make the school more pleasant than it was.

I was bowed down over my desk, writing out my plans for the government of the school which really consisted of the most outrageous ruffians, rollicking young women, and naughty children I had ever seen. I would occasionally, without looking up, cry out "Mind your books," to which they did not seem to pay any attention. I called them up to say their lessons; and to this part of the exercise I paid strict attention, prompting and instructing them in the kindest and friendliest terms possible, and encouraging them to be good and get their lessons well. And so it went on with many curious and disgusting occurrences until twelve o'clock Friday. I had by that time completed a constitution and set of by-laws which were intended to teach the poor untutored marauders to govern themselves.

As soon as they had got through with their dinner Friday, they came rushing, and one of the men said good humoredly, "What's up now, hoss?" I replied "It is Friday afternoon, and I am desirous of reading to you a set of rules for the school to go by. I have been engaged writing them all the week. Seeing the school is so large it is necessary that there should be some systematic regulations to insure and control the equal rights of each individual. If you will all be seated I will read what I have written that you may judge of its propriety and see what you think of it." They all took seats and became more and more attentive until I got through with the reading.

The constitution provided for a regularly organized court,—judge, clerk, jury, sheriff and a monitor. It made me the sheriff. It also specified the character and degrees of crime, terms of office, etc. The by-laws regulated the terms of courts, duty of the officers, modes of drawing jurors, and the manner of conducting trials, punishments, etc., etc.

I read it very distinctly, and when I had finished it I enquired: "Well, gentlemen and ladies, what is your opinion of the documents?" They unanimously exclaimed, "It is the best thing in the world." "With your permission," I said, "I will take the vote of the school on the subject." "Yes, go it, hoss, it's a good thing," one of the married men said. And I put the question "All you who are in favor of this constitution and accompanying by-laws for the government and regulation of this school will make it known by saying 'Aye.'" The vote was unanimous in its favor.

I expressed my gratification at the result, and told them that I looked upon it as a very favorable indication to find them all of one mind on a subject of so great importance to them; and that I hoped to be able to convince them thoroughly before the school term had expired that the vote they had given was on the right side of the question. I added "To certify your approbations, it is proper that you all put your names to the constitution. Let the married men sign first." Not more than half of the grown ones could write. They ordered me as sheriff to write their names. In the course of an hour all their names except those of the little ones who could not understand its nature, were on the paper.

One of the married men, whose name was Scatterwhite, exultingly remarked "I tell you what, folks, this is a big thing. We never had such sort of doings afore in these diggings. What next, old hoss?" My reply was, "The constitution provides that officers of the court should be appointed by election." I then moved that an election be held for judge, clerk and monitor, the sheriff being already appointed by the constitution. "Name your candidates; and as it is a part of my duty to appoint managers and superintend elections, we can hold one immediately. After a good deal of telling and directing and much awkwardness, we succeeded in bungling out the officers.

I made out the monitor's list and after explaining it to him, I seated them and read the constitution and by-laws to them again. They were all so much pleased that they fairly shouted, and said they had heard how "the great folks done away far off, but none of them have ever come here afore."

After telling them that the constitution and rules were to be read every day at 12 m. and that Friday was the regular court day, I dismissed them. They went off in great glee.

At an hour by sun Monday morning the whole number of pupils was present, and I thought I could discover a considerable change in their behavior. I concluded that it would be proper to read the constitution to them to start with. I assured them that I felt confident that with such a healthy, smart set of pupils as I had, that long before the nine months would expire, I would teach them and expand their minds to such a degree that it would excite the interest of their parents and other people to come and hear their court trials and their lawyers speak every Friday afternoon. To effectuate these great results the constitution and by-laws must be strictly adhered to, and they must pursue their studies industriously and earnestly. A number of them exclaimed that they believed what I said and were determined to do their best to follow my instructions. The effects of having put their names to the constitution on their general behavior was very visible. We got through the week without a fight, with but little talking in book time, and they got their lessons pretty well.

Friday came, and as soon as dinner was over they came into the house and demanded to have the court organized. I drew out a jury, and after some time got them to begin. The first case on the monitor's list was that of Stephen Herd, a grown man. The offense was throwing a little girl's bonnet into the branch. I appointed a lawyer for the defense, but being backward and awkward he and the solicitor said but few words. The judge read the law in such cases, and put the case to the jury. They returned in a few minutes with the verdict of guilty. The judge sentenced him with three lashes, well laid on with a hickory. I had cut and trimmed a number of nice hickory switches and had them sitting handy. I selected a good one and said "Come up, Stephen." Stephen came up smiling and looked as if he expected that as he was a grown man, I would just go through the motions with *him*. I laid my switch against his back to measure the distance, and then, with all the force I possessed, inflicted the three lashes, cutting the homespun back of his waistcoat into three ribbands. It surprised him so badly that he burst out crying, and said that he knew of some things that were not on the monitor's list which he could tell if he was a mind to. I said "Tell it to the court Stephen, and whatever the decision of that body may direct me to do, you may rest assured that I will faithfully execute it. I am an instrument in your hands; you have the laws and regulations in your own hands, and whatever in your deliberations you may order shall not fail on my part."

The next case was that of Elijah Scatterwhite, one of the jury. And drawing another to fill his place, I slipped in Stephen Herd, hoping that as he had just been punished he would be hard in the case and go for punishment. The crime was for willfully running over a little boy. In this trial the lawyers were a little bolder, understood it better and spoke more to the point. The trial was a little more interesting, and the case being put to the jury, they went out. There being nothing but the wall between the seat I occupied and where they were sitting, I could distinctly hear their deliberations. They were highly elated at the prompt and vigorous manner in which I had discharged the mandate of the court, and were loud for finding Scatterwhite guilty of a good deal of offence. They seemed to rejoice at the opportunity and power they possessed, and were in favor of putting it on to their criminal in good style, except Stephen Herd who had not as yet expressed himself either way, "Well, Steve, what's your verdict in this case?" they asked. "Well, boys," said he, "I have been thinking about the matter very seriously. In the first place I think we have an excellent chance with this man to learn a great deal, if we play our parts correctly. I also think that the regulations to which we have all signed our names is the best thing of the kind that could be made. It is liberal and just, placing the government of the school in our own hands, with the teacher to prompt, instruct and direct; and I am certain that if we perform our parts as well as I am now convinced he is sure to do, we shall all be proud of it. But if we all go for thrashing and punishment for every little offence, we shall soon all get up the spirit of spite among us and the school will go to nothing as all other schools have done in this settlement. I say, let us all try to do better, be more particular with the little ones, more respectful and polite to one another and as lenient in inflicting penalty as the law will allow us. In this case of Scatterwhite's it was not clearly proven that the act was willfully committed. The boy was not hurt, but made very angry and his clothes a little soiled. Mind you, I am not in favor of clearing Lige, but fine him. My verdict would be find him guilty of running over the boy, without the *willful* and fine him." Some of them said "Make out your verdict and let's see how it looks." So Stephen wrote "Guilty, but not willfully." They all agreed and brought it in. The judge sentenced him to pay three dozen good goose quills.

You will ask what they did with the fines. Well, the constitution recognized a treasury and an officer to take charge of and keep a regular book of all the receipts and disbursements. The treasury belonged to the school, the fines being all of a character suitable for school use. Any student could go with a lawful application and draw and receipt for anything he actually needed.

But Stephen Herd was the first and the last to receive corporal punishment. He was also the first to advocate its abolition. He afterwards became one of the most solid lawyers in my school. Green Wheeler and George Clayton were the other two. All three of them became distinguished lawyers of the State afterwards.

The school went on increasing in efficiency every day, and the interest that was excited among my employers filled the house every Friday afternoon with spectators. The boys borrowed law books and all of them were filled with the spirit of progress, and before the term was half out they were performing court action finely.

Several holidays occurred. At such times a very respectful petition was drawn by a committee appointed for the purpose, specifying its object, and praying for a few days of vacation for the purpose of recreation. This was always granted in a manner that delighted not only the pupils but their parents and guardians.

They had all, males and females, become tame and quite polite, and on the last two days of the term had an examination. At the conclusion of it, my employers declared it to be a complete success. They paid every dollar that was due me and offered me $1,000.00 to teach another session of ten months. I declined most respectfully; for father had sold out and was ready to take the road again.

My father loved a border life, and the place he had purchased on the Ocmulgee, as the people had already commenced settling on the opposite side of the river, was no longer looked upon as a border country. He sold his place and was soon equipped and geared up for the road, and so was I. I had been reared to a belief and faith in the pleasure of frequent change of country, and I looked upon the long journey, through the wilderness, with much pleasure.

Our company consisted of my father and mother and eight children, with six ne-groes; Joseph Bryan, my brother-in-law, and his wife and two negroes; my wife and me and two small sons and two negroes. We had good horses and wagons and guns and big dogs. We set out on the 10th of March, 1818. I felt as if I was on a big camp hunt.

The journey, the way we traveled, was about 500 miles, all wilderness; full of deer and turkeys, and the streams were full of fish. We were six weeks on the road; and, al-together it was, as I thought and felt, the most delightful time I had ever spent in my life. My brother Garland and I "flanked it" as the wagons rolled along and killed deer, turkeys, wild pigeons; and at nights, with pine torches, we fished and killed a great many with my bow and arrows, whenever we camped on any water course. Little creeks were full of fish in that season.

At length we reached Tuscaloosa, Ala. It was at that time a small log cabin village; but people from Tennessee were arriving daily, and in the course of that year it grew to be a considerable town.

I concluded to stop there, and my father and his family and Bryan and his fam-ily continued their journey to a small improvement eight miles below Tuscaloosa, on the river, where they settled, and, cutting down a canebrake, made corn; and killed bear, venison and fish enough to supply the family.

I fished and had as much as we needed of that kind of food, but there were no bear nor deer in reach of the town, and I had to buy provisions at enormous rates. Flour, $25 a barrel; corn, $2½ a bushel; sugar, 50 cents a pound; coffee, 62½ cents a pound; salt, $8 a bushel; bacon, 37½ cents a pound. There was no beef to be had.

I built a little clapboard house on the river side of the town, which had not yet been surveyed. The land hunters from Georgia found us and continued their friendly calls on us until what money I had left from the long journey was eaten up. This was a circumstance for which I had made no provisions. I felt no uneasiness on that ac-count; for I was as strong as two common men and could do anything from cutting and splitting fence rails to fine cabinet work. And in mercantile action was familiar with all the duties from the lumber house to the counting room. I could mix drugs and practice medicine as far as it was known in the interior of the country in those days. So I felt no alarm at the fact that my money was gone.

I started out early one morning, intending to accept an offer to engage in any kind of business that might present itself to me. I set my face towards Dr. Isbell's shop. It being midsummer, I thought I would try to make some kind of an arrangement with him. But before I reached the doctor's house, I met a very strong man, whose name was John Weeks—I was acquainted with him in Georgia—I asked him where he was going with his whipsaw. He informed me that he had been in partnership with a man that came with him from Tennessee, but that he was such a drunkard he had been forced to quit him.

I asked what he would think of me for a partner. "My friend," said he, "you have never been accustomed to work, and the whipsaw and summer heat will soon upset you."

I told him my money was out; that I must try to make more some way; and that I felt capable of performing any kind of work; that my family was composed of two women and three children, all equally helpless, and that they must be supported.

He did not think I would be able to stand the hot sun and the cutting, hewing and sawing with a whipsaw, and he suggested that the surest way for me to support my family would be a partnership with some of the doctors; or a position as salesman in one of the stores.

I replied that I liked the looks of *that* saw pretty well; and that if he had no other objections than those he had named, I would like to go in with him. I enquired where his family was.

"Well," said he, "if you go in with me I must go in with you. I left my wife and children in Tennessee and have no home here. Planks are worth four dollars a hundred and we can get the cash for all we can make. But it is heavy work I tell you."

So we went into partnership. He furnished the saw and all the tools and I was to let him live with me as one of my family. We divided the products of our labor equally.

We went to work the very next day. We hewed out stocks enough for 1,000 feet of inch planks which we had engaged to saw for Peter Remington, a Yankee who had brought a heavy stock of goods and was in a great hurry to set them up. We were to have the planks ready by Saturday evening. We had it done a day sooner. It was for a floor and counter; and he gave us twenty dollars to lay down the floor and make the counter, all rough. We completed the job Saturday, and I helped mark and put up goods all day Sunday, for which I received ten dollars.

We continued to saw about two months, averaging eight dollars a day, except a few days when we went hunting and fishing, and one day when we sawed planks and made a skiff.

About the last of August a party of Muscogee Indians who were passing through the country on their way to their country west of the Mississippi were fired on by some foolish Tennesseeans. The consequence was the Indians returned the fire and chased them a mile or more. The Tennesseeans hurried up to town and reported they had been fired on by some Indians twenty miles below Tuscaloosa, that there were four or five hundred of them, and that they were heading towards Tuscaloosa, and killing all who came in their way.

All the efficient men of the place made immediate preparation to go out and meet them. I also got my rifle ready. There were 25 or 30 men of us in a doctor's shop loading our guns. We were on the verge of setting off. I had loaded my gun, had laid it on the counter and was priming it from a paper that had two pounds of powder in it. Somebody had been tampering with the triggers, and when, after priming the gun, I shut the pan down the cock fell, fired off the gun, ignited the powder in my hands, which exploded and burnt me nearly half in two, even with the top of the counter; blew all the skin and some of the nails off my hands and burnt my face badly. I was badly injured, and was not able to use my hands in three weeks. This misfortune put an end to the whipsaw operations. Weeks hired to Captain Bakon on a keel boat, and I rented a billiard table for one month at $50. I attended to it myself. The billiard table supported my family, but it could not make money like the whipsaw.

About the time the month expired my father came to town, and informed me that he had just returned from exploring lands on the Tombecbee river and that he found it to be a more desirable country than that on the Tuscaloosa river. He said that the part he preferred was distant about 75 miles with no road to it, and that he was going to remove there immediately.

I was greatly pleased with his description of the country. He said there was not a house between Tuscaloosa and the Tombecbee, that the Choctaws were near the river on the opposite side, but that nowhere on the east side was to be found any signs that the country had ever been occupied. The forests were very densely timbered, and the bottom lands were covered with the heaviest kinds of cane. Altogether, he said, it was the wildest, least trodden and tomahawk marked country he had ever explored, and that the soil was rich enough.

His description of the dark, heavy forests, the wide thick cane-brakes and the clear, running river, full of fish put me into a perfect transport. I told my father that I owed nobody anything. I had nothing to hinder me from starting in two days, if he would be ready by that time; that I could take my effects in a boat down the river to his house where my wagon was.

He said that was what he came to see about; that he was glad to find me so little incumbered; and that he could be ready to move in three days.

I told him I would be with him before that time.

We had only our beds and wearing apparel to move, except a table and a very nice black walnut rocking crib I had made while I was keeping a free hotel during the first part of my sojourn at Tuscaloosa. I had thought of leaving the table and crib, but my wife said that she knew how to dispose of them. She brought Mrs. Bird, our nearest neighbor to see them. She was pleased with them, and gave my wife eight dollars in cash for them and a bread waiter I had made of white oak splits.

We had made every arrangement and packed our goods in our little boat by 4 p.m. the second day. We then bade adieu to Tuscaloosa and to a crowd of our newly made young friends, who had followed us down to the river, helping us to pack the boat.

We got to my father's house about dark. They were all delighted to see us, and we were in a perfect ecstasy over the prospect of a wagon journey through a roadless wilderness. We made the preparation and set out on the 1st day of November, 1818. The weather was fine. We were twelve days *en route* and the heavens were perfectly cloudless during the entire trip. The autumnal leaves and nuts were clattering down everywhere. Shellbarks, hickory nuts, and chestnuts strewed the ground, and grapes, muscadines, persimmons and various wild autumnal fruits were plentiful. It was delightful to observe the women and children wallowing in the dry leaves in the evening and gathering such quantities of nuts as to require assistance to get them into camp. Then such cracking and roasting nuts and loud merry talk till bedtime.

We killed plenty of deer, turkeys, ducks, wild pigeons, and had the music of great gangs of wolves around our camp every night. The entire trip was delightful beyond description.

Our wagons being the first that had ever traversed that unhacked forest, we, of course, had to make a sufficient road for them to pass. It fell to my lot to go in advance and blaze the way, and by taking advantage of the open spaces amongst the trees, I saved a great deal of time. The woods having been burnt every year by the Indian hunters, there were but few logs remaining, and we got along very nicely. Except when we came to the water-courses, we had but little difficulty. There are three little rivers and several creeks that crossed our path. We were forced to dig down the banks of these streams before crossing them.

In the afternoon of the twelfth day we landed on the banks of the Tombecbee river, three miles by land above where Columbus Miss., now stands. I was delighted with the appearance of the low bluff and the canebrake that came to a point where the river turned abruptly from the bluff a few steps above where we struck it. Here I made my camp. Father went four hundred yards lower down and pitched his tent. Three or four feet above low water mark, a flat rock that underlay the bluff projected six or eight feet into the river. Here a large sycamore tree had its roots fastened into the bluff immediately on top of the rock and from beneath these roots gushed a very bold spring of pure clear water. It flowed over the rock, falling into the river from its outer edge with a splashing sound that could be distinctly heard at the camp, which was not more than forty feet away. Everything about the place was beautiful and very convenient.

About sundown the day we arrived we heard a great number of turkeys flying up to roost not more than 100 yards from the camp. At daybreak next morning I crept out and shot one that weighed twenty-nine pounds. My wife couldn't handle it.

I on that day explored the river a few hundred yards above my camp, killed a wild goose and saw the beginning of a glorious canebrake, and plenty of bear and deer signs, and the banks of the river were strewn with holes that had been cut and barked by beavers. When I got back to the camp I told my wife what I had discovered. She was a very beautiful young woman then, and she put on one of her sweetest and most satisfied looking smiles and said, "You have found the right place for us to stop at."

I replied, "I am truly glad that you are pleased with the situation, it will be so encouarging to me in my effort to procure sustenance."

"Who," said she, "could look at this fat game, so easily obtained, this beautiful river with its handsome dry bluff, and gushing spring water and be otherwise? And that's not all that pleases me. While you were gone up the river, an hour ago, five very large deer passed lazily along in 30 yards of where Polly and I were standing, and they stared at us with their great black eyes as they passed and held their great chair frame looking horns so high that we were both frightened and didn't know whether to stand our ground or run to the camp. I have also been down to the spring and have examined that beautiful flat rock. It runs along under the bluff 30 or 40 yards above the spring, and in one place it is 20 feet wide. Oh! It is so pretty and I think there are plenty of fish. I have saved the turkey's liver for bait. Suppose you try for some after dinner."

I set out three or four hooks before dinner, and after eating dinner, went out into the upland hunting. I saw a great deal of deer sign, and several deer, but did not get a shot. When I got back in sight of camp my wife saw me, and, in the highest degree of delight, called to me to look what a fine fish she had caught. She had a blue cat weighing $25\frac{1}{2}$ pounds.

Suffice it to say, we were all greatly pleased, and supplied our table with a superabundance of fish, fowl and venison, and occasionally a glorious fleece of bear meat. The quantity of game that was found in that dark forest and the canebrakes was a subject of wonder to everybody. My brother Garland and I, after working all day, clearing up ground to plant corn, would go out nights on horseback, taking a big bag of nicely cut, rich pine and a frying pan tied on a stick, to burn the pine in. This pan full of pine, set on fire and carried on the shoulder, produced sufficient light to enable us to see the eyes of a deer 80 to 100 yards away. And with a big old shotgun that we had, we killed plenty of meat for all three of the families.

Three days after we came there I began to prepare for building me a house. I got the clapboards in one day, cut the logs in a day, hauled them together in a day; and the next day, by the aid of my brothers and Jo. Bryan, raised and covered it. The next day I floored it with linwood puncheons, and the day after I made a wooden chimney to it, and we left our camp and moved into it. The weather was getting cool, and with a rousing log fire fed with plenty of rich pine knots, the light was as bright as day, making the whole house which was lined with newly split board fairly glitter again. Having no bedstead yet, my wife made the bed on the floor. I never shall forget the encouraging remark she made when we lay down. After gazing for a moment on the shining walls of the little cabin she said, "This is fine, and it inspires me with confidence that we are capable of making our way and successfully meeting the exigencies of existence here. The quantity of venison, fish and fowl that we have on hand already, and the facility with which it is procured quiets all fears of scarcity of provisions."

Having no good place to keep our provisions, I then built a little smokehouse. My wife said, while she was placing the provisions in it, "This is very convenient." And then she remarked, "Notwithstanding the fact that we are surrounded with this wild impenetrable forest, we have nothing to fear." "No, dat we ha'n't," said Aunt Polly, who was young too then.

These little incidents tell the situation we occupied, and how little dread we entertained. We felt ourselves fully competent for the emergency.

Soon all the families had houses, and all hands went to work, cutting down and clearing the maiden forest to make fields to plant corn in. I cut down six acres of the canebrake that jammed itself almost down to the place where I built my house. I burnt off the cane on the 5th of May, and planted it with a sharp stick on the 6th. Twice while it was growing I cut and beat down the young cane that sprouted up from the old cane stumps. That was all the work the crop got. The bear and raccoons ate and destroyed a good deal of it, and yet I gathered 150 bushels of good corn.

As soon as I got my house done, I went over the river to see the Choctaws. They were not exceeding two miles distant. I also found there a white man by the name of John Pitchlynn. He had a large family of half breed children; was very wealthy; sixty-two years of age; possessed a high order of intelligence and was from every point of view, a clever gentleman. He was very glad to hear that we were settling so near to him, and he also said he must visit the place we had selected to see if we were building above the high water mark.

He asked my name, and when I told him, he enquired for the name of my father. I replied, "It is Hezekiah Lincecum." "Don't they call him Ky?" said he. "His familiar friends do," I replied. "I am a second cousin to your mother," said he. "I will go right over and see them this day." He was in a perfect ecstasy. He ordered his horse, and then turning to me said, "You were not born when I saw your father and mother last. I was on my return from Washington city. I had previously heard from my father, that I had relatives in Georgia; and turning my course down through that State, I was lucky enough to find them. I sojourned with them a month, and I look upon that time even now, as the most pleasant period of my life."

He went immediately over. I introduced him to my father and mother, and they were all overjoyed at meeting again. Twenty-five years had passed and they were all still healthy looking, and exceedingly rejoiced. Pitchlynn was a kind hearted man, and seemed willing to aid us every way that he could in making our new homes. We lived neighbors to him from 1818 to 1835; and he continued the same kind hearted gentleman all the time.

In 1819, the government marked or surveyed a road from Nashville, Tenn., to Natchez, Miss. It crossed the Tombecbee river where Columbus, Miss., now stands; ten miles by water, and three by land below where I had settled. I went down there to see what kind of a place it was. I found it a beautifully elevated situation, being about the head of navigation. I thought it was an eligible town site, and that it would be a town as soon as the country should settle up. I was so fully impressed with the belief that a big town would some day loom up on that beautiful bluff that I went home, sawed a thousand boards; put them on a raft and floated them down the river with the intention of building a snug little house on a nice place I had selected, hoping to be able to realize a profit from it, as soon as people should move into the country.

I was not the only person that had noticed the eligibility of that locality. When I got down to the place where I intended to land, a man by the name of Caldwell was about landing a keel boat at the same place. He was from Tuscaloosa, and he had a cargo of Indian goods which he intended to open on that bluff as soon as he could build a house to put them in.

I was acquainted with him while I resided in Tuscaloosa and was glad to see him, and thought I would sell my boards to him. *Friendship without interest.*

In the course of our conversation he enquired of me, if, while residing in Tuscaloosa, I had made the acquaintance of one Cornelius Schnider? "I knew him very well," said I. "And what kind of a man did you consider him?" I replied readily, that I did not think him a reliable man. "That is my opinion now," said Caldwell, "though I used to think him an honest man, but during the trip here, I have had reasons to change my good opinion of him."

I remarked to him, that had I been apprised of the fact that he had Schnider with him, I should not have been so careless in expressing my sentiments about him.

"My dear friend," said Caldwell, "I am truly obliged to you. I brought him with me to sell these goods for me, and now I don't know what in the world I shall do. He will ruin me if I leave him with them."

I replied, "I have a good notion to relieve you by buying out the entire stock, boat and all."

"I wish to the Lord you would," said he.

"But this raft of 1,000 clap-boards upon which I am standing, except my wagon and horses, is all the available means I possess. It is useless for me to talk about purchasing your goods; but you can give me $10 for these good boards to cover a house to put your goods in, and I'll go home."

"But," replied Caldwell, "I can make you able. I will expose my invoices to you. Let you have them at 10 per cent under cost and give you three, six and twelve months to pay it in; and you can cover your house with the boards you have."

I took the goods; hired his boat hands; went to work with them myself; and in three days had knocked up a pretty good shanty. We soon got the goods into it, and commenced opening boxes and taking account of the stock. But the Indians had heard of the arrival of the great supply of nice new goods and plenty of liquors, and they flocked in by hundreds. I began selling to them whiskey and such goods as we had marked; and this prevented us from work in the daytime. Having only night time to work on invoices, it took us ten days to get through with them. But I had by that time sold enough to pay the first installment, which I did, and Caldwell went home highly pleased.

I sent my boat immediately to Mobile for a cargo of sugar, coffee and whiskey. These were considered staple articles in the Indian trade. In due time the boat returned, and the business continued good. I paid the last installment at nine months.

The State line had not been run, and we were supposed to be in Alabama. It was not long until the line dividing the States of Alabama and Mississippi was laid off, and we found ourselves fifteen miles from the line on the Mississippi side; in a strip of country 80 miles long and averaging 20 miles in width, east of the Choctaw and Chickasaw Nations. The Tombecbee river was the line between us and the Indians; 200 miles from the other portion of the State. And thus cut off from the law, we were there 18 months before we saw an officer of any kind. At length, the Legislature recognized us as a portion of the State, and named that long strip of land Monroe county. They also appointed me chief justice, with authority to appoint all the officers necessary to organize the county. The land having been previously surveyed, it was found that Columbus was on a 16th section—school land.

The Legislature also appointed me chairman of the school commissioners, with power to appoint four associates; also to lay off the town and lease the lots for the term of 99 years, renewable forever.

I first appointed four other county justices and a county clerk, called a meeting, organized a county court and proceeded to appoint and commission the rest of the county officers. Everybody wanted office; and I found it a very difficult duty to get through with. I finally succeeded; and then turned my attention to surveying the town, and regulating all the school lands in the county. I had also to superintend the erection of two—male and female—academies.

On the first of August, I had all ready and in conformity to my advertisements, which had been published sixty days, a very large collection of people came to the leasing of the town lots. I leased in the two days I continued it, not more than half the lots that had been surveyed; but they brought in enough—$4,500—to commence building the academies.

Holding the courts, appointing the officers, surveying the town lots, appointing and regulating school commissioners at town, and all the other school sections in the county, procuring teachers, engaging workmen for the academies and opening the mail six times a week, consumed so much of my time, that my own business was badly neglected. The result of my firm, impartial action in appointing county officers had pleased the people so much that they began to talk of sending me to the Legislature.

To avoid such a dilemma, I immediately went over the river and entered into partnership with John Pitchlynn, Junior, a half-breed Chocktaw. He was a highly educated man and a very clever fellow; but a most incorrigible drunkard. That, however, made no difference; as according to our contract and the intercourse regulations, which forbade any white man with a white family from dwelling within the nation, he, Pitchlynn, was to have nothing in the management of the business. In the knowledge of all outsiders, I occupied the position of a superintending clerk. Pitchlynn had a pretty good storehouse at the ferry landing opposite Columbus, and four or five thousand dollars' worth of goods. I had about the same amount. We put them together. I moved my family into a room that was boarded in, of a large two story building he had commenced, and took possession of the goods and storehouse and ferry.

Pitchlynn's residence was two miles from the store,—a circumstance favorable to our business; for he was, when drunk, so abusive, and so often drunk, that he was not popular with the Indians.

I was known to almost every Indian in the Nation. My Indian name was, "Shappo Tohoba,"—"White hat." The first time they saw me, I had on a white hat. But my most popular name was, "Anumpatashula ebisya,"—"Interpreter's nephew." Sometimes, they called me "Hopigeh cheto"—"Big leader" because I took the lead and conducted a party of 100 of them out of a condition of starvation on our return from a failure in attempting to get some scalps from a large camp of Ooassashes, west of the Mississippi. All these and the fair, plain manner in which I traded with them, caused them to have full confidence in me, and they crowded my Pitchlynn establishment every day with their produce.

I bartered with them for every kind of produce, consisting of cowhides, deer skins, all kinds of fur, skins, buck horns, cow horns, peas, beans, peanuts, pecans, shellbarks, hickory nuts, honey, beeswax, blowguns and blowgun arrows, bacon and venison hams and big gobblers. I made it a rule to purchase, at some price, everything they brought to the store.

Every article I have named brought cash at 100 per cent on the cost. I dealt with a house—Willcox & Dallas, Philadelphia; and they were glad to get my Indian produce, for which they paid me well. I remember them as clever gentlemen.

BENJAMIN DRAKE

(1794–1841)

With his better known brother Dr. Daniel Drake, Benjamin Drake was brought to the west as a child and quickly embarked on a varied career as a founder and leader of various institutions in the Ohio valley. However, after a brief career as a lawyer and a businessman, Benjamin focused his energies almost entirely on the written word. As founder and editor of *The Cincinnati Chronicle,* Drake daily advocated causes that encouraged western economic and political autonomy. However, as a writer, Drake found his true calling. Aside from writing various promotional tracts as a younger man, Drake began writing books in the 1830s. He was most successful in the fields of short fiction and Native American biography. Encouraged in each by his friend (and later posthumous editor) James Hall, Drake sought and reached a popular audience in the west the way few other local writers could. Moreover, Drake's range of style demonstrates his skill and accomplishment as a literary voice.

The story reproduced here represents Drake's work in humorous short fiction. As is demonstrated elsewhere in this collection, a genre of local humor developed in the west, and often appeared first in newspapers, mostly in its southern areas, but also in northern outposts such as St. Louis and Cincinnati. Drake published a number of his pieces in the *Chronicle* and collected them in a book in 1835. This story stands out in the collection because it reminds us that the Ohio valley was characterized by an urban culture in which colleges and other institutions were commonplace. As Richard C. Wade first observed in 1958, the myth of the west as farm and wilderness was generated in the east to celebrate their own urbanity by contrast. Drake's humorous story, like most western humor, is geared toward deflating pomposity.

Drake's biographies of Native Americans, however, reflect a far more serious and confrontational tone. Along with *The Life of Black Hawk* (excerpted below), Drake wrote on Tecumseh (1841) and was planning a book on the Sioux at the time of his death in 1841. In these books, Drake was strikingly critical of the policies and practices of the American army in its conduct toward the west's Native Americans. Drake's consistent defense of Black Hawk in particular distinguishes western settlers from the army sent by the east. Drake directly refutes the official accounts of the war and questions the motives of the politicians and generals who conducted it. Written with clarity, concision, and a distinct sense of inclusive regional identity, *The Life of Black Hawk* stands as the most accomplished book to come out of antebellum Cincinnati.

Texts: "The Battle of Brindle and the Buck-Eyes" from *Tales and Sketches of the Queen City* (Cincinnati, 1835): 147–154. *The Life of Black Hawk* (Cincinnati, 1838; 8th ed., 1848): 91–117, 166–199.

THE BATTLE OF BRINDLE AND THE BUCKEYES (1835)

There is a tradition extant, that in the early dynasty of Cincinnati College, one of its worthy, painstaking Presidents, was a Doctor; not, however, of divinity or laws, nor yet a universal doctor, nor a quack doctor, nor a Brousais doctor, nor a homopathic doctor, nor a "No. 6," lobelia doctor, nor an animal magnetism doctor, but a regular, scientific electro-galvanic Doctor. Electricity and galvanism are reputed to have been his favorite hobby on which he frequently mounted in his laboratory and rode over the college grounds and into the college halls. These subtle and imponderable agents—were deemed by the president almost infallible in the cure of certain diseases, and he had a strong but vague belief, that their united power, could, under certain circumstances, restore vitality after it had been "squnched" in death. This point, he proposed to establish, on a certain occasion, but, unfortunately was prevented by the provoking obstinacy of an old criminal, convicted of murder, who positively and to the great disappointment of the President, declined being hung, when the choice was offered him, by the laws of the country, of either encountering atmospheric suspension—vulgarily called hanging—or being incarcerated in the Penitentiary for life. This unphilosophical decision of the old convict, led the President to pronounce him an obstinate and cowardly fellow, who was unwilling to make the smallest sacrifice, for the cause of science. His stubbornness was the more unaccountable, as he had been given to understand, that he would run very little risk in being hung, inasmuch, as the electro-galvanic battery of the President could, in all probability, restore him to life, so soon as his unnatural connection with the gallows was severed.

For some time after this disappointment, the President, put aside his aforesaid imponderable hobby, and betook himself to one of more tangible properties, in the shape of a little black horse, on which he was went to ride to market and to the college.—Now, it so happened, in the progress of events, that this little black horse, finding, it is supposed, more grains of literature than of corn, about "college commons" deliberately took leave of his *alma mater,* and went forth into the "city commons" to crop the green grass. At this exercise of free will, the President was sorely vexed, and his heart did yearn for the little horse, especially in a warm sunny day, when, in consequence of this love for foreign travels, he was compelled to walk to the chapel for prayers and recitations, whereby the perspiration did often times stand upon his expanded forehead, like the dew drops of the morning, on an opening cabbage. So the President forthwith resolved upon reclaiming his wandering pupil to collegiate duties, and accordingly made proclamation in the newspapers, that five dollars would be paid to whomsoever should return to his rightful owner, a little, black stray horse, with "rather a shortish tail;" but the promised reward was never claimed.

It has been said that misfortunes never come singly. Certain it is they did not with the worthy President, for during the absence of the aforesaid little black stray horse, with "rather a shortish tail," the internal economy of the college was sadly disturbed by the presence of a new and very extraordinary pupil, whereof tradition speaketh in this wise.

On a fine sunny morning in the month of September, the young Buckeyes of Cincinnati College assembled for prayers at an earlier hour than usual. They quietly arranged themselves in the lobby leading to the chapel, then in the second story, and when the well known thump of the Presidents' huge black cane, was heard upon the stairs, every Buckeye looked as grave, as if, in due time, he would make an excellent professor of *gravity*. When the President had unlocked the chapel door, behold! in the aisle, at the very foot of the pulpit, stood a large brindle cow, leisurely chewing her cud of contentment. Verily, if the President had suddenly encountered a certain other nameless animal who wears a "cloven foot," he would not have been more astounded. The young collegians, having neither the fear of their president nor his four footed competitor for the pulpit, before their eyes, broke into the most uproarious cachinnations, but their merriment was speedily nullified by a presidential threat of personal chastisement, against the perpetrators of this beastly outrage upon the discipline of the college and the sanctity of the chapel.

The assembled collegians were promptly ordered to drive the cloven-footed freshmen down stairs,—an order, as will appear in the sequel, more easily given than executed. They indeed, succeeded in getting brindle to the head of the stairs, but neither entreaties nor menaces, could induce her to make a single genuflection towards a descent. She was evidently enamoured of the college life, and altogether opposed to any step that would again place her upon a level with the beasts of the field. Whips were now applied to her legs and back, but to little purpose: the sturdy President in vain be-laboured her tough hide with his black cane; and, as his choler rose, his kicky fell, for it was a warm September morning. It being now obvious that her cowship was resolutely determined to make no demonstration of a problem, touching the angles of a stair-way, one of the stoutest of the senior class was directed to give the circumgyratory motion to her tail, an evolution, which the President had seen practised upon unruly calves: but the venerable maxim, "that sauce for the goose is sauce for the gander," did not hold good in this case, for the manipulations of the senior only aroused old brindle's warlike propensities, which were manifested by such a threatening flourish of horns as caused a sudden retreat of the assailants, in which, as a prudent general, the president, gallantly took the lead.

A council of war was now held in the chapel, and a new system of military operations agreed upon. At the suggestion of a senior, who had once been a cow boy up the valley of Mill-creek, a handful of salt, and a few nubbins of corn, were procured from a neighboring grocery, and with these, the obstinate old cud-chewer, was once more enveigled to the head of the stairs; but there she stopped, and thus declined even being bribed into a descent from her collegiate elevation. What was now to be done? Napoleon, when he first beheld the conflagration of Moscow gleaming upon the snows of a Russian winter,—the enemy in his rear and his army without provisions,—was not presented with a more perplexing problem. To have old brindle in the chapel at prayers, or in the recitation room among the young buckeyes, while translating Cæsar's Commentaries or demonstrating the properties of a right angled triangle, did not comport with collegiate regulations, more especially as she was likely to be the 'lion' of the day, an honor of which the president was not willing to be deprived. A second council of war was called, in which numerous measures for the dislogement of the enemy, were proposed and discussed. At length, upon the suggestion of a fierce little junior, all the way from Kentucky, who had often signalized himself on the banks of Licking river, as the "real thing" in hunting "coons" and "holeing 'possums," a new plan of military action was adopted. The president dispatched the janitor, in all haste, to his residence, for a bed-cord and a few more nubbins of corns: while he, with a determined and anxious expression of countenance, prepared for another attack.

It is related of the celebrated Tecumthe, that when about to engage in the battle of the Thames, he threw aside his British regimentals and all other unnecessary trappings. Following this aboriginal example, the president pulled off his silken canonicals, and assuming, as far as might be, the "cantankerous" air of the military chieftain, again placed himself at the head of his little corps of Buckeyes, and issued his orders with the firmness of a Jackson or a Wellington. The janitor having returned with the bed-cord, a slipping noose was formed at one end of it, and dexterously thrown over brindle's horns—the other end being placed in the hands of a party of the young assailants, planted at the bottom of the stairs: Other little detachments, armed with sticks and pebble stones, were stationed on the flanks of the enemy, while a few muscular seniors were placed in the rear. The commander-in-chief took his position on the top of a writing desk, near the chapel door, that he might not only overlook the whole field of battle, but in case of any great emergence, head a retreat into the Sanctuary. The necessary orders having been given, preceded by a very animating address from the President to his impatient troops, the battle was re-newed. The detachment below began to haul upon the bed-cord and the flankers to discharge their missiles, while the corps in the rear, once more gave the circumgyratory twist to old brindle's spinal elongation. The stentorian voice of the Presidential commander, urging his troops to feats of "noble daring," was distinctly heard above the loud din of battle. For a time the enemy gave way, and victory seemed about to crown the gallant collegians, but again brindle, came to a dead halt, at the top of the stairs, wheeled suddenly round, and with a furious toss of the horns, and a terrible whisk of the tail, the rope was snapped asunder: An awful bellowing ensued, which rang through the halls of the college, with such fearful clang, that the astounded president, who had hastily retreated to the chapel, had serious apprehensions of the same ruinous catastrophe, which in ancient times, was produced by the sound of the ram's horns on the walls of Jericho.

Once more hostilities ceased. Exhausted by his arduous duties and mortified by successive defeats, the President again seated himself in the chapel, with his little regiment of soldiers around him for new deliberations. It has been remarked that some men are great in proportion to the pressure of the circumstances by which they are surrounded.—The present case confirmed the truth of the maxim. There sat for a time, in "profound thought and deep meditation," the war-worn President, contemplating the field of battle, calling up his slumbering knowledge of strategy, and fixing, in his mind, upon the most approved plans of carrying out the assaults and retreats, the marches and counter-marches, which were likely to become necessary in the future operations of the campaign. Suddenly one of those happy thoughts which enable frail humanity to win its way to immortal renown, crossed his mind. As if rising at once above his misfortunes, he rose upon his feet, with a countenance lighted up with unwonted animation. His faithful troop of Buckeyes were again called to duty; and a small platoon of sophomores was ordered to bring to the field of battle, from the laboratory, the President's cherished galvanic battery. Meanwhile, as in earnest of a suspension of hostilities, a few more nubbins of corn were given to brindle, and while she was busily engaged in masticating this peace offering, the spliced bed-cord was re-attached to her horns, and the President, dexterously cleft, with a scalpel, the skin, on her back and tail, over the spinal nerves. The galvanic battery having now arrived, and the literary soldiers being displayed on the most approved system of military tactics, their commander once more addressed them in strains of sparkling eloquence. He spoke of the march of science in modern days—of the wonderful power of galvanism—of the varied improvements in the art of war. He depicted the dangers his gallant little army were about to encounter, the laurels which a successful battle would entwine around their brown—the imperishable glory that would forever play like an electrical atmosphere, around the names of those who might fall in fighting the battle of their revered *alma mater*. The address being concluded, at a concerted signal, a general assault was made.—Taken by surprize, old brindle suffered herself again to be forced to the top of the stairs, where; as in a former rencontre, she made a stand and prepared for the coming contest. At this critical juncture, the scientific President, adroitly touched the connecting galvanic wires of his battery, to the spinal wounds of his hitherto indomitable enemy. A tremendous shock ensued. With a bellicose bellow, forwards and downwards went the old sukey, while at the same instant, a grand flourish of her tail, freed it from the circumgyrators, but most unhappily brought it around the President's neck, to which it adhered with such pertinacity, as to drag both him and his battery, to the foot of the stairs. Here the furious and galvanized cud chewer, succeeded in dissolving the unnatural union between the president's upward and her downward spinal elongation, and eschewing forever, all further collegiate associations, she ran down Walnut street with the bed-cord dangling from her horns. It was some seconds before the overthrown but still viotorious Commander gave any signs of returning animation. Indeed, it was feared for a short time, that his earthly career was ended; and at the suggestion of a patriotic chum, the little army was about to promote the cause of science, by some galvanic experiments, upon the body of the President, when he suddenly sprung to his feet, and cried out, "where's my galvanic battery!"

FROM *THE LIFE OF BLACK HAWK* (1838)

CHAPTER IV

Building of Fort Armstrong—The good Spirit of Rock Island—Death of Black Hawk's children—Young Sac offers to die in place of his brother—Black Hawk's visit to Malden—Whipped by some whites—Whites settle at his village—Black Hawk's talk with Governor Coles and Judge Hall—Sale of the lands on Rock river—Indians ordered to remove—Agree-

ment to remove for six thousand dollars—Memorial of the white settlers to Governor Reynolds—The Governor's letters to General Clark and General Gaines—The latter leaves Jefferson Barracks with six companies of the United States troops for Rock Island—His interview with Black Hawk—Calls upon the Governor of Illinois for militia—The Indians abandon their village—treaty of peace made with them—Official letters to the war department—Summary of the causes which brought on this disturbance—Black Hawk's attempt to form an alliance with other tribes.

From the treaty of peace, between the United States and the Sac Indians of Rock river, in 1816, to the commencement of hostilities between these parties in 1832, the life of Black Hawk seems to have been quiet and monotonous, occasionally relieved by a warlike excursion, but generally spent in hunting, throughout the winter, and in loitering about his village, during the summer. Such, indeed, is the life of most Indians. Having no intellectual pursuits and little desire for the acquisition of property, beyond the supply of their immediate wants, they have in reality but two sources of excitement—war and the chase. They take no interest in the domestic affairs of their families, have little taste for the pursuits of agriculture, and, if not engaged in hostile excursions, in following the deer, or in trapping the beaver, they sink into listless inactivity. It is highly probable that many of their wars are undertaken, more for the gratification of that love of excitement, which is an indestructible element of the human mind, than from any constitutional proneness to cruelty and bloodshed. They need both physical and intellectual excitation, and having none of the resources which mental and moral culture throws open to civilized man, they seek it in making war upon each other or upon the wild animals which share with them the woods and the prairies.

Subsequently to the treaty of 1816, and perhaps in that year, the government of the United States built Fort Armstrong, upon Rock Island, in the Mississippi river, and but a few miles from the village where Black Hawk and his band resided. This measure, though not actually opposed, was by no means acceptable to them. They probably did not relish the gradual advances upon them, of the white population; but they entertained, moreover, a special regard for this beautiful island, which is justly considered one of the finest in the whole extent of the Mississippi. It is fertile, and produces many varieties of nuts and fruits, and being in the rapids of the stream, the waters which lave its shores, yield an abundance of excellent fish. In addition to all this, they have a traditionary belief, that the island was the favorite residence of a good spirit which dwelt in a cave in the rocks on which Fort Armstrong now stands. This spirit had often been seen by the Indians, but after the erection of the Fort, alarmed by the noise and intrusion of the white man, it spread its beautiful, swan-like wings, and disappeared. During the year 1817, the Sacs sent out some warriors against the Sioux, and succeeded in killing several of them, but Black Hawk was not of the party. About this time, his eldest son sickened and died, and within a short period afterwards, he lost his youngest daughter. This affliction seems to have made a deep impression upon him; and according to a custom common among the Indians, he blacked his face, and for the ensuing two years lived at home, in seclusion, drinking water at mid-day, and eating boiled corn but sparingly, in the evening. In the winter of 1819–20, there was a disturbance between the Sacs and Ioways, one of the latter having killed a young man belonging to the former. Under the agreement of a late council between these two tribes, the old custom of appeasing the friends of one who had been killed, by presents, had been abolished, and each party had promised, that in future, the murderer should be surrendered up, that he might be punished with death. A party of Sacs, of which Black Hawk was one, agreed to visit the Ioway village on this occasion, and when about to depart, called at the lodge of the young man who had committed the outrage, to take him along. He was sick, but still ready to accompany them. His brother interfered, and insisted that he was too unwell to travel; that he would himself go and die in his place, and finally set off with the party. On the seventh day, they reached the Ioway village. They dismounted a short distance from it, and bid farewell to their young brave, who went calmly forwards, alone, singing his death-song, and seated himself in the middle of the lodges. One of the Ioway chiefs went out to Black Hawk, who told him the brother had come in the place of the young man that had committed the murder, he being sick. Black Hawk and his party, now mounted their horses and set off on their return; and casting their eyes towards the village, saw the Ioways, armed with spears and clubs, gathering around the young prisoner. At night the returning party, having stopped and kindled a fire, were suddenly alarmed by the tramping of horses. They immediately stood to their arms, but were soon relieved, by finding, instead of a foe, their young brave, unhurt and in the possession of two horses. They ascertained that the Ioways, at first threatened him with instant death, but finally, changing their purpose, had given him something to eat, smoked the pipe with him, and presenting him with two horses, bid him return home in safety. The generous conduct of the Ioways is deserving of praise, but the genuine affection of this young brave, in nobly volunteering to die in place of his sick brother, presents one of those rare cases of self-devotion, which should be held in remembrance.

In the following autumn, Black Hawk and some of his band went on a visit to their British father at Malden and received presents from him. A medal was given to Black Hawk for his fidelity to the British in the late war, and he was requested to come up annually, to that place, with his band, and receive such presents, as had been promised them by Colonel Dixon, when they joined the English forces. These visits were regularly made, it is believed, from that time down to the year 1832. It is owing to this circumstance that Black Hawk's party has long been known by the appellation of the "British Band."

In the winter of 1822, Black Hawk and his party, encamped on the Two-rivers, for the purpose of hunting, and while there was so badly treated by some white men, that his prejudices against the Americans were greatly strengthened. He was accused of having killed the hogs of some settlers, who, meeting him one day in the woods, wrested his gun from his hands, and discharging it in the air, beat him so severely with sticks that for several nights he was unable to sleep. They then returned him his gun and ordered him to leave the neighborhood. Of the perpetration of this outrage, there is little doubt, while the fact of Black Hawk's having committed the offence charged upon him, rests, at best, upon suspicion. Supposing him to have been guilty, and the supposition is at variance with the whole tenor of his intercourse with the whites, i was on their part, one of those brutal appeals to *club* law, which are but too often practised towards the Indians; and which, when avenged by them, not unfrequently brings upon their nation, the power and the arms of the United States.

The ensuing summer, the expediency of a removal of the whole of the Sacs and Foxes, to the west side of the Mississippi, was urged upon them by the agent at Fort Armstrong. The principal Fox chief, as well as Keokuk, assented to the removal. The latter sent a messenger through the village informing the Indians that it was the wish of their great Father, the President, that they should remove, and he pointed out the Ioway river as presenting a fine situation for their new village. There was a party, however, among the Sacs, made up principally of the "British Band," who were decidedly opposed to a removal; and they called upon their old leader, Black Hawk, for his opinion on the question. He took the ground that the land on which their village stood had never been sold; that the Americans had, therefore, no right to insist upon the measure, and that as a matter of policy he was opposed to it. The old man was probably swayed in his decision by another cause. He felt that his power in the tribe was waning before the rising popularity of Keokuk. Here was a question on which their people differed in opinion. By placing himself at the head of one of the parties, he might recover his influence, or at least sustain himself against the overshadowing ascendancy of his rival. He had an interview with Keokuk to see if the matter could not be adjusted with the President, by giving him other lands in exchange for those on which their village stood; and the latter promised to see the great chief at St. Louis, on the subject. During the following winter, while Black Hawk and his party were absent on a hunting expedition, several white families arrived at their village, destroyed some of their lodges and commenced making fences over their corn-fields. Black Hawk upon hearing of this movement, promptly returned to Rock river, and found his own lodge occupied by the whites. He went to Fort Armstrong and complained to the interpreter, the agent being absent. He crossed the Mississippi and travelled several days to converse with the Winnebago sub-agent, who concurred with the interpreter in advising the Sacs to remove to Keokuk's settlement on the Ioway. He then visited the prophet, Wabokieshiek, or White-Cloud, whose opinions were held in much respect by the Sacs and Winnebagoes. He urged Black Hawk not to remove, but to persuade Keokuk and his party to return to Rock river, assuring them that if they remained quietly at their village, the whites would not venture to disturb them. He then rejoined his hunting party, and in the spring when they returned to their village, they found the white settlers still there, and that the greater part of their corn-fields had been enclosed by fences. About that time Keokuk visited Rock river and endeavored to persuade the remainder of the Sacs to follow him to the Ioway. He had accomplished nothing with the great chief at St. Louis, in regard to their remaining at their village, and as a matter of policy, that peace might be preserved, he was warmly in favor of the proposed removal. Black Hawk considered in an act of cowardice to yield up their village and the graves of their fathers, to strangers, who had no right to the soil, and the breach between Keokuk and himself was widened.

The white immigrants continued to increase, and the Sac village was the great point of attraction to them. It was situated on the neck of land formed by the junction of Rock river with the Mississippi, and had been the chief village of the tribe for sixty or seventy years. "Their women had broken the surface of the surrounding prairie with their hoes, and enclosed with a kind of flimsy pole fence, many fields, which were annually cultivated by them, in the raising of corn, beans, potatoes and squashes. They had also erected several hundred houses of various dimensions, some probably an hundred feet in length by forty or fifty broad; which were constructed of poles and forks, arranged so as to form a kind of frame, which was then enclosed with the bark of trees, which, being peeled off and dried under a weight for the purpose of keeping it expanded, was afterwards confined to the walls and roof by means of cords, composed of the bark of other trees. This indeed is a delightful spot:—on the north-west rolls the majestic Mississippi, while the dark forests which clothe the numerous islands of Rock river, with its several rippling streams on the south-east, form a delightful contrast, which is rendered still more pleasing from the general declivity of the surrounding country, as it sinks gradually away to the shores of these rivers. This ancient village had literally become the grave-yard of the nation. Scarcely an individual could be found in the whole nation, who had not deposited the remains of some relative, in or near to this place. Thither the mother, with mournful and melancholy step, annually repaired to pay a tribute of respect to her departed offspring; while the weeping sisters and loud lamenting windows, joined the procession of grief; sometimes, in accordance with their own feelings, no doubt, but always in pursuance of an established custom of their nation, from time immemorial. On these occasions they carefully clear away every spear of grass or other vegetable, which they find growing near the grave, and make such repairs as may be thought necessary. They also carry to the grave some kind of food, which they leave there for the spirit of the deceased: and before they conclude these ceremonies, they often, in a very melancholy and lamenting mood, address the dead, enquiring how they fare, and who, or whether any one performs for them the kind offices of mother, sister or wife; together with many other enquiries which a frantie imagination may happen to suggest. This being one of the most important religious duties, is scrupulously observed by all the better class of this people."[1]

The whites who established themselves at this place, in violation of the laws of congress, and the provisions of the treaty of 1804, committed various aggressions upon the Indians, such as destroying their corn, killing their domestic animals, and whipping the women and children. They carried with them, as articles of traffic, whiskey and other intoxicating liquors, and by distributing them in the tribe, made drunkenness and scenes of debauchery common. Black Hawk and the other chiefs of the band, remonstrated against these encroachments, and especially in regard to the introduction of spirituous liquors among their people: and, upon one occasion, when a white man continued, openly, to sell whiskey to them, the old chief, taking with him one or two companions, went to his house, rolled out the barrel of whiskey, broke in the head, and emptied its contents upon the ground, in presence of the owner. This was done, as he alleges, from the fear that some of the white persons would be killed by his people when in a state of intoxication. Thus things wore-on until 1827. During that winter, while the Indians were making their periodical hunt, some of the whites, in the hope of expediting their removal to the west side of the Mississippi, set on fire, in one day, about forty of their lodges, a number of which were entirely consumed. When the Indians returned in the spring and demanded satisfaction for the destruction of their property, they were met by new insults and outrages.

In the summer of 1829, Black Hawk happened to meet, at Rock island, with the late governor Coles, of whom he had heard as a great chief of Illinois, in company with "another chief" as he calls him—Judge Hall. Having failed in his appeals to the Indian agents, for redress of the grievances of his people, he determined to apply to these two chiefs, on the subject, and accordingly waited upon them for that purpose.

"He spoke of the indignity perpetrated upon himself, (his having been beaten with sticks by the whites,) with the feeling that a respectable person among us would have shown under such circumstances; and pointing to a black mark on his face, said that he wore it as a symbol of disgrace. The customs of his nation required, that he should avenge the wrong that he had received, but he chose rather to submit to it for

---

1. Chronicles of the North American Savages, No. 4. page 53.

the present than involve them in a war. And this was the only alternative, for if an Indian should kill, or even strike a white man, the aggression would be eagerly seized upon and exaggerated; the whole frontier population would rush to war, and the Indians would be hunted from their houses like wild beasts. He spoke of the intrusion upon their fields, the destruction of their growing corn, the ploughing up of the graves of their fathers, and the beating of their women; and added, "we dare not resent any of these things. If we did, it would be said that the Indians were disturbing the white people, and troops would be sent out to destroy us." We enquired, "why do you not represent these things to our government?—the President is a wise and a good ruler, who would protect you." "Our great father is too far off, he cannot hear our voice." "But you could have letters written and sent to him." "So we could," was his reply, "but the white men would write letters, and say that we told lies. Our great father would not believe an Indian, in preference to his own children."[2] Black Hawk in reference to this interview, says, "Neither of them could do any thing for us; but both evidently appeared very sorry. It would give me great pleasure at all times, to take these two chiefs by the hand."

Under the seventh article of the treaty made at St. Louis in 1804, it is provided that as long as the lands which are now ceded to the United States remain their property, the Indians belonging to the said tribes, shall enjoy the privilege of living and hunting upon them." It was not until the year, 1829, that any part of the lands upon Rock river, were brought into market by the United States. It follows as a matter of course, that all the white settlers upon them prior to this period, were trespassers, being there in violation of the laws of Congress, and the provisions of the treaty. Although the frontier settlements of Illinois, had not approached within fifty or sixty miles of Rock river, and the lands for a still greater distance around it, had not been offered for sale, yet in this year, government was induced to make sale of a few quarter sections, at the mouth of Rock river, including the Sac village. The reason for this uncalled for measure, is obvious—to evade the provisions of the foregoing treaty of cession, and create a pretext for the immediate removal of the Indians to the west side of the Mississippi.

In the spring of 1830, when Black Hawk and his band returned from their annual hunt, to occupy their lodges, and prepare as usual for raising their crop of vegetables, they found, that the land in and around their village, had been brought into market, and that their old friend, the trader at Rock Island had purchased a considerable part of it. Black Hawk, greatly disturbed at this new condition of things, appealed to the agent at that place, who informed him, that the lands having been sold by government to individuals, he and his party had no longer any *right* to remain upon them. Black Hawk was still unwilling to assent to a removal, and in the course of the summer, he visited Malden to consult his British father on the subject, and returned by Detroit to see the great American chief, Governor Cass, residing there. Both of these persons told him that if the Indians had not sold their lands and would remain quietly upon them, they would not be disturbed. Black Hawk, acting upon the assumption that the land on which their village stood, never had been legally sold to the United States, returned home determined to keep possession of it. It was late in the fall when he arrived: his people had gone to their hunting grounds for the winter and he followed them. They made an unsuccessful hunt and the season passed off in gloom. Keokuk again exerted his influence to induce them to desert Black Hawk and

2. History of the North American Indians, by James Hall, Esq.

remove to the Ioway. Such, however, was their attachment to their favorite village, that the whole band returned to it in the spring of 1831. The agent at Rock island forthwith notified them that if they did not remove from the land, troops would be sent by the United States to drive them off. Black Hawk says, he had a conference, about this time, with the trader at Rock Island, who enquired of him, if some terms could not be made, upon which he and his party would agree to remove to the west side of the Mississippi. To this he replied, that if his great father would do justice to them and make the proposition, they would remove. He was asked by the trader, "if the great chief at St. Louis would give six thousand dollars, to purchase provisions and other articles," if he would give up peaceably and remove. To this he agreed. The trader accordingly sent a message to the agent at St. Louis, that Black Hawk, and his whole band, could be removed for the sum of six thousand dollars, but the answer was, that nothing would be given, and that if they did not remove immediately, an armed force would be sent to compel them.

The squaws had now planted their corn, and it was beginning to grow, when the whites again commenced ploughing it up. Black Hawk at last determined to put a stop to these aggressions upon his people, and accordingly gave notice to those who were perpetrating them, that they must remove, forthwith, from his village. In the mean time, after the return of the Indians, which took place in April, eight of the white settlers united in a memorial to the Executive of the state of Illinois, in which they set forth that the Sac Indians of Rock river had "threatened to kill them; that they had acted in a most outrageous manner; threw down their fences, turned horses into their corn-fields, stole their potatoes, saying *the land was theirs and that they had not sold it,*—although said deponents had purchased the land of the United States' government: levelled deadly weapons at the citizens, and on some occasions hurt said citizens for attempting to prevent the destruction of their property," &c. &c. The memorial concludes with the still more startling outrage, that the said Indians went "to a house, rolled out a barrel of whiskey and destroyed it." One of these eight afflicted memorialists, swore the other seven to the truth of their statements, and with an earnest prayer for immediate relief, it was placed before his Excellency, on the 19th of May.

This long catalogue of outrages, backed by other memorials, and divers rumors of border depredations, committed by "General Black Hawk" and his "British Band," called into immediate action the patriotism and official power of the Governor. Under date of Bellville, May 26, 1831, he writes to the superintendent of Indian affairs, General William Clark, at St. Louis, that in order to protect the citizens of Illinois, which he considered in a state of "actual invasion," he had called out seven hundred militia to remove a band of Sac Indians, then residing at Rock river, and he pledges himself to the superintendent, that in fifteen days he will have a force in the field, sufficient to "remove them *dead* or *alive,* over to the west side of the Mississippi." But to save all this disagreeable business, his Excellency suggests to General Clark that perhaps a request from him to these Indians, to remove to the west side of the river, would effect the object of procuring peace to the citizens of the state. The letter concludes with the magnanimous declaration that there is no disposition on the part of the people of the state of Illinois to injure these unfortunate, deluded savages, "if they will let us alone."

General Clark, under date of St. Louis, 28 May, 1831, acknowledges the receipt of the above letter, and says, that he had already made every effort in his power, to get all the Indians who had ceded their lands to remove.

On the same day, 28th May, 1831, Governor Reynolds writes to General Gaines, then at St. Louis, that he had received information that Black Hawk and his band had invaded the state of Illinois; and that he had called out seven hundred troops to meet them. General Gaines, on the 29th of May, replies to his Excellency that he had ordered six companies of United States troops from Jefferson Barracks to Rock Island, and that they would be joined by four other companies from Prairie des Chiens, making in all ten companies; a force which he deemed sufficient to repel the invasion and give security to the frontier: That if the residue of the Sacs and Foxes, or other tribes should unite with the band of Black Hawk, he would call on his Excellency for some militia, but did not then deem it necessary.

On the 30th of May, the troops, accompanied by General Gaines, left Jefferson barracks, in a steam boat, for Fort Armstrong; and upon the 7th of June, the commanding general held a council on Rock island, at which Black Hawk and some of his braves were present. Keokuk, Wa-pel-lo and other chiefs from the west side of the Mississippi were also in attendance. When the council was opened, General Gaines rose and stated that the President was displeased with the refusal of the Sacs of Rock river, to go to the right bank of the Mississippi, that their great father wanted only that which was reasonable and right, and insisted that they should remove. Black Hawk replied, in substance, that the Sacs had never sold their lands and were determined to hold on to their village. General Gaines inquired, "who is Black Hawk? Is he a chief? By what right does he appear in council?"

No reply was made; Black Hawk arose, gathered his blanket around him, and stalked out of the council room. On the following morning he was again in his seat, and when the council was opened, he arose and said, "My father, you inquired yesterday, "who is Black Hawk? why does he sit among the chiefs?" I will tell you who I am. I am a Sac, my father was a Sac—I am a warrior and so was my father. Ask those young men, who have followed me to battle, and they will tell you who Black Hawk is—provoke our people to war, and you will learn who Black Hawk is." He then sat down, and nothing more was said on the subject. The result of this conference was, that Black Hawk refused to leave his village, and that General Gaines informed him and his party, if they were not on the West side of the Mississippi within a few days, he should be compelled to remove them by force. The General anxious, if possible, to effect the object without bloodshed, deemed it expedient to increase his forces, that the Indians might be intimidated, and thus induced to submit; or, in case of a resort to hostile measures, that he might be fully prepared to act with efficiency. He accordingly called upon the Governor of Illinois for some militia, to co-operate with the United States' troops under his command. On the 25th of June, Governor Reynolds, and General Joseph Duncan with 1600 mounted militiamen, principally volunteers, reached Rock river. On the morning of the 26th, General Gaines with his combined forces, took possession of the Sac village without firing a gun or finding an Indian; the whole party, with their wives and children, having crossed over the Mississippi the previous night. On the following day they were found on the west bank of that stream, encamped under the protection of a white flag.

On the 30th of June, General Gaines and Governor Reynolds signed a treaty of capitulation and peace, with Black Hawk, Pa-she-pa-how, Wee-sheat, Kah-ke-ka-mah, and other chiefs and head men of the British band of Sac Indians, and their old allies of the Winnebago, Pottawatamie and Kickapoo nations. The preamble to this treaty is worthy of preservation. It is in these words.

"Whereas, the British Band of Sac Indians, have in violation of the several treaties, entered into between the United States and the Sac and Fox nations, in the year 1804, 1816 and 1825, continued to remain upon and to cultivate the lands on Rock river, ceded to the United States by said treaties, after the said lands had been sold by the United States, to individual citizens of Illinois and other states: and whereas the said British Band of Sac Indians, in order to sustain their pretensions to continue upon said Rock river lands, have assumed the attitude of actual hostility towards the United States, and have had the audacity to drive citizens of the state of Illinois from their homes, destroy their corn, and invite many of their old friends of the Pottawatamies, Winnebagoes, and Kickapoos, to unite with them the said British band of Sacs, in war, to prevent their removal from said lands: and whereas many of the most disorderly of these several tribes of Indians, did actually join the said British band of Sac Indians prepared for war against the United States, and more particularly against the state of Illinois; from which purpose they confess nothing could have restrained them, but the apprehension of force far exceeding the combined strength of the said British Band of Sac Indians, with such of their aforesaid allies, as had actually joined them; but being now convinced that such a war would tend speedily to annihilate them, they have voluntarily abandoned their hostile attitude and sued for peace." Therefore, &c.

The first article stipulates that peace is granted by the United States to the British Band of Sac Indians—the second that they are required to submit to the chiefs of the Sac and Fox nations, who reside on the west side of the Mississippi—the third that the United States guaranty to them the integrity of their lands west of that river under the treaties of 1825 and 1830—the fourth that the said British Band shall not trade with any nation but the United States—that the United States have a right to establish military posts and roads within their country—the sixth that the chiefs and head men of the Sac and Fox nations shall enforce the provisions of this treaty—and finally that permanent peace and friendship be established between the United States and the said British Band of Sac Indians, and that the latter are not to return to the east side of the Mississippi without the permission of the former.

The commanding General, under date of sixth of July, 1831, informs the war department, that, "The mounted volunteers, the regulars, two pieces of artillery, and some musquetry and riflemen, induced the Indians to abandon the village before our arrival, without firing a gun. Deserted by their allies, this disorderly band was left alone to seek security in a speedy flight to the right bank of the Mississippi, where they were found the next day, under the protection of a white flag." Governor Reynolds in his official despatch to the same department, under date of Belleville. Ill. 7th July 1831, says:

"The Indians with some exceptions, from Canada to Mexico, along the northern frontier of the United States, are more hostile to the whites, than at any other period since the last war; particularly the band of Sac Indians, usually and truly called the "British Band," became extremely unfriendly to the citizens of Illinois and others. This band had determined for some years past to remain at all hazards, on certain lands which had been purchased by the United States, and afterwards some of them sold to private individuals by the general government. They also determined to drive off the citizens from this disputed territory. In order to effect this object, they committed various outrages on the persons and property of the citizens of this state. That this band might the more effectually resist all force that would be employed against them, they treated with many other tribes to combine together for the purpose of aiding this British Band to continue in possession of the country in question." General William Clark, the Indian agent at St. Louis, in his official communication to the department, says, "The disaffected Sacs were depending for an increase to their num-

ber from the discontented parts of the Kickapoos, Pottawatamies and Winnebagoes,"
and that they exhibited a daring opposition, &c. &c.

From the tone and pomposity of these documents, commencing with Governor
Reynold's annunciation to General Clark, that Illinois was in a state of "actual invasion," and ending with the letters to the war department, just cited, it might appear,
to one not familiar with the facts in the case, that a powerful confederacy of warlike
Indians, after years of secret preparation, had made a sudden and bold descent upon
the state of Illinois, and were about to carry war and desolation throughout the frontiers—to make the heavens lurid with the conflagration of dwelling houses, and the
air resonant with the wails of women and children sinking beneath the murderous
tomahawk: and, that this banded horde of northern savages, had been successfully
met, captured or dispersed, by the patriotism, valor and overwhelming power of the
combined army of the United States and the militia of Illinois! And yet, will it be
credited by posterity, that this "actual invasion" of the state, fierce and appalling as it
has been represented, consisted simply in this: a part of the Sac tribe of Indians, residing within the boundaries of Illinois, at their village on Rock river, where they were
born and had lived all their lives, refused to give up their corn-fields to some white
men, who had purchased the same, under a sale made by the government of the
United States for the purpose of a technical evasion of one of its own treaties. In short,
thus far, it was little more than a neighborhood quarrel between the squaws of the
"British Band" of Indians, and a few white settlers,—most of whom were there in violation of the laws of the country—about the occupancy of some corn-fields, which,
from time immemorial, had been annually cultivated by the Indian women. Black
Hawk became excited by these outrages, as he deemed them, upon the rights of his
people; but instead of killing every white man in his vicinity, which he could have
done in one night, he simply commanded them to leave his village: and threatened in
case they did not, to remove them by force. Such is the substance of the "actual invasion" of the state of Illinois, by the British Band of Sac Indians.

It is alledged, however, by the defenders of this memorable campaign, that this
band of Sacs had, in violation of the treaties of 1804, 1816 and 1825, continued to remain upon and cultivate the land on Rock river, ceded to the United States, after it
had been sold by the United States to individual citizens of Illinois and other states—
that they had refused positively to remove to the west side of the Mississippi—that
they had endeavored to persuade some of the neighboring tribes to unite with them
in defending this land against the rightful occupancy of the white purchasers—that
they had "threatened to kill" them—"thrown down their fences"—on "some occasions "hurt" said settlers—"stole their potatoes" saying they had not sold these lands—
otherwise "acted in a most outrageous manner," and finally, in the words of the capitulation on the 30th June, 1831, "assumed the attitude of actual hostility towards the
United States, and had the audacity to drive citizens of the state of Illinois, from their
homes." Admitting these allegations to be true, what may be said in behalf of the party
against which they are made? It may be replied, that under the treaty of 1804, the Indians had an undoubted right to "live and hunt" upon the land ceded by that treaty,
so long as it remained the property of the United States: that as early as 1823–4 the
whites had intruded upon the land on Rock river around the principal village of the
Sacs and Foxes—the United States neglecting to have these intruders removed, as by
the treaty they were solemnly bound to do: that these whites frequently beat the Indian men, women, and children with sticks, destroyed their corn fields, distributed
whiskey among them, cheated them out of their furs and peltries and on one occa-

sion, when the Indians were absent on a hunting excursion, set fire to some thirty or forty of their lodges, by which many of them were totally destroyed.

These outrages were perpetrated before a single acre of the land upon Rock river, had been sold by the United States, and when in fact, the regular frontier settlements of Illinois, had not approached within fifty miles of the Sac village. Consequently they were committed in express violation of the most solemn treaties and of the laws of the United States, for the protection of the Indians. In 1829, clearly with a view, on the part of those who brought about the measure, of evading the force of that article of the treaty of 1804, which permitted the Indians to live and hunt upon these lands, so long as they remained the property of the United States, a few quarter sections were sold, on Rock river, including the Sac village. New insults and outrages were now offered to the Indians, and they were again ordered to remove, not from the quarter sections which had actually been sold, but to the west side of the Mississippi. Against this, they remonstrated and finally refused, positively, to be driven away. The results of this refusal have already been shown in the narration which has been made of the events following upon the "actual invasion" of the state of Illinois, in the spring of 1831. But it has been said that these Indians endeavored to form an alliance with some of the neighboring tribes to defend their lands. There is no doubt that Black Hawk labored to persuade Keokuk and the Sac Indians residing with him, to return to the east side of the Mississippi and assist in defending their village. His effort to unite with him, in alliance against the United States, the Winnebagoes, Pottawotamies and Kickapoos, was probably for the same object, though the case is not so clearly made out. Mr. Schoolcraft in his "Narrative" speaks of a war message having been transmitted to the Torch lake Indians, by Black Hawk, or his counsellors, in 1830, and repeated in the two succeeding years; and adds that similar communications were made to other tribes. The message, continues Mr. Schoolcraft, was very equivocal. It invited these tribes to aid the Sacs in fighting their enemies. Whatever may have been the object, no success attended the effort. Other motives than that of retaining possession of these lands, may have prompted Black Hawk to seek this alliance. Being an ambitious, restless man, he may have thought it expedient to do something to keep himself in power with his people. A military campaign is occasionally a fortunate circumstance for a politician, whether his skin be red or white. Gunpowder-popularity is of equal importance to the chiefs of the Sacs and the chiefs of the Illini. An "actual invasion" of a state—which, in these modern times, is supposed to consist in "levelling deadly weapons" at the inhabitants thereof, and "stealing their potatoes," is quite a wind-fall to political aspirants.

That the British Band of Sac Indians cherished the feeling of active hostility towards the whites, that has been attributed to them, may well be questioned. That they were provoked to a feeble assertion of their rights by the injustice of our government and the lawless conduct of the white settlers among them, is unquestionably true. But it should be recollected, that from the period of their treaty with the United States, in 1816, to their capitulation in 1831, they had not killed one of our people. For a number of years prior to 1831, the Americans had constantly passed through their country, unarmed, carrying with them large amounts of money and of goods, for the trade at the lead mines: and yet not one of these travellers, sleeping in the woods and the Indian lodges, had been molested in person or property. For several years, the whites residing at and around the Sac village on Rock river were trespassing upon these Indians, for the purpose of driving them to the west side of the Mississippi, but still the tomahawk was not raised for retaliation. If Black Hawk and his party, had really intended to resort to arms, who that understands the Indian character, can doubt for a moment, that they would have struck a decisive blow, and murdered every white settler upon Rock river, before General Gaines ascended the Mississippi? After our army reached Fort Armstrong and General Gaines had been informed by Black Hawk that he would not remove, he gave orders to his braves, that if the American war chief came to the village to force them away, not a gun should be fired, nor any resistance offered; but that they must remain quietly in their lodges and let the war chief kill them if he chose. Under these circumstances, it is as difficult to believe that Black Hawk and his band seriously intended to make war upon the whites at that time, as it is to admit that the United States had a right to force the Indians to remove to the west side of the Mississippi, because a few quarter sections of the land at the mouth of Rock river, had been prematurely sold; while millions of acres around, were still the property of the United States, and as such, under the treaty of 1804, the Indians were expressly permitted to live and hunt upon them.

In the course of this narrative, frequent mention has been made of the leading chief of the Sac nation, who is highly distinguished by his influence, pacific character and fine talents. The relation he sustains to Black Hawk and his band, connects him directly with our narrative. On this account, as well as to gratify the interest which is felt in his history, the succeeding chapter will be occupied with a brief sketch of the life and adventures of Keokuk, the Watchful Fox.

CHAPTER VII

General Atkinson overtakes Black Hawk—Battle of the Bad Axe—Atkinson's official report—Incidents of the Battle—Capture of Black Hawk and the prophet—Naopope's statement to General Scott—General Scott and Governor Reynolds conclude a treaty with the Sacs, Foxes and Winnebagoes—Causes which led to the war—Motives for getting up Indian wars—First attack made by the Illinois militia—Report of the Secretary at War in regard to this campaign—General Macomb's letter to General Atkinson—Secretary Cass' statement of the causes which led to this war—Comments upon this statement, and its omissions pointed out.

AFTER the battle upon the Wisconsin, the whole army, under the command of General Atkinson, crossed to the north side of that river, at Helena, and on the twenty-ninth of July, commenced the pursuit of the Indians, by forced marches, over a rugged and mountainous country. On the morning of the second of August, while ten miles from the Mississippi, it was ascertained that the enemy were upon the bank of that stream, near the Bad-axe, and in the act of crossing to the west side. Arrangements were immediately made for an attack. Gen. Dodge's squadron was placed in front, followed by the infantry, and these by the brigades of Henry, Alexander, and Posey. The army had proceeded in this order about five miles, when some Indians were discovered and fired upon. They immediately retreated to the main body, on the bank of the river. To prevent the possibility of the escape of the enemy, Generals Alexander and

Posey, were directed to form the right wing of the army, and march to the river, above the Indian encampment, and then to move down along the bank. General Henry formed the left wing, and the United States' infantry and General Dodge's squadron, occupied the centre. In this order, the army descended a bluff bank into a river bottom, heavily timbered, and covered with weeds and brush-wood. General Henry first came upon a portion of the enemy, and commenced a heavy fire upon them, which was returned. General Dodge's squadron and the United States' troops, soon came into the action, and with General Henry's men, rushed upon the Indians, killing all in the way, except a few who succeeded in swimming a slough of the Mississippi, about a hundred and fifty yards wide. During this time the brigades of Alexander and Posey, in marching down the bank of the river, fell in with another party of Indians, and killed or routed the whole of them. When the Indians were driven to the brink of the river, a large number of men, women and children, plunged into the water to save themselves by swimming; but only a few escaped "our sharp-shooters." The battle lasted about three hours. In the afternoon, of the same day, Generals Atkinson, Dodge and Posey, descended the Mississippi, to Prairie des Chiens, in the Warrior, and there awaited the arrival of the mounted volunteers, who reached that place on the fourth. Among the Indians who escaped the slaughter was Black Hawk. Twelve of those who effected their escape, were captured on the fourth, by a party of whites, from Cassville, under the command of Captain Price, and most of those who succeeded in reaching the west side of the Mississippi, were subsequently attacked by a party of hostile Sioux, and either killed or taken prisoners. The brief, but official account of this battle is given by the commanding general, in these words.

Head Quarters, First Artillery Corps, North-western Army.

Prairie des Chiens, Augt. 25, 1832.

Sir: I have the honor to report to you that I crossed the Ouisconsin on the 27th and 28th ultimo, with a select body of troops, consisting of the regulars under Col. Taylor, four hundred in number, part of Henry's, Posey's and Alexander's brigades, amounting in all to 1300 men, and immediately fell upon the trail of the enemy, and pursued it by a forced march, through a mountainous and difficult country, till the morning of the 2d inst., when we came up with his main body on the left bank of the Mississippi, nearly opposite the mouth of the Ioway, which we attacked, defeated and dispersed, with a loss on his part of about a hundred and fifty men killed, thirtynine women and children taken prisoners—the precise number could not be ascertained, as the greater portion was slain after being forced into the river. Our loss in killed and wounded, which is stated below, is very small in comparison with the enemy, which may be attributed to the enemy's being forced from his positions by a rapid charge at the commencement, and throughout the engagement—the remnant of the enemy, cut up and disheartened, crossed to the opposite side of the river, and has fled into the interior, with a view, it is supposed, of joining Keokuk and Wapello's bands of Sacs and Foxes.

The horses of the volunteer troops being exhausted by long marches, and the regular troops without shoes, it was not thought advisable to continue the pursuit; indeed a stop to the further effusion of blood seemed to be called for, till it might be ascertained if the enemy would surrender.

It is ascertained from our prisoners, that the enemy lost in the battle of the Ouisconsin sixty-eight killed and a very large number wounded; his whole loss does not fall short of three hundred;—after the battle on the Ouisconsin, those of the enemy's women and children, and some who were dismounted, attempted to make their escape by descending that river, but judicious measures being taken by Captain Loomis and Lieut. Street, Indian agent, thirty-two women and children and four men have been captured, and some fifteen men killed by the detachment under Lieut. Ritner.

The day after the battle on this river, I fell down with the regular troops to this place by water, and the mounted men will join us to-day. It is now my purpose to direct Keokuk, to demand a surrender of the remaining principal men of the hostile party, which, from the large number of women and children we hold prisoners, I have every reason to believe will be complied with. Should it not, they should be pursued and subdued, a step Maj. Gen. Scott will take upon his arrival:

I cannot speak too highly of the brave conduct of the regular and volunteer forces engaged in the last battle and the fatiguing march that preceded it, as soon as the reports of officers of the brigades and corps are handed in, they shall be submitted with further remarks.

5 killed, 2 wounded, 6th inft.

2   do.   5th inft.

1 captain, 5 privates Dodge's Bat. mounted.

1 Lieut. 6 privates Henry's

1 private wounded, Alexander's

1 private,   Posey's.

I have the honor to be with great respect,

YR. OBT. SERVANT, H. ATKINSON,

BREVET BRIG. GEN. U. S. A.

MAJ. GEN. MACOMB, COM. IN CHIEF, WASHINGTON.

The destruction of life in the battle of the Badaxe, was not confined to the Indian warriors. Little discrimination seems to have been made between the slaughter of those in arms and the rest of the tribe. After they had sought refuge in the waters of the Mississippi, and the women, with their children on their backs, were buffeting the waves, in an attempt to swim to the opposite shore, numbers of them were shot by our troops. Many painful pictures might be recorded of the adventures and horrors of that day. One or two cases may be cited. A Sac women, named Na-ni-sa, the sister of a warrior of some note among the Indians, found herself in the hottest of the fight. She succeeded at length in reaching the river, and keeping her infant child, close in its blanket, by force of her teeth, plunged into the water, seized hold upon the tail of a horse, whose rider was swimming him to the opposite shore, and was carried safely across the Mississippi. When our troops charged upon the Indians, in their defiles near the river, men, women and children were so huddled together, that the slaughter fell alike upon all of them. A young squaw was standing in the grass, a short distance from the American line, holding her child, a little girl of four years old, in her arms. In this position, a ball struck the right arm of the child, just above the elbow, and shattering the bone, passed into the breast of its young mother, and instantly killed her. She fell upon the child and confined it to the ground. When the battle was nearly over, and the Indians had been driven from this point, Lieutenant Anderson of the United States army, hearing the cries of the child, went to the spot, and taking it from under the dead mother, carried it to the place for surgical aid. The arm was amputated, and during the operation, the half starved child did not cry, but sat quietly eating a piece of hard biscuit. It was sent to Prairie des Chiens, and entirely recovered from its wound.

When the fortunes of Black Hawk became desperate, his few straggling allies, from other tribes, not only deserted him, but joined his enemies. It is to two Winnebagoes, Decorie, and Chaetar, that the fallen chief is indebted for being taken captive. On the 27th of August, they delivered Black Hawk and the Prophet to the Indian agent, General Street, at Prairie des Chiens. Upon their delivery, Decorie, the One-eyed, rose and said:

"My father, I now stand before you. When we parted, I told you I would return soon; but I could not come any sooner. We have had to go a great distance [to the Dalle, on the Wisconsin, above the portage.] You see we have done what you sent us to do. These, (pointing to the prisoners) are the two you told us to get. We have done what you told us to do. We always do what you tell us, because we know it is for our good. Father, you told us to get these men, and it would be the cause of much good to the Winnebagoes. We have brought them, but it has been very hard for us to do so. That one, Black Hawk was a great way off. You told us to bring them to you alive: we have done so. If you had told us to bring their heads alone, we would have done so, and it would have been less difficult than what we have done. Father, we deliver these men into your hands. We would not deliver them even to our brother, the chief of the warriors, but to you; because we know you, and we believe you are our friend. We want you to keep them safe; if they are to be hurt we do not wish to see it. Wait until we are gone before it is done. Father, many little birds have been flying about our ears of late, and we thought they whispered to us that there was evil intended for us; but now we hope these evil birds will let our ears alone. We know you are our friend, because you take our part, and that is the reason we do what you tell us to do. You say you love your red children: we think we love you as much if not more than you love us. We have confidence in you and you may rely on us. We have been promised a great deal if we would take these men—that it would do much good to our people. We now hope to see what will be done for us. We have come in haste; we are tired and hungry. We now put these men into your hands. We have done all that you told us to do."

The agent, General Street, replied: "My children, you have done well. I told you to bring these men to me, and you have done so. I am pleased at what you have done. It is for your good, and for this reason I am pleased. I assured the great chief of the warriors, (General Atkinson) that if these men were in your country, you would find them and bring them to me, and now I can say much for your good. I will go down to Rock island with the prisoners, and I wish you who have brought these men, especially, to go with me, with such other chiefs and warriors as you may select. My children, the great chief of the warriors, when he left this place, directed me to deliver these and all other prisoners, to the chief of the warriors at this place, Col. Taylor, who is here by me. Some of the Winnebagoes, south of the Wisconsin, have befriended the Saukies, and some of the Indians of my agency have also given them aid. This displeases the great chief of the warriors, and your great father the President, and was calculated to do much harm. Your great father, the President at Washington, has sent a great war chief from the far east. General Scott, with a fresh army of soldiers. He is now at Rock Island. Your great father the President has sent him and the Governor and chief of Illinois to hold a council with the Indians. He has sent a speech to you, and wishes the chiefs and warriors of the Winnebagoes to go to Rock Island, to the council on the tenth of next month. I wish you to be ready in three days, when I will go with you. I am well pleased that you have taken the Black Hawk, the Prophet and other prisoners. This will enable me to say much for you to the great chief of the warriors, and to the president your great father. My children, I shall now deliver the two men, Black Hawk and the prophet, to the chief of the warriors here. He will take care of them till we start to Rock Island."

Col. Taylor upon taking charge of the prisoners made a few remarks to their captors, after which Chaetar, the associate of Decorie, rose and said,

"My father, I am young, and do not know how to make speeches. This is the second time I even spoke to you before people. I am no chief; I am no orator; but I have been allowed to speak to you. If I should not speak as well as others, still you must listen to me. Father, when you made the speech to the chiefs, Waugh Kon Decorie Carramani, the one-eyed Decorie, and others, I was there. I heard you. I thought what you said to them, you also said to me. You said if these two, (pointing to Black Hawk and the prophet) were taken by us and brought to you, there would never more a black cloud hang over your Winnebagoes. Your words entered into my ear, my brains and my heart. I left here that same night, and you know that you have not seen me since until now. I have been a great way; I had much trouble; but when I remembered what you said, I knew what you said was right. This made me continue and do what you told me to do. Near the Dalle on the Wisconsin, I took Black Hawk. No one did it but me. I say this in the ears of all present, and they know it—and I now appeal to the Great Spirit, our grandfather, and the Earth, our grandmother, for the truth of what I say. Father, I am no chief, but what I have done is for the benefit of my nation, and I hope to see the good that has been promised us. That one, Wabokieshiek, the prophet, is my relation—if he is to be hurt, I do not wish to see it. Father, soldiers sometimes stick the ends of their guns into the backs of Indian prisoners, when they are going about in the hands of the guard. I hope this will not be done to this man."

Naopope the second in command, with a few other Indians who escaped from the battle of the Bad-Axe, were also brought in by the Sioux, who being the ancient enemy of the Sacs and Foxes, seized upon this opportunity of waging war upon the remnant of Black Hawk's band. They were placed by General Street, in the custody of Colonel Taylor.

On the seventh of September, the prisoners were placed on board the steam boat Winnebago, and sent down to Jefferson Barracks, a few miles below St. Louis. The arrival of General Scott at the scene of action, was unfortunately delayed until after the campaign was closed, in consequence of the Asiatic cholera having broken out, among the troops under his command, while ascending the lakes. The disease continued to rage among them, with dreadful mortality, for some time after their arrival at Rock island. Of course, this campaign added no new laurels to the military reputation of General Scott; but, by his humane and tireless exertions for the alleviation of the sufferings of his soldiers, he won for himself more true glory, than the most brilliant victory, over an Indian enemy, could confer.

While at Rock Island, General Scott instituted some inquiries among the Indians, in regard to the difficulties between them and the whites. Among others interrogated was Naopope, the friend and counsellor of Black Hawk, who participated in the campaign, and on account of his courage and skill as a warrior, directed to a great extent, the movements of the band, from the period of their recrossing the Mississippi, until the battle of the Bad-Axe. His statement confirms the declaration of Black

Hawk, that in coming over to the east side of the river, there was no intention of making war upon the frontier settlers; and that they really intended to surrender to Major Stillman, upon Sycamore creek, on the 14th of May, and actually sent a white flag, in evidence of their submission, which was fired upon by the American troops.

"I always belonged to Black Hawk's band. Last summer I went to Malden; when I came back, I found that by the treaty with General Gaines, the Sacs had moved across the Mississippi. I remained during the winter with the Prophet, on Rock river, thirty-five miles above the mouth. During the winter the Prophet sent me across the Mississippi, to Black Hawk, with a message, to tell him and his band to cross back to his village and make corn: that if the Americans came and told them to remove again, they would shake hands with them. If the Americans had come and told us to move, we should have shaken hands, and immediately have moved peaceably. We encamped on Sycamore creek. We met some Pottowatomies and made a feast for them. At that time I heard there were some Americans [under Maj. Stillman] near us. I prepared a white flag to go and see them, and sent two or three young men on a hill to see what they were doing. Before the feast was finished, I heard my young men were killed. This was at sunset. Some of my young men ran out; two killed, and the Americans were seen rushing on to our camp. My young men fired a few guns, and the Americans ran off, and my young men chased them about six miles."

Naopope further stated that the Pottowatomies immediately left them, and that none of the Kickapoos ever joined them. A few of the Winnebagoes did, and brought in scalps at different times; but so soon as they discovered that the whites were too powerful for the Sacks, they turned round and fought against them. Some of the other witnesses examined on this occasion, testify, that when Black Hawk saw the steam boat Warrior approaching them, on the first of August, he said he pitied the women and children; and, having determined to surrender to the commander of the boat, raised a white flag which was immediately fired upon. This fact is stated in the letter of the Captain of the Warrior, and is corroborated by Lieutenant Kingsbury, who had charge of the troops on board.

Among the prisoners delivered to General Street, was the prophet Wabokieshiek, or the White Cloud, a stout, shrewd looking Indian about forty years of age. This individual exercised consider able influence over Black Hawk and his band. He had a village, called after him, upon Rock river, where he usually resided, and was recognized among the village chiefs. He claimed to be part Winnebago and part Sac, his father belonging to one and his mother to the other of these tribes. He wore a full suit of hair, with a white head-dress rising several inches above the top of his hair—a style of dress suited, it is supposed, to his profession. He seems to have had sagacity and cunning—two qualities essential to the character of a prophet, and without which they could not long retain their influence and sacred character. Wabokieshiek has been represented as the priest of assassination, but the evidence on which this charge is made, seems to be wanting. He was instrumental in persuading Black Hawk and his party to return to the east side of the Mississippi in 1832, and went down to the mouth of Rock river to meet them, and encourage the belief that the Americans would not interfere with them, so long as they refrained from any offensive operations. He made a speech to the braves and warriors of Black Hawk, in which he told them they had nothing to fear and much to gain: That the American war chief, would not molest them so long as they acted peaceably: That the time would come when they would be ready to pursue a different course; but that they must await such reinforcements as would enable them to resist the army of the whites. The Prophet was either duped himself, or playing upon the credulity of Black Hawk and Naopope. He was constantly giving them assurances of assistance from the other tribes and from their British Father at Malden. There may have been reason for expecting it from the former, but none from the latter. He entertained strong prejudices against the whites, and being naturally prone to mischief making, was willing to stir up the Indians to resistance, without caring for the results that would be likely to follow a border war. The likeness of him, which is here given, is said to convey a good idea of his style of dress and the expression of his face.

On the 21st of September, General Scott and Governor Reynolds concluded a treaty with the Winnebagoes, and the Sacs and Foxes; the provisions of which have been stated. For the faithful performance of it, on the part of the Indians, it was stipulated that Black Hawk and his two sons, Wabokieshiek the Prophet, Naopope and five other chiefs of the hostile band, should be retained as hostages during the pleasure of the President. The remainder of the prisoners, captured during the campaign, were set at liberty.

In recurring to the causes which led to this war and the spirit and military skill with which it was conducted, there is nothing on which a citizen of the United States can dwell with satisfaction. Looking alone to the official documents, that have been published on the subject, it would appear that the Indians were the aggressors—that they invaded the territory of the United States, marking their path with outrages upon the unoffending citizens; and that they were met, encountered, and defeated, under circumstances which shed renown upon the arms and humane policy of the government. But it is necessary, in doing justice to both parties in this contest, to destroy this flattering picture.

Some of the causes which operated to render Black Hawk and his band, discontented with the conduct of the United States, and with their condition upon the west side of the Mississippi, have been enumerated. Whatever may have been their ulterior views, in returning within the limits of the state of Illinois, in the spring of 1832, it cannot be supposed that they came with any immediate hostile intentions. Had they been determined upon war, they would neither have encumbered themselves with their wives and children, nor have openly re-crossed the Mississippi, near to Fort Armstrong, when they knew there was an officer of the United States army, with a body of troops, stationed at that point, for the express purpose of preserving peace upon the frontier. Such movements would have been at variance with the well known military policy of the Indians. Judging from the success of General Gaines, in removing this same band, in 1831, without blood shed, to the west side of the Mississippi, it has been supposed, that a pacific conference between the commandant of Fort Armstrong and Black Hawk, in 1832, before he had commenced his ascent up Rock river, would have resulted in the peaceable return of the Indians to their own hunting grounds. The condition of things at that time, warrants such a belief, and the subsequent declarations of the Indians, strengthen the opinion, that had the experiment been made, it would have been successful. It is true, that the commanding officer at Fort Armstrong, sent two messages to Black Hawk upon this subject; but the first is represented by the Indians to have been an *order* for them to return; and the second, that if they did not, they would be pursued and *forced* to re-cross the Mississippi. These efforts failed, but it does not follow that a friendly council upon the subject, would not have resulted differently.

Many causes operate in bringing about an Indian war, and in plunging the government of the United States, prematurely and unnecessarily, into it. There is generally upon the frontiers a class of persons who have nothing to lose, and much to gain by such a contest. It gives them employment and circulates money among them. With such pioneer loafers, an Indian war is always popular. Then there is the "Indian Hater,"[1] a numerous and respectable body of men, to be found upon the frontier settlements, who, from having suffered in their persons and property by the barbarities and plunder of the Indians, have come at length to look upon them as no better than the wild beasts of the forest, and whose many atrocities make it a moral duty, on the part of the whites, to exterminate by fire and the sword. Again there is the regular *squatter* and land speculator, whose interest is always promoted by a war, because it usually results in driving the Indians further back from the frontier. Intermixed with these classes, are many quiet and worthy citizens, who with their families, have been carried to the frontiers, in the ordinary course of events, by the tide of emigration. These may have neither a desire for war nor a feeling of hostility towards the Indians, but when the tomahawk is raised, they contribute to swell the alarum, and oftentimes, by their very fears of a war, do much to bring it about. Finally, it is not to be disguised, that there are many individuals, in the states, who are prone to look to an Indian war, as a means of gratifying their love for adventure and excitement; or who, having political aspirations, are disposed to make the military renown, which may be gained in a campaign, the means of attaining civic honors. It is obvious, if there be any foundation for these positions, that an Indian war may oftentimes be undertaken without any just cause, prosecuted without system and terminated in dishonor to our government.

When Black Hawk and his party rashly determined, in the spring of 1832, to recross the Mississippi, a fine opportunity was presented, for getting up a border war, and the necessary machinery was speedily put in motion. The old chief, with a few hundred braves and their women and children, carrying with them their cooking utensils and personal property, had no sooner reached the east bank of the Mississippi, than the alarm note was sounded upon the frontier, and echoed from cabin to cabin, until it was spread throughout the state of Illinois. The most dreadful anticipations of savage cruelty were indulged—the force of Black Hawk was greatly magnified—his thirst for vengeance upon the whites was only to be appeased by blood—the state was actually invaded by a powerful and remorseless enemy—and memorials and petitions, for an armed force to repulse the invaders and protect the frontiers, flowed in upon the Governor, from all quarters. Such was the excited state of public feeling, such the force of public sentiment, that little time was left for Executive deliberation. Governor Reynolds issued his proclamation, reiterating the dangers of the frontier, and calling for a body of the militia to march and protect it. A call under such circumstances was promptly responded to, and in a short time, a large body of mounted volunteers, embracing many of the most respectable and influential citizens of Illinois, were in the vicinity of the invading foe, and ready for co-operation with the regular troops under General Atkinson. A concentration of these two forces was made at Dixon's ferry, on Rock river, about thirty miles below the encampment of Black Hawk and his party. Had a conference now been sought with the Indians, their prompt submission cannot be doubted. Black Hawk, whatever might have been his previous expectations, had received no addition of strength from other tribes—he was almost destitute of provisions—had committed no act of hostility against the whites, and with all

---

1. This class is admirably described by the author of "Legends of the West."

his women, children and baggage, was in the vicinity of an army, principally of mounted volunteers, many times greater than his own band of braves. He would probably have been glad of any reasonable pretext for retracing his precipitate steps. Unfortunately no effort for a council was made. A body of impetuous volunteers dashed on, without caution or order, to Sycamore creek, within three miles of the camp of a part of Black Hawk's party. He instantly sent a white flag to meet them for the purpose of holding a council, and agreeing to return to the west side of the Mississippi. Unfortunately, for the cause of humanity, as well as the good faith of the United States, this flag was held to be but a decoy, and without waiting to ascertain its true character, the bearers of it were fired upon and one of them killed. An onset was immediately made by Maj. Stillman upon Black Hawk, who finding there was no alternative but war, met our troops, and put them to flight in the manner already described. Emboldened by his brilliant success in this engagement, and finding that he would not be permitted to capitulate, he sent out his war parties, removed his women and children up Rock river, and a regular border war was commenced. The murders which his men committed upon the frontier settlers, naturally increased the alarm throughout the state, additional volunteers rushed to the seat of war, and the commanding General commenced his military operations for a regular campaign. In about two months, Black Hawk, having lost many of his men, in the different skirmishes with the American troops, and not a few of his women and children by actual starvation, found himself upon the bank of the Mississippi, endeavoring to escape the pursuing enemy, by crossing to the west side of that stream. While engaged in this act, the steam boat Warrior, having an armed force on board, ascended the river for the purpose of cutting off his retreat. Once more Black Hawk raised the white flag, and sought to surrender himself and his whole band, to the whites. Again his flag was looked upon as a decoy, and in fifteen minutes, a round of canister shot, from the boat, was fired, with deadly fatality into the midst of his men, women and children. The following morning, the main army, under General Atkinson, reached the scene of action. His force must have been six or eight times greater than that of the Indians, and by a judicious movement, the latter was promptly surrounded on three sides by the pursuing army, while on the other, the steam boat Warrior, the waters of the Mississippi, and a band of hostile Sioux on its west bank, precluded all chance of escape in that quarter. A demand upon the Indians, at this time, to surrender, unconditionally, would undoubtedly have been most cheerfully acceded to. But it appears not to have been made. It is probable that General Atkinson whose character for humanity, has always stood high, could not restrain the impetuosity of his troops long enough to propose a capitulation. They had been deeply excited by the murders perpetrated by the Black Hawk band—had been harassed by a long and fatiguing march—and perhaps felt, that the results of the campaign, thus far, had been rather inglorious to their arms. These causes may have conspired to precipitate them into a battle, which had been better spared than fought, inasmuch as it resulted, necessarily, in the death of a great many miserable women and children, who were already on the brink of the grave, from hunger and exhaustion.

A brief recapitulation of a few of the events of this disastrous campaign, has thus been made, for the purpose of showing, that however hostile Black Hawk and his band may have been, originally, towards the whites, he did not make the first attack upon them; and that the war might in all probability have been prevented, or arrested in any stage of its progress, by the exercise of that forbearance, good faith and sound policy, which should ever be cherished by the United States.

The official report of General Atkinson to General Macomb, after the battle of the Bad-axe has been quoted in full. On the 25th of November 1832, the Secretary at War, Mr. Cass, in his annual report to the President, says, in speaking of this campaign,

"General Atkinson, with the regular troops and militia under his command, pursued the Indians through a country very difficult to be penetrated, of which little was known, and where much exertion was required to procure regular supplies. These circumstances necessarily delayed the operations, and were productive of great responsibility to the commanding officer, and of great sufferings and privations to all employed in this harassing warfare. The Indians, however, were driven from their fastnesses, and fled towards the Mississippi, with the intention of seeking refuge in the country west of that river. They were immediately followed by General Atkinson, with a mounted force, overtaken, and completely vanquished. The arrangements of the commanding general, as well in the pursuit as in the action, were prompt and judicious, and the conduct of the officers and men was exemplary. The campaign terminated in the unqualified submission of the hostile party, and in the adoption of measures for the permanent security of the frontiers, and the result has produced upon the Indians of that region, a salutary impression, which it is to be hoped will prevent the recurrence of similar scenes."

On the 25th of October 1832, General Macomb transmitted to General Atkinson, the following letter, from the Secretary at War.

Department at War, Oct. 24th. 1832.

SIR: The return of the President to the seat of government, enables me to communicate to you his sentiments in relation to the operations and result of the campaign, recently conducted under your orders, against the hostile Indians; and it is with great pleasure, I have received his instructions to inform you, that he appreciates the difficulties you had to encounter; and that he has been highly gratified at the termination of your arduous and responsible duties. Great privations and embarrassments, necessarily attend such a warfare, and particularly in the difficult country occupied by the enemy. The arrangements which led to the defeat of the Indians, were adopted with judgment and pursued with decision, and the result was honorable to yourself, and to the officers and men acting under your orders.

I will thank you to communicate to the forces that served with you, both regulars and militia, the feelings of the President upon this occasion. I have the honor to be very respectfully, your obt. servant.

LEWIS CASS.

GEN. H. ATKINSON, JEFFERSON BARRACKS, MISSOURI.

In the report of the Secretary at War which has just been referred to, there is the following statement of the causes which led to this contest. "The recent hostilities, commenced by the Sac and Fox Indians, may be traced to causes, which have been for some time in operation, and which left little doubt upon the minds of those acquainted with the savage character, that they were determined to commit some aggression upon the frontier. The confederated tribes of the Sacs and Foxes have been long distinguished for their daring spirit of adventure and for their restless and reckless disposition. At the commencement of the eighteenth century, one of these tribes made a desperate attempt to seize the post of Detroit; and during a period of forty years, subsequent to that effort, they caused great trouble and embarrassment to the French colonial government, which was only terminated by a most formidable military expedition, sent by that enterprizing people into their remote regions west of Green Bay. During the last war with Great Britain, this confederacy entered zealously into the contest, and was among the most active and determined of our enemies. After the peace their communication with the Canadian authorities was preserved; and, in every year, large parties of the most influential chiefs and warriors visited Upper Canada, and returned laden with presents. That this continued intercourse kept alive feelings of attachment to a foreign power and weakened the proper and necessary influence of the United States, is known to every one who has marked the progress of events and conduct of the Indians upon the north western frontier. The tribes upon the upper Mississippi, particularly the Sacs and Foxes and Winnebagoes, confident in their position and in their natural courage, and totally ignorant of the vast disproportion between their power, and that of the United States, have always been discontented, keeping the frontier in alarm, and continually committing some outrage upon the persons or property of the inhabitants. All this is the result of impulse, and is the necessary and almost inevitable consequence of institutions, which make war the great object of life. It is not probable, that any Indian seriously bent upon hostilities, ever stops to calculate the force of the white man, and to estimate the disastrous consequences which we know must be the result. He is impelled onward in his desperate career, by passions which are fostered and encouraged by the whole frame of society; and he is, very probably, stimulated by the predictions of some fanatical leader, who promises him glory, victory and scalps.

"In this state of feeling, and with these incitements to war, the Sacs and Foxes claimed the right of occupying a part of the country on Rock river, even after it had been sold to citizens of the United States, and settled by them. In 1829 and in 1830, serious difficulties resulted from their efforts to establish themselves in that section, and frequent collisions were the consequence. Representations were made to them, and every effort, short of actual hostilities, used by the proper officers, to induce them to abandon their unfounded pretensions, and to confine themselves to their own country on the west side of the Mississippi river. These efforts were successful, with the well disposed portion of the tribes, but were wholly unavailing with the band known by the name of the "British party." In 1831, their aggressions were so serious, and the attitude they assumed, so formidable, that a considerable detachment of the army, and of the militia of Illinois, was called into the field; and the disaffected Indians, alarmed by the preparation for their chastisement, agreed to reside and hunt, "upon their own lands west of the Mississippi river," and that they would not re-cross this river to the usual place of their residence, nor to any part of their old hunting grounds east of the Mississippi, without the express permission of the President of the United States, or the Governor of the state of Illinois.

"This arrangement had scarcely been concluded, before a flagrant outrage was committed, by a party of these Indians, upon a band of friendly Menomomies, almost under the guns of Fort Crawford. Twenty-five persons were wantonly murdered, and many wounded, while encamped in the Prairie du Chien, and resting in fancied security upon our soil, and under our flag. If an act like this, had been suffered to pass unnoticed and unpunished, a war between these tribes would have been the consequence, in which our frontiers would have been involved, and the character and influence of the government, would have been lost in the opinion of the Indians.

"Apprehensive, from the course of events already stated, and from other circumstances, that the disaffected band of Sacs and Foxes, would again harass and disturb the settlements upon our borders, and determined that the murderers of the Menomenies should be surrendered or taken, the department ordered General Atkinson, on the 7th of March last, to ascend the Mississippi with the disposable regular troops at Jefferson barracks, and to carry into effect the instructions issued by your direction. Still further to strengthen the frontiers, orders were given for the re-occupation of Chicago.

"The demand for the surrender of the Menomenie murderers was entirely disregarded: and the British party of the Sacs and Foxes re-crossed the Mississippi, and assuming a hostile attitude, established themselves upon Rock river. The subsequent events are well known, and the result has already been stated in this report."

In the annual report of Maj. General Macomb to Congress, of November 1832, very much the same positions are taken in regard to the causes which led to this contest with the Indians, that are contained in the report from the War Department. Its leading object seems to be to place the United States in the right—the Indians in the wrong.

It is to be regretted that the Honorable Secretary, whose opinions and statements on all subjects connected with the Indians, carry with them great weight, had not been more explicit, in assigning the causes which led to the late war, with a portion of the Sacs and Foxes. It is not to be supposed that the Secretary would designedly omit any thing, which in his opinion, was necessary, to a fair presentation of this matter; but as the case stands, his statement does not, it is believed, do justice to the Indians. The Secretary says the Sacs and Foxes "have always been discontented, keeping the frontier in alarm, and continually committing some outrage on the persons or property of the inhabitants." Between the treaty of peace at Portage des Sioux, in 1816, and the attack of Major Stillman, in 1832, it is supposed that the Sacs and Foxes never killed one American; and, their aggressions upon the persons and property of the whites, consisted principally, in an attempt to retain possession of their village and corn-fields, when pressed upon by the white settlers, who, in violation of the laws of Congress and express treaty provisions, were committing outrages upon the Indians: The report of the Secretary further states, that the Sacs and Foxes "claimed the right of occupying a part of the country upon Rock river, even after it had been sold to citizens of the United States, and settled by them." But the report does not state that under the treaty of 1804, by which these lands were ceded, it is expressly provided that so long as they remain the property of the United States, the Indians of said tribes shall enjoy the privilege of "living and hunting upon them;" it does not state that for six or eight years before the government had sold an acre of land upon Rock river, the white settlers were there, in violation of the laws, trespassing upon these Indians, and thus creating that very hostility of feeling, which, is subsequently cited as a reason for the chastisement inflicted upon them by the United States: it does not state, that in the year 1829, government, for the purpose of creating a pretext for the removal of the Indians from Rock river, directed a few quarter sections of land, including the Sac village, to be sold, although the frontier settlements of Illinois had not then reached within fifty or sixty miles of that place, and millions of acres of land around it, were unoccupied and unsold: it does not state that instead of requiring the Indians to remove from the quarter sections thus prematurely sold, to other lands on Rock river, owned by the United States, and on which, under the treaty, they had a right to hunt and reside, they were commanded to remove to the west side of the Mississippi: it does not state, that the "serious aggressions" and "formidable attitude" assumed by the "British party," in 1831, consisted in their attempt to raise a crop of corn and beans, in throwing down the fences of the whites who were enclosing their fields, in "pointing deadly weapons" at them and in "stealing their potatoes:" it does not state that the murder of the Menominie Indians, at Fort Crawford, by a party of the "British band," was in retaliation, for a similar "flagrant outrage," committed the summer previous, by the Menominies, upon Peah-mus-ka, a principal chief of the Foxes and nine or ten of his tribe, who were going up to Prairie des Chiens on business and were within one day's travel of that place: it does not state that one reason assigned by the "British party" for refusing to surrender the murderers of the Menominies, was the fact that the government had not made a similar demand of that tribe for the murderers of the Sacs: it does not state that the "hostile attitude" assumed by the Sacs and Foxes, in 1832, after recrossing the Mississippi, and their establishment on Rock river, simply amounted to this; that they came over with their women and children for the avowed purpose of raising a crop of corn with the Winnebagoes—were temporarily encamped on that stream—had committed no outrage upon person or property—and were actually engaged in entertaining some guests with a dog-feast, when the Illinois militia approached their camp, and killed the bearer of a white flag, which Black Hawk sent to them, in token of his peaceable disposition. These may be unimportant omissions, in the opinion of the Secretary, but in looking to the causes which led to this contest, and the spirit in which it was conducted, they have been deemed of sufficient importance, to receive a passing notice, when referring to his report.

The opinion has been expressed more than once in the course of this work, that there was in reality, no necessity for this war. A firm but forbearing course of policy, on the part of the United States, towards this discontented fragment of the Sacs and Foxes, would, it is believed, have prevented any serious aggression upon our people or their property. Certain it is, that a few thousand dollars, superadded to a humane spirit of conciliation, would have effected the permanent removal of Black Hawk and his band, to the west side of the Mississippi: and, as the government was not contending with them, in support of its national faith, nor about to punish them for an insult to its national honour, there could have been no disgrace in purchasing the settlement of the difficulty, on such terms. It has been stated that in the spring of 1831, Black Hawk agreed to remove his band to the west side of the Mississippi, and relinquish all claims to the lands upon Rock river, if the United States would pay him six thousand dollars, with which to purchase provisions and other necessaries for his people, and that the Indian agent at St. Louis, was informed of this fact. Moreover, it has been publicly alleged that before the campaign against Black Hawk, in the summer of 1832, the President and Secretary at War, were both informed, that the "British Band" of the Sacs and Foxes, could be peaceably removed to the west side of the Mississippi for six or eight thousand dollars. The secretary was assured, in the presence of a member of congress, that the inquiry had been made by a person familiar with the Indians, and the fact of their willingness to remove upon these terms distinctly ascertained.[2]

Under the treaty of 1804, the Sacs and Foxes ceded to the United States, more than twenty millions of acres of first rate land, for less than twenty thousand dollars. Black Hawk not only contended for the invalidity of this treaty, but insisted that the price paid by the United States was wholly below the value of the land. Under such circumstances, the course of the government was obvious—to have quieted the complaints of the Indians and secured their peaceable removal to the west, by a second

---

2. See St. Louis Times of 13th April, 1833.

purchase of their interest to the territory in question. Had it cost twenty, fifty or one hundred thousand dollars, to effect this object, our country would still have been the gainer, both by the preservation of the national faith and the national treasure—for the former was wantonly violated, and the latter uselessly squandered. The contest with Black Hawk and his party, destroyed the lives of four or five hundred Indian men, women and children—about two hundred citizens of the United States—and cost the government near two millions of dollars! Such are the results of a war commenced and waged by a great nation, upon a remnant of poor ignorant savages;—a war which had its origin in avarice and political ambition, which was prosecuted in bad faith and closed in dishonor.

34

WILLIAM CULLEN BRYANT

(1794–1878)

In the summer of 1832, the increasingly popular successful editor and poet, William Cullen Bryant, left New York to visit his brothers in Illinois. Steven Olson has meticulously traced the development of Bryant's impressions of his travels from their first appearance in his journals, then in letters he sent east to friends, and finally in poetic form. Olson finds that Bryant's initial engagement with the often tedious and drudging life in the settlement shifted to an increasingly romantic perspective. The poem "The Prairies" that resulted from this process, at first published in 1833, assumes a sweeping historical gaze. The poet looks over the pastures of Illinois and finds himself unable to find the words in English to describe them. By using a French word, Bryant engages a literary effort to move toward a uniquely American way of describing the nation's landscapes. However, Bryant still writes as an easterner, and tries, like Cooper, to write the history of the west as a continuation of the processes begun in the east. Bryant imagines a "disciplined and populous race" that inhabited the Mississippi valley prior to the Native Americans encountered by the Americans. This race, of course, more closely resembles the Yankee settlement of the west represented by Bryant's brothers, and, hence, white Americans are the natural inheritors of the land. Unlike many eastern writers, however, Bryant is deeply ambiguous about the process. The poem often reads more like an elegy than a celebration, and the poet ends up alone in the wilderness, unable to join the "advancing multitude" destined to inhabit the region. More like Joseph Snelling or Margaret Fuller—other easterners who wrote after brief stays in the west—Bryant reminds us that the process of the settlement of the west inspired in many Americans deep doubts and troubling notions of the legitimacy of the enterprise.

Text: "The Prairies" (*Poems*, 1834).

THE PRAIRIES (1833)

These are the gardens of the Desert, these
The unshorn fields, boundless and beautiful,
For which the speech of England has no name—
The Prairies. I behold them for the first,
5   And my heart swells, while the dilated sight
Takes in the encircling vastness. Lo! they stretch
In airy undulations, far away,
As if the Ocean, in his gentlest swell,
Stood still, with all his rounded billows fixed,
10 And motionless forever. Motionless?—
No—they are all unchained again. The clouds
Sweep over with their shadows, and, beneath,
The surface rolls and fluctuates to the eye;[1]
Dark hollows seem to glide along and chase
15 The sunny ridges. Breezes of the South!
Who toss the golden and the flame-like flowers,
And pass the prairie-hawk that, poised on high,
Flaps his broad wings, yet moves not—ye have played
Among the palms of Mexico and vines
20 Of Texas, and have crisped the limited brooks
That from the fountains of Sonora glide
Into the calm Pacific—have ye fanned
A nobler or a lovelier scene than this?
Man hath no part in all this glorious work:
25 The hand that built the firmament hath heaved
And smoothed these verdant swells, and sown their slopes
With herbage, planted them with island-groves,
And hedged them round with forests. Fitting floor
For this magnificent temple of the sky—
30 With flowers whose glory and whose multitude
Rival the constellations! The great heavens
Seem to stoop down upon the scene in love,—
A nearer vault, and of a tenderer blue,
Than that which bends above our Eastern hills.

35   As o'er the verdant waste I guide my steed,
Among the high rank grass that sweeps his sides
The hollow beating of his footstep seems

---

1. The prairies of the West, with an undulating surface, *rolling prairies,* as they are called, present to the unaccustomed eye a singular spectacle when the shadows of the clouds are passing rapidly over them. The face of the ground seems to fluctuate and toss like billows of the sea (Bryant's note).

A sacrilegious sound. I think of those
Upon whose rest he tramples. Are they here—
40   The dead of other days?—and did the dust
Of these fair solitudes once stir with life
And burn with passion? Let the mighty mounds
That overlook the rivers, or that rise
In the dim forest crowded with old oaks,
45   Answer. A race, that long has passed away,
Built them; a disciplined and populous race
Heaped, with long toil, the earth, while yet the Greek
Was hewing the Pentelicus² to forms
Of symmetry, and rearing on its rock
50   The glittering Parthenon. These ample fields
Nourished their harvests, here their herds were fed,
When haply by their stalls the bison lowed,
And bowed his manéd shoulder to the yoke.
All day this desert murmured with their toils,
55   Till twilight blushed, and lovers walked, and wooed
In a forgotten language, and old tunes,
From instruments of unremembered form,
Gave the soft winds a voice. The red-man came—
The roaming hunter-tribes, warlike and fierce,
60   And the mound-builders vanished from the earth.
The solitude of centuries untold
Has settled where they dwelt. The prairie-wolf
Hunts in their meadows, and his fresh-dug den
Yawns by my path. The gopher mines the ground
65   Where stood their swarming cities. All is gone;
All—save the piles of earth that hold their bones,
The platforms where they worshipped unknown gods,
The barriers which they builded from the soil
To keep the foe at bay—till o'er the walls
70   The wild beleaguerers broke, and, one by one,
The strongholds of the plain were forced, and heaped
With corpses. The brown vultures of the wood
Flocked to those vast uncovered sepulchres,
And sat, unscared and silent, at their feast.
75   Haply some solitary fugitive,
Lurking in marsh and forest, till the sense
Of desolation and of fear became
Bitterer than death, yielded himself to die.
Man's better nature triumphed then. Kind words
80   Welcomed and soothed him; the rude conquerors
Seated the captive with their chiefs; he chose

---

2. A mountain near Athens, famous for marble.

A bride among their maidens, and at length
Seemed to forget—yet ne'er forgot—the wife
Of his first love, and her sweet little ones,
85 Butchered, amid their shrieks, with all his race.

   Thus change the forms of being. Thus arise
Races of living things, glorious in strength,
And perish, as the quickening breath of God
Fills them, or is withdrawn. The red-man, too,
90 Has left the blooming wilds he ranged so long,
And, nearer to the Rocky Mountains, sought
A wilder hunting-ground. The beaver builds
No longer by these streams, but far away,
On waters whose blue surface ne'er gave back
95 The white man's face—among Missouri's springs,
And pools whose issues swell the Oregon—
He rears his little Venice. In these plains
The bison feeds no more. Twice twenty leagues
Beyond remotest smoke of hunter's camp,
100 Roams the majestic brute, in herds that shake
The earth with thundering steps—yet here I meet
His ancient footprints stamped beside the pool.

   Still this great solitude is quick with life.
Myriads of insects, gaudy as the flowers
105 They flutter over, gentle quadrupeds,
And birds, that scarce have learned the fear of man,
Are here, and sliding reptiles of the ground,
Startlingly beautiful. The graceful deer
Bounds to the wood at my approach. The bee,
110 A more adventurous colonist than man,
With whom he came across the eastern deep,
Fills the savannas with his murmurings,
And hides his sweets, as in the golden age,
Within the hollow oak. I listen long
115 To his domestic hum, and think I hear
The sound of that advancing multitude
Which soon shall fill these deserts. From the ground
Comes up the laugh of children, the soft voice
Of maidens, and the sweet and solemn hymn
120 Of Sabbath worshippers. The low of herds
Blends with the rustling of the heavy grain
Over the dark-brown furrows. All at once
A fresher wind sweeps by, and breaks my dream,
And I am in the wilderness alone.

35

THOMAS FORD

(1800–1850)

In 1839, Joseph Smith, founder and leader of the Church of Jesus Christ of Latter Day Saints, also known as the Mormons, arrived in the western Illinois town of Nauvoo, having been forcibly removed from previous settlements in Ohio and Missouri. The first west was home to many dissident religious sects and sites of socioreligious experimentation, from the Owenites at New Harmony, Indiana, to the Mennonites of Goshen, Indiana, to the Amish of southern Indiana and central Illinois. The antebellum west allowed many groups to practice their faith without fear of molestation or persecution. Such was not the case with the Mormons.

On June 27, 1844, Joseph Smith, his brother Hiram, and some of their followers were murdered by a mob in the jail in Carthage, Illinois. The governor of Illinois at the time was Thomas Ford. Ford had seen the crisis rising since the destruction of the Mormons' newspaper and its press on June 14, and had traveled to the area in an effort to keep the peace. His rather elliptical defense and explanation of his actions reveals much about the precariousness of government in the west.

First, Ford confesses to being poorly informed throughout about the nature of the Mormons and their response to their rejection by the other citizens of the state. Ford makes it clear that the "anti-Mormons'" objected to more than the Mormons' religious beliefs. The Mormons' sense of collective identity, as Ford explains it, was at the heart of the problems. Furthermore, despite his rank as governor, Ford is largely powerless against the mob, and fears for his own life from both the Mormons and the mob.

Actually, only Ford's political life ended in Nauvoo. He was not reelected in 1846, and he retired to write the book excerpted here. The Mormons left Nauvoo in 1846 and, under the leadership of Brigham Young, moved to Utah, where they established their permanent settlement.

Text: *A History of Illinois from Its Commencement as a State in 1818 to 1847* (Chicago, 1854): 330–356.

. . . These people had undertaken to innovate upon the established systems of religion. Their legal right to do so, no one will question. But all history bears testimony that innovations upon religion have always been attended by a hostility in the public mind, which sometimes has produced the most desolating wars: always more or less of persecution. Even the innocent Quakers, the unoffending Shakers, and the quiet and orderly Methodists in their origin, and until the world got used to them, had enough of persecution to encounter. But if either of these sects had congregated in one city where the world could never get to know them; could never ascertain by personal acquaintance the truth or falsity of many reports which are always circulated to the prejudice of such innovators; and moreover, if they had armed themselves and organized into a military legion as the citizens of Nauvoo, and had been guilty of high-handed proceedings carried on against the heretical press, the public animosity and their persecutions must have greatly increased in rancor and severity.

In addition to these causes of excitement, there were a great many reports in circulation, and generally believed by the people. These reports I have already alluded to, and they had much influence in swelling the public excitement.

It was asserted that Joe Smith, the founder and head of the Mormon church, had caused himself to be crowned and annointed king of the Mormons; that he had embodied a band of his followers called "Danites," who were sworn to obey him as God, and to do his commands, murder and treason not excepted; that he had instituted an order in the church, whereby those who composed it were pretended to be sealed up to eternal life against all crimes, save the shedding of innocent blood or consenting thereto. That this order was instructed that no blood was innocent blood, except that of the members of the church; and that these two orders were made the ministers of his vengeance, and the instruments of an intolerable tyranny which he had established over his people, and which he was about to extend over the neighboring country. The people affected to believe that with this power in the hands of an unscrupulous leader, there was no safety for the lives or property of any one who should oppose him. They affected likewise to believe that Smith inculcated the legality of perjury, or any other crime in defence, or to advance the interests of true believers; and that himself had set them the example by swearing to a false accusation against a certain person, for the crime of murder. It was likewise asserted to be a fundamental article of the Mormon faith, that God had given the world and all it contained to them as his saints; that they secretly believed in their right to all the goodly lands, farms, and property in the country; that at present they were kept out of their rightful inheritance by force; that consequently there was no moral offence in anticipating God's good time to put them in possession by stealing, if opportunity offered; that in fact the whole church was a community of murderers, thieves, robbers, and outlaws; that Joseph Smith had established a bogus factory in Nauvoo, for the manufacture of counterfeit money; and that he maintained about his person a tribe of swindlers, blacklegs, and counterfeiters, to make it and put it into circulation.

It was also believed that he had announced a revelation from heaven, sanctioning polygamy, by a kind of spiritual wife system, whereby a man was allowed one wife in pursuance of the laws of the country, and an indefinite number of others, to be employed in some mystical and spiritual mode; and that he himself, and many of his followers, had practiced upon the precepts of this revelation by seducing a large number of women.

It was also asserted that he was in alliance with the Indians of the western territories, and had obtained over them such a control, that in case of a war he could command their assistance to murder his enemies.

Upon the whole, if one-half of these reports had been true, the Mormon community must have been the most intolerable collection of rogues ever assembled; or, if one-half them were false, they were the most maligned and abused.

But the great cause of popular fury was, that the Mormons at several preceding elections, had cast their vote as a unit; thereby making the fact apparent, that no one could aspire to the honors or offices of the country within the sphere of their influence, without their approbation and votes. It appears to be one of the principles by which they insist on being governed as a community, to act as a unit in all matters of government and religion. They express themselves to be fearful that if division should be encouraged in politics, it would extend to their religion, and rend their church with schism and into sects.

This one principle and practice of theirs arrayed against them in deadly hostility all aspirants for office who were not sure of their support, all who have been unsuccessful in elections, and all who were too proud to court their influence, with all their friends and connections.

These also were the active men in blowing up the fury of the people, in hopes that a popular movement might be set on foot which would result in the expulsion or extermination of the Mormon voters. For this purpose, public meetings had been called, inflammatory speeches had been made, exaggerated reports had been extensively circulated, committees had been appointed, who rode night and day to spread the reports, and solicit the aid of neighboring counties. And at a public meeting at Warsaw, resolutions were passed to expel or exterminate the Mormon population.

This was not, however, a movement which was unanimously concurred in. . . .

A system of excitement and agitation was artfully planned and executed with tact. It consisted in spreading reports and rumors of the most fearful character.

As examples: On the morning before my arrival at Carthage [June 21, 1844], I was awakened at an early hour by the frightful report, which was asserted with confidence and apparent consternation, that the Mormons had already commenced the work of burning, destruction, and murder, and that every man capable of bearing arms was instantly wanted at Carthage for the protection of the country. We lost no time in starting; but when we arrived at Carthage we could hear no more concerning this story. Again: during the few days that the militia were encamped at Carthage, frequent applications were made to me to send a force here and a force there, and a force all about the country, to prevent murders, robberies, and larcenies, which it was said were threatened by the Mormons. No such forces were sent, nor were any such offences committed at that time, except the stealing of some provisions, and there was never the least proof that this was done by a Mormon. Again: on my late visit to Hancock county, I was informed by some of their violent enemies that the larcenies of the Mormons had become unusually numerous and insufferable. They indeed admitted that but little had been done in this way in their immediate vicinity; but they insisted that sixteen horses had been stolen by the Mormons in one night, near Lima, in the county of Adams. At the close of the expedition, I called at this same town of Lima, and upon inquiry was told that no horses had been stolen in that neighborhood, but that sixteen horses had been stolen in one night in Hancock county. This last informant being told of the Hancock story, again changed the venue to another distant settlement in the northern edge of Adams.

As my object in visiting Hancock was expressly to assist in the execution of the laws, and not to violate them, or to witness or permit their violation, as I was convinced that the Mormon leaders had committed a crime in the destruction of the press and had resisted the execution of process, I determined to exert the whole force of the state, if necessary, to bring them to justice. But seeing the great excitement in the public mind, and the manifest tendency of this excitement to run into mobocracy, I was of opinion that before I acted I ought to obtain a pledge from the officers and men to support me in strictly legal measures, and to protect the prisoners in case they surrendered. For I was determined, if possible, that the forms of law should not be made the catspaw of a mob, to seduce these people to quiet surrender, as the convenient victims of popular fury. I therefore called together the whole force then assembled at Carthage, and made an address, explaining to them what I could, and what I could not, legally do; and also adducing to them various reasons why they, as well as the Mormons, should submit to the laws, and why, if they had resolved upon revolutionary proceedings, their purpose should be abandoned. The assembled troops seemed much pleased with the address, and upon its conclusion the officers and men unanimously voted, with acclamation, to sustain me in a strictly legal course, and that the prisoners should be protected from violence. Upon the arrival of additional forces from Warsaw, McDonough, and Schuyler, similar addresses were made, with the same result.

It seemed to me that these votes fully authorized me to promise the accused Mormons the protection of the law in case they surrendered. They were accordingly informed that if they surrendered they would be protected, and if they did not, the whole force of the state would be called out, if necessary, to compel their submission.

On the 23rd or 24th of June, Joe Smith, the mayor of Nauvoo, together with his brother Hiram, and all the members of the council, and all others demanded, came into Carthage and surrendered themselves prisoners to the constable on the charge of riot. They all voluntarily entered into a recognizance before the justice of the peace for their appearance at court to answer the charge, and all of them were discharged from custody except Joe and Hiram Smith, against whom the magistrate had issued a new writ, on a complaint of treason. They were immediately arrested by the constable on this charge, and retained in his custody to answer it.

The overt act of treason charged against them consisted in the alleged levying of war against the state by declaring martial law in Nauvoo, and in ordering out the Legion to resist the *posse comitatus*. Their actual guiltiness of the charge would depend upon circumstances. If their opponents had been seeking to put the law in force in good faith, and nothing more, then an array of military force in open resistance to the *posse comitatus* and the militia of the state most probably would have amounted to treason. But if those opponents merely intended to use the process of the law, the militia of the state, and the *posse comitatus,* as catspaws to compass the possession of their persons for the purpose of murdering them afterwards, as the sequel demonstrated the fact to be it might well be doubted whether they were guilty of treason.

After the Smiths had been arrested on the new charge of treason, the justice of the peace postponed the examination, because neither of the parties were prepared with their witnesses for trial. In the meantime he committed them to the jail of the country for greater security.

In all this matter the justice of the peace and the constable, though humble in office, were acting in a high and independent capacity, far beyond any legal power in me to control. I considered that the executive power could only be called in to assist, and not to dictate or control their action; that in the humble sphere of their duties they were as independent, and clothed with as high authority by the law, as the executive department, and that my province was simply to aid them with the force of the state. It is true, that so far as I could prevail on them by advice, I endeavored to do so. The prisoners were not in military custody, or prisoners of war, and I could no more legally control these officers than I could the superior courts of justice.

Some persons have supposed that I ought to have had them sent to some distant and friendly part of the state for confinement and trial and that I ought to have searched them for concealed arms; but these surmises and suppositions are readily disposed of by the fact, that they were not my prisoners, but were the prisoners of the constable and jailor, under the direction of the justice of the peace. And also by the fact that by law they could be tried in no other county than Hancock.

The jail in which they were confined, is a considerable stone building containing a residence for the jailer, cells for the close and secure confinement of the prisoners, and one larger room, not so strong, but more airy and comfortable than the cells. They were put into the cells by the jailer; but upon their remonstrance and request, and by my advice, they were transferred to the larger room; and there they remained until the final catastrophe. Neither they nor I, seriously apprehended an attack on the jail through the guard stationed to protect it, nor did I apprehend the least danger on their part of an attempt to escape. For I was very sure that any such attempt would have been the signal for their immediate death. Indeed, if they had escaped, it would have been fortunate for the purposes of those who were anxious for the expulsion of the Mormon population. For the great body of that people would most assuredly have followed their prophet and principal leaders, as they did in their flight from Missouri.[1]

The force assembled at Carthage amounted to about twelve or thirteen hundred men, and it was calculated that four or five hundred more were assembled at Warsaw. Nearly all that portion resident in Hancock were anxious to be marched into Nauvoo. This measure was supposed to be necessary to search for counterfeit money and the apparatus to make it, and also to strike a salutary terror into the Mormon people by an exhibition of the force of the State, and thereby prevent future outrages, murders, rob-

---

1. I learned afterwards that the leaders of the anti-Mormons did much to stimulate their followers to the murder of the Smiths in jail, by alleging that the governor intended to favor their escape. If this had been true, and could have been well carried out, it would have been the best way of getting rid of the Mormons. These leaders of the Mormons would never have dared to return, and they would have been followed in their flight by all of their church. I had such a plan in my mind, but I had never breathed it to a living soul, and was thus thwarted in ridding the State of the Mormons two years before they actually left, by the insane frenzy of the anti-Mormons. Joe Smith, when he escaped from Missouri, had no difficulty in again collecting his sect about him at Nauvoo; and so the twelve apostles, after they had been at the head of affairs long enough to establish their authority and influence as leaders, had no difficulty in getting nearly the whole body of Mormons to follow them into the wilderness two years after the death of their pretended prophet.

beries, burnings, and the like, apprehended as the effect of Mormon vengeance, on those who had taken a part against them. On my part, at one time, this arrangement was agreed to. The morning of the 27th day of June was appointed for the march; and Golden's Point, near the Mississippi river, and about equidistant from Nauvoo and Warsaw, was selected as the place of rendezvous. I had determined to prevail on the justice to bring out his prisoners, and take them along. A council of officers, however, determined that this would be highly inexpedient and dangerous, and offered such substantial reasons for their opinions as induced me to change my resolution.

Two or three days' preparation had been made for this expedition. I observed that some of the people became more and more excited and inflammatory the further the preparations were advanced. Occasional threats came to my ears of destroying the city and murdering or expelling the inhabitants.

I had no objection to ease the terrors of the people by such a display of force, and was most anxious also to search for the alleged apparatus for making counterfeit money; and, in fact, to inquire into all the charges against that people, if I could have been assured of my command against mutiny and insubordination. But I gradually learned, to my entire satisfaction, that there was a plan to get the troops into Nauvoo, and there to begin the war, probably by some of our own party, or some of the seceding Mormons, taking advantage of the night, to fire on our own force, and then laying it on the Mormons. I was satisfied that there were those amongst us fully capable of such an act, hoping that in the alarm, bustle, and confusion of a militia camp, the truth could not be discovered, and that it might lead to the desired collision.

The officers insisted much in council upon the necessity of marching to that place [Nauvoo] to search for apparatus to make counterfeit money, and more particularly to terrify the Mormons from attempting any open or secret measures of vengeance against the citizens of the county, who had taken a part against them or their leaders. To ease their terrors on this head, I proposed to them that I would myself proceed to the city, accompanied by a small force, make the proposed search, and deliver an address to the Mormons, and tell them plainly what degree of excitement and hatred prevailed against them in the minds of the whole people, and that if any open or secret violence should be committed on the persons or property of those who had taken part against them, that no one would doubt that it had been perpetrated by them, and that it would be the sure and certain means of the destruction of their city and the extermination of their people.

I ordered two companies, under the command of Captain R. F. Smith, of the Carthage Grays, to guard the jail. In selecting these companies, and particularly the company of the Carthage Grays for this service, I have been subjected to some censure. It has been said that this company had already been guilty of mutiny, and had been ordered to be arrested whilst in the encampment at Carthage; and that they and their officers were the deadly enemies of the prisoners. Indeed it would have been difficult to find friends of the prisoners under my command, unless I had called in the Mormons as a guard; and this I was satisfied would have led to the immediate war, and the sure death of the prisoners.

Although I knew that this company were the enemies of the Smiths, yet I had confidence in their loyalty and integrity; because their captain was universally spoken of as a most respectable citizen and honorable man. The company itself was an old independent company, well armed, uniformed, and drilled; the members of it were the elite of the militia of the county. I relied upon this company especially, because it was an independent company, for a long time instructed and practiced in military discipline and subordination. I also had their word and honor, officers and men, to do their duty according to law. Besides all this, the officers and most of the men resided in Carthage, in the near vicinity of Nauvoo; and, as I thought, must know that they would make themselves and their property convenient and conspicuous marks of Mormon vengeance, in case they were guilty of treachery.

I had at first intended to select a guard from the country of McDonough, but the militia of that county were very much dissatisfied to remain; their crops were suffering at home; they were in a perfect fever to be discharged; and I was destitute of provisions to supply them for more than a few days. They were far from home, where they could not supply themselves. Whilst the Carthage company could board at their own houses, and would be put to little inconvenience in comparison.

It is true, also, that at this time I had not believed or suspected that any attack was to be made upon the prisoners in jail. It is true that I was aware that a great deal of hatred existed against them, and that there were those who would do them an injury if they could. I had heard of some threats being made, but none of an attack on the prisoners whilst in jail. These threats seemed to be made by individuals not acting in concert. They were no more than the bluster which might have been expected, and furnished no indication of numbers combining for this or any other purpose.

I must here be permitted to say, also, that frequent appeals had been made to me to make a clean and thorough work of the matter, by exterminating the Mormons, or expelling them from the State. An opinion seemed generally to prevail, that the sanction of executive authority would legalize the act; and all persons of any influence, authority, or note, who conversed with me on the subject, frequently and repeatedly stated their total unwillingness to act without my direction, or in any mode except according to law.

Having ordered the guard [of the jail], and left General Deming in command in Carthage, and discharged the residue of the militia, I immediately departed for Nauvoo, eighteen miles distant, accompanied by Colonel Buckmaster, Quartermaster-General, and Capt. Dunn's company of dragoons.

After we had proceeded four miles, Colonel Buckmaster intimated to me a suspicion that an attack would be made upon the jail. He stated the matter as a mere suspicion, arising from having seen two persons converse together at Carthage with some air of mystery. I myself entertained no suspicion of such an attack; at any rate, none before the next day in the afternoon; because it was notorious that we had departed from Carthage with the declared intention of being absent at least two days. I could not believe that any person would attack the jail whilst we were in Nauvoo, and thereby expose my life and the life of my companions to the sudden vengeance of the Mormons, upon hearing of the death of their leaders. Nevertheless, acting upon the principle of providing against mere possibilities, I sent back one of the companies with a special order to Capt. Smith to guard the jail strictly, and at the peril of his life, until my return.

We proceeded on our journey four miles further. By this time I had convinced myself that no attack would be made on the jail that day or night. I supposed that a regard for my safety and the safety of my companions would prevent an attack until those to be engaged in it could be assured of our departure from Nauvoo. I still think that this ought to have appeared to me to be a reasonable supposition.

I therefore determined at this point to omit making the search for counterfeit money at Nauvoo, and defer an examination of all the other abominations charged on that people, in order to return to Carthage that same night, that I might be on the ground in person, in time to prevent an attack upon the jail, if any had been meditated. To this end we called a halt; the baggage wagons were ordered to remain where they were until towards evening, and then return to Carthage.

Having made these arrangements we proceeded on our march and arrived at Nauvoo about four o'clock of the afternoon of the 27th day of June. As soon as notice could be given, a crowd of the citizens assembled to hear an address which I proposed to deliver to them. The number present has been variously estimated from one to five thousand.

In this address I stated to them how, and in what, their functionaries had violated the laws. Also, the many scandalous reports in circulation against them, and that these reports, whether true or false, were generally believed by the people. I distinctly stated to them the amount of hatred and prejudice which prevailed everywhere against them, and the causes of it, at length.

I also told them, plainly and emphatically, that if any vengeance should be attempted openly or secretly against the persons or property of the citizens who had taken part against their leaders, that the public hatred and excitement was such, that thousands would assemble for the total destruction of their city and the extermination of their people; and that no power in the state would be able to prevent it. During this address some impatience and resentment were manifested by the Mormons, at the recital of the various reports enumerated concerning them; which they strenuously and indignantly denied to be true. They claimed to be a law-abiding people, and insisted that as they looked to the law alone for their protection, so were they careful themselves to observe its provisions. Upon the conclusion of this address, I proposed a vote on the question, whether they would strictly observe the laws, even in opposition to their prophet and leaders. The vote was unanimous in favor of this proposition.

The anti-Mormons contended that such a vote from the Mormons signified nothing; and truly the subsequent history of that people showed clearly that they were loudest in their professions of attachment to the law whenever they were guilty of the greatest extravagances; and in fact that they were so ignorant and stupid about matters of law, that they had no means of judging the legality of their conduct, only as they were instructed by their spiritual leaders.

A short time before sundown we departed on our return to Carthage. When we had proceeded two miles we met two individuals, one of them a Mormon, who informed us that the Smiths had been assassinated in jail, about five or six o'clock of that day. The intelligence seemed to strike every one with a kind of dumbness. As to myself, it was perfectly astounding; and I anticipated the very worst consequences from it. The Mormons had been represented to me as a lawless, infatuated, and fanatical people, not governed by the ordinary motives which influence the rest of mankind. If so, most likely an exterminating war would ensue, and the whole land would be covered with desolation.

Acting upon this supposition, it was my duty to provide as well as I could for the event. I therefore ordered the two messengers into custody, and to be returned with us to Carthage. This was done to get time to make such arrangements as could be made, and to prevent any sudden explosion of Mormon excitement before they could be written to by their friends at Carthage. I also dispatched messengers to Warsaw, to advise the citizens of the event. But the people there knew all about the matter before my messengers arrived. They, like myself, anticipated a general attack all over the country. The women and children were removed across the river; and a committee was dispatched that night to Quincy for assistance. The next morning by daylight the ringing of bells in the city of Quincy, announced a public meeting. The people assembled in great numbers at an early hour. The Warsaw committee stated to the meeting that a party of Mormons had attempted to rescue the Smiths out of jail; that a party of Missourians and others, had killed the prisoners to prevent their escape; that the governor and his party were at Nauvoo at the time when intelligence of the fact was brought there; that they had been attacked by the Nauvoo legion, and had retreated to a house where they were then closely besieged. That the governor had sent out word that he could maintain his position for two days, and would be certain to be massacred if assistance did not arrive by the end of that time. It is unnecessary to say that the entire story was a fabrication. It was of a piece with the other reports put into circulation by the anti-Mormon party, to influence the public mind and call the people to their assistance. The effect of it, however, was that by ten o'clock on the 28th of June, between two and three hundred men from Quincy, under the command of Major Flood, embarked on board of a steamboat for Nauvoo, to assist in raising the siege, as they honestly believed.

As for myself, I was well convinced that those, whoever they were, who assassinated the Smiths, meditated in turn my assassination by the Mormons. The very circumstances of the case fully corroborated the information which I afterwards received, that upon consultation of the assassins it was agreed amongst them that the murder must be committed whilst the governor was at Nauvoo; that the Mormons would naturally suppose that he had planned it; and that in the first outpouring of their indignation they would assassinate him, by way of retaliation. And that thus they would get clear of the Smiths and the governor, all at once. They also supposed, that if they could so contrive the matter as to have the governor of the State assassinated by the Mormons, the public excitement would be greatly increased against that people, and would result in their expulsion from the State at least.

Upon hearing of the assassination of the Smiths, I was sensible that my command was at an end; that my destruction was meditated as well as that of the Mormons; and that I could not reasonably confide longer in the one party or in the other.

The question then arose, what would be proper to be done. A war was expected by everybody. I was desirous of preserving the peace. I could not put myself at the head of the Mormon force with any kind of propriety, and without exciting greater odium against them than already existed. I could not put myself at the head of the anti-Mormon party, because they had justly forfeited my confidence, and my command over them was put an end to by mutiny and treachery. . . .

For these reasons I determined to proceed to Quincy, a place favorably situated. . . . But first, I determined to return back to Carthage, and make such arrangements as could be made for the pacification and defence of the country. . . .

Here also I found Dr. Richards and John Taylor, two of the principal Mormon leaders, who had been in the jail at the time of the attack, and who voluntarily addressed a most pacific exhortation to their fellow citizens, which was the first intelligence of the murder which was received at Nauvoo. I think it very probable that the subsequent good conduct of the Mormons is attributable to the arrest of the messengers, and to the influence of this letter.

It was many days after the assassination of the Smiths before the circumstances of the murder fully became known. It then appeared that, agreeably to previous orders, the posse at Warsaw had marched on the morning of the 27th of June in the direction of Golden's Point, with a view to join the force from Carthage, the whole body then to be marched into Nauvoo. But by the time they had gone eight miles, they were met by the order to disband; and learning at the same time that the governor was absent at Nauvoo, about two hundred of these men, many of them being disguised by blacking their faces with powder and mud, hastened immediately to Carthage. There they encamped, at some distance from the village, and soon learned that one of the companies left as a guard had disbanded and returned to their homes; the other company, the Carthage Grays, was stationed by the captain in the public square, a hundred and fifty yards from the jail. Whilst eight men were detailed by him, under the command of Sergeant Franklin A. Worrell, to guard the prisoners. A communication was soon established between the conspirators and the company; and it was arranged that the guard was to have their guns charged with blank cartridges, and fire at the assailants when they attempted to enter the jail. Gen. Deming, who was left in command, being deserted by some of his troops, and perceiving the arrangement with the others, and having no force upon which he could rely, for fear of his life retired from the village. The conspirators came up, jumped the slight fence around the jail, were fired upon by the guard which, according to arrangement, was overpowered immediately, and the assailants entered the prison, to the door of the room where the two prisoners were confined, with two of their friends, who voluntarily bore them company. An attempt was made to break open the door; but Joe Smith being armed with a six-barrelled pistol, furnished by his friends, fired several times as the door was bursted open, and wounded three of the assailants. At the same time several shots were fired into the room, by some of which John Taylor received four wounds, and Hiram Smith was instantly killed. Joe Smith now attempted to escape by jumping out of the second-story window; but the fall so stunned him that he was unable to rise; and being placed in a sitting posture by the conspirators below, they dispatched him with four balls shot through his body.

Thus fell Joe Smith, the most successful impostor in modern times; a man who, though ignorant and coarse, had some great natural parts, which fitted him for temporary success, but which were so obscured and counteracted by the inherent corruption and vices of his nature, that he never could succeed in establishing a system of policy which looked to permanent success in the future. His lusts, his love of money and power, always set him to studying present gratification and convenience, rather than the remote consequences of his plans. It seems that no power of intellect can save a corrupt man from this error. The strong cravings of the animal nature will never give fair play to a fine understanding, the judgment is never allowed to choose that good which is far away, in preference to enticing evil near at hand. And this may be considered a wise ordinance of Providence, by which the counsels of talented but corrupt men, are defeated in the very act which promised success.

It must not be supposed that the pretended prophet practiced the tricks of a common impostor; that he was a dark and gloomy person, with a long beard, a grave and severe aspect, and a reserved and saintly carriage of his person; on the contrary, he was full of levity, even to boyish romping; dressed like a dandy, and at times drank like a sailor and swore like a pirate. He could, as occasion required, be exceedingly meek in his deportment; and then again rough and boisterous as a highway robber; being always able to satisfy his followers of the propriety of his conduct. He always quailed before power, and was arrogant to weakness. At times he could put on the air of a penitent, as if feeling the deepest humiliation for his sins, and suffering unutterable anguish, and indulging in the most gloomy forebodings of eternal woe. At such times he would call for the prayers of the brethren in his behalf, with a wild and fearful energy and earnestness. He was full six feet high, strongly built and uncommonly well muscled. No doubt he was as much indebted for his influence over an ignorant people, to the superiority of his physical vigor, as to his greater cunning and intellect.

His followers were divided into the leaders and the led; the first division embraced a numerous class of broken down, unprincipled men of talents, to be found in every country, who, bankrupt in character and fortune, had nothing to lose by deserting the known religions, and carving out a new one of their own. They were mostly infidels, who holding all religions in derision, believed that they had as good a right as Christ or Mahomet, or any of the founders of former systems, to create one for themselves; and if they could impose it upon mankind, to live upon the labor of their dupes. Those of the second division, were the credulous wondering part of men, whose easy belief and admiring natures, are always the victims of novelty, in whatever shape it may come, who have a capacity to believe any strange and wonderful matter, if it only be new, whilst the wonders of former ages command neither faith nor reverence; they were men of feeble purposes, readily subjected to the will of the strong, giving themselves up entirely to the direction of their leaders; and this accounts for the very great influence of those leaders in controlling them. In other respects some of the Mormons were abandoned rogues, who had taken shelter in Nauvoo, as a convenient place for the head-quarters of their villainy; and others were good, honest, industrious people, who were the sincere victims of an artful delusion. Such as these were more the proper objects of pity than persecution. With them, their religious belief was a kind of insanity; and certainly no greater calamity can befall a human being, than to have a mind so constituted as to be made the sincere dupe of a religious imposture.

CAROLINE KIRKLAND

(1801–1864)

Many eastern and European women wrote of their travels in the west. Aside from Kirkland, Eliza Farnham and Margeret Fuller are represented in the current volume. Unlike those women, however, Caroline Kirkland intended to settle on the frontier, specifically near the site of present-day Pinckney, Michigan. Nonetheless, unlike Rebecca Burlend, Kirkland was representative of the elite, landowning class of settlers. As a gentlewoman on the frontier, Kirkland manages to blend the subtle feminism of Farnham and Fuller with the direct eyewitness integrity of Burlend.

Kirkland constructs very loosely a narrative in the form of an epistolary novel telling of the arrival of her family in the township they had purchased from land speculators. Like the immigrant easterners of the fictions of Gilbert Imlay and James Fenimore Cooper, Kirkland's narrator is more concerned with the white settlers she encounters than with the natives lingering in the region. Like all representatives of the literate east, Kirkland is concerned with policing the distance the settlers have traveled, figuratively, from the standards of civility and material comfort established in the east. Her concern is with establishing a sense of order in the community of white settlers—who become her husband's tenants—by starting in the home. Her push toward establishing what Linda Kerber calls "republican motherhood" is met with resistance from the settlers, who reject her airs of condescension.

In the novel, Mrs. Clavers, the narrator, learns to compromise with western lifeways and is able to narrate stories such as that of the Beckwith family reproduced here, from something other than the metropolitan voice with which she began her sojourn on the frontier. However, in fact, when Kirkland herself returned east to publish her book in New York, her neighbors in Michigan read it, and discouraged a return visit. Kirkland herself stayed in New York and pursued a long and successful career as a writer and teacher. Nonetheless, long hailed as an important forerunner to nineteenth-century realism—a tradition continued by her son, the novelist Joseph Kirkland—A New Home is an important book for its recognition annd fictionalization of the growing divergence of the "West" in 1838 from its origin as site of violence and adventure. In fact, by taming the frontier, Kirkland heralds a new way of understanding interregional tensions through the lenses of domesticity and sentimentality.

Text: *A New Home, Who'll Follow?* (New York, 1838; rpt. New Brunswick, N.J., 1996, ed. Sandra A. Zaggarall): 1–8, 86–107.

FROM *A NEW HOME, WHO'LL FOLLOW?*

CHAPTER I

Here are seen
No traces of man's pomp and pride; no silks
Rustle, nor jewels shine, nor envious eyes
Encounter***
    Oh, there is not lost
One of earth's charms; upon her bosom yet
After the flight of untold centuries
The freshness of her far beginning lies.

—BRYANT

Our friends in the "settlements" have expressed so much interest in such of our letters to them, as happened to convey any account of the peculiar features of western life, and have asked so many questions, touching particulars which we had not thought worthy of mention, that I have been for some time past contemplating the possibility of something like a detailed account of our experiences. And I have determined to give them to the world, in a form not very different from that in which they were originally recorded for our private delectation; nothing doubting, that a veracious history of actual occurrences, an unvarnished transcript of real characters, and an impartial record of every-day forms of speech (taken down in many cases from the lips of the speaker) will be pronounced "graphic," by at least a fair proportion of the journalists of the day.

'Tis true there are but meagre materials for anything which might be called a story. I have never seen a cougar—nor been bitten by a rattlesnake. The reader who has patience to go with me to the close of my desultory sketches, must expect nothing beyond a meandering recital of common-place occurrences—mere gossip about every-day people, little enhanced in value by any fancy or ingenuity of the writer; in short, a very ordinary pen-drawing; which, deriving no interest from colouring, can be valuable only for its truth.

A home on the outskirts of civilization—habits of society which allow the maid and her mistress to do the honours in complete equality, and to make the social tea visit in loving conjunction—such a distribution of the duties of life as compels all, without distinction, to rise with the sun or before him—to breakfast with the chickens—then,

"Count the slow clock and dine exact at noon"—

to be ready for tea at four, and for bed at eight—may certainly be expected to furnish some curious particulars for the consideration of those whose daily course almost reverses this primitive arrangement—who "call night day and day night," and who are apt occasionally to forget, when speaking of a particular class, that "those creatures" are partakers with themselves of a common nature.

I can only wish, like other modest chroniclers, my respected prototypes, that so fertile a theme had fallen into worthier hands. If Miss Mitford, who has given us such charming glimpses of Aberleigh, Hilton Cross and the Loddon, had by some happy chance been translated to Michigan, what would she not have made of such materials as Tinkerville, Montacute, and the Turnip?

When my husband purchased two hundred acres of wild land on the banks of this to-be-celebrated stream, and drew with a piece of chalk on the bar-room table at Danforth's the plan of a village, I little thought I was destined to make myself famous by handing down to posterity a faithful record of the advancing fortunes of that favoured spot.

"The madness of the people" in those days of golden dreams took more commonly the form of city-building; but there were a few who contented themselves with planning villages, on the banks of streams which certainly never could be expected to bear navies, but which might yet be turned to account in the more homely way of grinding or sawing—operations which must necessarily be performed somewhere for the well-being of those very cities. It is of one of these humble attempts that it is my lot to speak, and I make my confession at the outset, warning any fashionable reader who may have taken up my book, that I intend to be "decidedly low."

Whether the purchaser of *our* village would have been moderate under all possible circumstances, I am not prepared to say, since, never having enjoyed a situation under government, his resources have not been unlimited;—and for this reason any remark which may be hazarded in the course of these my lucubrations touching the more magnificent plans of wealthier aspirants, must be received with some grains of allowance. "Il est plus aisé d'être sage pour les autres, que de l'être pour soi-même."

When I made my first visit to these remote and lonely regions, the scattered woods through which we rode for many miles were gay in their first gosling-green suit of half-opened leaves, and the forest odours which exhaled with the dews of morning and evening, were beyond measure delicious to one "long in populous cities pent." I desired much to be a little sentimental at the time, and feel tempted to indulge to some small extent even here—but I forbear; and shall adhere closely to matters more in keeping with my subject.

I think, to be precise, the time was the last, the very last of April, and I recollect well that even at that early season, by availing myself with sedulous application, of those times when I was fain to quit the vehicle through fear of the perilous mud-holes, or still more perilous half-bridged marshes, I picked upwards of twenty varieties of wild-flowers—some of them of rare and delicate beauty;—and sure I am, that if I had succeeded in inspiring my companion with one spark of my own floral enthusiasm, one hundred miles of travel would have occupied a week's time.

The wild flowers of Michigan deserve a poet of their own. Shelley, who sang so quaintly of "the pied wind-flowers and the tulip tall," would have found many a fanciful comparison and deep-drawn meaning for the thousand gems of the road-side. Charles Lamb could have written charming volumes about the humblest among them. Bulwer would find means to associate the common three-leaved white lily so closely with the Past, the Present, and the Future—the Wind, the stars, and the tripod of Delphos, that all future botanists, and eke all future philosophers, might fail to unravel the "linked sweetness." We must have a poet of our own.

Since I have casually alluded to a Michigan mud-hole, I may as well enter into a detailed memoir on the subject, for the benefit of future travellers, who, flying over the soil on rail-roads, may look slightingly back upon the achievements of their predecessors. In the "settlements," a mud-hole is considered as apt to occasion an unpleasant jolt—a breaking of the thread of one's reverie—or in extreme cases, a temporary stand-still or even an overturn of the rash or the unwary. Here, on approaching one of these characteristic features of the "West"—(How much does that expression mean to include? I never have been able to discover its limits)—the driver stops—alights—walks up to the dark gulf—and around it if he can get round it. He then seeks a long pole and sounds it, measures it across to ascertain how its width compares with the length of his wagon—tries whether its sides are perpendicular, as is usually the case if the road is much used. If he find it not more than three feet deep, he remounts cheerily, encourages his team, and in they go, with a plunge and a shock rather apt to damp the courage of the inexperienced. If the hole be narrow the hinder wheels will be quite lifted off the ground by the depression of their precedents, and so remain until by unwearied chirruping and some judicious touches of "the string" the horses are induced to struggle as for their lives; and if the fates are propitious they generally emerge on the opposite side, dragging the vehicle, or at least the fore wheels after them. When I first "penetrated the interior" (to use an indigenous phrase) all I knew of the wilds was from Hoffman's tour or Captain Hall's "graphic" delineations: I had some floating idea of "driving a barouche-and-four anywhere through the oak-openings"—and seeing "the murdered Banquos of the forest" haunting the scenes of their departed strength and beauty. But I confess, these pictures, touched by the glowing pencil of fancy, gave me but incorrect notions of a real journey through Michigan.

Our vehicle was not perhaps very judiciously chosen;—at least we have since thought so. It was a light high-hung carriage—of the description commonly known as a buggy or shandrydan—names of which I would be glad to learn the etymology. I seriously advise any of my friends who are about flitting to Wisconsin or Oregon, to prefer a heavy lumber-waggon, even for the use of the ladies of the family; very little aid or consolation being derived from making a "genteel" appearance in such cases.

At the first encounter of such a mud-hole as I have attempted to describe, we stopped in utter despair. My companion indeed would fain have persuaded me that the many wheel tracks which passed through the formidable gulf were proof positive that it might be forded. I insisted with all a woman's obstinacy that I could not and would not make the attempt, and alighted accordingly, and tried to find a path on one side or the other. But in vain, even putting out of the question my paper-soled shoes—sensible things for the woods. The ditch on each side was filled with water and quite too wide to jump over; and we were actually contemplating a return, when a man in an immense bear-skin cap and a suit of deer's hide, sprang from behind a stump just within the edge of the forest. He "poled" himself over the ditch in a moment, and stood beside us, rifle in hand, as wild and rough a specimen of humanity as one would wish to encounter in a strange and lonely road, just at the shadowy dusk of the evening. I did *not* scream, though I own I was prodigiously frightened. But our stranger said immediately, in a gentle tone and with a French accent, "Me watch deer—you want to cross?" On receiving an answer in the affirmative, he ran in search of a rail which he threw over the terrific mud-hole—aided me to walk across by the help of his pole—showed my husband where to plunge—waited till he had gone safely through and "slow circles dimpled o'er the quaking mud"—then took himself off by the way he came, declining any compensation with a most polite "rien, rien!" This instance of true and genuine and generous politeness I record for the benefit of all bearskin caps, leathern jerkins and cowhide boots, which ladies from the eastward world may hereafter encounter in Michigan.

Our journey was marked by no incident more alarming than the one I have related, though one night passed in a wretched inn, deep in the "timbered land"—as all woods are called in Michigan—was not without its terrors, owing to the horrible drunkenness of the master of the house, whose wife and children were in constant fear of their lives, from his insane fury. I can never forget the countenance of that desolate woman, sitting trembling and with white, compressed lips in the midst of her children. The father raving all night, and coming through our sleeping apartment with the earliest ray of morning, in search of more of the poison already boiling in his veins. The poor wife could not forbear telling me her story—her change of lot—from a well-stored and comfortable home in Connecticut to this wretched den in the wilderness—herself and children worn almost to shadows with the ague, and her husband such as I have described him. I may mention here that not very long after I heard of this man in prison in Detroit, for stabbing a neighbour in a drunken brawl, and ere the year was out he died of delirium tremens, leaving his family destitute. So much for turning our fields of golden grain into "fire water"—a branch of business in which Michigan is fast improving.

Our ride being a deliberate one, I felt, after the third day, a little wearied, and began to complain of the sameness of the oak-openings and to wish we were fairly at our journey's end. We were crossing a broad expanse of what seemed at a little distance a smooth shaven lawn of the most brilliant green, but which proved on trial little better than a quaking bog—embracing within its ridgy circumference all possible varieties of

"Muirs, and mosses, slaps and styles"—

I had just indulged in something like a yawn, and wished that I could see our hotel. At the word, my companion's face assumed rather a comical expression, and I was so preparing to inquire somewhat testily what there was so laughable—I was getting tired and cross, reader—when down came our good horse to the very chin in a bog-hole, green as Erin on the top, but giving way on a touch, and seeming deep enough to have engulfed us entirely if its width had been proportionate. Down came the horse—and this was not all—down came the driver; and I could not do less than follow, though at a little distance—our good steed kicking and floundering—covering us with hieroglyphics, which would be readily deciphered by any Wolverine we should meet, though perchance strange to the eyes of our friends at home. This mishap was soon amended. Tufts of long marsh grass served to assoilize our habiliments a little, and a clear stream which rippled through the marsh aided in removing the eclipse from our faces. We journeyed on cheerily, watching the splendid changes in the west, but keeping a bright look-out for bog-holes.

CHAPTER II

Think us no churls, nor measure our good minds
By this rude place we live in.

—SHAKESPEARE, *CYMBELINE*

The sun had just set when we stopped at the tavern, and I then read the cause of my companion's quizzical look. My Hotel was a log-house of diminutive size, with corresponding appurtenances; and from the moment we entered its door I was in a fidget to know where we could possibly sleep. I was then new in Michigan. Our good hostess rose at once with a nod of welcome.

"Well! is this Miss Clavers?" (my husband had been there before.) "well! I want to know! why do tell if you've been upsot in the mash? why, I want to know!—and didn't ye hurt ye none? Come, gals! fly round, and let's git some supper."

"But you'll not be able to lodge us, Mrs. Danforth," said I, glancing at three young men and some boys, who appeared to have come in from their work, and who were lounging on one side of the immense open chimney.

"Why, bless your heart! yes I shall; don't you fret yourself: I'll give you as good a bed as any-body need want."

I cast an exploring look, and now discovered a door opposite the fire.

"Jist step in here," said Mrs. Danforth, opening this door, "jist come in, and take off your things, and lop down, if you're a mind to, while we're a getting supper."

I followed her into the room, if room it might be called, a strip partitioned off, just six feet wide, so that a bed was accurately fitted in at each end, and a square space remained vacant between the two.

"We've been getting this room made lately, and I tell you it's real nice, so private, like!" said our hostess, with a complacent air. "Here," she continued, "in this bed the gals sleeps, and that's my bed and the old man's; and then here's a trundle-bed for Sally and Jane," and suiting the action to the word, she drew out the trundle-bed as far as our standing-place would allow, to show me how convenient it was.

Here was my grand problem still unsolved! If "me and the old man," and the girls, and Sally and Jane, slept in this strip, there certainly could be no room for more, and I thought with dismay of the low-browed roof, which had seemed to me to rest on the tops of the window-frames. And, to make a long story short, though manifold were the runnings up and down, and close the whisperings before all was ready, I was at length ushered up a steep and narrow stick-ladder, into the sleeping apartment. Here, surrounded by beds of all sizes spread on the floor, was a bedstead, placed under the peak of the roof, in order to gain space for its height, and round this state-bed, for such it evidently was, although not supplied with pillows at each end, all the men and boys I had seen below stairs, were to repose. Sundry old quilts were fastened by forks to the rafters in such a way as to serve as a partial screen, and with this I was obliged to be content. Excessive fatigue is not fastidious. I called to mind some canal-boat experiences, and resigned myself to the "honey-heavy dew of slumber."

I awoke with a sense of suffocation—started up—all was dark as the Hall of Eblis. I called—no answer came; I shrieked! and up ran one of the "gals."

"What on airth's the matter?"

"Where am I? What ails me?" said I, beginning to feel a little awkward when I heard the damsel's voice.

"Why, I guess you was scairt, wa' n't ye?"

"Why am I in the dark? Is it morning?"

"Morning? why, the boys has been gone away this hour, and, you see, there ain't no winder up here, but I'll take down this here quilt, and then I guess you'll be able to see some."

CHAPTER XXIII

I boast no song in magic wonders rife,
But yet, oh nature! is there nought to prize
Familiar in thy bosom-scenes of life?
And dwells in day-light truth's salubrious skies
No form with which the soul may sympathize?

—CAMPBELL

We returned by a different and less lonely route, the Tinkervillians having very civilly directed us to one on which we should not at any point be far distant from a dwelling. The single Indian we had encountered in the morning had been quite sufficient to spoil Mrs. Rivers' ride; and we hurried on at the best pace of our sober steeds.

The country through which we were passing was so really lovely that even my timid little friend forgot her fears at times and exclaimed like a very enthusiast. At least two small lakes lay near our way; and these, of winding outline, and most dazzling brightness, seemed, as we espied them now and then through the arched vistas of the deep woods, multiplied to a dozen or more. We saw grape-vines which had so embraced large trees that the long waving pennons flared over their very tops; while the lower branches of the sturdy oaks were one undistinguishable mass of light green foliage, without an inch of bark to be seen. The road side was piled like an exaggerated velvet with exquisitely beautiful ferns of almost every variety; and some open spots gleamed scarlet with those wild strawberries so abundant with us, and which might challenge the world for flavour.

Birds of every variety of song and hue, were not wanting, nor the lively squirrel, that most joyous of nature's pensioners; and it cost us some little care to keep D'Orsay in his post of honour as sole escort through these lonely passes. But alack! "'t was ever thus!" We had scarcely sauntered two miles when a scattered drop or two foretold that we were probably to try the melting mood. We had not noticed a cloud, but thus warned we saw portentious gatherings of these bug-bears of life.

Now if our poneys would only have gone a little faster! But they would not, so we were wet to the skin—travelling *jets d' eau*—looking doubtless very much like the western settler taking his stirrup-cup in one of Mrs. Trollope's true pictures.

When we could be no further soaked we reached a farm-house—not a Michigan farm-house, but a great, noble, yankee "palace of pine boards," looking like a cantle of Massachusetts or Western New-York dropped *par hazard,* in these remote wilds. To me who had for a long while seen nothing of dwelling kind larger than a good sized chicken-coop, the scene was quite one of *Eastern* enchantment. A large barn with shed and stables and poultry-yard and all! Fields of grain, well fenced and stumpless, surrounded this happy dwelling; and a most inviting door-yard, filled to profusion with shrubs and flowers, seemed to invite our entrance.

"A honey-suckle! absolutely a honey-suckle on the porch!" Mrs. Rivers was almost too forlorn to sympathize with me: but then she had not been quite so long from home. I have been troubled with a sort of home calenture at times since we removed westward.

As we were about to dismount, the sun shone out most provokingly: and I was afraid there would be scarce the shadow of an excuse for a visit to the interesting inmates, for such I had decided they must be, of this delicious home-like spot; but, as we wavered, a young man as wet as ourselves, came up the road, and, opening the gate at once, invited us to enter and dry our dripping garments.

We stayed not for urging, but turned our graceless steeds into the shady lane, and dismounting, not at the front entrance, but, *à la Michigan,* at the kitchen door, we were received with much grave but cordial politeness by the comely mistress of the mansion, who was sharing with her pretty daughter the after-dinner cares of the day. Our upper garments were spread to dry, and when we were equipped, with urgent hospitality, in others belonging to our hostesses, we were ushered into the parlor or "keeping room."

Here, writing at an old-fashioned *secretary,* sat the master of the house, a hearty, cheerful-looking, middle-aged man; evidently a person of less refinement than his wife, but still of a most prepossessing exterior. He fell no whit behind in doing the honours, and we soon found ourselves quite at ease. We recounted the adventures of our tiny journey, and laughed at our unlucky over-running of the game.

"Ah! Tinkerville! yes, I think it will be some time yet before those dreams will come to pass. I have told Mr. Jephson there was nothing there to make a village out of."

"You are acquainted then with the present proprietors?"

"With one of them I have been acquainted since we were boys; and he has been a speculator all that time, and is now at least as poor as ever. He has been very urgent with me to sell out here and locate in his village, as he calls it; but we knew rather too much of him at home for that," and he glanced at his fair spouse with some archness. I could scarcely believe that any man could have been impudent enough to propose such an exchange, but nothing is incredible in Michigan.

Mrs. Beckworth was now engaged in getting tea, in spite of our hollow-hearted declarations that we did not wish it. With us, be it known to new comers, whatever be the hour of the day, a cup of tea with *trimmings,* is always in season; and is considered as the orthodox mode of welcoming any guest, from the clergyman to "the maid that does the meanest chores." We were soon seated at a delicately-furnished table.

The countenance of the good lady had something of peculiar interest for me. It was mild, intelligent, and very pleasing. No envious silver streaked the rich brown locks which were folded with no little elegance above the fair brow. A slight depression of the outer extremity of the eyelid, and of the delicately-pencilled arch above it, seemed to tell of sorrow and meek endurance. I was sure that like so many western settlers, the fair and pensive matron had a story; and when I had once arrived at this conclusion, I determined to make a brave push to ascertain the truth of my conjecture.

I began, while Mrs. Beckworth was absent from the parlour, by telling every thing I could think of; this being the established mode of getting knowledge in this country. Mr. Beckworth did not bite.

"Is this young lady your daughter, Mr. Beckworth?"

"A daughter of my wife's—Mary Jane Harrington?"

"Oh! ah! a former marriage; and the fine young man who brought us into such good quarters is a brother of Miss Harrington's I am sure."

"A half brother—Charles Boon."

"Mrs. Beckworth thrice married! impossible!" was my not very civil but quite natural exclamation.

Our host smiled quietly, a smile which enticed me still further. He was, fortunately for my reputation for civility, too kindly polite not to consent to gratify my curiosity, which I told him sincerely had been awakened by the charming countenance of his wife, who was evidently the object of his highest admiration.

As we rode through the freshened woods with Mr. Beckworth, who had, with ready politeness, offered to see us safely a part of the way, he gave us the particulars of his early history; and to establish my claim to the character of a physiognomist, I shall here recount what he told me; and, as I cannot recollect his words, I must give this romance of rustic life in my own, taking a new chapter for it.

CHAPTER XXIV

> Sudden partings, such as press,
> The life from out young hearts; and choking sighs
> Which ne'er might be repeated, who could guess
> If ever more should meet those mutual eyes—
>
> —BYRON

Henry Beckworth, the eldest son of a Massachusetts farmer, of small means and many mouths, was glad to accept a situation as clerk in the comprehensive "variety store" of his cousin Ellis Irving, who was called a great merchant in the neighbouring town of Langton. This cousin Ellis had fallen into the dangerous and not very usual predicament of having every body's good word; and it was not until he had failed in business, that any one discovered that he had a fault in the world.

While he was yet in his hey-day, and before the world knew that he had been so good-natured as to endorse for his wife's harum-scarum brother, his clerk, Henry Beckworth, had never dared to acknowledge, even in his dreams, that he loved to very dizziness his sweet cousin Agnes Irving. But when mortification and apoplexy had done their work upon Mr. Irving, and his delicate wife had ascertained that the remnant of her days must pass in absolute poverty, dependant for food and raiment upon her daughter's needle, Henry found his wits and his tongue, and made so good use of both, that, ere long, his cousin Agnes did not deny that she liked him very well.

Now young ladies who have been at boarding-school and learned to paint water-melons in water colours, and work Rebecca at the well in chenille and gold thread, find real, thrifty, housewifely sewing, very slow and hard work, to earn even bread and salt by; but the dove-eyed Agnes had been the sole care and pride of a genuine New England housewife, who could make hard gingerbread as well as soft, and who had plumed herself on being able to put every stitch into six fine shirts between Sunday evening and Saturday night. And so the fair child, though delicately bred, earned her mother's living and her own, with cheerful and ungrudging industry; and Henry sent all the surplus of his clerkly gains to his father, who sometimes found the cry of "crowdie, crowdie, a' the day," rather difficult to pacify.

But by-and-bye, Mrs. Irving became so feeble that Agnes was obliged to nurse her instead of plying her skilful needle; and then matters went far astray, so that after a while the kind neighbours brought in almost all that was consumed in that sad lit-tle household; Henry Beckworth being then out of employ, and unable for the time to find any way of aiding his cousin, save by his personal services in the sick-room.

He grew almost mad under his distress, and the anxious, careful love which is the nursling of poverty, and at length seeing Mrs. Irving's health a little amended, he gave a long, sad, farewell kiss to his Agnes, and left her with an assurance that she should hear from him soon. He dared not tell her that he was quitting her to go to sea, in order that he might have immediate command of a trifling sum which he could de-vote to her service.

He made his way to the nearest sea-port, secured a berth before the mast in a ves-sel about to sail for the East Indies; and then put into a letter all the love, and hope, and fear, and caution, and encouragement, and resolution, and devotedness, that one poor sheet could carry, giving the precious document into the care of a Langton man, who was returning "direct," as he said, to the spot where poor Henry had left his senses.

This said letter told Agnes, among other things, how and when to draw on Messrs. ———, for Henry's wages, which were left subject to her order—and the lover went to sea, with a heavy heart indeed, but with a comforting security that he had done all that poverty would let him, for the idol of his heart.

An East India voyage is very long, and most people experience many a changing mood and many a wayward moment during its course; but Henry Beckworth's heart beat as if it would burst his blue jacket, when he found himself on shore again, and thought of what awaited him at Langton.

He called on Messrs. ———, to ascertain whether any thing remained of his pay, and found that every dollar was untouched. At first this angered him a little; "for," as he justly argued, "if Agnes loved me as I love her—but, never mind!" This I give as a fair specimen of his thoughts on his homeward journey. All his contemplations, how-ever incoherent or wide of the mark, came invariably to one conclusion—that Agnes would surely be willing to marry him, poor as he was, rather than he should go to sea again.

It was evening, and a very dull, lead-coloured evening, when the stage that con-tained our lover stopped at the only public-house in Langton. The True Blue Hotel, kept, as the oval sign which creaked by its side informed the grateful public, by Job

Jephson, (at this moment J. Jephson, Esquire, of Tinkerville, in Michigan,) the very Job Jephson to whose kindly care Henry had committed his parting letter. The stage passed on, and Mr. Beckworth paced the tesselated floor of Mr. Jephson's bar-room, until the worthy proprietor and himself were left its sole occupants.

"Why, Henry, my boy, is that you? Do tell! Why your hat was slouched over your eyes so, that I did not know you! Why, man! where on *airth* have you sprung from!'"

Henry asked after every body, and then after Agnes Irving and her mother.

"Agnes Irving!"

"Dead!" said Henry, wildly enough.

"Dead! no, married to be sure! three months ago; and this very day a week ago, her mother was buried."

It is really surprising how instantaneously pride comes to one's aid on some occasions. The flashing thought of the loved one's death, had been anguish intolerable and inconcealable; the certainty of what was far worse only blanched Henry's cheek, and set his teeth firmly together while his lips questioned on, and the loquacious host of the True Blue proceeded.

"Poor Agnes saw hard times after you went away. She had to give up the house you left her in, and take a room at Mr. Truesdell's. And then Mrs. Irving did nothing but pine after the comforts she had lost, for her mind was kind o'broke up by trouble. And Agnes tried to find some other place to board, because her mother took such an awful dislike to Mrs. Truesdell; but there was n't nobody willing to take them in, because the old lady was so particular. And so, John Harrington—you know John?—made up to her again, though she'd refused him two or three times before; and said he loved her better than ever, and that he would take her mother home and do for her as if she was his own. Now, you see, the neighbours had got pretty much tired of sending in things, because they thought Aggy ought n't to refuse such a good offer, and so after a while John got her. After all the poor old lady did not seem to enjoy her new home, but pined away faster than ever, and said she knew Aggy had sold herself for her sake, but that was only a notion you know, for John was an excellent match for a poor ———"

"Did you give my cousin the letter I handed you?" interrupted Henry.

"I'll just tell you all about that," responded Mr. Jephson, complacently drawing a chair for Henry, and inviting him to sit, as if for a long story. "I'll just tell you how that was. When you and I parted that time, I thought I was all ready for a start home; but there was a chance turned up to spekilate a little, and arter that I went down South to trade away some notions, so that when I got back to Langton it was quite cold weather, and I took off my best coat and laid it away, for where's the use of wearing good clothes under a great coat, you know? and there, to be sure was your letter in the pocket of it. Well, before I found it again Agnes was getting ready to be married; and, thinks I to myself, like enough it's a love-letter, and might break off the match if she got it, gals are so foolish! so I just locked up the letter and said nothing to nobody and"—there lay Mr. Jephson on his bar-room floor.

Henry turned from the place with some glimmering of an intention to seek his lost love and tell her all, but one moment's lapse cured this madness; so he only sat down and looked at Job, who was picking himself up and talking all the while.

"Man alive! what do you put yourself into such a plaguy passion for? I done it all for the best; and as to forgetting, who does not forget sometimes? Plague take you! you've given my back such a wrench I sha'n't be able to go to trainin' to-morrow, and tore my pantaloons besides; and, after all, you may likely thank me for it as long as you live. There's as good fish in the sea as ever was caught—but I swan! you're as white as the wall, and no mistake," and he caught the poor soul as he was falling from his chair.

"Well, now, if this does n't beat cock-fighting!" muttered he, as he laid his insensible guest at full length on the floor and ran to the bar for some "camphire," which he administered in all haste, "to take on so about a gal without a cent, but he wont come to after all, and I shall have to bleed him:" saying which he pulled off one sleeve of Henry's jacket and proceeded in due form to the operation.

"He wont bleed, I vow! Hang the fellow! if he dies, I shall be took up for manslaughter. Why, Harry, I say!" shaking him soundly, and dragging at his arm with no gentle force. At last blood came slowly, and Beckworth became once more conscious of misery, and Mr. Jephson's tongue set out as if fresh oiled by the relief of his fears for his own safety.

"Now, Henry, do n't make such a fool of yourself! You always used to be a fellow of some sconce. What can't be cured must be endured." But as Henry's lips resumed their colour, and he raised himself from the floor, Mr. Jephson's habitual prudence urged him farther and farther from the reach of the well arm. His fears were groundless, however, for all that Henry now wanted was to be alone, that he might weep like a woman.

"Promise me that you will never tell any one that I have been here this night," said he at length; "this is all I ask. Since Agnes is another man's wife, God forbid I should wish my name mentioned in her presence."

"Why, law! I'll promise that, to be sure; but you should n't make so much out o' nothing: Aggy has got the best house in town, and every thing comfortable; and it a' n't no ways likely she would fret after *you*." And with this comforting assurance Henry prepared for departure.

"I say, Beckworth!" said Mr. Jephson as his guest left the room with his valise; "I sha'n't charge you anything for the bleeding."

CHAPTER XXV

> Now I will believe
> That there are unicorns; that in Arabia
> There is one tree the Phœnix' throne; one Phœnix
> At this hour reigning there.*** I'll believe both,
> And what else doth want credit, come to me
> And I'll be sworn 't is true.
>
> —SHAKESPEARE, *THE TEMPEST.*

The windows of heaven were opened that night. The rain descended in sheets instead of drops; and it was only by an occasional flash of pale lightning that our unfortunate was able to find the house which he well recollected for John Harrington's. There it was in all its fresh whiteness and greenness, and its deep masses of foliage, and its rich screens of honey-suckle and sweet-briar, meet residence for a happy bridegroom and his new-found treasure. The upper half of the parlour shutters was unclosed, and plainly by the clear bright lamp-light could Henry see the delicate papering of the walls, and the pretty French clock under its glass shade on the mantel-piece. Oh! for one glance at the table, near which he felt sure Agnes was sitting. Wild thoughts of the old song—

We took but ae kiss, an' we tore ourselves away,

Were coursing through his brain, and he was deliberating upon the chance that the end window, which looked on a piazza, might be free from the envious shutter, when a man ran against him in the dark. The next flash showed a great-coated figure entering the pretty rural gate to the little shrubbery; and in another moment the hall-door opened. Henry saw the interior, light and cheerful; and again all was dark.

It would have been very wrong to set the house on fire and then go and murder Job Jephson; and as Henry could not at the moment decide upon any other course of conduct, which would be at all in unison with his feelings, he set out, a human locomotive at the top-speed, in the very teeth of the storm, on his way towards the sea-port again. The worse one feels, the faster one travels, hoping to outrun sorrow; so it did not take Henry Beckworth long to reach a neighbouring town, where he could find a stage-coach; and he was far at sea again in the course of a very few days.

His *outre-mer* adventures are of no importance to my story—how, as he stood with two or three messmates, staring, like a true Yankee, at the Tower of London, a press-gang seized them all, and rowed them to a vessel which lay off the Traitors' Gate, the Americans protesting themselves such, and the John Bulls laughing at them;—how, when they got on board the man o' war, they showed their protections, and the officer of his Majesty's recruiting service said he could do nothing in the case till the ship returned from her cruize—and how the ship did not return from her cruize, but after cruizing about for some three years or more, was taken by a French first-rate and carried into Brest. All this is but little to the purpose. But when Henry was thrown into a French prison, his American certificate procured his release through the consul's good offices, and he shipped at once for New-York, somewhat weary of a sea life.

At New-York he learned from a townsman whom he met there that Agnes Harrington had been two years a widow.

"Is she rich?" asked Henry. A strange question for a true lover.

"Rich!—Lord bless ye! John Harrington was n't worth *that;*" snapping his fingers most expressively. "His property was under mortgage to such an extent, that all it would sell for would n't clear it. His widow and child will not have a cent after old Horner forecloses, as he is now about doing. And Mrs. Harrington's health is very poor, though to my thinking she's prettier than ever."

Henry's movements were but little impeded by baggage, and the journey to Langton was performed in a short time. Once more was he set down at Job Jephson's; and there was day-light enough this time to see, besides the oval sign before hinted at, which had for years held out hopes of "Entertainment for man and beast," a legend over the door in great white characters, "Post Office,"—"good business for Job," thought Henry Beckworth,—a board in one window setting forth, "Drugs and Medicines," and a card in the other, "Tailoring done here."

Slight salutation contented Henry, when the man of letters made his appearance, and he requested a horse to carry him as far as his father's, saying he would send for his trunk in the morning. Mr. Jephson made some little difficulty and delay, but Henry seemed in fiery haste. In truth he hated the sight of Job beyond all reason; but that complacent personage seemed to have forgotten, very conveniently, all former passages in that memorable bar-room.

"You do n't ask after your old friends, Harry," said he. "A good many things has altered here since I see you last. You came that time a little too late."

Henry looked dirks at the fellow, but he went on as coldly as ever.

"Now this time, to my thinkin', you've come a *leetle* too soon."

Henry tried not to ask him what he meant; but for his life he could not help it.

"Why, I mean, if John Harrington's widow has not more sense than I think she has, you've come in time to spoil a good match."

"A match!" was all Henry could say.

"Aye, a match; for Colonel Boon came from there yesterday, and sent for old Horner here to this blessed house, and took up the mortgage on Harrington's property; and every body knows he has been after Aggy this twelvemonth, offering to marry her and clear the property, and do well by the child. And if there's a good man on airth, Boon is that man, and every body knows it."

What did Henry Beckworth now? He un-ordered his horse, and went quietly to bed.

CHAPTER XXVI

There are thoughts that our burden can lighten,
    Though toilsome and steep be the way,
And dreams that like moon-light can brighten
    With a lustre far clearer than day.

Love nursed amid pleasures is faithless as they,
But the love born of sorrow, like sorrow, is true.

—MOORE

Henry Beckworth came from the hand of Nature abundantly furnished with that excellent qualification known and revered throughout New England, under the expressive name of "spunk." This quality at first prompted him, spite of the croakings of the ill-omened Job, to present himself before the one and only object of his constant soul, to tell her all, and to ask her to share with him the weal or wo which might yet be in store for him. But he had now seen a good deal of this excellent world, and the very indifferent people who transact its affairs. He had tasted the tender mercies of a British man of war, and the various *agrémens* of a French prison; and the practical conclusion which had gradually possessed itself of his mind, was, that money is, beyond all dispute, one of the necessaries of life.

No way of making money off-hand occurred to him as he tossed and groaned through the endless hours of that weary night. He had neither house nor land, nor yet a lottery ticket—nor a place under government—and the chest which stood at his bedside, though it contained enough of this world's goods to keep his fair proportions from the weather; and a sea-journal—a love-log—which he hoped might one day, by some romantic chance, come into the fair hands of his beloved, and give her to guess how his sad life had passed—held as he well knew, nothing which she could in anywise eat, or that she would be probably willing, under any contingency to put on.

I feel proud of my hero. He was "a man of deeds, not words." He loved Agnes so well, that before morning shone on his haggard cheek, he had determined to turn his back forever on the home of his youth, the scene of his first love-dream; and to seek his dark fortune far away from the place which held all that his heart prized on earth.

This resolution once taken, he arose and addressed himself to his sad journey, waiting only the earliest beam of light before he awakened Mr. Jephson. This worthy commended much his prudent course, and recommended a long voyage; an attempt to discover the North-West Passage, or to ascertain the truth of Capt. Symmes' theory; to take the nonsense out of him and make a little money.

For five long years did Henry Beckworth box the compass; five years of whaling voyages and all their attendant hardships—and when at the end of that time he retouched his native shore, richer than he had ever been before in his life, he heard, as the reader will no doubt anticipate, that Agnes Boon was again unmated; her worthy Colonel having been killed by a fall from his horse in less than two years from his marriage.

Yet did our phœnix of lovers approach the village which he had vowed never to see again, with many more misgivings than he had experienced on former occasions. Years and a rough life he was well aware had changed him much. He thought of his Agnes, fair and graceful as a snow-drop, and feared lest his weather-beaten visage might find no favour in her eyes. Yet he determined that this time nothing, not even that screech-owl Job Jephson, should prevent him from seeing her, face to face, and learning his fate from her own lips.

He approached Langton by a road that passed not near the detested house of man and horse entertainment, and was just emerging from a thick grove which skirted the village on that side, when he came near riding over a man who seemed crouched on the ground as if in search of something, and muttering to himself the while. The face that turned hastily round was Job Jephson's.

"Why, it a'n't! Yes, I'll be switched if it is n't Harry Beckworth rose from the dead!" said this fated tormentor; and he fastened himself on the bridle-rein in such sort, that Henry could not rid himself of his company without switching him in good earnest.

"Here was I, lookin' up some little things for my steam doctorin' business," said Mr. Jephson, "and little thinkin' of any body in the world; and you must come along jist like a sperrit. But I've a notion you've hit it about right this time. I s'pose you know Aggy's a rich widow by this time, do n't ye?"

Henry vouchsafed no reply, though he found it very difficult to maintain a dignified reserve, when so many questions were clustering on his lips. But it was all one to Job—question or no question, answer or no answer, he would talk on, and on, and on.

"I'll tell ye what," he continued, "I should n't wonder if Aggy looked higher now, for she's a good spec for any man. I see you've smarted up a good deal, but don't be cock-sure—for there's others that would be glad to take her and her two children. I've been a thinkin' myself—"

And now Henry gave Job such a switch across the knuckles as effectually cleared the bridle, and changed the current of the steam-doctor's thoughts. In half an hour he rang at Mrs. Boon's door, and was ushered at once into her presence.

"Mr. Beckworth, ma'am," said the little waiting-maid as she threw open the parlour door.

Agnes, the beloved, rose from her seat—sat down again—tried to speak, and burst into tears; while Henry looked on her countenance—changed indeed, but still lovely in matronly dignity—more fondly than in the days of his lighter youthful love; and seating himself beside her, began at the wrong end of the story, as most people do in such cases, talking as if it were a thing of course that his twice-widowed love should become his wife.

"Marry again! oh, never!"—that was entirely out of the question; and she wiped her eyes and asked her cousin to stay to dinner. But Henry deferred his ultimatum on this important point, till he should have ravelled out the whole web of his past life before the dewy eyes of his still fair mistress, till he should tell her all his love—no, that he could never fully tell, but some of the proofs of it at least, and that first horrible forget of Job Jephson's. And when this was told in many words, Agnes, all sighs and tears, still said no, but so much more faintly that Mr. Beckworth thought he would stay to dinner. And then—but why should I tell the rest, when the reader of my true-love story has already seen Mrs. Beckworth like a fair though full-blown China-rose—Mr. Beckworth with *bien content* written on every line of his handsome middle-aged face—Mary Jane Harrington a comely marriageable lass, and George Boon a strapping youth of eighteen—all flourishing on an oak opening in the depths of Michigan?

Let none imagine that this tale of man's constancy must be the mere dream of my fancy. I acknowledge nothing but the prettinesses. To Henry Beckworth himself I refer the incredulous, and if they do not recognize my story in his, I cannot help it. Even a woman can do no more than her best.

CHAPTER XXVII

Smelling so sweetly (all musk), and so rushling, I warrant you, in
silk and gold; and in such alligant terms.

—SHAKESPEARE, *THE MERRY WIVES OF WINDSOR.*

Art thou not Romeo, and a Montague?

—SHAKESPEARE

My brain's in a fever, my pulses beat quick
I shall die, or at least be exceedingly sick!
Oh what do you think! after all my romancing
My visions of glory, my sighing, my glancing—

—MISS BIDDY FUDGE.

An Addition to our Montacute first circle had lately appeared in the person of Miss Eloise Fidler, an elder sister of Mrs. Rivers, who was to spend some months "in this peaceful retreat,"—to borrow one of her favourite expressions.

This young lady was not as handsome as she would fain have been, if I may judge by the cataracts of ash-coloured ringlets which shaded her cheeks, and the exceeding straitness of the stays which restrained her somewhat exuberant proportions. Her age was at a stand; but I could never discover exactly where, for this point proved an exception to the general communicativeness of her disposition. I guessed it at eight-and-twenty; but perhaps she would have judged this uncharitable, so I will not insist. Certain it is that it must have taken a good while to read as many novels and commit to memory as much poetry, as lined the head and exalted the sensibilities of our fair visitant.

Her dress was in the height of fashion, and all her accoutrements *point de vice.* A gold pencil-case of the most delicate proportions was suspended by a kindred chain round a neck which might be called whity-brown; and a note-book of corresponding lady-like-ness was peeping from the pocket of her highly-useful apron of blue silk—ever ready to secure a passing thought or an elegant quotation. Her album—she was just the person to have an album—was resplendent in gold and satin, and the verses which meandered over its emblazoned pages were of the most unexceptionable quality, overlaid with flowers and gems—love and despair. To find any degree of appropriateness in these various offerings, one must allow the fortunate possessor of the purple volume, at least all the various perfections of an Admirable Crichton, allayed in some small measure by the trifling faults of coldness, fickleness, and deceit; and to judge of Miss Fidler's friends by their handwriting, they must have been able to offer an edifying variety of bumps to the fingers of the phrenologist. But here is the very book itself at my elbow, waiting these three months, I blush to say, for a contribution which has yet to be pumped up from my unwilling brains; and I have a mind to steal a few specimens from its already loaded pages, for the benefit of the distressed, who may, like myself, be at their wits' end for something to put in just such a book.

The first page, rich with embossed lilies, bears the invocation, written in a great black spattering hand, and wearing the air of a defiance. It runs thus:

> If among the names of the stainless few
> Thine own hath maintain'd a place,
> Come dip thy pen in the sable dew
> And with it this volume grace.
>
> But oh! if thy soul e'er encouraged a thought
> Which purity's self might blame,
> Close quickly the volume, and venture not
> To sully its snows with thy name.

Then we come to a wreath of flowers of gorgeous hues, within whose circle appears in a *miminee piminee* hand, evidently a young lady's—

THE WREATH OF SLEEP

> Oh let me twine this glowing wreath
> Amid those rings of golden hair,
> 'T will soothe thee with its odorous breath
> To sweet forgetfulness of care.
>
> 'T is form'd of every scented flower
> That flings its fragrance o'er the night;
> And gifted with a fairy power
> To fill thy dreams with forms of light.

'T was braided by an angel boy
   When fresh from Paradise he came
To fill our earth-born hearts with joy—
   Ah! need I tell the cherub's name?

This contributor I have settled in my own mind to be a descendant of Anna Matilda, the high-priestess of the Della Cruscan order. The next blazon is an interesting view of a young lady, combing her hair. As she seems not to have been long out of bed, the lines which follow are rather appropriate, though I feel quite sure they come from the expert fingers of a merchant's clerk—from the finished elegance, and very sweeping tails of the chirography.

MORNING

Awake! arise! art thou slumbering still?
When the sun is above the mapled hill,
And the shadows are flitting fast away,
And the dews are diamond beneath his ray,
And every bird in our vine-roofed bower
Is waked into song by the joyous hour;
Come, banish sleep from thy gentle eyes,
Sister! sweet sister! awake! arise!

Yet I love to gaze on thy lids of pearl,
And to mark the wave of the single curl
That shades in its beauty thy brow of snow,
And the cheek that lies like a rose below;
And to list to the murmuring notes that fall
From thy lips, like music in fairy hall.
But it must not be—the sweet morning flies
Ere thou hast enjoyed it; awake! arise!

There is balm on the wings of this freshen'd air;
'T will make thine eye brighter, thy brow more fair,
And a deep, deep rose on thy cheek shall be
The meed of an early walk with me.
We will seek the shade by the green hill side,
Or follow the clear brook's whispering tide;
And brush the dew from the violet's eyes—
Sister! sweet sister! awake! arise!

This I transcribe for the good advice which it contains. And what have we here? It is tastefully headed by an engraving of Hero and Ursula in the "pleached bower," and Beatrice running "like a lap-wing" in the background. It begins ominously.

TO—

Oh, look upon this pallid brow!
   Say, canst thou there discern one trace
Of that proud soul which oft ere now

Thou'st sworn shed radiance o'er my face?
Chill'd is that soul—its darling themes,
    Thy manly honour, virtue, truth
Prove now to be but fleeting dreams,
    Like other lovely thoughts of youth.

Meet, if thy coward spirit dare,
    This sunken eye; say, dost thou see
The rays thou saidst were sparkling there
    When first its gaze was turn'd on thee?
That eye's young light is quench'd forever;
    No change its radiance can repair:
Will Joy's keen touch relume it? Never!
    It gleams the watch-light of Despair.

I find myself growing hoarse by sympathy, and I shall venture only a single extract more, and this because Miss Fidler declares it, without exception, the sweetest thing she ever read. It is written with a crow-quill, and has other marks of femininity. Its vignette is a little girl and boy playing at battle-door.

BALLAD

The deadly strife was over, and across the field of fame,
With anguish in his haughty eye, the Moor Almanzor came;
He prick'd his fiery courser on among the scatter'd dead,
Till he came at last to what he sought, a sever'd human head.

It might have seem'd a maiden's, so pale it was, and fair;
But the lip and chin were shaded till they match'd the raven hair.
There lingered yet upon the brow a spirit bold and high,
And the stroke of death had scarcely closed the piercing eagle eye.

Almanzor grasp'd the flowing locks, and he staid not in his flight,
Till he reach'd a lonely castle's gate where stood a lady bright.
"Inez! behold thy paramour!" he loud and sternly cried,
And threw his ghastly burden down, close at the lady's side.

"I sought thy bower at even-tide, thou syren, false as fair!
"And, would that I had rather died! I found yon stripling there.
"I turn'd me from the hated spot, but I swore by yon dread Heaven,
"To know no rest until my sword the traitor's life had riven."

The lady stood like stone until he turn'd to ride away,
And then she oped her marble lips, and wildly thus did say:
"Alas, alas! thou cruel Moor, what is it thou hast done!
"This was my brother Rodriguez, my father's only son."

And then before his frenzied eyes, like a crush'd lily bell,
Lifeless upon the bleeding head, the gentle Inez fell.
He drew his glittering ataghan—he sheath'd it in his side—
And for his Spanish ladye-love the Moor Almanzor died.

This is not a very novel incident, but young ladies like stories of love and murder, and Miss Fidler's tastes were peculiarly young-lady-like. She praised Ainsworth and James, but thought Bulwer's works "very immoral," though I never could discover that she had more than skimmed the story from any of them. Cooper she found "pretty;" Miss Sedgwick, "pretty well, only her characters are such common sort of people."

Miss Fidler wrote her own poetry, so that she had ample employment for her time while with us in the woods. It was unfortunate that she could not walk out much on account of her shoes. She was obliged to make out with diluted inspiration. The nearest approach she usually made to the study of Nature, was to sit on the wood-pile, under a girdled tree, and there, with her gold pencil in hand, and her "eyne, grey as glas," rolled upwards, poefy by the hour. Several people, and especially one marriageable lady of a certain age, felt afraid Miss Fidler was "kind o' crazy."

And, standing marvel of Montacute, no guest at morning or night ever found the fair Eloise ungloved. Think of it! In the very wilds to be always like a cat in nutshells, alone useless where all are so busy! I do not wonder our good neighbours thought the damsel a little touched. And then her shoes! "Saint Crispin Crispianus" never had so self-sacrificing a votary. No shoemaker this side of New-York could make a sole papery enough; no tannery out of France could produce materials for this piece of exquisite feminine foppery. Eternal imprisonment within doors, except in the warmest and driest weather, was indeed somewhat of a price to pay, but it was un-grudged. The sofa and its footstool, finery and novels, *would* have made a delicious world for Miss Eloise Fidler, *if* ——

But, alas! "all this availeth me nothing," has been ever the song of poor human nature. The mention of that unfortunate name includes the only real, personal, pun-gent distress which had as yet shaded the lot of my interesting heroine. Fidler! In the mortification adhering to so unpoetical, so unromantic, so inelegant a surname—a name irredeemable even by the highly classical elegance of the Eloise, or as the fair lady herself pronounced it, "Elovees;" in this lay all her wo; and the grand study of her life had been to sink this hated cognomen in one more congenial to her taste. Per-haps this very anxiety had defeated itself; at any rate, here she was at—I did not mean to touch on the ungrateful guess again, but at least at mateable years; neither married, nor particularly likely to be married.

Mrs. Rivers was the object of absolute envy to the pining Eloise. "Anna had been so fortunate," she said; "Rivers was the sweetest name! and Harley was such an ele-gant fellow!"

We thought poor Anna had been any thing but fortunate. She might better have been Fidler or Fiddlestring all her life than to have taken the name of an indifferent and dissipated husband. But not so thought Miss Fidler. It was not long after the ar-rival of the elegant Eloise, that the Montacute Lyceum held its first meeting in Mr. Simeon Jenkins's shop, lighted by three candles, supported by a candelabra of scooped potatoes; Mr. Jenkins himself sitting on the head of a barrel, as president. At first the debates of the institute were held with closed doors; but after the youthful or less practised speakers had tried their powers for a few evenings, the Lyceum was thrown open to the world every Tuesday evening, at six o'clock. The list of members was not very select as to age, character, or standing; and it soon included the entire gentility of the town, and some who scarce claimed rank elsewhere. The attendance of the ladies was particularly requested; and the whole fair sex of Montacute made a point of showing occasionally the interest they undoubtedly felt in the gallant knights who tilted in this field of honour.

But I must not be too diffuse—I was speaking of Miss Fidler. One evening—I hope that beginning prepares the reader for something highly interesting—one evening the question to be debated was the equally novel and striking one which regards the comparative mental capacity of the sexes; and as it was expected that some of the best speakers on both sides would be drawn out by the interesting nature of the subject, every body was anxious to attend.

Among the rest was Miss Fidler, much to the surprise of her sister and myself, who had hitherto been so unfashionable as to deny ourselves this gratification.

"What new whim posseses you, Eloise?" said Mrs. Rivers; "you who never go out in the day-time."

"Oh, just *per passy le tong,*" said the young lady, who was a great French scholar; and go she would and did.

The debate was interesting to absolute breathlessness, both of speakers and hearers, and was gallantly decided in favour of the fair by a youthful member who occupied the barrel as president for the evening. He gave it as his decided opinion, that if the natural and social disadvantages under which woman laboured and must ever continue to labour, could be removed; if their education could be entirely different, and their position in society the reverse of what it is at present, they would be very nearly, if not quite, equal to the nobler sex, in all but strength of mind, in which very useful quality it was his opinion that man would still have the advantage, especially in those communities whose energies were developed by the aid of debating societies.

This decision was hailed with acclamations, and as soon as the question for the ensuing debate, "which is the more useful animal the ox or the ass?" was announced, Miss Eloise Fielder returned home to rave of the elegant young man who sat on the barrel, whom she had decided to be one of "Nature's aristocracy," and whom she had discovered to bear the splendid appellative of Dacre. "Edward Dacre," said she, "for I heard the rude creature Jenkins call him Ed."

The next morning witnessed another departure from Miss Fidler's usual habits. She proposed a walk; and observed that she had never yet bought an article at the store, and really felt as if she ought to purchase something. Mrs. Rivers chancing to be somewhat occupied, Miss Fidler did me the honour of a call, as she could not think of walking without a chaperon.

Behind the counter at Skinner's I saw for the first time a spruce clerk, a really well-looking young man, who made his very best bow to Miss Fidler, and served us with much assiduity. The young lady's purchases occupied some time, and I was obliged gently to hint home-affairs before she could decide between two pieces of muslin, which she declared to be so nearly alike, that it was almost impossible to say which was the best.

When we were at length on our return, I was closely questioned as to my knowledge of "that gentleman," and on my observing that he seemed to be a very decent young man, Miss Fidler warmly justified him from any such opinion, and after a glowing eulogium on his firm countenance, his elegant manners and his grace as a debater, concluded by informing me, as if to cap the climax, that his name was Edward Dacre.

I had thought no more of the matter for some time, though I knew Mr. Darce had become a frequent visitor at Mr. Rivers', when Mrs. Rivers came to me one morning with a perplexed brow, and confided to me her sisterly fears that Eloise was about to make a fool of herself, as she had done more than once before.

"My father," she said, "hoped in this remote corner of creation Eloise might for-

get her nonsense and act like other people; but I verily believe she is bent upon encouraging this low fellow, whose principal charm in her bewildered eyes is his name."

"His name?" said I, "pray explain;" for I had not then learned all the boundless
absurdity of this new Cherubina's fancies.

"Edward Dacre?" said my friend, "this is what enchants my sister, who is absolutely mad on the subject of her own homely appellation."

"Oh, is that all?" said I, "send her to me, then; and I engage to dismiss her cured."

And Miss Fidler came to spend the day. We talked of all novels without exception, and all poetry of all magazines, and Miss Fidler asked me if I had read the "Young
Duke." Upon my confessing as much, she asked my opinion of the heroine, and then
if I had ever heard so sweet a name. "May Dacre—May Dacre," she repeated, as if to
solace her delighted ears.

"Only think how such names are murdered in this country," said I, tossing carelessly before her an account of Mr. Skinner's which bore, "Edkins Daker" below the
receipt. I never saw a change equal to that which seemed to "come o'er the spirit of
her dream." I went on with my citations of murdered names, telling how Rogers was
turned into Rudgers, Conway into Coniway, and Montague into Montaig, but poor
Miss Fidler was no longer in talking mood; and, long before the day was out, she complained of a head-ache and returned to her sister's. Mr. Daker found her "not at
home" that evening; and when I called next morning, the young lady was in bed,
steeping her long ringlets in tears, real tears.

To hasten to the catastrophe: it was discovered ere long that Mr. Edkins Daker's
handsome face, and really pleasant manners, had fairly vanquished Miss Fidler's romance, and she had responded to his professions of attachment with a truth and sincerity, which while it vexed her family inexpressibly, seemed to me to atone for all
her follies. Mr. Daker's prospects were by no means despicable, since a small capital
employed in merchandize in Michigan, is very apt to confer upon the industrious and
fortunate possesser that crowning charm, without which handsome faces, and even
handsome names, are quite worthless in our Western eyes.

Some little disparity of age existed between Miss Fidler and her adorer; but this
was conceded by all to be abundantly made up by the superabounding gentility of the
lady; and when Mr. Daker returned from New-York with his new stock of goods and
his stylish bride, I thought I had seldom seen a happier or better mated couple. And
at this present writing, I do not believe Eloise, with all her whims, would exchange
her very nice Edkins for the proudest Dacre of the British Peerage.

37

INDIAN REMOVAL ACT AND CHEROKEE NATION V. GEORGIA

(1830 and 1831)

White settlement of the region between the Appalachian mountains and the Mississippi River exploded between 1815 and 1830. Despite many cases of biracial cohabitation, larger forces at both the state and federal levels came to see it as necessary that all Native Americans be "removed" west of the Mississippi and resettled on lands, in turn, from which trans-Mississipian natives had been removed. Advocates of removal ranged from Lewis Cass, the last territorial governor, to George Copway, the Ojibwa whose speech on the subject is included in this volume.

It was argued that removal would protect the natives from the uncontrollable persecution of the lawless settlers, as well as from their alcohol and diseases—that removal was a form of protection. Such a transparent sophistry was resisted by a long series of native speakers and white western writers (such as Benjamin Drake and James Hall). Nonetheless, the federal government insisted on removal, and the results included the Black Hawk War, the Trail of Tears, and the fragmentation of many tribes that were only partially removed (such as the Pottawattomi). Removal openly violated the contractual basis of treaty law, a process that would finally lead to the destructive Dawes Act of 1887.

The most flagrant case of the abuse of federal power in the enforcement of removal was in the case of the Cherokees of Georgia, as is documented elsewhere in this volume in the work of Elias Boudinot and the Treaty of 1791. In the early nineteenth century, the Cherokees had followed the terms of assimilation dictated by that and subsequent treaties. They had become agriculturalists and were so entangled in the economics of the region that they owned a great number of slaves. Whites wishing their removal were further motivated by the mining opportunities recently discovered on tribal lands, and so removal was enforced, in open violation of the treaties.

The Cherokees, thinking themselves aggrieved citizens whose rightful course of relief was the court system, pursued legal means of staying on their land, and their case was taken to the Supreme Court. The resulting decision in *Cherokee Nation v. Georgia* was rendered by Chief Justice John Marshall and stands with *Johnson and Graham's Lessee v. William McIntosh* (1823) and *Worcester v. Georgia* (1832) in what is known by legal scholars as "The Marshall Trilogy." While all of these decisions uphold the notions of tribal sovereignty and collectivity, as Marshall's opinion in *Cherokee Nation* makes clear, they render Native Americans as children, existing "in a state of pupilage" to the United States. Removal, then, is justified as a paternalistic attempt at kindness, protecting a childish race from the burdens of citizenship.

Text: Both reprinted from *Documents of United States Indian Policy,* ed. Francis Paul Prucha (Lincoln: University of Nebraska Press, 1975): 52–53, 58–60.

42. INDIAN REMOVAL ACT MAY 28, 1830

An Act to provide for an exchange of lands with the Indians residing in any of the states or territories, and for their removal west of the river Mississippi.

Be it enacted . . . , That it shall and may be lawful for the President of the United States to cause so much of any territory belonging to the United States, west of the river Mississippi, not included in any state or organized territory, and to which the Indian title has been extinguished, as he may judge necessary, to be divided into a suitable number of districts, for the reception of such tribes or nations of Indians as may choose to exchange the lands where they now reside, and remove there; and to cause each of said districts to be so described by natural or artificial marks, as to be easily distinguished from every other.

SEC. 2. *And be it further enacted,* That it shall and may be lawful for the President to exchange any or all of such districts, so to be laid off and described, with any tribe or nation of Indians now residing within the limits of any of the states or territories, and with which the United States have existing treaties, for the whole or any part or portion of the territory claimed and occupied by such tribe or nation, within the bounds of any one or more of the states or territories, where the land claimed and occupied by the Indians, is owned by the United States, or the United States are bound to the state within which it lies to extinguish the Indian claim thereto.

SEC. 3. *And be it further enacted,* That in the making of any such exchange or exchanges, it shall and may be lawful for the President solemnly to assure the tribe or nation with which the exchange is made, that the United States will forever secure and guaranty to them, and their heirs or successors, the country so exchanged with them; and if they prefer it, that the United States will cause a patent or grant to be made and executed to them for the same: *Provided always,* That such lands shall revert to the United States, if the Indians become extinct, or abandon the same.

SEC. 4. *And be it further enacted,* That if, upon any of the lands now occupied by the Indians, and to be exchanged for, there should be such improvements as add value to the land claimed by any individual or individuals of such tribes or nations, it shall and may be lawful for the President to cause such value to be ascertained by appraisement or otherwise, and to cause such ascertained value to be paid to the person or persons rightfully claiming such improvements. And upon the payment of such valuation, the improvements so valued and paid for, shall pass to the United States, and possession shall not afterwards be permitted to any of the same tribe.

SEC. 5. *And be it further enacted,* That upon the making of any such exchange as is contemplated by this act, it shall and may be lawful for the President to cause such aid and assistance to be furnished to the emigrants as may be necessary and proper to enable them to remove to, and settle in, the country for which they may have exchanged; and also, to give them such aid and assistance as may be necessary for their support and subsistence for the first year after their removal.

SEC. 6. *And be it further enacted,* That it shall and may be lawful for the President to cause such tribe or nation to be protected, at their new residence, against all interruption or disturbance from any other tribe or nation of Indians, or from any other person or persons whatever.

SEC. 7. *And be it further enacted,* That it shall and may be lawful for the President to have the same superintendence and care over any tribe or nation in the country to which they may remove, as contemplated by this act, that he is now authorized to have over them at their present places of residence: *Provided,* That nothing in this act contained shall be construed as authorizing or directing the violation of any existing treaty between the United States and any of the Indian tribes.

SEC. 8. *And be it further enacted,* That for the purpose of giving effect to the provisions of this act, the sum of five hundred thousand dollars is hereby appropriated, to be paid out of any money in the treasury, not otherwise appropriated to be paid out of any money in the treasury, not otherwise appropriated. . . .

[US Statutes at Large 4:411–12]

44. CHEROKEE NATION V. GEORGIA 1831

When Georgia extended her laws over the Cherokee lands, the Indians brought suit against the state. The Supreme Court refused to accept jurisdiction because it declared that the Cherokee Nation was not a "foreign nation" in the sense intended by the Constitution. John Marshall, who delivered the opinion, described the Indian tribes as "domestic dependent nations."

. . . . Mr. Chief Justice MARSHALL delivered the opinion of the Court.

This bill is brought by the Cherokee nation, praying an injunction to restrain the state of Georgia from the execution of certain laws of that state, which, as is alleged, go directly to annihilate the Cherokees as a political society, and to seize, for the use of Georgia, the lands of the nation which have been assured to them by the United States in solemn treaties repeatedly made and still in force.

If Courts were permitted to indulge their sympathies, a case better calculated to excite them can scarcely be imagined. A people once numerous, powerful, and truly independent, found by our ancestors in the quiet and uncontrolled possession of an ample domain, gradually sinking beneath our superior policy, our arts and our arms, have yielded their lands by successive treaties, each of which contains a solemn guarantee of the residue, until they retain no more of their formerly extensive territory than is deemed necessary to their comfortable subsistence. To preserve this remnant, the present application is made.

Before we can look into the merits of the case, a preliminary inquiry presents itself. Has this Court jurisdiction of the cause?

The third article of the constitution describes the extent of the judicial power. The second section closes an enumeration of the cases to which it is extended, with "controversies" "between a state or the citizens thereof, and foreign states, citizens, or subjects." A subsequent clause of the same section gives the Supreme Court original jurisdiction in all cases in which a state shall be a party. The party defendant may then unquestionably be sued in this Court. May the plaintiff sue in it? Is the Cherokee nation a foreign state in the sense in which that term is used in the constitution?

The counsel for the plaintiffs have maintained the affirmative of this proposition with great earnestness and ability. So much of the argument as was intended to prove the character of the Cherokees as a state, as a distinct political society, separated from others, capable of managing its own affairs and governing itself, has, in the opinion of a majority of the judges, been completely successful. They have been uniformly treated as a state from the settlement of our country. The numerous treaties made with them by the United States recognise them as a people capable of maintaining the relations of peace and war, of being responsible in their political character for any violation of their engagements, or for any aggression committed on the citizens of the United States by any individual of their community. Laws have been enacted in the spirit of these treaties. The acts of our government plainly recognise the Cherokee nation as a state, and the Courts are bound by those acts.

A question of much more difficulty remains. Do the Cherokees constitute a foreign state in the sense of the constitution?

The counsel have shown conclusively that they are not a state of the union, and have insisted that individually they are aliens, not owing allegiance to the United States. An aggregate of aliens composing a state must, they say, be a foreign state. Each individual being foreign, the whole must be foreign.

This argument is imposing, but we must examine it more closely before we yield to it. The condition of the Indians in relation to the United States is perhaps unlike that of any other two people in existence. In the general, nations not owing a common allegiance are foreign to each other. The term foreign nation is, with strict propriety, applicable by either to the other. But the relation of the Indians to the United States is marked by peculiar and cardinal distinctions which exist no where else.

The Indian territory is admitted to compose a part of the United States. In all our maps, geographical treatises, histories, and laws, it is so considered. In all our intercourse with foreign nations, in our commercial regulations, in any attempt at intercourse between Indians and foreign nations, they are considered as within the jurisdictional limits of the United States, subject to many of those restraints which are imposed upon our own citizens. They acknowledge themselves in their treaties to be under the protection of the United States; they admit that the United States shall have the sole and exclusive right of regulating the trade with them, and managing all their affairs as they think proper; and the Cherokees in particular were allowed by the treaty of Hopewell, which preceded the constitution, "to send a deputy of their choice, whenever they think fit, to Congress." Treaties were made with some tribes by the state of New York, under a then unsettled construction of the confederation, by which they ceded all their lands to that state, taking back a limited grant to themselves, in which they admit their dependence.

Though the Indians are acknowledged to have an unquestionable, and, heretofore, unquestioned right to the lands they occupy, until that right shall be extinguished by a voluntary cession to our government; yet it may well be doubted whether those tribes which reside within the acknowledged boundaries of the United States can, with strict accuracy, be denominated foreign nations. They may, more correctly, perhaps, be denominated domestic dependent nations. They occupy a territory to which we assert a title independent of their will which must take effect in point of possession when their right of possession ceases. Meanwhile they are in a state of pupilage. Their relation to the United States resembles that of a ward to his guardian.

They look to our government for protection; rely upon its kindness and its power; appeal to it for relief to their wants; and address the president as their great father. They and their country are considered by foreign nations, as well as by ourselves, as being so completely under the sovereignty and dominion of the United States, that any attempt to acquire their lands, or to form a political connexion with them, would be considered by all as an invasion of our territory, and an act of hostility.

These considerations go far to support the opinion, that the framers of our constitution had not the Indian tribes in view, when they opened the Courts of the union to controversies between a state or the citizens thereof, and foreign states.

In considering this subject, the habits and usages of the Indians, in their intercourse with their white neighbours, ought not to be entirely disregarded. At the time the constitution was framed, the idea of appealing to an American Court of justice for an assertion of right or a redress of wrong, had perhaps never entered the mind of an Indian or of his tribe. Their appeal was to the tomahawk, or to the government. This was well understood by the statesmen who framed the constitution of the United States, and might furnish some reason for omitting to enumerate them among the parties who might sue in the Courts of the union. Be this as it may, the peculiar relations between the United States and the Indians occupying our territory are such, that we should feel much difficulty in considering them as designated by the term foreign state, were there no other part of the constitution which might shed light on the meaning of these words. But we think that in construing them, considerable aid is furnished by that clause in the eighth section of the third article, which empowers Congress to "regulate commerce with foreign nations, and among the several states, and with the Indian tribes."

In this clause they are as clearly contradistinguished by a name appropriate to themselves, from foreign nations, as from the several states composing the union. They are designated by a distinct appellation; and as this appellation can be applied to neither of the others, neither can the appellation distinguishing either of the others be in fair construction applied to them. The objects, to which the power of regulating commerce might be directed, are divided into three distinct classes—foreign nations, the several states, and Indian tribes. When forming this article, the convention considered them as entirely distinct. We cannot assume that the distinction was lost in framing a subsequent article, unless there be something in its language to authorize the assumption. . . .

The Court has bestowed its best attention on this question, and, after mature deliberation, the majority is of opinion that an Indian tribe or nation within the United States is not a foreign state in the sense of the constitution, and cannot maintain an action in the Courts of the United States. . . .

If it be true that the Cherokee nation have rights, this is not the tribunal in which those rights are to be asserted. If it be true that wrongs have been inflicted, and that still greater are to be apprehended, this is not the tribunal which can redress the past or prevent the future.

The motion for an injunction is denied. . . .

[5 *Peters*, 15–20.]

ELIAS BOUDINOT (GALEGINA)

(1803?–1839)

Elias Boudinot was born Galegina ("Mule Deer" or "Buck") at Ooth-caloga in the Cherokee nation, near present-day Calhoun, Georgia, prob-ably in 1803 or 1804. His parents were Oo-watie (later David Watie), a Cherokee warrior, and Susannah Reese, the daughter of a Cherokee woman and a white trader. In 1818, when Galegina enrolled in the Corn-wall Foreign Mission School in Cornwall, Connecticut, he gave his name as Elias Boudinot after the president of the American Bible Society, who had provided his scholarship. Boudinot converted to Christianity in 1820.

In December 1822, Boudinot returned to the Cherokee nation where he became clerk of Cherokee National Council. At the time he passionately opposed Indian relocation, believing that Indians and whites might live together peacefully. He began to have doubts, however, fol-lowing the announcement of his engagement to Harriet Ruggles Gold, a young white woman he had met in Cornwall. The Connecticut town was outraged at the prospect of an interracial marriage, and Gold's brother burned the couple in effigy. In 1826, after tempers cooled, Boudinot and Gold were married in Cornwall, and they promptly left to live together in the Cherokee nation.

Boudinot was the first editor of the nation's first newspaper, the bilin-gual *Cherokee Phoenix,* beginning on February 21, 1828. In addition, he col-laborated on a translation of the Bible into Cherokee and also translated the first novel to be published in Cherokee, the pious *Poor Sarah, or The Indian Woman* (1831). By 1832 Boudinot had become convinced that the Chero-kees must relocate or face gradual genocide at the hands of the whites who were invading their land. He wanted to debate this issue in the pages of the *Phoenix* but could not, as he was forbidden to discuss any proposal that was contrary to the official positions of the tribal government.

Thus, Boudinot resigned from the *Cherokee Phoenix* and joined the Treaty party. This group negotiated the Treaty of Echota (1835), in which the Cherokees agreed to exchange their lands east of the Mississippi River for land in present-day Oklahoma. This agreement was endorsed by nei-ther the Cherokee government nor a majority of the Cherokee people. Furthermore, Cherokee law made it a capital crime to cede tribal land without government approval. In his preface to *Letters and Other Papers Relating to Cherokee Affairs* (1837), Boudinot defended his decision to sign the Treaty of Echota: "If one hundred persons are ignorant of their true situation, and are so completely blinded as not to see the destruction that awaits them, we can see strong reasons to justify the action of a minority of fifty persons—to do what the majority *would do* if they understood their condition—to save a *nation* from political thraldom and moral degradation."

In 1838, the Treaty of Echota led to the infamous Trail of Tears, the forced march to Oklahoma, during which 4,000 Cherokees—roughly 25% of the tribe—died. Boudinot avoided the Trail of Tears, having arrived in Oklahoma in 1837. On June 22, 1839, tribal law was enforced: an unknown band of Cherokees executed Boudinot and others for having signed the unauthorized treaty.

An Address to the Whites was published in Philadelphia in 1826, when Boudinot's public face still showed Enlightenment optimism. At the time he was lecturing throughout the country to raise money for the printing press and type that would be used to publish the *Cherokee Nation*.

Text: *An Address to the Whites* (Philadelphia, 1826) 15 pp.

AN ADDRESS TO THE WHITES

To those who are unacquainted with the manners, habits, and improvements of the Aborigines of this country, the term *Indian* is pregnant with ideas the most repelling and degrading. But such impressions, originating as they frequently do, from infant prejudices, although they hold too true when applied to some, do great injustice to many of this race of beings.

Some there are, perhaps even in this enlightened assembly, who at the bare sight of an Indian, or at the mention of the name, would throw back their imaginations to ancient times, to the ravages of savage warfare, to the yells pronounced over the mangled bodies of women and children, thus creating an opinion, inapplicable and highly injurious to those for whose temporal interest and eternal welfare, I come to plead.

What is an Indian? Is he not formed of the same materials with yourself? For "of one blood God created all the nations that dwell on the face of the earth." Though it be true that he is ignorant, that he is a heathen, that he is a savage; yet he is no more than all others have been under similar circumstances. Eighteen centuries ago what were the inhabitants of Great Britain?

You here behold an *Indian,* my kindred are *Indians,* and my fathers sleeping in the wilderness grave—they too were *Indians*. But I am not as my fathers were—broader means and nobler influences have fallen upon me. Yet I was not born as thousands are, in a stately dome and amid the congratulations of the great, for on a little hill, in a lonely cabin, overspread by the forest oak, I first drew my breath; and in a language unknown to learned and polished nations, I learnt to lisp my mother's name. In after days, I have had greater advantages than most of my race; and I now stand before you delegated by my native country to seek her interest, to labour for her respectability, and by my public efforts to assist in raising her to an equal standing with other nations of the earth.

The time has arrived when speculations and conjectures as to the practicability of civilizing the Indians must forever cease. A period is fast approaching when the stale remark—"Do what you will, an Indian will still be an Indian," must be placed no more in speech. With whatever plausibility this popular objection may have heretofore been made, every candid mind must now be sensible that it can no longer be uttered, except by those who are uninformed with respect to us, who are strongly prejudiced against us, or who are filled with vindictive feelings towards us; for the present history of the Indians, particularly of that nation to which I belong, most incontrovertibly establishes the fallacy of this remark. I am aware of the difficulties which have ever existed to Indian civilization, I do not deny the almost insurmountable obstacles which we ourselves have thrown in the way of this improvement, nor do I say that difficulties no longer remain; but facts will permit me to declare that there are none which may not easily be overcome, by strong and continued exertions. It needs not abstract reasoning to prove this position. It needs not the display of language to prove to the minds of good men, that Indians are susceptible to attainments necessary to the formation of polished society. It needs not the power of argument on the nature of man, to silence forever the remark that "it is the purpose of the Almighty that the Indians should be exterminated." It needs only that the world should know what we have done in the few last years, to foresee what yet we may do with the assistance of our white brethren, and that of the common Parent of us all.

It is not necessary to present to you a detailed account of the various aboriginal tribes, who have been known to you only on the pages of history, and there but obscurely known. They have gone; and to revert back to their days, would be only to disturb their oblivious sleep; to darken these walls with deeds at which humanity must shudder; to place before your eyes the scenes of Muskingum Sahta-goo and the plains of Mexico, to call up the crimes of the bloody Cortes and his infernal host; and to describe the animosity and vengeance which have overthrown, and hurried into the shades of death those numerous tribes. But here let me say, that however guilty these unhappy nations may have been, yet many and unreasonable were the wrongs they suffered, many the hardships they endured, and many their wanderings through the trackless wilderness. Yes, "notwithstanding the obloquy with which the early historians of the colonies have overshadowed the character of the ignorant and unfortunate natives, some bright gleams will occasionally break through, that throw a melancholy lustre on their memories. Facts are occasionally to be met with in their rude annals, which, though recorded with all the colouring of prejudice and bigotry, yet speak for themselves, and will be dwelt upon with applause and sympathy when prejudice shall have passed away."

Nor is it my purpose to enter largely into the consideration of the remnants, of those who have fled with time and are no more— They stand as monuments of the Indian's fate. And should they ever become extinct, they must move off the earth, as did their fathers. My design is to offer a few disconnected facts relative to the present improved state, and to the ultimate prospects of that particular tribe called Cherokees to which I belong.

The Cherokee nation lies within the chartered limits of the states of Georgia, Tennessee, and Alabama. Its extent as defined by treaties is about 200 miles in length from East to West, and about 120 in breadth. This country which is supposed to contain about 10,000,000 of acres exhibits great varieties of surface, the most part being

hilly and mountaneous, affording soil of no value. The vallies, however, are well watered and afford excellent land, in many parts particularly on the large streams, that of
the first quality. The climate is temporate and healthy, indeed I would not be guilty of
exaggeration were I to say, that the advantages which this country possess to render it
salubrious, are many and superior. Those lofty and barren mountains, defying the
labour and ingenuity of many, and supposed by some as placed there only to exhibit
omnipotence, contribute to the healthiness and beauty of the surrounding plains, and
give to us that free air and pure water which distinguish our country. These advantages, calculated to make the inhabitants healthy, vigorous, and intelligent, cannot fail
to cause this country to become interesting. And there can be no doubt that the
Cherokee Nation, however obscure and trifling it may now appear, will finally become, if not under its present occupants, one of the Garden spots of America. And
here, let me be indulged in the fond wish, that she may thus become under those who
now possess her; and ever be fostered, regulated and protected by the generous government of the United States.

The population of the Cherokee Nation increased from the year 1810 to that of
1824, 2000 exclusive of those who emigrated in 1818 and 19 to the west of the Mississippi—of those who reside on the Arkansas the number is supposed to be about
5000.

The rise of these people in their movement towards civilization, may be traced
as far back as the rilinquishment of their towns; when game became incompetent to
their support, by reason of the surrounding white population. They then betook
themselves to the woods, commenced the opening of small clearings, and the raising
of stock; still however following the chase. Game has since become so scarce that little dependence for subsistence can be placed upon it. They have gradually and I could
almost say universally forsaken their ancient employment. In fact, there is not a single
family in the nation, that can be said to subsist on the slender support which the
wilderness would afford. The love and the practice of hunting are not now carried to
a higher degree, than among all frontier people whether white or red. It cannot be
doubted, however, that there are many who have commenced a life of agricultural
labour from mere necessity, and if they could, would gladly resume their former
course of living. But these are individual failings and ought to be passed over.

On the other hand it cannot be doubted that the nation is improving, rapidly improving in all those particulars which must finally constitute the inhabitants an industrious and intelligent people.

It is a matter of surprise to me, and must be to all those who are properly acquainted with the condition of the Aborigines of this country, that the Cherokees
have advanced so far and so rapidly in civilization. But there are yet powerful obstacles, both within and without, to be surmounted in the march of improvement. The
prejudices in regard to them in the general community are strong and lasting. The evil
effects of their intercourse with their immediate white neighbours, who differ from
them chiefly in name, are easily to be seen, and it is evident that from this intercourse
proceed those demoralizing practices which in order to surmount, peculiar and unremitting efforts are necessary. In defiance, however, of these obstacles the Cherokees
have improved and are still rapidly improving. To give you a further view of their condition, I will here repeat some of the articles of the two statistical tables taken at different periods.

In 1810 there were 19,500 cattle; 6,100 horses; 19,600 swine; 1,037 sheep; 467
looms; 1,600 spinning wheels; 30 waggons; 500 ploughs; 3 saw-mills; 13 grist-mills
&c. At this time there are 22,000 cattle; 7,600 horses; 46,000 swine; 2,500 sheep; 762

looms; 2488 spinning wheels; 172 waggons; 2,943 ploughs; 10 saw-mills; 31 grist-mills; 62 Blacksmith-shops; 8 cotton machines; 18 schools; 18 ferries; and a number of public roads. In one district there were, last winter, upwards of 0000 volumes of good books; and 11 different periodical papers both religious and political, which were taken and read. On the public roads there are many decent Inns, and few houses for convenience, &c., would disgrace any country. Most of the schools are under the care and tuition of christian missionaries, of differenct denominations, who have been of great service to the nation, by inculcating moral and religious principles into the minds of the rising generation. In many places the word of God is regularly preached and explained, both by missionaries and natives; and there are numbers who have publicly professed their belief and interest in the merits of the great Saviour of the world. It is worthy of remark, that in no ignorant country have the missionaries undergone less trouble and difficulty, in spreading a knowledge of the Bible, than in this. Here, they have been welcomed and encouraged by the proper authorities of the nation, their persons have been protected, and in very few instances have some individual vagabonds threatened violence to them. Indeed it may be said with truth, that among no heathen people has the faithful minister of God experienced greater success, greater reward for his labour, than in this. He is surrounded by attentive hearers, the words which flow from his lips are not spent in vain. The Cherokees have had no established religion of their own, and perhaps to this circumstance we may attribute, in part, the facilities with which missionaries have persued their ends. They cannot be called idolaters; for they never worshipped Images. They believed in a Supreme Being, the Creator of all, the God of the white, the red, and the black man. They also believed in the existence of an evil spirit who resided, as they thought, in the setting sun, the future place of all who in their time had done iniquitously. Their prayers were addressed alone to the Supreme Being, and which if written would fill a large volume, and display much sincerity, beauty and sublimity. When the ancient customs of the Cherokees were in their full force, no warrior thought himself secure, unless he had addressed his guardian angel; no hunter could hope for success, unless before the rising sun he had asked the assistance of his God, and on his return at eve he had offered his sacrifice to him.

There are three things of late occurance, which must certainly place the Cherokee Nation in a fair light, and act as a powerful argument in favor of Indian improvement.

First. The invention of letters.

Second. The translation of the New Testament into Cherokee.

And third. The organization of a Government.

The Cherokee mode of writing lately invented by George Guest, who could not read any language nor speak any other than his own, consists of eighty-six characters, principally syllabic, the combinations of which form all the words of the language. Their terms may be greatly simplified, yet they answer all the purposes of writing, and already many natives use them.

The translation of the New Testament, together with Guest's mode of writing, has swept away the barrier which has long existed, and opened a spacious channel for the instruction of adult Cherokees. Persons of all ages and classes may now read the precepts of the Almighty in their own language. Before it is long, there will scarcely be an individual in the nation who can say, "I know not God neither understand I what thou sayest," for all shall know him from the greatest to the least. The aged warrior over whom has rolled three score and ten years of savage life, will grace the temple of God with his hoary head; and the little child yet on the breast of its pious mother shall learn to lisp its Maker's name.

The shrill sound of the Savage yell shall die away as the roaring of far distant thunder; and Heaven wrought music will gladden the affrighted wilderness. "The solitary places will be glad for them, and the desert shall rejoice and blossom as a rose." Already do we see the morning star, forerunner of approaching dawn, rising over the tops of those deep forests in which for ages have echoed the warrior's whoop. But has not God said it, and will he not do it? The Almighty decrees his purposes, and man cannot with all his ingenuity and device countervail them. They are more fixed in their course than the rolling sun—more durable than the everlasting mountains.

The Government, though defective in many respects, is well suited to the condition of the inhabitants. As they rise in information and refinement, changes in it must follow, until they arrive at that state of advancement, when I trust they will be admitted into all the privileges of the American family.

The Cherokee Nation is divided into eight districts, in each of which are established courts of justice, where all disputed cases are decided by a Jury, under the direction of a circuit Judge, who has jurisdiction over two districts. Sheriffs and other publice officers are appointed to execute the decisions of the courts, collect debts, and arrest thieves and other criminals. Appeals may be taken to the Superior Court, held annually at the seat of Government. The Legislative authority is vested in a General Court, which consists of the National Committee and Council. The National Committee consists of thirteen members, who are generally men of sound sense and fine talents. The National Council consists of thirty-two members, beside the speaker, who act as the representatives of the people. Every bill passing these two bodies, becomes the law of the land. Clerks are appointed to do the writings, and record the proceedings of the Council. The executive power is vested in two principal chiefs, who hold their office during good behaviour, and sanction all the decisions of the legislative counil. Many of the laws display some degree of civilization, and establish the respectability of the nation.

Polygamy is abolished. Female chastity and honor are protected by law. The Sabbath is respected by the Council during session. Mechanics are encouraged by law. The practice of putting aged persons to death for witchcraft is abolished and murder has now become a governmental crime.

From what I have said, you will form but a faint opinion of the true state of prospects of the Cherokees. You will, however, be convinced of three important truths.

First, that the means which have been employed for the christianization and civilization of this tribe, have been greatly blessed. Second, that the increase of these means will meet the final success. Third, that it has now become necessary, that efficient and more than ordinary means should be employed.

Sensible of this last point, and wishing to do something for themselves, the Cherokees have thought it advisable that there should be established, a Printing Press and a Seminary of respectable character; and for these purposes your aid and patronage are now solicited. They wish the types, as expressed in their resolution, to be composed of English letters and Cherokee characters. Those characters have now become extensively used in the nation; their religious songs are written in them; there is an astonishing eagerness in people of all classes and ages to acquire a knowledge of them;

and the New Testament has been translated into their language. All this impresses on them the immediated necessity of procuring types. The most informed and judicious of our nation, believe that such a press would go further to remove ignorance, and her offspring superstition and prejudice, than all other means. The adult part of the nation will probably grovel on in ignorance and die in ignorance, without any fair trial upon them, unless the proposed means are carried into effect. The simplicity of this method of writing, and the eagerness to obtain a knowledge of it, are evinced by the astonishing rapidity with which it is acquired, and by the numbers who do so. It is about two years since its introduction, and already there are a great many who can read it. In the neighbourhood in which I live, I do not recollect a male Cherokee, between the ages of fifteen and twenty five, who is ignorant of this mode of writing. But in connexion with those for Cherokee characters, it is necessary to have types for English letters. There are many who already speak and read the English language, and can appreciate the advantages which would result from the publication of their laws and transactions in a well conducted newspaper. Such a paper, comprising a summary of religious and political events, &c. on the one hand; and on the other, exhibiting the feelings, disposition, improvements, and prospects of the Indians; their traditions, their true character, as it once was and as it now is; the ways and means most likely to throw the mantle of civilization over all tribes; and such other matter as will tend to diffuse proper and correct impressions in regard to their condition—such a paper could not fail to create much interest in the American community, favourable to the aborigines, and to have a powerful influence on the advancement of the Indians themselves. How can the patriot or the philanthropists devise efficient means, without full and correct information as to the subjects of his labour. And I am inclinded to think, after all that has been said of the aborigines, after all that has been written in narratives, professedly to elucidate the leading traits of their character, that the public knows little of that character. To obtain a correct and complete knowledge of these people, there must exist a vehicle of Indian intelligence, altogether different from those which have heretofore been employed. Will not a paper published in an Indian country, under proper and judicious regulations, have the desired effect? I do not say that Indians will produce learned and elaborate dissertations in explanation and vindication of their own character; but they may exhibit specimens of their intellectual efforts, of their eloquence, of the their moral, civil and physical advancement, which will do quite as much to remove prejudice and to give profitable information.

The Cherokees wish to establish their Seminary, upon a footing which will insure to it all the advantages, that belong to such institutions in the states. Need I spend one moment in arguments, in favour of such an institution; need I speak one word of the utility, of the necessity, of an institution of learning; need I do more than simply to ask the patronage of benevolent hearts, to obtain that patronage.

When before did a nation of Indians step forward and ask for the means of civilization? The Cherokee authorities have adopted the measures already stated, with a sincere desire to make their nation an intelligent and virtuous people, and with a full hope that those who have already pointed out to them the road of happiness, will now assist them to pursue it. With that assistance, what are the prospects of the Cherokees? Are they not indeed glorious, compared to the deep darkness in which the nobler qualities of their souls have slept. Yes, methinks I can view my native country, rising from the ashes of her degradation, wearing her purified and beautiful garments, and taking her seat with the nations of the earth. I can behold her sons bursting the fetters of ignorance and unshackling her from the vices of heathenism. She is at this instant, risen like the first morning sun, which grows brighter and brighter, until it reaches its fulness of glory.

She will become not a great, but a faithful ally of the United States. In times of peace she will plead the common liberties of America. In times of war her intrepid sons will sacrifice their lives in your defence. And because she will be useful to you in coming time, she asks you to assist her in her present struggles. She asks not for greatness; she seeks not wealth; she pleads only for assistance to become respectable as a nation, to enlighten and ennoble her sons, and to ornament her daughters with modesty and virtue. She pleads for this assistance, too, because on her destiny hangs that of many nations. If she complete her civilization—then may we hope that all our nations will—then, indeed, may true patriots be encouraged in their efforts to make this world of the West, one continuous abode of enlightened, free, and happy people.

But if the Cherokee Nation fail in her struggle, if she die away, then all hopes are blasted, and falls the fabric of Indian civilization. Their fathers were born in darkness, and have fled in darkness; without your assistance so will their sons. You see, however, where the probability rests. Is there a soul whose narrowness will not permit the exercises of charity on such an occasion? Where is he that can withhold his mite from an object so noble? Who can prefer a little of his silver and gold, to the welfare of nations of his fellow beings? Human wealth perishes with our clay, but that wealth gained in charity still remains on earth, to enrich our names, when we are gone, and will be remembered in Heaven, when the miser and his coffers have mouldered together in their kindred earth. The works of a generous mind sweeten the cup of affliction; they enlighten the dreary way to the cold tomb; they blunt the sting of death, and smooth his passage to the unknown world. When all the kingdoms of this earth shall die away and their beauty and power shall perish, his name shall live and shine as a twinkling star; those for whose benefit he done his deeds of charity shall call him blessed, and they shall add honor to his immortal head.

There are, with regard to the Cherokees and other tribes, two alternatives; they must either become civilized and happy, or sharing the fate of many kindred nations, become extinct. If the General Government continue its protection, and the American people assist them in their humble efforts, they will, they must rise. Yes, under such protection, and with such assistance, the Indian must rise like the Phoenix, after having wallowed for ages in ignorance and barbarity. But should this Government withdraw its care, and the American people their aid, then, to use the words of a writer, "they will go the way that so many tribes have gone before them; for the hordes that still linger about the shores of Huron, and the tributary streams of the Mississippi, will share the fate of those tribes that once lorded it along the proud banks of the Hudson; of the gigantic race that are said to have existed on the borders of the Susquehanna; of those various nations that flourished about the Potomac and the Rhappahannoc, and that peopled the forests of the vast valley of Shenandoah. They will vanish like a vapour from the face of the earth, their very history will be lost in forgetfulness, and the places that now know them will know them no more."

There is, in Indian history, something very melancholy, and which seems to establish a mournful precedent for the future events of the few sons of the forest, now scattered over this vast continent. We have seen every where the poor aborigines melt away before the white population. I merely speak of the fact, without at all referring to the cause. We have seen, I say, one family after another, one tribe after another, nation after nation, pass away; until only a few solitary creatures are left to tell the sad story of extinction.

Shall this precedent be followed? I ask you, shall red men live, or shall they be swept from the earth? With you and this public at large, the decision chiefly rests. Must they perish? Must they all, like the unfortunate Creeks, (victims of the unchristian policy of certain persons,) go down in sorrow to their grave?

They hang upon your mercy as to a garment. Will you push them from you, or will you save them? Let humanity answer.

39

CONSTITUTION OF THE CHEROKEE NATION

(1839)

May 23, 1838: this was the deadline for Cherokee Indians to leave their homeland voluntarily and relocate to the Indian Territory in present-day Oklahoma. Of roughly 17,000 Cherokees, only 2,000 left on their own. The 15,000 Cherokees who remained were removed by U.S. forces under the command of General Winfield Scott. These Indians, who lived in North Carolina, Tennessee, Georgia, and Alabama, were stripped of their belongings and gathered in detention camps in Tennessee before they were forced to march 800 miles to the west. This journey became known as the Trail of Tears. On their way to the Indian Territory, 4,000 Cherokees died.

The Cherokees were one of the so-called Five Civilized Tribes—along with the Creeks, Choctaws, Chickasaws, and Seminoles—who, by the early part of the nineteenth century, had adopted many aspects of white culture. The Cherokee alphabet, developed by Sequoyah, was completed in 1821. For the first time Cherokees were able to fix tribal law in writing. Cherokees resistant to such "civilization" moved west and thus became known as Western Cherokees. In 1827 the remaining Eastern Cherokees adopted a written constitution, which they modeled on the Constitution of the United States. With their chief remaining their political leader, the Eastern Cherokees formally established an elective bicameral legislature similar to the United States Congress, with the National Committee as their Senate and the National Council as their House of Representatives.

In 1839 in the Indian Territory, the Eastern and Western Cherokees were reunited. After the majority of the tribe had arrived, they agreed to adopt the Constitution of 1839, which was nearly identical to the Constitution of 1827. Ironically, the "civilized" Eastern Cherokees had prevailed over their western counterparts, though their decision to "civilize" had not allowed them to coexist with white Americans.

Text: *Compiled Laws of the Cherokee Nation* (Tahlequah, I.T., 1881): 10–27.

CONSTITUTION OF THE CHEROKEE NATION
(1839)

The Eastern and Western Cherokees having again reunited, and become one body politic, under the style and title of the CHEROKEE NATION: Therefore,

We, the people of the Cherokee Nation, in National Convention assembled, in order to establish justice, insure tranquility, promote the common welfare, and to secure to ourselves and our posterity the blessings of freedom—acknowledging with humility and gratitude, the goodness of the Sovereign Ruler of the Universe; in permitting us so to do, and imploring His aid and guidance in its accomplishment—do ordain and establish this Constitution for the government of the Cherokee Nation.

Article I

SEC. 1. The boundary of the Cherokee Nation shall be that described in the treaty of 1833, between the United States and Western Cherokees, subject to such extension as may be made in the adjustment of the unfinished business with the United States.

SEC. 2. The lands of the Cherokee Nation shall remain common property; but the improvements made thereon, and in the possession of the citizens of the Nation, are the exclusive and indefeasible property of the citizens respectively who made, or may rightfully be, in possession of them: *Provided,* that the citizens of the Nation possessing exclusive and indefeasible right to their improvements, as expressed in this article, shall possess no right or power to dispose of their improvements, in any manner whatever, to the United States, individual states, or to individual citizens thereof; and that, whenever any citizen shall remove with his effects out of the limits of this Nation, and become a citizen of any other government, all his rights and privileges as a citizen of this Nation shall cease: *Provided, nevertheless,* that the National Council shall have power to re-admit, by law, to all the rights of citizenship, any such person or persons who may, at any time, desire to return to the Nation, on memorializing the National Council for such re-admission.

Moreover, the National Council shall have power to adopt such laws and regulations, as its wisdom may deem expedient and proper, to prevent citizens from monopolizing improvements, with the view of speculation.

Article II

SEC. 1. The power of this government shall be divided into three distinct departments:—the Legislative, the Executive, and the Judicial.

SEC. 2. No person or persons belonging to one of these departments shall exercise any of the powers properly belonging to either of the others, except in the cases hereinafter expressly directed or permitted.

Article III

Sec. 1. The legislative power shall be vested in two distinct branches:—a National Committee and Council, and the style of their acts shall be:—*Be it enacted by the National Council.*

Sec. 2. The National Council shall make provision, by law, for laying off the Cherokee Nation into eight districts; and, if subsequently it should be deemed expedient, one or two may be added thereto.

Sec. 3. The National Committee shall consist of two members from each district, and the Council shall consist of three members from each district, to be chosen by the qualified electors in their respective districts for two years; the elections to be held in the respective districts every two years, at such times and places as may be directed by law.

The National Council shall, after the present year, be held annually, to be convened on the first Monday in October, at such place as may be designated by the National Council, or, in case of emergency, by the Principal Chief.

Sec. 4. Before the districts shall be laid off, any election which may take place, shall be by general vote of the electors throughout the Nation for all officers to be elected.

The first election for all the officers of the government:—Chiefs, Executive Council, members of the National Council, Judges and Sheriffs,—shall be held at Tahlequah, before the rising of this convention; and the term of service of all officers elected previous to the first Monday in October, 1839, shall be extended to embrace, in addition to the regular constitutional term, the time intervening from their election to the first Monday in October, 1839.

Sec. 5. No person shall be eligible to a seat in the National Council but a free Cherokee male citizen, who shall have attained to the age of twenty-five years.

The descendants of Cherokee men by all free women except the African race, whose parents may have been living together as man and wife, according to the customs and laws of this Nation, shall be entitled to all the rights and privileges of this Nation as well as the posterity of Cherokee women by all free men. No person who is of negro or mulatto parentage, either by the father's or mother's side, shall be eligible to hold any office of profit, honor or trust, under this government.

Sec. 6. The electors and members of the National Council shall in all cases, except those of treason, felony, or breach of the peace, be privileged from arrest during their attendance at elections, and at the National Council, in going to and returning.

Sec. 7. In all elections by the people, the electors shall vote *viva voce.*

All free male citizens, who shall have attained to the age of eighteen years, shall be equally entitled to vote at all public elections.

Sec. 8. Each branch of the National Council shall judge of the qualifications and returns of its own members, and determine the rules of its proceedings, punish a member for disorderly behavior, and, with the concurrence of two-thirds, expel a member; but not a second time for the same offense.

Sec. 9. Each branch of the National Council, when assembled, shall choose its own officers; a majority of each shall constitute a quorum to do business, but a smaller number may adjourn from day to day, and compel the attendance of absent members, in such manner and under such penalty as each branch may prescribe.

Sec. 10. The members of the National Committee shall each receive from the public treasury a compensation for their services, which shall be three dollars per day during their attendance at the National Council; and the members of the Council shall each receive three dollars per day for their services during their attendance at the National Council; *provided,* that the same may be increased or diminished by law; but no alteration shall take effect during the period of service of the members of the National Council by whom such alteration may have been made.

SEC. 11. The National Council shall regulate by law, by whom and in what manner, writs of elections shall be issued to fill the vacancies which may happen in either branch thereof.

SEC. 12. Each member of the National Council, before he takes his seat, shall take the following oath or affirmation:

I, A. B., do solemnly swear (or affirm, as the case may be,) that I have not obtained my election by bribery, treats, or any undue and unlawful means, used by myself or others, by my desire or approbation for that purpose: that I consider myself constitutionally qualified as a member of ————, and that on all questions and measures which may come before me, I will so give my vote, and so conduct myself, as in my judgment shall appear most conducive to the interest and prosperity of this Nation, and that I will bear true faith and allegiance to the same, and to the utmost of my ability and power, observe, conform to, support and defend, the constitution thereof.

SEC. 13. No person who may be convicted of felony shall be eligible to any office or appointment of honor, profit, or trust, within this Nation.

SEC. 14. The National Council shall have power to make all laws and regulations which they shall deem necessary and proper for the good of the Nation, which shall not be contrary to this constitution.

SEC. 15. It shall be the duty of the National Council to pass such laws as may be necessary and proper to decide differences by arbitration, to be appointed by the parties who may choose that summary mode of adjustment.

SEC. 16. No power of suspending the laws of this Nation shall be exercised, unless by the National Council or its authority.

SEC. 17. No retrospective law, nor any law impairing the obligation of contracts, shall be passed.

SEC. 18. The National Council shall have power to make laws for laying and collecting taxes for the purpose of raising a revenue.

SEC. 19. All bills making appropriations shall originate in the National Committee, but the Council may propose amendments or reject the same. All other bills may originate in either branch, subject to the concurrence or rejection of the other.

SEC. 20. All acknowledged treaties shall be the supreme law of the land, and the National Council shall have the sole power of deciding on the construction of all treaty stipulations.

SEC. 21. The Council shall have the sole power of impeaching. All impeachments shall be tried by the National Committee. When sitting for that purpose, the member shall be upon oath or affirmation, and no person shall be convicted without the concurrence of two-thirds of the members present.

SEC. 22. The Principal Chief, Assistant Principal Chief, and all civil officers, shall be liable to impeachment for misdemeanor in office, but judgment in such cases shall not extend further than removal from office, and disqualification to hold any office of honor, trust or profit, under the government of this Nation.

The party, whether convicted or acquitted, shall, nevertheless, be liable to indictment, trial, judgment, and punishment, according to law.

Article IV

Sec. 1. The supreme executive power of this Nation shall be vested in a Principal Chief, who shall be styled "The Principal Chief of the Cherokee Nation."

The Principal Chief shall hold his office for the term of four years, and shall be elected by the qualified electors, on the same day, and at the places where they shall respectively vote for members to the National Council.

The returns of the election for Principal Chief shall be sealed up and directed to the President of the National Committee, who shall open and publish them in the presence of the National Council assembled. The person having the highest number of votes shall be Principal Chief, but if two or more shall be equal and highest in votes, one of them shall be chosen by joint vote of both branches of the Council. The manner of determining contested elections shall be directed by law.

Sec. 2. No person, except a natural born citizen, shall be eligible to the office of Principal Chief; neither shall any person be eligible to that office who shall not have attained to the age of thirty-five years.

Sec. 3. There shall also be chosen at the same time by the qualified electors in the same manner for four years, an Assistant Principal Chief, who shall have attained to the age of thirty-five years.

Sec. 4. In case of the removal of the Principal Chief from office, or of his death or resignation, or inability to discharge the powers and duties of the said office, the same shall devolve on the Assistant Principal Chief, until the disability be removed, or the vacancy filled by the National Council.

Sec. 5. The National Council may, by law, provide for the case of removal, death, resignation, or disability of both the Principal and Assistant Principal Chiefs, declaring what officer shall then act as Principal Chief until the disability be removed, or a Principal Chief shall be elected.

Sec. 6. The Principal and Assistant Principal Chief shall, at stated times, receive for their services a compensation which shall neither be increased or diminished during the period for which they shall have been elected; and they shall not receive, within that period, any other emolument from the Cherokee Nation or any other government.

Sec. 7. Before the Principal Chief enters on the execution of his office, he shall take the following oath or affirmation:

I do solemnly swear or affirm that I will faithfully execute the duties of Principal Chief of the Cherokee Nation, and will, to the best of my ability, preserve, protect, and defend the constitution of the Cherokee Nation.

Sec. 8. He may, on extraordinary occasions, convene the National Council at the seat of government.

Sec. 9. He shall, from time to time, give to the National Council information of the state of the government, and recommend to their consideration such measures as he may deem expedient.

SEC. 10. He shall take care that the laws be faithfully executed.

SEC. 11. It shall be his duty to visit the different districts at least once in two years, to inform himself of the general condition of the country.

SEC. 12. The Assistant Principal Chief shall, by virtue of his office, aid and advise the Principal Chief in the administration of the government at all times during his continuance in office.

SEC. 13. Vacancies that may occur in offices, the appointment of which is vested in the National Council, shall be filled by the Principal Chief during the recess of the National Council by granting commissions which shall expire at the end of the next session thereof.

SEC. 14. Every bill which shall pass both branches of the National Council shall, before it becomes a law, be presented to the Principal Chief; if he approve, he shall sign it; but if not, he shall return it, with his objections, to that branch in which it may have originated, who shall enter the objections at large on their journals, and proceed to re-consider it; if, after such re-consideration, two-thirds of that branch shall agree to pass the bill, it shall be sent, together with the objections, to the other branch, by which it shall likewise be re-considered, and, if approved by two-thirds of that branch, it shall become a law. If any bill shall not be returned by the Principal Chief within five days, (Sundays excepted), after the same has been presented to him, it shall become a law in like manner as if he had signed it, unless the National Council, by their adjournment, prevent its return, in which case it shall be a law, unless sent back within three days after their next meeting.

SEC. 15. Members of the National Council, and all officers, executive and judicial, shall be bound by oath to support the constitution of this Nation, and to perform the duties of their respective offices with fidelity.

SEC. 16. In case of disagreement between the two branches of the National Council with respect to the time of adjournment, the Principal Chief shall have power to adjourn the same to such a time as he may deem proper; *provided,* it be not a period beyond the next constitutional meeting thereof.

SEC. 17. The Principal Chief shall, during the session of the National Council, attend at the seat of government.

SEC. 18. There shall be a council composed of five persons, to be appointed by the National Council, whom the Principal Chief shall have full power at his discretion to assemble; he, together with the Assistant Principal Chief and the counselors, or a majority of them, may, from time to time, hold and keep a council for ordering and directing the affairs of the Nation according to law; *provided,* the National Council shall have power to reduce the number, if deemed expedient, after the first term of service, to a number not less than three.

SEC. 19. The members of the executive council shall be chosen for the term of two years.

SEC. 20. The resolutions and advice of the council shall be recorded in a register, and signed by the members agreeing thereto, which may be called for by either branch of the National Council; and any counselor may enter his dissent to the majority.

SEC. 21. The treasurer of the Cherokee Nation shall be chosen by a joint vote of both branches of the National Council, for the term of four years.

SEC. 22. The treasurer shall, before entering on the duties of his office, give bond to the Nation, with sureties to the satisfaction of the National Council, for the faithful discharge of his trust.

SEC. 23. No money shall be drawn from the treasury but by warrant from the Principal Chief, and in consequence of appropriations made by law.

SEC. 24. It shall be the duty of the treasurer to receive all public moneys, and to make a regular statement and account of the receipts and expenditures of all public moneys at the annual session of the National Council.

Article V

SEC. 1. The judicial powers shall be vested in a Supreme Court, and such circuit and inferior courts as the National Council may, from time to time, ordain and establish.

SEC. 2. The Judges of the Supreme and Circuit courts shall hold their commissions for the term of four years, but any of them may be removed from office on the address of two-thirds of each branch of the National Council to the Principal chief for that purpose.

SEC. 3. The Judges of the Supreme and Circuit Courts shall, at stated times, receive a compensation which shall not be diminished during their continuance in office, but they shall receive no fees or perquisites of office, nor hold any other office of profit or trust under the government of this Nation, or any other power.

SEC. 4. No person shall be appointed a judge of any of the courts, until he shall have attained the age of thirty years.

SEC. 5. The Judges of the Supreme and Circuit Courts shall be elected by the National Council, and there shall be appointed in each district as many justices of the peace as it may be deemed expedient for the public good, whose powers, duties and duration in office, shall be clearly designated by law.

SEC. 6. The Judges of the Supreme Court and of the Circuit Courts, shall have complete criminal jurisdiction in such cases, and in such manner, as may be pointed out by law.

SEC. 7. No judge shall sit on trial of any cause when the parties are connected [with him] by affinity or consanguinity, except by consent of the parties. In case all the judges of the Supreme Court shall be interested in the issue of any cause, or related to all or either of the parties, the National Council may provide by law for the selection of a suitable number of persons of good character and knowledge, for the determination thereof, and who shall be specially commissioned for the adjudication of such case by the Principal Chief.

SEC. 8. All writs and other process shall run "in the name of the Cherokee Nation," and bear test and be signed by the respective clerks.

SEC. 9. Indictments shall conclude—"against the peace and dignity of the Cherokee Nation."

SEC. 10. The Supreme Court shall, after the present year, hold its session annually at the seat of government, to be convened on the first Monday of October in each year.

SEC. 11. In all criminal prosecutions the accused shall have the right of being heard; of demanding the nature and cause of the accusation; of meeting the witnesses face to face; of having compulsory process for obtaining witnesses in his or their favor; and in prosecutions by indictment or information, a speedy public trial, by an impartial jury of the vicinage; nor shall the accused be compelled to give evidence against himself.

SEC. 12. The people shall be secure in their persons, houses, papers and possessions, from unreasonable seizures and searches, and no warrant to search any place, or to seize any person or things, shall issue, without describing them as nearly as may be, nor without good cause, supported by oath or affirmation.

SEC. 13. All persons shall be bailable by sufficient securities, unless for capital offenses, where the proof is evident or presumption great.

Article VI

SEC. 1. No person who denies the being of a God, or future state of reward and punishment, shall hold any office in the civil department in this Nation.

SEC. 2. The free exercise of religious worship, and serving God without distinction, shall forever be enjoyed within the limits of this Nation: *provided,* that this liberty of conscience shall not be so construed as to excuse acts of licentiousness, or justify practices inconsistent with the peace or safety of this nation.

SEC. 3. When the National Council shall determine the expediency of appointing delegates, or other public agents, for the purpose of transacting business with the government of the United States, the Principal Chief shall recommend, and, by the advice and consent of the National Committee, appoint and commission such delegates or public agents accordingly. On all matters of interest, touching the rights of the citizens of this Nation, which may require the attention of the United States government, the Principal Chief shall keep up a friendly correspondence with that government through the medium of its proper officers.

SEC. 4. All commissions shall be "in the name and by the authority of the Cherokee Nation," and be sealed with the seal of the Nation, and signed by the Principal Chief. The Principal Chief shall make use of his private seal until a National seal shall be provided.

SEC. 5. A sheriff shall be elected in each district, by the qualified electors thereof, who shall hold his office two years, unless sooner removed. Should a vacancy occur, subsequent to an election, it shall be filled by the Principal Chief, as in other cases, and the person so appointed shall continue in office until the next regular election.

SEC. 6. No person shall, for the same offense, be twice put in jeopardy of life or limb; nor shall the property of any person be taken and applied to public use without a just and fair compensation: *provided,* that nothing in this clause shall be so construed, as to impair the right and power of the National Council to lay and collect taxes.

SEC. 7. The right of trial by jury shall remain inviolate, and every person, for injury sustained in person, property or reputation, shall have remedy by due course of law.

SEC. 8. The appointment of all officers, not otherwise directed by this constitution, shall be vested in the National Council.

SEC. 9. Religion, morality and knowledge, being necessary to good government, the preservation of liberty, and the happiness of mankind, schools, and the means of education, shall forever be encouraged in this Nation.

SEC. 10. The National Council may propose such amendments to this constitution as two-thirds of each branch may deem expedient, and the Principal Chief shall issue a proclamation, directing all civil officers, of the several districts, to promulgate the same as extensively as possible within their respective districts at least six months previous to the next general election. And if, at the first session of National Council, after such general election, two-thirds of each branch shall, by ayes and noes, ratify such proposed amendments, they shall be valid to all intent and purposes, as parts of this constitution; *provided,* that such proposed amendments shall be read on three several days in each branch, as well when the same are proposed, as when they are ratified.

Done in Convention at Tahlequah, Cherokee Nation, this sixth day of September, 1839.

GEORGE LOWREY,

PRESIDENT OF THE NATIONAL CONVENTION.

HAIR CONRAD, his X mark,

JOHN BENGE, his X mark,

ARCHIBALD CAMPBELL, his X mark,

THOMAS CANDY, JOHN DREW,

GEORGE GUESS, his X mark,

WALTER SCOTT ADAIR,

YOUNG ELDERS, his X mark,

WILL SHOREY COODEY,

THOMAS FOREMAN, RICHARD TAYLOR,

THOMAS FOX TAYLOR,

O-KAN-STO-TAH LOGAN, his X mark,

JAMES SPEARS, his X mark,

JOHN SPEARS,

STEPHEN FOREMAN,

YOUNG GLASS, his X mark,

LOONEY PRICE,

TOBACCO WILL, his X mark,

MAJOR PULLUM, his X mark,

MOSES PARRIS,

GEORGE WASHINGTON GUNTER,

KENCH LOGAN, his X mark,

YOUNG WOLF, JOS. MARTIN LYNCH,

SAL-LA-TEE-SKEE WATTS, his X mark,

GEORGE BREWER, his X mark,

JOSHUA BUFFINGTON,

JESSE BUSHYHEAD, JESSE RUSSELL,

JOHN FLETCHER BOOT, his X mark,

CRYING BUFFALO, his X mark,

BARK FLUTE, his X mark,

OO-LA-YO-A, his X mark,

SOFT SHELL TURTLE, his X mark,

EDWARD GUNTER,

DANIEL COLSTON, his X mark,

LEWIS ROSS, GEORGE HICKS,

TURTLE FIELDS, his X mark,

ELIJAH HICKS,

TAH–LAH–SEE–NEE, his X mark,

JAMES BROWN, CHARLES COODEY,

RILEY KEYS, DANIEL MCCOY,

LEWIS MELTON.

40

JOSEPH SNELLING

(1804–1848)

The son of the chief of the American army in Minnesota, Joseph Snelling left the family home in Boston in 1820 to live with his father on the frontier at a fort situated between the Sioux to the west and the Algonquian Ojibway to the east. Educated at elite Boston schools and later at West Point, Snelling, like Hall, Flint, and others, came west as a Yankee. Unlike them, however, he could not stay in the west, and eventually moved back to Boston in 1828 to spend the remainder of his life there as a journalist. The book he published upon his return east, *Tales of the Northwest* (1830), is a series of stories, narratives, and novellas in which the lines between fact and fiction are difficult to ascertain. At times, these stories depict natives in the style of Cooper, as noble savages vanishing into both the west and the grave.

At other times, however, he finds the more accommodating voice of western writers such as Benjamin Drake or Hugh Henry Brackenridge. The story reprinted here, "The Devoted," like Brackenridge's "Trial of Mamachtaga," has to do with the relation of American and native notions of justice. Again, this story depicts the American justice system dealing fairly with a native but also portrays an alternative, and equally just, native means of reckoning punishment and retribution. Furthermore, the story depicts evil and good in both races. The Saques (Sauks, Black Hawk's tribe) and John Moredock (the noted Indian-hater depicted by James Hall and Herman Melville) are "fiendish." Other whites and the Dakotahs aspire to a more functional and fair cohabitation of the region. Like most western writers, Snelling rejects the imported images of both races and their interactions on the frontier.

Text: *Tales of the Northwest* (Boston, 1830; rpt. 1936, ed. John T. Flanagan): 39–49.

THE DEVOTED (1830)

Life has no joys for me. For me the streams,
The clear, sweet waters of my native woods
Are streams of bitterness. The glorious sun
Shines on my path in vain, since he, my boy,
My brave, my best beloved, my first born,
Was torn from these old arms. I'll reckless rush
Upon the foemen's ranks; and with this blade
Will dig my own red grave.

—UNPUBLISHED PLAY

In the year eighteen hundred and nineteen, or twenty, two soldiers belonging to the sixth regiment of United States' Infantry, then stationed at Council Bluffs, were shot by two Dahcotahs of the Susseton band. No provocation was given by the sufferers; at least none was alleged by the perpetrators of the crime. They were induced to do the deed by one of those unaccountable impulses that so often actuate Indians.

The Sussetons, or 'People who end by Curing,' inhabit the country on the St Peter's River. They dress in cloth and blankets. Their original vesture and implements have given place to articles manufactured by the whites, so that they are in a great measure dependent on the traders for the necessaries of life. An embargo on the Indian trade is therefore the greatest evil that can be inflicted on them.

In order to compel the surrender of the offenders, the Colonel commanding the post at the mouth of the St Peters stopped the trading boats. Notice was duly given to the Sussetons that an absolute non-intercourse would be enforced till the persons demanded should be given up to justice. The good policy that dictated the measure was soon apparent. No Indian on the St Peters could shoot a duck, or catch a muskrat. The bow and arrow, weapons long out of use, were put in requisition, but to little purpose. The game taken by their means was insufficient for the support of life. As no knives could be had, if a deer was killed it was flayed with a flint or a clam shell. Tired of enduring such privations the Sussetons took measures to terminate them.

A large camp was convened at Munday Ean Tonkinkee, or The Big Stone Lake. A solemn council was held on the green sward, to devise means to avert the consequences of the folly of their 'young men.'

'I am willing,' said Mahzah Khotah, (The Grey Iron,) one of the criminals, 'to give my life to the Big Knives, as a reparation for that I have taken. They will put me to death. What then? I am a man. Better that one should suffer than many. I have been a fool, but now I will act with wisdom.'

The guttural ejaculation peculiar to an Indian council put the stamp of approbation to these generous sentiments. But one of the assembled elders did not join in the general applause. It was Ahkitcheetah Dootah, (The Red Soldier,) the father of the speaker. His head drooped, and he hid his face in his hands.

651

'I too,' said the other person implicated, 'will go to the chief of the Big Knives. I will throw away my body also.'

'Not so my son,' cried an old Susseton. 'You are my only boy, and how will your mother, and your sisters, and your wife, and your children eat, if you should die? I have long been unable to hunt. I am old and useless. Life for life is all the Big Knives can ask. They shall have mine. Come, young men, let us start immediately.'

This reasoning appeared conclusive to the assembly. Two men were to die and it seemed to the Sussetons immaterial which. The son himself made no opposition. The next day after leaving some worn out clothing and a quantity of tobacco on a rock, as a tribute to the Great Spirit, Mahzah Khotah and his intended fellow sufferer started for Fort Snelling, attended by a numerous retinue of friends and relatives.

Arrived within a mile of the fort, the party halted, smoked, and sung a prayer, in a subdued and monotonous tone. If Handel could have heard, it is probable he would not have wished ever to hear a Dahcotah concert again. Then they smutted their faces anew, and wounded their arms with knives. The prisoners' elbows were secured with ropes of braided buffalo's hair, and great oaken skewers were thrust through their flesh. This unnecessary pain they bore without blenching in the least. The prisoners began to sing, and in this fashion the whole party advanced to the walls of the fort. A company was drawn up under arms, and the commanding officer came out to receive them.

The elders and warriors sat down in a circle on the ground, with the prisoners in the midst. The American officer was desired to take his place with them, and then the peace pipe was produced and smoked round the circle from left to right, or with the sun, as the Indians express it. This ceremony ended the elder of the prisoners rose and spoke.

'A cloud,' he said, 'has come between us and our father. We hope the beams of this day's sun will drive it away. Our hearts are sad that the chain of friendship has been broken. We wish to mend it. Two foolish young men have acted according to their folly, and the Master of Life is angry about it. One of them was my son. I am here to suffer for him. We throw away the other also. Have pity on us father, for we are onsheekah. (pitiable.) Our women and children are starving. We have come a long distance to see you, and the path was overgrown with weeds. Father, take pity on us, and let the road between your people and ours be cleared.'

The pipe of peace was accepted. The prisoners were taken into custody, and the other Sussetons dismissed. Colonel Snelling wrote to Washington for instructions, but it was long before he received them. At that time, the facilities of communication were not so great as at present. It was not then known that the Mississippi was navigable for steamboats to the falls of St Anthony, and mail stages did not then run between Peoria and the Lead Mines. The breath of civilization has at length blown away all obstacles. Steam has conquered the Father of Waters, to the astonishment of the savages and the terror of the catfishes. Keelboats and their concomitant 'Salt River Roarers,' are seen no more. So much for the tide of emigration.

When the instructions did arrive, they directed that the old Susseton should be set at liberty, and that the young one should forthwith be sent to St Louis, there to be prosecuted by the United States' attorney, and dealt with as the law directs. So was the proverbial wisdom of our government in the management of Indian affairs exemplified!

Mahzah Khotah was put on board a boat and conveyed to the capital of Missouri as fast as three pairs of oars and a current of two miles an hour could carry him. When he was brought before the court on whose verdict his fate was to depend, his counsel advised him to retract his confession. There was no doubt of his guilt, for he had avowed it again and again at St Peters. Here, however, he pleaded not guilty, and as no witness appeared against him he was acquitted and discharged.

In a few days he left the city and began his journey across the prairies, directing his course to the Teton villages on the Missouri. Probably, these were his reflections: 'I have killed an American, and gained the name of a warrior. The Big Knives have not dared to revenge it, and I will therefore slay another the first opportunity.' Whether these were his thoughts or not, it is certain such were the common opinions of the more remote Indians before they were acquainted with the power of the whites; and this belief still prevails in many tribes.

But in an evil hour for Mahzah Khotah, he encountered with John Moredock, called from his inextinguishable hatred to the Aborigines, the Indian Hater. This man came into Illinois when the descendants of the French emigrants were its only inhabitants. The fourth husband of his mother had died like her three former spouses, being killed by the Indians. Yet this woman, who seemed a mark for the shafts of border warfare, left Vincennes in order to settle in Illinois with her children. As she was ascending the Mississippi she and the whole party with which she travelled were surprised and butchered by the savages. Of all her family John Moredock only escaped, he having voyaged in other company. From the day he heard of this calamity, revenge on those who had destroyed his kindred became his ruling passion. The Indians who had been active in their extermination did not escape him. By unremitting pursuit, he achieved the destruction of every individual of them. His vengeance did not sleep here. Though irreproachable in his dealings with his fellows, and though he afterwards obtained a seat in the legislature of Illinois, and the rank of colonel of militia, he never let slip an opportunity to dip his hands in Indian blood. He was famous as a hunter and a partizan warrior, and in the course of his life was said to have killed thirteen Indians with his own hand, and it is probable the truth rather exceeds than falls short of report.

He had been at Chariton on business, when he met Mahzah Khotah; both being on foot and alone. His rifle was in his hand. At the sight of the savage, his eyes flashed fire and his face grew black with passion. He 'sot his triggers,' but the time required for this operation enabled Mahzah Khotah to get behind a tree. He too was armed with a gun, given him by the Indian agent at St Louis. Moredock gained a similar cover. There they stood, watching each other as the gladiator and the lion might do in the arena. Neither could raise his weapon, or take a more than momentary look, without exposing himself to certain death. But the fertile brain of Moredock suggested an expedient. He drew his ramrod, put his cap on the end of it, and protruded it from his cover at the height of his head. The Indian very naturally supposed that his head was in it. The lightning is not quicker than was the flash of his gun. The Indian Hater fell, and Mahzah Khotah, drawing his knife, rushed forward to take his scalp. But the white man was instantly on his feet again. 'Where are you going with your knife?' said he, with a fiendish laugh. He fired, and the Dahcotah dropped. 'That counts one more,' said Moredock, as he turned from the bleeding corpse to pursue his journey.

From the time his son was surrendered to the American officer at St Peters, Ahkitchetah Dootah pitched his tent in the vicinity of the garrison. He visited his offspring daily, wept over him, and asked many questions relative to his probable fate. When Mahzah Khotah was removed to St Louis, the old man lost hope. He became listless and inactive. He was no more seen spearing fishes in the river, nor did the echoes of his gun disturb the silence of the surrounding hills. To a white man, such a course would promise a speedy release from sorrow by starvation; but it was no great disadvantage to Ahkitchetah Dootah. Among Indians the indolent share the provision made by the industrious, and a refusal to give food or clothes, is a thing unheard of. This very generosity is the great bar to their improvement. Where the 'social system' prevails to its fullest extent, as with the Dahcotahs, it is not to be expected that any individual will exert himself more than is necessary to meet the wants of the hour. It is no benefit to a squaw to plant a cornfield, for the harvest must be reaped by hands that did not sow. It is useless for a hunter to kill more venison than is needed for the immediate consumption of his family, as the greater part will be eaten by those who have been smoking by the fireside, while he has been freezing his fingers and weary-ing his limbs in the chase. The obstacles to the civilization of the Aborigines are in-deed many; but in the opinion of one who has had many opportunities for observa-tion, this is the greatest. But, dear reader, we find we have been betrayed into a digression, and if it pleases thee we will return to our story.

Ahkitchetah Dootah continued his visits to the fort, and at last learned that his son had been tried. It was in vain to tell him that Mahzah Khotah had been acquitted and set at liberty, for no process of reasoning could make him believe it. 'He has been put to death,' he would answer to those who endeavored to convince him that his son might yet return. 'He has been killed, and you are afraid to acknowledge it. You think we might revenge him. But I will not long survive my boy.' Accordingly, he made a feast, at which he appeared as naked as he was born. No one spoke, for savages as the guests were, they respected the intensity of his grief. When the dog was devoured, and its bones burned in the fire, he broke silence. He recapitulated the circumstances of his case and declared his belief as above stated. His auditors heartily concurred in it, for the way in which Mahzah Khotah had come to his end was unknown to the whites, and therefore could not be communicated to the Dahcotahs. In the same faith they re-main to this day, and nothing can persuade them to the contrary.

'I have certainly,' said the old man, 'committed some heinous offence against the Master of Breath. I do not know in what it consists, but it is certain that his hand is laid heavily on me. He is angry, and it is useless to live any longer. I am alone of my race. I am *onsheekah*. I will throw away my body the first opportunity.' And his dis-course was applauded by all present.

He immediately removed, and pitched his lodge on the extreme verge of the Chippeway territory, where he was most likely to be visited by the enemy. But hav-ing thus devoted himself to destruction, he seemed to bear a charmed life. He could find no hand charitable enough to terminate his miserable existence. He twice joined the war parties of his people, but in neither instance did they find an enemy with whom to combat.

At last, in the year eighteen hundred and twenty-three, he joined a party of twenty of his tribe, which was going to the red pipe stone quarry. It has been said that this is holy ground, and that the savages forget their hostility there. But this is sheer fiction. No war parties have ever met at the quarry, and therefore no battle has ever taken place in its vicinity.

The companions of Ahkitchetah Dootah took as much of the stone as they needed, and then left the place. We will not follow them till we have attempted a de-scription of the spot.

The country on each side of the river is a bare prairie, in which the eye seeks in

vain for a tree or a shrub. The only objects perceptible are the countless herds of buffaloes, and their constant attendants the wolves. These last accompany them, patiently
waiting till one of them 'takes a hurt from the hunter's hand,' or falls exhausted by
sickness or old age. Then they hurry to the feast. Through this vast plain the river runs,
in a thousand crooks and windings, its banks thinly skirted with trees and shrubs. At
the quarry the pipe stone is found imbedded between strata of limestone. It is red and
friable, a kind of serpentine, easily cut with a knife when first taken from the earth,
though it grows harder by exposure to the air. Asbestos is also found in the quarry.
Here the bluff rises perpendicularly from the river, and directly in its front stands an
isolated portion, rent from the parent cliff by some convulsion of nature. It is about
twelve feet from the bluff, and the younger and more active Dahcotahs used to try
their nerves by jumping upon it across the awful chasm below.

On the present occasion our friends wasted no time in such feats, or in contemplating the scenery. A trail had been found, which their sagacity discovered to have
been made by the feet of Saques and Foxes, and it behoved them to make off with all
convenient alacrity, for no people better understood that discretion is the better part
of valor, than Indians. They travelled swiftly for two days, till they came to the north
branch of the river Terre Bleue, where they halted and pitched their lodges. Ahkitcheetah Dootah indeed, remonstrated against such unseemly haste, but as the others
were not so weary of life as he, his words were unheeded. Yet he followed a good distance in the rear, to give the Saques and Foxes an opportunity to take his scalp.

The Dahcotahs had gained their halting place unmolested, but not unobserved.
The Saques and Foxes had seen them, but though trebly superior in number, they resolved to attack with as little risk as might be to themselves. They followed at a wary
distance taking good care to keep out of sight. They were better armed too, than the
Sioux, for their proximity to the whites enables them to procure weapons at pleasure.
They had each a good rifle, whereas half their opponents had nothing but bows and
arrows.

At daybreak the next morning, the usual time for Indian attacks, they approached
the Siou camp, taking advantage of the trees and of the inequalities of the ground.
When near enough they raised the war whoop, and poured a shower of balls into the
lodges. Five men were killed by this first volley. The sleepers started, and boldly gave
back the exulting shout of the enemy. They made so good a use of their knives, that
in an incredibly short space of time each had dug a hole in the ground deep enough
to protect his body, and with such effect did they project their missiles that in a few
minutes the assailants were compelled to retire to a more respectful distance.

At the first fire Ahkitchetah Dootah sprang upon his feet, and exclaimed that his
time was come at last, and that he should now rejoin his son. He snatched up his tomahawk and ran out of the lodge. A bullet through his thigh did not check his career
in the least. He brained the Saque who had discharged it, and rushed upon the next
with his tomahawk uplifted. The enemy waited till the old man was within five paces,
and then fired his piece with a certain aim. The bullet struck the Siou between the
eyes, and he was a dead man before his face touched the ground. Thus did Ahkitchetah Dootah fulfil his vow to 'throw away his body.'

The Saques and Foxes showed less than their wonted courage and the strife was
soon over. They gave way before the Dahcotahs, and Keokok, their partizan, or war
chief, was the first to throw off all encumbrances and fly. The Sioux were too few to
urge the pursuit far. Seven of them had been killed, and twice that number of the enemies remained on the field of battle.

He whose avocations or pleasure may lead him to a wild and solitary glen on the north branch of the Terre Bleue, four or five miles from its junction with the other arm of the river, will there find the bones of the slain Saques and Foxes whitening on the earth. In the branches of the trees above, he will see the bodies of the fallen Dah-cotahs, carefully wrapped up in buffalo robes.

41

JAMES WILLIAMS

(1805–?)

Born into slavery in Powhattan County, Virginia, James Williams was raised to be a domestic servant. According to his slave narrative, the early years of his life "went by pleasantly." At the age of seventeen, he was permitted to have a white clergyman perform his marriage ceremony. He and his bride were then "allowed two or three weeks to [themselves], which they spent in visiting and other amusements." Their first two children died in infancy; their next two lived to adulthood. The younger of these, a son, was two months old when Williams saw him for the last time.

Upon the death of his master, Williams was inherited by one of his master's three sons, George. George's wife, whom Williams describes as "half woman, and half fiend," owned 1,500 acres of land in Greene County, Alabama, and Williams was among the 214 slaves who were sent west to begin working her land. Upon arriving in Alabama, Williams met the plantation's overseer, Huckstep. After Williams had been in Alabama for about a week, his new master informed him that the two of them would soon return to Virginia together. It was left to Huckstep to tell him the truth: Williams was to be the plantation's slave driver.

Williams was "horror-struck." He could not believe that he had been so deceived by a man he had served faithfully since they both were boys. His agony was compounded by the responsibility of his new job: "a driver set over more than one hundred and sixty of my kindred and friends, with orders to apply the whip unsparingly to every one, whether man or woman, who faltered in the task, or who was careless in the execution of it." Williams accepted this new responsibility. It was not until he was facing the lash himself that he felt compelled to run away. Thus, he again narrates his westward journey, though this time in reverse.

Williams's escape took him to New York, where he arrived on the first day of 1838. He found there a general interest in his story, which was soon taken down for publication by John Greenleaf Whittier. *Narrative of James Williams, an American Slave, Who Was for Several Years a Driver on a Cotton Plantation in Alabama* appeared in print by February 15. According to the book's preface, Whittier acted only as an amanuensis and "carefully abstained from comments of his own." But when the book reached Alabama, there were cries of protest in the pages of the *Alabama Beacon*: some of the events Williams describes could not have occurred at the times and place that he claims. Apparently this charge was not without merit, as the book's publisher, the American Anti-Slavery Society, temporarily withdrew it from circulation.

Text: *Narrative of James Williams, an American Slave* (New York, 1838): 36–39, 81–99.

FROM *NARRATIVE OF JAMES WILLIAMS, AN AMERICAN SLAVE* (1838)

Soon after the settlement of the estate, I heard my master speak of going out to Alabama. His wife had 1500 acres of wild land in Greene County, in that State, and he had been negotiating for 500 more. Early in the summer of 1833, he commenced making preparations for removing to that place a sufficient number of hands to cultivate it. He took great pains to buy up the wives and husbands of those of his own slaves who had married out of the estate, in order, as he said, that his hands might be contented in Alabama, and not need chaining together while on their journey. It is always found necessary by the regular slave-traders, in travelling with their slaves to the far South, to handcuff and chain their wretched victims, who have been bought up as the interest of the trader and the luxury or necessities of the planter may chance to require, without regard to the ties sundered or the affections made desolate by these infernal bargains. About the 1st of September, after the slaves destined for Alabama had taken a final farewell of their old home, and of the friends they were leaving behind, our party started on their long journey. There were in all 214 slaves, men, women, and children. The men and women travelled on foot—the small children in the wagons, containing the baggage, &c. Previous to my departure, I visited my wife and children, at Mr. Gatewood's. I took leave of them with the belief that I should return with my master, as soon as he had seen his hands established on his new plantation. I took my children in my arms and embraced them; my wife, who was a member of the Methodist church, implored the blessing of God upon me during my absence, and I turned away to follow my master.

Our journey was a long and tedious one, especially to those who were compelled to walk the whole distance. My master rode in a sulky, and I, as his body servant, on horseback. When we crossed over the Roanoke, and were entering upon North Carolina, I remember with what sorrowful countenances and language the poor slaves looked back for the last time upon the land of their nativity. It was their last farewell to Old Virginia. We passed through Georgia, and, crossing the Chattahooche, entered Alabama. Our way for many days was through a sandy tract of country, covered with pine woods, with here and there the plantation of an Indian or a half-breed. After crossing what is called Line Creek, we found large plantations along the road, at intervals of four or five miles. The aspect of the whole country was wild and forbidding, save to the eye of a cotton planter. The clearings were all new, and the houses rudely constructed of logs. The cotton fields were skirted with an enormous growth of oak, pine, and bass wood. Charred stumps stood thickly in the clearings, with here and there a large tree girdled by the axe and left to decay. We reached at last the place of our destination. It was a fine tract of land, with a deep rich soil. We halted on a small knoll, where the tents were pitched, and the wagons unladen. I spent the night with my master at a neighboring plantation, which was under the care of an overseer named Flincher.

Nothing more of special importance occurred until July, of last year, when one of our men, named John, was whipped three times for not performing his task. On the last day of the month, after his third whipping, he ran away. On the following morning, I found that he was missing at his row. The overseer said we must hunt him up; and he blew the "nigger horn," as it is called, for the dogs. This horn was only used when we went out in pursuit of fugitives. It is a cow's horn, and makes a short, loud sound. We crossed Flincher's and Goldsby's plantations, as the dogs had got upon John's track, and went off barking in that direction, and the two overseers joined us in the chase. The dogs soon caught sight of the runaway, and compelled him to climb a tree. We came up; Huckstep ordered him down, and secured him upon my horse by tying him to my back. On reaching home he was stripped entirely naked and lashed up to a tree. Flincher then volunteered to whip him on one side of his legs and Goldsby on the other. I had, in the mean time, been ordered to prepare a wash of salt and pepper, and wash his wounds with it. The poor fellow groaned, and his flesh shrunk and quivered as the burning solution was applied to it. This wash, while it adds to the immediate torment of the sufferer, facilitates the cure of the wounded parts. Huckstep then whipped him from his neck down to his thighs, making the cuts lengthwise of his back. He was very expert with the whip, and could strike, at any time, within an inch of his mark. He then gave the whip to me and told me to strike directly across his back. When I had finished, the miserable sufferer, from his neck to his heels, was covered with blood and bruises. Goldsby and Flincher now turned to Huckstep, and told him that I deserved a whipping as much as John did; that they had known me frequently disobey his orders, and that I was partial to the "Virginia ladies," and didn't whip them as I did the men. They said if I was a driver of theirs they would know what to do with me. Huckstep agreed with them; and after directing me to go to the house and prepare more of the wash for John's back, he called after me, with an oath, to see to it that I had some for myself, for he meant to give me, at least, two hundred and fifty lashes. I returned to the house, and, scarcely conscious of what I was doing, filled an iron vessel with water, put in the salt and pepper, and placed it over the embers.

As I stood by the fire watching the boiling of the mixture, and reflecting upon the dreadful torture to which I was about to be subjected, the thought of *escape* flashed upon my mind. The chance was a desperate one, but I resolved to attempt it. I ran up stairs, tied my shirt in a handkerchief, and stepped out of the back door of the house, telling aunt Polly to take care of the wash at the fire until I returned. The sun was about one hour high, but, luckily for me, the hands, as well as the three overseers, were on the other side of the house. I kept the house between them and myself, and ran as fast as I could for the woods. On reaching them I found myself obliged to proceed slowly, as there was a thick undergrowth of cane and reeds. Night came on; I straggled forward by a dim starlight, amidst vines and reedbeds. About midnight the horizon began to be overcast, and the darkness increased, until, in the thick forest, I could scarcely see a yard before me. Fearing that I might lose my way and wander towards the plantation, instead of from it, I resolved to wait until day. I laid down upon a little hillock and fell asleep.

When I awoke it was broad day. The clouds had vanished, and the hot sunshine fell through the trees upon my face. I started up, realizing my situation, and darted onward. My object was to reach the great road by which we had travelled when we came out from Virginia. I had, however, very little hope of escape. I knew that a hot pursuit would be made after me, and what I most dreaded was that the overseer would procure Crop's bloodhounds to follow my track. If only the hounds of our plantation were sent after me, I had hopes of being able to make friends of them, as they were always good-natured and obedient to me. I travelled until, as near as I could judge, about ten o'clock, when a distant sound startled me. I stopped and listened. It was the deep bay of the bloodhound, apparently at a great distance. I hurried on until I came to a creek about fifteen yards wide, skirted by an almost impenetrable growth of reeds and cane. Plunging into it, I swam across and ran down by the side of it a short distance, and, in order to baffle the dogs, swam back to the other side again. I stopped in the reed-bed and listened. The dogs seemed close at hand, and by the loud barking I felt persuaded that Crop's hounds were with them. I thought of the fate of Little John, who had been torn in pieces by the hounds, and of the scarcely less dreadful condition of those who had escaped the dogs only to fall into the hands of the overseer. The yell of the dogs grew louder. Escape seemed impossible. I ran down to the creek with a determination to drown myself. I plunged into the water and went down to the bottom, but the dreadful strangling sensation compelled me to struggle up to the surface. Again I heard the yell of the bloodhounds, and again desperately plunged down into the water. As I went down I opened my mouth, and, choked and gasping, I found myself once more struggling upward. As I rose to the top of the water and caught a glimpse of the sunshine and the trees, the love of life revived in me. I swam to the other side of the creek, and forced my way through the reeds to a large basswood tree, and stood under one of its lowest limbs, ready, in case of necessity, to spring up into it. Here, panting and exhausted, I stood waiting for the dogs. The woods seemed full of them. I heard a bell tinkle, and, a moment after, our old hound Venus came bounding through the cane, dripping wet from the creek. As the old hound came towards me, I called to her as I used to do when out hunting with her. She stopped suddenly, looked up at me, and then came wagging her tail and fawning around me. A moment after the other dogs came up hot in the chase, and with their noses to the ground. I called to them, but they did not look up, but came yelling on. I was just about to spring into the tree to avoid them, when Venus, the old hound, met them, and stopped them. They then all came fawning and playing and jumping about me. The very creatures whom a moment before I had feared would tear me limb from limb, were now leaping and licking my hands, and rolling on the leaves around me. I listened awhile in the fear of hearing the voices of men following the dogs, but there was no sound in the forest save the gurgling of the sluggish waters of the creek, and the chirp of black squirrels in the trees. I took courage and started onward once more, taking the dogs with me. The bell on the neck of the old dog I feared might betray me, and, unable to get it off her neck, I twisted some of the long moss of the trees around it, so as to prevent its ringing. At night I halted once more with the dogs by my side. Harassed with fear, and tormented with hunger, I laid down and tried to sleep. But the dogs were uneasy, and would start up and bark at the cries or the footsteps of wild animals, and I was obliged to use my utmost exertions to keep them quiet, fearing that their barking would draw my pursuers upon me. I slept but little, and as soon as daylight started forward again. The next day towards evening I reached a great road, which, I rejoiced to find, was the same which my master and myself had travelled on our way to Greene County. I now thought it best to get rid of the dogs, and accordingly started them in pursuit of a deer. They went off, yelling on the track, and I never saw them again. I remembered that my master told me, near this place, that we were in the Creek country, and that there were some Indian settlements not far distant. In the course of the evening I crossed the road, and, striking into a path through the woods, soon came to a number of Indian cabins. I went into one of them and begged for some food. The Indian women received me with a great deal of kindness, and gave me a good supper of venison, corn-bread, and stewed pumpkin. I remained with them till the evening of the next day, when I started afresh on my journey. I kept on the road leading to Georgia. In the latter part of the night I entered into a long low bottom, heavily timbered, sometimes called Wolf Valley. It was a dreary and frightful place. As I walked on, I heard on all sides the howling of the wolves, and the quick patter of their feet on the leaves and sticks, as they ran through the woods. At daylight I laid down, but had scarcely closed my eyes when I was roused up by the wolves snarling and howling around me. I started on my feet and saw several of them running by me. I did not again close my eyes during the whole day. In the afternoon, a bear with her two cubs came to a large chestnut tree near where I lay. She crept up the tree, went out on one of the limbs, and broke off several twigs in trying to shake down the nuts. They were not ripe enough to fall, and, after several vain attempts to procure some of them, she crawled down the tree again and went off with her young.

The day was long and tedious. As soon as it was dark I once more resumed my journey; but fatigue and the want of food and sleep rendered me almost incapable of further effort. It was not long before I fell asleep, while walking, and wandered out of the road. I was wakened by a bunch of moss which hung down from the limb of a tree and met my face. I looked up and saw, as I thought, a large man standing just before me. My first idea was that some one had struck me over the face, and that I had been at last overtaken by Huckstep. Rubbing my eyes once more, I saw the figure before me sink down upon its hands and knees; another glance assured me that it was a bear, and not a man. He passed across the road and disappeared. This adventure kept me awake for the remainder of the night. Towards morning I passed by a plantation, on which was a fine growth of peach-trees, full of ripe fruit. I took as many of them as I could conveniently carry in my hands and pockets, and, retiring a little distance into the woods, laid down and slept till evening, when I again went forward.

Sleeping thus by day and travelling by night, in a direction towards the North star, I entered Georgia. As I only travelled in the night-time, I was unable to recognise rivers and places which I had seen before, until I reached Columbus, where I recollected I had been with my master. From this place I took the road leading to Washington, and passed directly through that village. On leaving the village, I found myself, contrary to my expectation, in an open country, with no woods in view. I walked on until day broke in the east. At a considerable distance ahead, I saw a group of trees, and hurried on towards it. Large and beautiful plantations were on each side of me, from which I could hear dogs bark, and the driver's horn sounding. On reaching the trees, I found that they afforded but a poor place of concealment; on either hand, through its openings, I could see the men turning out to the cotton fields. I found a place to lie down between two oak stumps, around which the new shoots had sprung up thickly, forming a comparatively close shelter. After eating some peaches, which since leaving the Indian settlement had constituted my sole food, I fell asleep. I was waked by the barking of a dog. Raising my head and looking through the bushes, I found that the dog was barking at a black squirrel who was chattering on a limb almost directly above me. A moment after, I heard a voice speaking to the dog, and soon saw a man, with a gun in his hand, stealing through the wood. He passed close to the stumps, where I lay trembling with terror lest he should discover me. He kept his eye, however, upon the tree, and, raising his gun, fired. The squirrel dropped dead close by my side. I saw that any further attempt at concealment would be in vain, and sprang upon my feet. The man started forward on seeing me, struck at me with his gun, and beat my hat off. I leaped into the road, and he followed after, swearing he would shoot me if I didn't stop. Knowing that his gun was not loaded, I paid no attention to him, but ran across the road into a cotton field where there was a great gang of slaves working. The man with the gun followed, and called to the two colored drivers, who were on horseback, to ride after me and stop me. I saw a large piece of woodland at some distance ahead, and directed my course towards it. Just as I reached it, I looked back and saw my pursuer far behind me, and found, to my great joy, that the two drivers had not followed me. I got behind a tree, and soon heard the man enter the woods and pass me. After all had been still for more than an hour, I crept into a low place in the depth of the woods, and laid down amidst a bed of reeds, where I again fell asleep. Towards evening, on awaking, I found the sky beginning to be cloudy, and before night set in it was completely overcast. Having lost my hat, I tied an old handkerchief over my head, and prepared to resume my journey. It was foggy and very dark, and, involved as I was in the mazes of the forest, I did not know in what direction I was going. I wandered on until I reached a road, which I supposed to be the same one which I had left. The next day the weather was still dark and rainy, and continued so for several days. During this time I slept only by leaning against the body of a tree, as the ground was soaked with rain. On the fifth night after my adventure near Washington, the clouds broke away, and the clear moonlight and the stars shone down upon me.

I looked up to see the North star, which I supposed still before me. But I sought it in vain in all that quarter of the heavens. A dreadful thought came over me that I had been travelling out of my way. I turned round and saw the North star, which had been shining directly upon my back. I then knew that I had been travelling away from freedom, and towards the place of my captivity, ever since I left the woods into which I had been pursued on the 21st, five days before. Oh, the keen and bitter agony of that moment! I sat down on the decaying trunk of a fallen tree, and wept like a child. Exhausted in mind and body, nature came at last to my relief, and I fell asleep upon the log. When I awoke it was still dark. I rose and nerved myself for another effort for freedom. Taking the North star for my guide, I turned upon my track, and left once more the dreaded frontiers of Alabama behind me. The next night, after crossing a considerable river, I came to a large road crossing the one on which I travelled, and which seemed to lead more directly towards the North. I took this road, and the next night after I came to a large village. Passing through the main street, I saw a large hotel which I at once recollected. I was in Augusta, and this was the hotel at which my master had spent several days when I was with him on one of his southern visits. I heard the guards patrolling the town cry the hour of twelve; and, fearful of being taken up, I turned out of the main street, and got upon the road leading to Petersburg. On reaching the latter place, I swam over the Savannah river into South Carolina, and from thence passed into North Carolina.

Hitherto I had lived mainly upon peaches, which were plenty on almost all the plantations in Alabama and Georgia; but the season was now too far advanced for them, and I was obliged to resort to apples. These I obtained without much difficulty until within two or three days' journey of the Virginia line. At this time I had had nothing to eat but two or three small and sour apples for twenty-four hours, and I waited impatiently for night, in the hope of obtaining fruit from the orchards along the road. I passed by several plantations, but found no apples. After midnight, I passed near a large house, with fruit-trees around it. I searched under and climbed up and shook several of them to no purpose. At last I found a tree on which there were a few apples. On shaking it, half a dozen fell. I got down, and went groping and feeling about for them in the grass, but could find only two; the rest were devoured by several hogs, who were there on the same errand with myself. I pursued my way until day was about breaking, when I passed another house. The feeling of extreme hunger was here so intense, that it required all the resolution I was master of to keep myself from going up to the house and breaking into it in search of food. But the thought of being again made a slave, and of suffering the horrible punishment of a runaway, restrained me. I lay in the woods all that day without food. The next evening, I soon found a large pile of excellent apples, from which I supplied myself.

The next evening I reached Halifax Court House, and I then knew that I was near Virginia. On the 7th of October, I came to the Roanoke, and crossed it in the midst of a violent storm of rain and thunder. The current ran so furiously that I was carried down with it, and with great difficulty, and in a state of complete exhaustion, reached the opposite shore.

At about 2 o'clock, on the night of the 15th, I approached Richmond; but not daring to go into the city at that hour, on account of the patrols, I lay in the woods near Manchester, until the next evening, when I started in the twilight, in order to enter before the setting of the watch. I passed over the bridge unmolested, although in great fear, as my tattered clothes and naked head were well calculated to excite suspicion; and, being well acquainted with the localities of the city, made my way to the house of a friend. I was received with the utmost kindness, and welcomed as one risen from the dead. Oh, how inexpressibly sweet were the tones of human sympathy, after the dreadful trials to which I had been subjected, the wrongs and outrages which I witnessed and suffered! For between two and three months I had not spoken with a human being, and the sound even of my own voice now seemed strange to my ears. During this time, save in two or three instances, I had tasted of no food except peaches and apples. I was supplied with some dried meat and coffee, but the first mouthful occasioned nausea and faintness. I was compelled to take my bed, and lay sick for several days. By the assiduous attention and kindness of my friends, I was supplied with every thing which was necessary during my sickness. I was detained in Richmond nearly a month. As soon as I had sufficiently recovered to be able to proceed on my journey, I bade my kind host and his wife an affectionate farewell, and set forward once more towards a land of freedom. I longed to visit my wife and children in Powhatan County, but the dread of being discovered prevented me from attempting it. I had learned from my friends in Richmond that they were living and in good health, but greatly distressed on my account.

My friends had provided me with a fur cap, and with as much lean ham, cake, and biscuit as I could conveniently carry. I proceeded in the same way as before, travelling by night and lying close and sleeping by day. About the last of November I reached the Shenandoah river. It was very cold; ice had already formed along the margin, and in swimming the river I was chilled through; and my clothes froze about me soon after I had reached the opposite side. I passed into Maryland, and on the 5th of December stepped across the line which divided the free state of Pennsylvania from the land of slavery.

I had a few shillings in money, which were given me at Richmond, and after travelling nearly twenty-four hours from the time I crossed the line, I ventured to call at a tavern and buy a dinner. On reaching Carlisle, I inquired of the ostler in a stable if he knew of any one who wished to hire a house-servant or coachman. He said he did not. Some more colored people came in, and, taking me aside, told me that they knew that I was from Virginia, by my pronunciation of certain words—that I was probably a runaway slave—but that I need not be alarmed, as they were friends, and would do all in their power to protect me. I was taken home by one of them, and treated with the utmost kindness; and at night he took me in a wagon, and carried me some distance on my way to Harrisburg, where he said I should meet with friends.

He told me that I had better go directly to Philadelphia, as there would be less danger of my being discovered and retaken there than in the country, and there were a great many persons there who would exert themselves to secure me from the slaveholders. In parting he cautioned me against conversing or stopping with any man on the road, unless he wore a plain, straight collar on a round coat, and said "thee" and "thou." By following his directions I arrived safely in Philadelphia, having been kindly entertained and assisted on my journey by several benevolent gentlemen and ladies, whose compassion for the wayworn and hunted stranger I shall never forget, and whose names will always be dear to me. On reaching Philadelphia, I was visited by a large number of the Abolitionists, and friends of the colored people, who, after hearing my story, thought it would not be safe for me to remain in any part of the United States. I remained in Philadelphia a few days, and then a gentleman came on to New York with me, I being considered on board the steam-boat, and in the cars, as his servant. I arrived at New York on the 1st of January. The sympathy and kindness which I have every where met with since leaving the slave states, has been the more grateful to me because it was in a great measure unexpected. The slaves are always told that if they escape into a free state they will be seized and put in prison until their masters send for them. I had heard Huckstep and the other overseers occasionally speak of the Abolitionists, but I did not know or dream that they were the friends of the slave. Oh, if the miserable men and women, now toiling on the plantations of Alabama, could know that thousands in the free states are praying and striving for their deliverance, how would the glad tidings be whispered from cabin to cabin, and how would the slave-mother, as she watches over her infant, bless God, on her knees, for the hope that this child of her day of sorrow might never realize, in stripes, and toil, and grief unspeakable, what it is to be a slave!

42

WILLIAM GILMORE SIMMS

(1806–1870)

The dean of antebellum southern literature, William Gilmore Simms edited a dozen periodicals and published more than eighty books over the course of his forty-five-year career. Much of his poetry and several of his novels—notably *Guy Rivers* (1834), *The Yemassee* (1835), *Richard Hurdis* (1838), and *Border Beagles* (1840)—deal with the American border country and issues of western emigration. Simms was, after James Fenimore Cooper, the second great novelist of the American frontier.

Simms was born in Charleston on April 17, 1806. When he was but a year old, his mother died birthing another child. Simms's father then moved to the Mississippi frontier, leaving Simms in Charleston to be raised by his maternal grandmother. His lifelong literary ambitions were fired in the 1820s when he twice visited his father in Mississippi and the two explored the western wilderness together and visited the Creek and Cherokee nations. The poems "Written in Mississippi" and "To a Winter Flower, Written in the Creek Nation," which he would collect in *Lyrical and Other Poems* (1827), were written during these travels. His father urged him to stay in Mississippi, but Simms felt obliged to return to Charleston and his fiancée Anna Malcolm Giles, whom he married in 1826.

From the middle 1820s to the early 1830s, Simms embarked on his literary career editing and contributing to the *Album*, the *Southern Literary Gazette*, the *Cosmopolitan*, and the *Charleston City Gazette*. His first major novel and the first of his border romances appeared in 1834. Named for its chief villain, *Guy Rivers: A Tale of Georgia* portrays the lawlessness of the Georgia frontier. Simms had struggled in his years as an editor and poet; *Guy Rivers* began his literary ascendency. After the publication of two more long novels, *The Yemassee* and *The Partisan* (1835), one reviewer noted that the name of Simms "will hereafter be a sufficient guaranty to the recommendation of his works." Comparisons to Cooper were favorable.

The productivity, success, and happiness of Simms's early years found a sad balance beginning in the late 1850s. To keep the Woodlands, his South Carolina home, from falling into "utter dilapidation" took energy that Simms would rather have reserved for writing. In addition, he complained that "the business of the plantation . . . [was] enough to employ all of [his] thoughts and time." In 1862 the Woodlands burned in an accidental fire. The home was soon rebuilt, but in 1865 it burned again, this time at the hands of Union soldiers. But none of this compared with Simms's personal losses. With his second wife, Chevillette Eliza Roach, he had fourteen children, only five of whom would outlive him. Two sons, ages four and six, were felled by yellow fever on the same day in 1858.

Two young daughters died in 1861; their mother would follow them in 1863. Simms spent his last years struggling to support his family. He died of cancer on June 11, 1870.

Text: *Lyrical and Other Poems* (Charleston, 1827): "Written in Mississippi," 73–74; "To a Winter Flower, Written in the Creek Nation," 97–98. *Poems Descriptive, Dramatic, Legendary and Contemplative,* vol. 2 (Charleston, 1853): "The Traveller's Rest," 22–35; "The Western Emigrants," 163–168. *Guy Ricers: A Tale of Georgia* (New York, 1855): 154–186.

WRITTEN IN MISSISSIPPI (1827)

Oh! sweet among these spreading trees,
   In noon-day's fervor to recline,
Whilst arching in the cooling breeze,
   We watch the distant waving vine.
5 And at our feet the rippling stream,
   In gentle murmurs glides along,
Free from the sun's oppressive beam,
   We listen to the Mocker's song.
And nought disturbs the gentle lay,
10   Save thro' the pine-tops bending round,
The amorous wind pursues its way,
   Scattering their leaves upon the ground;
Whilst far removed from noise or care,
   Where man has scarcely ever come,
15 Borne swiftly on the drowsy ear,
   We hark the noisy bee-tree's hum.

Oh! thus remote from worldly strife,
   Without the toil that crowds await,
How sweet to rove the vale of life,
20   Unchanged by love, unharm'd by hate.
Where no extreme of joy or ill
   Can urge or clog the steps of youth;
Where all of life, the wild and still,
   But bears the impress stamp of truth.

25 Swift as the red-deer could my feet,
   Compass the wastes that now divide
Thy form from mine, my more than sweet!
   How soon I'd clasp thee to my side!
Here would we wing the fleeting hours—
30   Here taste each joy the heart can see—

Thou finding, at each step, but flow'rs,
And I, a fairer flow'r in thee!

TO A WINTER FLOWER

Written in the Creek Nation (1827)

When winter comes with icy mien,
   To silver o'er this brook,
Thy form in loneliness is seen,
   By all forsook.

5 No shrub upon the fields remains,
   To feed the watchful gaze,
Nor blade of grass the earth retains,
   Nor sprig of maize.

The Indian here shall rest his eye,
10   And meditate alone,
That thou, when all his race shall die,
   Will still be known.

Pensive in anxious, thoughtful mood,
   His rifle at his side,
15 He'll wonder how alone thou'st stood,
   When all have died.

What secret spring of life is thine,
   Or, what art thou, to gain,
Such partial favor, as to shine,
20   Last of thy train?

Methinks such lot can ne'er be blest,
   To feel ourselves alone,
On earth the latest, only guest,
   When all are gone.

25 Then looking up from thee to him,
   That made thy outcast leaf,
Shall wonder that his soul is dim,
   And being brief.

That cannot with the sedgy grass,
30   That skirts yon streamlet's blue,
Compare the Indian warrior's trace,
   When life was new.

THE TRAVELLER'S REST (1849, 1853)

For hours we wander'd o'er the beaten track,
A dreary stretch of sand, that, in the blaze
Of noonday, seem'd to launch sharp arrows back,
As fiery as the sun's. Our weary steeds
5   Falter'd, with drooping heads, along the plain,
Looking from side to side most wistfully,
For shade and water. We could feel for them,
Having like thirst; and, in a desperate mood,
Gloomy with toil, and parching with the heat,
10 I had thrown down my burden by the way,
And slept, as man may never sleep but once,
Yielding without a sigh,—so utterly
Had the strong will, beneath the oppressive care,
Fail'd of the needed energy for life,—
15 When, with a smile, the traveller by my side,
A veteran of the forest and true friend,
Whose memory I recall with many a tear,
Laid his rough hand most gently on mine own,
And said, in accents still encouraging:—

20   "Faint not,—a little farther we shall rest,
And find sufficient succor from repose,
For other travel: vigor will come back,
And sweet forgetfulness of all annoy,
With a siesta in the noontide hour,
25 Shelter'd by ample oaks. A little while
Will bring us to the sweetest spot in the woods,
Named aptly, 'Traveller's Rest.' There, we shall drink
Of the pure fountain, and beneath the shade
Of trees, that murmur lessons of content
30 To streams impatient as they glide from sight,
Forget the long day's weariness, o'er steppes
Of burning sand, with thirst that looks in vain
For the cool brooklet. All these paths I know
From frequent travail, when my pulse, like yours,
35 Beat with an ardor soon discomfited,
Unseason'd by endurance. Through a course
Of toil, I now can think upon with smiles,
Which brought but terror when I felt it first,
I grew profound in knowledge of the route,
40 Marking each wayside rock, each hill of clay,
Blazed shaft, or blighted thick, and forked tree,

With confidence familiar as you found
In bookish lore and company. Cheer up,
Our pathway soon grows pleasant. We shall reach—
45 Note well how truly were my lessons conn'd,—
A little swell of earth, which, on these plains,
Looks proudly like a hill. This having pass'd,
The land sinks suddenly—the groves grow thick,
And, in the embrace of May, the giant wood
50 Puts on new glories. Shade from these will soothe
Thy overwearied spirit, and anon,
The broad blaze on the trunk of a dark pine
That strides out on the highway to our right,
Will guide us where, in woodland hollow, keeps
55 One lonely fountain; such as those of yore,
The ancient poets fabled as the home,
Each of its nymph; a nymph of chastity,
Whose duty yet is love. A thousand times,
When I was near exhausted as yourself,
60 That gash upon the pine-tree strengthen'd me,
As showing where the waters might be found,
Otherwise voiceless. Thanks to the rude man—
Rude in the manners of his forest life,
But frank and generous,—whose benevolent heart—
65 Good kernel in rough outside,—counsels him,
As in the ages of the Patriarch,
To make provision for the stranger's need.
His axe, whose keen edge blazons on the tree
Our pathway to the waters that refresh,
70 Was in that office consecrate, and made
Holier than knife, in hands of bearded priest,
That smote, in elder days, the innocent lamb,
In sacrifice to Heaven!

               "Now, as we glide,
75 The forest deepens round us. The bald tracts,
Sterile, or glittering but with profitless sands,
Depart; and through the glimmering woods behold
A darker soil, that on its bosom bears
A nobler harvest. Venerable oaks,
80 Whose rings are the successive records, scored
By Time, of his dim centuries; pines that lift,
And wave their coronets of green aloft,
Highest to heaven of all the aspiring wood; •
And cedars, that with slower worship rise—
85 Less proudly, but with better grace, and stand
More surely in their meekness;—how they crowd,
As if 'twere at our coming, on the path!—

Not more majestic, not more beautiful,
The sacred shafts of Lebanon, though sung
90 By Princes, to the music of high harps,
Midway from heaven;—for these, as they, attest
His countenance who, to glory over all,
Adds grace in the highest, and above these groves
Hung brooding, when, beneath the creative word,
95 They freshen'd into green, and towering grew,
Memorials of his presence as his power!
—Alas! the forward vision! a few years
Will see these shafts o'erthrown. The profligate hands
Of avarice and of ignorance will despoil
100 The woods of their old glories; and the earth,
Uncherish'd, will grow barren, even as the fields,
Vast still, and beautiful once, and rich as these,
Which, in my own loved home, half desolate,
Attest the locust rule,—the waste, the shame,
105 The barbarous cultivation—which still robs
The earth of its warm garment and denies
Fit succor, which might recompense the soil,
Whose inexhaustible bounty, fitly kept,
Was meant to fill the granaries of man,
110 Through all earth's countless ages.

                              "How the sward
Thickens in matted green. Each tufted cone
Gleams with its own blue jewel, dropt with white,
Whose delicate hues and tints significant,
115 Wake tenderness within the virgin's heart,
In love's own season. In each mystic cup
She reads sweet meaning, which commends the flower
Close to her tremulous breast. Nor seems it there
Less lovely than upon its natural couch,
120 Of emerald bright,—and still its hues denote
Love's generous spring-time, which, like generous youth,
Clouds never the dear aspect of its green,
With sickly doubts of what the autumn brings."

      Boy as I was, and speaking still through books—
125 Not speaking from myself—I said: "Alas!
For this love's spring-time—quite unlike the woods,
It never knows but one; and, following close,
The long, long years of autumn, with her robes
Of yellow mourning, and her faded wreath
130 Of blighted flowers, that, taken from her heart,
She flings upon the grave-heap where it rots!"

"Ah! fie!" was straightway the reply of him,
The old benevolent master, who had seen,
Through thousand media yet withheld from me,
135 The life I had but dream'd of—"this is false!—
Love hath its thousand spring-times like the flowers,
If we are dutiful to our own hearts,
And nurse the truths of life, and not its dreams.
But not in hours like this, with such a show
140 Around us, of earth's treasures, to despond,
To sink in weariness and to brood on death.
Oh! be no churl, in presence of the Queen
Of this most beautiful country, to withhold
Thy joy,—when all her court caparison'd,
145 Comes to her coronation in such suits
Of holiday glitter. It were sure a sin
In sight of Heaven, when now the humblest shrub
By the maternal bounty is set forth,
As for a bridal, with a jewell'd pomp
150 Of flowers in blue enamel—lustrous hues
Brightening upon their bosoms like sweet tints,
Caught from dissolving rainbows, as the sun
Rends with his ruddy shafts their violet robes,—
When gay vines stretching o'er the streamlet's breast
155 Link the opposing pines and arch the space,
Between, with a bright canopy of charms,
Whose very least attraction wears a look
Of life and fragrance!—when the pathway gleams,
As spread for march of Princess of the East,
160 With gems of living lustre—ravishing hues
Of purple, as if blood-dipp'd in the wounds
Of Hyacinthus,—him Apollo loved,
And slew though loving:—now, when over all
The viewless nymphs that tend upon the streams,
165 And watch the upward growth of April flowers,
Wave ever, with a hand that knows not stint,
Yet suffers no rebuke for profligate waste,
Their aromatic censers, 'till we breathe
With difficult delight;—not now to gloom
170 With feeble cares and individual doubts,
Of cloud to-morrow. It were churlish here,
Ungracious in the sovereign Beauty's sight,
Who rules this realm, the dove-eyed sovran, Spring!
This hour to sympathy—to free release
175 From toil, and sorrow, and doubt, and all the fears
That hang about the horizon of the heart,
Making it feel its sad mortality,

Even when most sweet its joy—she hath decreed:
Let us obey her, though no citizens.

180   "How grateful grows the shade—mix'd shade of trees,
And clouds, that drifting o'er the sun's red path,
Curtain his awful brows! Ascend yon hill,
And we behold the valley from whose breast
Flows the sweet brooklet. Yon emblazon'd pine
185 Marks the abrupt transition to the shade,
Where, welling from the bankside, it steals forth,
A voice without a form. Through grassy slopes,
It wanders on unseen, and seems no more
Than their own glitter; yet, behold it now,
190 Where, jetting through its green spout, it bounds forth,
Capricious, as if doubtful where to flow,—
A pale white streak—a glimmering, as it were,
Cast by some trembling moonbow through the woods!

    "Here let us rest. A shade like that of towers,
195 Wrought by the Moor in matchless arabesque,
Makes the fantastic ceiling,—leaves and stems,
Half-form'd, yet flowery tendrils, that shoot out,
Each wearing its own jewel,—that above
O'erhangs; sustain'd by giants of the wood,
200 Erect and high, like warriors gray with years,
Who lift their massive shields of holiest green,
On fearless arms, that still defy the sun,
And foil his arrows. At our feet they fall,
Harmless and few, and of the fresh turf make
205 A rich mosaic. Tremblingly, they creep,
Half-hidden only, to the blushing shoots
Of pinks, that never were abroad before,
And shrink from such warm instance. Here are flowers,
Pied, blue, and white, with creepers that uplift
210 Their green heads, and survey the world around—
As modest merit, still ambitionless—
Only to crouch again; yet each sustains
Some treasure, which, were earth less profligate,
Or rich, were never in such keeping left.
215 And here are daisies, violets that peep forth
When winds of March are blowing, and escape
Their censure in their fondness. Thousands more,—
Look where they spread around us—at our feet—
Nursed on the mossy trunks of massive trees,
220 Themselves that bear no flowers—and by the stream—
Too humble and too numerous to have names!

    "There is no sweeter spot along the path,
In all these western forests,—sweet for shade,

Or beauty, or reflection—sights and sounds—
225 All that can charm the wanderer, or o'ercome
His cares of travel. Here we may repose,
Subdued by gentlest murmurs of the noon,
Nor feel its heat, nor note the flight of hours,
That never linger here. How sweetly falls
230 The purring prattle of the stream above,
Where, roused by petty strife with vines and flowers,
It wakes with childish anger, nor forbears
Complaint, even when, beguiled by dear embrace,
It sinks to slumber in its bed below!
235 The red-bird's song now greets us from yon grove,
Where, starring all around with countless flowers,
Thick as the heavenly host, the dogwood glows,
Array'd in virgin white. There, mid the frowns
Of sombrous oaks, and where the cedar's glooms
240 Tell of life's evening shades, unchidden shines
The maple's silver bough, that seems to flash
A sudden moonlight; while its wounded arms,
Stream with their own pure crimson, strangely bound
With yellow wreaths, flung o'er its summer hurts,
245 By the lascivious jessamine, that, in turn,
Capricious, creeps to the embrace of all.

"The eye unpain'd with splendor—with unrest
That mocks the free rapidity of wings,
Just taught to know their uses and go forth,
250 Seeking range but no employment—hath no quest
That Beauty leaves unsatisfied. The lull
Of drowsing sounds, from leaf, and stream, and tree
Persuades each sense, and to forgetfulness
Beguiles the impetuous thought. Upon the air
255 Sweetness hangs heavy, like the incense cloud
O'er the high altar, when cathedral rites
Are holiest, and our breathing for a while
Grows half suspended. Sullen, in the sky,
With legions thick, and banners broad unfurl'd,
260 The summer tempest broods. Below him wheels,
Like some fierce trooper of the charging host,
One fearless vulture. Earth beside us sleeps,
Having no terror; though an hour may bring
A thousand fiery bolts to break her rest.

265 "How natural is the face of woods and vales,
Trees, and the unfailing waters, spite of years,
Time's changes, and the havoc made by storm!
The change is all in man. Year after year,
I look for the old landmarks on my route,
270 And seldom look in vain. A darker moss

Coats the rough outside of the old gray rock;—
Some broad arm of the oak is wrench'd away,
By storm and thunder—through the hill-side wears
A deeper furrow,—and the streams descend,
275 Sometimes, in wilder torrents than before—
But still they serve as guides o'er ancient paths,
For wearied wanderers. Still do they arise,
In groups of grandeur, an old family,
These great magnificent trees, that, as I look,
280 Fill me with loftiest thoughts, such as one feels
Beholding the broad wing of some strong bird,
Poised on its centre, motionless in air,
Yet sworn its master still. Not in our life,
Whose limit, still inferior, mocks our pride,
285 Reach they this glorious stature. At their feet,
Our young, grown aged like ourselves, may find
Their final couches, ere one vigorous shaft
Yields to the stroke of time. Beneath mine eyes,
All that makes beautiful this place of peace,
290 Wears the peculiar countenance which first
Won my delight and wonder as I came—
Then scarcely free from boyhood,—wild as he,
The savage Muscoghee, who, in that day,
Was master of these plains. His hunting range
295 Grasp'd the great mountains of the Cherokee,
The Apalachian ridge—extended west
By Talladega's valleys—by the streams
Of Tallas-hatchie—through the silent woods
Of gray Emuckfau, and where, deep in shades,
300 Rise the clear brooks of Autossee that flow
To Tallapoosa;—names of infamy
In Indian chronicle! 'Twas here they fell,
The numerous youth of Muscoghee,—the strong—
Patriarchs of many a tribe—dark seers renown'd,
305 As deeply read in savage mystery—
The Prophet Monohōee—priest as famed,
Among his tribe, as any that divined
In Askelon or Ashdod;—stricken to the earth,
Body and spirit, in repeated strife,
310 With him, that iron-soul'd old chief, who came
Plunging from Tennessee.

                    "Below they stretch'd,
In sovran mastery o'er the wood and stream,
'Till the last waves of Choctawhatchie slept,
315 Subsiding, in the gulf. Such was the realm
They traversed, in that season of my youth,

When first beside this pleasant stream I sank,
In noontide slumber. What is now their realm,
And where are now their warriors? Streams that once
320 Soothed their exhaustion, satisfied their thirst—
Woods that gave shelter—plains o'er which they sped
In mimic battle—battle-fields whereon
Their bravest chieftains perish'd—trees that bore
The fruits they loved but rear'd not;—these remain,
325 But yield no answer for the numerous race,—
Gone with the summer breezes—with the leaves
Of perish'd autumn;—with the cloud that frowns
This moment in the heavens, and, ere the night,
Borne forward in the grasp of chainless winds,
330 Is speeding on to ocean.

          "Wandering still—
That sterile and most melancholy life,—
They skirt the turbid streams of Arkansas,
And hunt the buffalo to the rocky steeps
335 Of Saladanha; and, on lonely nooks,
Ridge-barrens, build their little huts of clay,
As frail as their own fortunes. Dreams, perchance,
Restore the land they never more shall see;
Or, in meet recompense, bestow them tracts
340 More lovely—vast, unmeasured tracts, that lie
Beyond those peaks, that, in the northern heavens,
Rise blue and perilous now. There, rich reserves
Console them in the future for the past;
And, with a Christian trust, the Pagan dreams
345 His powerful gods will recompense his faith,
By pleasures, in degree as exquisite
As the stern suffering he hath well endured.
His forest fancy, not untaught to soar,
Already, in his vision of midnight, sees
350 The fertile valleys; on his sight arise
Herds of the shadowy deer; and, from the copse,
Slow stealing, he beholds, with eager gaze,
The spirit-hunter gliding toward his prey,
In whose lithe form, and practised art, he views
355 Himself!—a noble image of his youth
That never more shall fail!

          "We may not share
His rapture; for if thus the might of change
Mocks the great nation, sweeps them from the soil
360 Which bore, but could not keep—what is't with us,
Who muse upon their fate? Darkly, erewhile,
Thou spok'st of death and change, and I rebuked

The mood that scorn'd the present good—still fond
To brood above the past. Yet, in my heart,
365 Grave feelings rise to chide the undesert,
That knew not well to use the power I held,
In craving that to come. Have these short years
Wrought thus disastrously upon my strength,
As on the savage? What have I done to build
370 My better home of refuge; where the heart,
By virtue taught, by conscience made secure,
May safely find an altar, 'neath whose base
The tempest rocks in vain? The red-man's fate
Belong'd to his performance. They who know
375 How to destroy alone, and not to raise,
Leaving a ruin for a monument,
Must perish as the brute. But I was taught
The nobler lesson, that, for man alone,
The maker gives the example of his power,
380 That he may build on him. What work of life—
The moral monument of the Christian's toil—
Stands, to maintain my memory after death,
Amongst the following footsteps? Sadly, the ear
Receives his question, who, with sadder speech,
385 Makes his own answer. Unperforming still,
He yet hath felt the mighty change that moves,
Progressive, as the march of mournful hours,
Still hurrying to the tomb. 'Tis on his cheek,
No more the cheek of boyhood—in his eye,
390 That laughs not with its wonted merriment,
And in his secret heart. 'Tis over all
He sees and feels—o'er all that he hath loved,
And fain would love, and must remember still!
Those gray usurpers, Death and Change, have been
395 Familiar in his household, and he stands,
Of all that grew around his innocent hearth,
Alone—the last! And this hath made him now
An exile,—better pleased with woods and streams,
Wild ocean, and the rocks that vex his waves,
400 Than, sitting in the city's porch, to hear
The hurry, and the thoughtless hum of trade!

"The charm is broken and the 'Traveller's Rest!'
The sun no longer beats with noonday heat
Above the pathway, and the evening bird,
405 Short wheeling through the air, on whirring wing,
Counsels our flight with his. Another draught—
And to these pleasant waters—to the groves
That shelter'd—to the gentle breeze that soothed,

Even as a breath from heaven—to all sweet sights,
410 Melodious sounds and murmurs, that arise
To cheer the sadden'd spirit at its need—
Be thanks and blessing; gratitude o'er all,
To God in the Highest! He it is who guides
The unerring footstep—prompts the wayward heart
415 To kindly office—shelters from the sun—
Withholds the storm,—and, with his leaves and flowers,
Sweet freshening streams and ministry of birds,
Sustains, and succors, and invigorates;—
To Him, the praise and homage—Him o'er all!"

THE WESTERN EMIGRANTS (1836; 1853)

AN aged man, whose head some seventy years
Had snow'd on freely, led the caravan;—
His sons and sons' sons, and their families,
Tall youths and sunny maidens—a glad group,
5   That glow'd in generous blood and had no care,
And little thought of the future—follow'd him;—
Some perch'd on gallant steeds, others, more slow,
The infants and the matrons of the flock,
In coach and jersey,—but all moving on
10 To the new land of promise, full of dreams
Of western riches, Mississippi-mad!
Then came the hands, some forty-five or more,
Their moderate wealth united—some in carts
Laden with mattresses;—on ponies some;
15 Others, more sturdy, following close afoot,
Chattering like jays, and keeping, as they went,
Good time to Juba's creaking violin.

I met and spoke them. The old patriarch,
The grandsire of that goodly family,
20 Told me his story, and a few brief words
Unfolded that of thousands. Discontent,
With a vague yearning for a better clime,
And richer fields than thine, old Carolina,
Led him to roam. Yet did he not complain
25 Of thee, dear mother—mother still to me,
Though now, like him, a wanderer from thy homes.
Thou hadst not chidden him, nor trampled down

His young ambition;—hadst not school'd his pride
By cold indifference; hadst not taught his heart
30 To doubt of its own hope, as of thy love,
Making self-exile duty. He knew thee not,
As I, by graves and sorrows. Thy bright sun
Had always yielded flowers and fruits to him,
And thy indulgence and continued smiles
35 Had made his pittance plenty—made his state
A proud one in the honors which thou gav'st,
Almost in's own despite. And yet he flies thee
For a wild country, where the unplough'd fields
Lie stagnant in their waste fertility,
40 And long for labor. His are sparkling dreams,
As fond as those of boyhood. Golden stores
They promise him in Mississippian vales,
Outshining all the past, compensating—
So thinks he idly—for the home he leaves,
45 The grave he should have chosen, and the walks,
And well-known fitness of his ancient woods.
Self-exiled, in his age he hath gone forth
To the abodes of strangers,—seeking wealth—
Not wealth, but money! Heavens! what wealth we give,
50 Daily, for money! What affections sweet—
What dear abodes—what blessing, happy joys—
What hopes, what hearts, what affluence, what ties,
In a mad barter where we lose our all,
For that which an old trunk, a few feet square,
55 May compass like our coffin! That old man
Can take no root again! He hath snapp'd off
The ancient tendrils, and in foreign clay
His branches will all wither. Yet he goes,
Falsely persuaded that a bloated purse
60 Is an affection—is a life—a lease,
Renewing life, with all its thousand ties
Of exquisite endearment—flowery twines,
That, like the purple parasites of March,
Shall wrap his aged trunk, and beautify
65 Even while they shelter. I could weep for him,
Thus banish'd by that madness of the mind,
But that mine own fate, not like his self-chosen,
Fills me with bitterer thoughts than of rebuke;—
He does not suffer from the lack of home,
70 And all the pity that I waste on him
Comes of my own privation. Let him go.

There is an exile which no laws provide for,
No crimes compel, no hate pursues;—not written

In any of the records! Not where one goes
75 To dwell in other regions—from his home
Removed, by taste, or policy, or lust,
Or the base cares of the mere creature need,
Or pride's impatience. Simple change of place
Is seldom exile, as it hath been call'd,
80 But idly. There's a truer banishment
To which such faith were gentle. 'Tis to be
An exile on the spot where you were born;—
A stranger on the hearth which saw your youth,—
Banish'd from hearts to which your heart is turn'd;—
85 Unbless'd by those, from whose o'erwatchful love
Your heart would drink all blessings:—'Tis to be
In your own land—the native land whose soil
First gave you birth; whose air still nourishes,—
If that may nourish which denies all care
90 And every sympathy,—and whose breast sustains,—
A stranger—hopeless of the faded hours,
And reckless of the future;—a lone tree
To which no tendril clings—whose desolate boughs
Are scathed by angry winters, and bereft
95 Of the green leaves that cherish and adorn.

FROM *GUY RIVERS: A TALE OF GEORGIA* (1834, 1855)

CHAPTER XII

Trouble Among the Trespassers

Ralph now made his way into the thick of the crowd, curious to ascertain the source of so much disquiet and tumult as now began to manifest itself among them. The words of peace which they had just heard seemed to have availed them but little, for every brow was blackened, and every tongue tipped with oaths and execrations. His appearance attracted no attention, if, indeed, it were not entirely unobserved. The topic in hand was of an interest quite too fresh and absorbing to permit of a single glance toward any other of more doubtful importance, and it was only after much delay that he was enabled at length to get the least insight into the mystery. All were speakers, counsellors, orators—old and young, big and little, illustrious and obscure— all but the legitimate and legal counsellor Pippin, who, to the surprise of the youth, was to be seen galloping at the uttermost stretch of his horse's legs toward the quiet of his own abode. The lawyer was known to have a particular care of number one, and such a movement excited no remark in any of the assembly. There was danger at hand, and he knew his value—besides, there might be business for the sessions, and he valued too highly the advantages, in a jury-case, of a clean conscience, not to be solicitous to keep his honor clear of any art or part in criminal matters, saving only such connection as might come professionally.

That the lawyer was not without reason for his precaution, Ralph had soon abundant testimony himself. Arms and the munitions of war, as if by magic, had been rapidly collected. Some of the party, it is true, had made their appearance at the place of prayer with rifles and fowlingpieces, a practice which occasioned no surprise. But the managers of the present movement had seemingly furnished all hands with weapons, offensive and defensive, of one kind or another. Some were caparisoned with pistols, cutlasses, and knives; and, not to speak of pickaxes and clubs, the array was sufficiently formidable. The attitude of all parties was warlike in the extreme, and the speeches of those who, from time to time, condescended to please themselves by haranguing their neighbors, teemed with nothing but strife and wounds, fight and furious performance.

The matter, as we have already remarked, was not made out by the youth without considerable difficulty. He obtained, however, some particulars from the various speakers, which, taken in connection with the broken and incoherent sentences of Forrester, who dashed into speech at intervals with something of the fury of a wounded panther in a cane-brake, contributed at length to his full enlightenment.

"Matter enough—matter enough! and you will think so too—to be robbed of our findings by a parcel of blasted 'coons, that haven't soul enough to keep them freezing. Why, this is the matter, you must know: only last week, we miners of Tracy's diggings struck upon a fine heap of the good stuff, and have been gathering gold pretty freely ever since. All the boys have been doing well at it; better than they ever did before— and even Munro there, and Rivers, who have never been very fond of work, neither of them, have been pretty busy ever since; for, as I tell you, we were making a sight of money, all of us. Well now, somehow or other, our good luck got to the ears of George Dexter and his men, who have been at work for some time past upon old Johnson's diggings about fourteen miles up on the Sokee river. They could never make much out of the place, I know; for what it had good in it was pretty much cleaned out of it when I was there, and I know it can't get better, seeing that gold is not like trees, to grow out every year. Well, as I say, George Dexter, who would just as lief do wrong as right, and a great deal rather, got tired, as well as all his boys, of working for the fun of the thing only; and so, hearing as I say of our good luck, what did they do but last night come quietly down upon our trace, and when Jones, the old man we kept there as a kind of safeguard, tried to stop 'em, they shot him through the body as if he had been a pig. His son got away when his father was shot, though they did try to shoot him too, and come post haste to tell us of the transaction. There stands the lad, his clothes all bloody and ragged. He's had a good run of it through the bushes, I reckon."

"And they are now in possession of your lands?"

"Every fellow of 'em, holding on with gun in hand, and swearing to be the death of us, if we try for our own. But we'll show them what's what, or I can't fling a hatchet or aim a rifle. This, now, Master Colleton, is the long and the short of the matter."

"And what do you propose to do?" asked Ralph, of his informant.

"Why, what should we do, do you think, but find out who the best men are, and put them in possession. There's not a two-legged creature among us that won't be willing to try that question, any how, and at any time, but more particularly now, when everything depends upon it."

"And when do you move, Forrester?"

"Now, directly—this very minute. The boys have just sent for some more powder, and are putting things in readiness for a brush."

The resolution of Ralph was at once adopted. He had nothing, it is true, to do with the matter—no interest at stake, and certainly no sympathy with the lawless men who went forth to fight for a property, to which they had not a jot more of right than had those who usurped it from them. But here was a scene—here was incident, excitement—and with all the enthusiasm of the southern temper, and with that uncalculating warmth which so much distinguishes it, he determined, without much regard to the merits of the question, to go along with the party.

"I'll ride with you, Forrester, and see what's going on."

"And stand up with us, 'squire, and join in the scuffle?" inquired his companion.

"I say not that, Forrester. I have no concern in this matter, and so long as I am let alone myself, I see no reason for taking part in an affair, of the merits of which I am almost entirely ignorant."

"You will take your arms with you, I suppose. You can lend them to those who fight, though you make no use of them yourself."

"Yes—I never go without arms in travelling, but I shall not lend them. A man should no more lend his arms than he should lend his coat. Every man should have his own weapons."

"Yes; but, 'squire, if you go along with us, you may be brought into the scrape. The other party may choose to consider you one of us."

"It is for this reason, not less than others, that I would carry and not lend my arms."

"Well, 'squire, you might lend them to some of us, and I would answer for them. It's true, as you say, that every man should have his own weapons; but some among us, you see, ha'n't got 'em, and it's for that we've been waiting. But come, it's time to start; the boys are beginning to be in motion; and here come Munro and that skunk Rivers. I reckon Munro will have the command, for he's thought to be the most cunning among us."

The party was now ready for departure, when a new interruption was experienced. The duties of the pastor were yet to begin, and, accordingly, sallying forth at the head of his remaining congregation, Parson Witter placed himself in front of the seceders. It is unnecessary that we should state his purpose; it is as little necessary that we should say that it was unavailing. Men of the kind of whom we speak, though perhaps not insensible to some of the bolder virtues, have no sympathy or love for a faith which teaches forbearance under wrong and insult, and meekness under blows. If they did not utterly laugh in his face, therefore, at his exhortations, it was because, at the very first, they had to a man turned their backs upon him, and were now generally mounted. Following the common lead, Ralph approached the group where stood his fair friend of the morning; and acknowledged, in an under-tone, to herself, the correctness of her opinion in regard to the merits of the sermon. She did not reply to the observation, but seeing his hand upon the bridle, asked hurriedly—

"Do you, sir—does Mr. Colleton go with this party?"

"I do; the circumstances are all so novel, and I am curious to see as much of manners and events foreign to those to which I have been accustomed, as may be practicable."

"I fear, sir, that those which you may behold on occasions such as these, and in this country, though they may enlighten you, will do little toward your gratification. You have friends, sir, who might not be willing that you should indulge in unnecessary exposure, for the satisfaction of a curiosity so unpromising."

Her manner was dignified, and though as she spoke a something of rebuke came mingled with the caution which her language conveyed, yet there was evidently such an interest in his fortunes embodied in what she said, that the listener whom she addressed could not feel hurt at the words themselves, or the accompanying expression.

"I shall be a mere looker-on, Miss Munro, and dare to disregard the caution which you bestow, though duly sensible of the kindness which gives it utterance. Perhaps, too, I may be of service in the way of peace-making. I have neither interest nor wish which could prompt me to any other course."

"There is every need for caution among young travellers, sir; and though no astrologer, it seems to me your planet is full of unfavorable auguries. If you will be headstrong, see that you have your eyes about you. You have need of them both."

This was all in by-play. The group had passed on, and a single nod of the head and a doubtful smile, on her part, concluded the brief dialogue we have just narrated. The youth was puzzled to understand the significant warnings, which, from time to time, she had given him. He felt unconscious of any foe in particular, and though at that time sojourning with a people in whom he could repose but little confidence, he yet saw no reason to apprehend any danger. If her manner and words had reference simply to the general lawlessness of the settlement, the precaution evidently conveyed no compliment to his own capacities for observation. Whatever might have been her motive, the youth felt its kindness; and she rose not a little in his esteem, when he reflected with how much dignity and ladylike propriety she had given, to a comparative stranger, the counsel which she evidently thought necessary to his well-being. With a free rein he soon overtook Forrester, and with him took his place in the rear of the now rapidly-advancing cavalcade.

As Forrester had conjectured, the command of the party, such as it was, was assigned to the landlord. There might have been something like forty or fifty men in all, the better portion of them mounted and well armed—some few on foot struggling to keep pace with the riders—all in high spirits, and indignant at the invasion of what they considered their own. These, however, were not all hunters of the precious metal, and many of them, indeed, as the reader has by this time readily conjectured, carried on a business of very mixed complexion. The whole village—blacksmith, grocer, baker, and clothier included, turned out *en masse,* upon the occasion; for, with an indisputable position in political economy, deriving their gains directly or indirectly from this pursuit, the cause was, in fact, a cause in common.

The scene of operations, in view of which they had now come, had to the eye all the appearance of a moderate encampment. The intruding force had done the business completely. They had made a full transfer, from their old to their new quarters, of bag and baggage; and had possessed themselves of all the log-houses in and about the disputed region. Their fires were in full heat, to use the frontier phrase, and the water was hissing in their kettles, and the dry thorns crackling under the pot. Never had usurpers made themselves more perfectly at home; and the rage of the old incumbents was, of course, duly heightened at a prospect of so much ease and felicity enjoyed at their expense.

The enemy were about equal in point of number with those whom they had so rudely dispossessed. They had, however, in addition to their disposable force, their entire assemblage of wives, children, slaves, and dependants, cattle and horses, enough, as Forrester bitterly remarked, "to breed a famine in the land." They had evidently settled themselves *for life,* and the ousted party, conscious of the fact, prepared for the *dernier* resort. Everything on the part of the usurpers indicated a perfect state of preparedness for an issue which they never doubted would be made; and all the useless baggage, interspersed freely with rocks and fallen trees, had been well-employed in increasing the strength of a position for which, such an object considered, nature had already done much. The defences, as they now stood, precluded all chance of success from an attack by mounted men, unless the force so employed were overwhelming. The defenders stood ready at their posts, partly under cover, and so arrayed as easily to put themselves so, and were armed in very nearly the same manner with the assailing party. In this guise of formidable defence, they waited patiently the onset.

There was a brief pause after their arrival, on the part of the invading force, which was employed principally in consultation as to the proper mode of procedure, and in examination of the ground. Their plan of attack, depending altogether upon the nature of circumstances yet to be seen, had not been deliberated upon before. The consultation lasted not long, however, and no man's patience was too severely tried. Having deputed the command to the landlord, they left the matter pretty much to that person; nor was their choice unhappy.

Munro had been a partisan well-taught in Indian warfare, and it was said of him, that he knew quite as well how to practise all their subtleties as themselves. The first object with him, therefore, in accordance with his reputation, was to devise some plot, by which not only to destroy the inequality of chances between the party assailing and that defending a post now almost impregnable, but to draw the latter entirely out of their defences. Still, it was deemed but courteous, or prudent at least, to see what could be done in the way of negotiation; and their leader, with a white handkerchief attached to a young sapling, hewn down for the purpose, by way of apology for a flag, approached the besieged, and in front of his men demanded a conference with the usurping chief.

The demand was readily and at once answered by the appearance of the already named George Dexter; a man who, with little sagacity and but moderate cunning, had yet acquired a lead and notoriety among his fellows, even in that wild region, simply from the reckless boldness and fierce impetuosity of his character. It is useless to describe such a person. He was a ruffian—in look and manner, ruffianly—huge of frame, strong and agile of limb, and steeled against all fear, simply from a brute unconsciousness of all danger. There was little of preliminary matter in this conference. Each knew his man, and the business in hand. All was direct, therefore, and to the point. Words were not to be wasted without corresponding fruits, though the colloquy began, on the part of Munro, in terms of the most accredited courtesy.

"Well, George Dexter, a pleasant morning to you in your new accommodations. I see you have learned to make yourself perfectly at home when you visit your neighbors."

"Why, thank you, Wat—I generally do, I reckon, as you know of old. It's not now, I'm inclined to think, that you're to learn the ways of George Dexter. He's a man, you see, Wat, that never has two ways about him."

"That's true, friend George, I must say that for you, were I to have to put it on your tombstone."

"It's a long ride to the Atlantic, Wat; and the time is something off yet, I reckon, when my friends will be after measuring me for a six-foot accommodation. But, look you, Wat, why are all your family here?—I did think, when I first saw them on the trail, some with their twisted and some with smooth bores, tomahawks, and scalping-knives, that they took us for Indians. If you hadn't come forward now, civilly, I should have been for giving your boys some mutton-chops, by way of a cold cut."

"Well, George, you may do that yet, old fellow, for here we have all come to take our Sunday dinner. You are not in the notion that we shall let you take possession here so easily, without even sending us word, and paying us no rent—no compensation?"

"Why, no, Wat—I knew you and your boys too well for that. I did look, you see, to have a bit of a brush, and have made some few preparations to receive you with warmth and open arms," was the response of Dexter, pointing as he spoke to the well-guarded condition of his intrenchments, and to his armed men, who were now thickly clustering about him.

Munro saw plainly that this was no idle boast, and that the disposition of his enemy's force, without some stratagem, set at defiance any attack under present circumstances. Still he did not despair, and taught in Indian warfare, such a position was the very one to bring out his energies and abilities. Falling back for a moment, he uttered a few words in the ear of one of his party, who withdrew unobserved from his companions, while he returned to the parley.

"Well, George, I see, as you have said, that you have made some preparations to receive us, but they are not the preparations that I like exactly, nor such as I think we altogether deserve."

"That may be, Wat—and I can't help it. If you will invite yourselves to dinner, you must be content with what I put before you."

"It is not a smart speech, Dexter, that will give you free walk on the high road; and something is to be said about this proceeding of yours, which, you must allow, is clearly in the teeth of all the practices prevailing among the people of the frontier. At the beginning, and before any of us knew the value of this or that spot, you chose your ground, and we chose ours. If you leave yours or we ours, then either of us may take possession—not without. Is not this the custom?"

"I tell you what, Munro, I have not lived so long in the woods to listen to wind-guns, and if such is the kind of argument you bring us, your dumpy lawyer—what do you call him?—little Pippin, ought to have been head of your party. He will do it all day long—I've heard him myself, at the sessions, from midday till clean dark, and after all he said nothing."

"If you mean to persuade yourself, George, that we shall do no more than *talk* for our lands and improvements, you are likely to suffer something for your mistake."

"Your 'lands and improvements!' Well, now, I like that—that's very good, and just like you. Now, Wat, not to put you to too much trouble, I'd like to look a little into your title to the lands; as to the improvements, they're at your service whenever you think proper to send for them. There's the old lumber-house—there's the squatter's house—there's where the cow keeps, and there's the hogsty, and half a dozen more, all of which you're quite welcome to. I'm sure none of you want 'em, boys—do you?"

A hearty laugh, and cries in the negative, followed this somewhat technical retort and reply of the speaker—since, in trespass, according to the received forms of law, the first duty of the plaintiff is to establish his own title.

"Then, George, you are absolutely bent on having us show our title? You won't deliver up peaceably, and do justice?"

"Can't think of such a thing—we find the quarters here quite too comfortable, and have come too far to be in a hurry to return. We are tired, too, Wat; and it's not civil in you to make such a request. When you can say 'must' to us, we shall hear you, but not till then; so, my old fellow, if you be not satisfied, why, the sooner we come to short sixes the better," was the response of the desperado.

The indifferent composure with which he uttered a response which was in fact the signal for bloodshed, not less than the savage ferocity of his preparations generally, amply sustained his pretension to this appellative. Munro knew his man too well not to perceive that to this "fashion must they come at last;" and simply assuring Dexter that he would submit his decision to his followers, he retired back upon the anxious and indignant party, who had heard a portion, and now eagerly and angrily listened to the rest of the detail.

Having gone over the matter, he proceeded to his arrangements for the attack with all the coolness, and certainly much of the conduct of a veteran. In many respects he truly deserved the character of one; his courage was unquestionable, and aroused; though he still preserved his coolness, even when coupled with the vindictive ferocity of the savage. His experience in all the modes of warfare, commonly known to the white man and Indian alike, in the woods, was complete; everything, indeed, eminently fitted and prepared him for the duties which, by common consent, had been devolved upon him. He now called them around him, under a clump of trees and brushwood which concealed them from sight, and thus addressed them, in a style and language graduated to their pursuits and understandings:—

"And now, my fine fellows, you see it is just as I told you all along. You will have to fight for it, and with no half spirit. You must just use all your strength and skill in it, and a little cunning besides. We have to deal with a man who would just as lief fight as eat; indeed, he prefers it. As he says himself, there's no two ways about him. He will come to the scratch himself, and make everybody else do so. So, then, you see what's before you. It's no child's play. They count more men than we—not to speak of their entrenchments and shelter. We must dislodge them if we can; and to begin, I have a small contrivance in my head which may do some good. I want two from among you to go upon a nice business. I must have men quick of foot, keen of sight, and cunning as a black-snake; and they mustn't be afraid of a knock on the head either. Shall I have my men?"

There was no difficulty in this, and the leader was soon provided. He selected two from among the applicants for this distinction, upon whose capacities he thought he could best rely, and led them away from the party into the recess of the wood, where he gave them their directions, and then returned to the main body. He now proceeded to the division, into small parties, of his whole force—placing them under guides rather than leaders, and reserving to himself the instruction and command of the whole. There was still something to be done, and conceiving this to be a good opportunity for employing a test, already determined upon, he approached Ralph Colleton, who surveyed the whole affair with intense curiosity.

"And now, young 'squire, you see what we're driving at, and as our present business wo'nt permit of neutrality, let us hear on which side you stand. Are you for us or against us?"

The question was one rather of command than solicitation, but the manner of the speaker was sufficiently deferential.

"I see not why you should ask the question, sir. I have no concern in your controversy—I know not its merits, and propose simply to content myself with the position of a spectator. I presume there is nothing offensive in such a station."

"There may be, sir; and you know that when people's blood's up, they don't stand on trifles. They are not quick to discriminate between foes and neutrals; and, to speak the truth, we are apt, in this part of the country, to look upon the two, at such moments, as the same. You will judge, therefore, for yourself, of the risk you run."

"I always do, Mr. Munro," said the youth. "I can not see that the risk is very considerable at this moment, for I am at a loss to perceive the policy of your making an enemy of me, when you have already a sufficient number to contend with in yonder barricade. Should your men, in their folly, determine to do so, I am not unprepared, and I think not unwilling, to defend myself."

"Ay, ay—I forgot, sir, you are from Carolina, where they make nothing of swallowing Uncle Sam for a lunch. It is very well, sir; you take your risk, and will abide the consequences though I look not to find you when the fray begins."

"You shall not provoke me, sir, by your sneer; and may assure yourself, if it will satisfy you, that though I will not fight for you, I shall have no scruple of putting a bullet through the scull of the first ruffian who gives me the least occasion to do so."

The youth spoke indignantly, but the landlord appeared not to regard the retort. Turning to the troop, which had been decorously attentive, he bade them follow, saying

"Come on, boys—we shall have to do without the stranger; he does not fight, it seems, for the fun of the thing. If Pippin was here, doubtless, we should have arguments enough from the pair to keep *them* in whole bones, at least, if nobody else."

A laugh of bitter scorn followed the remark of Munro, as the party went on its way.

Though inwardly assured of the propriety of his course, Ralph could not help biting his lip with the mortification he felt from this circumstance, and which he was compelled to suppress; and we hazard nothing in the assertion when we say, that, had his sympathies been at all enlisted with the assailing party, the sarcasm of its leader would have hurried him into the very first rank of attack. As it was, such was its influence upon him, that, giving spur to his steed, he advanced to a position which, while it afforded him a clear survey of the whole field, exposed his person not a little to the shot of either party, as well from without as from within the beleaguered district.

The invading force soon commenced the affair. They came to the attack after the manner of the Indians. The nature of forest-life, and its necessities, of itself teaches this mode of warfare. Each man took his tree, his bush, or stump, approaching from cover to cover until within rifle-reach, then patiently waiting until an exposed head, a side or shoulder, leg or arm, gave an opportunity for the exercise of his skill in marksmanship. To the keen-sighted and quick, rather than to the strong, is the victory; and it will not be wondered at, if, educated thus in daily adventure, the hunter is enabled to detect the slightest and most transient exhibition, and by a shot, which in most cases is fatal, to avail himself of the indiscretion of his enemy. If, however, this habit of life begets skill in attack and destruction, it has not the less beneficial effect in creating a like skill and ingenuity in the matter of defence. In this way we shall account for the limited amount of injury done in the Indian wars, in proportion to the noise and excitement which they make, and the many terrors they occasion.

The fight had now begun in this manner, and, both parties being at the outset studiously well sheltered, with little or no injury—the shot doing no more harm to the enemy on either side than barking the branch of the tree or splintering the rock behind which they happened individually to be sheltered. In this fruitless manner the affray had for a little time been carried on, without satisfaction to any concerned, when Munro was beheld advancing, with the apology for a flag which he had used before, toward the beleaguered fortress. The parley he called for was acceded to, and Dexter again made his appearance.

"What, tired already, Wat? The game is, to be sure, a shy one; but have patience, old fellow—we shall be at close quarters directly."

It was now the time for Munro to practise the subtlety which he had designed, and a reasonable prospect of success he promised himself from the bull-headed stupidity of his opponent. He had planned a stratagem, upon which parties, as we have seen, were despatched; and he now calculated his own movement in concert with theirs. It was his object to protract the parley which he had begun, by making propositions for an arrangement which, from a perfect knowledge of the men he had to deal with, he felt assured would not be listened to. In the meantime, pending the negotiation, each party left its cover, and, while they severally preserved their original relationships, and were so situated as, at a given signal, to regain their positions, they drew nearer to one another, and in some instances began a conversation. Munro was cautious yet quick in the discussion, and, while his opponent with rough sarcasms taunted him upon the strength of his own position, and the utter inadequacy of his strength to force it, he contented himself with sundry exhortations to a peaceable arrangement—to a giving up of the possessions they had usurped, and many other suggestions of a like nature, which he well knew would be laughed at and rejected. Still, the object was in part attained. The invaders, becoming more confident of their strength from this almost virtual abandonment of their first resort by their opponents, grew momently less and less cautious. The rifle was rested against the rock, the sentinel took out his tobacco, and the two parties were almost intermingled.

At length the hour had come. A wild and sudden shriek from that part of the beleaguered district in which the women and children were congregated, drew all eyes in that direction, where the whole line of tents and dwellings were in a bright conflagration. The emissaries had done their work ably and well, and the devastation was complete; while the women and children, driven from their various sheltering-places, ran shrieking in every direction. Nor did Munro, at this time, forget his division of the labor: the opportunity was in his grasp, and it was not suffered to escape him. As the glance of Dexter was turned in the direction of the flames, he forgot his precaution, and the moment was not lost. Availing himself of the occasion, Munro dashed his flag of truce into the face of the man with whom he had parleyed, and, in the confusion which followed, seizing him around the body with a strength equal to his own, he dragged him, along with himself, over the low table of rock on which they had both stood, upon the soft earth below. Here they grappled with each other, neither having arms, and relying solely upon skill and muscle.

The movement was too sudden, the surprise too complete, not to give an ascendency to the invaders, of which they readily availed themselves. The possession of the fortress was now in fact divided between them; and a mutual consciousness of their relative equality determined the two parties, as if by common consent, quietly to behold the result of the affair between the leaders. They had once recovered their feet, but were both of them again down, Munro being uppermost. Every artifice known to the lusty wrestlers of this region was put in exercise, and the struggle was variously contested. At one time the ascendency was clearly with the one, at another moment it was transferred to his opponent; victory, like some shy arbiter, seeming unwilling to fix the palm, from an equal regard for both the claimants. Munro still had the advantage; but a momentary pause of action, and a sudden evolution of his antagonist, now materially altered their position, and Dexter, with the sinuous agility of the snake, winding himself completely around his opponent, now whirled him suddenly over and brought himself upon him. Extricating his arms with admirable skill, he was enabled to regain his knee, which was now closely pressed upon the bosom of the prostrate man, who struggled, but in vain, to free himself from the position.

The face of the ruffian, if we may so call the one in contradistinction to the other, was black with fury; and Munro felt that his violation of the flag of truce was not likely to have any good effect upon his destiny. Hitherto, beyond the weapons of nature's furnishing, they had been unarmed. The case was no longer so; for Dexter, having a momentary use of his hand, provided himself with a huge dirk-knife, guarded by a string which hung around his neck, and was usually worn in his bosom: a sudden jerk threw it wide, and fixed the blade with a spring.

It was a perilous moment for the fallen man, for the glance of the victor, apart from the action, indicated well the vindictive spirit within him; and the landlord averted his eyes, though he did not speak, and upraised his hands as if to ward off the blow. The friends of Munro now hurried to his relief, but the stroke was already descending—when, on a sudden, to the surprise of all, the look of Dexter was turned from the foe beneath him, and fixed upon the hills in the distance—his blow was arrested—his grasp relaxed—he released his enemy, and rose sullenly to his feet, leaving his antagonist unharmed.

CHAPTER XIII

New Parties to the Conflict

This sudden and unlooked-for escape of Munro, from a fate held so inevitable as well by himself as all around him, was not more a matter of satisfaction than surprise with that experienced personage. He did not deliberate long upon his release, however, before recovering his feet, and resuming his former belligerent attitude.

The circumstance to which he owed the unlooked-for and most unwonted forbearance of his enemy was quickly revealed. Following the now common direction of all eyes, he discerned a body of mounted and armed men, winding on their way to the encampment, in whose well-known uniform he recognised a detachment of the "Georgia Guard," a troop kept, as they all well knew, in the service of the state, for the purpose not merely of breaking up the illegal and unadvised settlements of the squatters upon the frontiers, upon lands now known to be valuable, but also of repressing and punishing their frequent outlawries. Such a course had become essential to the repose and protection of the more quiet and more honest adventurer whose possessions they not only entered upon and despoiled, but whose lives, in numerous instances, had been made to pay the penalty of their enterprise. Such a force could alone meet the exigency, in a country where the sheriff dared not often show himself; and, thus accoutred, and with full authority, the guard, either *en masse,* or in small divisions like the present, was employed, at all times, in scouring, though without any great success, the infested districts.

The body now approaching was readily distinguishable, though yet at a considerable distance—the road over which it came lying upon a long ridge of bald and elevated rocks. Its number was not large, comprising not more than forty persons; but, as the squatters were most commonly distrustful of one another, not living together or in much harmony, and having but seldom, as in the present instance, a community of interest or unity of purpose, such a force was considered adequate to all the duties assigned it. There was but little of the pomp or circumstance of military array in their appearance or approach. Though dressed uniformly the gray and plain stuffs which they wore were more in unison with the habit of the hunter than the warrior; and, as in that country, the rifle is familiar as a household thing, the encounter with an individual of the troop would perhaps call for no remark. The plaintive note of a single bugle, at intervals reverberating wildly among the hills over which the party wound its way, more than anything beside, indicated its character; and even this accompaniment is so familiar as an appendage with the southron—so common, particularly to the negroes, who acquire a singular and sweet mastery over it, while driving their wagons through the woods, or poling their boats down the streams, that one might fairly doubt, with all these symbols, whether the advancing array were in fact more military than civil in its character. They rode on briskly in the direction of our contending parties—the sound of the bugle seeming not only to enliven, but to shape their course, since the stout negro who gave it breath rode considerably ahead of the troop.

Among the squatters there was but little time for deliberation, yet never were their leaders more seriously in doubt as to the course most proper for their adoption in the common danger. They well knew the assigned duties of the guard, and felt their peril. It was necessary for the common safety—or, rather, the common spoil—that something should be determined upon immediately. They were now actually in arms, and could no longer, appearing individually and at privileged occupations, claim to be unobnoxious to the laws; and it need occasion no surprise in the reader, if, among a people of the class we have described, the measures chosen in the present exigency were of a character the most desperate and reckless. Dexter, whose recent triumph gave him something in the way of a title to speak first, thus delivered himself:—

"Well, Munro—you may thank the devil and the Georgia guard for getting you out of that scrape. You owe both of them more now than you ever calculated to owe them. Had they not come in sight just at the lucky moment, my knife would have made mighty small work with your windpipe, I tell you—it did lie so tempting beneath it."

"Yes—I thought myself a gone chick under that spur, George, and so I believe thought all about us; and when you put off the finishing stroke so suddenly, I took it for granted that you had seen the devil, or some other matter equally frightful," was the reply of Munro, in a spirit and style equally unique and philosophical with that which preceded it.

"Why, it was something, though not the devil, bad enough for us in all conscience, as you know just as well as I. The Georgia guard won't give much time for a move."

"Bad enough, indeed, though I certainly ought not to complain of their appearance," was the reply of Munro, whose recent escape seemed to run more in his mind than any other subject. He proceeded:—

"But this isn't the first time I've had a chance so narrow for my neck; and more than once it has been said to me, that the man born for one fate can't be killed by another; but when you had me down and your knife over me, I began to despair of my charm."

"You should have double security for it now, Wat, and so keep your prayers till you see the cross timbers, and the twisted trouble. There's something more like business in hand now, and seeing that we shan't be able to fight one another, as we intended, all that we can do now is to make friends as fast as possible, and prepare to fight somebody else."

"You think just as I should in this matter, and that certainly is the wisest policy left us. It's a common cause we have to take care of, for I happen to know that Captain Fullam—and this I take to be his troop—has orders from the governor to see to us all, and clear the lands in no time. The state, it appears, thinks the land quite too good for such as we, and takes this mode of telling us so. Now, as I care very little about the state—it has never done me any good, and I have always been able to take care of myself without it—I feel just in the humor, if all parties are willing, to have a tug in the matter before I draw stakes."

"That's just my notion, Wat; and d—n 'em, if the boys are only true to the hub, we can row this guard up salt river in no time and less. Look you now—let's put the thing on a good footing, and have no further disturbance. Put all the boys on shares—equal shares—in the diggings, and we'll club strength, and can easily manage these chaps. There's no reason, indeed, why we shouldn't; for if we don't fix them, we are done up, every man of us. We have, as you see and have tried, a pretty strong fence round us, and, if our men stand to it, and I see not why they shouldn't, Fullam can't touch us with his squad of fifty, ay, and a hundred to the back of 'em."

The plan was feasible enough in the eyes of men to whom ulterior consequences were as nothing in comparison with the excitement of the strife; and even the most scrupulous among them were satisfied, in a little time, and with few arguments, that they had nothing to gain and everything to lose by retiring from the possessions in which they had toiled so long. There was nothing popular in the idea of a state expelling them from a soil of which it made no use itself; and few among the persons composing the array had ever given themselves much if any trouble, in ascertaining the nice, and with them entirely metaphysical distinction, between the *mine* and *thine* of the matter. The proposition, therefore, startled none, and prudence having long since withdrawn from their counsels, not a dissenting voice was heard to the suggestion of a union between the two parties for the purpose of common defence. The terms, recognising all of both sides, as upon an equal footing in the profits of the soil, were soon arranged and completed; and in the space of a few moments, and before the arrival of the newcomers, the hostile forces, side by side, stood up for the new contest as if there had never been any other than a community of interest and feeling between them. A few words of encouragement and cheer, given to their several commands by Munro and Dexter, were scarcely necessary, for what risk had their adherents to run—what to fear—what to lose? The courage of the desperado invariably increases in proportion to his irresponsibility. In fortune, as utterly destitute as in character, they had, in most respects, already forfeited the shelter, as in numberless instances they had not merely gone beyond the sanction, but had violated and defied the express interdict, of the laws: and now, looking, as such men are apt most usually to do, only to the immediate issue, and to nothing beyond it, the banditti—for such they were—with due deliberation and such a calm of disposition as might well comport with a life of continued excitement, proceeded again, most desperately, to set them at defiance.

The military came on in handsome style. They were all fine-looking men; natives generally of a state, the great body of whose population are well-formed, and distinguished by features of clear, open intelligence. They were well-mounted, and each man carried a short rifle, a sword, and pair of pistols. They rode in single file, following their commander; a gentleman, in person, of great manliness of frame, possessed of much grace and ease of action. They formed at command, readily, in front of the post, which may be now said to have assumed the guise of a regular military station; and Fullam, the captain, advancing with much seeming surprise in his countenance and manner, addressed the squatters generally, without reference to the two leaders, who stood forth as representatives of their several divisions.

"How is this, my good fellows? what is meant by your present military attitude? Why are you, on the sabbath, mustering in this guise—surrounded by barricades, arms in your hands, and placing sentinels on duty. What does all this mean?"

"We carry arms," replied Dexter, without pause, "because it suits us to do so; we fix barricades to keep out intruders; our sentinels have a like object; and if by attitude you mean our standing here and standing there—why, I don't see in what the thing concerns anybody but ourselves!"

"Indeed!" said the Georgian; "you bear it bravely, sir. But it is not to you only that I speak. Am I to understand you, good people, as assembled here for the purpose of resisting the laws of the land?"

"We don't know, captain, what you mean exactly by the laws of the land," was the reply of Munro; "but, I must say, we are here, as you see us now, to defend our property, which the laws have no right to take from us—none that I can see."

"So! and is that your way of thinking, sir; and pray who are you that answer so freely for your neighbors?"

"One, sir, whom my neighbors, it seems, have appointed to answer for them."

"I am then to understand, sir, that you have expressed their determination on this subject, and that your purpose is resistance to any process of the state compelling you to leave these possessions!"

"You have stated their resolution precisely," was the reply. "They had notice that unauthorized persons, hearing of our prosperity, were making preparations to take them from us by force; and they prepared for resistance. When we know the proper authorities, we shall answer fairly—but not till then."

"Truly, a very manful determination; and, as you have so expressed yourself, permit me to exhibit my authority, which I doubt not you will readily recognise. This instrument requires you, at once, to remove from these lands—entirely to forego their use and possession, and within forty-eight hours to yield them up to the authority which now claims them at your hands." Here the officer proceeded to read all those portions of his commission to which he referred, with considerable show of patience.

"All that's very well in your hands, and from your mouth good sir; but how know we that the document you bear is not forged and false—and that you, with your people there, have not got up this fetch to trick us out of those possessions which you have not the heart to fight for? We're up to trap, you see."

With this insolent speech, Dexter contrived to show his impatience of the parley, and that brutal thirst which invariably prompted him to provoke and seek for extremities. The eye of the Georgian flashed out indignant fires, and his fingers instinctively grasped the pistol at his holster, while the strongly aroused expression of his features indicated the wrath within. With a strong and successful effort, however, though inwardly chafed at the necessity of forbearance, he contrived, for a while longer, to suppress any more decided evidence of emotion, while he replied:—

"Your language, sirrah, whatever you may be, is ruffianly and insolent; yet, as I represent the country and not myself in this business, and as I would perform my duties without harshness, I pass it by. I am not bound to satisfy you, or any of your company, of the truth of the commission under which I act. It is quite enough if I myself am satisfied. Still, however, for the same reason which keeps me from punishing your insolence, and to keep you from any treasonable opposition to the laws, you too shall be satisfied. Look here, for yourselves, good people—you all know the great seal of the state!"

He now held up the document from which he had read, and which contained his authority; the broad seal of the state dangling from the parchment, distinctly in the sight of the whole gang. Dexter approached somewhat nearer, as if to obtain a more perfect view; and, while the Georgian, without suspicion, seeing his advance, and supposing that to be his object, held it more toward him, the ruffian, with an active and sudden bound, tore it from his hands, and leaping, followed by all his group, over his defences, was in a moment close under cover, and out of all danger. Rising from his concealment, however, in the presence of the officer, he tore the instrument into atoms, and dashing them toward their proprietor, exclaimed—

"Now, captain, what's the worth of your authority? Be off now in a hurry, or I shall fire upon you in short order!"

We may not describe the furious anger of the Georgian. Irritated beyond the control of a proper caution, he precipitately—and without that due degree of deliberation which must have taught him the madness and inefficacy of any assault by his present force upon an enemy so admirably disposed of—gave the command to fire; and after the ineffectual discharge, which had no other result than to call forth a shout of derision from the besieged, he proceeded to charge the barrier, himself fearlessly leading the way. The first effort to break through the barricades was sufficient to teach him the folly of the design; and a discharge from the defences bringing down two of his men, warned him of the necessity of duly retrieving his error. He saw the odds, and retreated with order and in good conduct, until he sheltered the whole troop under a long hill, within rifle-shot of the enemy, whence, suddenly filing a detachment obliquely to the left, he made his arrangements for the passage of a narrow gorge, having something of the character of a road, and, though excessively broken and uneven, having been frequently used as such. It wound its way to the summit of a large hill, which stood parallel with the defences, and fully commanded them; and the descent of the gorge, on the opposite side, afforded him as good an opportunity, in a charge, of riding the squatters down, as the summit for picking them off singly with his riflemen.

He found the necessity of great circumspection, however, in the brief sample of controversy already given him; and with a movement in front, therefore, of a number of his force—sufficient, by employing the attention of the enemy in that quarter, to cover and disguise his present endeavor—he marshalled fifteen of his force apart from the rest, leading them himself, as the most difficult enterprise, boldly up the narrow pass. The skirmishing was still suffered, therefore, to continue on the ground where it had begun, whenever a momentary exposure of the person of besieged or besieger afforded any chance for a successful shot. Nor was this game very hazardous to either party. The beleaguered force, as we have seen, was well protected. The assailants, having generally dismounted, their horses being placed out of reach of danger, had, in the manner of their opponents, taken the cover of the rising ground, or the fallen tree, and in this way, awaiting the progress of events, were shielded from unnecessary exposure. It was only when a position became awkward or irksome, that the shoulder or the leg of the unquiet man thrust itself too pertinaciously above its shelter, and got barked or battered by a bullet; and as all parties knew too well the skill of their adversaries, it was not often that a shoulder or leg became so indiscreetly prominent.

As it was, however, the squatters, from a choice of ground, and a perfect knowledge of it, together with the additional guards and defences which they had been enabled to place upon it, had evidently the advantage. Still, no event, calculated to impress either party with any decisive notion of the result, had yet taken place; and beyond the injury done to the assailants in their first ill-advised assault, they had suffered no serious harm. They were confident in themselves and their leader—despised the squatters heartily—and, indeed, did not suffer themselves for a moment to think of the possibility of their defeat.

Thus the play proceeded in front of the defences, while Fullam silently and industriously plied his way up the narrow gorge, covered entirely from sight by the elevated ridges of rock, which, rising up boldly on either side of the pass, had indeed been the cause of its formation. But his enemy was on the alert; and the cunning of Munro—whom his companions, with an Indian taste, had entitled the "Black Snake"—had already prepared for the reception of the gallant Georgian. With a quick eye he had observed the diminished numbers of the force in front, and readily concluded, from the sluggishness of the affair in that quarter, that a finesse was in course of preparation. Conscious, too, from a knowledge of the post, that there was but a single mode of enfilading his defences, he had made his provision for the guardianship of the all-important point. Nothing was more easy than the defence of this pass, the ascent being considerable, rising into a narrow gorge, and as suddenly and in like manner descending on the point opposite that on which Fullam was toiling up his way. In addition to this, the gulley was winding and brokenly circuitous—now making a broad sweep of the circle—then terminating in a zigzag and cross direction, which, until the road was actually gained, seemed to have no outlet; and at no time was the advancing force enabled to survey the pass for any distance ahead.

Everything in the approach of the Georgian was conducted with the profoundest silence: not the slightest whisper indicated to the assailants the presence or prospect of any interruption; and, from the field of strife below, nothing but an occasional shot or shout gave token of the business in which at that moment all parties were engaged. This quiet was not destined to continue long. The forlorn hope had now reached midway of the summit—but not, as their leader had fondly anticipated, without observation from the foe—when the sound of a human voice directly above warned him of his error; and, looking up, he beheld, perched upon a fragment of the cliff, which hung directly over the gorge, the figure of a single man. For the first time led to anticipate resistance in this quarter, he bade the men prepare for the event as well as they might; and calling out imperatively to the individual, who still maintained his place on the projection of the rock as if in defiance, he bade him throw down his arms and submit.

"Throw down my arms! and for what?" was the reply. "I'd like to know by what right you require us to throw down our arms. It may do in England, or any other barbarous country where the people don't know their rights yet, to make them throw down their arms; but I reckon there's no law for it in these parts, that you can show us, captain."

"Pick that insolent fellow off, one of you," was the order; and in an instant a dozen rifles were lifted, but the man was gone. A hat appearing above the cliff, was bored with several bullets; and the speaker, who laughed heartily at the success of his trick, now resumed his position on the cliff, with the luckless hat perched upon the staff on which it had given them the provocation to fire. He laughed and shouted heartily at the contrivance, and hurled the victim of their wasted powder down among them. Much chagrined, and burning with indignation, Fullam briefly cried out to his men to advance quickly. The person who had hitherto addressed him was our old acquaintance Forrester, to whom, in the division of the duties, this post had been assigned. He spoke again:—

"You'd better not, captain, I advise you. It will be dangerous if you come farther. Don't trouble us, now, and be off, as soon as you can, out of harm's way. Your bones will be all the better for it; and I declare I don't like to hurt such a fine-looking chap if I can possibly avoid it. Now take a friend's advice; 'twill be all the better for you, I tell you."

The speaker evidently meant well, so far as it was possible for one to mean well who was commissioned to do, and was, in fact, doing ill. The Georgian, however, only the more indignant at the impertinence of the address, took the following notice of it, uttered in the same breath with an imperative command to his own men to hasten their advance:—

"Disperse yourselves, scoundrels, and throw down your arms!—on the instant disperse! Lift a hand, or pull a trigger upon us, and every man shall dangle upon the branches of the first tree!"

As he spoke, leading the way, he drove his rowels into the sides of his animal; and, followed by his troop, bounded fearlessly up the gorge.

CHAPTER XIV

Catastrophe—Colleton's Discovery

It is time to return to Ralph Colleton, who has quite too long escaped our consideration. The reader will doubtless remember, with little difficulty, where and under what circumstances we left him. Provoked by the sneer and sarcasm of the man whom at the same moment he most cordially despised, we have seen him taking a position in the controversy, in which his person, though not actually within the immediate sphere of action, was nevertheless not a little exposed to some of its risks. This position, with fearless indifference, he continued to maintain, unshrinkingly and without interruption, throughout the whole period and amid all the circumstances of the conflict. There was something of a boyish determination in this way to assert his courage, which his own sense inwardly rebuked; yet such is the nature of those peculiarities in southern habits and opinions, to which we have already referred, on all matters which relate to personal prowess and a masculine defiance of danger, that, even while entertaining the most profound contempt for those in whose eye the exhibition was made, he was not sufficiently independent of popular opinion to brave its current when he himself was its subject. He may have had an additional motive for this proceeding, which most probably enforced its necessity. He well knew that fearless courage, among this people, was that quality which most certainly won and secured their respect; and the policy was not unwise, perhaps, which represented this as a good opportunity for a display which might have the effect of protecting him from wanton insult or aggression hereafter. To a certain extent he was at their mercy; and conscious, from what he had seen, of the unscrupulous character of their minds, every exhibition of the kind had some weight in his favor.

It was with a lively and excited spirit that he surveyed, from the moderate eminence on which he stood, the events going on around him. Though not sufficiently near the parties (and scrupulous not to expose himself to the chance of being for a moment supposed to be connected with either of them) to ascertain their various arrangements, from what had met his observation, he had been enabled to form a very correct inference as to the general progress of affairs. He had beheld the proceedings of each array while under cover, and contending with one another, to much the same advantage as the spectator who surveys the game in which two persons are at play. He could have pointed out the mistakes of both in the encounter he had witnessed, and felt assured that he could have ably and easily amended them. His frame quivered with the "rapture of the strife," as Attila is said to have called the excitation of battle; and his blood, with a genuine southern fervor, rushed to and from his heart with a bounding impulse, as some new achievement of one side or the other added a fresh interest to, and in some measure altered the face of, the affair. But when he beheld the new array, so unexpectedly, yet auspiciously for Munro, make its appearance upon the field, the excitement of his spirit underwent proportionate increase; and with deep anxiety, and a sympathy now legitimate with the assailants, he surveyed the progress of an affray for which his judgment prepared him to anticipate a most unhappy termination. As the strife proceeded, he half forgot his precaution, and unconsciously continued, at every moment, to approach more nearly to the scene of strife. His heart was now all impulse, his spirit all enthusiasm; and with an unquiet eye and restless frame, he beheld the silent passage of the little detachment under the gallant Georgian, up the narrow gorge. At some distance from the hill, and on an eminence, his position enabled him to perceive, when the party had made good their advance nearly to the summit, the impending danger. He saw the threatening cliff, hanging as it were in mid air above them; and all his sympathies, warmly excited at length by the fearfulness of the peril into a degree of active partisanship which, at the beginning, a proper prudence had well counselled him to avoid, he put spurs to his steed, and rushing forward to the foot of the hill, shouted out to the advancing party the nature of the danger which awaited them. He shouted strenuously, but in vain—and with a feeling almost amounting to agony, he beheld the little troop resolutely advance beneath the ponderous rock, which, held in its place by the slightest purchase, needed but the most moderate effort to upheave and unfix it for ever.

It was fortunate for the youth that the situation in which he stood was concealed entirely from the view of those in the encampment. It had been no object with him to place himself in safety, for the consideration of his own chance of exposure had never been looked to in his mind, when, under the noble impulse of humanity, he had rushed forward, if possible, to recall the little party, who either did not or were unwilling to hear his voice of warning and prevention. Had he been beheld, there would have been few of the squatters unable, and still fewer unwilling, to pick him off with their rifles; and, as the event will show, the good Providence alone which had hitherto kept with him, rather than the forbearance of his quondam acquaintance, continued to preserve his life.

Apprized of the ascent of the pass, and not disposed to permit of the escape of those whom the defenders of it above might spare, unobserved by his assailants in front, Dexter, with a small detachment, sallying through a loophole of his fortress, took an oblique course toward the foot of the gorge, by which to arrest the flight of the fugitives. This course brought him directly upon, and in contact with, Ralph, who stood immediately at its entrance, with uplifted eye, and busily engaged in shouting, at intervals, to the yet advancing assailants. The squatters approached cautiously and unperceived; for so deeply was the youth interested in the fate of those for whom his voice and hands were alike uplifted, that he was conscious of nothing else at that moment of despair and doubt. The very silence which at that time hung over all things, seemed of itself to cloud and obstruct, while they lulled the senses into a corresponding slumber.

It was well for the youth, and unlucky for the assassin, that, as Dexter, with his uplifted hatchet—for fire-arms at that period he dared not use, for fear of attracting the attention of his foes—struck at his head, his advanced foot became entangled in the root of a tree which ran above the surface, and the impetus of his action occurring at the very instant in which he encountered the obstruction, the stroke fell short of his victim, and grazed the side of his horse; while the ruffian himself, stumbling forward and at length, fell headlong upon the ground.

The youth was awakened to consciousness. His mind was one of that cast with which to know, to think, and to act, are simultaneous. Of ready decision, he was never at a loss, and seldom surprised into even momentary incertitude. With the first intimation of the attack upon himself, his pistol had been drawn, and while the prostrate ruffian was endeavoring to rise, and before he had well regained his feet, the unerring ball was driven through his head, and without word or effort he fell back among his fellows, the blood gushing from his mouth and nostrils in unrestrained torrents.

The whole transaction was the work of a single instant; and before the squatters, who came with their slain leader, could sufficiently recover from the panic produced by the event to revenge his death, the youth was beyond their reach; and the assailing party of the guard, in front of the post, apprized of the sally by the discharge of the pistol, made fearful work among them by a general fire, while obliquing to the entrance of the pass just in time to behold the catastrophe, now somewhat precipitated by the event which had occurred below. Ralph, greatly excited, regained his original stand of survey, and with feelings of unrepressed horror beheld the catastrophe. The Georgian had almost reached the top of the hill—another turn of the road gave him a glimpse of the table upon which rested the hanging and disjointed cliff of which we have spoken, when a voice was heard—a single voice—in inquiry:—

"All ready?"

The reply was immediate—

"Ay, ay; now prize away, boys, and let go."

The advancing troop looked up, and were permitted a momentary glance of the terrible fate which awaited them before it fell. That moment was enough for horror. A general cry burst from the lips of those in front, the only notice which those in the rear ever received of the danger before it was upon them. An effort, half paralyzed by the awful emotion which came over them, was made to avoid the down-coming ruin; but with only partial success; for, in an instant after, the ponderous mass, which hung for a moment like a cloud above them, upheaved from its bed of ages, and now freed from all stays, with a sudden, hurricane-like and whirling impetus, making the solid rock tremble over which it rushed, came thundering down, swinging over one half of the narrow trace, bounding from one side to the other along the gorge, and with the headlong fury of a cataract sweeping everything from before its path until it reached the dead level of the plain below. The involuntary shriek from those who beheld the mass, when, for an instant impending above them, it seemed to hesitate in its progress down, was more full of human terror than any utterance which followed the event. With the exception of a groan, wrung forth here and there from the half-crushed victim, in nature's agony, the deep silence which ensued was painful and appalling; and even when the dust had dissipated, and the eye was enabled to take in the entire amount of the evil deed, the prospect failed in impressing the senses of the survivors with so distinct a sentiment of horror, as when the doubt and death, suspended in air, were yet only threatened.

Though prepared for the event, in one sense of the word, the great body of the squatters were not prepared for the unusual emotions which succeeded it in their bosoms. The arms dropped from the hands of many of them—a speechless horror was the prevailing feature of all, and all fight was over, while the scene of bloody execution was now one of indiscriminate examination and remark with friend and foe. Ralph was the first to rush up the fatal pass, and to survey the horrible prospect.

One half of the brave little corps had been swept to instant death by the unpitying rock, without having afforded the slightest obstacle to its fearful progress. In one place lay a disembowelled steed panting its last; mangled in a confused and unintelligible mass lay beside him another, the limbs of his rider in many places undistinguishable from his own. One poor wretch, whom he assisted to extricate from beneath the body of his struggling horse, cried to him for water, and died in the prayer. Fortunately for the few who survived the catastrophe—among whom was their gallant but unfortunate young leader—they had, at the first glimpse of the danger, urged on their horses with redoubled effort, and by a close approach to the surface of the rock, taking an oblique direction wide of its probable course, had, at the time of its precipitation, reached a line almost parallel with the place upon which it stood, and in this way achieved their escape without injury. Their number was few, however; and not one half of the fifteen, who commenced the ascent, ever reached or survived its attainment.

Ralph gained the summit just in time to prevent the completion of the foul tragedy by its most appropriate climax. As if enough had not yet been done in the way of crime, the malignant and merciless Rivers, of whom we have seen little in this affair, but by whose black and devilish spirit the means of destruction had been hit upon, which had so well succeeded, now stood over the body of the Georgian, with uplifted hand, about to complete the deed already begun. There was not a moment for delay, and the youth sprung forward in time to seize and wrest the weapon from his grasp. With a feeling of undisguised indignation, he exclaimed, as the outlaw turned furiously upon him—

"Wretch—what would you? Have you not done enough? would you strike the unresisting man?"

Rivers, with undisguised effort, now turned his rage upon the intruder. His words, choked by passion, could scarce find utterance; but he spoke with furious effort at length, as he directed a wild blow with a battle-axe at the head of the youth.

"You come for your death, and you shall have it!"

"Not yet," replied Ralph, adroitly avoiding the stroke and closing with the ruffian—"you will find that I am not unequal to the struggle, though it be with such a monster as yourself."

What might have been the event of this combat may not be said. The parties were separated in a moment by the interposition of Forrester, but not till our hero, tearing off in the scuffle the handkerchief which had hitherto encircled the cheeks of his opponent, discovered the friendly outlaw who collected toll for the Pony Club, and upon whose face the hoof of his horse was most visibly engraven—who had so boldy avowed his design upon his life and purse, and whom he had so fortunately and successfully foiled on his first approach to the village.

The fight was over after this catastrophe; the survivors of the guard, who were unhurt, had fled; and the parties with little stir were all now assembled around the scene of it. There was little said upon the occasion. The wounded were taken such care of as circumstances would permit; and wagons having been provided, were all removed to the village. Begun with too much impulse, and conducted with too little consideration, the struggle between the military and the outlaws had now terminated in a manner that left perhaps but little satisfaction in the minds of either party. The latter, though generally an unlicensed tribe—an Ishmaelitish race—whose hands were against all men, were not so sure that they had not been guilty of a crime, not merely against the laws of man and human society, but against the self-evident decrees and dictates of God; and with this doubt, at least, if not its conviction, in their thoughts, their victory, such as it was, afforded a source of very qualified rejoicing.

43

WILLIAM DAVIS GALLAGHER

(1808–1894)

There was perhaps no better chronicler and publicist for western writing, particularly of the literary scene in Cincinnati, than William Davis Gallagher. Gallagher was brought west by his widowed mother in 1814. His father, an Irish rebel forced to flee to Philadelphia after the 1798 uprising, died when Gallagher was young, yet seems to have imparted to his son his antiauthoritarian views. Starting in 1830, Gallagher began publishing a long series of doomed journals that endeavored to espouse both western politics and literature. At the same time, he published similarly inflected poetry. The best of his writing in each area is reflected here.

The essay, "Sketches of the Literature of the West," is a variant on an essay he often used in the first edition of his journals. In it he demonstrates an awareness of the forces impeding the progress of western writing and finds the causes, both internal and external. Like James Hall and others, Gallagher blames the east for monopolizing the American publishing industry. However, looking ahead to his protegé, William T. Coggeshall, or even Hamlin Garland, Gallagher also blames western readers for their acquiescence in their own misrepresentation, a subject he takes up more directly in "Thoughts of My Own," purportedly a correspondent's response to the first essay but, far more likely, the work of Gallagher's own pen, since sections of it are reproduced from an earlier essay, "East and West," he had published in 1834.

In 1841, Gallagher published what he thought would be the first in a series of anthologies of writings from the west. In this volume he published some of his own work but also that of dozens of others from the Ohio valley. While the other planned collections never appeared, the poms in *Selections from the Poetical Literature of the West* stand as the first significant and self-conscious effort to celebrate western writing. Gallagher's own poetry ranges from the descriptive romanticism of "The Miami Woods" to the labor-activist haranguing of "Radicalos." Gallagher's increasing attachment to radical political causes, such as feminism and women's rights, further demonstrate his iconoclasm and his belief in the power of poetry as a political force.

Gallagher's literary career was effectively ended when Senator Thomas Corwin of Ohio, best known for his resistance to the Mexican-American War, brought him east to manage his office as he ran for president in 1852. Long an abolitionist, Gallagher was witness to the death of the Whigs and the rise of the Republican party. In fact, in 1853 he accepted the editorship of an abolitionist paper in Louisville and was subsequently challenged to duels and threatened with tarring and feathering. During the war he served as a customs agent on the Ohio, in charge of preventing the flow of materials to the South. While he continued in government after the war, he still published poetry. None of it, however, achieved the power and the clarity of his earlier work. His continued residence in Kentucky also demonstrates that he, unlike many others, clung to the unified American west on each side of the Ohio long after most had abandoned that vision at the coming of the war.

Texts: "Sketches and Response," *Western Literary Journal and Monthly Review* (Cincinnati, August 1836; December 1836): 210–214, 283–284. "The Miami Woods" and "The Mothers of the West" in *Selections from the Poetical Literature of the West,* ed. Gallagher (Cincinnati, 1841): 13–20, 53–54. "Song of the Pioneers," "The Laborer," and "Radicalos" in *Poets and Poetry of the West,* ed. William T. Coggeshall (Cincinnati, 1860): 141–143, 147–148.

SKETCHES OF THE LITERATURE OF THE WEST

NUMBER ONE

We do not know that we can make up a portion of our BUDGET, in a manner likely to be more acceptable to the generality of our readers, than by giving an occasional article on the Literature of the West, to consist in great part of extracts from the uncollected writings of this region. The caption which we have chosen for these articles, may excite a smile in some, even among ourselves; for it is notorious that several of our writers are better known at the East and the South, and more correctly appreciated, than here where they look for and ought to receive encouraging consideration and solid support. This fact applies to the editorial fraternity, with particular pertinance.

How many of the conductors of our numerous public journals, are aware that the West has supplied some of the most zealous and distinguished votaries of Science which the United States can boast? How many of them are aware, that the West has sent forth treatises in the medical and physical departments of scientific knowledge, that have been republished in Europe, frequently referred to and quoted from by her most eminent *savans,* and secured for their authors distinction and respect? How many of them are aware, that the West has produced several fictions that as far surpass nine-tenths of the foreign-spun and home-woven novels and romances of the day, as they are in turn surpassed by the 'Abbottsford Magician' in his better and greater efforts? How many of them are aware, that from the wilds of the West has issued one of the most gorgeous, majestic, ingenious and impressive poems—a Tale of Faery—that the literature of the nineteenth century can as yet shew?—nearly as much superior, in some respects, to the long-talked-about 'Lillian' of England, or the recently much-lauded 'Culprit Fay' of America, as it is surpassed in everything by 'Comus' or the 'Red-Cross Knight.' How many of them are aware, that throughout the fresh and wild and romantic regions of the West, Poetry is scattered in 'golden ingots,' bright from the mint of genius, and glowing with the all-worshipful spirit of truth and the all-lovely impress of beauty and purity?—and this in quantities sufficient, were it known and appreciated, as it would be known and appreciated in other countries, and even in other sections of our own country,—demagogue-ridden and collar-marked and politico-huckstered as it is, and stock-jobbing and calculating and heartless as are the times,—to secure us an honorable reputation throughout the world? And finally, how many of them are aware, that there are among us tens and scores of souls charged with the electric spark, and of spirits thirsting for the waters of Castaly, whose possessors prey on themselves, and fold the wings of their genius, because of the seldom and faint praise that chills, and the cold and heartless neglect that freezes? How many among the conductors of our numerous public journals, we ask, and with respect, are aware of these things? Perhaps one or two! And yet are they facts, as it is our purpose to show in the course of these papers.

The few here who have for a length of time persevered in their young passion and their early love, are, as we have intimated, better known and more correctly appreciated East than West. We have sometimes been surprised, at the inquiries after and intelligent remarks upon some of our writers, by eastern gentlemen and ladies of literary taste and acquirements; and we have been almost as often chagrined by learning the answers such individuals had previously received to like inquiries; such as: 'O, he's some young Kentucky preacher, I believe, or a farm-boy in the interior, or a strolling printer, or a journeyman shoemaker or carpenter, or a poor shop-keeper down street, or a briefless lawyer about town, or a clodhopper who has quit hoeing corn and digging potatoes, and connected himself with a weekly paper to tell love-stories and scribble verses for the ladies.' Respectful inquiries have more than once met with responses similar to these. And if a stranger happen to have had his curiosity awakened respecting some literary backwoodsman, whose occasional productions he had met with success in eastern periodicals, where portions of the polite literature of the West are frequently to be found accompanied with introductory, critical, and commendatory remarks, and refer for gratification to current western papers, or even to files of our public journals for years, he will stand fifty or a hundred chances to one of being disappointed. Western Periodicals, in reality, with one or two exceptions, afford no evidence of the western literary character.—We mention this not in the way of fault-finding—for it would not become us to complain—but merely for the purpose of calling the attention of our editorial friends to a subject, which has perhaps never occurred to them, or at least upon which they have never bestowed any thought. Still less would it become us to dictate; we may, however, be permitted to suggest, that it would not detract from the interest of their papers, nor lessen them in the esteem of their business patrons or in general value, did they not give up their columns so entirely to editorial vituperation, political slang, and the disgusting details of crime in its various manifestations.

One object of this magazine, as set forth in our Introductory, is to represent to ourselves and our neighbors, correctly and thoroughly, the literary character of the Great West.[1] A surprising degree of ignorance prevails, as respects our productions in

---

1. Wherever we speak of *western* literature, it is not in a spirit that would separate it from *eastern* or *southern* literature, but merely as a matter of convenience. Though, as we conceive, we surpass our neighbors in freshness and energy, we are far behind them in scholarship, polish, and general perfection. But we dislike, as much as any one can, all sectional lines and distinctions; and when, in speaking of the literature of this section of the Union, we use the term *western,* it is merely to distinguish it as a young and rising province of our great Republic of Letters.

the several departments of literature. Circumstances, in a measure, have rendered this state of the matter inevitable. Most of our writings, have been either produced for a particular occasion, with the ceremonies of which they went to rest; or, have been published carelessly in newspapers of slight merit and limited circulation, where they were not likely to be noticed themselves, much less to call attention to their authors: and as no periodical of character, with the exception of one with which the editor of this magazine was formerly connected, has hitherto made it its business to call these occasional productions to light and present them to the public in a manner calculated to secure them notice, they still remain, for the most part, scattered about in their original obscurity. We have but few writers who pursue authorship as a means of support, and whose productions have been published in a collected form. Our poetry, especially, is the mere mometary outgushing of irrepressible feeling, and has proceeded from the hearts of individuals who were daily and hourly subjected to the perplexities and toils of business, and the cares and anxieties inseparable from the procuring of one's daily bread by active occupation. The consequences of this state of things, are as already mentioned. We have however taken up the pen for *our brethren in sorrow and tribulation,* and it shall go hard with us but we will find opportunities to secure them a hearing, and language to plead their cause.

The grass of the field, and the flowers of the wilderness, are growing over the bones of some whose aspirations were boundless, and whose genius was undoubted. Such were Hainey, the author of 'Crystalina' and the 'Fever Dream,' Robinson, the author of 'The Savage,' Little, the sweet and tender poet of homely truth and christian feeling, Godman, the greatly beloved and universally respected student of Nature, and one or two others. To these, our first duties are due. With one exception, their literary remains are almost wholly unknown; and with that exception, likewise, their very *names* will sound strange even to western ears. Ours be the task,—a holy one it is, and a pleasant one will it prove,—to rescue there names from oblivion, and their works from unmerited neglect. But first a few moments to the living—as some time must elapse before their merits and faults can be the subject of eulogy and animadversion in our pages.

We have a word or two of advice, which we wish here to impress upon the young writers of the West. There is among us, an abundance of poetical talent—some of it of a high order, and very considerable compass—but there is great danger of its being rendered of no account, if not worse than useless, for want of proper direction. Our poetry,—and indeed it is the fault of the poetry of the age,—reminds one not of the blue sky or the green earth—of babbling brooks or singing waterfalls—of the quiet hamlet, embowered in trees and covered with vines, or the peaceful landscape—of the velvet valley or the rock-ribbed mountain—of Nature's magnificent repose, or her awful awakenings to earthquake and tempest: but of the wealthy city, where thought is sicklied with sentiment—of the splendid mansion, where too frequently sloth prevails, and the high aims and glorious impulses of life are examinate—of the rich hall, carpeted, and picture hung, and glittering with mirrors—of the green-house, with its varied and beautiful but forced and unhealthy flowers. To say nothing of breadth or compass, philosophical depth or intellectual elevation, compare the simple *character* of the poetry of to-day with that of the masters of the English lyre: pretty conceits, beautiful turns of expression, and monotonous smoothness and regularity of versification, have taken the place of manly ideas, abrupt and thrilling transitions, and sonorous lines; and for the rush, and energy, and wholesomeness of a former day, we look in vain.

This ought not to be—it need not be. We do not expect ever to see the fathers of English Poetry surpassed, or often equalled; yet they may be *approached;* and the *nearer* they are so, the greater will be the success of that individual who fixes his eye on the mountain, and attempts the ascent. To approach them, need not be to *imitate* them. The study of a model does not necessarily force imitation, except upon inferior minds. Mediocrity may not be able to comprehend the *soul* that stirred them; and consequently may be led into an imitation of the mere body: but genius will approach them only to light its torch at their altar; its future course will have no relation to the paths they trod, other than being guided by the same light.—Let us, then, who are in the enjoyment of a tri-youthfulness,—being young as a people, young in years, and young as a literary community,—endeavor to approach them. Let us discard the affectation of parlor prettinesses, waxwork niceties, and milliner-like conceits. Let us turn our lady-pegasuses out to pasture, and mount coursers of speed and mettle. Let us give over our pacing and ambling, and dash off with a free rein. Let us abandon the luxurious couch, and the glittering hall, and the garden of exotics—and away to the grassy meadows, and the breezy slopes, and the inspiring hills. And above all, let us strike at once for the 'wells undefiled' of English Poetry, and not pause by the way to quench our thirst at the many puny fountains that shall beset our paths, decked out with all manner of gaudy trappings, in the miserable taste of an effeminate day.

As we have said, there is among us an abundance of poetical talent; and occasionally we find it walking in the right path; but for the most part it has received a wrong direction; and constant watching, and repeated efforts, will be necessary to set it aright. We cannot go to work in this respect, a moment too soon. Habits are stubborn things; and habits of writing after a bad model, when once confirmed, are quite beyond the reach of reform. Let us, therefore, begin now to ask ourselves, Is there nothing beautiful, but the face of woman? nothing to apostrophize, but a penciled eyebrow? nothing symmetrical, but a female form? nothing worth praising, but a well-turned ancle? nothing that *floats upon the heart,* but disheveled tresses? nothing whose touch thrills us, but the soft white hand? Is the *soul,* which animates all these, a cipher? is the *heart,* which alone can make them lastingly beautiful, unworthy of a thought? And finally, is this wide earth so glorious, and not made for our worship? Let us,—and we seriously urge it upon our young writers,—let us answer these questions in a right spirit, and, as poets, we shall soon do something of which we may well be proud. We have the power within us: the inspiration is around.

In our search after the evidences of that poetical talent which we have heretofore claimed for the West, we have met with but little to discourage us, and much to stimulate and cheer us. We have now a mass of material collected, in this department of our literature, which we shall from time to time present to the literary public with much pride and confidence, and but slight misgivings. In our next, we contemplate giving a brief sketch of Dr. Hainey, with extensive extracts from 'Crystalina,' and such an abstract of the entire poem, which contains about three thousand five hundred lines, as will substantiate its claims to all the consideration that we have asked for it.

Confident that these numbers will afford intrinsic evidence of high poetic capacity among the western people,—(whether this be the result of our origin, our situation in a vast and till recently solemn and lonely wilderness, our peculiar habits of life, or other causes combined with these, we shall not pretend to discuss,)—we doubt not that they will receive respectful attention abroad; and we conclude this introductory paper, by asking for them like attention at home.

THOUGHTS OF MY OWN

The first number of the "Western Literary Journal and Monthly Review" lately fell under my eye, and itself gave the first announcement I had of its entrance on the theatre of existence. I was glad that this fact, so pleasing in itself, was not published in the usual manner of the newly born, namely, by piteous cries for pap, and pressing demands for a wet nurse. The manly tone of Number One was sufficient to challenge admiration. That must be a brave production—a perfect Pallas among periodicals—that can make its entry upon life boasting of matured parts, and vitality enough for twelve months' animation. Success to the Journal!

As much, however, as the growth and prosperity of the Journal may be desired, the event thereof must be granted to be somewhat problematical. There are many "lions in the way" of its advancement, and there is some reason to apprehend that the Journal will pause in its course, and—ashamed to go backwards, afraid to go forwards—perish by mere atrophy. It is true that in number One, we have given us from an able pen, a history of the "decline and fall" of all preceding monthly periodicals that have risen in the West; and this history seems intended as a sort of chart for the regulation of the Journal's course. But one who has been wrecked on Scylla can not always tell how we may indubitably avoid Charybdis. And though, by the light and teaching of experience, the Journal may be saved from destruction in the form in which it befel others, we need not therefore conclude that it will measure many centuries by its monthly periods. This proposition is applicable to all journals, and its truth will not be disputed. I am willing to admit, however, that should one Literary Journal escape the ordinary fatalities of similar works that have sprung up in the West, and should live and prosper for the limited term of one hundred years, its lease on life will be a good one—sufficiently sound to justify a prudent man in the investment of a year's subscription, at least.

As I am friendly to the Journal, and desirous to see it creditably serve out its short probation, I will proceed to set forth some thoughts of my own with regard to the difficulties in the way.

1. The extent, productiveness and scenic variety and magnificence of the great West is, at present, a serious obstacle to the cultivation of literature, and must therefore operate to the disadvantage of the Literary Journal.

In this life, we are taught there is a continual struggle for the upper-hand between the "flesh and the spirit"—the physical and the mental man. The physical man loves to eat, and if the appetite be not duly guarded, it will soon have the mind exhausting its energies in the invention and comparison of the merits of culinary preparations, rather than employing it in the investigation of its own nature, and the exercise of its creative power. All men have naturally a love of eating. Eve was appealed to through the palate, and with Adam, forfeited Paradise for eating; and their descendants, all, inherit this weakness. The stomach, in the hour of temptation, has always proved too strong for the spirit, and hence it is a lamentable thing to live in a fertile land, and quite impossible that literature should flourish there.

The people of the West live in the midst of temptation, and, as might be expected, the fruitfulness of their country is their cause of weakness. They are apt to cultivate their fields in preference to their minds; to regard the coming of the new moon—the season of sowing—rather than the arrival of the "Monthly," and to prefer the production of edibles to that of essays. Their barns are always full, and their poultry fat. They live in the midst of oil and fatness. How can such a people be literary? When did the fat ever become the favorite of literature? Or, rather, when did literature ever become the favorite of the fat?

The physical man loves to hunt, too, and to enjoy the free exercise of his lungs, legs, and all other limbs and parts. The love of this physical exercise often becomes a strong passion, and the mind soon forgets its varied capacities, and its employment becomes as monotonous and restricted as that of a pilot to a boat. In the West there is too much temptation for the physical man—too much scope for gymnastics. The physical too easily gains the advantage, and leads the mental off hundreds of miles to deer licks, buffalo ranges, &c. whereby dangers, perils and privations—the glory of the physical—may be incurred; and the mental becomes but the pilot of the physical in its restless, roving, adventurous life.

These reflections lead me to the conclusion, no longer novel to the reader, I hope, that the growth of literature in the West must be necessarily hindered in consequence of our rich and expansive territory, and the profuse fruitfulness of its soil.

Some persons no doubt will object to the deductions from my mode of reasoning, and contend that the circumstances of life in the West, such as I have mentioned, are of the very kind to give vigor to the mind and buoyancy to the spirits, and that these are essential to the production of sound and wholesome literature. To this position it is not convenient for me at present to reply. But this much, in passing, I will say: it is inconsistent with all the original and preconceived notions of mankind. Who ever conceived a poet to be a big, portly, or puncheon-shaped man—Who ever conceived a writer of fiction to be fat or full-bodied? Or who ever conceived a writer of any kind to be a sleek and well-fed waiter on his physical wants? No one, I will venture. Leave any one to his natural, spontaneous suggestions, and he invariably associates the idea of "pale and intellectual" with his conceptions of literary men. All this proves the position to be wrong.

But indeed the position is absurd in itself. Can *pork eaters* ever be poets? Impossible. The lard fumes of Porkopolis would stifle any one whose organs were fitted for snuffing the ambrosial airs of Parnassus. Can the careless, roving hunters of the West ever become writers of fact or fiction? Impossible. Nature did not so ordain. Some men were made to write—others to be written about. These men of the West are the fancied heroes of fiction, the real heroes of history. They *act,* and leave it for the cooped up denizens of cities, and those who have nothing else to do, to write.

The conclusion on this point is, that the mental and physical are not so exactly alloyed in the composition of man, but that the one and then again the other may prevail, and give character to the whole. And the West is too great, too fruitful, too spacious, and offers too many occasions and inducements for the physical activity of man, to allow of immediate encouragement to literature and the Literary Journal. The appeal of the Journal to sectional pride may possibly ensure success, for certainly the West has as much pride as another portion of the Union of "peculiar institutions," lately appealed to on that score by its leading and distinguished magazine, which, as descriptive probably of its political cast, styles itself the "*Blackwood* of America."

2. But another great obstacle to the growth and well-being of a Western Journal, is the intimate association of Western writers with circumstances and scenes that naturally inspire men with lofty thought, philosophic reflection, or poetic feeling. This

would seem a singular proposition, but for the acknowledged truth that "distance lends enchantment to the view."

The Western people have always recognized this truth fully, and have acted on it. Hence we see them seek with great avidity and hugely admire descriptions of "Scenes in the West," "Western Life and Manners," and many other works of similar titles—all written by strangers to us and our country, who have no other lights to guide them in their compositions than fall upon the picture of the varied and expansive West, when they take the enchanting "view" that "distance" lends. This course of the Western people is so sensible in itself, and their homage to Eastern literature so honorable, that no surprise will be excited in the minds of the thoughtful on hearing it stated. For who so well prepared to dwell, in immortal verse, on the glowing, glorious themes of the West, as those who know them only by report, and whose bosoms have never throbbed under their influence? Who should sketch Western character—its boldness and sectional peculiarities—and describe the generous, hospitable nature, and direct, practical character of our people, but the writer of Europe or the Atlantic States, who trembles at the thought of treading our soil, and sits secure in his garret, while he pictures our people rude, ignorant and savage? And who should philosophize on the political destiny of the West, in view of its physical advantages, but he whose foot has never stirred a gravel on our soil—who knows it but by its paper cities, its Cairo schemes, and other inventions of speculation?

The conclusion, then, is, that the familiarity of western men with grand subjects of composition, breeds contempt therefor; that strangers and distant persons write about them better, their ignorance of the subject matter giving an originality to their statements, quite novel and pleasing; and finally, that the people of the West acquiesce in and encourage the state of things brought about by this faith, by neglecting western literary enterprizes, and giving their money for the periodicals and papers of the east. Here is an evil which the Journal must rectify, before it can reign over the empire of western mind.

3. The last obstacle in the way of the Journal which I shall notice, is the one which I fear must finally overthrow it:—it is *the poverty of the western population.* This may be an unexpected announcement to some, but it is lamentably true.—The whole West may be canvassed and its people questioned, and with one accord they will avow themselves to be in the direst straits and necessities. Ninety-nine out of a hundred will be found absolutely too "poor" to take any periodical whatever. And the reason for this wide-spread poverty is obvious enough. It is a well-ascertained fact, that, with us, a man can, by the employment of one-third of the time usually allotted to labor, produce what will support himself and a moderate family in comfort and comparative luxury. It follows then that for two-thirds of their time, our people are *out of work—idle—unemployed!* Such a state of things in England would fill that island with wailing, starvation, and death. It brings *our* people to hard-griping poverty and fills their hearts with sorrow. In their misfortune they are often driven to the extremities of distress, and in the narcotic influence of the James River weed or the fumes of the fine scented Spanish, they seek alleviation of their sorrows. How could an agent of the Journal have the heart to harrow up their feelings and revive fearful images of want, by the cruel request to 'subscribe'?

Just consider the effect of this state of things on the prospects of the Journal. The people are too poor to pay the publishers for the periodical—the publishers are too poor to pay writers to fill its columns—the writers are too poor to write for nothing—and so the Journal comes to an end.—Alas, the fatality of poverty! The con-

templation of such melancholy consequences is nearly sufficient to drive the disconsolate publishers to the indulgence of "honey-dew," or "half Spanish." As for myself,
though very poor, I will light this "Regalia," and while I smoke away the sad thoughts
I have conjured up, think of the propriety of subscribing.

A. S. M.

MIAMI WOODS (1841)

THE Autumn Time is with us!—Its approach
Was heralded, not many days ago,
By hazy skies, that veil'd the brazen sun,
And sea-like murmurs from the rustling corn,
And low-voiced brooks, that wandered drowsily
By purpling clusters of the juicy grape,
Swinging upon the vine. And now, 'tis here!
And what a change hath pass'd upon the face
Of Nature, where the waving forest spreads,
Then robed in deepest green! All through the night
The subtle frost hath plied its mystic art;
And in the day the golden sun hath wrought
True wonders; and the winds of morn and even
Have touch'd with magic breath the changing leaves.
And now, as wanders the dilating eye
Athwart the varied landscape, circling far,
What gorgeousness, what blazonry, what pomp
Of colors, bursts upon the ravish'd sight!
Here, where the maple rears its yellow crest,
A golden glory: yonder, where the oak
Stands monarch of the forest, and the ash
Is girt with flame-like parasite, and broad
The dogwood spreads beneath, a rolling field
Of deepest crimson; and afar, where looms
The gnarléd gum, a cloud of bloodiest red!

Out in the woods of Autumn!—I have cast
Aside the shackles of the town, that vex
The fetterless soul, and come to hide myself,
Miami! in thy venerable shades.
Low on thy bank, where spreads the velvet moss,
My limbs recline. Beneath me, silver-bright,

Glide the clear waters, with a plaintive moan
For summer's parting glories. High o'erhead,
Seeking the sedgy lakes of the warm South,
Sails tireless the unerring waterfowl,
Screaming among the cloud-racks. Oft from where,
Erect on mossy trunk, the partridge stands,
Bursts suddenly the whistle clear and loud,
Far-echoing through the dim wood's fretted aisles.
Deep murmurs from the trees, bending with brown
And ripened mast, are interrupted now
By sounds of dropping nuts; and warily
The turkey from the thicket comes, and swift
As flies an arrow darts the pheasant down,
To batten on the autumn; and the air,
At times, is darkened by a sudden rush
Of myriad wings, as the wild pigeon leads
His squadrons to the banquet. Far away,
Where the pawpaw its mellow fruitage yields,
And thick, dark clusters of the wild grape hang,
The merry laugh of childhood, and the shout
Of truant schoolboy, ring upon the air.

  Deep in the solemn forest!—From the tops
Of these old trees, swept by the evening wind,
Which swells among their leaves, and dies away,
And gathers strength again, float softly down
Strange, wild, deep harmonies. And I have been
All day among the Voices of the Wood,
That are but echoes of perpetual tones
With which God fills the universe. The noon,
Gairish and still, and midnight's calm repose,
And dewy eve, and blue rejoicing morn,
Are full of them. I hear them in the breeze
That stirs the reed to music. In the faint,
Sad murmur of the stream that glides below,
Bearing away the fallen leaves, as pass
The dreams of childhood and the hopes of life,
I hear them. And I hear them in the spring
That, bubbling from beneath you dark old root,
Falls tinkling o'er the mossy rock below.
And in the billowy ehimes that wake aloft
When gale-like breezes sweep the ancient trees,
They speak with organ-tones, that reach the depths
Stirring within me, and an echo find
In the roused soul . . . O God! Thou art in all
I now behold! the essence and the life,
The germ and the vitality! the birth,

The being, and the end! Else Reason gropes
In darkness all her days, and Knowledge dies.
What but the high intelligence, the hand
Almighty, and the sempiternal life—
What but the omnipresence, and the will,
All which we feel Thou art, and all which fills
Our great Idea of a primal cause
And final end, could speak this glorious world
From wildest Chaos and profoundest Night?
What poise the planets in the void, and set
The infinite stars in order, and confine
Each in its separate path on high? What fill
Earth with its countless forms of Life, and raise
Eternally, as ages glide along,
New being from the ashes of decay?

    Alone, with God and Nature!—Round me now
Is pressing onward the eternal change.
And here, where all is seen, but nought reveal'd,
I contemplate the mysteries sublime
Of birth, and life, and death . . . From the dark womb
Of winter, comes the spring, with mild, warm breath;
And instantly the chains that bound the streams
Are loosen'd, and the waters leap to light,
And shout with gladness. Soon the spell that long
Has held the earth, is broken; and the grass
Pierces the sod, and from the sheltering leaves
That strew the ground, look out the fresh, young flowers,
Smiling to heaven. Then the gray, leafless trees,
Long desolate in their utter nakedness,
Feel the new presence; and, although no sign
Of life is visible, a delicate green
Creeps out along the tender twigs, where swell
The germ-infolding buds; and in the warm
And sunny day, and through the breezy night,
Come forth the myriad leaves, courting the light
And wantoning with the zephyr, till a robe
Of brightest green bursts on the wondering eye.
O'er the cold bosom of the sluggish clod
Soon steals the influence; and from the broad
And seeded field shoots up the waving grain,
Till spreads a sea of verdure far around,
Toss'd by the winds, and with the clouds at play.
Then comes the long and sunny summer time,
And for the garners of the husbandman
Ripens, and to the sickle lays, the grain;
And for the cherish'd tribes of air, that make

The cool groves vocal, strews the briery glebe
With berries; and for the innumerous flocks
That shun the haunts of men, and hang their nests
High in the endless wood, or in the low
Dark thicket build, matures the beechen mast;
And takes the worm upon the leaf, and wraps
A silken tissue round it; and prepares
For all the insect race befitting tombs,
Where each shall sleep the winter hours away.
Then comes the lone and quiet autumn on,
With tinckling water-falls, and moaning woods,
And arid wastes, o'er which the night-winds sigh.
And this is here; and still the eternal round
Of change goes on—beginning, being, ending;
And still the mystery proclaims a Hand
Omnipotent—an Eye that never sleeps.

   End of the vernal year!—The flower hath closed
And cast its petals, and the naked stalk
Stands shrivelling in the frost; the feathered grass
Is heavy in the head; the painted leaf
Flies twittering on the wind; and to the earth
Falls the brown nut, with melancholy sound.
Yet the low, moaning autumn wind, that sweeps
The seeded grass and lately-blossoming flower,
Bears the light germs of future life away,
And sows them by the gliding rivulet,
And o'er the plain, and on the mountain side,
To clothe anew the earth, when comes again
The quickening breath of spring. And on the place
Where fall the ripened nuts, the frosty night
Will heap the stricken leaves; and thence shall spring,
In many an after age, another growth
Of stately trees, when those around me now,
Fallen with eld, shall moulder, and enrich
The ground that now sustains their lofty pride.

   Changing, forever changing!—So depart
The glories of the old majestic wood;
So pass the pride and garniture of fields;
The growth of ages, and the bloom of days,
Into the dust of centuries; and so
Are both renewed. The scattered tribes of men,
The generations of the populous earth,
All have their seasons too. And jocund Youth
Is the green spring-time—Manhood's lusty strength
Is the maturing summer—hoary Age
Types well the autumn of the year—and Death
Is the real winter, which forecloses all.

And shall the forests have another spring,
And shall the fields another garland wear,
And shall the worm come forth renew'd in life
And clothed with highest beauty, and not man?
No!—in the Book before me now, I read
Another language; and my faith is sure,
That though the chains of death may hold it long,
This mortal will o'ermaster them, and break
Away, and put on immortality.

    Almighty Father! such the lesson is,
That, in these cool and venerable woods,
I con to-day; and firmer in my breast,
By every syllable, these truths are fixed:
That Thou art the beginning, and the end,
Of all this wondrous work; and that Thy love
Pervades the universe; and that Thy smile
Seeketh all hearts to sun them; and that Thou,
In every glorious thing we here behold,
Declarest and reveal'st Thyself to be
The Majesty Supreme—Eternal God.

THE MOTHERS OF THE WEST (1841)

The Mothers of our Forest-Land!
    Stout-hearted dames were they;
With nerve to wield the battle-brand,
    And join the border-fray.
Our rough land had no braver,
    In its days of blood and strife—
Aye ready for severest toil,
    Aye free to peril life.

The mothers of our Forest-Land!
    On old Kan-tuc-kee's soil,
How shared they, with each dauntless band,
    War's tempest and Life's toil!
They shrank not from the foeman—
    They quailed not in the fight—
But cheered their husbands through the day,
    And soothed them through the night.
The Mothers of our Forest-Land!
    Their bosoms pillowed *men!*

And proud were they by such to stand,
  In hammock, fort, or glen.
To load the sure old rifle—
  To run the leaden ball—
To watch a battling husband's place,
  And fill it should he fall.

The Mothers of our Forest-Land!
  Such were their daily deeds.
Their monument!—where does it stand?
  Their epitaph!—who reads?
No braver dames had Sparta,
  No nobler matrons Rome—
Yet who or lauds or honors them,
  E'en in their own green home!

The Mothers of our Forest-Land!
  They sleep in unknown graves:
And had they borne and nursed a band
  Of ingrates, or of slaves,
They had not been more neglected!
  But their graves shall yet be found,
And their monuments dot here and there
  "The Dark and Bloody Ground."

SONG OF THE PIONEERS (1841)

A SONG for the early times out West,
  And our green old forest home,
Whose pleasant memories freshly yet
  Across the bosom come:
A song for the free and gladsome life,
  In those early days we led,
With a teeming soil beneath our feet,
  And a smiling Heav'n o'erhead!
Oh, the waves of life danced merrily,
  And had a joyous flow,
In the days when we were Pioneers,
  Fifty years ago!

The hunt, the shot, the glorious chase,
  The captur'd elk, or deer;

The camp, the big, bright fire, and then
    The rich and wholesome cheer:—
The sweet, sound sleep, at dead of night,
    By our camp-fire, blazing high—
Unbroken by the wolf's long howl,
    And the panther springing by.
Oh, merrily pass'd the time, despite
    Our wily Indian foe,
In the days when we were Pioneers,
    Fifty years ago!

We shunn'd not labor: when 'twas due
    We wrought with right good will;
And for the homes we won for them,
    Our children bless us still.
We lived not hermit lives, but oft
    In social converse met;
And fires of love were kindled then,
    That burn on warmly yet.
Oh, pleasantly the stream of life
    Pursued its constant flow,
In the days when we were Pioneers,
    Fifty years ago!

We felt that we were fellow-men;
    We felt we were a band,
Sustain'd here in the wilderness
    By Heaven's upholding hand.
And when the solemn Sabbath came,
    We gathered in the wood,
And lifted up our hearts in prayer
    To God, the only Good.
Our temples then were earth and sky;
    None others did we know,
In the days when we were Pioneers,
    Fifty years ago!

Our forest life was rough and rude,
    And dangers clos'd us round;
But here, amid the green old trees,
    Freedom was sought and found.
Oft through our dwellings wint'ry blasts
    Would rush with shriek and moan;
We cared not—though they were but frail,
    We felt they were our own!
Oh, free and manly lives we led,
    Mid verdure, or mid snow,
In the days when we were Pioneers,
    Fifty years ago!

But now our course of life is short;
   And as, from day to day,
We're walking on with halting step,
   And fainting by the way,
Another Land more bright than this,
   To our dim sight appears,
And on our way to it we'll soon
   Again be pioneers!
Yet while we linger, we may all
   A backward glance still throw,
To the days when we were Pioneers,
   Fifty years ago!

THE LABORER (1860)

STAND UP—erect! Thou hast the form,
   And likeness of thy God!—who more?
A soul as dauntless mid the storm
Of daily life, a heart as warm
   And pure, as breast e'er bore.

What then?—Thou art as true a Man
   As moves the human mass among;
As much a part of the Great Plan
That with creation's dawn began,
   As any of the throng.

Who is thine enemy?—the high
   In station, or in wealth the chief?
The great, who coldly pass thee by,
With proud step and averted eye?
   Nay! nurse not such belief.

If true unto thyself thou wast,
   What were the proud one's scorn to thee?
A feather, which thou mightest cast
Aside, as idly as the blast
   The light leaf from the tree.

No:—uncurb'd passions—low desires—
   Absence of noble self-respect—
Death, in the breast's consuming fires,
To that high nature which aspires
   Forever, till thus check'd:

These are thine enemies—thy worst:
   They chain thee to thy lowly lot—
Thy labor and thy life accurst.
Oh, stand erect! and from them burst!
   And longer suffer not!

Thou art thyself thine enemy!
   The great!—what better they than thou?
As theirs, is not thy will as free?
Has God with equal favors thee
   Neglected to endow?

True, wealth thou hast not: 'tis but dust!
   Nor place; uncertain as the wind!
But that thou hast, which, with thy crust
And water may despose the lust
   Of both—a noble mind.

With this, and passions under ban,
   True faith, and holy trust in God,
Thou art the peer of any man.
Look up, then—that thy little span
   Of life may be well trod!

RADICALOS (1860)

IN the far and fading ages
   Of the younger days of earth,
When man's aspirations quicken'd,
   And his passions had their birth—
When first paled his glorious beauty,
   And his heart first knew unrest,
As he yielded to the tempter
   That inflamed and fill'd his breast—
When the Voice that was in Eden
   Echoed through his startled soul,
And he heard rebuking anthems
   Through the heavenly arches roll—
When he fell from the high promise
   Of his being's blesséd morn,
To a night of doubt and struggle—
   Radicálos then was born.

Through the ages long and dreary
   That since then have dawn'd on earth,
Man has had but feeble glimpses
   Of the glory of his birth:
Catching these, his soul, aspiring
   To its morning light again,
Hard has upward toil'd, and often
   Fill'd with hope, but still in vain.
Many a blessed song comes stealing
   Downward from the Eden aisles,
Whence the light of heavenliest beauty
   Still upon the banish'd smiles;
But the harmonies are broken
   Of each sounding choral hymn,
And the gloom that vails his spirit
   Makes e'en heavenly splendor dim.

Faint revealings, thwarted hopings,
   Wearying struggles, day by day—
So the long and dreary ages
   Of his life have worn away.
War, and rapine, and oppression,
   Early in his course he found—
Brother against brother striving—
   By the few the many bound.
And in patience, and in meekness,
   To the galling chain resign'd,
Thus the fettered limbs have rested—
   Thus both slept the darkened mind.
But it wakens now!—it flashes
   Like the lightning ere the rain;
And those limbs grow strong;—when ready.
They can rend the mightiest chain.

Through the slow and stately marches
   Of the centuries sublime,
Radicalos hath been strengthening
   For the noblest work of Time,
And he comes upon the Present
   Like a god in look and mien,
With composure high surveying
   All the tumult of the scene:
Where obey the fettered millions;
   Where command the fettering few;
Where the chain of wrong is forging,
   With its red links hid from view;
And he standeth by the peasant,
   And he standeth by the lord,

And he shouts "Your rights are equal!"
    Till earth startles at the word.

He hath seen the record written,
    From the primal morn of man,
In the blood of battling nations
    O'er ensanguined plains that ran;
In the tears of the deluded,
    In the sweat of the oppress'd,
From Ind's farthest peopled borders
    To the new worlds of the West.
And he cometh with deliverance!
    And his might shall soon be known,
Where the wrong'd rise up for justice,
    And the wrongers lie o'erthrown.

Wo! the pride that then shall scorn him:
    He will bring it fitly low!
Wo! the arm that shall oppose him:
    He will cleave it at a blow!
Wo! the hosts that shall beset him:
    He will scatter them abroad!
He will strike them down forever!
    Radicálos is of God.

44

MINOR POETS OF CINCINNATI:

Laura M. Thurston (?–?) Charles Jones (?–?), Frederick Thomas (1811–1866)

During the decades leading up to the Civil War, Cincinnati produced dozens of poets, short-story writers, playwrights, and novelists. While much of their work was derivative and imitative of British and eastern models, certain writers produced works of significant quality and polish. The scene itself was nurtured by more prolific figures such as the Drake brothers, Edwin Mansfield, James Hall, Timothy Flint, and William Gallagher. Lesser known writers often found publication in their journals and collections. Each was introduced as expressing specifically regional sentiments, and a similar sentiment has guided the selections reproduced here.

Little is known about Laura Thurston. The poems of hers published by Gallagher in 1841, along with other of her poems, had been earlier printed in local periodicals. All of these reflect the emigrant's perspective upon coming to the west from a woman's point of view, similar to that of Rebecca Burlend, likewise an emigrant from the British Isles, who found the freedom and opportunity in the west that had been lost in both Europe and the east. Of Charles Jones as well, the historical record holds little save these poems. From their content and sentiment, however, it might be surmised that he was a colleague of Benjamin Drake. They share Drake's interest in including the Native American presence in the construction of regional identity. Nonetheless, like many white writers, Jones gives in to the temptation to reconstruct Tecumseh as an embodiment of European virtues.

Frederick Thomas was a prolific writer of very mundane novels. Among these, *East and West* is typical: a formulaic romance set against the move of elite eastern settlers from Philadelphia to Louisville. In it, Louisville's frontier qualities are wholly lacking. In a longer poem-cycle, "The Emigrants" (available only in extracted form), Thomas works toward but never fully achieves a more cogent view of the west. For example, his contradictory representations of the Native Americans in this poem suggests an unresolved, or perhaps transitional, condition.

An immigrant to Cincinnati from South Carolina as an adult, Thomas's engagement with the west ultimately suggests the perspective reflective of the ambivalence held by most Americans toward the frontier. Not surprisingly, Thomas left Cincinnati for the east in 1840 and returned only once. Nonetheless, in the poem, Thomas, as well as Thurston and Jones in their poems, articulates the unsettled nature in the minds of many whites on the frontier, caught between the received images of eastern writing and their own divergent experiences in the west.

Text: Thurston and Jones are in *Selections from the Poetical Literature of the West,* ed. William D. Gallagher (Cincinnati, 1841): Thurston, 59–60; 101–103; Jones, 40–42, 76–77. While a shorter version of Thomas's "Extracts" is also in Gallagher's collection, a longer version was published in *Poets and Poetry of the West,* ed. William T. Coggeshall (Cincinnati, 1860):186–189.

THURSTON, ON CROSSING THE ALLEGHANIES

THE broad, the bright, the glorious West,
   Is spread before me now!
Where the gray mists of morning rest
   Beneath yon mountain's brow!
The bound is past—the goal is won—
The region of the setting sun
   Is open to my view.
Land of the valiant and the free—
My own Green Mountain land—to thee,
   And thine, a long adieu!

I hail thee, Valley of the West,
   For what thou yet shalt be!
I hail thee for the hopes that rest
   Upon thy destiny!
Here—from this mountain height, I see
Thy bright waves floating to the sea,
   Thine emerald fields outspread,
And feel that in the book of fame,
Proudly shall thy recorded name
   In later days be read.

Yet while I gaze upon thee now,
   All glorious as thou art,
A cloud is resting on my brow,
   A weight upon my heart.
To me—in all thy youthful pride—
Thou art a land of cares untried,
   Of untold hopes and fears.
Thou art—yet not for thee I grieve;
But for the far-off land I leave,
   I look on thee with tears.

O! brightly, brightly, glow thy skies,
   In summer's sunny hours!

The green earth seems a paradise
   Arrayed in summer flowers!
But oh! there is a land afar
Whose skies to me are brighter far
   Along the Atlantic shore!
For eyes beneath their radiant shrine,
In kindlier glances answered mine—
   Can these their light restore?

Upon the lofty bound I stand,
   That parts the East and West;
Before me—lies a fairy land;
   Behind—*a home of rest!*
Here, hope her wild enchantment flings,
Portrays all bright and lovely things,
   My footsteps to allure—
But *there,* in memory's light, I see
All that was once most dear to me—
   My young heart's cynosure!

THURSTON, THE GREEN HILLS OF MY FATHERLAND

THE green hills of my father-land
   In dreams still greet my view;
I see once more the wave-girt strand—
   The ocean-depth of blue—
The sky—the glorious sky, outspread
   Above their calm repose—
The river, o'er its rocky bed
   Still singing as it flows—
The stillness of the Sabbath hours,
   When men go up to pray—
The sun light resting on the flowers—
The birds that sing among the bowers,
   Through all the summer-day.

Land of my birth!—mine early love!
   Once more thine airs I breathe!
I see thy proud hills tower above—

Thy green vales sleep beneath—
Thy groves, thy rocks, thy murmuring rills,
  All rise before mine eyes,
The dawn of morning on thy hills,
  Thy gorgeous sunset skies,—
Thy forests, from whose deep recess
  A thousand streams have birth,
Glad'ning the lonely wilderness,
And filling the green silentness
  With melody and mirth.

I wonder if my home would seem
  As lovely as of yore!
I wonder if the mountain stream
  Goes singing by the door!
And if the flowers still bloom as fair,
  And if the woodbines climb,
As when I used to train them there,
  In the dear olden time!
I wonder if the birds still sing
  Upon the garden tree,
As sweetly as in that sweet spring
Whose golden memories gently bring
  So many dreams to me!

I know that there hath been a change,
  A change o'er hall and hearth!
Faces and footsteps new and strange,
  About my place of birth!
The heavens above are still as bright
  As in the days gone by,
But vanished is the beacon light
  That cheered my morning sky!
And hill, and vale, and wooded glen,
  And rock, and murmuring stream,
That wore such glorious beauty then,
Would seem, should I return again,
  The record of a dream!

I mourn not for my childhood's hours,
  Since, in the far-off West,
'Neath sunnier skies, in greener bowers,
  My heart hath found its rest.
I mourn not for the hills and streams
  That chained my steps so long,
Yet still I see them in my dreams,
  And hail them in my song;
And often by the hearth-fire's blaze,
  When winter eves shall come,

We'll sit and talk of other days,
And sing the well-remembered lays
  Of my green mountain home.

JONES, TECUMSEH

WHERE rolls the dark and turbid Thames
  His consecrated wave along,
Sleeps one, than whose, few are the names
  More worthy of the lyre and song;
Yet o'er whose spot of lone repose
  No pilgrim eyes are seen to weep;
And no memorial marble throws
  Its shadow where his ashes sleep.

Stop, stranger! there Tecumseh lies;
  Behold the lowly resting place
Of all that of the hero dies;
  The Cæsar—Tully—of his race:
Whose arm of strength, and fiery tongue,
  Have won him an immortal name,
And from the mouths of millions wrung
  Reluctant tribute to his fame.

Stop—for 'tis glory claims thy tear!
  True worth belongs to all mankind:
And he whose ashes slumber here,
  Though man in form was god in mind.
What matter he was not like thee,
  In race and color—'tis the soul
That marks man's true divinity—
  Then let not shame thy tears control.

Art thou a patriot?—so was he!
  His breast was Freedom's holiest shrine;
And as thou bendest there thy knee,
  His spirit will unite with thine.
All that a man can give, he gave—
  His life—the country of his sires
From the oppressor's grasp to save:
  In vain—quench'd are his nation's fires.

Art thou a soldier? dost thou not
  O'er deeds chivalric love to muse?

Here stay thy steps—what better spot
　　Couldst thou for contemplation choose?
The earth beneath is holy ground;
　　It holds a thousand valiant braves;
Tread lightly o'er each little mound,
　　For they are no ignoble graves.

Thermopylæ and Marathon,
　　Though classic earth, can boast no more
Of deeds heroic than yon sun
　　Once saw upon this lonely shore,
When in a gallant nation's last
　　And deadliest struggle, for its own,
Tecumseh's fiery spirit pass'd
　　In blood, and sought its Father's throne.

Oh, softly fall the summer dew,
　　The tears of heaven, upon his sod,
For he in life and death was true,
　　Both to his country and his God;
For oh, if God to man has given,
　　From his bright home beyond the skies,
One feeling that's akin to heaven,
　　'Tis his who for his country dies.

Rest, warrior, rest!—Though not a dirge
　　Is thine, beside the wailing blast,
Time cannot in oblivion merge
　　The light thy star of glory cast;
While heave yon high hills to the sky,
　　While rolls yon dark and turbid river,
Thy name and fame can never die—
　　Whom Freedom loves will live forever.

THOMAS, EXTRACTS FROM THE EMIGRANT

THE PIONEER HUNTERS

HERE once Boone trod—the hardy Pioneer—
The only white man in the wilderness:
Oh! how he loved, alone, to hunt the deer,
Alone at eve, his simple meal to dress;
No mark upon the tree, nor print, nor track,

To lead him forward, or to guide him back:
He roved the forest, king by main and might,
And looked up to the sky and shaped his course aright.

That mountain, there, that lifts its bald, high head
Above the forest, was, perchance, his throne;
There has he stood and marked the woods outspread,
Like a great kingdom, that was all his own;
In hunting-shirt and moccasins arrayed,
With bear-skin cap, and pouch, and needful blade,
How carelessly he lean'd upon his gun!
That scepter of the wild, that had so often won.

Those western Pioneers an impulse felt,
Which their less hardy sons scarce comprehend;
Alone, in Nature's wildest scenes they dwelt;
Where crag, and precipice, and torrent blend,
And stretched around the wilderness, as rude
As the red rovers of its solitude,
Who watched their coming with a hate profound,
And fought with deadly strife for every inch of ground.

To shun a greater ill sought they the wild?
No, they left happiér lands behind them far,
And brought the nursing mother and her child
To share the dangers of the border war.
The log-built cabin from the Indian barred,
Their little boy, perchance, kept watch and ward,
While father plowed with rifle at his back,
Or sought the glutted foe through many a devious track.

How cautiously, yet fearlessly, that boy
Would search the forest for the wild beast's lair,
And lift his rifle with a hurried joy,
If chance he spied the Indian lurking there:
And should they bear him prisoner from the fight,
While they are sleeping, in the dead midnight,
He slips the thongs that bind him to the tree,
And leaving death with them, bounds home right happily.

Before the mother, bursting through the door,
The red man rushes where her infants rest;
O God! he hurls them on the cabin floor!
While she, down kneeling, clasps them to her breast.
How he exults and revels in her woe,
And lifts the weapon, yet delays the blow;
Ha! that report! behold! he reels! he dies!
And quickly to her arms the husband—father—flies.

In the long winter eve, their cabin fast,
The big logs blazing in the chimney wide—

They'd hear the Indian howling, or the blast,
And deem themselves in castellated pride:
Then would the fearless forester disclose
Most strange adventures with his sylvan foes,
Of how his arts did over theirs prevail,
And how he followed far upon their bloody trail.

And it was happiness, they said, to stand,
When summer smiled upon them in the wood,
And see their little clearing there expand,
And be the masters of the solitude.
Danger was but excitement; and when came
The tide of emigration, life grew tame;
Then would they seek some unknown wild anew,
And soon, above the trees, the smoke was curling blue.

THE RED MAN

How patient was that red man of the wood!
Not like the white man, garrulous of ill—
Starving! who heard his faintest wish for food?
Sleeping upon the snow-drift on the hill!
Who heard him chide the blast, or say 'twas cold?
His wounds are freezing! is the anguish told?
Tell him his child was murdered with its mother!
He seems like carved out stone that has no woe to smother.

With front erect, up-looking, dignified—
Behold high Hecla in eternal snows!
Yet while the raging tempest is defied,
Deep in its bosom how the pent flame glows!
And when it bursts forth in its fiery wrath!
How melts the ice-hill from its fearful path,
As on it rolls, unquench'd, and all untamed!—
Thus was it with that chief when his wild passions flamed.
Nature's own statesman—by experience taught,
He judged most wisely, and could act as well;
With quickest glance could read another's thought,
His own, the while, the keenest could not tell;
Warrior—with skill to lengthen, or combine,
Lead on or back, the desultory line;
Hunter—he passed the trackless forest through,
Now on the mountain trod, now launch'd the light canoe,

To the Great Spirit, would his spirit bow,
With hopes that Nature's impulses impart;
Unlike the Christian, who just says his vow
With heart enough to say it all by heart.
Did we his virtues from his faults discern,
'Twould teach a lesson that we well might learn:

An inculcation worthiest of our creed,
To tell the simple truth, and do the promised deed.

How deeply eloquent was the debate,
Beside the council-fire of those red men!
With language burning as his sense of hate;
With gesture just; as eye of keenest ken;
With illustration simple but profound,
Drawn from the sky above him, or the ground
Beneath his feet; and with unfalt'ring zeal,
He spoke from a warm heart and made e'en cold hearts feel.

And this is eloquence. 'Tis the intense,
Impassioned fervor of a mind deep fraught
With native energy, when soul and sense
Burst forth, embodied in the burning thought;
When look, emotion, tone, are all combined—
When the whole man is eloquent with mind—
A power that comes not to the call or quest,
But from the gifted soul, and the deep feeling breast.

Poor Logan had it, when he mourned that none
Were left to mourn for him;—'twas his who swayed
The Roman Senate by a look or tone;
'Twas the Athenian's, when his foes, dismayed,
Shrunk from the earthquake of his trumpet call;
'Twas Chatham's, strong as either, or as all;
'Twas Henry's holiest, when his spirit woke
Our patriot fathers' zeal to burst the British yoké.

LOVE

O, Love! what rhymer has not sung of thee?
And, who, with heart so young as his who sings,
Knows not thou art self-burdened as the bee,
Who, loving many flowers, must needs have wings?
Yes, thou art wing'd, O, Love! like passing thought,
That now is with us, and now seems as naught,
Until deep passion stamps thee in the brain,
Like bees in folded flowers that ne'er unfold again.

TO THE OHIO

Auspicious Time! unroll the scroll of years—
Behold our pious pilgrim fathers, when
They launch'd their little bark, and braved all fears,
Those peril-seeking, freedom-loving men!
Bless thee thou stream! abiding blessings bless
Thy farthest wave—Nile of the wilderness!
And be thy broad lands peopled, far and wide,
With hearts as free as his who now doth bless thy tide.

And may new States arise, and stretch afar,
In glory, to the great Pacific shore—
A galaxy, without a falling star—
Freedom's own Mecca, where the world adore.
There may Art build—to Knowledge there be given,
The book of Nature and the light of Heav'n;
There be the statesman's and the patriot's shrine,
And oh! be happy there, the hearts that woo the nine.

There is a welcome in this western land
Like the old welcomes, which were said to give
The friendly heart where'er they gave the hand;
Within this soil the social virtues live,
Like its own forest trees, unprun'd and free—
At least there is one welcome here for me:
A breast that pillowed all my sorrows past,
And waits my coming now, and lov'd me first and last.

$$\mathcal{Q} \quad 45 \quad \mathcal{Q}$$

JOSEPH HOLT INGRAHAM

(1809–1860)

In the 1840s, Joseph Holt Ingraham was the most prolific, most commercially successful novelist in the United States. The first edition of his first novel, *Laffite: The Pirate of the Gulf* (1836), sold its 2,500 copies almost immediately and earned him $1,350, the equivalent of more than $20,000 today. Over the next decade, Ingraham fine-tuned a formula that he would use to write and sell as many as twenty books in a year.

Ingraham was born on January 26, 1809, in Portland, Maine. He claimed to have attended Bowdoin, though his name does not appear in that college's records. Ingraham dedicated *Laffite* to Henry Wadsworth Longfellow—a Portland native who unquestionably *did* attend Bowdoin—though Longfellow apparently had not yet met him.

In 1830, Ingraham took a sea voyage to New Orleans, and he settled soon thereafter near Natchez, Mississippi, where he married Mary Brooks, the daughter of a local planter. He taught there at Washington College, thus earning the title "Professor Ingraham," which he sometimes attached to his novels.

The Ingraham assembly line peaked between 1842 and 1847, when he published eighty short paperback romances with such titles as *Frank Rivers, or, The Dangers of the Town: A Story of Temptation, Trial and Crime* (1843, 32 pages) and *Arnold, or, The British Spy: A Tale of Treason and Treachery* (1844, 39 pages). In all, Ingraham wrote more than 10 percent of all the American novels published in the 1840s. Longfellow noted in his journal on April 6, 1846, "[Ingraham] says he has written eighty novels, and of these twenty during the last year; till it has grown to be merely mechanical with him. These novels are published [first] in the newspapers. They pay him something more than three thousand dollars a year."

The floodgates closed in 1847 when Ingraham joined the Protestant Episcopal church and became headmaster of a school for girls in Tennessee. In 1851 he became a deacon, and in 1853 he joined the priesthood. But Ingraham could not stop writing, so he turned to novels based on religious subjects. Surprisingly, the first of these, *The Prince of the House of David* (1855), was the best-selling novel of his career. It sold several million copies and remained in print until 1975. Ingraham died on December 18, 1860, nine days after he shot himself when he accidentally dropped a loaded gun.

Written before he turned to fiction, *The South-West* (1835), published anonymously by "A Yankee," chronicles Ingraham's initial journey south. The book's epigraph comes from the opening lines of Samuel Rogers's *Italy* (1822–1828):

Day glimmer'd in the east, and the white Moon
Hung like a vapor in the cloudless sky,
Yet visible, when on my way I went,
Glad to be gone—a pilgrim from the north,
Now more and more attracted as I drew
Nearer and nearer.

In quoting Rogers, Ingraham deleted the phrase "Glad to be gone," an understandable decision if only because *The South-West* was to be published in New York. With his bushels of novels yet to be written, Ingraham was already mindful of his audience.

Text: *The South-West,* vol. 1 (New York, 1835): 117–127.

FROM *THE SOUTH-WEST* (1835)

XI. [NEW ORLEANS]

I HAVE endeavoured to give you, in my hastily written letters, some notion of this city—its streets, buildings, inhabitants and various novelties, as they first struck my eye; and I apprehend that I have expanded my descriptions, by minuteness of detail, to a greater length than was necessary or desirable. But the scenes, individuals, and circumstances I meet with in my erranting expeditions through the city, are such as would attract, from their novelty, the attention of a traveller from the North, and, consequently, a description of them is neither unworthy a place in his letters, nor too inconsiderable to detain the attention of an inquisitive northern reader, vegetating "at home."

On entering, from the dimly lighted lobby, the spacious and brilliant hall, illuminated with glittering chandeliers, where the beauty, and fashion, and gallantry of this merry city were assembled, I was struck with the spirit, life, and splendour of the scene. From alcoves on every side of the vast hall, raised a few steps from the floor, and separated from the area for dancing by an estrade of slender columns which formed a broad promenade quite around the room, bright eyes were glancing over the lively scene, rivalling in brilliancy the glittering gems that sparkled on brow and bosom.

There were at least five hundred persons in the hall, two-thirds of whom were spectators. On double rows of settees arranged around the room, and bordering the area, were about one hundred ladies, exclusive of half as many, seated in the alcoves. In addition to an almost impenetrable body of gentlemen standing in the vicinity of the grand entrance, the promenade above alluded to was filled with them, as they lounged along, gazing and remarking upon the beautiful faces of the dark-eyed Creoles,[1] as their expressive and lovely features were lighted up and instinct with the animation of the moment; while others, more enviable, were clustered around the alcoves—most of which were literally and truly "bowers of beauty,"—gayly conversing with their fair occupants, as they gracefully leaned over the balustrade. There were several cotillions upon the floor, and the dancers were young masters and misses—I beg their pardon—young gentlemen and ladies, from four years old and upward—who were bounding away to the lively music, as completely happy as innocence and enjoyment could make them. I never beheld a more pleasing sight. The carriage of the infantile gentlemen was graceful and easy: and they wound through the mazes of the dance with an air of manliness and elegance truly French. But the tiny demoiselles moved with the lightness and grace of fairies. Their diminutive feet, as they glided through the figure, scarcely touched the floor, and as they sprang flying away to the livelier measures of the band, they were scarcely visible, fluttering indistinctly like humming birds' wings. They were dressed with great taste in white frocks, but their hair was so arranged as completely to disfigure their heads. Some of them, not more than eight years of age, had it dressed in the extreme Parisian fashion; and the little martyrs' natural deficiency of long hair was amply remedied by that sovereign mender of the defects of nature, Monsieur le friseur. The young gentlemen were dressed also in the French mode; that is, in elaborately embroidered coatees, and richly wrought frills. Their hair, however, was suffered to grow long, and fall in graceful waves or ringlets (French children always have beautiful hair) upon their shoulders; very much as boys are represented in old fashioned prints. This is certainly more becoming than the uncouth round-head custom now prevalent in the United States, of clipping the hair short, as though boys, like sheep, needed a periodical sheering; and it cannot be denied that they both—sheep and boys—are *equally* improved in appearance by the operation.

Turning from the bright and happy faces of the children, we met on every side the delighted looks of their parents and guardians, or elder brothers and sisters, who formed a large portion of the spectators.

As I promenaded arm in arm with Monsieur D. through the room, I noticed that at one end of the hall many of the young misses (or their guardians) were so unpardonably unfashionable as to suffer their hair to float free in wild luxuriance over their necks, waving and undulating at every motion like clouds; and many of the cheerful

---

1. There is at the North a general misconception of the term "CREOLE." A friend of mine who had visited Louisiana for his health, after a residence of a few months gained the affections of a very lovely girl, and married her. He wrote to his uncle in Massachusetts, to whose large estate he was heir-expectant, communicating the event, saying that he "had just been united to an amiable *Creole*, whom he anticipated the pleasure of introducing to him in the Spring." The old gentleman, on receiving the letter, stamped, raved, and swore; and on the same evening replied to his nephew, saying, that as he had disgraced his family by marrying a *Mulatto*, he might remain where he was, as he wished to have nothing to do with him, or any of his woolly-headed, yellow skinned brats, that might be, henceforward." My friend, however, ventured home, and when the old gentleman beheld his lovely bride, he exclaimed, "The d—l, nephew, if you call this little angel a *Creole*, what likely chaps the real ebony Congos must be in that country." The old gentleman is not alone in his conception of a *Creole*. Where there is one individual in New England correctly informed, there are one hundred who, like him, know no distinction between the terms *Creole* and *Mulatto*. "Creole" is simply a synonym for "native." It has, however, only a local, whereas "native" has a general application. To say "He is a *Creole* of Louisiana," is to say "He is a *native* of Louisiana." Contrary to the general opinion at the North, it is seldom applied to coloured persons. *Creole* is sometimes, though not frequently, applied to Mississippians; but with the exception of the West-India Islands, it is usually confined to Louisiana.

joyous faces I gazed upon, forcibly reminded me of those which are to be met with, trudging to and from school, every day at home.

"These are the American children," observed my companion; "one half of the hall is appropriated to them, the other to the French." "What!" I exclaimed, "is there such a spirit of rivalry, jealousy, or prejudice, existing between the French and American residents here, that they cannot meet even in a ball-room without resorting to so singular a method of expressing their uncongeniality of feeling, as that of separating themselves from each other by a line of demarcation?"

"By no means," he replied; "far from it. There is, I believe, a universal unanimity of feeling among the parties. There is now no other distinction, whatever may have existed in former days, either known or admitted, than the irremediable one of language. This distinction necessarily exists, and I am of opinion ever will exist in this city in a greater or less degree. It is this which occasions the separation you behold; for, from their ignorance of each other's language,—an ignorance too prevalent here, and both inexcusable and remarkable, when we consider the advantages mutually enjoyed for their acquisition,—were they indiscriminately mingled, the result would be a confusion like that of Babel, or a constrained stiffness and reserve, the natural consequence of mutual inability to converse,—instead of that regularity and cheerful harmony which now reign throughout the crowded hall."

During our promenade through the room I had an opportunity of taking my first survey of the gay world of this city, and of viewing at my leisure the dark-eyed fascinating Creoles, whose peculiar cast of beauty and superb figures are everywhere celebrated. Of the large assembly of ladies present,—and there were nearly two hundred, "maid, wife, and widow,"—there were many very pretty, if coal-black hair, regular features, pale, clear complexions, intelligent faces, lighted up by

"Eyes that flash and burn
Beneath dark arched brows,"

and graceful figures, all of which are characteristic of the Creole, come under this definition. There were others who would be called "handsome" anywhere, except in the Green Mountains, where a pretty face and a red apple, a homely face and a lily, are pretty much synonymous terms. A few were eminently beautiful; but there was one figure, which, as my eye wandered over the brilliant assembly, fixed it in a moment. I soon learned that she was the most celebrated belle of New-Orleans.

I have certainly beheld far more beauty among the same number of ladies in a northern ball-room, than I discovered here. Almost every young lady in New-England appears pretty, with her rosy cheeks, intelligent face, and social manners. The style of beauty at the south is of a more passive kind, and excitement is requisite to make it speak to the eye; but when the possessor is animated, then the whole face, which but a few moments before was passionless and quiet, becomes radiant and illuminated with fire and intelligence; and the indolent repose of the features becomes broken by fascinating smiles, and brilliant flashes from fine dark eyes. Till this change is produced, the face of the southern lady appears plain and unattractive; and the promenader through a New-Orleans assembly-room, where there was no excitement, if such could be the case, would pronounce the majority of the ladies decidedly wanting in beauty; but let him approach and enter into conversation with one of them, and he would be delighted and surprised at the magical transformation,

"From grave to gay, from apathy to fire."

It is certain, that beauty of features and form is more general in New-England; though in grace and expression, the south has the superiority.

The difference is usually attributed to climate; but this never has been demonstrated, and the cause is still inexplicable. You are probably aware that the human form, more particularly the female, is here matured three or four years sooner than at the north. At the age of thirteen or fourteen, before their minds are properly developed, their habits formed, or their passions modified, the features of young girls become regular, their complexions delicate, and their figures attain that *tournure* and womanly grace, though "beautifully less" in their persons, found only in northern ladies, at the age of seventeen or eighteen. The beauty of the latter, though longer in coming to maturity, and less perfect, is more permanent and interesting than the infantile and bewitching loveliness of the former. In consequence of this early approach to womanhood, the duration of their personal loveliness is of proportional limitation. Being young ladies at an age that would entitle them to the appellation of children in colder climates, they must naturally retire much sooner than these from the ranks of beauty. So when northern ladies are reigning in the full pride and loveliness of their sex— every feature expanding into grace and expression—southern ladies, of equal age, are changing their premature beauty for the faded hues of premature old age.

The joyous troops of youthful dancers, before ten o'clock arrived, surrendered the floor to the gentlemen and ladies, who, till now, had been merely spectators of the scene, and being resigned into the hands of their nurses and servants in waiting, were carried home, while the assembly-room, now converted into a regular ball-room, rang till long past the "noon of night" with the enlivening music, confusion, and revelry of a complete and crowded rout. Introductions for a partner in the dance were not the "order of the day," or rather of the night. A gentleman had only to single out some lady among the brilliant assemblage, and though a total stranger, solicit the honour of dancing with her. Such self-introductions are of course merely *pro tem.*, and, like fashionable intimacies formed at Saratoga, never after recognised. Still, to a stranger, such absence of all formality is peculiarly pleasant, and, though every face may be new to him, he has the grateful satisfaction of knowing that he can make himself perfectly at home, and form innumerable delightful acquaintances for the evening, provided he chooses to be sociable, and make the most of the enjoyments around him. We left the hall at an early hour on our return to the hotel.

Crowds of mulatto, French and English hackdrivers were besieging the door, shouting in bad French, worse Spanish, and broken English—

"Coachee, massas! jontilhomme ridee!" "Caballeros, voulez vous tomer mé carriage?" "Wooly woo querie to ride sir?" "Fiacre Messieurs!" "By St. Patrick jintilmen—honie, mounseers, woulee voo my asy riding coach?"—et cetera, mingled with execrations, heavy blows, exchanged in the way of friendship, laughter, yells and Indian whoops, composing a "concord of sweet sounds" to be fully appreciated only by those who have heard similar concerts. We, however, effected our escape from these pupils of Jehu, who, ignorant of our country, in a city where all the nations of the earth are represented, wisely addressed us in a Babelic medley of languages, till we were out of hearing.

Returning, as we came through Rues Royale and St. Pierre, past the quarter of the "gens d'armes," we entered Chartres-street, which was now nearly deserted. Proceeding through this dark, narrow street on our way home, meeting now and then an individual pursuing his hasty and solitary way along the echoing pavé, we arrived at the new Exchange alluded to in my first letter, which served the double purpose of gentlemen's public assembly-room and *café*. As we entered from the dimly lighted street, attracted by the lively crowd dispersed throughout the spacious room, our eyes were dazzled by the noon-day brightness shed from innumerable chandeliers. Having lounged through the room, filled with smokers, newspaper-readers, promenaders, drinkers, &c. &c., till we were stunned by the noise of the multitude, who were talking in an endless variety of languages, clattering upon the ear at once, and making "confusion worse confounded," my polite friend suggested that we should ascend to "the rooms," as they are termed. As I wished to see every thing in New-Orleans interesting or novel to a northerner, I readily embraced the opportunity of an introduction into the penetralium of one of the far-famed temples which the goddess of fortune has erected in this, her favourite city. We ascended a broad flight of steps, one side of which exhibited many lofty double doors, thrown wide open, discovering to our view an extensive hall, in which stood several billiard tables, surrounded by their "mace and cue" devotees.

But as my letter is now of rather an uncharitable length, I will defer till my next, farther description of the deeds and mysteries and unhallowed sacrifices connected with these altars of dissipation.

46

ABRAHAM LINCOLN

(1809–1865)

Undoubtedly the best-known denizen of the first west was Abraham Lincoln. Lincoln was born in Kentucky in 1809 to an impoverished family from Virginia that soon moved to Indiana and then to central Illinois. Like most white immigrants to Illinois, Lincoln's family represented the non-Yankee yeoman class, many of whom were from the South. Excluded from the academies and other social institutions Yankee settlers established for their own children, Lincoln came to view the professional gentility on the frontier as an outsider. As a young Whig politician, Lincoln was consistently among the minority in the Illinois legislature.

As such, much of his professional career was as a lawyer riding circuit, and not as a politician. The first writing reproduced here is a private letter to a friend in Louisville, Joshua Speed. While written for private consumption, it demonstrates Lincoln's mastery of the syles of frontier humor more usually visible in his expository and improvised speeches in the courtroom, on the legislative floor, or on the stump. The letter's literary qualities in particular demonstrate his familiarity with the southern writers of the west. The second document reproduced here is the draft of a campaign speech Lincoln gave in various forms in support of the Republican nominee for president in 1856, John C. Fremont. Here, Lincoln very carefully distinguishes sectionalism from nationalism. Like Daniel Drake, Lincoln was a nationalist but was cognizant of the need for local self-determination. However, localism must still correspond to constitutional order, and Lincoln rejects sectionalism, particularly Southern sectionalism, for refusing to do so.

When he became president in 1860, Lincoln's Republican administration included many westerners, such as William D. Gallagher, Salmon P. Chase, and William T. Coggeshall, all participants in the Cincinnati literary scene of the 1830s and 1840s. As the first president born and raised in the west (Andrew Jackson, Zachary Taylor, and William Henry Harrison were all eastern by birth), Lincoln stands as the greatest achievement of the culture of the west.

Text: *Speeches and Writings, 1832–1858* (New York: Library of America, 1989): 69–73, 370–374.

TO JOSHUA F. SPEED (1841)

DEAR SPEED:

We have had the highest state of excitement here for a week past that our community has ever witnessed; and, although the public feeling is now somewhat allayed, the curious affair which aroused it, is verry far from being, even yet, cleared of mystery. It would take a quire of paper to give you any thing like a full account of it; and I therefore only propose a brief outline. The chief personages in the drama, are Archibald Fisher, supposed to be murdered; and Archibald Trailor, Henry Trailor, and William Trailor, supposed to have murdered him. The three Trailors are brothers; the first, Arch: as you know, lives in town; the second, Henry, in Clary's Grove, and the third, Wm., in Warren county; and Fisher, the supposed *murderee,* being without a family, had made his home with William. On saturday evening, being the 29th. of May, Fisher and William came to Henry's in a one horse dearborn, and there staid over sunday; and on monday all three came to Springfield, Henry on horseback, and joined Archibald at Myers' the dutch carpenter. That evening at supper Fisher was missing, and so next morning. Some ineffectual search was made for him; and on tuesday at 1 o'clock PM. Wm. & Henry started home without him. In a day or so Henry and one or two of his Clary Grove neighbours came back and searched for him again, and advertised his disappearance in the paper. The knowledge of the matter thus far, had not been general; and here it dropped entirely till about the 10th. Inst. when Keys received a letter from the Post Master in Warren stating that Wm. had arrived at home, and was telling a verry mysterious and improbable story about the disappearance of Fisher, which induced the community there to suppose that he had been disposed of unfairly. Key's made this letter public, which immediately set the whole town and adjoining country agog; and so it has continued until yesterday. The mass of the People commenced a systematic search for the dead body, while Wickersham was dispatched to arrest Henry Trailor at the Grove; and Jim Maxey, to Warren to arrest William. On monday last Henry was brought in, and showed an evident inclination to insinuate that he knew Fisher to be dead, and that Arch: & Wm. had killed him. He said he guessed the body could be found in Spring Creek between the Beardstown road bridge and Hickoxes mill. Away the People swept like a herd of buffaloes, and cut down Hickoxes mill dam *nolens volens,* to draw the water out of the pond; and then went up and down, and down and up the creek, fishing and raking, and ducking and diving for two days, and after all, no dead body found. In the mean time a sort of scuffling ground had been found in the brush in the angle or point where the road leading into the woods past the brewery, and the one leading in past the brick-yard join. From this scuffle ground, was the sign of something about the size of a man having been dragged to the edge of the thicket, where it joined the track of some small wheeled carriage which was drawn by one horse, as shown by the horse tracks. The carriage track led off towards Spring Creek. Near this drag trail, Dr. Merryman found *two hairs,* which after a long scientific examination, he pronounced to be triangular human hairs, which term, he says includes within it, the whiskers, the hairs growing under the arms and on other parts of the body; and he judged that these two were of the

whiskers, because the ends were cut, showing that they had flourished in the neighbourhood of the razor's operations. On thursday last, Jim: Maxey brought in William
Trailor from Warren. On the same day Arch: was arrested and put in jail. Yesterday (friday) William was put upon his examining trial before May and Lavely. Archibald and
Henry were both present. Lamborn prossecuted, and Logan, Baker, and your humble
servant, defended. A great many witnesses were introduced and examined; but I shall
only mention those whose testimony seemed to be the most important. The first of
these was Capt. Ransdell. He swore, that when William and Henry left Springfield for
home on the tuesday before mentioned, they did not take the direct route, which, you
know, leads by the butcher shop, but that they followed the street North until they
got opposite, or nearly opposite May's new house, after which he could not see them
from where he stood; and it was afterwards proven that in about an hour after they
started, they came into the street by the butcher's shop from towards the brick yard.
Dr. Merryman & others swore to what is before stated about the scuffle-ground, drag-
trail, whiskers, and carriage tracks. Henry was then introduced by the prossecution.
He swore, that when they started for home, they went out North as Ransdell stated,
and turned down West by the brick yard into the woods, and there met Archibald;
that they proceeded a small distance further, where he was placed as a sentinel to
watch for, and announce the approach of any one that might happen that way; that
William and Arch: took the dearborn out of the road a small distance to the edge of
the thicket, where they stopped, and he saw them lift the body of a man into it; that
they then moved off with the carriage in the direction of Hickoxes mill, and he loitered about for something like an hour, when William returned with the carriage, but
without Arch: and said that they had put *him* in a safe place; that they then went some
how, he did not know exactly how, into the road close to the brewery, and proceeded
on to Clary's Grove. He also stated that sometime during the day, William told him,
that he and Arch: had killed Fisher the evening before; that the way they did it was by
him (William) knocking him down with a club, and Arch: then choking him to death.
An old man from Warren, called Dr. Gilmore, was then introduced on the part of the
defence. He swore that he had known Fisher for several years; that Fisher had resided
at his house a long time at each of two different spells; once while he built a barn for
him, and once while he was doctored for some chronic disease; that two or three years
ago, Fisher had a serious hurt in his head by the bursting of a gun, since which he has
been subject to continual bad health, and occasional abberations of mind. He also
stated that on last tuesday, being the same day that Maxey arrested William Trailor, he
(the Dr) was from home in the early part of the day, and on his return about 11 o'-
clock, found Fisher at his house in bed, and apparantly verry unwell; that he asked
how he had come from Springfield; that Fisher said he had come by Peoria, and also
told several other places he had been at not in the direction of Peoria, which showed
that he, at the time of speaking, did not know where he had been, or that he had been
wandering about in a state of derangement. He further stated that in about two hours
he received a note from one of William Trailor's friends, advising him of his arrest,
and requesting him to go on to Springfield as a witness, to testify to the state of
Fisher's health in former times; that he immediately set off, catching up two of his
neighbours, as company, and riding all evening and all night, overtook Maxey &
William at Lewiston in Fulton county; that Maxey refusing to discharge Trailor upon
his statement, his two neighbors returned, and he came on to Springfield. Some question being made whether the doctor's story was not a fabrication, several acquaintances of his, among whom was the same Post Master who wrote to Key's as before

mentioned, were introduced as sort of compurgators, who all swore, that they knew the doctor be of good character for truth and veracity, and generally of good character in every way. Here the testimony ended, and the Trailors were discharged, Arch: and William expressing, both in word and manner their entire confidence that Fisher would be found alive at the doctor's by Galaway, Mallory, and Myers, who a day before had been dispatched for that purpose; while Henry still protested that no power on earth could ever show Fisher alive. Thus stands this curious affair now. When the doctor's story was first made public, it was amusing to scan and contemplate the countenances, and hear the remarks of those who had been actively engaged in the search for the dead body. Some looked quizical, some melancholly, and some furiously angry. Porter, who had been very active, swore he always knew the man was not dead, and that *he* had not stirred an inch to hunt for him; Langford, who had taken the lead in cutting down Hickoxes mill dam, and wanted to hang Hickox for objecting, looked most awfully wo-begone; he seemed the *"wictim of hunrequited haffection"* as represented in the comic almanic we used to laugh over; and Hart, the little drayman that hauled Molly home once, said it was too *damned* bad, to have so much trouble, and no hanging after all.

I commenced this letter on yesterday, since which I received yours of the 13th. I stick to my promise to come to Louisville. Nothing new here except what I have written. I have not seen Sarah since my long trip, and I am going out there as soon as I mail this letter. Yours forever

ON SECTIONALISM (1856)

It is constantly objected to Fremont & Dayton, that they are supported by a *sectional* party, who, by their *sectionalism,* endanger the National Union. This objection, more than all others, causes men, really opposed to slavery extension, to hesitate. Practically, it is the most difficult objection we have to meet.

For this reason, I now propose to examine it, a little more carefully than I have heretofore done, or seen it done by others.

First, then, what is the question between the parties, respectively represented by Buchanan and Fremont?

Simply this: *"Shall slavery be allowed to extend into U.S. teritories, now legally free?"* Buchanan says it *shall;* and Fremont says it shall *not.*

That is the *naked* issue, and the *whole* of it. Lay the respective platforms side by side; and the difference between them, will be found to amount to precisely that.

True, each party charges upon the other, *designs* much beyond what is involved in the issue, as stated; but as these charges can not be fully proved either way, it is probably better to reject them on both sides, and stick to the naked issue, as it is clearly made up on the record.

And now, to restate the question *"Shall slavery be allowed to extend into U.S. teritories, now legally free?"* I beg to know *how one* side of that question is more sectional than the other? Of course I expect to effect nothing with the man who makes this charge of sectionalism, without caring whether it is just or not. But of the *candid, fair,* man who has been puzzled with this charge, I do ask how is *one* side of this question, more *sectional,* than the other? I beg of him to consider well, and answer calmly.

If one side be as sectional as the other, nothing is gained, as to sectionalism, by changing sides; so that each must choose sides of the question on some other ground—as I should think, according, as the one side or the other, shall appear nearest right.

If he shall really think slavery *ought* to be extended, let him go to Buchanan; if he think it ought *not* let him go to Fremont.

But, Fremont and Dayton, are both residents of the free-states; and this fact has been vaunted, in high places, as excessive *sectionalism.*

While interested individuals become *indignant* and *excited,* against this manifestation of *sectionalism,* I am very happy to know, that the Constitution remains calm—keeps cool—upon the subject. It does say that President and Vice President shall be resident of different states; but it does not say one must live in a *slave,* and the other in a *free* state.

It has been a *custom* to take one from a slave, and the other from a free state; but the custom has not, at all been uniform. In 1828 Gen. Jackson and Mr. Calhoun, both from slave-states, were placed on the same ticket; and Mr. Adams and Dr. Rush both from the free-states, were pitted against them. Gen: Jackson and Mr. Calhoun were elected; and qualified and served under the election; yet the whole thing never suggested the idea of sectionalism.

In 1841, the president, Gen. Harrison, died, by which Mr. Tyler, the Vice-President & a slave state man, became president. Mr. Mangum, another slave-state man, was placed in the Vice Presidential chair, served out the term, and no fuss about it—no sectionalism thought of.

In 1853 the present president came into office. He is a freestate man. Mr. King, the new Vice President elect, was a slave state man; but he died without entering on the duties of his office. At first, his vacancy was filled by Atchison, another slave-state man; but he soon resigned, and the place was supplied by Bright, a free-state man. So that right now, and for the year and a half last past, our president and vice-president are both actually free-state men.

But, it is said, the friends of Fremont, avow the purpose of electing him exclusively by free-state votes, and that this is unendurable *sectionalism.*

This statement of fact, is not exactly true. With the friends of Fremont, it is an *expected necessity,* but it is not an "*avowed purpose,*" to elect him, if at all, principally, by free state votes; but it is, with equal intensity, true that Buchanan's friends expect to elect him, if at all, chiefly by slave-state votes.

Here, again, the sectionalism, is just as much on one side as the other.

The thing which gives most color to the charge of Sectionalism, made against those who oppose the spread of slavery into free teritory, is the fact that *they* can get no votes in the slave-states, while their opponents get all, or nearly so, in the slave-states, and also, a large number in the free States. To state it in another way, the Extensionists, can get votes all over the Nation, while the Restrictionists can get them only in the free states.

This being the fact, *why* is it so? It is not because one *side* of the question dividing them, is more sectional than the *other;* nor because of any difference in the mental or moral structure of the people North and South. It is because, in that question, the people of the South have an immediate palpable and immensely great pecuniary interest; while, with the people of the North, it is merely an abstract question of moral right, with only *slight,* and *remote* pecuniary interest added.

The slaves of the South, at a moderate estimate, are worth a thousand millions of dollars. Let it be permanently settled that this property may extend to new teritory, without restraint, and it greatly *enhances,* perhaps quite *doubles,* its value at once. This immense, palpable pecuniary interest, on the question of extending slavery, unites the Southern people, as one man. But it can not be demonstrated that the *North* will gain a dollar by restricting it.

Moral principle is all, or nearly all, that unites us of the North. Pity 'tis, it is so, but this is a looser bond, than pecuniary interest. Right here is the plain cause of *their perfect* union and *our want* of it. And see how it works. If a Southern man aspires to be president, they choke him down instantly, in order that the glittering prize of the presidency, may be held up, on Southern terms, to the greedy eyes of Northern ambition. With this they tempt us, and break in upon us.

The democratic party, in 1844, elected a Southern president. Since then, they have neither had a Southern candidate for *election,* or *nomination.* Their Conventions of 1848–1852 and 1856, have been struggles exclusively among *Northern* men, each vieing to out-bid the other for the Southern vote—the South standing calmly by to finally cry going, going, gone, to the highest bidder; and, at the same time, to make its power more distinctly seen, and thereby to secure a still higher bid at the next succeeding struggle.

"Actions speak louder than words" is the maxim; and, if true, the South now distinctly says to the North "Give us the *measures,* and you take the *men.*"

The total withdrawal of Southern aspirants, for the presidency, multiplies the number of Northern ones. These last, in competing with each other, commit themselves to the utmost verge that, through their own greediness, they have the least hope their Northern supporters will bear. Having got committed, in a race of competetion, necessity drives them into union to sustain themselves. Each, at first secures all he can, on personal attachments to him, and through *hopes* resting on him personally. Next, they unite with one another, and with the perfectly banded South, to make the offensive position they have got into, "a party measure." This done, large additional numbers are secured.

When the repeal of the Missouri compromise was first proposed, at the North there was litterally "*nobody*" in favor of it. In February 1854 our Legislature met in call, or extra, session. From them Douglas sought an indorsement of his then pending measure of Repeal. In our Legislature were about 70 democrats to 30 whigs. The former held a caucus, in which it was resolved to give Douglas the desired indorsement. Some of the members of that caucus bolted—would not stand it—and they now divulge the secrets. They say that the caucus fairly confessed that the Repeal was wrong; and they placed their determination to indorse it, solely on the ground that it was *necessary* to sustain Douglas. Here we have the direct evidence of how the Nebraska-bill obtained it's strength in Illinois. It was given, not in a sense of right, but in the teeth of a sense of wrong, to *sustain Douglas.* So Illinois was divided. So New England, for Pierce; Michigan for Cass, Pensylvania for Buchanan, and all for the Democratic party.

And when, by such means, they have got a large portion of the Northern people into a position contrary to their own honest impulses, and sense of right; they have the impudence to turn upon those who do stand firm, and call them *sectional.*

Were it not too serious a matter, this cool impudence would be laughable, to say the least.

Recurring to the question *"Shall slavery be allowed to extend into U.S. teritory now legally free?"*

This *is* a sectional question—that is to say, it is a question, in its nature calculated to divide the American people geographically. Who is to *blame* for that? *who* can help it? Either side *can* help it; but how? Simply by *yielding* to the other side. There is no other way. In the whole range of *possibility,* there is no other way. Then, which side shall yield? To this again, there can be but one answer—the side which is in the *wrong.* True, we differ, as to which side *is* wrong; and we boldly say, let all who really think slavery ought to spread into free teritory, openly go over against us. There is where they rightfully belong.

But why should any go, who really think slavery ought not to spread? Do they really think the *right* ought to yield to the *wrong?* Are they afraid to stand by the *right?* Do they fear that the constitution is too weak to sustain them in the right? Do they really think that by right surrendering to wrong, the hopes of our constitution, our Union, and our liberties, can possibly be bettered?

47

MARGARET FULLER

(1810–1850)

After publishing her most famous pamphlet, "The Great Lawsuit," in the spring of 1843, Margaret Fuller toured the west, traveling in Illinois, Wisconsin, and Michigan. She traveled mostly with friends and was generally more interested in traveling to the small towns and native settlements than in staying in the polite circles of western cities favored by her friends. She managed to find her way to quite a few western places usually overlooked by polite eastern travelers and she observed western lifeways with a keen eye. Along the way as well, Fuller read what had been written about the west and its peoples and generally found them wanting. In the section reproduced below, she criticizes, among others, Washington Irving and Henry Rowe Schoolcraft for their small-mindedness when describing the west.

As is true in virtually all of Fuller's work, in *A Summer on the Lakes* she aspires to test and challenge the ways in which things have always been done. The book itself is mostly autobiographical, but often is digressive, exploring other subjects and relating the anecdotes she hears from fellow travelers. In the second chapter, reprinted here, Fuller describes traveling from Buffalo to Chicago. This early in the book she has not yet fully encountered the space between the actual west and its accepted description. However, late in this sequence, while in Chicago, she becomes increasingly aware of the need to create a text that represents the west more accurately.

She finds that the image of the west as land of opportunity, the transplanted east promoted by so many eastern writers, has lured settlers west on false pretenses and, as a result, the west is in danger of becoming a tragically lost opportunity to build a better American community than the one she has left in New England. For example, she encourages the smudging of gender roles on the frontier, an aspect of the famous feminism Fuller endorsed that might be easily contrasted with Caroline Kirkland's efforts at domestication. Soon after publishing *A Summer on the Lakes* in 1844, Fuller moved from New England to New York and published her masterwork, *Women in the Nineteenth Century.* While it is difficult to tell if her time in the west influenced her feminism, it is not difficult to see how the same iconoclastic perspective allowed her to critique how Americans thought about both women and the west.

Text: *A Summer on the Lakes* (Boston, 1844; rpt. *The Portable Margaret Fuller,* ed. Mary Kelley, New York, 1994,): 77–94.

CHAPTER II

The Lakes

Scene, Steamboat

About to leave Buffalo—Baggage coming on board—Passengers bustling for their berths—Little boys persecuting everybody with their newspapers and pamphlets—J., S. and M. huddled up in a forlorn corner, behind a large trunk—A heavy rain falling.

M.: Water, water everywhere. After Niagara one would like a dry strip of existence. And at any rate it is quite enough for me to have it under foot without having it over head in this way.

J.: Ah, do not abuse the gentle element. It is hardly possible to have too much of it, and indeed, if I were obliged to choose amid the four, it would be the one in which I could bear confinement best.

S.: You would make a pretty Undine, to be sure!

J.: Nay, I only offered myself as a Triton, a boisterous Triton of the sounding shell. You, M. I suppose, would be a salamander, rather.

M.: No! that is too equivocal a position, whether in modern mythology, or Hoffman's tales. I should choose to be a gnome.

J.: That choice savors of the pride that apes humility.

M.: By no means; the gnomes are the most important of all the elemental tribes. Is it not they who make the money?

J.: And are accordingly a dark, mean, scoffing,—

M.: You talk as if you had always lived in that wild unprofitable element you are so fond of, where all things glitter, and nothing is gold; all show and no substance. My people work in the secret, and their works praise them in the open light; they remain in the dark because only there such marvels could be bred. You call them mean. They do not spend their energies on their own growth, or their own play, but to feed the veins of mother earth with permanent splendors, very different from what she shows on the surface.

Think of passing a life, not merely in heaping together, but making gold. Of all dreams, that of the alchymist is the most poetical, for he looked at the finest symbol. Gold, says one of our friends, is the hidden light of the earth, it crowns the mineral, as wine the vegetable order, being the last expression of vital energy.

J.: Have you paid for your passage?

M.: Yes! and in gold, not in shells or pebbles.

J.: No really wise gnome would scoff at the water, the beautiful water. "The spirit of man is like the water."

S.: Yes, and like the air and fire, no less.

J.: Yes, but not like the earth, this low-minded creature's chosen dwelling.

M.: The earth is spirit made fruitful,—life. And its heart-beats are told in gold and wine.

J.: Oh! it is shocking to hear such sentiments in these times. I thought that Bacchic energy of yours was long since repressed.

M.: No! I have only learned to mix water with my wine, and stamp upon my gold the heads of kings, or the hieroglyphics of worship. But since I have learnt to mix with water, let's hear what you have to say in praise of your favorite.

J.: From water Venus was born, what more would you have? It is the mother of Beauty, the girdle of earth, and the marriage of nations.

S.: Without any of that high-flown poetry, it is enough, I think, that it is the great artist, turning all objects that approach it to picture.

J.: True, no object that touches it, whether it be the cart that ploughs the wave for sea-weed, or the boat or plank that rides upon it, but is brought at once from the demesne of coarse utilities into that of picture. All trades, all callings, become picturesque by the water's side, or on the water. The soil, the slovenliness is washed out of every calling by its touch. All river-crafts, sea-crafts, are picturesque, are poetical. Their very slang is poetry.

M.: The reasons for that are complex.

J.: The reason is, that there can be no plodding, groping words and motions, on my water as there are on your earth. There is no time, no chance for them where all moves so rapidly, though so smoothly, everything connected with water must be like itself, forcible, but clear. That is why sea-slang is so poetical; there is a word for everything and every act, and a thing and an act for every word. Seamen must speak quick and bold, but also with utmost precision. They cannot reef and brace other than in a Homeric dialect—therefore,—(Steamboat bell rings.) But I must say a quick good-by.

M.: What, going, going back to earth after all this talk upon the other side. Well, that is nowise Homeric, but truly modern.

J.: is borne off without time for any reply, but a laugh—at himself, of course.

S. and M. retire to their state-rooms to forget the wet, the chill and steamboat smell in their just-bought new world of novels.

Next day, when we stopped at Cleveland, the storm was just clearing up; ascending the bluff, we had one of the finest views of the lake that could have been wished. The varying depths of these lakes give to their surface a great variety of coloring, and beneath this wild sky and changeful lights, the waters presented kaleidoscopic varieties of hues, rich, but mournful. I admire these bluffs of red, crumbling earth. Here land and water meet under very different auspices from those of the rock-bound coast to which I have been accustomed. There they meet tenderly to challenge, and proudly to refuse, though not in fact repel. But here they meet to mingle, are always rushing together, and changing places; a new creation takes place beneath the eye.

The weather grew gradually clearer, but not bright; yet we could see the shore and appreciate the extent of these noble waters.

Coming up the river St. Clair, we saw Indians for the first time. They were camped out on the bank. It was twilight, and their blanketed forms, in listless groups or stealing along the bank, with a lounge and a stride so different in its wildness from the rudeness of the white settler, gave me the first feeling that I really approached the West.

The people on the boat were almost all New Englanders, seeking their fortunes. They had brought with them their habits of calculation, their cautious manners, their love of polemics. It grieved me to hear these immigrants who were to be the fathers of a new race, all, from the old man down to the little girl, talking not of what they should do, but of what they should get in the new scene. It was to them a prospect, not of the unfolding nobler energies, but of more ease, and larger accumulation. It wearied me, too, to hear Trinity and Unity discussed in the poor, narrow doctrinal way on these free waters; but that will soon cease, there is not time for this clash of opinions in the West, where the clash of material interests is so noisy. They will need the spirit of religion more than ever to guide them, but will find less time than before for its doctrine. This change was to me, who am tired of the war of words on these subjects, and believe it only sows the wind to reap the whirlwind, refreshing, but I argue nothing from it; there is nothing real in the freedom of thought at the West, it is from the position of men's lives, not the state of their minds. So soon as they have time, unless they grow better meanwhile, they will cavil and criticise, and judge other men by their own standard, and outrage the law of love every way, just as they do with us.

We reached Mackinaw the evening of the third day, but, to my great disappointment, it was too late and too rainy to go ashore. The beauty of the island, though seen under the most unfavorable circumstances, did not disappoint my expectations. But I shall see it to more purpose on my return.

As the day has passed dully, a cold rain preventing us from keeping out in the air, my thoughts have been dwelling on a story told when we were off Detroit, this morning, by a fellow passenger, and whose moral beauty touched me profoundly.

Some years ago, said Mrs. L., my father and mother stopped to dine at Detroit. A short time before dinner my father met in the hall Captain P., a friend of his youthful days. He had loved P. extremely, as did many who knew him, and had not been surprised to hear of the distinction and popular esteem which his wide knowledge, talents, and noble temper commanded, as he went onward in the world. P. was every way fitted to succeed; his aims were high, but not too high for his powers, suggested by an instinct of his own capacities, not by an ideal standard drawn from culture. Though steadfast in his course, it was not to overrun others, his wise self-possession was no less for them than himself. He was thoroughly the gentleman, gentle because manly, and was a striking instance that where there is strength for sincere courtesy, there is no need of other adaptation to the character of others, to make one's way freely and gracefully through the crowd.

My father was delighted to see him, and after a short parley in the hall—"We will dine together," he cried, "then we shall have time to tell all our stories."

P. hesitated a moment, then said, "My wife is with me."

"And mine with me," said my father, "that's well; they, too, will have an opportunity of getting acquainted and can entertain one another, if they get tired of our college stories."

P. acquiesced, with a grave bow, and shortly after they all met in the dining-room. My father was much surprised at the appearance of Mrs. P. He had heard that his friend married abroad, but nothing further, and he was not prepared to see the calm, dignified P. with a woman on his arm, still handsome, indeed, but whose coarse and imperious expression showed as low habits of mind as her exaggerated dress and gesture did of education. Nor could there be a greater contrast to my mother, who, though understanding her claims and place with the certainty of a lady, was soft and retiring in an uncommon degree.

However, there was no time to wonder or fancy; they sat down, and P. engaged in conversation, without much vivacity, but with his usual ease. The first quarter of an hour passed well enough. But soon it was observable that Mrs. P. was drinking glass after glass of wine, to an extent few gentlemen did, even then, and soon that she was actually excited by it. Before this, her manner had been brusque, if not contemptuous towards her new acquaintance; now it became, towards my mother especially, quite rude. Presently she took up some slight remark made by my mother, which, though it did not naturally mean anything of the sort, could be twisted into some reflection upon England, and made it a handle, first of vulgar sarcasm, and then, upon my mother's defending herself with some surprise and gentle dignity, hurled upon her a volley of abuse, beyond Billingsgate.

My mother, confounded, feeling scenes and ideas presented to her mind equally new and painful, sat trembling; she knew not what to do, tears rushed into her eyes. My father, no less distressed, yet unwilling to outrage the feelings of his friend by doing or saying what his indignation prompted, turned an appealing look on P.

Never, as he often said, was the painful expression of that sight effaced from his mind. It haunted his dreams and disturbed his waking thoughts. P. sat with his head bent forward, and his eyes cast down, pale, but calm, with a fixed expression, not merely of patient wo, but of patient shame, which it would not have been thought possible for that noble countenance to wear, "yet," said my father, "it became him. At other times he was handsome, but then beautiful, though of a beauty saddened and abashed. For a spiritual light borrowed from the worldly perfection of his mien that illustration by contrast, which the penitence of the Magdalen does from the glowing earthliness of her charms."

Seeing that he preserved silence, while Mrs. P. grew still more exasperated, my father rose and led his wife to her own room. Half an hour had passed, in painful and wondering surmises, when a gentle knock was heard at the door, and P. entered equipped for a journey. "We are just going," he said, and holding out his hand, but without looking at them, "Forgive."

They each took his hand, and silently pressed it, then he went without a word more.

Some time passed and they heard now and then of P., as he passed from one army station to another, with his uncongenial companion, who became, it was said, constantly more degraded. Whoever mentioned having seen them, wondered at the chance which had yoked him to such a woman, but yet more at the silent fortitude with which he bore it. Many blamed him for enduring it, apparently without efforts to check her; others answered that he had probably made such at an earlier period, and finding them unavailing, had resigned himself to despair, and was too delicate to meet the scandal that, with such a resistance as such a woman could offer, must attend a formal separation.

But my father, who was not in such haste to come to conclusions, and substitute some plausible explanation for the truth, found something in the look of P. at that trying moment to which none of these explanations offered a key. There was in it, he felt, a fortitude, but not the fortitude of the hero, a religious submission, above the penitent, if not enkindled with the enthusiasm of the martyr.

I have said that my father was not one of those who are ready to substitute specious explanations for truth, and those who are thus abstinent rarely lay their hand on a thread without making it a clue. Such an one, like the dexterous weaver, lets not one color go, till he finds that which matches it in the pattern; he keeps on weaving, but chooses his shades, and my father found at last what he wanted to make out the pattern for himself. He met a lady who had been intimate with both himself and P. in early days, and finding she had seen the latter abroad, asked if she knew the circumstances of the marriage. "The circumstances of the act I know," she said, "which sealed the misery of our friend, though as much in the dark as any one about the motives that led to it."

We were quite intimate with P. in London, and he was our most delightful companion. He was then in the full flower of the varied accomplishments, which set off his fine manners and dignified character, joined, towards those he loved, with a certain soft willingness which gives the desirable chivalry to a man. None was more clear of choice where his personal affections were not touched, but where they were, it cost him pain to say no, on the slightest occasion. I have thought this must have had some connexion with the mystery of his misfortunes.

One day he called on me, and, without any preface, asked if I would be present next day at his marriage. I was so surprised, and so unpleasantly surprised, that I did not at first answer a word. We had been on terms so familiar, that I thought I knew all about him, yet had never dreamed of his having an attachment, and, though I had never inquired on the subject, yet this reserve, where perfect openness had been supposed, and really, on my side, existed, seemed to me a kind of treachery. Then it is never pleasant to know that a heart, on which we have some claim, is to be given to another. We cannot tell how it will affect our own relations with a person; it may strengthen or it may swallow up other affections; the crisis is hazardous, and our first thought, on such an occasion, is too often for ourselves, at least, mine was. Seeing me silent, he repeated his question.

To whom, said I, are you to be married?

That, he replied, I cannot tell you. He was a moment silent, then continued with an impassive look of cold self-possession, that affected me with strange sadness.

"The name of the person you will hear, of course, at the time, but more I cannot tell you. I need, however, the presence, not only of legal, but of respectable and friendly witnesses. I have hoped you and your husband would do me this kindness. Will you?"

Something in his manner made it impossible to refuse. I answered before I knew I was going to speak, "We will," and he left me.

I will not weary you with telling how I harassed myself and my husband, who was, however, scarce less interested, with doubts and conjectures. Suffice it that, next morning, P. came and took us in a carriage to a distant church. We had just entered the porch when a cart, such as fruit and vegetables are brought to market in, drove up, containing an elderly woman and a young girl. P. assisted them to alight, and advanced with the girl to the altar.

The girl was neatly dressed and quite handsome, yet something in her expression displeased me the moment I looked upon her. Meanwhile the ceremony was going on, and, at its close, P. introduced us to the bride, and we all went to the door.

Good-by, Fanny, said the elderly woman. The new-made Mrs. P. replied without any token of affection or emotion. The woman got into the cart and drove away.

From that time I saw but little of P. or his wife. I took our mutual friends to see her, and they were civil to her for his sake. Curiosity was very much excited, but entirely baffled; no one, of course, dared speak to P. on the subject, and no other means could be found of solving the riddle.

He treated his wife with grave and kind politeness, but it was always obvious that they had nothing in common between them. Her manners and tastes were not at that time gross, but her character showed itself hard and material. She was fond of riding, and spent much time so. Her style in this, and in dress, seemed the opposite of P.'s; but he indulged all her wishes, while, for himself, he plunged into his own pursuits.

For a time he seemed, if not happy, not positively unhappy; but, after a few years, Mrs. P. fell into the habit of drinking, and then such scenes as you witnessed grew frequent. I have often heard of them, and always that P. sat, as you describe him, his head bowed down and perfectly silent all through, whatever might be done or whoever be present, and always his aspect has inspired such sympathy that no person has questioned him or resented her insults, but merely got out of the way, so soon as possible.

Hard and long penance, said my father, after some minutes musing, for an hour of passion, probably for his only error.

Is that your explanation? said the lady. O, improbable. P. might err, but not be led beyond himself.

I know his cool gray eye and calm complexion seemed to say so, but a different story is told by the lip that could tremble, and showed what flashes might pierce those deep blue heavens; and when these over intellectual beings do swerve aside, it is to fall down a precipice, for their narrow path lies over such. But he was not one to sin without making a brave atonement, and that it had become a holy one, was written on that downcast brow.

The fourth day on these waters, the weather was milder and brighter, so that we could now see them to some purpose. At night was clear moon, and, for the first time, from the upper deck, I saw one of the great steamboats come majestically up. It was glowing with lights, looking many-eyed and sagacious; in its heavy motion it seemed a dowager queen, and this motion, with its solemn pulse, and determined sweep, becomes these smooth waters, especially at night, as much as the dip of the sailship the long billows of the ocean.

But it was not so soon that I learned to appreciate the lake scenery; it was only after a daily and careless familiarity that I entered into its beauty, for nature always refuses to be seen by being stared at. Like Bonaparte, she discharges her face of all expression when she catches the eye of impertinent curiosity fixed on her. But he who has gone to sleep in childish ease on her lap, or leaned an aching brow upon her breast, seeking there comfort with full trust as from a mother, will see all a mother's beauty in the look she bends upon him. Later, I felt that I had really seen these regions, and shall speak of them again.

In the afternoon we went on shore at the Manitou islands, where the boat stops to wood. No one lives here except woodcutters for the steamboats. I had thought of such a position, from its mixture of profound solitude with service to the great world, as possessing an ideal beauty. I think so still, after seeing the woodcutters and their slovenly huts.

In times of slower growth, man did not enter a situation without a certain preparation or adaptedness to it. He drew from it, if not to the poetical extent, at least, in some proportion, its moral and its meaning. The woodcutter did not cut down so many trees a day, that the hamadryads had not time to make their plaints heard; the shepherd tended his sheep, and did no jobs or chores the while; the idyl had a chance to grow up, and modulate his oaten pipe. But now the poet must be at the whole expense of the poetry in describing one of these positions; the worker is a true Midas to the gold he makes. The poet must describe, as the painter sketches Irish peasant girls and Danish fishwives, adding the beauty, and leaving out the dirt.

I come to the west prepared for the distaste I must experience at its mushroom growth. I know that where "go ahead" is the only motto, the village cannot grow into the gentle proportions that successive lives, and the gradations of experience involuntarily give. In older countries the house of the son grew from that of the father, as naturally as new joints on a bough. And the cathedral crowned the whole as naturally as the leafy summit the tree. This cannot be here. The march of peaceful is scarce less wanton than that of warlike invasion. The old landmarks are broken down, and the land, for a season, bears none, except of the rudeness of conquest and the needs of the day, whose bivouac fires blacken the sweetest forest glades. I have come prepared to see all this, to dislike it, but not with stupid narrowness to distrust or defame. On the contrary, while I will not be so obliging as to confound ugliness with beauty, discord with harmony, and laud and be contented with all I meet, when it conflicts with my best desires and tastes, I trust by reverent faith to woo the mighty meaning of the scene, perhaps to foresee the law by which a new order, a new poetry is to be evoked from this chaos, and with a curiosity as ardent, but not so selfish as that of Macbeth, to call up the apparitions of future kings from the strange ingredients of the witch's caldron. Thus, I will not grieve that all the noble trees are gone already from this island to feed this caldron, but believe it will have Medea's virtue, and reproduce them in the form of new intellectual growths, since centuries cannot again adorn the land with such.

On this most beautiful beach of smooth white pebbles, interspersed with agates and cornelians, for those who know how to find them, we stepped, not like the Indian, with some humble offering, which, if no better than an arrow-head or a little parched corn, would, he judged, please the Manitou, who looks only at the spirit in which it is offered. Our visit was so far for a religious purpose that one of our party went to inquire the fate of some Unitarian tracts left among the woodcutters a year or two before. But the old Manitou, though, daunted like his children by the approach of the fire-ships which he probably considered demons of a new dynasty, he had suffered his woods to be felled to feed their pride, had been less patient of an encroachment, which did not to him seem so authorized by the law of the strongest, and had scattered those leaves as carelessly as the others of that year.

But S. and I, like other emigrants, went not to give, but to get, to rifle the wood of flowers for the service of the fire-ship. We returned with a rich booty, among which was the uva ursi, whose leaves the Indians smoke, with the kinnick-kinnick, and which had then just put forth its highly-finished little blossoms, as pretty as those of the blueberry.

Passing along still further, I thought it would be well if the crowds assembled to stare from the various landings were still confined to the kinnick-kinnick, for almost all had tobacco written on their faces, their cheeks rounded with plugs, their eyes dull with its fumes. We reached Chicago on the evening of the sixth day, having been out five days and a half, a rather longer passage than usual at a favorable season of the year.

Chicago, June 20

There can be no two places in the world more completely thorough-fares than this place and Buffalo. They are the two correspondent valves that open and shut all the time, as the life-blood rushes from east to west, and back again from west to east.

Since it is their office thus to be the doors, and let in and out, it would be unfair to expect from them much character of their own. To make the best provisions for the transmission of produce is their office, and the people who live there are such as are suited for this; active, complaisant, inventive, business people. There are no provisions for the student or idler; to know what the place can give, you should be at work with the rest, the mere traveller will not find it profitable to loiter there as I did.

Since circumstances made it necessary for me so to do, I read all the books I could find about the new region, which now began to become real to me. All the books about the Indians, a paltry collection, truly, yet which furnished material for many thoughts. The most narrow-minded and awkward recital still bears some lineaments of the great features of this nature, and the races of men that illustrated them.

Catlin's book is far the best. I was afterwards assured by those acquainted with the regions he describes, that he is not to be depended on for the accuracy of his facts, and, indeed, it is obvious, without the aid of such assertions, that he sometimes yields to the temptation of making out a story. They admitted, however, what from my feelings I was sure of, that he is true to the spirit of the scene, and that a far better view can be got from him than from any source at present existing, of the Indian tribes of the far west, and of the country where their inheritance lay.

Murray's travels I read, and was charmed by their accuracy and clear broad tone. He is the only Englishman that seems to have traversed these regions, as man, simply, not as John Bull. He deserves to belong to an aristocracy, for he showed his title to it more when left without a guide in the wilderness, than he can at the court of Victoria. He has, himself, no poetic force at description, but it is easy to make images from his hints. Yet we believe the Indian cannot be looked at truly except by a poetic eye. The Pawnees, no doubt, are such as he describes them, filthy in their habits, and treacherous in their character, but some would have seen, and seen truly, more beauty and dignity than he does with all his manliness and fairness of mind. However, his one fine old man is enough to redeem the rest, and is perhaps the relic of a better day, a Phocion among the Pawness.

Schoolcraft's Algic Researches is a valuable book, though a worse use could hardly have been made of such fine material. Had the mythological or hunting stories of the Indians been written down exactly as they were received from the lips of the narrators, the collection could not have been surpassed in interest, both for the wild charm they carry with them, and the light they throw on a peculiar modification of life and mind. As it is, though the incidents have an air of originality and pertinence to the occasion, that gives us confidence that they have not been altered, the phraseology in which they were expressed has been entirely set aside, and the flimsy graces, common to the style of annuals and souvenirs, substituted for the Spartan brevity and sinewy grasp of Indian speech. We can just guess what might have been there, as we can detect the fine proportions of the Brave whom the bad taste of some white patron has arranged in frock-coat, hat, and pantaloons.

The few stories Mrs. Jameson wrote out, though to these also a sentimental air has been given, offend much less in that way than is common in this book. What would we give for a completely faithful version of some among them. Yet with all these drawbacks we cannot doubt from internal evidence that they truly ascribe to the Indian a delicacy of sentiment and of fancy that justifies Cooper in such inventions as his Uncas. It is a white man's view of a savage hero, who would be far finer in his natural proportions; still, through a masquerade figure, it implies the truth.

Irving's books I also read, some for the first, some for the second time, with increased interest, now that I was to meet such people as he received his materials from. Though the books are pleasing from their grace and luminous arrangement, yet, with the exception of the Tour to the Prairies, they have a stereotype, second-hand air. They lack the breath, the glow, the charming minute traits of living presence. His scenery is only fit to be glanced at from dioramic distance; his Indians are academic figures only. He would have made the best of pictures, if he could have used his own eyes for studies and sketches; as it is, his success is wonderful, but inadequate.

McKenney's Tour to the Lakes is the dullest of books, yet faithful and quiet, and gives some facts not to be met with elsewhere.

I also read a collection of Indian anecdotes and speeches, the worst compiled and arranged book possible, yet not without clues of some value. All these books I read in anticipation of a canoe-voyage on Lake Superior as far as the Pictured Rocks, and, though I was afterwards compelled to give up this project, they aided me in judging of what I afterwards saw and heard of the Indians.

In Chicago I first saw the beautiful prairie flowers. They were in their glory the first ten days we were there—

"The golden and the flame-like flowers."

The flame-like flower I was taught afterwards, by an Indian girl, to call "Wickapee;" and she told me, too, that its splendors had a useful side, for it was used by the Indians as a remedy for an illness to which they were subject.

Beside these brilliant flowers, which gemmed and gilt the grass in a sunny afternoon's drive near the blue lake, between the low oakwood and the narrow beach, stimulated, whether sensuously by the optic nerve, unused to so much gold and crimson with such tender green, or symbolically through some meaning dimly seen in the flowers, I enjoyed a sort of fairyland exultation never felt before, and the first drive amid the flowers gave me anticipation of the beauty of the prairies.

At first, the prairie seemed to speak of the very desolation of dullness. After sweeping over the vast monotony of the lakes to come to this monotony of land, with all around a limitless horizon,—to walk, and walk, and run, but never climb, oh! it was too dreary for any but a Hollander to bear. How the eye greeted the approach of a sail, or the smoke of a steamboat; it seemed that any thing so animated must come from a better land, where mountains gave religion to the scene.

The only thing I liked at first to do, was to trace with slow and unexpecting step the narrow margin of the lake. Sometimes a heavy swell gave it expression; at others, only its varied coloring, which I found more admirable every day, and which gave it an air of mirage instead of the vastness of ocean. Then there was a grandeur in the feeling that I might continue that walk, if I had any seven-leagued mode of conveyance to save fatigue, for hundreds of miles without an obstacle and without a change.

But after I had rode out, and seen the flowers and seen the sun set with that calmness seen only in the prairies, and the cattle winding slowly home to their homes in the "island groves"—peacefullest of sights—I began to love because I began to know the scene, and shrank no longer from "the encircling vastness."

It is always thus with the new form of life; we must learn to look at it by its own standard. At first, no doubt my accustomed eye kept saying, if the mind did not, What! no distant mountains? what, no valleys? But after a while I would ascend the roof of the house where we lived, and pass many hours, needing no sight but the moon reigning in the heavens, or starlight falling upon the lake, till all the lights were out in the island grove of men beneath my feet, and felt nearer heaven that there was nothing but this lovely, still reception on the earth; no towering mountains, no deep tree-shadows, nothing but plain earth and water bathed in light.

Sunset, as seen from that place, presented most generally, low-lying, flaky clouds, of the softest serenity, "like," said S., "the Buddhist tracts."

One night a star shot madly from its sphere, and it had a fair chance to be seen, but that serenity could not be astonished.

Yes! it was a peculiar beauty of those sunsets and moonlights on the levels of Chicago which Chamouny or the Trosachs could not make me forget.

Notwithstanding all the attractions I thus found out by degrees on the flat shores of the lake, I was delighted when I found myself really on my way into the country for an excursion of two or three weeks. We set forth in a strong wagon, almost as large, and with the look of those used elsewhere for transporting caravans of wild beastesses, loaded with every thing we might want, in case nobody would give it to us—for buying and selling were no longer to be counted on—with a pair of strong horses, able and willing to force their way through mud holes and amid stumps, and a guide, equally admirable as marshal and companion, who knew by heart the country and its history, both natural and artificial, and whose clear hunter's eye needed neither road nor goal to guide it to all the spots where beauty best loves to dwell.

Add to this the finest weather, and such country as I had never seen, even in my dreams, although these dreams had been haunted by wishes for just such an one, and you may judge whether years of dullness might not, by these bright days, be redeemed, and a sweetness be shed over all thoughts of the West.

The first day brought us through woods rich in the moccasin flower and lupine, and plains whose soft expanse was continually touched with expression by the slow moving clouds which

> "Sweep over with their shadows, and beneath
> The surface rolls and fluctuates to the eye;
> Dark hollows seem to glide along and chase
>   The sunny ridges,"

to the banks of the Fox river, a sweet and graceful stream. We reached Geneva just in time to escape being drenched by a violent thunder shower, whose rise and disappearance threw expression into all the features of the scene.

Geneva reminds me of a New England village, as indeed there, and in the neighborhood, are many New Englanders of an excellent stamp, generous, intelligent, discreet, and seeking to win from life its true values. Such are much wanted, and seem like points of light among the swarms of settlers, whose aims are sordid, whose habits thoughtless and slovenly.

With great pleasure we heard, with his attentive and affectionate congregation, the Unitarian clergyman, Mr. Conant, and afterward visited him in his house, where almost everything bore traces of his own handywork or that of his father. He is just such a teacher as is wanted in this region, familiar enough with the habits of those he addresses to come home to their experience and their wants; earnest and enlightened enough to draw the important inferences from the life of every day.

A day or two we remained here, and passed some happy hours in the woods that fringe the stream, where the gentlemen found a rich booty of fish.

Next day, travelling along the river's banks, was an uninterrupted pleasure. We closed our drive in the afternoon at the house of an English gentleman, who has grat-ified, as few men do, the common wish to pass the evening of an active day amid the quiet influences of country life. He showed us a bookcase filled with books about this country; these he had collected for years, and become so familiar with the localities that, on coming here at last, he sought and found, at once, the very spot he wanted, and where he is as content as he hoped to be, thus realizing Wordsworth's description of the wise man, who "sees what he foresaw."

A wood surrounds the house, through which paths are cut in every direction. It is, for this new country, a large and handsome dwelling; but round it are its barns and farm yard, with cattle and poultry. These, however, in the framework of wood, have a very picturesque and pleasing effect. There is that mixture of culture and rudeness in the aspect of things as gives a feeling of freedom, not of confusion.

I wish it were possible to give some idea of this scene as viewed by the earliest freshness of dewy dawn. This habitation of man seemed like a nest in the grass, so thoroughly were the buildings and all the objects of human care harmonized with what was natural. The tall trees bent and whispered all around, as if to hail with shel-tering love the men who had come to dwell among them.

The young ladies were musicians, and spoke French fluently, having been edu-cated in a convent. Here in the prairie, they had learned to take care of the milk-room, and kill the rattlesnakes that assailed their poultry yard. Beneath the shade of heavy curtains you looked out from the high and large windows to see Norwegian peasants at work in their national dress. In the wood grew, not only the flowers I had before seen, and wealth of tall, wild roses, but the splendid blue spiderwort, that or-nament of our gardens. Beautiful children strayed there, who were soon to leave these civilized regions for some really wild and western place, a post in the buffalo coun-try. Their no less beautiful mother was of Welsh descent, and the eldest child bore the name of Gwynthleon. Perhaps there she will meet with some young descendants of Madoc, to be her friends; at any rate, her looks may retain that sweet, wild beauty, that is soon made to vanish from eyes which look too much on shops and streets, and the vulgarities of city "parties."

Next day we crossed the river. We ladies crossed on a little foot-bridge, from which we could look down the stream, and see the wagon pass over at the ford. A black thun-der cloud was coming up. The sky and waters heavy with expectation. The motion of the wagon, with its white cover, and the laboring horses, gave just the due interest to the picture, because it seemed as if they would not have time to cross before the storm came on. However, they did get across, and we were a mile or two on our way before the violent shower obliged us to take refuge in a solitary house upon the prairie. In this country it is as pleasant to stop as to go on, to lose your way as to find it, for the vari-ety in the population gives you a chance for fresh entertainment in every hut, and the luxuriant beauty makes every path attractive. In this house we found a family "quite above the common," but, I grieve to say, not above false pride, for the father, ashamed of being caught barefoot, told us a story of a man, one of the richest men, he said, in one of the eastern cities, who went barefoot, from choice and taste.

Near the door grew a Provence rose, then in blossom. Other families we saw had brought with them and planted the locust. It was pleasant to see their old home loves, brought into connection with their new splendors. Wherever there were traces of this tenderness of feeling, only too rare among Americans, other things bore signs also of prosperity and intelligence, as if the ordering mind of man had some idea of home beyond a mere shelter, beneath which to eat and sleep.

No heaven need wear a lovelier aspect than earth did this afternoon, after the clearing up of the shower. We traversed the blooming plain, unmarked by any road, only the friendly track of wheels which tracked, not broke the grass. Our stations were not from town to town, but from grove to grove. These groves first floated like blue islands in the distance. As we drew nearer, they seemed fair parks, and the little log houses on the edge, with their curling smokes, harmonized beautifully with them.

One of these groves, Ross's grove, we reached just at sunset. It was of the noblest trees I saw during this journey, for the trees generally were not large or lofty, but only of fair proportions. Here they were large enough to form with their clear stems pillars for grand cathedral aisles. There was space enough for crimson light to stream through upon the floor of water which the shower had left. As we slowly plashed through, I thought I was never in a better place for vespers.

That night we rested, or rather tarried at a grove some miles beyond, and there partook of the miseries so often jocosely portrayed, of bedchambers for twelve, a milk dish for universal handbasin, and expectations that you would use and lend your "hankercher" for a towel. But this was the only night, thanks to the hospitality of private families, that we passed thus, and it was well that we had this bit of experience, else might we have pronounced all Trollopian records of the kind to be inventions of pure malice.

With us was a young lady who showed herself to have been bathed in the Britannic fluid, wittily described by a late French writer, by the impossibility she experienced of accommodating herself to the indecorums of the scene. We ladies were to sleep in the bar-room, from which its drinking visiters could be ejected only at a late hour. The outer door had no fastening to prevent their return. However, our host kindly requested we would call him, if they did, as he had "conquered them for us," and would do so again. We had also rather hard couches; (mine was the supper table,) but we yankees, born to rove, were altogether too much fatigued to stand upon trifles, and slept as sweetly as we would in the "bigly bower" of any baroness. But I think England sat up all night, wrapped in her blanket shawl, and with a neat lace cap upon her head; so that she would have looked perfectly the lady, if any one had come in; shuddering and listening. I know that she was very ill next day, in requital. She watched, as her parent country watches the seas, that nobody may do wrong in any case, and deserved to have met some interruption, she was so well prepared. However, there was none, other than from the nearness of some twenty sets of powerful lungs, which would not leave the night to a deadly stillness. In this house we had, if not good beds, yet good tea, good bread, and wild strawberries, and were entertained with most free communications of opinion and history from our hosts. Neither shall any of us have a right to say again that we cannot find any who may be willing to hear all we may have to say. "A's fish that comes to the net," should be painted on the sign at Papaw grove.

48

JOHN BEAUCHAMP JONES

(1810–1866)

On March 6, 1810, John Beauchamp Jones was born in Baltimore. Though little is known for certain about Jones's early life, much can be inferred from his autobiographical novel *The Western Merchant* (1849). Here he indicates that when he was six his family moved to Kentucky, and that as a young man he joined his brother in a move to Missouri frontier.

The banks of the Missouri River would serve as the setting for Jones's most popular novel, the episodic *Wild Western Scenes: A Narrative of Adventures in the Wilderness* (1841). The novel's hero, Charles Glenn, was modeled after Jones himself. Jones explained, referring to himself in the third person,

> Like the hero of this book, the author had his vicissitudes in boyhood, and committed such indiscretions as were incident to one of his years and circumstances, but nevertheless only such as might be pardoned by the charitable. Like Glenn, he submitted to a voluntary exile in the wilds of Missouri. Hence the description of scenery is a true picture, and several characters were real persons. Many of the occurrences actually transpired in his presence, or had been enacted in the vicinity at no remote period.

One real person who appears in the book is Daniel Boone. It seems unlikely, however, that Boone and Jones were acquainted, since Boone died when Jones was ten years old.

Jones had ended his voluntary exile by 1840, when he began in earnest to pursue his ambition to be a writer. He edited the *Baltimore Saturday Visiter,* and he would later edit papers in Washington and Philadelphia as well. His first novel was *Wild Western Scenes,* which he was initially forced to publish at his own expense. Jones followed with a dozen other titles including two sequels, *Wild Western Scenes, Second Series: The War Path* (1856) and *Wild Western Scenes: or, The White Spirit of the Wilderness* (1863). Perhaps his most interesting later work is *Border War: A Tale of Disunion* (1859), a foretelling of the Civil War.

When the war actually came, Jones served as a clerk in the Confederate War Department. Here he was privy to many of the inner workings of the Southern government, which he recorded and analyzed and often criticized in a lengthy diary. In 1866, this work was published in two volumes as *A Rebel War Clerk's Diary.* Though Jones was acknowledged by some as "the Confederate Pepys," his portrayal of the late rebel government was not well received in the South. Jones, however, lived to hear neither the praise nor the criticism. He died on February 4, 1866, as *A Rebel War Clerk's Diary* was going to press.

Text: *Wild Western Scenes: A Narrative of Adventures in the Wilderness* (Philadelphia, 1856): 32–48, 99–121.

FROM *WILD WESTERN SCENES:* *A NARRATIVE OF ADVENTURES IN THE* *WESTERN WILDERNESS* (1841, 1856)

CHAPTER III

Some weeks had passed since the bear hunt. The emigrants had crossed the river, and selected their future homes in the groves that bordered the prairie, some miles distant from the ferry. Glenn, when landed on the south side of the Missouri, took up his abode for a short time with Jasper Roughgrove, the ferryman, while some half dozen men, whose services his gold secured, were building him a novel habitation. And the location was as singular as the construction of his house. It was on a peak that jutted over the river, some three hundred feet high, whence he had a view eight or ten miles down the stream, and across the opposite bottom-land to the hills mentioned in the preceding chapter. The view was obstructed above by a sudden bend of the stream; but on the south, the level prairie ran out as far as the eye could reach, interrupted only by the few young groves that were interspersed at intervals. His house, constructed of heavy stones, was about fifteen feet square, and not more than ten in height. The floor was formed of hewn timbers, the walls covered with a rough coat of lime, and the roof made of heavy boards. However uncouth this abode appeared to the eye of Glenn, yet he had followed the instructions of Boone, (to whom he had fully disclosed his plan, and repeated his odd resolution,) and reared a tenement not only capable of resisting the wintry winds that were to howl around it, but sufficiently firm to withstand the attacks of any foe, whether the wild beast of the forest or the prowling Indian. The door was very narrow and low, being made of a solid rock full six inches in thickness, which required the strength of a man to turn on its hinges, even when the ponderous bolt on the inside was unfastened. There was a small square window on each side containing a single pane of glass, and made to be secured at a moment's warning, by means of thick stone shutters on the inside. The fire-place was ample at the hearth, but the flue through which the smoke escaped was small, and ran in a serpentine direction up through the northern wall; while the ceiling was overlaid with smooth flat stones, fastened down with huge iron spikes, and supported by strong wooden joists. The furniture consisted of a few trunks, (which answered for seats,) two camp beds, four barrels of hard biscuit, a few dishes and cooking utensils, and a quantity of hunting implements. Many times did Joe shake his head in won-derment as this house was preparing for his reception. It seemed to him too much danger was apprehended from without, and it too much resembled a solitary and se-cure prison, should one be confined within. Nevertheless, he was permitted to adopt his own plan in the construction of a shelter for the horses. And the retention of these animals was some relief to his otherwise gloomy forebodings, when he beheld the erection of his master's suspicious tenement. He superintended the building of a sub-stantial and comfortable stable. He had stalls, a small granary, and a regular rack made for the accommodation of the horses, and procured, with difficulty and no little ex-pense, a supply of provender. The space, including the buildings, which had been cleared of the roots and stones, for the purpose of cultivating a garden, was about one hundred feet in diameter, and enclosed by a circular row of posts driven firmly in the ground, and rising some ten feet above the surface. These were planted so closely to-gether that even a squirrel would have found it difficult to enter without climbing over them. Indeed, Joe had an especial eye to this department, having heard some awful tales of the snakes that somewhat abounded in those regions in the warm seasons.

One corner of the stable, wherein a quantity of straw was placed, was appropri-ated for the comfort of the dogs, Ringwood and Jowler, which had been presented to Glenn by his obliging friend, after they had exhibited their skill in the bear hunt.

When every thing was completed, preparatory for his removal thither, Glenn dis-missed his faithful artisans, bestowing upon them a liberal reward for their labour, and took possession of his castle. But, notwithstanding the strange manner in which he proposed to spend his days, and his habitual grave demeanour and taciturnity, yet his kind tone, when he uttered a request, or ventured a remark, on the transactions pass-ing around him, and his contempt for money, which he squandered with a prodigal hand, had secured for him the good-will of the ferrymen, and the friendship of the surrounding emigrants. But there was one whose esteem had no venal mixture in it. This was Mary, the old ferryman's daughter, a fair-cheeked girl of nineteen, who never neglected an opportunity of performing a kind office for her father's tempo-rary guest; and when he and his man departed for their own tenement, not ventur-ing directly to bestow them on our hero, she presented Joe with divers articles for their amusement and comfort in their secluded abode, among which were sundry live fowls, a pet fawn, and a kitten.

The first few days, after being installed in his solitary home, our hero passed with his books. But he did not realize all the satisfaction he anticipated from his favourite authors in his secluded cell. The scene around him contrasted but ill with the cre-ations of Shakspeare; and if some of the heroes of Scott were identified with the wildest features of nature, he found it impossible to look around him and enjoy the magic of the page at the same time.

Joe employed himself in attending to his horses, feeding the fowls and dogs, and playing with the fawn and kitten. He also practiced loading and shooting his musket, and endeavoured to learn the mode of doing execution on other objects without committing violence on himself.

"Joe," said Glenn, one bright frosty morning, "saddle the horses; we will make an excursion in the prairie, and see what success we can have without the presence and assistance of an experienced hunter. I designed awaiting the visit of Boone, which he promised should take place about this time; but we will venture out without him; if we kill nothing, at least we shall have the satisfaction of doing no harm."

Joe set off towards the stable, smiling at Glenn's joke, and heartily delighted to exchange the monotony of his domestic employment, which was becoming irksome, for the sports of the field, particularly as he was now entirely recovered from the effects of his late disasters, and began to grow weary of wasting his ammunition in firing at a target, when there was an abundance of game in the vicinity.

"Whoop! Ringwood—Jowler!" cried he, leading the horses briskly forth. The dogs came prancing and yielding round him, as well pleased as himself at the prospect of a day's sport; and when Glenn came out they exhibited palpable signs of recognition and eagerness to accompany their new master on his first deer-hunt. Glenn stroked their heads, which were constantly rubbed against his hands, and his caresses were gratefully received by the faithful hounds. He had been instructed by Boone how to manage them, so as either to keep them at his side when he wished to approach the game stealthily, or to send them forth when rapid pursuit was required, and he was now anxious to test their sagacity.

When mounted, the young men set forward in a southern direction, the valley in which the ferryman's cabin was situated on one hand, and one about the same distance above on the other. But the space between them gradually widened as they progressed, and in a few minutes both disappeared entirely, terminating in scarcely perceptible rivulets running slowly down from the high and level prairie. Here Glenn paused to determine what course he should take. The sun shone brightly on the interminable expanse before him, and not a breeze ruffled the long dry grass around, nor disturbed the few sear leaves that yet clung to the diminutive clusters of bushes scattered at long intervals over the prairie. It was a delightful scene. From the high position of our hero, he could distinguish objects miles distant on the plain; and if the landscape was not enlivened by houses and domestic herds, he could at all events here and there behold parties of deer browsing peacefully in the distance. Ringwood and Jowler also saw or scented them, as their attention was pointed in that direction; but so far from marring the sport by prematurely running forward, they knew too well their duty to leave their master, even were the game within a few paces of them, without the word of command.

"I see a deer!" cried Joe, at length, having till then been employed gathering some fine wild grapes from a neighbouring vine.

"I see several," replied Glenn; "but how we are to get within gun shot of them, is the question."

"I see them, too," said Joe, his eyes glistening.

"I have thought of a plan, Joe; whether right or wrong, is not very material, as respects the exercise we are seeking; but I am inclined to believe it is the proper one. It will at all events give you a fair opportunity of killing a deer, as you will have to fire as they run, and the great number of bullets in your musket will make you more certain to do execution than if you fired a rifle. You will proceed to yon thicket, about a thousand yards distant, keeping the bushes all the time between you and the deer. When you arrive at it dismount, and after tying your pony in the bushes where he will be well hid, select a position whence you can see the deer when they run; I think they will go within reach of your fire. I will make a detour beyond them, and approach from the opposite side."

"I'd rather not tie my pony," said Joe.

"Why? he would not leave you, even were he to got loose," replied Glenn.

"I don't think he would—but I'd rather not leave him yet awhile, till I get a little better used to hunting," said Joe, probably thinking there might be some danger to himself on foot in a country where bears, wolves, and panthers were sometimes seen.

"Can you fire while sitting on your pony?" inquired Glenn.

"I suppose so," said Joe; "though I never thought to try it yet."

"Suppose you try it now, while I watch the deer, and see if what I have been told is true, that the mere report of a gun will not alarm them."

"Well, I will," said Joe. "I think Pete knows as well as the steed, that shooting on him won't hurt him."

"Fire away, then," said Glenn, looking steadfastly at the deer. Joe fired, and none of the deer ran off. Some continued their playful sports, while others browsed along without lifting their heads; in all likelihood the report did not reach them. But Glenn heard a tremendous thumping behind, and on turning round, beheld his man quietly lying on the ground, and the pony standing about ten paces distant, with his head turned towards Joe, his ears thrust forwards, his nostrils distended and snorting, and his little blue eyes ready to burst out of his head.

"How is this, Joe?" inquired Glenn, scarce able to repress a smile at the ridiculous posture of his man.

"I hardly know myself," replied Joe, casting a silly glance at his treacherous pony; and after examining his limbs and finding no injury had been sustained, continued, "I fired as you directed, and when the smoke cleared away, I found myself lying just as you see me here. I don't know how Pete contrived to get from under me, but there he stands, and here I lie."

"Load your gun, and try it again," said Glenn.

"I'd rather not," said Joe.

"Then I will," replied Glenn, whose horsemanship enabled him to retain the saddle in spite of the struggles of Pete, who, after several discharges, submitted and bore it quietly.

Joe then mounted and set out for the designated thicket, while Glenn galloped off in another direction, followed by the hounds.

When Joe arrived at the hazel thicket, he continued in the saddle, and otherwise he would not have been able to see over the prairie for the tall grass which had grown very luxuriantly in that vicinity. There was a path, however, running round the edge of the bushes, which had been made by the deer and other wild animals, and in this he cautiously groped his way, looking out in every direction for the deer. When he had progressed about halfway round, he espied them feeding composedly, about three hundred paces distant, on a slight eminence. There were at least fifteen of them, and some very large ones. Fearful of giving the alarm before Glenn should fire, he shielded himself from view behind a cluster of persimmon bushes, and tasted the ripe and not unpalatable fruit. And here he was destined to win his first trophy as a hunter. While bending down some branches over head, without looking up, an opossum fell upon his hat, knocking it over his eyes, and springing on the neck of Pete, thence leaped to the ground. But before it disappeared Joe had dismounted, and giving it a blow with the butt of his musket it rolled over on its side, with its eyes closed and tongue hanging out, indicating that the stroke had been fatal.

"So much for you!" said Joe, casting a proud look at his victim; and then leaping on his pony, he gazed again at the deer. They seemed to be still entirely unconscious of danger, and several were now lying in the grass with their heads up, and chewing the cud like domestic animals. Joe drew back once more to await the action of Glenn, and turning to look at the opossum, found to his surprise that it had vanished!

"Well, I'm the biggest fool that ever breathed!" said he, recollecting the craftiness imputed to those animals, and searching in vain for his game. "If ever I come across another, he'll not come the 'possum over me, I'll answer for it!" he continued, somewhat vexed. At this juncture Glenn's gun was heard, and Joe observed a majority of the deer leaping affrighted in the direction of his position. The foremost passed within twenty yards of him, and, his limbs trembling with excitement, he drew his gun up to his shoulder and pulled the trigger. It snapped, perhaps fortunately, for his eyes were convulsively closed at the moment; and recovering measurably by the time the next came up, this trial the gun went off, and he found himself once more prostrate on the ground.

"What in the world is the reason you won't stand still!" he exclaimed, rising and seizing the pony by the bit. The only answer Pete made was a snort of unequivocal dissatisfaction. "Plague take your little *hide* of you! I should have killed that fellow to a certainty, if you hadn't played the fool!" continued he, still addressing his pony while he proceeded to load his gun. When ready for another fire, he mounted again, in quite an ill humour, convinced that all chance of killing a deer was effectually over for the present, when, to his utter astonishment, he beheld the deer he had fired at lying dead before him, and but a few paces distant. With feelings of unmixed delight he galloped to where it lay, and springing to the earth, one moment he whirled round his hat in exultation, and the next caressed Pete, who evinced some repugnance to approach the weltering victim, and snuffed the scent of blood with any other sensation than that of pleasure. Joe discovered that no less than a dozen balls had penetrated the doe's side, (for such it was,) which sufficiently accounted for its immediate and quiet death, that had so effectually deceived him into the belief that his discharge had been harmless. He now blew his horn, which was answered by a blast from Glenn, who soon came up to announce his own success in bringing down the largest buck in the party, and to congratulate his man on his truly remarkable achievement.

An hour was consumed in preparing the deer to be conveyed to the house, and by the time they were safely deposited in our hero's diminutive castle, and the hunters ready to issue forth in quest of more sport, the day was far advanced, and a slight haziness of the atmosphere dimmed in a great measure the lustre of the descending sun.

Animated with their excellent success, they anticipated much more sport, inasmuch as neither themselves nor the hounds (which hitherto were not required to do farther service than to watch one of the deer while the men were engaged with the other) were in the slightest degree fatigued. The hours flew past unnoticed, while the young men proceeded gayly outward from the river in quest of new adventures.

Glenn and his man rode far beyond the scene of their late success without discovering any new object to gratify their undiminished zest for the chase. It seemed that the deer which had escaped had actually given intelligence to the rest of the arrival of a deadly foe in the vicinity, for not one could now be seen in riding several miles. The sun was sinking low and dim in the west, and Glenn was on the eve of turning homeward, when, on emerging from the flat prairie to a slight eminence that he had marked as the boundary of his excursion, he beheld at no great distance an enormous mound, of pyramidical shape, which, from its isolated condition, he could not believe to be the formation of nature. Curious to inspect what he supposed to be a stupendous specimen of the remains of former generations of the aborigines, he resolved to protract his ride and ascend to the summit. The mound was some five hundred feet in diameter at the base, and terminated at a peak about one hundred and fifty feet in height. As our riders ascended, with some difficulty keeping in the saddle, they observed the earth on the sides to be mixed with flint-stones, and many of them apparently having once been cut in the shape of arrow-heads; and in several places where chasms had been formed by heavy showers, they remarked a great many pieces of bones, but so much broken and decayed they could not be certain that they were particles of human skeletons. When they reached the summit, which was not more than twenty feet in width and entirely barren, a magnificent scene burst in view. For ten or fifteen miles round on every side, the eye could discern oval, oblong, and circular groves of various dimensions, scattered over the rich virgin soil. The gentle undulations of the prairie resembled the boundless ocean entranced, as if the long swells had been suddenly abandoned by the wind, and yet remained stationary in their rolling attitude.

"What think you of the view, Joe?" inquired Glenn, after regarding the scene many minutes in silence.

"I've been watching a little speck, way out toward the sun, which keeps bobbing up and down, and gets bigger and bigger," said Joe.

"I mean the prospect around," said Glenn.

"I can't form an opinion, because I can't see the end of it," replied Joe, still intently regarding the object referred to.

"That is an animal of some kind," observed Glenn, marking the object that attracted Joe.

"And a wapper, too; when I first saw it I thought it was a rabbit, and now it's bigger than a deer, and still a mile or two off," said Joe.

"We'll wait a few minutes, and see what it is," replied Glenn, checking his steed, which had proceeded a few steps downward. The object of their attention held its course directly towards them, and as it drew nearer it was easily distinguished to be a very large buffalo, an animal then somewhat rare so near the white man's settlement, and one that our hero had often expressed a wish to see. Its dark shaggy sides, protuberant back and bushy head, were quite perceptible as it careered swiftly onward, seemingly flying from some danger behind.

"Down, Ringwood! Jowler!" exclaimed Glenn, preparing to fire.

"Down, Joe, too," said Joe, slipping down from his pony, preferring not to risk another fall, and likewise preparing to fire.

When the buffalo reached the base of the mound, it saw for the first time the objects above, and halted. It regarded the men with more symptoms of curiosity than alarm, but as it gazed, its distressed pantings indicated that it had been long retreating from some object of dread.

Meantime both guns were discharged, and the contents undoubtedly penetrated the animal's body, for he leapt upright in the air, and on descending, staggered off slowly in a course at right angles from the one which he was first pursuing. Glenn then let the hounds go forth, and soon overtaking the animal, they were speedily forced to act on the defensive; for the enormous foe wheeled round and pursued in turn. Finding the hounds were too cautious and active to fall victims to his sharp horns, he pawed the earth, and uttered the most horrific bellowings. As Glenn and Joe rode by the place where he had stood when they fired, they perceived large quantities of frothy blood, which convinced them that he had received a mortal wound. They rode on and paused within eighty paces of where he now stood, and calling back the baying hounds, again discharged their guns. The buffalo roared most hideously, and making a few plunges towards his assailants, fell on his knees, and the next moment turned over on his side.

"Come back, Joe!" cried Glenn to his man, who had mounted and wheeled when the animal rushed towards them, and was still flying away as fast as his pony could carry him.

"No—never!" replied Joe; "I won't go nigh that awful thing! Don't you see it's getting dark? How'll we ever find the way home again?"

The latter remark startled Glenn, for he had lost all consciousness of the lateness of the hour in the excitement, and to his dismay had also lost all recollection of the direction of his dwelling, and darkness had now overtaken them! While pausing to reflect from which quarter they first approached the mound, the buffalo, to his surprise and no little chagrin, rose up and staggered away, the darkness soon obscuring him from view altogether. Glenn, by a blast of his horn, recalled the dogs, and joining Joe, set off much dispirited, in a course which he feared was not the correct one. Night came upon them suddenly, and before they had gone a mile the darkness was intense. And the breathless calm that had prevailed during the day was now succeeded by fitful winds that howled mournfully over the interminable prairie. Interminable the plain seemed to our benighted riders, for there was still no object to vary the monotony of the cheerless scene, although they had paced briskly, and, as they supposed, far enough to have reached the cliffs of the river. Nor was there even a sound heard as they rode along, save the muffled strokes of their horses' hoofs in the dry grass that covered the earth, the low winds, and an occasional cry of the dogs as they were trodden upon by the horses.

Ere long a change came over the scene. About two-thirds of the distance round the verge of the horizon a faint light appeared, resembling the scene when a dense curtain of clouds hangs over head, and the rays of the morning sun steal under the edge of the thick vapour. But the stars could be seen, and the only appearance of clouds was immediately above the circle of light. In a very few minutes the terrible truth flashed upon the mind of Glenn. The dim light along the horizon was changed to an approaching flame! Columns of smoke could be seen rolling upwards, while the fire beneath imparted a lurid glare to them. The wind blew more fiercely, and the fire approached from almost every quarter with the swiftness of a race horse. The darkened vault above became gradually illuminated with a crimson reflection, and the young man shuddered with the horrid apprehension of being burnt alive! It was madness to proceed in a direction that must inevitably hasten their fate, the fire extending in one unbroken line from left to right, and in front of them; and they turned in a course which seemed to place the greatest distance between them and the furious element. Ever and anon a frightened deer or elk leaped past. The hounds no longer noticed them, but remained close to the horses. The leaping flames came in awful rapidity. The light increased in brilliance, and objects were distinguishable far over the prairie. A red glare could be seen on the sides of the deer as they bounded over the tall, dry grass, which was soon to be no longer a refuge for them. The young men heard a low, continued roar, that increased every moment in loudness, and looking in the direction whence they supposed it proceeded, they observed an immense, dark, moving mass, the nature of which they could not divine, but it threatened to annihilate every thing that opposed it. While gazing at this additional source of danger, the horses, blinded by the surrounding light, plunged into a deep ditch that the rain had washed in the rich soil. Neither men nor horses, fortunately, were injured; and after several ineffectual efforts to extricate themselves, they here resolved to await the coming of the fire. Ringwood and Jowler whined fearfully on the verge of the ditch for an instant, and then sprang in and crouched trembling at the feet of their master. The next instant the dark, thundering mass passed over head, being nothing less than an immense herd of buffalo driven forwards by the flames! The horses bowed their heads as if a thunderbolt was passing. The fire and the heavens were hid from view, and the roar above resembled the rush of mighty waters. When the last animal had sprung over the chasm, Glenn thanked the propitious accident that thus providentially prevented him from being crushed to atoms, and uttered a prayer to Heaven that he might by a like means be rescued from the fiery ordeal that awaited him. It now occurred to him that the accumulation of weeds and grass in the chasm, which saved them from injury when falling in, would prove fatal when the flames arrived! And after groping some distance along the trench, he found the depth diminished, but the fire was not three hundred paces distant! His heart sank within him! But when on the eve of returning to his former position, with a resolution to remove as much of the combustible matter as possible, a gleam of joy spread over his features, as, casting a glance in a contrary direction from that they had recently pursued, he beheld the identical mound he had ascended before dark, and from which his unsteady and erratic riding in the night had fortunately prevented a distant separation. They now led their horses forth, and mounting without delay, whipped forward for life or death. Could the summit of the mound be attained they were in safety—for there the soil was not encumbered with decayed vegetation—and they spurred their animals to the top of their speed. It was a noble sight to see the majestic white steed flying towards the mound with the velocity of the wind, while the diminutive pony miraculously followed in the wake like an inseparable shadow. The careering flames were not far behind; and when the horses gained the summit and Glenn looked back, the fire had reached the base!

"I thank all the saints at once!" exclaimed Joe, dismounting and falling on his knees.

"Thank your pony's legs, also," remarked Glenn, smiling.

"Was there ever such a blessed deliverance!" said Joe, panting.

"Was there ever such a lucky tumble into a ditch!" replied Glenn, with spirits more buoyant than usual.

"Was there ever an old hunter so much deceived!" said a voice a few paces down that side of the cone least exposed to the glare of the fire, and so much in the shadow of the peak that the speaker was not perceived from the position of the young men. But as soon as the words were uttered, Ringwood and Jowler sprang from the horses' heels where they had lain panting, and rushed in the direction of the speaker, whom they accosted with marks of joyful recognition.

"It is Boone!" exclaimed Glenn, leaping from his horse, and running forward to his friend, who was now seen to rise up, and a moment after his horse, that had been prostrate and still, was likewise on his feet.

"Ha! ha! ha! You have played me a fine trick, truly," laughingly remarked Boone, returning their hearty salutations.

"How?" inquired Glenn.

"In the first place, to venture forth before my arrival; in the next to inspire me with the belief that I was on the eve of encountering a brace of Indians. But I will begin at the beginning. When I crossed the river and reached your hut, (which is indeed impregnable,) I was astonished to find you had gone forth to hunt without a guide; and not so much fearing you would be lost, should night overtake you, as apprehending serious danger from the fire, the approach of which I anticipated long before night, from the peculiar complexion of the atmosphere, I set out on your trail, in hopes of overtaking you before the shades of evening set in; but darkness coming on, I could trace you no farther than to this mound. In vain did I endeavour to ascertain which direction you then travelled; but resolving not to abandon the search, I continued cruising about the prairie until the near approach of the fire forced me to retreat hither. It was when urging my horse to his utmost speed that I beheld you and your bear-hunter charging from another direction, and from the partial view, as we were all under whip, (and knowing the Osages were not far off,) I was instantly convinced that you were savages. Arriving first, I made my sagacious horse lie down, and then concealed myself behind his body."

"I am not only rejoiced that we were not the savages you supposed, (for then Joe and I must have perished in the flames somewhere,) on our own account, but for the sake of the only man who can possibly extricate us from this dilemma," replied Glenn.

"You are somewhat wide of the mark as respects my jeopardy, my lad," said Boone; "for had you been hostile Osages, most assuredly ere this you had both been killed."

"Good gracious!" exclaimed Joe, whose predicament suddenly flashed upon his mind; "for Heaven's sake let us get home as fast as possible! He says the Indians are about! Do let us go, Mr. Glenn; we can travel now out yonder where the grass has all been burnt."

"Pshaw! You seem more alarmed now, Joe, than when there really was danger. Are the Osages truly hostile?" continued Glenn, addressing Boone.

"They are not at war with the whites, as a nation," replied Boone, ever and anon looking towards the only point from which the fire now approached; "but in thin settlements, where they may easily be the strongest party, as roving brigands, they may be considered extremely dangerous. Your man's advice is not bad."

"There! Don't you hear that? Now, *do* let's go home!" continued Joe, with increased alarm.

Fortunately, that portion of the plain over which the scathing element had spent its fury was the direction the party should pursue in retracing their way homeward.

The light dry grass had been soon consumed, and the earth wore a blackened appearance, and was as smooth as if vegetation had never covered the surface. As the party rode briskly along, (and the pony now kept in advance,) the horses' hoofs rattled as loudly on the baked ground as if it were a plank floor. The reflection of the fire in the distance still threw a lurid glare over the extended heath. As the smoke gradually ascended, objects could be discerned at a great distance, and occasionally a half-roasted deer or elk, was seen plunging about, driven to madness by its tortures. And frequently they found the dead bodies of smaller animals that could find no safety in flight.

"What's that?" cried Joe, reining up his pony, and gazing at a huge dark object ahead.

"A prize, to which we are justly entitled!" exclaimed Glenn, riding forward, on discovering it to be the buffalo (now dead) that they had fired upon early in the evening, and which circumstance he was relating to Boone at the moment of the discovery by Joe.

"You have not only been lucky as hunters," said Boone, as they dismounted to inspect the animal, (which was an enormous bull,) "but, what is extraordinary indeed, when you find your fallen game, it is already cooked!"

"Huzza for us!" cried Joe, momentarily forgetting the Indians, in his extravagant joy of having aided in killing the animal, and at the same time leaping astride of it.

"The wolves have been here before us," observed Boone, seeing a large quantity of the buffalo's viscera on the ground, which he supposed had been torn out by those ravenous animals.

"Oh! oh! oh! oh!" exclaimed Joe, leaping up, and running a few steps, and then tumbling down and continuing his cries.

"What has hurt the fellow so badly?" inquired Glenn, walking round from the back of the animal to the front. The words were scarcely uttered before he likewise sprang away, hastily, as he beheld a pronged instrument thrust from the orifice in the body whence the bowels had been extracted!

"Dod! I wonder if it's wolves or Injins!" exclaimed a voice within the cavity of the huge body.

"I've heard that voice before—it must be Sneak's," said Boone, laughing heartily.

Now the buffalo was observed to quiver slightly, and after some exertion to extricate himself, the long snake-like form of the redoubtable "Hatchet-face" came forth and stood erect before the gaping mouth and staring eyes of Joe.

"If I didn't hear a white man speak, I wish I may be singed!" exclaimed Sneak, wiping the moisture from his face, and rolling his eyes round.

"What did you stick that sharp thing in the calf of my leg for?" demanded Joe, shaking his head threateningly, and coming forward.

"He! he! he! That's revenge for shooting my pups," replied Sneak.

"But how came you here?" inquired Boone.

"I was taking a hunt"—here Boone interrupted him by asking where his gun was. "I had no gun," said Sneak; and then stooping down and running his arm into the body of the buffalo, he produced a pronged spear, about four feet in length; "this," he continued, "is what I hunted with, and I was hunting after muskrats in the ponds out here, when the fire came like blazes, and like to 'ave ketched me! I dropped all the muskrats I had stuck, and streaked it for about an hour towards the river. But it gained on me like lightning, and I'd 'ave been in a purty fix if I hadn't come across this dead bull. I out with my knife and was into him in less than no time—but split me, if I didn't feel the heat of the fire as I pulled in my feet! I knew the Injins was about, by the buffalo; and the tarnation wolves, too, are always everywhere, and that accounts for my jobbing that feller's leg when he sot down on top of me."

Glenn's laughter at the above narration was arrested by Boone, who placed one hand on his shoulder, and with the other pointed out towards the fire about a mile distant, before which and thrown in relief by the flames could be distinctly discerned the flitting forms of a band of savages! A number were mounted, and others could be seen on foot, and all moving about in various directions round a large herd of buffalo, which occasionally made a stand to resist the foe that harassed them on all sides, but were soon driven forward again by the flames. Now a mounted chief could be seen to ride boldly up within a few paces of the dark mass of animals, and drawing his arrow to the head, discharge it, shaft and all, into the defenceless side of his victim. The enraged animal thus pursued either fell or rushed furiously on its foe; but the skilful savage, by a dexterous turn or sudden leap, seemed to avoid him with ease, and flying round, sent forth another barbed messenger as he careered at full speed.

"As I'm afoot, I'll go ahead!" cried Sneak, starting off at a gait that verified his words.

"Good gracious!" exclaimed Joe, leaping on his pony and whipping after Sneak, while Boone and Glenn followed in a brisk gallop.

CHAPTER VIII

The night was beautiful. The moon sailed through a cloudless sky, and the north wind, which had whistled loudly among the branches of the trees in the valley at the close of day, was hushed, and a perfect calm pervaded the scene.

"What're you leaving your post for?" asked Sneak, as Joe suddenly abandoned his watch on the west side of the inclosure, and tripped across to Roughgrove.

"Mr. Roughgrove—Mr. Roughgrove," said Joe, in a low tone.

"Well, what do you want with me?" responded the old ferryman.

"I wanted to tell you that your two oarsmen are forgotten, and to ask you if we hadn't better call to them to come up here, where they'll be out of danger?"

"They are *not* forgotten," said Roughgrove; "I sent them over the river to procure assistance, if possible."

"Thank you. I'm glad they're out of danger. I couldn't rest till I found out something about them," said Joe, retiring; but instead of resuming his watch, he slipped into the house.

"He's at his old tricks agin," said Sneak, when he observed him stealthily enter the door. "Come out, I say!" he continued, in a loud voice.

"What is the matter?" interrogated Glenn, from his station on the north.

"Why, that feller's crept into the house agin, replied Sneak."

"Well, but he's come out again," said Joe, reappearing, and walking reluctantly to his loophole.

"What did you go in for?" demanded Glenn.

"I just wanted to tell Miss Mary that the two oarsmen that helped us to bury Posin were gone over the river, and were safe."

"Did she ask for this information?" inquired Glenn.

"No, not exactly," responded Joe; "but I thought if I was uneasy about the young men myself, that she, being more delicate than a man, must be considerably distressed."

"A mere subterfuge! See that you do not leave your post in future, under any circumstances, without permission to do so."

"I won't," replied Joe, peering through his loophole.

Matters remained quiet for a great length of time, and Glenn began to hope that even Boone had been mistaken. But Boone himself had no doubts upon the subject. Yet he seemed far more affable and cheerful than he did before the plan of resistance was formed in his mind. Occasionally he would walk round from post to post, and after scanning the aspect without, direct the sentinels to observe closely certain points, trees or bushes, where he thought the enemy might first be seen. He never hinted once that there was a possibility of escaping an attack, and the little party felt that the only alternative was to watch with diligence and act with vigor and resolution when assailed.

"Do you think they are now in this immediate neighbourhood?" inquired Glenn.

"They are not far off, I imagine," replied Boone; and calling the hounds from the stable, he continued, "I can show you in which quarter they are." The hounds well understood their old master. At his bidding they snuffed the air, and whining in a peculiar manner, with their heads turned towards the west, the vicinity of the savages was not only made manifest, but their location positively pointed out.

"I was not aware, before, of the inestimable value of your gift," said Glenn, gazing at the hounds, and completely convinced that their conduct was an unerring indication of the presence of the foe.

"Eh! Ringwood!" exclaimed Boone, observing that his favorite hound now pointed his nose in a northern direction and uttered a low growl. "Indeed!" he continued, "they have got in motion since we have been observing the hounds. I was not mistaken. Even while we were speaking they divided their strength. One party is even now moving round to the east, and at a given signal the other will attack us on the west, precisely as I predicted. See! Ringwood turns gradually."

"And you think the greatest danger is to be apprehended from those on the east?" said Glenn.

"Yes," said Boone, "for the others cannot approach near enough to do much injury without exposing themselves to great peril."

"But how can you ascertain that they will cut a passage under the snow, and the precise direction in which they will come?"

"Because," said Boone, "we are situated near the cliff on the east, to the summit of which they can climb, without being exposed to our fire, and thence it is likewise the shortest distance they can find to cut a passage to us under the snow. Mark Ringwood!" he continued, as the hound having made a semicircle from the point first noticed, became at length stationary, and crouching down on the earth, (where the snow had been cleared away at Boone's post,) growled more angrily than before, but so low he could not have been heard twenty paces distant.

"This is strange—very strange," said Glenn.

A sound resembling the cry of an owl was heard in the direction of the cliff. It was answered on the west apparently by the shrill howl of a wolf.

"The signal!" said Boone. "Now let us be on *the* alert," he continued, "and I think we will surprise *them,* both on and under the snow. Let no one fire without first consulting me, even should they venture within the range of your guns."

The party resumed their respective stations, and once more not a sound of any description was heard for a considerable length of time. Roughgrove was at the side of Boone, and the other three men were posted as before described. The hounds had been sent back to their lair in the stable. Not a motion, animate or inanimate, save the occasional shooting of the stars in the begemmed firmament, could be observed.

While Glenn rested upon his gun, attracted ever and anon by the twinkling host above, a throng of unwonted memories crowded upon him. He thought of his guileless youth; the uncontaminated days of enjoyment ere he had mingled with the designing and heartless associates who strove to entice him from the path of virtue; of the hopes of budding manhood; of ambitious schemes to win a name by great and honourable deeds; of parents, kindred, home; of *her,* who had been the angel of all his dreams of paradise below: and then he contemplated his present condition, and notwithstanding his resolution was unabated, yet in spite of all his struggles, a tear bedewed his cheek. He felt that his fate was hard, but he *knew* that his course was proper, and he resolved to fulfil his vow. But with his sadness, gloomy forebodings, and deep and unusual thoughts obtruded. In the scene of death and carnage that was about to ensue, it occurred to him more than once that it might be his lot to fall. This was a painful thought. He was brave in conflict, and would not have hesitated to rush reckless into the midst of danger; but he was calm now, and the thought of death was appalling. He would have preferred to die on a nobler field, if he were to fall in battle. He did not wish to die in his *youth,* to be cut off, without accomplishing the many ends he had so often meditated, and without reaping a few of the sweets of life as the reward of his voluntary sacrifice. He also desired to appear once more in the busy and detracting world, to vindicate the character that might have been unjustly aspersed, to reward the true friendship of those whose confidence had never been shaken, and to rebuke, perhaps forgive, the enemies who had recklessly pursued him. But another, and yet a more stirring and important thought obtruded upon his reflections. It was one he had never seriously considered before, and it now operated upon him with irresistible power. It was a thought of things *beyond* the grave. The stillness of midnight, the million stars above him, the blue eternal expanse through which they were distributed—the repose of the invisible winds, that late had howled around him—the never-ceasing flow of the ice-bound stream before him, and the continual change of hill and valley—now desolate, and clothed in frosty vestments, and anon teeming with verdure and variegated beauty—constrained him to acknowledge in the secret portals of his breast that there was a great, ever-existing Creator. He then called to mind the many impressive lessons of a pious mother, which he had subsequently disregarded. He remembered the things she had read to him in the book of books—the words of prayer she taught him to utter every eve, ere he closed his eyes in slumber—and he *now* repeated that humble petition with all the fervency of a chastened spirit. He felt truly convinced of the fallacy of setting the heart and the affections altogether on the things of this world, where mortals are only permitted to abide but a brief space; and a hearty repentance of past errors, and a firm resolve to obey the requisitions of the Omnipotent in future, were in that hour conceived and engraven indelibly upon his heart.

"Mr. Boone—Mr. Boone—Mr. Boone!" cried Joe, softly.

"Dod! don't make sich a fuss," said Sneak.

"Be silent," whispered Boone, gliding to Joe, and gazing out on the snow, where he beheld about twenty savages standing erect and motionless, not eighty paces distant.

"I came within an ace of shooting," said Joe, "before I thought of what you had said. I pulled the trigger with all my might before I remembered that you said I mustn't shoot till you told me, but as good luck would have it, my musket wasn't cocked." Boone went to each of the other loopholes, and after scrutinizing every side very closely, he directed Sneak and Glenn to abandon their posts and join him at Joe's stand, for the purpose of discharging a deadly volley at the unsuspecting foe.

"Does it not seem cruel to spill blood in this manner?" whispered Glenn, when he viewed the statue-like forms of the unconscious Indians.

"Had you witnessed the barbarous deeds that *I* have seen *them* perform—had you beheld the innocent babe ruthlessly butchered—your children—your friends maimed, tomahawked, scalped, *burned* before your eyes—could you know the hellish horrors they are *now* meditating—you would not entertain much pity for them," said Boone, in a low tone, evidently moved by terrible memories, the precise nature of which the one addressed could not understand. But Glenn's scruples vanished, and as a matter of necessity he determined to submit without reserve to the guidance of his experienced friend.

"I should like to know how them yaller rascals got up here so close without being eyed sooner," said Sneak to Joe.

"That's what's been puzzling me, ever since I first saw them," said Joe, in scarce audible tones.

"Split me if you havn't been asleep," said Sneak.

"No indeed I havn't," said Joe. "I'll declare," he continued, looking out, "I never should have thought of *that*. I see now, well enough, how they got there without my seeing them. They've got a great big ball of snow, half as high as a man's head, and they've been rolling it all the time, and creeping along behind it. They're all standing before it now, and just as I looked one moved his leg, and then I saw what it was. This beats the old boy himself. It's a mercy they didn't come all the way and shoot me in the eye!"

"Hush!" said Boone. "They must have heard something, or supposed they did, or else your neglect would have been fatal to you ere this. They are now waiting to ascertain whether they were mistaken or not. Move not, and speak no more, until I order you."

"I won't," said Joe, still gazing at the erect dark forms.

"See how many there is—can't you count 'em?" said Sneak, in a whisper, leaning against Joe, and slyly taking a cartridge from his belt, slipped it in the muzzle of the musket which was standing against the palisade.

"What're you doing with my gun?" asked Joe, in a very low tone, as he happened to turn his head and see Sneak take his hand away from the muzzle of the musket.

"Nothing—I was only feeling the size of the bore. It's big enough to kick down a cow."

"What are you tittering about? you think it's a going to kick me again, but you're mistaken—it ain't got two loads in this time."

"Didn't Mr. Boone jest tell you to keep quiet?" said Sneak.

"Don't you speak—then I won't," responded Joe.

The moon had not yet reached the meridian, and the dark shadow of the house reaching to the palisade on the west, prevented the Indians from observing the movements of the whites through the many slight apertures in the inclosure, but through which the besieged party could easily observe them.

After a long pause, during which neither party had uttered a word or betrayed animation by the least movement, Glenn felt the weight of a hand laid gently on his shoulder, and turning beheld Mary at his side. Without a motion of the lips, she placed in his hand some bullets she had moulded, and then passing on to the other men, gave each a like quantity.

"Retire, now, my lass," said Boone; and when she returned to the house, he continued, addressing Glenn—"If they do not move one way or the other very soon, we will give them a broadside where they are."

"And we could do execution at this distance," observed Glenn.

"I'd be dead sure to kill one, I know I would," said Sneak.

"Let me see if I could take aim," said Joe, deliberately pointing his musket through the loophole. The musket had inadvertently been cocked, and left in that condition, and no sooner did Joe's finger gently press upon the trigger, than it went off, making an astounding report, and veiling the whole party in an immense cloud of smoke.

"Who did that?" cried Boone, stamping with vexation.

"Was that you, Joe?" demanded Glenn.

Joe made no answer.

"Oh, dod! my mouth's smashed all to pieces!" said Sneak, crawling up from a prostrate position, caused by the rebound of the musket, for he was looking over Joe's shoulder when the gun went off.

"Where's Joe?" inquired Glenn, pushing Sneak aside.

"He's dead, I guess—I believe the gun's busted," said Sneak.

"Now, sir! why did you fire?" cried Glenn, somewhat passionately, stumbling against Joe, and seizing him by the collar. No answer was made, for poor Joe's neck was limber enough, and he quite insensible.

"He's dead in yearnest, jest as I told you," said Sneak; "for that gun kicked him on the shoulder hard enough to kill a cow—and the hind side of his head struck my tooth hard enough to've kilt a horse. He's broke one of my upper fore-teeth smack in two."

"Every man to his post!" exclaimed Boone, as a shower of arrows rattled about the premises.

Sneak now occupied Joe's station, and the first glance in the direction of the savages sufficed to determine him how to act. Perhaps no one ever discharged a rifle more rapidly than he did. And a brisk and well-directed fire was kept up for some length of time, likewise, by the rest of the besieged.

It was, perhaps, a fortunate thing that Joe *did* fire without orders, and without any intention of doing so himself. It seemed that the savages had been meditating a desperate rush upon the fort, notwithstanding Boone's prediction; for no sooner did Joe fire, than they hastily retreated a short distance, scattering in every direction, and, without a moment's consultation, again appeared, advancing rapidly from every quarter. It was evident that this plan had been preconcerted among them; and had all fired, instead of Joe only, they might easily have scaled the palisade before the guns could have been reloaded. Neither had the besiegers been aware of the strength of the garrison. But they were soon made to understand that they had more than Glenn and his man to contend against. The discharges followed in such quick succession that they paused, when but a moment more would have placed them within the inclosure. But several of them being wounded, and Boone and Glenn still doing execution with their pistols, the discomfited enemy made a precipitate retreat. An occasional flight of arrows continued to assail the besieged, but they came from a great distance, for the Indians were not long in scampering beyond the range of the loopholes.

When Glenn could no longer see any of the dark forms of the enemy, he turned round to contemplate the sad condition of Joe. Joe was sitting up, with his hands locked round his knees.

"Well, split me in two!" cried Sneak, staring at his companion.

"What's the matter, Sneak?" asked Joe, with much simplicity.

"That's a purty question for *you* to ask, after laying there for dead this half-hour almost."

"Have the Indians been here?" asked Joe, staring round wildly.

"Hain't you heard us shooting?"

"My goodness," cried Joe, springing up. "Oh! am I wounded? say!" he continued, evincing the most lively alarm.

"Well, if this don't beat every thing that ever I saw in all my life, I wish I may be shot!" said Sneak.

"What is it?" asked Joe, his senses yet wandering.

"Jest feel the back of your head," said Sneak. Joe put his hand to the place indicated, and winced under the pain of the touch. He then looked at his hand, and beholding a quantity of clotted blood upon it, fell down suddenly on the snow.

"What's the matter now?" asked Glenn, who had seen his man sitting up, and came swiftly to him when he fell.

"I'm a dead man!" said Joe, mournfully.

"That's a lie!" said Sneak.

"What ails you, Joe?" asked Glenn, his tone much softened.

"I'm dying—oh! I'm shot through the head!"

"Don't believe him, Mr. Glenn—I'll be smashed if its any thing but my tooth," said Sneak.

"Oh—I'm dying!" continued Joe, pressing his hand against his head, while the pain and loss of blood actually produced a faintness, and his voice became very weak.

"Are you really much hurt?" continued Glenn, stooping down, and feeling his pulse.

"It's all over!" muttered Joe. "I'm going fast. Sanete Petre!—Pater noster, qui es in cœlis, sanctificeter nomen tuum; adveniat regnum tu—"

Here Joe's voice failed, and, falling into a syncope, Glenn and Sneak lifted him up and carried him into the house.

"Is he shot?" exclaimed Mary, instantly producing some lint and bandages which she had prepared in anticipation of such an event.

"I fear he has received a serious hurt," said Glenn, aiding Mary, who had proceeded at once to bind up the wound.

"I'll be split if he's shot!" said Sneak, going out and returning to his post. Glenn did likewise when he saw the first indications of returning consciousness in his man; and Mary was left alone to restore and nurse poor Joe. But he could not have been in better hands.

"I should like to know something about them curious words the feller was speaking when he keeled over," said Sneak, as he looked out at the now quiet scene from the loophole, and mused over the events of the night. "I begin to believe that the feller's a going to die. I don't believe any man could talk so, if he wasn't dying."

"Have you seen any of them lately?" inquired Boone, coming to Sneak's post and running his eye along the horizon through the loophole.

"Not a one," replied Sneak, "except that feller laying out yander by the snowball."

"He's dead," said Boone, "and he is the only one that we are sure of having killed to-night. But many are wounded."

"And smash me if Joe didn't kill that one when his musket went off before he was ready," said Sneak.

"Yes, I saw him fall when Joe fired; and that accident was, after all, a fortunate thing for us," continued Boone.

"But I'm sorry for poor Joe," said Sneak.

"Pshaw!" said Boone; "he'll be well again in an hour."

"No, he's a gone chicken."

"Why do you think so?"

"Didn't he say so himself? and didn't he gabble out a whole parcel of purgatory talk? He's as sure gone as a stuck pig, I tell you," continued Sneak.

"He will eat as hearty a breakfast to-morrow morning as ever he did in his life," said Boone. "But let us attend to the business in hand. I hardly think we will be annoyed any more from this quarter, unless yonder dead Indian was a chief, and then it is more than probable they will try to steal him away. However, you may remain here. I, alone, can manage the others."

"Which others?" inquired Sneak.

"Those under the snow," replied Boone; "they are now within twenty paces of the palisade."

"You don't say so?" said Sneak, cocking his gun.

"I have been listening to them cutting through the snow a long while, and it will be a half hour yet before I spring the mine," said Boone.

"I hope it will kill 'em all!" said Sneak.

"Watch close, and perhaps *you* will kill one yet from this loophole," said Boone, returning to his post, where the slow-match was exposed through the palisade near the ground; and Roughgrove stood by, holding a pistol, charged with powder only, in readiness to fire the train when Boone should give the word of command.

Boone applied his ear to a crevice between the timbers near the earth, where the snow had been cleared away. After remaining in this position a few moments, he beckoned Glenn to him.

"Place your ear against this crevice," said Boone.

"It is not the Indians I hear, certainly!" remarked Glenn. The sounds resembled the ticking of a large clock, differing only in their greater rapidity than the strokes of seconds.

"Most certainly it is nothing else," replied Boone.

"But how do they produce such singular sounds? Is it the trampling of feet?" continued Glenn.

"It is the sound of many tomahawks cutting a passage," replied Boone.

"But what disposition do they make of the snow, when it is cut loose."

"A portion of them dig, while the rest convey the loose snow out and cast it down the cliff."

While the above conversation was going on, a colloquy of a different nature transpired within the house. Joe, after recovering from his second temporary insensibility, had sunk into a gentle doze, which lasted many minutes. Mary had bathed his face repeatedly with sundry restoratives, and likewise administered a cordial that she had brought from her father's house, which seemed to have a most astonishing somniferous effect. When the contents of the bottle were exhausted, she sat silently by, watching Joe's apparent slumber, and felt rejoiced that her patient promised a speedy recovery. Once, after she had been gazing at the fawn, (that had been suffered to occupy a place near the wall, where it was now coiled up and sleeping,) on turning her eyes towards the face of Joe, she imagined for a moment that she saw him close his eyelids quickly. But calling him softly and receiving no answer, she concluded it was a mere fancy, and again resigned herself to her lonely watch. When she had been sitting thus some minutes, watching him patiently, she observed his eyes open slowly, and quickly smack to again, when he found that she was looking at him. But a moment after, conscious that his wakefulness was discovered, he opened them boldly, and found himself possessed of a full recollection of all the incidents of the night up to his disaster.

"Have they whipt all the Indians away that were standing out on the snow, Miss Mary?"

"Yes, long ago—and none have been seen, but the one you killed, for some time," she replied, encouragingly.

"Did I kill one sure enough?" asked Joe, while his eyes sparkled exceedingly.

"Yes, indeed," replied she; "and I heard Mr. Boone say he was glad it happened, and that the accident was, after all, a fortunate thing for us."

"*Accident!*" iterated Joe; "who says it was an accident?"

"Wasn't it an accident?" asked the simple girl.

"No, indeed!" replied Joe. "But," he continued, "have they blown up the other Indians yet?"

"Not yet—but I heard them say they would do it very soon. They can be heard digging under the snow now, very plainly," said Mary.

"Indeed!" said Joe, with no little terror depicted in his face. "I wish you'd go and ask Mr. Boone if he thinks you'll be entirely safe, if you please, Miss Mary," said Joe beseechingly.

"I will," responded Mary, rising to depart.

"And if they ask how I am," continued Joe, "please say I am a great deal better, but too weak yet to go out."

Mary did his bidding; and when she returned, what was her astonishment to find her patient running briskly across the room from the cupboard, with a whole roasted prairiehen in one hand, or at least the body of it, while he tore away the breast with his teeth, and some half dozen crackers in the other! In vain did he attempt to conceal them under the covering of his bed, into which he jumped as quickly as possible. Guilt was manifest in his averted look, his trembling hand, and his greasy mouth! Mary gazed in silent wonder. Joe cowered under her glance a few moments, until the irresistible flavour of the fowl overcame him, and then his jaws were again set in motion.

"I fear that eating will injure you," remarked Mary, at length.

"Never fear," replied Joe. "When a sick person has a good appetite, it's a sure sign he's getting better."

"If you think so you can eat as much as you please," said Mary; "and you needn't hide any thing from me."

Joe felt a degree of shame in being so palpably detected, but his appetite soon got the better of his scruples, and he gratified the demands of his stomach without reserve.

"But what did Mr. Boone say?" asked he, peeping out.

"He says he thinks there is no danger. But the Indians are now within a few feet of the palisade, and the explosion is about to take place."

CHAPTER IX

"DON'T you think I know who you are, and what you're after?" said Sneak, as he observed a large black sow, or what seemed to be one, rambling about on the snow within a hundred paces of him. "If that ain't *my* sow! She's gone, that's dead sure; and if I don't pepper the red rascal that killed her I wish I may be split. That Indian 'll find I'm not such a fool as he took me for. Just wait till he gits close enough. I ain't to be deceived by my own sow's dead skin, with a great big Osage in it, nohow you can fix it." Sneak's conjecture was right. The Indian that Joe had killed was a chief, and the apparent sow was nothing more than a savage enveloped in a swine's skin. The Indian, after reconnoitering the premises with some deliberation, evidently believed that his stratagem was successful, and at length moved in the direction of his dead comrade, with the manifest intention of bearing the body away.

"I'll let you have it now!" said Sneak, firing his rifle, when the seeming sow began to drag the fallen chief from the field. The discharge took effect; the savage sprang upright and endeavoured to retreat in the manner that nature designed him to run; but he did not go more than a dozen paces before he sank down and expired.

"That's tit for tat, for killing my sow," said Sneak, gazing at his postrate foe.

"Come here, Sneak," said Boone, from the opposite side of the inclosure.

"There was but one, and I fixed him," said Sneak, when they asked him how many of the enemy were in view when he fired.

"They heard the gun," said Glenn, applying his ear to the chink, and remarking that the Indians had suddenly ceased to work under the snow.

"Be quiet," said Boone; "they will begin again in a minute or two."

"They're at it a'ready," said Sneak, a moment after, and very soon they were heard again, more distinctly than ever, cutting away with increased rapidity.

"Suppose the match does not burn?" observed Glenn, in tones betraying a fearful apprehension.

"In such an event," said Boone, "we must retreat into the house, and fasten the door without a moment's delay. But I do not much fear any such failure, for the dampness of the snow cannot so soon have penetrated through the dry reeds to the powder. Still we should be prepared—therefore, as there is no necessity that more than one of us should be here now, and as I am that man, withdraw, all of you, within the house, and remain there until your ears and eyes shall dictate what course to pursue." Boone's command was promptly obeyed, and when they reached the house and looked back, (the door was kept open,) they beheld the renowned pioneer standing erect, holding a pistol in his right hand (which he pointed at the cotton that connected with a train of powder running along a short plank to the reed that reached the buried keg,) while the moon, now midway in the heavens, "and beautifully bright," revealed the stern and determined expression of his pale brow and fixed lip. Thus he stood many minutes, and they seemed hours to those who gazed upon the breathless scene from the house. Not a sound was heard, save the rapid ticking of tomahawks under the snow outside of the inclosure, or the occasional hasty remark of those who were looking on in painful and thrilling suspense. Once Boone bowed his head and listened an instant to the operations of the savages, and when he rose erect again, the party looking on confidently expected he would fire the train. But the fatal moment had not yet arrived. Still he pointed the pistol at the combustible matter, and his eye glanced along the barrel; but he maintained a statue-like stillness, as if awaiting some preconcerted signal.

"Why don't he fire?" inquired Glenn, in a whisper.

"It is not quite time yet," responded Roughgrove.

"Dod! they'll crawl up presently, and jump over the fence," said Sneak.

"Oh, goodness! I wish he'd shoot!" said Joe, in low, sepulchral tones, his head thrust between Sneak's legs, whither he had crawled unobserved, and was now peering out at the scene.

"Who are you?" exclaimed Sneak, leaping away from Joe's bandaged head, which he did not recognize at the first glance.

"It's nobody but me," said Joe, turning his face upward, that his friend might not suppose him an enemy.

"Well, what are you doing here? I thought you was a dying."

"I'm a good deal better, but I'm too weak to do any thing yet," said Joe, in piteous tones, as he looked fearfully at Boone, and listened to the strokes of the Indians without, which became louder and louder.

"Stand back a little," said Boone to those in the doorway, "that I may enter when I fire—the match may burn more briskly than I anticipated."

A passage was opened for him to enter. He pulled the trigger—the pistol missed fire—he deliberately poured in fresh priming from his horn, and once more taking aim, the pistol was discharged, and, running to the house, and entering a little beyond the threshold, he paused, and turned to behold the realization of his hopes. The light combustible matter flashed up brightly, and the blaze ran along the ground a moment in the direction of the end of the reed, but at the instant when all expected to see the powder ignited, the flames seemed to die away, and the darkness which succeeded impressed them with the fear that the damp snow had, indeed, defeated their purpose.

"Split me if it *shan't* go off!" cried Sneak, running out with a torch in his hand, that he snatched from the fireplace. When he reached the trench that had been dug along the palisade, and in which the slow match was placed, he looked down but once, and dashing his fire-brand behind him, sprang back to the house, with all the celerity of which he was capable. "Dod!" said he, "it's burning yet, but we couldn't see it from here. It'll set the powder off in less than no time!"

"I trust it will!" said Boone, with much anxiety. And truly the crisis had arrived, beyond which, if it were delayed a single minute, it would be too late! The *voices* of the Indians could now be heard, and the sounds of the tomahawks had ceased. They were evidently on the eve of breaking through the icy barrier, and rushing upon their victims. Boone, with a composed but livid brow, placed his hand upon the ponderous door, for the purpose of retreating within, and barring out the ruthless assailants. The rest instinctively imitated his motions, but at the same time their eyes were yet riveted on the dimly burning match. A small flash was observed to illumine the trench— another and a larger one succeeded! The first train of powder was ignited—the Indians were bursting through the snow-crust with direful yells—the blaze ran quickly along the plank—it reached the end of the reed—a shrill whizzing sound succeeded—a sharp crash under the snow—and then all was involved in a tremendous chaotic explosion! An enormous circular cloud of smoke enveloped the scene for a moment, and then could be seen tomahawks, bows, and arrows, and even *savages,* sailing through the air. The moon was darkened for the space of several minutes, during which time immense quantities of snow poured down from above. The startling report seemed to rend both the earth and the heavens, and rumbled far up and down the valley of the Missouri, like the deep bellowing of a coruscant thunder-cloud, and died away in successive vibrations until it finally resembled the partially suppressed growling of an angry lion.

When the inmates of the house sallied forth, the scene was again quiet. After clearing away the enormous masses of snow from the palisade, they looked out from the inclosure through the loophole on the east, and all was stillness and silence. But the view was changed. Instead of the level and smooth surface, they now beheld a concave formation of snow, beginning at the earth, which was laid bare where the powder had been deposited, and widening, upward and outward, till the ring of the extreme angle reached a height of fifteen or twenty feet, and measured a circumference of fifty paces. But they did not discover a single dead body. On the contrary, they soon distinguished the sounds of the savages afar off, in fiendish and fearful yells, as they retreated in great precipitation.

"Dod! none of 'em's killed!" exclaimed Sneak, looking about in disappointment.

"Hang it all, how could they expect to kill any, without putting in some lead?" replied Joe, standing at his elbow, and evincing no symptoms of illness.

"What're *you* a doing out here? You'd better go in and finish dying," said Sneak.

"No, I thank you," said Joe; "my time's not come yet; and when it does come, I'll know what to do without your instructions. I'm well now—I never felt better in my life, only when I was eating."

"Go to the horses, Joe, and see if they have suffered any injury," said Glenn. "I don't believe a single Indian was killed by the explosion," he continued, addressing Boone.

"The snow may have preserved them," replied Boone; "and yet," he continued, "I am sure I saw some of them flying up in the air."

"I saw them too," said Glenn, "but I have known instances of the kind, when powder-mills have blown up, where men were thrown a considerable distance without being much injured."

"It answered our purpose, at all events," said Boone, "for now, no inducement whatever can ever bring them back."

"If I were sure of that," replied Glenn, "I would not regret the bloodless result of the explosion."

"You may rely upon it implicitly," said Boone; "for it was a surprise they can never understand, and they will attach to it some superstitious interpretation, which will most effectually prevent them from meditating another attack."

"Goodness gracious alive!" exclaimed Joe, nimbly springing past Boone and Glenn, and rushing into the house.

"What can be the matter with the fellow, now?" exclaimed Glenn.

"He was alarmed at something in the stable—see what it is, Sneak," said Boone.

"I've got you, have I? Dod! come out here!" exclaimed Sneak, when he had been in the stable a few moments.

"Who are you talking to?" asked Glenn.

"A venimirous Osage smutty-face!" said Sneak, stepping out of the stable door backwards, and dragging an Indian after him by the ears.

"What is that?" demanded Glenn, staring at the singular object before him. The question was by no means an unnatural one, for no being in the human shape ever seemed less like a man. The unresisting and bewildered savage looked wildly round, displaying a face as black as if he had just risen from the bottom of some infernal lake. His tattered buckskin garments had shared the same fate in the explosion; his eyebrows, and the hair of his head were singed and crisped; and, altogether he might easily have passed for one of Pluto's scullions. He did not make resistance when Sneak led him forth, seeming to anticipate nothing else than an instantaneous and cruel death, and was apparently resigned to his fate. He doubtless imagined that escape and longer life were utterly impossible, inasmuch as, to his comprehension, he was in the grasp of evil spirits. If he had asked himself *how* he came thither, it could not have occurred to him that any other means than the agency of a supernatural power threw him into the hands of the foe.

"I thought I saw one of them plunging through the air over the inclosure," said Boone, smiling.

"Hanged if I didn't think so too," said Joe, who had at length returned to gaze at the captive, when he ascertained that he was entirely meek and inoffensive.

"Have you got over your fright already?" asked Sneak.

"What fright?" demanded Joe, with affected surprise.

"Now, *can* you say you weren't skeered?"

"Ha! ha! ha! I believe you really thought I *was* frightened. Why, you dunce, you! I only ran in to to tell Miss Mary about it."

"Now go to bed. Don't speak to me agin to night," said Sneak, indignantly.

"I'll go and get something to eat," said Joe, retreating into the house.

"Tell Roughgrove to come here," said Boone, speaking to Joe.

"I will," said Joe, vanishing through the door.

When the old ferryman came out, Boone requested him (he being the most familiar with the Osage language,) to ask the savage by what means he was enabled to get inside of the inclosure. Roughgrove did his bidding; and the Indian replied that the Great Spirit *threw* him over the palisade, because he once killed a friend of Boone's at the cave-spring, and was now attempting to kill another.

"Why did you wish to kill us?" asked Roughgrove.

The Indian said it was because they thought Glenn had a great deal of money, many fire weapons, and powder and bullets, which they (the savages) wanted.

"Was it *right* to rob the white man of these things, and then to murder him?" continued Roughgrove.

The savage replied that the prophet (Raven) had told the war-party it was right. Besides, they came a long and painful journey to get (Glenn's) goods, and had suffered much with cold in digging under the snow; several of their party had been killed and wounded, and he thought they had a good right to every thing they could get.

"Did the whites ever go to your village to rob and murder?" inquired the old ferryman.

The Indian assumed a proud look, and replied that they *had*. He said that the buffalo, the bear, the deer, and the beaver—the eternal prairies and forests—the rivers, the air and the sky, all belonged to the red men. That the whites had not been *invited* to come among them, but they had intruded upon their lands, stolen their game, and killed their warriors. Yet, he said, the Indians did not hate Boone, and would not have attacked the premises that night, if they had known he was there.

"Why do they not hate Boone? He has killed more of them than any one else in this region," continued Roughgrove.

The Indian said that Boone was a great prophet, and was loved by the Great Spirit.

"Will the war-party return hither to-night?" asked Roughgrove.

The Indian answered in the negative; and added that they would never attack that place again, because the Great Spirit had fought against them.

Boone requested Roughgrove to ask what would be done with the false prophet who had advised them to make the attack.

The savage frowned fiercely, and replied that he would be tied to a tree, and shot through the heart a hundred times.

"What do you think we intend to do to *you?*" asked Roughgrove.

The savage said he would be skinned alive and put under the ice in the river, or burned to death by a slow fire. He said he was ready to die.

"I'll be shot if he isn't a spunky fellow!" said Sneak.

"Do you desire such a fate?" continued the old ferryman.

"The Indian looked at him with surprise, and answered without hesitation that he *did*—and then insisted upon being killed immediately.

"Would you attempt to injure the white man again if we were not to kill you?"

The Indian smiled, but made no answer.

"I am in earnest," continued Roughgrove, "and wish to know what you would do if we spared your life."

The Indian said such talk was only trifling, and again insisted upon being dispatched.

After a short consultation with Boone and Glenn, Roughgrove repeated his question.

The savage replied that he did not believe it possible for him to escape immediate death—but if he were not killed, he could never think of hurting any of those, who saved him, afterwards. Yet he stated very frankly that he would kill and rob any *other* pale-faces he might meet with.

"Let me blow his brains out," said Sneak, throwing his gun up to his shoulder. The Indian understood the movement, if not the words, and turning towards him, presented a full front, without quailing.

"He speaks the truth," said Boone; "he would never injure any of us himself, nor permit any of his tribe to do it, so far as his influence extended. Yet he will die rather than make a promise not to molest others. His word may be strictly relied upon. It is not fear that extorts the promise never to war against us—it would be his gratitude for sparing his life. Take down your gun, Sneak. Let us decide upon his fate. I am in favour of liberating him."

"And I," said Glenn.

"And I," said Roughgrove.

"I vote for killing him," said Sneak.

"Hanged if I don't, too," said Joe, who had been listening from the door.

"Spare him," said Mary, who came out, and saw what was passing.

"We have the majority, Mary," said Glenn; "and when innocence pleads, the generous hand is stayed."

Roughgrove motioned the savage to follow, and he led him to the gate. The prisoner did not understand what was to be done. He evidently supposed that his captors were about to slay him, and he looked up, as he thought, the last time, at the moon and the stars, and his lips moved in deep and silent adoration.

Roughgrove opened the gate, and the savage followed him out, composedly awaiting his fate. But seeing no indication of violence, and calling to mind the many wild joys of his roving youth, and the horrors of a sudden death, he spoke not, yet his brilliant eyes were dimmed for a moment with tears. His deep gaze seemed to implore mercy at the hands of his captors. He would not utter a petition that his life might be spared, yet his breast heaved to rove free again over the flowery prairies, to bathe in the clear waters of running streams, to inhale the balmy air of midsummer morning, to chase the panting deer upon the dizzy peak, and to hail once more the bright smiles of his timid bride in the forest-shadowed glen.

"Go! thou art free!" said Roughgrove.

The Indian stared in doubt, and looked reproachfully at the guns in the hands of his captors, as if he thought they were only mocking him with hopes of freedom, when it was their intention to shoot him down the moment he should think his life was truly spared.

"Go! we will not harm thee!" repeated Roughgrove.

"And take this," said Mary, placing some food in his yielding hand.

The Indian gazed upon the maiden's face. His features, by a magical transition, now beamed with confidence and hope. Mary was in tears—not tears of pity for his impending death, but a gush of generous emotion that his life was spared. The savage read her heart—he knew that the white woman never intercedes in vain, and that no victim falls when sanctified by her tears. He clasped her hand and pressed it to his lips; and then turning away in silence, set off in a stately and deliberate pace towards the west. He looked not back to see if a treacherous gun was pointed at him. He knew that the maiden had not trifled with him. He knew that she would not mock a dying man with bread. He neither looked back nor quickened his step. And so he vanished from view in the valley.

"Dod! he's gone! We ought to've had his sculp!" said Sneak, betraying serious mortification.

"We must give it up, though—we were in the minority," said Joe, satisfied with the decision.

"In the what?" asked Sneak.

"In the minority," said Joe.

"Let's go in the house and git something to eat," said Sneak.

"Hang me if I ain't willing to be with you there," said Joe.

The whole party entered the house to partake of a collation prepared by the dainty hands of Mary. Mary had frequently insisted upon serving them with refreshments during the night, but hitherto all her persuasions had been unavailing, for the dangers that beset them on every hand had banished all other thoughts than those of determined defensive operations.

Boone was so certain that nothing farther was to be apprehended from the enemy, that he dispensed with the sentinels at the loopholes. He relied upon Ringwood and Jowler to guard them through the remainder of the night; and when a hearty meal was eaten he directed his gallant little band to enjoy their wonted repose.

49

WILLIAM TAPPAN THOMPSON

(1812–1882)

William Tappan Thompson, a literary protégé of Augustus Baldwin Longstreet, was born on August 31, 1812, in the frontier village of Ravenna, Ohio. Orphaned at fourteen, Thompson struck out for Philadelphia, where he became a printer's devil at the *Daily Chronicle.* He left Philadelphia about 1830 to become the personal assistant of James D. Westcott, secretary of the territory of Florida.

After four years with Westcott, Thompson moved to Augusta, Georgia, to study law with Longstreet. At that time Longstreet was editing and publishing the Augusta *States' Rights Sentinel,* where his literary sketches, the "Georgia Scenes," were then appearing. Thompson probably set type for the *Sentinel,* and may have helped to set type for the first edition of Longstreet's *Georgia Scenes* (1835).

In early 1836 Thompson left Augusta with the Richmond Blues, a unit of volunteers for the Second Seminole War (1835–1842) in Florida. This conflict was a result of the Indian Removal Act of 1830, which had called for the relocation of all natives to west of the Mississippi River. Understandably, many Seminoles did not want to move. Between February 2 and March 29, 1836, the *Sentinel* published fifteen unsigned reports from a member of the Blues; most, if not all, were by Thompson. The Blues returned to Augusta in May.

In 1838 Thompson and James McCafferty, a fellow veteran of the Blues, founded the *Augusta Mirror,* Georgia's first literary magazine. The mission of the *Mirror* was "to afford a suitable medium through which the productions of southern talent and genius, may find their way into the literary world." Among the talented southerners whose fiction appeared in the *Mirror* was Thompson himself. In early 1842 the *Mirror* merged with and took the name of the Macon (Georgia) *Family Companion and Ladies' Mirror.* In June 1842, *The Family Companion* published the first of Thompson's Major Jones letters.

Thompson did not get along with his co-editor at *The Family Companion,* which prompted him to leave after the July 1842 issue. Beginning the next month, Thompson edited the Madison (Georgia) *Southern Miscellany,* where additional Major Jones letters appeared. The first edition of *Major Jones' Courtship,* Thompson's best-known work, was published in 1843 as a premium for *Southern Miscellany* subscribers. In 1850 Thompson helped to establish the Savannah *Morning News,* which he edited until his death on March 24, 1882.

"The Seminole Dance," the first of Thompson's published literary sketches, appeared in the Augusta *State Rights' Sentinel* on July 8, 1836. It is based on his experiences while working for Westcott, with whom he twice visited the Seminole reservation in central Florida. Thompson's biographer Herbert Shippey notes that in 1843 Thompson wrote of having once danced with the Seminoles. It is impossible to say, however, whether "The Seminole Dance" is strictly autobiographical.

Text: "The Seminole Dance," *Augusta State Rights' Sentinel* (July 8, 1836): 2.

THE SEMINOLE DANCE (1836)

An Extract from the Journal of a Private Secretary

"Nae cotillion brent new frae France,
But hornpipes, jigs, strathspies and reels,
Put life and mettle in their heels."

—BURNS

"And a change came o'er the spirit of my dream."

—BYRON

"It was just in the *edge* of a fine summer's evening," as N. P. Willis would say, or (in plain English) it was about 5 o'clock on just such an evening, that an Indian came to the fort, with a message from the head chief to the Governor. The payment of the annuity had just been completed, and the Indians, who had all returned to their villages, were now about to celebrate that important event with a grand national dance, and it was for the purpose of inviting us to attend, that the young Indian just mentioned had been sent to Fort King. From the moment I learned the purport of his message I was all anxiety to go. To see the *Indians at home,* and to witness what I had heard so much spoken of, an Indian dance, was what I had ardently desired from the first day we arrived in the nation; and when I heard the Governor say we would go, I felt that the first wish of my heart was about to be gratified.

A few hurried arrangements were made, such as putting up a few provisions, and selecting a small parcel of presents, to be distributed among the women and children who had not been at the cantonment, and consequently had not yet tasted the bounty of their *affectionate father* at Washington. Our horses were saddled, and being joined by most of the officers at the fort, we set off for the town of the head chief of the Seminoles.

Our little cavalcade made quite a respectable appearance as we moved gallantly over the beautiful green plain that skirted the fort;[1] but striking a trail which led through the wood, it was impossible longer to preserve any thing like order, and dropping into Indian file, as it is called, we journeyed on towards the Indian villages.

The wood through which we travelled was a specimen of that delightful country which composes the greater part of the original Indian reserve, and is not surpassed either in beauty or fertility, by any other portion of the "land of flowers." The scenery was varied and beautiful. At one moment we moved through some deep shaded grove of live-oak, studded with the fragrant magnolia, wild orange and olive trees, interspersed with sundry species of evergreens and flower-bearing shrubbery; which, with the cool scented breeze that softly rustled the deep green foilage, would almost persuade one that he was traversing some eastern garden or enchanted grove. Now we stood upon the summit of some beautiful undulating hill, and now our passing forms were reflected in the smooth surface of some miniature lake, or the hoofs of our horses dashed through the chrystal waters of some meandering rivulet.

We had not journeyed long, however, before the barking of the Indian dogs announced that we were not far distant from our place of destination; and advancing a little farther, we were enabled to see the little cluster of hovels which compose the great Seminole metropolis. We were met at a little distance from the town by the *big Micco* himself, accompanied by all the *distingui* of the nation, who with no little formality conducted us to the council house. According to ancient custom, the *"big chief"* then lighted his pipe, and after raising a young volcano of smoke, enough to strangle a man of moderate lungs, passed it round to the whites, who had previously disposed themselves upon the platform of canes, which are used as seats in the council house. Each in his turn gave it "a whiff or two," and then passed it among their red brethren, who, as I considered it, *"repeated the doss."* After this ceremony was concluded, several orators addressed the concourse, eliciting frequent bursts of applause from their hearers, which demonstrated itself in sudden growls, very like the simultaneous *"ugh?"* usually uttered by a gang of wild hogs, when suddenly surprized.

It was now fast approaching to the shades of evening, and as the convention at the council-house dispersed, all seemed busy in preparation for the coming revels. Being now left somewhat to ourselves, we also commenced a little preparation. We repaired to the dance ground, which was situated a few hundred yards distant from the town, in a beautiful grove of live oak; and selecting a tree near the place, deposited our provisions, saddles, bridles, &c., hobbled our horses, and putting all under the charge of *Peter,* a trusty black, we took a survey of the scene, which was now increasing in life and interest as the shades of night hastened on.

By the time it was quite dark, the Indians had assembled, men, women and children, to the number of three or four hundred, and only waited the presence of the great chief, to commence the dance. This distinguished personage shortly arrived, attended as before by a host of *Tustonuggies,* or law-givers, and took his seat on the logs which encircled the dance-fire. I noticed that particular regard was paid to rank in the distribution of the company: the Chief and his *cabinet* took their station in the East,

---

1. Fort King at this time, is very unlike what it was at the time of which I write (1832). It was then the abode of peace and tranquillity—it is now the camp of war. The pleasant little cottages that then stood in its immediate vicinity, are now strewed upon the ground,—the white-washed buildings of the Fort are now enclosed by rude pine pickets—the young orange groves are cut down,—'the beautiful green plain that skirted the fort' is now strewed with rubbish, and on the very spot where I once beheld an Indian game at ball, a small enclosure now encompasses the graves of Thompson, Rogers, and Smith.

the females in the West, while the *plebians* filled up the space on either side. We were invited to a seat next the chief.

When the company had all got quietly seated on the logs, the chief rose and made his speech, in true Indian style, using all the emphasis and impassioned gesticulation which characterises the Indian orator.—He was followed by the second in power, an old skinny-faced fellow, who spoke as fluently as though he had committed his speech for the occasion.

All the preliminaries being arranged, the dance was commenced. This was done by ten or a dozen men forming a circle round the fire, and chaunting a wild chorus, during which they frequently gave utterance to yells such as made the blood chill in my veins.—After the opening chorus had been completed, one of the number, an old chief, who held in his hand a cocoanut shell, containing several shot, with which he kept regular time by beating it against his hand, commenced trotting slowly round the fire, at the same time uttering in a low gutteral tone something like

"Yah-ah ugh,
E-ah-yah-ugh," &c.

The rest of the company about the fire followed his example, and as they continued to grow warmer and louder, they were joined by group after group from the surrounding company, till the number of the dancers was augmented to more than a hundred, who all swept round the fire in a double circle, dancing and singing as they went. It seemed that the leader composed his poetry on the spur of the moment, and from his frequent pointing and inclination of his body towards us, it was evident that we were often the theme of his muse. The chorus was led by the one next the leader, who varied the key as well as the words, to suit the verse, in which he was joined by all the dancers save the *hoketuckies,* who danced in perfect silence. At the end of each verse or figure, the leader gave a yell, which was followed by a hundred boistrous throats, that made the "welkin ring," and doubtless started the birds from their roosts for miles around. All were dressed in their best—and as they moved round the bright lightwood fire that illumined the grove, their appearance was truly imposing. The fantastic dresses of the men—their waving plumes and grotesquely painted faces, formed a striking contrast to the neat and strictly modest appearance of the females, many of whom were truly beautiful, and dressed like princesses. Their long raven hair was handsomely combed back, and tied with ribbons that trailed to the ground—around their necks hung innumerable strings of beads, while their breasts were literally covered with jewellery of every variety of shape,—which, as it caught the rays of the fire, sent back a gleam that dazzled the eyes of the beholder, and enlivened the whole scene.

Never in my life had I witnessed a scene bearing any resemblance to the one now acting before me.—I gazed upon the wild revellers with the intensest curiosity;—and as they wheeled round the blazing pile, my mind was filled with a thousand strange fancies. At one moment I imagined them to be so many goblin sprites, rather than human beings; and again as they passed in review before me, I beheld a personification of all the heroes and heroines of romance.

I would have longer continued a silent looker on, but for the interruption of one of the masters of ceremonies, an old chief with whom I had contracted a slight acquaintance, while at the fort, who now came up and tapping me familiarly on the shoulder, requested that I should join in the dance. To this I most unequivocally demurred. I had never attempted to dance but once in my life—and I shall never forget

the pretty fist I made of it—it was a most woeful failure, and I for once in my life edified a whole company. On this subject my memory was particularly retentive, and I
had no disposition a second time to render myself ridiculous—and most especially in
a company where I had so little to expect from charity.

But I was not to get off so easily—the old man pressed his suit with an earnestness that forbade denial—and as the rest of the whites had acceded to his request, and
being informed that it would be considered a most flagrant violation of etiquet,
should I persist in refusing, I at length consented. This was a special occasion, and in
compliment to us, the *big micco* himself was to lead the dance. Not having partners to
solicit, we were soon upon the *ground*—the old chief commenced his song, and led
off the dance. We all fell in, and commenced jumping and kicking about the fire at a
great rate, much to the amusement of the Indians, whose frequent exclamations of *I-
e-lah!* sufficiently satisfied me that there was something about our dancing that attracted no little attention. But for the life of me, "I could not get the hang of it," as
the boy said of the school-house. When I attempted to mind the chorus, I was sure
to forget the accompanying motion of my feet—and when I took particular pains to
jump when the rest did, I forgot to sing—and then the herd of little half naked urchins
that paced round on the outside, would eye the red tops of my boots, and when I
stepped out of order, or mashed the toes of him in my rear, or yelled when the rest
were done yelling (all of which errors I frequently committed) they would set up a
laugh at my awkwardness, that was not a little annoying. In short, I longed for the termination of the Black-snake dance, as they called it, as earnestly as I ever did for the
end of a hard day's march, or the last name of the muster-roll at tattoo. One or two
of our party had participated in this sort of cotillion parties before, and of course had
the advantage of me, but there were others who were equally as awkward as myself,
so that there was some consolation in having the sympathies of one another, even
though the more accomplished did laugh at us. In a short time however, I began to
feel less restraint, and determining to "go ahead," I soon began to understand it, and
finally to contract quite a partiality for that mode of exercise, and before the dance
was ended had became a perfect amateur.

At length a loud yell from the dancers, and a simultaneous *"Matto!"* from the
spectators, announced the dance to have drawn to a close, and we hurried to our seats,
leaving the dance-fire to be occupied by a fresh party.

I had not long been seated, before my copper colored friend took his seat beside
me. He evidently wished to enter into conversation; but there was a lack of medium
through which to convey our ideas to one another. He first tried Indian, but he found
me too illiterate to converse with much fluency in that language; he next tried English, and then I had the advantage of him. I remember one of his old speeches, which
made me laugh at the time, in spite of good manners:

"Where you lib?" said he.

"Away north," I replied, pointing with my hand in that direction.

"Eh-hem, eh-hem," grunted he, "New York—lib town—toder side—white man
too much—me see 'em."[2]

After a litte pantomimic conversation, he pressed me to dance again; and placing
his turban upon my head, at the same time appropriating my hat to his own, he ex-

---

2. The large silver medal which hung suspended from his neck by a small silver chain, bearing the
inscription of "John Q. Adams, President of the United States," denoted that he had been a member of
some treaty delegation; and the purport of his speech was that he had seen New York.

claimed, as he played with the black ostrich plumes that shaded my brow, "*Cheme Este-chati inclis che!*" He then drew my arm through his, and after gallanting me proudly round the circle led me again to the dance, where I capered for another twenty minutes, much better pleased with the amusement than I had been at first.

For several hours the dance was kept up with spirit. As fast as one company became fatigued, and retired, a fresh one supplied its place, in such quick succession, that scarce a moment elapsed when the fire was unoccupied. Our party, in good keeping with the spirit of revelry that animated the whole of the red assemblage, partook in almost every dance, until one by one, they dropt off, and repairing to the place where we had deposited our baggage, sought refreshment in sleep. My highest ambition was gratified when I saw the last of the whites retire, yielding the victory to me; and I felt not a little proud of the fact that I had vanquished the whole party, particularly when I remembered how they had laughed at my awkwardness in the early part of the evening.

At length, having sated my appetite for dancing, and having more curiosity to see the termination of the revels, than desire to sleep, I stole away from the dance-fire, and seated myself upon the logs, where I could conveniently watch the movements of the dancers.

It was past midnight,—and the dance began to wane. The revellers had grown weary of its enjoyment; and, as they seated themselves round the amphitheatre, seemed to prefer the society of one another to the mazes of the dance. The night, which had been very dark in the early part of the evening, had now much changed. The moon had risen high in the heavens, and yielded a bright but fickle light, as the large masses of rugged clouds flitted in hurried throngs across her pale face. At times she shed a silver light upon the scene, that penetrated the gloomy shade of the thick branches of the live-oak, and showed every form that thronged about the dance-ground in bold relief; and then, as if some sable curtain had been drawn, to hide her pale disk from mortal gaze, all was dark. The wind, which had scarce rustled the branches of the fragrant orange, and had stolen through the vale with a silent whisper, had now risen high, and rushed in rude gusts above our heads, tossing to and fro the tops of the largest trees.

I rose from the log where I had seated myself, and went to the place where my companions had nestled themselves together, and were all fast asleep, save Peter, who had been commissioned guard of our effects, and who seemed laboring under a very severe fit of drowsiness.

"Massa William," said he, as I drew near, "I speck' dem Ingens mus be too sleepy to steal. May I jus drap down here and take a little snooze—I's be nodin dis long time; and if de *mus*-keeters did'nt bite so much, I'd drap't long afore dis."

As I did not feel sleepy, I told him I would take his office for a time, and when I wished to sleep I would wake him. Peter had hardly heard his release before he was snoring melodiously. I then sat myself down at the root of the tree which had been chosen as the resting place of my companions, and sitting with my face towards the smouldering embers of the dance-fire, watched the movements of the dingy concourse.

The dancing had entirely subsided—the boistrous song and chorus was hushed, and the loud finale no longer waked the echo. All was silent; save where a group of young people were assembled round some songster, who sang in a low sleepy strain some ditty, or where another party were discussing the common topics of the day, or amusing each other by relating the wild legions of their tribe. Then too might be heard the chaunt of some more lonely spirit, who, as he lay by his solitary fire, accompanied his song by drumming with his hands upon his naked breast.

The scene and the hour were eminently calculated to induce the meditative mood, and as I looked upon the jaded and drowsy multitude, my mind was busied in retracing the history of the Indian race and contrasting the miserable creatures now before me with the once proud lords of the forest from whom they emanated. Alas, thought I, how degenerate, how fallen. But a century ago, the red man knew no control; but free as air, he reigned lord of his native wilds, nor knew any bounds to his vast possessions. How changed his lot;—of this vast continent, how small a portion now belongs to him—scarce room is left to lay his bones. Pent up, persecuted, robbed of his liberty and defrauded of his hunting grounds, he has dwindled away before the approach of civilization, till scarce a trace is left of his once numerous people. Where will another century find him? He will be numbered among the 'things that were;'— his wrongs forgotten, and his name unheard.

At length, however, I began to feel a strong sympathy with the slumbering multitude around me. A dreamy feeling stole over me, which I tried in vain to shake off, and I was about to yield myself into the arms of the drowsy god, when the sharp crack of a rifle roused me to my feet. A deep groan was heard—then the loud shrill scream of a female voice rose high upon the midnight air, and was echoed back in a thousand mimic tones. A moment more and all was wild confusion. The Indians were to be seen running in every direction, while the air was filled with their tumultuous yells. What could be the occasion of this excitement? A thousand vague suspicions rushed through my mind in an instant. Our little party were soon huddled together, all equally amazed at what was passing. Was an attack meditated upon us? Who was shot? was in every mouth. Another moment and our speculations were put at rest: An Indian approached, and desired the surgeon who had accompanied us from the fort to follow him; we all approached to the opposite side of the amphitheatre, where the first object that met our eyes was one of horror.

A young chief lay weltering in his gore; while his young and beautiful wife, in the mad frenzy of her grief, clung screaming to his lifeless body, with a tenacity that defied separation. The assassin had fled the moment the deed was done, and the Indians were now in hot pursuit. The whole wood resounded with their yells, as they bounded through the brush like hounds in full chase of their prey. Fifteen minutes, perhaps, had elapsed, when they returned bringing with them the murderer, who though a stout able bodied man, had not been able to effect his escape. His hands were pinioned behind him, and an Indian on either side led him into the arena, which had but a short time before been occupied with the dance.

Aware that the Indian law was blood for blood, and that any interference on our part to prevent its execution would be of no avail, we resolved to remain quiet spectators of their proceedings.

A short consultation took place among the principal men of the nation, during which the prisoner stood erect and motionless, his lips compressed, and his eyes raised towards the heavens. He regarded no one;—and as the bright moon-beams played upon his manly face, I thought I could perceive an air of proud disdain depicted in his countenance, that spoke how little he regarded his approaching doom; and when the plaintive moan of the yet frantic wife fell upon his ear, his stern features relaxed into a smile of fiendish satisfaction. The Indians were gathered in groups in every direction, and were conversing with one another, doubtless concerning the melancholy event, but not a word was addressed to the murderer.

While the preparations were making for the execution, an aged chief was seen to approach the prisoner—he was his father. The old man drew close to his son, and continued to speak in a low tone for some minutes, but received not a word in reply. The father evidently endeavored to conceal his emotion and when he had taken a last farewell, retired to some distance.

In the mean time, the rifle with which the murder had been committed, was reloaded and placed in the hands of a small boy, the nearest blood relative of the murdered man present, who, according to Indian custom, was to be the executioner. The boy, under the guidance of two chiefs, approached the prisoner, who as he preserved his erect position and inflexible manner, rather resembled a statue of stone than a human being. He moved not a muscle as the fatal muzzle was pointed at his breast. Never shall I forget that hour. The moon shone bright, and one might perceive even the expression of every face.—The boy seemed unconscious of what he was about to do—the aim was directed by one of the chiefs—a moment elapsed—the fatal trigger was pulled—the murderer reeled and with a deep groan fell to the ground. The piece had been well aimed; the ball penetrated the left breast, and passing through the heart, came out at the right shoulder. He was then removed to a little distance, and interred in the same grave with him who had but an hour before fallen by his hand.

Thus in the space of half an hour after the commission of the horrid crime, the slayer and the slain were deposited side by side in the same grave, with the weapon that had taken the lives of both between them. The Indians would not permit us to approach the grave until after the burial ceremony was completed. Curiosity then led us to visit the place. We paused in silence, for a few moments, to view the little mound which had been raised over them; then returning to the place where we had deposited our baggage, we mounted our horses and directed our course towards Fort King.

It was a lovely morning. The sun just rising from his eastern couch, poured forth his broad streams of airy light, reflecting the tall trees in the mirror lakes, and tipping the dewy leaves with gold; while the fresh scented breeze came laden with the mingled notes of the thousand feathered songsters, as they sported from bower to bower. All nature seemed to have just awoke from a refreshing sleep. At any other time I would have been transported with the beauty of the surrounding scenery, but my mind was too much engrossed with the recollections of the past to leave room for the contemplation of the present. I could scarce realize that what I had witnessed was reality, and more than once I was inclined to doubt if it were not all a dream. The minds of the whole company must have been equally absorbed, for scarce a word was uttered during our ride, but following at a little distance apart, we jogged slowly on till we reached Fort King. I soon found my bed and tried to sleep, but the tragedy of the night was constantly acting before me.

From an Indian who visited the fort the next day, I learned something of the history of this sad affair:—Love, love, that tyrant king of passions was at the bottom of all: The murderer had long loved the wife of his victim, but she preferred his rival. Seeing her preference, he threatened her lover's death, if she married him until he should consent to their union. He then went upon a long hunt, endeavoring by absence and lively pursuit, to banish from his heart a passion which he was too well aware could never be reciprocal, and which, should he cherish it, could only entail misery upon himself. Upon his return, he found her whom he had so fondly loved already the wife of his rival. Stung with jealousy and rage, he resolved at once to put his threat into execution, and not being able to forego his revenge until some more favorable opportunity should present itself, chose a time when detection was inevitable, and consequently forfeited his own life.

The beautiful *Echoe* became a maniac from the moment of her husband's death, and died a few months after that sad event.

50

JOHNSON JONES HOOPER

(1815—1862)

"IT IS GOOD TO BE SHIFTY IN A NEW COUNTRY." This is the motto of Simon Suggs, confidence man, who ranks among the most memorable of all literary rogues. In *Some Adventures of Captain Simon Suggs* (1845), a satire of nineteenth-century campaign biographies, Suggs roams the frontier swindling all comers while the book's narrator begs for votes: "His military services; his numerous family; his long residence among you; his gray hairs—all plead for him! Remember him at the polls!" Readers then and now might feel an odd temptation to vote "Suggs for Sheriff"; his character both repulses and attracts.

The creator of Simon Suggs, Johnson Jones Hooper, was born on June 9, 1815, in Wilmington, North Carolina. The Hoopers were a prominent family in increasingly dire financial straits. As Johnson entered his teens, there was no hope of sending him to college. Rather, he was expected to help the family financially, which he did to a limited extent working part time as a printer's devil. Johnson, however, gave his family less comfort than concern. They fretted in particular over his habit of keeping questionable hours with questionable company.

For some time the Hoopers had considered migrating west to improve their fortunes. Finally Johnson's eldest brother, George, took the plunge. He established a law practice in Lafayette, Alabama, and in early 1834 he wrote to his brother D. B. that Johnson should be sent to read law with him: "if he can be made steady he is just the fellow to advance in the practice of law in this part of the country where a fluent tongue & abundant assurance invariably succeed with any modicum of talent." Johnson was sent, but he was not soon "made steady." Instead, he wandered the frontier, traveling as far west as Texas. He admitted, "I have been a dependent all my life and it is mortifying to sponge on my brother's liberality when I am twenty years old. But I can't help myself." In his willingness to take advantage of others, young Hooper resembles Simon Suggs.

It was not until 1842, some seven years after moving to the frontier, that Johnson finally settled down in the same town as George. There he began to pursue a legal career, and he began editing the Lafayette *East Alabamian,* the local Whig newspaper. Simon Suggs debuted in the pages of the *East Alabamian* in December 1844. The Suggs stories were quickly reprinted by William T. Porter in his influential New York paper *The Spirit of the Times,* and it was Porter who arranged to have *Some Adventures of Captain Simon Suggs* published by Carey and Hart of Philadelphia.

Hooper published one other work of fiction, *A Ride with Old Kit Kuncker* (1849), which contained only two Simon Suggs tales. After this,

his life was dominated by journalism and politics. He died on June 7, 1862, probably from tuberculosis, while serving the Confederate government as editor of the records of the Provisional Congress.

Text: *Some Adventures of Captain Simon Suggs* (Philadelphia, 1845): "Simon Speculates Again," 69–81; "Simon Becomes Capain," 82–95; "The 'Tallapoosy Vallantares' Meet the Enemy," 111–117.

SIMON SPECULATES AGAIN (1845)

THERE are few of the old settlers of the Creek territory in Alabama, who do not recollect the great Indian Council held at Dudley's store, in Tallapoosa county, in September of the year 1835. In those days, an occasion of the sort drew together white man and Indian from all quarters of the "nation"—the one to cheat, the other to be cheated. The agent appointed by the Government to "certify" the sales of Indian lands was always in attendance; so that the scene was generally one of active traffic. The industrious speculator, with his assistant, the wily interpreter, kept unceasingly at work in the business of fraud; and by every species and art of persuasion, sought—and, sooner or later, succeeded—in drawing the untutored children of the forest into their nets. If foiled once, twice, thrice, a dozen times, still they kept up the pursuit. It was ever the constant trailing of the slow-track dog, from whose fangs there was no final escape!

And where are these speculators NOW?—those lords of the soil!—the men of dollars—the fortune-makers who bought with hundreds what was worth thousands!—they to whom every revolution of the sun brought a reduplication of their wealth! Where are they, and what are they, now! They have been smitten by the hand of retributive justice! The curse of their victims has fastened upon them, and nine out of ten are houseless, outcast, bankrupt! In the flitting of ten years, the larger portion have lost money, lands, character, every thing! And the few who still retain somewhat of their once lordly possessions, mark its steady, unaccountable diminution, and strive vainly to avert their irresistible fate—an old age of shame and beggary. They are cursed, all of them—blighted, root and trunk and limb! The Creek is avenged! Avenged, and for *what!* ask you, reader? Let us tell you a little story!

We knew, at the period to which this chapter refers, an Indian who refused to sell his land on any terms. He was a sturdy, independent fellow; one of the few who would not be contaminated by intercourse with the whites. His land was very valuable, and many speculators were, therefore, anxious to purchase it. So desirable was it, that several would, perhaps, have paid the "Sky chief" half its actual value to obtain it; but the "Sky chief" resolutely persisted in resisting all their arts; and he was too well known to make it practicable to get it, by hiring some thieving Indian to personate him before the certifying agent. But "Sudo Micco" had a daughter, a very pretty girl of fifteen—slightly made, with a Grecian face, and long coal-black hair; and her name was Litka. Well! Litka went to a dance—the green corn dance of her people—and it was conceded, that in her new calico frock and profusion of blue and red ribbons, and her silver buckles, she was the handsomest girl on the ground. Among her admirers was a young man named Eggleston—a sub-partner, or "striker," of the great Columbus Land Company. Eggleston told a sweet tale to the Indian girl, and she—as he was a very handsome young man—believed it all. He told her that he would marry her and take care of her, and of her father; and that when the rest of the tribe should be forced to Arkansas, *they* could stay with him in their old home, by the graves of their fathers. The "long and short" of all this was, that the white man and Indian girl were married according to the Creek custom; Sudo Micco having willingly assented to an arrangement by which he expected to be permitted to remain upon the soil which contained the bones of his ancestors. For a few months Eggleston treated Litka and Sudo Micco very well, and they confided in him implicitly. Then he told his wife that her father must "certify" his land to him, or "bad white men" might contrive to get it. Litka told the old "Sky chief" what her husband said, and the simple-minded Indian said it was "a good talk," and that his "white man son" should do as he pleased. So the "Sky chief" "certified" his land to his son-in-law; and the certifying agent saw a thousand silver dollars paid to the Indian, who within ten minutes afterwards returned them. Then Eggleston deserted Litka, and sold the land for three thousand dollars. Sudo Micco fumed and raved—but what good could that do? And Litka, poor thing! was almost broken-hearted. And last of all, Sudo Micco begged his son-in-law, as he had got his land for nothing, and his daughter was too near her confinement to travel on foot, to get him a little wagon and a horse to take them to Arkansas. But Eggleston laughed in his face, and told him that a wagon would cost too much money. So Sudo Micco was compelled to wait until the Government removed his people; and then he went in one of the "public" wagons, among the "*poor*" of his tribe. FOR THIS, AND SUCH AS THIS—as we have shown—IS THE CREEK AVENGED!

But we set out to tell about the council at Dudley's, and here we are writing episodes about Creek frauds, as long almost, as the catalogue of Creek wrongs! We will come back to the starting point. It was a right beautiful sight to look at—the camp-fires of five thousand Indians, that burned at every point of the circular ridge which enclosed Dudley's trading establishment; and it was thrilling to hear the wild whoopings, and wilder songs of the "natives," as they danced and capered about their respective encampments—on the first night of the council. It was a little alarming too, to witness the occasional miniature battle between "towns" which, like the Highland clans, had their feuds of immemorial date.

"Coop! coop! hee!" shouts a champion of the Cohomutka-Gartska town, the principal family of which was that which rejoiced in the name of "Deer." "The Oak-fuskee people are all cowards—they run like rabbits! They are liars! They have two tongues! Coop! coop! hee-e-e! the Alligator family is mixed-blooded! they come from the runaway Seminole and the runlet-making Cherokee! The "Deer" people can beat the Alligator people till they beg for their hides!" Then the representative of the chivalrous "Deer" people struts before his camp-fire, gesticulating violently, and expressing his contempt of his Alligator brethren, by all sorts of grotesque attitudes; while the women and children about the fire, declare that Cho-yoholo, (the Screaming Deer,) is a great warrior, and can flog every Alligator of them all by himself.

Presently, a representative of the Oakfuskee town, and the Alligator family, strides out in front of his temporary lodge, which is about a hundred yards from the encampment of his hostile neighbours.

"Eep! eep! e-e-e-yah!" he shouts, so shrilly that your "skin creeps." "The dog of Cohomutka-Gartska brags like a child, but his heart is the heart of the poor little toad, that tries to hop away at dusk from the black-snake! The Alligators are brave; their hearts are big and full of red blood. If the thieving Deer people will send one of their best warriors half-way, the Alligator people will send an old woman to meet him! Eep! eep! e-e-e-yah!" And then Hulputta Hardjo (Mad Alligator,) slaps his hands upon his hips, and turns contemptuously away.

In a few moments the "Alligators" and "Deer," and all their friends, are engaged pell mell, in a fight with clubs, rocks, knives, teeth, hands and toes; while the Indians in their neighbourhood, who have no particular interest in the affray, hold torches to enable the combatants on both sides, to deal their blows more effectively.

As a matter of course, our friend and hero the Captain, was at the council. He was never known to absent himself from any such congregation. If out of funds, he went to "recruit;" if he had a "stake," he attended that the "Tiger"—which then was peripatetic and almost omnipresent, because at that time our supreme court judges had not muzzled him—might have an opportunity of devouring it. On the present occasion he really had business; for he had brought with him to be "certified"—that is, to submit for the approval of the government agent, a contract for the sale of her land—an Indian woman, whose "reserve" was an excellent one. Simon had contracted to pay her two hundred dollars and three blankets for it; and as she happened to take a liking to him, she preferred that he should have it at that price, to selling to others who were offering her a thousand. In this, the "Big Widow" but illustrated a waywardness, amounting to absolute stupidity, which was common among the Creeks. It was in vain that she was assailed on all hands, and persuaded to accept a larger price. "The Mad Bird,"—so was the Captain called by the Indians—she would observe, "would give her three blankets and two hundred dollars, and she would give him her land. The Mad Bird was a good friend, and had a sweet tongue; and if she gave her land to any body else, he would have the "big mad," and then he wouldn't give her tobacco and *sweet water* any more.

There was but one obstacle in the way of the Captain's making a very handsome speculation; but that was a very serious one under present circumstances: he did't happen to have the money. True, we have said in another chapter, that the Captain disdained to embark in speculations requiring the investment of cash capital; but the reader must do us the justice to recollect, that "there is no rule without an exception." *In a general way,* we know we have asserted, and we here reassert, that Simon Suggs could, by the force of his own genius, speculate without funds; but we would like to know how any reasonable man could expect Captain Suggs, or any one else, to purchase an Indian's land without money, when by an act of Congress it was requisite that the appraised price should be paid *in the presence of the agent.* Could the Captain but have had the use, for only ten minutes, of two hundred dollars, he could easily have owned the Big Widow's "low grounds," and paid the money back, too, had he chosen so to do. Unfortunately, however, such a loan was not to be obtained, and his efforts to "make the raise," caused it to be known that he had no means of paying the widow for her land at that time. This fact—for it was so regarded, very correctly—gave each of a half-dozen other speculators on the ground, encouragement to hope that *he* might be the lucky purchaser. They then beset the old woman, one after another, so that she had scarcely time to cook the sophky for her children, or drink a spoonful herself. Still she resolutely adhered to her promise to the Mad Bird, and would *not* sell to any other. At length the Captain hit upon an expedient, and calling together his rivals at the widow's camp, he harangued them:

"Gentle*men,*" said he, "you all know this here old widder Injun is under promise to me, to sell me her land! Now I takes it to be d—d ongentlemanly, gentle*men,* that you all, bein' in the same line o' business with myself, should endeavour to take advantage of a feller's bein' a leetle low down, and steal his *honest* contract. But, hows'ever, gentle*men,* that's not the pint of my discourse, which are shortly this: ef any of you, gentle*men,* will shell out the necessary trimmins, so's that the old lady, here, can pass muster before the agent, I'll let him have an even intrust with me in the land! Which of you'll do it, gentle*men?*—don't all speak at oncet!"

Colonel Bryan whispered to General Lawson, and Major Taylor whispered to Mr. Goodwin; and then they all whispered together, and then they all stopped and looked at one another, as not knowing what to say.

"Out with it, gentle*men,*" exclaimed Simon, "don't spile the shape on it, by keepin' it in!"

"Can't stand it, Simon," said Lawson.

"As good as wheat!" replied Simon; "but I'll eat Satan raw and onsalted, ef any of you ever git a foot of that land. I'm not quite as fur down as you think. There's an old friend of mine not twenty mile from here, that's got three or four hamper baskets-full o' Mexicans, and I guess I can git a bushel or so, jist to ease the pain, twell a feller can git the chance to have the tooth drawd!" Then turning to the Big Widow, and indicating with his finger the point in the heavens at which the sun would be the next morning at ten o'clock, he told her, if he was not back by the time it got there, she might believe that he had failed to procure the money, and sell to whom she pleased. He then mounted his pony and galloped off.

The next day, at a very early hour, the speculators were tugging at the Big Widow, each striving to induce her to sell to himself in case Simon should not return, upon which they all confidently calculated. Each made so tempting an offer, that the poor woman knew not which to accept; or rather, she accepted them all in turn. The land was worth fifteen hundred dollars, and eight hundred were already bid when Simon's limit was within a half hour of its expiration. At length the sun reached the ten o'-clock point, and the Captain not appearing, the rivals, among them, pushed and pulled the old squaw up to the shed under which the agent was "certifying." Here a general fight ensued; Colonel Bryan striking Major Taylor across the nose in the enthusiasm of the moment; and General Lawson doing something of the same sort for Mr. Goodwin, because he apprehended that the row would become general, and that those would fare best, who struck soonest and hardest.

Just at this moment Simon dashed up at full speed.

"Don't break *all* the crockery, gentle*men,*" he shouted. "Jist give a poor man a chance to make an honest contract, won't ye!"

"The Mad Bird has come back, I will give my land to him," said the Big Widow, approaching Simon, who had dismounted, and was bending beneath the weight of a very plethoric pair of saddle-bags.

The fighting ceased when Suggs made his appearance, and there was a moment's silence. The first to break it was General Lawson. "Mr. Suggs," said he, "I'd like to have an interest in your contract, and I'm willing to pay for it. I'll find the money to pay the Indian, and give you an interest of one-third."

"Not 'thout I was willing—would ye?" asked Suggs jeeringly.

"I'll do better than that," said Taylor, wiping the blood from his nose; "I'll furnish the money and give you half the land sells for when we part with it!"

"Very proverbly," remarked Simon, "very proverbly! But onless some on ye counts me out five hundred, and furnishes your own money to buy the land, I shall have to onlock these here," patting his saddle-bags, "and buy it for myself."

"I'll do it!" said Colonel Bryan, who had been making a calculation on the inside of the crown of his hat—"I'll do it!"

"Ah!" said Suggs, "*that's* what made the chicken's squall! *You're* the man I'm a-huntin'! Draw your weepins!"

The land was forthwith "certified" to Suggs, who immediately transferred it to Bryan.

"Now, gentle*men,*" said the Captain, every body's satisfied—aint they?"

"If they *aint,* they *ought* to be," replied Colonel Bryan, who was delighted with his bargain.

"I think so too," remarked Suggs, "and bein' as that's the case," he continued, opening his saddlebags, "I'll throw out these here *rocks and old iron,* for its *mighty* tiresome to a horse!" and the Captain *did* throw out the rocks and old iron!

The speculators vanished!

"This here's a mighty hard world," murmured the Captain to himself, musingly, "to git along in. Ef a feller don't make every aidge cut, he's in the background directly. It's tile and strive, and tussle every way, to make an honest livin'. Well!" he continued, in a strain of unusual piety, as he threw up and caught again, a rouleau of dollars; "Well! thar *is* a Providence that purvides; and ef a man will *only* stand squar' up to what's right, it *will* prosper his endeavours to make somethin' to feed his children on! Yes, thar *is* a Providence! I should like to see the man would say thar aint. I don't hold with no sich. Ef a man says thar aint no Providence, you may be sure thar's something wrong *here;*" striking in the region of his vest pocket—"and *that* man will swindle you, ef he can—CERTIN!"

SIMON BECOMES CAPTAIN (1845)

By reference to memoranda, contemporaneously taken, of incidents to be recorded in the memoirs of Captain Suggs, we find that we have reached the most important period in the history of our hero—his assumption of a military command. And we beg the reader to believe, that we approach this portion of our subject with a profound regret at our own incapacity for its proper illumination. Would that thy pen, O! Kendall, were ours! Then would thy hero and ours—the nation's Jackson and the country's Suggs—go down to far posterity, equal in fame and honors, as in deeds! But so the immortal gods have not decreed! Not to Suggs was Amos given! Aye, jealous of his mighty feats, the thundering Jove denied an historian worthy of his puissance! Would that, like Cæsar, he could write himself! Then, indeed, should Harvard yield him honors, and his country—justice!

Early in May of the year of grace—and excessive bank issues—1836, the Creek war was discovered to have broken out. During that month several persons, residing in the county of Tallapoosa, were cruelly murdered by the "inhuman savages;" and an exceedingly large number of the peaceful citizens of the state—men, women and children—excessively frightened. Consternation seized all! "Shrieks inhuman" rent the air! The more remote from the scenes of blood, the greater the noise. The yeomanry of the country—those to whom, as we are annually told, the nation looks with confidence in all her perils—packed up their carts and wagons, and "incontinently" departed for more peaceful regions! We think we see them now, "strung along the road," a day or two after the intelligence of the massacres below had reached the "settlement" of Captain Suggs! There goes old man Simmons, with his wife and three daughters, together with two feather beds, a few chairs, and a small assortment of pots and ovens, in a cart drawn by a bob-tail, gray pony. On the topmost bed, and forming the apex of this pile of animate and inanimate "luggage," sits the old tom-cat, whom the youngest daughter would not suffer to remain lest he might come to harm. "Who knows," she exclaims, "*what* they might do to the poor old fellow?" On they toil! the old man's head, ever and anon, turned back to see if they are pursued by the remorseless foe; while the wife and daughters scream direfully, every ten minutes, as they discover in the distance a cow or a hog—"Oh, they'll kill us! they'll skelp us! they'll tar us all *to* pieces! Oh, Lord! daddy! oh, Lord!" But the old tom-cat sits there, gravely and quietly, the very incarnation of tom philosophy!

It was on Sunday that the alarm was sounded in the "Suggs settlement," and most of the neighbours were in attendance upon the "preaching of the word" by brother Snufflenosey, at Poplar Spring meeting-house, when the "runner" who brought the woful tidings, disclosed them at old Tom Rollins', by yelling, as he sat on his horse before the door,—"the Injuns is a-killin every body below! I aint got time to stop! tell the neighbours!" Now, old Mr. Rollins and the "gals" were already at meeting, but the old lady, having staid behind "to fix up a leetle," was, at the identical moment of the messenger's arrival, *en chemise* before a very small glass set in a frame of red paper, preparing to adorn her person with divers new articles of apparel, inclusive of a new blue-and-red-calico gown. But no sooner did her mind comprehend the purport of the words from without, than she sprang out of the house, "accoutred as she was," shrieking at every bound, "the Injuns! the Injuns!"—nor stopped until with face, neck, and bosom crimson as a strutting gobbler's snout, she burst into the meeting-house, and having once more screamed "the Injuns!" fell exhausted, at full length, upon the floor. "Will any of the breethring lend me a horse?" asked the Reverend Mr. Snufflenosey, wildly, as he bounded out of the pulpit, in very creditable style—"Wont *none* of you lend me one?" he repeated emphatically; and obtaining no answer, dashed off precipitately afoot! Then went up to Heaven the screams of fifty frightened women, in one vast discord, more dreadful than the war-squalls of an hundred cats in fiercest battle. Men, too, looked pale and trembled; while, strange to relate, all of the dozen young babies in attendance silently dilated their astonished eyes—struck utterly dumb at being so signally beaten at their own peculiar game!

At length an understanding was somehow effected, that Taylor's store, five miles thence, should be the place of rendezvous, for that night at least; and then Mr. Snufflenosey's congregation tumbled itself forth as expeditiously as was possible.

Simon was "duly" at the store with his family, when the wagon, cart, and pony loads of "badly-scared" mortality began to arrive in the afternoon. He was there of course, and he was in his element. Not that Suggs is particularly fond of danger—albeit, he is a hero—but because he delighted in the noise and confusion, the fun and the free drinking, incident to such occasions. And he enjoyed these to the uttermost now, because he was well informed as to the state of feeling of the Indians, in all the country for ten miles around, and knew there was no danger. But Simon did not disclose this to the terrified throng at the store. Not he! Suggs was never the man to destroy his own importance in that sort of way. On the contrary, he magnified the danger, and endeavoured to impress upon the minds of the miscellaneous crowd "then and there" assembled, that he, Simon Suggs, was the only man at whose hands they could expect a deliverance from the imminent peril which impended.

"Gentle*men,*" said he impressively, "this here is a critercle time; the wild savage of the forest are beginnin' of a bloody, hostile war, which they're not a-goin' to spar nither age nor sek—not even to the women and children!"

"Gracious Lord above! what *is* a body to do!" exclaimed the portly widow Haycock, who was accounted wealthy, in consideration of the fact that she had a hundred dollars in money, and was the undisputed owner of one entire negro—"we shall all be skelped, and our truck all burnt up and destr'yed! What shall we do!"

"That's the question," remarked Simon, as he stooped to draw a glass of whiskey from a barrel of that article—the only thing on sale in the "store"—"that's the question. Now, as for you women-folks"—here Suggs dropped a lump of brown sugar in his whiskey, and began to stir it with his finger, looking intently in the tumbler, the while—"as for you women-folks, it's plain enough what *you*'ve got to do"—here Simon tasted the liquor and added a little more sugar—"plain *enough!* You've only got to look to the Lord and hold your jaws; for that's all you *kin* do! But what's the 'sponsible *men*"—taking his finger out of the tumbler, and drawing it through his mouth— "of this crowd to do? The inemy will be down upon us right away, and before mornin'"—Simon drank half the whiskey—"blood will flow like—like"—the Captain was bothered for a simile, and looked around the room for one, but finding none, continued—"like all the world! Yes, like all the world"—an idea suggested itself— "and the Tallapussey river! It'll pour out," he continued, as his fancy got rightly to work, "like a great guljin ocean!—d—d ef it don't!" And then Simon swallowed the rest of the whiskey, threw the tumbler down, and looked around to observe the effect of this brilliant exordium.

The effect was tremendous!

Mrs. Haycock clasped her hands convulsively, and rolled up her eyes until the "whites" only could be seen. Old Mrs. Rollins—who by this time was fully clothed— and her two daughters had what Simon termed the "high-strikes" in one corner of the room, and kicked up their heels at a prodigious rate; while in another, a group of young women hugged one another most affectionately, sobbing hysterically all the time. Old granny Gilbreth sat in the middle of the floor, rocking her body back and forth, striking the palms of her hands on the planks as she bent forward, and clapping them together as she re-attained the perpendicular.

"My apinion," continued Simon, as he stooped to draw another tumbler of whiskey; "my apinion, folks, is this here. We ought to form a company right away, and make some man capting that aint afeard to fight—mind what I say, now—*that-aint-afeard-to-fight!*—some sober, stiddy feller"—here he sipped a little from the tumbler— "that's a good hand to manage women and keep 'em from hollerin—which they're a-needin' somethin' of the sort most damdibly, and I eech to git holt o' that one a-making that devilish racket in the corner, thar"—the noise in the corner was suddenly suspended—"and more'n all, a man that's acquainted with the country and the ways of the Injuns!" Having thus spoken, Suggs drank off the rest of the whiskey, threw himself into a military attitude, and awaited a reply.

"Suggs is the man," shouted twenty voices.

"Keep close to *him,* and you'll never git hurt," said a diminutive, yellow-faced, spindle-legged young man.

"D'ye think so now?" exclaimed Simon furiously, as he "planted" a tremendous kick on that part of the joker's person at which the boot's point is most naturally directed. "D'ye think so, now? Take *that* along, and next time keep your jaw, you slink, or I'll kick more clay outen you in a minute, than you can eat again in a month, you durned, little, dirteatin' deer-face!"

"Keep the children outen the way," said the little fellow, as he lay sprawling in the farthest corner of the room; "ef you don't, *Cap'en* Suggs will whip 'em all. He's a sight on children and people what's got the *yaller janders!*"

Simon heeded not the sarcasm, but turning to the men he asked—

"Now gentle*men,* who'll you have for capting?"

"Suggs! Suggs! Suggs!" shouted a score and a half of masculine voices.

The women said nothing—only frowned.

"Gentle*men,*" said Simon, a smile of gratified, but subdued pride playing about his mouth; "Gentle*men,* my respects—ladies, the same to you!"—and the Captain bowed—"I'm more'n proud to sarve my country at the head of sich an independent and patriotic cumpany! Let who will run, gentle*men,* Simon Suggs will allers be found sticking thar, like a tick onder a cow's belly—"

"Whar do you aim to bury your dead Injuns, Cap'en?" sarcastically inquired the little dirt-eater.

"I'll bury *you,* you little whifflin fice," said Captain Suggs in a rage; and he dashed at yellow-legs furiously.

"Not afore a body's dead, I reckon," replied the dirt-eater, running round the room, upsetting the women and trampling the children, in his efforts to escape. At last he gained the door, out of which he bounced and ran off.

"Durn the little cuss," said the Captain, when he saw that pursuit would be useless; "I oughtent to git aggravated at him, no how. He's a poor signifiken runt, that's got the mark of the huckle-berry ponds on his legs yit, whar the water come to when he was a-getherin 'em, in his raisin' in Northkurliny. But I must put a stop to sich, and that right away;" and striding to the door, out of which he thrust his head, he made proclamation: "Oh yes! gentle*men!* Oh yes! This here store-house and two acres all round is now onder *martial law!* If any man or woman don't mind my orders, I'll have 'em shot right away; and children to be whipped accordin' to size. By order of me, Simon Suggs, Capting of the"—the Captain paused.

"Tallapoosy Vollantares," suggested Dick Cannifax.

"The Tallapoosy Vollantares," added Suggs, adopting the suggestion; "so let every body look out, and walk the chalk!"

Thus was formed the nucleus of that renowned band of patriot soldiers, afterwards known as the "FORTY THIEVES"—a name in the highest degree inappropriate, inasmuch as the company, from the very best evidence we have been able to procure, never had upon its roll, at any time, a greater number of names than *thirty-nine!*

As became a prudent commander, Captain Suggs, immediately after the proclamation of martial law, set about rendering his position as strong as possible. A rude rail fence near by was removed and made to enclose the log store, and another building of the same sort, which was used as a stable. The company was then paraded, and a big drink dealt out to each man, and five men were detailed to serve as sentinels, one at each corner of the enclosure, and one at the fence in front of the store door. The Captain then announced that he had appointed Andy Snipes, "fust lewtenant," Bird Stinson "sekkunt ditto," and Dave Lyon "sarjunt."

The guard was set, the women summarily quieted, the mass of the company stowed away in the stable for the night; and the Captain and "Lewtenant Snipes" sat down, with a bottle of bald-face between them, to a social game of "six cards, seven up," by a fire in the middle of the enclosure. About this time, the widow Haycock desired to possess herself of a certain "plug" of tobacco, wherewithal to supply her pipe during the watches of the night. The tobacco was in her cart, which, with a dozen others, stood in the road twenty steps or so from the front door. Now, as the widow Haycock was arrayed rather grotesquely—in a red-flannel wrapper, with a cotton handkerchief about her head—she did not wish to be seen as she passed out. She therefore noiselessly slipped out, and, the sentinel having deserted his post for a few moments to witness the playing between his officers, succeeded in reaching the cart unobserved. As she returned, however, with the weed of comfort in her hand, she was challenged by the sentinel, who, hearing a slight noise, had come back to his post.

"Stand!" said he, as the old lady was climbing the fence.

"Blessed Master!" exclaimed Mrs. Haycock; but the soldier was too much frightened to observe that she spoke English, or to recognize her voice.

"Give the counter-sign or I'll shoot," said he, bringing his gun to a "present," but receding towards the fire as he spoke.

Instead of the counter-sign, Mrs. Haycock gave a scream, which the sentinel in his fright, mistook for the war-whoop, and instantly fired. The widow dropped from the fence to the ground, on the outside, and the sentinel ran to the Captain's fire.

In a moment was heard the thundering voice of Captain Suggs:

"Turn out, men! Kumpny fo-r-m!"

The women in the store screamed, and the company formed immediately in front of the door. The Captain was convinced that the alarm was a humbug of some sort; but keeping up the farce, kept up his own importance.

"Bring your guns to a level with your breasts, and fire through the cracks of the fence!" he ordered.

An irregular volley was fired, which brought down a poney and a yoke of steers, haltered to their owner's carts in the road; and frightened "yellow-legs," (who had slyly taken lodgings in a little wagon,) nearly to death.

"Over the fence now! Hooraw! my galyunt voluntares!" shouted the Captain, made enthusiastic by the discharge of the guns.

The company scaled the fence.

"Now charge baggonets! Hooraw! Let 'em have the cold steel, my brave boys!"

This manœuvre was executed admirably, considering the fact, that the company was entirely without bayonets or a foe. The men brought their pieces to the proper position, ran ten steps, and finding nothing else to pierce, drove the long, projecting ram-rods of their rifles deep in the mellow earth!

"Pickle all them skelps, Cap'en Suggs, or they'll *spile!*" said a derisive voice, which was recognized as belonging to Yellow-legs, and a light form flitted from among the wagons and carts, and was lost in the darkness.

"Somebody kill that critter!" said Suggs, much excited. But the "critter" had "evaporated."

A careful examination of the field of battle was now made, and the prostrate bodies of the pony, the oxen, and the widow Haycock discovered, lying as they had fallen. From the last a slight moaning proceeded. A light was soon brought.

"What's the matter, widder—hurt?" inquired Suggs, raising up one of Mrs. Haycock's huge legs upon his foot, by way of ascertaining how much life was left.

"Only dead—that's all," said the widow as her limb fell heavily upon the ground, with commendable resignation.

"Pshaw!" said Suggs, "you aint bad hurt. Wharabouts did the bullet hit?"

"All over! *only* shot all to pieces! It makes *no* odds tho'—kleen through and through—I'm a-goin' mighty fast!" replied the widow, as four stout men raised her from the ground and carried her into the house, where her wounds were demonstrated to consist of a contusion on the bump of philo-progenitiveness, and the loss of a half square inch of the corrugated integument of her left knee.

Captain Suggs and Lieutenant Snipes now resumed their game.

"Lewtenant,"—said Suggs, as he dealt the cards—"we must—there's the tray for low—we must *court-martial* that old 'oman in the mornin'."

"'Twon't do, Capting—the tray I mean—to be sure we must! She's vierlated the rules of war!"

"And Yaller-legs, *too!*" said Suggs.

"Yes, yes; and Yaller-legs too, ef we kin ketch him," replied Lewtenant Snipes.

"Yes, d—d ef I don't!—court-martial 'em both, as sure as the sun rises—*drumhead* court-martial at that!"

THE "TALLAPOOSY VOLLANTARES" MEET THE ENEMY (1845)

Captain Suggs, with the troops under his command, remained, we believe, during the entire continuance of the "war," in garrison at the Fort. The reason for this was obvious. The object of our hero was to protect that portion of the country which had the strongest claims upon his affection—his own neighbourhood. It was beyond human knowledge to foretell how soon the wily savage might raise the tomahawk and scalping knife in the immediate vicinity of Fort Suggs. Why then should any body ever have expected, or desired the Captain to leave that important post and the circumjacent country in a state of absolute defencelessness? Suggs was too prudent for that: he remained snug enough at the Fort, subsisting comfortably upon the contributions which he almost daily levied from wagons passing with flour, bacon, and whiskey, from Wetumpka eastward. In his own energetic language, "he had tuk his persition, and d—d ef he didn't keep it as long as he had yeath enough to stand upon!"

In spite of the excitement of frequent *sorties* upon ox-wagons; of dollar-pitching, and an endless series of games of "old sledge;" as well as the occasional exhibition of a chuck-a-luck table, at which the Captain himself presided; time at last began to hang heavily upon the hands of the inmates of Fort Suggs. At length, however, an event occurred which dispelled the *ennui* of the "Vollantares," for a season at least. An Indian *ball-play* was announced to "come off" within a few days, at the ball-ground near the river, and only three miles from the fort, though on the opposite side of the Tallapoosa. It was decided that Captain Suggs and his company should attend and witness the sport; and as both the towns engaged in the game were reputed to be "friendly," not the slightest danger was anticipated. Had there been, from our knowledge of the prudence of Captain Suggs, we do not hesitate to say, that he would never have jeoparded his own invaluable life, not to speak of those of his comparatively insignificant soldiers, by appearing on the ball-ground. Tire-some as was the monotony of Fort Suggs, he would have remained there indefinitely, ere he had done his country such wrong!

Early on the day appointed for the trial of skill between the copper-coloured sportsmen of the towns of Upper and Lower Oakfuskee, the "Vollantares" and their illustrious Captain had crossed the river at the ferry which lay between the fort and the ball-ground, and soon they had reached the long, straight pine ridge upon which the game was to be played. Already two or three hundred Indians had assembled, and the Captain also found there some ten or a dozen white men. A stake was set up close to the goal which was nearest the river, and from its top hung a huge shot-bag of crimson cloth, covered with beautiful bead-work, and filled with the silver money which was bet on the result of the game. At the foot of the stake, on the ground, were blankets, shawls, guns, bolts of cotton goods, and all sorts of trumpery; all of which was also bet on the result. The "odds" were in favour of the Lower Oakfuskees, among whom were some of the best players in the "nation," and Captain Suggs quickly backed them to the amount of ten dollars, and the money was added to that already in the shot-pouch.

The Indian game of ball is a very exciting one, and the Creeks gamble furiously at it. To play it, a level piece of ground, some two or three hundred yards long, is selected, and the centre ascertained. Goals are designated at each end, and the ball—very like that used in games among the whites, but not so elastic—is thrown up at the centre. One side endeavours to get it to one "base," while their antagonists strive to carry it to the other. The players are armed with two short sticks, each of which is bent and tied at one end, so as to form a sort of spoon; and when these ends are placed together they make an oval cup in which the ball is caught, and then hurled to a surprising distance. Every time the ball is carried to a goal, it counts one for the side who take it there. No idea of the furious excitement into which the players are worked, can be conceived by one who has never witnessed a scene of the kind. They run over and trample upon each other; knock down their antagonists with their ball-sticks; trip them as they are running at full speed; and, in short, employ all kinds of force and foul playing to win the game. Generally there are two or three hundred—often five—engaged in the sport at once; all naked except the "flap," and in most instances the affair ends in a terrible *melée,* in which the squaws on each side supply their male friends with missiles, such as rocks and light-wood knots. The betting is often high; the main bet being, not uncommonly, five hundred dollars.

On the present occasion the game was "twenty-one up." The playing commenced, and the woods resounded with the fierce yells of the naked savages. The first run was gained by the upper town, but the next, and the next, and the next, were won with ease by the lower. The Captain was exultant, and whooped loudly at every winning.

At length, when it was seen that the upper town must lose, one of the white men whom Captain Suggs found on the ground when he arrived—and who was the heaviest better against the lower town—approached our hero, and informed him that he had discovered the astounding fact, that both parties of Indians were determined to make a sudden attack upon all the white men present, and kill them to a man. He stated farther, that he had overheard a conversation between Cocher-Emartee, the chief of the upper town, and Nocose Harjo, the principal man of the lower, in which it was agreed between them, that the signal for attack should be the throwing of the ball straight up into the air. In view of these facts, he advised the Captain to leave at once, whenever he should see the signal given.

Captain Suggs is human, and "*as sich*" is liable to err, but it isn't *often* that he can be "throwed" by ordinary men. He "saw through the trap" that was set for him in a minute. He did not doubt that an attack would be made, he knew that a *feigned* one would be made by Cocher-Emartee's Indians, and he was well convinced that its only object would be to frighten the "Vollantares" from the ground, and give the upper town an opportunity, with the assistance of their white confederates, to beat the lower town Indians and seize the stakes. He determined therefore to "watch out," and keep himself "whole" in a pecuniary point of view if possible. Calling his trusty lieutenant to his side, he discovered to him the machinations against them, and directing him to keep the company—most of whom were a-foot—in the neighbourhood of a number of ponies that were hitched near the upper end of the ball-ground; he himself walked to the lower end, and bringing his pony close to the post from which the shot-pouch was suspended, he hitched him and sat down.

Suddenly, when most of the Indians were collected near the centre of the ground, the ball was seen to ascend high into the air. Simon was watching for it, and before it had risen twenty feet, had loosed his pony, flung the reins over his neck, cracked him smartly across the rump, and so started him home by himself. The next moment he was mounted on a fine blood bay, belonging to Cocher-Emartee, which wheeling under the post, he took off the shot-bag containing the stakes with the muzzle of his rifle, and in less time than we have taken to describe his movements, was thundering at full speed through the woods towards the ferry, the silver in the pouch giving a responsive jingle to every bound of the gallant bay.

At the same moment that Captain Suggs mounted and dashed off, most of the "Vollantares," under the lead of Snipes, jumped upon the ponies of the upper Oak-fuskees and made for the river. A volley of rifle shots was discharged over their heads, and with furious yells the Indians pursued. Only a few, however, could muster ponies; and such was the promptness with which the Captain's orders were executed, that the "Vollantares" arrived at the ferry full five minutes in advance of their pursuers. Here a difficulty presented itself. The flat would not carry across more than a fourth of the company at once. Time was precious—the enemy was rushing onward, now fully determined to recover their ponies or die in the attempt. Suggs, equal to any emergency, cut loose the flat and started it down the river. Then holding his gun aloft, he dashed his spurs into his horse's flanks and plunged into the stream, and his men followed. As they ascended the opposite bank, Cocher-Emartee, foaming and furious, rode up on the side they had just left. He was mounted on a borrowed horse, and now loudly howled forth his demand for the restoration of his gallant bay and the shot-bag of silver; protesting that the whole affair was a joke on his part to try the spunk of the "Vollantares"—that he was "good friends" to the white people, and didn't wish to injure any of them.

"Go to h-ll! you d—d old bandy-shanked redskin!" shouted back Simon; "I know the inemies of my country better'n that!"

Cocher danced, shouted, raved, bellowed, and snorted in his boundless rage! Finally, he urged his pony into the water with the intention of swimming across.

"Kumpny form!" shouted Simon—"blaze away at the d—d old *hostile!*" A volley was fired, and when the smoke cleared away, the pony was seen struggling in the river, but there were no Indians in sight.

Captain Suggs never recovered the pony which he turned loose in the woods; and notwithstanding this loss was incurred while in the discharge of his duties as one of the defenders of his country, the state legislature has *thrice* refused to grant him any remuneration whatsoever. Truly "republics *are* ungrateful!"

51

ELIZA W. FARNHAM

(1815–1864)

Eliza Farnham spent three and and half years in central Illinois in the late 1830s. Born and raised in upstate New York, however, she returned there in 1840 and remained there most of the rest of her life. After returning east, although married to a noted travel writer (John Farnham, *Travels in the Great Western Prairies* [1841]), she initiated a successful career as a penologist, advocate, and, finally, feminist. Early in that process, she published her first book, *Life In Prairie Land*. This book combines much of the best of her two most obvious forerunners and fellow travelers—Caroline Kirkland and Margaret Fuller, the latter a close friend of Farnham's during the 1840s.

Her book, then, reflects two stages of her life: her life in Illinois as a young woman and bride and her more mature perspective as a professional woman in a troubled marriage. As such, it combines the domesticating, Yankee ideology espoused by Kirkland with the iconoclastic feminism of Fuller. Linking the two, however, is a more general romanticism, most visible in the book's final chapter, reproduced here. Nonetheless, in the book's earlier sections, Farnham ventures a more personal and revealing voice, which comes closer to that of Rebecca Burlend. Furthermore, Farnham's awareness of the west's complex regional identity is announced from the opening of our selection. Her observation that the "Yankees" from New England used various technicalities of the law to displace earlier western and southern settlers in Illinois was a story told often in the upper midwest during the 1830s and 1840s.

Farnham's own ambiguous position as a member of the "universal Yankee Nation," perhaps, is what finally motivated her to leave Illinois and return to New York. Her ability to understand the many cultural presences of the region without aligning herself solely with one or the other makes *Life in Prairie Land* an extraordinary book. For Farnham, the frontier is both squalor and majesty, the site of both magnificent opportunity and tragic deception.

Text: *Life in Prairie Land* (New York, 1846; rpt. Urbana, Illinois: 1988, ed. John Hallwas): 98–116, 259–269.

CHAPTER XVI

But it is time I left my domestic circle, and introduced to the reader some of our neighbors and fellow citizens, and their doings. Our town had been settled two years before, by a colony compounded of New-Yorkers, Bostonians, Providence people, and a few random Yankees and adventurers, that were said by an ancient *Sucker* lady in the neighborhood to have been "hove in to fill up." They had organized in the east and come to the west at random, knowing that there was plenty of territory there whereof to manufacture farms, cities, et cet. The honor of being the shire-town of this large and wealthy county was then vibrating between two villages, both of which were settled mostly by western people. The Yankee colony came, took this tract of unbroken prairie, laid out a square mile into lots (the wealthiest men holding the contiguous farms under promise not to refuse room in case the town should outgrow its original boundaries); and by the aid of a little capital, some notes of hand, more brains, and still more cunning, bore off the prize for which the open-mouthed Kentuckians, Tennesseeans, and Buckeyes were disputing. What equivalent was offered the Commissioners, who were appointed to select the most eligible spot, for their choice of this, was never known to the public; but it has since appeared that they were pretty "*shrewdly done*" to a considerable amount in promises, the payment of which was afterward refused on the plea of want of consideration! One may guess, therefore, that we have a pretty sharp population, and he will not very widely err. It is but rendering honor where it is due, however, to say that most of this kind of public spirit dwells in a few of the original company. The majority are thriving, industrious mechanics, farmers, and tradesmen, who, possibly, contributed their quota for such purposes when called upon, but otherwise pursued their occupation peaceably—content with their daily gains and the prospect of a rise in the price of property. The latter formed by far the largest item in their expectations of becoming capitalists. The most matter-of-fact citizen who had paid six hundred dollars for a choice lot at the sales, could not but see his money doubled, interest included, within the first two years. Nearly every citizen owned one, two, or three such lots, besides farms of immense value in the vicinity, so that we had also a wealthy population.

In politics the balance was pretty nearly equal in point of numbers between the two great parties. The four leading spirits, those on whom the responsibility of public efforts rested, were equally divided. But like true men and patriots, they suffered no party questions to divide or weaken their efforts in the common cause of personal aggrandizement. In truth, political considerations among them were rarely suffered to outrun community of interest. Not that men were less rank politicians there than elsewhere, but causes that affected the price of town lots were superior to all other considerations; and as this was the great point on which golden expectation turned, nothing was allowed to interfere with it. Our religious zeal was much more heated and less suppressed. Sectarian piety ran high among the professing heads of the community; and, as people who buy town property, et cet., for the most part care little whether a man has any religion, and still less what particular sect he adopts (his choice in these matters not affecting his vote) we were less restrained in the expression of these opinions than of those which bore on the more embarrassing question of politics *Orthodox* and *heterodox,* therefore, were terms in frequent use among us. The precise meaning attached to each was known only to the initiated (if indeed to them); but this very indefiniteness was one of their greatest charms. Nothing more restrains vituperation and combat than an exact use of words. A term which has great latitude of meaning is much more easily hurled at an antagonist, than if it were precisely defined and did not touch his case. As in metaphysics, imagination is made to cover every phenomenon for which no other cause can be assigned; so in our discussions of character and morals, orthodoxy and heterodoxy were made the sources of all sin, or the parents of all virtue. Unlike political opinions, these extended to the feminine population, and were, I rejoice to say, the single cause of whatever dissension or difficulty existed among us. Let me not be understood to rejoice that this existed, but that it was the only one known among us.

The most important personage in all village affairs was one of our nearest neighbors, who, for certain good and sufficient reasons, I shall call Mrs. Esculapius. The reader will suppose now, that Mrs. Esculapius was the wife of the physician, but his sagacity is entirely at fault in the supposition. The occupation of her husband is a matter of no moment whatever to us. If it were, it would exceed his own importance in his family, for never man had less. The law that size is, *cæteris paribus,* a measure of power, has been much discussed of late years; I only wish those who doubt its truth could have seen the complete illustration of it afforded by these worthy citizens. In no fact that ever fell under my observation was it more fully demonstrated, than in the relative size and power of Mrs. Esculapius and her husband. Both these qualities were in the extreme of contrast in them. He was the smallest of men, she at the opposite end of the scale among women. He was less of a master in his household than any other man, she quite the reverse. He was good-natured; this did not spoil the contrast. He was submissive, she imperative. He was timid and retiring, she was always foremost in every domestic movement. But beside these points of difference, Mrs. Esculapius possessed some other peculiarities which will, if permitted, stand alone. She was endowed with a sense of hearing, the acuteness of which was perfectly astounding: neither walls nor distance offered any impediment to it. She knew as well the topics under discussion at her neighbor's houses, and the opinions expressed upon them, as if she had been present. She could report all these opinions the next day with as much certainty as if she had participated in the utterance of them herself. Her optical sense was equally keen; and, what was still more extraordinary, both these wondrous powers could be used at once; and hence she could report the expressed opinions, and the unuttered thoughts, of persons in any part of the town. We should have voted the phenomenon magnetic, but for two reasons; first, we were all unbelievers; and, secondly, a stronger faith in the possible than any of her friends exercised, would have been necessary to believe that she was ever in a magnetic state. For no one ever saw her asleep. But all conjecture and speculation of this sort were rendered superfluous by reference to the plain demonstrable fact, that, at the time when she was taking notes for these reports, she was always pursuing her ordinary household avocations; to all appearance as unabstracted by such employment, as any person to whom this power was denied.

The only circumstance which threw any light upon this wonderful faculty, was the necessity of waiting till the next day, and possibly till the second, before she proceeded to report. It was suggested, that a troop of fairies had chosen her for their general post-office, and were making her the victim of their harmless pranks. If any more ingenious solution can be offered, the case still waits for its light. Passing these peculiarities, this lady is a pattern housekeeper, a kind friend to those whom she likes, a sympathetic woman at a sick bed, a hospitable and generous hostess in her own house. She takes pleasure in sending specimens of her excellent cookery to neighbors who are less skilful in the art, or less favored with conveniences for plying it. I take pleasure in acknowledging myself still her debtor for many such little kindnesses.

In the front ranks of our religious community stands Deacon Cantwyne—a man celebrated in all the "country side" for his piety, his love of money, and his affectation of philosophy. Deacon Cantwyne's house is the resort of all the clergy of his own denomination; and the philosophy which he affects, leads him to extend his hospitalities to many others. So that he lives in a theological atmosphere, so to speak, an atmosphere musical with expressions of the religious feelings. This is his chosen condition. But if denied him in the presence of others, he is capable of creating it to a great extent for himself. He prays three times a day, and reads the Scriptures each time. He never neglects religious worship, takes an active part in the orthodox Sabbath-schools, frowns on open vice or dishonesty in any shape, is scrupulous in the observance of the Sabbath, even to leaving the room in which so profane a thing as the Pilgrim Fathers is sung on that day, and loses no opportunity of exhorting his non-professing neighbors to "come out from the world," and "fight the good fight of faith." Deacon Cantwyne is a business man, and he declares that a profession of religion, so far from interfering with success in business, as many worldly-minded but mistaken individuals think, is no little aid to it. He speaks from experience, for his religious pretensions have enabled him to pray his way to the bottoms of hundreds of pockets, which he could never otherwise have approached. All the while that he is doing it, he will lavish the most hearty expressions of esteem on you—esteem grounded on the virtues which he has discovered in you, for, as a Christian, he can admire no other qualifications. If you are in affliction, he will console you, pray with you and for you, commend you to the Bible, and to those sources of comfort which he has found so potent, and in the next moment, count the dollars which some proposed operation will enable him to make out of the confidence his speech was designed to create. When any special enterprise of this kind is in prospect, he prays longer and more fervently than usual; and if the victim is present, in the shape of a purchaser, or a debtor whose all lies under a mortgage which he holds, he is apt to be quite overpowered with his love of duty and his charity for his neighbor. Ten chances to one but he makes you the subject of a special petition, and closes with a request that you may be preserved from the devouring influences of the carnal appetites, from vanity, and from love of riches. He feels for you already, and wishes that your sufferings may be light when he shall have sounded your purse. His piety is never more apparent than on these occasions. If the operation is one of considerable magnitude, he solicits the brethren of the neighborhood to unite in a protracted meeting, for he feels that the gospel is losing its influence on the hearts of men. When he has consummated the affair, he will meet you with the blandest face, and enter into a conversation on electricity, the aurora borealis, or the last Arctic expedition. But he never fails to turn to the pole of his thoughts before he leaves you, and exhort you to remember that all these "phenomeny," wonderful as they are, are the handiwork of a power to whom your highest services are due, and that the best of us can but poorly glorify Him. Or perhaps he reads you a page from his own experience, telling you how, when he was a young man, he began life with the hope of achieving some worldly honors and possessions, but soon found that to do so, he *"should have to set his face like a flint,"* and close his ears to all the petitions of mercy; how this struggle between his better nature and the desire to do his duty had almost ended in the triumph of Satan; how thankful he is that it did not, and how much he hopes that every young man whom he sees entering life may be preserved as he was. And all this is said with a grave face as if he had not just defrauded you of your last penny, and were not ready to do you the like favor to-morrow.

Deacon Cantwyne's exhortations are uttered with a face and tone that would subdue a Philadelphia mob. These are natural gifts—at least I set them down as such. If they are not, they must have been cultivated in early life; for nothing of the kind can be more perfect. The face leads you to anticipate the voice, and vice versa. Deacon Cantwyne has been pretty intimately connected with the affairs of the colony, and some of his transactions would edify men whose kindred genius is restrained by stone walls and sheriff's processes.

He was originally from one of the principal cities of the east. While there he was employed in a highly useful trade, from which he seems to have realized a handsome equivalent for his labors. To this he has added whatever has fallen in his way, beside several things that have not been able to get out of it since he came west; and he is now one of our wealthiest men. He is not so ardently beloved in the neighborhood as many persons I could designate, but he never discovers this unless it is forced on his attention; and when it is, he sets it down to the account of his rigid piety. "How shall a devoted christian expect to command the love of the children of darkness? He ought to glory in their hatred, and would if it did not argue such deplorable wickedness in them"—and show that they would be on their guard against his long prayers. His piety is embellished by a liberality as striking as itself. This, however, partakes more of a public than a private character. Any public bequest which will enhance the value of property, he makes freely, provided it be expended in the vicinity of his own possessions. There are many little tales afloat in the village and country, illustrative of Deacon Cantwyne's peculiarities, which his biographer will doubtless gather for the purpose of doing justice to his memory. If I have drawn his picture correctly enough to have it recognized by himself and his friends, I have done all that I proposed to do on this page. If occasion to refer to him again should arise, a single stroke will bring him before the reader. That is a principal advantage in having his character well defined at the outset.

CHAPTER XVII

Our village abounded in professional men. Not to mention the youthful Cokes and the unassuming Blackstones, who asked no loftier place for their names than gilt or gamboge letters on a black shingle nailed beside their office-doors; we had magistrates, judges of law and probate, retired counsellors, waiting a favorable opportunity to embellish some of the more elegant walks of life. But most indispensable and popular of all was our doctor. He was the ornament not only of our professional classes, but of the village. His personal appearance is worthy a livelier pen than mine. He is actually of middle stature, but seems considerably below it, from the excessive deficiency of anything like hauteur in his character. His head projects well over the eyes, and towers above the forehead into an immense table-land, on which you might heap offences that would outnumber the hairs that cover it, and yet find forgiveness. This preponderance brings the head forward and upward in a right line, but it is the most graceful departure from a perpendicular that could be imagined. His strong perceptions leave about him no air of stumbling abstraction, but, combined with a boundless benevolence, lend the delightful expression one wears when looking for objects of sympathy or admiration. Leaving the doctor's head, the next most striking thing about him is his gait. Various were the attempts at description which this wonderful gait elicited from his fellow citizens. A walk it certainly was not, if by this term is meant a straightforward, or indeed almost any other use of the limbs given for that purpose. I do not mean to say that he performed locomotion without the use of these organs at all, because that would imply that he walked upon his hands or head—arts which I am not aware that he ever cultivated; and which it will be conceded must have been extremely inconvenient, unless his pockets had been made to correspond, for they were his medicine-chests. If he had been an importer of drugs, he would never have wanted any storehouse but these, and the privilege of depositing samples that were unsaleable, or robbed of their virtues by age, upon the shelves of his wife's closets.

But to go back to his gait. It certainly was a curious one. It was made up of incredibly short steps, that followed so fast upon one another as to give the idea of a man with two pairs of legs, each running on a wager against the other. If one could conceive a sheep with his two fore-legs lengthened so as to give him an erect attitude, yet still preserving his peculiar motion, with a perfect resemblance to the human figure in all other respects, he might have a tolerable idea of the doctor's gait. I am aware that this is a labored illustration, and that the idea at best is complicated; but no one knows how difficult the subject is, nor how long I might search the whole kingdom of animate nature in vain, for something whereunto to liken this motor phenomenon. It is true, that the terms "*nudge*," "*shuffle*," "*trot*," and sundry others were used among the puzzled villagers to designate it; but they are all feeble, and so I believe will be anything I can add to them. There are things in nature which words hover around in vain: they never touch them.

The other eccentricities of our Galen were not so indescribable. He had a versatility of genius, which never failed to respond to any appeal. An Indian war-dance, or the amputation of a limb; the old woman in Robin Roughhead at a private theatrical entertainment, or a post at the couch of prostrating, withering disease, were matters of equal facility—I had almost said of pleasure; for the warm exercise of his sympathies on the painful occasions, and the relief which his skill and tenderness often enabled him to afford, were high sources of pleasure. As might be expected with such a constitution, our doctor had been a merry youth. He had spent a very considerable fortune in early life, for the purpose of reducing himself to terms of equality with necessity, whom he could not coax to his acquaintance in any other way. And he seemed even now to have a fear that she would forsake him again, for he never collected his dues, never informed any one that his services were to be paid for, unless by way of assent when the proposition originated with themselves. When he returned from a ball one winter morning with his splendid wife and brother, and found the house which they had jointly occupied burned to the ground, with everything it had contained, he stood a moment, and then said, "There are plenty of houses about here whose inmates will receive Mary for a few days, and there will be sick enough this season, heaven help them, to whom I can do some good, in return for which they shall enable me to build her a better home. I'll have it all right in a year or so, except the little mementos and trifles endeared by association and otherwise. Those cannot be replaced, so I suppose we must mourn over them a little." And the doctor kept his word; catching the means which fortune threw at him for his poorly-paid, arduous, and ceaseless labors, he purchased a beautiful building-spot in "Court-end;" build a cottage with a roof so sharp that it was described by a stage-driver, who had a passenger to set down there, as "the house with a ruff that split the rain-drops," made a sort of bird's nest of it, whose chief ornament was his peerless wife: and there he lives, or rather, the lady and her babes; for he is too much abroad during the warm season to have a proper residence anywhere. And there a hospitality and social charm are offered to guests, which is rarely surpassed in more elegant mansions.

At this time the doctor is accompanied in his professional visits by a faithful old horse, who is known throughout the country by the name of "Pomp." It would, perhaps, be as correct to say that the doctor accompanies Pomp; for the latter, if harnessed and left loose, under the false impression that his friend was in the seat, would doubtless have gone alone to visit their patients. I say *their* patients, because it always seemed to me that the doctor and Pomp were partners. What share the latter had in the profits was never know, though his share in the labors was, for he sometimes traveled sixty or seventy miles a day, beside stopping for calls. The estimation in which the doctor held Pomp was very high. To have struck him would have been treason; yet I ought to add, as an evidence of the inconsistency of man, that he would allow him to be driven till his bay coat was white with foam. But how could Pomp complain when his master treated himself in the same manner! Seated in his light waggon, reins in hand, the doctor announced his readiness to set off by speaking the name of his four-footed friend, in an tone which seemed to be agreed on between them as a signal for moving; and away they went; never a blow was struck, nor a harsher word spoken. I apprehend it would not have been safe for any person to have attemped either. I remember riding out with the doctor once, to see a sick friend. On our arrival, a coarse fellow came up, and seizing Pomp by the head, called out to know whether he should "*ondo him?*"

"Ondo him!" exclaimed the doctor. "Ondo Pomp!" and he cast a look at him which might have been translated into a volume; but, passing on, he merely said "No! you may give him some fresh grass, if you have any here. I should like to see the man," he added, in a muttered parenthesis, "who would dare ondo Pomp!"

The doctor's mode of communicating his opinions and wishes to Pomp is very convenient and pleasant, not only to themselves, but to the settlers whose habitations they visit. You may foretell their approach when two miles distant on the prairies, at any hour of the night, by listening to the mono-syllable Pomp! Pomp! And pleasant sounds they are to those who leave the bedside of languishing pain, and step forth an instant into the cool silent night, to breathe and catch the signal of the visit so ardently longed for.

In sickly seasons they travel all night. The doctor moves the seat of his waggon back, has an extra cloak or buffalo robe, of which he makes a bed, and, when he leaves a house, curls himself up in it, gives Pomp the signal, and starts on, leaving the latter pretty much to his own choice about the road. And they thus go on admirably; for the doctor has such a habit of speaking to Pomp, that, though fast asleep, he articulates his name in the usual tone, about once in twenty minutes, and the latter knows the roads so well that he always goes right, if not left to his own pleasure too long. In those latter cases the doctor is likely, on awaking, to find himself before the sharp-roofed cottage, for Pomp, among his other virtues, is eminent for his love of home. This goes on till poor Pomp is incapable of traveling longer at such rate, and then a stranger is hired for day-driving, and Pomp kept for night-driving.

For himself the doctor has no substitute. He goes night and day for weeks, snatching rest as I have described, and sometimes, when he goes into a house, after examining his patient, lying down upon the floor, or on three chairs, with a strict injunction to the watchers not to let him sleep over half an hour. This and a cup of tea twice a day, strong enough for the brother of the Sun or Moon himself, were all that the doctor required to keep him going till the pestilence abated. It is only in rare seasons, however, that their duties are so arduous. Ordinarily, the "sickly season," as it is termed, extends through some two or two months and a half at the close of the summer and opening of the autumn. During those weeks bilious fevers prevail more or less through the whole country; but especially in the vicinity of streams and low grounds. Here they are very general, and more malignant than in the prairies and higher regions. In many cases, where the medical adviser is unskilful, or proper care is not bestowed, the patient is left with the "*shakes,*" this term being merely a shorter name for the disease which others choose to call "*Fever Ragy.*" Exclusive of the short period just specified, little sickness prevails. More than half the numerous forms of disease which poison society and baffle the physician here are there unknown. And, judging from my own experience, I should say that a large proportion of those which do prevail, might be avoided, by ordinary attention to the laws of health. Regularity in sleep, temperance in diet, personal cleanliness, and due share of exercise at proper seasons, would reduce materially the frightful amount of disease which now makes these western summers alarming. A residence of nearly five years, with only a tolerable attention to diet and regimen, brought me not a week's indisposition from the causes incident to the country.

But I have left our doctor to speak a word of caution to settlers. I know his good-nature so well however, that I am assured of pardon, even though my advice should shorten his bills. And why not, since the length of so few of them is ever estimated? In periods when his professional cares relax, the doctor is the most efficient of our village sociables. Always ready to converse well with those who wish to do so, or play the mountebank for those who prefer amusement; ready to flatter a lady into good-nature with herself, if it be necessary, or argue political tendencies with her husband, if this be more agreeable; he was indispensable in all social meetings, and nowhere a more delightful companion than at his own table or fireside. Though not an accomplished singer, he was sometimes prevailed upon to do his devoir even in this behalf. I never heard but one or two exhibitions of his vocal powers, and these were made at the pressing instance of friends who could not be refused. He had one favorite piece which served on both occasions, though doubtless he was master of others equally elegant in diction and charming in composition. I more than half suspected that he had played Mozart himself to the following lines—

> "At the battle of the Nile,
> I was there all the while."

These lines were burthen, chorus, and all: they comprised the entire piece. And the third or fourth repetition, in a tone incomparably more monotonous than the words, generally drew such peals of applause from the gentlemen and such a waving of handkerchiefs from the ladies, that the doctor was quite overcome, and took his seat in a very interesting state of confusion. As a mere artist the doctor was rarely excelled in what he undertook. A negro dance or a lofty flight of admiration for the works of nature, with which he was so continually conversant, were executed with nearly equal excellence, except that to the latter he brought the strength of a fine mind, as well as a high degree of artistic skill. In short our doctor was a rare character, and we prized him as such. His very faults and weaknesses, and he had plenty of them, only made us pity him and wish they were not—one could scarcely be indignant at them.

CHAPTER XVIII

Summer had worn away, with its wealth of golden grains and flowers. The luxuriant harvest had disappeared from the farms in the adjacent country, the tall corn was in its sere and yellow leaf, the late fruits began to ripen, the prairies faded from their rich green, save where here and there a "*late burn*" showed the tender grass, like an emerald island in the vast brown ocean. Autumn in the prairie land is scarcely excelled for the richness of its charms by any other season. Coupled with the perfection of the wide vegetable world is an idea of repose which fills the soul. An immense country, whose energies have been springing all the previous months with ceaseless toil, whose rank luxuriance evinces the employment of tremendous powers, now lies all around you in the deep quiet which ushers in a truly natural death. The sun pours forth a rich, mellow light; dim and soft, as if like a tender nurse he watched over this sleep of nature. The native birds, happy in the abundance which they cannot consume, fly cheerfully but quietly about, as if, their labor done, the season of rest had come to them also. The quail whistles and dances among the brown hazel thickets; the grouse flies from field to field, dividing his depredations through the neighborhood, and bearing off, when unmolested, a full crop to the plains, which he loves better than the abodes of man. The crow calls from the wood top, or wheels his long and lazy flights above the naked prairies, seeming really more amiable than at any other season. The air is filled with the smoke of distant fires; some day they creep up into your own neighborhood, and when night comes, light the heavens and the earth as far as the eye can reach. These are magnificent spectacles. I have stood upon the roof of our large hotel in the evening, and looked into a sea of fire which appeared to be unbroken for miles. These incidents occasionally interrupt the dreamy rest to which everything tends, but they pass away in a few hours, and the next day is as quiet as before. Sporting parties are made up among the gentlemen, and fruit parties, including ladies, to visit the nearest groves in search of haws, nuts, et cet.; or if any orchard has been cultivated in the vicinity by some ancient settler, this is resorted to, and small parcels of its rare fruit purchased and taken home. Our fruit parties usually resorted to a grove about a mile distant, on the west, and returned after an hour or two of delightful rambling, with baskets laden with the delicious haw-berry, a feast for many days. The pawpaw and persimmon did not flourish in our vicinity. They love the bottom lands of streams.

The groves at this season are indescribably charming. There is not in the large foliage that gorgeous variety which we find in the eastern forest. The trees wear a more sober and uniform complexion; but there are a thousand minuter beauties which touch the heart. A few flowers linger in the borders of the woodland and skirt the small streams. In the deeper recesses some sprightly ones are found, indicating by their vigor and freshness that they belong to the season of frost. Among these is one which I dearly love. It grows upon a tall stalk sparsely set with leaves, and forms near the top a beautiful shaft, studded with myriads of small flowers of the most exquisite hue and loveliness. They are like so many bright eyes looking gaily out into the pleasant world around. This flower does not belong to the deep groves, but is found in the little glades or openings in the woodside. And there, when October winds play among the leaves, and the bright sunshine pours through a sea of mist and smoke, into little nooks and corners, by decaying logs and upturned roots, where it has not gained admittance during all the leafy reign of summer, this bright flower is seen nodding and dancing merrily in the breeze as if it rejoiced in the approaching gloom. The squirrel searches timidly about among the fallen leaves, making provision for the winter; and the hare, whom he often meets, skips by him, half in sport, half in earnest, seeking the tender twigs whereof to make her dinner. The ripened nuts dropping among the leaves often startle her from her contemplations, and drive her to seek refuge in the nearest clump of grass or bushes.

These wood-parties are delightful recreations. Armed with thick shoes and provided with a basket each, for trophies of all descriptions—or if the distance be too great to be traversed on foot, mounted, as we could be best provided (the reader will remember pony), without our riding dresses, that we may not be cumbered with them when we reach the wood—away we go, free as the winds. North, south, east, or west, the way is equally open. The wild Indian, mounted on his hunting horse, has scarcely a larger liberty than we. We scour the plain, leap or plough the "slues," and gain the grove. Here our steeds are fastened to trees and boughs, and we scatter. Oh what a joyous afternoon is before us! And some at least know it, though all do not seem to do so. Toward evening, when the shadows begin to lengthen on the turf, and the winds to sweep more chillingly through the grove, we gather at the rendezvous; bring forth the shawls and other cautionary articles, spring into our saddles, give free rein, and after a swift and exhilarating ride, stop at our own doors filled with happy recollections, and made better in spirit and body by a day in the woods.

About three miles from our village is an orchard, which has been cultivated these many years by the widow of the original proprietor. It is the only one in the vicinity, and the old lady's name is therefore well known. And though no two words could be more unlike in orthography and sound than her own name and that of the fruit she sold, yet to me the former was always synonymous with apples. You could not hear or speak it without having your mouth water for the delicious fruit with which it thus became associated. The old lady was much patronized by our villagers and the settlers on adjacent farms. She lived quite neatly in a half-framed house, which you had to circumvent in order to enter it, there being three doors in the rear, but none on the roadward-side. (I avoid saying front, to be exact in the use of words.) The grounds contiguous to the house had at certain seasons of the year rare beauty and richness. A stream of some magnitude swept in a crescent form around the orchard-clad hill, on which it stood. Across the road this hill sloped downward to the stream in a smooth green lawn, dotted with trees. On either hand from the house and skirting the bank of the stream in front of it, was a dense grove of the peach, the apple, and wild-crab apple-trees. About the first of June these were in full bloom, and no perfume of Araby could excel their sweetness, no floral display, their beauty. As you approached the spot after sunset, when the light dews just moistened the blooming boughs, and the evening winds swept over them, the whole air was laden with their fragrance; and when you gained the summit of the hill and looked down upon the nodding clusters of blossoms, set, as it were, in the tender green of the forest trees towering above them, nothing could be conceived more beautiful. Many a pleasant twilight ride have we enjoyed, lingering through the paths of this blossoming wilderness, inhaling its delicious odors, and gazing on its unequaled beauty. I remember one evening, when the sounds of bells seemed coming up from the grove below our path to greet us; they advanced slowly; and we almost stopped in admiration of the gorgeous sunset above and the wealth of the foliage lavished around. Presently the sounds became more distinct, and a large Pennsylvania waggon with a top of snowy whiteness emerged from the green wood. It was an emigrant family—a group of the happiest faces and the cleanest persons one often finds among them. This was a favorite camping ground,— and we lingered watching them till their supper fires shone in the advancing darkness, and then reluctantly turned our horses' heads homeward. How I envied those people!—to lie down there, bathed in the calm, pure air of a June night, the dropping petals strewing their place of rest, the clear brooklet murmuring to their sleep; who could submit patiently to imprisonment within four walls, as dull then as if nature were not doing her best in grove, plain, and sky to induce us to leave them!

But here lived the old lady of apple memory, and here amid all this beauty had she lived from time immemorial among the Yankee settlers. Her spirit had partaken of the scene. She lived neatly in doors, and there was an air of comfort about the exterior of her home quite in harmony with the feelings awakened by the surrounding scenery. How indeed could she have violated so beautiful a sanctuary, by a life altogether coarse and unlovely. But she was not proof against the pernicious influences which the possession of absolute power works in the mind which exercises it. Being for many years the sole dispenser of apples to a large region round her, she had grown capricious in her tastes, and now cared little to accommodate those whom she did not like. If you were one of her favorites, and called on her in the fruit season, either by way of compliment, or as a purchaser, she always presented you a dish of the choicest productions of her orchard to eat in her house, and made her happiest selection for your purchase. We were fortunately of this class. She regarded it as an evidence of kind and friendly interest, to inquire after the prosperity of her place, and usually tendered some hints gratis, on the cultivation of fruit trees. In one of these familiar lessons, she remarked that there was a way to make trees bear much earlier than most persons supposed they would.

"Prey how is that, Mrs. S———?"

"Why, when we was a settin out the last of our trees, them in the orchard down thar," pointing out of the door, "the man we got 'em of, told my old man that if he wanted 'em to bear early he must set 'em out when the moon was in *parrighee.*"

"When is that, Mrs. S———?" said I, making a violent effort to preserve my gravity, for her keen eyes were fixed on my face.

"O, I reckon folks that's college larnt as you be, needn't ax me when the moon's in *parrighee.* I expect you can tell any time when you look at it."

"I am not college learned," I replied, "you know ladies never are, and I presume my husband has forgotten all about the *parrighee* of the moon long since."

"Well you can find it any time by looking in a *nalmanic;* that's whar we found it. Some folks," added the old lady, "don't allow there's anything in the moon about fruit

and so on, but I reckon they don't know so much more than other folks as they think
they do. I know a heap of things that does better when they're planted at sartin times
o' the moon, and there can't nobody make me think 'tain't so, 'cause I've tried it.
'Tain't so much account about some things; I reckon taters does as well planted one
time as another, and so does beets and so on, but cabbages and onions and all them
'dought to be planted in the new o' the moon, if you want 'em to be of any 'count."

Such edifying conversation usually occupied the time spent at the old lady's
house. If you were particularly deferential and received instructions meekly, you were
always rewarded by having your pockets or basket filled with the choicest apples for
your own especial gratification. I know of no other way in which the good woman
ever corrupted the morals of her visitors, but this was bad enough. Whose integrity
could stand unshaken before a dish heaped with apples such as money could not buy?
Who would venture to correct the friendly old woman's orthoëpy at such a risk? Certainly not one who had such a longing for the apple bins of eastern cellars as I had.

Such were some of the many excursions of autumn days which we shared. Then,
as I intimated, the gentlemen more frequently went out in small companies to shoot
the quail, grouse, hare, and squirrel. These parties were generally equestrian and very
jocose among themselves, though the whole mass of female nerves in the village was
in a flutter till they returned. Because it had been found that in the absence of game
they shot each other! My husband had joined one of these parties and came home
with shot enough in his limbs to make us count it quite a serious affair, though it only
resulted in his giving two or three days' exclusive attention to books within doors.

Later in the season an occurrence under similar circumstances robbed us of one
of our worthiest young mechanics, and produced a most melancholy feeling throughout in our little community. Two young men, intimate friends, had left the village together on Saturday evening, to spend the Sabbath at the house of a friend six miles
away. On Monday morning they started for home, each with his rifle and game-bag,
intending to search the groves and thickets on their way down for game. Near sunset
they had reached the skirt of the grove about a mile and a half from the village, and
discovering some quail in one of the hazel thickets which bordered it, they parted to
"beat" the thicket. Stealing cautiously around, one raised his rifle and fired at a bird
that was just tripping into his place of concealment. The bird fell, but a spring and a
dismal groan at the same instant made his blood curdle. He dropped his rifle and ran
to the other side. Judge of his feelings when he saw his friend lying on the ground, a
crimson stream sprouting from his breast; and heard him exclaim in a faint voice,
"C———, you have shot me!" In three minutes he was dead! The ball had passed
through the heart! His remains were borne to the village on the waggon of a neighboring farmer, a coroner's inquest was held, and on the second day they were followed
to the grave by the mourning citizens. The unfortunate man was a son of New
Hampshire, the pride of his aged father and mother, whom he had left to seek a more
promising home in the richer regions of the west. His friend, scarcely less an object
of sympathy, took a vow never again to handle fire-arms; but so completely had the
horrors of the scene fastened upon his mind, that he never recovered his former calmness. He brooded over the dreadful event with a morbid kind of self-accusation, abandoned his business, and at length wandered away melancholy, abstracted, miserable.
This was a painful tragedy for our little community, and lasting and deep was the sympathy it created for the two unfortunate young men.

The reader will remember I informed him that our next door on the left was a
grocery—(groggery would be the truer name, but what lady can ever make up her
mind to write it). If he has heard nothing from this place before, it is not because I have

not. Many a day's tranquillity and many a night's rest did this horrid place destroy. All the influence which the respectable portion of the community could bring to bear upon it, failed to mitigate its character or check the abominations daily enacted in it. The sights and sounds of the poor wretches who frequented it often compelled me to forsake and close the front of my house; but it was vain to seek seclusion from them in my small tenement; their sickening shouts and groans reached one everywhere. Sometimes these diabolical orgies lasted two or three days and nights without pause, and then a time of comparative quiet followed. The master-spirit among those who shared in their scenes, was the individual who kept the shop. His ceaseless habits of drunkenness had made him one of the most disgusting of human spectacles. With a face enormously bloated beyond its natural proportions, eyes bleared and watery, white lips, parched and mottled with bright red spots, and palsied limbs, the miserable wretch, not yet thirty-five years of age, crept about, a warning, one would have thought, to those who congregated about him. But here they assembled, two or three miserably lost spirits from the eastern states, and as many Kentuckians of the lowest class; and here, hand in hand, they led each other to ruin. Sometimes the citizens would acquire influence enough over one of the band to keep him from the spot for a period, but they seized on him again at the first opportunity, and made him pay for his respite by a deeper plunge than ever. There was one unfortunate man highly connected in one of the principal cities of the east, where he had left a wife and two interesting children. He had fallen among these wretches soon after his arrival, but had several times been restrained, partly by his better feelings, partly by the remonstrances of his friends. Every one who knew him mourned over the waste of a man who possessed so many of the elements of usefulness and happiness. Early in the autumn, he received a letter from his wife, appealing to him, as her husband and the father of his children, to return to them or make provision for them to come to him. It touched the right chord in him; he resolved to become a temperate man. And he preserved in this resolution till the beginning of November with every promise of success. Accident at length threw him into the clutches of these fiends. They dragged him to their place of sacrifice, and compelled him to taste, nay, to drink; till he was again without self-control or reason. His friends, who had watched him with deep interest, seizing every opportunity to strengthen his good resolutions, called on the master demon, and begged that he would let him go; that he would not supply him with the means of self-destruction. He answered their remonstrances with curses, and assured them that as long as he had liquor and "Mac" had money, the latter should have what he wanted. On Saturday evening there was deep drinking in this miniature hell. The carousal held till morning opened, and at a late hour the various inmates set out reeling and stumbling toward home, or whatever lodging chance might bring them. The Sabbath opened clear and bright. A light frost had crisped the grass; the red sun came up the eastern sky, curtained with mist and smoke; soft winds crept over the embrowned forests and plains, and all nature seemed to be filled with a kind of sad joy. I shall never forget that morning. The holy quiet which rested on the earth contrasted strongly with the fierce and harrowing sounds of the previous night. I looked out just as the sun was rising. The smoke began to curl slowly upward from various chimneys, and a few early risers were abroad inhaling the air freshened by the frost which yet lay upon the grass. They looked as if care were dismissed, and man as well as nature was to enjoy a holy day. When the family who had sheltered poor "Mac," notwithstanding his many deviations, ascertained that he had not returned to the house, they dispatched a person to the grocery, to bring him home. But he was not there! The miserable proprietor reported as nearly as his half conscious state and drunken recollections would permit, that he left there about two o'clock.

"You'll find him," said he, "under some fence or the side of a house, fast enough, I'll warrant you; for he was drunk when he went away; he wanted to git off afore he took the last drink, but we made him go it!"

There was an unfinished house some distance below, and thither they went, thinking it probable that he had crept in there to sleep. But he was not to be found. They were wondering where he could have gone, when one of them, happening to pass near the open well, glanced into it, and was horrified to discover the figure of the lost man in the bottom, partly covered with water. He was immediately removed, and measures taken to resuscitate him, but life was utterly quenched. Another coroner's inquest was held. A rude coffin was nailed together, and the remains were deposited the same day in the earth. I see now before me the thrilling events of that day, faint as is this picture of them. I feel again the overpowering emotions we experienced when reflecting on the fate of this unwilling victim to the vices of others. The poor wretch, half conscious, notwithstanding the maddening potations that had been forced upon him, stumbling along in the dark night for a place of rest, thinking possibly of his broken vows, and of the faithful wife and children whose hearts would bleed could they know his situation; half resolving, perhaps, that he would still save himself, and never touch again the fire that had so nearly consumed his soul—all these thoughts and feelings, faintly recognized, passing through the mind that had bowed reluctantly to its renewed degradation, and all cut short by the brief and sudden plunge which ended in almost instant death! What an entrance into eternity! what a fearful leave-taking of the fair earth! what an introduction to the mighty future! For days my mind was busied with his last thoughts, and the fearful struggles he must have made to recover his hold upon life. I could not dismiss them.

If everything connected with this terrible place had been painful and disgusting before, it will readily be conceived that they were incomparably more so now. The groans seemed the dying agonies of fiends, the shouts their exultations. The reeling forms and bloated faces seemed more deeply lost than ever. But they did not remain long: public indignation was so roused at the destruction of a man who had naturally so much to win esteem and respect, that the grocery was doomed from the day of his death. Pity it could not have been before; but people require something which would startle the blind and deaf, to rouse them to action in such matters. Even now public opinion barely permitted individual action, but did not aid it. The license which conferred the power to do all these things was revoked, the shop broken up, and the miserable wretch who had kept it driven to seek another place of abode. He lingered about some time in his degradation, till at last one of his brother masons took him to his house in a neighboring town, and by some means induced his reformation. When I last saw him, I scarcely recognized him. But improved as he was, he still bore the stamp of a degraded, wretched man.

CHAPTER XXV

The return of my husband was now *the event* to which I looked forward. Sixteen months of perilous wanderings in the wilderness, and upon the ocean, were now drawing to a close. His arrival had been joyfully heralded by letters from California, and last of all, by the public prints, announcing that it had been in his power to save the lives, and restore the liberties of several of his countrymen and Englishmen, prisoners to the authorities of that misgoverned, but beautiful country. The period of waiting was prolonged much beyond what I had anticipated. Days ran into weeks, and summer was drawing to a close, and still he came not. At last the third anniversary of our departed boy's birth, among the last days of August, brought him. It was early one morning, just after breakfast, that he came into my friend's house, following one of the villagers whom he had met in the street, and who could not forbear playing the startling office of usher on the occasion.

I pass over all that followed, the thousand interesting things to be heard and communicated; the welcomes and congratulations of friends, and come to the time but a few weeks forward, when we were preparing to leave prairie land and sever all the sacred ties that bound us to those who were sleeping in its quiet bosom, and those who still trod its beautiful surface, full of life and hope.

We visited Prairie Lodge and the resting-place of those who had been laid in the quiet graves near it, two long years before. At that distance of time, I could look calmly upon those hallowed spots, regarding them as what they really were—one, the tomb of a woman who had lived, loved, and suffered—the other, the tiny couch of an infant, whose tender bud of being scarce opened ere it closed again, to bloom in a more genial world. They were now objects of faith and hope, not of harrowing grief; and it was not altogether painful to linger over them, and train the evergreens and other plants which I had placed there long before. The foliage of the surrounding trees and shrubs had already faded from the high vigor and pomp of summer into the sober and gentle beauty of autumn—the season Mary had so much loved. A few short weeks, and the leaves would no more rustle to the gentle winds, the birds would no more dance in the boughs above, the mellow sunshine would no longer stream through the trembling canopy that softened its stronger glare into a tone harmonious with the hallowed character of the spot. All were departing; and we were going too; a few days would see us bid farewell to the country in which we had enjoyed and suffered so much; which still contained so much of life and death, to enchain our affections, and draw from our hearts in after times strong longings to behold it once more.

It was late in autumn when we bade adieu to the little village in which our home had been, and to the few faithful and beloved friends it contained. Yet late as it was, nature was still clothed with the full majesty of her departing grandeur. As we rode slowly over the high rolling prairies of the north toward our point of embarkation, I thought I had never seen the country more magnificent. It seemed inviting us to return. Distant fires, scarcely kept alive by the gentle winds, crept lazily over the great brown meadows, curtaining them from the flood of sunlight that filled the upper air, and just veiling the line of the horizon, so that it seemed an interminable distance away from us, and from all mortal care and toil—a quiet and holy region, where, indeed, earth and heaven might meet without exalting the loveliness and peace of the one or lessening those of the other. Never was prairie land more beautiful to us, than in her farewell smiles. Never were our hearts more deeply touched by her charms, than in those days when we were passing away from them all.

The surface of the river, till our steamer broke it into foam, was smooth as the skies it reflected, and even then its agitated waters fell off, as soon as we had passed away, into a soft undulating motions that died upon the sleeping shore, as if the repose of nature were too deep to be broken by man. Trees, half disrobed of their trembling leaves and bathed in sunshine, swayed softly to and fro, their long arms reflected from the still waters with a distinctness that suggested the idea of another creation slumbering beneath!

Myriads of wild fowl sat upon the tranquil stream, chattering in low tones, and lazily disporting themselves in the genial elements. They had been arrested in their migratory flight by the wondrous beauty and softness of those days, and now lingered in the still waters, their dreamy rest broken occasionally by the panting steamers and the more cruel gun of the sportsman on the shore. At long intervals, these merciless sounds boomed over the surface, and sent thousands of geese, brant, and ducks screaming into the air, till the silent woods and long line of water reëchoed to the cry. These were the only painful features of the scene. Nature would have been altogether lovely and gentle in her repose; but man was there with his selfishness and cruelty, to mar it!

Our route lay through the theatre of many of the most interesting scenes and events in the history of the race that has now almost disappeared from these lands—the classic ground of the west! Legends of mighty deeds, such as make the boast of prouder nations fierce hatreds, undying loves, such as troubadours delighted to sing of the knights of olden times, float over all these beautiful realms.

There is the "Starved Rock;" its frowning sides overhanging the quiet waters—its half-naked surface strown with the bones of brave men, tender women, and help-less children! The storms of near a century have bleached and wasted them into crumbling fragments for here, so long ago, a band of warriors retreating with their wives and little ones, took refuge from their more powerful enemies thinking to make their defence good on the small area, which could only be approached by one narrow passage connecting it with the mainland. Here they spent many days, defying their besiegers, and laughing at their efforts to drive them from their shelter. Food they had in plenty, and water ran at the foot of their fort, two hundred and fifty feet below them, which they raised in buckets attached to bark ropes. One afternoon, however, a bucket was let down, but when the Indian would draw it up, it was strangely light! Twice or thrice, after shooting it a few feet, he returned it to the stream, wondering that it did not dip! At length, weary at being thus foiled, he drew it hastily to the top of the rock. Consternation seized every bosom! The rope had been severed, and the bucket was gone! The experiment was repeated at another and another point with the same result! Where now was their hope? The base of their rocky fortress was surrounded by the canoes of their enemies! If they remained, a death more terrible than the tomahawks and scalping knives of their foes could inflict was before them. Yet, with their small numbers, and their wives and children there, it were madness to venture a sally. A council was held, at which it was determined by the warriors to await some relaxation on the part of their besiegers, or some interposition of the Great Spirit in their behalf. Days passed in this fearful condition. Mothers with their nursing infants were famishing of thirst. Their babes were starving for the food which their exhausted systems could no longer furnish! Strong warriors began to look aghast, and tremble, as they walked about! The Great Spirit was angry with them; for clouds, charged with the blessing they so much craved, floated over them, and poured out their delicious treasures on the senseless plains and woods around, but never there. The clear river lay stretched for miles before them, its waters glancing in the sun, or maddening their thirst more fearfully when clouds darkened its checkered surface, making them look still more cool and inviting. Nay, it ran at their very feet. When the gusty night-wind swept over it, they could hear the waters faintly plash and chime below, and could almost in their madness have precipitated themselves into them, from the fearful height, to revel for one brief moment in their abundance. Sometimes, at the deepest hour of night, a vessel would descend the rock, stealthily and slowly, that no untoward contact might arouse their cruel watchers, if haply they slumbered. But vain and infuriating the hope and effort. It resulted only in the loss of the vessel, and the more dreadful aggravation of their sufferings. The terrible watch was never relaxed for a moment of the day or night, and the stern sufferer, at every failure, could hear the exulting laugh and the fierce congratulation of those who had caused it. Then they would heighten his agonies by toying idly with the water, making it splash and leap till the victim could almost see the light bubbles dancing on its cool dark surface. Some of the feeble women and the children died. But they could not be buried. Their bodies were laid decently away on the verge of the rock, and then the friends sat down to wait till they should follow!

Oh! what days and nights were those. Manacles on the limbs of the free, proud warrior, the lighted deathfire, the flashing tomahawk would have been his paradise, could he but have thrown himself upon them. To sit in miserable inaction all the day, he who was like the wind in swiftness and love of motion; to endure the raging torments of thirst and hunger (for the latter had at length been added to their sufferings); to see his wives and his young warriors sinking and dying around him; to make trial after trial for their relief, each ending in failure, more exasperating than before—was one of those fearful conditions of human being, which occur but once in the history of ages, and form in the annals of nations the proverbial evidences of bravery and fortitude, to which countless ages turn back with pride and exultation.

At length, when the exquisite torture could be no longer borne, and the prospect of an ignominious death by slow degrees was the only certainty before them, they determined on a sally. Seizing an hour, when those stationed on the landward side would least expect a movement after their long repose, and causing their women and children to render redoubled vigilance necessary at the base of the rock, they armed themselves, and, strong in the fury which their fearful suffering had provoked, issued silently from the retreat and fell upon their foes.

The contest that followed was bitter as Indian hatred and cruelty could make it. It resulted in the total route and destruction of the Illinois. From that day they were no more seen in council-house or battle field. Their name became extinct or was borne only by a few miserable wanderers from tribe to tribe. Their bones were left to crumble on the field, and their enfeebled women and children slain within the fortress, whence they watched the fatal struggle.

Such is the legend of the "Starved Rock!" It is now, in these tamer days, a curious and interesting object to visitors. Surrounded on three sides by the waters of the Illinois, it rears its frowning summit two hundred and fifty feet above them. The sides are smooth in many places and overhang the base, looking into the dark mirror below, as tranquilly as if they had never formed an impassable barrier between mortal agony and all that earth could afford to relieve it. The summit of the rock is crowned with vegetation; rich grasses and a light growth of young trees render its surface a more agreeable resting-place now than when the wretched Indian pined and famished there in the noonday sun. From its top it commands a view of the river for many miles, broken only here and there, by interposing trees or the gigantic vegetation that crowds its banks. One can imagine the unfortunate savage standing on it and looking out upon those waters which his light canoe had so often parted around him, with a desperation and agony that only the strong pride of his race could prevent him from uttering in tones of inexpressible anguish. To me it was a thrilling and fearful spot.[1]

But here is Mont Joliet with its fair proportioned valley, and swift running stream—the theatre where the good French père planted the first cross ever reared in these sublime solitudes. The tale is longer than I can tell, but it is a beautiful one— beautiful in its exhibition of exalted virtue, and its connexion with this lovely spot. It is one of the most glowing of those old legends that enrich the past. The past in the prairie land! What romance, what mystery, what uncounted volumes of thrilling interest sleep in its mighty bosom! Into these majestic solitudes, ages ago, came the wandering trapper and the solitary, self-sacrificing missionary. Here they lived, alone and humbly, among the proud sovereigns of the land. Their rude cabins were constructed beneath the forests that bordered the streams, and there, upon the margin of the still waters, the former sprung his trap, and the latter, clad in his long, coarse gown, the symbol of his faith and calling pendent at his girdle, preached, for the first time in these vast domains of nature, the doctrines of the Cross.

Seasons came and went; tender spring, glowing summer, ripening autumn, stern winter; and in them all was wondrous beauty or impressive majesty! From fort to solitary fort they floated on streams, thousands of miles in length, winding their lazy ways through a country unparalleled in fertility, beauty, and grandeur. Forests, magnificent in their richness, sublime in their loveliness, hung upon the margins of these rivers, their dense foliage peopled with myriad of gay, glancing birds, their dark mazes occasionally threaded the startling catamount and panther! Passed these! and plains, no less impressive in their vastness, stretched out before the eyes of the *voyageur,* dotted with countless herds of the buffalo, the elk the deer, and the antelope, feeding upon their peaceful bosoms. The gaunt wolf, stealing silently among them, hiding by day, and sending his dismal howl into the silent hours of night, added a striking feature to the strange joyousness of such wanderings.

Nor were these journeys less impressive when undertaken by land. Their way from post to post lay in the narrow trail which the Indian had trod from time immemorial. Day after day they wandered over these plains, and night after night slept upon their bosoms, beneath soft skies and gentle winds. Sunset and twilight such as Italy would boast, ushered in their slumbers; and the grouse with his mournful matin song, aroused them with the dawn, and sent them on their way with hearts swelling in unison with the world-wide peace and joy of nature!

What marvel, if they never wearied with telling the wonders of their new home! What marvel, if they spread its fame to far lands and were content to die, away in its deep solitudes? What marvel was all this? Streams, whose course was equal to a quarter of the diameter of the globe, were stretched around them; storms, whose fearful wrath made the firm earth tremble, gathered and burst over them; sunshine and winds, birds and animals, flowers and fruits, such as only the fairest regions of the old world would return to unsparing labor, were here spread over half a continent! What

---

1. This rock is about six miles below Ottawa, on the east side of the Illinois. It projects far into the stream, and is connected with the mainland by a narrow passage which could be defended by a few men against thousands. Thither a band of the Illinois retreated, after a severe engagement at the north, when pursued by their more powerful and numerous enemies, the Pottowatamies, and then occurred the painful scene described above.

marvel, if, amid these, they felt that language was too poor for their emotions, that fable could not exaggerate them?

Amid this magnificence they lived—alone with the "untutored Indian," sole lord and sovereign of it all. And wild and free was their life, with its abundance—its great untried resources—its boundless variety. One may well conceive that, with minds such as they possessed, it was the realization of their highest ideal. But it was destined to vanish! The second era of civilization dawned over these majestic realms, and its light dispelled their dream.

While the streams were yet unvexed by the impetuous steamer and the beaver and otter dwelt unscared in their early homes; while the forest tracts were yet dark with the unbroken foliage, and wide plains, over which ages were destined to roll before plow or spade should mar their beauty, lay spread around them; came softly, one by one, the white-topped waggons of the early emigrants. They had left the dense forests of Ohio and Pennsylvania, the undulating hills of Kentucky, and the old homes of Virginia, for the new and more hopeful country which adventurers assured them lay beyond. Before them the Indian would retreat, and his white friend must follow. The bond that linked him to his kind was between him and the red man. He had lived in his lodge, shared his hospitality, smoked his pipe, united in his hunts, scalped his enemies, and cemented still more strongly their bond of union, by marrying his daughters. What had he in common with the cultivator of the soil, though wearing a skin of the same color? What had he not in common with those who retired to make way for him?

Here nature would be herself no longer. All her former aspect would fade away beneath the despoiling hand that labor would lay upon her charms; and they must flee to other regions where the spoilers had not come; their old haunts by stream and woodside were forsaken; the smoke no longer ascended from their solitary forts and villages; the rank grass overgrew their well worn trails, and the solitude of their familiar places was deepened by every object which showed that man had been there and departed.

Slowly, and with many regrets and painful yearnings toward the land which time and association had so much endeared, they wended their way to the yet unbroken realms between them and the setting sun.

Scarcely less a distinct race than these, were their successors. Their former lives—exposed as some of them had been by contiguity to savage neighbors, reared as others were in dependence upon slave labor, and accustomed as all were to the plain subsistence afforded by only partial industry—had begotten in them a love of ease, an unrestrained freedom which the new country was well calculated to foster.

To labor with the steady perseverance which anticipates its reward—to toil for the grain which, slow in accumulating, smiles only on the later years of life, was not their mission. Why should freemen do this, when nature was inviting them by such pomp and fascination, to come abroad with her, and enjoy every passing hour. The first settler could not live far from her; a rude cabin and a single field were all that he could brook of separation; more than these were burthensome to the spirit, and reduced freemen to slaves; more was unnecessary in his new condition. We have already beheld him living thus, content as if palaces rose around him. But a dark shadow soon fell upon his home. Files of earnest men, with hard hands and severe, calculating faces, pressed toward it from the east. Tales of its beauty, its grandeur, its freedom, its wondrous fertility, have reached their far firesides and rocky fields; and they are pressing forward to see if such things really are. When their eyes rest upon the glorious plains and gigantic forests, they exclaim, "This was no dream! Here is all that we looked for, and more than can be described! We will build our homes here."

They sat down beside the second son of nature. They fenced the plain adjacent to his field; they built a cabin, more finished than his; its smoke was continually ascending before him; their axe was heard in the neighboring grove, and the brave old trees, that had tossed their arms in the storms of ages, fell and were piled into lofty barns, that were visible wherever he went. If he chased the deer or hunted the grouse, or was returning from a visit to a neighboring settlement, there they stood, the first objects that greeted his vision; a blight upon the fair scene whose free aspect he had never thus marred. They struck his sight unpleasantly. He liked not these crowded ways of living, nor the busy sounds that floated with the morning light from his neighbor's home, nor his earnest toil in field and wood, nor his large crops, nor anything, in short, pertaining to his toilsome life. The country was less pleasant than it used to be, when there were no buildings, no fences, no living things in sight but his own and nature's.

He begins now to contemplate the possibility of following those who fled before him, and even while he is doing it, comes his neighbor's friend or brother, and proposes to bargain with him for his cabin and field! Now indeed, it is time for him to betake himself to a land of liberty. When the Yankees, not content with curtailing his freedom, his very breath of life—not content with crowding around him, and making a prison of his home, come and ask for that home itself—there is no longer any alternative. Everything admonishes him that the time of his departure has come! He therefore gathers his few worldly goods, and these, except his horses and rifle, are more than he wishes they were, and turns from his deserted hearthside to seek a more congenial spot, where industry and trade have not yet despoiled the fair earth, or crowded it with busy, thriving homes.

And now in his place succeeds a permanent population. His old haunts and pleasant ways are trodden by men, who, while they cast a careless eye upon the flying deer, count the resources of every acre which he scorns.

Broad farms open as by magic on the blooming plain; stately houses take the place of the solitary cabin; and industry, that counts her gains, has stretched her transforming arm over all the fair land. The wild, the free, the mysterious, are fading beneath her touch. But a power is growing up where they vanish, before whose might a continent may tremble. Who shall define the limits of its growth? Who shall conceive what intelligence and moral purpose may do, when they seize upon resources such as these, wherewith to consummate their energies.

Lands, boundless in extent, exhaustless in fertility, lying under every variety of climate from the tropical to the arctic; accessible in all their parts by continuous watercourses of magnitude unparalleled on the globe, containing so much to stimulate the nobler faculties and gratify the senses; so much that is calculated to induce a high state of physical development and fine perceptions of the beautiful, the grand, and the true; lands whose primeval glory, when it shall have become ancient, will form the theme of the poet and glow on the page of the historian; though too feebly sung and written to convey to future ages what the present feels. It must be the theatre of a life larger than human prophecy can foretell!

When the tide of intelligence shall have swept from the green barrier on the east, to the bald, heaven-reared wall that stretches along the west, and from the northern lakes to the gulf; when the remote tributaries of the great streams shall have become the commercial channels of the vast regions which they drain; and territories equal in extent to empires renowned in history, and surpassing the gardens of the old world in fertility, shall be overspread by a free brotherhood, united as to the great purposes of life, and pursuing them under a liberal and fostering policy—then will be presented the phenomenon of a life, of which we can have now but a faint conception. The pent-up, famishing legions of Europe may find room and abundance here, when they shall have burst the fetters that bind them there! And here may future tyrants behold how great, and good, the strong, is man when left to govern himself; free from want, from oppression, from ignorance, from fear!

But we are departing from prairie land! The bright waters of Lake Michigan dance around our steamer. Blue and dim in the distance, fades the mellow-tinted shore, its long faint outline trembling in the golden haze of the Indian summer! Farewell! land of majestic rivers and flowering plains—of fearful storms and genial sunshine—of strong life and glowing beauty! Glorious in thy youth—great in thy maturity—mighty in thy age—thou shalt yet rival the eastern lands of heroism and song, in the worship and affection of man! Thy free plains and far-reaching streams shall be the theatre of a power and intelligence never yet witnessed! Thy countless acres shall glow with checkered beauty and hum with busy life, where the generations of those who love thee now, sleep in thy peaceful bosom! Land of the silent past and stirring future, farewell!

52

JOSEPH GLOVER BALDWIN

(1815–1864)

Like Johnson Jones Hooper, Joseph Glover Baldwin was born into a prominent family on the wane. After his birth in Friendly Grove Factory, Virginia, on January 25, 1815, Jo, as his friends and family called him, had a few years of schooling before necessity forced him to work. At fourteen he became a deputy clerk in the Old Chancery Court, in Staunton, Virginia, and three years later he began to study law with a cousin, Alexander H. H. Stuart, and an uncle, Judge Briscoe G. Baldwin. His legal education was complete when he was twenty, but he could not receive his license to practice until he was twenty-one. Thus, in 1835–1836, Baldwin passed time working for newspapers in Lexington, Virginia, and Buchanan, Virginia. When he turned twenty-one, he headed for the frontier. He counted as his belongings "a pony valued at $35, a pair of saddle bags and contents, a new razor not much needed at that early day, and $75 in Virginia Bank bills."

Baldwin worked briefly as a lawyer in DeKalb, Mississippi, before relocating his practice to Gainesville, Alabama, in 1837, and then Livingston, Alabama, in 1850. In 1851 he began to publish in the *Southern Literary Messenger* essays and anecdotes based on his experiences in the legal profession. Seventeen of these items were among the twenty-six pieces collected in the hodgepodge *The Flush Times of Alabama and Mississippi* (1853), the first of his two books. His second book, *Party Leaders* (1855), consisting of biographies of Thomas Jefferson, Alexander Hamilton, Andrew Jackson, and others, is rarely read today.

By 1854 the flush times of which Baldwin had written were gone, and he was again lured west, this time to California, where he was elected an associate justice of the California Supreme Court in 1858. On a business trip to the east in 1863, he wanted to visit his family in Virginia, but he could not gain permission to cross Confederate lines. He did, however, gain an audience with President Lincoln, who told Baldwin that he counted *Flush Times* among his favorite books.

Following minor surgery, Baldwin developed tetanus and died on September 30, 1864.

Text: *The Flush Times of Alabama and Mississippi* (New York, 1853): 223–249.

822

THE BAR OF THE SOUTH-WEST (1853)

THE citizens of an old country are very prone to consider the people of a newly set-tled State or Territory as greatly their inferiors: just as old men are apt to consider those younger than themselves, and who have grown up under their observation, as *their* inferiors. It is a very natural sentiment. It is flattering to pride, and it tickles the vanity of senility—individual and State—to assign this status of elevation to self, and this consequent depression to others. Accordingly, the Englishman looks upon the American as rather a green-horn, gawky sort of a fellow, infinitely below the standard of John Bull in every thing, external and internal, of character and of circumstance; and no amount of licking can thrash the idea out of him. As Swedenborg says of some religious dogmas held by certain bigots—it is glued to his brains. So it is with our own people. The Bostonian looks down upon the Virginian—the Virginian on the Ten-nesseeian—the Tennesseeian on the Alabamian—the Alabamian on the Mississip-pian—the Mississippian on the Louisianian—the Louisianian on the Texian—the Texian on New Mexico, and, we suppose, New Mexico on Pandemonium.

It may be one of the perversions of patriotism, to create and foster invidious and partial discriminations between different countries, and between different sections of the same country: and especially does this prejudice exist and deepen with a people stationary and secluded in habit and position. But travel, a broader range of inquiry and observation, more intimate associations and a freer correspondence, begetting larger and more cosmopolitan views of men and things, serve greatly to soften these prejudices, even where they are not entirely removed. That there is *some* good coun-try even beyond the Chinese wall, and that all not within that barrier are not quite "outside barbarians," the Celestials themselves are beginning to acknowledge.

There is no greater error than that which assigns inferiority to the bar of the South-West, in comparison with that of any other section of the same extent in the United States. Indeed, it is our honest conviction that the profession in the States of Tennessee, Alabama, Mississippi and Louisiana, are not equalled, as a whole, by the same number of lawyers in any other quarter of the Union,—certainly in no other quarter where commerce is no more various and largely pursued.

The reasons for this opinion we proceed to give. The most conclusive mode of establishing this proposition would probably be by comparison; but this, from the na-ture of the case, is impossible. The knowledge of facts and men is wanting, and even if possessed by any capable of instituting the comparison, the decision would, at last, be only an opinion, and would carry but little weight, even if the capacity and fair-ness of the critic were duly authenticated to the reader.

It is a remarkable fact, that the great men of every State in the Union, were those men who figured about the time of the organization and the settling down of their several judicial systems into definite shape and character. Not taking into the account the Revolutionary era—unquestionably the most brilliant intellectual period of our history—let us look to that period which succeeded the turmoil, embarrassment and confusion of the Revolution, and of the times of civil agitation and contention next following, and out of which arose our present constitution. The first thing our fathers did was to get a country; then to fix on it the character of government it was to have;

then to make laws to carry it on and achieve its objects. The men, as a class, who did all this, were lawyers: their labors in founding and starting into motion our constitutions and laws were great and praiseworthy: but after setting the government agoing, there was much more to do; and this was to give the right direction and impress to its jurisprudence. The Statutes of a free country are usually but a small part of the body of its law—and the common law of England, itself but a judicial enlargement and adaptation of certain vague and rude principles of jurisprudence to new wants, new necessities and exigencies, was a light rather than a guide, to the judges of our new systems, called to administer justice under new and widely different conditions and circumstances. The greatest talent was necessary for these new duties. It required the nicest discrimination and the soundest judgment to determine what parts of the British system were opposed to the genius of the new constitution, and what parts were inapplicable by reason of new relations or differing circumstances. The great judicial era of the United States—equally great in bar and bench—was the first quarter of this century. And it is a singular coincidence that this was the case in nearly every, if not in every, State. Those were the days of Marshall and Story and Parsons, of Kent and Thompson and Roane, of Smith and Wythe and Jay, and many other fixed planets of the judicial system, while the whole horizon, in every part of the extended cycle, was lit up by stars worthy to revolve around and add light to such luminaries. Mr. Webster declared that the ablest competition he had met with, in his long professional career, was that he encountered at the rude provincial bar of back-woods New Hampshire in his earlier practice.

And this same remarkable preëminence has characterized the bar of every new State when, or shortly after emerging from, its territorial condition and first crude organization; the States of Tennessee, Kentucky, Alabama, Mississippi and Louisiana forcibly illustrate this truth, and we have no question but that Texas and California are affording new expositions of its correctness.

A fact so uniform in its existence, must have some solid principle for its cause. This principle we shall seek to ascertain. It is the same influence, in a modified form, which partly discovers and partly creates great men in times of revolution. Men are fit for more and higher uses than they are commonly put to. The idea that genius is self-conscious of its powers, and that men naturally fall into the position for which they are fitted, we regard as by no means an universal truth, if any truth at all. Who believes that Washington ever dreamed of his capacity for the great mission he so nobly accomplished, before with fear and trembling, he started out on its fulfilment? Probably the very ordeal through which he passed to greatness purified and qualified him for the self-denial and self-conquest, the patience and the fortitude, which made its crowning glory. To be great, there must be a great work to be done. Talents alone are not distinction. For the Archimedean work, there must be a fulcrum as well as a lever. Great abilities usually need a great stimulus. What dormant genius there is in every country, may be known by the daily examples of a success, of which there was neither early promise nor early expectation.

In a new country the political edifice, like all the rest, must be built from the ground up. Where nothing is at hand, every thing must be made. There is work for all and a necessity for all to work. There is almost perfect equality. All have an even start and an equal chance. There are few or no factitious advantages. The rewards of labor and skill are not only certain to come, but they are certain to come at once. There is no long and tedious novitiate. Talent and energy are not put in quarantine, and there is no privileged inspector to place his *imprimatur* of acceptance or rejection upon them. An emigrant community is necessarily a practical community; wants come before luxuries—things take precedence of words; the necessaries that support life precede the arts and elegancies that embellish it. A man of great parts may miss his way to greatness by frittering away his powers upon non-essentials—upon the style and finish of a thing rather than upon its strength and utility—upon modes rather than upon ends. To direct strength aright, the aim is as essential as the power. But above all things, success more depends upon self-confidence than any thing else; talent must go in partnership with will or it cannot do a business of profit. Erasmus and Melancthon were the equals of Luther in the closet; but where else were they his equals? And where can a man get this self-reliance so well as in a new country, where he is thrown upon his own resources; where his only friends are his talents; where he sees energy leap at once into prominence; where those only are above him whose talents are above his; where there is no *prestige* of rank, or ancestry, or wealth, or past reputation—and no family influence, or dependants, or patrons; where the stranger of yesterday is the man of mark to-day; where a single speech may win position, to be lost by a failure the day following; and where amidst a host of competitors in an open field of rivalry, every man of the same profession enters the course with a race-horse emulation, to win the prize which is glittering within sight of the rivals. There is no stopping in such a crowd: he who does not go ahead is run over and trodden down. How much of success waits on opportunity! True, the highest energy may make opportunity; but how much of real talent is associated only with that energy which appropriates, but which is not able to create, occasions for its display. Does any one doubt that if Daniel Webster had accepted the $1,500 *clerkship* in New Hampshire, he would not have been *Secretary* of State? Or if Henry Clay had been so unfortunate as to realize his early aspirations of earning in some backwoods county his $333 33 per annum, is it so clear that Senates would have hung upon his lips, or Supreme Courts been enlightened by his wisdom?

The exercise of our faculties not merely better enables us to use them—it strengthens them as much; the strength lies as much in the exercise as in the muscle; and the earlier the exercise, after the muscle can stand it, the greater the strength.

Unquestionably there is something in the atmosphere of a new people which refreshes, vivifies and vitalizes thought, and gives freedom, range and energy to action. It is the natural effect of the law of liberty. An old society weaves a network of restraints and habits around a man; the chains of habitude and mode and fashion fetter him: he is cramped by influence, prejudice, custom, opinion; he lives under a feeling of *surveilance* and under a sense of *espionage*. He takes the law from those above him. Wealth, family, influence, class, caste, fashion, coterie and adventitious circumstances of all sorts, in a greater or less degree, trammel him; he acts not so much from his own will and in his own way, as from the force of these arbitrary influences; his thoughts and actions do not leap out directly from their only legitimate head-spring, but flow feebly in serpentine and impeded currents, through and around all these impediments. The character necessarily becomes, in some sort, artificial and conventional; less bold, simple, direct, earnest and natural, and, therefore, less effective.

What a man does well he must do with freedom. He can no more speak in trammels than he can walk in chains; and he must learn to think freely before he can speak freely. He must have his audience in his mind before he has it in his eye. He must hold his eyes level upon the court or jury—not raised in reverence nor cast down in fear. For the nonce, *the* speaker is the teacher. He must not be sifting his discourse for deprecating epithets or propitiating terms, nor be seeking to avoid being taken up and

shaken by some rough senior, nor be afraid of being wearisome to the audience or disrespectful to superiors: bethinking him of exposure and dreading the laugh or the
sneer, when the bold challenge, the quick retort, the fresh thought, the indignant crim-
ination, the honest fervor, and the vigorous argument are needed for his cause. To illustrate what we mean—let us take the case of a young lawyer just come to the bar of
an old State. Let us suppose that he has a case to argue. He is a young man of talent, of
course—*all* are. Who make his audience? The old judge, who, however mild a man-
nered man he may be, the youth has looked on, from his childhood, as the most awful
of all the sons of men. Who else? The old seniors whom he has been accustomed to
regard as the ablest and wisest lawyers in the world, and the most terrible satirists that
ever snapped sinews and dislocated joints and laid bare nerves on the rack of their merciless wit. The jury of sober-sided old codgers, who have known him from a little boy,
and have never looked on him except as a boy, most imprudently diverted by parental
vanity from the bellows or the plough-handles, to be fixed as a cannister to the dog's
tail that fag-ends the bar:—that jury look upon him,—as he rises stammering and
floundering about, like a badly-trained pointer, running in several directions, seeking
to strike the cold trail of an idea that had run through his brain in the enthusiasm of
ambitious conception the night before:—these, his judges, look at him or from him
with mingled pity and wonder; his fellow-students draw back from fear of being
brought into misprision and complicity of getting him into this insane presumption;
and, after a few awkward attempts to propitiate the senior, who is to follow him, he
catches a view of the countenances of the old fogies in whose quiet sneers he reads his
death-warrant; and, at length, he takes his seat, as the crowd rush up to the veteran who
is to do him—like a Spanish rabble to an *auto da fe*. What are his feelings? What or who
can describe his mortification? What a vastation of pride and self-esteem that was? The
speech he made was not the speech he had conceived. The speech he had in him he
did not *deliver;* he "aborted" it, and, instead of the anticipated pride and joy of mater-
nity, he feels only the guilt and the shame of infanticide.

Alack-a-day! Small is the sum of sympathy which is felt by the mass of men for
the woes and wounds of juvenile vanity and especially for the woes of professional
vanity. From the time of Swift, who pilloried Bettsworth to eternal ridicule, and of
Cobbett, who, with rude contempt, scoffed at the idea of being blamed for "crushing
a lawyer in the egg," but few tears of commiseration have been shed for the poor
"Wind-seller," cut down in his raw and callow youth. And, yet, I cannot help, for the
soul of me, the weakness which comes into my eyes, when I see, as I *have* seen, a gallant youth, full of ardor and hope, let down, a dead failure,—on his first trial over the
rough course of the law. The head hung down—the cowed look of timid depreca-
tion—the desponding carriage—tell a story of deep wounds of spirit—of hopes overcast, and energies subdued, and pride humbled—which touches me deeply. I picture
him in the recesses of his chamber, wearing through the weary watches of the night—
grinding his teeth in impatient anguish,—groaning sorrowfully and wetting his pillow with bitter tears—cursing his folly, and infatuation, and his hard fate—envying
the hod-carrier the sure success of his humbler lot, and his security against the ill fortune of a shameful failure, where failure was exposed presumption.

I have felt, in the intensity of my concern for such an one, like hazarding the of-
ficiousness of going to him, and advising him to abandon the hang-dog trade, and
hide his shame in some obscurer and honest pursuit.

And, rough senior, my dear brother, think of these things when your fingers itch
to wool one of the tender neophytes—and forbear. I crave no quarter for the lawyer,

full-grown or half-grown; he can stand peppering—it is his vocation, Hal—he is paid for it; but for the lawyerling I plead; and to my own urgency in his behalf, I add the pathetic plea of the gentle Elia in behalf of the roast-pig—"Barbecue your whole hogs to your palate, steep them in shalots, stuff them with the plantations of the rank and guilty garlic; you cannot poison *them* or make them stronger than they are—but consider, *he* is a weakling—a flower."

But *revenons à nos moutons.*

But suppose the debutant does better than this; suppose he lets himself out fully and fearlessly, and has something in him *to* let out; and suppose he escapes the other danger of being ruined by presumption, real or supposed; he is duly complimented:— "he is a young man of promise—there is some 'come out' to that young man; some day he will be something—if—if" two or three preadventures don't happen to him. If he is proud,—as to be able to have accomplished all this he must be,—such compliments grate more harshly than censure. He goes back to the office; but where are the clients? They are a slow-moving race, and confidence in a young lawyer "is a plant of slow growth." Does he get his books and "scorn delights and live laborious days," for the prospect of a remote and contingent, and that at best, but a poorly remunerating success? Does he cool his hot blood in the ink of the Black-letter, and spin his toils with the industry and forethought of the patient spider that is to be remunerated *next* fly-season, for her pains, and sit, like *that* collecting attorney, at the door of the house, waiting and watching until *then,* for prey? If so, he is a hero indeed; but what years of the flower of his life are not spent in waiting for the prosperous future, in the vague preparation which is not associated with, or stimulated by, a present use for, and direct application to a tangible purpose of what he learns! Where one man of real merit succeeds, how many break down in the training; and even where success *is* won, how much less that success than where talent, like Pitt's, takes its natural position at the start, and, stimulated to its utmost exercise, fights its way from its first strivings to its ultimate triumphs—each day a day of activity and every week a trial of skill and strength; learning all of law that is evolved from its practice, and forced to know something, at least, of what the books teach of it; and getting that larger and better knowledge of men which books cannot impart, and that still more important self-knowledge, of which experience is the only schoolmaster.

In the new country, there are no seniors: the bar is all Young America. If the old fogies come in, they must stand in the class with the rest, if, indeed, they do not "go foot." There were many evils and disadvantages arising from this want of standards and authority in and over the bar—many and great—but they were not of long continuance, and were more than counterbalanced by opposite benefits.

It strikes me that the career of Warren Hastings illustrates my idea of the influence of a new country and of a new and responsible position over the character of men of vigorous parts. In India, new to English settlement and institutions, he well earned the motto, "*Mens æqua in arduis,*" inscribed over his portrait in the council chamber of Calcutta: but after he returned to England, amidst the difficulties of his impeachment, his policy ignored all his claims to greatness, had it alone been considered: the genius that expatiated over and permeated his broad policy on the plains of Hindostan seemed stifled in the conventional atmosphere of St. Stephen's.

While we think that the influence of the new country upon the intellect of the professional *emigré* was highly beneficial, we speak, we hope, with a becoming distrust, of its moral effect. We might, in a debating club, tolerate some scruple of a doubt, whether this violent disruption of family ties—this sudden abandonment of the associations and influence of country and of home—of the restraints of old authority and of opinion—and this sudden plunge into the whirling vortex of a new and seething population—in which the elements were curiously and variously mixed with free manners and not over-puritanic conversation—were efficient causes of moral improvement: we can tolerate a doubt as to whether the character of a young man might not receive something less than a pious impression, under these circumstances of temptation, when that character was in its most malleable and fusible state. But we leave this moral problem to be solved by those better able to manage it, with this single observation, that if the subject *were* able to stand the trial, his moral constitution, like his physical after an attack of yellow fever, would be apt to be the better for it. We cannot, however, in conscience, from what we have experienced of a new country with "flush fixins" annexed, advise the experiment. We *have* known it to fail. And probably more of character would have been lost if more had been put at hazard.

In trying to arrive at the character of the South-Western bar, its opportunities and advantages for improvement are to be considered. It is not too much to say that, in the United States at least, no bar ever had such, or so many: it might be doubted if they were *ever* enjoyed to the same extent before. Consider that the South-West was the focus of an emigration greater than any portion of the country ever attracted, at least, until the golden magnet drew its thousands to the Pacific coast. But the character of emigrants was not the same. Most of the gold-seekers were mere gold-diggers—not bringing property, but coming to take it away. Most of those coming to the South-West brought property—many of them a great deal. Nearly every man was a speculator; at any rate, a trader. The treaties with the Indians had brought large portions of the States of Alabama, Mississippi and Louisiana into market; and these portions, comprising some of the most fertile lands in the world, were settled up in a hurry. The Indians claimed lands under these treaties—the laws granting preemption rights to settlers on the public lands, were to be construed, and the litigation growing out of them settled, the public lands afforded a field for unlimited speculation, and combinations of purchasers, partnerships, land companies, agencies, and the like, gave occasion to much difficult litigation in after times. Negroes were brought into the country in large numbers and sold mostly upon credit, and bills of exchange taken for the price; the negroes in many instances were unsound—some as to which there was no title; some falsely pretended to be unsound, and various questions as to the liability of parties on the warranties and the bills, furnished an important addition to the litigation: many land titles were defective; property was brought from other States clogged with trusts, limitations, and uses, to be construed according to the laws of the State from which it was brought: claims and contracts made elsewhere to be enforced here: universal indebtedness, which the hardness of the times succeeding made it impossible for many men to pay, and desirable for all to escape paying: hard and ruinous bargains, securityships, judicial sales; a general looseness, ignorance, and carelessness in the public officers in doing business; new statutes to be construed; official liabilities, especially those of sheriffs, to be enforced; banks, the laws governing their contracts, proceedings against them for forfeiture of charter; trials of right of property; an elegant assortment of frauds constructive and actual; and the whole system of chancery law, admiralty proceedings; in short, all the flood-gates of litigation were opened and the pent-up tide let loose upon the country. And such a criminal docket! What country could boast more largely of its crimes? What more splendid rôle of felonies! What more terrific murders! What more gorgeous bank robberies! What more magnificent operations in the land offices! Such McGregor-like levies of black mail, individual and corporate! Such superb forays on the treasuries, State and National! Such expert transfers of balances to undiscovered bournes! Such august defalcations! Such flourishes of rhetoric on ledgers auspicious of gold which had departed for ever from the vault! And in INDIAN affairs!—the very mention is suggestive of the poetry of theft—the romance of a wild and weird larceny! What sublime conceptions of super-Spartan roguery! Swindling Indians by the nation! (*Spirit of Falstaff, rap!*) Stealing their land by the township! (*Dick Turpin and Jonathan Wild! tip the table!*) Conducting the nation to the Mississippi river, stripping them to the flap, and bidding them God speed as they went howling into the Western wilderness to the friendly agency of some sheltering Suggs duly empowered to receive their coming annuities and back rations: What's Hounslow heath to this? Who Carvajal? Who Count Boulbon?

And all these merely forerunners, ushering in the Millennium of an accredited, official Repudiation; and IT but vaguely suggestive of what men could do when opportunity and capacity met—as shortly afterwards they did—under the Upas-shade of a perjury-breathing bankrupt law!—But we forbear. The contemplation of such hyperboles of mendacity stretches the imagination to a dangerous tension. There was no end to the amount and variety of lawsuits, and interests involved in every complication and of enormous value were to be adjudicated. The lawyers were compelled to work, and were forced to learn the rules that were involved in all this litigation.

Many members of the bar, of standing and character, from the other States, flocked in to put their sickles into this abundant harvest. Virginia, Kentucky, North Carolina and Tennessee contributed more of these than any other four States; but every State had its representatives.

Consider, too, that the country was not so new as the practice. Every State has its peculiar tone or physiognomy, so to speak, of jurisprudence imparted to it, more or less, by the character and temper of its bar. That had yet to be given. Many questions decided in older States, and differently decided in different States, were to be settled here; and a new state of things, peculiar in their nature, called for new rules or a modification of old ones. The members of the bar from different States had brought their various notions, impressions and knowledge of their own judicature along with them; and thus all the points, dicta, rulings, off-shoots, quirks and quiddities of all the law, and lawing, and law-mooting of all the various judicatories and their satellites, were imported into the new country and tried on the new jurisprudence.

After the crash came in 1837—(there were some *premonitory fits* before, but *then* the *great convulsion* came on)—all the assets of the country were marshalled, and the suing material of all sorts, as fast as it could be got out, put into the hands of the workmen. Some idea of the business may be got from a fact or two: in the county of Sumpter, Alabama, in one year, some four or five thousand suits, in the common-law courts alone, were brought; but in some other counties the number was larger; while in the lower or river counties of Mississippi, the number was at least double. The United States Courts were equally well patronized in proportion—indeed, rather more so. The white *suable* population of Sumpter was then some 2,400 men. It was a merry time for us craftsmen; and we brightened up mightily, and shook our quills joyously, like goslings in the midst of a shower. We look back to that good time, "now past and gone," with the pious gratitude and serene satisfaction with which the wreckers near the Florida Keys contemplate the last fine storm.

It was a pleasant sight to profesional eyes to see a whole people let go all holds and meaner business, and move off to court, like the Californians and Australians to the mines: the "pockets" were picked in both cases. As law and lawing soon got to be the staple productions of the country, the people, as a whole the most intelligent—in the wealthy counties—of the rural population of the United States, and, as a part, the *keenest* in all creation, got very well "up to trap" in law matters; indeed, they soon knew more about the delicate mysteries of the law, than it behooves an honest man to know.

The necessity for labor and the habit of taking difficulties by the horns is a wonderful help to a man; no one knows what he can accomplish until he tries his best; or how firmly he can stand on his own legs when he has no one to lean on.

The range of practice was large. The lawyer had to practise in all sorts of courts, State and Federal, inferior and Supreme. He had the bringing up of a lawsuit, from its birth in the writ to its grave in the sheriff's docket. Even when not concerned in his own business, his observation was employed in seeing the business of others going on; and the general excitement on the subject of law and litigation, taking the place, in the partial supension of other business, of other excitements, supplied the usual topics of general, and, more especially, of professional conversation. If he followed the circuit, he was always in law: the temple of Themis, like that of Janus in war, was always open.

The bar of every country is, in some sort, a representative of the character of the people of which it is so important an "institution." We have partly shown what this character was: after the great Law revival had set in, the public mind had got to be as acute, excited, inquisitive on the subject of law, as that of Tennessee or Kentucky on politics: every man knew a little and many a great deal on the subject. The people soon began to find out the capacity and calibre of the lawyers. Besides, the multitude and variety of lawsuits produced their necessary effect. The talents of the lawyers soon adapted themselves to the nature and exigencies of the service required of them, and to the tone and temper of the juries and public. Law had got to be an every-day, practical, common-place, business-like affair, and it had to be conducted in the same spirit on analogous principles. Readiness, precision, plainness, pertinency, knowledge of law, and a short-hand method of getting at and getting through with a case, were the characteristics and desiderata of the profession. There was no time for wasting words, or for manœuvring and skirmishing about a suit; there was no patience to be expended on exordiums and perorations: few jurors were to be humbugged by demagogical appeals; and the audience were more concerned to know what was to become of the negroes in suit, than to see the flights of an ambitious rhetoric, or to have their ears fed with vain repetitions, mock sentimentality, or tumid platitudes. To start *in medias res*—to drive at the centre—to make the home-thrust—to grasp the hinging point—to give out and prove the law, and to reason strongly on the facts—to wrestle with the subject Indian-hug fashion—to speak in plain English and fervid, it mattered not how rough, sincerity, were the qualities required: and these qualities were possessed in an eminent degree.

Most questions litigated are questions of law: in nine cases out of ten tried, the jury, if intelligent and impartial, have no difficulty in deciding after the law has been plainly given them by the court: there is nothing for a jury to do but to settle the facts, and these are not often seriously controverted, in proportion to the number of cases tried in a new country; and the habit of examining carefully, and arguing fully, legal propositions, is the habit which makes the lawyer. Nothing so debilitates and corrupts a healthy taste and healthy thought, as the habit of addressing ignorant juries; it corrupts style and destroys candor; it makes a speech, which ought to be an enlightened exposition of the legal merits of a cause, a mere mass of "skimble skamble stuff," a compound of humbug, rant, cant and hypocrisy, of low, demagoguism and flimsy perversions—of interminable wordiness and infinite repetition, exaggeration, bathos and vituperation—frequently of low wit and buffoonery—which "causes the judicious to grieve," "though it splits the ears of the groundlings." I do not say that the new bar was free from these traits and vices: by no manner of means: but I do say that they were, as a class, much freer than the bar of the older States out of the commercial cities. The reason is plain: the new dogs hadn't learned the old tricks; and if they had tricks as bad, it was a great comfort that they did not have the same. If we had not improvement, we had, at least, variety; but, I think, we had improvement.

There was another thing: the bar and the community—as all emigrant communities—were mostly young, and the young men cannot afford to play the pranks which the old fogies safely play behind the domino of an established reputation. What is ridiculous, in itself or in a young man, may be admired, or not noticed, in an older leader with a prescriptive title to cant and humbug; it is *lese majesty* to take him off, but the juniors with us had no such immunity. If he tried such tricks he heard of it again; it was rehearsed in his presence for his benefit—if he made himself *very* ridiculous, he was carried around the circuit, like a hung jury in old times, for the especial divertisement of the brethren. A respectable old snob like Mr. Buzzfuz, shrouded like Jack the Giant Killer, in a mantle of dignity that forbade approach, if it did not hide the wearer from attack, never could hear what his "d—d good-natured friends" thought of his performances in the department of humbug or cant; but this was, by no means, the case with such an one in our younger community.

Again, it is flattering to human nature to know that these forensic tricks are not spontaneous but acquired, and a young bar cannot, all at once, acquire them. It requires experience, and a monstrous development of the organs of Reverence and Marvellousness in the audience to practise them with any hope of success, and these bumps were almost entirely wanting in the craniums of the new population around, all of whose eye-teeth were fully cut, and who, standing knee-deep in exploded humbugs, seemed to wear their eyes stereotyped into a fixed, unwinking *qui vive:* the very expression of their countenances seemed to be articulate with the interrogatory, "who is to be picked up next?" It stops curiously the flow of the current when the humbugger sees the intended humbuggee looking him, with a quizzical 'cuteness in the eye, and seeming to say by the expression of his own, "Squire, do you see any thing green here?"

The business of court-house speaking began to grow too common and extensive to excite public interest; the novelty of the thing, after a while, wore off. A stream of sound poured over the land like the trade winds; men now, as a general thing, only came to court because they had business there, and staid only until it was accomplished. It is otherwise in the old country as it had been in the new. It is one of the phenomena of mind that quiet and otherwise sensible men, come from their homes to the county seat to listen to the speeches of the lawyers,—looking over the bar and dropping the under jaw in rapt attention, when some forensic Boreas is blowing away at a case in which they have no interest or concern, deserting, for this queer divertisement, the splitting of their rails and their attention to their bullocks; or, if they needed some relaxation from such pursuits, neglecting their arm-chairs in the passage with the privilege of reading an old almanac or listening to the wind whistling through the key-hole. When a thing gets to be a work-day and common-place affair, it is apt to be done in a common-place way, and the parade, tinsel, and fancy fireworks of a holiday exercise or a gala-day fête are apt to be omitted from the bill and the boards.

It is a great mistake to suppose that a lawyer's strength lies chiefly in his tongue;

it is in the preparation of his case—in knowing what makes the case—in stating the case accurately in the papers, and getting out and getting up the proofs. It requires a good lawyer to make a fine argument; but he is a better lawyer who saves the necessity of making a fine argument, and prevents the possibility of his adversary's making one.

These practical requirements and habits had the effect of driving from the bar that forensic nuisance, "a pretty speaker;" Fourth-of-Julyisms fled to the stump or the national anniversary barbecues; they were out of place in those prosaic times and proceedings. A veteran litigant having a tough lawsuit, had as little use for a flowery orator, letting off his fancy pyrotechnics, as he had for Juno's team of peacocks for hauling his cotton to market.

Between the years 1833 and 1845, the bar was most numerous, and, we think, on the whole, most able. The Supreme Court bar of Mississippi was characterized by signal ability. It may well be doubted if so able and efficient a bar ever existed at any one period of the same duration, in a Southern State: not that the bar was made up of Wickhams, Leighs, Johnsons, and Stanards, nor of Clays, Crittendens, Rowans, and Wickliffes; nor, possibly, that there were any members of the Jackson bar equal to these great names of the Richmond and Frankfort bars; yet those who have heard the best efforts of Prentiss, Holt, Walker, Yerger, Mays, and Boyd, may be allowed to doubt the justness of that criticism which would deny a place to them among lawyers even so renowned as the shining lights of the Virginia and Kentucky forums. But we meant to say, that if this claim be ignored, yet the Mississippi bar, if not so distinguished for individual eminence, made up the deficiency by a more generally-diffused ability, and a larger number of members of inferior, though only a shade inferior, distinction.

As some proof of the ability of the South-western bar, it may be stated, that we had not unfrequently an advent into the new country of lawyers of considerable local reputation in the older States—men who, in their own bailiwicks, were mighty men of war—so distinguished, indeed, that on the first bruiting of a lawsuit, the litigants, without waiting for the ferry-boat, would swim Tar river, or the Pedee, or French Broad, to get to them, under the idea that who got to them first would gain the case. But after the first bustle of their coming with the fox-fire of their old reputations sticking to their gowns, it was generally found, to the utter amazement of their friends who had known them in the old country, that the new importation would not suit the market. They usually fell back from the position at first courteously tendered them, and, not unfrequently, receded until, worked out of profitable practice, they took their places low down in the list, or were lost behind the bar, among the spectators. There is something doubtless in transplantation—something in racing over one's own training paths—something in first firing with a rest, and then being compelled to fire off-hand amid a general flutter and confusion; but, making all this allowance, it hardly accounts fully for the result. For we know that others, against these disadvantages, sustained themselves.

Nor was there, nor is there, any bar that better illustrates the higher properties or nobler characteristics which have, in every State, so much ennobled the profession of the law, than that of the South-West, a class of men more fearless or more faithful, more chivalrous, reliable or trustworthy, more loyal to professional obligations, or more honorable in inter-professional intercourse and relations. True, there were exceptions, as, at all times and every where, there are and will be. Bullying insolence, swaggering pretension, underhanded arts, low detraction, unworthy huckstering for fees, circumvention, artful dodges, ignoring engagements, facile obliviousness of arrangements, and a smart sprinkling, especially in the early times of pettifogging, quibbling and quirking, but these vices are rather of persons than of caste, and not often found; and, when they make themselves apparent, are scouted with scorn by the better members of the bar.

We should be grossly misunderstood if we were construed to imply that the bar of the South-West, possessing the signal opportunities and advantages to which we have adverted, so improved them that all of its members became good lawyers and honorable gentlemen. Mendacity itself could scarcely be supposed to assert what no credulity could believe. All the guano of Lobos could not make Zahara a garden. In too many cases there was no sub-soil of mind or morals on which these advantages could rest. As Chief Justice Collier, in Dargan and Waring, 17 Ala. Reports, in language, marrying the manly strength and beauty of Blackstone to the classic elegance and flexible grace of Stowell, expresses it, "the claim of such," so predicated, "would be *pro tanto* absolutely void, and, having nothing to rest on, a court of equity" (or law) "could not impart to it vitality. Form and order *has* been given to chaos, but an appeal to equity" (or law) "to breathe life into a nonentity, which is both intangible and imperceptible, supposes a higher power—one which no human tribunal can rightfully exercise. *Æquitas sequitur legem.*" This view is conclusive.

We should have been pleased to say something of the bench, especially of that of the Supreme Court of Alabama and Mississippi, but neither our space nor the patience of the reader will permit.

A writer usually catches something from, as well as communicates something to, his subject. Hence if, in the statements of this paper, we shall encounter the incredulity of some old fogy of an older bar, and he should set us down as little better than a romancer in prose, we beg him to consider that we have had two or three regiments of lawyers for our theme—and be charitable.

THOMAS BANGS THORPE

(1815–1878)

Though he served in the Union army during the Civil War, Thomas Bangs Thorpe is usually remembered as a southern writer. Thorpe was born in Westfield, Massachusetts, on March, 1, 1815. In 1818 Thorpe's family moved to New York City. The following year, when Thorpe was four, his father, a circuit-riding Methodist minister, died of tuberculosis. Thorpe's mother was pregnant at the time, and she moved the family to Albany, New York, to live with her parents.

The Thorpes eventually moved back to New York City, where, about 1830, Thorpe began to study figure painting with John Quidor, a local artist who made his living painting the panels of fire engines. In 1833 Thorpe exhibited his first painting, *Ichabod Crane,* which had been in-spired by the works of Washington Irving. Thorpe so admired Irving that he claimed once to have memorized *A History of New York* (1809) and *The Sketch Book* (1820–1821).

Thorpe could not afford to travel to Europe to study art, so in 1834 he enrolled at Wesleyan University in Middletown, Connecticut, where he studied almost every subject except for art. He had hoped to graduate in 1837, but in late 1836 he moved to Louisiana in the belief that frontier life would improve his health. Leaving college had another attraction as well: again Thorpe could devote his time to painting.

In Louisiana, when painting portraits proved not as lucrative as he had hoped, Thorpe turned to writing. On July 27, 1839, his first effort, "Tom Owen, the Bee-Hunter," appeared in *The Spirit of the Times,* the New York paper that would soon become the nation's leading publisher of frontier humor. Thorpe's story was credited to "a New Yorker in Louisiana."

In the 1840s, Thorpe continued to publish sketches in *The Spirit of the Times* and elsewhere. Too, he edited five Louisiana newspapers between 1843 and 1847. In 1854 Thorpe moved back to New York. He returned south for the last time during the Civil War to serve the Union as a colonel in the military government of New Orleans. He returned to New York in October 1864. In his later years, he suffered from chronic Bright's disease, which probably caused his death on September 20, 1878.

"The Big Bear of Arkansas," Thorpe's masterpiece, appeared in *The Spirit of the Times* on March 27, 1841. Many critics consider it the finest story written on the antebellum southern frontier. Leo Lemay has argued that the story of the bear represents "the end of the Eden-like wilderness of the Old Southwest." William Faulkner said simply, "A writer is afraid of a story like that. He's afraid he'll try to rewrite it. A writer has to learn when to run from a story."

Text: *The Hive of "The Bee-Hunter"* (New York, 1854): 72–93.

THE BIG BEAR OF ARKANSAS (1841, 1854)

A STEAMBOAT on the Mississippi, frequently, in making her regular trips, carries between places varying from one to two thousand miles apart, and, as these boats advertise to land passengers and freight at "all intermediate landings," the heterogeneous character of the passengers of one of these up-country boats can scarcely be imagined by one who has never seen it with his own eyes.

Starting from New Orleans in one of these boats, you will find yourself associated with men from every State in the Union, and from every portion of the globe; and a man of observation need not lack for amusement or instruction in such a crowd, if he will take the trouble to read the great book of character so favorably opened before him.

Here may be seen, jostling together, the wealthy Southern planter and the pedler of tin-ware from New England—the Northern merchant and the Southern jockey—a venerable bishop, and a desperate gambler—the land speculator, and the honest farmer—professional men of all creeds and characters—Wolvereens, Suckers, Hoosiers, Buckeyes, and Corncrackers, beside a "plentiful sprinkling" of the half-horse and half-alligator species of men, who are peculiar to "old Mississippi," and who appear to gain a livelihood by simply going up and down the river. In the pursuit of pleasure or business, I have frequently found myself in such a crowd.

On one occasion, when in New Orleans, I had occasion to take a trip of a few miles up the Mississippi, and I hurried on board the well-known "high-pressure-and-beat-every-thing" steamboat "Invincible," just as the last note of the last bell was sounding; and when the confusion and bustle that is natural to a boat's getting under way had subsided, I discovered that I was associated in as heterogeneous a crowd as was ever got together. As my trip was to be of a few hours' duration only, I made no endeavors to become acquainted with my fellow passengers, most of whom would be together many days. Instead of this, I took out of my pocket the "latest paper," and more critically than usual examined its contents; my fellow-passengers, at the same time, disposed of themselves in little groups.

While I was thus busily employed in reading, and my companions were more busily still employed, in discussing such subjects as suited their humors best we were most unexpectedly startled by a loud-Indian whoop, uttered in the "social hall," that part of the cabin fitted off for a bar; then was to be heard a loud crowing, which would not have continued to interest us—such sounds being quite common in that *place of spirits*—had not the hero of these windy accomplishments stuck his head into the cabin, and hallooed out, "Hurra for the Big Bear of Arkansaw!"

Then might be heard a confused hum of voices, unintelligible save in such broken sentences as "horse," "screamer," "lightning is slow," &c.

As might have been expected, this continued interruption, attracted the attention of every one in the cabin, all conversation ceased, and in the midst of this surprise, the "Big Bear" walked into the cabin, took a chair, put his feet on the stove, and looking back over his shoulder, passed the general and familiar salute—"Strangers, how are you?"

He then expressed himself as much at home as if he had been at "the Forks of Cypress," and "perhaps a little more so."

Some of the company at this familiarity looked a little angry, and some astonished, but in a moment every face was wreathed in a smile. There was some thing about the intruder that won the heart on sight. He appeared to be a man enjoying perfect health and contentment; his eyes were as sparkling as diamonds and good-natured to simplicity. Then his perfect confidence in himself was irresistibly droll.

"Prehaps," said he, "gentlemen," running on without a person interrupting, "prehaps you have been to New Orleans often; I never made *the first visit before,* and I don't intend to make another in a crow's life. I am thrown away in that ar place, and useless, that ar a fact. Some of the gentlemen thar called me *green*—well prehaps I am said I, *but I arn't so at home;* and if I aint off my trail much, the heads of them perlite chaps themselves wern't much the hardest; for according to my notion, they were *real know nothings,* green as a pumpkin vine—couldn't, in farming, I'll bet, raise a crop of turnips; and as for shooting, they'd miss a barn if the door was swinging, and that, too, with the best rifle in the country. And then they talked to me 'bout hunting, and laughed at my calling the principal game in Arkansaw poker, and high-low-jack.

"'Prehaps,' said I, 'you prefer checkers and roulette;' at this they laughed harder than ever, and asked me if I lived in the woods, and didn't know what *game* was?

"At this, I rather think *I* laughed.

"'Yes,' I roared, and says, I, 'Strangers, if you'd asked me *how we got our meat* in Arkansaw, I'd a told you at once, and given you a list of varmints that would make a caravan, beginning with the bar, and ending off with the cat; that's *meat* though, not game.

"Game, indeed,—that's what city folks call it; and with them it means chippen-birds and shite-pokes; may be such trash live in my diggins, but I arn't noticed them yet: a bird anyway is too trifling. I never did shoot at but one, and I'd never forgiven myself for that, had it weighed less than forty pounds. I wouldn't draw a rifle on any thing less heavy than that; and when I meet with another wild turkey of the same size, I will drap him."

"A wild turkey weighing forty pounds!" exclaimed twenty voices in the cabin at once.

"Yes, strangers, and wasn't it a whopper? You see, the thing was so fat that it couldn't fly far; and when he fell out of the tree, after I shot him, on striking the ground he bust open behind, and the way the pound gobs of tallow rolled out of the opening was perfectly beautiful."

"Where did all that happen?" asked a cynical looking Hoosier.

"Happen! happened in Arkansaw: where else could it have happened, but in the creation State, the finishing up country—a State where the *sile* runs down to the centre of the arth, and government gives you a title to every inch of it? Then its airs—just breathe them, and they will make you snort like a horse. It's a State without a fault, it is."

"Excepting mosquitoes," cried the Hoosier.

"Well, stranger, except them; for it ar a fact that they are rather *enormous,* and do push themselves in somewhat troublesome. But stranger, they never stick twice in the same place; and give them a fair chance for a few months, and you will get as much above noticing them as an alligator. They can't hurt my feelings, for they lay under the skin; and I never knew but one case of injury resulting from them, and that was to a Yankee and they take worse to foreigners, any how, than they do to natives. But the way they used that fellow up! first they punched him until he swelled up and busted; then he sup-per-a-ted, as the doctor called it, until he was as raw as beef; then, owing to the warm weather, he tuck the ager, and finally he tuck a steamboat and left the country. He was the only man that ever tuck mosquitoes at heart that I knowd of.

"But mosquitoes is nature, and I never find fault with her. If they ar large, Arkansaw is large, her varmints ar large, her trees ar large, her rivers ar large, and a small mosquito would be of no more use in Arkansaw than preaching in a cane-brake."

This knock-down argument in favor of big mosquitoes used the Hoosier up, and the logician started on a new track, to explain how numerous bear were in his "diggins," where he represented them to be "about as plenty as blackberries, and a little plentifuller."

Upon the utterance of this assertion, a timid little man near me inquired, if the bear in Arkansaw ever attacked the settlers in numbers?

"No," said our hero, warming with the subject, "no, stranger, for you see it ain't the natur of bear to go in droves; but the way they squander about in pairs and single ones is edifying.

"And then the way I hunt them—the old black rascals know the crack of my gun as well as they know a pig's squealing. They grow thin in our parts, it frightens them so, and they do take the noise dreadfully, poor things. That gun of mine is a perfect *epidemic among bear:* if not watched closely, it will go off as quick on a warm scent as my dog Bowieknife will: and then that dog—whew! why the fellow thinks that the world is full of bear, he finds them so easy. It's lucky he don't talk as well as think; for with his natural modesty, if he should suddenly learn how much he is acknowledged to be ahead of all other dogs in the universe, he would be astonished to death in two minutes.

"Strangers, that dog knows a bear's way as well as a horse-jockey knows a woman's: he always barks at the right time, bites at the exact place, and whips without getting a scratch.

"I never could tell whether he was made expressly to hunt bear, or whether bear was made expressly for him to hunt; any way, I believe they were ordained to go together as naturally as Squire Jones says a man and woman is, when he moralizes in marrying a couple. In fact, Jones once said, said he, 'Marriage according to law is a civil contract of divine origin; it's common to all countries as well as Arkansaw, and people take to it as naturally as Jim Doggett's Bowieknife takes to bear.'"

"What season of the year do your hunts take place?" inquired a gentlemanly foreigner, who, from some peculiarities of his baggage, I suspected to be an Englishman, on some hunting expedition, probably at the foot of the Rocky Mountains.

"The season for bear hunting, stranger," said the man of Arkansaw, "is generally all the year round, and the hunts take place about as regular. I read in history that varmints have their fat season, and their lean season. That is not the case in Arkansaw, feeding as they do upon the *spontenacious* productions of the sile, they have one continued fat season the year round; though in winter things in this way is rather more greasy than in summer, I must admit. For that reason bear with us run in warm weather, but in winter they only waddle.

"Fat, fat! its an enemy to speed; it tames every thing that has plenty of it. I have seen wild turkeys, from its influence, as gentle as chickens. Run a bear in this fat condition, and the way it improves the critter for eating is amazing; it sort of mixes the ile up with the meat, until you can't tell t'other from which. I've done this often.

"I recollect one perty morning in particular, of putting an old he fellow on the stretch, and considering the weight he carried, he run well. But the dogs soon tired him down, and when I came up with him wasn't he in a beautiful sweat—I might say fever; and then to see his tongue sticking out of his mouth a feet, and his sides sinking and opening like a bellows, and his cheeks so fat that he couldn't look cross. In this fix I blazed at him, and pitch me naked into a briar patch, if the steam didn't come out of the bullet-hole ten foot in a straight line. The fellow, I reckon, was made on the high-pressure system, and the lead sort of bust his biler."

"That column of steam was rather curious, or else the bear must have been very *warm,*" observed the foreigner, with a laugh.

"Stranger, as you observe, that bear was WARM, and the blowing off of the steam show'd it, and also how hard the varmint had been run. I have no doubt if he had kept on two miles farther his insides would have been stewed; and I expect to meet with a varmint yet of extra bottom, that will run himself into a skinfull of bear's grease: it is possible; much onlikelier things have happened."

"Whereabouts are these bears so abundant?" inquired the foreigner, with increasing interest.

"Why, stranger, they inhabit the neighborhood of my settlement, one of the prettiest places on old Mississipp—a perfect location, and no mistake; a place that had some defects until the river made the 'cut-off' at 'Shirt-tail bend,' and that remedied the evil, as it brought my cabin on the edge of the river—a great advantage in wet weather, I assure you, as you can now roll a barrel of whiskey into my yard in high water from a boat, as easy as falling off a log. It's a great improvement, as toting it by land in a jug, as I used to do, *evaporated* it too fast, and it became expensive.

"Just stop with me, stranger, a month or two, or a year, if you like, and you will appreciate my place. I can give you plenty to eat; for beside hog and hominy, you can have bear-ham, and bear-sausages, and a mattrass of bear-skins to sleep on, and a wild-cat-skin, pulled off hull, stuffed with corn-shucks, for a pillow. That bed would put you to sleep if you had the rheumatics in every joint in your body. I call that ar bed, a *quietus.*

"Then look at my 'pre-emption'—the government aint got another like it to dispose of. Such timber, and such bottom land,—why you can't preserve any thing natural you plant in it unless you pick it young, things that will grow out of shape so quick.

"I once planted in those diggins a few potatoes and beets; they took a fine start, and after that, an ox team couldn't have kept them from growing. About that time I went off to old Kaintuck on business, and did not hear from them things in three months, when I accidentally stumbled on a fellow who had drapped in at my place, with an idea of buying me out."

"'How did you like things?' said I.

"'Pretty well,' said he; 'the cabin is convenient, and the timber land is good; but that bottom land aint worth the first red cent.'"

"'Why?' said I.

"'Cause,' said he.

"'Cause what?' said I.

"'Cause it's full of cedar stumps and Indian mounds, and *can't be cleared.'*

"'Lord,' said I, 'them ar "cedar stumps" is beets, and them ar "Indian mounds" tater hills.'

"As I had expected, the crop was overgrown and useless: the sile is too rich, *and planting in Arkansaw is dangerous.*

"I had a good-sized sow killed in that same bottom land. The old thief stole an ear of corn, and took it down to eat where she slept at night. Well, she left a grain or two on the ground, and lay down on them: before morning the corn shot up, and the percussion killed her dead. I don't plant any more: natur intended Arkansaw for a hunting ground, and I go according to natur."

The questioner, who had thus elicited the description of our hero's settlement, seemed to be perfectly satisfied, and said no more; but the "Big Bear of Arkansaw" rambled on from one thing to another with a volubility perfectly astonishing, occasionally disputing with those around him, particularly with a "live Sucker" from Illinois, who had the daring to say that our Arkansaw friend's stories "smelt rather tall."

The evening was nearly spent by the incidents we have detailed; and conscious that my own association with so singular a personage would probably end before morning, I asked him if he would not give me a description of some particular bear hunt; adding, that I took great interest in such things, though I was no sportsman. The desire seemed to please him, and he squared himself round towards me, saying, that he could give me an idea of a bear hunt that was never beat in this world, or in any other. His manner was so singular, that half of his story consisted in his excellent way of telling it, the great peculiarity of which was, the happy manner he had of emphasizing the prominent parts of his conversation. As near as I can recollect, I have italicized the words, and given the story in his own way.

"Stranger," said he, "in bear hunts *I am numerous,* and which particular one, as you say, I shall tell, puzzles me.

"There was the old she devil I shot at the Hurricane last fall—then there was the old hog thief I popped over at the Bloody Crossing, and then—Yes, I have it ! I will give you an idea of a hunt, in which the greatest bear was killed that ever lived, *none excepted;* about an old fellow that I hunted, more or less, for two or three years; and if that aint a *particular bear hunt,* I ain't got one to tell.

"But in the first place, stranger, let me say, I am pleased with you, because you aint ashamed to gain information by asking and listening; and that's what I say to Countess's pups every day when I'm home; and I have got great hopes of them ar pups, because they are continually *nosing* about; and though they stick it sometimes in the wrong place, they gain experience any how, and may learn something useful to boot.

"Well, as I was saying about this big bear, you see when I and some more first settled in our region, we were drivin to hunting naturally; we soon liked it, and after that we found it an easy matter to make the thing our business. One old chap who had pioneered 'afore us, gave us to understand that we had settled in the right place. He dwelt upon its merits until it was affecting, and showed us, to prove his assertions, more scratches on the bark of the sassafras trees, than I ever saw chalk marks on a tavern door 'lection time.

"'Who keeps that ar reckoning?' said I.

"'The bear,' said he.

"'What for?' said I.

"'Can't tell,' said he; 'but so it is: the bear bite the bark and wood too, at the highest point from the ground they can reach, and you can tell, by the marks,' said he, 'the length of the bear to an inch.'

"'Enough,' said I; 'I've learned something here a'ready, and I'll put it in practice.'

"Well, stranger, just one month from that time I killed a bar, and told its exact length before I measured it, by those very marks; and when I did that, I swelled up considerably—I've been a prouder man ever since.

"So I went on, larning something every day, until I was reckoned a buster, and allowed to be decidedly the best bear hunter in my district; and that is a reputation as much harder to earn than to be reckoned first man in Congress, as an iron ramrod is harder than a toadstool.

"Do the varmints grow over-cunning by being fooled with by greenhorn hunters, and by this means get troublesome, they send for me, as a matter of course; and thus I do my own hunting, and most of my neighbors'. I walk into the varmints though, and it has become about as much the same to me as drinking. It is told in two sentences—

"A bear is started, and he is killed.

"The thing is somewhat monotonous now—I know just how much they will run, where they will tire, how much they will growl, and what a thundering time I will have in getting their meat home. I could give you the history of the chase with all the particulars at the commencement, I know the signs so well—*Stranger, I'm certain*. Once I met with a match, though, and I will tell you about it; for a common hunt would not be worth relating.

"On a fine fall day, long time ago, I was trailing about for bear, and what should I see but fresh marks on the sassafras trees, about eight inches above any in the forests that I knew of. Says I, 'Them marks is a hoax, or it indicates the d———t bear that was ever grown.' In fact, stranger, I couldn't believe it was real, and I went on. Again I saw the same marks, at the same height, and *I knew the thing lived*. That conviction came home to my soul like an earthquake."

"Says I, 'Here is something a purpose for me: that bear is mine, or I give up the hunting business.' The very next morning, what should I see but a number of buzzards hovering over my corn-field. 'The rascal has been there,' said I, 'for that sign is certain:' and, sure enough, on examining, I found the bones of what had been as beautiful a hog the day before, as was ever raised by a Buckeye. Then I tracked the critter out of the field to the woods, and all the marks he left behind, showed me that he was *the bear*.

"Well, stranger, the first fair chase I ever had with that big critter, I saw him no less than three distinct times at a distance: the dogs run him over eighteen miles and broke down, my horse gave out, and I was as nearly used up as a man can be, made on *my* principle, *which is patent*.

"Before this adventure, such things were unknown to me as possible; but, strange as it was, that bear got me used to it before I was done with him; for he got so at last, that he would leave me on a long chase *quite easy*. How he did it, I never could understand.

"That a bear runs at all, is puzzling; but how this one could tire down and bust up a pack of hounds and a horse, that were used to overhauling every thing they started after in no time, was past my understanding. Well, stranger, that bear finally got so sassy, that he used to help himself to a hog off my premises whenever he wanted one; the buzzards followed after what he left, and so, between *bear and buzzard,* I rather think I got *out of pork.*

"Well, missing that bear so often took hold of my vitals; and I wasted away. The thing had been carried too far, and it reduced me in flesh faster than an ager. I would see that bear in every thing I did: *he hunted me,* and that, too, like a devil, which I began to think he was.

"While in this shaky fix, I made preparations to give him a last brush, and be done with it. Having completed every thing to my satisfaction, I started at sunrise and to my great joy, I discovered from the way the dogs run, that they were near him. Finding his trail was nothing, for that had become as plain to the pack as a turnpike road.

"On we went, and coming to an open country, what should I see but the bear very leisurely ascending a hill, and the dogs close at his heels, either a match for him this time in speed, or else he did not care to get out of their way—I don't know which. But wasn't he a beauty, though! I loved him like a brother.

"On he went, until he came to a tree, the limbs of which formed a crotch about six feet from the ground. Into this crotch he got and seated himself, the dogs yelling all around it; and there he sat eyeing them as quiet as a pond in low water.

"A greenhorn friend of mine, in company, reached shooting distance before me, and blazed away, hitting the critter in the centre of his forehead. The bear shook his head as the ball struck it, and then walked, down from that tree, as gently as a lady would from a carriage.

"'Twas a beautiful sight to see him do that—he was in such a rage, that he seemed to be as little afraid of the dogs as if they had been sucking pigs; and the dogs warn't slow in making a ring around him at a respectful distance, I tell you; even Bowieknife himself, stood off. Then the way his eyes flashed!—why the fire of them would have singed a cat's hair, in fact, that bear was in a *wrath all over.* Only one pup came near him, and he was brushed out so totally with the bear's left paw, that he entirely disappeared; and that made the old dogs more cautious still. In the mean time, I came up, and taking deliberate aim, as a man should do, at his side, just back of his foreleg, *if my gun did not snap,* call me a coward, and I won't take it personal.

"Yes, stranger, *it snapped,* and I could not find a cap about my person. While in this predicament, I turned round to my fool friend—'Bill,' says I, 'you're an ass— you're a fool—you might as well have tried to kill that bear by barking the tree under his belly, as to have done it by hitting him in the head. Your shot has made a tiger of him; and blast me, if a dog gets killed or wounded when they come to blows, I will stick my knife into your liver, I will—.' My wrath was up. I had lost my caps, my gun had snapped, the fellow with me had fired at the bear's head, and I expected every moment to see him close in with the dogs and kill a dozen of them at least. In this thing I was mistaken, for the bear leaped over the ring formed by the dogs, and giving a fierce growl, was off—the pack, of course, in full cry after him. The run this time was short, for coming to the edge of a lake, the varmint jumped in, and swam to a little island in the lake, which it reached, just a moment before the dogs.

"'I'll have him now,' said I, for I had found my caps in the *lining of my coat*—so, rolling a log into the lake, I paddled myself across to the island, just as the dogs had cornered the bear in a thicket. I rushed up and fired—at the same time the critter leaped over the dogs and came within three feet of me, running like mad; he jumped into the lake, and tried to mount the log I had just deserted, but every time he got half his body on it, it would roll over and send him under; the dogs, too, got around him, and pulled him about, and finally Bowieknife clenched with him, and they sunk into the lake together.

"Stranger, about this time I was excited, and I stripped off my coat, drew my knife, and intended to have taken a part with Bowieknife myself, when the bear rose to the surface. But the varmint staid under—Bowieknife came up alone, more dead than alive and with the pack came ashore.

"'Thank God!' said I, 'the old villain has got his deserts at last.'

"Determined to have the body, I cut a grape-vine for a rope, and dove down where I could see the bear in the water, fastened my rope to his leg, and fished him, with great difficulty, ashore. Stranger, may I be chawed to death by young alligators, if the thing I looked at wasn't a *she bear, and not the old critter after all.*

"The way matters got mixed on that island was on accountably curious, and thinking of it made me more than ever convinced that I was hunting the devil him self. I went home that night and took to my bed—the thing was killing me. The entire team of Arkansaw in bear-hunting acknowledged himself used up, and the fact sunk into my feelings as a snagged boat will in the Mississippi. I grew as cross as a bear with two cubs and a sore tail. The thing got out 'mong my neighbors, and I was asked how come on that individ-u-al that never lost a bear when once started? and if that same individ-u-al didn't wear telescopes when he turned a she-bear, of ordinary size, into an old he one, a little larger than a horse?

"'Prehaps,' said I, 'friends'—getting wrathy—'prehaps you want to call somebody a liar?'

"'Oh, no,' said they, 'we only heard of such things being *rather common* of late, but we don't believe one word of it, oh, no,'—and then they would ride off, and laugh like so many hyenas over a dead nigger.

"It was too much, and I determined to catch that bear, go to Texas, or die,—and I made my preparations accordin."

"I had the pack shut up and rested. I took my rifle to pieces, and iled it.

"I put caps in every pocket about my person, *for fear of the lining.*

"I then told my neighbors, that on Monday morning—naming the day—I would start THAT B(E)AR, and bring him home with me, or they might divide my settlement among them, the owner having disappeared.

"Well, stranger, on the morning previous to the great day of my hunting expedition, I went into the woods near my house, taking my gun and Bowieknife along, just *from habit,* and there sitting down, also from habit, what should I see, getting over my fence, but *the bear!* Yes, the old varmint was within a hundred yards of me, and the way he walked *over that fence*—stranger; he loomed up like a *black mist,* he seemed so large, and he walked right towards me.

"I raised myself, took deliberate aim, and fired. Instantly the varmint wheeled, gave a yell, and *walked through the fence,* as easy as a falling tree would through a cobweb.

"I started after; but was tripped up by my inexpressibles, which, either from habit or the excitement of the moment; were about my heels, and before I had really gathered myself up, I heard the old varmint groaning, like a thousand sinners, in a thicket near by and, by the time I reached him, he was a corpse.

"Stranger, it took five niggers and myself to put that carcass on a mule's back, and old long-ears waddled under his load, as if he was foundered in every leg of his body; and with a common whopper of a bear, he would have trotted off, and enjoyed himself.

"'Twould astonish you to know how big he was I made a *bed-spread of his skin,* and the way it used to cover my bear mattress, and leave several feet on each side to tuck up, would have delighted you. It was, in fact, a creation bear, and if it had lived in Samson's time, and had met him in a fair fight, he would have licked him in the twinkling of a dice-box.

"But, stranger, I never liked the way I hunted him *and missed him*. There is something curious about it that I never could understand,—and I never was satisfied at his giving in so *easy at last*. Prehaps he had heard of my preparations to hunt him the next day, so he jist guv up, like Captain Scott's coon, to save his wind to grunt with in dying; but that ain't likely. My private opinion is, that that bear was an *unhuntable bear, and died when his time come*."

When this story was ended, our hero sat some minutes with his auditors, in a grave silence; I saw there was a mystery to him connected with the bear whose death he had just related, that had evidently made a strong impression on his mind. It was also evident that there was some superstitious awe connected with the affair,—a feeling common with all "children of the wood," when they meet with any thing out of their every day experience.

He was the first one, however, to break the silence, and, jumping up, he asked all present to "liquor" before going to bed,—a thing which he did, with a number of companions, evidently to his heart's content.

Long before day, I was put ashore at my place of destination, and I can only follow with the reader, in imagination, our Arkansas friend, in his adventures at the "Forks of Cypress," on the Mississippi.

54

JAMES L. SCOTT

(?–?)

Many of the books published about the west during the antebellum decades addressed the activities of missionaries in the west. Various groups spanning the range of Protestant denominations sent missionaries west, first with the intent to convert the "heathen" Native Americans but later, once most of the natives had been removed, to bring the word of God to frontier whites whose distance from the east and whose exposure to the barbarity of settlement and conquest had taken them far from the fold. In this collection, Timothy Flint and George Copway first traveled west as missionaries, and others, such as Peter Cartright and Joseph Badger— among dozens of others—published their memoirs upon their return to the east.

The Seventh-Day Adventist missionary James L. Scott traveled west from Pennsylvania during 1842 in an effort to preach his sect's version of Christianity to the settlers. While the majority of published missionaries were either Presbyterian or Methodist, Scott's distance from those faiths matters little in his description: like them, he records the west as deeply in need of proselytizing and civilization. In his travels from Michigan to Indiana to Iowa and then back east to New York, Scott records the various threats to the establishment of the civilizing influence of the Church in the west.

Nonetheless, Scott's keen powers of observations and his passionate abolitionism make *A Missionary Tour* a book worth reading. Ironically, one of its most valuable qualities as well is its demonstration of Yankee naiveté concerning the west. Scott is repeatedly surprised by the settler's unwillingness to listen to his preaching and is constantly disappointed by their resistance to his putative scriptual and social authority.

Text: *A Journal of a Missionary Tour* (Providence, Rhode Island, 1843): 9–18, 60–89.

FROM *A JOURNAL OF A MISSIONARY TOUR* (1843)

CHAPTER I

Reflections on the Western Valley—Anxieties to visit that section—Engagement for the Missionary Society—Departure—The Mormon Temple at Kirtland, Ohio—Man sick with the Ague and Fever—The Phrenologist.

I entered the Gospel Ministry with a resolution that my mind should be all absorbed in that subject. A world, deluged in iniquity with its millions floating down the current of time, and plunging over the cataract into the burning billows below, aroused the energies of the soul, and caused a renunciation of the world for the sake of the destitute and the requirements of God. Of the different fields of labor that I had in view, the valley of the Mississippi occupied most of my moments of secret meditation. Long had I wept and prayed over the destitute condition of that wild scattered waste, and for a long time no way opened through which I might call the attention of the wandering probationers *there,* to the all absorbing subject of their soul's eternal interest. But notwithstanding my feeble health, when I received the appointment from the Executive of the Missionary Society, I was ready to comply, assured that He who was willing to die for the sinner and was able to conquer death, hell, and the grave, was capable of sustaining and conducting his servants to the end. Not knowing how long duty would detain me in the valley, I resolved on having my family (consisting of Mrs. Scott and a son of six years of age,) accompany me. Accordingly on the sixth of January, 1842, we, after pledging our mutual prayers, took leave of the Church, and our friends. This was a season of the deepest feeling to us all. But feelings were not to be substituted for duty, and often during our absence did we feel that the parting pledge was redeemed. Oh what a boon bestowed from heaven is that blessing of prayer. By it the saints are brought in unison at the throne, and there they meet, though mountains rise and waters roll between. Through this channel saints terrestial hold converse with those of the celestial world, and with the God of eternity. Heaven be praised for this inestimable treasure, and may I ever hold it dear as the blessings it brings. Thus in the midst of a cold winter, we left our fireside and the bosom of the Church to face the stormy blasts, and the frowns of a wicked world, the latter being far the most intolerable. At first when suffering intensely from the inclement weather, nature would recoil; but one reflection of the Savior's pangs for a guilty world would quell each rising thought, and faith would take hold of eternal rest beyond this vale of tears.

7th. Called at Olean Point. Here, in this flourishing village are two families, and although lonely situated as to society, yet persevering in the cause of truth, fully resolved to obey God at the risk of all things. From thence we came to Great Valley— called on a brother, who, without interrogation, acknowledged his convictions of the justice of our cause, and of his becoming a member of some S. D. Baptist Church. From that we passed on to Mansfield, where we spent the Sabbath with first day people, the thaw preventing our reaching the Church at Persia.

9th. Called at Persia, and spent only one evening with the friends there, as our instructions required us to hasten to some remote portion of the Mission, and visit nearer home on our return route.

12th. In North East, Erie County, Pa., called at Br. Abel Babcock's, who had for a long season lived without any knowledge of the prosperity of his covenant brethren. He said "our visit was to him as cold water to a thirsty soul," and wished to express his thankfulness to the society for looking after him. He was in the enjoyment of religion—strong upon the bible Sabbath, and shunned not to defend its cause.

15th. Being Sabbath, spoke to an audience whose number amounted to six, two of them were first day people. Our friends here are faithful soldiers in the cause of God, and an ornament to the society. Our Br. Julius Todd, is trying to publish salvation in this place—preaches each Sabbath to three persons, except on accidental occasions, he also preaches in the country around; his example is worthy of imitation.

16th. Spent the day as usual in travelling, and at night called at Father Bailey's and although his head is silvered over with the frosts of eighty-seven winters, yet he was strong in the Lord, and a bold advocate for the doctrines of the bible. May he live to bring in his centenary offering.

17. We came to Gerard. Enquired for a brother Langworthy, but he was not known by any until morning: When after we had spent the night, and the Landlord had obtained a heavy bill, he was well known!! and our Host gave correct direction to the very house !!! a distance of some seven miles.—With Br. L———, we dined, and continued our journey, through Coneaut to Kingsville, O. While passing through Coneaut we conversed about the Lady, Mrs. Applebee, who had been shipwrecked opposite the town on Lake Erie, and lived seven days in the cabin which was nearly full of water. But God was with her, nor suffered the floods to overflow her soul, and she was preserved to glorify His name. On the day appointed for the funeral discourse she was restored to her weeping husband, to his astonishment and inexpressible joy. While reflecting upon the Omnipotence of Jehovah's arm, we were encouraged with the reflection that *that* arm could sustain *us,* and if so, "why art thou cast down, oh my soul, trust thou in God, for he is thy hope and salvation."

Leaving Kingsville we passed on to Kirtland where we took a survey of the "Morman Temple." Of the Mormons, there were left to guard the Temple, about five hundred in all, their main body having taken their pilgrimage to Nauvoo, the promised inheritance of the latter day saints. The Temple is a huge stone edifice, standing on the brink of a towering bank, overlooking the surrounding country. High upon its front is written in large capitals,

THE TEMPLE
OF THE LIVING GOD.
DEDICATED TO HIM
BY THE LATTER
DAY SAINTS.
1835.

It is kept locked, and may not be entered free of cost, or without a guide. After engaging our conductor we passed through the broad hall into the main body. Each door is as carefully bolted as those in a prison. One room embraces the whole basement story, with the exception of the hall, or entry, and I should judge the room was thirty feet between floors, and but for its architecture it would appear like a cavern. On each end was a pulpit containing four seats, each of which as it rose above, receded from the other until the last was much elevated, and placed against the wall. The seats in the east end was for the presiding officers in the priesthood of Aaron. Each seat is calculated for three persons, each person occupying a seperate niche in the form of a segment of a circle. In the centre sits the presiding officer, who has on either side a counsellor. The pulpits are decorated with carved work of the most costly workmanship. In front of each appears three initials. Those on the front of the lowest seat were P. D. A. I inquired of my guide for their fullest meaning, and was informed as follows: The initials on the first seat were

1. P. D. A.—President, Deacon of Aaron.

2. P. T. A.—President, Teacher of Aaron.

3. P. A. P.—President of the Aaronic Priesthood.

4. B. P. A.—Bishop of the Priesthood of Aaron.

"Those in the west end are," said he, "for the presiding officers in the Melchisedec Priesthood."

1. P. E. M.—Presiding Elder of Melchisedec.

2. P. M. H.—President of Melchisedec's High Priest.

3. M. H. P.—President of the High Priesthood of Melchisedec.

4. M. P. C.—Melchisedec's President Senior.

My guide said, "Sometimes these men of God shine with dazzling splendor." I looked on him with pity. Each of the seats of these pulpits could be shut in entire by pasteboard curtains, suspended from the upper ceiling, thus completely secluding each seat with its occupant from every other object in the Temple. Besides this, there are curtains to inclose the whole at once. Here (my skepticism suggested) they can dress their Angels at will. There was a curtain suspended, which when dropped would divide the congregation in the centre.

This is but one of the deceptive machines invented by the adversary of souls to their evarlasting destruction. From this apartment we ascended two flights of stairs which led us into a school room, which contained the same number of pews and pulpits as did the basement story, but not so costly, and without curtains. Ascending another flight of stairs we come to another loft which was subdivided into study rooms, some of these were so destitute of light that they appeared fitted for deeds of darkness.

Ascending another flight of stairs, we stood in the belfry, the base of which was ninety-four feet from the ground. This was the most interesting position in, or about the Temple. From it we could survey the village and many of the plantations, with the hills and dales which beautify the surrounding country. But all was mingled with sorrowful reflections, as beneath our feet were those rooms which, to us appeared fitted for deceptive purposes, and where it is feared, almost all manner of sinful gratifications were indulged. They were *then* beneath our feet, and may Heaven grant, that such delusions with there kindred spirits, may always remain there. In view of the thousands thus deluded, how gloomy the thought. In the blaze of Gospel truth how easily men are blinded and led into fatal delusions. The soul sunk still lower than in the beginning, the mind still more degraded and yet they hope for a being with the blest!

How awfully accountable then, are those who lead them thus astray. This is as concise a description as I am able to give, and although my notes are somewhat defaced I believe it is correct. I have noticed "The Temple," not because its merits demand it, but to show how far delusion may go, even in this our enlightened land.

Leaving the Mormon Temple, we resumed our journey. It being very warm and pleasant, the frozen ground began to soften, and it was very soon exceeding bad travelling. Our course led us through Cleaveland which is a splendid city indeed. It is surrounded with a beautiful and fertile country. Above and below the city on the lake road, the country seats were surpassingly elegant. At Cleaveland we took the pike road for Columbus, which led us from the lake; and notwithstanding the wheeling was intolerable, they exacted an extravagant toll. When we came to Medina, the wheeling was so heavy that we left the turnpike for back roads, at which time we thought our troubles had begun.

Part of the time we ploded on through mud knee deep, and so frosty that all the turbid soil adhering to the carriage wheels congealed. Sometimes we were hobbling over the hubs, at others trundling the crazy log and rail bridges, in which the country greatly abounds. Through swamps and lonely deserts much of our pathway lay. Twice we broke our carriage, costing much time and money to get it repaired again. The charity of many of these people begins at home, and we should judge was scarcely ever found wandering abroad.

Our way, however, was through a very pleasant country newly settled from almost every nation on the globe. The productions of the soil, though not extravagant, will reward the husbandman for his toil.

Thus we urged our way on, and although we could make but little progress, we felt it our duty to pursue the journey.

Jan. 18. We called at Harrisville, and from appearances I thought they were sometimes visited by the ague and fever; but when I enquired concerning it, the keeper of the Inn declared emphatically *that it was not the case.* Shortly after a gentleman came in, and drawing up to the stove, said, "I guess, Landlord, my fit is coming on again." After he had shaken sometime, I enquired if that man was a resident of that town. My host answered "*he is sir.*" "Has he been absent recently?" "No sir." "Well sir," I replied "he must have the disease from his own climate;" I mention this as a specimen of the smuggling spirit of the inhabitants in unhealthy countries.

At Sullivan my carriage was broken, by which I was detained about a day; there I found a Phrenological Lecturer, who was making extravagant strides in the business of his profession. At about eleven, A. M., a company was gathered in the bar-room, and I was invited to a seat with the spectators. From their manner, I discovered that it was their intention to have a little sport at my expense. Sin appeared their chief delight, and a *minister* the object of their greatest envy. I had desired a privilege to preach to them, and when I entered the room which was crowded, I thought a way might then open. Soon after entering, a rusty looking man took the seat and the exhibition commenced. At the first onset, the actor fastened his eyes upon the object of their anticipated sport, remarking as follows: "This gentleman [?] can never be a christian, not having sufficient organs for marvellous conceptions." Then with a haughty air proceeded, "That is the case with *me, I* cannot believe in ghosts and hobgoblins, neither can I bring before my mind the form of *your christians God*. If I could only see his shape, his feet, hands, eyes, &c.; how he looked, walked, talked, and appeared, I should take *the greatest pleasure in worshipping him.*" At the close of the last sentence, I remarked, "that, sir, is intended for me." To which he pompously replied, "Indeed it is, sir." Approaching him, and placing my hand on his head, I said, "sir, you have informed us, that these organs are the seat of the *mind.* Tell us if you please how that mind looks, its form, features, &c., and we will believe you." He saw that with his own weapons he was slain. His hands lazily fell from the cranium, and all was silent. I then remarked, "Establish holiness as a common centre, and cluster around it the other attributes of Deity, then you *might* worship. Add to that a renewed heart, which you very much need, and you would *delight* to worship." This is only noticed to show that truth, if brought to bear, will ever triumph over the advocates of error. Surely "our weapons are not carnal but mighty— through God to the pulling down of the strong holds of Satan."

"How happy is the Christian's lot."

CHAPTER V

Idiomatic expressions—Shattered dwellings—Cookery—Danger of Popery—Extract from Pollok.

In many places in the south of Ohio and Indiana, the English Language is put upon the rack and very much mangled. The affirmative answer to a question is "Well I reckon." The negative "All but that." For instance: "Are you going to Town today?" "Well I reckon." "Did you accomplish your object yesterday?" "All but that." When an answer is thus given no more is to be said, as a repetition required is esteemed dishonorable.

When in an office one day a gentleman came in, and the following conversation ensued.

"Well Doctor, how are you to-day?"

DOCT.: "Tolerable like."

VISIT.: "How are your concerns?" (family.)

DOCT.: "Tolerable like, how did you leave your concerns at home?"

VISIT.: "Tolerable like."

DOCT.: "We had a powerful rain yesterday."

VISIT.: "Lots and slathers of it."

A short pause ensues, when the visitor interrupts the silence by saying, "Well Doctor, I reckon you'd like dearly well to see a coming a little of that are corn?"

DOCT.: "Well I reckon. Did you raise quite powerful of it this year?"

VISIT.: "Well I reckon, quite a smart chance of it." The visitor continues, "I have a smart chance of it in my barn, and lots and slathers in the field that hasn't its jacket torn off it yet."

DOCT.: "Well I should be mighty glad to see it. When will you *haul* it."

(He designs to say in the course of this month.)

VISIT.: "Well I reckon in all this month."

DOCT.: "Well, I have now a pretty smart chance of corn, but last week I was pretty tight on't until Mr. ———— hauled me a powerful load of the smartest corn I've had in many a day."

When one wishes to say he is not well, it is "I am sort of donsey."

At one time a gentleman came where we were to get some one to convey the corpse of a deceased friend to the grave, when after the usual compliments, he began:

"Well I have come to get you to *haul* the corpse of my brother's wife to the grave."

"Well I reckon I can *haul* it as well as any one in the State, for I have a powerful team."

When they wish to speak of a large assembly they say "a smart sprinkle of people." The word balance comes into almost every transaction. "To make out the balance he ate a smart chance of baked pig." "To make out the balance of a night's rest he slept until eight in the morning." If they refer to the intelligence of an individual they say "He knows a heap." If they conceive a good quality in any thing, they say, "It's jam up." For instance, "That's a jam up friend or a jam up dinner," &c.

If a large amount is expressed, it is "a smart chance." "What did you get for your ox at the sale?" "Quite a smart chance," &c. &c. &c.

Many live in shattered, leaky, log huts, or shanties, and much of their wearing apparel compares well with the hovels in which they stay. We often slept or rather made an attempt, in rooms where the snow, rain, and sleet, would sift through the crevices and give us as they say, "a smart sprinkle." It is common to see the women in the field, attending to the farming business. Tidiness is a stranger to many of them. I have often been obliged to walk about the yard while meals were preparing, and then, while receiving my repast, labor to see nothing but what was on my plate, and sometimes shut my eyes while conveying the food to my mouth. "Corn dodgers" is a sort of indian bread. "Corn bread and common doings" constitute commonplace fare. "Wheat bread and chicken fixings," "stewed crab-apples," "pickled eggs," &c. &c. comprise the *extra* repasts. These things are only mentioned to open the eyes of the more enlightened, that they may not neglect their duty to the wretched in our own land, while devoting so much time and expense to the diffusion of light and education in other portions of the world. How far into ignorance people may fall, and not be "heathen" is not for me to judge, but one thing I *do* know, that such society demands the sympathies of the enlightened, religious portion of community. In *that* society what is there to hinder Romanism from having its designed effect, if promulgated. If the Protestant Churches do not send teachers to those destitute regions, as far as in them lie, they must be in a measure, at least, responsible for the neglect and consequent results. And if the Papal yoke is fastened upon that people, the sin may be found at our own door. That Romanism is rapidly increasing in those parts is too obvious to require an argument. And but give the power to her, and she will, as she always has done, wreak her vengeance on the meek followers of the Lamb. Popery is the same *now* as when she established that horrid tribunal, and, in the burning words of Pollok:

"With horrid relish drank the blood
Of God's peculiar children—and was drunk;
And in her drunkenness dreamed of doing good.
The supplicating hand of innocence,
That made the tiger mild, and in his wrath
The lion pause—the groans of suffering most
Severe, were nought to her: she laughed at groans;
No music pleased her more; and no repast
So sweet to her as blood of men redeemed
By blood of Christ. Ambition's self, though mad,
And nursed on human gore, with her compared
Was merciful. Nor did she always rage;
She had some hours of meditation, set
Apart, wherein she to her study went,
The Inquisition, model most complete
Of perfect wickedness, where deeds were done,
Deeds! let them ne'er be named—and sat and planned
Deliberately and with most musing pains,
How, to extremest thrill of agony,
The flesh, and blood, and souls of holy men,
Her victims might be wrought; and when she saw
New tortures of her laboring fancy born,
She leaped for joy, and made great haste to try
Their force—well pleased to hear a deeper groan."

CHAPTER VI

President Harrison's Homestead—North Bend—Tunnel through the Hill—Big Miami—Kentucky Tavern—Flood in 1832—Arrival at Milan—The Country—Inhabitants—Young Gallant.

Much has been said of President Harrison's Homestead at North Bend. It is surely a splendid country seat, but aside from this, in connection with the mound, on which his remains are entombed, North Bend would present any thing but an interesting scene. The mound and farm are situated within an amphitheatre of forest crowned hills. The mound presents a conical form, carpeted with an indigenous sward of green grass, and upon the very pinnacle is the tomb of the illustrious William H. Harrison, over which is erected a monument to his memory.

The mound is about one hundred rods from the bank of the river. I was informed that after the tomb was commenced, it was struck by lightning, which was most likely attracted by some mineral substance exposed by the excavation. Leaving the mound, we crossed an adjoining hill, through which a canal was tunnelled. Passing from the Ohio to the Big Miami river, we were soon on its Bank.—The surrounding plains presented a pleasing aspect. The ungathered corn still standing (as in many places they leave it until spring,) and the large cribs indicated a rich soil.

Passing through Lawrenceburg we called at a Tavern kept by a Kentuckian. Those people almost disgust one with their unnecessary attention. In that country in the warm seasons, a lad is kept at the table with a flag of Peacock's feathers to fight the flies.—Their charges however, are moderate. One thing I have learned in travelling, the poorer the fare at a public house, the greater the bills. Near this Tavern a large Distillery had just been burned down.

After leaving we crossed a river, and high over our heads was a board nailed to a tree, at the high water mark of the flood in the winter of 1832. This flood caused much damage in the lower country. We then ascended a mountain, as we left the low land of the Ohio river. At evening we arrived at Milan, Ripley Co., Ia., and were gladly received by the inhabitants, most of whom had emigrated from the East. The soil in that section was very unproductive, and I often wondered how they ever passed over so much good country, to locate in a region which is much poorer than the one they left.

In that section are many who were once in covenant relation with the Sabbath Baptist, but now are in different circumstances, having mingled with other societies and the majority left the Sabbath. But they wish us to notice that their practice and not their doctrine was changed! and a part of them expressed deep regret for their apostacy. Some, however, remain permanent, but their number is comparatively small. We believe that with sufficient time, and proper means, good might be done there by us as a Denomination. Our friends there have been many years *isolated,* and destitute of the privileges of society. And although they have groaned, and repeatedly called for help, no minister was ever sent there before, and we at too late an hour to be successful in the time allotted to us. They were exceedingly lonesome, and thought that they and their petitions had been too much neglected. But this is no apology for the violation of God's law. The churches may consider whether they have done their duty in this particular, and many others, or not. If in this case it should prove too late to accomplish what we might have done, it is not in many others. And shall we suffer the numerous groups, settled in those western countries to relax, and be scattered like sheep without a shepherd? As God has prospered us, and we are able, let us forbid it, and send to them, and sustain among them competent ministers, who shall instruct, encourage, and reprove, thus leading them along in the paths of peace. As we considered our mission of an exploring rather than a local nature, we thought not best to stay long in Ripley. And if it had been otherwise, our appointed time was too short to accomplish much, as there were numerous obstacles to remove before we could establish upon a good foundation.

April 9. Attended our last meeting in Milan.

I was informed that about the time *that* people left the Sabbath, many were about to join them in their opinions and practice. They now mourn when too late their apostacy. The people were unanimous in attending meeting while we were there. One day while there, I stood upon the steps of the meeting house, as the people were gathering; one circumstance arrested my attention. A gentleman with four ladies in his wagon, (or as they term it "carry-all") came up with much pomp, he on the horses back and they setting so low in the wagon, that I at first did not discover them. When at the door they alighted, and he rode off to the "*hitching post.*" When he first came up I expected a general smile, but the audience appeared as indifferent as though nothing had transpired, and I could only laugh in my sleeves. At the close of the meeting I saw the fashion out. The Gallant unfastened his horse, placed himself as before, then flourished around to the steps of the house, when the four ladies hopping into the wagon, seated themselves as before, and he turning his eye over his shoulder to see if all was right, galloped off in all the pride of a gallant youth.

CHAPTER VII

Leave Milan—Michigan Road—Beach Woods—Gang of "Hoosiers"—Family from Delaware—Indianapolis—Drove of Buffalo—Manner of taking them—Country from Indianapolis to Terre Haute—Emigrants in the Forest—Stranger in the Thicket—Emigrants with an Ox Cart—Terre Haute—High Water—Grand Prairie, Ill.—Its Features—Paris— Measles in the Town—Trouble in obtaining entertainment.

April 10. Left Milan for a band of brethren located on the Wabash river, forty-four miles below Terre Haute, near Bussron's Mills, Sullivan Co., Ia. In consequence of the roughness of the way we were obliged to go by Indianapolis.

In the after part of the day came to Flat Rock Creek, Shelby Co. In that region are some who observe the Sabbath according to the commandment, but are united with first-day people, and they, together, style themselves the separate Baptists.

The first day the roads were quite dry, and we advanced encouragingly. But at night it rained, and much of the next day, which caused exceeding bad going. And when we struck the Michigan road, we found it almost impassable. But we had before this, learned to be patient under such circumstances. Stopping at one Tavern we learned the corn was all planted, and was informed that one man had planted about forty acres in March.

On our way we found three teams stalled in the mire. The drivers said we could not pass, but letting my family go over on foot, I, with a quick motion, plunged my team through, and the carriage being very light, did not sink as did their loaded wagons. We called for dinner at a Tavern in one of the beach swamps, and about the time it was ready, a company of "*Hoosiers*" (a term applied to the lower class in Ia.,) came for dinner, and their common language was that of profane songs, vulgar jokes, and low ribaldry. I discovered preparations were making for *all,* and asked the Landlord if those vulgar-mouthed fellows were to be our companions at the table. He answered in the affirmative, to which I replied I would not dine with such a corrupt set. He was somewhat surprised to think I considered *these gentlemen* anything but respectable. He finally gave the table to myself and family.

Six miles before we entered Indianapolis, we stopped for the night, and found in those lonely beach woods a family from Delaware. The man was contented, but we found his wife, like the most of the women we had seen, "home-sick." For what was there to cheer a person in that swampy, lonely wilderness? Doomed to wear out a life in such eternal solitude, must be a prison indeed. The reader will remember that these lonely regions are not the "entire west."

It was rainy, and their location may have appeared more gloomy than it would in a different atmosphere. I could but admire the taste of the original owner of this isolated mansion. Shade trees of almost every description were planted around the dwelling. The house was well furnished, and although we regreted their solitude, we were happy to find in that wilderness such entertainment. This night wore off with delight and astonishing rapidity. Morning came, and we struck the graded, but unfinished National Pike, about two miles from Indianapolis. This city is located on a very beautiful, but rather low plain. It rather scatteringly spreads over much territory. Its prospects have been somewhat blighted by the injudicious management of the State, and the general *hard times* which have widely spread their withering influence over the western country. I was informed that many of the main men of this city had utterly failed. As we entered the city, we saw on the left a group of men, women, and children, and turned to find out the cause of this collection. Here were twenty-five young Buffaloes, and an Elk, directly from the Rocky Mountains. The owner informed me that he had been one year gathering them in their native country, and preparing them for the journey, and driving them thus far. He said he drove cows to the hunting ground, and in the Spring caught the Buffalo Calves, and killing the Calves of his Cows, filled their place by young Buffaloes, thus rearing and taming them. His price was six hundred dollars a pair. But I did not hear of his making any sales. And since my return, I have heard that the same number was seen on the Mohawk, on their way to New-York city. When I saw them they were poor and very shabby. In Indianapolis, they have a very costly State House, which does not very well compare with their hard times. It was however, built when they enjoyed brighter prospects. The National Pike forms "broad street," with magnificent buildings on either side. We then followed the great National high way, as it led to Terre Haute, on the Wabash. By this time the rain had fallen in such torrents, as to make it almost impossible to travel on any other road. I have before noticed that there are but few bridges in all the western country. One thing makes it more difficult in these lower countrys, when the river once rises, they retain their height a long time. From Indianapolis to Terre Haute there is some very beautiful undulating country, and some that is rough and unproductive. Almost every house is a tavern, or at least, holds out a sign. There are also many little villages. One evening just before dark, we found in the midst of an extensive forest, a company of emigrants, who had stopped for the night, and had a good fire on the ground. Around it, reclining upon the grass, were the men and boys. Some were preparing their rifles, others had turned nurses and were dandling about the unconcious infant. The women were gathering the cooking utensils, and preparing for supper. All was jollity among them. They had two large covered wagons, or "travelling hotels." I stopped and inquired if I could get entertainment. They at first appeared surprised, but consented. On asking their number, they said "only nineteen!" We bade them good night, and drove on. About one mile from this, we passed a huge looking man, sitting in the edge of the thicket, by the root of a tree, holding in his hand a rifle. What was his object, I could not imagine, he was some considerable distance from any house in this dense forest. We that night stopped at a widow's tavern. She had recently lost many of her family by the diseases of this low land country.

Before we came to the Wabash, we passed a man with his wife and two children. They had one ox in the thills of a two wheeled cart, in which was one or two boxes, and a mat or bed. This was all we could see that they possessed. And from their appearance, I should judge they had but little money. They told me they were "GOING TO IOWA." We then came to a ferry, where I left him with the ferryman, bantering over six cents difference on the price of crossing. This I thought, was travelling poverty indeed. But they were elated with the prospect of one day treading the rich soil, and gazing upon the unbounded plains of "IOWA."

15. We came in sight of Terra Haute, situated on the margin of a prairie which skirted the Wabash river. The prairie was enchanting in its aspect. It was unlike the low marshy prairies in Ohio, which are interspersed with shrubbery. It was completely adapted to the plough, and its blac soil bespoke its richness and strength. When we came to this place, we soon learned that the river was too high to be passed, nor could we reach those brethren at Bussron's Mills in Sullivan Co., Ia. In that place are six or seven families, who have long wished for an administrator to constitute them into a church in connection with the S. D. Baptists. The *custom beggars* flocked around us, and began their skill for the purse, saying, that very likely we should be obliged to tarry in the town, *weeks* before we could cross. We soon learned that up the river there was a ferry, but they very much doubted our reaching it if we made the attempt. We set off, and hired a pilot to ride on horse back before us in the water, the river having overflowed its banks. As I left Terre Haute, I thought the French name appropriate, for it was truly a beautiful "*high bank.*" We then followed our guide through the water, and Sycamore woods, until we came to the bank of the river, seven miles above Terre Haute, where we crossed over and were soon on our way again.

Calling for refreshment at a private house we found a Connecticut man, beautifully situated and contented. Though far from the land of his nativity, he said he was happy. Left him and soon drove on to the grand prairie in Illinois.

When we first entered this great plain it was interspersed with little groups of small bushes of various kinds. But soon we were on an almost unbounded, uninterrupted sea of green grass. This was rather low and wet, and much of it unfit for cultivation. I looked upon it and reflected upon its vast expanse, spreading over much of the "far west," interrupted only by interspersing groves of thrifty timber, adapted to the wants of the tenants of its rich soil. A stretch of thought, like contemplating infinity, was required, which can measure only by succession, its expansion and sublimity. Like the vanishing lines in prospect, so is contemplation lost in this expanded prairie.

"In it we see no barren or rocky wastes, no frozen mountains. Destitute of prominent land-marks to catch the eye of the traveller, he sees in the wide distance before him, only, the almost horizontal lines of level or rolling meadow. No one points him to the peaks of dim mountains, and tells him that the range divides two sister states, or separates two noble rivers. He sees no clouds resting on the shoulders of lofty Butes, and blending their neutral tint, with the hazy blue of the landscape before them, nor Tentons rearing their heads into the regions of perpetual snow. Day after day he pursues his journey without any thing to create in his bosom emotions of the grand and sublime, unless it be the vastness of the expanse."—PARKER.

We arrived at a town called Paris, just as the sun was sinking in the western bounds of the prairie. On entering the village, we found the black measles had made great ravages with the people. My family had never had the disease, and we were driven from house to house, and could find no place to lay our weary heads. We at last went through the place and expected to have the bounds of the prairie our room walls, the earth our bed, and the heavens our shelter. But happily after getting out about one mile, we met a man, startled at our preposterous course. Being informed of our success, he took us and entertained us for the night.

CHAPTER VIII

Flat roofed tavern—tavern in the grove—cross a large Prairie—Grave in the midst—returning emigrants—story of Missouri—Kaskaskia—stolen team—more returning omigrants—their manner of travelling—Springfield—Sangermon river—call for refreshment— "Pigs in the parlor"—Havanah—begging emigrants—Illinois river—Spoon river—profanity in the South— Lewistown—arrival at widow Hull's—Religion of the people—skeleton of a sermon—gentleman from Philadelphia.

Ten miles from Paris, are two flat roofed cottages, together forming the two apartments of a tavern. Near by stands a straw covered hovel for a barn. An old shattered bureau on which lay Scott's Bible, as I entered met my view. I enquired if they loved and obeyed God? to which the old man said "sometimes a little." On leaving he said he wanted three cents for the pail of water. This family had thus stayed twelve years, ten miles from any inhabitants, and I was afterwards informed that he always charged for water, and so I should think, if he ever obtained money, for this was all I could see that was worth buying.

At about two P. M. we came to a small cluster of houses, in a little grove, where we called for dinner. On first seeing the inhabitants I wondered how so many dirty, disgusting creatures, inclining to human, could have got together.

But I conducted Mrs. Scott into the "sitting room," which was about twelve feet square, and had in it two beds. It was also the bar-room and druggist shop. As it was about twenty miles across to the next grove we had expected to tarry for the night. But what a place was this to abide! The company in the sitting room was about half a dozen, half drunken fellows, and a tipsy quack doctor, and of course not very genteel. I made my way to the barn and fed my team, and then those "horse jockeys" eagerly flocked to see them, and their eulogies were amusing indeed. They bantered for an exchange, saying they would give me for my horses another span that was worth fifty dollars more. I told them I was not after their charity. But nothing would do— *trade I must.* I wish all horse traders could have seen this chattering group as they flocked around me, and each patting me on the shoulder, was to appearance, the best friend I ever had. After they found I would not exchange, they said with emphasis, "*your horses, sir, we will have at all events.*" I replied that they appeared as though they could *steal* a horse, but I had hardly thought they would tell a man of it beforehand. We then made preparations to leave the place, in which I considered not only a den of thieves but a vile banditti. When we were about to start they appeared somewhat surprised, saying, we could not reach the other grove, for the most of the way the prairie was inundated, and in some places for eighty rods, the water was four feet deep. I enquired if the roads were more wet than those I had just been travelling? They replied "*far more difficult,*" and more, that strangers would need a pilot. It being so very early in the season I feared there might be something in it, as before the water runs off in the spring many of these prairies are not capable of being traversed by a team.

The country is so level and the soil so rich, that in some places, it is very miry, and more especially while crossing the "slues" as they term them. These are where there would be rivulets in a hard soil country, but owing to the loamy nature of the soil these small streams ooze through the ground beneath the thick matted turf, and are often rods in width. In the spring these passages are flowed with water, but in mid-summer they are dry, or nearly so on the surface, and can be crossed with little diffi-culty before the turf is broken. Before we left this tavern I inquired of the lady of the house if she was happily situated? The gushing tear told her unreconciliation to her wretched fate.

We at length "made off," and concluded we had rather spend the night in the open air, on the prairie, than in that loathesome place. My team exhibited their speed, and we were soon "out of sight of land" as the inhabitants say, that is, out of sight of every thing but green grass, and the broad plains. On our way we passed a grave in the prairie, and surely thought *that* a gloomy grave-yard. I afterwards learned that the man who was buried there, was, in company with others, caught on the prairie in the night, and losing the road about one half mile from the grove, he left the waggon, and felt for the road on his hands and knees. When he found the path he called to the company, and evidently supposed he was going to the grove, when he took the back track. The remnant of the company found the grove, but he in consequence of his mistake and the chilly weather, perished where we saw his grave.

> "Here lies the relics of some stranger one,
>   Who rests afar from his own native plain;
> His grave's been warmed by many a summer sun,
>   Bedew'd full oft by spring's refreshing rain.
> But yet has not appear'd a mourning train,
>   No flowers have sprung upon this silent mound,
> No tears have fall'n to damp this spot again,
>   No vigils made it consecrated ground;
>   But man has often strode, unfeelingly around."

Night was approaching, and yet we could not discover the grove to which we were bending our course, but was disappointed in the road, for it was the best we had yet found in the state. At length we came in sight of the timber that skirted the Kaskaskia river, and was soon safely moored in the comfortable dwelling of a chris-tian farmer. The cold wind began to blow, the sleet to fall, and we were thankful that the Lord had thus led our steps to a comfortable abode and shelter from the stormy blast. How sweet that promise, "I will never leave nor forsake thee." Just before dusk a covered waggon stopped a little below the house, and a poor ragged set of movers commenced a fire in the midst of the rain. The benevolent master of the house opened his door to them, but they said they were too "ragged" to accept the offer. There were besides men and children, three young ladies, and the grief worn mother. I could not refrain the tear, for it would fall, while gazing on such suffering humanity. This family had been to Missouri Territory—spent all they had, and were on their way back, dressed in poverty's poorest garb. They said that the country was a poor, muddy region, but they were "homesick" and by that disease I always weigh the relation of such histories, for they are generally dressed in despair and most commonly come from a cowardly fountain.

It is worthy of notice that a storm soon passes by in this country, and it is considered somewhat remarkable to have three days of gloomy weather in succession.

Crossing the Kaskaskia river we found on the opposite bank, a family of emigrants, who, two nights before, had their four-horse-team stolen, and as yet had found no traces of them. *How barbarous a deed! and can it be so in Christian America?* If I had been in the old world among the mountains that swarm with robbers, or on the sandy deserts of Arabia, I should not have wondered. But to find it thus in my own country, was astonishing to me. But the reason is obvious. Many who run away from the East to shun the penalty of a violated law, locate in clubs in these newly settled countries. So here is the *scum* and *dregs* of many societies. During this day we passed Mount Auburn. It is an elevation in the centre of a large Prairie, gradually rising from the base to the summit in a conical form. It contained in all about two hundred acres of land, and sloped off in every direction just enough to give it beauty. I thought I should like to cast anchor there for life. There were a few buildings already on the mount. I often wished my friends could get a glance at this, for surely, I thought it *did* exceed, even in its wildest state, any landscape I ever saw, being covered with green shade trees, well arranged. At noon, after travelling thirty-one miles, we called at a Kentucky tavern, where I inquired after the health of the lower country, as I often did, and found by these people that it had been very sickly. At night we stopped at the house of a good old Presbyterian, on whose premises two loads of emigrants that were on their return from Missouri Territory had stopped for the night. These emigrants in the Mississippi valley almost invariably lodge in their covered waggons, cook upon the ground, and feed their teams in a box fastened to the side of the waggon. Thus they travel great distances with but little disadvantage to their purse. We kept the main road towards Springfield, and stopped the next night at a widow's, where I was compelled to hitch my team under an open shed with a herd of smoking swine. She was very anxious that I should converse and pray with her unconverted, uncultivated family, which I always rejoiced to do when an opportunity occurred. She kept us until nine in the morning, and then said she would *help the cause* by taking a very small bill, after which she charged me more than they would at the best Hotel in Springfield. I notice this to show that all which is called religion does not exhibit its principles of benevolence.

19. We drove into the Capital of Illinois, and I went from store to store to see their inland treasures. Their goods were old, rusty, and exceedingly dear. They were building a very costly Capitol. I passed the grave-yard, and it looked like a newly ploughed field, in which four hundred had been buried during the winter and spring thus far. The most died by what was denominated the "French measles." I did not fancy the location for the Metropolis of this State, it being a perfect level prairie, and rather inclined to a wet soil. While I was running about, Mrs. Scott saw a man with a load of corn for sale at six cents a bushel, but had found no purchaser, for which there were

two causes; first, it was too low down in the country for Eastern market, and corn was raised in abundance, costing but little labor; secondly, times were then unusually hard, and grain could be obtained for barter pay. We then bent our course direct for Havana, on the Illinois river, and at night put up with a very good christian man, whose heart was warm with the love of God. I found by him, that the religious state of society there was good, to what it had been in other places where I had passed. Fifteen miles from there we came to the Sangamon river. I had already become weary of waiting for a ferry "flat," however, we crossed after a long time, and through much difficulty forded the inundated bottoms to the rising bank, about one and a half miles from the river. Here we were on a sandy plain, surrounded by a rich fertile country, which reminded us of the Arabian desert. The sand was in drifts, and had on its bosom but few shrubby burr oaks. This continued about ten miles, and we were again on a green carpeted prairie. Time was at hand for refreshments and I called at one house, but to no purpose.

I soon stopped again, went into a hut where I saw a woman with some small children. The dogs, hens, and pigs, were playing round the door, and some were already in quiet possession of the house. In the ashes was baking a "corn dodger." It was enough! I asked not to stay for refreshment. I drove across the prairie about eight miles to Havana, which has a *great* name for a *small* place. Here was a man from Rochester, very sick with the ague and fever, and wished himself back to his native State. He kept store, tavern, and the ferry across the Illinois river, which lazily meanders its way through the beautiful prairie country. As to the state of society through Indiana and this portion of Illinois, the reader will have already anticipated. As a general thing, religion is not a welcome guest, and, if a man introduces it, he is considered obtrusive. But profanity is considered no obtrusion. It is always in time, and always in place. Christians must keep religion out of sight and hearing, but the wicked may be as open and obtrusive as they please, nor would they have Christians cast their pearls before swine. Gambling is practised to a very great extent, and is a favorite amusement with those whose minds are not sufficiently cultivated to find satisfaction in reading or intelligent conversation. The number of "black-legs" that make gambling their business of life is great, more particularly up and down the Ohio river, and they are adepts in the profession. I often thought, while on the bank of the Ohio river, that the society in many places was heathenish enough to require Missionary stations, yet some portions of the country are well supplied with faithful ministers. While I was in Havana two men came along, moving to Iowa, with an ox-team, and a prairie cart. For fellies and tyre, they had the half of a hickory sapling bent around the ends of the spokes, which formed the wheels. They begged a free ferriage across the river, and plead as a reason their poverty, saying they had but "six bits" (seventy five cents,) to carry them to Iowa. From what we saw we all agreed they had no small amount of money. I was informed that many, who were afterwards found to possess wealth, took this means to travel cheap. When we crossed the Illinois, we landed below the mouth of Spoon river, a sluggish stream up which we passed four miles to Waterford, and ferried across. This was a new settlement in the woods. It might be proper to notice, that the most of these streams are clothed on one side at least, with a dense forest, Rock river being the only exception I saw while traveling on the western prairies.

Leaving Waterford, we took the road to Lewistown, the Shire town of Fulton Co. The road led through the woods until we arrived at that place, a distance of about four miles. Here I was exceedingly disappointed. From information, I had expected to find a very pleasing location. But it was in the woods, surrounded with bluffs and hills, nor are their appearances pleasingly romantic. We passed through without a call, and bent our way towards Milton. The road led over bluffs and hillocks, and through gulfs, and when we arrived at the top of the hill, above the little town, it looked like a dark chasm below. Down we went, crossed over, and ascended the bank as soon as possible, and pursued our way toward widow Hull's, about two miles distant. It was growing dark and we were weary, having then travelled four hundred miles since we left Milan, Ia.

When near the widow's we took a bye path, which led us into the wilderness, which I followed on foot, by moonlight, and Mrs. Scott drove until we run the road entirely out. The shrill note of the nightingale was echoing through the woods on every hand. We turned to retrace our steps and found it difficult to find the way back again. We at length found the road, and soon after the family of our pursuit, and we were happy to hope for a few days rest on our part, and to cheer the friends thus destitute. O what a meeting we had! how joyfully received. They praised God for answers to prayer. We bowed around the throne of Grace, and in melting thankfulness adored the God of heaven, the melting scene was enough to repay us for all our toils in reaching those five families that ought to have been, long before this time, bound in one covenant.

We passed through several neighborhoods where it does appear that the people must not be neglected, and to say the least of Ohio, we think that one missionary should be kept there by us, and Illinois is still more destitute, for the calls were from every direction. There is also a great excitement upon the subject of difference between us and other denominations, and the people wished us to plead their cause. If it was for ourselves, or for riches, or worldly emoluments for others, we would lay aside our pen. The needy are calling. Parents are weeping for themselves and their children. The cry has gone up before God. Shall *we* heed or not? If the church could but realize the condition of these people, we believe she would, (in addition to what has been done,) supply them with proper instruction.

May God send his spirit through the Churches, from house to house, and heart to heart, until this subject is sufficiently realized, and from the cause we see, and enjoy the happy effect. The Lord knows, and eternity will unfold their destitute condition, together with the groans and tears lodged in the bosom of our heavenly Father. Friends of Jesus, will you let them plead in vain? Shall they imploringly cling to the last lingering gleam of hope, and die in despair? Our life will soon be gone, and with it the privilege to do good. The harvest is now ripe—tares are sown—false reapers are plundering the field—darkness, error, and superstition are rushing forth—Infidelity is getting deep root—Satan's kingdom is fortifying, and souls are deceived. O! for able gospel ministers who shall come forth like flaming seraphs with the sword of the Spirit. May all consider this subject well, and not wait *too* long before they act.

Meetings soon commenced, and the people gathered from far and near. There are many preachers of the Gospel by profession, but they are Mormons, "Two Seed-ites,"[1] "Bride the Lamb's wife,"[2] "Campbellites," "Non-Resistants," and "many others too numerous to mention," and although I wish not to judge, yet I thought they had an unwholesome influence on community, and were too combative for success. If they can raise a dispute with the different denominations, they appear to be in their ele-

---

1. These hold that Cain was literally the child of the Devil, and all his posterity are doomed to Hell. While Abel was the son of Adam, and his posterity are the elect by grace.

2. This sect have seceded from the Mormons.

ments. I will here give a skeleton of one sermon I heard delivered in Fulton Co., founded on Matt, xiii. 31, 32. "Parable of the Mustard seed."

1st. Stalk was Jesus Christ.

2d. Planted in the earth, and springing up at His resurrection.

3d. The Apostles were the different branches.

4th. All denominations were the different branchlets springing from the Apostles.

5th. Leaves, the consciences of the people, which are often fanned by the breezes of heaven.

6th. The fowls of the air, the redeemed souls lodged in the branches of the tree.

7th. Then all should live in peace.

But in the conclusion he anathematized all who did not agree with him. During our stay in this region, which was about five weeks, I held meetings in Fulton and Peoria Counties, and I found people of all denominations very friendly, and attentive to the ministrations of the word. In this vicinity are people from almost every state in the Union, but the majority are from the Eastern and Middle States. Here was a Mr. Ingalls, who was once a man of business in Philadelphia, but had sought this retirement for the express purpose of securing, in Christ, his soul's salvation. He had found favor and was happy. Well would it be for many, if they would abandon the world for heaven, which is simply secured in obedience to God. And if our present pursuits any way prevent our securing a well grounded hope in Christ, or entangle our feet that we walk not meekly and perseveringly in the paths of religious duties, we had better give them up—for we are bound and do wickedly if we do not abandon such engagements at once. What is our will that it should contend with the will of God. What is time's transitory bliss, to the permanent joys of religion—a well grounded hope in Christ—a home in heaven above. "O that men would be wise! that they would consider this, their "best good" and latter end. "But the ox knoweth his owner, and the ass his master's crib, but my people do not know, they will not consider."

Reader! are you willing to leave, if necessary, the busy affairs of life and the prospects of temporal bliss, and wealth, for obedience to God, and eternal life? If you are, God speed you on your way; if not, pause a moment, consider it well—throw into the scale, Time and Eternity, with their relative interests.

Jehovah calls! "Give me thy heart
   Nor turn thy feet astray
From wisdom's paths, and let thine eye
   Observe the better way."

"Obey! though time's tempestuous sea
   With boisterous wind contend,
The mountain waves I'll calm for thee,
   I've sworn, and I'll defend."

55

KAH-GE-GAH-GAH-BOWH
(GEORGE COPWAY)

(1818–1869)

Kah-ge-gah-gah-bowh was born on the north shores of Lake Ontario to an Ojibway band still living by traditional lifeways, despite the fact that for two centuries they had been trading with the French. When he was an adolescent his family was converted by Methodist missionaries, and he soon traveled west to Lake Superior with the missionaries to work as a translator and teacher for the western Ojibways. A few years later, George Copway, as he now called himself, was educated in the otherwise all-white Ebenezar Seminary in Jacksonville, Illinois, and thereafter began a career as a missionary. It would not last. More established Ojibway missionaries such as Peter Jones soon perceived Copway's overarching ambition and corruption, and in 1847 Copway was forced to flee to New York City and remake himself.

In 1851, a newspaper appeared in New York City calling itself *Copway's American Indian*. Copway was already known as the Ojibway author of two books, an autobiography and *The Traditional History of the Ojebwe People*. Since publishing those books, he had toured state legislatures throughout the eastern United States and gone on a speaking tour of the European capitals. Copway presented himself both as educated and cosmopolitan and as native and primitive. Even as he advocated removal for the protection of the natives, he yearned to represent the sophistication and assimilability of his race.

Ultimately, again, Copway's façade collapsed, and he was forced to flee New York, having associated himself with the Know-Nothing party and Francis Parkman, two sources of anti-Indian racism. Copway's goals in doing so were entirely selfish: he aspired to be viewed as a cosmopolitan, rather than as a native or a westerner. Finally, he retreated to a life of obscurity and disgrace.

The Address reproduced here reveals Copway at his best. Having shed his past as a missionary, he aspires here to have it both ways: he presents himself as both a leader of the natives and a member of the eastern intelligentsia. The plan he submits is designed to ingratiate himself to removalist whites and to aggrandize himself. His impossible hopes for pan-Indian unity and a separate homeland with the rights of a state reflect his own ultimate and tragic naiveté concerning the motives of the white American culture that he so wanted to join.

Text: Address before the Legislature of Pennsylvania (New York, 1850; rpt. *Life, Letters, and Speeches of George Copway,* ed. A Lavonne Brown Ruoff and Donald B. Smith. Lincoln, Nebraska, 1997): 175–188.

ADDRESS BEFORE THE LEGISLATURE OF PENNSYLVANIA (1849)

The following is an address delivered before the Legislature of Pennsylvania, on the 25th of January last, by Mr. George Copway, (or Kah-ge-ga-gah-bowh,) a chief of the Chippewa tribe. Mr. Copway has recently been in this City and lectured before respectable and interested audiences. We presume all feel an interest in the welfare of the Indians—and we place this address before our readers, feeling that they will be instructed in its reading.

GENTLEMEN OF THE LEGISLATURE OF PENNSYLVANIA:

My limited knowledge of your language will render it somewhat difficult for me to be understood this evening, as I speak a tongue which is not my own—which is not my native language. Permit me, however, to ask your indulgence while I endeavor to present to you the claims of the Indian, and at the same time, I solicit you to extend to me, personally, your sympathy, as well as to the cause in which I am engaged. Besides the embarrassments under which I labor at the present moment, I have had for several days past a severe cold, which, in a great degree, incapacitates me from speaking with that ease and freedom that I could wish, in order to lay my heart open to you.

In presenting the claims of my unfortunate race, I cannot resist recurring to the period when the Indian and the white man first commenced their intercourse, three hundred and fifty-six years ago. The Indian was then an inhabitant of all the Eastern Countries on which rests the different cities of the Atlantic States. The Indian was the sovereign of the whole country; the mountain echoed with his voice, and all he saw was his. The game of the forest he claimed as his own, the fish of the waters and the course of the rivers were also his. Proudly he then roamed through the country where now stand your farms and your mighty cities. There was then no cloud that the heathen saw portending his danger. The heavens were clear before his eye. He knew no bounderies; he knew no limits to his desire. And when he was found in this country, he had no extent of society, he had no extensive institutions, which have since been established where he then lived. There were no palaces, with their gaudy attendants; but, wherever you now see the mountains of your State, whether in the north, the south, or the west, you may picture to your mind's eye the noble form of the Indian standing on one of their lofty peaks. He made his native mountains his throne, and it was from thence he could see, to a limited extent, his boundless empire.

While the paleface trembled on Plymouth Rock, shivering there with cold, his billow-tossed limbs were gathered by our fathers, who brought him to their firesides, and introduced him to their people. The palefaces were then a small nation, but they have since become a great one, and the proud sons of the forest have, one by one, fallen away, like the stars that die at a distance in the skies. In return for our kindness and friendly feeling towards you, we look to you for protection, for guardianship, for instruction, as we protected and taught your fathers in the early history of this country. Several years back, with much solicitude, I endeavored to study the peculiar wants of my poor people, as well as the condition of the emigrants west-ward; and in order to promote the welfare and interests of both, I attempted, to the best of my ability, to mature a plan which, I think, if carried into effect, will prove highly beneficial and advantageous to both people, the whites as well as the Indians, gentlemen, I feel assured that when you shall have heard all my remarks on this important and interesting subject, you will not accuse me of selfishness on this occasion, as I have not overlooked your nation in advocating the claims of my own.

In presenting my plan before you this evening, gentlemen, permit me to state, in as few words as possible, what I have to say, as I wish to accomplish my visits to the different State Legislatures now in session, on this errend, with as little delay as possible. On the 31st of March last, you may remember that a meeting was held in the city of Philadelphia, where I attended for the first time, and broached the subject of civilization among the Indians in a more extensive and elaborate manner than on the present occasion. I found however, that it was done at a consumption of a great deal more time and an expenditure of money than I could conveniently afford. I found that the getting up of meetings in cities was a more tardy and inefficient method of obtaining the action of Congress in the matter than in personally soliciting and enlisting the aid, influence and action of the Legislatures of the several States. I have visited the different States of the Union, presented to them my views in relation to saving the Indians, and, if possible, to get their expressions of approbation of my plan, in order that their resolutions might be addressed to Congress, in the hope that they may set apart a territory in the West, in which all the Indian tribes shall be collected, and there remain unmolested for ever. Gentlemen, I have found this project, as far as I have gone, meet the views of those who have counselled me in the matter.

The object I have in view, is to call upon the General Government to grant to the Indians a part of the north western territory, west of the Iowa territory, and between the Nebraska and Minesotta territories, for the use and occupancy of all those Indians who are living there in a scattered condition, where they can enjoy permanent homes, the advantages of education and agricultural instruction, so that, after a time, when they shall have become Christianized and enlightened, they may be incorporated into the Federal Union as a State. Before we can do much good for the Indians, we must, as I have already said, provide them *permanent* homes, and by that means, secure to them peace of mind, which is absolutely necessary to ensure their improvement and progress in the arts of civilization. Much good can be effected in this way; and all the Indian tribes will assemble together, and go to their new and permanent homes, there to live in peace and harmony.

But the Indians, in their present isolated condition, are eternally at war with each other, and every influence is now brought to bear upon them, that is calculated to increase their revengeful feelings towards one another. I do not refer to the civilized, educated and enlightened portion of the Indians that are now living in different parts of the United States, as, for instance, the Indians of the State of New York, and those in Michigan, and the States of North and South Carolina, as well as Georgia. All these Indians, however, will go to the far West, and there join their brethren and form one family. I repeat, that I do not mean that the more improved and educated portion of them, will remove from their present homes but only those who are not so advanced in civilization. Let them remain where they are, and go on improving and enjoying all the blessings of civilization. I mean that those Indians that are scattered in Michigan, the territory of Iowa, and on the banks of the Mississippi, shall go to one place, and form a great settlement among themselves.

Gentlemen, in advocating this plan in the different States of the Union, I have been asked the question—'Have not the Indians now homes in the West, which the United States have granted them, on the other side of the Mississippi?' Those Indians in Arkansas—the Chickasaws and Creeks, and several other nations have homes there, and the same kind that they had when they were east of the Mississippi river. It is said that their homes have been so secured to them that no one can buy their homes from them. That, gentlemen, is our present version of the acts of the general government with the Indians; but have they not been violated in bygone ages? Have not the laws which have been secured to this people, been violated by those who succeeded to the law-making power. Most assuredly they have. Unfortunately for the government of the United States, the commissioners appointed by it to select a territory for the Indians, selected the best portions of the west, and the consequence has been that circumstances have rendered it impossible—and unfortunately—for them to hold their lands.

In the first place, their position is such that their land extends all the way from Texas to the North, like a barrier through which emigration must press. There, roads are to be constructed and canals opened through their country. Military roads, too, will be opened for emigrants; and, no sooner do you propose to go and buy one acre of land to open those highways, than the eye of the Indian will be directed with suspicion to their Great Father, and the Indians will be removed from the last acre of land that they hold.

2. The quality of their land is another great inducement to deprive them of it, and they never can hold it. Several months ago, I was conversing on the subject with Mr. Albert Gallatin, of New York, when he remarked 'that is one of the greatest reasons why the Indians can never hold the lands which the United States has ceded to them. The quality is such, that the people living out West will tease the Indian, and also the government of the United States, that in the end the land will be bought again from the Indians by the government. Then, again, the day will come when we will see trouble, as in the State of Georgia.'

3. The quantity of the land is so great that they cannot hold it. And what do the Indians want with so much land when we are attempting to teach them the science of agriculture? for, the having so much land begets a feverish anxiety on their part for deer hunting; and, as long as there is a deer on their territory, so long will they let fall every agricultural implement from their hand and take their guns in order to maintain themselves by hunting.

4. They have no means of educating their children, because they are inhabiting so broad an extent of country, that it is impossible for the people of the United States to supply them with schools, and teachers of morality, and the arts and sciences, which are necessary to elevate their condition.

5. They depend upon the proceeds of the sales of their lands, and having a great quantity for sale, they dispose of it and will reason thus: 'my children will fare no

worse than I have fared. I was living yonder; my father sold a portion of the territory, which we occupy, to the United States, upon the proceeds of which I and my children have lived, and now the United States will buy this land from us. My children will fare the same as I fared ever since I sold it to the United States. Therefore, it will not be worth while to have plantations, because they will only be a loss to us; for, no sooner have we our plantations and our farms, than we must be compelled to sell them through necessity. This moving, then, must still go on westwardly, till the last Indian shall stand on the barren peaks of the Rocky Mountains, and gaze on the land which has been taken from him. The kind-hearted, then, will drop a tear for the fate of that race which was once noble and free as the eagle that soars in the skies.

6. The scarcity of food which must follow, will produce trouble between the Indians and the government of the United States; for, as long as there is a deer or a buffalo on this side of the Rocky Mountains, no cloud of discord will be over the head of the Indian and the white man. But, no sooner will the last resource of the Indian be gone, than he will nerve himself for the worst, and take up his weapons of warfare. He will feed for a time upon the cattle on the frontier, and no sooner has he killed a bullock or a steer for his subsistence, than the newspapers abroad will proclaim that 'the Indians are coming against us, that they are killing our cattle by hundreds;' and the while country is in danger, and soon the soldiers will be on the spot, and the rattling of their firearms be heard, giving proof of the destruction of a race that once lived in this country. And when, gentlemen, that day comes, the Indian will die with his weapons of war—for he will not die but at the mouth of the cannon, when desperation has driven him to it. In order to avert this state of things, I have addressed the Legislatures of the several States. I love peace—I am for peace.

7. The Indians in their present distinctive position—in the isolated condition in which they are found—will perpetuate the peculiarities which characterize them as a nation apart from others. The Sioux, the Winnebagoes, the Pottawatamies, the Osages, and the rest of the Indians have their several peculiarities, but when you come to throw their interest in the centre, the effect will be to unite the one tribe to the other—an interest which the United States alone is capable of giving and controlling. What, I ask, would be the natural results of such an arrangement, if carried into operation? In the first place, there would be a perceptible improvement in the physical, intellectual and moral condition of the Indians. Their seminaries of learning would be permanent. There is now annually appropriated by the generosity of the people of the United States, for the purpose of educating the Indians, the sum of $10,000 and that is so divided in the West, that some times two or three dollars of it come to us at the head waters of the Mississippi and the Lake Superior. The money, in short, is so scattered along the banks of the Mississippi river, and the banks of the great Northern Lakes, as not to be of any perceptible advantage to those for whom it is intended. The small sum of $10,000 circulated over so extensive a country, and intended to be used in paying teachers to educate the Indians, does little or no good.

Suppose you were to go and sow seed on the ground, putting two grains there, and one here, and another yonder, when the ground was rich to produce fruit; and, in the spring of the year, on going to it, you would find but a very sparse crop—a little stick here and another there only—the little birds having had access to the seed at all times, and much of which would be destroyed by disease. This by way of illustration. But, gentlemen, put the Indians on one territory, in a central position, and use the fund now set apart for school purposes and you will have schools and seminiaries of learning that shall reflect credit alike upon the Indians as the government of the

United States, the benefits and good effects of which will be felt for ages to come. Wherever the government and the missionaries have succeeded in educating the Indians, they have become an industrious, moral, and well-behaved people. We have learned to read and write. We have tried to become like the white people, but when the Indian sees the deer bounding before him, he will let drop all his implements of husbandry, and follow the chase.

But no sooner have the Indians gone on and made improvements and our children began to like to go to the school houses which have been erected, than we hear the cry of the United States government 'We want your lands;' and, in going from one place to another, the Indian looses all that he had previously learned. But were they to be placed in a position, where they would forever be free from molestation, then they would profit by the establishment of schools among them, and religion and piety would increase and flourish among that people. The disastrous effects of removing the Indians has been shown on the banks of the Ohio and the Sandusky, and in Georgia and New York, where the Presbyterians, labored hard to make the Indians what they were twenty-five or thirty years ago. And no sooner did the tree of piety begin to expand its limbs, than comes the request, 'We want you to go Westward. We want your lands.' The Indian reluctantly gives up his land to the American government, not believing, at first, that they were in earnest; but, when he was convinced of the fact, and his soul being almost teased out of him, and the soldiers having dug up the trees, and taking it to the woods of Arkansas, there to plant it, he surrendered.

We have ever been told that while the eye of philosophy has ever looked on, that under all favorable circumstances, the Indian would be Indian still. And, I would ask, who, under such circumstances would improve? We cannot find institutions of learning, even among the whites, cherished though they may be to a greater extent, always patronized according to their worth.

2. When the Indians have a permanent home given, then what they did on their plantations would of course be permanent. When you give them a home, you will find contentment around their fire-sides; but, if they see a probability of their being removed still further westward, the Indians will act as they have always done, showing that they have no faith in the government of the United States.

Yes! when I went to Washington last April, I saw there a Chief from Green Bay, whose name was John Quincy, to whom I opened my heart as to what I intended, if possible to accomplish. No sooner did he learn what my object was, than he rose from his seat, and stretching forth his hands—the tears running from his eyes—he said, 'I hope the Great Spirit will preserve your life till you accomplish this object, for if the day shall come when the United States shall grant to the Indians a country to the West, I will be the first one to move there, for I am tired of moving about from place to place; for, when we came from the State of New York to Green Bay, we were told that we should not have to remove again; and now, again, Col. Medilly will not settle with us for $7,000, in order that we might sell our lands again, as we did several years ago.' The poor man then sat down.

Ah, my dear friends, if there be any one here who calls himself a man, I would ask him if he would not feel for any one placed in such circumstances as these.

3. By circumscribing the domains of the Indians, you will make agriculturists of them. Twenty-five years ago, in Canada, we were all hunters and it is now 17 or 18 years since we become agriculturists. So long, as there was a deer to hunt, within a range of 18 or 20 miles, we did not regard agricultural pursuits; but no sooner was the country cleared and settled, than we became agriculturists. No sooner did they find

that they could raise grain in the quantity of 1,000 bushels a year, than they were encouraged to labor.

4. The Indians are a social race. They are social among themselves, and were they to be placed in a central position, the intimacy between the several nations would soon become strong, and they would be on the most friendly terms. Their respective nationalities would, before the lapse of many years, be lost, and they would become social and kind towards each other, and thus would be brought about a peaceful state of society which is necessary in order to their improvement.

5. Contentment would be followed by all its attendant blessings. The missionary societies would have great influence, and one school teacher can be employed in educating hundreds; but, while the Indians are in a separate and isolated condition, they cannot avail themselves of these advantages. So that in forty or fifty years hence, the condition of the Indians will be greatly ameliorated and improved. I say it is impossible for you, according to your present system, to succeed in converting the whole of the North American Indians.

6. You must convince the Indians that it is for their good and their salvation—that it will be just and right. The Indian is not a stupid being. When he is to be convinced by the advice and arguments of some kind-hearted man, that his home is never to be touched again—that his children are never to be removed, and that the fruit of his labor is never to be blasted as heretofore,—then will he accept it and act upon it.

7. The improvement of which I speak cannot be accomplished in one day, or in one year, or five years. The elements are now ripening in the far West. If the government of the United States would look to the example of Wm. Penn, and assure the Indians that their new home should be permanent, then they need never fear that one arrow is ever to be directed against it, or the people of the United States. So long as the people follow the example of that kind and good-hearted man, William Penn, towards the Indians of Delaware, when he first came to this country, they need never be at war with the Indian tribes.

8. Emulation would spring up all around them. Some may do well, and thus set an example to those who are not doing well. We do not expect much from the old men, but after they shall have passed away—have ceased to exist—their children will imbibe a different spirit from them. They will be guided and governed by Christianity on the one hand, and education on the other.

9. Your government expenses would become less. Now you are trying to fortify the whole of the West by means of barracks and garrisons. You have spent thousands upon thousands and millions upon millions of dollars, for the last 40 or 50 years, and what has it been for? Because, it is said, it is necessary to defend the frontier settlements from the encroachments of the Indians. Therefore it is, that you have sent your soldiers to your garrison from Arkansas away down to the North. Now all that we have to ask is to have but one garrison in the central part of the territory. If there is any bad feeling among the Indians, that will be a check upon them, instead of incurring so much expense and trouble in undertaking to fortify the entire far West with barracks and garrisons. I would ask the government to give us four or five hundred soldiers, to go (not as a great many have done to break down and overawe the Indian spirit, under pretext that they are encroaching upon the white people) to ward off the hard-hearted white men, who disturb the peace of the Indians by selling them liquors—for many of them are worse than the worst kind of Indians I ever did see. (*Applause and Laughter.*)

10. In buying up the country which lies on this side of the Rocky Mountains, I

would have given but one price for it—for, according to Col. McKenney's statement, you have given a quarter of a center per acre for the land to the Indians, who have afterwards sold it to the government for half a cent, by having to purchase it so often.

11. The expense of sending agents to reside among the Indians, has become a loss on the part of the government, for we would ask but one or two. You have got ten or fifteen among the Chippewas, and ten or fifteen among other nations, and consequently you have expended thousands of dollars needlessly. And some of these agents do not know the Indian character, and are, therefore, unfit to be agents. We want agents who would keep the door, and all the whites that should come among us, would have to come through them. By this means we would ward off a great many wicked men; and when there are any offenders against the laws of the United States, we will hand them over for punishment, and when also, there should happen to be any offenders against our own laws we will punish them. If there is any misunderstanding between the Indians and the agents, then the difficulty can be adjusted between the parties.

12. The expense of transporting the Indians has been great to the government, but as soon as you give a country to the Indians, you will be relieved from the trouble of removing them, for they will go there of themselves.

13. The missionary labors there would become permanent, which has not been the case since their labors have been broken up. And the Indian has always been the sufferer.

14. Gentlemen, in conclusion, I deem it necessary to give the reasons why the Indians have decreased and not improved—why they decreased in a vastly greater proportion since the introduction of the white race on this continent, than before. Prior to their landing on these shores, the small pox and many other virulent and noxious diseases, were unknown among the Indians.

The wars that have raged among themselves. Before the discovery of America, and before the introduction of fire-arms from Europe, the wars among the Indians were not so fatal and destructive as they are now. They have been taught to handle fire-arms with a great deal of skill. The history of Pennsylvania—the history of the New England States, and the history of the South, all tells in what manner those wars were conducted. Champlain, in 1612, supplied the the Indians in the North with fire arms, to oppose the Six Nations in that part of Canada, now composing a portion of the State of New York, who at length became so reduced in numbers, that they were compelled to give up the contest. And so it was with the Spaniards in the South, who, as well as the French and English, also furnished arms to the Indians. In all the wars that have been waged in this country among the European powers, the Indian was always asked to show his fearless nature on the battle field, in behalf of the English, French, Spaniards and Americans. And when the Indian has received these weapons of war from them, his heart has bled, and he has suffered. Yes! look towards the South. In 1763, the Spaniards were waging war against the French. Look in the state of New York, among that class of people, who were of German descent, who encouraged the Indian to war against each other. Look, too, among the people of the North, in Canada, where the British government furnished the Indians with munitions of war, and encouraged them to fight against the North Americans. Sometimes the Indian has been called a savage, because he has been called upon to go and show his bravery in the field.

I ask you, gentlemen, as intelligent men—men who live in an enlightened age, which was the most savage, the ones who knew not the origin of these wars, or those who did? Spirituous liquor has been the great cause of the decrease of the Indians of this country. Disease, war, and famine, have alike preyed upon the life of the Indian. But, ah, alcoholic spirits have cut off the existance of those nations who have left the records of their existence upon their rivers and their mountains. I remember well when I was but a child, that my mother related to me the introduction of liquor on the shores of Lake Superior. Some young men (said she,) were urged to go down to Montreal. They went, and returned late in the year; a council of the nation was called, and one of the men seized a war club and knocked down another. He then fled into the woods, and his brother took the place of the murderer, ordered the men to make two fires, and place a post behind him; then to paint his bare breast black, and put a white spot near the place where he felt his heart beating. And when all these things had been done, twelve warriors came forth with their bows and arrows to shoot him in the breast as soon as he was ready. 'Don't shoot me,' he said, 'till I have sung the death song.' When he was ready, he called out to his brother, 'I am now ready to die in your stead, and if you can live to endure the idea, that the world shall look upon you as a coward, you will not disgrace the clan to which you belong, but shrinking from that which you merit; and then he began to sing. The murderer now ran to him and pushing him aside, pointed to his breast, and made a white spot where he felt his heart beating. He then exclaimed, 'I am not a coward—I am not afraid to die—I went to the woods to get sober for I would not die drunk.' After saying this, he commenced singing the death song, and when he gave the signal that he was ready to die, twelve arrows pierced his heart, and he fell, one of the first victims to alcohol.

'Ah! brandy, brandy, bane of life,
Spring of tumult, source of strife;
Could I but half thy curses tell,
The wise would wish the safe in hell.'

[Here Mr. Copway read the series of resolutions which had been passed, by the Legislatures of North Carolina and South Carolina, respectively.]

Mr. C. resumed, saying—In conclusion, gentlemen, I will say that I have detained you too long. I ask nothing more than what is reasonable, and in asking this of the people of the United States, I feel more confident that my humble petition will be granted by this Legislature, at least, on account of Pennsylvania's early history, in connection with the Indians, I am convinced that there has been friendly relations existing between the Indians and the people of the Pennsylvania particularly. Oh, when I think of that day when peace reigned between the Indians and William Penn. That was a glorious period, and he was a kind-hearted and humane man.

I have ever venerated the name of William Penn, and whenever I thought of the tree under which he made his treaty, which never has been broken, I have often thought if I had only been under the boughs of that old elm tree, I should have been satisfied. I sent to Philadelphia three or four years ago, the endeavor to procure a little piece of that tree, but I failed to obtain it. And I never succeeded in getting hold of any of it until yesterday. Yesterday I received a card from a lady in Philadelphia, requesting me to call at her house. I did so, and, on entering one of the rooms, I saw a picture of the old tree. After salutation, she said, 'there is the tree under which William Penn made his treaty with the Indians. I have understood that you were inquiring for a piece of it, and many have tried to get it from me; and I do not know why I have not parted with it before; and now, it seems to me is the proper time to part with it. I will give it to you.'

And, I took it in my hand and pressed it to my bosom. There it is, and I hope as long as I live, and venerate the name of William Penn, that I shall keep it close to where my heart beats, for I revere the memory of that old man. I venerate the very day when he first came to negotiate with the Indians of this country. For seventy years not a cloud in the Heavens portended danger and discord. The Great Spirit even smiles upon the wild Indian and the white man, as they smoked the pipe of peace. Oh, last summer, when I was in the city of Washington, on the 4th of July, I thought to myself, when I saw the people enjoying themselves, and flocking around at the laying of the corner-stone of the monument to the memory of Washington, that if the day came when the Indians shall have peaceable possession of their homes in the West, I would get my people to raise another monument to the memory of George Washington. We will point our children to his noble form, and speak of his exalted character, and love of country, in the hope that they may emulate his spirit, and follow his glorious examples in all that was great and good.

We trust that the time may come when the Indians of the far West will have it in their power as it is their inclination, to erect a monument as well to the memory of Gen. Washington as to that of William Penn. The eagle of liberty is stretching forth his wings all over the earth, and the mountains of France and Germany have received him. The isles of the sea are celebrating their songs of liberty; and will not, I ask, the Indian participate in the glorious jubilee? You, gentlemen, have too much patriotism in your hearts,—you have too much love in your hearts, to let the Indian die without being lamented.

Many have asked—'Who is that Indian? Where has he come from, and where was he born? And what is he about?' They have asked one another these questions when I have been endeavoring to explain my views in relation to the salvation of my poor countrymen. Thank Heaven, I am an Indian. Yes; were I to be the last to stand on the peaks of the Rocky Mountains, I would still raise my hand to the world as a part of a noble speciment of humanity, the representative of the Indians who once lived in this country. I heard one gentleman say to another—'Who is that?' [Alluding to myself] 'Who is he?' Now if he is in this Hall at the present time, tell him 'I am a native American.' [Applause and laughter.]

Mr. C. in conclusion, said—'I beg this audience—highly inteligent and respectable as it is—to receive my warm acknowledgments for your kind attention this evening; and I pray the Great Spirit that you and I may, while we live, do something for the benefit of the world—that, when we are about to visit the world to come, and the Angel of Death appears to sever our bodies from our souls, that the latter may fly, like an eagle, to mansions in the skies. I trust that the white man and the Indian may meet where they shall swear eternal friendship before their God.

56

HORACE SMITH FULKERSON

(1818–1891)

Horace Smith Fulkerson was born on April 18, 1818, in Harrodsburg, Kentucky, which had once been the site of violent battles between Native Americans and European settlers. By the time of Fulkerson's birth, however, the natives were mostly gone. In 1836, when Fulkerson was eighteen, he moved west to Mississippi, where the human landscape was much different: "One of the novelties to me, of my new home," he recalled, "was the frequent sight in the streets of small bands of Indians, belonging to the Choctaw tribe. I had heard such blood-curdling and *hair-lifting* stories in my boyhood days from the old hunters and Indian fighters of Kentucky."

Mississippi had been admitted to the Union in 1817, only one year before Fulkerson's birth. Had Fulkerson arrived there much later than 1836, he might have missed encountering its natives, too. In treaties of 1830 and 1832, the Choctaws and Chickasaws had ceded their lands in the northern half of the state, and the opening of this territory prompted a deluge of settlers. In the decade from 1830 to 1840, the white population of the state more than doubled, and the slave population nearly tripled. Fulkerson was there to watch as the frontier disappeared.

Fulkerson initially settled in Rodney, Mississippi. In 1840, he moved to Port Gibson, where he was employed as Deputy United States Marshall. He remained in Port Gibson until 1858, when he relocated to New Orleans. After the outbreak of the Civil War, he served the Confederacy in several civil offices before reporting to a conscript camp and then guarding a post in Meridian, Mississippi. After the war, Fulkerson moved his family from New Orleans back to Mississippi, where he worked in the mercantile business in Vicksburg. While in Vicksburg he published a series of historical and autobiographical sketches, some of which he would collect in *Random Recollections of Early Days in Mississippi* (1885).

Like Augustus Baldwin Longstreet before him, Fulkerson fancied himself an historian, yet felt free to take artistic license with his material. In the preface to his *Random Recollections* he wrote, "It is fragmentary history; very many of the incidents related being literally true, while all of them rest upon a foundation of truth, receiving only such exaggeration of finish in their statement as accorded with the taste of the writer, and as was needed to make them, in his judgment, more acceptable to the public." Fulkerson also published *A Civilian's Recollection of the War between the States* (1886) and *The Negro: As He Was, As He Is, As He Will Be* (1889). He died in Vicksburg on April 5, 1891.

Text: *Random Recollections of Early Days in Mississippi* (Vicksburg, 1885): "Shocco Jones in Mississippi," 66–75; "Hanging the Gamblers," 95–97.

SHOCCO JONES IN MISSISSIPPI (c. 1868, 1885)

The successful cultivation of cotton and the profitableness of the pursuit, in Mississippi and Louisiana, in the years from 1834 to 1838, had led to so much speculation in wild lands, and such a rapid advance in them, that anybody with a little money had only to buy a tract of land, put a few negroes on it, and deaden the timber, to grow rich—*on paper.* The sales were all on a credit; but the banks discounted paper freely and every man was ready to endorse every other man's paper.

The country was apparently so prosperous and everybody was growing rich so fast, that every little town had its bank, and the bigger ones had two or more. Vicksburg had several of these "institutions," and Natchez, the oldest town in the State, had two, the Agricultural Bank and Planters' Bank, old banks, which had existed for a number of years and had been very successful. The celebrated Union Bank was chartered in 1838, and was in operation the following year. The "boom" in every branch of business was immense, and everything was aglow with speculation.

It was just anterior to this period that General Jackson, as President of the United States, had his successful fight with the old United States Bank. The withdrawal of the public deposits from this bank had so deranged the finances of the country as to bring on a great financial crisis, which involved the Southern State banks in the ruin that followed.

It was at the height of the distress and anxiety growing out of this state of things, in the Fall of 1839, that that wonderful genius and Prince of Humbuggers, Shocco Jones, of North Carolina, burst upon the vision of the distressed Mississippians. He came unheralded, arriving in Jackson, the Capital of the State, by stage from Columbus, at which latter point he had created quite a flutter in the little coterie of bank officials and directors who controled the fiscal institution of the city on the banks of the Tombigbee; making a soft place in the circle of its officers for an impecunious relative who dwelt in their midst, by sheer force of his unrivaled genius and unparalleled impudence, and strange to say only for the sake of a love of fun which was all-devouring with him and which he indulged alone for his personal gratification, for he never divulged to any one of his boon companions, attracted by his captivating manners, that *fun* was his prime, and in fact, his only object. In his intense love of it he was unwilling to share it with others. He was a veritable hoarder of fun. Imperturbable impudence, a gracious manner, bright intelligence, and the business air of a monied man without solicitude for the future, made up his stock in trade, and were the tools with which he forged his fun. The gullible trait in human character was the field of his operations, and he had unbounded confidence in its resources, in its capacity to yield him an abundant harvest of fun under his skillful cultivation. A crisis in public affairs, a period of anxiety when everybody was on the *qui vive* for strange and startling things, was his fit occasion. His advent in Mississippi was opportune, and his knowledge of human nature and the condition of affairs told him so.

So soon after reaching Jackson as he made himself as presentable as becomes a man of affairs and a man of means, he got directions to the office of Dr. Wm. M. Gwin who was then U. S. Marshal for the District of Mississippi, and proceeded thither, carrying under his arm a large bundle of papers carefully wrapped up, tied with red tape, and having on it seals done in red wax.

Arriving at the Marshal's office, he introduced himself as a confidential agent of the United States Treasury Department, and informed the Marshal that he had authority from the Secretary of the Treasury to enquire into the condition of the Southern banks in which Government funds had been deposited. This information was imparted in the quiet tone and with the mysterious air of one charged with valuable State secrets; the agent meantime, carelessly turning about and thrumming upon the ominous looking package bound in red tape. The high functionary of the Marshal's office took in the situation promptly, and tendered his services to the agent. Dr. Gwin was himself a man of affairs and a man of parts, and he had a high place in the confidence of the Government.

The agent scanned the office of the Marshal in search of a strong box wherein to deposit his valuable papers, and seeing none, enquired of the Marshal if he knew of one. Certainly he did. The Receiver at the Land Office had the finest one in the State. They went thither; the agent was introduced to the Receiver; the safe was carefully inspected by the agent, and the package locked up. Then the Receiver was taken into confidence and had the high State secret imparted to him. And it is said he had an armed watchman on duty all night over the safe containing the package.

Before separating, Shocco said he desired to consult them about a legal adviser; that besides the need of one in the affairs of Government, he thought it not unlikely he would need one to examine land titles, as the cashier of the Cape Fear Bank of North Carolina had requested him, as he passed through on his way from Washington, to invest a large surplus of gold which the bank held, in Mississippi land mortgages, on one to three years; that the sum was great enough to meet the wants of many persons, and he would likely have to pass upon a number of titles. He had heard of a Mr. Prentiss, of Vicksburg, as being a very superior lawyer and desired to know if he would be a proper person for so important a trust. The Marshal and Receiver agreed that he could do no better than to employ that distinguished gentleman, and the Marshal was requested to invite him to Jackson, by letter, which he did.

The great lawyer, promptly obeying the summons, repaired to the Capital and was presented to the great fiscal agent. A single look at each other and they were as firmly knit together as were Jonathan and David. "As face answereth to face in water," genius answers to genius when meeting. Until this meeting the agent had not been seen to smile. The weight of great cares was upon him, and his bearing and expression were altogether such as became the occasion. But a magician was before him now with the rod of a Moses. One stroke—a single flash of wit from the great lawyer—and the flinty face of the financier broke into smiles, and a flash went back. The grave Marshal and Receiver heard explosion after explosion as the rockets of wit flashed thick and fast, and the Treasury agent rose higher and higher in their estimation. What! a wit, a poet, a philosopher and an orator, as well as an astute sober-minded business man! What an acquisition to the State! He must be held. And they went off, the lawyer on the agent's arm, with his eloquent hobble— there was nothing about him that was not eloquent—the Marshal and Receiver following.

Who that having seen and heard the great orator in his convivial moods, at the bar, on the hustings, or the platform, would part with the memory? Heathen sages and philosophers would have worshipped him as the god of eloquence. Having once seen it, who can forget that wonderful face, with its varied expression, running the whole gamut of the passions, from that gentle love which "worketh no ill to its neighbor," to a hissing scorn and look as fatal to the adversary as that of the fabled basalisk's.

The boon and genial companions soon reached the point of intimacy which drops the formalities of social intercourse, and "Prent and Shoc" became the terms in which their reciprocal endearment was expressed. Prentiss for once had met his match, in some points—in *all* points he was *matchless*. A trip to Vicksburg was arranged for; the package with the dynamite load, which was to blow up the banks, was withdrawn from the Receiver's strong box, and they started off to storm Vicksburg, the stronghold of speculators in lands and negroes, and shaky banks. The news of the contemplated visit by the Treasury agent and money lender had preceded them. The bank officers were shaking in their shoes, and the speculators were busy perfecting their titles.

It must be remembered that at this early day the telegraph was not in operation, and there were no fast mails. A man of Shocco's genius could have his game played to the end before evidence that he was a fraud could be furnished, and so anxious was everybody to believe that relief to the distressed was at hand, and so busy were the bank officers with their financial entanglements and getting ready for the expected examination by the so-called agent, that nobody thought to ask for his authority. His native shrewdness told him as much, and besides he knew that he was equal to any such emergency as a demand for his authority should it be made. The town was all agog with the news of the arrival of the great financier accompanied by their distinguished townsman, who they knew had been closeted with him long enough to detect the imposter if such he was. As soon as he became separated from his attorney, after having been freely introduced, he assumed his most rigid business air and called at the banks, carrying the red tape package under his arm. His visits were expected and were prepared for, and most of the Directors were in attendance. He was introduced and treated with marked courtesy. The financial crisis in which the country was involved soon became the topic of conversation. He hadn't a doubt but that it would pass away speedily under the skillful management of the great man then Secretary of the U. S. Treasury, who combined in his person the financial skill of a Hamilton and a Morris, adding that the President had given the highest evidence of his fitness for his exalted position in calling this eminent citizen to his council board; that the mantle of the retiring President would certainly fall upon the shoulders of the great Secretary. From that topic he passed on to the resources of the great State of Mississippi; how that her soil surpassed the fertile valley of the Nile in the days when the sons of Jacob went down to Egypt for corn, and saying further that he had been besieged by his monied friends in his native State, as he passed through it, to make investments for them in Mississippi real estate securities. And all of this with the seriousness and knit brow of a veteran financier.

Meantime, a messenger had been dispatched to a favorite resort on Main street with orders for a liberal lunch to be set, and another was sent for the genial and witty Maj. C., and other vivacious and convivial friends. Adjournment to the lunch room was proposed, and was assented to by the agent without reluctance or surprise, and as though it belonged to his business mission. Before leaving he took the cashier aside, whispered a few words to him, and after making, in pencil, in few cabalistic marks on the valuable package tied up with red tape, and a duplicate of the same in his memorandum book, with the name of the bank added, placed it in the hands of the cashier, and then informed the gentlemen that he was at their service.

Arrived at the lunch room, it was observed that the business cloud which had overshadowed the countenance of the agent began to pass away and was followed by a sunny smile that betokened hilarity and appreciation of life's enjoyments. He apparently partook freely of the tempting viands, but it was observed by a few persons that he had left more than he partook of; that he never refused to "fill" his glass at the call, but he only "sipped." The merriment ran high. Maj. C. was at his best, and his sallies of wit drew from the distinguished guest shot after shot of the most telling reparte and appropriate anecdote.

At the height of the fun the great lawyer came limping in, and the lunch room rang again and again with applause, for help was needed. The Major's fund of wit, and that of others of no mean quality, was becoming exhausted, while that of Shocco had only been whetted up to an easy-going point: no strain, no spurring. The great lawyer threw off one of his telling impromptus, aimed at the agent, who caught it, and sent it back with a new and glittering point, which drew forth a round of applause as it struck. The floor was then given to the two champions. The hilarious crowd that surrounded them, now considerably augmented, had naught to do but hurrah, applaud and laugh. Shakespeare and Byron and Scott, were freely quoted in illustration of the happier things said by the champions. Round after round of applause was given. One enthusiastic business man was heard to say, "we *must* capture him. With such a lawyer and such a financier Vicksburg's fame will cover the continent."

But the end came, and with it the struggle for the honor of privately entertaining the guest. Major C. won it. The baggage was sent up and the agent made his affable bow to the hostess. He was soon surrounded by the children, whose eyes and ears he as soon captured, for he knew all the stories they had heard, and many more, of a highly marvelous character. They followed him over the house and never seemed to tire of him. The day following the lunch, he appeared upon the streets wearing his gravest business aspect, but courteously bowing to all, and as applicants for loans would approach him with their papers he would quietly say "take your papers to Mr. Prentiss, there is money enough for all," and tradition says that a leading family in the city gave him a great banquet next day, where wine flowed freely, and many title deeds were spread out. At night, he, on invitation, met some leading gentlemen in a social game, but got in late, after the game had been made up. Looking on for a while, he said to his leading friend: "Get up; give me your hand; you don't understand the game." He soon passed over a handsome sum to his friend as his winnings and pocketed enough for expenses. He then visited a cock-pit, walked in and up to the master of ceremonies, who held a high bred game cock in his hands, saying, with an authoritative composure, "give me that bird, I will teach you how to tie on a gaff." He did it and the bird won.

In a day or two Shocco informed his attorney of his purpose to visit Natchez by the first packet going South; that he should stop off a day or two at Grand Gulf and Port Gibson to look after his banking matters; that he hoped he would push the examination of the numerous titles then in his hands, and requested him to follow him by the next packet, as he should need his services at Natchez. Withdrawing the red tape parcel from the bank, he proceeded to the boat, accompanied by numerous friends and admirers, to see him off. On the boat he was the "cynosure of all eyes," and was overwhelmed with attentions by the numerous planters on board going to

New Orleans. He bore himself with becoming business dignity and social unreserve. He was at home with them, and entertained them with high talk on finance and many interesting anecdotes, for which latter mental exercise the planters had a high relish.

At Grand Gulf and Port Gibson he created a great sensation in business and banking circles. An old friend of the writer was cashier of the Bank of Port Gibson. The old gentleman, in his white roundabout and gold rimmed spectacles had occasion to wipe off much perspiration from his noble brow with his red bandana at Shocco's pointed interrogatories, and it was said that Shocco was the first man he ever met with whom he failed to differ. The agent returned to the river after having exhorted the banks to set their houses in order, saying he should return in a week to make a final examination.

The next packet came along. The agent was at the landing and as the boat rounded to, the great lawyer emerged from the social hall, followed by boon companions. When Shocco was spied, the welkin rang again with three cheers for the great deliverer. The scene on board, as the boat wended her way to Natchez, is past describing. The gentle reader must draw his own picture as best he can by the light of what has been said already in that line. Shocco went to the barkeeper, after greeting the party, and in his lordliest way ordered that functionary to let the little lame man (meaning Prentiss) have anything he called for, adding, "I will make it all right!" Arrived at Natchez, the banks were visited immediately by the prompt Treasury agent, and the great lawyer was taken charge of by his friends—the friends of his earliest Southern days. Natchez, at that day, was the seat of wealth and refinement and high aristocratic tendencies. It was the oldest city in the State, and had two banks, which were presided over by some of her wealthiest resident planters, and transacted a very large business. Shocco was not wanting in the needed resources of mind in meeting these magnates and notables. In their presence he rose to sublimest heights and discoursed eloquently of the noted citizen then at the head of the Treasury Department. The details of what tradition has handed down as having been said and done by him would weary the reader.

The red tape package with the broad seal was duly deposited in bank, and the day after his arrival a dray backed up to the door of the bank, having on it boxes of specie, marked "S. Jones, U. S. T. Agent, care of the bank." The boxes were deposited in the vault of the bank.

Numerous interviews of a private and confidential character were held with the bank officers, by the agent, and the attorney was besieged by parties with papers—in want of accommodations. A great dinner party was given the two distinguished visitors by one of the citizens. But Shocco had an almanac, and a good memory besides, and these told him that his time was nearly up. It was nearing the time when somebody might be receiving an answer to a letter which may have been mailed to Washington. A return to Vicksburg to finish up business there, and then a return to Natchez, was determined on. The first boat up conveyed the two great men to Vicksburg, the specie having been left and the red tape package withdrawn and carried off. Arrived at Vicksburg, hurried business interviews followed the next day, and much high merriment the following night. Late in the next forenoon, the revellers of the night before called at his lodgings, but Shocco was *gone!* and the country was *sold!* The red tape package was found on the table in his room. The seals were broken—contents, old *newspapers!* The news flew to Natchez. The specie boxes were opened—contents, *scrap iron!*

HANGING THE GAMBLERS (c. 1868, 1885)

This tragical incident—the hanging of the gamblers in the year 1835—serves to illustrate the desperate character of Vicksburg's population, in the period of 1830 to 1840. The dreadful vice of gambling, encouraged by some of the most prominent people, had taken a deep hold upon the community, and these dens or "hells" as they were called, wherein the nefarious business was pursued, were numerous on every business thoroughfare of the city, conducted openly by day and night, and all day of Sundays. They were a shocking scandal and disgrace in the eyes of the better part of the people, but the gamblers and their patrons were so numerous, and were such reckless and desperate characters, that the better class stood in awe of them, much as they loathed and condemned the vice.

But submission in this case, like submission and intolerance in every case of outrage and wrong, only tended to stimulate the insolence of the offenders. The law was resorted to, but its "delay," together with the money of its violators, rendered it inoperative. The question—a grave one—of the right of any whole community, organized under the legal sanctions common to all civilized countries, to its life, when in peril, and to its preservation by taking the law into its own hands, began to move the people, and was decided in the affirmative.

Self-preservation is a law of God, a law of nature, and a law of man, and who shall say that a community, after exhausting all legal remedies, and failing of protection, from defects of law, or from its perversion to evil ends, by corruption or intimidation, *may not* resort to this higher law as a remedy? Under these named circumstances, *good ends* are always the aim. And though it may be an evil, may not a community, under an inexorable necessity, make a choice of evils? Every community which holds this right in reserve, has served notice upon evil doers, and notice often acts as an ounce of prevention, and saves a resort to the pound of cure.

The trouble with the gamblers at Vicksburg culminated to the unendurable point, on the 4th of July, 1835, when one of their number, uninvited, in his insolence, disturbed the festivities of the day as they were being conducted by Capt. Brungard's military company, in the Springfield portion of the city. His conduct was wholly that of a ruffian and blackguard, under the influence of strong drink. He was put under guard, but was released in the evening, when he made threats of dire vengeance. When the company returned to the Court House, he was there, heavily armed, prepared to execute his threats. He was seized, disarmed, and carried to the outskirts of the town, where he was whipped, and a coat of tar and feathers applied, and was ordered to leave immediately, which he did, and has never been heard of since.

Soon it was seen that there was great firment amongst the gamblers. They were loud in their denunciations and threats of revenge, for the treatment received by their comrade. At night a public meeting of citizens, largely attended, was held at the Court House. Resolutions were adopted ordering all gamblers to leave town in six hours, under penalty of being roughly handled, and notices to that effect were posted by 9 o'clock next morning.

At 9 o'clock the following morning, (Monday) the military and citizens to the number of four hundred, well armed, assembled on Main street, when committees were appointed to visit every gambling house, which was done, and all the furniture and implements used by the gamblers, were collected in the streets and burned. One of the houses was found to be fortified and barricaded, and armed men were in it. It was immediately surrounded by the angered citizens, when the door was broken in, and a gun was fired from within, whose contents, a load of buckshot, entered the breast of Dr. Bodley, a prominent and highly esteemed citizen, killing him almost instantly. Some dozen or more other shots were fired, from within and without, but without effect, when the beseigers made a rush, and getting inside, captured and bound the inmates. Two escaped from the house, but were soon overtaken and brought back. All of the inmates, five in number, were then pinioned, and led out to execution in the eastern portion of the city, where a gallows had been speedily erected, and where they were as speedily launched into eternity.

Thus ended the short but long growing war with the gamblers, and the city "had rest" from the fraternity for a period of not less than a quarter of a century. The names of the hung men, though of record, are not here given. It is enough to charge the memory and these pages with the sickening event. Some of them may have borne honored names, and it is certain all of them had fathers and mothers who may have been as virtuous as yours or mine, reader. And rather than blazon their names to the world, let us remember that innocent tears were shed for them, and let us rather ourselves drop a tear over their wrecked lives, remembering that they were once as innocent as that natural depravity in which we are all involved, will allow.

ALICE CARY

(1820–1871)

Poet, novelist, and short-story writer Alice Cary, and her sister Phoebe, a poetess, were born in southern Ohio in the early 1820s. Although coming from impoverished but gentile backgrounds, they quickly found themselves publishing in the vibrant Cinicinnati literary scene in the 1840s. Encouraged by such figures as William D. Gallagher, they published prose and poetry in the local journals and had access to eastern literary celebrities passing through the region. Encouraged by Rufus Griswold's republication of their poetry in his *The Female Poets of America* (1847)—as well as by Edgar Allen Poe's very positive review of their work—they moved to New York in 1850.

Alice found most of her success in the field of short-story writing. Her first collection, *Clovernook; or Recollections of Our Neighborhood in the West,* appeared in 1851 and was popular enough to merit a second, and more artistically successful, sequel, *Clovernook, Second Series,* in 1853. These collections stand as important forerunners to the emergent field of women's local color writing, a genre developed by such figures as Harriet Beecher Stowe and Mary Wilkins Freeman in the years following the Civil War. In their stories and those of the many writers working in the area, the most consistent theme is the picturesque ways in which rural places might be contrasted with the model of American metropolitan society familiar to eastern readers and publishers. The realism and attention to dialect in these stories largely follow Caroline Kirkland's model of an ambiguous collision between local and national cultures, with the latter emerging, eventually, as preferable.

The main subject of the particular story reprinted here is the difficult class politics of the west as reflected through issues of gender. Most recently, Timothy Mahoney has studied how easterners and westerners who aspired to eastern models of social order and hierarchy in the west often imposed their notions of gentility on a local population ill-suited to managing the forms and expectations of nineteenth-century manners. In "Charlotte Ryan," the eponymous title character's final disappointment and sense of loss reflect Cary's ambivalence concerning her own departure from the west. While the east represented opportunities for publishing and the metropolitanism impossible even in Cincinnati, the west was more than primitive backwater.

Text: "Charlotte Ryan" (*Clovernook, Second Series,* New York, 1853; rpt. in *Clovernook Sketches and Other Stories,* ed. Judith Fetterley. New Brunswick, New Jersey: 1987): 105–137.

CHARLOTTE RYAN (1853)

I

AS THERE IS in every neighborhood a first family, so there is a last family—a family a little behind everybody else—and in Clovernook this family was named Ryan. They did not indeed live very near the village, but rather on the very verge of our neighborhood. A little dingy house, off the main road, and situated in a hollow, was their habitation, and, though they were intelligent, they had no ideas of the elegancies of life, and but meagre ones, indeed, of its comforts.

Charlotte, the eldest daughter, inherited all the cleverness of her parents, with few of their prejudices against modern improvements, so that, now and then, her notions ran out into a sort of flowery border along the narrow way in which she had been taught to walk. Small opportunities had she for the indulgence of refined or elegant tastes, but sometimes, as she brought home the cows at night, she lingered to make a "wreath of roses," or to twist the crimson tops of the iron-weeds with her long black hair; and once I remember seeing her, while she was yet a little girl, with a row of maple leaves pinned to the bottom of her skirt; she was pretending they were the golden fringe of her petticoat.

Clovernook boasted of one or two select schools even at that time, to which most of the people, who were not very poor, contrived to send their daughters: but little Charlotte went down the hollow, across a strip of woods, to the old schoolmaster, who taught in a log house and in an obscure neighborhood for the summer, and made shoes in the winter, and I suspect he was but imperfectly skilled in either vocation, for I remember it used to be said that he had "taken up both trades out of his own head." The girls of the "high school" were in her eyes "privileged beyond the common run—quite on the verge of heaven." And no wonder she regarded them so: the ribbons that tied their braids, were prettier than the two or three teeth of horn comb that fastened her own hair, and her long checked-apron compared unfavorably with their white ones. But with this period of her life I have little to do, as the story I am going to relate is limited to the circle of a few days, when Charlotte had ceased to pin maple leaves on her petticoat, and wore instead ornaments of glass and pinchbeck.[1]

"Here is a letter for Miss Ryan: it will not be much out of your way, if you will be so kind," said the post-master to me one evening, as I received my own missives, for at that time the postmaster of Clovernook knew all the persons in the habit of receiving letters, and as one for Miss Ryan had never been there before, I as well as he, naturally supposed it would be a surprise, probably an agreeable one to her, and I therefore gladly took charge of it, choosing instead of the dusty highway, a path through the meadows, and close under the shadow of the woods, which brought the home of Charlotte directly in my way, though the duty I undertook added more than a mile to my walk homeward. It was in the late autumn, and one of those dry, windy, uncomfortable days which brings thought from its wanderings to hover down about

---

1. Pinchbeck is an alloy of zinc and copper used to imitate gold.

one's home; so, as the night fell, I quickened my steps, pausing now and then to listen to the roar down deep in the woods, which seemed like the moan of the sea—which I had heard only in imagination then—or to mark the cabin homes, peering out of the forest, and calculate the amount of comfort or discomfort in them or about; and I remember to this day some particular facts from which inferences were drawn. Before one door, a dozen dun and speckled pigs were feeding from a trough, and sunken in mud knee deep, and near them, barefooted, and wearing a red flannel shirt, stood a ragged urchin, whose shouts of delight would have been pleasant to hear, but for the harsh, scolding voice that half drowned them. Both the joy and the anger were a mystery at first, but I presently saw by what they were caused.

"I'll come out and settle with you, my boy, if you don't quit that—mind I tell you!" screamed an old woman, leaning over the low rail fence of the door-yard, her cap-border flapping like a flag of war, and with one foot on the ground and one in the air, as she bent eagerly forward, gesticulating vehemently, but chiefly in the direction of an old cat, which the boy had put in a slender harness of twine—his own ingenious workmanship, I suspect. He laughed heartily, in spite of the threatened settlement, calling out in high glee, as pussy ran up a tree to escape him, "Jementallies! how she goes it!"

"I'll go you," continued the monitor, "as sure as you're born, if you don't ungear the poor sarpent before you're a minute older!" And so I passed out of hearing and out of sight, and I have never since been enlightened as to the adjustment of the pending difficulty.

It was quite night, and the candle-light streamed bright through the dead morning-glory vines which still hung at the window, when my rap at the door of Mr. Ryan was answered by a loud and clear "Come in!" so earnest that it seemed half angry.

Homely, but still home-like, was the scene that presented itself—the hickory logs were blazing in the deep wide fire-place, the children were seated quietly on the trundle-bed, for their number had grown faster than that of the chairs, and talking in an under-tone about "choosing sides" at school, and what boys and girls were "first-rate and particular" as choosers, and what ones were big dumb-heads: they presently changed their tone from a low key to a sharp whisper, much more distinct, but my entrance did not interrupt their discussion.

Mr. Ryan, wearing a coat and trowsers with patches at elbow and knee of a dissimilar color, was seated on a low stool in the corner, engaged in softening with melted tallow the hard last year's shoes of the children, which had been put aside during the summer season.

"A young winter," he said, by way of welcoming me, and then continued apologetically, and as though it was almost a disgrace to wear shoes, "the wind to-day makes a body feel like drawing their feet in their feathers."

I said the winter brought its needs, or something of that sort, implying that we regarded things in the same way, and he resumed and continued the mollifying process without speaking another word.

Golden rings of dried pumpkins hung along the ceiling, bags of dried apples and peaches, bunches of herbs, and the like, and here and there from projections of framework, hung stockings, by dozens, and other garments suited to the times. A limb of bright red apples, withering in the warmth and smoke, beautified the jamb, beneath the great "bake oven," and such were all the ornaments of which the room could boast, I think.

Mrs. Ryan was busy at the kneading trough, making shortcakes for breakfast—

silent mostly, and wearing a look of severity, as though she knew her duty and did it. Only Charlotte came forward to meet me, and smiled her welcome. The Methodist "Advocate" lay open on the table, and some sewing work dropped from her lap as she rose. She politely offered me the chair with the leather bottom, and added to the sticks on the fire, manifesting her good will and courtesy in the only ways possible.

She had grown beautifully into womanhood, and though her dress was neither of choice material, nor so made as to set off her person very advantageously, it was easy to perceive that under the hands of an artist in waists, skirts, &c., her form would seem admirable for its contour and fine proportion, while her face should be a signal for envy or for admiration to youthful women and men, if she were "in society." And she had in some way acquired, too, quite an agreeable manner of her own, only wanting a freedom from restraining influences to become really graceful and captivating; and I could not help wishing, as I looked on her, that she could find a position better suited to her capacities and inclinations. A foolish wish.

The letter elicited expressions of surprise and curiosity from all members of the family, except Charlotte, who suppressed her interest for the time. "Let me see it, let me see it," exclaimed the children, but the stamp of the father's foot brought silence into the room, on which he arose, and wiping his hands on his hair, prepared to read the letter, for Charlotte did not think of breaking the seal herself.

"It's from down the river I reckon," said the mother, "and tells us all about Peter's folks." Charlotte blushed and looked annoyed. "I'll just bet!" said one of the boys, a bright-looking lad of nine or ten years, "that a queen gets letters every day; yes, and written on gold paper, likely enough," he continued, after a moment, and in response to himself as it were.

"I wish I was there," said a younger sister, smiling at the pleasant fancy, "and I'd climb away up on her throne some time when she was gone to meeting, and steal some of her things."

"And you would get catched and have your head chopped off with a great big axe," replied the brother.

The little girl continued musingly, "I expect Charlotte's new Sunday dress is no finer than a queen wears every day."

"Every day!" exclaimed the mother in lofty contempt, "she wears as good washing-day in the kitchen." In the midst of these speculations I took leave. A day or two afterwards, I learned that Charlotte was gone to pass a month or two with some relations near the city.

II

THESE RELATIVES were but recently established in a country home, having belonged originally to one of the northern seaport towns. The family embraced but three persons, the father, whose life had in some capacity been passed mostly at sea, and two daughters—all unfitted by education and habit for their new position.

Of course Charlotte had heard much of her uncle, Captain Bailey, and his daughters, and in childish simplicity supposed them to be not only the grandest but also the most excellent people in the world. They dwelt in her thoughts on a plane of being so much above her, that she involuntarily looked up to them and reverenced them as if they were of a fairer and purer world.

Through all her childhood it had been a frequent wish that some of uncle John's folks would come, but uncle John's folks never came, and so she grew into womanhood without being much disenchanted. Nobody about Clovernook was at all comparable to them in any respect, as they lived in the beautiful region of her dreams.

Mrs. Ryan and Mrs. Bailey were sisters, who in early life were all in all to each other. Marriage had separated them, by distance much, by circumstances more. Mrs. Bailey went to an establishment in town, and after a round of dissipations and gaieties, became a small link in the chain of fashion, having married out of, and above her previous and fit position. Mrs. Ryan, who as a girl was the less dashing and spirited of the two, became a farmer's wife, and with the energy and determination which characterized her always, struck at once into the wilderness in search of a new home.

Sad enough was the parting of the sisters, and many the promises to write often, and to visit each other as soon as might be; but these promises were never kept, and perhaps it was well they never were, for far outside of the blessed oneness of thought and feeling in which they parted, would have been their meeting! Absence, separate interests, different ways of life, soon did their work.

As I said, they never met, and so never knew that they had grown apart, but each lived in the memory of the other, best and most beautiful to the last. But though each mother taught her children to love and reverence the good aunt that lived far away, and whom possibly they would see some time, the young Baileys failed to be impressed with that respect and admiration for their country relations, which the country relations felt for them.

After a series of successes came adverse fortune to the Baileys, then the death of the wife and mother, and so, partly in the hope of bettering their condition, and partly to escape mortification, the broken and helpless family removed from their statelier home and settled in the neighborhood of our beautiful city in the west. For they fancied, as many other people do who know nothing about it, that the farmer's is a sort of holiday life; that after planting the crop he may sleep or play till the harvest time; that then the labor of a day or two fills the barn with bright sheaves and sweet hay; and that all the while, and without any effort, cattle and sheep and horses are growing and fattening, and plenty flowing in. A little experience sufficed to cure the Baileys of this pleasant conceit. In truth, they didn't go to work in the right way, with an honest determination that compels success. Farming and housekeeping were begun as delightful experiments, and when the novelty was lost, they fell back into lamentations and repinings for the opulence they had lost. Briers made sorry work with Captain Bailey's ruffles, and the morning dew was unfavorable to the polish of his boots; the corn didn't fall into baskets of itself, nor the apples come home without having been first shaken from the trees, and picked up, one by one. Weeds and burs ran over the garden and choked the small vegetables; the cows grew lean, and their milk dried away, to the astonishment of all parties—for nobody suspected they were not milked regularly and rightly, or that their wants were not attended to, and some fearful distemper was supposed to have attacked them, as day after day flocks of buzzards and crows were seen settling in hollows where the poor creatures had died. But Captain Bailey's troubles were trifles compared with the afflictions of his daughters, who not only sighed and cried, but wished themselves dead, a dozen times a day. The hard, yellow balls of butter, which they fancied would be so nice, required more labor and care in the making than they were willing to bestow; bread was taken from the oven black and heavy; and, in fact, the few things that were done at all were not done well, and general weariness and dissatisfaction was the consequence.

"I wish I was in heaven!" exclaimed Miss Sally Bailey, one day, more wrathfully than piously, turning at the same time from the churn and hiding her eyes from the great splash of cream that soiled the front of her lavender colored silk.

"It's no use for us to try to live like anybody," answered Kate, "and we might as well give up first as last, and put on linsey, and work, and work, and work till we die!"

And both girls sat down and bent their eyes on the floor, either not seeing, or affecting not to see, the discomfort in which their father was; poor man, he had come in from the field with a thorn in his hand, and with the blood oozing from the wound, was vainly searching under chairs and tables, and shoving his hand one way and the other across the carpet, for the needle lost in his endeavor to perform with it a surgical operation.

"*I do* wish," he said at last, a little petulantly, "I could ever have any body to do any thing for me."

"I am sure I am sorry for the accident," said one of the girls, "if that will do you any good."

"I don't think it will," was the reply; and the other sister offered assistance, assuring her father, and as though he were responsible for it, that she could feel nothing less than the broomstick in her clumsy fingers, so it was useless to try to handle a needle.

Having survived the operation, Captain Bailey, who was really disposed to do the best he could, pinned a towel against his vest, and took hold of the churn, saying, "Now, my dears, I'll make the butter, while you arrange the dinner."

"I would like to know what we are to arrange," said Kate, tossing her head, "there is nothing in the house that I know of."

"Surely there is something," the father said, working the dasher most energetically; "there is pork, and flour, and apples, and cream, and butter, and potatoes, and coffee, and tea, and sugar"—there the girls interrupted him with something about a meal suitable for wood-choppers.

Captain Bailey was now seriously discouraged, and without speaking again, continued to churn for two hours, but the cream was cold and thin, and at the end of that time looked no more likely to "come" than at first, so giving the churn a jostle to one side, with something that sounded very like an oath, the gentleman removed the towel which had served him for an apron, and taking down his gun from the wall, walked hurriedly in the direction of the woods. But he was one of those men who are called good-hearted, and though he managed badly, never doing either himself or anybody else any good, still, every one said, "he means well," and "what a good-hearted fellow he is." So, of course, his amiability soon returned, and having brought down two squirrels and a wood-cock, whistling out the hope and good-nature that were in his heart. "Well, Sally," he said, throwing down the game, "here is something for dinner."

"Very well," she replied, but without looking up, or ceasing from her work of rubbing chalk on the cream-spot of her dress.

Kate, since her father's departure, had bestirred herself so much as to pin a towel about the churn, set it one side, and fill the tea-kettle, after which she seated herself with the last new novel.

"Well my dear, what is the news with you?" asked the captain, punching the fire at the same time, in an anxious way.

"The news is," she answered, "that two chickens have drowned themselves in a pail of dish-water, and the pig you bought at the vendue is choked to death with a

loaf of burnt bread—when I found it, it was in the last agonies," she continued, laughing, "and I don't see what we *are* to do."

"An idea strikes me," answered the father, in no wise discouraged. "Write to your
cousin—what's her name? who lives out in Clovernook—she's a housekeeper, I'll
warrant you; write to her to come and visit you for a month or two, and initiate you
in the ways of the woods."

"A good notion," said Kate, throwing down her book, and the dinner went forward better than any one had done since the housekeeping began.

The farm selected by Captain Bailey, was east of the Queen City—not so far,
however, but that some of the spires, and it is a city of spires, were clearly visible from
its higher elevations. Both house and grounds were seriously out of repair, having
been abandoned by the person who purchased and fitted them up, and sold ultimately
at a sacrifice. They were well suited for the present proprietor; the spirit of broken-
down assumption reigned supreme everywhere: you might see it perched on the leaning posts of the gateway, and peering from under the broken mullions of the great
windows. It had been a fine place, when the forest land was first trimmed up and
cleared, when pebbles and flowers bordered the rivulets, and the eminence on which
stood the house was terraced into green stairs. The tall red chimneys were some of
them fallen partly down now, and the avenue leading from the gate to the hall was
lost in weeds and grass, through which only a wagon-track was broken.

One or two trellised summer-houses stood pitching down the hill, and here and
there a rose-bush or lilac lopped aside devoid of beauty, except the silver sieves woven
amongst them by the black and yellow spiders.

III

THE LITTLE CART in which Charlotte Ryan rode with her father rattled terribly; it
seemed never to have made so much noise till then; it would betray their poverty, but
if her father would only drive softly and leave the cart at the gate, it doubtless would
be supposed that they had come in a more stylish way. Mr. Ryan, however, was a plain
blunt farmer, and would have driven his little cart up to the White House, and elbowed his way through the Cabinet without a fear or a blush for his home-spun dress
or country breeding, if he had felt inclined to pay his respects to the President—and
why indeed should he not? He was a yeoman, and not ashamed of being a yeoman—
what cause had he to be? But a pride of despising all innovation, all elegance, were
peculiarities that stood in his light. So, as I said, he dashed forward at a rapid and noisy
rate, feeling much, honest man, as though the sound of his wagon wheels would be
the gladdest one his friends ever heard. Nor did he slacken rein till the feet of his work
horses struck on the pavement before the main entrance of the house, and with their
sides panting against the wide bands of faded leather composing their harness, stood
champing the bit, and foaming as though they had run a race.

Poor Charlotte! she could scarcely rise out of the straw in which she was imbedded, when the hall-door opened, and Captain Bailey, followed by his two daughters,
came forward to meet her and her father, with self-possession and well-bred cordiality. The young women not only kissed her, but imposed a similar infliction on the dear
uncle, making many tender inquiries about the aunt and sweet little cousins at home;
but when Captain Bailey offered his arm, saying, "This way, my dear," the discomfiture of the niece was completed, and slipping two fingers over his elbow, and at arm's

length from him, she entered the hall, trying her best not to hear her father say—
"Bless your souls, gals, I don't want your sarvant man," as he went lustily to unharness
his horses, just as he would have done at home.

"We are so glad you are come," said the cousins; "we want you to teach us so
many things," but Charlotte felt that though the last part of the sentence might be
true, the first was not—for we instinctively recognize the difference between formal
politeness and real heartiness. Partly because she thought she ought to do so, and
partly because her conflicting emotions could find vent in no other way, she began to
cry.

"Are you sick?" asked the girls, really concerned, for their sense of propriety
would not have allowed of such an ebulition of feeling on any occasion, much less on
one so trivial. They could not imagine why she cried—models of propriety that they
were—unless indeed, she were in great bodily pain.

Presently Mr. Ryan, having attended to the duties of the groom, came in, bearing in each hand a small budget,[2] containing presents of his choicest apples, saying as
he presented them, "These apples my daughter here helped me to gather, and we have
a hundred bushels as fine at home."

The father was now appealed to for an explanation of Charlotte's conduct, for
she had covered her face with her hands, and sat in an obscure corner, sobbing to
herself.

"She sees so many strange, new, and fine things that she is not used to," he said,
for he could understand her; "they make her feel kind of bad and home-sick like.
Charlotte," he continued, speaking as he would to a child, "wipe up your eyes, and
let's see how much better your uncle's stock is than ours."

Glad of any excuse to escape from the cold speculation of the eyes that were on
her, the daughter obeyed, making neither excuse nor apology for the abrupt and
somewhat inquisitive procedure.

The sunshine soon dried up her tears, for her spirit was healthful, and though she
had given way to a brief impulse of sorrow, it was not an expression of habitual sick-
liness of feeling. Her father's repeated exclamations of surprise and contempt for the
bad culture and bad stock, helped, too, to reassure her, and she returned at length to
the house, her crushed self-esteem built up in part, at least; but contrasts unfavorable
to herself would present themselves, in spite of efforts to keep them down, whenever
her brown hands touched the lily ones of her cousins, or when the noise of her coarse
shoes reminded her of their delicate slippers; and when toward sunset the horses were
brought out, feeling smart, for they had had a visitor's portion of oats, she half wished
she was to go back, especially when she remembered the contents of the little bundle she had brought with her, containing what she considered the choice portion of
her wardrobe.

But I need not dwell longer on this phase of her experience. In education, in
knowledge of the world, in the fashionable modes of dress, the Misses Bailey were in
the advance of her, as much as she, in good sense, natural refinement, and instinctive
perceptions of fitness, was superior to them. But unfortunately she could see much
more clearly their advantages than her own. Falling back on the deficiencies of which
she was so painfully aware, she could not think it possible that she possessed any advantage whatever, much less any personal charms.

---

2. A budget is a workman's bag, pack, or wallet, generally made of leather; the leather pouch in
which a mower carries his whetstone; a bag or wallet in which Indians carried their totems, weapons, etc.

All the while the envied cousins were envious of her roseate complexion, elasticity of movement, and black heavy braids of hair, arranged, though they were, something ungracefully. The books which they kept, to be admired rather than read, afforded her much delight, and alone with these or with her uncle, the homesick and restless feeling was sometimes almost forgotten; for Captain Bailey was kind from the impulses of his nature, and not because he thought it duty or policy. The cheerful and natural aspect which things assumed under the transforming hands of Charlotte gave him excessive delight, and then when her work was done, she would tie on her sunbonnet, and accompany him in his walks through the fields and woods, making plans with him for the next year's culture and improvements. In the evenings she read to him, or listened to stories of the sea, which it gave him pleasure to relate; while the young ladies mourned at one side of the room over their hapless fate—wishing themselves back in their old home, or that Mrs. so, or so, would come out to the West, and give such parties as she used.

"But then," said they, "there is nobody here that is anybody," and so the mere supposition that a fashionable lady might come West and give parties, hops, re-unions, &c., was but a new source of discontent.

Sometimes they recounted, partly for the pleasure of hearing themselves, and partly to astonish and dazzle their country cousin, the various elegant costumes they had worn, on what, to them, were the most interesting occasions of their lives; and after all, they were not so much to blame—it was natural that they should pine for their native air, and for the gaieties to which they had been accustomed. But to Charlotte, whose notions of filial respect were almost reverent, it was a matter of painful surprise that they never mentioned their mother, or in any way alluded to her, except in complaints of the mourning clothes, which compelled them to be *so* plain. Neither brain nor heart of either was ample enough for a great sorrow.

At first Charlotte had lent her aid in the management and completion of household affairs with hearty good will, but the more she did the more seemed to be expected of her—the ladies couldn't learn because they paid no attention to her teaching, and took no interest in it, though never was there a more painstaking instructor. All persons are not gifted alike, they said, "it seems so easy for you to work." But in what their own gifts consisted it were hard to tell.

"Really, cousin Charlotte is quite companionable sometimes," said Sally, one day—laying emphasis on the word cousin—after partaking of some of her fresh-baked pumpkin pies.

"But it's a pity," replied Kate, "that she only appears to advantage in the kitchen. Now what in the *world* would you do if Dr. Opdike, or Lawyer Dingley, or any of that set were to come?"

"Why," said Sally, laughing, "I always think it's as well to tell the truth, when there is no particular advantage to be gained by telling anything else, so I should simply say—'A country cousin, whom father has taken a fancy to patronize.'"

Kate laughed, and taking with them some light romance, fit suited to wile the way into dreamland, they retired to their chamber.

"Suppose we steal a march on the girls," said Captain Bailey, entering the room where Charlotte was engaged in idle endeavors to make her hair curl—"what say you to riding into town?"

Charlotte hesitated, for nothing called her to town except the search for pleasure, and she had been unaccustomed to go out of her way for that; but directly yielding to persuasion, she was tying on her bonnet, when the Captain, desirous of improving her toilet, suggested that she should not wear her best hat, but the old hack of Kate or Sally. The little straw bonnet, which looked smart enough at the prayer meetings and "circuit preachings" of the log school-house, became suddenly hateful, and the plain white ribbon, crossed about the crown, only in keeping with summer, and seventy years. Her cheeks flushed as her trembling hands removed her favorite bonnet, and the uncle continued—"just bring along Kate's white cashmere, while you are about it—yours will be too warm to-day, I think."

The shawl which Charlotte proposed to wear was a coarse black woolen one, which had already been worn by her mother for twenty years, or thereabouts, and though she had never looked so well in her life, as in the old bonnet and shawl belonging to Kate, still she felt ill at ease, and could not suppress a wish that she had at once declined the invitation. Captain Bailey, who was really a kind-hearted man, exerted himself to dissipate the cloud which weighed down her spirit, but ever and anon she turned aside to wipe the tears away. My wish was being fulfilled—Charlotte had attained a new position.

"Now, my dear," said the uncle, as he assisted Charlotte out of the carriage, before the most fashionable dry-goods shop of the city, "you must favor me by accepting a new gown and hat, and whatever other trifles you may fancy to have."

"Oh, no, no!" she said, blushing, but dissent was not to be listened to—she was merely desired to select one from among the many varieties of silks thrown on the counter.

Now the purchasing of a silk dress was in the estimation of Charlotte, a proceeding of very grave importance, not to be thus hastily gone into. She would consent to accept of a calico—positively of nothing more—and on being assured by the clerks, as they brought forward some highly colored prints, that they were the patterns most in vogue, she selected one of mingled red and yellow, declined to receive anything further, and returned home, saddened and injured, rather than glad and grateful. She could not help wishing she had remained in her old haunts instead of going where people were ashamed of her—and then would come the more crushing and bitter thoughts which justified the feelings with which they regarded her; and so, in alternate emotions of self-contempt and honest and indignant pride, she continued to think and think—sometimes disregarding and sometimes answering briefly and coldly the various remarks of her kind relative. The sun had set an hour when the white walls of his house appeared in the distance, and as they approached nearer, it was evident from the lights and laughter within, that the occasion with the inmates was an unusually joyous one.

At the sound of footsteps in the hall, Kate came hurriedly forth to communicate the intelligence of the arrival of a friend, "Mr. Sully Dinsmore, a young author of rising eminence, and a man whose acquaintance was worth having"—and she continued, as her father observed—"glad to have you know him, Charlotte"—"Of course you will like to make some change in your toilet—the dress you have on affects your complexion shockingly."

Charlotte assented, not knowing how she was to improve her appearance, inasmuch as she then wore the best clothes she possessed.

Once in the dressing room, she threw indignantly aside what appeared to her but borrowed finery, and gave way to such a passion of tears as never before had dimmed her beautiful eyes.

She was disturbed at length by a light tap at the door, followed by an inquiry of her uncle whether she were not ready to go below. "Thank you, I don't wish to go," she replied, with as much steadiness of voice as she could command; but her sorrow betrayed itself, and the kindly entreaties which should have soothed, only aggravated it.

"Well, my dear," said the uncle, as if satisfied, seeing that she was really unpresentable, "if you will come down and make a cup of tea, you and I will have the pleasure of partaking of it by ourselves."

This little strategem succeeded in part, and in the bustling preparation of supper, the smile of resignation, if not of gaiety, came back; for Charlotte's heart was good and pure, and her hands quick always in the service of another. The benevolent uncle prudently forbore any reference to guest or drawing-room for the evening, and leading the conversation into unlooked-for channels, only betrayed by unusual kindness of manner a remembrance of the unhappy incidents of the day. A practiced observer, however, might have detected the tenor of his thoughts, in the liberal amount of cream and sugar—twice as much as she desired—infused into the tea of the gentle niece, whose pained heart throbbed sensitively, while her lips smiled thanks.

IV

THE ORANGE LIGHT of the coming sunrise was widening among the eastern clouds, and the grass that had till then kept green, stood stiff in the white frost, when the quick step of Charlotte broke rather than bent it down, for she had risen early to milk the spotted heifer ere any one should be astir. She tripped gracefully along, unconscious that earnest eyes were on her, singing snatches of rural songs, and drinking the beauty of the sunrise with the eyes of a poet. Half playfully, and half angrily, the heifer shook her horns of pearly green for such untimely rousing from the warm grassy hollow in which she lay, but the white pine pail was soon brimming with milk.

The wind blew aside Charlotte's little hood, and with cheeks, flushed with the air, and the exercise, gleaming through the tangles of her black hair, she really presented a picture refreshing to look on, especially to eyes wearied with artificial complexions and curls. As she arose the hues deepened, and she drew the hood quickly forward—for standing midway in the crooked path leading from the door-yard to the cow-yard, and shelling corn to a flock of chickens gathered about him, was Mr. Sully Dinsmore—a rather good looking, pleasant-faced young man of thirty or thereabout. He bowed with graceful ease as the girl approached, and followed his salutation by some jest about the fowl proceeding in which he had been detected, and at the same time took from her hand the pail with an air and manner which seemed to say he had been used to carrying milk-pails all his life—there was nothing he liked so well, in fact. Charlotte had no time for embarrassment—deference was so blended with familiarity—and beside, the gentleman apologized so sweetly and sadly for the informal introduction he had given himself; the young lady looked so like one—he hesitated—like his own dear wife—and he continued with a sigh, "she sleeps now among the mountains." He was silent a moment, and then went on as if forcibly rallying, "This is a delightful way to live, is it not? We always intended, poor Florence and I, to come to the West, buy a farm, and pass the evening of our days in quiet independence; but," in a more subdued tone, "I had never money enough till dear Florence died, and since that I have cared little about my way of life—little about life at all."

Charlotte's sympathies were aroused. Poor man, his cheek did look pale, and doubtless it was to dissipate his grief that he was there; and with simple earnestness she expressed a hope, that the bright hills and broad forests of the West might restore something of the old healthiness of feeling in his heart.

His thanks were given with the tone and manner of one sincerely grateful; the gay worldlings, he said, with whom he had been fated mostly to mingle, could not appreciate his feelings. All this required much less time than I have taken to record it, for the gentleman made the most of the brief walk.

At the door Captain Bailey met them, and with a look of mingled surprise and curiosity, was beginning a formal presentation, when Mr. Dinsmore assured him such ceremony was quite unnecessary—each had recognized a friend in the other, he said, and they were already progressing toward very intimate relations. No sooner had Charlotte disappeared, with her pail and strainer, than, abruptly changing tone and manner, he exclaimed, "Dev'lish pretty girl—I hope she remains here as long as I do!"

The Captain, who was displeased, affected ignorance of what had been said, and bent his steps in rather a hurried way toward the barn.

"Propose to fodder the stock, eh?" called out Mr. Dinsmore: "allow me to join you—just the business I was brought up to do." And coming forward, he linked his arm through that of the stout Captain, and brought him to a sudden standstill, saying, with the delightful enthusiasm of a voyager come to the beautiful shore of a new country, "What a wonderful scene—forest and meadow, and orchards and wheat-fields! why, Captain, you are a rich man; if I owned this place I shouldn't want any-thing beside—no other place half so good about here, I suppose?—in fact, it seems to me, in all my travels, I never saw such a farm—just enough of it—let's see, what's its extent? Yes, I thought you must have just about that much; and, if I had never seen it, I could have sworn it was the best farm in the country, because I know the soundness of your judgment, you see!"

The Captain drew himself up, and surveyed the prospect more proudly than he had done before, saying he ought to know something of good land, and favorable lo-calities—he had seen something of the world.

"Why," answered Mr. Sully Dinsmore, as though his host had not done half jus-tice to himself, "I guess there is not much of the world worth seeing that you have not seen; you have been a *great* traveler, Captain; and you know what you see, too," he added in a tone acceptably insinuating.

"Yes, yes, that is true: few men know better what they see than Captain Bailey," and he began pointing out the various excellencies and attractions of his place which the young man did not seem to have observed.

"No wonder," Mr. Dinsmore proceeded, "my vision was too much dazzled to take all in at once; you must remember, I am only used to rugged hills and bleak rocks, where the farmers fasten the grain down with stones, lest being indignant at the poor soil, it should *scrabble* out, you see." This word was coined with special reference to the Captain, who sometimes found himself reduced to such necessities. An approving peal of laughter rewarded his pains, and he repeated it, "Yes, the grain would actually scrab-ble out but for the stones; so you see it's natural my eyes failed to perceive all those waves of beauty and plenty." Where he saw the waves referred to, only himself could have told, for the stubble land looked bleak enough, and the November woods dark and withered to dreariness. "Well, Captain," he said at last, as though the scene were a continual delight to his eyes, "it's of no use—I could stand gazing all day—so let us fodder those fine cattle of yours."

With good will he entered upon the work—seizing bundles of oats and corn-blades, and dusty hay, regardless of broadcloths and linen; now patting the neck of some clumsy-horned, long-legged steer, calling to the Captain to know if he were not of the full blood; and now, as he scattered the bushel of oats among the little flock of thin and dirty sheep, inquiring, with the deepest interest apparently, if they were not something superior to the southdowns or merinos—for the wool was as fine as could be.

The "chores" completed, they returned to the house, but Mr. Dinsmore found so many things to admire by the way that their progress was slow; now he paused at the gateway to remark what nice strong posts they were—he believed they were of cedar; and now he turned in admiration of the smoke-house—a ruinous and exceedingly diminutive building of bricks, of which the walls were overgrown with moss, the roof sunken, and the door off its hinges: they seemed to him about the best bricks he ever saw—moss wouldn't gather over them if they were not solid as a rock—"what a pleasing effect it has," he said.

"A little out of repair," said the Captain, "and too small—too small! I think of enlarging," and he attempted to urge his companion forward.

"But," interposed the guest, still gazing at the smoke-house, "that is one of your few errors of judgment: I wouldn't have it an inch bigger, nor an inch less; and besides, the moss is prettier than any paint."

"I must put up the door, at least," interrupted the Captain.

"Ay, no sir, let me advise you to the contrary. Governor Patterson, of New Jersey, smokes all his meat, and has for twenty years, in a house without a door—it makes the flavor finer—I thought it was built so on purpose—if ever I have a farm I should make your smoke-house a model."

This morning all the household tasks had fallen on Charlotte. "She went to bed early," said the cousins, "and can afford to get up early—besides, she has no toilet to make, as we have."

But though they gave her the trouble of delaying the breakfast, after she had prepared it, Charlotte was amply repaid for all, in the praises bestowed on her coffee and toast by Mr. Sully Dinsmore. Her uncle, too, said she had never looked so pretty, that her hair was arranged in most becoming style, and that her dress suited her complexion.

"Really, Lotty, I am growing jealous," said Kate, tossing her head in a way meant to be at once irresistibly captivating, and patronizing.

Kate had never said "Lotty" before, but seeing that Mr. Dinsmore was not shocked with the rural cousin, she thought it politic to make the most of her, and from that moment glided into the most loving behavior. Lotty was a dear little creature, in her way, quite pretty—and she was such a housekeeper! Finally, it was concluded to make a "virtue of necessity," and acknowledge that they were learning to keep house themselves—in truth, they thought it fine fun, and preferred to have as few troublesome servants about as possible.

So a few days glided swiftly and pleasantly to Charlotte, notwithstanding that most of the household labor—all its drudgery—devolved on her. What cared she for this, while the sunrise of a paradisal morning was glorifying the world. Kate and Sally offered their assistance in making the new dress, and contrived various little articles, which they said would relieve the high colors, and have a stylish effect. These arts, to the simpleminded country girl, were altogether novel—at home she had never heard of "becoming dress." She, as well as all the girls whom she knew, had been in the habit of going to town once or twice a year, when the butter brought the best price, or when a load of hay or a cow was sold, and purchasing a dress, bonnet, &c., without regard to color or fashion. A new thing was supposed to look well, and to their unpractised eyes always did look well.

"Come here, Lotty," said Kate, one evening, surveying her cousin, as she hooked the accustomed old black silk. "Just slip off that old-womanish thing," she continued, as Charlotte approached—and ere the young girl was aware, the *silk* dress that had been regarded with so much reverence was deprived of both its sleeves. "Oh mercy! what will mother say?" was her first exclamation; but Kate was in no wise affected by the amputation she had effected, and cooly surveying her work, said, "Yes, you look a thousand dollars better." And she continued, as Charlotte was pinning on the large cape she had been used to wear, "Have you the rheumatism in the shoulders, or anything of that sort, or why do you wrap up like a grandmother at a woods-meeting?"

Charlotte could only say, "Just because"—it was, however, that she desired to conceal as much of her bare arms as possible; and it was not without many entreaties and persuasions that she was induced to appear with arms uncovered and a simple white frill about her neck.

"What a pity," said the cousins, as they made up the red calico, "that she had not consulted us, and spent her money the other day for ruffles and ribbons instead of this fantastic thing!"

They regarded her in a half-pitying, half-friendly light, and, perhaps, under the circumstances, did the best they could; for though Charlotte had many of the instincts of refinement, she had been accustomed to a rude way of living, and a first contact with educated society will not rub off the crust of rusticity which has been years in gathering.

"I have been too sensitive," thought Charlotte, or she tried to think so, and if her heart ever throbbed wildly against some delicate insinuation or implied rebuke, she crushed it down again, blaming her own awkwardness and ignorance rather than the fine relations who had stood preeminent in her childish imagination. She might not so readily have reconciled herself to the many mortifications she endured, but for the sustaining influence of Mr. Dinsmore's smiles and encouraging words. Ever ready to praise, and with never a word of blame, he would say to the other ladies, "you are looking shocking to-night," and they could afford to bear it—they never did look so; but whatever Charlotte wore was in exquisite taste—at least he said so. And yet Mr. Dinsmore was not really and at heart a hypocrite, except indeed in the continued and ostentatious display of private griefs. Constitutionally, he was a flatterer, so that he could not pass the veriest mendicant without pausing to say, "Really, you are as fine a looking old beggar-man as I have met this many a day!" Whether he was disinterested and desired only to confer pleasure upon others, or whether he wished to win hearts to himself, I know not—I only know, no opportunity of speaking gracious words ever escaped him.

However or whatever this disposition was, Charlotte interpreted all his speeches kindly. "She had eyes only for what was good," he said, and the sombre shadow of affliction in which he stood, certainly gave him an appearance of sincerity. When the Misses Bailey were thrown, or rather when they threw themselves in his way, he said his delight could not be expressed—they seemed to have the air of the mountain maids about them that made him feel at home in their presence. But when he praised one, generally, he disparaged another, and he not unfrequently said on these occasions, "I have been sacrificing an hour to that country cousin of yours," or, "I have been benevolently engaged," pointing toward Charlotte. Then came exchanges of smiles and glances, which seemed to say, "We understand each other perfectly—and nobody else understands us." One day; while thus engaged in playing the agreeable, Charlotte having finished her dish-washing, came in, her hands red and shining from the suds. Mr. Dinsmore smiled, and, with meaning, added, "Do you remember where Elizabeth tells some clodhopper, the reputed husband of Amy Robsart, I think, that his boots well nigh overcame my Lord of Leicester's perfumery!"[3] and in the burst of laughter which followed, the diplomatist rose and joined the unsuspecting girl, saying, as he seated himself beside her, and playfully took two of her fingers in his, "You have been using yellow soap, and the fragrance attracted me at once—there is no perfume I like half so well. Why, you might spend hundreds of dollars for essential oils, and nice extracts, and after all, if I could get it, I would prefer the aroma of common yellow soap—it's better than that of violets."

"I have been talking to those frivolous girls," he continued, after a moment, and with the manner of one who had been acting a part and was really glad to be himself again: "rather pretty," in a soliloquising sort of way, "but their beauty is not of the fresh, healthful style I admire."

"I thought," said Charlotte, half pettishly, "you admired them very much!"

"Yes, as I would a butterfly," he said, "but they have not the thrifty and industrious habits that could ever win my serious regard—my love;" and his earnest tone and admiring look were more flattering than the meaning of his words. Charlotte crushed her handkerchief with one hand and smoothed her heavy black hair with the other, to conceal the red burning of her cheek. Mr. Dinsmore continued, "Yes, I have been thinking since I came here, that this is the best way in the world to obtain health and happiness—this rural way of life, I mean. Just see what a glorious scene presents itself!" and he drew the young girl to the recess of a window, and talked of the cattle and sheep, the meadow and woodland, with the enthusiasm of a devoted practical farmer.

"Of course," said Charlotte, "my predilections are all in favor of the habits to which I have been used."

"Another proof of your genuine good sense," and Mr. Dinsmore folded close both the little red hands of Charlotte within his own soft white ones, but with less of gallantry than sincere appreciation of her sweet simplicity and domestic excellencies. And he presently went on to say, that if he ever found any happiness again, it must be with some such dear angel as herself, and in the healthful, inspiriting occupation of a farmer. True, he did not say in so many simple words, "I should like to marry you, Charlotte," but the nameless things words cannot interpret, said it very plainly to the unsophisticated, simple-minded, true-hearted Charlotte. Poor man, he seemed to her so melancholy, so shut out from sympathy, it was almost a duty to lighten the weary load that oppressed him.

But I cannot record all the sentiment mingled in the recess of that window. I am ignorant of some particulars; and if I were not, such things are interesting only to lovers. But I know a shadow swept suddenly across the sweetest light that for Charlotte had ever brightened the world. The window, beside which these lovers sat, if we may call them lovers, over-looked the highway for half a mile or more; and as they sat there it chanced that a funeral procession came winding through the dust and under the windy trees far down the hill. It was preceded by no hearse or other special carriage for the dead, for in country places the coffin is usually placed in an open wagon, and beneath a sheet, carried to the grave-yard. So, from their elevated position, they could see, far off, the white shape in the bottom of the wagon. Mr. Dinsmore's attentions became suddenly abstracted from the lady beside him, and the painful con-

---

3. The reference is to a scene from Sir Walter Scott's *Kenilworth* (1821).

sciousness of bereavement, from which he had almost escaped, weighed on him with tenfold violence. "Hush, hush," he said, in subdued and reproachful accents, as she made attempts to talk of something besides shrouds. "Florence," he continued, burying his face in his hands, and as though swept by a sudden passion from the consciousness of a living presence, "why was I spared when you were taken, and why am I not permitted to go voluntarily"—he abruptly broke off the sentence, and, rising, rushed from the house. Charlotte arose, too, her heart troubled and trembling, and followed him with her eyes, as he staggered blindly forward to obtain a nearer view of the procession, every now and then raising himself on tiptoe, that he might see the coffin more distinctly.

In the suburbs of the city, and adjoining the grounds of Captain Bailey, lay the old grave-yard termed the Potter's Field, and across the sloping stubble land, toward this desolate place, Charlotte bent her steps, and seated on the roots of a blasted tree, on a hill-side, waited for the procession. Gloomy enough was the scene, not relieved by one human figure, as perhaps she had hoped to find it. To the South hung clouds of smoke over crowded walls, with here and there white spires shooting upward, and in one opening among the withered trees, she caught a glimpse of the Ohio, and over all and through all sounded the din of busy multitudes. In the opposite direction were scattered farm-houses, and meadows, and orchards, with sheep grazing and cattle pasturing, and blue cheerful columns of smoke drifted and lifted on the wind. And just at her feet, and dividing the two pictures, lay this strip of desolated and desecrated ground, the Potter's Field. It was inclosed by no fence, and troops of pigs and cows eked out a scanty sustenance about the place. One of these starved creatures, having one horn dangling loosely about her ear—in consequence of some recent quarrel about the scanty grass perhaps—drew slowly toward the hollow nearest the place where Charlotte sat, and drank from a little grave which seemed to have been recently opened. The soil was marshy—so much so that the slightest pit soon filled with water. The higher ground was thickly furrowed with rows of graves, and two or three, beside this open one, had been made in the very bottom of the hollow. Nearer and nearer came the funeral train. It consisted of but few persons—men, and women, and children—the last looking fearfully and wonderingly about, as led by the hands of their parents they trod the narrow path between the long lines of mounds. Forward walked a strong stalwart middle-aged man, bearing in his arms the coffin—that of a little child; and Charlotte shuddered to think of the cold damp bed which was waiting for it. There seemed to be no clergyman in attendance; and without hymn or prayer, the body that had slept always in its mother's arms till now, was laid in the earth, and in the obscurest and lonesomest corner of the lonesomest of all burial places, left alone. Closer than the rest, even pressing to the edge of the grave, was a pale woman, whose eyes looked down more earnestly than the eyes of the others; and that it was, and not the black ribbon crossed plainly about the straw bonnet—which indicated the mother. Hard by, but not so near the grave, stood a man holding in his arms a child of some two years, very tightly, as though the grave should not get that; and once he put his hand to his eyes; but he turned away before the woman, and as he did so, kissed the cheek of the little child in his arms— she thought only of the dead.

The sun sunk lower and lower, and was gone; the windy evening came dimly out of the woods, shaking the trees and rustling the long grass; the last lengths of light drew themselves from the little damp heap, and presently the small grey headstones were lost from view. And, scarcely disturbing the stillness, the funeral people returned to their several homes—for the way was dusty and they moved slowly—almost as slowly as they came. There were no songs of birds in the twilight—not even a hum of insects; the first were gone, and the last, or such of them as still lived, were crept under fallen leaves, and were quietly drowsing into nothingness. No snakes slipt noiselessly along the dust-path, hollowing their slow ways. They too were gone— some dropping into the frosty cracks of the ground, and others, pressed flat, lay coiled under decaying logs and loose stones. So, at such a time and in such a place, the poor little baby was left alone, and the parents went to their darkened cottage, the mother to try to smile upon the child that was left, while her eyes are tearful and she sees only the vacant cradle,—and the father to make the fire warm and cheerful, and essay with soft words to win the heavy-hearted wife from their common sorrow. They are poor, and have no time to sit mourning, and as the mother prepares the scanty meal, the fa- ther will deal out to the impatient cows hay and corn, more liberally than his garners can well afford, for to-night he feels like doing good to everything.

Something in this way ran the thoughts of Charlotte, as slowly and sadly she re- traced her steps, trying to make herself believe she would have felt no less lonely at any other time if she had witnessed so mournful a scene. And in part she deceived herself: not quite, however, for her eyes were wandering searchingly from side to side of the path, and now and then wistfully back, though she could scarcely distinguish the patches of fading fennel from the thick mounds of clay. Perhaps she fancied Mr. Sully Dinsmore still lingered among the shadows to muse of the dead.

Nothing like justice can here be done to the variously accomplished Sully Dins- more. Charlotte requires no elaborate painting; a young and pretty country girl—with a heart, except in its credulity, like most other human hearts, yearning and hopeful— as yet she had distilled from no keen disappointment a bitter wisdom. Little joys and sorrows made up the past; her present seemed portentous of great events.

"Where is Kate?" she asked one day, in the hope of learning what she did not dare to ask; and Sally replied in a way that she meant to be kindly, and certainly thought to be wise, by saying, "She is in some recess, I suppose, comforting poor Mr. Dinsmore, who seems to distribute his attentions most liberally. It was only this morn- ing," she added, "that against a lament for the dead Florence, he patched the story of his love for me."

Charlotte joined in the laugh, but with an ill grace, and still more reluctantly fol- lowed when Sally led the way toward the absentees, saying in a whisper, "Let us re- connoitre—all stratagems fair in war, you know."

But whether the stratagem was fair or not, it failed of the success which Sally had expected, for they no sooner came within hearing of voices than Mr. Dinsmore was heard descanting in a half melancholy, half enthusiastic tone, of the superiority of all western products. "Why, Captain Bailey," said he, speaking more earnestly than be- fore, "I would not live east of the mountains for anything I can think of—not for hardly anything in the world!" Such childish simplicity of speech made it difficult to think him insincere; and Charlotte, at least did not, but was the more confirmed in her previous notions, that he was a weary, broken-hearted man, sick of the world and pining for some solitude, "with one sweet spirit for his minister."

Whether Sally's good intentions sprang from envy and jealousy, it might be dif- ficult to decide; but Charlotte attributed only these feelings to her, as she petulantly turned away with the exclamation—"Pshaw! Kate has left him, and he is trying to make father believe the moon is made of green cheese!"

From that day the cousins began to be more and more apart; the slight disposi- tion to please and be pleased, which had on both sides been struggling for an exis- tence, died, and did not revive again.

It was perhaps a week after this little scene, and in the mean time Mr. Dinsmore had been no unsuccessful wooer; in truth, Charlotte began to feel a regret that she had not selected a white instead of a red dress; all the world looked brighter to her than it had ever done before, dreary as the season was.

The distance between the cousins and herself widened every day; but what cared she for this, so long as Mr. Dinsmore said they were envious, selfish, frivolous, and unable to appreciate her. I cannot tell what sweet visions came to her heart; but whatever they were, she found converse with them pleasanter than friends—pleasanter than the most honeyed rhymes poet ever syllabled. And so she kept much alone, busy with dreams—only dreams.

V

IT WAS ONE of the mildest and loveliest of all the days that make our western autumns so beautiful. The meadow sides, indeed, were brown and flowerless; the lush weeds of summer lopped down, black and wilted, along the white dry dust of the roadside; the yellow mossy hearts of the fennel were faded dry; the long, shriveled iron-weeds had given their red bushy tops for a thin greyish down, and the trees had lost their summer garments; still, the day was lovely, and all its beauties had commended themselves with an unwonted degree of accuracy to the eyes of Charlotte—Mr. Dinsmore had asked her to join him in an autumn ramble and search for the last hardy flowers. All the morning she was singing to herself,

"Meet me by moonlight alone,
And then I will tell thee a tale."

It had been stipulated by Mr. Dinsmore, "so as not to excite observation," he said, that they should leave the house separately, and meet at an appointed place, secure from observation. Why a ramble in search of flowers should be clandestine, the young lady did not pause to inquire, but she went forth at the time appointed, with a cheek bright almost as the calico she wore.

On the grassy slope of a hollow that ran in one direction through a strip of partly cleared woodland, and in the other toward an old orchard of low heavy-topped trees, she seated herself, fronting the sun, which was not shining, but seemed only a soft yellow spot in the thick haze that covered all the sky. A child might have looked on it, for scarcely had it more brightness than the moon. The air was soft and loving, as though the autumn was wooing back the summer. The grass was sprouting through the stubble, and only the clear blue sky was wanting to make the time spring-like, and a bird or two to sing of "April purposes." It was full May-time in the heart of Charlotte, and for a time, no bird could sing more gaily than she, as she sat arranging and disarranging the scarlet buds she had twined among her hair; now placing them on one side, now on the other: now stripping off a leaf or two, and now adding a bud or blades of grass.

So an hour was wiled away; but though it seemed long, Charlotte thought perhaps it was not an hour after all; it could not be, or surely Mr. Dinsmore would have joined her. The day was very still, and she knew the time seemed longer when there were no noises. And yet when she became aware of sounds, for a cider-mill was creaking and grating in the edge of the orchard, they seemed only to make the hours more long and lonesome.

Round and round moved the horse, but she could not hear the crushing and grinding of the apples—only the creaking of the mill. Two or three little boys were there, whistling and hopping about—now riding the horse, and now bending over the tub and imbibing cider with a straw. An old man was moving briskly among bundles and barrels, more from a habit of industry, it seemed, than because there was anything to do. But, try as she would, Charlotte could not interest herself in their movements. An uneasy sensation oppressed her—she could not deceive herself any longer—it was time, and long past the time appointed. At first she looked back on the way she had come, long and earnestly; then she arose and walked backward and forward in the path, with a quick step at first, then more irresolutely and slowly. The yellow spot in the clouds had sunken very low and was widening and deepening into orange, when she resumed the old seat, folded her hands listlessly in her lap, and looked toward the cider-mill. The creaking was still, the horses harnessed, and barrels, and bundles of straw, and boys, all in the wagon. The busy farmer was making his last round, to be sure that nothing was amiss, and this done he climbed before the barrels and bundles and boys, cracked his whip, and drove away toward the orange light in the clouds. Mr. Dinsmore was not coming—of that she was confident, and anger, mortification, and disappointment, all mingled in her bosom, producing a degree of misery she had never before experienced.

Not till night had spread one dull leaden color all over the sky, did she turn her steps homeward, in her thoughts bitterly revolving all Mr. Dinsmore had said, and the much more he had suggested. And, as she thus walked, a warm bright light dried up the tears, and she quickened her step—she had fallen back on that last weakness—some unforeseen, perhaps terrible event, had detained him, and all the reproaches she had framed were turned upon herself; she had harshly blamed him, when it was possible, even probable, that he could not come. The world was full of accidents, dangers, and deaths—some of these might have overtaken him, and he perhaps had been watching as anxiously for her as she for him. At this thought she quickened her steps, and was soon at the house. The parlor was but dimly lighted, and, with a trembling and anxious heart, she entered, and recognizing Mr. Dinsmore in one of the recesses of the windows, she obeyed the first impulse, hurried toward him, and parting the heavy and obscuring draperies, said, in an earnest whisper, "Why did you not come?"

"Come—where?" he replied, indolently; and added, in a moment, "Ay, yes, really, I forgot it."

A half sigh reached her, and turning, she became aware that a young and pretty lady occupied the corner of the window opposite. No further explanation was needed.

With feelings never known before, pent in her heart, Charlotte sought the chamber in which she was used to sleep—the lamp was faintly burning, and the bright carpet and the snowy counterpane and curtains, and low cushioned seats, looked very comfortable; and as Charlotte contrasted all with the homely garret in which she had slept at home, the contrast made it luxury.

In her heart, she wished she had never slept any where else but under the naked rafters of her father's house. "I should have known better than to come," she thought; "it is no wonder they think the woods the best place for me." Now, no one had said this, but she attributed it and many such thoughts to her *rich* friends, as she called them, and then set herself as resentfully against them as though they had said they despised her.

Her eyes turned toward the night; she was sitting very still, with all bitter and resentful and sorrowful feelings running through her heart, when a soft tap on the door summoned her to answer. With a haughty step and repellant manner she went forward; and when, opening the door, she saw before her the pleasant-faced little lady she had seen in the window, below, she said, very coldly, "you have mistaken the apartment, I think," and was turning away, when the intruder eagerly but artlessly caught up both her hands, saying, in a tone of mingled sweetness and heartiness, "No, I am not mistaken; I know you, if you do not know me—I could not wait for a formal introduction, but commissioned myself to bring you down to tea. My name," she added, "is Louise—Louise Herbert."

Charlotte bowed stiffly, and saying, "You are very obliging, but I don't want any tea," closed the door abruptly, and resumed her old seat, looking out into the night as before.

"I suppose it was mere curiosity that brought her here," she said, by way of justifying her rudeness; "of course, she could feel no interest in me." And further, she even tried to approve of herself by saying she always hated pretence, and for a fine lady like Miss Herbert, who had evidently been accustomed to all the refinements of wealth, to affect any liking for a poor ignorant country girl, as she chose to call herself, was absurd. In truth, she was glad she had shown independence at least, and let the proud creature know she would not cringe because of her silk dress, or white hands, or pretty face. She didn't want anything of her—she could live without her, and she would. And rising and pacing the room, she made what she thought a very wise and dignified resolve. When they were asleep she would tie in a bundle what few things she had, and walk home; she would not ask her uncle to take her—she would not tell him she was going—he might find it out the best way he could. This decision made, she undressed and went to bed, as usual, and tried to compose herself to sleep by thinking that she was about as ugly and ill-bred, and unfortunate in every way, as she could be; that everybody disliked and despised her, and that all who were connected with her were ashamed of her. There was one thing she could do, nevertheless, and that she would do—go back and remain where she belonged. Thus she lay tossing and tumbling, and frightening the drowsy god quite from the neighborhood of her pillow, when Kate entered, accompanied by the agreeable looking little woman, who, being introduced, begged in a jocular way, that she would afford her sleeping-room for only one night. "I could not," she added very sweetly, "give my friends the trouble of making an extra bed, if you would allow me to share yours."

Charlotte answered, coldly and concisely, that she was ready to do anything to oblige, and placing herself close against the wall, buried her face in the pillow, and lay stiff and straight and still. But Miss Herbert, singularly oblivious of the young woman's uncivil behavior, prepared for sleep,

"And lay down in her loveliness."

"How cold you are," she said, creeping close to her companion, and putting her arm around her. Charlotte said nothing, and gave a hitch, which she meant to be from, but, somehow, it was toward the little woman. "Oh, you are quite in a chill," she added, giving her an embrace, and in a moment she had hopped from the bed, and in her clean, white, night dress, was fluttering out of the room.

"I never had such a night-gown," thought Charlotte, "with its ruffles and lace trimming—I never had any at all," and she resumed her old position, which, however, she had scarcely gained, when the guest came fluttering back, and folding off the counterpane, wrapt, as though she were a baby, her own nicely warmed woollen pet-ticoat about her feet, and having tucked the clothing down, slipt under it and nestled Charlotte in her arms, as before, saying, "There, isn't that better?"

"Yes—thank you," and her voice trembled, as she yielded to this determined kindness.

"Another night we must have an additional blanket," said the lady; "that is, if I succeed in keeping you from freezing to-night," and pressing the chilly hands of Charlotte close in her bosom, she fell asleep. And Charlotte, thinking she would be at home the next night, fell asleep too, and woke not till along the counterpane ran the shadows of the red clouds of morning.

But I am lingering, and must hasten to say, that Louise Herbert was one of the most lovable, generous, and excellent of women; that she had been accustomed to affluence was true, and that she could not know the feelings of Charlotte, who had been born and bred in comparative poverty, was not her fault; from her position in life, she had naturally fallen into certain agreeing habits and ways of thinking, but her soul was large, her heart was warm, and her apprehensions quick; and when she saw Charlotte, and heard the trembling inquiry, and the answer of indifference, she read the little history, which to the young girl was so much, and appreciating, so far as she might, her sor-rows, determined to win her love; for at once her heart went out toward her—for she was unsuspicious and unhesitating, always ready to find something good in every one.

Even Charlotte found it impossible not to love her. She didn't know why, but she could get on a stool at her feet, lay her head on her lap, and forget that Louise was not as poor and humble as herself; or, if she remembered it, the silks and plumes and jew-elry worn by her, didn't make her envious or jealous—it gave her pleasure to see Louise look pretty.

Mr. Dinsmore, after some vain attempts to coquette and flirt with Miss Herbert, who had too much tact, or was too indifferent to him, to pay much regard to his over-tures, departed rather abruptly, merely sending his adieus to Charlotte, who was en-gaged in the kitchen at the time, and who had been in the shade since the coming of Miss Herbert.

And after a month of eating and sleeping, talking and laughing, baking and mak-ing and mending, Louise was joined by her party, who had left her with her friends, the Baileys, while they continued a ruralizing tour through the West, and Charlotte's heart grew desolate at the thought of separation from her. But such a misfortune was not yet to be; for before the departure of the young lady, she persuaded the parents of Charlotte (who could not help liking, though they regarded her very much as they would a being from another sphere) to allow their daughter to accompany her home.

With a heart full of curious joy, but with tears in her eyes, Charlotte took leave of the old home that she had so despised, and yet loved so well.

VI

A YEAR or two afterwards, changes and chances brought me for a moment within the circle in which she moved as the admired star. The rooms were brilliant with lights and flowers, and gaiety and beauty, and intellect; and the lately shrinking country girl was the cynosure of all eyes—the most envied, the most dreaded, the most admired, the most loved.

When my attention was drawn first toward her, there were some voices that had sounded at least through the length and breadth of their own country, softened to the most dulcet of tones, for her sake; and she seemed to listen indifferently, as though her thoughts were otherwhere.

I naturally recalled the humble life she had led—my walk to her house along the autumn woods—the letter which had been the key opening a new life to her—and while I was thus musing, I heard a voice which seemed not altogether unfamiliar—so low, and soft, and oily,—"Really, Miss Herbert, I was never so proud as to-night—that *you* should have remembered me on such an occasion as this! I cannot express the honor I feel, the obligations you have placed me under."

And then, as if constrained to throw aside all formality, and express himself with simple sincerity, he continued—"Why, how in the world did you get all these great folks together! I don't believe there is a house in the United States, except yours, that ever held at once so many celebrities."

Before my eye fell on him, I recognized Mr. Dinsmore, and observed him with increasing interest as he made his way to Miss Ryan, who appeared not to see him, till having pushed and elbowed his way, he addressed her with the familiarity of an old and intimate friend, and as though he were not only delighted himself, but felt assured that she must be much more so. But she hesitated—looked at him inquiringly—and seemed to say by her manner, as plainly as possible, "What impudent fellow are you—and what do you want?"

"Surely, you remember meeting with me," the gentleman said, a little discomfited, but in his most insinuating tone.

"When—where?" she asked, as if she would remember him if she could.

"Don't you remember," he said, "a month with Sully Dinsmore at Captain Bailey's?"

"Ah, yes," she replied, quoting his own words on a former occasion; "Really, I had forgotten it."

He shrunk a head and shoulders in stature, and slipt aside like a detected dog; and after one or two ineffectual attempts to rally, took leave in modest and becoming silence.

An hour afterward we sat alone—Charlotte and I—in the dim corner of a withdrawing room; and as I was congratulating her on her new position, especially on the beauty of her appearance that night, she buried her face in my lap, and burst into tears; and when I tried to soothe her, but wept the more. At length, lifting herself up, and drying her eyes, she said: "What would mother think, if she saw me here, and thus?"—And she scanned her gay dress, as though it were something neither right nor proper for her to wear. "And dear little Willie and sturdy Jonathan," she continued: "I suppose they sleep in their little narrow bed under the rafters yet, and I—I—would I not feel more shame than joy if they were to come in here to-night! Oh, I wish I had staid at home and helped mother spin, and read the sermon to father when the weekly paper came. His hair is getting white, isn't it?" she asked, pulling the flowers out of her own, and throwing them on the ground.

My wish was fulfilled—Charlotte had attained the position I had thought her so fitted to adorn; but was she happier? In the little gain was there not much loss—the fresh young feeling, the capacity to enjoy, the hope, the heart, which, once gone, never come back.

I cannot trace her biography all out: since that night of triumph and defeat, our paths have never crossed each other.

58

WILLIAM WARREN

(1825–1853)

William Warren's brief biography brings together an incredible variety of the issues facing the antebellum west as a whole. Warren could trace his ancestry to Ojibway, French, and Puritan sources and leaders. Like the sons of many wealthy westerners, he was educated at a New York preparatory school but was bilingual and also spent many nights collecting tribal history from his elders in traditional settings and in the Ojibway language. At the age of twenty-five, he was elected by white voters to the Territorial Legislature of Minnesota from the entire, sparsely populated northern half of the state. While in St. Paul he began writing and publishing the essays that would become his book. Unfortunately, during a trip to New York to meet with publishers, he contracted tuberculosis, and was dead at age twenty-eight. His book was finally published in 1885.

Gerald Vizenor and Roger Buffalohead have recently recovered Warren and his *History* not only as an important source of information on the Ojibways but also as an important voice in "crossblood" writing. Warren embodies a multiracial experience that resists the categories of racial identity both during his own life and during our own. While he writes mostly within the straightforward method of Euroamerican historiography, his sources are the authentic and legitimate Ojibway voices unavailable to any other informant. Nonetheless, his refusal to identify himself as strictly Ojibway has often left him excluded from the current reconsideration of nineteenth-century native voices.

In any case, a complex subjectivity emerges in an otherwise objective account. Warren tells and gives voice to the complexity of the racial, tribal, and national politics of the fur trade, distinguishing between French, British, and American presences within the white groups he describes and among the Iroquois, Ojibway, and Sioux presences among the natives. His Ojibway align themselves with various groups not by race but rather by a commonality of interests and values. His refusal of the simple categories usually employed to describe the frontier is also demonstrated in his direct refutation of such eastern American writers as George Catlin, George Bancroft, and Henry Rowe Schoolcraft. Like other western figures from Daniel Drake to George Washington Harris, he resists the eastern assumption of the mantle of national identity and seizes the terms of representation they sought to monopolize.

The sections reproduced here demonstrate Warren's deft interculturalism, interracialism, and intertextuality. In the end, Warren must be considered simply as a western writer, since no other category—race, class, and so on—is applicable to him. Furthermore, unlike other literate "native" voices from the region such as Boudinot or Copway, Warren clings to the notion that "race" itself is a construct imported to northern Minnesota and demands a sensitivity that does more than simply pit each race against the other.

Text: *A History of the Ojibway People* (Minnesota Historical Society, 1885, ed. Fletcher Williams): 23–27, 113–124, 368–394.

FROM *A HISTORY OF THE OJIBWAY PEOPLE* (1852, 1885)

Preface[1]

THE red race of North America is fast disappearing before the onward resistless tread of the Anglo-Saxon. Once the vast tract of country lying between the Atlantic seaboard and the broad Mississippi, where a century since roamed numerous tribes of the wild sons of Nature, but a few—a very few, remnants now exist. Their former domains are now covered with the teeming towns and villages of the "pale face" and millions of happy free-men now enjoy the former home of these unhappy and fated people.

The few tribes and remnants of tribes who still exist on our western frontiers, truly deserve the sympathy and attention of the American people. We owe it to them as a duty, for are we not now the possessors of their former inheritance? Are not the bones of their ancestors sprinkled through the soil on which are now erected our happy homesteads? The red man has no powerful friends (such as the enslaved negro can boast), to rightly represent his miserable, sorrowing condition, his many wrongs, his wants and wishes. In fact, so feebly is the voice of philanthropy raised in his favor, that his existence appears to be hardly known to a large portion of the American people, or his condition and character has been so misrepresented that it has failed to secure the sympathy and help which he really deserves. We do not fully understand the nature and character of the Red Race. The Anglo-Americans have pressed on them so unmercifully—their intercourse with them has been of such a nature, that they have failed to secure their love and confidence.

The heart of the red man has been shut against his white brother. We know him only by his exterior. We have judged of his manners and customs, and of his religious rights and beliefs, only from what we have seen. It remains yet for us to learn how

---

1. Written in 1852, before the emancipation of negroes in the Southern States of the Republic.— E. D. N.

these peculiar rites and beliefs originated, and to fathom the motives and true character of these anomalous people.

Much has been written concerning the red race by missionaries, travellers and some eminent authors; but the information respecting them which has thus far been collected, is mainly superficial. It has been obtained mostly by transient sojourners among the various tribes, who not having a full knowledge of their character and language, have obtained information through mere temporary observation—through the medium of careless and imperfect interpreters, or have taken the accounts of unreliable persons.

Notwithstanding all that has been written respecting these people since their discovery, yet the field for research, to a person who understands the subject, is still vast and almost limitless. And under the present condition of the red race, there is no time to lose. Whole tribes are daily disappearing, or are being so changed in character through a close contact with an evil white population, that their history will forever be a blank. There are but a few tribes residing west of the Mississippi and over its headwaters, who are comparatively still living in their primitive state—cherishing the beliefs, rites, customs, and traditions of their forefathers.

Among these may be mentioned the Ojibway, who are at the present day, the most numerous and important tribe of the formerly wide extended Algic family of tribes. They occupy the area of Lake Superior and the sources of the Mississippi, and as a general fact, they still live in the ways of their ancestors. Even among these, a change is so rapidly taking place, caused by a close contact with the white race, that ten years hence it will be too late to save the traditions of their forefathers from total oblivion. And even now, it is with great difficulty that genuine information can be obtained of them. Their aged men are fast falling into their graves, and they carry with them the records of the past history of their people; they are the initiators of the grand rite of religious belief which they believe the Great Spirit has granted to his red children to secure them long life on earth, and life hereafter; and in the bosoms of these old men are locked up the original causes and secrets of this, their most ancient belief.

The writer of the following pages was born, and has passed his lifetime, among the Ojibways of Lake Superior and the Upper Mississippi. His ancestors on the maternal side, have been in close connection with this tribe for the past one hundred and fifty years. Speaking their language perfectly, and connected with them through the strong ties of blood, he has ever felt a deep interest in their welfare and fate, and has deemed it a duty to save their traditions from oblivion, and to collect every fact concerning them, which the advantages he possesses have enabled him to procure.

The following pages are the result of a portion of his researches; the information and facts contained therein have been obtained during the course of several years of inquiry, and great care has been taken that nothing but the truth and actual fact should be presented to the reader.

In this volume, the writer has confined himself altogether to history; giving an account of the principal events which have occurred to the Ojibways within the past five centuries, as obtained from the lips of their old men and chiefs who are the repositories of the traditions of the tribe.

Through the somewhat uncertain manner in which the Indians count time, the dates of events which have occurred to them since their discovery, may differ slightly from those which have been given us by the early Jesuits and travellers, and endorsed by present standard historians as authentic.

Through the difficulty of obtaining the writings of the early travellers, in the wild country where the writer compiled this work, he has not had the advantage of rectifying any discrepancies in time or date which may occur in the oral information of the Indians, and the more authentic records of the whites.

The following work may not claim to be well and elaborately written, as it cannot be expected that a person who has passed most of his life among the wild Indians, even beyond what may be termed the frontiers of civilization, can wield the pen of an Irving or a Schoolcraft. But the work does claim to be one of truth, and the first work written from purely Indian sources, which has probably ever been presented to the public. Should the notice taken of it, by such as feel an interest in the welfare of the red race, warrant a continuation of his labors in this broad field of inquiry, the writer presents this volume as the first of a series.

He proposes in another work to present the customs, beliefs, and rites of the Ojibways as they are, and to give the secret motives and causes thereof, also giving a complete exposition of their grand religious rite, accompanied with the ancient and sacred hieroglyphics pertaining thereto, with their interpretation, specimens of their religious idiom, their common language, their songs. Also their creed of spiritualism or communion with spirits, and jugglery which they have practised for ages, and which resembles in many respects the creed and doctrines of the clairvoyants and spiritualists who are making such a stir in the midst of our most enlightened and civilized communities. Those who take an interest in the Indian, and are trying to study out his origin, will find much in these expositions which may tend to elucidate the grand mystery of their past.

Succeeding this, the writer proposes, if his precarious health holds out, and life is spared to him, to present a collection of their mythological traditions, on many of which their peculiar beliefs are founded. This may be termed the "Indian Bible." The history of their eccentric grand incarnation—the great uncle of the red man—whom they term Man-abo-sho, would fill a volume of itself, which would give a more complete insight into their real character, their mode of thought and expression, than any book which can be written concerning them.

A biography of their principal chiefs, and most noted warriors, would also form an interesting work.

The writer possesses not only the will, but every advantage requisite to procure information for the completion of this series of works. But whether he can devote his time and attention to the subject fully, depends on the help and encouragement he may receive from the public, and from those who may feel an anxiety to snatch from oblivion what may be yet learned of the fast disappearing red race.

CHAPTER VII

Era of the Discovery

Preliminary remarks—Visit of Claude Allouez to the Bay of Shag-a-waum-ikong, as known to the Ojibways—Definition of "Wa-me-tig-oshe," the Ojibway name for Frenchman—Antique silver crucifix found near La Pointe—Ancient prophecy foretelling the coming of the white race—The singular dream of Ma-se-wa-pe-ga—He goes in search of the white spirits—Finds

them and returns to his people with presents—He makes a second journey and returns with the
fire-arms and fire-water—Anecdote of the first trial and effect of fire-water—Anecdote of the ef-
fect of the fire-arm among the Dakotas—Two white traders found starving on the island of La
Pointe—First white visitors to the Ojibways in the Bay of Shag-a-waum-ik-ong—Two hun-
dred years ago—Establishment of traders and priests at the Ojibway village—Remarks, etc.

THE ERA of their first knowledge of, and intercourse with the white race, is one of
most vital importance in the history of the aborigines of this continent.

So far as their own tribe is concerned, the Ojibways have preserved accurate and
detailed accounts of this event; and the information which their old men orally give
on this subject, is worthy of much consideration, although they may slightly differ
from the accounts which standard historians and writers have presented to the world,
and which they have gleaned from the writings of the enterprising and fearless old
Jesuit missionaries, and from the published narratives of the first adventurers who
pierced into the heart of the American wilderness. This source of information may be
considered as more reliable and authentic than the oral traditions of the Indians, but
as we have undertaken to write their history as they themselves tell it, we will do so
without respect to what has already been written by eminent and standard authors.
The writer is disposed to consider as true and perfectly reliable, the information
which he has obtained and thoroughly investigated, on this subject, and which he will
proceed in this chapter to relate in the words of his old Indian informants.

A few preliminary remarks are deemed necessary, before fully entering into the
narrative of the Ojibway's first knowledge and intercourse with his white brother.

Those who have carefully examined the writings of the old Jesuit missionaries
and early adventurers, who claim to have been the first discoverers of new regions,
and new people, in the then dark wilderness of the west, or central America, have
found many gross mistakes and exaggerations, and their works as a whole, are only
tolerated and their accounts made matters of history, because no other source of information has ever been opened to the public

It is a fact found generally true, that the first adventurer who is able to give a flaming account of his travels, is handed down to posterity as the first discoverer of the
country and people which he describes as having visited, when mayhap, that same region, and those same people had been, long previous, discovered by some obscure and
more modest man, who, because he could not blazon forth his achievements in a
book of travels, forever loses the credit of what he really has performed.

Many instances of this nature are being daily brought to light, and might be enumerated. Among others, Mr. Catlin claims in his book (and is believed by all who do
not know to the contrary), to have been the first white man who visited the Dakota
pipestone quarry, when in fact, that same quarry had been known to, and visited by
white traders for nearly a century before Catlin saw it and wrote his book.

In the same manner also, Charles Lanman, of later notoriety, claims to have been
the first white man who visited the Falls of the St. Louis River, when in fact Aitkin,
Morrison, Sayer, and a host of others as white as he, had visited, and resided for fifty years
within sound of those same falls.[2] It is thus that a man who travels for the purpose of

_____

2. The allusion is to Lanman's *Summer in the Wilderness,* published in New York, 1847.—E. D. N.

writing a book to sell, and who, being a man of letters, is able to trumpet forth his own fame, often plucks the laurels due to more modest and unlettered adventurers.

Mr. Bancroft in his standard "History of the United States," mentions that in the year 1665, the enterprising and persevering Jesuit missionary, Claude Allouez, with one companion, pushed his way into Lake Superior and discovered the Ojibways congregated in a large village in the Bay of Shag-a-waum-ik-ong, and preparing to go on a war party against the Dakotas; that he resided two years among them, and taught a choir of their youths to chant the *Pater* and *Ave*.

This is the first visit made by white men to this point on Lake Superior, of which we have any reliable *written* testimony. The account as given in Bancroft's "History" is not altogether corroborated by the Ojibways. It is only through minute and repeated inquiry, that I have learned the fact from their own lips, of this early visit of a "black gowned priest," but not of his having resided with them for any length of time. And they assert positively that it was many years after the first visit of the white men to their village in the Bay of Shag-a-waum-ik-ong, that the "priest" made his appearance among them. And I am disposed to doubt that as long a stay as two years was made by Father Allouez among their people, or that any of them learned to chant canticles, for the reason that the Ojibways, who are so minute in the relation of the particulars of any important event in their history, comprised within the past eight generations, do not make any mention of these facts. It is probable that the two years stay of this Jesuit in the Bay of Shag-a-waum-ik-ong, amounted to an occasional visit from Sault Ste. Marie, or Quebec, which place had already at this period, become the starting and rallying point of Western French adventurers.[3]

In those days there appears to have been a spirit of competition and rivalry among the different sects of the Catholic priesthood, as to who would pierce farthest into the western wilderness of America to plant the cross.

Imagination in some instances, outstripped their actual progress, and missionary stations are located on Hennepin's old map, in spots where a white man had never set foot. That the Catholic priests appeared amongst their earliest white visitors, the Ojibways readily acknowledge. And the name by which they have ever known the French people is a sufficient testimony to this fact, Wa-me-tig-oshe. For many years this name could not be translated by the imperfect interpreters employed by the agents of the French and English, and its literal definition was not given till during the last war, at a council of different tribes, convened by the British at Drummond's Isle. The several Ojibway interpreters present were asked to give its definition. All failed, till John Baptiste Cadotte, acknowledged to be the most perfect interpreter of the Algies in his time, arose and gave it as follows: "Wa-mit-ig-oshe is derived from wa-wa, to wave, and metig, wood or stick, and means literally, people or 'men of the waving stick,' de-

---

3. Mr. Bancroft erroneously wrote in the 14th edition of the History of the United States, that Allouez "on the first day of October arrived at the great village of the Chippewas in the Bay of Chagouamigon," but Mr. Warren is also wrong in his supposition.

Allouez upon invitation of traders, came with them to Chagouamigon Bay in October, 1665. At that time there was no permanent Ojibway village beyond Sault Ste. Marie. He built a bark chapel on the shores of the Bay between a village of Petun Hurons, and a village comprised of three bands of Ottawas. On the 30th of August, 1667, he returned to Montreal, and in two days departed again for Lake Superior, where he remained until 1669, when a mission was established among the Ojibways at Sault Ste. Marie. In 1669 Marquette succeeded Allouez, in the words of the Relation of 1669–70, "at Chagouamigong where the Outaouacs and Hurons dwell." He remained with them until they were driven out of Lake Superior in 1671 by the Sioux.—E. D. N.

rived from the fact that when the French first appeared among the Algonquins who have given them this name, they came accompanied with priests who waved the Cross over their heads whenever they landed at an Indian village."

The circumstance also is worthy of mention, that a few years ago, an old Indian woman dug up an antique silver crucifix on her garden at Bad River near La Pointe, after it had been deeply ploughed. This discovery was made under my own observation, and I recollect at the time it created quite a little excitement amongst the good Catholics of La Pointe, who insisted that the Great Spirit had given this as a token for the old woman to join the church. The crucifix was found about two feet from the surface of the ground, composed of pure silver, about three inches long and size in proportion. It has since been buried at Gull Lake, in the grave of a favorite grandchild of the old Indian woman, to whom she had given it as a plaything.

The Ojibways affirm that long before they became aware of the white man's presence on this continent, their coming was prophesied by one of their old men, whose great sanctity and oft-repeated fasts, enabled him to commune with spirits and see far into the future. He prophesied that the white spirits would come in numbers like sand on the lake shore, and would sweep the red race from the hunting grounds which the Great Spirit had given them as an inheritance. It was prophesied that the consequence of the white man's appearance would be, to the An-ish-in-aub-ag, an "ending of the world." They acknowledge that at first their ancestors believed not the words of the old prophet foretelling these events; but now as the present generation daily see the foretold events coming to pass in all their details, the more reflective class firmly believe that they are truly a "doomed race." It was through harping on this prophecy, by which Te-cum-seh and his brother, the celebrated Show-a-no prophet, succeeded so well in forming a coalition among the Algic and other tribes, the main and secret object of which, was the final extermination of the white race from America.

The account which the Ojibways give of their first knowledge of the whites, is as follows:—

While still living in their large and central town on the Island of La Pointe, a principal and leading Me-da-we priest, whose name was Ma-se-wa-pe-ga (whole ribs), dreamed a dream wherein he beheld spirits in the form of men, but possessing white skins and having their heads covered. They approached him with hands extended and with smiles on their faces. This singular dream he related to the principal men of the Ojibways on the occasion of a grand sacrificial feast to his guardian dream-spirit. He informed them that the white spirits who had thus appeared to him, resided toward the rising sun, and that he would go and search for them. His people tried to dissuade him from undertaking what they termed a foolish journey, but firm in his belief, and strong in his determination, he was occupied a whole year in making preparations for his intended journey. He built a strong canoe of birch bark and cedar wood; he hunted and cured plenty of meat for his provisions; and early in the spring when the ice had left the Great Lakes, and he had completed his preparations, Ma-se-wa-pe-ga, with only his wife for a companion, started on his travels in quest of the white spirits whom he had seen in his dream.

He paddled eastward down the Great Lakes in the route of the former migration of his tribe, till he entered into a large river which flowed in the direction of the rising sun. Undiscovered he passed through the hostile tribes of the Naud-o-ways. At last when the river on which he floated, had become wide and like a lake, he discovered on the banks, a hut, made of logs, and he noticed the stumps of large trees which had been cut by sharper instruments than the rude stone axes used by the Indians.

The signs were apparently two winters old, but satisfied that it was the work of the spirits, for whom he was in search, Ma-se-wa-pe-ga proceeded on his journey, and he soon came to another hut and clearing, which though deserted, had been built and occupied during the previous winter. Much encouraged, he paddled on down stream till he discovered another hut from the top of which arose a smoke. It was occupied by the "white spirits," who, on his landing, cordially welcomed him with a shake of the hand.

When about to depart to return home, presents of a steel axe, knife, beads, and a small strip of scarlet cloth were given him, which, carefully depositing in his medicine bag, as sacred articles, he brought safely home to his people at La Pointe. Ma-se-wa-pe-ga again collected the principal men of his tribe in council, and displaying his curious presents, he gave a full narrative of his successful journey and the fulfilment of his dream. The following spring a large number of his people followed him on his second visit to the supposed "white spirits." They carried with them many skins of the beaver, and they returned home late in the fall with the dread fire-arm, which was to give them power over their much feared enemies. It is on this occasion also, that they first procured the fire-water which was to prove the most dreadful scourge and curse of their race.

It is related that on the arrival of this party at La Pointe, with the fire-water, none dare drink it, thinking it a poison which would immediately cause death. They, however, to test its virtues, made an experimental trial on a very aged woman who—as they reasoned—had but a short time to live at all events, and whose death would be a matter of no account. The old woman drank it, appeared perfectly happy and in ecstasies, got over the effects of it, and begged for more. On which the men took courage, and drank up the remainder themselves. From that time, fire-water became the mammon of the Ojibways, and a journey of hundreds of miles to procure a taste of it, was considered but as boy's play.

They tell, also, the effect of the first gun, which they procured from the whites and introduced among the more remote and ignorant Dakotas, with whom at this time they happened to be on terms of peace. A peace party of the Ojibways visited a village of these people on the St. Croix river, and took with them as a curiosity, the dreadful weapon they had procured. While enjoying their peaceful games, the young men of the Ojibways informed the Dakotas of the fearful and deadly effects of the gun; but they, thinking that the Ojibways wished to intimidate them with an imaginary fear, reviled and laughed at the instrument, and in their disbelief they even offered to bet against its deadly effects. The dispute becoming high, the bet was taken, and a Dakota brave in utter derision, insisted on offering the back part of his body as a prominent mark. He was shot dead on the spot. With difficulty the peaceparty succeeded in returning safely home, for the wrath of the Dakotas was aroused at the death of their warrior, and the old feud was again renewed, though from this time they evinced a mortal fear of the gun, which their remoteness from the white strangers precluded them from obtaining, till many years after the Ojibways had been fully supplied.

About this time, the old men of the tribe date the sudden evacuation of their town on the island of La Pointe, and the planting of their lodges in the adjoining Bay of Shag-a-waum-ik-ong, which occurrence I have fully mentioned in the preceding chapter. The first white men whom they tell of having visited them, came after this dispersion, and while they were congregated on the shores of the Bay.

One clear morning in the early part of winter, soon after the islands which are clustered in this portion of Lake Superior and known as the Apostles, had been locked in ice, a party of young men of the Ojibways started out from their village in the Bay of Shag-a-waum-ik-ong, to go, as was customary, and spear fish through holes in the ice, between the island of La Pointe and the main shore, this being considered as the best ground for this mode of fishing. While engaged in their sport, they discovered a smoke arising from a point of the adjacent island, toward its eastern extremity.

The island of La Pointe was then totally unfrequented, from superstitious fears which had but a short time previous led to its total evacuation by the tribe, and it was considered an act of the greatest hardihood for any one to set foot on its shores. The young men returned home at evening and reported the smoke which they had seen arising from the island, and various were the conjectures of the old people respecting the persons who would dare to build a fire on the spirit-haunted isle. They must be strangers, and the young men were directed, should they again see the smoke, to go and find out who made it.

Early the next morning, again proceeding to their fishing ground, the young men once more noticed the smoke arising from the eastern end of the unfrequented island, and led on by curiosity, they ran thither and found a small log cabin in which they discovered two white men in the last stages of starvation. The young Ojibways filled with compassion, carefully conveyed them to their village, where, being nourished with great kindness, their lives were preserved.

These two white men had started from Quebec during the summer with a supply of goods, to go and find the Ojibways who every year had brought rich packs of beaver to the sea-coast, notwithstanding that their road was barred by numerous parties of the watchful and jealous Iroquois. Coasting slowly up the southern shores of the Great Lake late in the fall, they had been driven by the ice on to the unfrequented island, and not discovering the vicinity of the Indian village, they had been for some time enduring the pangs of hunger. At the time they were found by the young Indians, they had been reduced to the extremity of roasting and eating their woollen cloth and blankets as the last means of sustaining life.

Having come provided with goods they remained in the village during the winter, exchanging their commodities for beaver skins. The ensuing spring a large number of the Ojibways accompanied them on their return home.

From close inquiry, and judging from events which are said to have occurred about this period of time, I am disposed to believe that this first visit by the whites took place about two hundred years ago. It is, at any rate, certain that it happened a few years prior to the visit of the "Black gowns" mentioned in Bancroft's History, and it is one hundred and eighty-four years since this well-authenticated occurrence.

If thorough inquiry were to be made, it would be found that the idea which is now generally believed, that the pious missionaries of those olden times, were the first pioneers into the Indian country about the great chain of Lakes, and Upper Mississippi, and were only followed closely by the traders, is a mistaken one. The adventurous, but obscure and unlettered trader, was the first pioneer. He cared only for beaver skins, and his ambition not leading him to secure the name of a first discoverer by publishing his travels, this honor naturally fell to those who were as much actuated by a thirst for fame, as by religious zeal.

The glowing accounts given by these traders on their return with their peltries to Quebec, their tales of large villages of peaceable and docile tribes, caused the eager Jesuit and Franciscan to accompany him back to the scene of his glowing accounts, and to plant the cross amongst the ignorant and simple children of the forest.

In making these remarks, we do not wish to deteriorate from the great praise which is nevertheless due to these pious and persevering fathers, who so early attempted to save the souls of the benighted Indians.

In the separation of the Ojibway tribe into two divisions, upwards of three centuries ago at the outlet of Lake Superior, which has been fully treated of in a previous chapter, a considerable band remained on their ancient village site at Bow-e-ting or Falls of St. Marie; and here, some years prior to the first visit of the white men and "Black Gowns" to the greater village in the Bay of Shag-a-waum-ik-ong, traders and priests had established themselves, and this circumstance naturally conduced to draw thither from their more western and dangerously situated villages, many families of this tribe, till they again numbered many wigwams, on this, the site of their ancient town. It was the first discovery of this tribe, at this point, which has given them the name, by the French, of Saulteaux, from the circumstance of their residing at the "Falls."

This band have ever since this period, remained detached by the intervening southern shores of Lake Superior, from the main body of the tribe who have radiated northward, westward and southward, from their central town of La Pointe.

Aided by the French, Ottawas, Potawatumies, and Wyandots, they succeeded in checking the harassing incursions of the war-like Iroquois, and as they became equally possessed of the fire-arm, instead of being pressed west-ward, as they had been for centuries before, they retraced the eastern track of their ancestors' former emigration, and rejoined the remnants of their race who had been for many years cut off from them by the intervening Iroquois, and who had first greeted the French strangers who landed in the river St. Lawrence, and who termed them Algonquins.

From this period, the communication between the eastern section or rear of the Algic tribes, occupying the lower waters of the River St. Lawrence, and the great western van who occupied the area of Lake Superior, became comparatively free and open, for villages of the Algic tribes lined the shores of the great chain of Lakes and also the banks of the great river which forms the outlet into the "salt water."

In one of their traditions it is stated that "when the white man first came in sight of the 'Great Turtle' island of Mackinaw, they beheld walking on the pebbly shores, a crane and a bear who received them kindly, invited them to their wigwams, and placed food before them." This allegory denotes that Ojibways of the Crane and Bear Totem families first received the white strangers, and extended to them the hand of friendship and rites of hospitality, and in remembrance of this occurrence they are said to have been the favorite clans with the old French discoverers.

CHAPTER XXXIII

Endeavors of the British to Entice the Ojibways of Lake Superior and Mississippi to Join Their Arms in the War of 1812.

Mistaken impression respecting the position of the Ojibways during the last war—Efforts of British agents to induce them to break their neutrality—Col. Dickson sends a messenger to the Pillagers to induce them to join the British—Laconic reply of Flat Mouth—Great Cloud, an Ojibway warrior, helps the arms of Great Britain—Anecdote of his first acquaintance with Col.

*Dickson, who makes him a chief—Michel and John Baptiste Cadotte, Jr., act as British inter-
preters—Ojibways collect in large numbers at Mackinaw—British attempts to induce them to
fight the Americans—Opposition of the chieftain Keesh-ke-mun—He is called to council, and
reprimanded by the British commandant—The chieftain's answer—We-esh-coob, the Pillager
war-chief—He refuses to join the British—His bitter reply to their taunt of cowardice.*

It has been a general impression throughout the United States, that the Ojibways, as
a tribe, fought under the flag of Great Britain, during the war of 1812. It is not so;
and it can be stated as a fact, that of the nine thousand which this tribe number on
Lake Superior, and the Mississippi, not more than one or two warriors are mentioned
as having joined the British. There are several villages of Indians in Upper Canada,
who are sometimes denominated as Ojibways, but who are more properly the remnants of the original Algonquins who have always been in the interest of the British,
and aided them in their wars. The connection existing between these and the Lake
Superior and Mississippi Ojibways, is not very close, though they speak the same language, and call one another relatives.

If any of the Ojibways living within the boundaries of the United States fought
for the British during the last war, it was more through coercion than otherwise, and
they belonged to small bands who lived among the Ottaways at Mackinaw, and who
were scattered in Michigan among the Pottawatumies and other tribes. The main
body of the tribe occupying Lake Superior, and the waters of the Mississippi firmly
withstood every effort made by the British to induce them to enter into the war, and
it is thus they have succeeded in holding their own in numbers, and in fact, gradually
increasing, while other tribes, who have foolishly mingled in the wars of the whites,
have become nearly extinct.

Agents were sent by the British government to the principal villages of the Ojibways, to invite them to join their arms against the Americans. Col. Dickson,[1] who
had long been a trader amongst the Dakotas, and northern Ojibways, is mentioned as
one of the most prominent and active of the British agents in levying the savage
tribes, in an exterminating warfare against the men, *women, and children* of the United
States.

He sent the British interpreter, St. Germain, in a light canoe, fully manned with
Canadian voyageurs, from Fort William to Leech Lake, to obtain the co-operation of
the Pillagers. He gave presents to Esh-ke-bug-e-coshe (Flat Mouth), the chief of the
warlike band, and in public council he presented the wampum belts of the British
agent, and delivered his message. The Pillager chieftain sent back the belts with the laconic answer: "When I go war against my enemies, I do not call on the whites to join
my warriors. The white people have quarrelled among themselves, and I do not wish
to meddle in their quarrels, nor do I intend ever, even to be guilty of breaking the
window-glass of a white man's dwelling."

St. Germain next urged him to visit Col. Dickson at Ft. William, but the chief refused to go, and of all his warriors, but one obeyed the summons of the British agent.
This one was a noted warrior named Ke-che-aun-o-guet, or Great Cloud, whose attachment had been secured by Col. Dickson, in the following characteristic manner:—

---

1. For notices of Dickson, see Neill's *History of Minnesota,* 5th edition, 1883, Minnesota Historical
Collections, Vol. I. p. 390.

Great Cloud was one time, early in the spring, hunting in company with a Frenchman near Leaf Lake, while the Dakotas still claimed the country about it as their own. Early one morning, hearing the report of a gun towards Leaf Lake, Great Cloud told his comrade that he knew it must be the Dakotas, and he must go and see what they were about. Bidding the Frenchman good-bye, saying that he would try and return during the night, but not to wait for him longer than noon the next day, the Indian started on his dangerous expedition. Arriving at the outlet of Leaf River from the lake, he noticed some maple trees freshly tapped, and he soon fell on a beaten path, following which he soon discovered a log house, surrounded by a fence of felled trees. He hid by the roadside between the forks of a fallen tree, and there patiently awaited the appearance of some Dakota, whose scalp would add another eagle plume to his head-dress.

A woman came from the house to examine the maple trees, and gather the sap. She was dressed like a white man's squaw, and not wishing to kill a woman, Great Cloud did not molest her, but still continued in his ambush. Soon after, two other women, apparently mother and daughter, issued from the hut, came close to his hiding place, to gather sap. They were both apparently the women of some white man, as they were much cleaner and dressed far better than squaws usually are, and again the warrior refrained from attacking them. Towards evening he saw a man going towards the house, carrying some swans and ducks on his back, and Great Cloud prepared for an onset, but the hunter passed close to the lake shore, and out of bullet range. Tired of waiting, he at last crawled up to the house and posted himself directly in front of the gateway, amongst a clump of stumps. He saw a lodge standing within the inclosure on the other side of the house, and this he determined to watch till a Dakota should issue from it. It was now dusk, and he had remained in his new position but a moment, in fact had but just lighted his pipe, when the two women he had seen in the afternoon again came out of the house, and were examining a canoe which lay close to him, when they discovered the ambushed warrior. They immediately ran screaming into the house, from whence a white man with a large head of red hair soon issued, carrying a tremendous sword under his arm, and a gun in his hand. This was Col. Dickson. He walked up to Great Cloud, who was quietly smoking his pipe, and presenting his gun to his breast, demanded in broken Ojibway, "who he was, and what he wanted?"

The Indian answered, that "he was Great Cloud, an Ojibway warrior, and he had come to look for Dakota scalps." The trader then told him that the Dakotas were all gone, and that there was no one with him but a Menominee Indian. He inquired if there were any more of his people with him, and on answering in the negative, Dickson laughed, took Great Cloud by the hand, called him a brave man, and invited him into his house, where he was well treated. The Menominee Indian soon came in, and together they took a social smoke. Great Cloud related his adventures, and so pleased was his host at his having spared his women, that he gave him a flag and placed a medal on his breast, besides loading him with a present of goods.

On his return, Great Cloud found his French comrade had fled to Leech Lake, where he himself soon arrived, dressed as a chief, and instead of fur, loaded with merchandise, to the great surprise and wonder of his people. From this time he always showed a deep attachment to Col. Dickson, and though his people refused to recognize him as a chief, yet he always assumed the dignity and was treated as such by the British. Great Cloud proceeded to Fort William with St. Germain, and he was in nearly all the principal battles which took place between the British and Americans, during the last war, in Canada. He remained in the east some time after the closing of the war, and we find his name attached to most of the treaties which from this time the United States government made with the allied Ottaways, Pottawatumies, and eastern Ojibways, at Detroit, Vincennes, and Sault Ste. Marie.

Of the Ojibway half-breeds, John Baptiste and Michel, sons of Michel Cadotte, Sr., of La Pointe, were captured or enticed by the British of Isle Drummond, and there given the option, either to go into confinement during the war, or act as interpreters, and use their influence to collect the Ojibways. They accepted the latter alternative, and were actors in all the principal Canadian battles, and were present on the occasion of Tecumseh's death. John Baptiste was severely wounded, and is now[2] a pensioner on the British government. Michel is also living, minus one arm, at La Pointe, on Lake Superior.

After the taking of Fort Howard, on the island of Mackinaw, the Ojibways of Lake Superior and the inland country towards the Mississippi, being deprived of their usual resident traders and supplies, congregated in unusual numbers on the island. The British took this occasion again to renew their attempts to induce them to join their arms. They, however, signally failed to make an impression on their minds, as the Ojibways were influenced by one of their principal chiefs, who was noted both for wisdom and great firmness of character. His name was Keesh-ke-mun, already mentioned in a previous chapter. On discovery that the councils of this chief was the cause of the failure of their attempts to induce the Ojibways to war against the Americans, the British officers sent for him to come to their council room. The chief obeyed the summons, accompanied by a numerous guard of his warriors. Michel Cadotte, Jr., acted as interpreter, and from his lips have these items and speeches been obtained by the writer.

The British officers, in full uniform, were all collected in the council room, when the Ojibway chieftain and his train entered and silently took the seats allotted to them. Mr. Askin, a British agent, opened the council by stating to the chief that his British father had sent for him, understanding that his councils with his red brethren had shut their ears against his words, and cooled their hearts towards him. "Your British father wishes to know who you are, that you should do these things—that you should dare to measure yourself against him." After an interval of silence, during which the chieftain quietly smoked his pipe, he at last arose, and shaking hands with the British commandant, he answered as follows:—

"Englishman! you ask me who I am. If you wish to know, you must seek me in the clouds. I am a bird who rises from the earth, and flies far up, into the skies, out of human sight; but though not visible to the eye, my voice is heard from afar, and resounds over the earth!

"Englishman! you wish to know who I am. You have never sought me, or you should have found and known me. Others have sought and found me. The old French sought and found me. He placed his heart within my breast. He told me that every morning I should look to the east and I would behold his fire, like the sun reflecting its rays towards me, to warm me and my children. He told me that if troubles assailed me, to arise in the skies and cry to him, and he would hear my voice. He told me that his fire would last forever, to warm me and my children.

---

2. A. D. 1852.

"Englishman! you, Englishman, you have put out the fire of my French father. I became cold and needy, and you sought me not. Others have sought me. Yes, the *Long Knife* has found me. He has placed his heart on my breast. It has entered there, and there it will remain!"

The chieftain here pulled out from his decorated tobacco pouch, an American George Washington medal, which had been given him by a former commandant of Fort Howard, and placing it around his neck, it lay on his breast, as he quietly returned to his seat.

Somewhat excited at the vehement address of the chief, and at the act of seeming bravado which closed his harangue, the British officer replied to him:—

"You say true. I have put out the fire of the French men; and in like manner am I now putting out the fire of the Long Knife. With that medal on your breast, you are my enemy. You must give it up to me, that I may throw it away, and in its stead I shall give you the heart of your great British father, and you must stand and fight by his side."

Keesh-ke-mun, without arising from his seat, answered:

"Englishman! the heart of the Long Knife, which he placed on my breast, has entered my bosom. You cannot take it from me without taking my life."

The officer, exasperated at the unflinching firmness of the chieftain, now exclaimed, in anger, addressing the interpreter: "Tell him, sir, that he must give up his medal, or I shall detain him a prisoner within the walls of this fort." This threat, being duly interpreted to him, the chief grasped his medal in his hand, and once more arising from his seat, he addressed the excited officer, himself not showing the least marks of emotion:—

"Englishman! I shall not give up this medal of my own will. If you wish to take it from me, you are stronger than I am. But I tell you, it is but a mere bauble. It is only an emblem of the heart which beats in my bosom; to cut out which you must first kill me! Englishman! you say, that you will keep me a prisoner in this your strong house. You are stronger than I am. You can do as you say. But remember that the voice of the Crane echoes afar off, and when he summons his children together, they number like the pebbles on the Great Lake shore!"

After a short consultation between the officers and Mr. Askin, the commandant again addressed the chief:—

"Your words are big, but I fear them not. If you refuse to give up the medal of the Long Knives, you are my enemy, and you know I do not allow my enemies to live."

The chief answered: "Englishman! you are stronger than I am. If you consider me an enemy because I cherish the heart which has been placed on my bosom, you may do so. If you wish to take my life, you can take it. I came into your strong house because you sent for me. You sent for me wishing to set me on to my father the Long Knife, as a hunter sets his dogs on a deer. I cannot do as you wish. I cannot strike my own father. He, the Long Knife, has not yet told us to fight for him. Had he done so, you Englishmen would not now be in this strong house. The Long Knife counsels us to remain quiet. In this do we know that he is our own father, and that he has confidence in the strength of his single arm."

After some further consultation among the officers, who could not help admiring his great firmness, the chief was dismissed. The next morning, Michel Cadotte (his grandson), was again sent to him to call him to council. Keesh-ke-mun, with a score of his warriors again presented themselves. A large pile of goods and tobacco was placed before him. Mr. Askin addressed him as follows:—

"Your English father has not sent for you to take your life. You have refused to accept the badge of his heart. You have refused to join him in putting out the fire of the Long Knives who are stealing away your country. Yet he will not detain you. He will not hurt a hair of your head. He tells you to return to your village in peace. He gives you wherewith to warm your children for the coming winter. But he says to you, remain quiet—remember if you join the Long Knives, we shall sweep your villages from the earth, as fire eats up the dry grass on the prairie."

Keesh-ke-mun, without answering a word, accepted the presents and returned to his village. To his influence may be chiefly attributed the fact that the Ojibways of Lake Superior and Mississippi remained neutral during the progress of the last war.

Another anecdote is told by my informant, who acted as the British interpreter for the Ojibways during the last war; which further illustrates the attachment which this tribe had conceived for the American people.

About the same time that Keesh-ke-mun so firmly withstood the inducements and threats of the British officers at Fort Howard, We-esh-coob, the war-chief of the Pillagers, with a party of his people from Leech Lake, happened to be present at the island of Michilimacinae. He was vainly urged by the British agents to join their arms with his band of warriors, who were noted as being the bravest of the Ojibway tribe. At a council held within the fort, this chief was asked, for the last time, by the British commandant, to array himself under their flag. We-esh-coob, in more decided terms than ever, refused, and his words so exasperated the commandant, that he rose from his seat, and forgot himself so far as to say to the Pillagers:—

"I thought you were men, but I see that you are but women, not fit even to wear the breech-cloth. Go back to your homes. I do not wish the assistance of women. Go, put on the clothing which more befits you, and remain quiet in your villages."

As he delivered this violent speech, he was proceeding to leave the council room, when We-esh-coob, having quietly listened to the interpretation thereof, rose to his feet, and approaching the angry Englishman, he put his hand on his epaulette and gently held him back. "Wait," said he, "you have spoken; now let me speak. You say that we should not wear the breech-cloth, but the dress of women." Then pointing to the opposite shore of the lake, towards the site of the old English fort which the Ojibways had taken in 1763, We-esh-coob exclaimed:—

"Englishman! have you already forgotten that we once made you cry like children? yonder! who was the woman then?

"Englishman! you have said that we are women. If you doubt our manhood, you have young men here in your strong house. I have also young men. You must come out on some open place, and we will fight. You will better know, whether we are fit, or not, to wear the breech-cloth.

"Englishman! you have said words which the ears of We-esh-coob have never before heard," and throwing down his blanket in great excitement, he pointed to different scars on his naked body, and exclaimed: "I thought I carried about me the marks which proved my manhood."

The English officer whose irritation had somewhat abated during the delivery of this answer, grasped the unusually excited Indian by the hand, and requested the interpreter to beg him to forget his hasty words. Peace and good-will were thus restored, but this bitter taunt tended greatly to strengthen the minds of the Ojibways against the agents who were continually engaged amongst them, to draw them into the war.

A Brief Sketch of the Fur Trade and Fur Traders Among the Ojibways from the Formation of the Northwest Company in 1787 to 1834.

Origin of the Northwest Fur Company—Departments of their trade in the Ojibway country—Depot at Grand Portage—Yearly meetings of the partners—Names of the original partners—Sir Alex. McKenzie—He forms the X. Y. Company, and opposes the Northwest—The two companies join issues—Opposition of the Hudson's Bay Co.—Bloody struggle between the two rival companies—Northwest becomes merged in the Hudson's Bay Co.—Names of their Ojibway traders—Astor's American Fur Co.—Amount of their outfits in 1818—Policy of their trade—Names of their principal traders—W. A. Aitkin—Lyman W. Warren—Names, motives, and conduct of the American traders.

AMONG the first traders who pushed their enterprise to the villages of the Ojibways on Lake Superior, after France had ceded the Canadas to Great Britain, the names of Alexander Henry and the Cadottes appear most conspicuous. The Northwest Fur Company was not formed till the year 1787. It originated in the following manner:—

Three or four rival traders, or small companies, had proceeded from Montreal and Quebec, and located trading posts on the north coast of Lake Superior, about the mouth of Pigeon River, up which stream they sent outfits to the "Bois Fort" and Muskego Ojibways, and then to the Kenisteno and Assineboines of Red River. The rivalry between these different traders became extremely bitter, and at last resulted in the murder of Waddon, who was shot in cold blood, within his trading house, at Grand Portage. This outrage brought the most sensible portion of the traders to their senses, and they immediately made efforts to compromise their difficulties, and to join their interests into one. These efforts resulted in the formation of the Northwest Company, which soon became so rich and powerful that for a long time they were enabled to monopolize the northern fur trade, and cope with the most powerful and favored combinations which the capitalists of Great Britain could bring against them.

In the year 1792, immediately after the noted expedition of John Baptiste Cadotte to the Upper Mississippi, the Northwest Company extended their operations over the whole Ojibway country within the limits of the United States, on Lake Superior and the Mississippi. Their trade in these regions was divided into four departments:—

The Fond du Lac department consisted of the country at the head of Lake Superior, and the sources of the St. Louis and Mississippi Rivers. The Folle Avoine department consisted of the country drained by the waters of the St. Croix. The Lac Coutereille department covered the waters of the Chippeway; and the Lac du Flambeau department, the waters of the Wisconsin.

The depot for this portion of their trade was located at Fond du Lac, but their great depot was at Grand Portage on the north coast of Lake Superior and within the limits of what is now known as Minnesota Territory. From this point they sent their outfits up Pigeon River, towards the northwest, and occupied the country of the Kenisteno and Assineboines. Here, each summer, the partners and clerks of the company, who had passed the winter amongst the inland posts, collected their returns of fur, and were met by the partners from Montreal with new supplies of merchandise. These yearly meetings were enlivened with feastings, dancing, and revelry, held in the great hall of the company. In the style of the feudal barons of old, did these prosperous traders each year hold their grand festival surrounded by their faithful and happy "coureurs du bois" and servitors. The eyes of an "old northwester," while relating these happy scenes of by-gone times, will sparkle with excitement—his form will become momentarily erect as he imagines himself moving off in the merry dance, and his lips will water, as he enumerates the varied luxuries under which groaned long tables in the days of these periodic feastings.

Amongst the different partners of this company on its first formation, the names of Frobisher, McTavish, Pond, Gregory, and Pangman are mentioned as most conspicuous. In their future operations, the names of Sir Alex. McKenzie and McGilvray soon became prominent as the most active partners. They were early opposed at some of their northern posts by the Forsyths and Ogilvys, but were not much troubled by the rivalry of these men till, through some unfortunate misunderstanding with members of the company, Sir Alex. McKenzie was forced to draw out his means and leave the firm. He thereupon joined with the Forsyths, and under the denomination of the X. Y. Company, through his great tact and experience in the trade, he caused the Northwest for several years to suffer severe losses. After his death, the two rival companies came to an amicable understanding, and joined as partners.

It is about this time that the Northwest first began to be materially harassed by the Hudson's Bay Company, who not only met them in their most lucrative northern posts, from the direction of Hudson's Bay, but followed them up, through their usual route from Canada. This company, formed principally of influential lords and gentlemen in England, supported by the favor of government and possessing a charter, eventually proved too powerful for the old Northwest. They, however, did not crush this old firm till after a protracted and severe struggle. The Northwest Company, by the honorable and humane course which they are noted as having pursued towards the Indians, and also towards their numerous Canadian and half-breed servitors and dependants, were, in return, loved by them, and in the efforts of these people to retain them in their country, blood was unfortunately made to flow.

On the 17th of June, 1816, Governor Semple, of the Hudson's Bay Company, with some British troops, in trying to prevent the march of a body of mounted half-breeds, was suddenly cut down, and his troops killed, by a sweeping charge of these hardy buffalo hunters. A bloody partisan warfare was only prevented by the strong interference of the British government. In 1819 the Northwest became merged into the Hudson's Bay Company, and ceased to exist. With it may be said to have ended the Augustan age of the fur trade. With deep regret do the old voyageurs and Indians speak of the dissolution of this once powerful company, for they always received honorable and charitable treatment at their hands. The principal traders who operated among the Ojibways during the era of the Northwest Company, and who may be mentioned as contemporary with John Baptiste and Michel Cadotte, are Nolin, Gaulthier, McGillis, St. Germain, Bazille Beauleau, Chabolier, Wm. Morrison, Cotte, Roussain, Bonga, J. B. Corbin, and others. These early pioneer traders all intermarried in the tribe, and have left sons and daughters to perpetuate their names. Wm. Morrison of Montreal, and J. B. Corbin, of Lac Coutereille, are now[1] the only survivors of all these old traders.

For the above brief account of the early fur trade, I am indebted to Hon. Allan Morrison of Crow Wing, who has been for upwards of thirty years a trader among the Ojibways, and who is a grandson of Waddon, whose murder led to the formation of the Northwest Company.

To Mr. Bruce, of St. Croix Lake, now in his seventy-ninth year, mostly passed in the northwest, I am also indebted for information. At the dissolution of the Northwest Company, citizens of the United States began seriously to turn their attention to the Ojibway fur trade, and from this time a new class of individuals, as traders, began to penetrate to the remotest villages of this tribe. In the year 1818, the Astor Fur Company first commenced their operations on Lake Superior. They confined themselves, however, during the years 1816 and 1817, to trading posts at Sault Ste. Marie, Grand Island, and Ance-ke-we-naw. John Johnston, with a capital each year, of $40,000, managed this portion of their trade.

In 1818, the company sent outfits to cover the whole Ojibway country, within the limits of the United States. William Morrison, Roussain, Cotte, and others, as traders on salary, with an outfit amounting to $23,606, were sent to the Fond du Lac department, which included the Upper Mississippi country. These traders continued during the years 1819-20-21-22, with small increase of capital. The department of Lac du Flambeau was placed in charge of Bazil Beauleau and Charatte as traders, on salary, in 1818, with a capital of $5100; Hawley and Durant, with a capital of $5299.

For the Lac Coutereille department, the company outfitted John Baptiste Corbin, as a trader on salary, with goods to the amount of $5328. For the St. Croix district, Duchene acted as trader, on salary, for the company in 1818. Capital $3876.

In 1822, the capital of the Lac Coutereille and St. Croix departments amounted to $19,353, in charge of Duchene as trader. In 1818, the Ance department was placed in charge of John Holliday as trader on salary; his capital, or amount of outfit, averaged till 1822, $6000 per annum.

In 1822, the Astor Fur Company made a slight change in the system of their trade in the Ojibway country. The Fond du Lac department was given to Wm. Morrison on halves, and this arrangement continued to 1826, when Messrs William A. Aitkin and Roussain took charge with a share of one-sixth each. In 1820, Mr. Aitkin bought out Roussain, and for one year he had charge, with a share of one-third. In 1831, Mr. Aitkin took charge of this important department on halves with the Astor Company, and continued thus till 1834.

In 1824, Lyman M. Warren, after having traded in opposition to the American Fur Company for six years, in the Lac du Flambeau, Lac Coutereille and St. Croix departments, entered into an arrangement with them, and took charge as a partner, and under a salary of these three departments, making his depot at La Pointe. He continued with the same arrangement till the year 1834.

These items respecting the fur trade are here introduced to give the reader an idea of the importance of the trade amongst the Ojibways, and to introduce the names of the principal traders who, at this time, were remaining in the country. The Astor Fur Company followed the example of the Northwest Company in hiring as traders, men whom they found already in the country, holding influential positions among the

---

1. A. D. 1852.

Ojibways, and in some cases connected with them by marriage. Some of these men had traded in connection with the old Northwest Company, as William Morrison, Cotte, Roussain, Corbin, and others, while others of more recent date had traded as opposition traders, and distinguished themselves by their success. Among these may be mentioned Wm. A. Aitkin, Esq., who first came into the Chippeway country about 1815, a mere boy, and as a servant for a trader named John Drew. Intermarrying into an influential Indian family, he was soon enabled to trade on his own account, and he gradually increased his business till, in 1831, he takes charge of the important department of Fond du Lac, on halves, with John Jacob Astor. Mr. Aitkin's name is linked with the history of the Upper Mississippi Ojibways for the last half century. He was one of the old pioneers of the northwest. He died in the fall of the year 1851, and lies buried at Aitkinsville (Swan River), on the banks of the Upper Mississippi.

Among others may be mentioned the names of Lyman M. and his brother Truman A. Warren. They first came into the Ojibway country from Vermont, in 1818. They hired the first year in charge of small outfits, to Charles Ermitinger, at the rate of $500 per annum. They soon took outfits on their own account, and traded with great success in the Lac Coutereille and Lac du Flambeau departments. In 1821, they married each a daughter of the old trader Michel Cadotte, and their trade increased to such a degree that in 1824, Lyman Warren made an apparently advantageous arrangement with the Astor Fur Company, becoming a partner thereof, besides receiving a handsome salary. Truman died in 1825, on board a vessel bound from Mackinaw to Detroit, from a severe cold caused by the extreme exposure incident to an Indian trader's life. He died much lamented by the Ojibways, who had already learned to love him for his many gentle and good traits of character.

Lyman M. Warren, the elder brother, located his permanent residence on La Pointe Island, and continued with slight interruptions and varied success, to trade with the Ojibways till his death in 1847. He lies buried at La Pointe, and his name may now well be mentioned among the early American pioneers of the northwest. Half a century hence, when the scenes of their wild adventures and hardships shall be covered with teeming towns and villages, these slight records of individuals who still live in the memory of the present generation, will be read with far greater interest than at the present day.

Samuel Ashmun, Daniel Dingley, Charles H. Oakes, and Patrick Conner, may be mentioned as prominent traders among the Ojibways during the early part of the nineteenth century. Some of these gentlemen commenced their career in opposition to the Astor Fur Company, but in accordance to the policy of this rich firm, they were soon bought out and engaged in its service.

When John Jacob Astor entered into arrangements with the British Fur Companies for the monopoly of the Ojibway trade within the United States territory, a new era may be said to have occurred in the fur trade. The old French Canadian traders so congenial to the Indians, who had remained in the country after the closing of the French supremacy, had all nearly died away, and disappeared from the stage of active life, and a new class of men, of far different temperaments, whose chief object was to amass fortunes, now made their appearance among the Ojibways. They were of the Anglo-Saxon race, and hailed from the land of the progressive and money-making "Yankee." To some degree the Indian ceased to find that true kindness, sympathy, charity, and respect for his sacred beliefs and rites, which he had always experienced from his French traders.

The Ojibways were more deserving of respect in those days, while living in their natural state, and under the full force of their primitive moral beliefs, than they are at the present day, after being degenerated by a close contact with an unprincipled frontier white population. The American fur traders, many of whom were descended from respectable New England families, did not consider their dignity lessened by forming marital alliances with the tribe, and the Ojibway women were of so much service to their husbands, they so easily assimilated themselves to their modes of life, and their affections were so strong, and their conduct so beyond reproach, that these alliances, generally first formed by the traders for present convenience, became cemented by the strongest ties of mutual affection. They kindly cherished their Indian wives, and for their sakes, as well as for the sake of children whom they begat, these traders were eventually induced to pass their lifetime in the Ojibway country. They soon forgot the money-making mania which first brought them into the country, and gradually imbibing the generous and hospitable qualities of the Indians, lived only to enjoy the present. They laid up no treasure for the future, and as a general fact, which redounds to the honor of this class of fur traders, they died poor. The money which has been made by the fur trade has been made with the sweat of their brows, but it has flowed into the coffers of such men as John Jacob Astor.

It is a fact worthy of notice, that the Anglo-Saxon race have mingled their blood with the Ojibways to a much greater extent than with any other tribe of the red race.

It reflects honor on this tribe, as it tends greatly to prove the common saying, that they are far ahead of other tribes in their social qualities, and general intelligence and morality. Of French and American extraction, the Ojibways number about five thousand persons of mixed blood, who are scattered throughout Canada, Michigan, Wisconsin, Minnesota, and the British possessions. Many of the Ojibway mixed bloods are men of good education and high standing within their respective communities.

The American Board of Foreign Missions early established a mission school on the island of Mackinaw, to which most of the Ojibway traders sent their half-breed children. The school was sustained on the manual labor system, and great good was disseminated from it, which spread over the whole northwest country. Many of our most prominent half-breeds, now engaged as missionaries, or in mercantile pursuits, and women who figure in the best of civilized society, received their education at the Mackinaw mission. After its dissolution, such of the traders as were pecuniarily able, usually sent their children to receive an education in some of the Eastern States.

CHAPTER XXXV

Events from 1818 to 1826.

In 1818, Black Dog, a Pillager war-leader, marches into the Dakota country, with a party of sixteen warriors—Desperate fight, from which but one Pillager escapes death—In 1824, four white men are murdered on the shores of Lake Pepin by an Ojibway war party—Unsuccessful pursuit of the murderers—The traders demand them at the hands of their chiefs—Chief of Lac

du Flambeau delivers three of the ring-leaders into the hands of Truman A. Warren—The prin-
cipal murderer is secured by Wm. Holliday—They are taken to Mackinaw and confined in jail,
from which they make their escape—Convention at Fond du Lac in 1826, between commis-
sioners on the part of the United States, and the Ojibways—Objects thereof.

FOR several years after the closing of the last war between Great Britain and the United States, no event of sufficient importance to deserve record, occurred to the Ojibways. Their warfare continued with the Dakotas, but no important battle was fought, nor striking acts of valor and manhood performed, such as find a durable place in the lodge tales and traditions of the tribe, till the year 1818, when the hardy Pillagers again lost a select band of their bravest warriors.

A noted war-leader, Black Dog, having lately lost some relatives, at the hands of the Dakotas, raised a small but select band of warriors to go with him in pursuit of vengeance. They numbered but sixteen men, but being all of determined character, they marched westward, and proceeded further into the country of their enemies, than any Ojibway war party had ever done before them. After having travelled all one night in crossing a wide prairie, early in the morning they discovered a large encampment of Dakotas, whose lodges were located on a prairie, close by the banks of a small river. The Ojibways were unfortunately discovered by a party of buffalo hunters who were scouring the prairie on horseback, and their presence was immediately reported to the grand encampment, whose warriors prepared to turn out in irresistible numbers against them. It was useless for them to think of flight, for their enemy, being on horseback, would soon overtake and surround them. They could but sell their lives as dearly as possible.

The leader lost not his presence of mind, though perfectly satisfied that the fate of his party was fully sealed. Addressing a few words of encouragement to his warriors, he led them to a small clump of poplar trees which grew on a knoll on the prairie, in plain view of the Dakota encampment. Here, they each dug a hole in the ground, from which they determined to keep up the fight with their numerous enemies, as long as their ammunition might last. They had hardly finished their preparations, when the Dakota warriors made their appearance in a formidable array on the open prairie. They were fully painted and dressed for battle, and a large number were on horseback, who quickly rode forward and completely surrounded the knoll of trees in which the Ojibways had taken shelter. The battle commenced, and lasted without intermission till midday, the Dakotas suffering a severe loss from the unerring aim of their desperate enemies, who threw not a single shot away. So well were they posted, that it was impossible to approach or dislodge them. At last their scanty supply of ammunition gave out, and the Dakotas discovering it by the slackening of their fire, and by one of their number being wounded with a stone which an Ojibway had substituted in his gun for a bullet, a simultaneous rush was made on them, and after a short hand to hand struggle, the sixteen Pillager warriors, with but one exception, were killed. This one, named Bug-aun-auk, returned safely to his people, but he never would give but the most supernatural account of his manner of escape—tales that were not believed by his own people. It was at first the general impression that he had deserted his party before the fight came on, but the Dakotas, at a future peace-meeting with the Ojibways, stated that there were sixteen warriors who went into the poplar grove, as counted by their scouts, and there were found sixteen holes from which the warriors fought, in one of which remained only the bundle of the man who had so miraculously escaped. The

Dakotas acknowledged that they lost thirty-three of their warriors in this desperate engagement, besides many maimed for life.

Since the execution of the Indian at Fond du Lac in 1797, by the northwestern traders for killing a Canadian "coureur du bois," the life of a white man had been held sacred by the Ojibways, and one could traverse any portion of their country, in perfect safety, and without the least molestation. In the year 1824, however, four white men were killed by the Ojibways, under circumstances so peculiar, as to deserve a brief account in this chapter.

An Ojibway named Nub-o-beence, or Little Broth, residing on the shores of Lake Superior near the mouth of Ontonagun River, lost a favorite child through sickness. He was deeply stricken with grief, and nothing would satisfy him but to go and shed the blood of the hereditary enemies of his tribes, the Dakotas. He raised a small war party, mostly from the Lac du Flambeau district, and they floated down the Chippeway River to its entry, where, for several days they watched without success on the banks of the Mississippi, for the appearance of an enemy. The leader had endured hardships, and came the great distance of five hundred miles to shed blood to the manes of his dead child, and long after his fellows had become weary of waiting and watching, and anxious to return home, did he urge them still to continue in their search. He had determined not to return without shedding human blood.

Early one morning, as the warriors lay watching on the shores of Lake Pepin, they saw a boat manned by four white men land near them, and proceed to cook their morning meal. Several of the party approached the strangers, and were well received. The white men consisted of a Mr. Finley, with three Canadian boat men, who were under the employ of Mons. Jean Brunet, of Prairie du Chien, an Indian trader. They were proceeding up the Mississippi to Ft. Snelling on some urgent business of their employer, and Mr. Finley had with him a number of account books and valuable papers.

The assault and massacre of these men was entirely unpremeditated by the Ojibway war party, and contrary to the wishes of the majority. They had paid them their visit and begged some provisions, receiving which, they retired and sat down in a group on a bank immediately above them. The leader here commenced to harangue his fellows, expressing a desire to shed the blood of the white man. He was immediately opposed, on which he commenced to talk of the hardships he had endured, the loss of his child, till, becoming excited, he wept with a loud voice, and suddenly, taking aim at the group of white men, who were eating their breakfast, he fired and killed one. Eight of his fellows immediately followed his example, and rushing down to the water-side, they quickly dispatched the whole party, and tore off their scalps. Taking the effects of their victims, they returned towards their homes. At Lac Coutereille they attempted to dance the scalp dance before the door of J. B. Corbin, the trader, who immediately ran out of his house, and forcibly deprived them of the white men's scalps which they were displaying, ordering them at the same time to depart from his door. The trader was supported by the Indians of his village, and the murderers now for the first time beginning to see the consequences of their foolish act, skulked silently away, very much crestfallen.

The remains of the murdered white men were soon discovered, and the news going both up and down the river, a boat load of fifty soldiers was sent from Prairie du Chien to pursue the murderers. At Lake Pepin they were met by three boats laden with troops from Ft. Snelling, and the party, including volunteers, numbered nearly two hundred men. Mons. Jean Brunet was along, and had been most active in raising this force. They followed the Ojibway war-trail for some distance, till, coming to a place where the warriors had hung up their usual thanksgiving sacrifices for a safe return to their homes, a retreat was determined on, as the party had not come prepared to make a long journey, and it was folly to think of catching the murderers, scattered throughout the vast wilderness which lay between Lake Superior and the Mississippi.

The matter was subsequently left in the hands of the traders among the Ojibways. Truman A. Warren, the principal trader of the Lac du Flambeau department, demanded the murderers, at the hands of the chiefs of this section of the tribe. The celebrated Keesh-ke-mun had died a short time previous, and had left his eldest son Mons-o-bo-douh to succeed. This man was not a whit behind his deceased father in intelligence and firmness of character. He called a council of his band, and insisted on the chief murderers being given up by their friends. He was opposed in council by a man noted for his ill-tempered and savage disposition, who even threatened to take his life if he attempted to carry his wishes into effect. A brother of this man had been one of the ring-leaders in the murder, and now stood by his side as he delivered his threats against the young chief. As they again resumed their seats, Mons-o-bo-douh arose, and drawing his knife, he went and laid hold of the murderer by the arm and intimated to him that he was his prisoner. He then ordered his young men to tie his arms. The order was immediately obeyed, and accomplished without the least resistance from the prisoner or his brother, who was thunderstruck at the cool and determined manner of the chief.

Shortly after, two more of the murderers were taken, and Mons-o-bo-douh delivered them into the hands of the trader. The leader of the party, who lived on the shores of Lake Superior, was secured by Mr. William Holliday, trader at Ance Bay. The four captives were sent to Mackinac, and confined in jail. While orders were pending from Washington respecting the manner of their trial, they succeeded in making their escape by cutting an aperture through the logs which formed their place of confinement.

The ensuing year (1826), the Hon. Lewis Cass was commissioned by the United States, to proceed to Lake Superior, and convene the Ojibways in council, to treat with them for the copper and other mineral, which was now found to abound in their country. This important convention was held at Fond du Lac, which was then considered as about the centre of the Ojibway country. Boat loads of provisions were taken from Mackinaw and collected at this point, to feed the assembly of Indians, who were notified through messengers to collect. The Ojibways had not collected in such large numbers for a long time. Delegations arrived from their most remote villages towards the north. Shin-ga-ba-ossin, chief of the Crane family, from Sault Ste. Marie, was also present, and took a most prominent part in the proceedings, in behalf of his tribe. He is said to have made a speech to his fellows, wherein he urged them to discover to the whites their knowledge of the minerals which abounded in their country. This, however, was meant more to tickle the ears of the commissioners and to obtain their favor, than as an earnest appeal to his people, for the old chieftain was too much imbued with the superstition prevalent amongst the Indians, which prevents them from discovering their knowledge of mineral and copper boulders to the whites. The objects of the commissioners were easily attained, but the Ojibways, who felt a deep love for the offspring of their women who had intermarried with the whites, and cherished them as their own children, insisted on giving them grants of land on the Sault Ste. Marie River, which they wished our government to recognize and make good. These stipulations were annexed by the commissioners to the treaty, but were never ratified by the Senate of the United States. It is merely mentioned here to show the great affection with which the Ojibways regarded their half-breeds, and which they have evinced on every occasion when they have had an opportunity of bettering their condition.

A stipulation was also annexed to the treaty, wherein some of the relatives of the murderers of Finley and his party, agreed to deliver them within a given time. This, however, was never carried into effect, and as the traders took no further interest in the matter, the murderers were allowed to run at large. The leader is still[1] living at Ontonagun, and another named "the Little Eddy," is living[1] at La Pointe. Both are noted for their quiet and peaceable disposition.

At the treaty of Fond du Lac, the United States commissioners recognized the chiefs of the Ojibways, by distributing medals amongst them, the size of which were in accordance with their degree of rank. Sufficient care was not taken in this rather delicate operation, to carry out the pure civil polity of the tribe. Too much attention was paid to the recommendation of interested traders who wished their best hunters to be rewarded by being made chiefs. One young man named White Fisher, was endowed with a medal, solely for the strikingly mild and pleasant expression of his face. He is now a petty sub-chief on the Upper Mississippi.

From this time may be dated the commencement of innovations which have entirely broken up the civil polity of the Ojibways.

---

1. A. D. 1852.

59

WILLIAM T. COGGESHALL

(1824–1867)

William T. Coggeshall was best known in his lifetime for saving the life of Abraham Lincoln. Lincoln picked up Coggeshall, who had campaigned for him in Ohio, in Cincinnati on his inaugural train from Springfield to Washington. In Pennsylvania, a bomb was thrown onto the train; Coggeshall grabbed it and threw it off before detonation. During the Civil War, Coggeshall served the Union as a scout in Virginia and, after, was appointed the American emissary to Peru. During the war, Coggeshall had contracted tuberculosis, and soon after he arrived in Quito, he died.

With his death, in many ways, the vibrant literary scene that had characterized antebellum Cincinnati died as well. Coggeshall had moved to southern Ohio in 1850. In the decade that followed, he assumed the mantle of his forerunners in establishing the need for a western regional literature and culture. Like James Hall, Daniel and Benjamin Drake, and William D. Gallagher, Coggeshall saw a number of impediments to the region's ability to develop a distinct and appropriate voice to counter the east's domination of the publishing industry. His work in this area took many forms: as an activist, he worked for temperance and abolition; as an editor, he published the massive *Poets and Poetry of the West* (1860), which brought into print poets from Iowa to Tennessee; and as an author, he wrote short fiction (*Easy Warren and his Contemporaries* [1854]). In all these ways, Coggeshall explored the need for regional culture to be the basis for a larger cultural self-exploration.

His most important contribution, however, was the essay reprinted here. Early in the essay, Coggeshall lays forth an agenda for regional culture that would serve as the blueprint for post–Civil War regionalists such as Hamlin Garland and Edward Watson Howe. Coggeshall's recognition that "Western literature . . . has been disregarded, as a distinct power, in the general interest for welcome to whatever, springing out of the seaboard cities, has been creditable as the national character" informs the motivation for this collection itself. Unlike his predecessors, however, Coggeshall blamed both easterners for their ambition and westerners for their passivity for the asymmetry of regional contributions to the national culture.

Coggeshall argues, in essence, that one can be an American without being a Yankee. The essay ranges from a history of western writing to an ironic and sarcastic analysis of western reading habits. Ultimately a literary critic, Coggeshall deftly uncovers the east's attempts to represent itself as the nation through the politics of anthology selection. W. H. Venable, the historian of the Cincinnati scene, suggests that Coggeshall would have returned to Cincinnati after serving in Peru and continued to foster and redirect the careers of young writers like himself, William Dean Howells, and others whose work he had already edited and published. After the war, though, the first west was irretrievably divided into north and south, and Coggeshall might have had a hard time reassembling the sense of coherent regional identity he so hoped to nurture.

Text: "The Protective Policy in Literature" (Columbus, Ohio: 1859). Published as a pamphlet.

THE PROTECTIVE POLICY IN LITERATURE (1859)

The West and its Literature

When I was invited to stand in this place to-night, distrusting my fitness for such a position, I could not accept the responsibility it would impose, until I had determined the purpose of a Discourse.

It was with great diffidence and deep embarrassment, I seriously took up that question. I could not be mistaken in the character of the audience to which I would speak. I was invited by a Literary Society composed of young men, who are soon, with cultivated minds and willing hands, to go forth into the world to forge out careers for themselves. I knew that my voice would be heard within the walls of the first general Institution of Learning provided for, by the liberal foresight of Congress, in the Great West. Bearing in mind that this Institution seeks to develop character becoming the vigor and independence of prosperous intelligence, I was led to reflect whether it would not be peculiarly appropriate to plead before the Students and Teachers, the thinkers and workers, here assembled, the advantages of cultivating a Literature in the West, which will represent its history and its capacities—its people, their opportunities and their purposes.

When I had decided upon that theme, I did not fear an imputation of "sectionalism." Literature which lives represents the spirit of a people. In that sense it must be "sectional," or local; in a word, native.

From the earliest Hebrew, Chaldaic, or Egyptian records, through Grecian, Roman, German, Spanish, French or English, "sectionalism" has been a vitalizing power—sectionalism, not as a subservient spirit devoted to selfish purposes for narrow ends, but truthfulness to the animating characteristics of thought and action among an individual people.

Plato and Demosthenes, Cæsar and Cicero, Luther and Calvin, Shakspeare and

Gœthe, Voltaire and Calderon, Milton and Moliere, were "sectionalists." So are Bryant and Longfellow, Bancroft and Irving, Willis and Cooper. American literature was unrecognized, in the world's highest courts of criticism, half a century ago, because it was not pervaded with the special characteristics of the forming nation. Western literature, though in a lively degree representing Pioneer men and Pioneer times, has been disregarded, as a distinct power, in the general interest for welcome to whatever, springing out of seaboard cities, has been creditable to the national character.

Let us inquire why.

It is a law of mental and physical philosophy, that the character of a people depends greatly upon the advantages, or disadvantages, of the country it inhabits.

The most favorable natural condition for the healthful development of a people, is in a climate and upon a soil which require, but which generously reward, judicious industry.

That is the character, preëminently, of the soil and climate which have attracted emigrants from all quarters of the globe to

"The land of the West, green forest land,"

fitly apostrophized by William D. Gallagher as the

"Clime of the fair and the immense,
Favorite of Nature's liberal hand,
And child of her munificence."

Its mountains and valleys and plains—its great rivers and inland seas, bless a people, whose ancestry had peculiar incentives to industry—who, with mental cultivation, braving peril and deprivation, vigorously started a new life. Having no use for the conventionalities to which they had been accustomed, they could afford manners and customs becoming their new relations, and consequently, it is said with truth, that western men are frank, generous, prompt; perhaps rude; it may be rough, according to the rules of polite society.

Daniel Boone and Simon Kenton, Davy Crockett and George Rogers Clark, Rufus Putnam and William Henry Harrison, were types of the character which fought the Indians, hunted the bear and the deer and the buffalo, conquered the wilderness, and organized States.

The antithesis of characteristics which distinguished their public lives, were not more deeply marked than the contrasts to have been met, in camps and circles, never known out of the forest or the settlement. Heroism, in the sense of self-sacrificing devotion to a definite purpose, was a necessity of pioneer life; and self-reliance shone as an eminent characteristic of Western Society, when general observation was first attracted to it as an element in national councils.

The social history of the early West exposes need of culture, but it evinces virtue, and its political history evinces wisdom. Consequently its amazingly augmenting power can be explained as clearly as a mathematical problem. Self-reliant industry upon a generous soil, shaded by hills and forests, brightened by navigable rivers—social virtue and political wisdom—these won the epithet *great* for the West, and upon these does security for the worthiness of that epithet depend, in whatever respect it may be used, not implying extent of domain.

It is said that a frontier merchant is at once recognized in New York, by his self-reliance, his independence; it may be, his rude generosity. The half-horse, half-alligator caricatures of Western peculiarities which have prevailed, had a natural significance in the stamp pioneer life gave its inheritors.

When a thorough-bred Yankee, a regular down-Easter, comes "out west," with his cautious care of sixpences, he is as surely known as a fresh Hollander, or an Irishman with brogans; and, not until he is so transformed that he can speak as if he were not afraid of wasting his voice, does he cease to be an object of scrutiny.

It is well worthy of remark, that while Western Society is required to harmonize countless conflicting peculiarities, which accompany emigrants from all quarters of the globe, it so far preserves its original force of character, that it is competent to liberalize the shrewd New Englander, who, after forty years' wear and tear on a sterile farm, or in a narrow counting-house, comes West, with a long face, deploring the necessity of relinquishing good society for the companionship of wide corn-fields, fat oxen, big pigs and land warrants, or town lots and railway scrip.

But the modification of character which overcomes the immigrant in the West, is owing in a great degree to an influence which always underlies progress. It exists in distrust for the past and hope for the future, inspiring a willingness to adopt and encourage whatever promises prosperity.

This influence led the earliest pioneer, and it leads the latest immigrant, if he comes hither for good purpose. In the language of a writer who has studied the history of the West, and who appreciates her opportunities:[1]

What, till within a few years past, the onward-coming multitudes have found on arriving here, has been, chiefly, physical sufficiency, great intellectual expertness, a degree of moral independence wholly new to them, and capacity for almost indefinite extension, either morally, intellectually or physically. Coming in upon us by hundreds and thousands, as they now are and for years have been, their gentler and fiercer passions, like meadow rivulets and mountain torrents, mixing in with and modifying our own, and their art, science and literature, their hard-handedness and willing-heartedness, and their experiences of life generally giving to and receiving from ours new impulses and new directions, the whole soon to flow together in one common stream of Humanity, which will be found irresistible by any barriers that may oppose its course, must inevitably give new and peculiar aspects to the region and the era wherein it holds its way.

"Out of the crude materials, collected and collecting in the North-West—materials that are just now taking forms of symmetry, and exhibiting a homogeneousness that has not heretofore belonged to them—are to come arts and institutions and educations better fitted for the uses and enjoyments of man, and more promotive of those high developments that are within the capacities of his nature, than anything which the world has yet seen.

"Here, on this magnificent domain—this undulating plain—that extends from the beautiful bases of the Allegheny Mountains to the broad, fertile shores of the Mississippi River, and stretches its arms from near the 36th quite to the 42d degree of north latitude—are in time to be witnessed the freest forms of social development, and the highest order of human civilization."

Enthusiasm animated the pen of the writer whose words I have quoted, but it was enthusiasm tempered by judgment; it grew out of a liberal estimate of natural opportunity.

---

1. William D. Gallagher—Historical Address, 18—.

The conditions of the superior human advancement, possible, in the lapse of time, through that opportunity, depend on well-directed industry, humanitary ingenuity and political wisdom; but all of these depend upon social characteristics, for upon social characteristics—upon domestic life—in the widest degree, rest the morals of a people; and the morals of a people are purified or corrupted by their literature—the literature they produce.

The world's history is marked by periods to which literature gave character, and these periods are among the brightest on the scroll of Time. Songs and Poems, Orations and Histories, with their encouragements and warnings, are valued in all influential society, with higher and deeper reverence than whatever else the proudest nations produced. They are not only inspiring for themselves, but they preserve whatever was inspiring among the people from whom they proceeded.

The record of the world's action, as it appears in monuments or mausoleums, in pagodas or palaces, in pyramids or temples, does not teach that honor and usefulness are what men should have ambition for. These noble lessons lie in the literature, spoken from the pulpit, on the rostrum or in the forum, upon the highway or in the cloister, which, through its agents, that now search every cabin, the Printing Press, reproduces and renews.

Books are the most enduring of human possessions. Literature is alone, of human instrumentalities, a pervading spirit which Time cannot destroy—a spirit which animated tradition when time, with man, was young, and took form and comeliness in poetry and history—a spirit for which ingenuity has toiled through all the centuries of the past, and to which the highest forms of human aspiration now do reverence.

Nature's affinities are not monopolized in the natural sciences. The mental as well as the material world has its attractions and its repulsions. Literature, in the broadest sense, is the medium of their transmission from one man—from one age or from one nation to another.

Music has tones which act responsive to peculiar human emotions, and so has Literature; but there are melodies which inspire all humanity, and there are literary utterances which find echo wherever there is a human heart. These utterances are among the surest evidences of the cultivation of the right spirit of literature by a people, but often they burst forth in signal rebuke of indifference to that spirit.

Greece and Rome, England and France, Germany and Spain, through their authors, have quiet homes of love and respect in the hearts of the cultivated every where. Neither successful warriors, nor shrewd diplomats, nor wise statesmen, have as general respect as standard writers; nor does mechanism, nor even the art of the printer or the sculptor, hold rank, in universality of recognition, with literature. It is the servant of the Statesman and the Artist, the Artisan and the Agriculturist; and that their uses and purposes, their glories and beauties, may be fully appreciated, every people aspiring to greatness must cultivate literature. Just appreciation will prevent it from becoming the slave of whatever is bad in politics or war, of whatever is a defamation of Art; consequently all the questions which affect the prosperity and happiness of a people, enter into their cultivation of a literature.

The citizen who is sensitive to his varied obligations, recognizes a duty in the support of all the instrumentalities of instruction, and he knows literature, in even its technical sense, to be among the most important. The good man lives in consciousness of obligations to good literature, which cannot be dissevered from his duties to family, church, and government.

The solidarity of a literature is not established in a generation. Poetry, History, or Romance, Science or Belles Lettres, may have representatives, within the first age of a people, whose individuality is distinct; but each and all must gain recognition, independently of the people from which they spring, before it can be said that a national literature exists. It is not enough, either, that a national literature exists. It is required of a nation, which combines wide differences of characteristics, that each shall have its own representation.

A Republic of letters may be a confederacy of individualities, as well as that a Republic in politics may be a confederacy of States.

In Commerce, in Mechanics, in Agriculture, in Politics, the West has recognized individuality; but the poetry, romance, and history peculiar to it—inspired by its natural advantages—woven into its traditions—developed in its settlement—do not significantly animate a literature which the popular will accredits.

Tomahawks and wigwams, sharp-shooting and hard fights, log cabins, rough speech, dare-devil boldness, bear-hunting and corn-husking, prairie flowers, bandits, lynch-law and no-law-at-all, miscellaneously mixed into "25 cent novels," printed on poor paper and stitched between yellow covers, represent the popular idea of Western Literature.

Two years ago, on a steamboat trip down the Ohio River, I met a young man fresh from a counting-house in Rhode Island. He was a very intelligent young man, in the general acceptation of that phrase, but he had many stupid opinions about the West. He learned that I was from Cincinnati, and he was curious to know all about Porkopolis. In perfect candor, and "only for information," he deliberately asked me whether the noise and stench, occasioned by the immense slaughter of hogs, did not make life in the city almost intolerable. I discovered, in conversation with him, that he imagined Porkopolis to be composed, in about equal proportion, of pig pens and poorly constructed business and dwelling houses. Reasoning from what he had seen of hog-killing in the town-yards of Yankee land, he supposed that the citizens of the great metropolis for ham and bacon, must dwell in the midst of alarms to eye and ear and nose. His idea of Cincinnati was just about as intelligent as that entertained by most people concerning what literature the West has failed to encourage.

For the popular opinion, that whatever individuality Western Literature has, belongs to the shock-your-nerves, excite-your-wonder school, there are two prominent reasons: First, because that opinion agrees with the popular idea of pioneer life; second, because the descendants, or successors, of the early pioneers have not endeavored to maintain an individual or home literature of a higher character.

If any poem, or oration, or history, or romance, or essay, has given honor to the West, it was a spontaneous production, in defiance to public indifference, and it failed to disturb that indifference until New York or London had pronounced upon it.

The pioneers were not always men of culture; but they were not merely hunters, who could only appreciate the merits of a rifle, or take delight in "bear signs" and "deer tracks." They were brave, intelligent men, capable of culture, and when social circles could be encouraged in their settlements, they demanded literature. In young cities, men of hope and trust presumed upon this demand, and newspapers were issued, and magazines were printed, and books were published; but the pioneer looked out of the woods for every thing which his simple habits required, excepting grain and meat. He would not believe that the forest could give him literature. His affections were with the bookstores, and at the printing offices he had known in his youth;

consequently the western authors, printers and publishers, were left to act the part of pioneers, in fields supporting a thick growth of prejudice, which had to be cleared away before confidence could be cultivated.

The society of young towns and cities and farms waited to see whether young newspapers and young editors and young publishers would succeed or not, and it witnessed melancholy failures which but served to confirm the prejudice that crushed out hope and paralyzed enterprise.

Many of the unsuccessful did not understand their own powers, nor what their enterprises required; but there were among them men and women, who, with fair encouragement, would long ago have secured the West a recognized place of honor in the literary history of America.

The first literary center in the West was Cincinnati. There the first newspaper ever published in our great inland valley made its appearance on the 9th day of November, 1793. Cincinnati was then five years old, and contained about 500 inhabitants. The first book written and printed in the North-West was published at Cincinnati in 1809. Between the years 1811 and 1815, there were twelve books, averaging about 200 pages each, printed in the Queen City. In 1819 the North-West had its first literary journal. It was called the *Literary Cadet,* and appeared on the 22d day of November, in the year mentioned, (1819). Only twenty-three numbers of the *Cadet* were issued. In 1824 Cincinnati had a second literary paper, and it has had thirteen since, all of which are dead.

The first literary magazine of the Great West appeared at Lexington, Kentucky, in 1819, and in 1827 the second was projected at Cincinnati, in which city seventeen have since died.

Of all the books published in the West between 1800 and 1854, not one attained national success; but works by western authors, published at the east, have been universally popular. To the present generation there is not known one in a hundred of the names that have been linked with the valuable in the writings of the valley of the Ohio and Mississippi during thirty years past.

Those who are familiar with the magazines and newspapers *that failed,* or those whose experiences of life reach into the pioneer period, have recollections of which they are proud; but a majority of the present citizens of Ohio or Kentucky or Indiana or Illinois or Michigan, have quite as little knowledge of the real merit of the literature of the past in the West as they have of the color or condition of the people who constructed the mounds of

"The region of sunset."

Within a period of ten years, counting backward and forward from 1830, there existed a literary circle of which Cincinnati was the center, which, as a whole, has never had a superior in America.

Among those who were influential in that circle, I may mention the names of William Henry Harrison, Timothy Flint, Micah P. Flint, Daniel Drake, James Hall, Jacob Burnet, Benjamin F. Drake, Edward D. Mansfield, William D. Gallagher, Otway Curry, S. P. Hildreth, L. A. Hine, Caroline Lee Hentz, Rebecca S. Nichols, Thos. H. Shreve, F. W. Thomas, Lyman Beecher, Charles Hammond, Elisha Whittlesey, Albert Pike, L. J. Cist, James H. Perkins, Harriet Beecher Stowe, Eliza A. Dupuy, Amelia Welby, Sarah T. Bolton, and John B. Dillon.

These names, and others I could call, are familiar to all intelligent persons, but that their owners made valiant, though vain effort for literary support in the West twenty-five years ago, is a fact unacknowledged in the public mind. It is a popular saying that

"Westward the star of Empire takes its way."

The history of the world shows that he who uttered that saying was a philosopher as well as a poet. But literary history in the West teaches that the westward marching look back for civilization, and that by example, if not by precept, they teach their children to look for literary as well as natural light toward sunrise. Therefore does it happen now-a-days, that stars which rise with a dim lustre in the literary or dramatic or artistic world of the east, become luminaries of the first magnitude when they deign to shine on our valleys.

The religion of the Persians, who worship the god of day, has devotees in show, if not in substance, in the western hemisphere, for though we do not worship the sun as a divine emblem, we cultivate the idea of an association of mental with material illumination in our disparagement of the occidental and our expectancy concerning the oriental.

There is a popular notion that the western sections of a city are more healthful than the eastern, because currents of air are continually wafting the smoke and dust eastward. Whether this be true as a principle of hygiene or not, it is true that currents of thought run eastward which carry reward and encouragement away from the toiling in shops and offices, in studios and libraries, to the detriment, not only of literature in the ideal, but of morals and industry in the actual.

In the year 1839, James H. Perkins contributed to the New York Review an article on "Western Literature," in which he said:

"The first thing that strikes us is the amount of foreign literature. Not a novel of any note comes from the London press but may be met with everywhere, from Pittsburgh to the Yellowstone—from New Orleans to the falls of St. Anthony. Byron thought it something like fame to be read in America, but in our day it proves no merit in a writer that his works circulate to the Rocky Mountains. ★ ★ ★ ★ Most of this foreign literature comes from eastern publishers, and is, of course, the same which they circulate in the Atlantic States.

"The chief reading of the stirring men of the West relates to stirring men. ★ ★ ★ Western taste demands something which tells of men of life, of battle, of suffering, of heroism, skill and wisdom, or else something which addresses man's highest nature, his holiest and deepest feelings. ★ ★ ★ The western people love western history, not the history of the common events of civil life, of laws, treaties and humdrum times of peace; but of the stirring frontier incidents; of the struggles of the backwoodsman. ★ ★ ★ Having a knowledge of the prevalent love of the mass, western writers have almost buried the truly noble leaders of the pioneer bands under reiterated accounts of their doings, and yet, a full, living, trustworthy account of those men, such an one as ought to be written, is wanting."

Mr. Perkins wrote truly, and the want to which he referred has not yet been supplied, chiefly because the people have oftenest applauded and most liberally rewarded those of their own authors, who aim to construct highly-wrought legends or romances, or who speculate glowingly upon astonishing statistics which entice capital.

Cotemporaneous with Mr. Perkins's article, William D. Gallagher published one, in which he said:

"To supply the demand for select current reading, the Eastern States have four quarterly reviews, twelve or fifteen monthlies, and something like a score of weekly literary papers, together with twenty or thirty large miscellaneous sheets of the family class. The Western States, with an equal population, have—what? Three specimens of the family class, one weekly literary paper, and three monthly magazines. ★ ★ ★ Eight millions of people, one in soil, territory and government, looking to another eight millions to furnish a literature. Independent in every thing else, the West relies upon the Eastern States and upon the old world for literary aliment."

These words of complaint, from Mr. Gallagher's pen, apply with more significance to the year 1859 than they did to 1839. With our increase of population, with the development of our material resources, Atlantic literary preponderance keeps pace. Markets for our grain and salt and iron are not only brought near to us, but literary circles are made our immediate neighbors, and without taking the trouble to ask whether the ability to supply our literary demands exists, if we want a poem, an address, or a lecture, our first impulse is to telegraph for second-hand wares, which some society over the mountains or over the ocean has put aside.

If our best policy requires that writers and preachers and lecturers for the West should have a seaboard indorsement, why does it not require that we should send to salt water for our Governors, our Senators and Representatives. Doughfaces are at a discount now, and specimens plastic enough to answer any tone in the public voice anxiously await orders.

Popular sentiment requires that those who come among us with strange words in their mouths and strange manners and customs and opinions in their daily work and pleasure, should adapt themselves to their new relations, forgetting not home and country, but prejudices and preferences which better life and wider opportunity rebuke. Why has not the same policy application to him who crosses only mountains as well as to him who crosses oceans; not to disparagement of what is beyond mountains or seas, that is worthy of regard, but only in rebuke of neglect of what is here, simply because it "comes out of Nazareth?"

It cannot be argued, that absence of liberal encouragement demonstrates unworthiness in the literature which the West has inspired. That argument would condemn the opinions of the present, upon many standard works of art and literature, and it would overthrow established doctrines of philosophy and religion.

Posterity takes delight in reversing the judgments which cotemporary jealousy or partiality placed upon the efforts of notorious or obscure men. It is full time that, out of self-respect, the West awarded to its pioneer writers the poor justice of acknowledgment of service, and encourage thereby strivings of Genius, which shall accomplish what is worthy of the example of the past, the inspiration of the present, and the promise of the future.

Periodical literature in the West twenty years ago was superior, incomparably, in all most-to-be-desired qualities, to that which, associated with fashion plates and baby dresses, with patterns for night-caps and recipes for the toilet, may now be found on the center tables of every model parlor in any western town; and yet the "WESTERN REVIEW," projected at Lexington, Kentucky, in 1819, by William Gibbes Hunt, a scholar and an industrious, tasteful writer; the "WESTERN MONTHLY REVIEW," by Timothy Flint, begun in Cincinnati in 1827; the "ILLINOIS MAGAZINE," started at Vandalia, Illinois, by James Hall, in 1829; the "HESPERIAN," conducted by Wm. D. Gallagher and Otway Curry, at Columbus, Ohio, in 1828; the "LITERARY REVIEW," at Cincinnati, by L. A. Hine and E. Z. Judson, in 1844; the "WESTERN LITERARY MES-

SENGER," by George Brewster, at Columbus, Ohio, in 1850; the "GENIUS OF THE WEST," by Howard Durbin, in 1854; and all of later date, "good, bad, and indifferent," whether of Ohio, Indiana, Illinois, Kentucky, or Michigan, failed *for want of support,* within three years of their origin, excepting the "LADIES' REPOSITORY," of Cincinnati, first published in 1841; which, indeed, is not to be considered independently a literary magazine, because it is the favorite of a powerful church.

It is universally conceded among those who know the character of literary enterprises in the West, that had merit been all that was needed to insure success, the editors and proprietors of at least half a score of magazines and newspapers had been handsomely rewarded. With them were associated, as writers, all the men and women whose names I have mentioned, and many others worthy to be mentioned; and in their columns were published Essays, Reviews, Tales, Sketches, and Poems, which were not only indorsed by New York and Boston, but which were republished in Europe, and have found their way into school books that are universally popular.

If neither ability, scholarship, industry, enthusiasm nor tact was wanting, why have literary enterprises, on the sunset side of the Alleghanies, been signally disastrous? It cannot be denied, that a majority of the projectors of these enterprises did not command the pecuniary resources necessary to establish a business requiring the cultivation of confidence; but, after all, the chief cause lies where I have, more than once, traced it—in servile dependence upon the Atlantic States, and in ungenerous distrust of home energy, home honesty, and home capacity.

Now, I protest against the thoughtlessness, or selfishness, or jealousy, which exemplifies, in modern times, the New Testament axiom, that "a prophet is not without honor save in his own country," with full knowledge that home missions are now neglected for foreign ones, in a variety of forms and circumstances; but I am persuaded that literature bears such relations to society, that home encouragement may enlarge enjoyment of the remote in origin, and while affording gratification of curiosity for what comes to us from abroad, correct tastes, and develop faculties which can reciprocate borrowed blessings.

Literature, in the most enlarged sense, is cosmopolitan. It is a law of its encouragement, that home attention prepares most directly and thoroughly for just appreciation of whatever another people produces.

The association may appear odd, indeed incongruous, but whenever I see a farmhouse in one of our western valleys without the protecting shade of a native tree, to tell, in its silent majesty, how the wilderness and its traditions have passed away, I am reminded of that spirit of indifference which has chilled the development of an individual literature, fitly representing not only the stirring times when the Hunter and the Indian watched each other, or the Pioneer took his rifle into his new fields, when he had seed to sow or grain to reap; but later times, in which a society, composed of conflicting elements of character, needs the guidance of genius, that has studied its peculiarities, and appreciates its opportunities.

I knew a farmer in Northern Ohio, who had a promising son-in-law, on whom he wished to make a marriage settlement. Accordingly he presented him with a corner lot, on which the native forest yet stood. The young man, wanting to build a house on his property, made a "clearing." When the house was ready to be occupied it was thickly surrounded with stumps of trees, which may have sheltered the moundbuilders, who perhaps roamed these valleys before the red man twanged his bow in their solitudes. Where checkered shadows had changed and mingled for centuries, not a foot of shade protected the intruding house. Contemplating the ruin he had made, and knowing what the example of his father and his father-in-law had been, he planted a few puny shade and fruit trees in his garden and before his door; and consoled with the attention they required, the young man did not once think what a fool he had been, when, without forecast, he destroyed the monarchs of the woods, among whose boughs the winds of ancient time had sighed.

He was a blockhead, to be sure; but he was as wise as his neighbors, among whom forethought had been wanting, for material beauty and the enjoyment of natural poetry.

Destruction, as well as cultivation, was a law of necessity in the pioneer period; but, while one was exercised without judgment in the material world, the other, without discretion, has been neglected in the mental; and, therefore, precedent leads social circles to overlook what would win them honor and confer happiness, as precedent led the young man, of whom I complain, to be wasteful of what would have afforded his home generous protection, and himself refined satisfaction.

Everybody says, "A narrow man is the fancy farmer who removes the monarch oak, or beech, or elm, to surround his residence with the alianthus, the catalpa, and other exotics;" but quite as narrow is the fashionable hero-worshiper, who encourages support in literature, of that for which curiosity is the chief stimulus, while native talent and ingenuity go abroad begging.

The spreading catalpa, the tall poplar, the luxuriant alianthus, adorn our country gardens and beautify our town walks; but he who would strip all our hills of their native crowns and plant upon them these exotics, would act the part of a lunatic. Yet he would be no more insane than is he who, in art and literature, worships strange models, with affected or acquired contempt for whatever originates among his own people.

Why does America hold high rank for native ingenuity in mechanism, and for energy in trade and commerce? Reward waits upon effort. Honor and fame offer immediate premiums for triumphs. It was logical that the most direct needs of the nation should first gain satisfaction; but every energy of every circle in America, need not now be wholly and exclusively devoted to what will augment material wealth and power. The amenities of life, the quiet advantages of contemplative pursuits, are more valuable, though less imperative, than material wealth or power—more valuable not only to individuals but to communities, because what they accomplish has perennial significance for good, furnishing the standards by which the future always estimates the real greatness of the past.

If we trace the paths along which the literary hopes of the past in the West are buried, we find numerous neglected graves, around which long processions have gathered. The characteristics, trials, failures, or successes of even the chief mourners in these processions, I will not be permitted to sketch in this Lecture. Several evenings would be required to present a satisfactory review of the poetical, historical, legendary, legal, medical, theological, and political literature, which has been creditable to our society. Only in a course of Lectures, would I undertake to mention, with the thinnest outline of their productions, all the respectable writers of the West. I refer to them in a body now for the purpose of connecting the present with the past, in a few general facts which, in my opinion, possess distinct importance.

From Rufus Wilmot Griswold's "Survey of the Literature of the United States," in three volumes, regarded by the most influential critics as standard authority, the analytic inquirer learns, that whatever forms of inspiration may repose in the grand old forests, or along the mighty rivers, or upon the solemn mountains, or on the broad plains of the West—however frequently, in the old time gone, its groves may have been made musical with the unwritten cadences of aboriginal poetry, it has not yet been productive of pale-faced writers.

In his volume on "The Prose Writers of America," Mr. Griswold recognizes, with biographical notices, only two men who are identified with Western Literature.

First: Timothy Flint, born in Massachusetts, who came to the West as a Missionary; and after ten years' hard service in that capacity, chose Literature as his profession—his exclusive vocation—and wrote and published with such poor pecuniary success, though a man of industry and rare ability, with a glow of poetic fervor in his style, that he has never had a legitimate successor.

Second: James Hall, born in Pennsylvania, who, like Mr. Flint, was a magazine editor and a writer of romances, and valuable works of history and statistics; but, unlike him, chose banking instead of writing for his vocation, and has had many successors, legitimate and illegitimate.

Incidentally, Mr. Griswold mentions F. W. Thomas, author of the novel, "Clinton Bradshaw," and other works of merit; and Morgan Neville, author of "Mike Fink, the Boatman," a forgotten romance. But, with these exceptions, the student of Literature could never ascertain, form "standard authority," that there had been prose writers in Ohio, or Indiana, or Kentucky, or Illinois, or Michigan.

Toward the Poets of the West, Mr. Griswold has been more liberal. He recognizes Micah P. Flint and Albert Pike, from Massachusetts; F. W. Thomas, from Rhode Island; G. D. Prentice, from Connecticut; Wm. D. Gallagher, from Pennsylvania; F. Casby, born in Kentucky, and Otway Curry and G. W. Cutter, born in Ohio; Annie P. Dinnies, from South Carolina; Laura M. Thurston and Lydia Jane Pierson, from Connecticut; Rebecca S. Nichols, from New Jersey; Amelia Welby and Margaret S. Bailey, from Virginia; Sophia H. Oliver and Sarah T. Bolton, born in Kentucky; Frances A. and Metta Victoria Fuller, from New York, and Alice and Phebe Cary, born in Ohio.

It will be observed, that among twenty poets, Ohio has original claim to four—two of the masculine and two of the feminine gender—while Kentucky has one masculine and two feminine; but that neither Indiana, Illinois, Michigan, or Missouri, is recognized as having either a native prose writer or poet.

Only those men who, writing prose in the West, *published it at the East,* have been considered by Mr. Griswold worthy of notice; consequently a large number, whom the people of the West should honor and respect, and who deserve to be introduced to every student of American Literature, are grossly slighted. Among them, I may take time to mention Daniel Drake, the first student of medicine in Cincinnati, and the first man who, from the West, called the aid of Literature to the development of the natural resources of the Ohio basin—who, during a long life of remarkable activity, was the earnest friend of all intellectual progress; and who, besides an invaluable work on the "Diseases of the Mississippi Valley," left influences which must exert great force in the settlement of the principles which are, hereafter, to guide the mental and physical life of our people;—James H. Perkins, a man of great soul and high poetic temperament, who did signal service to the historical literature of America, and who was the author of Tales and Sketches, which have had as wide circulation as the American press could give them;—Benjamin F. Drake, author of a "Life of Black Hawk," and a "Life of Tecumseh;" requiring laborious research, and throwing much light upon the careers and characters of the great representative men of the forest;—E. D. Mansfield, whose works on Politics, Education and Biography, entitle him to most respectful consideration: not to speak of Burnet and Hildreth of Ohio, Marshall and Butler of Kentucky, Dillon of Indiana, Ford of Illinois, and others, in a list longer than

I dare now repeat, who have made contributions to history no less important than many to which the "standard authority" I have spoken of, pays respectful deference.

But Mr. Griswold is not alone in his disregard of the literary claims of the West.

A "Cyclopedia of American Literature" was published in New York in 1855.[2] Its editors are Everet A. and G. L. Ducykink, who for several years conducted the *Literary World,* a recognized organ of literary information and discussion. They claim most decidedly to represent the literature of the nation, past and present. Let us inquire into their fairness respecting "out West."

Twenty-three persons, whose names are, or have been, identified with western literature, are recognized in the Cyclopedia—sixteen as prose writers, and seven as poets. Among these persons are Lewis Cass, Thos. H. Benton, Henry Clay, Dr. Chas. Caldwell and Bishop Philander Chase, but neither Otway Curry, George W. Cutter, E. D. Mansfield, John B. Dillon, Thos. H. Shreve, Judge Jacob Burnet, S. P. Hildreth, Timothy Walker of Cincinnati, I. B. Walker the theologian, Rev. Edward Thomson of Delaware, W. W. Fosdick, Rebecca S. Nichols, Sarah T. Bolton, Metta Victoria Fuller, Mrs. Ruter Defour, or Annie P. Dinnies, are regarded with the briefest mention. They, and all of lesser note who write "out West," independent of certain city cliques, are even behind Franklin Pierce, whose name indeed appears in the index, because Nathaniel Hawthorne wrote his biography.

The Cyclopedia recognizes two poets native to Ohio—Alice and Phebe Cary; one poet native to Kentucky—William Ross Wallace; one prose writer native to Illinois—John L. McConnell, author of the novel "Talbot and Vernon," and one prose writer native to Kentucky—C. W. Webber, the "Hunter Naturalist;" but with these exceptions, the world is left in ignorance, so far as the Cyclopedia of American Literature can leave it, of native talent for authorship in any Western State.

The Ducykinks have done justice to a few men and women whom Griswold overlooks, and they have slighted others whom he recognizes. But, without fear of successful contradiction, I affirm that neither Griswold's Survey of American Literature, in three volumes, nor Ducykink's Cyclopedia, in two volumes, nor both together, can be given credit for due respect to western authorship, while they exhibit active diligence in "making a good show" for all the giants and many of the dwarfs of eastern authordom.

Looking outside of mere literary circles, let us inquire of eastern fairness toward western men. In 1857, Appleton's publishing house of New York issued two *American* Cyclopedias—one of Eloquence, one of Wit and Humor.

In the Cyclopedia of American Eloquence, the only western man mentioned, excepting Henry Clay, is Tecumseh, but eastern men not half so well known for eloquence as Tecumseh's conqueror at Tippecanoe, have the honor of biographical notices, with select passages from their speeches.

In the Cyclopedia of "Wit and Humor," something nearer justice is done western talent, because Micah P. Flint, Geo. W. Bradbury, James Hall, Sol. Smith, Geo. D. Prentice, J. M. Field (Everpoint), J. S. Robb (Solitaire), J. L. McConnell, and J. V. Watson are honorably mentioned; but had the same diligence in the pursuit of wit and humor been exercised for the west that has been for the east, I could quote other names from Mr. Burton's Cyclopedia.

Permit still another illustration of the fact that either on account of ignorance or of illiberal spirit, critics and compilers "down east" do injustice to the "great west."

---

2. By Charles Scribner.

In 1858, D. Appleton & Co. published "*The Household Book of Poetry,*" compiled and edited by Charles A. Dana, one of the editors of the *New York Tribune.* In his preface the editor says that he undertook to "comprise within the bounds of a single volume whatever is truly beautiful and admirable among the minor poems of the English language," and he claims to have developed "a considerable store of treasures hitherto less known to the general public than to scholars and to limited circles," from "careful and prolonged research in the current receptacles of fugitive poets." He claims, also, that it has been his constant endeavor "to exercise a catholic as well as a severe taste; and to judge every piece by its poetical merit solely, without regard to the name, nationality or epoch of the author."

It is not too much to say that the people of the West who are expected—at least several thousand of them—to be purchasers of Mr. Dana's book, are familiar with poems, from writers within their circle of acquaintance, which are quite as good as many of those that have been selected by him as poems of Nature—of Childhood—of Friendship—of Love—of Ambition—of Comedy—of Tragedy and Sorrow—of the Imagination—of Sentiment and of Reflection—or of Religion.

The poems for which we make this claim are not "fugitive pieces," merely, that have gone the "rounds of the papers," but may be found in books with which, it is fair to presume, Mr. Dana, as an editor of a leading journal, if not as the editor of a book of household poetry, ought to be familiar. Alice Cary, Mrs. R. S. Nichols, Mrs. S. T. Bolton, Geo. D. Prentice, W. D. Gallagher, James II. Perkins, John B. Dillon, Geo. W. Cutter, Otway Curry, F. W. Thomas, and others we might name, who are yet young, are not poets of mere local reputation, or authors of "fugitive pieces," only. None of them are quoted by Mr. Dana. The only person quoted who is recognized as western, is Mrs. Amelia Welby. Her "Old Made" is given as a poem of sentiment and reflection.

We invite the curious to look at Mr. Dana's book, and then consider whether Alice Cary's "Pictures of Memory"—George D. Prentice's "Lines to my Wife," or "The Closing Year"—Otway Curry's "Kingdom Come," or "The Goings Forth of God"—F. W. Thomas's song, "Tis said that Absence Conquers Love"—W. D. Gallagher's "August," or his lines to Autumn, in his poem on "The Miami Woods," or his "Conservative," or "Laborer," or Coates, Kinney's "Rain on the Roof," are not quite as good as much written in New York or Boston, or there-abouts, to which "Household Poetry" gives consideration.

While making these analyses of unfairness to talent identified with the West, I do not forget that whatever may be true respecting lack of information, or partiality, on the part of "standard authorities" for American literature, the fact remains clear that the great central valley has not been signally distinguished by native genius in poetry, romance, or history, not because talent or genius has been wanting—not because inspiration has been absent, but chiefly because repose has been denied—time to individuals for study and labor—time to the people for mellowing influences which impress popular opinion with respect for the noblest forms of mental force, and stimulate inquiry for delights from a calm and lofty sphere.

The pioneer period of the North-west was remarkably a period of all-absorbing material demand, and it was brief.

Sixty-six years ago[3] the first newspaper was published in the North-west; fifty years ago the first book was printed here. Of all the men and women who have, labored significantly for literature in the great valley, not ten have been called to the

---

3. 1793.

higher life. The others are yet with us, and it is not too late to show them that they are cherished, and will be remembered with gratitude.

We may regret that our literary pioneers did not meet wider encouragement and ampler reward, but we need not complain, unless we take care that the future does not have reason to complain of us. Knowing what the past has been, we may confidently appeal to the present for the future.

What *has* the past been? Discouraging, as I have shown it—disheartening, unjust to enterprise and industry which aimed to enrich its mental character, but opulent, bountiful in all materials for poetry, for romance, and for history.

The west has a new opportunity. This central valley is the heart of the Republic, and it may give tone to the entire system.

It is the glory of our institutions, not only that they open opportunity for the forming hand, but that they educate the informing spirit. Removed from the direct influences of the old world—with intimate relations to the South, to the East, and to the Great West, beyond the Mississippi—with a past mysterious, awe-inspiring—remarkable for potent results—with a present active, buoyant, intelligent—with a future full of promise, if the central valley, of the heart of which the homes of this audience are a part, must continue subordinate in any of the fundamental activities of civilization, it will only be because the people are untrue to themselves.

I speak advisedly when I say there is brilliant promise for noble achievement in all the highest walks of literature, in native mind which now asks direction.

As citizens, as friends, best policy and noblest principle demand of us that we require society to begin to make whomever has a thought of value, understand that *at home* recognition will be given it, whether it is good for the soil, or the shop, the office or the parlor—whether it shall culminate in a plow, a new motor, a poem, an oration, a history or a statue.

Provided with capabilities for equal rights, in opportunity, for all its citizens, let the West aspire to set the glorious example which just Republicanism contemplates—the successful working of a social system based on goodness and truth among men, who cultivate the "memorable, the progressive, and the beautiful," whether they are what the world calls workers or thinkers.

If tradition be credited, there was a literature in the West before the rifle's report and the woodman's ax displaced the war-whoop and the twang of the bow—before smiling fields appeared, where deep groves had for centuries welcomed sunshine, and invited showers.

If the red men had a touch of poetry in their manners and customs, as well as oratory in their councils, from character stamped by the inspiration of nature, shall white men fail, out of civilization, to attract regard for higher achievements than those which satisfy mere physical necessities?

The West has now shaping for homogeneousness, elements of character impressed with the individuality of its own early period, and with ancient civilization from the maturest nations, and all being quickened by the spirit of modern progress—commerce having its pressing demands satisfied, trade and manufactures enjoying far-reaching triumphs of genius—circumstances conspire to demand of the people of today, literary development which shall bring to us honor and respect as abundantly as notoriety for wheat and whisky, for corn and pork, brings now to us dollars and dimes.

The epic, the lyric, the pastoral, repose in tradition, and in legend and story—in groves and prairies—in rivers and cascades—in fruitful valleys, and on picturesque hills: history lives in our progress; romance is an ever-pervading spirit of our valleys and water-courses and hill-sides; but it will remain unwritten history, or poetry, or romance, except under spasmodic influences, or with spasmodic effort, and the people of the West will win scornful censure, unless they encourage, with pen and purse, and good will and good words, instrumentalities which are competent to individualize a Western Literature.

Literature is chief among teachers; it preserves the past and cultivates the present. Its development is highest among a people's honors. That people which invites rich gifts, in poetry and history and romance, from all other people, taking no pains to reciprocate favors and cancel obligations, is weaker and meaner than an individual who will accept presents, to which neither courtesy nor charity entitles him.

Young Men's Literary Societies, with libraries and lectures, discussions and essays, have been organized in nearly all of our towns and cities. They are an outgrowth of intelligent sentiment, fostered in our colleges, seminaries, and high schools. Professors and Teachers, in a large degree, command their interest and usefulness for the future.

From college halls and school rooms, in which compositions are read and discussions and declamations are heard, convictions and incentives may go out, which, in the next generation, can accomplish for a home literature all I have demanded—all I have hoped—in this Discourse.

May I not appeal to this audience for thoughtful consideration of what I have urged—for executive interest and local pride in a local Literature? Societies, such as that I now address, are potent for literary culture. They have weighty responsibility. They can stimulate local pride in local poetry, and romance and history. Let each member bear actively in mind, that it is nobler to develop new thought than to circulate old; that the capacity which produces is grander than that which enjoys.

Suggestions for Further Reading

Aaron, Daniel. *Cincinnati: Queen City of the West, 1819–1838.* Columbus: Ohio State University Press, 1992.

Aron, Stephen. *How the West Was Lost: The Transformation of Kentucky from Daniel Boone to Henry Clay.* Baltimore: Johns Hopkins University Press, 1996.

Bergland, Renee L. *The National Uncanny: Indian Ghosts and American Subjects.* Hanover, N. H.: University Press of New England, 2000.

Bodley, Temple. *Our First Great West in the Revolutionary War, Diplomacy, and Politics.* Louisville: Morton, 1938.

Brown, Carolyn S. *The Tall Tale in American Folklore and Literature.* Knoxville: University of Tennessee Press, 1987.

Calloway, Colin G. *The American Revolution in Indian Country: Crisis and Diversity in Native American Communities.* New York: Cambridge University Press, 1995.

Cash, W. J. *The Mind of the South.* New York: Knopf, 1941.

Cashin, Joan E. *A Family Venture: Men and Women on the Southern Frontier.* New York: Oxford University Press, 1991.

Cayton, Andrew R. L. *Frontier Ohio.* Bloomington: Indiana University Press, 1998.

———. and Fredrika J. Teute, eds. *Contact Points: American Frontiers from the Mohawk Valley to the Mississippi, 1750–1830.* Chapel Hill: University of North Carolina Press, 1997.

Clark, Thomas D. *Frontier America: The Story of the Westward Movement.* New York: Scribner, 1959.

———. *Travels in the Old South: A Bibliography. Volume Three: The Ante Bellum South, 1825–1860: Cotton, Slavery, and Conflict.* Norman: University of Oklahoma Press, 1959.

———. *Travels in the Old South: A Bibliography. Volume Two: The Expanding South, 1750–1825: The Ohio Valley and the Cotton Frontier.* Norman: University of Oklahoma Press, 1956.

———. *The Rampaging Frontier: Manners and Humors of Pioneer Days in the South and Middle West.* Bloomington: Indiana University Press, 1939.

Clark, Thomas D., and John D. W. Guice. *The Old Southwest, 1795–1830: Frontiers in Conflict.* Norman: University of Oklahoma Press, 1996. [Originally published in 1989 as *Frontiers in Conflict: The Old Southwest, 1795–1830*]

Cohen, Hennig, and William B. Dillingham, eds. *Humor of the Old Southwest.* 3rd ed. Athens: University of Georgia Press, 1994.

Davis, James E. *Frontier Illinois.* Bloomington: Indiana University Press, 1998.

Dippie, Brian W. *The Vanishing American: White Attitudes and U.S. Indian Policy.* Middleton, Conn.: Wesleyan University Press, 1982.

Drinnon, Richard. *Facing West: The Metaphysics of Indian-Hating and Empire Building.* Minneapolis: University of Minnesota Press, 1980.

Dunaway, Wilma A. *The First American Frontier: Transition to Capitalism in Southern Appalachia, 1700–1860.* Chapel Hill: University of North Carolina Press, 1996.

Eblen, Jack Ericson. *The First and Second American Empires: Governors and Territorial Government, 1784–1912.* Pittsburgh: University of Pittsburgh Press, 1968.

Garland, Hamlin. *Crumbling Idols: Twelve Essays on Art Dealing Chiefly with Literature, Painting and the Drama.* Ed. Jane Johnson. Cambridge, Mass.: Harvard University Press, 1960.

Georgi-Findlay, Brigitte. *The Frontiers of Women's Writing: Women's Narratives and the Rhetoric of Westward Expansion*. Tuscon: University of Arizona Press, 1996.

Goldman, Anne. *Continental Divides: Revisioning American Literature*. New York: Palgrave, 2000.

Grant, Mary Susan. *North over South*. Lawrence: University of Kansas Press, 2000.

Gray, Susan E. *The Yankee West: Community Life on the Michigan Frontier*. Chapel Hill: University of North Carolina Press, 1996.

Griffith, Nancy Snell. *Humor of the Old Southwest: A Bibliography of Primary and Secondary Sources*. New York: Greenwood Press, 1989.

Grossman, James R., ed. *The Frontier in American Culture*. Berkeley: University of California Press, 1994.

Guilds, John Caldwell, and Caroline Collins, eds. *William Gilmore Simms and the American Frontier*. Athens: University of Georgia Press, 1997.

Hinsdale, B. A. *The Old Northwest with a View of the Thirteen Colonies as Constituted by the Royal Charters*. New York: Townsend, 1888.

Hinderaker, Eric. *Elusive Empires: Constructing Colonialism in the Ohio Valley, 1673–1800*. Cambridge: Cambridge University Press, 1997.

Holman, David Marion. *A Certain Slant of Light: Regionalism and the Form of Southern and Midwestern Fiction*. Baton Rouge: Louisiana State University Press, 1995.

Hoxie, Frederick E., et al., eds. *Native Americans and the Early Republic*. Charlottesville: University Press of Virginia, 1999.

Hubbell, Jay B. *The South in American Literature, 1607–1900*. Durham: Duke University Press, 1954.

Hudson, Arthur Palmer, ed. *Humor of the Old Deep South*. New York: Macmillan, 1936.

Hurt, James. *Writing Illinois: The Prairie, Lincoln, and Chicago*. Urbana: University of Illinois Press, 1992.

Hurt, R. Douglas. *The Ohio Frontier: Crucible of the Old Northwest, 1720–1830*. Bloomington: Indiana University Press, 1996.

Inge, M. Thomas, ed. *The Frontier Humorists: Critical Views*. Hamden, Conn.: Archon, 1975.

Inge, M. Thomas, and Edward J. Piacentino, eds. *The Humor of the Old South*. Lexington: University Press of Kentucky, 2001.

Jones, Dorothy V. *Licence for Empire: Colonialism by Treaty in Early America*. Chicago: University of Chicago Press, 1982.

Jordan, David M. *New World Regionalism: Literature in the Americas*. Toronto: University of Toronto Press, 1993.

Kolodny, Annette. *The Land before Her: Fantasy and Experience of the American Frontier, 1630–1860*. Chapel Hill: University of North Carolina Press, 1984.

———. *The Lay of the Land: Metaphor as Experience and History in American Life and Letters*. Chapel Hill: University of North Carolina Press, 1975.

Krupat, Arnold. *The Voice in the Margin: Native American Literature and the Canon*. Berkeley: University of California Press, 1989.

Littlefield, Daniel F., Jr., and James W. Parins. *A Bibliography of Native American Writers, 1772–1924: A Supplement*. Metuchen, N.J.: Scarecrow, 1985.

———. *A Bibliography of Native American Writers, 1772–1924*. Metuchen, N.J.: Scarecrow, 1981.

Lynn, Kenneth. *Mark Twain and Southwestern Humor*. Boston: Little, Brown, 1959.

Mahoney, Timothy. *Provincial Lives: Middle Class Experience in the Antebellum Middle West*. Cambridge: Cambridge University Press, 1999.

McDermott, John Francis, ed. *Travelers on the Western Frontier*. Urbana: University of Illinois Press, 1970.

Michaelsen, Scott. *The Limits of Multiculturalism: Interrogating the Origins of American Anthropology*. Minneapolis: University of Minnesota Press, 1999.

Nobles, Gregory H. *American Frontiers: Cultural Encounters and Continental Conquest*. New York: Hill and Wang, 1997.

Nordholt, Jan Willem Schulte. *The Myth of the West: America as the Last Empire*. Trans. Herbert H. Rowen. Grand Rapids, Mich.: Eerdmans, 1995.

Odum, Howard W., and Harry Estill Moore. *American Regionalism: A Cultural-Historical Approach to National Integration*. New York: Holt, 1938.

Pearce, Roy Harvey. *Savagism and Civilization*. 2nd ed. Baltimore: Johns Hopkins University Press, 1965.

Perdue, Theda, and Michael D. Green, eds. *The Cherokee Removal: A Brief History with Documents*. Boston: Bedford/St. Martin's, 1995.

Perkins, Elizabeth A. *Border Life: Experience and Memory in the Revolutionary Ohio Valley*. Chapel Hill: University of North Carolina Press, 1998.

Peyer, Bernd C. *The Tutor'd Mind: Indian Missionary-Writers in Antebellum America*. Amherst: University of Massachusetts Press, 1997.

Power, Richard Lyle. *Planting Corn Belt Culture: The Impress of the Upland Southerner and Yankee in the Old Northwest*. Indianapolis: Indiana Historical Society, 1953.

Riley, Glenda. *Women and Indians on the Frontier, 1825–1915*. Albuquerque: University of New Mexico Press, 1984.

Rohrbaugh, Malcolm. *The Trans-Appalachian Frontier: People, Societies, and Institutions, 1775–1850*. New York: Oxford University Press, 1978.

Rubin, Louis D., Jr. *The Edge of the Swamp: A Study in the Literature and Society of the Old South*. Baton Rouge: Louisiana State University Press, 1989.

Rusk, Ralph Leslie. *The Literature of the Middle Western Frontier*. 2 vols. New York: Columbia University Press, 1926.

Savage, W. Sherman. *Blacks in the West*. Westport, Conn.: Greenwood Press, 1976.

Scheckel, Susan. *The Insistence of the Indian: Race and Nationalism in Nineteenth-Century American Culture*. Princeton, N.J.: Princeton University Press, 1998.

Seelye, John. *Beautiful Machine: Rivers and the Republican Plan, 1755–1825*. New York: Oxford University Press, 1991.

Shortridge, James R. *The Middle West: Its Meaning in American Culture*. Lawrence: University of Kansas Press, 1989.

Slaughter, Thomas P. *The Whiskey Rebellion: Frontier Epilogue to the American Revolution*. New York: Oxford University Press, 1986.

Smith, Henry Nash. *Virgin Land: The American West as Symbol and Myth*. Cambridge, Mass.: Harvard University Press, 1950.

Snodgrass, Mary Ellen. *Encyclopedia of Frontier Literature*. New York: Oxford University Press, 1997.

Taylor, Alan. *William Cooper's Town: Power and Persuasion on the Early American Frontier*. New York: Vintage, 1995.

Taylor, Quintard. *In Search of the Racial Frontier: African Americans in the American West, 1528–1990*. New York: Norton, 1998.

Turner, Frederick Jackson. *The Frontier in American History*. New York: Holt, 1947.

Venable, W. H. *Beginnings of Literary Culture in the Ohio Valley: Historical and Biographical Sketches*. Cincinnati: Clarke, 1891.

Wade, Richard C. *The Urban Frontier: The Rise of Western Cities, 1790–1830*. Urbana: University of Illinois Press, 1959, rev. ed. 1991.

Walker, Cheryl. *Indian Nation: Native American Literature and Nineteenth-Century Nationalisms*. Durham: Duke University Press, 1997.

Wallace, Anthony F. C. *The Long, Bitter Trail: Andrew Jackson and the Indians*. New York: Hill & Wang, 1993.

Weber, Ronald. *The Midwestern Ascendancy in American Writing*. Bloomington: Indiana University Press, 1992.

White, Richard. *The Middle Ground: Indians, Empires, and Republics in the Great Lakes Region, 1650–1815*. New York: Cambridge University Press, 1991.

Wyatt-Brown, Bertram. *Southern Honor: Ethics and Behavior in the Old South*. New York: Oxford University Press, 1982.

Yates, Norris W. *William T. Porter and The Spirit of the Times*. New York: Arno, 1977.